LAROUSSE

Wines AND *Vineyards* OF FRANCE

LAROUSSE

Wines AND *Vineyards* OF FRANCE

EBURY PRESS
LONDON

Published by Ebury Press
an imprint of the Random Century Group Limited
Random Century House, 20 Vauxhall Bridge Road
London SW1V 2SA

French edition, *Vins et Vignobles de France*, first published
in 1987 by Librairie Larousse

English language editor: Andrew Jefford

Translation: Rosetta Translations and Andrew Jefford

British Library Cataloguing in Publication Data
Larousse wines and vineyards of France,
1. French wines
641,2'2'0944

ISBN 0-85223-860-6

Computerset by MFK Typesetting Ltd, Hitchin, Herts
Printed and bound in Italy by New Interlitho S.p.a., Milan

CONTENTS

Panorama of the Life of Wine

The various stages in the biography of wine are described in articles at the end of each letter in the dictionary, appearing on the following pages:

CONTRIBUTORS TO *WINES AND VINEYARDS OF FRANCE*

Managing Editor: Pierre Anglade
Editorial Adviser: Jacques Puisais, *Director of the Laboratoire Départementale et Régionale d'Analyses et de Recherches, Tours*
President of the Académie Internationale du Vin
Member of the Académie d'Agriculture
Honorary President of the Unions Françaises et Internationales des Oenologues

OUR THANKS ARE DUE TO ALL THE CONTRIBUTORS WHOSE WORK MADE THIS BOOK POSSIBLE:

Barrier, Charles, *Restaurateur at Saint-Cyr-sur-Loire (Indre)*
Bartoli, Guy, *Restaurateur at Guagno (Corsica)*
Bazin, Jean-François, *Journalist and writer*
Berger, Alain, *Head of the Economics and Promotions Section, INAO*
Bergeret, Jacques, *Professor of Oenology*
Honorary Director of the Centre d'Expérimentation Viticole et Oenologique, University of Dijon
Bidan, Pierre, *Professor of Technology and Oenology, École Nationale Supérieure Agronomique, Montpellier*
Bienaymé, Marie-Hélène, *Head of the Foreign and Legal Section, INAO*
Bise, Françoise, *Restaurateur at Talloires (Haute-Savoie)*
Bocuse, Paul, *Restaurateur at Collonges-au-Mont-d'Or (Rhône)*
Boidron, Jean-Noël, *Oenologist*
Lecturer at the Institut d'Oenologie, Talence
Boyer, Gérard, *Restaurateur at Reims (Marne)*
Braitberg, Jean-Moïse, *Journalist*
Brun, Suzanne, *Professor*
Cabanis, Jean-Claude, *Professor at the Centre de Formation et de Recherche en Oenologie, University of Montpellier*
Carre, Étienne, *Doctor of Oenology*
Oenologist Technician at the Laboratoire Départementale et Régionale d'Analyses et de Recherches, Indre-et-Loire
Castets, Michel, *Marketing BSN*
Charnay, Pierre, *Agricultural engineer*
Oenologist
Cordonnier, Robert, *DSc, Agricultural engineer*
Director of the Laboratoire des Arômes et des Substances Naturelles of the Institut des Produits de la Vigne, INRA
Culas, Gabriel, *Oenologist*
Engineer at the Institut Technique de la Vigne et du Vin, Chambéry
Dubernet, Marc, *DChem, Oenologist*
Dubois, Jean, *Professor, Director of Research, INRA*
Expert in the service of CEE, OIV and FAO
President of the Groupe de Recherches Interuniversitaires d'Économie Viti-Vinicole, Toulouse (GRIEVIT)
Dumay, Raymond
Duprat, Jean-Claude, *Oenologist of the Chambre d'Agriculture, Agen*
Expert, Jacques, *Journalist*
Foulon, Dominique, *Director of an oenological service*
Galet, Pierre, *DSc, Agricultural engineer*
Assistant Head of Viticultural Studies at the École Nationale Supérieure Agronomique, Montpellier

Gastaud-Gallagher, Patricia, *Director, Académie des Vins*
Gay-Bellile, Francis, *Oenologist*
Agricultural engineer at ENSA, Montpellier
Gérardin, Martine, *Journalist*
Guimberteau, Guy, *Institut d'Oenologie, University of Bordeaux-II*
Haeberlin, Jean-Pierre and Paul, *Restaurateurs, Illhaeusern (Haut-Rhin)*
Hecquet, Daniel, *Oenologist*
CIVRB Technical Service representative
Hiély, Pierre, *Restaurateur, Avignon (Vaucluse)*
Huglin, Pierre, *Honorary Director of Research at the Institut National de la Recherche Agronomique*
Jambon, Jean-Claude, *World Champion Sommelier, 1986*
Jeunet, André, *Restaurateur, Arbois (Jura)*
Lacoste, Jacques, *Technician*
Oenologist at the Institut Technique de la Vigne et du Vin
Laguiche, Comte Alain de
Laporte, Pierre, *Restaurateur, Biarritz (Pyrénées-Atlantiques)*
Le Cannelier, Yves, *Le Savour Club*
Léglise, Max, *Oenologist*
Lemonnier, Michel, *Wine Columnist*
Member of the Académie Internationale du Vin
Martin, Jean-Louis, *Director of the Bureau National Interprofessionnel de l'Armagnac*
Meneau, Marc, *Restaurateur, Saint-Père-sous-Vézelay (Yonne)*
Mercury, François, *President of the Syndicat des Coteaux d'Ajaccio (Corsica)*
Meyer, Henri, *Vice-President of the Union Française des Oenologues*
Oliver, Raymond, *Restaurateur*
Orizet, Louis, *Honorary Inspector-General, INAO*
Outhier, Louis, *Restaurateur, la Napoule (Alpes-Maritimes)*
Pagès, Patrick, *Restaurateur, Vialas (Lozère)*
Pierre, Catherine, *Journalist and Writer*
Pijassou, René, *DLit, Associate Professor in geography*
Professor, University of Bordeaux-III
Poirier, Louis, *Agricultural engineer*
Oenologist
Honorary director of the Laboratoire Régionale d'Analyses Agricoles, Corsica
Puisais, Jacques
Puisais-Ponsain, Maryvonne
Quittanson, Charles, *Technician in the agricultural and food and drink industries*
Oenologist
Rejalot, Jacques, *Oenologist*
Roger, Jean, *Adviser to Anivit and the Comité du Vin de Saumur*
Sarthou, Philippe, *Oenologist*
Lecturer at the Faculty of Pharmacy, Toulouse
Schaeffer, Alex, *Agricultural engineer, Oenologist*
Simon, François, *Journalist*
Souzenelle, Annick de, *Writer*
Taransaud, Jean, *Cooper*
Tinlot, Robert, *Director of the Office International de la Vigne et du Vin*
Torres, Pierre, *Agricultural engineer*
Director of the Station Viti-Vinicole, Roussillon
Troisgros, Pierre, *Restaurateur, Roanne (Loire)*
Vagny, Pierre, *Head of the Viticultural Equipment Service of the ITV*
Wouttaz, Fernand, *Journalist and writer*

FOREWORD

From antiquity, wine has held a distinguished place in human societies. Homer was already able to describe people of good taste 'who draw produce of great worth from the vine, thanks to their skill in husbandry and to the care they bestow on vineyards and wines.' Down the centuries, and through all the civilizations it helped to expand and enhance, the vine has continually conquered new territories, despite all the snares that history has laid for it. In France, the vine found a propitious land that was especially welcoming and, thanks to a favourable geographical situation, one that was well suited to make the most of the vine's potential.

The vine is consequently rooted in French history, and is an integral part of French culture; it is of incontestable symbolic richness; and the wine made from it soon came to play a privileged role in French society, as national and regional traditions testify.

At the same time, wines proliferated in France, offering the consumer a subtle and almost infinite range of tastes; so the consumer has found it ever more difficult to comprehend fully all the complexities — and pitfalls — of a subject made even more intricate by advertising that has not always been of the first quality. It is with these difficulties in mind that *Wines and Vineyards of France* sets out to explore every aspect of the rich world of French wine.

There are few fruits of the earth, the climate and the toil of men that have as elusive and fugitive an image as wine does. It has as many forms and expressions as there are *terroirs*, grape varieties, microclimates and wine growers. Like all living things, it has its own breadth, its own areas of light and shade, making it something unique and irreducible.

The writers who have contributed their scientific expertise to the creation of this reference book have nevertheless endeavoured to give a rigorously objective picture of wine.

Thus *Wines and Vineyards of France* renders an account of the life of wine in France today, but against the background of its tremendous past and with a degree of scrutiny of its future perspectives.

To carry out this immense task, some fifty writers have been required: technicians, oenologists, researchers, university lecturers, historians, geographers, authors and restaurateurs, all of them eminent specialists in their fields. Under the leadership of Jacques Puisais, they have put their knowledge at the service of wine . . . and of readers, making this work an indispensable tool of reference.

To make the book easy to use, *Wines and Vineyards of France* has been conceived both as a dictionary and as an encyclopedia of French wine. All the names of *appellation* wines, grape varieties and viticultural regions and districts appear in alphabetical order, forming the dictionary component. 'Scenes' from the biography of the vine and of wine are given in the form of detailed close-ups, interspersed throughout the dictionary in chronological order, from the planting of the vine to the drinking of the wine, and these supply the reader with an encyclopedic perspective.

Dictionary of French wines, wine regions and grape varieties

For each wine, from the most humble to the most renowned, the contributors have compiled an 'identity card' that sets out all its particulars and features: the date of its ratification as an *appellation d'origine contrôlée* (AOC) or *vin délimité de qualité supérieure* (VDQS), the area of the *appellation*, average production, the grape varieties it comes from, its organoleptic characteristics — the qualities that can be discerned by sight, smell and taste and give the wine its style — and, where space allows, its history and the type of soils and climate found in the area from which it comes. The grape variety entries, meanwhile — whether describing the little-grown Bachet or the famous Gamay — list first the many different synonyms for each variety found in various parts of France. Then follows a botanical description, sufficiently detailed to enable identification, together with an indication of the soils each is planted in, the diseases that affect it, and the character of the wines that can be made from it.

Each wine-growing area, whether of regional or national importance, is the subject of a study detailing its history, geography, soils, prevailing climate, vineyard area, characteristic grape varieties, methods of harvesting, vinification and *élevage* of its wines, production statistics, economic and commercial structure, and the cultural and social activities that distinguish its viticultural life. . . . In addition, famous restaurateurs write affectionately about the wines of their regions, how they set about tasting and enjoying them, and how they partner them with food.

Scenes from the biography of the vine and of wine

This picture of the wines of France and the areas in which they are grown would be incomplete, however, without a thorough, detailed description of everything that has so far constituted the biography of the vine and of wine. In a series of lavishly illustrated and documented panoramas, from *terroir* to tasting, the reader may take part in the grape harvest, in vinification, and in the many forms and metamorphoses of wine. He or she will learn of wine diseases, and of the way that wine is kept and aged; as well as how to buy and taste in a knowledgeable and informed manner.

At this stage in its biography, wine assumes a cultural and social dimension, and this is evoked in a collection of articles dealing with its history, its symbolic role, its place in art and in museums, its effect on our health, its economic importance and its future.

A fully illustrated work

A large number of illustrative aids have been put at the reader's disposal to help convey ideas that are sometimes complex, and to facilitate absorption of the vast amount of information the book contains. There are some 25 maps in colour, drawn by a specialist wine cartographer, that show each region in detail, and that locate each *appellation* accurately. There are more than a dozen geological sections and diagrams to help explain why a particular grape variety performs better in one *terroir* than in another. A number of illustrations reveal details that photography is unable to show with the same precision.

The many photographs — about 500, all of them in colour — are relevant and telling. They are an indispensable accompaniment to the text, not only illustrating it but constituting a supplementary source of information.

Finally, economic and scientific data are presented in charts and diagrams that make them easier to grasp than if they had been immersed in continuous text.

The book has three essential appendices: a Glossary of French Tasting Terms contains all the French words, with English equivalents, that are used to define the sensory characteristics of wine, its savours, aromas, tastes and faults; a Technical Glossary explains all the technical terms that the reader is likely to encounter in reading the work; and the Index will enable the reader to refer rapidly to any grape variety, *appellation*, vineyard area, town, *cru*, *climat*, technique or any other element required.

This, then, is *Wines and Vineyards of France*, a book whose encyclopedic scope will, it is hoped, earn the approval of all its readers, whether professionals, informed amateurs, or newcomers to the appreciation of wine.

PIERRE ANGLADE

List of Maps and Sections

The maps in this book have been produced with the aid of cartographic reference material supplied by the French Institut Géographique National.

The boundaries of the wine-growing areas have been determined by means of a communal survey. The whole area of any commune has been included when any part of its territory is entitled to benefit from the appellation *in question, whether AOC, VDQS or* vin de pays.

For ease of reading, only information directly relating to the wine-growing areas and their geographical location is included in the maps.

MAPS OF THE WINE-GROWING AREAS

GEOLOGICAL MAPS AND SECTIONS

FRENCH WINE-GROWING AREAS

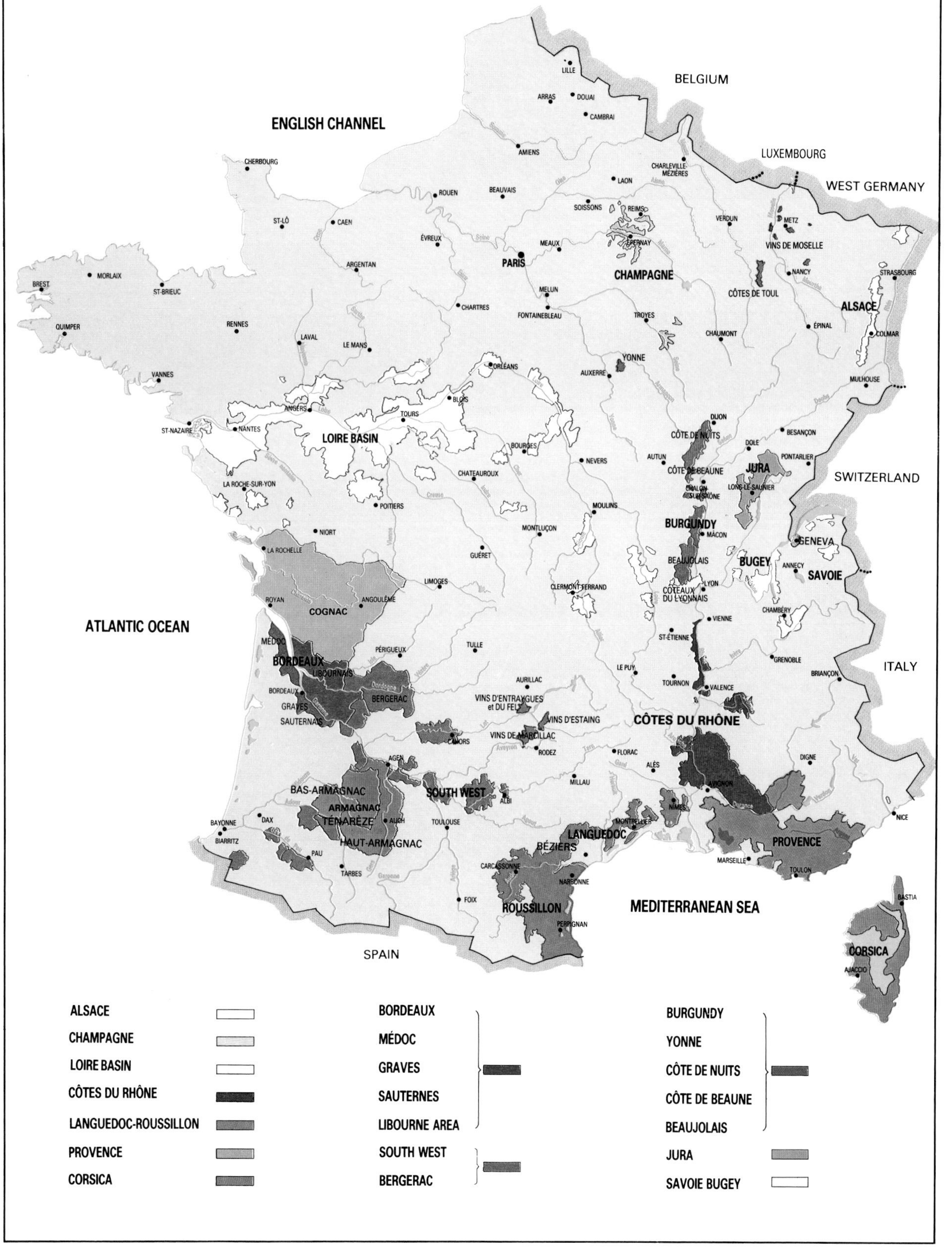

A

Abondance Noir

Synonyms: *Abondance de Doui, Gamay d'Orléans, Pineau Rouge, Plant de Bazouge.*

Bunches large, 20–25cm, winged, conical, compact; grapes spherical, black, small, 10–12mm, juicy; ripening period: second epoch.

A very vigorous, productive variety, the Abondance Noir produces a *vin ordinaire*, with little colour and low alcohol content; formerly used for making sparkling wines. It is grown throughout the Loire valley.

Abondant Blanc

Crossing of the Steinschiller or Kövdinka Rose × Sylvaner, classed as an 'authorized' variety in Alsace and Moselle. Gives a *vin ordinaire*, low in alcohol and rather flat.

Abouriou Noir

Synonyms: *Plant Abouriou, Beaujolais* in Lot-et-Garonne, *Gamay du Rhône* in Lot, *Précoce Naugé, Précoce Dordogne, Noir Hâtif* in Dordogne, *Malbec Argenté* in the Médoc, *Gamay-Beaujolais* in Entre-Deux-Mers, *Négret de la Conourgue, Gamay Saint-Laurent.*

Growing tips felty white with carmine margins. Young leaves downy with bronze areas. Leaves medium sized, orbicular, contorted, finely bullate, lobes convex; lateral sinus of medium depth and pointed at bottom, petiolar sinus lyrate; dentation convex, medium sized; underside of blade pubescent, rough.

Green shoots ribbed, with pink nodes. Bunches medium sized, compact; grapes spherical, medium sized, black, juicy; ripening period: first epoch, early.

Vigorous, fertile, with early budbreak, this variety was discovered in Lot-et-Garonne in 1882. It is relatively resistant to oidium (powdery mildew), downy mildew and to grey rot (botrytis). Its wine has a rich colour but is flat and lacking in character. Grown on 600ha in the South West (Lot-et-Garonne, Tarn-et-Garonne, Haut-Garonne) and in Loire-Atlantique. It is classed as a 'recommended' variety in many *départements*, and has three registered clones: numbers 539, 603 and 604.

Ahumat

Synonym: *Enfumé* in the Béarn region.

Bunches medium sized, conical; grapes spherical or slightly ovoid, small, golden white to bronze-pink, a colour which, in combination with the bloom, gives the fruit a smoky appearance; ripening period: second epoch, late.

This is a Jurançon variety, unclassified and therefore with a limited future. In the past it was stake-trained, and pruned long and lightly. It is vulnerable to oidium (powdery mildew).

Ajaccio

The wine-growing area of this Corsican *appellation*, classified as an AOC on 3 April 1984, covers 220ha out of a total potential growing zone of 22,620ha. Its production at present remains comparatively steady: 7,429hl of classified wines in 1979–80 and 6,914hl in 1983–4. Two thirds of this production comes from private growers, the remaining third from a small cooperative. The *appellation* area stretches over a large region of dry hills of granitic sand, with a lot of clay in places.

The grape varieties planted in this *appellation* zone are the most typically Corsican of any on the island, with 46.29 per cent Sciaccarello, 5.11 per cent Nielluccio, 12 per cent Vermentino, and 3.91 per cent of various reds and whites - in fact 67.31 per cent of the vines are purely Corsican.

The white wines, based on the Vermentino grape variety, are dry, fruity, full bodied, with an aftertaste reminiscent of hazelnuts. The straightforward, well-structured rosés age well. The reds, ranging in colour from a clear ruby to a deep purple-red, have a good deal of tannin and need at least three years' ageing. They have an aroma in which pepper, redcurrant, blackcurrant and almond scents are combined.

A wine-growing estate in the Ajaccio **appellation**, *where long-lasting red and rosé wines are produced. The white wines are dominated by the characteristics of the Vermentino grape.*

Leaf of the Alicante Bouschet, a productive red-wine variety with deeply coloured juice.

Leaf of the white-wine variety Aligoté, grown mainly in Burgundy.

Aleatico Noir

A Tuscan grape variety, musky, very close to the Muscat à Petits Grains Rouges; it is grown to a modest extent (26ha) on Corsica.

Alicante Bouschet

A Teinturier (red-fleshed) crossing, Petit Bouschet × Grenache, made by Henri Bouschet.

Growing tips felty white with notably carmine margins.

Young leaves downy, bullate, with red on bulges; underside of blade felty, pink-white. Leaves orbicular, thick, glossy, bullate with margins of blade markedly convex, either without lobes or only slightly three-lobed; petiolar sinus lyrate and practically closed; dentation convex, medium sized though not very noticeable because of the curling margins of the blade, which has white down on underside, with arachnoid and pubescent principal veins. The foliage turns completely red in autumn.

Green shoots ribbed, downy at the tip, with red-brown striations; long tendrils.

Bunches large, winged, conical, loose; grapes spherical, medium sized, black with abundant bloom; richly coloured juice; ripening period: second epoch, early.

A productive variety, budbreak midseason, generally pruned short, with some resistance to oidium (powdery mildew) but vulnerable to downy mildew, phomopsis, anthracnose, and much affected by bacterial infections. There are three registered clones: numbers 262 (the most important), 540 and 620.

The wine of the Alicante Bouschet has a fine bright red colour and attains high alcohol levels when the grapes have ripened on favourable hill slopes; it is often used in blending to add colour to wines from flat sites, which lack it.

Alicante Bouschet is classed as 'recommended' in most wine-growing *départements* and the variety is grown on a total area of 22,000ha, putting it in 11th place among French varieties. Of this total, the Languedoc vineyards account for 15,000ha, Provence and Corsica together for 4,600ha and the vineyards of the Aquitaine area for 1,200ha.

Aligoté

Synonyms: *Giboudot Blanc* in Rully, *Griset Blanc* at Beaune, *Plant Gris* on the Côte de Nuits, *Plant de Trois Raisins* north of Dijon, *Chaudenet Gras* on the Côte Chalonnaise, *Vert Blanc* in Jura.

Growing tips downy white with pink margins. Young leaves arachnoid, pale green. Leaves orbicular, medium sized, without lobes, bullate with convex edges; petiolar sinus lyrate; dentation pointed, medium sized; underside of blade arachnoid and pubescent. Green shoots ribbed, reddish or purplish; tendrils brown, short and thin. Bunches small, cylindrical or conical, loose; grapes spherical, small, orange-white and flecked with brown; ripening period: first epoch.

The Aligoté is a white Burgundy grape, vigorous, with early budbreak, hardy and thriving on slopes where it regularly yields 50hl/ha. Affected little by oidium (powdery mildew), it is vulnerable to downy mildew, black rot, anthracnose and grey rot (botrytis). Five registered clones have been approved: numbers 263, 402, 264, 591 and 651.

The wine of the Aligoté is light, slightly acid, fresh, low in tannins and with little scent. It is entitled to a special *appellation*: that of Bourgogne Aligoté. It is a wine that is best drunk as young as possible. It is often mixed with Crème de Cassis and drunk as an aperitif — Kir, named after Canon Kir, deputy mayor of Dijon, who made it fashionable after 1945.

With its 1,128ha the Aligoté is only the 52nd most grown variety in France, and its cultivation is very largely a Burgundian affair: 550ha in Côte-d'Or, 345ha in Saône-et-Loire, 212ha in Yonne. There are also a few small areas planted with it in Ain, Allier, Savoie, Drôme, Ardèche, Isère, Rhône and the Loire valley.

Aloxe-Corton

This wine-growing village in Burgundy's Côte de Beaune received its *appellation d'origine contrôlée* on 11 March 1938, extending over sites totalling 87ha within the commune boundaries of Aloxe-Corton, Pernand-Vergelesses and Ladoix-Serrigny. It should be noted, however, that in addition to this commune *appellation* there is another, Aloxe-Corton Premier Cru, covering a total area of 29ha. Its mostly red wines — whites make up only 1 per cent of production — come from Pinot Noir vines. The official minimum alcoholic strength is 10.5°, with 11° set for the Premiers Crus; and the maximum yield is fixed at 40hl/ha. Wines from the Corton, Corton-Charlemagne and Charlemagne vineyards can be included in the Aloxe-Corton *appellation*, using the Premier Cru title, if they do not fulfil all the conditions of their own Grand Cru status requirements (under which no village name need be mentioned). Aloxe-Corton wines are generally powerful, soundly constituted and agreeable, but without the breadth found in the wines of the very best neighbouring sites. They are somewhat hard and unyielding to begin with, but fill out and mellow with age.

Alsace *See* the following page.

Alsace

This AOC is governed by an edict of 2 November 1945 that defined the statutes of Alsace wines, supplemented by further legislation, the latest dating from 19 October 1974.

The Alsace *appellation* can be followed by grape names: Gewürztraminer, Muscat, Pinot Blanc, Pinot Gris or Tokay d'Alsace, Pinot Noir, Riesling, Sylvaner, Chasselas or Gutedel; or by that of the 'noble mixture': Edelzwicker.

Alsace Grand Cru

This comparatively recent AOC was defined by the decree of 23 November 1975, listing the first of the approved vineyards. (*See* the panel opposite and the regional entry on the following page.)

Altesse

Synonyms: *Roussette* in Savoie, *Roussette Haute* at Seyssel, *Mâconnais, Petit Mâconnais, Prin Blanc* in Savoie, *Ignan Blanc* at Bourgoin, *Arin* at Chabons, *Sérène Blanche* at Voreppe.

Bunches small to medium sized, cylindrical, quite compact, often winged, on a peduncle that is rather long and slender, holding the grapes away from the branch; grapes spherical or slightly ovoid, small, with thick skins, reddish yellow when ripe, becoming bronze-pink, almost lilac, when the fruit wrinkles and shrinks as a result of *pourriture noble* (noble rot); flesh juicy; ripening period: second epoch, late.

This Savoie variety, producing wines of quality, appears to have been brought back from the island of Cyprus by a duke of Savoy in the 15th century. Three registered clones have been approved: numbers 265, 403 and 404. This vine is very susceptible to downy mildew, but resists oidium (powdery mildew) and grey rot (botrytis) well, and can therefore be late-harvested.

Various kinds of wine are made from the Altesse (or Roussette) in Savoie. By itself, it produces a full-bodied dry white wine, 10–13° alcohol, very fragrant and of great distinction when well made. This wine is produced in the *appellation* of Seyssel. The Altesse can also be mixed with other grape varieties (like the Chardonnay or the Mondeuse Blanche) to produce Vin de Savoie, Roussette de Savoie or Roussette de Bugey, with or without a *cru* name; these wines can be dry or sweet, *pétillant* or sparkling. The Altesse is grown on 130 ha, divided between Ain and Savoie.

Stake-trained vines at Hunawihr, near Riquewihr in Alsace.

THE ALSACE GRAND CRU AOC

Vineyard Sites	Communes
Altenberg de Bergbieten	*Bergbeiten*
Altenberg de Bergheim	*Bergheim*
Brand	*Turckheim*
Eichberg	*Eguisheim*
Geisberg	*Ribeauvillé*
Gloeckelberg	*Rodern & Saint-Hippolyte*
Goldert	*Gueberschwihr*
Hatschbourg	*Hattstatt & Voegtlinshoffen*
Hengst	*Wintzenheim*
Kanzlerberg	*Bergheim*
Kastelberg	*Andlau*
Kessler	*Guebwiller*
Kirchberg de Barr	*Barr*
Kirchberg de Ribeauvillé	*Ribeauvillé*
Kitterlé	*Guebwiller*
Moenchberg	*Andlau & Eichhoffen*
Ollwiller	*Wuenheim*
Rangen	*Thann & Vieux-Thann*
Rosacker	*Hunawihr*
Saering	*Guebwiller*
Schlossberg	*Kaysersberg Kientzheim*
Sommerberg	*Niedermorschwihr & Katzenthal*
Sonnenglanz	*Beblenheim*
Speigel	*Bergholts & Guebwiller*
Wiebelsberg	*Andlau*

***Only wines made from the Riesling, Muscat, Pinot Gris and Gewürztraminer grape varieties enjoy the right to this* appellation.**

ALSACE

The Alsace wine-growing region is the only one in France to have named its wines after their grape varieties, thus giving happy expression to the maxim of Olivier de Serres (1539–1619): 'The genius of a wine lies in its vine.' More recently Alsace has linked its name to its* crus *and so has paid merited homage to the sites that delineate one of the most beautiful of France's wine routes.

The geographical situation of the Alsace wine region makes it one of the most northerly in France. Set in the far north-east of the French hexagon, it stretches over the two *départements* of Bas-Rhin and Haut-Rhin, between the Vosges mountains and the plain of Alsace: a narrow corridor of land running from Marlenheim in the north to Thann in the south. It is 120km long and nowhere more than 4km wide. In the north of Bas-Rhin, separated from the main wine-growing area, there is a small 200 ha enclave formed by the Wissembourg wine-growing district. Apart from a little red or rosé wine from the Pinot Noir, Alsace is distinguished by its remarkable white wines, each with very specific characteristics.

***R**iquewihr boasts a remarkable number of beautifully preserved 16th-century houses. In this period, wine growing in Alsace was thriving.*

The history of wine growing in Alsace

Although fossilized grape pips and vine wood dating from about 3000 BC have been discovered in Alsace — probably remains of the wild wine *Vitis silvestris* — it is generally agreed that the cultivation of the European vine *Vitis vinifera* began in Alsace with the Roman invasion of the Rhine valley. There is, however, much less certainty about when commercial wine growing started here. The impetus for this would have come in the 3rd century AD, the period during which Romans officially authorized the cultivation of the vine in Alsace. Except in the 5th century, when Germanic invasions took place, the vine became increasingly important, reaching its zenith in the 16th century. The origin of this development lay, without any doubt, in the opening up of the Rhine as a waterway. This allowed the export of Alsace wines to all the countries through whose territories the river flowed — and to others that could be reached by waterborne trade, such as England.

This was, consequently, the era that made the fortunes of the great Rhineland towns, Strasbourg among them, as well as those of the wine-growing communities. Many of the houses of the period, now the pride of Alsatian villages, bear witness still to this prosperity. However, the Thirty Years War, in the 17th century, checked the expansion of wine growing, and it was not until the 19th century that security and prosperity returned fully to the region. Unfortunately, wine growing with the aim of mass production now made its appearance and after the annexation of Alsace by Germany in 1871, this policy was further encouraged. The phylloxera blight aggravated the situation still more, for the grower of this period generally replaced his ravaged vines with direct producing (ungrafted) hybrids with some resistance to this parasite, even though the wine they gave was of miserable quality. Only after 1918 and the return of Alsace to France was there any move back towards quality wines: the task of restoring health and individuality to the vineyards was a long one, ending only after 1945 with the establishment of the present regulations.

The Alsace wine laws

There are three *appellations d'origine contrôlée* in Alsace: AOC Alsace, AOC Alsace Grand Cru and AOC Crémant d'Alsace. To the first two, the qualifications Vendange Tardive and Sélection de Grains Nobles can be added. These terms are defined in the legislation of 1 March 1984. In particular, the musts have to contain the minimum sugar content shown below.

MINIMUM NATURAL SUGAR CONTENT OF MUSTS		
Wines	Vendange Tardive	Sélection de Grains Nobles
Gewürztraminer	243 g/l	279 g/l
Pinot Gris	243 g/l	279 g/l
Riesling	220 g/l	256 g/l
Muscat	220 g/l	256 g/l

Crémant d'Alsace is a sparkling wine obtained by secondary fermentation in bottle.

For each of the *appellations*, the area of production is defined, and also the authorized grape varieties, conditions of production and legal requirements in so far as they affect the pruning of the vines, minimum alcohol content and the yield. It should also be pointed out that Alsace is the only French region that insists on its wines being bottled in the two *départements* where they are produced, Bas-Rhin and Haut-Rhin.

For all three *appellations* the regional committee of the Institut National des Appellations d'Origine (INAO) fixes the date for the start of the grape harvest — the *ban des vendanges* — as well as the annual production conditions.

The geography and climate of the Alsace wine-growing region

Vines are planted on the foothills of the Vosges, as well as on the lower slopes of the mountains themselves. They rise in terraces from the Alsatian plain, at 180m, to 380m. The latter height is the upper limit for the vine in Alsace. Grown on the eastern slopes of the Vosges, preferably in south- or southeast-facing situations, the vines benefit from the natural screen provided by the mountains, which partly protect them from the otherwise maritime climatic influences. Rainfall varies between 500 and 700mm a year (500mm at Colmar), whereas the tops of the Vosges experience 2,000mm of rain a year.

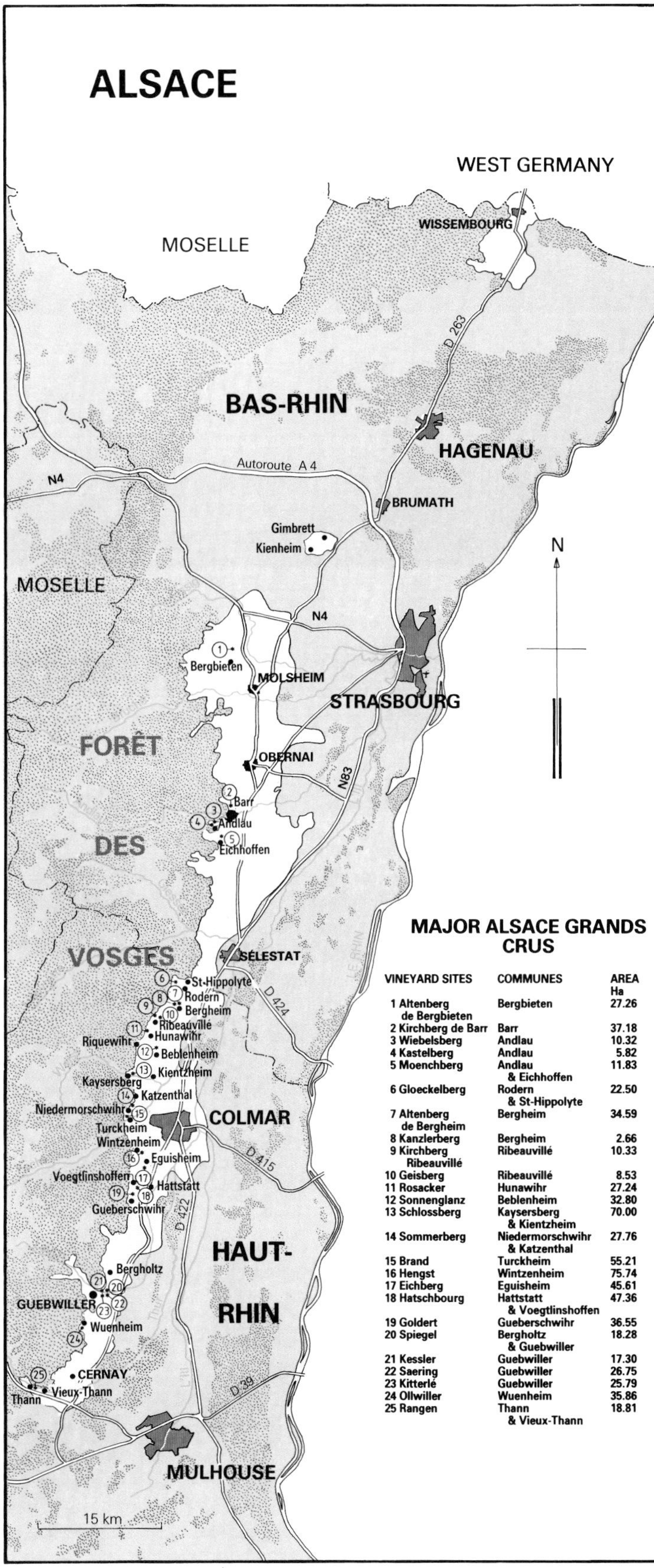

MAJOR ALSACE GRANDS CRUS

VINEYARD SITES	COMMUNES	AREA Ha
1 Altenberg de Bergbieten	Bergbieten	27.26
2 Kirchberg de Barr	Barr	37.18
3 Wiebelsberg	Andlau	10.32
4 Kastelberg	Andlau	5.82
5 Moenchberg	Andlau & Eichhoffen	11.83
6 Gloeckelberg	Rodern & St-Hippolyte	22.50
7 Altenberg de Bergheim	Bergheim	34.59
8 Kanzlerberg	Bergheim	2.66
9 Kirchberg Ribeauvillé	Ribeauvillé	10.33
10 Geisberg	Ribeauvillé	8.53
11 Rosacker	Hunawihr	27.24
12 Sonnenglanz	Beblenheim	32.80
13 Schlossberg	Kaysersberg & Kientzheim	70.00
14 Sommerberg	Niedermorschwihr & Katzenthal	27.76
15 Brand	Turckheim	55.21
16 Hengst	Wintzenheim	75.74
17 Eichberg	Eguisheim	45.61
18 Hatschbourg	Hattstatt & Voegtlinshoffen	47.36
19 Goldert	Gueberschwihr	36.55
20 Spiegel	Bergholtz & Guebwiller	18.28
21 Kessler	Guebwiller	17.30
22 Saering	Guebwiller	26.75
23 Kitterlé	Guebwiller	25.79
24 Ollwiller	Wuenheim	35.86
25 Rangen	Thann & Vieux-Thann	18.81

THE ALSACE PLAIN IN THE QUATERNARY PERIOD

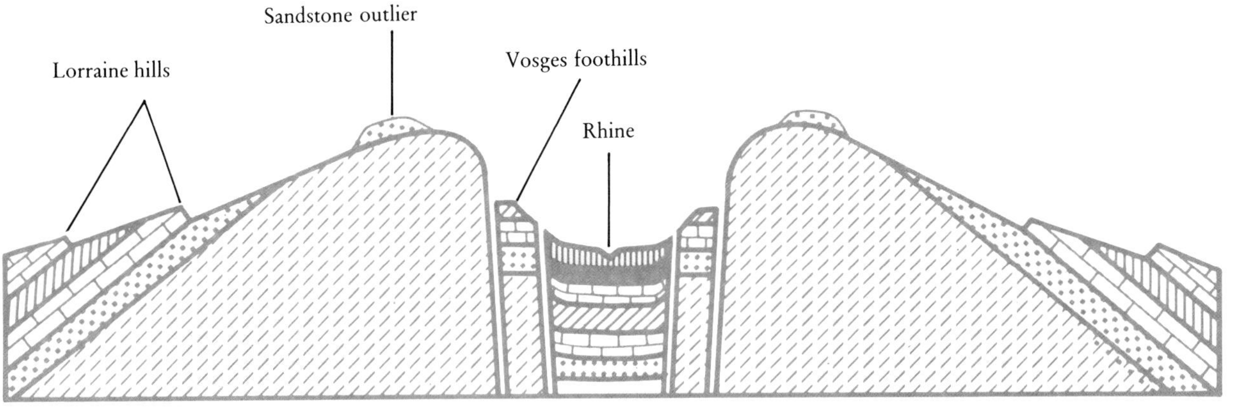

The 0°C isotherm runs wholly to the east of the Rhine, and does not include Alsace. The swift rise in temperature in the spring is due to the influence of the mild *föhn* wind that blows over the Alsatian plain from north to south and brings on the opening of the vine buds. The warm summers are often conducive to abundant leaf and plant growth. Autumns tend to be long and mild, and these conditions are favourable to a slow and perfect ripening of the grapes.

Geological structure of the wine-growing area

The Rhine plain has its origin in the collapse, some 50 million years ago, of the highest part of a former massif that had joined the Vosges to the Black Forest. The vines are grown in the areas of these ancient fractures. The rocky or stony outcrops here are very varied, revealing nearly all the ground formations that have appeared in the course of the various geological periods. In the flatter areas, the terrain consists mainly of sediments, some of them alluvial.

Detail from a carved stone façade at Mittelbergheim.

Production

The Alsace *appellation* extends over 56 communes in Haut-Rhin and 64 in Bas-Rhin. The present area of wine growing is 12,600 ha and total production averages between 900,000 and 1,000,000 hl a year, with about the same quantity being sold each year (in 1985 the figure was 950,000 hl).

The grape varieties and their taste characteristics

The wines of Alsace have a twofold originality: they are characterized by an aromatic richness that is remarkable in its finesse and its style; and, with one exception, they bear the name of the grape variety they are made from. Only Edelzwicker is made from a blend of grape varieties.

It is customary to classify the different grape varieties into two groups, according to the degree of impact, potential for longevity and intensity of aroma possessed by each.

The first group comprises the Chasselas, Sylvaner, Pinot Blanc and Auxerrois grapes, which give light, very drinkable and agreeably fruity wines.

The second group includes the varieties from which the greatest wines of Alsace are made, namely the Riesling, Muscat, Pinot Gris or Tokay d'Alsace, Pinot Noir and Gewürztraminer.

Chasselas This grape variety represents 2.15 per cent of production. Few wines are sold under this name, but wines made from the Chasselas go into the Edelzwicker blend. It is in a steady decline as it is very liable to *coulure* (flower abortion) and its yield therefore fluctuates greatly; in addition, the wine it produces, although very agreeable, does not have the same richness of taste when grown in Alsace as the other varieties.

Sylvaner A variety that, with its very regular yield (providing 20 per cent of total production), is gradually replacing the Chasselas to form an important proportion of the region's vines. Along with Edelzwicker it has the highest immediate consumption rate: this is the 'wine for everyday and every moment'. It is a pleasantly fruity wine with appealing freshness; when grown on a good site, it can achieve a remarkable combination of strength, fruit and body.

Pinot Blanc (Klevner) and Auxerrois With 18.7 per cent of total production between them, these two grape varieties are the origin of the wine customarily called Pinot Blanc (or Klevner, a local name; Pinot Auxerrois is also seen). They also make up the larger part of the wines used in making Crémant d'Alsace. For this reason planting has increased strikingly over the last decade. Pinot Blanc wine possesses agreeable fruit, set off by a very pleasing freshness and body.

Riesling This grape represents 20.17 per cent of production and its wines are among the most prestigious and renowned of Alsace. The often fine autumn weather of the region, contributing to slow, full ripening, suits the variety perfectly. The wine often achieves a perfect balance between exquisite fruit that can be of either a vegetal or a mineral character, acidity that is fresh and vivacious, and great fullness of body. In a remarkable way, too, Riesling can express the distinctive aromas of overripened grapes.

Muscat This is a dry wine accounting for 3 per cent of production, delicately musky, with — at best — a fullness of body in unison with its seductive aromatic richness.

Pinot Gris or Tokay d'Alsace This variety makes up 4.19 per cent of production. The traditional understanding was that the grape came to Alsace from Hungary, hence the name 'Tokay'. However, there are strong reasons today for presuming the variety came from Burgundy.

Compared to the other fine wines of the region, the aromatic character of the Pinot Gris is subdued. Its fragrance may be floral (sometimes reminiscent of violets), or suggest dried fruit or even hazelnuts. On the palate the wine is full bodied, with perfect harmony between its component parts. It is an alcoholic, heady wine when it has been made from very ripe grapes (Vendange Tardive) becoming sweeter and unctuous when made from carefully picked grapes affected by *pourriture noble* or noble rot (Sélection de Grains Nobles). This is a wine that must be well-made: mediocre examples are invariably disappointing. When well made and well aged, Pinot Gris is one of the greatest wines of Alsace.

Pinot Noir This variety constitutes 6.14 per cent of production; giving rosé and red wines only, it is the exception to the white-wine rule of Alsace wine growing. However, Pinot Noir wines have been produced for many decades at Marlenheim, Ottrott, Saint-Hippolyte, Rodern and Turckheim, a tradition that has been perpetuated and developed in recent years. Deliciously fresh and fruity rosés, and aromatic red wines with the potential for ageing, are the result.

Guwürztraminer This grape variety, representing 19.18 per cent of production, has undoubtedly found its favourite environment in Alsace. It offers complex nuances of aroma and taste, according to the microclimates and *terroirs* in and on which it is grown. With time, it can become a delicate, even lacy, wine. The power and generosity of its body lifts its aroma into prominence: it can be deliciously spicy, very floral, or it may even recall certain dried fruits, especially when the grapes it is made from reach a high degree of ripeness.

THE CONFRÉRIE SAINT-ÉTIENNE D'ALSACE

Ninety per cent of the town of Ammerschwihr, a true jewel of the Middle Ages, was destroyed in 1945. Resolutely the inhabitants rebuilt their home, giving priority to wine cellars and to rebuilding work connected with wine production — one of the main reasons for the town's existence. One citizen of an old local family, Joseph Dreyer, made up his mind to take a direct part in this renewal, and in the advancement of local wine. He revived an ancient and forgotten guild of townsmen that went under the name of 'Herrenstubengesellschaft'; this guild had, of old, watched over the quality of wines leaving Ammerschwihr. The great annual meeting of the society was always held on 26 December, the Feast of Saint Stephen, and it finally came to be known by this saint's name ('Étienne' is the French form of 'Stephen'). The name was adopted by the revived fraternity, which soon represented the whole of Alsace wine growing.

In 1957 the confrérie *created its own Sigille de Qualité, guaranteeing the merit of the wines that pass its examination, and in awarding it, the* confrérie *recalls its precursor's original role.*

The administration of the distinction has placed a considerable burden of responsibility on the confrérie, *but it has also brought with it the honour of presenting to the customer and connoisseur the best and most characteristic wines of the Alsace vineyards.*

Since 1976, the Confrérie Saint-Étienne d'Alsace has been based at the Château de Kientzheim, a superb historic building that houses a remarkable museum of Alsace wines, making it doubly attractive to the members and public. With the many activities it has in hand, the fraternity contributes greatly to the widening appreciation and understanding of Alsace and its wines.

Costume of the Confrérie Saint-Étienne d'Alsace.

Edelzwicker This wine is sold in relatively large quantities and is made by blending various grape varieties. There is no specific rule governing this but the general recommendation is that the characteristics of any one of the grape varieties used in the blend should not predominate over the others.

Vines near Kientzheim. As in most northern wine regions, the vines are pruned long in Alsace.

The Monument du vigneron alsacien *(the Alsatian Wine Grower Monument), Colmar, by Frédéric Auguste Bartholdi, sculptor of New York's famous Statue of Liberty ('Liberty Enlightening the World').*

Making and ageing the wines

White wines, which represent about 94 per cent of total production from the Alsace vineyards, are made according to the customary principles of white wine vinification. Maceration and oxidization are avoided as far as possible during harvesting and the must is pressed out as quickly as possible. After the primary, alcoholic fermentation has occurred, secondary or malolactic fermentation is prevented from taking place. Bottling the wine follows, six to eight months after the harvest, and is generally completed before the following year's vintage.

The wines are therefore kept for a relatively short time in vats or large casks, so they acquire the aromas of maturity for the most part in bottle. Generally they attain the full development of their qualities after two to five years, and they will remain at a peak for a comparatively long time subsequently — five to ten years on average. The very greatest Alsace wines, those of exceptional quality, can be aged for much longer. Some of them maintain their qualities for decades, the length of the ageing period being a function of the initial constitution of the vintage in question.

Selling the wines

According to harvest declaration figures, the average area of holdings in Alsace is about 1.15 ha, leading to the conclusion that many wine growers have more than one job and that viticulture is not their main occupation. It also shows that land ownership in the Alsace wine region is very fragmented, with relatively few holdings of large size.

The whole wine-growing and -marketing fraternity has been grouped together in the Comité Interprofessionnel des Vins d'Alsace (CIVA), and the various branches of the profession are each represented on the Comité.

VINTAGES

Like all wine-growing areas, Alsace experiences good or very good years as well as less good ones. Vintages since 1945 worthy of mention are: 1947, 1949, 1953, 1959, 1961*, 1964, 1971*, 1976*, 1983*, 1985 (asterisks signal years considered exceptionally good).*

Sales of Alsace wines are secured by three categories of vendor, in the following percentages:

▷ wine growers: 25 per cent;
▷ wine cooperatives: 34 per cent;
▷ *négociants* (shippers or merchants): 41 per cent.

The annual volume exported is nearly 300,000 hl, which is about 31 per cent of all sales of Alsace wine.

Wine's role in Alsatian life

Thanks to the unceasing efforts of local *viticulteurs*, Alsace wine growing occupies a

Grape harvest at Riquewihr. In Alsace, grapes are often picked by hand rather than mechanically because of the steepness of the slopes.

L'AUBERGE DE L'ILL

I was familiar with vines long before I knew about wine. I went to school at Ribeauvillé, the old château of the lords of Ribeaupierre, with its vineyards all around. While playing there I discovered, quite physically, the grapes, the foliage and the soil of our hillsides. My first gourmet memories also date from this time, when I came to realize how the scent from the wine press heralded the sweet nectar of fresh grape juice. Sharper, but no less distinctive, was the odour of the wine that the great wooden casks seemed steeped in ... I was small then, and the only one able to climb, through a tiny door, into the casks to clean each out with a brush. Every autumn, I too was entitled to the threefold treat of our part of the world: country bread, newly shelled nuts and a little Fatterwisse — heady new wine with a milky appearance.

Strangely enough it was a Burgundian grower who introduced me to wine tasting. He came to Alsace every year to hunt and was at pains to acquaint me with the wines of Burgundy. One day I found him in spirited discussion with his wife about how to match the freshly skinned rabbit he held in his hand with an appropriate wine — and I became aware of the importance of wine in gastronomy, and from that, of the immense depth of France's culinary riches.

What a wonderful country I live in, where the preparation of a dish is a subject for endless discussion!

After the war, my brother and I took over our family inn. We worked hard at perpetuating our ancestral recipes: fried dishes, frogs' legs, crayfish, and above all matelote of eels in Riesling. I had previously studied at the Beaux Arts, so I was able to apply my aesthetic training both to the décor and the dishes themselves. Gradually our inn and our menu became more amply furnished. However, we always took care that secondary matters did not usurp primary concerns: in our trade, the pleasures of the palate come before those of the eyes.

The Riesling is held to be the king of Alsace wines — and justly so, in my opinion, for it has the merit of combining a crisp dryness with great fruit. I find that no other white wine goes so well with chicken (as in poulet au Riesling), white meats, sea or river fish, or crustaceans. Aged Riesling, in particular, lends itself marvellously to sauces.

I never despise a simple little Pinot Blanc, fresh and gulpable, as a start to a meal or to accompany our Alsace charcuteries; but to my taste the most delicious pairing is that of the Tokay (Pinot Gris) with fresh Alsace foie gras en terrine. The success of this partnership lies in the balance between the slightly acidulated sweetness of the Tokay and the rich aromatic quality of the foie gras.

There are, of course, a host of other happy marriages between Alsace wines and the subtle preparations of French cuisine, for everyone to appreciate according to his own particular desires and sensibilities. For wine can only speak to responsive spirits, as the following anecdote shows.

Alsace wine is reputed not to age well. We were able to demonstrate quite the contrary recently when, with a number of friends, we tasted bottles of Riesling and Gewürztraminer more than 100 years old, discovered in a cellar in Riquewihr. Before opening them, we were afraid we should find water. There was none; and as we drank we all experienced a deep, indeed almost religious emotion; so much so that there were tears in our eyes. Proof, if such were needed, that Alsace wine, even of a great age, keeps all its powers.

Jean-Pierre Haeberlin

An Alsace wine merchant's traditional wrought-iron sign.

Itterswiller: this village, situated on a hillside near Andlau, reveals the characteristic harmony of architecture and vineyard in Alsace.

The long, tapering, green flûte is the only bottle type authorized for Alsace wines.

favoured position both within the region and in the wider French context. Alsace wine growers, deeply attached to their province, have managed to keep their traditions very much alive. These are embodied in numerous celebrations and events held in villages as renowned for the riches of their history and architecture as they are for their wines. A wine route, picturesque throughout the year, but particularly splendid in autumn colours, enables the traveller to discover a succession of these charmingly spruce old wine villages.

Detail of a large cask dating from 1751, in the Musée Unterlinden in Colmar, where the Issenheim Altarpiece can also be seen.

Viticultural tradition is also evident in museums that give prominence to wine-growing collections, in particular the Musée Unterlinden in Colmar and the Musée du Vin in Kientzheim. Although the former, one of the most visited of all French museums, has been made famous by its paintings, including Grünewald's Issenheim Altarpiece, it also devotes generous space to the history of wine growing in Alsace. The Kientzheim museum is in the precincts of the château there. It traces the history of wine growing in Alsace in the context of more general viti- and vinicultural evolution over the last few centuries.

The Alsace wine region is divided into subdistricts and each in its turn shows its products to the public — essentially the wines of the current year. Wine Fairs (Foires aux Vins) are generally also organized in the bigger centres: Ammerschwihr, in April; Molsheim, 1 May; Guebwiller, Ascension Day; Barr, around 14 July; Ribeauvillé, the last weekend in July. Colmar, acknowledged capital of the wine region, holds a great Foire aux Vins for all Alsace wines during the ten days before 15 August.

Anjou *See* the following page.

Anjou

This wine region was classified as an AOC in legislation dated 31 December 1957. It covers some 8,000 ha with an average annual production over the last ten years of 85,000 hl of white, 73,000 hl of red and 216,000 hl of rosé wine. The area extends over 198 communes in Maine-et-Loire, Deux-Sèvres and Vienne.

The white wines come mainly from the Chenin Blanc grape (80 per cent), with the Chardonnay and Sauvignon Blanc varieties making up the balance. The reds are made from the Cabernet Franc and Cabernet Sauvignon grapes, as well as the Pineau d'Aunis. The Gamay is reserved exclusively for the Anjou Gamay *appellation* among the red wines. For the rosé wines, the Cabernet Franc, Cabernet Sauvignon, Pineau d'Aunis, Gamay, Côt and Grolleau varieties are all used.

The white wines are quite full in colour, with a straw-yellow hue tending towards gold in wines that have been aged. Aromas are striking, with a vegetal character. On the palate they are off-dry to semi-sweet, balanced by well-developed acidity, the consequence of their not undergoing a malolactic fermentation. They have a persistent finish, and a remarkable capacity for ageing in bottle.

The characteristic colour of the rosés is called *oeil-de-perdrix* (literally 'partridge eye'), understood as being a brilliant pale red in this region. They are just off-dry to semi-sweet in type. Their finesse is brought them by the Grolleau grape, and this characteristic underlies their prominent fruitiness. They finish well on the palate and can be aged.

The Cabernet Franc and Sauvignon grapes distinguish the red wines. These wines are slightly tannic, but full, with fruit in their bouquets. They are best drunk young. (*See* Anjou and Saumur.)

Anjou-Coteaux de la Loire

This district, classified as an AOC in legislation dated 26 August 1946, covers an area of 50 ha with the Chenin Blanc as the only grape variety. Production over the last five years has been around 1,200 hl per year. The wine-growing area stretches over 11 communes or parts of communes. The wines are full in colour, yellow with a slight green glint; as they age they tend towards gold. The nature of the schistous soil the vines grow in marks the wines' bouquet. They are strong and firm on the palate, but at the same time supple, and they finish well. They are suitable for ageing.

Anjou Gamay

A wine produced in the Anjou *appellation*, exclusively from the Gamay Noir à Jus Blanc grape variety.

Anjou Mousseux

The area of production of this sparkling wine AOC extends over the same communes as are grouped in the Anjou *appellation*. An average annual 3,000 hl has been produced in recent years from grape varieties identical to those of the Anjou Pétillant *appellation*.

Anjou Mousseux is gently sparkling. It is a full, lively wine with some firmness, and can age well.

Anjou Pétillant

The potential of this *appellation* is considerable, but not many growers lay claim to this *pétillant* (very slightly sparkling) wine AOC, defined by the decree of 31 December 1957. Its area of production extends over the same communes as are grouped in the Anjou *appellation*.

The white wine comes from the Chenin Blanc, supplemented by the two Cabernet varieties, Côt, Gamay, Grolleau and Pineau d'Aunis grapes (vinified without maceration in the case of the red varieties). The rosé is made from the two Cabernets, Côt, Gamay, Grolleau and Pineau d'Aunis. Anjou Pétillant is full in colour: straw yellow for the whites, pale pink for the rosés. These are fairly full-bodied and characterful wines with a discreet sparkle.

Pressing grapes by traditional methods at Saint-Lambert du Lattay, near Rochefort-sur-Loire.

ANJOU AND SAUMUR

This wine-growing area occupies the meeting point of a number of natural regions: those of the Armorican and Vendée Massifs, Poitou, Touraine and the border of the Paris Basin. This explains why so many different soils are found here and, as a result, so many subtly differing styles of wine; including, when climatic conditions permit, wines of exceptional longevity.

The longer wine growing has been practised in a region, the harder it is to pinpoint its actual date of origin. So it is with this region. There are, nevertheless, many facts that bear witness to an important viticultural past in Anjou and Saumur: the conversion of the area to Christianity by St Martin in the 3rd century; the founding of an enclosed monastic house in the 9th century to which Guy de Fougereuse granted rights in regard to wine dues; the gift by Alain III, king of Brittany, of the abbey of Saint-Serge with its vines to the bishop of Angers in the 10th century . . .

However, it was in the 13th century that Anjou wines began to be famous, for it was at this time that the Plantagenets took to shipping them to England. For two centuries the best wines, those that could stand the sea voyage, were loaded up at Chalonnes, Rochefort-sur-Loire or les Ponts-de-Cé. The rest, except for the most fragile, which stayed in the region, were dispatched to Paris. Over the centuries since then, the situation changed greatly and the wines have now acquired a solid reputation across the whole French market.

At Montsoreau, in the Val d'Anjou, the Saumur-Champigny vineyards benefit from the gentle influence of the river Loire on climatic conditions.

The wine-growing area and the soils

The wine-growing area takes the form of a cross, with the town of Angers at its centre. Flowing from east to west, the river Loire divides the area into two parts, which are in turn cut by a north-south line that passes slightly to the east of Angers. Vineyards to the west of this line are on soils originating from the Palaeozoic era or earlier, while those to the east are on soils of Mesozoic era or Tertiary period origin. In the northwest quarter, growers around Bouchemaine, Épiré, Savennières, la Possonnière, Saint-Georges-sur-Loire and Ingrandes cultivate their vines on Silurian schist. In the northeast quarter, the Anjou *appellation* area around Trélazé, Fontaine-Milon, Pellouailles-les-Vignes and Montreuil-sur-Loir is on soils from the Cenomanian and Turonian stages of the Upper Cretaceous period.

In the southwest quarter there are hard siliceous and schistous rocks. It is here that the river Layon flows, and so some vineyards are sited on alluvial soils at Nueil-sur-Layon and les Verchers-sur-Layon. The area of Concourson-sur-Layon and Saint-Georges-Châtelaison is on a massif of the Carboniferous period. At Martigné-Briand the soil is again Cenomanian (Upper Cretaceous) in origin, while a little further on Perray is on Jurassic period limestone. The Silurian schist shapes not only the landscape but the wines at Chavagnes, before reaching the prestigious *crus* of Bonnezeaux and Quarts de Chaume and, similarly, those of Faye d'Anjou, Beaulieu-sur-Layon, la Pierre-Bise, Saint-Aubin-de-Luigné and Rochefort-sur-Loire. Adjacent to these villages, along the river Aubance, the distinguished vineyards of Coteaux de l'Aubance, between Soulaines, Mozé-sur-Louet and Mûrs-Erigné lie on schist.

The southeast quarter is dominated by the Thouet valley where the wines are more delicate, made from vines growing in limestone soils.

The grape varieties

The Chenin Blanc is pre-eminent in the production of white wines in this part of the Loire valley. The Grolleau is the principal grape variety for Anjou rosé. The red wines have the Cabernet Franc as their basis, often in association with the Cabernet Sauvignon.

The climate

The Anjou climate, characterized by its overall mildness or *douceur*, gives winters that are never harsh, warm summers and — crucially — fine autumns. These last favour the development of *pourriture noble* (noble rot) on the grapes — particularly on schistous terrains, which do not cool down much at night, and thus create a microclimate favourable to the growth of this fungus. The numerous small rivers and streams of the region are also beneficial, providing perfect drainage, and the many south-facing slopes are another positive factor.

The wines of Saumur

The white wines of Saumur, made from a single grape variety, the Chenin Blanc, are dry or off-dry, lively, with a supple structure and straightforward, predominantly vegetal aroma.

The red wines are made mostly from the Cabernet Franc, to which the Cabernet Sauvignon and even the Pineau d'Aunis may be added. They are wines that are at once smooth and firm; they have astringency, but it is of a rounded and developed kind. Their aromas are characterized by fruit scents.

The white sparkling wines, mainly from the Chenin Blanc, but sometimes also from the Sauvignon Blanc, Gamay, Grolleau, Pineau d'Aunis or Pinot Noir, are elegant, particularly when the Grolleau is present. They are generally dry or medium dry, and are also produced in *pétillant* (slightly sparkling) form.

Saumur-Champigny

This red wine is made from the Cabernet Franc, complemented by the Cabernet Sauvignon. Saumur-Champigny wines are generally lively and light. The tannins are not aggressive and are incorporated smoothly into the structure of the wine. There is a lot of fruit in their aroma. Drunk young, these wines have striking sprightliness; those of superior quality can also be aged successfully.

Coteaux de Saumur

Production of this dry or off-dry white wine, made from the Chenin Blanc, is tiny.

Cabernet de Saumur

This lively rosé wine is made from the Cabernet Franc and Cabernet Sauvignon grape varieties.

The wines of Anjou

The red wines are made from the Cabernet Franc, Cabernet Sauvignon and Pineau d'Aunis grape varieties. They are quite fleshy, full in colour, tannic but with a rounded sweetness to them, and with pronounced primary fruit aromas. The rosé wines, from the Grolleau, Cabernet Franc, Cabernet Sauvignon, Côt and Gamay varieties, are medium dry, soft and pleasant to drink. The whites come from the Chenin Blanc, with the Sauvignon Blanc and Chardonnay in subsidiary roles up to a limit of 20 per cent. Generally off-dry to medium dry, these wines are lively and full.

Anjou-Coteaux de la Loire

From a single grape variety, the Chenin Blanc, this district makes a small quantity of dry or medium dry wine.

Cabernet d'Anjou

This delicate rosé wine is made from the Cabernet Franc and Cabernet Sauvignon grape varieties. It ages well.

Savennières

Made from the Chenin Blanc grape variety, this white wine is particularly known for its dry style, though it can be supple and full. It has a fine mineral aroma.

Coteaux du Layon

This white wine comes solely from the Chenin Blanc. Medium dry to sweet, rarely dry, its style is pleasingly delicate, yet lively too. Coteaux du Layon-Chaume and Coteaux du Layon + commune name are made from musts with a high natural sugar content.

Quarts de Chaume

Also made exclusively from the Chenin Blanc grape, this is a white wine distinguished by its breeding. It is the finest expression of Anjou wine making, semi-sweet to sweet in style.

Bonnezeaux

This ample white wine from the Chenin Blanc

THE ANJOU GLASS AND BOTTLE

Anjou wanted to drink wine out of a glass of its own; so in 1914 a competition to select one was launched. Events, however, held up the realization of the scheme and the glasses were not set before the jury until 1920. What was wanted was a 12 cl glass, elegant, not too fragile, and easy to clean. Three hundred designs were submitted before one, from a wine grower from Rochefort-sur-Loire, was chosen: it has a high stem and a conical bowl.

Anjou had its glass; now it wanted a bottle of its own. The royal glassworks at Ingrandes - already important in 1755 - created a bottle with a deep colour, sturdy in form but with a slender, graceful neck. It features a seal with three fleur-de-lys motifs, a crown and a star, enclosed by laurel branches.

Annual production per *appellation* in hl	White	Red	Rosé	Sparkling
Anjou	83 700	73 000	216 000	3 000
Anjou Gamay		15 000		
Anjou-Coteaux de la Loire	1 200			
Savennières	1 800			
Coteaux du Layon	44 000			
Coteaux du Layon-Chaume	1 500			
Bonnezeaux	1 200			
Quarts de Chaume	700			
Coteaux de l'Aubance	2 000			
Coteaux de Saumur	100			
Saumur	39 000	11 000		100 000 (as rosé 5 800)
Cabernet d'Anjou			135 000	
Cabernet de Saumur			2 000	
Rosé de Loire			19 000	
Saumur-Champigny		40 000		
Crémant de Loire				19 000
Vins du Thouarsais	450	350		
Total	175 650	139 350	372 000	127 800

The windmill at Brissac, in the Coteaux de l'Aubance vineyards, where elegant dry and medium dry white wines are produced from Chenin Blanc grapes.

grape is medium dry to sweet, and can be lusciously sweet after very sunny years. It has an excellent length of life in bottle.

Coteaux de l'Aubance

This dry to medium dry wine comes from the Chenin Blanc and is elegant and fresh; the aroma has great finesse, with hints of verbena.

Crémant de Loire

This is a white sparkling wine from a blend of grape varieties that may include the Chenin Blanc, Sauvignon Blanc, Cabernet Franc, Pineau d'Aunis, Pinot Noir, Chardonnay and Arbois, supplemented by the Grolleau. It should combine liveliness and firmness with delicacy and charm.

Rosé de Loire

A dry rosé wine made from a mixture of grape varieties: at least 30 per cent Cabernet Franc and Cabernet Sauvignon, with the balance made up by Gamay, Grolleau, Pineau d'Aunis and Pinot Noir. It is dry and lively in style and pale pink in colour.

Vins du Thouarsais

The vineyards of this VDQS produce a very small volume of wine. The red, from the Cabernet Franc, Cabernet Sauvignon and Gamay varieties, is a pleasant and sometimes distinctive wine. The rosé is dry and delicate. The white, made from the Chenin Blanc and the Chardonnay, is dry to medium dry and can be a characterful light wine.

Vinification of Anjou and Saumur wines

For white wines, vinification follows classic lines: the grapes are harvested when ripe, or even overripe in sweet-wine areas. Mechanical harvesting is not possible in the latter case. After the must (grape juice) has been pressed, the wines are put to ferment in casks, in cellars. For the simpler wines, fermentation takes place in stainless steel vats.

The wines are usually racked (transferred off their lees) three times; on each of these occasions the level of sulphur dioxide is checked and adjusted so as to prevent the risk of re-fermentation in wines with residues of sugar. The wine is fined with gelatine after it has been treated with tannin, then bottled in March.

Vinification of rosé wines

The rosé wines of Anjou are made, unlike some others, by pressing red grapes. From that point on, they are vinified in the same way as the whites. The level of ripeness at which the grapes are picked varies from year to year, so the fruit is macerated for some hours before it is pressed, to obtain the correct colour. Like the whites, the rosé wines are bottled in the spring.

Vinification of red wines

The grape varieties used for red wines in Anjou

are generally tannic. As the grape stalks do not always reach full maturity in the region, the crop is destalked. Fermentation and vatting of the red wines take place using grapes more or less thoroughly crushed by the picking process, transportation and destalking.

Today fermentation temperatures are carefully monitored and controlled throughout, and this means that the process lasts for around 10 to 15 days, according to the type of wine and the characteristics of the particular vintage. After the usual racking procedures have been carried out, the very finest wines are matured further in wood, for up to a year.

Anjou wines in general, though, undergo most of their maturation in bottle. For the simpler wines, bottle life is a few years; for the best (*cru*) white wines from very sunny years it may be more than half a century. These are wines whose style is brought to a refined perfection by the tranquil passage of time.

The manufacture of sparkling wines

All the sparkling wines of this region enjoying *appellation contrôlée* status are produced by secondary fermentation in bottle. The prescribed technique is, for the moment, termed the *méthode champenoise*, though this description will become illegal for any EC wine not produced in Champagne, from 1989 onwards. The important point is the length of this secondary fermentation, i.e. the amount of time during which there is contact between the wine and the lees or deposit: the method requires there to be one year between bottling and disgorgement. But in many cases this minimum period is exceeded, which allows more rounded and full-flavoured wines to be obtained.

The wines can be Brut, with a maximum 15g of sugar per litre, or Sec, in which case the amount of sugar can rise to 30g per litre.

The economic structure of the Anjou wine trade

Financially, this is the most important sector of the Loire wine region. It produces an annual average of 831,200 hl.

The wine-growing economy divides up as follows: 85 per cent of production comes from private holdings and 15 per cent from cooperatives. Direct sales to consumers are around 30 per cent, while the activity of *négociants-éleveurs* (merchants with their own wine-making facilities) has remained very dynamic. They have an 80 per cent share in the production and marketing of sparkling wines and they therefore play a dominant role in this subsector.

Export figures average 30 per cent of total annual production.

THE CONFRÉRIE DES CHEVALIERS DU SACAVIN

The name 'sacavin' *(literally 'winebag', and by extension 'belly' or 'gut') comes from Rabelais, who was born locally. So does the fraternity's solemn promise:*

'When my glass is full I empty it
And when it is empty I fill it ...'

Despite these brave 16th-century words, the Confrérie des Chevaliers du Sacavin (Fraternity of the Knights of the Winebag) was not founded until 1947, rising then from the ashes of a cheerful Angevin association, the Dévôts Oenophiles, formed in 1909 but dispersed at the time of the First World War.

Today, in association with all the appropriate professional organizations, the confrérie *sets itself the task of informing amateurs about the pleasures and advantages they will derive from attentive drinking of the very wide range of splendid Anjou wines. It holds spirited chapter meetings in the magnificent cellars built in the 12th century by Henry II, Plantagenet King of England and Count of Anjou.*

The Angevin vineyards now cover more than 35,000 ha, with a total annual production of nearly 1 million hl. For some decades, the growers have been looking to quality production, particularly with regard to red and dry white wines, both suited to the developing tastes of customers today. Although, fortunately, there are always connoisseurs to appreciate the sweet and luscious grands vins *of Coteaux du Layon, Quarts de Chaume and Bonnezeaux, the choice of the average wine lover inclines more to fresh, dry wines for drinking young. Another of the roles the* confrérie *has given itself is to make the whole spectrum of present-day Anjou wines better known to those interested, and to help newcomers discover the truly great wines of Angevin tradition.*

Leaf of the Aramon, the world's most productive wine grape variety.

Green shoot of the Aramon vine.

A bunch of Aramon grapes.

Aramon

Synonyms: *Plant Riche, Rabalaïré, Réballaïré, Révalaïré* in Hérault, *Pisse-vin* at Hyères, *Gros Bouteillan* at Draguignan, *Ugni Noir* in Provence.

Growing tips flattened, with white down. Young leaves arachnoid, bullate, yellowish on the bulges.

Leaves large, cuneiform, thin, yellowish green, three-lobed but not markedly, sometimes five-lobed on leaves at the base of the shoots; V-shaped petiolar sinus; dentation pointed, in two unequal series; underside of blade either glabrous or pubescent according to the clone.

Green shoots weakly ribbed, arachnoid at ends, green with light, brown-red striations on the side exposed to the sun. Spreading habit in *gobelet* (bush) shape with shoots curving upwards on contact with the soil.

Bunches very large, bulky, conical, with the peduncle remaining green until grapes are ripe, often provided with a well-developed shoulder, weighing on average 400–600g, with bunches sometimes exceeding 1kg. Grapes large, 15–20mm in width and sometimes more, blue-black; skin very thin and splitting easily; flesh very juicy, the juice produced being colourless and abundant; ripening period: third epoch.

The Aramon has early budbreak, which makes it very vulnerable to spring frosts. It always has to be pruned short: being very fertile and productive (up to 8kg of grapes per vine) it would be quickly exhausted if pruned long. Planted on hill slopes, its production varies between 60 and 80hl/ha, providing wines of from 10° to 12° alcohol, without much colour but pleasant to drink. However, it is on the plains that the Aramon shows what it can achieve with yields of 120hl/ha to more than 250hl/ha, at 7–9° alcohol. Yields of juice are good: from 115 to 120kg for 1hl of wine.

The Aramon has to be grafted on to vigorous rootstocks. It is very vulnerable to downy mildew, phomopsis, grey rot (botrytis), grape worm and yellow spider mite; on the other hand it is resistant to oidium (powdery mildew). It is probably the world's most fertile vine. For three or four generations it has been the basis of wine growing, together with Aramon hybrids made by Louis and Henri Bouschet, in the plains of Languedoc. Classed only as an 'authorized' variety, it has greatly declined in importance since 1958, a time when it grew on more than 150,000ha, and has now dropped to 4th place among French grape varieties, with around 64,000ha. Six registered clones have been approved: numbers 204 and 266 (the most useful), 323, 324, 325 and 401.

This grape variety so typical of the Midi is grown mainly in Languedoc (Hérault, Gard, Aude, Ardèche) on almost 60,000ha, with a smaller quantity — 4,000ha — in Provence (Var, Bouches-du-Rhône and Vaucluse).

The grey variety, Aramon Gris, is grown on 400ha in Languedoc and its grapes are mixed with other white varieties to make white wines there. The Aramon Blanc is also little grown, and plays the same role as the Aramon Gris.

Arbane

Synonyms: *Arbanne, Arbone, Albane* in Aube and Haute-Marne, *Arbenne* at Riceys and around Tonnerre, *Crène* at Polisot (Aube), and *Crénillat* in the Gier valley (Loire).

Bunches small, conical, medium compact; grapes small, spherical, with high sugar levels; ripening period: second epoch.

This is an Aube variety, long grown in the Bar-sur-Aube area, but only on the most favourable sites as it ripens late for this area, and its budbreak is early, which exposes it to spring frosts. It is a modest producer, pruned long, and little grown today because of its vulnerability to downy mildew and oidium (powdery mildew).

Its wines are dry, firm and sinewy, with considerable aroma and alcohol in good years. Classed as 'recommended' in Aube and Marne, it is one of the listed champagne grapes but grows on no more than 2ha in the Aube winegrowing area. An Arbane Noir and an Arbane Rouge, described at the beginning of this century, have now disappeared.

Arbois

Synonyms: *Herbois* in Jullien, *Orbois, Orboué, Orboé* (in dialect), *Menu Pineau* (as distinct from Gros Pineau, another name for Chenin Blanc), *Menu Pineau de Vouvray, Petit Pineau* in Loir-et-Cher, *Verdet* or *Pinot Verdet*.

Growing tips flattened, open, felty white with carmine margins. Young leaves downy, yellowish green; underside of blade felty.

Leaves small, orbicular, blue-green, thick, bullate, without lobes; petiolar sinus lyrate and virtually closed, sometimes naked at the base; petiolar junction pink; dentation convex, medium sized; underside of blade downy in tufts.

Green shoots ribbed, red-brown with pink nodes; tendrils small and thin.

Bunches small, conical, tightly packed; grapes golden white, ovoid, small, juicy; ripening period: second epoch.

In spite of its name, this variety did not originate in the Arbois vineyards of Jura, where it is unknown. Very vigorous, it was formerly planted in the Orléans area and the Cher valley, to the extent of forming a quarter of all white vine stocks there, thanks to its contribution of suppleness to blends. Its wine, in fact, is rather softer and more delicate than that of the Chenin Blanc. Yields are between 40 and 80 hl/ha. Three registered clones have been approved: numbers 205, 206 and 504.

This grape variety is classed as 'recommended' in the Loire valley, where it is one of the varieties for the Crémant de Loire AOC, as well as for the Cheverny and Valençay VDQS categories. The Arbois is ranked in 56th place among French grape varieties, with 1,145 ha planted, 1,060 ha of which are in Loir-et-Cher and the rest in Indre and Vienne.

The Arbois Rose, found at Oisly (Loir-et-Cher), is distinguished from the Arbois only by its pink grapes. It is not grown commercially.

Arbois and Arbois-Pupillin

Together these two *appellations*, ratified by the decrees of 15 May 1936 and 12 June 1970 respectively, form a large zone, their 700 ha covering nearly half of Jura's wine-growing area. Total production over the last 20 years has been around 25,000 hl per year on average, with a yield of 38 hl/ha. Red and rosé wines are mainly produced, from the Trousseau grape variety — which performs better here than anywhere else — and the Poulsard. Other more specialized Jura wine types (such as white wines from the Savagnin grape) are also produced in this district.

The Trousseau thrives on marly soils and gives a wine with an attractive colour, plenty of body, and with good ageing potential. Sometimes a little hard in its youth, it mellows and softens as it ages.

The Poulsard thrives on rich, well-exposed soils. It produces a delicate but alcoholic red wine with a beautiful colour that acquires an elegant onionskin tint as it ages. At its peak, it has a bouquet of great finesse.

It was at Arbois that the first cooperative in Jura was set up in 1906. This 'Fruitière Vinicole', like the other five in Jura, sells most of its wine to private customers.

Arbois today enjoys as good a reputation as at any time in its history, and this is largely due to the energetic efforts of the largest merchant house of the region, which owns important vineyards in Arbois itself.

Arbois Mousseux

To qualify for the Arbois Mousseux *appellation contrôlée*, wines have to be made from grapes picked when well ripened and have a minimum natural alcohol content of 10 per cent by volume. These sparkling wines have to be made exclusively by secondary fermentation in bottle, and within the Jura *département*.

Ardonnet

Synonyms: *Ardounet* (Béarnais word for *arrondi*, 'rounded'), *Ardonnenc* in Pyrénées-Atlantiques, *Acheria Moyeta*.

Bunches small, very tightly packed; berries small, spherical, blue-black; ripening period: second epoch, late.

This is a Jurançon variety, unclassified, and giving wines without much colour.

Argant

Synonyms: *Margillien, Gros Margillien* at Arbois, *Rouillot* at Poligny.

Leaves large, truncate, thick, dark green, with concave edges, five-lobed with lateral sinuses acute at base, petiolar sinus V-shaped; dentation large and pointed, very narrow; underside of blade almost glabrous.

Green shoots ribbed with longitudinal red-brown striations and slightly pinkish nodes; tendrils large, fleshy.

Bunches medium, conical, compact; grapes spherical, small, black, with soft pulp, little juice; ripening period: second epoch, late.

This is an old Jura variety, grown particularly in the Poligny district, and also to a modest extent in the Doubs *département*; it has a limited future, however, not having been classified. As it is very vigorous it has to be pruned long, with three or four canes of 40cm in length. Yields reach 100 hl/ha. Its wine is a rich red oxblood colour, well constituted, but of middling quality. Its relative resistance to downy mildew meant that it became popular around 1885, when this disease became widespread.

Arinarnoa

Crossing of Merlot × Petit Verdot, made at the Institut Nationale de la Recherche Agronomique (INRA) at Bordeaux in 1956.

Bunches large, semi-compact on long peduncles; grapes spherical, black, medium sized; ripening period: second epoch, late.

The budbreak of this variety is late, and it produces well and consistently. Its wine has plenty of alcohol and great depth of colour, is fruity and fine, sometimes with a grassy or leafy taste. It has good resistance to grey rot (botrytis). Classified as 'authorized' in 1980 with one approved clone: number 723.

Armagnac *See* the following page.

ARMAGNAC

A wine-based **eau-de-vie** *known as* **'Aygue ardent'** *has been produced in Gascony since the beginning of the 15th century. The centuries of experience that have followed, combined with a great respect for tradition, a profound knowledge of the soil and a search for the most suitable grape varieties are reflected in the range of armagnacs that Gascon growers offer us today.*

Armagnac lies in the South West of France, midway between Bordeaux and Toulouse, facing the Pyrenees and in an area channelled by valleys fanning out from this mountain range.

It was through the river routes provided by two of these valleys that the spendours of Armagnac first attracted outside attention. The valley of the Baïse in the north enabled the local brandy to be shipped to Bordeaux; that of Midouze in the south gave access to Bayonne.

The area was overrun by the Gascons towards the end of the 6th century AD. They appear to have been a mountain people, and they gave their name to this region: in 670 it became the first duchy of Gascony. The early counts of Armagnac entered record books in the 10th century.

The name 'Armagnac' goes back to Gallo-Roman times. A certain Arminius had an estate there, and in the local dialect his name was modified to Armagnac.

Excavations carried out on the site of a Gallo-Roman villa have uncovered mosaics depicting bunches of grapes — evidence of the presence of the vine in this region from classical times.

Manor house in the heart of the Armagnac vineyards, not far from Condom, in the Gers **département.**

The history of Armagnac brandy

The first known text describing the distilling of spirits is found in the writings of the Persian Rhazes, or Rasis (AD 865–928). A number of texts subsequent to the Persian's works mention early examples of alcohols, used as perfumes in the Arab world, and medicines in the West.

It was in the 12th century that Gerard of Cremona (1114–1187) translated works by Arab and Oriental scholars on the distilling process, thus ensuring their diffusion in the Western world. Armand de Villeneuve described the process as it was practised around 1300: 'Take black or white wine, clear and aromatic, and distil all the ardent water from it over a gentle fire, refining it until no phlegmy matter remains.' It was under the name *Aygue ardent* ('ardent water') that this brandy appeared in the Saint-Sever market in the Landes in 1461. Earlier still than this, in 1411, the records of a Toulouse lawyer were already listing a certain Antoine as an *ayga ardenterius*: a distiller.

By 1730, brandy was a commodity that knew good and bad years. Some were so bad that merchants were obliged to put brandy into storage — in wooden casks. It was then discovered that the brandy appeared to acquire colour and roundness when in wood; and that the qualities that ageing gave it were pleasing to the eye and nose, and to taste.

The 17th and 18th centuries saw an extension of Armagnac's trade via Bordeaux and Bayonne, thanks to fluctuating political trends and a number of military occupations.

The Gers vineyards, where the grapes for armagnac are grown, were devastated by phylloxera around 1870. Little by little, the vines were grafted and replaced. Armagnac, though, did not benefit from the considerable growth in trade of the end of the 19th and the beginning of the 20th century: the area was too remote, with too few people, and its manufacturing capabilities were too localized. The first steps towards organization of the vineyards were taken, however, and a decree of 25 May 1909 defined the area of production of Armagnac brandy; that of 6 August 1936 defined the Armagnac, Bas-Armagnac, Haut-Armagnac and Ténarèze *appellations contrôlées.*

The Armagnac vineyards

Lying north of the Pyrenees, between the

Adour and Garonne rivers, the production area takes in a large part of the Gers *département*, as well as some *cantons* of the Landes *département* to the west and of Lot-et-Garonne to the north. The wine-growing area is divided into three regions:

Bas-Armagnac
Set in the west of the production area, this region has many small valleys. It produces the best-known and finest of all armagnacs, from the 7,500 ha of vines grown for this purpose.

Ténarèze
This region consists of a narrow corridor in the centre of the *appellation*. The hills here are steeper than in Bas-Armagnac and the vineyards cover 5,500 ha.

Haut-Armagnac
This part of the wine-growing area lies to the south and east of the other two zones and its relief is even more marked than theirs. However, the quality of the armagnac produced in this area is inferior, and the vines grown for armagnac production have dwindled to such an extent that very little is now made here.

The division of Armagnac into these three regions is justified by the distinctive geological features of each.

The *terroir*

The mixture of subsoils in the area is the outcome of marine, lacustrine and fluvial deposits laid down at the end of the Oligocene and the beginning of the Miocene epochs in the course of marine transgressions. The last of these advances of the sea over the land left behind a deposit of tawny sand in Landes and the western part of Gers in the Bas-Armagnac region.

In Bas-Armagnac, most of the slopes are covered by fine quartz sands, mixed with ferruginous elements that colour them the tawny shade indicated by their French name: *sables fauves*. These sand and alluvial terrains are relatively poor in acids and hence well suited to wine growing.

In Ténarèze, the calcareous clay soils are the product of chemical and mechanical decomposition of Miocene deposits (termed *terreforts* and *peyrusquets*). These shallow deposits, too, are suitable for vines.

In Haut-Armagnac, the more exclusively calcareous soils occur in association with aspects favourable to the cultivation of cereal crops as well as vines.

Climate

The climate in this part of Gascony is predominantly maritime: temperatures are moderate and humidity is high. These characteristics, coupled with moderate sunshine, are responsible for the production of white wine that is low in alcohol — often less than 10° — and is thus ideal for producing high-quality brandy.

High-trellis or pagoda vine training (called taille en sylvos *in French) is more and more widespread in Ténarèze. It makes picking easier, whether by hand or machine.*

The grape varieties

Some ten different grape varieties are authorized for the production of armagnac. Today, however, two dominate: the Ugni Blanc at 55 per cent of the total and the Baco Blanc at 35 per cent. The Folle Blanche (or Picpoul) is armagnac's traditional grape variety, but great vulnerability to grey rot (botrytis) has contributed to its very marked decline: it now represents no more than 2 per cent of the vines grown. The Colombard is relatively widespread in Gers, but virtually all its production is used for table wine.

The different varieties are not evenly distributed across the Armagnac vineyards. For example, the Ugni Blanc accounts for about 80 per cent of plantings in Ténarèze, whereas the Baco Blanc dominates plantings in Bas-Armagnac.

Characteristics of the brandies of each subregion

In Armagnac, it is the *terroir* that is chiefly responsible for giving each brandy made there

Ripe bunches of armagnac grapes ready for harvesting.

its distinguishing characteristics.

The tawny sands of Bas-Armagnac enable a fruity, light, very delicate brandy to be produced.

In Ténarèze, the vines grow in calcareous clay soils, so the resulting armagnacs are richer, more full-bodied and imposing, suitable for a longer ageing period.

Each of the two subregional brandies has its own appeal, but it is often a blend of both that produces the best commercial armagnacs.

Distilling armagnac

This process is started as quickly as possible after the grape harvest and has to be completed by 30 April of the following year.

Distilling is carried out mainly by means of the *alambic armagnacais*, which is a particular type of continuous-flow still. It is gradually replacing the double-distilling pot still, which continues to predominate in the Cognac area.

Between 10 and 15 per cent of armagnac is produced in the ordinary pot stills introduced into the region in 1972.

The *alambic armagnacais* type of still is made of pure copper, hammered and laminated. It is an apparatus comprising two or three linked heaters working on the continuous-flow princi-

On leaving the still, the armagnac is poured into hand-made oak casks to mature.

ARMAGNAC CONTINUOUS STILL

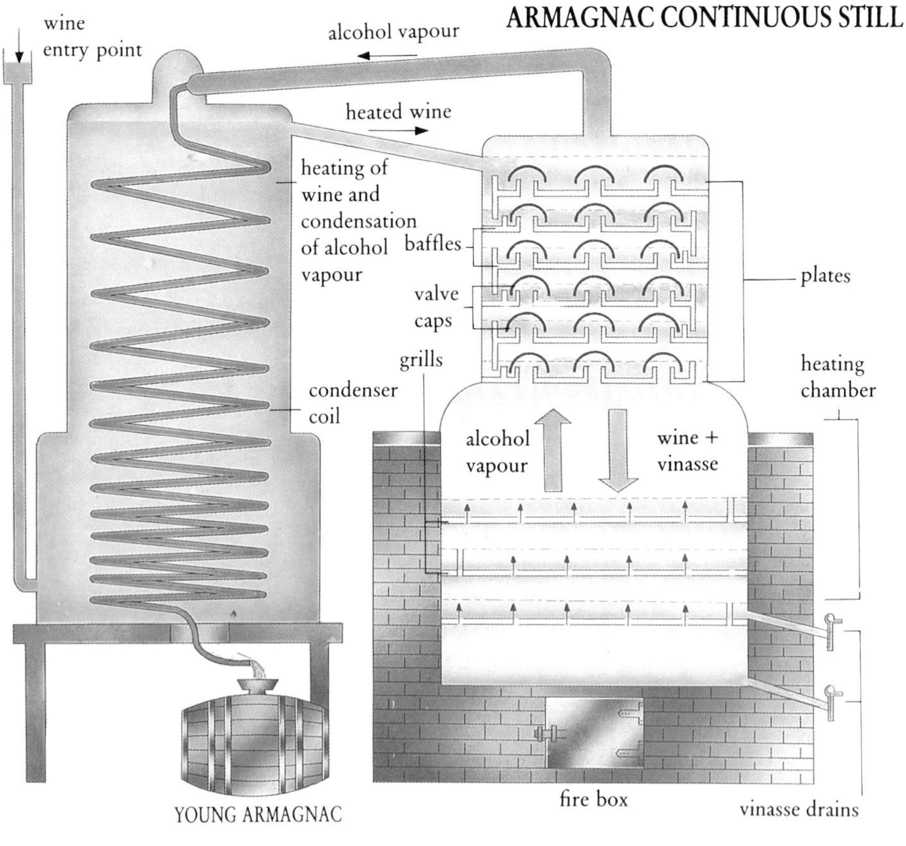

ple, with nothing circulating through the system more than once.

The still is fed continuously with wine from a vat. This enters the apparatus at the bottom of the wine heater, in the centre of which the new brandies circulate through the spiral coil in which condensation of the spirit takes place.

The wine moves through the apparatus in the opposite direction to the brandy. It is fed into the heating chamber, where it vaporizes. This chamber is heated by a naked flame fuelled by wood or gas (oil is banned because of its odour). The vapour rises through a series of plates, where it becomes mixed with the precipitated and descending wine, absorbing its aromas. The vaporized spirit leaves the top of the heating chamber, and condenses in the coil. At no point in the process must there be sudden temperature changes. On leaving the still the brandy is raw in flavour but very aromatic; it should have an alcohol content of between 50° and 72°.

Armagnac is bottled at a strength of 40°. The bottles are stored upright so that the alcohol does not attack the corks.

Ageing

After distillation, the armagnac is put to age in 400-litre, hand-made oak casks, called *pièces*. (No machine has so far succeeded in producing casks of equal quality.) These casks are stored in above-ground *chais*.

It is only at this point that the *maître de chais* (cellarmaster) takes charge of the armagnac. He jealously watches over the ageing process, making sure that nothing disturbs the slow development of the spirit. In contact with the wood, the brandies become impregnated with the scents of earth and forest, taking on the pungent, fiery aroma and beautiful amber colour that characterize them.

As the armagnac ages in oak casks, contact with the wood impregnates the brandy with tannins, giving it its aroma and its beautiful amber colour.

Evaporation — called, as in Cognac, 'the angels' share' — is around 3 per cent per year of all stocks.

Surveillance of the ageing process is constant and checks are frequently made on the spirit to determine the moment when the transfer of tannins and essences from the wood has reached its optimum level. The armagnac is then either transferred to old casks — those that will contribute no further tannin to the brandy — or blended in vats.

The required alcoholic strength (40°) is reached in successive stages by the addition of *petites eaux* — mixtures of distilled water and armagnac. When this has been done, the *maître de chai* can begin making the *coupes*: blends of a number of armagnacs of different ages and origins so as to achieve a consistent product that upholds the good name of the marque. In marrying two or more brandies, the *coupe* has as its aim the combination of the respective qualities and characteristics of each, so that they find better expression in one whole than as individual parts.

The age of the blend is taken to be that of the youngest armagnac in it when the blend was assembled. If a 30-year-old brandy is blended with a four-year-old one, the result will be a 'four-year-old armagnac'.

When the legally stipulated alcoholic strength (40°) is reached, and any blending is completed, the armagnac is bottled. It ages no further, but stabilizes and evolves discreetly. One might say that it 'blossoms'.

Bottles of armagnac are kept upright so that the alcohol does not attack the corks; they are stored in cellars in which the ideal temperature is 12°C.

Arriloba

Crossing of the Raffiat de Moncade × Sauvignon Blanc, made by INRA at Bordeaux in 1960. This fertile variety produces consistently, giving a wine that is fine, with a light bouquet, less heavy than that of the Sauvignon Blanc. Classed as an 'authorized' grape variety with one approved clone: number 762.

Arrouya

Synonyms: *Aroyat, Aruya, Arhuya.*

Bunches medium sized, pyramidal, compact, with two small shoulders; grapes medium sized, ovoid, blue-black; ripening period: third epoch.

This grape variety, in the past stake-trained, produces large quantities of rather pale red wine. It is, though, late ripening for the Béarn area and the Basque country where it is grown. Prone to downy mildew and black rot, growers have increasingly forsaken it and it now occupies only a hundred or so hectares in the two Pyrenean *départements*, where it is classified as 'authorized'.

Arrufiac

Synonyms: *Arufiat, Arrefiac, Arrefiat, Raffiat, Ruffiac, Rouffiac Femelle, Ambré* at Monein.

Bunches small to medium in size, cylindrical; grapes spherical, small, yellowish white, juicy; ripening period: second epoch.

This variety is quite susceptible to downy mildew and oidium (powdery mildew), and in addition its fruit is sometimes affected by *millerandage* (shot berries: the failure of certain berries in a bunch to develop properly). Categorized as 'recommended' in Gers and the two Pyrenean *départements*, where it is stake-trained, on about 100 ha.

Wine made from the Arrufiac has a high alcohol content and a pronounced and distinctive aroma, similar to that of madeira.

Leaf of the Aubun, a late-ripening and vigorous variety originally from the Vaucluse area.

Aspiran Noir

Synonyms: *Spiran, Espiran, Epiran, Pirans* in Gard and Hérault, *Ribeyrenc, Riveyrenc, Riveyrène* in Aude, *Verdaï, Verdal.* The name should really be *Espiran*, as cited by Pierre Magnol in 1686.

Bunches medium sized, conical, winged, quite loose; grapes medium, ovoid to ellipsoidal, black, bloomy, fine but delicate skin; very juicy; ripening period: third epoch.

This ancient Languedoc grape variety was quite widespread in the past in the quality vineyards of Hérault (Pignan, Saint-Georges-d'Orques, Villeveyrac) and of Gard (Langlade, Uchaud, Nages), where it accounted for a fifth to a quarter of the vines. A small producer, thriving particularly in stony soils, it gives a light, rather pale wine, delicate and lightly perfumed. Its importance has greatly diminished with the recent reorganization of these vineyards. It now grows on no more than a few hectares and even these will soon disappear as it has not been given a classification, except in Minervois when it forms part of an existing stock of vines. In old vineyards there are sometimes isolated Aspiran vines whose grapes are generally eaten, as they make very pleasant table grapes when they ripen at the end of August or the beginning of September.

There is an Aspiran Blanc, and an Aspiran Gris or Rosé, also called Aspiran Verdal.

In 1865, Henri Bouschet created the Aspiran-Bouschet, a crossing of the Gros Bouschet (Aramon × Teinturier du Cher) × Aspiran Noir; it was a grape with richly coloured juice and foliage closely resembling that of the Aspiran.

Aubin Blanc

Synonyms: *Blanc de Creuë* in Meuse; *Blanc de Magny, Pétracine* (erroneously, as this refers to Riesling).

Bunches small to medium sized, conical, winged, very compact; grapes spherical, small, golden white, not very juicy; ripening period: first epoch. This grape variety, with 'recommended' status only in Lorraine, is among the vines planted in the Côtes de Toul for the production of its VDQS white wines.

Aubin Vert

Synonyms: *Vert Blanc, Blanc d'Euvézin.*

Bunches small, cylindrical, loose, sometimes winged; grapes small, ovoid, pink white, with very small pips; ripening period: first epoch.

This grape variety differs from the Aubin Blanc in certain of its characteristics, and it has only been categorized as 'authorized' in Lorraine, as its wine is very ordinary. At the École Nationale Supérieure d'Agriculteurs (ENSA) at Montpellier, it readily develops *millerandage* and is susceptible to oidium (powdery mildew).

Aubun

A grape that originated in the Mont Ventoux area in Vaucluse. It is sometimes called *Carignan de Bédoin* or *Carignan de Gigondas*. From the older collections of ENSA at Montpellier, we know it was called *Moustardier* or *Counoise* in Vaucluse; and *Grosse Rogettaz* in Savoie.

Growing tips felty white with carmine margins.

A bunch of Aubun grapes.

Young leaves downy, yellowish with bronze patches.

Leaves orbicular, blue-green, dull, finely bullate, slightly concave, deeply five-lobed with the base of the sinuses wide, concave and often dentate, the upper lateral sinuses often closed up and club-shaped; petiolar sinus lyrate and more or less closed; dentation convex, large; underside of leaf felty-pubescent. There is extensive reddening of the foliage in autumn.

Green shoots ribbed, arachnoid at ends, with red-brown longitudinal striations on the side exposed to the sun; tendrils long, fleshy.

Bunches medium to fairly large, with little branching of stalks, cylindrical, compact; grapes medium sized, spherical or slightly ovoid, black, firm, tough skinned, fleshy and not very juicy; ripening period: third epoch.

The Aubun has late budbreak, which enables it to escape spring frosts. It also has good resistance to oidium (powdery mildew) and downy mildew. Its grapes are moderately resistant to grey rot (botrytis).

This vigorous vine of erect habit produces 60 to 80 hl/ha on hillside positions, and even more on flat ground.

The wine the Aubun gives is rather pale, quite alcoholic, of moderate quality. This grape variety is inferior to the Carignan as it is susceptible to *coulure* (flower abortion) and *millerandage*, and because its shoots break more easily in strong winds, such as the *mistral* or *tramontane*. It was thought that the variety had a measure of resistance to phylloxera, but this was simply because in the Ventoux area the vine happened to be planted in rich, light soils, and phylloxera did not spread as quickly in these as elsewhere. Two registered clones have been approved: numbers 168 and 350. The Aubun has 'recommended' status in Provence and Languedoc, and is planted on a total of 5,821 ha, mainly in Gard, Aude, Vaucluse and Bouches-du-Rhône.

Auxerrois

Synonyms: *Auxerrois Blanc de Laquenexy* in Moselle, *Pinot Auxerrois* in Alsace.

The identifications by 19th-century ampelographic experts of this variety with the Chardonnay, Sylvaner, Melon or the Meslier Saint-François varieties were mistaken.

Growing tips downy, greenish white.

Young leaves arachnoid, bronze coloured.

Leaves orbicular, large, finely bullate, slightly crimped at the petiolar junction, without lobes or very slightly three-lobed, petiolar sinus in open V-shape; dentation pointed, medium sized; underside of blade pubescent, rough.

Green shoots green with brown longitudinal striations, pink nodes; tendrils long, fleshy.

Bunches small to medium, compact; grapes ovoid, small, dull golden white, skin fine, pulp soft; ripening period: first epoch.

This is essentially an Alsace variety, grown on an area of 1,190 ha, but it has been classified as 'recommended' in a number of *départements* in the Loire valley and the Centre-Ouest, as well as in Lorraine, the area where it originated.

Two registered clones have been approved: numbers 56 and 57. As its budbreak is late and the variety is therefore little threatened by untimely frosts, the Auxerrois is planted on unpromising sites. Its wine is of the second rank and is often sold blended with that of the Pinot Blanc as Pinot Blanc (or Klevner).

There is also an Auxerrois Gris, distinguished from the Auxerrois by the grey colour of its berries, but it is hardly grown today.

Green shoot of the Auxerrois vine.

Auxey-Duresses

This Côte de Beaune village gives its name to an *appellation* that was ratified by decree on 21 May 1970. Its vineyards are divided into 138 ha of AOC Auxey-Duresses and 32 ha of Auxey-Duresses Premier Cru, apportioned between nine different *crus*. The wine law distinguishes between the two categories in terms of minimum alcoholic strength as well as *terroir*: 10.5° for red wines with the 'village' classification and 11° for the Premiers Crus; 11° for white wines with the 'village' classification and 11·5° for the Premier Cru whites. The base yield for all the wines is 35 hl/ha. Average annual production of red wines is around 3,300 hl, while 1,100 hl of white wine is produced.

The red wines of Auxey-Duresses are firm but well balanced, and are comparable to the reds of Volnay or Monthélie in longevity and ageing potential. The white wines are reminiscent of those of Meursault in terms of vigour and aromatic quality, though they are not their equals in overall distinction.

The Vine

From the fossil seeds of wild vines of the Tertiary period in Transcaucasia, from the sun-drenched vineyards of Homeric Greece to the enclosed vineyards of the richly endowed monastaries of pre-Revolutionary France, down through all the vicissitudes of history, climate and parasite invasions, the vine, that wonderful, abundant climber, has evolved, adapted and survived to bring us greater pleasure than ever today.

The vine belongs to the *Vitaceae* or *Ampelidaceae* family, which includes a large number of climbing or creeping plants; only the genus *Vitis* concerns us here. This is divided into two subgenera, *Muscadiniae* and *Euvites*. The majority of cultivated vines belong to the *Euvites* subgenus, within which three groups are distinguished. The first, called the Eurasian, contains only one species: *Vitis vinifera, Linnaeus* and its progenitor *Vitis vinifera silvestris*. This species, sometimes termed the European vine, comprises some thousands of varieties: these are our *cépages*, or grape varieties. The second, known as the Asiatic group, is made up of about a dozen species. The third, the American group, embraces a further score of species, several of which serve to provide phylloxera-resistant rootstocks and in the development of hybrid varieties.

The domestication of the wild vine

The discovery of fossil leaves of *Vitaceae* dating from the Eocene and Pliocene epochs proves the existence of this family since the first half of the Tertiary era, in other words for some 50 million years. Some of these leaf remains, however, are controversial, as they could equally well have come from other species. Fossilized pips found in Greenland, Britain, France, Central Europe and in North America, though, constitute absolute proof of the existence of the vine at this time.

The great cooling that caused the formation of huge glaciers in North America and Europe (about 650,000 BC to 15,000 BC) is one of the salient features of the Quaternary period. In Europe, this climatic upset brought about the disappearance of the American *Vitis* species, which had adapted to warm conditions. *Vitis vinifera*, however, partly recolonized the northern regions, moving up from its southern refuges. These were, in fact, varieties of *Vitis vinifera silvestris* that had developed unhindered as climbing vines in forest environments which remained untouched until relatively recently.

The accumulations of grape pips, dating from the European Neolithic period (5000–2500 BC), found in many European sites show that the fruits of these wild vines were already being consumed by prehistoric populations. Archaeological and ethnographic data, however, indicate that the beginning of viticulture should be placed prior to 4000 BC in Transcaucasia, where wild vines were plentiful in the forests. In fact the

'Dionysus Crossing the Sea', detail of a kylix (shallow drinking cup) by Exekias, 1st century BC. It illustrates the importance of the vine in Greek civilization.

Tomb of Sennufer (18th dynasty) in the Valley of the Nobles, Egypt.

first vineyards would have been obtained simply by clearing undergrowth and thinning out the trees that acted as natural supports for the wild vines. It would seem, too, that the keeping of goats made a great contribution to the development of wine growing! The goat was the first animal to be domesticated by man on a large scale; it browsed on the vines so thoroughly that it pruned them, which helped them to thrive and be fruitful. In time, the Asiatic tribes inhabiting these regions migrated, taking with them the first rudiments of the vine culture that was, little by little, to take over the Near East, then the western Mediterranean basin and Central Asia.

Written and pictorial records relating to the vine show the importance of wine growing in Mesopotamia and Egypt from 1700 BC. In turn, this wine-based civilization spread to Greece. It was already flourishing there in about 800 BC, during the Homeric period. The Greek navigators who founded many cities around the margins of the Mediterranean probably introduced not only the wild vine into these regions, but also varieties in the modern sense, selected from the wild stock for their qualitative and productive attributes.

It was in Italy that viticulture became most fully developed. We can see from the writings of Pliny and Columella, authors of treatises on natural sciences and agriculture, that at the beginning of our own era the cultivation of the vine was already based on sound techniques with regard to selection, pruning, manuring and harvesting. From this period on, the success of the wine producers led the authorities to resort to fairly severe measures from time to time, to reap benefits for themselves in taxes, or to check the expansion of wine growing at the expense of corn crops, or to combat fraud.

The development of wine growing in France

As happened elsewhere throughout Europe, the fruit of the wild vine was gathered and made into 'wine' by the earliest peoples of Gaul, particularly the Celts. However, it was probably the Phocaeans who, in the 6th century BC, brought the cultivation of vine, in the true sense of the word, to the south of France. There it developed in parallel with the cultivation of the olive.

In other areas of France, the establishment of vineyards followed soon after the conquest of Gaul by Julius Caesar (58–51 BC). The Gallo-Roman period, which lasted until the 5th century AD, was marked by a considerable expansion of the French area under vines.

After declining somewhat due to barbarian invasions and the disturbed times that followed them, wine growing was once more encouraged by Charlemagne (742–814). It then experienced mixed fortunes through the Middle Ages. During the whole of this period the Church, and in particular the monasteries, became the privileged centres for the development of wine growing and making. There can be no doubt that it was the monks who developed viticulture to the stage at which it could be commercially exploited. Contrary to popular belief, this was by no means due to an excessive fondness on their part for the pleasures of the table. For many centuries, in fact, the monks did not even drink the wine. They were content to sell it and devote the profits to charity or to the upkeep of their estates. Their influence on the development of French wine growing as a whole was considerable, but their greatest success was probably the development of the Burgundian vineyards.

In the course of the following centuries, the often thoughtless extension of the vineyards forced the authorities to intervene many times to curb wine production by limiting new plantings, by grubbing up vines — and even by forbidding manuring! But all in vain: towards the end of the 17th century the total French vineyard area was in the neighbourhood of 2.3 million ha. This situation, linked with extreme poverty in the rural population, worsened to the point where a royal edict was necessary, in 1731, to institute various restrictive measures. These, it seems, were successful, for nearly 700,000 ha of vineyards disappeared within 50 years. After the French Revolution, however, all restraints of this kind were removed, so that by 1865 the total vineyard area had once more reached its peak of 2.3 million ha, distributed across most of the country's *départements*.

Monk filling a cask. Illustration from the register of the abbey of Saint-Germain-des-Prés, 15th century.

The dark years

What man had not been able to achieve — a permanent reduction in the wine-growing acreage — nature brought about, in a most radical manner. Until about the middle of the 19th century, it was only occasionally necessary to do battle with vine parasites and, properly speaking, these did not represent an obstacle to production. But, around 1850, a parasitic fungus — oidium (powdery mildew), which had arrived from Britain — began to spread in France and cause serious reductions in the grape harvest. The use of sulphur in the vineyards, however, quickly neutralized this scourge.

Some 15 years later, a withering of vine stems was noticed in Gard and Gironde. This proved to be due to the destruction of their roots by a plant louse, named *Phylloxera vastatrix*, introduced from North America, where it lived on resistant species of *Vitis*. This was the start of the 'phylloxera invasion', which in a few years was to wipe out many French vineyards.

Fortunately, it was soon realized that the way to save the French and other European vineyards affected by phylloxera lay in grafting *Vitis vinifera* vines on to American *Vitis* species rootstocks. Even then, new difficulties lay ahead: this American rootstock material served as a means of transport to Europe for a new and formidable parasitic fungus: downy mildew (also known as peronospora). This made its appearance in France in 1878. Treatment based on copper salts was proposed in 1884, but systematic countermeasures did not become general until much later. These natural calamities enforced a radical change in viticultural techniques and it is not surprising that the rebuilding of vineyards by means of grafted plants was only carried through in regions that were strongly and traditionally given over to wine growing. The disappearance of the vines from marginal growing zones in many northern *départements*, further accentuated by the growth of rail transport (which enabled wine to be supplied to Paris and other larger northern towns from sources far to the south) finally reduced the French wine-producing area to around 1.7 million ha. The years 1870 to 1890 are certainly the darkest and most eventful in the history of *Vitis vinifera*.

The French vineyards today

The success that has been achieved — fairly easily, on the whole — by crossing different species of *Vitis* to obtain rootstocks well adapted to specific situations has encouraged researchers to seek viticultural salvation not in chemical combat with cryptogamic afflictions but in the creation of hybrid direct producers: ungrafted 'ideal' vines that combine the quality of French grape varieties with the resistance to downy mildew, phylloxera and oidium (powdery mildew) possessed by American species. But the efforts of the plant breeders have come up against the difficulty of uniting in a single variety organoleptic qualities suitably close to those of *vinifera*, with good resistance to parasites. This is the reason why direct producer (ungrafted) hybrids have never seriously threatened grafted traditional varieties in the areas that produce fine wines. Nevertheless, these hybrids spread considerably in the southwest and west of France, in the Rhône valley, and in the mixed-farming areas where wine growing was under threat. They ended by accounting for 30 per cent of the total French wine-growing area, and it is only since 1980 that plantings of these hybrids have undergone a rapid decline.

PHYLLOXERA

In France and most other wine-growing countries today, phylloxera is no longer considered to be a dangerous vine parasite, thanks to the more or less general practice of grafting fruiting varieties on to resistant rootstocks.

It can never be forgotten, however, that in the 19th century this insect came close to totally destroying the vineyards of Europe planted with Vitis vinifera, *and that it caused a crisis without parallel in the history of viticulture, the effects of which are still felt around the wine-growing world today.*

Phylloxera vastatrix *(now sometimes called* Dactylosphaera vitifoliae*) is a plant louse originating in the eastern United States, where it lives almost exclusively on the vine. Its life cycle is complex as it can develop in either of two forms, one affecting the leaves, the other the roots.*

In summer the winged phylloxera that have reached the surface of the soil take flight and lay three to eight eggs on the bark of vines. Some of the insects lay eggs that will produce female individuals, others the smaller ones from which males will emerge. After mating the female lays a single egg on two-year-old wood. The female larva that emerges in early spring attaches herself to the underside of young foliage and causes a gall to form. There she lays parthenogenetic eggs, which will be the start of three to five more generations of phylloxera that, in their turn, will be capable of producing galls. This gall-producing form is not particularly dangerous for the vine. It is found especially on certain varieties of American Vitis *and on hybrids. It is rare on* vinifera *vines.*

Towards autumn, certain of the larvae enter the soil, where they hibernate. These are very prolific, and are the originators of multiple parthenogenetic generations of the phylloxera that attack roots; they can, furthermore, continue to reproduce indefinitely without needing to pass through the gall-producing form.

These larvae attach themselves to young vine roots, which they pierce with their rostra. In the resistant species, i.e. most of the American Vitis, *the multiplication of these parasites is reduced and the lesions they cause are benign. On the roots of* Vitis vinifera, *on the other hand, their density can be very great and the numerous punctures they make induce cellular disorders, which produce tubercles, and these first restrict and then block the circulation of the sap. The vine stocks become progressively weaker and usually die within the space of 3 to 10 years. The damage can be noticed spreading in the form of blemishes on the leaves that increase in number from year to year.*

Introduced into France with Vitis *cuttings from the United States between 1858 and 1862, the parasite multiplied unrecognized, for several years. Around 1869 the withering of vines in parts of Hérault, Gard and Gironde proved to be due to the insect, by this time named* Phylloxera vastatrix. *By 1880, the situation seemed catastrophic: most of the French vineyards were infested. This is still the case — but without damage to the vines, thanks to grafting, which brought about a swift reconstitution of the affected vineyards. This process has led to a considerable geographical movement of grafts and rootstocks, which in turn has been one of the main factors in the spread of virus diseases — one of the unfortunate consequences of the phylloxera invasion.*

The containment of parasites within acceptable limits, and the general progress that has affected wine growing as well as all the other sectors of agriculture, led after the First World War to a new crisis of overproduction, due this time not to an increase in the total vineyard area but to bigger yields. This situation, in which the ill-considered development of Algerian viticulture played an important part, not only provoked an economic crisis but also serious social troubles in many wine-growing regions. All this forced governments to bring in a succession of legal measures, such as halting or regulating new vine planting, blocking part of the grape harvest, or getting rid of surplus wine through distillation. A consequence of these measures was the establishment of uniform pricing for basic table wines, based on yield and alcoholic content. This had some positive results in the Midi, but led to no improvement in the quality of the harvest. The fact that there are good and less good grape varieties, and that the quality of wine should be paramount, had simply been forgotten; so eventually this solution was seen to have been a disastrous one.

The general levelling of the price of wine severely penalized the production of fine wines. The old wine-growing areas, the glory of French viticulture, saw their existence threatened. Happily they were saved by the introduction of *appellations d'origine contrôlée*, gradually established from 1935 onwards, and still being introduced in our own times.

Among the various *appellation* requirements, those relating to grape varieties are of particular importance: what would bordeaux be without its Cabernet Sauvignon, burgundy and champagne without their Pinot Noir and Chardonnay, the wines of the Côtes du Rhône without their Syrah, the wines of Alsace without Gewürztraminer?

Today, the total French wine-growing area covers 1.1 million ha: about one tenth of the world total. But France is not alone; viticulture in the countries of the European Community accounts for 60 per cent of world wine production, from 50 per cent of the world's total vineyard area. Bearing in mind the overproduction that is once again rampant, the land given over to wine growing can only diminish. It is to be hoped that this will work to the detriment of the lesser *vins ordinaires* and to the profit of those striking and individual wines that, in parallel with the great French *crus*, will prove attractive enough to draw tomorrow's consumers.

Grape Varieties

There are, around the world, some 5,000 grape varieties — without counting hybrids! Ampelography, the science of vine description, has the difficult task of bringing order into this world of proximity and confusion. It is an important task, for wine quality depends on a thorough knowledge of grape varieties, and on their intelligent utilization.

In viticulture, the term 'grape variety' indicates the kind of vine plant used to make a particular wine. Thus red burgundy is made from the Pinot Noir grape variety, whereas white burgundy comes from Chardonnay. From a strictly botanical viewpoint, however, a 'grape variety' is not a true variety at all, as it does not reproduce itself identically from seed and can only be perpetuated through vegetative propagation, i.e. through taking cuttings, grafting or layering. Nor is the term 'cultivar' appropriate since it indicates a clone raised from seed then subsequently propagated vegetatively, so that all its descendants are identical to it. Vines can be true cultivars when they result from artificial hybridization; one example is the Alicante Bouschet, from the Petit Bouschet × Grenache cross. But most of our grape varieties are in reality an 'assemblage' of apparently closely similar clones lumped together under the same name. Practitioners down through the centuries have often managed to spot differences between these closely related clones and named them accordingly. These names may reflect those of the selective breeder, as in Pinot Liébault, Pinot Pansiot, Pinot Renevey; or of the place of origin, as in Pinot de Pernand, or Pinot Maltais.

Variations between grape varieties are of three kinds:

▷ morphological characteristics: hairiness, leaf shape, sex of the flowers, dimensions of the bunches or of individual grapes, colour of the grapes;

▷ physiological or cultural characteristics: budbreak or ripening time, fertility and size of yield, amount of sugar and acidity in the musts, quality of the wines obtained, colour of wines, taste of wines;

▷ health profile of the plants.

The origins of grape varieties

French grape varieties all belong to the botanical species *Vitis vinifera, Linnaeus*, which is distributed across the whole central area of Europe and the Mediterranean countries as well as in western Asia, the region that is thought to be the cradle of the vine. The first grapes gathered by men in antiquity came from vines that had developed naturally among other kinds of vegetation. Very probably they resulted from natural propagation, growing from seeds distributed at random after passing

GRAPE RIPENING PERIODS

Grape ripening periods vary according to latitude, climate and the soil a particular variety is growing in. The exact moment of ripening also changes every year as a function of differing spring and autumn temperatures. It has nevertheless been possible to compile a scale of ripeness for all varieties, using the Chasselas, a variety grown throughout the world, as a reference point.

EPOCH		RIPENING PERIOD	GRAPE VARIETY
Early-ripening grapes		15 days before	Baco Noir
First-epoch grapes	early	5 days before	Chasselas
	middle	Ripening of the Chasselas	
	late	5 days after	
Second-epoch grapes	early	12 days after	Cinsaut
	middle	17days after	Sauvignon Blanc
	late	22 days after	Cabernet Sauvignon
Third-epoch grapes		25 – 35 days after	Aramon Carignan Grenache
Fourth-epoch grapes		40 – 45 days after	Muscat d'Alexandrie

undamaged through the digestive tracts of men and animals who had eaten the grapes. These wild vines, belonging to a morphological class described as Labruscoid, often survived in forests until the arrival of the phylloxera in Europe in the 19th century. Nowadays, they are only encountered in certain isolated regions or in areas as yet untouched by phylloxera, such as Nuristan in Afganistan, the Crimea, Austria or Yugoslavia.

In France, one can find 'pseudo-wild' vines in woods or by rivers: these are vineyard escapes resulting from the consumption of dessert or wine grapes by animals or by Sunday picnickers.

Identifying grape varieties

It is not known exactly how many cultivated grape varieties there are, but the number must be around 5,000, not including hybrids, which on their own must number several thousand. The difficulties involved in making an inventory on a world scale are of several kinds.

In each wine-producing region, the vines bear traditional names that have sometimes been in use for centuries: in Burgundy, for example, the Chardonnay is also known as the Pinot Chardonnay or even the Pinot Blanc. But there is a true Pinot Blanc, grown most notably in Alsace. Its foliage is identical to that of the Pinot Noir, but its grapes are white. In the Loire valley, the leading quality white grape is the Chenin Blanc, which is also referred to locally as the Pinot (or Pineau) de la Loire, even though it does not belong to the Pinot family. Thus in France the name Pinot Blanc can lead to the confusion of three different varieties.

Matters are further complicated at the international level. Not only are these three varieties also found outside France under the same name — the Chenin Blanc is known in Argentina and Chile, for example, as the Pinot Bianco — but so are other vines of French origin. The Melon is called the Pinot Blanc in California. There is, then, a 'global synonymy', in which one name may refer to separate varieties of vines that differ greatly in the quality of wine they produce.

Each variety may have a number of different names given it by growers down the years. To identify them, lists of synonyms have to be compiled. To resume with the example of the Chardonnay, we find that it is called the Melon Blanc in Arbois, Petite Sainte-Marie in Savoie, Rousseau or Roussot in Yonne, Beaunois around Tonnerre, Plant de Tonnerre in Yonne, Noirien Blanc on the Côte d'Or, Chablis in the Paris area, Luisant at Besançon, Épinette in the Marne, Auvergnat Blanc in Moselle, Weiss Clevner, Klevner or Klewner in Alsace, and so on. This degree of synonymy makes any tally of the precise number of varieties difficult, the more so since voluntary or involuntary errors have arisen in the course of trade. There would need to be a complete catalogue of syn-

AMPELOGRAPHY

The study of grape varieties is called ampelography, a term coined in 1661 by Sachs, a doctor of medicine at Leipzig. He published a work on vine varieties entitled Ampelographia. *Today the purpose of ampelography is the botanical description of all the key parts of the vine: leaves, green shoots and fruit, to enable correct identification of varieties, and recognition of these varieties wherever they grow and whatever their local names may be. Recognizing grape varieties (there are about 5,000 of them) is a problem the world over, as is disentangling their synonyms (there are at least 40,000 names for the 5,000 varieties - an average of eight names each!).*

Ampelography is also concerned with knowing the physiological characteristics of each variety and the features of its cultivation: budbreak, flowering, ripening, qualities of the grape and the wine, methods of pruning and training, vulnerability to vine diseases and parasites, and those things that determine the grower's choice of variety in terms of what he wants to produce - grapes for the table or the fermenting vat, varieties for quality or quantity, resistance to winter or spring cold, or resistance to cryptogamic diseases.

The Syrah has been an increasingly planted variety in recent years.

The Chenin Blanc is the fourth most widely grown white grape variety in France.

The Carignan is the most widely grown grape variety in France.

The Ugni Blanc is chiefly grown in the Cognac and Armagnac regions.

REGIONAL PLANTINGS OF GRAPE VARIETIES IN FRANCE
in hectares

ALSACE	BORDEAUX	BURGUNDY & BEAUJOLAIS	CHAMPAGNE	COGNAC	CORSICA
Pinot Noir 700 Oberlin Noir 50	Merlot 36 000 Cabernet Sauv. 18 000 Cabernet Franc 11 000 Malbec/Côt 2 200 Petit Verdot 450 Bouchalès 400 Villard Noir 275 Garonnet 50 Plantet 40 Baco Noir 30 various 629	Gamay 25 600 Pinot Noir 9 000 Gamay Teint. 500 Syrah 100 Plantet 80 Oberlin Noir 80 Baco Noir 40 Maréchal Foch 25 Florental 10 various 235	Meunier 10 500 Pinot Noir 7 800 various 61	Merlot 700 Cabernet Franc 200 Cabernet Sauv. 100 Jurançon Noir 50 Villard Noir 30 Plantet 20 Baco Noir 10	Carignan 3 500 Cinsaut 2 600 Nielluccio 2 550 Grenache 2 000 Alicante B. 1 550 Sciaccarello 730 Syrah 300
Total red 750	**Total red 69 074**	**Total red 35 670**	**Total red 18 361**	**Total red 1 110**	**Total red 13 230**
Gewürztraminer 2 700 Sylvaner 2 650 Riesling 2 500 Auxerrois 1 200 Pinot Blanc 900 Chasselas 600 Pinot Gris 600 Muscat Ottonel 400 Muscat Blanc 100 various 707	Sémillon 16 700 Ugni Blanc 6 500 Colombard 3 600 Sauvignon Blanc 2 500 Muscadelle 2 400 Merlot Blanc 1 800 Baco Blanc 125 Villard Blanc 75 various 100	Chardonnay 6 700 Aligoté 1 100 Pinot Blanc 100 Melon 50 Chasselas 20 Viognier 10 various 277	Chardonnay 7 000	Ugni Blanc 90 300 Colombard 1 000 Folle Blanche 50 Baco Blanc 30 Villard Blanc 15 various 5	Vermentino 1 000 Ugni Blanc 600 various 501
Total white 12 357	**Total white 33 800**	**Total white 8 257**	**Total white 7 000**	**Total white 91 400**	**Total white 2 101**
Plantings 1985 13 107	**Plantings 1985 102 874**	**Plantings 1985 43 927**	**Plantings 1985 25 361**	**Plantings 1985 92 510**	**Plantings 1985 15 331**

LANGUEDOC-ROUSSILLON

Carignan	170 200
Aramon	54 000
Grenache	34 800
Cinsaut	34 500
Alicante B	15 000
Couderc Noir	3 150
Aubun	3 000
Merlot	2 300
Syrah	2 000
Cabernet Sauv.	1 500
Terret Noir	1 100
Villard Noir	1 000
Mourvèdre	600
Tempranillo	500
Counoise	400
Piquepoul Noir	350
Cabernet Franc.	200
Garonnet	150
Varousset	100
Colobel	50
various	189
Total red	**325 089**
Grenache Blanc	15 300
Terret	9 000
Macabeu	7 000
Ugni Blanc	4 000
Muscat Blanc	3 700
Muscat d'Alex	3 400
Villard Blanc	3 000
Carignan Blanc	2 300
Clairette	2 300
Mauzac	2 000
Aramon Gris	1 100
Piquepoul Blanc	600
Listan	410
Bourboulenc	200
Chardonnay	200
Chenin Blanc	60
Total white	**54 570**
Plantings 1985	**379 659**

PROVENCE

Grenache	40 500
Carignan	25 500
Cinsaut	13 500
Aramon	4 400
Aubun	2 600
Alicante B	2 500
Mourvèdre	2 400
Couderc Noir	1 500
Tibouren	500
Villard Noir	250
Cabernet Franc.	100
Varousset	15
various	574
Total red	**94 339**
Ugni Blanc	10 500
Clairette	2 100
Roussanne	1 000
Villard Blanc	500
Muscat Blanc	300
Rolle	200
Sémillon	100
Sauvignon Blanc	50
various	50
Total white	**14 800**
Plantings 1985	**109 139**

RHÔNE-ALPES JURA & SAVOIE

Grenache	10 000
Carignan	4 500
Syrah	4 000
Cinsaut	2 500
Couderc Noir	2 500
Aramon	2 000
Villard Noir	1 700
Gamay	1 300
Alicante B	1 000
Mourvèdre	300
Poulsard	300
Mondeuse	250
Pinot Noir	250
Plantet	250
Aubun	100
Merlot	100
Trousseau	100
Valdiguié	100
Varousset	100
Cabernet Sauv	80
Chambourcin	50
Baco Noir	35
Seinoir	25
Cabernet Franc.	20
Garonnet	20
various	2 115
Total red	**33 695**
Clairette	1 000
Jacquère	1 000
Chardonnay	850
Muscat Blanc	500
Villard Blanc	450
Chasselas	350
Marsanne	250
Savagnin	250
Altesse	200
Ugni Blanc	200
Aligoté	50
Molette	40
Roussanne	40
Viognier	28
Rayon d'Or	18
various	2 042
Total white	**7 268**
Plantings 1985	**40 963**

SOUTH WEST PYRENEES

Jurançon Noir	7 500
Merlot	6 000
Villard Noir	4 000
Cabernet Franc	3 700
Malbec/Côt	3 500
Tannat	3 500
Cabernet Sauv	1 900
Gamay	1 800
Alicante B.	1 700
Syrah	1 700
Bouchalès	1 600
Couderc Noir	1 200
Portugais Bleu	1 200
Négrette	1 150
Plantet	1 000
Valdiguié	900
Mansenc Noir	800
Mérille	750
Chambourcin	700
Abouriou Noir	600
Duras	400
Fer	300
Milgranet	300
Cinsaut	200
Garonnet	150
Aramon	100
Carignan	100
various	934
Total red	**47 684**
Ugni Blanc	12 500
Baco Blanc	9 500
Sémillon	7 000
Mauzac	4 500
Baroque	1 700
Villard Blanc	1 600
Muscadelle	1 400
Colombard	1 300
Sauvignon Blanc	1 100
Jurançon Blanc	700
Petit Manseng	600
Graisse	500
Len de l'El	500
Listan	360
Folle Blanche	300
Meslier St-François	200
Ondenc	150
Arrufiac	100
Clairette	100
Merlot Blanc	100
various	1 510
Total white	**45 720**
Plantings 1985	**93 404**

LOIRE VALLEY

Cabernet Franc	10 500
Gamay	6 500
Grolleau	6 000
Plantet	3 800
Chambourcin	3 000
Cabernet Sauv	1 800
Pinot d'Aunis	1 500
Villard Noir	900
Malbec/Côt	500
Pinot Noir	500
Seinoir	500
Gamay Teint	300
Landal	300
Meunier	250
Léon Millot	150
Oberlin Noir	80
Abouriou	40
Colobel	35
Couderc Noir	30
Garonnet	20
various	6 615
Total red	**43 320**
Chenin Blanc	9 700
Melon	9 700
Folle Blanche	4 000
Sauvignon Blanc	3 500
Arbois	1 200
Baco Blanc	1 200
Meslier St-François	600
Pinot Blanc	500
Romorantin	400
Rayon d'Or	350
Grolleau Gris	250
Chardonnay	200
Chasselas	150
Seyval	100
Villard Blanc	50
Pinot Gris	30
Rubilande	30
Aligoté	10
various	4 018
Total white	**35 988**
Plantings 1985	**79 308**

onyms for each wine-producing country before any global tally of varieties could be made.

The universal language of botanists and, in a more general sense, of all educated people, used to be Latin; and the use of Latin has been maintained for the description of new species. French also played an important part in botanical literature up to the end of the 19th century. The misfortunes of the French wine industry following the arrival of the American diseases led to the publication of many works on these disorders and means of combating them, as well as on the grape varieties that were resistant to the parasites. Since then, English has taken over as the chief language used in such works. Since 1945, however, numerous books about grape varieties have been published in various other languages, making ampelography something of a Tower of Babel, and rendering clear identification of vines and their synonyms still more difficult.

Classifying grape varieties

Vines can be classified in a number of ways:

▷ The botanical characteristics of foliage and fruit can be utilized — this ampelographic approach enables grape varieties to be arranged into groups and families: Muscats, Pinots, Malvoisies, etc.

▷ Geographical distinctions can be taken as primary, with vines divided into French, German, Spanish, Italian, Portuguese varieties, etc. However, it should be remembered that at the moment some 30 high-quality varieties are found in many wine-growing countries of the world, and that most of these are of French origin.

▷ A further basis of classification is the purpose the fruit is intended for: vinification, distillation or the table.

Varieties suitable for wine making have grapes with high levels of sugar and juice. A distinction is made between 'noble' varieties that provide wines of high quality, such as the Pinot Noir, Chardonnay, Cabernet Sauvignon, Riesling, Syrah or Grenache; and the 'ordinary' grape varieties with high yields for quantity production of table wines, such as the Aramon or the Ugni Blanc.

Varieties destined for distilling are productive white grapes. Wines made from grapes such as these are thin and acid, both desirable qualities in base wines for distilling into spirits. The Folle Blanche, Ugni Blanc, Baco Blanc and Colombard are all typical distilling varieties.

Dessert grape varieties bear bunches of good appearance with well-separated grapes; these are often large, juicy and fleshy, according to taste. Customer preference is for white grapes rather than black or pink ones. The flavour of table grapes may be neutral, musky or 'foxy'.

Varieties meant for drying to provide raisins and sultanas are generally seedless (termed *apyrène* in French). Among them are the Sultana (known as the Sultanine in France, and as the Thompson Seedless in California), Corinthe Noir and Perlette; but seedlessness is not essential — the Rosaki and Muscat d'Alexandrie grapes have pips.

It will be clear that the above classification is less than rigorous and that some varieties can be used in more than one way, according to the locality and the economic circumstances under which they are grown. Thus in some countries unsold table grapes end in the fermenting vats, and wine-making varieties may have multiple functions. The Muscat d'Alexandrie has four uses: as a table grape, as dried fruit, to make muscat wine, and to provide wine for distilling into pisco (Peruvian brandy). Similarly, the Sultanine can be used as a table grape, as dried fruit, vinified into wine, and sometimes even distilled to make arak.

This system of classification by purpose has been adopted by the European Community. The EC, however, distinguishes between two further subcategories of its own for wine grapes, namely 'recommended' grape varieties, which provide wines of recognized good quality; and 'authorized' grape varieties giving straightforward, marketable wines whose quality, although satisfactory, is below that of the 'recommended' category. The cultivation of these less desirable 'authorized' grapes is limited to a maximum of 50 per cent of the total vineyard area of each grape-growing country.

As a result, a list of 'recommended' and 'authorized' grapes has been drawn up for each French *département* (and for each province in other EC countries).

With regard to the French AOC or VQPRD wines (*vin de*

GRAPE VARIETIES AND WINE QUALITY

Every grape variety has its own particular characteristics, manifested in the dimensions of the bunches and the size and shape of the grapes, the amount of juice produced, the thickness of the skins and in their chemical composition — sugars, organic acids, polyphenols, anthocyanins, aromatic elements, etc. Every variety therefore has a specific purpose, as a wine grape of quality, as a wine grape of quantity, or as a table grape.

Certain growing techniques, such as the choice of rootstock, density of planting, methods of pruning and training, irrigation and manuring affect the initial chemical composition of the berries. All techniques aimed at significantly increasing the yield of a vine are bound to entail a lowering of the quality of the resulting wine. This is the main reason for the often poor quality of wine from new vineyard areas of the world; in general, these growers seek the greatest possible yields without consideration of the quality characteristics of the variety.

In old French vineyards there was often a tradition of planting two or more varieties together, each with slightly different attributes: one type would give colour and tannins; another finesse and bouquet; a third, possibly with a higher yield, would be introduced into the final mix to ensure consistency of production.

It is the choice of grape variety that, after due allowance is made for the methods of cultivation and vinification employed, conditions the basic quality of the wine obtained.

The Merlot is a vigorous and, at present, fashionable grape variety that thrives in well-watered ground.

qualité produit dans une région déterminée: 'quality wine produced within a defined area', an EC term), legally approved varieties of vines have been set out in the legislation governing each *appellation*, with in some cases the maximum percentage allowed, or a minimum threshold of planting of a particular variety to be reached within a stipulated period.

The vines planted in a given vineyard or vineyard region may be of one variety only: for example, the Muscat à Petits Grains for the Muscat de Frontignan, Lunel, Mireval, Beaumes de Venise or Saint-Jean de Minervois AOCs. Sometimes, as in Alsace, wines are sold under the names of the grape varieties they are made from: Riesling, Gewürztraminer, Sylvaner. Often, however, the name of a single grape variety is not given, but it is implied by mention of the place of origin: Beaujolais (Gamay), Vouvray (Chenin Blanc), Sancerre (Sauvignon Blanc) or Hermitage (Syrah).

Plantings of two kinds of vines are more often encountered in France, though, their fruits being complementary in terms of quality and of yield; better still, three kinds; and sometimes even greater complexity is found: 13 different grape varieties are permitted for Châteauneuf-du-Pape.

Before the phylloxera epidemic, there was a tradition of planting several varieties of vine within one vineyard, providing a mixture of grapes to be taken to the vats to ferment together. In the vineyard, cross-fertilization between the varieties ensured good fertility, lessened the ravages of *coulure* (flower abortion) and divided the risk of disease attendant on frost, drought or attacks of grey rot (botrytis).

ROOTSTOCKS

Following the phylloxera invasion in the second half of the 19th century, wine growers almost everywhere, except in those areas of sand where the vines are trained part-buried, and where phylloxera itself cannot survive, had to resort to grafting French vines on to resistant American varieties. The latter are termed rootstocks.

The qualities required of a good rootstock in the French context are, firstly, that it should be resistant to the form of phylloxera that destroys the roots of vulnerable varieties; secondly, that it should be well adapted to the limestone soils so prevalent in France; and thirdly, that it should, when necessary, be resistant to certain nematode worms or eelworms that infest light, sandy soils.

Other criteria may be involved in rootstock choice: acidity of soils; presence of salt (sodium chloride) in soils; adaptability to drought or humidity; sensitivity to mineral deficiency; vigour; the incompatibility of certain rootstock clones with some clones of wine or table grape varieties; the quest for rootstocks of early-ripening varieties for growing early table grapes, or for advancing the ripening time of wine grapes in unfavourable geographical situations. In the case of late-ripening varieties, the choice of rootstock should be from among those that are vigorous, with long vegetative cycles.

For the nurseryman other factors come into play: productivity of canes for rootstock material, which varies from one variety to another; ease of recovery from cutting and grafting in the nursery; total national demand, differing as it does from one region to another; and, finally, trends in foreign markets which regulate the export of vine plants and cuttings.

Under EC regulations, 29 registered varieties of rootstock have been listed for use in France: Rupestris du Lot (also known as Rupestris St George), Riparia Gloire de Montpellier, 34 EM, 333 EM, 3309 Couderc, 1616 C, 161–49 C, 420 A Mgt, 101–114 Mgt, 41 B Mgt, 99 & 110 Richter, SO4, 4453 Malègue, 196–17 Castel, 2163 Cl, 4010 Cl, 140 Ruggeri, 1103 & 1447 Paulsen, Kober 5 5B, Kober 125 AA, Teleki 8B, 5C, Vialla, Grézot 1, Berlandieri-Colombard no. 2, Fercal & RS (Resseguier sélection Birolleau no. 1).

Since the American vine diseases became generalized in France, the preference has been for growing different varieties separately so as to be better able to combat these scourges. Lastly, legal requirements also necessitate one-variety planting, which makes it easier to check the amount of vineyard area devoted to 'recommended' or 'authorized' grape varieties.

Wine-Growing Soils And Environments

Wine draws its greatness from the terroir *that has given it birth. The alchemy of light, temperature, water and earth determines a wine's qualities and particular features. Science has begun to penetrate these mysteries, but as yet offers no more than the beginning of an explanation. Wine-growing* terroirs *are jealous of their secrets . . .*

A *terroir* may be defined as a stretch of land with specific agricultural attributes resulting from the combination of local climate factors and the nature of the soil. A viticultural *terroir*, however, is rather more than this. There is a good deal of man's handiwork in it. Through a whole series of interventions, in the methods of nurturing the vines and the soil, the wine grower is in fact able to change the natural environment into a managed one that is generally favourable to the quality of its products. The reputation of a particular *terroir* may depend in the first instance on its natural potential, but it also depends to a considerable extent on the skill of the wine grower, and then on that of the wine maker.

The idea of a wine-growing *terroir* necessarily implies a degree of affinity between the characteristics of the environment and the potential of the grape varieties grown there. The grapes should not only be able to reach a satisfactory degree of ripeness, but should also exhibit pleasing organoleptic characteristics, subtle, nuanced, and varying according to the *terroir* they are grown in.

The study of a *terroir* requires analysis and knowledge of both climate and soil.

Climatic factors and the vine

Three types of climate can be distinguished, according to the size of the *terroir* under consideration. The macroclimate, or regional climate, is the average climate of a fairly extensive stretch of land. The local climate, or mesoclimate, corresponds to a particular part of a macroclimate, as, for example, a series of slopes facing the same way. In everyday language, the mesoclimate or local climate is often confused with the microclimate, a term that should really be applied only to a small and clearly delimited area.

There are three basic climate factors: light, temperature and water.

Light is the source of photosynthesis. This is the very complex process that enables green plants to synthesize sugars. In the great majority of the wine-growing regions of the world, enough intense light is radiated naturally to produce this phenomenon in vines. In northern regions, the longer hours of summer daylight offset the decrease in light intensity.

Temperature exerts a prime influence on the growth of the vine and the ripening of the grapes. The distribution of different *Vitis* species around the world is due to a great extent to temperature factors. And the specific temperature requirements of different grape varieties are the most important element governing their distribution within natural or national wine regions.

For a long time now, researchers have been trying to establish in numerical terms some degree of correlation between temperature and the growth of plants. Taking mean temperatures over a period of six months in certain wine-growing

Seasonal heat summations are used to evaluate the thermal potential of a wine-growing environment. Their method of calculation is as follows. Vines only grow and develop fruit when the temperature is above 10°C. Seasonal heat summations are therefore based on 'degree days': days when the average daily temperature is above 10°C. The amount by which the average daily temperature exceeds 10°C during the growing season (April to November) is totalled to give the heat summation for a particular area.

RIPENING ZONES FOR FRENCH GRAPE VARIETIES

Zone	Average daily temperature 0°C during growing season	Seasonal heat summation	Varieties	Towns
Cool temperate	< 17	< 1 290	Sauvignon Blanc, Chardonnay, Gewürztraminer, Gamay, Pinot Noir	Dijon Nantes
Temperate	17.1 to 18.5	1 300 to 1 560	Sémillon, Cabernet Sauvignon, Merlot	Bordeaux
Warm temperate	18.6 to 20	1 570 to 1 840	Syrah, Grenache, Cinsaut, Carignan, Ugni Blanc, Clairette	Montpellier
Warm	20.1 to 21.5	1 850 to 2 120		Perpignan

environments, they have arrived at a classification of the French viticultural regions into four zones where different grape varieties can each enjoy satisfactory conditions (see below left).

The ripeness of the fruit is another rather complex matter, and does not only relate to the development of the sugar content of the berries. It is also governed by levels of acids, aromatic elements and phenolic compounds in the fruit.

From the wine-growing point of view, it is 'technological' ripeness that counts most. 'Technological' in this context refers to the optimum time for picking, with a view to obtaining a given type of wine. Thus the optimum technological ripeness of the Pinot Noir, for example, differs according to whether the grapes are required for making champagne or red burgundy. Physiological ripeness, on the other hand, corresponds more simply to a maximum natural sugar content. Overripeness (as required for certain dessert wines) is a purely physical phenomenon whereby increased sugar content results from evaporation of water in the berries.

Temperature is also a critical factor with regard to the acidity of wine, its colour and its aromatic potential. For example, bunches of grapes exposed to direct sunlight exhibit a lower malic acid content than those shaded by clouds or leaf cover. The breakdown of this acid is accelerated by heat.

It is difficult to obtain red wines of deep colour in cool climatic conditions. This is why, in cool wine-growing regions like Alsace, growers produce mainly white wines.

It has been possible to establish quality wine growing in northern regions or high-altitude areas largely due to certain mesoclimates, and a good many microclimates, being favourable in terms of warmth. Such sites may owe their potential to south or southwestern aspects, to the slope of the vineyard, or to the presence of lakes or of rivers: all these factors improve not only the ripening process but the whole unfolding of the vegetative cycle.

Water — a prime factor

Water occupies a prime place among the climatic factors affecting wine-growing environments. It may be considered the most important constituent of the organs of healthy plants. It ensures their multiple metabolic functioning, being an essential part of biochemical reactions, and conveying materials and synthesized products. In evaporating, it protects plants from overheating. In the soil, water plays an important role in the absorption of minerals by the plant.

In France, where irrigation is only authorized in certain Mediterranean areas, the vineyards' water needs are met almost exclusively by local rainfall. However, knowledge of the amount and distribution of rainfall does not indicate whether the requirements of the vines are in reality being supplied. In fact, given that evaporation of water from the soil and transpiration from the plants is more intensive in a warm climate than in a cool one, the same amount of rainfall may be broadly sufficient for a northern wine area but inadequate in the Midi.

The concept of potential evapotranspiration (*évapotranspiration potentielle*, or ETP in French) enables a more precise analysis to be made of the water situation in a given environment. Potential evapotranspiration can be defined as the total evaporation from the soil and total transpiration from plants within a given period, where the vegetation is in active growth and the soil amply provided with water. The result is given in millimetres. Thanks to this notion of potential evapotranspiration, the theoretical water balance sheet of a given environment can be defined in relation to the nature of its soil, of its relief, the presence of ground water beneath the water table, and so on. All the studies carried out in this area, however, have shown that the best wine-growing *terroirs* are often characterized by a water balance that is either in deficit or only just in credit.

The supply of water to a vine plays an important part in the development of its fruit. Yields, in particular, are influenced by the amount of water available during the period between flowering and *véraison* (when the grapes begin to colour and ripen). Ripening demands, above all, plenty of light and not very much water. Trials have shown that copious watering during the ripening process nearly always exerts, regardless of the sugar content of the fruit, a negative influence on the organoleptic quality of the resulting wines. Severe drought during the ripening period, however, is prejudicial to good ripening. Such situations are exceptional in France.

The soil and the quality of wines

The soil is a complex medium in which physical structure, chemical composition, water and temperature each play important parts. The yield of a vine is essentially dependent on the nutritive content of the soil. Traditionally, the ideal plot for wine growing is thought to be sloping, infertile, and well drained. But there are famous *crus* that come from naturally fertile soils. It should, however, be stressed that among cultivated plants the vine is unusual in having such a low fertilizer requirement and that it is good for putting poor land to use; indeed, too much manuring is certainly detrimental to the quality of the vintage.

In France, the potential quality of a wine-growing plot is attributed in large measure to the soil. From the outset, the soil plays an important role in the hierarchy of French wine. In a certain type of soil, a certain grape variety is always thought to

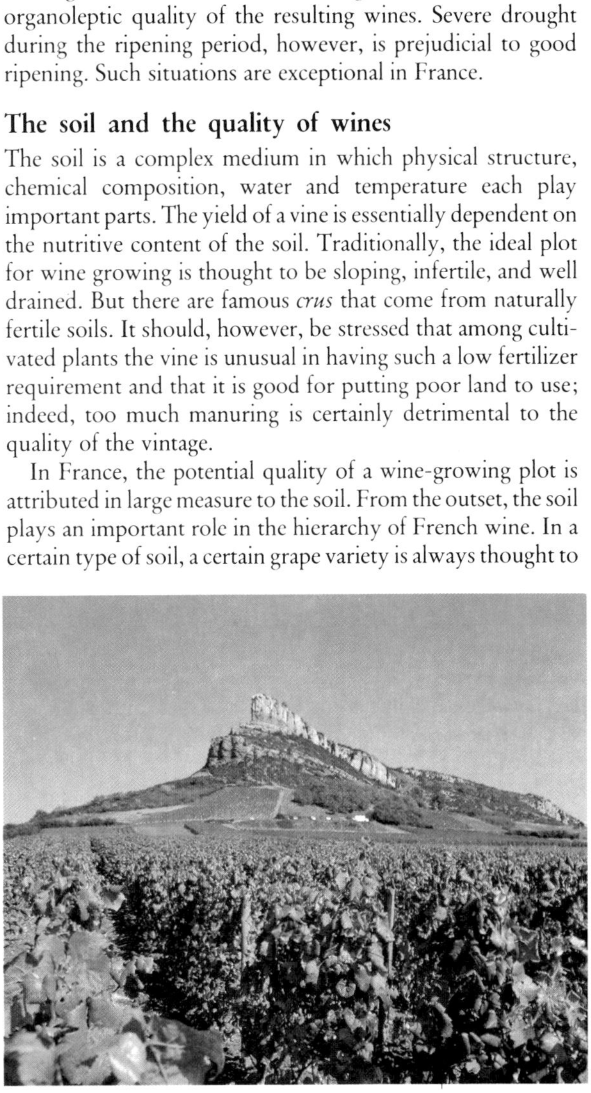

The rock of Solutré in the Mâconnais. The vineyards shown above, planted on layers of limestone rubble, produce the famed wine of Pouilly-Fuissé.

The depth of soil conditions root development and can affect the quantity of wine produced. The vine responds to the soil through the intermediary of its rootstock. Soil is a complex medium: it is generally recognized that its character influences the quality of wines, their aromas and colour, though exactly how is not yet known.

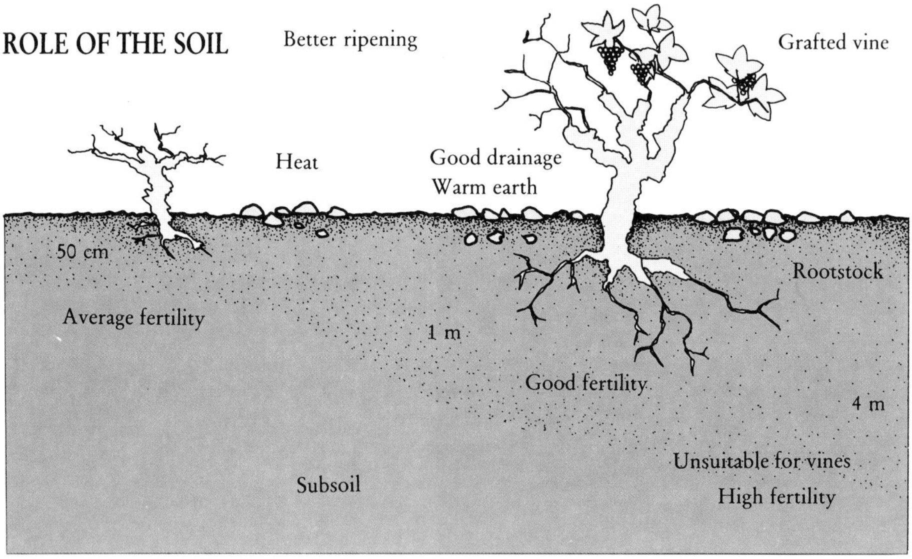

give a product that is organoleptically better, or less good, than it would be in other soils. The boundaries of all French *appellations d'origine contrôlée* are drawn up on this principle.

The soil also exerts its influence on specific features of wines from the same grape variety. Two such wines can be of equivalent quality yet, depending on the soil they were grown in, display differences that are regularly noted by good tasters.

Our knowledge of the specific role of the soil with regard to the quality of wines is still based largely on practical experience. However, numerous studies carried out in this field lead to certain conclusions.

In the first place, any difference in the geological character of the land (whether a plot contains clay, limestone or sandy soils, for example) exerts an influence on the wine produced. It appears that wines grown in light soils, such as granitic gravels and sands, have a floral character and reach full maturity more quickly than those from heavy soil. There are, however, many exceptions to this rule, due notably to the method of ageing.

Each soil, too, satisfies a predilection on the part of certain grape varieties. Thus in Burgundy the best location of varieties is as follows:

▷ Gamay on granitic sand (as in Beaujolais);
▷ Chardonnay on soils with a clay admixture, derived from marl;
▷ Pinot Noir on more fully evolved soils, derived from limestone.

Each of these varieties can be grown on other soils, but the quality is then diminished.

Based on minor differences of soil structure, very fine differentiations can be made out within a single category of wine. On the wine-growing slopes of the Côte d'Or, for example, there are two limestone-based soils of which one is characterized by pebbly surface deposits and the other by a much higher proportion of fine elements or clay. They are situated at comparable heights and with similar exposures. The first soil gives Pinot Noir wines that are very perfumed, relatively light and supple; the second produces much more tannic wines, with a different bouquet, less rounded on the palate than the former kind. There is, thus, a noticeable relationship between the amount of clay in the soil and the level of astringency in the resulting wine.

Finally, it has been shown that it is possible to distinguish between wines grown on sites very close together, with apparently identical soils. Experienced local tasters are able to differentiate between them to identify them. This phenomenon seems to defy logic. In such instances the notion of soil must generally defer to the concept of *terroir*, which implies the hand of man complementing the gifts of nature.

A possible hypothesis, however, attributes these differences to the chemical composition of the soil. We know that the richness of the soil in fertilizing elements affects yields and the quality of the wine. But the vine needs twelve mineral elements for its growth: nitrogen (N), phosphorus (P), calcium (Ca), magnesium (Mg), sulphur (S), iron (Fe), zinc (Zn), boron (B), manganese (Mn), molybdenum (Mo) and copper (Cu). The first six are macro-elements, the other six micro-elements.

Vineyards at Châteauneuf-du-Pape. The soil is made up of large quartzite pebbles washed down by the river Rhône. These absorb the sun's heat during the day and return it to the vines at night.

Along with the grape variety and the climatic conditions, the originality of a wine seems to be caused by the pattern and concentration of mineral elements penetrating the roots of the vine from the soil mixture. It has not, however, been possible to verify this hypothesis experimentally. Viable correlations between the levels of macro-elements in different soils, in the vegetative organs of the vines and in the resulting musts or wines are difficult to draw.

However, it does seem that in very many cases a regular water supply at relatively deep level is an extremely important quality factor. The regulation of this supply is largely due to the hydromorphic characteristics of the soils, and the many edaphic microclimates that result lead to specific qualities of taste. The level of concentration of mineral elements in the soil is evidently implicated in this process but, except in the case of deficiency or excess, it does not seem to be determinant.

This line of thought is supported by the results of recent research showing that the mineral content of the leaves of the same kind of vine grown on the same soil can vary considerably according to the rootstock used. Rootstocks, in fact, show very variable capacity for mineral absorption. If organoleptic differences between certain wines can be attributed to the minerals that have been absorbed (macro- or micro-elements) by the vine, then the rootstocks themselves must be the origin of an organoleptic variability at least as important as that due to the soil.

The zoning of wine-growing *terroirs*

In traditional wine-growing regions, where the cultivation of the vine has been practised for centuries, the preferred sites have, so to speak, individualized themselves over the years. This process started as soon as it had been ascertained that wines from these sites were of remarkable or special quality. Such sites went on to acquire a certain reputation, and the wines they produced were designated by the name of their place of origin. They were, of course, sold at prices higher than those of more anonymous wines. In the absence of any legal protection, a situation like this inevitably led to frauds, and it was not until the establishment, from 1935 onwards, of *appellations d'origine contrôlée* that such frauds were brought under control. Under the system then established the boundaries of the *appellation* zones were defined and each zone was, according to the *appellation* category given it, classed within a certain hierarchical group. The task of delimitation was — and still is — entrusted to a group of experts who went to the area in question and studied its every aspect (climate, topography, geology, pedology, orography, and so on). Account was taken of the traditional local grape varieties, methods of cultivation, and the limits on yields necessary for reaching the required standard of quality. Tastings of wines of different ages from the area being defined were also very helpful. This approach, combining a scientific basis with enlightened empiricism, has on the whole produced very good results.

For some time now, however, efforts have been made to establish more precise methods of evaluating wine-growing *terroirs*.

In the Aude *département*, some zoning work has recently been carried out. The methodology employed comprised:

▷ a climatological study that was further refined by noting the distribution of the natural vegetation and an examination of the phenology of the vine varieties;

▷ geological, pedological and physiochemical analysis of the soils;

▷ an agronomic study, ranging from tests on vine productivity through to cultivation and vinification methods prevalent in the area.

Similarly, researchers in the red wine vineyards of the Loire valley are in the process of working out a method of characterizing the wine-growing zones based on similarity of ecological conditions (climate, relief, natural vegetation), and of geology and pedology. They are trying to arrive at an objective, hierarchical arrangement of the Saumur-Champigny, Chinon and Bourgueil *appellations*.

These various projects constitute a scientific approach to the principles of delimitation and definition in viticulture. It is likely that the future will see the development of other initiatives of this kind. They will, no doubt, lead to a better knowledge of wine and ensure its quality — indeed improve it.

Vineyards at Ay in Champagne. The vine roots have difficulty penetrating the chalk, but pump up the water stored in tiny pores in this rock type.

B

Bachet

Synonyms: *Bachey* in the Aube and Aujon valleys; *Gris Bachet* in Maranville (Haute-Marne); *François Noir* in Aube.

Bunches small, tightly packed, shouldered; grapes ovoid, small blue-black, juicy; ripening period: first epoch.

The Bachet is an old grape variety from Aube, where it remains 'authorized' on about 1 ha of vineyard only. It was formerly used to give colour and sweetness to Gamay wines.

Baco Blanc

Synonyms: *22A Baco, Maurice Baco*. This is a crossing of Folle Blanche × Noah (a *labrusca* × *riparia* direct producer).

Growing tips felty white with slightly carmine edges.

Young leaves downy, yellowish, bullate on underside of felty white blade.

Leaves cuneiform, deep green, bullate, generally without lobes but sometimes deeply three-lobed, petiolar sinus in open V; dentation pointed, small and wide; underside of blade felty, white to light beige; petioles glabrous.

Green shoots finely ribbed, glabrous, light green; tendrils discontinuous (compared with subcontinuous on the Noah). Bunches medium sized, loose, cylindrical; grapes spherical, medium sized, golden white, pulp soft and flavour foxy; ripening period: second epoch, late.

A bunch of Baco Blanc grapes. This variety is classed as 'recommended' for making armagnac.

This hybrid variety has been classed as 'recommended' for the Armagnac AOC and as 'authorized' for table wines from Gers, Landes and Lot-et-Garonne. It is a vine that is vulnerable to phylloxera and does not flourish if there is lime in the soil. It therefore has to be grafted, except in the sandy areas of Bas-Armagnac. Its budbreak is early, it has an average resistance to downy mildew and grey rot (botrytis), but is vulnerable to oidium (powdery mildew) and *flavescence dorée*. It yields abundantly, being capable of 100 to 150 hl/ha, and gives a white wine that is foxy, but less so than that of the Noah. Its brandy matures more quickly than that from the Folle Blanche, and is less fine. At around 10,000 ha, its area of cultivation is considerable (ranking 16th among French grape varieties), but is declining because of the problems caused by its susceptibility to *flavescence dorée*.

Baco Blanc leaf.

Baco Blanc green shoot.

Baco Noir

Synonym: *Baco*.

Growing tips downy white.

Young leaves arachnoid, bronze coloured. Leaves large, cuneiform, dull, finely bullate, slender, slightly three-lobed, the upper lateral sinuses not very deep; petiolar sinus lyrate; dentation convex, narrow; underside of blade lightly pubescent; veins almost glabrous, with setose tufts at points of bifurcation of primary and secondary veins; petioles glabrous.

Green shoots glabrous, well developed, smooth, with long internodes, reddish.

Grape bunch of the Baco Noir, a vigorous variety giving wine high in colour and alcohol.

Baco Noir leaf.

Bunches medium sized, cylindrical, compact; grapes small, spherical, black with soft pulp and herbaceous taste; ripening period: early.

This hybrid, a crossing of Folle Blanche × *riparia*, produces very early ripening grapes, which means that it can be grown at altitude or at the northern limit of grape cultivation. On the other hand it has early budbreak, which exposes it to spring frosts. It is a very vigorous plant, with long, strong shoots. These can readily be trained long, or arched — necessary to stimulate fruit development in order to obtain satisfactory yields, for bunches seldom exceed 150g. The foliage of the Baco Noir is very resistant to downy mildew and oidium (powdery mildew), but its grapes are slightly susceptible to grey rot (botrytis). Wine from the Baco Noir is strong in alcohol and colour, with a leafy or grassy taste.

Baco Noir green shoot.

Balzac Blanc

Synonyms: *Balzat, Balzard Blanc, Blanc Limousin, Margnac Blanc, Plant de Saint-Jean, Chigné, Ressière* or *Dressière*.

Bunches conical, compact, quite large; grapes spherical, small, white, flecked with orange; ripening period: second epoch.

This former Charente vine, now disappearing, has not been classified. Its budbreak is a little later than that of the Folle Blanche and it is irregular in its yields. Its wine is of reasonable quality, though it was traditionally vinified together with other varieties.

Bandol

The Bandol vineyards were planted by the Romans who, after creating the city of Taurocentum, settled in the hinterland towards today's le Castellet and grew vines there.

Bandol owes its success in the first instance to its port. Shallow initially, the port harboured tartans and feluccas — small sailing craft that carried wine for export out to the many larger ships anchored offshore. The village of Bandol dates from 1715. In 1734, a deep-water port was constructed and, a century later, Bandol wines were leaving it for the far waterfronts of the Americas and Indies.

On 11 November 1941 Bandol was officially classed as an AOC, covering six communes.

In a setting that is happily protected from the assaults of urbanization, the Bandol vineyards cover more than 600 ha and produce an average of 30,000 hl annually. The climate is dry, but the heat is moderated by the marked relief of the area, and by maritime influences. The most widespread kind of soil is very poor and thin (termed '*squelettique*' or 'skeletal'), and is whitish in colour: it results from the degradation of calciferous sandstones and sandy marls.

The vines here are of classical Mediterranean type, with the Mourvèdre dominant — the wines contain a minimum 50 per cent of this variety.

Bandol produces red, white and rosé wines. The whites and rosés have a marked bouquet and a refreshing taste, when well made, that the drinker will note with pleasure. The red wines, Bandol's speciality, are of average alcoholic content and have a spicy bouquet, with aromas of black cherry and ripe plum. They take on a fine balance after a few years' storage, and are never heavy or coarse.

Banyuls and Banyuls Grand Cru

These two AOCs, in which some of the most beautiful vineyards for *vins doux naturels* are to be found, cover about 2,000 ha. The *appellation* area rises in terraces on schistous hills that plunge steeply into the Mediterranean, in the far southwest of France near the Spanish border. Four communes benefit from the *appellations*: Banyuls, Cerbère, Collioure and Port-Vendres. Annual production is around 45,000 hl. The basic grape variety is the Grenache, with the Carignan also playing a part. Vinification takes place with maceration, and *mutage* — stopping the fermentation, in this case by fortification — is often carried out directly on to the macerated grape matter (*sur grain*). The minimum ageing requirement is one year.

The Cadière d'Azur vineyards produce AOC Bandol wines.

The Banyuls Grand Cru *appellation* stipulates a total of five days' maceration and a minimum period of 30 months' ageing in wood.

The wines of Banyuls are characterized by aromas of great complexity, developing hints of red summer fruits when young, and scents of almond, prune and vanilla when older; they are rich and mouth-filling; their colour evolves with age from ruby red to tile red or onionskin.

These two *appellations d'origine contrôlée* were classified on 19 May 1972.

Banyuls Rancio and Banyuls Grand Cru Rancio

The term *rancio* (meaning that the wines possess a slightly rancid, oxidized aroma, much prized locally) is added to these two *vins doux naturels*, produced in the Banyuls AOC area and under the same conditions, on account of their age. These wines, which undergo oxidization in air, light and heat, are characterized by heady yet harmonious aromas.

Barbarossa

Italian vine found on Corsica, where it has been classed as 'recommended'. It is one of the grape varieties permitted for the Ajaccio and Vin de Corse AOCs, though it is not widely grown.

Barbaroux

Grape variety classed as 'recommended' in Var, Vaucluse and Bouches-du-Rhône. It is grown on about 100 ha.

Baroque

Synonyms: *Baroque, Baroca* in the Tursan region, *Plant Bordelais, Bordelais (Bourdalès* in Gascon dialect), *Bordeleza Zuria* in the Basque country, *Escripet* at Saint-Boès (Pyrénées-Atlantiques), *Sable Blanc* in southern Landes, at Capbreton.

Bunches medium sized, cylindrical, small shouldered, compact; grapes spherical, medium sized, dull pink-white, pulp juicy; ripening period: second epoch, late.

A Landes variety from the Tursan district. Long ignored, it is gradually replacing the Claverie, which is too susceptible to oidium (powdery mildew). It has a measure of resistance to downy mildew and black rot, and takes well to grafting. Its wine is strong in alcohol, pleasant and aromatic. It is the basic grape variety used for Tursan white wines, and has been classed as 'recommended' for the whole of the South West. It is grown on 1,575 ha, concentrated in Landes (with 1,360 ha), Gers and Pyrénées-Atlantiques. Four registered clones have been approved: numbers 351 (the most useful), 390, 391 and 392.

Barras

Black grape variety from Tarn, very similar to the Malpé, and unclassified.

Barsac

The Barsac *appellation d'origine contrôlée*, created by decree on 11 September 1936, is reserved for wines made from grapes harvested within the boundaries of the Barsac commune, which lies on the left bank of the Garonne, some 40km southeast of Bordeaux, and north of the Sauternes commune.

The Barsac *appellation* area is officially encompassed by that of Sauternes. This is why the growers of Barsac can lay claim to either one of the *appellations*. Rules governing production are precisely the same as those for Sauternes.

In 1985, Barsac's vineyard area was 560 ha with an annual production of 14,186 hl, which represents a yield of 25.3 hl/ha.

The wines of Barsac are as exceptional in quality as those of Sauternes, from which they are distinguished by subtle differences. In youth they are racier, fruitier, less fat; they develop more quickly and acquire elegance with age.

Two out of the eleven Sauternes *premiers crus classés,* and eight of the thirteen *deuxièmes crus classés,* come from Barsac.

BARSAC CRUS CLASSÉS

Premiers Crus Classés
Château Climens
Château Coutet

Deuxièmes Crus Classés
Château Broustet
Château Caillou
Château Doisy-Daëne
Château Doisy-Dubroca
Château Doisy-Védrines
Château Myrat
Château Nairac
Château Sau

Bâtard-Montrachet

This Côte de Beaune Grand Cru covers 12 ha, 6 in the commune of Chassagne and 6 in Puligny. Almost the twin of Chevalier-Montrachet, it illustrates well the magnificence of the great white wines of Burgundy.

Bâtard-Montrachet without doubt owes a good deal of its renown to its *terroir*, a site made up of siliceous and clayey soils, with lime covering a magnesian subsoil. The Chardonnay is at its best here.

In addition, the wine benefits from an excellent situation on a smooth, even slope that faces east and then south in sequence. Production methods enhance these natural advantages, with alcoholic strength fixed at a minimum 12° and base yield at 30 hl/ha. Average annual production is around 550 hl.

Like Montrachet and Chevalier-Montrachet, this wine is distinguished by its liveliness and its delicate, nutty bouquet, with perhaps more robustness and less finesse on the palate than either of its peers.

Banyuls vineyard on the slopes of the Albères, near Cerbère.

Béarn

This little wine district rises in pebbly terraces around Bellocq and its *gave* (or Pyrenean mountain stream), halfway between Biarritz and Pau. It obtained *appellation contrôlée* status for its rosé, red and white wines on 17 October 1975.

It was Roman colonists, those expert wine growers, who discovered that the hills around Bellocq were especially favourable for cultivating vines. Later, the abbeys and monasteries of the region contributed to the development of the vineyards and the improvement of the wines grown there. In the 17th century it was expatriate French Protestants who negotiated the export of these full-bodied wines to Holland and England. When shipping these consignments abroad, the growers would load their precious casks on to *gabarres*, a kind of primitive raft, securing them with clematis creeper. These loads were hauled down the river Adour to Bayonne, where they were transferred on to waiting schooners.

The soils are made up of materials resulting from glacial erosion. They are largely based on marl, clay or limestone, with considerable quantities of large, water-rolled pebbles among them.

The wine district, along with all those of the Basque country, enjoys a relatively temperate climate, Pyrenean and maritime at the same time. It is characterized by good rainfall distribution, hot summers and outstandingly warm, bright autumns that favour perfect ripening of grapes. The small vineyard plots, with vines trained high or on Italian-style pergolas, are tucked away in little valleys or on hillsides, sheltered from winds and spring frosts.

Besides the basic grape varieties in use throughout the Pyrenees, the Béarn-Bellocq district benefits from a particularly rich range of varieties of its own. For red wines the Tannat, with its ample tannin, and the Cabernet Franc (locally termed the Bouchy), with its taste and its aroma of red berries, are both grown; so too are the Mansenc Noir, the Courbu Noir and the Fer (locally termed the Pinenc), each contributing the authentic aromas of traditional regional grape varieties.

For whites there are, in addition to the Petit and the Gros Manseng, the Raffiat de Moncade, the Courbu Blanc, the Lauzet and the Camaralat de Lasseube; each adds its own note to a harmonious blend that is as alluring as it is complex.

Yields are low: an average of 50 hl/ha. Average annual production of rosés, reds and whites in 4,600, 1,100, and 300 hl respectively. But this modest production means that the wines are able to retain all their rich authenticity of taste and savour.

Béarn's bright, luminous rosé was greatly appreciated by Jeanne d'Albret, Queen of Navarre. Its brilliant colour varies from pale

The Salies hills, in the Béarn wine district, produce rosé, red and white wines with great richness of flavour.

rosewood to a light redcurrant. Its floral aromas are delicate and persistent. This dry rosé is frank, elegant, supple and silky, with a lingering aftertaste.

The red wine is distinguished by its beautiful purple colour and its aromas of black- and redcurrant. It is a wine lover's wine: sincere, original, particularly well balanced, well fleshed and full, with agreeably rounded tannins and a long finish. Although it is very pleasant as a young wine, its bouquet develops exciting toasted, spicy notes after two or three years in bottle.

The white wine, with its remarkable complexity of aromas, is a beautifully delicate green with gold glints. Its aroma suggests gorse, acacia and ripe fruit. Both lively and elegant, its firm structure ensures it a good length of life.

Beaujolais *See* the following page.

Beaujolais

This regional *appellation d'origine contrôlée*, ratified by decree on 12 September 1937, is also referred to as Beaujolais *tout court* ('simple Beaujolais').

The *appellation* is mainly used for red and rosé wines from the Gamay Noir à Jus Blanc, with a minimum alcoholic strength of 9°. White wines are also produced, from the Chardonnay, Pinot Blanc and Aligoté grape varieties.

An area of 9,100 ha is covered by this appellation, which is a little less than half that of the whole wine region.

Annual average production amounts to 550,000 hl, of which 5,000 hl are white wines made from Chardonnay grapes. Two thirds of the white wine total is produced at the local centre of la Chapelle-de-Guinchay in northern Beaujolais.

Beaujolais Supérieur

This AOC covers the same geographical area as AOC Beaujolais, but its wines have an alcoholic strength 1° above that of Beaujolais. Annual production is around 10,000 hl.

Beaujolais-Villages

This regional *appellation*, ratified as an AOC by decree on 12 September 1937, produces red wines almost exclusively, made from the Gamay Noir à Jus Blanc and with an alcoholic strength of 10°. It covers 6,300 ha, which is one third of the entire wine region, and average annual production is 350,000 hl.

If wished, wines from the region may use the 'simple' Beaujolais *appellation*, followed by the name of a commune. Those communes enjoying this privilege in Saône-et-Loire include Leynes, Saint-Amour-Bellevue, La Chapelle-de-Guinchay, Romanèche-Thorins, Pruzilly, Chânes, Saint-Amour-Vérand and Saint-Symphorien d'Ancelles. In Rhône, they include Juliénas, Jullié, Émeringes, Chénas, Fleurie, Chiroubles, Lancié, Villié-Morgon, Lantignié, Beaujeu, Régnié-Durette, Cercié, Quincié, Saint-Lager, Odenas, Charentay, Saint-Étienne-la-Varenne, Vaux, le Perréon, Saint-Étienne-des-Ouillières, Blacé, Salles-Arbuissonnas, Saint-Julien, Montmelas, Rivolet, Dencié, les Ardillats, Marchampt and Vauxrenard.

In fact, these wines are known and marketed simply as Beaujolais-Villages. As with Beaujolais Supérieur, the alcoholic strength of the wines has to be 1° above that of Beaujolais.

A hilly landscape near Jarnioux, typical of the Beaujolais region.

Traditional dwelling at Juliénas in the Beaujolais wine district.

BEAUJOLAIS

Over the last 30 years the vogue for Beaujolais Nouveau has created a simplified and universal image of the region's viticultural production: that of an infant wine, eager, joyous and gulpable. Although it corresponds to some extent to reality, this hastily drawn portrait has the disadvantage of disguising the true diversity of Beaujolais wines, as well as their potential for ageing, and sometimes leads to the quality of the Beaujolais* crus *being forgotten.

Cherub with grapes, at Morgon.

If Léon Daudet (1867–1942) is to be believed, Lyon is watered by the Saône, the Rhône and a third river — the Beaujolais, which never grows muddy and never dries up. What might be termed the upper valley of this river stretches 55 km from south of Mâcon to Villefranche-sur-Saône, and is 12 to 15 km across from the Beaujolais hills to the river Saône, at an average altitude of 300 m.

By a decision of the civil court taken at Dijon on 29 April 1930, this wine district forms part of the Burgundy region. At that time Beaujolais enjoyed no more than a modest reputation and the Burgundian link seemed logical. Things are different today; for although reference is still made to 'greater Burgundy', taking in the *départements* of Yonne, Côte-d'Or, Saône-et-Loire and Rhône, Beaujolais has acquired full and entire autonomy centred on Villefranche-sur-Saône. Furthermore, the general lie of the land slopes down towards Lyon rather than up towards Beaune.

So is Beaujolais really Burgundian? History has always linked it with the Lyonnais area. On the other hand, its geographical features are akin to those of Burgundy, and in particular those of the Mâconnais. The Gamay grape, the sole Beaujolais variety, is also Burgundian in origin. And finally, although the larger part of the Beaujolais area comes within the Rhône *département*, the Beaujolais canton of La Chapelle-de-Guinchay belongs to Saône-et-Loire, which is in Burgundy. Such is the waywardness of departmental boundaries . . . and heed was not paid to viticultural subtleties at the time of the French Revolution, when they were drawn up.

The vineyards

The vine is grown on 22,000 ha in Beaujolais, which is a greater vineyard area than is found in the three Burgundian *départements* together. This was already the extent of the vineyards in 1876, on the eve of the phylloxera invasion. It reached 30,000 ha at the beginning of the 20th century, its greatest-ever area, before being fixed within its present limits. The *appellations* cover an even larger total area — 35,000 ha — but planting all of this is hardly feasible or necessary.

Chiroubles and its vineyards. The wines of this well-known cru *are appreciated for their finesse and fruit.*

Climate

The temperate climate mingles maritime, continental and Mediterranean influences. The north wind brings fine weather, the south wind rain, and storms come with the west wind. These storms, often spectacular, cause the Beaujolais wine growers many anxieties, as does cold weather in May, which can bring on *coulure* (flower abortion). Although in winter temperatures rarely drop below −10°C, in summer they can rise to 40°C, with the risk of storms and hail.

The soils

In Bas-Beaujolais, between Villefranche-sur-Saône and the Azergues valley, the soils are calcareous, pebbly and light, sometimes stained a reddish colour from the iron in what are termed *pierres dorées*. *Primeur* wines are well suited by the sedimentary deposits here, of clay or clay and limestone.

North of Villefranche, the Haut-Beaujolais results from the Hercynian folding of ancient terrains formed mainly of granite debris, of porphyry, diorite or schists. At the bases of the hills these siliceous, stony, sandy soils change into *gore*, a clay layer with an ashy appearance. This is the kind of earth found at Chiroubles or Fleurie, whereas the heavy soils of Morgon are derived from schists. At Brouilly they are stonier and full of metallic oxides and limestone rubble. Manganese is noticeable at Moulin-à-Vent. This is the country of the *crus*.

This geological diversity shows that there is no single Beaujolais but several, with perceptible differences from area to area, and sometimes even within the same *appellation*.

The Gamay grape

The grape grown here — the Gamay Noir à Jus Blanc, not to be confused with the only rather middling Gamay Noir à Jus Rouge, or Gamay Teinturier — does, though, give the Beaujolais district a unity. This variety has early budbreak and does not tolerate frosts well, but if affected is able to recover well afterwards. The wine acquires its beautiful red colour during fermentation and vatting in the presence of the grape skins. Burgundy opted for the Pinot Noir, Beaujolais for the Gamay, a fertile vine that accounted for 90 per cent of plantings here by the beginning of the 19th century. Today 98 per cent of the Beaujolais area is planted with the Gamay; the remainder with Chardonnay and Pinot Noir.

The vines and vinification

The *crus* and Beaujolais-Villages areas grow their vines low and prune them short; those in the south train their plants high, on wires, and prune long. Vines are planted at a density of

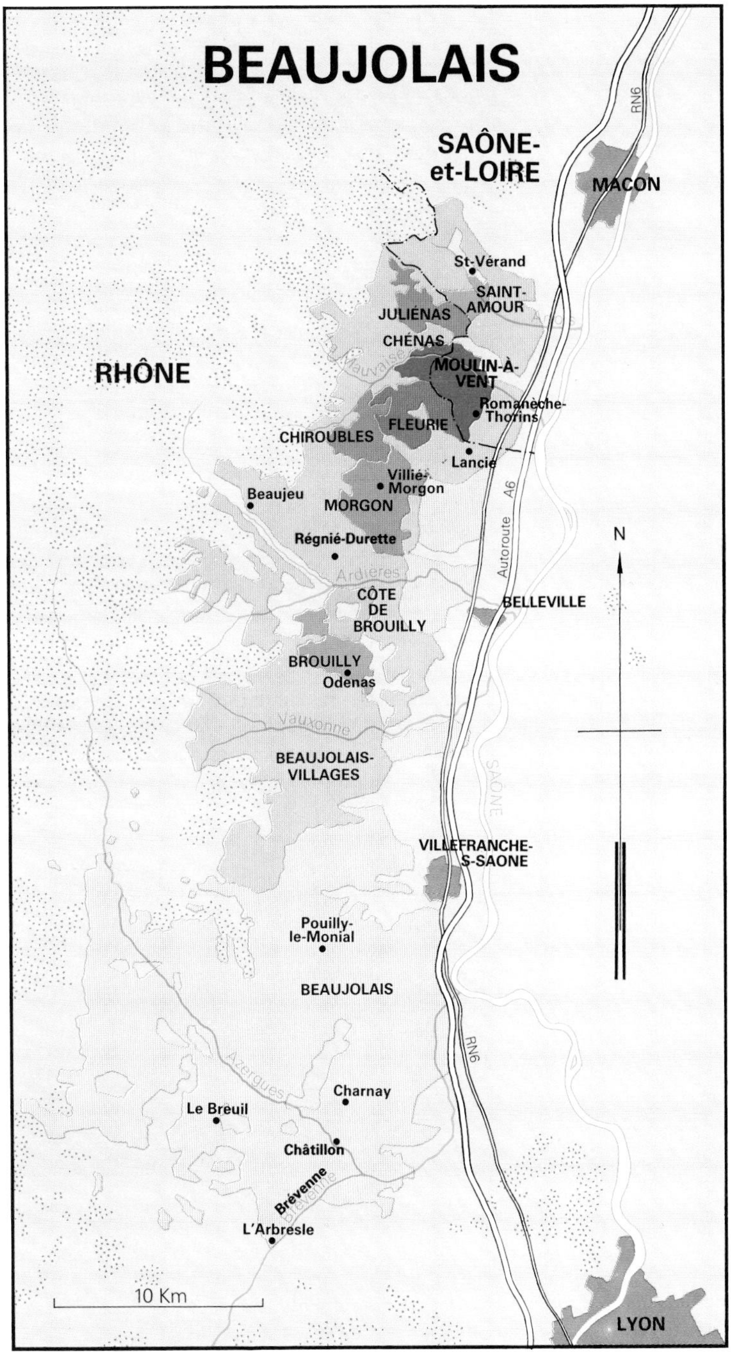

9,000 to 13,000 per hectare. Mechanical harvesting has so far been excluded from the Beaujolais. Vinification here is of whole grapes — the bunches are not crushed — and as they ferment, they undergo a period of maceration lasting three to four days. The *crus* and wines for ageing are vatted for a longer period, but fermentation time is reduced to a minimum for the *primeurs*.

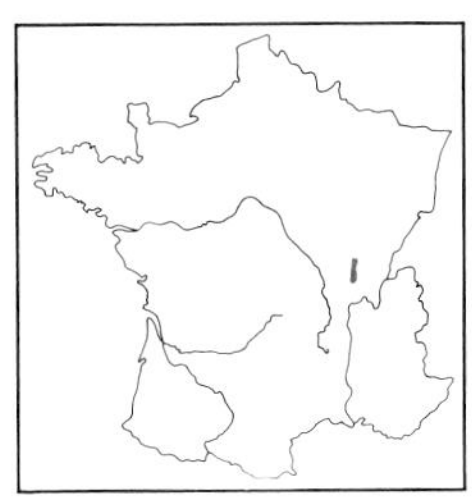

Yields

The base yield is 40 hl/ha for the *cru* wines, 50 hl/ha for Beaujolais, Beaujolais Supérieur and

Beaujolais-Villages. These rates can be adjusted in accordance with the size of the actual harvest; the annual yield can be increased by up to 20 per cent above the base yield for the relevant category. Yields can thus go up to 60 or 70hl/ha in an abundant year. Preliminary tasting, already in force for the *primeurs*, has now become obligatory for all Beaujolais.

Costume of the Compagnons du Beaujolais.

The structure of Beaujolais wine growing

There are some 7,000 wine-growing estates at present in the Beaujolais, most of them family owned. Thirty years ago, 23,000 individual harvest declarations were registered. Since then, the average area of the holdings has gradually risen to between 2 and 10ha. There were only 30 holdings with more than 10ha in 1955; today there are more than 200, due to a continuing tendency towards increasing the size of holdings and abandoning mixed cultivation.

The territory is still, though, greatly fragmented. It is made up of nearly 60,000 individual plots with an average area of 0.35ha.

About 40 per cent of the holdings are worked by tenant growers: *métayage* here (known locally as *vigneronnage*) is under a form of contract that goes back to the 16th century and involves sharecropping, with half the fruit going to the owner of the site. The 'hired hand' or *gagné* will be a vineyard worker given accommodation and heating, and paid monthly.

Sales and production

The selling of Beaujolais wines is conducted mainly through Villefranche-sur-Saône, with many Burgundian *négociant* firms involved.

Average annual production of Beaujolais and Beaujolais-Villages from 1981 to 1985 was 875,000hl. The annual average for the whole Beaujolais area is around 1,200,000hl.

THE COMPAGNONS DU BEAUJOLAIS

Love of work well done, fraternity, and respect for tradition are some of the qualities of the spirit of compagnonnage *(a* compagnon *is both a craftsman and a companion, and* compagnonnage *is a trade guild), which lives on proudly today in the Beaujolais country. There is even a museum dedicated to this subject at Romanèche-Thorins.*

The craftsman's spirit, like the craftsman's costume, quite naturally prevailed when the Confrérie was formed in 1947, a time when Beaujolais wines did not benefit from the fame they have today!

The Parisian branch of the Confrérie, which links Beaujolais devotees in the capital, attracts attention through the quality of its organized events. The same is true of the British or Italian branches who, far away, uphold the reputation of this welcoming province and its wines.

The solemn promise every new Compagnon has to make sums up the society's purpose:

'I swear before St Vincent to be a true and faithful Compagnon and to practise the virtues of my order. My duty is to love our region; to work to maintain its tradition of hospitality, wisdom and good humour; to make known the beauty of its scenery and the interest contained in its ancient churches and its old châteaux — witnesses to a past suffused with the spirit of artists and master craftsmen; to value and make valued the products of our vines; and to honour the rugged wine growers who, by their stoutheartedness, build the prosperity and renown of the Beaujolais country.'

The Fleurie wine harvest. Fleurie's landscape epitomizes the undulating harmony of the Beaujolais countryside.

Cooperatives have made good progress in the Beaujolais. This contrasts with the situation further north in Burgundy, where there are few cooperatives, and those that do exist are mainly established in the south of the region. Whereas there were only 10 or so cooperatives in Beaujolais in 1955, today there are 18 with a combined membership of more than 4,000 growers, representing 6,000ha of vines and a total annual production of 350,000 hl — a little more than a quarter of the region's output.

In 1985, half of Beaujolais wine production — nearly 600,000 hl — was exported. Switzerland was the largest importer, with 20 per cent of the total; then West Germany with 18 per cent; the United Kingdom with 14 per cent; the United States with 12 per cent; and Belgium and Luxembourg with 6 per cent.

Wine's role in Beaujolais life

The Beaujolais wine-growing area has a very strongly developed local character and sense of identity. The roots of the vine go deep into the past here: documents show that in AD 956 the lord of Beaujeu was already engaged in selling a Morgon vineyard. Yet the wines of the region were not widely known elsewhere in France until half a century ago. Its gastronomic and literary fame came about in the 1930s, thanks to the Lyonnais writers Marcel E. Grancher, Léon Daudet, Henri Béraud and Gabriel Chevallier, as well as through the political and gastronomic influence of Édouard Herriot.

The transfer to Lyon of several Parisian newspapers between 1940 and 1942 further developed the reputation of Beaujolais. After the Second World War the *Canard Enchaîné* made it the almost exclusive inspiration of its satirical zest, thereby offering it Parisian homage and glory. San Antonio and René Fallet (*Le Beaujolais nouveau est arrivé*) have subsequently assured its literary celebrity.

Corks on sale in the market at Juliénas.

Cafés and restaurants soon grasped the

WHAT IS BEAUJOLAIS NOUVEAU?

A wine is termed nouveau *during the period between its own and the following grape harvest. It is termed* primeur *during the period between its harvest and a date in the following spring, fixed by French national or European rules. Therefore Beaujolais Nouveau is, technically speaking, Beaujolais Primeur. The AOC wines of Beaujolais have to wait until 15 December before venturing out into the world. By law the Primeurs are allowed out from 15 November — a date sometimes altered, but only by a few days.*

*Beaujolais Primeurs have to be analysed and tasted blind by an official jury. Their vinification demands very rapid centrifugation and filtering before sale. A short vatting time (*cuvaison*) is used. Grapes are kept whole and the Beaujolais, or carbonic, system of fermentation — sometimes rather drastic in its realization — is applied in order to bring out the aromas of the young fruit.*

Before the Second World War, and before the AOCs were established, the wines could be freely sold once their vinification was complete: they were called vins bourrus *(literally 'gruff wines': cloudy new wines). In 1951, a number of wines were allowed to leave the* chais *before 15 December, the date that had been fixed for their unrestricted sale. The wines concerned were Beaujolais, Côtes du Rhône, Mâcon Blanc, Gaillac, and Muscadet, all of them dubbed 'café wines': they were not held in very high regard! The date chosen then for their release was 15 November. In 1967 new, precisely detailed rules affecting* primeurs *were brought in: volatile acidity below 0.6g/litre: less than 2g sugar; and tasting obligatory. To these were added, in the case of Beaujolais, a maximum alcohol content of 13°; stability; and a terminated malolactic fermentation. Beaujolais grasped this opportunity as a miraculous opening. Of course many wine regions have now joined it in the field, but it has had a good start . . .*

The Beaujolais Primeurs originated in the granitic soils of the Beaujolais-Villages and Haut-Beaujolais vineyards, but then growers turned to the Bas-Beaujolais to meet demand.

The Primeur phenomenon has profoundly altered the market and the general economy of this wine region.

Every November, these posters announcing the arrival of the Beaujolais Nouveau appear on café windows all over France.

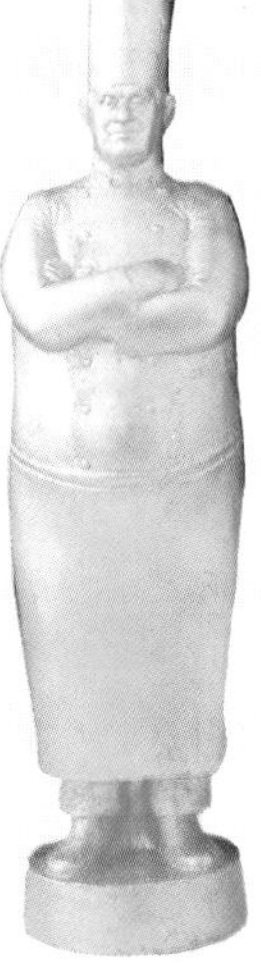

BEAUJOLAIS – THE GREATEST OF LITTLE WINES

The most vivid memory marking my first contacts with wine is without doubt my discovery of the existence of Beaujolais.

Even as a child the word intrigued me when it passed to and fro over my head; happily I was soon able to recognize it. I must have been about six when I accompanied my father to Beaujolais for the first time to buy the famous pièces, *or casks. My mother had been 'putting money by' in expectation of this annual purchase. From September onwards all conversation centred on the phenomenon of 'Beaujolais'. Weather conditions were of supreme importance. My father watched the smallest puff of cumulus that could have presaged storms and thwarted the grape harvest.*

It took me several years to sort out my ideas, drawn from many observations, and understand something of the behaviour of this famous Beaujolais, who could be none other than a great personage since we were going to pay him a visit, and we feared that he might get wet, and we were saving hard on his account!

So, one morning in October, very excited, the two of us set off on our bicycles to make a visit to Beaujolais. After riding along the Saône as far as Villefranche we branched off towards Morgon, following a road hedged by vineyards that were taking on the colours of copper and purple, dotted here and there with houses made of the local pierres dorées. *My first impressions were favourable.*

My father was in the habit of buying his wine from his friend Aufran of Morgon, a former cellarman at the famous Léon de Lyon restaurant. At that time its founder, Léon Déan, had been running a wine business as well as his restaurant. They had worked side by side for 11 years, my father and Aufran, my father having been the chef there during that period. Daily consumption of Beaujolais touched 220 litres — the contents of one pièce *— divided between the morning snack, lunch, dinner and sales by the glass at the counter.*

We reached our destination. After the customary politenesses had been exchanged (health, rain, fine weather), discussion of the subject in hand began: what the Beaujolais was like that year and, most crucial of all, what the price per pièce *would be.*

Buying these casks was a huge capital outlay for my father, for they had to be paid for in cash. In years when the restaurant was not doing well, he would be forced, much against his will, to ask his brother to help him finance the purchase.

We then entered the sanctuary where Lord Beaujolais presided. A smell of wood, mixed with that of the mould on the stone walls and the damp earth floor, engulfed us, wrapping us in its striking coolness. There the tasting began. One of the sausages that hung from a beam at the entrance was sacrificed to the occasion accompanied by the goat's milk cheeses that were finishing drying off in a meshed food safe. This mixture of odours made me a little queasy, but fascinated me at the same time.

Finally, we reached agreement on the price and the delivery date for the casks. Some years earlier, in my grandfather's time, casks and barrels were conveyed by a paddleboat, Le Parisien *by name, which plied the Saône between Mâcon and Lyon, delivering its precious cargoes on the way.*

All these transactions led us to the bistrot in the village square. It was a café-tabac-épicerie, *the forerunner of the* 'drugstores' *of today, where the documentation concerning the delivery of the casks was drawn up. It was not uncommon for local wine growers to bring out a Beaujolais from the year of their birth on such occasions. Then the men would clink glasses once more, enthusing over the 'flinty' taste of this Beaujolais from Clos du Py, as the place was called. The toast would be to whoever told the tallest story or, better still, an actual experience they'd been through. Often it was the same story year after year, but everyone would enjoy it once again.*

After these excesses my father and I returned to Collonges. The very next day, in anticipation of the imminent arrival of the casks, I would help my father to begin to get the cellar ready.

Going down into the cellar was always a moment of some emotion for me on account of the shadows that peopled its gloom. A smell of mould and sulphur caught me by the throat, particularly on the day when the barrels were sulphured, an operation that amazed me. A little blue flame danced at my father's fingertips, which he directed deftly around the inside of each barrel.

At last the delivery day arrived. A rope had to be secured around each cask before it was let down the steps that led to the cellar. My father, down below, had to check the descent of each cask. I thought this a very dangerous way of doing things and always feared that he might be crushed by the load.

From this moment onwards the Beaujolais required a good deal of care. Each cask had to be inspected regularly, for the wood absorbed liquid. This loss had to be made up and the cask racked to remove the lees that formed.

Then came the bottling. To distinguish between casks from the different Beaujolais crus, *my father put elastic bands of different colours around the necks of the bottles.*

Beaujolais began by being a little wine, a petit vin *known only to the people of Lyon and its region. It was much appreciated by* boules *players. I recall those sunny Sundays of my childhood when my father used to stand out 46 cl jugs of it in buckets of cool water in the shade of the plane trees. The players used to come over after a fiercely disputed game to quench their thirsts, and were served by women in light summer dresses.*

For Beaujolais, the moment of glory came on the day a group of astute growers went up to Paris with it. It was adopted by Paris immediately. Ever since that time, the arrival of the Beaujolais Nouveau has been greeted and celebrated like a family birth. Every year it has taken on more importance, its reputation crossing more and more frontiers. Today it is known all around the world. We, the chefs of the region, have held it as a dear duty to honour Beaujolais by using it in our specialities: coq au vin de Juliénas, oeufs pochés beaujolaise aux croûtons à l'ail, boeuf au Moulin-à-Vent, andouillettes au Beaujolais, *and many other succulent dishes.*

Finally, I am proud to have been born so near to the Beaujolais region, and of having helped to make it better known. As a wholehearted partisan of Beaujolais, several years ago I acquired a small vineyard at Létra and have since been able to further improve my knowledge of this, le plus grand des petits vins*!*

Paul Bocuse

commercial value of the famous poster that went up in November announcing the arrival of that year's Beaujolais Nouveau: townsfolk need their dreams. With Beaujolais Nouveau, 'Saint Primeur' became a date on the calendar, like Candlemas or May Day. On foot or on horseback, in trucks or cargo planes, first Europe and then the entire planet set about competing in the Beaujolais race (*la course au Beaujolais*). Lyon's third river broke its banks and changed its course: it is now an Amazon flooding the whole world from November to December.

In 1956, the first year of this innovation, 13,000 hl of Beaujolais wines were sold *en primeur*. The annual volume now exceeds 500,000 hl. In 30 years, sales have risen from 1.7 to more than 65 million bottles. Beaujolais Nouveau now disposes of around half of the region's total harvest within a few weeks, without the costs of *élevage* or storing the wine. No more spectacular triumph could be imagined for a product, particularly as exports account for more than half of this sales blitz.

Local traditions

Every year since 1864, Romanèche-Thorins has celebrated the Raclet festival, on the last weekend in October. It honours the memory of Benoît Raclet (1780–1844). He discovered a way of getting rid of the mealmoth caterpillars that were devastating the vineyards — by scalding them. Victor Vermorel, a manufacturer of agricultural equipment at Villefranche-sur-Saône, played a large part in the fight against phylloxera at the end of the 19th century. He also invented and manufactured the portable spraying apparatus containing Bordeaux mixture for combating downy mildew. This apparatus became famous throughout the world, to the extent that people referred to it as a 'vermorel'.

Chiroubles has not forgotten Victor Pulliat (1827–1896), an ampelographer with a private collection of 2,000 varieties of vines, and a pioneer of grafting on to American rootstocks at the time of the struggle against phylloxera.

The Hospices de Beaujeu are the Beaujolais equivalent of the Hospices de Beaune in Burgundy. Founded in 1240, they own a 63 ha wine estate (Beaujolais-Villages, Pisse-Vieille at Brouilly). The auction of the Hospices wines takes place on the second Sunday in December.

Besides the Compagnons du Beaujolais, there is also a Confrérie des Grapilleurs de Pierres Dorées (Fraternity of the *Pierres Dorées* Gleaners), created in 1986, which celebrates the wines of the region with equal gusto.

And, finally, every year in mid-November, Juliénas awards the Victor Peyret prize to the writer, journalist or artist who has best expressed an appreciation of the local *cru* wines.

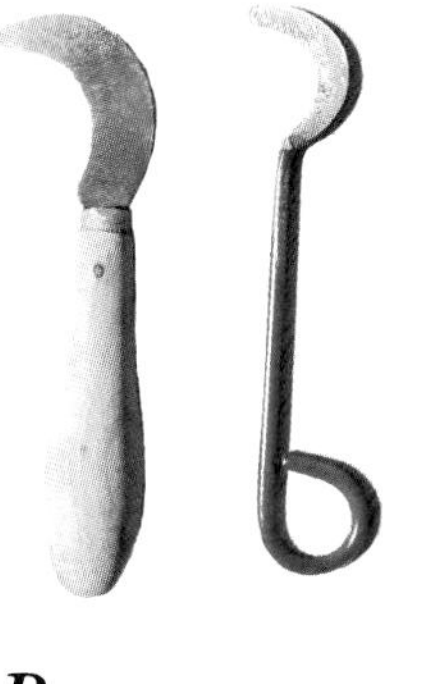

Beaujolais pruning and harvest knives, ancient and modern.

Beaune

Under the terms of the legislation of 5 December 1972, wines from the Beaune *appellation d'origine contrôlée* either enjoy 'village' classification, or may be followed by the name of their vineyard and by Premier Cru, or by one or other of these two terms alone. The vineyard area, on the slopes of the Beaune hills, is divided in two by the D970; different microclimates affect the vineyards on each side of the road, with the most favourable sites and plots lying to the north.

The total vineyard area covers nearly 530 ha, with a maximum yield of 35 hl/ha, and an average annual production of 540 hl of white and 11,000 hl of red wine. Minimum alcoholic strength is 10.5° for red wines and 11° for white. Premiers Crus have to have an alcoholic strength of 11° if red, 11.5° if white. Chardonnay and small quantities of Pinot Blanc grapes for white wines, and Pinot Noir for reds, all prosper in the soils here.

The red wines of Beaune are delicate, silky smooth and aromatic. They are not as highly valued as their quality merits. The whites, produced only in small quantities, are worth seeking out for their alluring nose and their delicacy. However, they reach their peak comparatively quickly and are never likely to equal the great white burgundies of Chassagne, Montrachet and Meursault.

Tapestry by Jean Lurçat (1882-1966) entitled 'Le Vin', at Beaune.

Beaunoir

Synonyms: *Cep Gris* or *Seau Bris* in the Seine valley, *Pinot d'Orléans* at les Riceys.

Bunches small, cylindrical, very compact; grapes small, spherical, blue-black.

The Côte de Beaune produces supple, smooth and aromatic red wines, as well as delicate white wines.

This hardy, vigorous vine, which ripens during the second epoch, is known only in Aube (Bar-sur-Seine *arrondissement*) and Côte-d'Or (Châtillon-sur-Seine *arrondissement*). It gives ordinary wines and is unclassified.

Béclan

Synonyms: *Petit Béclan* in Jura, *Baclan, Baccalan, Bécclan, Petit Margilien* in Arbois, *Seaut Noir, Saunoir* at Saint-Amour, *Roussette Noire* at Lons-le-Saunier. Its name comes from *bècle*, meaning 'trellis, arbour' in local Jura dialect.

Growing tips open in form, slightly downy, white with carmine borders. Young leaves arachnoid, bronze in colour, five-lobed.

Leaves small, thick, orbicular, bullate, dark green, deeply five-lobed with lobes pointed at base, petiolar sinus lyrate; dentation convex, medium sized; veins and underside of blade pubescent, rough to the touch. The whole of the foliage turns red in autumn.

Green shoots glabrous, finely ribbed, with a purplish hue; tendrils small, thin.

Bunches small, cylindrical, compact; grapes small, spherical to ovoid, blue-black, pulp juicy; ripening period: second epoch, late.

The Béclan is a fine grape variety, giving wine that is strong in colour and high in alcohol, of good quality. As it ages it takes on a slight raspberry perfume. It is classified as 'authorized' in Jura.

Bellet

This *appellation d'origine contrôlée*, ratified by decree on 11 November 1941, lies within the Nice commune, around the hamlet of Saint-Romain-de-Bellet.

The landscape is splendid. The land rises up very steeply from the Var fault to the Serre-Long hill, so steeply that the soil has been laid out in terraces, which are mainly given over to flower growing.

The tiny Bellet wine district — 30 ha producing an annual average of 900 hl — is situated chiefly in the Saint-Isidore and Saint-Antoine areas at a height of 350 m, and is on gravelly pudding-stone soils. The châteaux of Crémat and Bellet are the *appellation* landmarks.

The proximity of Italy and its vineyards has given local plantings a certain originality. Although here, as elsewhere, the Clairette, Bourboulenc, Grenache, Cinsaut and Mourvèdre are grown, vines of Italian origin predominate: the Rolle (Ligurian Rollo) with a little Chardonnay for the white wines; Fuella Nera (Folle Noire) and the Brachet (Braquet or Brachetto) for the rosés and reds. To these are added the rare Roussan, Spagnol and Pignerol.

The altitude and soil conditions in which they are grown make the white wines very different from those produced in the country around: they have an elegant floral bouquet and a light, fresh character. The rosé wines, thanks to the Grenache, Cinsaut and, above all, Brachet grape varieties, have aromas of fruit and almond that linger in the mouth. The red wines also have characteristics very much of their own: an intense bouquet of fruit with vegetal hints, and a remarkable gracefulness of form.

Beni-Carlo

Synonyms: *Carignan Espagnol, Terret d'Espagne, Mourvèdre* (erroneously).

Bunches voluminous, conical with two shoulders, compact; grapes large, spherical or ovoid, blue-black, very juicy; ripening period: third epoch, late.

A grape of Spanish origin giving a wine that is low in alcohol and colour, and that tends to be acid because its late ripening means that it rarely achieves maturity. There are some unclassified plantings in Aude and Hérault.

Béquignol

Synonyms: *Petit Bec, Béquignaou* in Gascon dialect, *Balouzat* in Cussac, *Béguinols, Chalosse Noire* in Blaye, *Béquin Rouge* in Saint-Macaire, *Camerouge* in Margaux, *Chausset* or *Chaussé* at Saint-Loubès; *Egrenant* and *Prunelard* in Dordogne, *Fer* (erroneously) in Gironde, *Hère, Grosse Hère* in Buzet and in the Marmandais, *Enrageat Rouge* at Saint-Pierre d'Aurillac.

Leaves medium, orbicular, dull green, paler than those of the Fer, bullate, contorted, five-lobed with lateral sinuses narrow or overlapping at ends, petiolar sinus lyrate; dentation convex, narrow; veins pale green, but petiolar junction pink; underside of blade arachnoid, with pubescent veins; foliage turns partly red in autumn. Bunches small to medium sized, winged, compact; grapes ellipsoidal, medium, blue-black, juicy, readily dropping from stalks; ripening period: second epoch.

This Bordeaux vine has often been confused with the Fer, from which it differs in having young leaves that are more bronze in hue, with a red petiolar junction, narrower dentation and deeper lateral sinuses. The Béquignol is susceptible to oidium (powdery mildew), but relatively resistant to downy mildew. Not very productive, it gives a wine light in alcohol, well coloured but a little acid. It has been classified as 'recommended' in Gironde and Vienne.

There is a grey Béquignol, called the Gros Gris, that is found in Indre and the Landes, with grapes that are part-grey and part-black.

Berdomenel

A variety from the Ariège *département* where (especially at Pamiers) it is sometimes called the *Berdanel*.

Bunches small, cylindrical, loose; grapes ovoid, white; ripening period: second epoch.

This is an old variety from the Pamiers vineyards, vigorous but a small producer and now disappearing, not having been classified. It is susceptible to oidium (powdery mildew) and to grey rot (botrytis).

Bergerac, Bergerac Sec, Côtes de Bergerac and Côtes de Bergerac Moelleux

Bergerac was one of the first wine regions to achieve *appellation d'origine contrôlée* status, in 1936. All the wines, red and white, grown in the 93 communes of the Bergerac *arrondissement* are entitled to the Bergerac *appellation*, providing they satisfy certain criteria.

Bergerac Rouge wines must have a minimum alcoholic strength of 10°. The legally defined maximum yield is 55 hl/ha. Total annual production is on average around 225,000 hl. This is a fine, generous, aromatic wine, very easy to drink. Generally destalked before vinification, the fruit is macerated for 8 to 15 days — even longer in some years. These wines do not lend themselves to prolonged ageing and gain by being drunk fairly young, after two to three years.

Côtes de Bergerac Rouges have an alcoholic strength of 11°, and a maximum yield of 50 hl/ha, so they are fuller bodied than the Bergerac Rouges — and sometimes better suited to ageing. Annual production is 25,000 hl. Bergerac Rouge and Côtes de Bergerac Rouge are both made from Merlot grapes (40–50 per cent), Cabernet Sauvignon and Cabernet Franc (40–60 per cent), with just a little Côt (Malbec).

Bergerac Rosé has a small annual production of 3,000 hl (400,000 bottles). These wines, made with 75 per cent Cabernet Franc and Cabernet Sauvignon grapes, are obtained by direct pressing in years when the fruit is very ripe, or by draining the must off the skins after a maceration period of about 10 hours in less generous years. These wines are for drinking young.

Bergerac Sec is a dry white wine that is traditionally low in acid and rich on the palate with light, floral aromas. This profile reflects the predominance of the Sémillon grape in the blend, at 50–60 per cent, complemented usually by the Sauvignon Blanc, and sometimes the Muscadelle. Research into new vinification techniques, together with increasing efforts by the growers with regard to equipment, explains the steadily improving quality of these wines, which should preferably be drunk within 18 months of vintage.

Bergerac Sec has to have a minimum alcoholic strength of 10° and must not contain more than 4g per litre of residual sugar. If this same kind of wine has between 5 and 17g of sugar per litre, then it carries the *Côtes de Bergerac appellation*. If the sugar content is higher still, between 17 and 54g per litre, the wine is classed as *Côtes de Bergerac Moelleux* (sweet).

These latter wines are made from between 80 and 100 per cent Sémillon grapes, harvested in a slightly overripe condition, with *Botrytis cinerea* (noble rot) affecting a possible 50 per cent of the berries. The alcoholic strength of these wines must not be below 11°, while the total alcohol plus potential alcohol in the form of residual sugar should not exceed 14.5°.

Bergerac region

See the following page.

Bia Blanc

Synonyms: *Biard* in Isère, *Béar, Béard* in Rhône.

Bunches medium, cylindrical, narrow, compact; grapes medium, ellipsoidal, white, juicy; ripening period: second epoch.

This vine was formerly grown in the Isère valley around Saint-Marcellin, as well as in the la Tronche vineyards, near Grenoble. In the Rhône valley it is known in the Côte Rôtie area and around Lyon at Chandieu-Toussieu, Feyzin and Saint-Romain-du-Mont-d'Or. A modest producer, but of vigorous growth, it has to be pruned long.

It gives a distinguished wine, perfumed and recalling the taste of the Sauvignon Blanc. However, it is unclassified and hence has a limited future.

Biancone

Several white, late-ripening varieties are grown under this name, especially in the north of Corsica.

Bunches large, winged, tightly packed; grapes slightly ovoid or spherical, medium sized, white; ripening period: fourth epoch.

This is a productive variety, or group of varieties, contributing quantity to the grape harvest, and also adding a measure of acidity by reason of its late ripening. The group is unclassified, and is now grown on just under 60 ha.

Biancu Gentile

Also known under the name Biancone Gentile, this unclassified white grape is grown to a small extent in the higher parts of Corsica.

Bienvenues-Bâtard-Montrachet

Adjoining the Bâtard-Montrachet vineyards on the Côte de Beaune, the Bienvenues-Bâtard-Montrachet *appellation d'origine contrôlée* covers only 3.5 ha, most of it in the commune of Puligny-Montrachet. This *appellation*, ratified by decree on 31 July 1937, produces an annual average of 150 hl of wine with a minimum alcohol level of 11° and a maximum yield of 30 hl/ha.

The only grape variety authorized here is the Chardonnay, and this rather poor, arid plot provides the most favourable conditions for its successful growth. In this prestigious white wine are found all the qualities for which the Montrachet Grands Crus are renowned: a light, brilliant and delicate colour, unforgettable panache and subtle harmony.

The famous white wine Grands Crus of Chevalier-Montrachet and Bienvenues-Bâtard-Montrachet are grown at Puligny-Montrachet.

Blagny

Ratified by decree on 21 May 1970, this small, red wine *appellation d'origine contrôlée* is the only one in Burgundy with the name not of a commune but of a hamlet, whose territory is divided between that of Meursault and Puligny-Montrachet. The wines are made from the Pinot Noir. White wines produced in the hamlet take the name of their commune of origin (Meursault or Puligny). Minimum alcoholic strength is fixed at 10.5° and the base yield is limited to 35 hl/ha. The Blagny soils are similar to those of Meursault - they are rich in ferruginous magnesian limestone. Every year about 210 hl are produced of a fine, flowery wine, both vigorous and distinguished.

Blanc Auba

Synonym: *Blanc Aouba*, in Entre-Deux-Mers.

Bunches small, winged, cylindrical, compact; grapes spherical, medium sized, white, not very juicy; ripening period: third epoch.

A Bordeaux grape variety formerly grown in Entre-Deux-Mers, notably at Sainte-Croix-du-Mont, as well as in the area of Libourne, Bazas and into the Marmandais. This vine is very susceptible to downy mildew and *coulure* (flower abortion), but is less seriously affected by oidium (powdery mildew) and grey rot (botrytis). It is said to give quite a fine wine. It is unclassified and plantings have now largely been replaced by the Ugni Blanc.

Blanc Cardon

Synonyms: *Blancardon, Mauzac Blanc* (erroneously).

Bunches cylindrical, narrow, small; grapes spherical, white, not very juicy; ripening period: second epoch, late.

This is a former Lot-et-Garonne grape, productive but susceptible to grey rot (botrytis). It gives very average wines, is unclassified and has now almost disappeared.

Blanc Dame

Synonyms: *Blanc Madame* in Jurançon, *Clairette de Gascogne* or *Claret de Gascogne, Blanquette Grise* in Gers.

Growing tips felty white.

Bunches large, winged, conical, fairly loose; grapes medium sized, spherical or slightly ellipsoidal, white to russet-white; ripening period: second epoch, late.

This vine is classed as 'authorized' and is grown on a few hectares in Gers and Pyrénées-Atlantiques. It is susceptible to oidium (powdery mildew) and to grey rot (botrytis). Its wine is average in quality.

Blanc Fumé de Pouilly *See* Pouilly-Fumé.

Blanc Verdet

Synonyms: *Blanc Berdet, Petit Blanc Verdet.*

Bunches large, conical, winged; grapes medium sized, spherical or slightly ovoid, white; ripening period: third epoch.

This minor grape variety of the Gironde area has not been classified as it provides only wines of poor quality, chiefly because it ripens too late for the Bordeaux region.

THE BERGERAC REGION

From the period of Roman presence in this region to today, through all the vicissitudes of history — English occupation, the oppressive feudal system, religious wars — and through much change, the wines of Bergerac have never ceased to maintain their originality and quality.

Wine growing made its appearance in Périgord at the end of the 1st century AD, as part of the wider viticultural expansion of the time centred on Bordeaux. The vine, which had been brought to Bordeaux down the Garonne by the Romans, made its way back up the Dordogne to give birth to the wines of Montravel, then to those of Sainte-Foy, Bergerac and Monbazillac. Later this progress was continued into the higher parts of Périgord towards the Massif Central.

Vines at Thénac, a commune included in the Bergerac appellation.

Appellations and production

Today production in the Bergerac *arrondissement* embraces the major part of Dordogne wine growing. The number of *appellations* in the region bears witness to the richness and diversity of its *terroirs*. Red and rosé wines are produced: Bergerac Rouge, Côtes de Bergerac Rouge, Pécharmant, Bergerac Rosé. There are dry white wines — Bergerac Sec, Montravel; rich white wines — Côtes de Bergerac Moelleux, Rosette, Côtes de Montravel, Haut-Montravel, Saussignac; or dessert wines — like Monbazillac. These wines can be grouped into four large districts: Bergerac, Monbazillac, Montravel, Pécharmant.

The region as a whole has mainly produced white wines over recent decades, but it is now effecting a return to the configurations seen there at the beginning of the 20th century. A balance between the production of white and red wine has been achieved; while production of Bergerac Sec has increased in response to the general trend of the market towards increased consumption of dry white wines.

The soils

The Bergerac wine region is fundamentally one of *coteaux*, of slopes. The plateaux on either side of the valley do not share the same geological structure, so two zones can be distinguished, based on the soils of the right and left banks.

If the Dordogne is followed upstream, the first soils on the left bank are those of Montravel. These are predominantly Agenais molasse, a very variable Tertiary period formation consisting of sandstones and sands mixed with clay and gravel, with occasional outcrops of tufa. Although the clay component dominates, the fundamental diversity of these soils makes them an excellent medium for wine growing.

The hills continue east to Bergerac but their geological structure changes profoundly, to a different kind of Tertiary formation: the rather poor sands and gravels of Périgord. The Pécharmant and Rosette *appellations* are largely based on soils that are reddish in colour from the presence of iron. Further upstream on the right bank the slopes face north and drop in a series of shelves down to the valley floor. This zone of hills and slopes is that of the Monbazillac wine district and is made up of clay and limestone

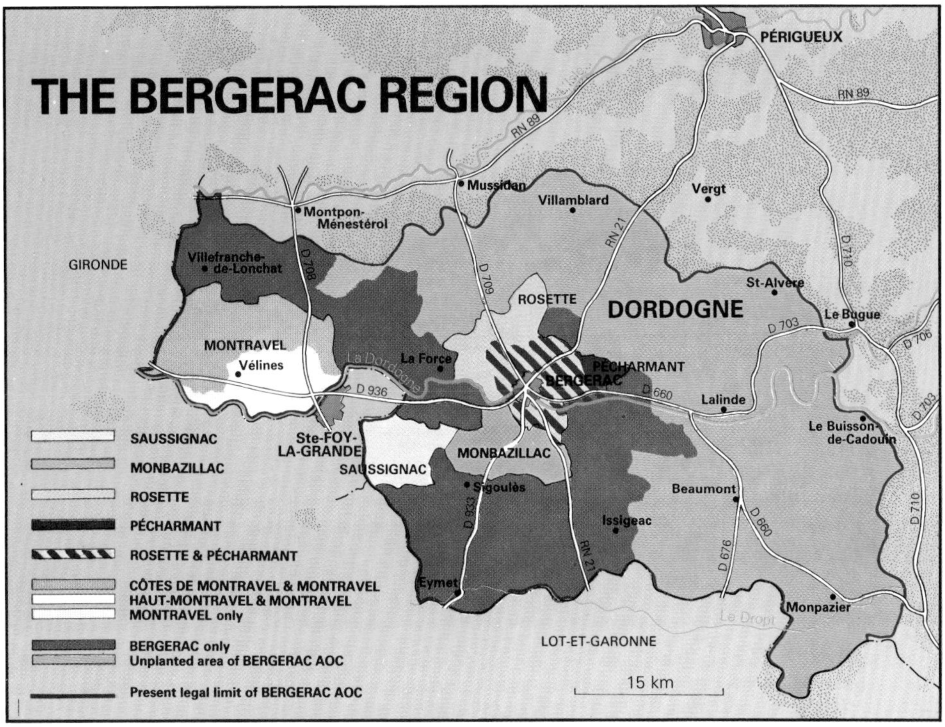

soils, the former being dominant. The system of valleys provides natural drainage which, by removing excess water from the soil, makes it suitable for wine growing. At the same time, the colloidal structure of the clay means that there is sufficient humidity for *Botrytis cinerea* (noble rot) to develop when the grapes are overripe.

Climate

The maritime climate with meridional features that prevails here is particularly favourable to wine growing. Mean temperatures are mild, and the annual rainfall of 770mm is usefully distributed over 153 days of the year. Average annual sunshine, calculated over the last 15 years, is 1,845 hours.

These weather conditions encourage vine budbreak between 20 and 26 April, and flowering between 10 and 20 June. *Véraison* for most of the grape varieties occurs at about the same time, in mid-August, and this allows harvesting between 10 September and the beginning of October, depending on the variety and the overall warmth of the summer.

The grape varieties

Wine growing in Bergerac is based on three main grape varieties. Each makes a characteristic contribution to the wines of the region.

White wines

With 75 per cent of total plantings, the Sémillon is an essential component of white-wine growing in this region. This predominance is explained by the considerable production of rich and sweet white wines — Côtes de Bergerac Moelleux, Haut-Montravel, Côtes de Montravel, Saussignac — and dessert wines such as Monbazillac. This grape variety responds very favourably to overripening and acquires, when changes due to the action of *Botrytis cinerea* have taken place, excellent aromatic qualities. If dry white wine is being made, wine from other varieties is added to that from the Sémillon.

The Sauvignon Blanc, a vigorous variety that ripens earlier than the Sémillon, is an average producer in terms of yield. Sauvignon Blanc

Merlot vines planted in clay soils produce powerful, well-structured wines.

A Bergerac wine grower studies the new vintage before sampling its taste and assessing its character.

BERGERAC REGIONAL PRODUCTION IN HECTOLITRES	1965	1975	1985
Bergerac Sec	209 375	49 911	84 253
Montravel	13 204	16 757	17 566
Côtes de Bergerac Moelleux	5 296	78 877	65 207
Rosette	1 293	570	60
Saussignac	7 120	4 885	300
Côtes de Montravel	10 790	5 854	4 997
Haut-Montravel	8 548	2 168	792
Monbazillac	76 903	73 194	45 490
Bergerac Rosé	2 666	—	—
Bergerac Rouge	28 985	84 401	227 203
Côtes de Bergerac Rouge	—	13 953	25 519
Pécharmant	1 237	3 125	11 642
	365 417	333 695	483 029

The Sauvignon Blanc variety expresses its qualities best when grown in predominantly limestone soils.

wines possess a special, slightly musky bouquet, much sought after in white-wine making. Its planting is now encouraged and the Sauvignon Blanc represents at present 20 per cent of the Bergerac region's white grape stocks.

The Muscadelle grape produces wines with a Muscat-like perfume. It is a grape that can make a useful contribution to both dry and dessert wines. However, its great susceptibility to grey rot (botrytis) and to *millerandage* (failed grape development), and its low productivity, have led some growers to abandon it.

The tower where Montaigne lived, in the heart of 'his' vineyards at Montravel.

Red wines

The Merlot produces wines that are supple, rich in colour and ready for drinking sooner than those from the Cabernet Sauvignon. It is the earliest ripening of the red varieties used in Bergerac and is the basic grape for Bergerac Rouge.

The Cabernet Sauvignon is quite widely planted in the Bergerac region. It is not a large producer and it ripens late. On its own, it produces soundly structured, balanced wines for keeping, but it is most often used to balance other varieties. The Cabernet Franc gives very perfumed red wines, finer and more delicate than those from the Cabernet Sauvignon. The Côt grape produces a smoother, still more delicate wine than the two Cabernets. It is found chiefly in the Pécharmant wine district.

Professional organization

The Conseil Interprofessionnel des Vins de la Région de Bergerac (the Bergerac Region Interprofessional Wine Council), established in 1953, represents all the different Bergerac wine trades and professions. The CIVRB has a threefold role: it shows the way in both the technical and economic spheres and it helps promote the region's wines.

Visiting Bergerac

Any wine lover touring the region should visit the Franciscan friary, built between the 12th and 17th centuries, which houses the Maison du Vin. Here he or she will be able to get to know all of Bergerac's wines. Other places of interest in Bergerac are the Museum of Wine and the Museum of Tobacco, both housed in the Maison de Peyrarède. Out of town, the Château de Monbazillac, Montaigne's Tower and the Gallo-Roman remains at Montcaret will repay the visitor's attention.

Blanc Vert

Synonyms: *Plant Notre-Dame* at Fronton, *Oeil de Crapaud* in Tarn-et-Garonne.

Bunches fairly short, compact, with two shoulders; grapes ovoid, medium sized, yellowish white, skin rather thick, flavour grassy or leafy; ripening period: second epoch.

This is a secondary variety in the vineyards of Lavilledieu (Tarn-et-Garonne) as well as of Fronton (Haut-Garonne). It has not been classified and produces a *vin ordinaire*, low in alcohol.

Blanqueiron

Synonyms: *Blanquerio, Blanqueirol, Blanquerel.*

An old grape variety of the Nice area, grown at Saint-Jeannet and la Gaude. Closely related to the Bouteillan Blanc and the Pignerol, it gives a strong white wine that is well regarded locally.

Blanquette de Limoux

This *appellation* zone, situated on the hillsides bordering the Aude valley south of Carcassonne, is the only one in Languedoc-Roussillon producing traditional sparkling wine. Blanquette de Limoux is made by the *méthode champenoise*, undergoing secondary fermentation in bottle, with disgorgement after not less than nine months.

Eighty per cent of plantings are given over to the Mauzac, making it the basic grape variety for Blanquette. Some Chenin Blanc and Chardonnay are also used.

Two other kinds of wines are produced: a still wine, Limoux, formerly called Limoux Nature; and another form of sparkling wine, Vin de Blanquette. The latter is made by an ancient method, termed the *méthode rurale*, which involves bottling the wine while it still contains both yeast and unfermented sugar. Once in the bottle, the yeast continues to ferment the sugar, giving off carbon dioxide as it does so, and thus producing a sparkle. This method gives an original wine characterized by its fruitiness. The *appellation d'origine contrôlée*, classified under legislation of 13 April 1981, is available to 45 communes and covers an area of 5,500 ha, of which 2,000 ha are planted, giving an annual production of 80,000 hl.

A **hotte** *full of Mauzac grapes, the main grape variety used in making Blanquette de Limoux.*

Blayais or Blaye, Côtes de Blaye, Premières Côtes de Blaye

This is a vast wine-growing district situated on the right bank of the Gironde about 50km north of Bordeaux, at the gateway to the Charente, around the little town of Blaye, famous for its citadel built by Vauban. It is divided into three *appellations*: Blaye or Blayais, Côtes de Blaye, and Premières Côtes de Blaye.

These *appellations* are reserved for grapes picked in the cantons of Blaye, Saint-Savin-de-

The vineyard of the citadel in Blaye, a district where the wines are divided among three appellations.

Blaye and Saint-Ciers-sur-Gironde. The hilly, green landscape of this area overlooking the Gironde is dotted with small or medium-sized estates.

To be sold under the ***Blaye*** or ***Blayais*** *appellation d'origine contrôlée*, defined by legislation of 11 September 1976, red wines must be made from the following grape varieties only: Cabernet Sauvignon, Cabernet Franc, Merlot, Côt (Malbec), Arrivet or Franc Noir de l'Yonne (Cahors), Bouchalès (Prolongeau), Béquignol, and Petit Verdot. Minimum sugar content of the musts has to be 162g per litre and the wines have to have an alcohol content of between 9.5° and 12.5°. Base yield is 55 hl/ha.

The grapes stipulated for the white wines are: Merlot Blanc, Folle Blanche, Colombard, Chenin Blanc (Pineau de la Loire), Monbadon (Frontignan), Sémillon, Sauvignon Blanc and Muscadelle. The musts have to contain a minimum sugar level of 170g per litre and the minimum alcoholic strength of the wines has to be 10°. Base yield is 65 hl/ha.

The ***Côtes de Blaye*** AOC is reserved solely for dry white wines. Grape varieties are the same as for the Blaye *appellation*. Minimum sugar content of the musts has to be 144g per litre and the wines must have an alcohol content of between 10° and 13°. Base yield is 60 hl/ha.

The ***Premières Côtes de Blaye*** AOC is restricted to red wines made from the Cabernet Franc, Cabernet Sauvignon, Côt (Malbec) and Merlot grapes; and to white wines from the Muscadelle, Sauvignon Blanc and Sémillon. For the red wines the minimum sugar content of the musts has to be 162g per litre. Minimum alcoholic strength required for the wines is 10° and the maximum 13°. Base yield is 50 hl/ha. For the white wines 144g per litre is stipulated for the musts; minimum alcoholic strength for the wines is 10°. Base yield is 60 hl/ha.

Under legislation of 23 September 1970, wines from the Côtes de Blaye and Premières Côtes de Blaye *appellations* cannot be sold without a certificate issued by an official tasting panel.

These *appellations* cover an area of about 3,000 ha. In 1985, production was 127,910 hl of red wines (nearly all of it of the Premières Côtes de Blaye *appellation*), of which 15,126 hl was produced by six cooperatives. White wine production in the same year was 13,933 hl for the Blayais *appellation* and 8,557 hl for the Côtes de Blaye. About a third of the white wines are made by cooperatives.

As in many of the Bordeaux districts, there is a marked trend at the moment towards increasing red wine production at the expense of white wines. Those white wines still produced tend more and more to the dry, lively, fruity style. Production of rich or dessert white wines with high sugar levels is in decline.

The red wines are light, supple and aromatic, and for drinking young. The white wines, sometimes marked by the characteristic aroma of the Colombard grape, are at their best in the year after bottling.

A Côte de Nuits cellar.

Bobal

Synonym: *Carignan Espagnol*.

Bunches medium sized, compact; grapes oblate, medium sized, blue-black with a slight grey hue, skins thick, taste tart; ripening period: third epoch, late.

A Spanish variety from the Requena region, introduced into France at the time of the phylloxera crisis. Unclassified, it lingers on in the Midi on a few hectares — waiting for total demise.

Bonnes Mares

This great red wine vineyard of the Côte de Nuits is divided between villages, with 1.84 ha in Morey-Saint-Denis and 13.70 ha in Chambolle-Musigny. Annual production amounts to 400 hl.

The Bonnes Mares *appellation d'origine contrôlée* was ratified by decree on 8 December 1936. The minimum alcoholic strength required of the wine is 11° and the yield is restricted to 35 hl/ha.

This Grand Cru is a model of balance. It ranks among the greatest wines of the Côte de Nuits by reason of its power, its texture and its structure, allied to an exquisite bouquet in which flowers and ripe red fruits — strawberry and blackcurrant — can both be found.

Bonnezeaux

This wine district, classified as an AOC by decree on 6 November 1951, covers an area of 20 ha, with the Chenin Blanc as its only grape variety. Average annual production is around 1,200 hl. The area of production stretches over part of the commune of Thouarcé.

The wines may come from grapes affected by *pourriture noble* (noble rot). The fruit has to have a sugar content of 230g per litre. The wines range in colour from yellow to a distinctly golden hue; they are sweet and mellow in style. Their aroma is characterized by floral scents and by the odour of very ripe, exotic fruit.

The wines have a great capacity for ageing in bottle, even for a hundred years or more. The best are exquisite, thoroughbred examples of fine Loire wine making.

Bordeaux and Bordeaux Sec

The generic Bordeaux *appellation d'origine contrôlée*, established by decree on 14 November 1936, can be claimed — subject to certain conditions — by all the red and white wines made from grapes harvested in the Gironde *département*, excluding those from the low-lying, marshy and forested areas bordering the Atlantic close to the Landes *département*.

To be entitled to the Bordeaux *appellation*, the red wines must be made from the following grape varieties: Cabernet Sauvignon, Cabernet Franc, Carmenère, Merlot, Côt (Malbec) or Petit Verdot. Minimum sugar content of the musts has to be 162g per litre and an alcoholic strength of between 9.5° and 12.5° is required for the wines. Base yield is 55 hl/ha.

Since 1967, Bordeaux *appellation* red wines have not been allowed on to the market without a certificate of quality issued by a tasting panel.

White wines making use of the Bordeaux *appellation* have to be made from the Sauvignon Blanc, Sémillon and Muscadelle as the main grape varieties, with Merlot Blanc, Colombard, Mauzac, Ondenc and Ugni Blanc in a secondary role (as *cépages accessoires*). The proportion of these minor varieties must not exceed 30 per cent of the total.

Legislation of 14 December 1977 made precise stipulations concerning white wines of the generic Bordeaux *appellation*. Those with an alcoholic strength of between 9.5° and 13°, and with a sugar content below 4g per litre, carry the obligatory description ***Bordeaux Sec***; they have to have come from musts with a minimum 144g of sugar per litre. In the case of richer white wines, the ***Bordeaux*** *appellation* is open to those with between 10.5° and 13.5° of alcohol and a sugar content of more than 4g per litre. They

Château Dudon, near Langoiran in Gironde, within the Bordeaux **appellation.**

have to be made from musts with a minimum sugar content of 161g per litre. Production of this kind of white wine has decreased rapidly in recent years. Growers of sweet white wines now prefer to work within the framework of the Bordeaux Supérieur *appellation*.

The base yield for dry or sweet Bordeaux wines is 65 hl/ha. Since 1974, white wines of the Bordeaux *appellation* have not been allowed on to the market without a certificate of quality from a tasting panel appointed by the INAO.

In 1985 the area covered by the Bordeaux Rouge *appellation* was 21,836 ha and production stood at 1,493,426 hl, of which 486,084 hl was made in 40 regional cooperatives. The Bordeaux Blanc area was 9,421 ha and production 635,828 hl, with 236,243 hl coming from 35 cooperatives.

The dry white wines are generally bottled very early, sometimes only two to three months after the vintage. They are always at their best in the year following bottling. However, certain growers with the advantage of a favoured *terroir*, and in particular those using only the best grape varieties, do produce wines with a longer lifespan.

In most cases, red wines of the Bordeaux *appellation* are quickly put on sale and please customers with their suppleness and their fruity aroma. Few of them, however, will continue to improve after four to five years in bottle.

Bordeaux Clairet

Red wines with a light structure and very pale colour that otherwise fulfil all the requirements laid down for the Bordeaux Rouge category (grape varieties, alcohol level, base yield, etc.) can claim the generic *appellation* Bordeaux Clairet. The area under vines used for growing this wine is 252 ha, and the 1985 production total of Bordeaux Clairet was 4,873 hl.

Bordeaux-Côtes de Castillon

Under legislation of 15 July 1955, modified by that of 27 January 1976, 'Côtes de Castillon' can be added to the Bordeaux name for red wines grown in the area covered by the communes of Castillon-Saint-Magne, Monbadon, Belvès, Saint-Genès-de-Castillon, Gardegan, Saint-Philippe-d'Aiguille, les Salles and Sainte-Colombe, providing that they comply with all the conditions laid down for the Bordeaux Supérieur *appellation* with regard to grape varieties, minimum sugar content in the musts, alcoholic strength, base yield, and so on.

In 1985, the Bordeaux-Côtes de Castillon area was 2,343 ha and production stood at 135,031 hl, of which 27,696 hl came from three cooperatives.

Bordeaux-Côtes de Francs

Legislation of 26 March 1967, modified by that of 27 January 1976, enables 'Côtes de Francs' to be added to the Bordeaux name for red wines and dry and sweet white wines from the area covered by the communes of Francs, Saint-Cibard, Salles-de-Castillon and Tayac.

The red wines have to fulfil the conditions laid down for red wines of the Bordeaux Supérieur *appellation* regarding grape variety, minimum sugar content in the musts, alcoholic strength and base yield.

The white wines may be made only from the Sauvignon, Sémillon and Muscadelle varieties. In the case of the dry whites, the minimum sugar content of the musts has to be 153g per litre and the wines have to have a minimum of 10° and a maximum of 12.5° of alcohol. For the sweet white wines, the musts are required to have a minimum sugar content of 187g per litre. Minimum sugar content of the wines has to be 27g per litre and alcoholic strength has to be between 12° and 15°. Base yield is 50 hl/ha.

In 1985, the area growing red Bordeaux-Côtes de Francs was 234 ha and production was 14,004 hl. The area declared by growers for white wines came to a total of 4 ha!

Bordeaux-Haut-Benauge

Under legislation dated 15 July 1955, the name of the Haut-Benauge *appellation d'origine contrôlée* can be added to that of Bordeaux for sweet white wines grown in the area occupied by the communes of Arlis, Cantois, Escoussans, Gornac, Ladaux, Mourens, Saint-Pierre-de-Bat, Soulignac and Targon, in the south of the Entre-Deux-Mers region, provided that they are made

Saint-Cibard in the Bordeaux-Côtes de Francs appellation.

from the Sémillon, Sauvignon Blanc and Muscadelle grapes only. Minimum sugar content of the musts should be no less than 195g per litre and the alcohol content of the wines must lie between a minimum of 11.5° and a maximum of 13.5°.

Bordeaux Mousseux

Wines of the Bordeaux Mousseux *appellation d'origine contrôlée*, established by legislation of 28 March 1962, are grown in the Bordeaux *appellation* area. The major grape varieties used for these wines are the Sémillon, Sauvignon Blanc and Muscadelle.

The secondary varieties, which must not exceed 30 per cent of the total, are the Ugni Blanc, Merlot Blanc, Colombard, Mauzac and Ondenc. Cabernet Sauvignon and Cabernet Franc, Carmenère, Merlot, Côt (Malbec) and Petit Verdot grapes are used to produce Bordeaux Mousseux Rosé.

Bordeaux Rosé

Rosé wines that fulfil all the production requirements laid down for red wines of the Bordeaux *appellation*, and which have an alcoholic strength of 11°, are entitled to the Bordeaux Rosé *appellation*.

In 1985, the production total for Bordeaux Rosé was 8,518hl, with 165hl of Bordeaux Supérieur Rosé.

Bordeaux Sec *See* Bordeaux and Bordeaux Sec.

Bordeaux Supérieur and Bordeaux Supérieur Clairet

The Bordeaux Supérieur *appellation*, created by legislation of 14 October 1943, is reserved for certain wines entitled to the Bordeaux family of *appellations* that also comply with certain more stringent quality criteria.

For the red and *clairet* wines, minimum sugar content of the musts has to be 212g per litre and a minimum of 10.5° and a maximum of 13° of alcohol is required for the wines. Base yield is 50hl/ha. Since 1965, the wines have not been allowed into circulation without a certificate of quality issued by a tasting panel.

The château at Benauge.

White wines can claim the Bordeaux Supérieur *appellation* providing they are made exclusively from the Sauvignon, Sémillon, Muscadelle and Merlot Blanc grapes; this last-named variety must not exceed 15 per cent of the total. The minimum sugar content of the musts is stipulated at 212g per litre and the total potential alcoholic strength has to lie between 12.5° and 15°, with a minimum of 11.5° of actual alcohol in the finished wine. Base yield is 50hl/ha. Since 1973, the wines have been submitted to official tasting panels before being allowed to go on sale.

In 1985 the area planted with vines producing Bordeaux Supérieur red wines was 10,251ha and 539,388hl was put on sale; for Bordeaux Supérieur whites, the area was 214ha and production amounted to 9,232hl.

Compared with AOC Bordeaux, the Bordeaux Supérieur reds have greater longevity. The Bordeaux Supérieur whites, rich rather than sweet in taste, enjoy popularity on certain export markets on account of their aromatic freshness, which they only possess when young.

BORDEAUX

The wines of Bordeaux offer an enormous and subtle range of tastes to enchant the connoisseur. The grape varieties grown here may well play a leading role in this appeal, but no one should overlook the influence of the various regional* terroirs, *the part played by the local climate and the contribution that Bordelais wine growers have made, generation after generation, in creating and improving the great wines of Bordeaux.

When speaking of the kinds of soils a wine-growing district has, it is advisable to distinguish between soil in its simplest, most literal sense, and what the French term *terroir*. In agronomic terms the type of soil, the cultivable top layer, is determined by the composition of the materials present in it. Texture and structure are specified, in other words how the various elements in the soil combine and interact; and also the coefficient of fertility, which refers to the proportion of the constituent parts that conditions growth and production.

There can certainly be no question of neglecting the soil sciences in the context of Bordeaux wine growing, but it is imperative that these should be included in the whole geographical setting of the *terroir*. This concept, so fundamental to an understanding of French viticulture, links together the relief of the site, the circulation of water from above and below, and the nature of the underlying bedrock — the geological framework of the *terroir*. Seen in this way, the notion of *terroir* will include the lie of the land and its system of slopes, the permeability or impermeability of the substratum, the availability or otherwise of fertilizing elements and the capacity for biological exchange. It also takes into account the depth of roots of the vines, from which can be inferred the varying potential for bringing water and nutrients, by stages, to the plants. Too much water, it should be remembered, is not favourable to the quality of the fruit, which in the 1820s led Lamothe, *régisseur* (steward) of Château Latour in the Médoc, to describe water as 'that poisoner of vines'.

Between the sands of the Landes and the borders of Charente

Figure 1 shows the general disposition of the wine-growing *terroirs* of Bordeaux. From west to east there are, successively, the Landes plateau, with its dark sands (*sables noirs*) unsuitable for quality wine growing, and instead a forest area with sea pines; then the narrow strip of gravels on the left bank of the Garonne-Gironde, shaped in ridges that are planted with vines. Here, from north to south, lie the great

Château Margaux, classed as a Premier Cru in 1855, lies in the Médoc, on the gravels of the left bank of the Garonne. The splendid château building dates from the beginning of the 19th century.

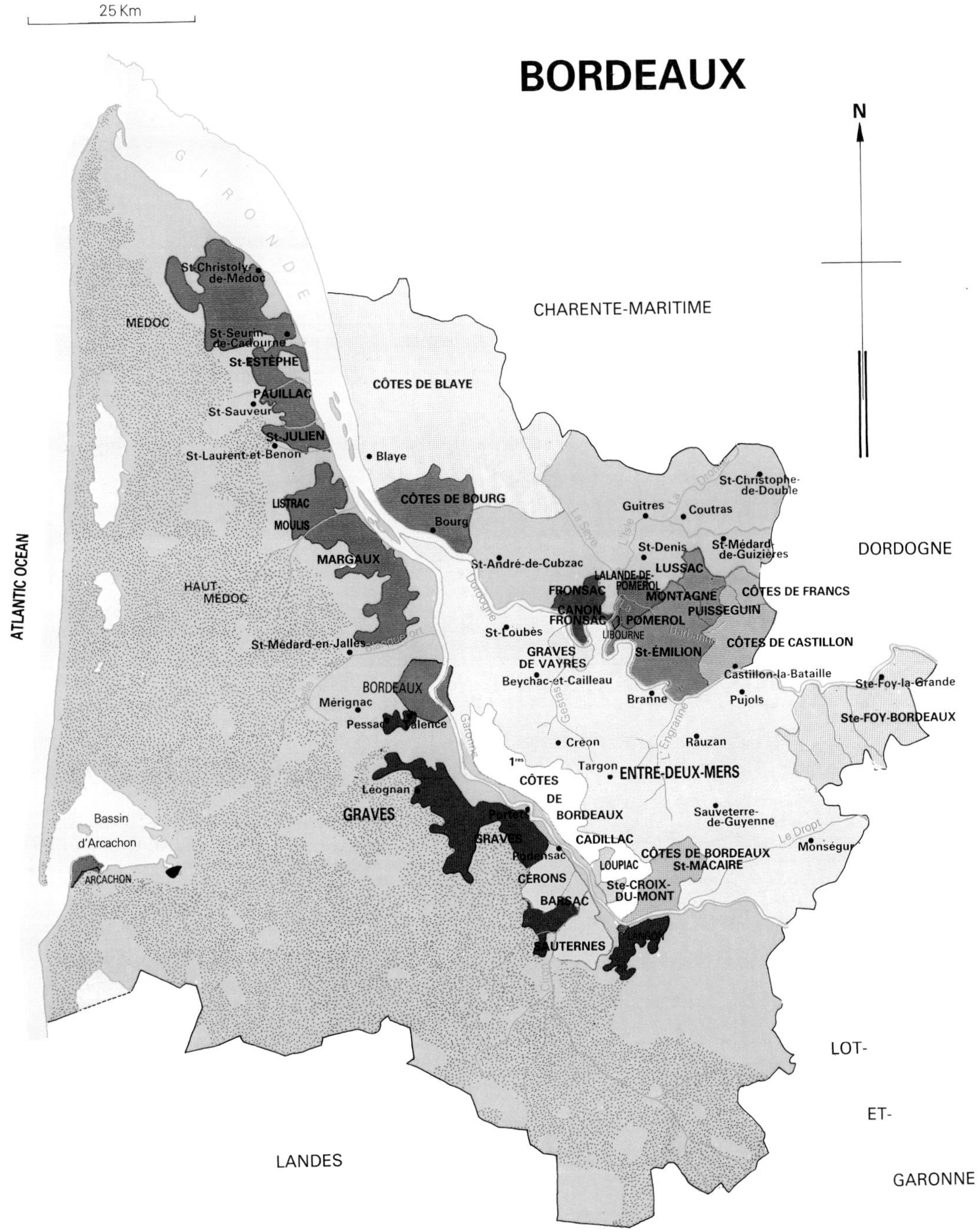

AOC wine areas of Haut- and Bas-Médoc, then the Graves and Sauternes areas. These *graves* (gravel banks) dominate — from a height of 20m to 40m, seldom more — the low-lying clay and alluvium of the marshland bordering the Gironde, downstream from the Dordogne and Garonne. These fertile stretches, which need to be artificially drained, used to be planted with vines, but viticulture has given way to other forms of cultivation here in recent years.

Between the rivers Garonne and Dordogne there is the Entre-Deux-Mers platform, a uniform feature consisting of asteriated limestones from the Stampian stage (Oligocene epoch) in the Tertiary period. This undulating plateau is covered, particularly in its northern and central sectors, by a layer of clay with gravels from the Pliocene epoch. This area, which constitutes the backbone of the Bordeaux region, is furrowed with sunken valleys that make its topography broken and hilly. The plateau overlooks the right bank of the Garonne from a steep escarpment, which provides the soils and relief for the AOC vineyards of the Premiers Côtes de Bordeaux and Sainte-Croix-du-Mont. These hillsides are covered with layers of siliceous alluvium and capped with *vieilles graves* ('old gravels') formed of clays and sands, relatively thick and suitable for quality white wines, sweet or dry. To the east and southeast the plateau connects with the molasse of la Réole and Marmande.

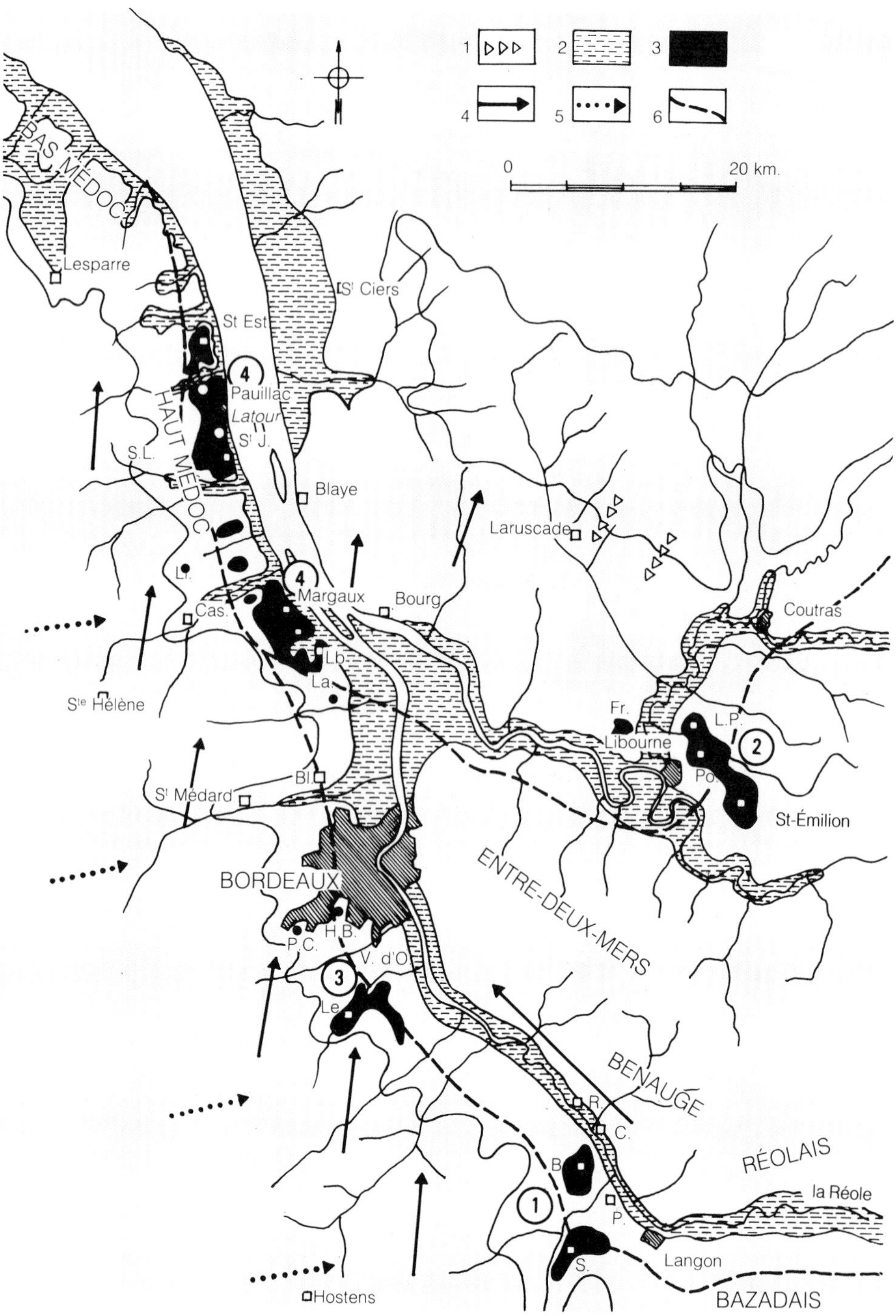

(1) Sauternes-Barsac
(2) Saint-Émilion, Pomerol, Fronsac
(3) Graves
(4) Haut-Médoc

These favoured zones are spread about within the large wine district that takes up the whole Gironde countryside except for the Landes forests, and the low-lying, marshy areas along the rivers and estuary (although even here, some vines are still planted).

KEY

1 Direction of spread of gravels, from Limousin (dissipating area).
2 Low-lying, marshy areas (*palus*).
3 Quality vineyards.
4 Direction of spread of gravels, from the Pyrenees and the older Garonne (dissipating area).
5 Direction of spread of Landes sands (dissipating area).
6 Southern limit of the fluvial gravels of the early Quaternary period.

Figure 1 : THE WINE-GROWING *TERROIRS* OF BORDEAUX

Beyond the Dordogne valley and the Gironde estuary the limestone plateau reappears in the Blayais, but is broken up into raised blocks and made uneven by a series of fractures or faults, as is shown in Figure 2. Travelling down the Dordogne into the Gironde estuary, wine districts based around the towns of Sainte-Foy-la-Grande, Castillon-la-Bataille and Libourne succeed each other, with the famous Saint-Émilion, Pomerol and Fronsac areas radiating from Libourne. Saint-André-de-Cubzac marks a break in the *appellation* zones, before the large area of Bourg and Blaye on the right bank of the Gironde, completes Bordeaux's vineyards. Each of these districts has its particular geological characteristics; but two common features are the wine-growing plateau, hillside or ridge and then the lower-lying, sandy parts. The Saint-Émilion and Pomerol *terroirs* are more varied, in fact, for they also have ridges of gravel and hollows thickly covered with rubified sands, as well as abundant molasse. The vineyards situated on asteriated limestone are planted on thin clay and sand soils, or thicker sand soils, resting on top of the limestone. The Bordeaux region does not have chalky soils of the kind seen in Champagne or Cognac. Further still in a northwest direction are the heathlands of the Gironde-Charente borders, where very few vines are grown.

The left-bank group of gravels: Médoc, Graves, Sauternes

Gravel-based *terroirs* serve as a growing medium for the vines of the most famous of the Bordeaux wine districts (although they are not the only soil type to do so). The great red wines from the Médoc and the Graves, as well as the golden dessert wines from Sauternes, come from vines planted on knolls and the brows of low hills. These features have been formed of alluvial layers made up of pebbles, particularly of quartz, of varying sizes, contained in a siliceous and clayey matrix. The beautiful vineyard slopes run down either to the river or to the *jalles*, the little tributary streams of the Garonne and Gironde. Good drainage is thus assured, and the circulation of the water through the soil structure generally facilitated.

This particular kind of relief has often escaped the notice of otherwise sound writers, for whom all the Bordeaux gravels (or *graves*) look alike; to the extent that they do not register the true reason for the diversity of Bordeaux's wine-growing areas. This was the case with Roger Dion, who wrote: 'Why is is that the *graves*, which stretch the length of the Garonne in continuous, very homogeneous strips, lose their exceptional viticultural qualities beyond a certain distance from Bordeaux?'

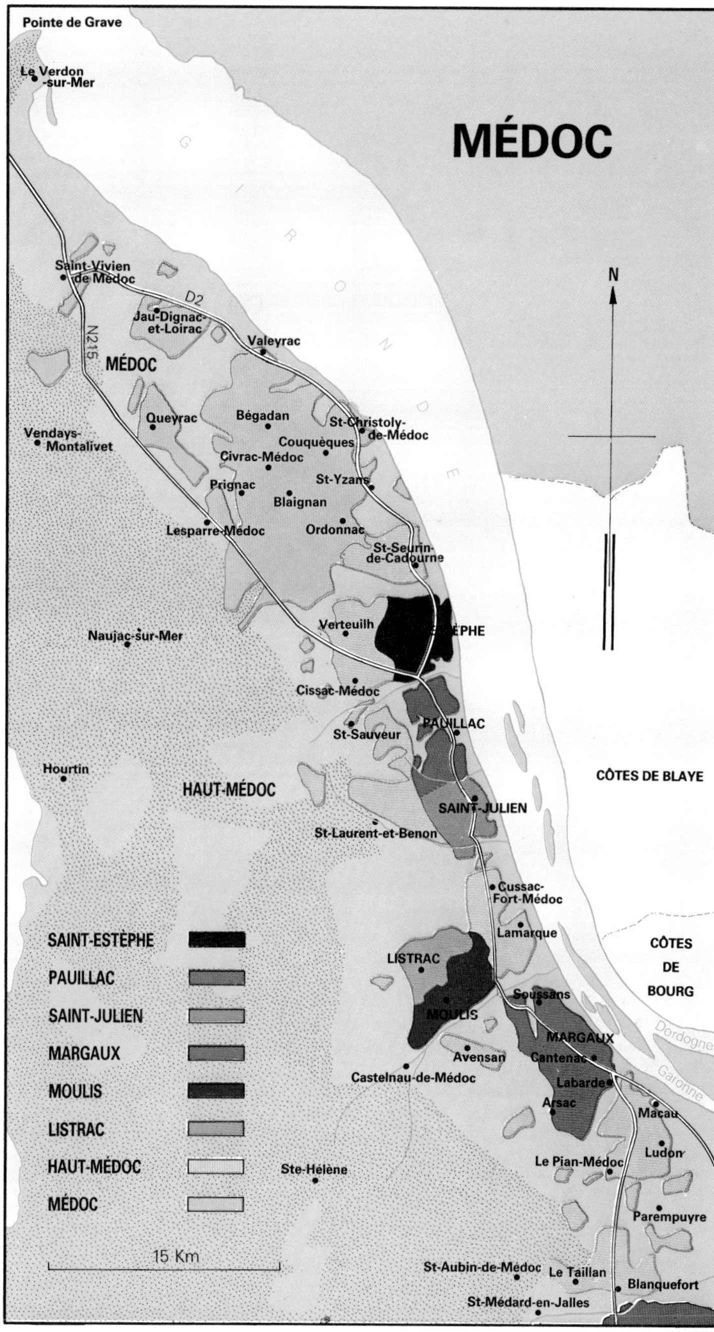

This question, difficult to answer on the face of it, pays no heed to regional or local conditions. It is certainly true that the Toulouse and Aquitaine parts of the French South West, from the Pyrenean piedmont at Saint-Gaudens and Pamiers as far as la Réole, have the finest series of gravel terraces in the whole of Europe. They are formed of Pyrenean gravels, with gravels from the southern Central Massif added by the rivers Tarn and Agout. But there are no famous wine districts in this sector. The main reason is that these terraces have remained intact, and

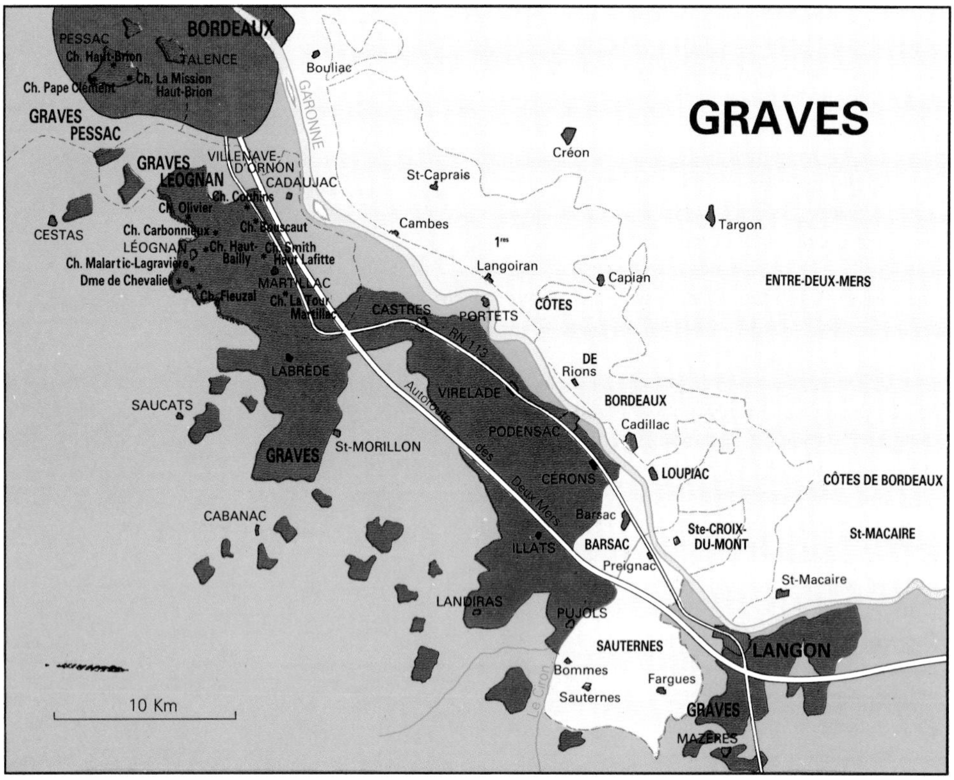

are largely covered with fine alluvium and silt, giving the soil type known as *boulbènes*. The vine can be grown here — but it will give wines of only average quality. From Langon downstream, on the other hand, the gravel terraces and beds have been severely damaged by erosion. They have been divided up into more or less rounded low hills, without a covering of alluvium. And it is on these alluvium-free gravel soils that some of Bordeaux's greatest quality vineyards have been established.

There are three advantages to the conditions found here. They offer soil and subsoil that together are poor enough for the vine to have to struggle and therefore produce small crops, always an assurance of quality; secondly, they offer a healthy, permeable terrain in which old vines are able to extend their roots to a depth of five or six metres; thirdly, this great permeability means that water does not linger and stagnate in the soil, even at some depth — and the air circulates through at the same time, so that the soil dries out quickly. The vine has to struggle to adapt itself to this drying out of the soil: another fundamental precondition for small quantity and high quality.

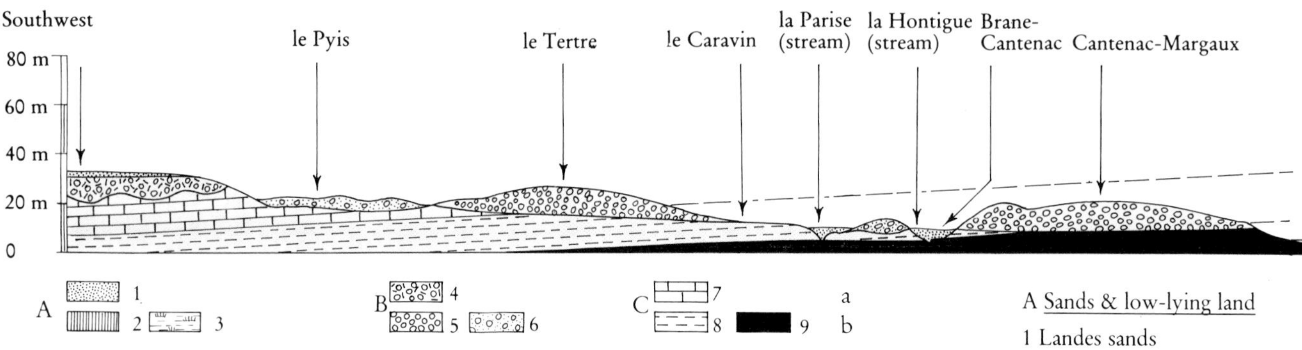

Figure 2: **CROSS SECTION SOUTH, SOUTHWEST, EAST, NORTHEAST, OF THE MARGAUX-CANTENAC-ARSAC REGION: THE GIRONDIAN DISSYMMETRY**

A Sands & low-lying land
1 Landes sands
2 Blayais alluvium
3 Marshes of the Flandrian transgression

These details permit a better understanding of how favoured the Gironde districts are in their soils. The gravel terrains are too poor and too easily dried out for commercial agriculture; but when it comes to viticulture, the soils are remarkable in terms of the quality of their wines, especially their red wines. Since the beginning of the 18th century it has been the great good fortune of Bordeaux to possess and make the best use of *terroirs* of this kind. This has enabled the region to set standards and offer itself as a model for other wine-growing areas: its estates were pioneers in producing fine wines capable of ageing, and in achieving ever more careful and polished vinification techniques that are the basis of the very best that is achieved in viticulture today.

The Bordeaux gravels differ from one another both in the time at which they were formed and in their composition. The earliest of them belong to the Pyrenean layer dating from the Pontian stage of the Miocene epoch, at the end of the Tertiary period. They spread themselves out over fairly level ground, before the great hollowing out of the Gironde. This type of gravel is small in size, without the pebbles originating from the Massif Central, and is fairly fertile. Deposits are discontinuous and occur on the Sauternes 'heights', in most of the Graves district and in the hinterland of the Haut-Médoc.

The main dispersal of the gravels, and their dissection into low hills, dates from the Günz glaciation of the Pleistocene epoch in the Quaternary period. Also added at this time are the large or medium-sized pebbles from the Pyrenees, and old stocks of pudding stone from the Albi region, from the southern Massif Central, from Limousin and from the northeast of the Aquitaine basin. This layer was spread by the Garonne and Dordogne and their tributaries.

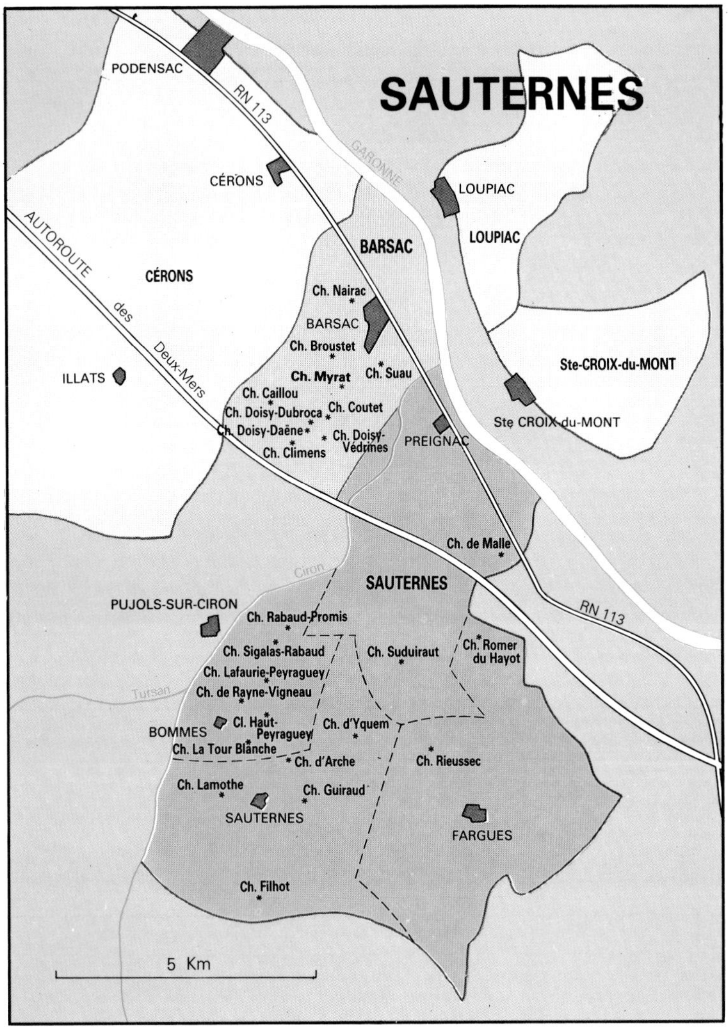

White or pink quartzes predominate and there are also crystalline agatoids from the Albi region, black lydite, greenish Pyrenean sandstones, Périgord flintstones, and flints and

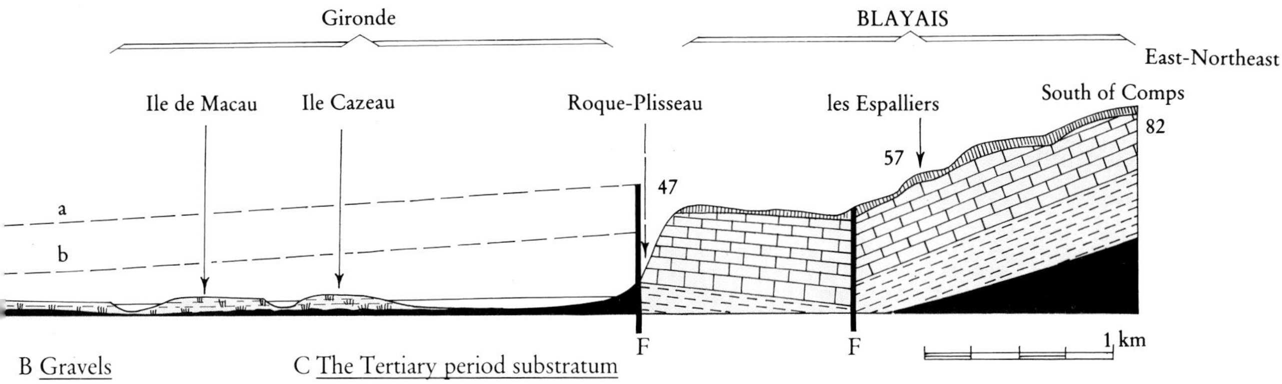

B Gravels

4 Pyrenean gravels
5 Garonne gravels type 1
6 Garonne gravels type 2

C The Tertiary period substratum

7 Asteriated limestone : Stampian stage
8 Sannoisian stage molasse
9 Fronsac molasse
a) base line of Asteriated limestone
b) base line of Sannoisian molasse

buhrstones from northeast Aquitaine. This coarse layer, drastically broken up in the Quaternary period by the Mindel glaciation, when slightly less coarse gravels were added, is the basis of the *crus classés* of Sauternes, of Château Haut-Brion and, in particular, of the great Médoc *crus classés*. Outliers are found at Saint-Émilion and Pomerol. Certain low hills, such as that of la Lagune at Ludon in the Médoc, are composed solely of gravels deposited during the Mindel glaciation. Also worthy of note is the singularity of the soils at Barsac-Preignac, in Sauternes, which resulted from the powerful Mindelian dissection. This hollowed out a large depression in the asteriated limestone substratum. There were some deposits of gravels and sands here and there; but these were immediately destroyed. All that remained were some large, sometimes very large pebbles. They can be seen dotted about among the plots of vines in the Barsac vineyards. At the end of the Mindelian 'crisis', strong winds brought about a partial accretion, covering the limestone platform with coarse sands. These have developed a red colour *in situ*. Such is the soil component of the wine-growing *terroir* at Barsac-Preignac: an excellent substratum of permeable limestone and a red sandy soil with numbers of large or medium-sized stones, and the wherewithal to support its ten *grands crus* with ease.

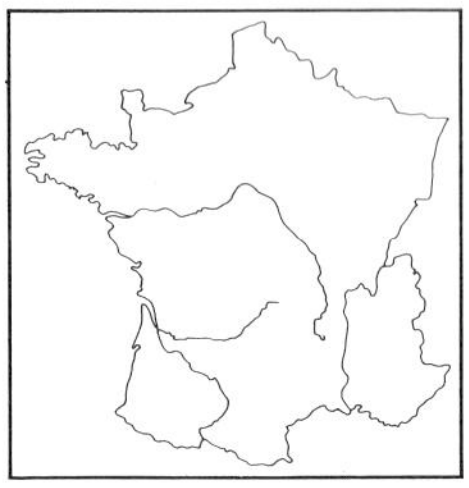

The most recent Quaternary-Pleistocene glaciations (Riss and Würm) brought only a little gravel to the Gironde; the Rissian gravel has more or less disappeared today, and the Würmian gravel is now submerged by the estuary.

On the other hand these two geological stages saw the completion of the present Bordeaux relief, and stopped the extension of the characteristic gravel hillocks. During both the Riss and Würm glaciations the Landes sands, blown by very strong west winds, came to cover the western edge of the gravels; and after the end of the Würm glaciation, in Holocene times, the Flandrian transgression drowned the eastern base of the gravel hills, forming the estuarine marshes.

The Saint-Émilion, Pomerol and Fronsac soils

The soils of the Libournais, another great area for high-quality wines, are more varied than is generally realized. This explains the finely nuanced tastes of its products. The Isle and Dordogne rivers reach their confluence after crossing the northern edge of the marine or lacustrian terrains of Aquitaine, those being composed of asteriated limestone or Fronsac molasse. Alternating with these Tertiary period strata to the north and northeast is a detrital system with a fairly high proportion of clay, resulting from the movement of terrains from the Massif Central. French geologists use the

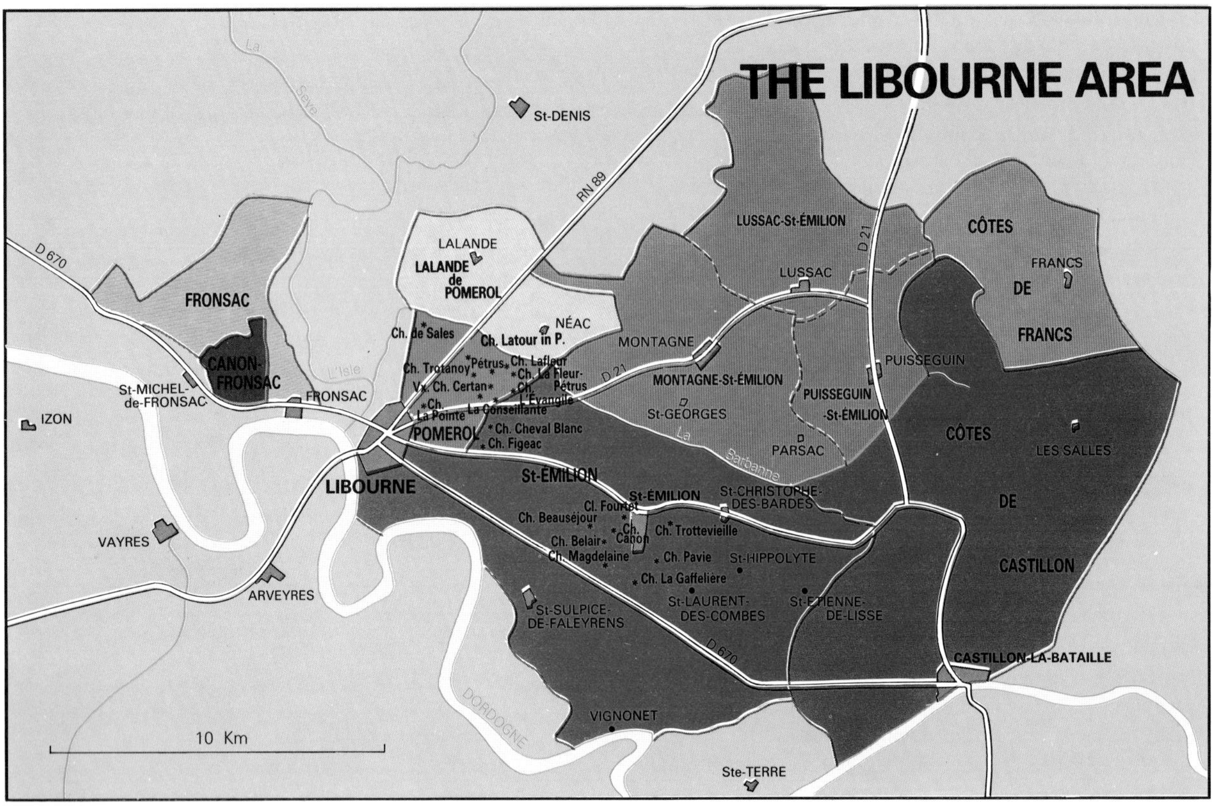

Figure 3: THE WINE-GROWING *TERROIRS* OF SAINT-ÉMILION

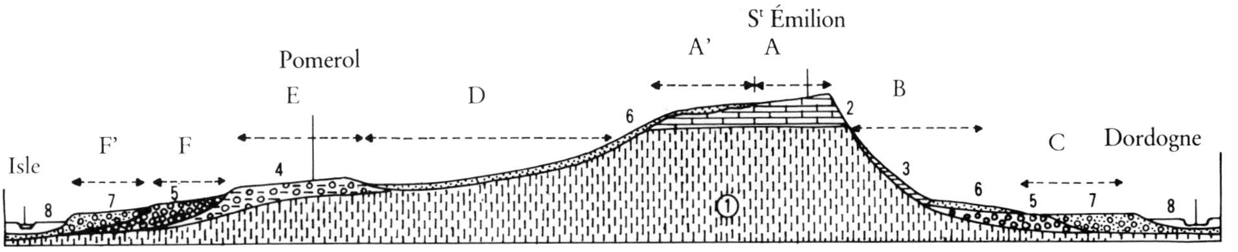

There are vines everywhere in Saint-Émilion, which is truly a single-crop district. The terroirs, *however, are very varied. They are also markedly hierarchical. One of the best is on the asteriated limestone plateau (2), where the small town of Saint-Émilion is situated. The vines grow sometimes on the limestone itself (A), and sometimes on the sands that cap it (A[1]). These siliceous sands belong either to a residual formation from the end of the Tertiary period (there are some gravels among them) or represent wind-blown Mindelian deposits. There are also some highly respected* crus *(B) on the steep gradients of the southern slope cut into the molasse (1). Debris (3) covers the bottom of the slope. This is mixed with sands and siliceous alluvium (6), situated on top of Mindelian gravels (5). On the plain, Rissian gravels (7) overlap the banks of Mindelian gravels. They have more sand mixed in with them and carry vineyards (C) of good quality, though no more. Further down, there is marshy land (8). To the northwest, good vineyards (D) extend over the sands and siliceous alluvium of the Mindel glaciation (6) that cover the molasse base (1). At Pomerol and to the northwest of Saint-Émilion, the Günzian gravels (4) carry a vineyard area (E) of very high quality. Growing conditions become slightly less favourable further down, on further deposits of Mindelian gravels (5), and again on more Rissian gravels (7) — vineyards F and F' of Lalande-de-Pomerol.*

term *sables de Périgord* for these sands and gravels, although they originated in Limousin and merely moved across Périgord. During the Quaternary period the Dordogne and Isle also brought in coverings of gravels of the Médoc kind, formed into fairly sandy terraces during the Riss and Würm glaciations. Wind-blown rubified sands also became trapped in hollows and small valleys at this time. Dissection by erosion and the succession of morphological changes in the Quaternary period has shaped the Libourne *terroirs*, as is shown in Figure 3.

The main features of the Fronsac and Saint-Émilion terrain, its plateaux and slopes, have been determined by the prominent position of the asteriated limestone strata. This explains names such as Tertre de Fronsac, de Mazerat, and so on (*tertre* means 'mound' or 'knoll') for premier wine sites where the vines are planted in thin, clayey and siliceous soils that rest on the underlying limestone, where quartz is often in evidence. These areas of higher ground, sometimes divided up into isolated knolls by small valleys, dominate the Dordogne river plain and their slopes are often very steep. This is the countryside of the *côte*, the hillside or slope, as in the *côte de Saint-Émilion*, or the *côte de Canon-Fronsac*, for example. The limestone outcrops of the hilltops overhang slopes formed of subjacent molasse. The outlines are often broken up by re-entrant *combes* or small valleys. Another kind of wine-growing terrain, the *pied de côte*, occurs where the slopes meet the sandy terraces of the Dordogne. These sites have been enriched by sand and clay that has slid down the slopes and by a covering of wind-blown sands.

At a lower level, to the north and northeast of Saint-Émilion towards Grâce-Dieu, there is a sloping valley filled with rubified wind-blown sand from the Quaternary period. Towards the northwest and the river Isle, there are low gravel knolls, as in the Médoc: these make up a good part of the Pomerol *terroir*. It is not by chance that they are the soil type in which the vines of such very great *crus* as Château Figeac or Château Cheval-Blanc are rooted. These gravels certainly bear a resemblance to those of the Médoc: they date from the same Günz glaciation in the early Quaternary period; they are of a similar thinness since all the non-siliceous rocks, the limestones, and the granites too, have disappeared; and lastly they have large-sized pebbles. Nevertheless, they differ in some ways from the Médoc gravels. In the first place the subsoil, which in the Pomerol and Saint-Émilion area consists solely of molasse, takes the form of alternating limestones, clays and molasse in the Médoc, from Margaux to Saint-Estèphe. In the second place, the gravels of the lower Isle, in the Libourne area, are slightly less varied than those of the mid-Gironde, in the Médoc. In the Pomerol and Saint-Émilion gravels a good proportion of Périgord flintstones are found, whereas their percentage is reduced in the Médoc. Pyrenean deposits, on the other hand, are missing from the Isle, in particular the black lydite. The fact and manner of the confluence of the two rivers means that the Médoc gravels come mainly from the Garonne with only a small contribution from the Dordogne, and this has had the effect of increasing the variety of materials

WEATHER CONDITIONS BEFORE AND DURING THE BORDEAUX HARVEST						
	Before the harvest[1]			During the harvest[2]		
Year	Sum of average temperatures (°C)	Hours of sunshine	Rainfall (mm)	Sum of average temperatures (°C)	Hours of sunshine	Rainfall (mm)
1976	326	100	126	183	48	10
1977	320	91	39	160	81	0
1978	320	121	9	139	44	4
1979	311	99	38	168	42	23
1980	298	69	105	116	61	30
1981	350	118	70	167	43	40
1982	410	157	7	173	37	48
1983	377	158	22	180	61	1
1984	302	94	169	132	53	15
1985	412	181	1	192	60	11
1986	373	110	125	189	70	0

1. During the 20 days preceding the approx. date of start of harvest.
2. During the 10 days following the approx. date of start of harvest.

found within the gravels downstream of the Bec d'Ambès.

The terrace of gravels from the Günz glaciation at Pomerol is formed into low knolls (except for the *terroir* of Château Pétrus, which is the result of an upward movement of expanded molasse). Its gentle slope rises above the later Mindelian terrace of sandy gravels, which also has good wine-growing sites. Finally the more recent sandy gravels of the Riss glaciation stretch towards the Isle and the Dordogne. The northern part of the Rissian gravels were formed by the action of the Isle and the Dronne; the southern part by the Dordogne river plain. These recent, rather flat gravels are occupied by the Lalande-de-Pomerol *appellation*. On the southern slope of the Saint-Émilion district stretches the Rissian terrace of the Dordogne, occupied by the wine-growing plain of Saint-Pey-d'Armens, Vignonet and Saint-Sulpice. This alluvial feature is made up of small sandy gravels and coarse sands brought down by the Dordogne.

These three features — plateaux, slopes and gravel banks — give the wine-growing sites of Bordeaux their essential character. However, the combination of the three geological forms differs in each of the various wine districts. They are also to be found in the Bourg, Blaye and Entre-Deux-Mers areas. But again there are differences, with gravels almost completely absent in certain sites, and siliceous alluvium present in greater quantities in others.

A maritime climate

Montesquieu was among the first to consider that the whole of the Bordeaux region benefited from climatic advantages, for he wrote to the Intendant of Bordeaux saying: 'Long experience has led me to note that when the wines were in a poor state in Bordeaux, they were worse in the rest of the kingdom; and that, often, they were good here when they were bad in most of the the other provinces.'

That there is a 'Bordeaux climatic region' is undeniable, one that is characterized by mild winters, early springs, customarily hot summers and very fine, long, gentle autumns — attributes that suit the vine perfectly and enable it, in combination with the soil and other aspects of the *terroir*, to produce great wines. This favoured situation of the Gironde, quite remarkable in world terms, is connected with the fact that the Gulf Stream and the North Atlantic Drift bring warm water from the tropics to the coasts of Europe. California experiences the reverse of this, for there the Pacific currents bring cold water down from Alaska.

Neither the mean annual temperature of 12.5°C nor the average yearly rainfall of 850–900mm are sufficient in themselves to make a link between climate and quality wine growing. A better approach is to emphasize how seldom really bad weather, such as severe cold, or excessive rainfall, affects the region. Spring frosts do occur, but they are not a serious threat, and especially not for vineyards facing the rivers. Hailstorms are exceptional occurrences — a scourge limited to small areas. These are the real factors that promise viticultural success.

The climatic problem for most vineyards sited near to the Atlantic lies in the ripening of the grapes. Therefore April to October is the crucial period, corresponding as it does to the vegetative cycle of the vine; the overall balance in Bordeaux generally proves favourable. There is relatively little rainfall in spring and summer, though the moderate rains experienced in July favour the ripening and swelling of the fruit. August is generally dry and warm — *Août fait le moût* (August makes the must), as they say in the Médoc. Early autumn, from 15 September to 15 October, is usually dry and sunny, allowing the grapes to complete their ripening suitably slowly; and harvesting in the latter half of September or the early days of October generally proceeds untroubled by persistent rain.

The whims and freaks of a maritime climate can, however, cause considerable annual variations in this general weather pattern. Another factor of the concern is that the Bordeaux vineyards include many 'noble' grape varieties, like Cabernet Sauvignon and Franc, Merlot, Côt (Malbec), Sauvignon Blanc and Muscadelle, that bud at different times and thus react in different ways to the caprices of the local climate. A few late spring frosts can seriously affect the early-budding Merlot, but the later-budding Cabernets much less so. Flowering in June, in a cool, damp period, can mean many vine flowers abort and fail to develop fruit (*coulure*), which reduces harvest prospects. A warm, bright, dry summer prepares the way for a great vintage. A cool, wet summer, like those of 1965, 1968 and 1972, and late, damp harvests favour the development of grey rot (botrytis), especially on the delicate Merlot. The crop will be small in consequence. It has been shown that in years when there are around 15 to 20 very hot days during the year, with maximum temperatures at or above 30°C, wines of very high quality will result. These favourable or unfavourable weather patterns in Bordeaux can be traced through more than two centuries of observation and record-taking.

Year-by-year variations in the quantity and quality of the vintages, then, can on the whole be put down to the kind of weather Bordeaux has had. But the climate is only one in a complex of natural factors that act upon, and find their realization in, the vines themselves. And behind the vines' presence lie the choices of men.

Man's role

No one can dispute the fact that vines have been cultivated for a very long time in Bordeaux. There is no need, however, to accept the colourful legends that have surrounded the origins of the great quality wines of the region with a thick, gilded haze. Numerous writers have painstakingly reproduced them — encouraged, it must be said, by château owners obsessed with the antiquity of their wines, who push the genesis of these noble products back into the remotest past. Back to the 4th century AD, for apocryphal sayings attributed to the Bordeaux poet and rhetorician Ausonius (310–395) are legion. Is there not a Saint-Émilion Premier Grand Cru bearing his prestigious name? Then there was John Talbot, Earl of Shrewsbury, mortally wounded in the Battle of Castillon in 1453 — did he not found the Saint-Julien *cru classé* that bears his name? But anyone who

The vineyards of Château Cos d'Estournel border the Gironde estuary and are directly subject to the climatic influences of the Atlantic Ocean.

wants to understand the real origin of the *grands crus* must resolutely put aside such legends. More than 20 years of research, both archaeological and in well-stocked public and private archive collections, now enable a more securely based view of this remarkable ampelographic and viticultural story to be put forward. In reality, the Bordeaux *grands crus* had their birth at the beginning of the 18th century.

The legacy of antiquity

Tired or angry at having to pay dearly for wines imported by Roman merchants from Italy's Campania or the Narbonne area, the *negotiatores vinearum* established at Burdigala (Bordeaux) — the wealthy and notable *Bituriges Vivisques* — decided in the 1st century AD to create vineyards of their own. They believed that in this way they would be able to shake off the commercial tutelage of the Roman traders and, in particular, benefit from the profitable export trade in wine to Britain, newly conquered by the legions of the Emperor Claudius.

The establishment of commercial wine growing in the Bordeaux area depended on the choice of a grape variety well adapted to local conditions. The men of Bordeaux developed a variety for this purpose that they called the *biturica*. The origin of this vine is much disputed by experts. In Roger Dion's view, it must have been imported from the Cantabrian region of northern Spain. The historian Robert Étienne has a more alluring theory. Pointing out that there were no vineyards in the Cantabrian region in Roman times, he produced evidence to show that the *biturica* came from the Durazzo region in Epirus, on the eastern shore of the Adriatic. Durazzo, Roman Dyrrhachium, is the modern Durrës, in Albania. The variety had been developed, through selection, from another vine of this district, the *balisca*, which was subsequently introduced into Italy.

Small glazed earthenware figure of Bacchus, at Château Haut-Brion.

The *balisca*, progenitor of the *biturica*, was probably a variety well adapted to geographical conditions similar to those of Bordeaux. Henri Enjalbert, taking up the thread, observed that the essential point of the story was that the 'climatic threshold had been crossed'. So what kind of wine did the merchants of Burdigala and their customers have to drink? No one knows. At most, taking into account habits of the time documented from other sources, it may be supposed that their wine, stored in amphoras, would have been a decent everyday kind, but not a *grand cru* as we would understand it today. Apart from this, did the *biturica* give rise to any of the modern 'noble' grape varieties? Documents proving a definite relationship are lacking. A tentative hypothesis could be advanced: might not the Cabernet Sauvignon, the basic vine of the Bordeaux vineyards today, and called the *vidure* in the 18th century, be the distant descendant of the *biturica*?

From this rather speculative theory, two essential facts relating to the period when the great Bordeaux growths had their birth need to be retained. Firstly, that the *biturica* was a selected variety, meant for producing good *vins de pays*, but not *grands crus*. Secondly, that the selection of this grape variety took place in the economic perspective of the deliberate creation of a commercial wine-growing zone developed by the leading citizens of an Atlantic port.

The Middle Ages

What became of these first vineyards, of uncertain boundaries, after the Roman world had collapsed under the barbarian onslaughts? More than six centuries of Bordeaux wine growing are shrouded in total darkness. It is probable that the vineyards survived around Bordeaux on the estates of the archbishop, the spiritual and temporal ruler of the city, and on those of the other ecclesiastical or secular lords. The latter, in particular, liked to be able to drink wine from their own vineyards and offer it to their guests. Besides this, the vineyards provided the wine needed in Christian worship.

Glimmers of light appear during the course of the 12th century. The situation in the wine trade was profoundly altered. The decline in importance of the Mediterranean countries was balanced by the rise of those in the north. In addition, Aquitaine became an English duchy through the marriage of Eleanor of Aquitaine to Henry Plantagenet, Count of Anjou, who became Henry II of England. Progress in the Bordeaux vineyards, however, did not really take place until the 13th century, after the French king Louis IX had taken la Rochelle, in 1226; this had been the main port for the export of wines from Bordeaux, Gascony and the former province of Saintonge (now Charente-Maritime). Bordeaux, a modest-sized city, then became the entrepôt licensed for the export of Gascon wines to English markets. The king-duke (king of England and duke of Guyenne or Aquitaine) granted important fiscal and commercial privileges to the Bordeaux citizens. Bordeaux assumed the position of 'England's cellar in the Middle Ages'; in other words, it became the premier wine-exporting region of the medieval world.

The people of Bordeaux were now seized by the first *'fureur de planter'* ('planting mania') in their history. By clearing land, the vineyards were extended on to the areas of sandy or pebbly terraces around the city, into Saint-Émilion and the Libournais, on both banks of the Garonne upstream from Bordeaux, in the

Bourg and Blaye areas, downstream on the low-lying marshy *palus* — but all this still did not hint at the present extent of the wine region. More particularly, there was little wine growing in the Médoc, on the left bank of the Gironde estuary, at this time, and throughout the Middle Ages.

It is a very tricky matter to estimate the surface area of this large, exporting wine region, the most important in the world at the time, ahead of the German Rhineland. A figure of 20,000 to 25,000 ha has been suggested, which is about a quarter of the present area. On the other hand, the volume of Bordeaux exports is quite well known, thanks to English documents and Gascon lists. At the beginning of the 15th century, for example, the port was shipping out an average 100,000 casks a year, which is almost 900,000 hl, a considerable amount if it is related to the vineyards within the immediate environs of Bordeaux. In fact, this total includes wines from 'the high country' (*vins du Haut Pays*), meaning the products of vineyards around the Garonne upstream of Sainte-Foy-la-Grande. The merchants of Bordeaux tolerated the 'incursion' of these up-country wines, transported as they were in casks of a different size and shape to the Bordeaux *barriques*, when their own vintage was insufficient to meet the needs of their English customers. When this was not the case, they forbade the entry of wines from the interior either before mid-November or before Christmas. At that period, the wine fleet would have sailed for England by the end of October or the beginning of November. By this means, the men of Bordeaux made rigorous use of their great commercial privileges, to the wrath of citizens of the towns upstream.

The presence of that autumn fleet in the Port de la Lune, as the curve of the Garonne at Bordeaux was called at the time, symbolized the fact that the direction of the main international trade in wine, unaltered since antiquity, had completely changed. Along the coasts of the English Channel, the North Sea and the Baltic, the great ports of the Hanseatic League had a virtually monopoly of trade. English and Breton seamen, and boatmen from the island of Oléron, came to join in the great maritime effort each autumn to transport the *vins gascons* abroad, mainly to English markets.

Bordeaux wine in the Middle Ages was still not a *grand cru* in the sense that this would be understood today. The buyers called it 'claret' — as the British still do. It was a *clair* or 'light' wine, the *vinum clarum* of medieval texts, and probably rosé in colour, for fermentation periods were short and maceration of the skins in the must hardly existed. In addition, 'claret' came from a mixture of red and white grapes, pressed and vinified together.

***A** 19th-century engraving of the port of Bordeaux. From the beginning of the 17th century, businessmen and* **négociants** *(shippers or merchants) established their stores and warehouses here, making this one of the great centres of world trade.*

What grape varieties were planted at this time is not known in any detail, but 18th-century texts suggest that they were very mixed. Claret was a 'new' wine, and was drunk as such. Medieval documents always refer to a claret as 'good, pure, clear, new and saleable'. This is not surprising when it is considered that at this time no one knew how to age wines, lacking the necessary techniques. For people in the 14th and 15th centuries, an old wine was one of eight to nine months that, still unsold, was worth half the price of a newer one. Claret was, in fact, a 'Bordeaux Primeur' that, from the May or June after its harvest, tended to turn sour.

Finally, the idea of a particular *terroir*, of a *cru*, was unknown to the people of the Middle Ages. At most, reference was sometimes made in the 15th century to wines from gravels (*graves*) or marshes (*palus*). Sometimes an English buyer might want a wine made by this or that *seigneur*, or from this or that estate. But *grands crus* did not exist; and in the *Bataille des Vins*, a 13th-century literary text, Saint-Émilion was considered a white wine!

The birth of the great wines

The situation developed slowly in the 16th and the first half of the 17th centuries. What happened was that *bourdieux* were created in the marshy areas of the Gironde. These were specialized holdings with the vines planted in rows, that is to say in furrows or *règes*. The grape variety that now appeared was the Petit Verdot, which produced red wines known as *'cargaison'* ('cargo'). These were wines designed to furnish ship's crews on the high seas with enough to drink. These *bourdieux* were the property of Bordeaux citizens, who ran them through the agency of a steward or *régisseur*.

At the beginning of the 17th century the arrival of Dutch traders and engineers upset once again the inherited notions of Bordeaux wine growing and commerce. At that time the Dutch, the 'carriers of the high seas', dominated world trade. Establishing themselves in Bordeaux during the early decades of the 18th century, the Dutch merchants transformed business methods. Their commercial activity in this period led to an economic renewal that was experienced first in the coastal ports and then in the Aquitaine hinterland. At Bordeaux, they established warehouses where they stored and blended wines. In France, England, and the northern countries they spread the habit of taking 'colonial infusions': chocolate, coffee, and tea a little later. They offered their European customers other drinks, such as strong beers made with plenty of hops, and gin; they greatly improved the latter, making it from grain alcohol and steeping juniper berries in it.

These new drinks competed seriously with the Gascon clarets, even though the Dutch were instrumental in the expansion of the *palus* vineyards. But the crisis that hit Bordeaux exports at this time originated principally from the new kinds of wine the Dutch were encouraging the growers to produce: sweet white wines, much liked by Flemish customers — wines that were *mutés et frelatés* (the fermentation checked by the addition of spirit, with sweetening and flavourings added). This '*façon hollandaise*' favoured the extension of peasant vineyards, bulk producers of lesser wines, red and white, for distilling. It is true that, in parallel with this, the Dutch developed the production of *brandewijn* (known as *brandevin* locally), the brandy that was drunk in large quantities by the crews of their ships. As a result, there was an expansion of the vineyards producing wines for distilling (*vins de chaudière*), not only in Cognac and Armagnac, but also in Bordeaux, especially in the Entre-Deux-Mers. They also promoted the production of red wines with more alcohol and colour than the clarets; these were known as *vins noirs*, 'black wines', at the time. In fact they were red wines, as the term would be understood today. The Dutch encouraged their production in the Cahors region — but also in the Iberian peninsula, where they were exploring commercial possibilities, especially in Portugal. Early ports were strong 'black wines', as yet unfortified, of this sort.

This diversification of the sources of supply, and the fashion for 'black wines', particularly in England, could not fail to put up serious competition to the Gascon clarets. Furthermore, the wars of the 17th century, the period of Louis XIV, had economic repercussions as well as affecting customs barriers, with serious consequences for the export market in wines. In 1688, William of Orange became king of England and assumed a protectionist policy that was extremely unfavourable to French supplies, and to Bordeaux clarets in particular, but favoured the 'black wines' of Spain and Portugal.

Haut-Brion and the Médoc's 'Princes of the Vines'

How did the Bordeaux growers react to this? Some of them remained faithful to 'claret'. Others strove to create a different kind of wine, the more so since there was a well-to-do English clientele already very well disposed towards Bordeaux wines. These claret lovers were to be found among the newer aristocracy. Under the prevailing circumstances, offering them a more expensive product of better quality seemed to be an appropriate course.

The great genius of the Pontacs, owners of Château Haut-Brion at Pessac in the Graves region, lay in their having recognized the potential of the English market. Besides the lordship of Haut-Brion, which had been theirs since the 16th century, the Pontacs held huge estates in Aquitaine and received substantial revenues. Having become rich, they had soon been absorbed into the local parliamentary aristocracy; in the 1660s the head of the family, Arnaud de Pontac, was elevated to the high office of First President of the Bordeaux *parlement*. A man of substance as well as eminence, he was particularly fond of his château of Haut-Brion and the promotion of its wines. In 1663 Samuel Pepys, that convivial Londoner, noted in his diary that he had just been at the Royal Oak tavern in the City of London, where he had drunk a 'sort of French wine called Ho Bryen that hath a good and most particular taste that I ever met with.' Besides establishing that Haut-Brion was known in London in 1663, this quotation provides the first written mention of an individual Bordeaux *cru*.

In 1666, Arnaud de Pontac had the inspired idea of sending his son, François-Auguste, to establish a fashionable restaurant in London, the 'New Eating House', under the Pontac name. There the Pontacs served meals at one guinea and sold their Haut-Brion wine, often referred to as 'M. de Pontac's wine'. They catered for a select clientele, which included writers such as Saint-Évremond, Daniel Defoe and Jonathan Swift; the philospher John Locke; rich merchants and businessmen; and the aristocracy. Patrons of this calibre were responsible for establishing an incomparable reputation for M. de Pontac's wines. John Locke in fact visited Haut-Brion in April 1667; he left a remarkable description of the vineyards of this great growth and emphasized the quality of its wines, rating them more highly than those from the neighbouring vineyards. It is known from other

Château Haut-Brion in the Graves, the first creation of the Bordeaux parliamentary elite, played a decisive part in the development of the wine region as a whole.

sources that these wines, the immediate forerunners of the Bordeaux *grand crus*, were carefully nurtured in new oak casks. At Haut-Brion it was known how to rack the wines and, no doubt, how to clarify them. And they sold at two to three times the price of ordinary clarets. The Pontacs had thus shown the way towards a renaissance in wine growing.

Pontac enterprise at Haut-Brion served as a model and a spur to the wealthy parliamentarians of Bordeaux, often kinsmen or friends of the family, as well as to the affluent middle class of the city. They all aimed to acquire, and to plant with vines, estates in the Médoc, an area that had hitherto been mainly given over to growing rye rather than wine — and had in consequence been less affected by the devastation caused by the 'great winter' of 1709. A vast pioneering effort began from Margaux, the district nearest to Bordeaux, and spread gradually towards Pauillac and Saint-Estèphe a little further north. Before long it had reached the Bas-Médoc, the northernmost part of the present Médoc *appellation*.

In 1725 Boucher, Intendant of Bordeaux, denounced this new *'fureur de planter'* that had taken hold of the city's bourgeoisie, and the aristocratic members of its parliament.

By the middle of the 18th century, not only were most of the Médoc sites now under vines, but so were other areas of Bordeaux: the Graves, Sauternes, the country around Bourg and Blaye, the Gironde *palus* and, to a lesser extent, the districts of Fronsac, Saint-Émilion and Pomerol.

Among the leading figures in this founding of the *grands crus*, mention should be made of those remarkable Médocains of the time of Louis XI, the 'Princes of the Vines' as they were called: the Marquis d'Aulède de Lestonnac, creator of the Château Margaux vineyards and joint owner of Haut-Brion; and the de Ségur family, which owned the domains of Lafite and Latour at Pauillac and established the renowned vineyards of those names. Most illustrious of all was the Marquis Nicolas Alexandre de Ségur, First President of the Parliament of Bordeaux. At the time of his death in 1755 his fortune was reckoned, in today's terms, to be worth several millions.

Many other aristocratic or wealthy middle-class families imitated these great initiators. Thus from the start the pioneering Médoc, where the Bordeaux *grands crus* were truly born, was organized around a small circle of dominant properties — the great wine châteaux.

Saint-Émilion, Pomerol and Fronsac

By contrast, the vineyard areas of Saint-Émilion, Pomerol and Fronsac made their transition to wine growing later and less completely. The outlines of these vineyards emerged only in the years 1760 to 1780, and then not fully. The innovative work was done by several leading Libourne families, notably the Fontémoings, the Boyers and the de Carles.

There are a number of reasons for this time lag between the development of the Médoc and that of Saint-Émilion, Pomerol and Fronsac. To begin with, a different basic farming system was

'Wine-tasting in London docks'; English engraving of the early 19th century. British fondness for the wines of Bordeaux contributed greatly to their fame.

Montesquieu (1689-1755), the famous thinker, writer and member of the parliamentary aristocracy of Bordeaux, was also a wine grower.

in operation: *métayage* (tenant farming or sharecropping), unknown in the Médoc, persisted for a long time in the Libourne district. Then, too, the local people of substance were less wealthy or less enterprising than those of Bordeaux. Any they did not benefit from the support of the big Bordeaux *négociants* (shippers or merchants). The Libourne wine trade, although active, was undoubtedly less dashing and less successful than that based in Bordeaux. It opened up different markets — in Brittany, the north of France, in what is now Belgium, and in Holland; but it never succeeded in penetrating the English market — the only one ready to pay the higher prices demanded for great wines.

Later, however, from the time of the Second Empire, the great red wines of Saint-Émilion, Pomerol and Fronsac put themselves in the front rank of Bordeaux wine growing, thanks to the coming of the railway and consequent innovative action by the big growers. Later still, the same process took place with the great sweet white wines of Sauternes. In fact the way had already been shown by M. Sauvage of Yquem in 1770–80; it was he who laid the foundations for the future Château d'Yquem in Sauternes.

Merchants, brokers and sophisticated society

At the beginning of the 18th century, the great Médoc red wines were being sold on the London market as 'New French Clarets' — witness the many small announcements in the *London Gazette* between 1704 and 1711–12. This fact is corroborated by other British sources of the period, including the diary of John Hervey, 1st Earl of Bristol, and bills paid by Robert Walpole, effectively Britain's first prime minister (as first lord of the Treasury and Chancellor of the Exchequer, 1721–42).

In this same period, a new form of wine growing was being established on the gravel soils of the Médoc. The big châteaux began to arrange their vines in large *plantiers*, that is to say planted in straight lines in plots neatly ploughed by teams of oxen. This new viticulture, managed by important *régisseurs* and worked by teams of wine growers, strove gradually to select and improve the grape varieties. In the technical documents of the time, the gradual appearance of today's 'noble' varieties can be noted, slowly emerging from the great mass of local types: Cabernet Sauvignon, Petit Verdot, Côt (as Malbec) and, a little later, Merlot and Cabernet Franc. These vines were trained low, at a density of 8,000 to 10,000 to the hectare. The *régisseurs* of the day were always careful to apply manure sparingly and at long intervals. Their concern, above all else, was with having low yields — around 15 to 16 hl/ha. And, finally, it was always found expedient to have a good stock of old vines, those 'mothers of great *crus*', as a Château Latour *régisseur* wrote at the end of the 18th century. These laborious and expensive operations presupposed regular investment and a long-term policy; high revenues, and the permanence of the founding families at the helm of each *grand cru*, certainly made it easier for these requirements to be fulfilled.

This renewal and reform of viticulture in Bordeaux was completed by the development of new techniques for vinifying and ageing the great wines. These were gradually worked out at the time in the *chais* of the big châteaux by the cellarmasters and their workmen, and in those of the merchants of the Chartrons area of Bordeaux. Fermentation times were shortened; and after the new wine had finished fermentation and been racked off its sediment, there followed a rigorous selection process from the various lots of wine. For the good of their product the *régisseurs*, 'cup in hand', would set aside the best wines, the premier category that alone bore the château name, then the second, less successful grade, as well as the 'bottom of the vat', for selling to different markets under other names.

From all this, the fundamental importance of Bordeaux in the creation of great wines emerges clearly, as does the vital influence of the city's merchants in the worldwide distribution of these great wines. The last decades of the 17th century and, especially, the first decades of the following century were notable for the establishment of many Bordeaux wine-trading houses. It was then that the new quarter of Chartreux, to the north of the old city, took the name 'Chartrons' and became the symbol as well as the district of residence of the new commercial aristocracy of the Bordeaux wine trade.

Most of these new *négociants* originated from the British Isles — such as the Bartons, who arrived in 1725, and the Johnstons, whose firm was founded in 1734, as well as many others. A little later, firms from the German states, from Denmark and from Holland were established.

Relations between these merchants and the estate owners were secured by a new generation of wine brokers, again mostly from the British Isles. These, too, set themselves up in Chartrons. There was, for example, Abraham Lawton, born in Cork in Ireland into a family of wine merchants. He established himself in Bordeaux at the end of 1739. He founded one of the most famous of the Bordeaux brokerage firms, and his direct descendants still follow the same profession today.

The 18th century was Bordeaux's golden age, one when trade flourished and a new society emerged, rich and sophisticated. This is borne out by the founding in 1705 of the Chamber of Commerce, and the creation in 1712–13 of the Académie Royale des Sciences, Belles-Lettres et Arts de Bordeaux. For a while the latter was presided over by Charles-Louis Secondat, Baron de La Brède: the future Montesquieu. This young President of the Bordeaux Parliament was himself a wine grower. The building of fine, stone town houses and the monumental architecture of the old commercial city testify, in their splendour, to the increasing wealth of the Bordeaux élite of the period, and to their new *art de vivre*.

In fact this new society, rich and elegant, with refined tastes and in love with beautiful things, modelled itself on London rather than Paris. London high society appreciated great wines, which it served in cut glass. It frequented the coffee houses, which were multiplying in number and where the 'New French Clarets' were served. But the birth of the Bordeaux *grands crus* has also to be placed in the larger framework of the new civilization of early 18th-century Europe, closely knit and wealthy. In this fortunate Europe, the rich at their tables could eat more delicately than hitherto, and savour new drinks, among them the great, rare and expensive wines of Bordeaux.

The creation of the *grands crus* was accompanied by the gradual sifting of these superior wines into a quality hierarchy. Thus a reading of the early books (1740–75) of the Tastet-Lawton firm of brokers confirms that there was already a classification of the great wines of the Médoc in existence in the 1770s. Some 15 years later, Thomas Jefferson, the future president of the United States and personal friend of George Washington, also confirmed that there was such a classification in his travel journal; what the *négociants* had given him was an outline of the subsequent 1855 classification. It distinguished — more particularly in the red wines — three grades: the four classics of the first rank, Haut-Brion, Lafite, Latour and Margaux, then a second and third class, at this stage somewhat incomplete. Jefferson was a loyal customer of the great wines of the Médoc, and of Château d'Yquem.

Gradually the art of tasting the fine wines of

The vineyards of Château d'Yquem, Sauternes' only Premier Cru Classé Supérieur, owned by the Lur-Saluces family. Tremendous care is taken to ensure the exceptional quality of the wines of this great cru.

Bordeaux came into being — then the art of talking about them. In the past, people had been content to quaff their wines 'by the potful', drawn straight from the cask, without analysing their special qualities. The development of Venetian crystal glasses encouraged wine lovers to study both the glass and its contents, as in Veronese's 'Marriage at Cana', or in a number of Hogarth's pictures from the first half of the 18th century. It was not only the '*robe*', the colour of the *grands crus*, that was admired, but also their qualities of body, taste and bouquet. By the late 18th century the fact that great wines could now be kept in corked bottles made it easier to make comparisons between vintages on the one hand, and between *crus* on the other. Bordeaux merchants and brokers, and the *régisseurs* and owners of the big Médoc châteaux, created a marvellously rich vocabulary of wine tasting in this period, one not without a certain resemblance to that of today's experts.

Little by little, from the 1680s to the 1750s, the great vineyards of Bordeaux were established. The pioneering role in matters of quality fell to Haut-Brion and the big Médoc châteaux. They put a premium on new ideas: the use of a particular soil type — gravel; the use of grape varieties selected and adapted to the qualities of the particular site; rigorous methods of selection, vinification and ageing; and, above all, the application of a long-term quality policy, backed up by regular and substantial investments. Such was the origin of the threefold base on which all fine wine is founded: a great growth, a *terroir*, a name. Thus the 'New French Clarets' consigned the light and anonymous 'clarets' of times past to oblivion.

The Bordeaux grape varieties

The search for quality starts in the vineyard. The first choice to be made is that of the grape variety. A region cannot hope to produce great wines if it does not have superior varieties, with fruit that comes to perfect ripeness under local conditions. In the most renowned French vineyards, the grape varieties are the result of empirical choices made by generations of growers. Out of a very large number of varieties, whether native or imported from abroad at various times, they have kept only those that have shown themselves to be suitable from both the growing and the wine-making viewpoint. The Bordeaux region has had the good fortune of being able to bring together several good varieties that are perfectly suited to its climate.

Today the main red varieties are the Cabernet Sauvignon, Cabernet Franc and Merlot, to which are added the Petit Verdot and the Côt (locally called the Malbec); the main white varieties are the Sémillon, Sauvignon Blanc, and Muscadelle, with in addition the Ugni Blanc, Colombard and Merlot Blanc.

Cabernet Sauvignon, the main grape of the Médoc, gives a wine of deep garnet red, strongly constituted and rich in tannin, with characteristic vegetal aromas.

These vines differ from one another in their general appearance, the shape of their leaves, bunches and grapes, and also in the biochemical and chemical make-up of the grapes, skins and pips. The musts from the various Bordeaux grape varieties thus show important differences in composition, particularly in acidity.

The Bordeaux grape varieties, in fact, are classified according to their degree of acidity. How considerable these differences are depends on how the vine is trained, the soil's composition and the climatic conditions of the year; but a general classification holds good regardless of these local modifying factors. The same principle would apply if the proportions of phenolic compounds and aromatic substances were taken into consideration.

The present choice of red varieties undoubtedly inclines towards those from which supple wines with tannin and good colour can be made. Plantings of the two Cabernet varieties, which both give wines a special aromatic character, as well as of the Merlot, which contributes suppleness, are spreading. By contrast the Côt (Malbec), with less sugar and higher acidity than the Merlot, is being less widely planted. The same is true for the Petit Verdot, which has difficulty in regularly producing ripe grapes under today's conditions. This used to be the main grape variety used in certain *crus*, but today it remains on only a few Médoc estates, where it represents a very small percentage of the planted area.

At the beginning of the century, vineyards growing white grapes were planted with a view to the production of semi-dry, sweet or very sweet wines. Sémillon, Muscadelle and Sauvignon Blanc grapes combine to produce wines of this last category that take on a characteristic bouquet as they age in cask and then in bottle.

Since the 1950s, however, tastes have been changing. The great sweet white wines are still in demand, but this is not true of the lesser ones. The present taste is for dry white wines rich in primary aromas — and the stock of varieties in its present proportions is less well adapted to producing this sort of wine. Only the Sauvignon Blanc has adequate aromatic potential.

The combination of varieties, found in varying proportions according to district, enables each *cru* to produce an original, harmonious, complex, yet balanced wine. In addition, having several varieties to draw on means that a certain consistency of quality and quantity can be achieved.

The red grape varieties

The Merlot is the most widely grown red grape variety in the Bordeaux region, where it accounts for about half of all plantings. It thrives in soils with moderate moisture levels in summer. It is an early-budding variety and is therefore sometimes affected by spring frosts; it is also susceptible to *coulure* (flower abortion) so, if weather conditions are unfavourable at the time of flowering, yields are very low. Thus it is an inconsistent producer. Merlot grapes are rich in sugar and give supple wines that often gain by being blended with those of the Cabernet Sauvignon.

The Cabernet Sauvignon, one of the great French grape varieties, is undoubtedly of Bordeaux origin. It is now present in most wine-growing countries, as wines of high quality can always be made from it. In the Bordeaux region, it grows on almost 25 per cent of the total red-wine vineyard area. It is the main variety in the Médoc.

A late-budding variety, which saves it from the menaces of spring frosts, it requires good weather in the autumn if it is to ripen fully. Thanks to the thickness of its grape skins, the Cabernet Sauvignon offers good resistance to grey rot (botrytis) and its yield is consistent.

Wines made from the Cabernet Sauvignon are deep in colour, with plenty of body and tannin, and with a distinctive aroma. These characteristics are refined in the ageing process and the wine develops a remarkable bouquet.

The Cabernet Franc, widely grown in the wine-growing parts of the west of France, from the Loire to the Pyrenees, accounts for about 16 per cent of the area planted with red vines in the Bordeaux region. It has a particularly strong presence in the Libourne district. It is a moderately early variety, budding and eventually ripening after the Merlot. It gives aromatic, supple wines, less full-bodied than those from the Cabernet Sauvignon and generally developing more quickly in bottle.

The Côt, most often called the Malbec (or Pressac in the Libourne district), is the earliest of all the red varieties. It is susceptible to *coulure* (flower abortion) and its production is therefore irregular. For the last 20 years, cultivation of the Côt has been in decline in the Bordeaux region because its wines are rather thin and do not improve much with age. It is now grown on only about 3 per cent of the area devoted to red wine. Its wine is at best supple, but with an aroma that often lacks finesse; its colour depends on the yield.

The Petit Verdot is the vine of the low-lying, marshy areas, the *palus*, and of the areas with alluvial soils. It grows in some Médoc sites, but its presence in the vineyards of the Bordeaux region is very modest: it occupies less than 2 per cent of the plantings of red grape varieties. It is a late budding and ripening variety that gives wines with a lot of colour and tannin when autumn weather conditions are favourable.

The white grape varieties

The Sémillon is the most widely planted of the white grape varieties of Bordeaux. It accounts for about half of the vineyard area given over to white wine growing. A very productive variety, it has good resistance to *coulure* (flower abortion), but poor resistance to grey rot (botrytis). Its grapes have a high sugar content. Sémillon wines are generally low in acidity, and have a discreet but fine aroma.

The Sémillon has the special quality of being able, under certain conditions, to profit from being attacked by *pourriture noble* (noble rot), which enables great sweet wines to be made from it. Its main failing is that it is not very suitable for the production of high-quality dry white wines.

The Sémillon is a white grape variety with high natural sugar levels. When affected by pourriture noble *(noble rot, shown above), this variety produces the great sweet white wines of Sauternes.*

The Sauvignon Blanc is one of the finest of the 'noble' grape varieties. Its cultivation is increasing and it now represents about 20 per cent of Bordeaux white wine plantings. There is at present as much Sauvignon Blanc in the Bordeaux region as there is in the Loire valley vineyards. It is not generally a very productive vine. It gives very aromatic, full-bodied, dry wines that acquire great complexity as they age. High-quality sweet wines can be obtained from it in combination with other varieties.

The Ugni Blanc is the most widely grown white grape variety in France. In the Bordeaux region, where it is known as Saint-Émilion-des-Charentes, it takes up roughly one fifth of the white vineyard area. It is a late-budding and -ripening variety that is highly and consistently productive. Wine from the Ugni Blanc is light, not very aromatic and possesses moderate acidity levels. It is primarily used for making sparkling wines. When blended with wine from other white grape varieties it can give agreeably racy dry white wines, but of limited lifespan.

The Colombard is a white grape variety in decline in Bordeaux: it now accounts for no more than 9 per cent of the white-wine-growing vineyards. It is mainly planted in the districts on the right bank of the Gironde, notably Blaye and Bourg. This grape variety is susceptible to grey rot (botrytis). Its wine has a distinctive aroma, but lacks finesse.

For the last 20 years, the area devoted to plantings of the Muscadelle has been decreasing. Today it takes up only 5 per cent of the white wine area, the reason being its susceptibility to diseases, particularly grey rot (botrytis). The Muscadelle gives a wine with an aroma that is fine and lightly reminiscent of the Muscat. It is mainly used for making sweet wines.

The Merlot Blanc (which, despite its name, is not a close relative of the red Merlot) has been planted in the area because of its great productivity. At present it occupies about 5 per cent of the white vineyard area. It gives large quantities of wine of poor quality, low in alcohol.

The elimination of hybrid varieties

Thirty years ago the Bordeaux Institut d'Oenologie showed that hybrid red grape varieties — obtained by crossing a *Vitis vinifera* vine with a variety not on its own suitable for producing wine — synthesize certain anthocyanins. These pigments are in fact diglucosides and are never present in *vinifera* vines. The properties of these diglucosides enable a wine from a hybrid to be distinguished from one from a pure *vinifera*. It is now possible to detect even very small percentages of 'hybrid' wine in a *vin d'appellation d'origine contrôlée*, all of which should come only from 'noble' *vinifera* grape varieties. This kind of fraud, which had been spreading in an alarming manner in Bordeaux, was checked by this discovery. Since 1959 it has been possible to ban hybrid vines, *appellation* by *appellation*, from properties laying claim to an AOC.

Vinification

The wine of Bordeaux has probably changed more than any other in France since the 19th century. There are a number of reasons for this phenomenon: the progress achieved in growing techniques; the expansion of the wine-growing area and of its production; the development of taste in wine drinking; and, most of all, the influence from the 1950s onwards of modern oenology on wine making. Today Bordeaux can boast of being one of the best-endowed wine regions in an oenological sense.

Red wine vinification

The red wines of the Médoc and the Graves were, in the past, characterized by their acidity and high tannin content, and by their low levels of alcohol.

The high level of tannin was a consequence of lengthy vatting time (*cuvaison*). This period, far from being fixed, is now adjusted according to the type of wine desired. There are in fact a multiplicity of tannic substances with various tastes in the different parts of the grape. By carefully calculating the intensity and length of vatting time, the wine maker can extract beneficial tannins in the quantities he wants. In addition, the traditional oak vats have gradually been replaced, for most producers, by cement or metal ones, which have the virtues of being clean, watertight and neutral with regard to taste. Finally, the length of time the wine is kept in cask has been cut down to a period between 12 and 16 months — whereas, until a few decades ago, this period often lasted several years. These important modifications of the vinification process have not come about without some resistance; but they do correspond to recent developments in taste, which tend towards wines that are less hard and astringent than formerly. At the moment, there is a counter-reaction among oenologists who believe that most Bordeaux wines should be richer in tannins and deeper in colour than they have recently become.

Another considerable transformation has been the noticeable reduction in the acidity of wines, resulting in an improvement in their qualities of taste and aroma, with more emphasis on fruit and freshness. This is consequent on a greater understanding of and insistence on seeing the malolactic fermentation through — a necessary stage in the refining of a wine, and for its biological stability. Another cause of lower acidity is that the grapes arrive for fermentation in a riper state, having been picked later than used to be the case.

Today the average alcohol content of Bordeaux red wines is between 11° and 12°, thanks to a more general use of chaptalization (sugaring of musts to increase alcohol levels) and to the improved ripeness of the grape harvest. This has also softened and mellowed the flavour of the wines.

Dry white wine vinification

For this type of vinification, technological progress has been just as remarkable as in the red wine area, most particularly in the prevention of oxidization at the time of picking, running off of the free-run juice, and even during pressing and the other stages of wine making.

The quality of dry white wine depends to a large extent on the state of health of the grapes at harvest time and, Bordeaux being a warm region, it is not absolutely necessary for the grapes to be fully ripe. Picking is therefore often done early; in many instances the grapes are sorted to remove any affected by rot. Bringing in the harvest in baskets or tubs is done with great care so as not to damage the grapes.

The grapes then go through crushers but are not stripped from the bunches, as is the case when red wines are made. The juice that runs off at this point — the *jus de goutte* or free-run juice — represents about 70 per cent of the must used. When grapes in very large quantities are being vinified this process is carried out by mechanical means.

Pressing takes place next, enabling the rest of the juice to be extracted. The Bordeaux region today is mainly equipped with horizontal or pneumatic presses. The search for quality means that the must from the final pressing is generally discarded. The tendency now is to have a very short, mechanically assisted run from grape harvest to vinification, enabling any maceration of the must with the skins and stalks — which would impart an astringent quality to the wine — to be minimized.

Before fermentation takes place, *débourbage* is carried out: the removal of impurities that might leave unpleasant tastes in the wine. Usually preceded by treatment with sulphur dioxide, *débourbage* is done by drawing off the must that has been left to rest and deposit its impurities in a special 'settling vat' (*cuve de décantation*), or by centrifuging it using a clarifier with an automatic run-off facility. Another technique, in which the temperature of the must is lowered to below 15°C, is generally applied when *débourbage* involves a prolonged period of rest, as this cooling allows better clarification of the wine. It is at this stage that any necessary corrections to the musts can be made, especially increasing or decreasing their acidity levels.

Finally the various musts are poured into casks or, increasingly, into large metal vats which are positioned outside. There, fermentation can begin at temperatures maintained at between 17°C and 20°C by continually running water over the outsides of the vessels. The wine finally undergoes malolactic fermentation, required to improve and stabilize it.

Sweet white wine vinification

The vinification of *moelleux* or sweet wines, those that contain up to 36g of sugar per litre, is quite similar to that of dry white wines. Vinification of the sweeter *liquoreux* or dessert wines proceeds differently.

To start with, the harvesting of the grapes is radically different as it entails selective picking of very ripe and overripe fruit, especially those grapes affected by *pourriture noble* (noble rot). Extraction of the must is governed by the same need for speed, so as to avoid maceration with the skins and stalks, and oxidization. But, unlike the vinification of dry white wines, there is no *égouttage* or collection of free-run juice before pressing. The reason is that in this case the pressed musts are superior to the free run. They are obtained by means of horizontal presses, well adapted to grapes attacked by *pourriture noble* and hence low in juice.

Débourbage following treatment with sulphur dioxide is no longer practised, for this could compromise the fermentation process. The 'fermentability' of the musts varies according to whether they are pressed from the first or the final sweeps through the vineyards. To get fermentation started, yeasts and other substances, such as ammonium salts and thiamine, are added.

The most characteristic quality of this type of vinification is the process of *mutage*, the halting of fermentation. This is achieved in different ways. When the musts are rich in sugar it occurs naturally, provided ambient temperature is low enough. Artificial cooling to below 10°C, accompanied by treatment with sulphur dioxide, or heating of the must to 45°C, produces the same result. However, adding a massive 80mg of sulphur dioxide per litre of wine remains the surest, and therefore the most widespread, method. Even this does not ensure complete sterilization of the wine, and so it has to be followed by racking, centrifugation or filtering.

Vintages in the Bordeaux region

In the Bordeaux region, as in all European wine-producing areas in the fringe beyond the Mediterranean belt, the quality of a crop is closely linked to the climatic conditions between the spring and the autumn. The temperature, the amount of sunshine and the rainfall all play an essential part in the growth of the vine,

SWEET WINES AND POURRITURE NOBLE

A bunch of Sémillon grapes infected by Botrytis cinerea.

The great sweet wines of Bordeaux are produced from grapes that have undergone a particular form of over-ripening called pourriture noble *(noble rot). This is caused by the growth of a microscopic fungus, called* Botrytis cinerea, *on the grape. In certain favourable climatic conditions, an improvement in the quality of grapes affected by this fungus takes place, caused by a concentration of grape sugars without a corresponding increase in acidity. These grapes produce wines which, when mature, develop a characteristic aromatic profile. However, if the climate is not favourable, this same fungus — or a closely related form of it — develops* pourriture vulgaire *or* pourriture grise *('vulgar' rot or grey rot, also known as botrytis) on the grapes, which leads to a decrease in the quality of the grape harvest and consequently of the wine.*

The development of Botrytis

If the Sémillon grapes contaminated by Botrytis cinerea *are observed through an electronic microscope, it can be seen that the fungus penetrates the grape through small lesions in the skin which are invisible to the naked eye. These microscopic fissures occur when tension, caused by the grape's increasing volume while maturing, causes the skin to crack. The grapes also have microscopic openings in their skins called stomata, which allow the passage of gases; when the grapes ripen fully, a circular crack forms all around these stomata.*

The fungal spores, which are disseminated by the wind or the rain, germinate on the surface of the grape. Embryonic tubes then penetrate the grape through the various microscopic lesions and disrupt the cell walls of the skin. At this stage, some of these fungal tubes or filaments cause the skin to burst and form clumps on the outside of the grape, loaded with numerous spores which propagate the rot further.

When Botrytis cinerea *attacks a grape, small brown circular speckles are the first visible sign of the growth: this is the* 'grains tachetés' *('speckled grape') stage. Then, within a few days, the whole of the grape is invaded; it turns a purple-brown colour, becomes thinner and extremely fragile. At this stage, the fruit is described as being at the* 'grains pourris pleins' *('full rotted grape') stage. If the temperature and humidity conditions are favourable,* Botrytis cinerea *develops further and the grape withers. In this case, the grapes are referred to as* 'grains rôtis ou confits' *(literally 'roasted' or 'preserved' grapes). It is from grapes like these that sweet, rich, unctuous wines are obtained, with characteristically complex aromas and flavours, notably that special flavour called* 'goût de rôti' *in French (meaning literally a 'roasted' taste, but referring to the slightly bitter flavour of sweet wines made from* Botrytis*-affected grapes). As the wine matures, the* goût de rôti *becomes more refined and nuanced.*

Grapes affected by noble rot to the rôti *stage are formed over a long period, generally of several weeks. This means in practice that the grapes must harvested in several sweeps. Only the bunches, or parts of bunches, that are in the desired state are harvested. Grapes that have been spoiled by the development of various alien moulds or bacteria are first removed from the vines: this is called the cleaning sweep* ('la trie de nettoyage'). *The workforce charged with picking grapes affected by noble rot must be familiar with that task. This is vital to the quality of the wines. Only local workers can therefore be used.*

The action of Botrytis cinerea on the composition of the must

The growth of Botrytis cinerea *causes a profound change in the chemical composition of the grape. The sugars and acids are both 'burnt' by the fungus. The latter diminish in a much greater proportion than the sugars, and more than half of them may disappear. It should be noted that the tartaric acid decreases to a much greater extent than malic acid. Glycerol, polysaccharides, and acetic, citric and gluconic acids are formed.* Botrytis cinerea *also secretes numerous enzymes. Some of these break up the cell walls in the grape skins. The structure of the grape is broken, and therefore exchanges with the mother vine come to a halt, so that the grape behaves exactly as if it were detached from the stock. Only climatic conditions are then significant. In dry and hot weather, the grape rapidly looses water and becomes concentrated. The sugar level increases considerably. The acids are also concentrated but, because they are 'burnt' to a greater degree than the sugars, the acidity of the must from grapes affected by botrytis is more or less the same as that of healthy grapes. In rainy or very humid weather, the grape absorbs water and the sugar content diminishes rapidly. In the course of the same day, the sugar levels can therefore vary greatly. Even morning mists, which are very common in Sauternes in October and November, are enough to reduce the sugar content. To produce the richest must, therefore, the grapes are harvested in the afternoon.*

The role of climate, soil and water

The development of Botrytis cinerea *in the form of* pourriture noble *can only take place on ripe grapes, and in particular grapes that have not burst; the vine should therefore not receive too much water. It has been noted that, after substantial summer rain, grapes from some plots were more likely to burst than grapes from other plots. This may be explained by the physical properties of the soil. The soil in the Sauternes region is very heterogeneous, with great variations in the amounts of clay and of coarse stones it contains. In very permeable, gravelly, sandy areas, natural drainage allows the water to disappear very quickly. On the other hand, in areas where the soil has a greater quantity of clay, artificial drainage often has to be arranged to limit the water supply to the vines, and hence the risk of the grapes bursting.*

During the overripening phase, climatic conditions play an essential role. In fact, the development of Botrytis cinerea *as* pourriture noble *is only possible when there is an alternation between short humid spells, which are favourable to the development of the fungus, and longer dry spells, which accelerate the concentration of sugars in the grapes. It is therefore clear that, because of natural climatic differences from autumn to autumn in the Bordeaux region, it is not possible to obtain* pourriture noble *on all of the crop, every year.*

The production of Sauternes requires grapes harvested selectively, in several sweeps, and overall yields are very low. More than any other type of wine, Sauternes is subject to the hazards of the climate, and growers here run considerable risks in competing with similar products that have a lower cost price, thanks to less stringent production methods.

the maturation of the grape and, in consequence, the quality of the wine. Since no two years are meteorologically similar, no two vintages are ever completely identical.

For the grapes to attain proper maturity in Bordeaux, the climatic conditions should be as follows:

▷ a temperature total, calculated for the vegetative period from April to September inclusive, greater than 3,100°C;
▷ more than 15 very hot days during this time, with maximum temperatures equal or superior to 30°C;
▷ a rainfall level for this period between 250mm and 350mm, that is to say 250 – 350mm per square metre or, approximately, per vine;
▷ luminosity between April and September corresponding to at least 1,250 hours of direct sunshine.

If the conditions are other than as described above, the grapes on the vine will have difficulty in ripening properly. The wines made from these grapes will lack character and be ill-suited to ageing. One of these conditions on its own is insufficient to ensure quality; it is important that all should prevail for a good vintage.

Exceptional years, producing wines of great longevity, require still more sun and less rain than the standards given above. More exactly, the best vintages result from hot, largely dry summers and bright autumns. Good years are generally years in which the vegetative and fruiting cycle is early. The reason for this is that good maturity can more easily be attained if the maturation takes place over the course of long summer days which allow the vine to receive the maximum light and heat and thus to produce very ripe grapes.

It is very rare for a late year to yield a good vintage. On the other hand, early years may still prove poor if, for example, a lot of rain falls at the end of September, as this will mean that the grapes have an inadequate concentration of sugars and other elements. As this last observation suggests, statistical equations based on climatic totals only bear a schematic relationship to wine quality. This is because quality is influenced much less by the sum of temperatures or the level of rainfall than by the time at which heat occurs or rain falls. It is well known that the weather at harvest time can radically change the quality of the grapes on the vines.

Since weather forecasts are not very reliable beyond five days, it is impossible to know in advance how good a vintage will be. Likewise, only ignorance of the nature of the vine or dishonesty could lead someone to pass judgment on the quality of a vintage before it is ready for consumption. In fact, as Emile Peynaud has

A bottle of 1893 Château d'Yquem. As it matures, this — Sauternes' only Premier Cru Supérieur — takes on a warm amber colour.

PHENOLOGICAL OBSERVATIONS OF THE LAST TWENTY-THREE YEARS IN THE BORDEAUX REGION

Vintage	Mid-flowering	Mid-ripening	Full-maturity	Longevity of vintage in years	
				Red	Sweet white
1964	9 June	14 August	26 September	30	15
1965	22 June	27 August	6 October	10	15
1966	9 June	13 August	26 September	30	35
1967	12 June	19 August	2 October	30	35
1968	19 June	23 August	8 October	20	25
1969	22 June	24 August	4 October	30	35
1970	15 June	21 August	2 October	40	50
1971	15 June	21 August	1 October	30	35
1972	26 June	1 September	16 October	20	25
1973	10 June	13 August	2 October	20	25
1974	15 June	19 August	6 October	10	25
1975	14 June	20 August	1 October	40	35
1976	4 June	7 August	18 September	30	25
1977	27 June	2 September	12 October	20	25
1978	26 June	2 September	12 October	30	20
1979	21 June	25 August	8 October	20	25
1980	25 June	3 September	13 October	10	15
1981	12 June	20 August	5 October	30	35
1982	5 June	9 August	23 September	30	35
1983	13 June	19 August	28 September	30	35
1984	18 June	20 August	6 October	10	15
1985	15 June	16 August	1 October	30	35
1986	20 June	19 August	3 October	30	35

written, 'each vintage has its own character, its own development, its own reputation and its own price. A vintage is part of the personality of a wine. It is sometimes said that it dominates the *cru*, meaning that there is more similarity between wines from different vineyards made in the same year than there is between wines from the same vineyard made in different years.'

The consumer often attaches too much importance to the relative reputations of vintages. Present-day wine-making technology mitigates or even eliminates 'bad' vintages. In Peynaud's succinct phrase, 'there are no more bad years; there are just difficult years'.

This does not mean that all wines now resemble each other, but it shows that there are well-structured, rich wines which need several years to reach their peak, and stay there for a long time; and that there are light but well-balanced wines which develop more quickly. It is thus wrong to separate vintages into two categories, the good and the bad. The reality of things is different.

In the Bordeaux region, the wine comes from several different grape varieties and the degree of success, depending on the weather conditions of the year, is different for each. Sometimes the Merlot ripens best, but on other occasions the quality of the wines is due to the high standard reached by the Cabernet Sauvignon and Cabernet Franc. Moreover, in the same vintage, one *appellation* may be more successful than another according to the grape variety dominant in that area. In difficult years, some châteaux are more successful than others thanks to a more judicious or fortunate choice of day for the start of the harvest, to a more rigorous selection of grapes and to the use of wine-producing techniques appropriate to the difficulty in question.

Therefore, in the vast Bordeaux region, in a year that is said to be mediocre, there will always be a greater or lesser number of wines that, though they do not have great longevity, are none the less rewarding to drink.

It is, for the reasons cited above, difficult to establish a hierarchy of vintages. A wine cannot be graded according to a scale of absolute value but only in relation to other wines of the same year and the same origin. How can the taste of a wine in ten or more years' time be forecast? What sort of memory is necessary to remember the organoleptic characteristics that a wine more than 20 years old possessed when it came out of the vinification vat? Vintage charts and comparative tables abound, without always bringing satisfaction to wine lovers, as Alexis Lichine writes: 'Misled by vintage tables, too many people think that they should only buy wines from good years . . . By doing this, they most often buy wines which should be kept for a long time. All too often they drink these wines before they have reached full maturity. If they had chosen a wine from a less bountiful year, they would have paid less and, at the moment when they drank it, would have had a better bottle.'

The Code de l'Académie des Vins de Bordeaux (Code of the Academy of Bordeaux Wine) is original in that it does not classify the vintages hierarchically. It uses symbols to give information on each vintage: its general character, the level of success achieved by the growers with the vintage, and the degree of development of the wines. The use of this chart permits consumers to enjoy the wines of each vintage at their optimum stage of development.

The *crus classés* of the Bordeaux region

For many years, the hierarchy of Bordeaux *crus* was only known to the large vineyard owners, the *négociants* (shippers or merchants) and the wine brokers. Lovers of these great wines remained in semi-ignorance until a series of books started to lift the corner of the veil.

The first of these books was by Jullien, *Topographie de tous les vignobles connus*, followed by a *Classification générale des vins*, the first edition of which appeared 1816, and the second revised and enlarged edition in 1822. The author obtained his information from *négociants* and vineyard owners, but also from restaurateurs. In his classification outline, he distinguished between the four red wine *premiers crus*, already well known: Lafite, Latour, Margaux and Haut-Brion; then between seven *deuxièmes crus*: Rauzan, Gorce, Léoville, Larose, Brane-Mouton, Pichon-Longueville and Calon. As far as further classifications were concerned, the author was more evasive; he did not refer to any named *crus* but just to parishes and communes.

Jullien's work served as a basis for his successors, who repeated him and sometimes even plagiarized him without quoting him. Wilhelm Franck, in his *Traité sur les vins du Médoc et les autres vins rouges du département de la Gironde*, published in 1824, gives Lafite, Latour and Margaux as the three *premiers crus* of the Médoc. He cites only four *deuxièmes crus*, Brane-Mouton, Rauzan, Léoville and Gruaud-Larose. Next came eight *troisièmes crus*: Bergeron (Ducru-Beaucaillou), Calon, Cos d'Estournel, Branes-Arbouet (Lagrange), Gorce, Lascombes, Pichon-Longueville, Pontet-Langlois (Langoa). The group of *quatrièmes crus* numbered 18: Boyd, Durfort (Durfort-Vivens), Duluc (Branaire-Ducru), Duhart-Milon, Desmirail, Ferrière, Giscours, Malescot-Saint-Exupéry, Saint-Pierre, Pouget, de Terme, Pontet-Canet, Grand-Puy-Lacoste, la Colonie, Tronquoy, Kirwan and Issan.

From 1838 to 1841, Lecoultre de Beauvais and the editors of the monthly journal *le Producteur* took an interest in the *crus* of the Bordeaux region. They published a series of detailed maps of the communes of the Médoc in particular, but also of other wine-producing areas of the Gironde, accompanied by a precise commentary on the *crus* and their classification. As far as *crus classés* were concerned, *le Producteur* seems, from today's perspective, to have given way to a sort of galloping inflation. The editors of the magazine, evidently influenced by their informants, arrive at a total of 210 *crus classés*: 3 *premiers*, 14 *deuxièmes*, 28 *troisièmes* (twice the total later arrived at in 1855), and, in particular, 46 *quatrièmes* and 119 *cinquièmes*. This classification is not without interest, however, for Montrose appears for the first time as a *deuxième cru* and Palmer is mentioned among the *troisièmes*. Whatever the differences between these classifications and the exaggerations of *le Producteur*, these works show that the châteaux owners at this time were greatly concerned with classification.

The classification of the *grands crus* of the Médoc was also of interest to British authors of the period, as is witnessed by *The History of Ancient and Modern Wines*, by Dr Alexander Henderson, published in 1824, and *A History and Description of Modern Wines*, by Cyrus Redding, published in 1833. These English-language works show that, on the other side of the Channel, consumers and readers were very attentive to what was being written in Bordeaux on matters to do with wine growing and vinification. All these factors demonstrate that, between 1840 and 1850, the need for a more or less official publication on the classification of the *grands crus* was being felt.

The 1855 classification

A little before 1855, a number of initiatives taken in the Médoc modified somewhat the order that had been established for 50 years. As far as the *premiers crus* were concerned, only questions of precedence were being asked: Lafite had put itself forward as a candidate for the title of the first of all the *crus* of the Médoc!

Among the *deuxièmes*, Brane-Mouton was trying to get itself elevated to the ranks of the *premiers crus*.

The Bordeaux Wine Brokers' Union was the only organization capable of objectively working out a classification. The occasion that was to provoke this group into drawing up a public

Château Lafite-Rothschild at Pauillac. The fine wine of this Médoc Premier Cru Classé is tannic, distinguished and vigorous, developing a scent of violets with time.

list of the *grands crus* was the Exposition Universelle, organized in Paris in 1855.

In a letter to the Wine Brokers' Union on 5 April 1855, the Gironde Chamber of Commerce explained that it had had a wine map drawn up to accompany the samples of wine that would appear at the Exhibition, and it went on to formulate the fateful request: 'We kindly ask you to send us an exact and complete list of all the red *crus classés* of the *département*, specifying to which of the five categories each belongs, and indicating which commune each comes from.'

On the 8 April 1855, the Wine Brokers Union sent off the famous 'list of the classified red wines of the Gironde'. In fact, this only included the *crus classés* of the Médoc, to which the Union had added Haut-Brion, from the Graves. It cited 58 *crus* by name: 4 *premiers*, 12 *deuxièmes*, 14 *troisièmes*, 11 *quatrièmes* and 17 *cinquièmes*. This list was accompanied by another: that of the sweet white wines coming exclusively from the five communes that today enjoy the Barsac or Sauternes *appellation*.

The famous emblem of Château Latour, one of the five red Premiers Crus Classés.

The wine brokers were well aware of the risk they had taken by drawing up this exclusive list. They accompanied it with a letter in which they said: 'In order to conform with your desires, we have gathered together all the possible information and we are honoured in imparting to you, by means of the enclosed table, the results of our investigations. You know as well as we do, gentlemen, how delicate a matter this classification is and how much it can arouse sensitivities; therefore, instead of drawing up an official register of all our great wines, we are rather submitting for your attention a simple piece of work researched from the best sources.' The wine brokers were, in fact, merely ratifying an old situation and did not want to take upon themselves the responsibility of giving it official status.

Since this date, the classification has undergone only one significant modification: by decree of 21 June 1973, Château Mouton-Rothschild, which was classified as a *deuxième cru* in 1855, was promoted to the rank of *premier cru*, and the *premiers crus* of the Médoc were henceforth to be classified in alphabetical order. No changes have been made to the other *crus* classified in 1855, apart from those caused by the division or regrouping of properties.

Since 1855, many *crus* have changed hands, sometimes several times. This means that the skills of the managers and the means at their disposal could have changed the quality of the wines for better or for worse. It is a strong probability that the plots of vines of some châteaux do not occupy the same positions as they did in 1855. In many cases, there have only been minor modifications, but in other cases, plots have been bought to increase the area of the *cru*. All this is true, but is it enough to call into question the 1855 classification? We do not think so. In fact, with a few slight exceptions, today's sale prices accurately reflect the classification of 1855. If some adjustments are necessary, they are made naturally and justly by the fact that some *crus* attain higher prices than those corresponding to their position in the classification. Equally justly, the reverse is true.

The classification of the Graves

Apart from Château Haut-Brion, the 1855 classification did not take into account the wines of the Graves district. With much difficulty the Wine Growers' Union (Syndicat Viticole), in conjunction with the Institut National des Appellations d'Origine, established a classification that became official by ministerial decree on 16 February 1959. It applies to both red and white wines, which means that some châteaux are mentioned twice, once in each category.

The classification of Saint-Émilion

No Saint-Émilion *cru* is mentioned in the 1855 classification. The Saint-Émilion Wine Growers' Union decided to establish its own classification but, so as to prevent it becoming rigid and outdated, agreed that it should be revised every ten years (a term that is lengthened by administrative delays). The first classification dates from 1954, the second from 1969 and the third came into effect with the 1985 harvest, the decree itself dating from 23 May 1986.

The Crus Bourgeois of the Médoc

A first classification of the Crus Bourgeois of the Médoc was made in 1932 by a commission of wine brokers, under the authority of the Gironde Chamber of Commerce and the Gironde Chamber of Agriculture. A total of 444 properties were classified into three groups: Crus Bourgeois Supérieurs Exceptionnels, Crus Bourgeois Supérieurs and Crus Bourgeois.

In 1962, the Union of Crus Bourgeois was formed. The first task its committee undertook was to summon all the vineyard owners listed in 1932. Only 210 of them remained, of whom 94 had already joined the new union; today 140 are members. In 1966 and in 1978, the Union drew up a fresh list of the *crus bourgeois* and renamed the three categories: they are now Crus Grands Bourgeois Exceptionnels, Crus Grands Bourgeois and Crus Bourgeois.

Bordeaux wine production

The vineyards of the Bordeaux region, mostly given over to fine wine production, are characterized by their diversity and quality. Some 100,000 ha, divided among 20,000 wine growers, produce on average 500 million bottles per year, about 65 per cent of them containing red

OFFICIAL CLASSIFICATIONS OF THE WINES OF BORDEAUX

Region	AOC	Date	Crus classés	Colour	Communes
Graves	Graves	1855	Ch. Haut-Brion (1er)	R	Pessac
		1959	Ch. Bouscaut	R & W	Cadaujac
			Ch. Carbonnieux	R & W	Léognan
			Dm de Chevalier	R & W	Léognan
			Ch. Couhins	W	Villenave-d'O.
			Ch. Couhins-Lurton	W	Villenave-d'O.
			Ch. Fieuzal	R	Léognan
			Ch. Haut-Bailly	R	Léognan
			Ch. Haut-Brion	R	Pessac
			Ch. Laville-Haut-Brion	W	Talence
			Ch. Malartic-Lagravière	R & W	Léognan
			Ch. La Mission-Haut-Brion	R	Talence
			Ch. Olivier	R & W	Léognan
			Ch. Pape-Clement	R	Pessac
			Ch. Smith-Haut-Lafitte	R	Martillac
			Ch. La Tour-Haut-Brion	R	Talence
			Ch. La Tour-Martillac	R & W	Martillac
Médoc	Haut-Médoc	1855 (1973 for the *premiers crus classés*)	Ch. La Tour-Carnet (4e)	R	Saint-Laurent
			Ch. Belgrave (5e)	R	Saint-Laurent
			Ch. Camensac (5e)	R	Saint-Laurent
			Ch. La Lagune (5e)	R	Ludon
			Ch. Cantemerle (5e)	R	Macau
	Margaux		Ch. Margaux (1er)	R	Margaux
			Ch. Durfort-Vivens (2e)	R	Margaux
			Ch. Lascombes (2e)	R	Margaux
			Ch. Rauzan-Ségla (2e)	R	Margaux
			Ch. Rauzan-Gassies (2e)	R	Margaux
			Ch. Desmirail (3e)	R	Margaux
			Ch. Ferrière (3e)	R	Margaux
			Ch. Malescot-Saint-Exupéry (3e)	R	Margaux
			Ch. Marquis d'Alesme-Becker (3e)	R	Margaux
			Ch. Marquis de Terme (4e)	R	Margaux
			Ch. Brane-Cantenac (2e)	R	Cantenac
			Ch. Boyd-Cantenac (3e)	R	Cantenac
			Ch. Cantenac-Brown (3e)	R	Cantenac
			Ch. d'Issan (3e)	R	Cantenac
			Ch. Kirwan (3e)	R	Cantenac
			Ch. Palmer (3e)	R	Cantenac
			Ch. Pouget (4e)	R	Cantenac
			Ch. Prieuré-Lichine (4e)	R	Cantenac
			Ch. Giscours (3e)	R	Labarde
			Ch. Dauzac (5e)	R	Labarde
			Ch. du Tertre (5e)	R	Arsac
	Pauillac		Ch. Lafite-Rothschild (1er)	R	Pauillac
			Ch. Latour (1er)	R	Pauillac
			Ch. Mouton-Rothschild (1er)	R	Pauillac
			Ch. Pichon-Longueville (2e)	R	Pauillac
			Ch. Pichon-Longueville-Lalande (2^{e})	R	Pauillac
			Ch. Duhart-Milon (4e)	R	Pauillac
			Ch. Batailley (5e)	R	Pauillac
			Ch. Haut-Batailley (5e)	R	Pauillac
			Ch. Clerc-Milon (5e)	R	Pauillac
			Ch. Croizet-Bages (5e)	R	Pauillac
			Ch. Grand-Puy-Ducasse (5e)	R	Pauillac
			Ch. Grand-Puy-Lacoste (5e)	R	Pauillac
			Ch. Haut-Bages-Libéral (5e)	R	Pauillac
			Ch. Lynch-Bages (5e)	R	Pauillac
			Ch. Lynch-Moussas (5e)	R	Pauillac
			Ch. Mouton-Baronne Philippe (5e)	R	Pauillac
Médoc (cont'd)			Ch. Pédesclaux (5e)	R	Pauillac
			Ch. Pontet-Canet (5e)	R	Pauillac
	Saint-Estèphe		Ch. Cos d'Estournel (2e)	R	Saint-Estèphe
			Ch. Montrose (2e)	R	Saint-Estèphe
			Ch. Calon-Ségur (3e)	R	Saint-Estèphe
			Ch. Lafon-Rochet (4e)	R	Saint-Estèphe
			Ch. Cos-Labory (5e)	R	Saint-Estèphe
	Saint-Julien		Ch. Ducru-Beaucaillou (2e)	R	Saint-Julien
			Ch. Gruaud-Larose (2e)	R	Saint-Julien
			Ch. Léoville-Las-Cases (2e)	R	Saint-Julien
			Ch. Léoville-Poyferré (2e)	R	Saint-Julien
			Ch. Léoville-Barton (2e)	R	Saint-Julien
			Ch. Lagrange (3e)	R	Saint-Julien
			Ch. Langoa-Barton (3e)	R	Saint-Julien
			Ch. Beychevelle (4e)	R	Saint-Julien
			Ch. Branaire-Ducru (4e)	R	Saint-Julien
			Ch. Saint-Pierre-Sevaistre (4e)	R	Saint-Julien
			Ch. Talbot (4e)	R	Saint-Julien
Libourne area	Saint-Émilion (for the *grands crus classés*, see p.486)	1986	A: Ch. Ausone (1er)	R	Saint-Émilion
			Ch. Cheval-Blanc (1er)	R	Saint-Émilion
			B: Ch. Beauséjour (Duffau-Lagarrosse) (1er)	R	Saint-Émilion
			Ch. Belair (1er)	R	Saint-Émilion
			Ch. Canon (1er)	R	Saint-Émilion
			Ch. Fourtet (1er)	R	Saint-Émilion
			Ch. Figeac (1er)	R	Saint-Émilion
			Ch. La Gaffelière (1er)	R	Saint-Émilion
			Ch. Magdelaine (1er)	R	Saint-Émilion
			Ch. Pavie (1er)	R	Saint-Émilion
			Ch. Trottevieille (1er)	R	Saint-Émilion
Sauternes area	Barsac	1855	Ch. Climens (1er)	W	Barsac
			Ch. Coutet (1er)	W	Barsac
			Ch. Broustet (2e)	W	Barsac
			Ch. Caillou (2e)	W	Barsac
			Ch. Doisy-Daëne (2e)	W	Barsac
			Ch. Doisy-Dubroca (2e)	W	Barsac
			Ch. Doisy-Védrines (2e)	W	Barsac
			Ch. Myrat (2e)	W	Barsac
			Ch. Nairac (2e)	W	Barsac
			Ch. Suau (2e)	W	Barsac
	Sauternes		Ch. d'Yquem (1er cru supérieur)	W	Sauternes
			Ch. Guiraud (1er)	W	Sauternes
			Ch. d'Arche (2e)	W	Sauternes
			Ch. Filhot (2e)	W	Sauternes
			Ch. Lamothe-Despujols (2e)	W	Sauternes
			Ch. Lamothe-Guignard (2e)	W	Sauternes
			Ch. Lafaurie-Peyraguey (1er)	W	Bommes
			Clos Haut-Peyraguey (1er)	W	Bommes
			Ch. de Rayne-Vigneau (1er)	W	Bommes
			Ch. Rabaud-Promis (1er)	W	Bommes
			Ch. Sigalas-Rabaud (1er)	W	Bommes
			Ch. La Tour Blanche (1er)	W	Bommes
			Ch. Rieussec (1er)	W	Fargues
			Ch. Romer du Hayot (2e)	W	Fargues
			Ch. Romer (2e)	W	Fargues
			Ch. Suduiraut (1er)	W	Preignac
			Ch. de Malle (2e)	W	Preignac

A BORDEAUX CHÂTEAU

Château Carbonnieux in Léognan dates from the 14th century. The estate of this Graves Cru Classé covers 172ha, sited on hilltop gravels mixed with sand, or gravel over a clay-limestone base. Both red and white wines are produced here, and all the vinification operations take place within the château itself.

Building A
1. Grape reception area. **2.** Destalker.
3. Presses. **4.** Red-wine fermentation vats. **5.** Settling pit (*puits de débourbage*).
Building B: **1** and **2.** Red-wine fermentation tanks.
Building C: White-wine fermentation tanks.
Building D: White-wine maturation *chai.*
Building E: **1.** White-wine maturation *chai.* **2.** Bottle store for older vintages.
Building F: Red-wine maturation *chai.*
Building G: Warehouse for cased wines ready for dispatch.
Building H: Bottling plant.
Building I: Warehouse for one-year-old wines in cask.
Building J: Office.
Buildings K and L: Living quarters.

K
J
E
I
H
G
F

wine and 35 per cent white wine.

Since the first cooperative was created in Saint-Émilion in 1932, the cooperative movement in Bordeaux has developed considerably.

The wholesale wine trade (*le négoce*), that other important partner of wine growing in the Bordeaux area, and the motor force behind the reputation of the wines, continues to play a dynamic role with 400 commercial firms and 150 wine brokers' offices active at present.

Professional structures and marketing

Interprofessional collaboration in Bordeaux was born in the form of an association, the Union de la Propriété et du Commerce (Union of Vineyard Ownership and Commerce), after the First World War, on the initiative of M. Fernand Ginestet, a vineyard owner and *négo-*

In Gironde, 59 cooperatives produce nearly one third of the département's *total AOC production.*

RECENT HARVESTS OF AOC RED WINES IN GIRONDE

	1981	1982	1983	1984	1985
BORDEAUX GROUP					
Bordeaux Rouge	845 324	1 229 593	1 099 361	779 055	1 493 426
Sainte-Foy-Bordeaux	2 615	5 745	2 362	1 714	3 226
Bordeaux Rosé	12 184	16 420	15 892	12 255	15 856
Bordeaux Supérieur	374 228	441 570	405 634	251 029	539 388
CÔTES GROUP					
Bordeaux-Côtes de Castillon	91 081	124 060	105 175	44 426	135 031
Bordeaux-Côtes de Francs	8 754	9 769	9 295	5 653	14 004
1res Côtes de Blaye	87 254	124 015	131 669	66 156	127 910
Côtes de Bourg	127 585	174 676	139 280	85 040	171 677
1res Côtes de Bordeaux	49 419	82 046	65 500	42 965	78 242
Graves de Vayres	8 527	10 769	8 438	6 464	14 579
MÉDOC AND GRAVES GROUP					
Médoc	123 990	172 866	158 628	94 158	208 725
Haut-Médoc	117 730	156 097	144 543	97 932	172 376
Listrac	22 534	31 633	29 500	13 328	23 669
Moulis	13 307	20 676	21 680	14 262	21 339
Margaux	38 569	30 913	58 226	34 046	53 375
Saint-Julien	29 209	40 835	45 940	24 574	42 444
Pauillac	35 397	44 440	48 505	38 071	60 944
Saint-Estèphe	50 311	58 071	60 411	39 161	71 525
Graves	66 469	100 869	94 868	60 073	98 585
SAINT-ÉMILION-POMEROL-FRONSAC GROUP					
Saint-Émilion	201 151	390 091	261 838	104 944	278 621
Montagne-Saint-Émilion	53 322	76 522	74 625	26 238	70 802
Saint-Georges-Saint-Émilion	5 568	9 054	8 991	2 934	8 022
Lussac-Saint-Émilion	42 307	61 237	57 694	22 397	64 212
Puisseguin-Saint-Émilion	25 140	35 832	35 054	10 619	36 540
Pomerol	23 720	38 626	30 073	14 683	35 565
Lalande-de-Pomerol	32 661	45 871	35 642	20 100	29 461
Fronsac	30 028	40 514	36 317	13 187	45 759
Canon-Fronsac	9 911	15 555	12 004	5 116	17 298
Total in hectolitres	**2 528 295**	**3 508 365**	**3 197 145**	**1 930 580**	**3 932 601**

RECENT HARVESTS OF AOC WHITE WINES IN GIRONDE

DRY WHITES	1981	1982	1983	1984	1985
Bordeaux	460 480	629 593	543 064	566 035	636 728
Blayais	27 133	18 329	11 186	18 942	13 933
Côtes de Blaye	10 898	11 487	11 834	12 166	8 557
Côtes de Bourg	5 139	5 129	3 989	3 401	3 576
Entre-Deux-Mers	99 854	150 797	140 452	118 581	129 995
Graves de Vayres	11 254	8 459	6 613	11 843	9 370
Graves	22 469	64 043	43 202	48 708	48 814
SWEET WHITES					
Bordeaux Supérieur	12 989	16 900	17 064	12 889	9 232
Sainte-Foy-Bordeaux	4 424	9 197	6 114	2 848	4 082
Côtes de Bordeaux-Saint-Macaire	4 625	3 711	2 982	1 336	2 298
1res Côtes de Bordeaux	23 456	24 279	25 789	19 934	24 343
Cadillac	2 318	2 329	1 772	1 475	3 279
Graves Supérieures	12 356	20 100	25 953	19 434	14 516
Cérons	6 271	5 706	4 870	4 121	2 676
Loupiac	10 252	10 696	10 597	9 170	6 320
Sainte-Croix-du-Mont	13 092	16 294	16 059	14 885	16 021
Barsac	12 890	14 794	14 461	13 809	14 186
Sauternes	28 290	30 076	31 306	28 252	30 363
Total in hectolitres	768 190	1 041 919	917 307	907 829	978 289

THE MARKETING OF RED BORDEAUX WINES

1984–1985 Campaign	Total	France	Exports
Bordeaux	1 022 954	635 580	387 374
Bordeaux Superieur	409 952	310 480	99 472
Bordeaux-Côtes de Castillon	90 876	76 268	14 608
1res Côtes de Blaye	98 176	79 340	18 836
Côtes de Bourg	138 390	106 768	31 622
1res Côtes de Bordeaux	56 914	45 681	11 233
Graves de Vayres	2 014	1 709	305
Bordeaux Rosé	15 339	12 090	3 249
Graves	75 706	44 662	31 044
Haut-Médoc	134 457	75 286	59 171
Médoc	137 524	64 581	72 943
Moulis	15 227	4 911	10 316
Listrac	24 770	13 341	11 429
Margaux	46 539	10 983	35 556
Saint-Julien	32 680	8 848	23 832
Pauillac	39 435	9 906	29 529
Saint-Estèphe	53 258	29 978	23 280
Saint-Émilion	227 318	129 326	97 992
Montagne-Saint-Émilion	57 895	43 800	14 095
Lussac-Saint-Émilion	49 746	32 705	17 041
Saint-Georges-Saint-Émilion	6 459	3 674	2 785
Pomerol	33 165	16 901	16 264
Puisseguin-Saint-Émilion	28 791	18 247	10 544
Fronsac + Canon-Fronsac	39 361	24 377	14 984
Lalande-de-Pomerol	35 035	25 446	9 589

Exports of Bordeaux's wines are constantly increasing, and now approach 40 per cent of total production. The chief export markets are Great Britain, the Netherlands and the United States.

ciant. After the end of the Second World War, the authorities created, with the law of 18 August 1948, the Comité Interprofessionnel du Vin de Bordeaux (Bordeaux Interprofessional Wine Committee).

The Comité Interprofessionel du Vin de Bordeaux

It is possible from today's viewpoint to distinguish three main stages in the development of interprofessional relations in Bordeaux.

From 1948 to 1965, the professionals were solely concerned with stimulating, by means of publicity and advertising, the general sales of Bordeaux wines. During this postwar period, the leading châteaux had the necessary weight to force through measures of replanting and renewal in the vineyards, and they played an important role in the politics of wine production at that time.

At the end of this period, a crisis in the sales of generic wines made the interprofessional collaborators realize the need for a better organizational structure, and the necessity of equipping themselves with greater powers and financial resources. Thus, on 8 December 1965, the Protocol of Bordeaux Wines was signed; this signalled a resolve to acquire a better knowledge of the market and initiated a policy of establishing contractual relations between producers and *négociants*.

The years 1966 to 1975 were marked by the reorganization of the professional structure of the CIVB, and by attempts to put into practice the ideas developed in the Protocol of Bordeaux Wine. These attempts resulted in a wider understanding of the market for all the different *appellations* and, for the Bordeaux Rouge *appellation*, in a number of control measures: obligatory contractural agreements and obligatory registering of bulk transactions.

After a period of euphoria, the interprofessional collaborators were forced into a realization that they were powerless to avoid crises: they lacked solid economic power and the financial muscle necessary to ensure complete command of the market.

However, it was during this period that the professionals gave much thought to their future and refined for themselves the functioning of their new profession. Thanks to a proposal from the Bordeaux region to Paris, the law of 10 July 1975 gives agricultural interprofessional collaborators the economic powers and the financial means that they previously lacked.

From 1976 onwards, after a further reorganization of the professional structure following the decree of 15 February 1976, the professional collaborators have instituted a viable and successful policy for the command and development of the Bordeaux wine market.

Since 1977, a marketing strategy has been in operation, based on three-year interprofessional agreements and a flexible economic approach, designed to regulate the volume of wine marketed and maintain prices within a campaign. Voluntary and incentive measures are used to achieve this with price margins that are satisfactory to the producer, reasonable within

Château Barreyres, a Médoc Cru Bourgeois, at Arcins.

the market context and acceptable to the consumer.

In 1979, a promotion policy based on contemporary marketing principles was launched. The notion of expansion of the market was henceforth built into that of economic control: the CIVB's promotional budget was quickly quadrupled and a medium-term campaign — first national, then international — was initiated, based on the slogan *'Bordeaux, la couleur du bon goût'* ('Bordeaux — the colour of good taste').

In this same period, efforts were redoubled to promote white Bordeaux wines and improve their production techniques, with the aim of making them internationally recognized and competitive.

The CIVB thus fulfils its three specific tasks: the organization of the market for Bordeaux wine; the development of the reputation of AOC Bordeaux wines both in France and abroad; and the control of the application of AOC decrees, to ensure that the quality level achieved always corresponds to the *appellation* requirements.

The Académie du Vin de Bordeaux

No other region of France has been more completely and deeply imbued with, and fashioned by, the vine than the Bordeaux region. It is therefore not surprising that a particular sort of spirit was born in Bordeaux, giving rise to the creation, among other institutions, of the Académie du Vin de Bordeaux (Academy of Bordeaux Wine).

Like the Académie Française founded by Richelieu, the Académie du Vin de Bordeaux, created on 18 December 1947, numbers 40 members chosen from among the most highly qualified people in the realms of science, literature, the arts and wine growing — 'all that is beautiful and true'.

The aims of the Académie du Vin de Bordeaux are the following:

▷ the establishment of rules of gastronomic savoir-faire, and of a *savoir-boire* for the enjoyment of great Bordeaux wine;

▷ the matching of regional dishes and *crus*;

▷ the publication of monographs by or about great gastronomes and great restaurants that have demonstrated a proper knowledge of Bordeaux wines;

▷ the publication of a *Bulletin*;

▷ the annual publication of a Vintage Chart.

In addition to the full members, there are also honorary members, emeritus members, associate members (owners of a *cru* that has been classified), registered members (owners of unclassified *crus*) and *correspondants* (persons or vineyard owners with an interest in Bordeaux wine).

The Jurade de Saint-Émilion

In 1199, the king of England, John Lackland, signed a charter at Falaise giving Saint-Émilion its communal freedom. For six centuries, this charter governed the *jurade*, which was a working 'municipal council' for Saint-Émilion. The *jurats* were simultaneously magistrates, administrators, tax collectors and distributors of

THE GRAND CONSEIL DE BORDEAUX

In the days when the vine reigned supreme, Bordeaux would, on important occasions, call a meeting of the Grand Conseil (or Grand Council), which was formed of representatives of all the constituent bodies administering the vineyards. The same is true today for all those persons and organizations for whom the vine remains sovereign. The Grand Conseil de Bordeaux is the conciliar meeting place of delegations from all the confréries *of the Bordeaux region: the Jurade de Saint-Émilion, the Commanderie du Bontemps de Médoc et des Graves, the Connétablie de Guyenne and the Hospitaliers de Pomerol, together with the Académie du Vin de Bordeaux.*

As a true synthesis of all the confréries, *the Grand Conseil de Bordeaux undertakes foreign visits as a dignified representative of all the* appellations *of the Bordeaux region, which, by their very multiplicity, might otherwise distract attention one from another or engender confusion among themselves.*

The Grand Conseil also receives foreign delegations or important visitors at Bordeaux's Maison du Vin: all are impressed by the quality of the welcome and the tone of the receptions, which are in every way worthy of the city; and a few rare and privileged visitors will be made Conseillers du Vin de Bordeaux (Bordeaux Wine Councillors).

The Grand Conseil is not a sort of 'super-confrérie', *though, so chapter meetings are not held at a fixed date, but only when opportune and convenient for those visitors to be honoured. With the emphasis it places on regional unity, the Grand Conseil is a reminder that the prestige of Bordeaux wine belongs to all the* appellations, *and that it is primarily under the name of Bordeaux that these wines have acquired their glory.*

WINE — AN UNALLOYED PLEASURE

It gives me pleasure to talk informally about wine, that jewel of gastronomy, which has always had a powerful influence on my cooking. But, at the risk of shocking a few people, I must tell you that, although I taste and appreciate wine as a connoisseur, I buy it above all to drink it, and to drink it from large glasses — from glasses large enough to quench my thirst!

It is often said that, to bring your children up well, you should live closely with them. It must be the same for wines. The discovery and appreciation of a wine is, in fact, an eminently intimate and personal affair. This is why I think that the institution of grades and charts was a stupid idea: how can a whole harvest be stamped with the same seal of quality or rejected out of hand?

My youth spent in the Bordeaux region, cradled by wine growers' stories, and the trade I conducted with many wine growers have strengthened me in my opinion that tasting a wine should be an unalloyed pleasure which you should discover strictly on your own. No one can taste for you. The merchant, wine taster, or wine club can, at the very most, advise us, but it is up to us to check the validity of their judgments and to bring the light of our own taste and our personal sensibility to bear on them.

Similarly, no peremptory decrees can be issued as to how to drink a wine or as to what part of a meal it should be served at. Finally, I do not believe that there is such a thing as a 'cooking' wine to be used only in the kitchen.

I consider that white wines should not be drunk exclusively with fish, nor burgundies with game. Moreover it is not obligatory to serve white wine cool and red wine at room temperature. As for rosé, as far as I am concerned, it is nothing but a whim. But whatever the wine chosen, the important thing is always to taste it at the moment you feel like it, depending on your mood and temperament.

Although, in my opinion, no wine needs to be 'brought up to room temperature', all wines gain from being decanted. Great wines are always decanted in the place they have matured, and will be served at the temperature of the cellar. Very young wines often benefit from being cooled, i.e. simply placed in a bucket of very cold water for 20 minutes. White wines should only be chilled, if possible in ice, a few hours before being served. In general, I advise against using the refrigerator.

I like all wines, but I prefer two of them above all the others: champagne and bordeaux. Among the bordeaux, I love Sauternes in particular, because it evokes the days of my youth. Thus, when I am far from home, when melancholy gets the better of my habitual optimism and I seem to be at a permanently low ebb, only Sauternes can bring back my lust for life.

I have often experienced a feeling of separation during the course of my many travels; it would become still stronger if I tasted foreign wines, even though these wines are very appealing. But I have never tried to compare them to our French wines; at the very most, I have tried to take as much pleasure as possible in drinking (and not tasting) them. In my cooking, I have used the most diverse wines in order to find the ones that, when married with a dish, produce the most authentic sensations of pleasure. I have been able to establish that some of them did not produce happy marriages. Those that did not were never the great ones, because the great ones are in general guarantors of success in culinary matters.

Even great wines are only the sum of their qualities, as is proved by the following story heard in a speech at an agricultural show. The old Marquis de Lur-Saluces, owner of Château d'Yquem, decided to go fishing. So he set out for the estuary, leaving from Château Beychevelle, which dominates the Gironde so splendidly. The boat was entrusted to a sailor who was evidently a freshwater specialist, because this is what happened. When the fishing was well under way, it was time for a snack. The Marquis had brought a bottle of Yquem with him. Everyone drank copiously from it. But the weather got worse and the swell made the boat pitch, so much so that the sailor ended up bringing up his meal for the fish. Having carried out this formality, he regained his position at the helm, looking somewhat dazed but nevertheless grateful, and he said to the Marquis: 'It's really good, that Yquem, even when it comes back up again!'

Raymond Oliver

The 'legs' or 'tears' in a glass of Château d'Yquem.

public funds. But it was in the wine-growing domain that the actions of the *jurade* were most significant and long-lasting.

By virtue of their office, the *jurats* would proclaim the annual start of the grape harvest (*le ban des vendanges*). As soon as the wine was removed from the fermentation vats, they would visit the cellars; the Grand Vinetier (Grand Wine Master) would brand the casks of good wine; the wine judged to be unworthy was destroyed. Not one barrel was dispatched to a customer without being checked by the *jurade*.

The French Revolution of 1789 put an end to these practices. Nevertheless, thanks to the clearsightedness and vigilance of the owners of the *grands crus*, quality was maintained. But by the 20th century a return to legislation had now become necessary. The law relating to *appellations d'origine contrôlée* had beneficial effects. But no law could replace an inspection that was freely accepted and administered by one's wine-growing peers. Therefore, after the Second World War, a number of producers decided to resurrect the *jurade* and to proclaim their adhesion to its noble traditions; on 16 September 1948 the *jurade* was reborn. In 1949, the seal of the *jurade* was restored; it was not marked on the barrels as in former days, but was labelled on any wine felt to be worthy of château-bottling (uncommon at the time). Since 1954, all Saint-Émilion wines without exception have been submitted to quality inspection by a tasting panel, under the authority of the INAO.

Today the *jurade* is composed of 40 members. They wear a red robe and a hat decorated with ermine. Solemn torch-lit chapters are held in the famous monolithic church dug from the rock at the occasion of the spring festival and the grape harvest; then it is that the *jurats* proclaim the *ban des vendanges* from the top of the Tour du Roi (King's Tower).

From the top of the Tour du Roi (King's Tower), the **jurats** *of Saint-Émilion proclaim the beginning of the grape harvest each year.*

The Commanderie du Bontemps de Médoc et des Graves

Founded in 1949 by a small, dynamic group of Médoc inhabitants, this *confrérie* is named partly in memory of a Commanderie des Templiers de l'Order de Malte, created at Bénon-Saint-Laurent, which greatly influenced the development of wine growing in the Médoc, and partly after the *bontemps*, a traditional wooden receptacle in which egg whites, to be used for fining wines, were beaten.

This *bontemps* is called a *desquet* in local dialect. The invention of the receptacle is attributed to Jehan Odule Paulin d'Esquet, a wine grower who lived in the Médoc around AD 1000. Thanks to this invention, he has the honour of being the patron of the *commanderie*.

The *commanderie* originally drew its membership only from the Médoc, but later it expanded to include members from the area of the Graves *appellation*. It now has 160 members. The dignitaries of the *confrérie* assume the titles of Grand Maître (Grand Master), Grand Chancelier (Grand Chancellor), Grand Argentier (Grand Superintendent of Finance), Vinothécaire (Vinothecary), Porte-desquet (Desquet Carrier), Pipetier (Pipette Handler), Massier (Mace Bearer) and Commandeurs (Commanders).

The costume is a claret-coloured robe with a cloak that is green for the Médoc and yellow for the Graves. The headdress is round, in the shape of a *bontemps*, and decorated with a white muslin ruffle representing the egg whites used to clarify the wines.

The Commanderie du Bontemps de Sauternes et de Barsac

The great sweet wines of Sauternes and Barsac emulated their neighbours from Médoc and Graves on 6 June 1959. In this way, these two prestigious regions strengthened the geographical and historical links that had existed between them for a long time, and that were made official in the 1855 classification.

The statutes, spirit and activities of the *commanderie* are the same as in the Médoc. The robe and the headdress reflect the colour of the great sweet wines — old gold; the bottom of the headdress, which is shaped like a *bontemps*, is white. The insignia is a bronze medal bearing the arms of the Commanderie: an Aquitaine leopard and two ships; it is inscribed with the motto: '*Le soleil est mon reflet*' ('The sun is my reflection').

Coat of arms of the Commanderie du Bontemps de Sauternes et de Barsac.

Green shoot of the Bouchalès vine.

Bouchalès leaf. This extremely productive variety is confined to the South West, and is in decline.

Underside of the leaf blade.

Bunch of Bouchalès grapes.

Bouchalès

Synonyms: *Boucharès* in Gironde, *Bouscalès* in Haute-Garonne, *Bouchedy, Boucherès* in Agen and Nérac, *Gros de Judith* around Bordeaux, *Grapput, Grappu, Gros Grappu, Prolongeau* in Médoc and in the Blaye region, *Toussan* or *Touzan* in the Agen region, *Aubet and Calya* in the ENSA collections at Montpellier, *Cujas, Gros Marty, Jeanjean* at Saint Loubès (Gironde), *Esparbasque* at Orthez, *Gros Mol* or *Gros Maure* at Villeneuve-sur-Lot, *Négrasse* at Biasse and Sainte-Maure (Lot-et-Garonne).

Young leaves downy, rapidly becoming arachnoid, green and glossy.

Leaves orbicular, dark green, glossy, flat or only slightly bullate, contorted, usually five-lobed with narrow lateral sinuses, petiolar sinus lyrate or with overlapping edges; dentation convex, wide; blade arachnoid in tufts on the underside. In the autumn, the leaves turn partly red.

Green shoots ribbed, pale green, coloured slightly pink at the nodes, with a slight mauve bloom.

Bunches medium sized, winged, cylindrical to conical, compact; grapes spherical, blue-black, small, with thick skin; ripening period: third epoch.

This is a vine-group and includes several distinct types; one registered clone has been approved: number 406. Bouchalès is a high-producing vine, sensitive to disease and requiring considerable exposure to heat to bring its late-ripening grapes to maturity. Its wine is flat, light in colour and acid.

Classified as 'recommended' in the South West, today it only occupies 49th place among French varieties with 1,400 ha, compared to 5,000 ha in 1958. The main plantings are in Lot-et-Garonne (926 ha), Gironde (408 ha), Gers and Dordogne.

Bouillenc

Synonym: *Plant de Larroque*.

A grape variety from the South West, not very productive, related to Milgranet. It is sensitive to oidium (powdery mildew). Unclassified.

Bouillet Noir

Synonyms: *Quillard* in Lot, *Plant Dame Noir* at Lauzerte (Tarn-et-Garonne), *Fouine* and *Plant de Mérille* in Lot.

This grape variety, related to the Jurançon Noir, is classed as 'recommended' in Lot-et-Garonne and 'authorized' in Dordogne, but it is not widely cultivated in either *département* (60 ha total). It is a productive variety, but its wine is flat, light in colour and low in alcohol.

Bouquet Blanc

Synonyms: *Bouquettraube, Sylvaner Musqué*.

Bunches small, cylindrical; grapes spherical, white, aromatic, more or less musky; ripening period: second epoch, early.

This vine, which is grown a little in Alsace, is said to come from Würzburg in Germany. Its wine is ordinary, although the grapes are aromatic. It is susceptible to grey rot (botrytis).

Bourboulenc

Synonyms: *Bourboulenque, Bourboulenco, Clairette Dorée, Grosse Clairette* in Var, *Clairette à Grains Ronds* at Aigues-Mortes, *Clairette Blanche* or *Clairette Dorée* at Paulhan, *Malvoisie* in Aude, *Mourterille* and *Blanquette* in Pyrénées-Orientales, *Clairette Productive* in Bouches-du-Rhône, *Blanquette du Gard, Clairette Menue* and *Roussette* in Vaucluse.

Growing tips open, felty white with carmine margins, downy stem.

Young leaves downy, yellowish with bronze-coloured bands, underside of blade felty white.

Leaves orbicular, thick, bullate, contorted, five-lobed with elongated central lobes, deep lateral upper sinuses often with overlapping edges, open lower lateral sinuses, petiolar sinus lyrate with overlapping edges; dentation convex, wide, not clearly visible; underside of blade downy-pubescent with main veins strongly pubescent, the whole having a whitish felty appearance like the Clairette variety.

Green shoots ribbed, purplish on the side exposed to the sun.

Bunches medium sized, cylindrical to conical; grapes ovoid or slightly ellipsoidal, medium sized, pink-white with a dull grey bloom which appears orange-russet in the sun; ripening period: third epoch.

The Bourboulenc grape variety is said to be of Greek origin and is spread throughout Provence (AOC Bandol, Cassis, Coteaux d'Aix-en-Provence), as well as Languedoc, especially in Gard, where it is one of the white grape varieties of the AOCs of Côtes du Rhône, Coteaux du Languedoc, Corbières and Minervois, covering a total area of about 400 ha. This vine is classified as 'recommended' in all the Mediterranean *départements* and a registered clone has been approved: number 541.

This is a vigorous and hardy grape variety, sensitive to downy mildew, a little less so to oidium (powdery mildew), more productive than the Clairette variety, but it has to be harvested late, sometimes after all the other varieties, if the wine is to be as good as it can be. It is frequently vinified together with the grapes of other white varieties.

Bourg or Côtes de Bourg

The Côtes de Bourg vineyard is situated about 30km north of Bordeaux, on the right bank of the Dordogne. It covers the hills surrounding the town of Bourg-sur-Gironde which, as its name suggests, used to lie on the Gironde. Because of the accumulation of silt, the confluence of the Dordogne and the Gironde moved towards the river mouth and Bourg, despite its name, now finds itself on the Dordogne.

The *appellation d'origine contrôlée* of Bourg or Côtes de Bourg was created by the decree of 11 September 1936 for red wines and by the decree of 14 May 1941 for white wines. It can only be used for wines coming from grapes harvested in a number of demarcated plots in the canton of Bourg.

To be entitled to the *appellation*, the red wines must be made from Cabernet Sauvignon, Cabernet Franc, Merlot or Côt (Malbec) grape varieties. The must has to contain 172g of sugar per litre and the wines should have a minimum alcohol content of 10° and a maximum of 13°. The base yield is 50 hl/ha.

Since 1974, the wines are not allowed to proceed for sale without a certificate of quality from an official tasting panel appointed by the INAO.

White wines of this *appellation* may only be made from the following grape varieties: Sauvignon Blanc, Sémillon, Muscadelle and Merlot Blanc; the Chenin Blanc is allowed as a secondary variety so long as it does not exceed 20 per cent of the total. The must should contain a minimum of 187g of sugar per litre and the wines should have a total alcohol content of 11 per cent, of which 10.5 per cent is acquired alcohol. The base yield is 60 hl/ha.

The area under cultivation for white wines is very small: in 1985, it covered 84 ha and the production was 3,576 hl, three quarters of which was produced by three cooperatives.

In 1985, the area under cultivation for red wines was 31,017 ha and the production was 171,677 hl, a quarter of which was produced by seven cooperatives.

The red wines are richly coloured, full bodied and well structured. They are at their best after four or five years in bottle. Château-bottling has become widespread in this region during the 1970s and 1980s. There are about 30 châteaux with vineyards of over 30 ha, and these leading *crus* are responsible for the reputation of the *appellation*.

Bourgogne *See* page 116 for the Burgundy regional entry.

Château Guerry, in the Bourg vineyard area, adjacent to the Gironde.

Bourgogne

This regional *appellation d'origine contrôlée* was ratified by the decree of 31 July 1937. This decree limited the area of production to the Burgundy region and stated that red, rosé and white wines claiming this *appellation* should be harvested in the *départements* of Yonne, Côte-d'Or and Saône-et-Loire and, under certain conditions, in the *arrondissement* of Villefranche-sur-Saône in the Rhône *département*. In addition, the Beaujolais *cru appellations* of Saint-Amour, Juliénas, Fleurie, Chénas, Moulin-à-Vent, Chiroubles, Morgon, Brouilly and Côte de Brouilly may — under certain conditions — also claim the Bourgogne Rouge *appellation* for their wines.

As far as grape varieties are concerned, only the Pinot Noir and Pinot Gris (Pinot Beurot), and a clone of the Pinot Noir called Pinot Liébault, are authorized for Bourgogne Rouge and Rosé, with a special authorization in the Yonne for the César and Tressot varieties. For Bourgogne Blanc, Chardonnay and Pinot Blanc are authorized.

Finally, the Bourgogne *appellation* requires a minimum alcohol content of 10° for the red and rosé wines and 10.5° for the white wines. Base yields are 55 hl/ha for red and rosé wines and 60 hl/ha for whites.

If they are well made, these generally light wines may spring some pleasant surprises, especially if they are the result of the downgrading of a superior *appellation*. But it is advisable to choose them with care, according to their producer, merchant or place of origin, for these are the determining factors with regard to quality.

Bourgogne Aligoté

This regional AOC, ratified by decree on 31 July 1937, governs white wines produced from the Aligoté grape variety, grown in the production zone of Burgundy. This zone stretches over numerous plots situated in Yonne, Côte-d'Or and Saône-et-Loire. Following the decree of 7 March 1979, the commune of Bouzeron in Saône-et-Loire can join its name to that of the main *appellation* for Aligoté wines produced there.

The Aligoté is, of course, the principal variety used for this *appellation*. It is only cultivated in Burgundy. However, the Chardonnay is still provisionally authorized in Burgogne Aligoté blends up to a limit of 15 per cent.

The minimum alcohol content for Bourgogne Aligoté is 9.5°; its maximum yield has been fixed at 55hl/ha. Average harvests are in the order of 45,000hl.

Bourgogne Aligoté, which is often combined with Crème de Cassis (blackcurrant liqueur) to make Kir, deserves better than this secondary role. The best examples of this *appellation* reveal the wine to be fine, lively, dry, and pleasantly fresh, especially in its early years.

Bourgogne Aligoté de Bouzeron

This white wine from the Côte Chalonnaise is governed by the decree of 31 July 1937, but it has only enjoyed its individual *appellation d'origine contrôlée* status since 1979.

The decree fixes, apart from other conditions of production, minimum alcohol content at 9.5° and maximum yield at 50hl/ha. Produced exclusively from the Aligoté grape variety, these white wines are harvested on plots situated in the commune of Bouzeron in Saône-et-Loire, to the south of the Côte d'Or, between Santenay and Rully.

Each year, some 1,000hl of Bourgogne Aligoté de Bouzeron are produced. The wine is appreciated and sought out for its subtle, vanilla-tinged taste and its overall distinction.

Bourgogne Clairet

See Bourgogne Rosé.

Bourgogne-Hautes Côtes de Beaune

Governed by the *appellation d'origine contrôlée* decree of 4 August 1961, the wines of Bourgogne-Hautes Côtes de Beaune are produced to the west of the Côte de Beaune at a higher altitude (300 to 400m), on terrain based on several levels of limestone cliff formation. The area of the *appellation* covers 14 communes of Côte-d'Or and 7 communes of Saône-et-Loire. The production of red wines (16,291hl in 1983) is greater than that of whites (598hl in 1983). Chardonnay is the chief grape variety used for the white wines and Pinot Noir for the reds. The minimum alcohol content is 10° for the reds and 10.5° for the whites. Half of the production of these light, clear wines, with their fine bouquet, is in the hands of the cooperative Caves des Hautes Côtes at Beaune.

Bourgogne-Hautes Côtes de Nuits

In the past known simply as the *vins fins* (fine wines) of the Hautes Côtes de Nuits, Bourgogne-Hautes Côtes de Nuits wines have only been precisely regulated since 4 August 1961. This *appellation d'origine contrôlée* was then authorized only for wines produced on the edge of the plateau dominating the Côtes de Nuits from the west, and mainly to the west of Nuits-Saint-Georges itself, covering about 100ha in the following communes: Arcenant, Bévy, Chaux, Chevannes, Collonges-lès-Bévy, Marey-lès-Fussey, Messanges, Meuilley, Reulle-Vergy, Segrois, Villars-Fontaine and Villers-la-Faye. The chief grape varieties specified are Pinot Noir for the red wines and Chardonnay for the whites. The minimum alcohol content is 10° for the reds and 10.5° for the whites. The maximum yield permitted is 50hl/ha. The very low production — 1,000hl of mainly white wine — gives these light, fresh, delicate burgundies something of a rarity value.

Bourgogne-Irancy

Spread over the commune of Irancy in Yonne, this *appellation* covers 85ha, and was ratified as an AOC by decree on 14 December 1977. It also includes vineyard parcels in the neighbouring villages of Cravant and Vincelottes, and produces about 3,500hl (2,635 hl in 1985) of red wine from the following grape varieties: Pinot Noir, Tressot and César. Despite a marked decline in plantings the César has always provided much of the character of the wines of Irancy. These wines have been known and appreciated since the 11th century, thanks to the efforts of local wine-making monks. Alcohol content is fixed at 10°, and yields should not exceed 55hl/ha.

These remarkable wines are a dark red colour; they tend to be a little hard in their first years, because of high tannin levels, but they soon loosen up and reveal themselves as wines of structure and personality. They tend to become smoother with age and to acquire a bouquet of violets and raspberries. They can be kept for more than 20 years. The rosés, which are pale in colour, have a surprisingly full and vigorous flavour.

Bourgogne Mousseux

Governed by the decree of 16 March 1943, Bourgogne Mousseux wines used to be based on the same range of grape varieties as those used for Bourgogne Grand Ordinaire: César, Tressot and Sacy in Yonne, and Pinot Noir, Pinot Gris, Gamay Noir à Jus Blanc, Chardonnay, Aligoté, Pinot Blanc and Melon in Côte-d'Or. Since 31 December 1985, however, this AOC can only be used for sparkling red wines, the whites and rosés being included in the Crémant de Bourgogne *appellation*.

Bourgogne Mousseux wines can come from anywhere in the AOC Bourgogne area. They can also come from the Beaujolais *cru* zones, and be made with the Gamay Noir à Jus Blanc, provided that they have been vinified according to the *méthode champenoise* (with secondary fermentation in bottle). Maximum yield is fixed at 60hl/ha and the alcohol content at 8.5°. These wines are not made in large quantities but are greatly appreciated abroad. They are lively, fruity and crisp.

Bourgogne Ordinaire or Bourgogne Grand Ordinaire

This curiously named AOC, created by decree on 31 July 1937, covers red, white and rosé wines made from vineyards from all over the Burgundy region. The grape varieties authorized by law have been modified according to the demands of the *terroirs* as well as to local tradition, which is why, in Yonne, César and Tressot are used for the reds and Sacy for the whites. In the rest of Burgundy, the usual varieties are authorized: Pinot Noir, Pinot Gris and Gamay Noir à Jus Blanc for the reds; Chardonnay, Aligoté, Melon and Pinot Blanc for the whites.

The minimum alcohol content authorized by the decree is 9° for the red wines and 9.5° for the whites. The base yield has been fixed at 60hl/ha, and annual production is at present about 4,400hl of white wine and 15,000hl of red wine. These rustic wines are often very pleasant.

Bourgogne Passetoutgrains

The decree of 31 July 1937 authorized the use of the Bourgogne Passetoutgrains AOC for red wines made under certain conditions. First of all, the grapes must come from Burgundy's regional vineyards. Secondly, the wine must be composed of a mixture of two thirds Gamay Noir à Jus Blanc and one third Pinot Noir.

The grape harvest on the Côte d'Or, near Marsannay-la-Côte.

Bourgogne Passetoutgrains wines must also have a minimum alcohol content of 9.5° and result from a basic yield of 55hl/ha. Average annual production is 50,000hl.

Bourgogne Rosé (or Clairet), Bourgogne Rosé-Hautes Côtes de Beaune, -Hautes Côtes de Nuits and Bourgogne Rosé de Marsannay

Following the decree of 14 October 1943, rosé wines produced in the Burgundy *appellation d'origine contrôlée* zone can claim the Bourgogne Rosé or Bourgogne Clairet *appellation*. The same applies to rosé wines made in the area of the Hautes Côtes de Beaune and Hautes Côtes de Nuits *appellations*, and in the communes of Marsannay-la-Côte and Couchey. The rosé wines of these *appellations*, when well made, have a characteristic aroma of summer fruits.

Bourgueil

This *appellation*, classed by decree on 31 July 1937, covers 1,000ha. The main grape variety is the Cabernet Franc (locally called the Breton); Cabernet Sauvignon is also permitted up to a limit of 10 per cent. The average production is about 40,000hl. A small quantity of rosé Bourgueil (between 2 and 5 per cent of the red wine production figure) is also made.

The area of production covers the following communes or parts of communes: Bourgueil, Saint-Nicolas-de-Bourgueil, Restigné, Ingrandes-de-Touraine, Saint-Patrice, Benais, la Chapelle-sur-Loire, Chouzé-sur-Loire.

The wine has a strong, deep colour when it is made from grapes grown on calcareous soils, while it is lighter in colour when the grapes have been grown on gravel terraces. In either case, the wine may have attractive garnet or redcurrant glints.

The aroma is floral and fruity, becoming animal and mineral with age. The wine is full-bodied, with soft tannins and a lively balance. It is very well suited to ageing.

Bouteillan Blanc

Synonyms: *Colombaud, Colombeau, Couloumbaou, Colomba, Couroumbaou* in Var, *Aubié, Aubier* in Bouches-du-Rhône, *Grègues* at Marseillan, *Psalmodi Blanc* in Gard, *Saint Pierre* in Charente, *Mellenc* in Tarn-et-Garonne, *Mouilla* in Pyrénées-Atlantiques, *Lubaou, Cérès, Salem.*

Bunches medium sized, cylindrical and very compact; grapes spherical or slightly ovoid, large, white; ripening period: third epoch.

This Provençal grape variety has late budbreak, and is very strong and hardy; it became popular during the phylloxera crisis by resisting the insect for several years. Its tightly packed bunches of fruit, though, are very susceptible to grey rot (botrytis).

Its wine has little colour, is very dry, and is generally vinified together with other white varieties. The Bouteillan Blanc has been classed as 'authorized' in Var, where it survives in isolated plantings.

The vineyards of Bourgueil produce deeply coloured wines with a floral and fruity aroma.

Bouteillan Noir

Synonyms: *Fouiral* or *Esfouiral* in Hérault, *Sigoyer* or *Sigotier* in Alpes-de-Haute-Provence, *Petit Bouteillan* at Draguignan, *Cayau, Cargomuou, Moulas* in Vaucluse, *Plant de Psalmodi* or *Psalmodi Noir* from the name of the abbey where it was found at Saint-Laurent-d'Aigouze.

This vine is often confused with the Calitor because of two identical synonyms — *Fouiral* and *Cargo-Muou* — but its leaves are morphologically very different. Nor is it truly a 'Noir' version of Bouteillan Blanc, as the latter has felty growing tips, young leaves with bronze patches and mature leaves that are arachnoid-pubescent on the underside of the blade. The growing tips, young leaves and mature leaves of the Bouteillan Noir contrast with those of the Bouteillan Blanc in each of these respects.

Bunches medium sized, cylindrical and compact; grapes spherical, large, black; ripening period: third epoch.

The Bouteillan Noir, which has an upright habit and late budbreak, is fertile, but its production is irregular because it is susceptible to *coulure* (flower abortion). Its grapes are also very susceptible to oidium (powdery mildew) and to grey rot (botrytis). During the phylloxera crisis, it became moderately widespread in the Midi under the local name of Psalmodi Noir, as its great strength enabled it to resist the insect for longer than other vine varieties. Not classified.

Brachet

Synonym: *Braquet* in Nice.

Bunches medium sized, winged, conical, loose; grapes spherical, medium sized, blue-black, fairly juicy; ripening period: third epoch.

This old grape variety from the Var *département* is one of those used for the AOC wine of Bellet. It produces very fine, high quality wines that are strong in alcohol and improve with age. It has been classed as 'recommended' in Alpes-Maritimes.

Brégin Noir

This old grape variety from Doubs is disappearing, because it has not been classified. It produces an unexceptional wine, not deeply coloured but with a vivid hue. (*Brégin* means 'purple red' in the Celtic spoken in this part of France.)

Brouilly

Brouilly, which produces one of the easiest and most accessible Beaujolais *cru* wines to appreciate, was classed as an AOC by decree on 19 October 1938. The crop is harvested on fairly high land — the peak of Mont Brouilly is at 483m — and the soils are formed of a mixture of hard green-blue schist (known as *cornes vertes* or 'green horns' to the locals) and granite. The chapel of the appropriately named Notre-Dame-du-Raisin (Our Lady of the Grape) looks out from its position on Mont Brouilly on to the vineyards of this *appellation* and of Côte de Brouilly AOC.

The surface area of 900ha produces on average 70,000hl (9,000,000 bottles) per year. The wine is made in six different villages — Cercié, Odenas, Saint-Lager, Charentay, Quincié-en-Beaujolais and Saint-Étienne-la-Varenne — and for this reason Brouilly is not homogeneous in character. It does, though, have a full, firm colour, and its aroma recalls bilberries, apples and blackberries. It keeps well. When grown on soils in which granite predominates, the wine is more precocious than when grown on predominantly schistous soils.

The Château de la Chaize estate on the Mont de Brouilly in Beaujolais.

Brumeau Noir

An old grape variety from the Brioude area of Haute-Loire, where it used to produce deeply coloured wines, strong in alcohol but not without finesse. It has a certain similarity to the Arrivet or Franc Noir de l'Yonne (*see* Blayais or Blaye, page 72) but the leaves of the Brumeau are deeply five-lobed while those of the Arrivet are without lobes or three-lobed. Not classified.

Brun Argenté

Synonyms: *Camarèse, Camarézo, Camères du Gard, Vacarèze Blanc* or *Madeleine, Vaccarèse, Vaccareso.*

Bunches medium sized, cylindrical, compact; grapes medium sized, spherical or slightly ovoid, blue-black, not very juicy; ripening period: third epoch, late.

This grape variety has late budbreak, and is one of the vines used in Châteauneuf-du-Pape and Côtes du Rhône. It has been classed as 'recommended' in the Gard, Hérault, Vaucluse, Ardèche and Drôme *départements,* where it occupies a total of about 40ha. It is rarely vinified on its own, but when it is, it produces a very freshly flavoured wine with a floral aroma.

Brun Fourca

Synonyms: *Brunfourka, Brun d'Auriol, Brun de Farnous, Farnous* (meaning 'floury') in Var, *Floura* (meaning 'flowery') or *Mourrastel Floura* in Languedoc, *Morrastel Fleuri, Flouron* in Drôme, *Moulan, Moulard, Moureua, Mouzeau* in Gard, *Caula Noir* in Vaucluse.

Bunches medium sized, cylindrical-conical, compact; grapes spherical, large, ovoid, blue-black, with a lot of bloom (hence 'floury' or 'flowery'), juicy; ripening period: second epoch, late.

This Provençal variety has late budbreak, like the Mourvèdre; it is very susceptible to downy mildew, a little less so to oidium (powdery mildew); the grapes are quick to drop off the bunch when mature, and they rot easily. It is also said to be sensitive to winter frosts, and to develop burrs easily. The yields are satisfactory and the wines are of good quality, with a fine colour. The variety is not classified, but it is nonetheless used for the Palette AOC, and about 30ha are planted in Provence.

Brustiano

A white grape variety peculiar to Corsica, where it is sometimes called *Calitrano* or *Colitrano* in Sartène. Its bunches have fairly large, white, ellipsoidal grapes, which may also be eaten. Not classified.

Bugey

See Vins du Bugey.

BURGUNDY

The reputation of this region's wines, whose pedigree was first established by the Grand Dukes of Burgundy, has never faltered. It is this hallmark of excellence that unites the multitude of different wines to be found in this vast and many-faceted province.

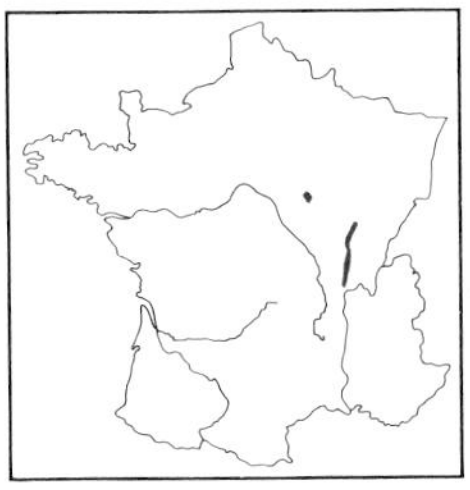

In Gaulish Burgundy, as in Gaul as a whole, the origin of the vine is misty and confused. Was it imported or is it native? No one is yet able to prove the case either way. What is incontestable is that the Gauls made and drank wine, and that the Romans traded wine with them. The remains of numerous amphoras have been found in Burgundy. The amphora was not a receptacle used by the Gauls, who developed and perfected the barrel, made from a clever assembly of staves; but staves, unlike amphoras, are perishable . . .

Wine growing flourished in the Gallo-Roman period and the Romans had a determining influence on the organization of vineyards in Burgundy. After the departure of the Romans, the Celts and the Burgundians worked their vineyards according to the needs of the local communities or those of the nearest towns. River transport later played an important role in Burgundy. This is how wine from the Yonne was able to find a market in the future capital of France, and wine from Beaujolais a market in Lyon.

The introduction of Christianity to the region greatly encouraged the extension of the vineyards as well as the creation of large estates attached to and run by abbeys. This was the case for Cîteaux (Clos de Vougeot) and Cluny, for example. The wines of Burgundy had pride of place on the tables of the nobility and casks were often given as presents; several popes received and enjoyed them. In 1395, Philip the Bold made an effort to improve the quality of the wines by ordering the uprooting of the 'vile' Gamay! This duke had obviously not taken into account the quality of wine made from the Gamay in the area now known by the name of Beaujolais . . . In sum, a great vineyard area flourished in Burgundy and its surroundings until the end of the 19th century.

The phylloxera crisis

In 1874, a devastating root-living insect arrived from America and slowly but inexorably spread across France from the South and South West: this was the phylloxera. All vines had to be uprooted and replanted. The figures shown on page 118 illustrate the extent of this national and regional catastrophe.

It is clear from these figures that the marginal vineyards producing *vins ordinaires* were only partially replanted. This is what typically happened in the Auxerre and Dijon areas, where

The Château du Clos de Vougeot, headquarters of the Confrérie des Chevaliers du Tastevin. It is situated in the middle of the Clos de Vougeot, a renowned 60ha vineyard in the heart of the Côte de Nuits.

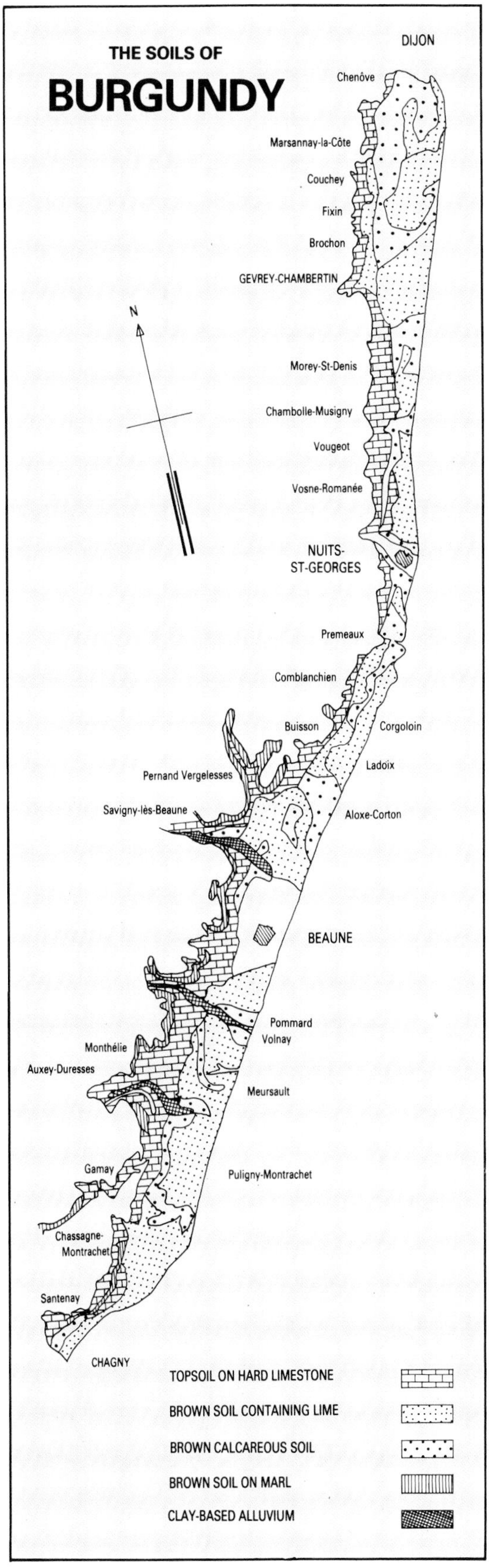
THE SOILS OF
BURGUNDY
DIJON
Chenôve
Marsannay-la-Côte
Couchey
Fixin
Brochon
GEVREY-CHAMBERTIN
N
Morey-St-Denis
Chambolle-Musigny
Vougeot
Vosne-Romanée
NUITS-
ST-GEORGES
Premeaux
Comblanchien
Buisson
Corgoloin
Ladoix
Pernand Vergelesses
Savigny-lès-Beaune
Aloxe-Corton
BEAUNE
Pommard
Volnay
Monthélie
Auxey-Duresses
Meursault
Gamay
Puligny-Montrachet
Chassagne-
Montrachet
Santenay
CHAGNY
TOPSOIL ON HARD LIMESTONE
BROWN SOIL CONTAINING LIME
BROWN CALCAREOUS SOIL
BROWN SOIL ON MARL
CLAY-BASED ALLUVIUM

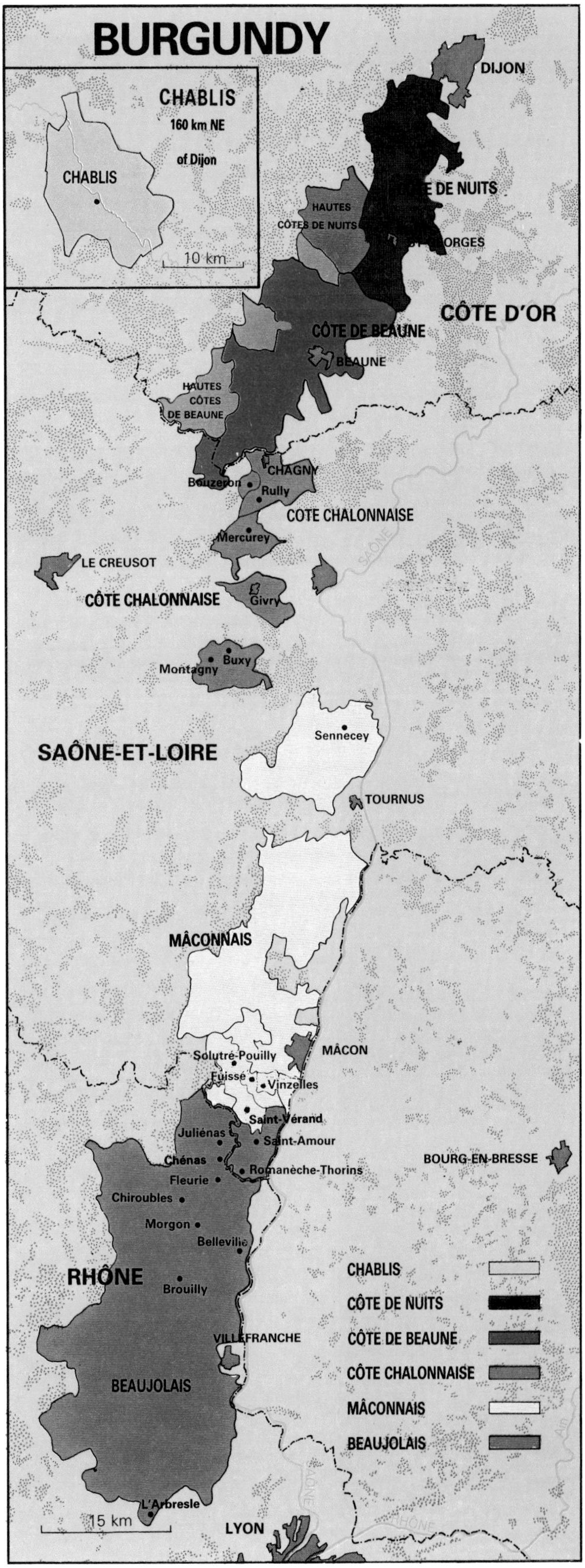
BURGUNDY
CHABLIS
160 km NE
of Dijon
CHABLIS
10 km
DIJON
HAUTES
CÔTES DE NUITS
CÔTE D'OR
CÔTE DE BEAUNE
BEAUNE
HAUTES
CÔTES
DE BEAUNE
CHAGNY
Bouzeron
Rully
COTE CHALONNAISE
Mercurey
LE CREUSOT
CÔTE CHALONNAISE
Givry
Buxy
Montagny
Sennecey
SAÔNE-ET-LOIRE
TOURNUS
MÂCONNAIS
MÂCON
Solutré-Pouilly
Fuissé
Vinzelles
Saint-Vérand
Juliénas
Saint-Amour
Chénas
Romanèche-Thorins
Fleurie
BOURG-EN-BRESSE
Chiroubles
Morgon
Belleville
RHÔNE
Brouilly
VILLEFRANCHE
BEAUJOLAIS
L'Arbresle
15 km
LYON
CHABLIS
CÔTE DE NUITS
CÔTE DE BEAUNE
CÔTE CHALONNAISE
MÂCONNAIS
BEAUJOLAIS

THE CONSEQUENCES OF THE PHYLLOXERA CRISIS				
Changes to Burgundy's vineyards in hectares				
	Yonne	Côte-d'Or	Saône-et-Loire	Rhône
Before 1875	37 500	33 700	43 600	46 700
The 1920s, after replanting	6 700	12 100	13 700	20 300

Painted wooden statue of a wine grower, 18th century.

the vine was grown amid other crops. Highly specialized areas exclusively given over to viticulture, such as the Côte de Nuits and the Côte de Beaune, found almost all of their land replanted with high quality varieties.

Much research was undertaken before it was discovered that only grafting resistant American rootstocks on to native European varieties would enable the vine to flourish in soils still infested by phylloxera. This research, and the replanting of grafted vines, took more than a quarter of a century, and it was not until after the First World War that the vineyards of Burgundy started to flourish once more and regained their age-old rhythm.

During the Second World War, a lack of manpower and shortage of materials, especially copper (the active ingredient of bordeaux mixture and its Burgundian counterpart *bouillie bourguignonne*), as well as a lack of fertilizer and of draught animals, resulted in a net drop in production.

The almost total mechanization of all vineyard work, apart from pruning, has revolutionized the lives of the wine makers of today. It has enabled the cultivable area of a property to be increased, the least accessible plots to be worked more efficiently, and allowed more time to be devoted to the care and nurturing of the wine after its initial fermentation (*élevage*). The wine maker is no longer exclusively a man of the soil. Nowadays he travels in search of customers both at home and abroad.

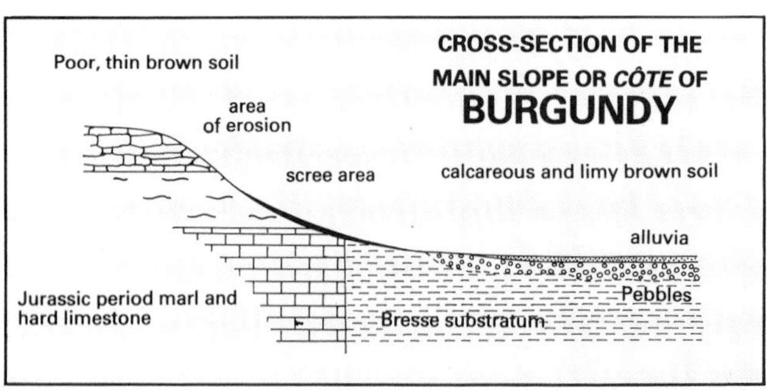

The climate and the soil

The geographical diversity of Burgundy results quite naturally in a diversity of climates and mesoclimates, the existence of numerous microclimates, and an equally disparate soil structure and topography. A mosaic of wines, extremely different from each other in character, parallels this physical diversity.

We may, however, make two general statements. Firstly, the climate of Burgundy is situated at the limit of continental and maritime influences. The former ensures that the vines receive enough dry weather and sunshine; the latter that the vines receive adequate rainfall. Secondly, the structure of the soil in Burgundy influences the growth of the vine more than the soil's biochemical composition does.

Apart from these two statements, it would be idle to attempt a complete description of the climate and soil of such a large region as Burgundy under a single heading. It is better to deal with each subregion separately, and precise descriptions of climate and soil will be found in each of the regional entries that comprise greater Burgundy. The following should therefore be referred to: *Beaujolais, Chablis and Auxerre, The Côte Chalonnaise, The Côte d'Or* and *The Mâcon Region*.

The limits and divisions of the region

Burgundy extends from north to south over four *départements*: Yonne, whose main centre is Chablis; Côte-d'Or, from Dijon to Chagny; Saône-et-Loire; and Rhône, for the Villefranche district. It should, though, be realized that the wine-producing area of Burgundy is geographically different from administrative Burgundy, the latter including the Nièvre *département*, but not the Rhône *département*.

The Beaujolais region follows on without a break from Mâcon, in a southerly direction. This is a natural continuation, though the two are very different from the geological point of view. Beaujolais is thus placed in the wine-producing context of Burgundy, and some of its wines are able to carry the Bourgogne Rouge *appellation*, following a ruling by the civil court of Dijon in 1930.

The* département *of Yonne

Some 150 km north of Dijon, half way to Paris, lies the Auxerre-Chablis vineyard complex, which for centuries produced red and white wines destined for the capital, thanks to the confluence of waterways converging on the Seine.

The* département *of Côte-d'Or

Lying south-southwest of Dijon is the 'Côte d'Or' ('golden slope') itself, often also called 'Haute Bourgogne'. It is situated entirely inside the *département* of Côte-d'Or, and is about 65km long and between 500m and 1.5km wide, down to its southern limit marked by Chagny. This thin band, with its very varied terrain caused by discontinuous soil layers, is arbitrarily but not unreasonably divided into the Côte de Nuits and the Côte de Beaune.

The Côte de Nuits extends from Dijon to Corgoloin, while the Hautes Côtes de Nuits lies to the west of this strip, at a higher altitude. The Côte de Beaune stretches from Ladoix-Serrigny as far south as Chagny, with the Hautes Côtes de Beaune again to the west, and again at a higher altitude (see the maps of each area in the Côte d'Or regional entry).

The Chablis vineyards are found in the north of Burgundy, on the banks of the Serein, in the* département *of Yonne.

The* département *of Saône-et-Loire

Going south from Chagny as far as Mâcon and then just beyond, over a distance of about 65km, are situated first the Côte Chalonnaise then the Mâconnais itself, mainly to the west of the Chagny-Mâcon axis.

The* département *of Rhône

In the Villefranche *arrondissement*, covering around 50km from north to south, and lying west of the town of Villefranche, is the Beaujolais region, a vast area of vineyards with the largest surface area and production of any in greater Burgundy. It is divided into Haut- and Bas-Beaujolais, this distinction being based on differences in the soils of each area.

Burgundy's vineyard area

The round numbers shown in the table below represent figures averaged out over a period of three years — 1981, 1982 and 1983 — and are thus indicative of the present situation in Burgundy.

These statistics and those on the following pages are taken from documents published by the French tax office, and are based on the harvest declarations made in November each year at the *mairie* of the place where the wine was produced or put into storage.

The size of individual properties

It is difficult, working from the above-mentioned documents, to gain an exact idea of the size and importance of individual properties in Burgundy. The number of harvest declarations signed is an unreliable indicator, since there are several categories of declarers:

▷ The owner-grower, who works the whole of his property, directly and exclusively, makes a declaration of the surface area and volume produced;

More vines are grown in the Beaujolais region than in the whole of the département *of Saône-et-Loire, two and a half times more than in the* département *of Côte-d'Or, and six times more than in the* département *of Yonne.*

AREA COVERED BY VINEYARDS IN BURGUNDY

	Yonne	Côte-d'Or	Saône-et-Loire	Rhône
Area in hectares	3 200	8 500	10 000	21 000
A O C	75 %	90 %	85 %	93 %
V D Q S	2 %	—	—	1 %
Vins de table	23 %	10 %	15 %	6 %

The total area is nearly 43 000 ha of vines or 4.3 per cent of the total area occupied by vineyards in France.

The village of Fixin, whose wines can be sold under the Côtes de Nuits-Villages **appellation,** *is noted for its church steeple decorated with Burgundian glazed tiles.*

▷ The owner who lets his vines on the *métayage* system, usually receiving one third of the fruit himself, with the farmer receiving two thirds, does not declare the surface area but only the volume of wines corresponding to his own share, stocked at his home or that of his farmer (declaration by *métayage*);

▷ The owner who lets his complete property to a tenant farmer, declares neither surface nor volume since no fruit is shared out.

To complicate matters further, various permutations of the above are possible: owner-growers doubling as *métayage* tenants or owners; *métayage* with a tenancy arrangement for one or more leaseholders . . . The sum of the surface areas declared divided by the declarations gives an average holding of 1.3 ha in the Beaujolais area, 1 ha in Côte-d'Or, 0.9 ha in Yonne and 0.85 ha in Saône-et-Loire, which is neither indicative nor representative of the true average size of properties in Burgundy.

Production patterns in Burgundy

The facts given in the table below require some comment.

▷ The production of the Beaujolais area (in the Rhône *département*) is almost constant, whereas Yonne, by virtue of occupying the northernmost position in Burgundy, suffers the consequences of winter and, in particular, spring frosts: its production may vary by up to 400 per cent.

▷ Production in Côte-d'Or also fluctuates, but to a lesser extent: by 200 per cent or, very occasionally, 300 per cent.

▷ Yonne produces on average nine times more white wine than red, Côte-d'Or three times more red than white and the Beaujolais area 700 times more red than white.

Quantity and quality of a given harvest are not closely linked in the Burgundy region. Over a long period, it is undeniable that good and very good quality white-wine vintages are two to three times more frequent than red-wine vintages of equal quality. Fine red wines require hot, sunny summers; fine white wines less so. A more extensive analysis of the situation is needed to provide an explanation of the qualitative differences observed, in the same

BURGUNDY WINE PRODUCTION

Year	Harvest characteristics	YONNE	CÔTE-D'OR	SAÔNE-ET-LOIRE	RHÔNE
1981	*Very meagre harvest*				
	Hectolitres produced	65 970	171 970	281 500	1 004 225
	of which: white AOC	49 445	41 416	92 994	1 351
	red AOC	5 095	119 787	160 212	951 581
	French Total: 57 010 712				
1982	*Very plentiful harvest*				
	Hectolitres produced	233 951	576 220	846 661	1 477 684
	of which: white AOC	152 678	119 119	300 990	2 024
	red AOC	21 498	293 679	380 917	1 213 574
	French Total: 79 229 938				
1983	*Harvest of average size*				
	Hectolitres produced	238 665	335 995	568 428	1 268 685
	of which: white AOC	173 286	78 096	221 082	1 728
	red AOC	19 476	243 225	281 146	1 185 915
	French Total: 68 123 339				

THE GRAPE VARIETIES OF BURGUNDY

Distribution of grape varieties in the four département *zones of Burgundy expressed as an approximate percentage of the total area under vines.*

	YONNE	CÔTE-D'OR	SAÔNE-ET-LOIRE	RHÔNE
White varieties				
Main				
— Chardonnay	more than 90%	from 10 to 20 %	from 40 to 50%	less than 10%
— Aligoté	less than 10%	from 10 to 20%	from 10 to 20%	—
Secondary				
— Pinot Blanc	—	less than 10%	—	—
— Melon	—	—	less than 10%	—
— Sauvignon Blanc	less than 10%	—	—	—
Red varieties				
Main				
— Pinot Noir	less than 10%	from 50 to 70%	from 10 to 20%	—
— Gamay	from 10 to 20%	from 10 to 20%	from 40 to 50%	more than 90%
Secondary				
— César	less than 10%	—	—	—
— Tressot	less than 10%	—	—	—

year, between the wines of two neighbouring subregions, such as the Côte de Nuits and the Côte de Beaune. In this case, mesoclimates play a decisive role.

Vinification patterns in Burgundy

A small percentage of the total grape harvest is bought by *négociants* for vinification and *élevage* in their own cellars. The rest, in other words the main part of the annual harvest, is treated by the producers themselves or by cooperatives. Yonne has only one cooperative, though this is an important one: it vinifies 16 per cent of the entire production of the *département*. There are seven in Côte-d'Or, vinifying 7 per cent of the harvest. In Saône-et-Loire, 19 cooperatives vinify 46 per cent of production and in Rhône, 18 of them vinify 30 per cent of the annual crop. The storage capacity of most cooperatives is about twice the volume vinified in a year of average production.

The grape varieties of Burgundy

The vineyards of Burgundy consist of vines classified in the great *Ampelidaceae* family, or more precisely, the *Vitis* genus of viniferous European vines. These are botanically heterogeneous populations, and differences can be found from one vine to another within what is ostensibly the same grape variety. In a plot of Pinot Noir, for example, it is possible to find stocks having different physiological and botanical characteristics (e.g. the outline of the leaf or the shape of the bunches), and these consequently modify the yield and its quality.

In greater Burgundy, four main types of grape variety are grown — Pinot Noir, Chardonnay, Aligoté and Gamay — and their grapes are generally vinified separately, without blending in the vat. An exception to this is Bourgogne Passetoutgrains, which includes both Gamay and Pinot Noir; where secondary grape varieties are grown, they, too, are vinified with the major varieties. This particularly applies to Yonne vineyards, where a number of very old grape varieties are still to be found.

All the principal grape varieties have a vegetative cycle that is perfectly adapted to the prevailing climatic conditions in the Burgundy area. In each case, their ripening period is during the first epoch.

The beginning of the annual growth cycle varies by several days according to the weather conditions of the year and the microclimatic conditions of the locale, as well as the large climatic differences between the south of the Beaujolais region and those found in Yonne. The first sign of the vines' awakening is the formation of drops of sap at the end of a cut vine shoot: sap rises in the vine in March during the spring pruning, and the vine is then said to 'cry'. A little later, budbreak occurs: bud down appears within the scale leaves protecting the buds in the first week of April. Flowering occurs around 15 June and, on average, 100 days pass between this point and the harvest.

Pinot Noir

This ancient vine, cultivated by the Gauls, is the

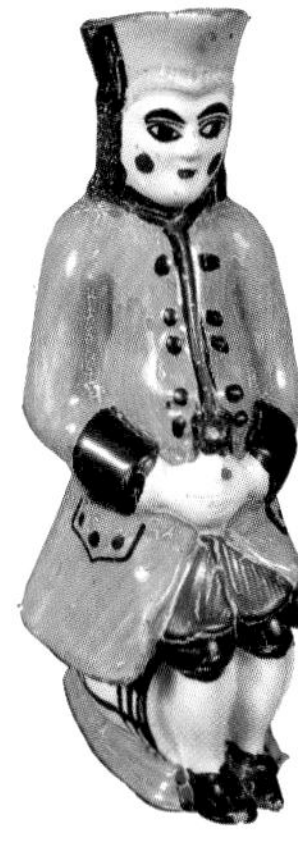

A glazed earthenware wine jug, early 19th century, in the Musée de la Vie Bourguignonne, Dijon.

'noble' grape variety *par excellence*. It is of average robustness. Mixed-length pruning, according to the Guyot system, allows the buds situated half way along the fruit-bearing cane (or *baguette*) to achieve maximum fruiting potential — an average of one and a half bunches of grapes per bud.

The bunches, however, are given to *millerandage* (or shot berries). This condition means that the development of the grapes in the bunch is not regular: normal grapes and aborted grapes are both produced. The yield is obviously affected by this.

The skin of the Pinot Noir is not thick, and all the colouring material is found within it, the juice being colourless. The wine's intensity of colour will therefore depend to a large extent on the ratio of the volume of juice to the total weight of the harvest. This ratio can vary from 65 to 80 per cent according to the year.

Pinot Noir is the grape variety used exclusively for all the 'village', Premier Cru and Grand Cru *appellations* of Burgundy, wines whose bouquet and flavour are incomparable, as well as playing the dominant role in the *appellations* of Bourgogne, Bourgogne-Hautes Côtes de Nuits and Bourgogne-Hautes Côtes de Beaune. It is worth noting that this variety, when it has been transplanted to other, warmer countries, has never produced wines of such good quality. The Pinot Noir in Burgundy is a typical case of perfect harmony between vine and natural environment.

Chardonnay

The Chardonnay is often confused with, and erroneously thought to be synonymous with, the Pinot Blanc. It is in fact a distinctive type of vine, identifiable by its leaves whose lyrate petiolar sinus has a naked base.

A Pinot Noir vine stock. This 'noble' grape variety produces its greatest wines only in Burgundy.

The vine stock, which is fairly robust and fertile, should be cut in such a way that there is a framework of old wood to hold back the flow of sap in the spring. The very old, traditional way of pruning known as the *système à traîne* (tow system), still applied in Chablis, meets this need.

This grape variety, which is remarkably well adapted to the continental climates of both Burgundy and Champagne, produces high class wines with an incomparable aroma. It provides the fruit for all the 'village', Premier and Grand Cru white wines of Burgundy, as well as for the Bourgogne Blanc *appellation* and for Burgundy's sparkling wines.

It is not widely grown in France other than in the two above-mentioned regions, but it has crossed the Atlantic and the American continent and settled in California. The average fertility of a 'well-placed' Chardonnay bud is two bunches of grapes.

Gamay Noir à Jus Blanc or Gamay du Beaujolais

This 'noble' grape variety produces wines with a remarkable bouquet and sumptuous colour when grown in the granite and schist soils found at the heart of the Beaujolais region. The wines produced are less typical and not of such high quality in marlacious or calcareous clay soils. As a variety, it has a surprising degree of adaptability. It is found practically everywhere in France: in the valley of the Loire, in the South West, in the Auvergne, in the Bugey region and in the most remote Alpine valleys. Its fruitiness means it is much sought after as a *primeur*, along the lines of the Beaujolais Nouveau which has been so successful. However, it has not always occupied a place of honour; as a 'disloyal' competitor to the Pinot Noir, it was banned from Burgundy, or rather from the hills of Burgundy, by the edict of Philip the Bold. Gamay vines produce reliably and regularly, and their secondary buds are also fertile, giving two bunches per bud: this is why the variety was widespread in the marginal areas of the Côte d'Or and Côte Chalonnaise and in the Mâcon area until the middle of the 19th century.

Aligoté

This vine is also planted in other wine-producing regions of France, although not in southern ones. It is cultivated in the Côte d'Or, in Saône-et-Loire and in the Hautes Côtes, where it produces a pleasant and fresh wine which should be drunk young. Its production is irregular. Along with the Chardonnay, it is used for the production of sparkling wines (Bourgogne Mousseux, Crémant de Bourgogne). Its wines can only claim the specific regional *appellation* of Bourgogne Aligoté.

Sauvignon Blanc

This is a white grape variety with pronounced

aromatic qualities, though it is not as aromatic as the Muscat. It is not a native of Burgundy. It may be found in the Bordeaux and Sancerre regions planted in marlacious soils, geologically identical to those of Saint-Bris-le-Vineux in Yonne. In this latter area, it produces pleasant, perfumed and fresh wines, classified as VDQS.

César

This red grape variety is still cultivated in the Auxerre region; when vinified on its own, it produces robust, strongly coloured wines, very rich in tannins. However, it is more usually blended with Pinot Noir, to provide the wine of the latter variety with stiffening and keeping qualities, and sold under the Bourgogne Irancy *appellation*.

Tressot

This grape variety has now all but disappeared from the Auxerre region. Its red wine is pleasant and keeps well.

Melon

This vine is native to Burgundy and used to be grown in the plains of Saône-et-Loire, on the borders of *appellation* vineyard areas. Its wine was not very good. The variety, which is very productive despite its susceptibility to cryptogamic diseases, was then introduced to the vineyards of Loire-Atlantique, where it was, and is, used to produce Muscadet. It thus had to emigrate in order to gain its reputation.

Since the reconstruction of the Burgundy vineyards at the end of the last century, all these varieties have been grafted on to rootstocks of American origin, the exact choice of which has been dictated by the chemical nature of the soil. The level of active lime (called *CA*, or *calcaire actif* in French), a factor causing chlorosis in vines, is decisive. It is essential to analyse the soil before any planting takes place.

If the level of active lime is almost zero, as is the case in the granitic soil of the Beaujolais area, the Vialla rootstock, which has an excellent affinity with the Gamay, is used. If the level is less than ten per cent, the rootstock 3309C (*riparia* × *rupestris*) is suitable. If the level is above ten per cent, rootstocks *riparia* × *berlandieri* 161–49 and SO4 are required. All these rootstocks graft well on to the *vinifera* varieties with which they are combined; they intrude only slightly in the development of the vegetative cycles, and leave all the fruit characteristics of the French vines intact. There is renewed interest in the rootstock Riparia Gloire, which is planted in soil having less than six per cent active lime. It has a very good affinity with Pinot Noir, in addition to being a quality grafting stock in its own right.

Vine training systems in Burgundy

The average age of a vine stock in Burgundy is

Tying young vines to trellises in the Hautes Côtes de Beaune, during May.

about 35 years. Within a property, it is sensible to plan to uproot a certain percentage of the vines grouped together in a plot at regular intervals, so as to spread out the loss in income resulting from unplanted vineyards or from young plantings which will be unproductive for four to five years. In a vineyard of medium age, a certain number of vines must be replaced each year if productivity is not to suffer. Replanting and bedding out call for rooted grafts obtained by wine growers from professional nurserymen. These are either one-year-old grafts taken from a nursery and planted in the spring, before vegetation has begun to form, or new grafts prepared in plastic pots in the vegetative period and planted in July or August. The latter technique is very successful, though it requires the use of more labour and materials at a time of year when the wine grower is exceptionally busy anyway. Planting from pots brings good results if the team charged with the planting is competent; a year can be saved in this way.

During the previous year, the soil which is to receive the plants will first have been deep-ploughed to a depth of 40 to 50cm, manured and chemically disinfected to kill off virus-carrying nematodes or eelworms.

The density of planting

In Yonne, the density of planting is about 10,000 vines/ha. The orientation of the rows depends on the shape of the vineyard plots and is decided upon so as to facilitate their cultivation and reduce the amount of time lost in turning, if mechanical cultivation and harvesting is adopted. On a hillside, rows or lines of vines following the gradient of the slope are generally adopted, thereby allowing the use of powerful machines. On the other hand, the soil is eroded more in this way than is the case if the rows are planted following level, horizontal contours.

Pruning methods

In lower Burgundy (Yonne), the old Chablis 'tow' system of pruning (*le systeme à traîne*), though modified, remains widespread. The vine stock is composed of two frame arms, of old wood, each carrying a fruit branch with six buds, on opposite sides to one another and vertically spaced. Nowadays, vegetation forms a curtain that is sufficiently far away from the soil to allow mechanical cultivation, which was not previously the case with this system. In the Côte d'Or, the Pinot Noir, Chardonnay and Aligoté are all pruned in one of two different ways: either by Guyot pruning, which is the most common, and the only system used on the Côte de Nuits — it consists of a short cane (or *courson*) with two buds and a long fruit-bearing cane (or *baguette*) of six to eight buds, depending on the vine's strength; or by the Cordon de Royat system, which has four or five short canes (*coursons*) with two buds each, growing from a spur of older wood, trained at a right angle to the vine trunk. The Gobelet system, now modified to form a 'fan' system of pruning (*en eventail*) is the classic method of pruning the Gamay in Beaujolais: four arms are left on the trunk, and each carries a short cane with two buds. (The Gamay bears more fruit than the other vines.) Finally, in the Mâcon region, the Chardonnay is pruned by the 'tail' system (*en queue*), whereby two long, fruit-bearing canes are arched in each direction from the main trunk.

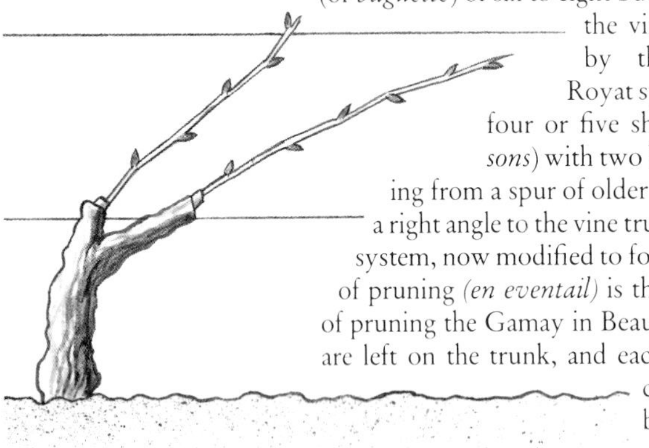

The 'Chablis' or 'tow' system of pruning Chardonnay.

Pruning begins as soon as the leaves fall in the autumn and continues through to the end of March, except in case of great cold. It can either be accomplished in two stages — a first preparatory pruning leaving only the main shoots, which will later provide the short and long canes (*coursons et baguettes*), followed by a final pruning in the spring; or in one single operation.

The decrees fixing the conditions of production for AOC wines specify the number of buds it is advisable to leave on each vine. Pruning in general is a manual operation that calls for thought and intelligence on the part of the wine grower; it is made easier by the use of pneumatic secateurs. The pruned wood is either burned on the spot — it is at this time that a delicate wisp of smoke may be seen rising from the vineyard — or it is chopped up. The vine cuttings are still occasionally left lying on the ground between the rows to reduce soil erosion.

The importance of the way the vine is pruned cannot be overemphasized. It is first of all pruned for structure, then pruned for fruit. Each vine presents the wine grower with a unique case which should be carefully considered before the secateurs are applied.

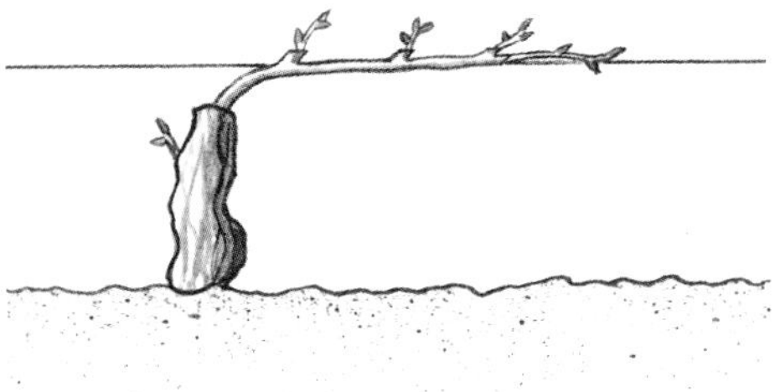

Cordon de Royat pruning of Pinot Noir and Chardonnay vines.

Vineyard work

After pruning, the wine grower removes any sterile shoots (or *gourmands*) that have grown from the eyes of the old wood, thus freeing the vine for its productive growth. This operation takes place after budding, when there is no more risk of frost. The grower then trains the new shoots of the vine to a system of parallel wires of which the middle two are detachable; finally, he trims the shoots along the sides and above the last wire, often mechanically.

From May to mid-September, the wine grower applies pesticide treatments against vegetal parasites (downy mildew, oidium or powdery mildew, grey rot or botrytis) and animal parasites (grape worms, spider mites). He ceases treatment two to three weeks before the harvest.

On the ground, the work consists either of loosening the soil by earthing up around the vines in the autumn and unearthing again in the

Burning the vine shoots. This operation takes place in autumn or spring, during pruning.

spring, together with superficial tilling in the summer, allowing weeds to be physically eradicated; or it consists of leaving the soil unworked and chemically treating weeds either before or after they emerge. This type of weeding has become more common from year to year. Chemical weeding has both advantages and disadvantages, and a certain amount of flexibility seems to be necessary. Vineyards planted with young vines, in particular, have to be ploughed and not chemically treated.

Organic fertilizers and farmyard manure are used to manure soils before they are planted with vines. Mineral fertilizers based on nitrogen and potash are also used, generally every two or three years.

The evolution of vineyard techniques

Evolution or revolution? Enormous transformations have taken place in Burgundian vineyards since the end of the Second World War. Until then, animal traction by horses or mules was the rule. In Côte-d'Or, vine-growing was, and still is, a monoculture. Only the large estates had traction animals; the smaller estates had to hire horses or mules by the day. The situation was different in Yonne and Saône-et-Loire, where there was permanent livestock on most holdings.

Between 1940 and 1950, motorized cultivators started to appear. These individually operated machines of modest power allowed small wine growers a certain independence, but could not satisfy all needs, particularly the application of pesticides.

Guyot pruning of Pinot Noir, Chardonnay and Aligoté vines.

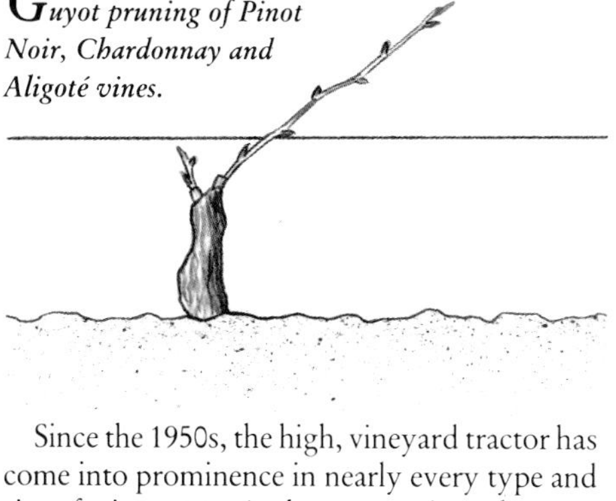

Since the 1950s, the high, vineyard tractor has come into prominence in nearly every type and size of wine estate. At the present time, there are no more horses in the vineyard. This *tracteur enjambeur* is a multipurpose vehicle that helps with, among other things, transportation and harvesting, and is marvellously well adapted to both soil and plant work. It must, however, be admitted that Burgundy's vineyards are over-equipped with them. Where a horse was once needed full time to maintain eight hectares of vines, a tractor of 40 to 50 horsepower is now only used part time; there are often two for the same piece of land.

'Fan' or 'eventail' *pruning of Gamay vines, in the Beaujolais area.*

Mechanization of harvesting has become very popular by necessity, because of the lack of manpower in the region and the constraints imposed when manpower is available. A machine is only economically viable for more than 20 ha, otherwise wine growers must form an association to purchase and use equipment, or apply to contractors, who generally follow the harvest through several subregions, from Mâcon up to Chablis, according to the staggered harvest dates. But some structural modifications have to be made to the machine so that it is equally effective in each region, where access to the plots of land may be different, as will the shape of plots, methods of pruning and the physical shapes of the vines . . .

The mechanization of work on the soil has had another consequence: that of erosion of vineyard slopes. The removal of supporting walls to provide easier mechanical access to vineyards has greatly disrupted the rainwater drainage system. Significant work has been carried out to collect this water in order to limit the loss of fine, fertilizing elements from the arable layer. Neither whole or partial non-cultivation, nor intentional grassing over between the vines, can offer a complete cure for this.

The harvest

The fixing of the harvest date — which is made official by the publication of the *ban*, an order made by the prefect of the *département* on the advice of the INAO, and in agreement with the producers' unions — follows a preliminary study of the maturity of grapes in the region over a period of about three weeks.

Teams take samples and measure the sugar and acidity levels in the grape juice; the results are interpreted and commented on by specialists of the INAO and official laboratories, and then published in the local press. The wine growers base their harvest

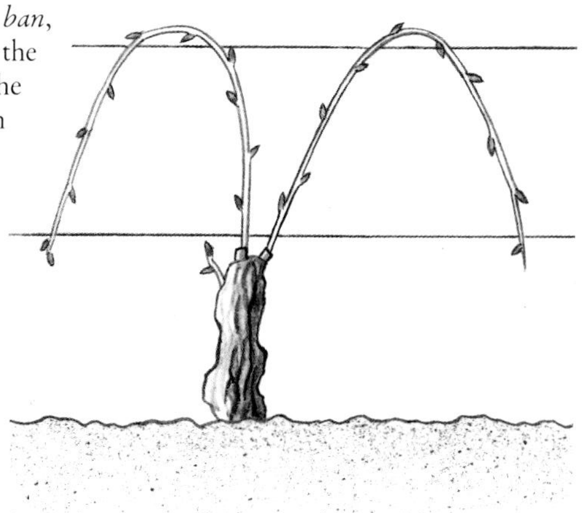

Pruning Chardonnay vines by the 'tail' system ('en queue'*) in the Mâcon region.*

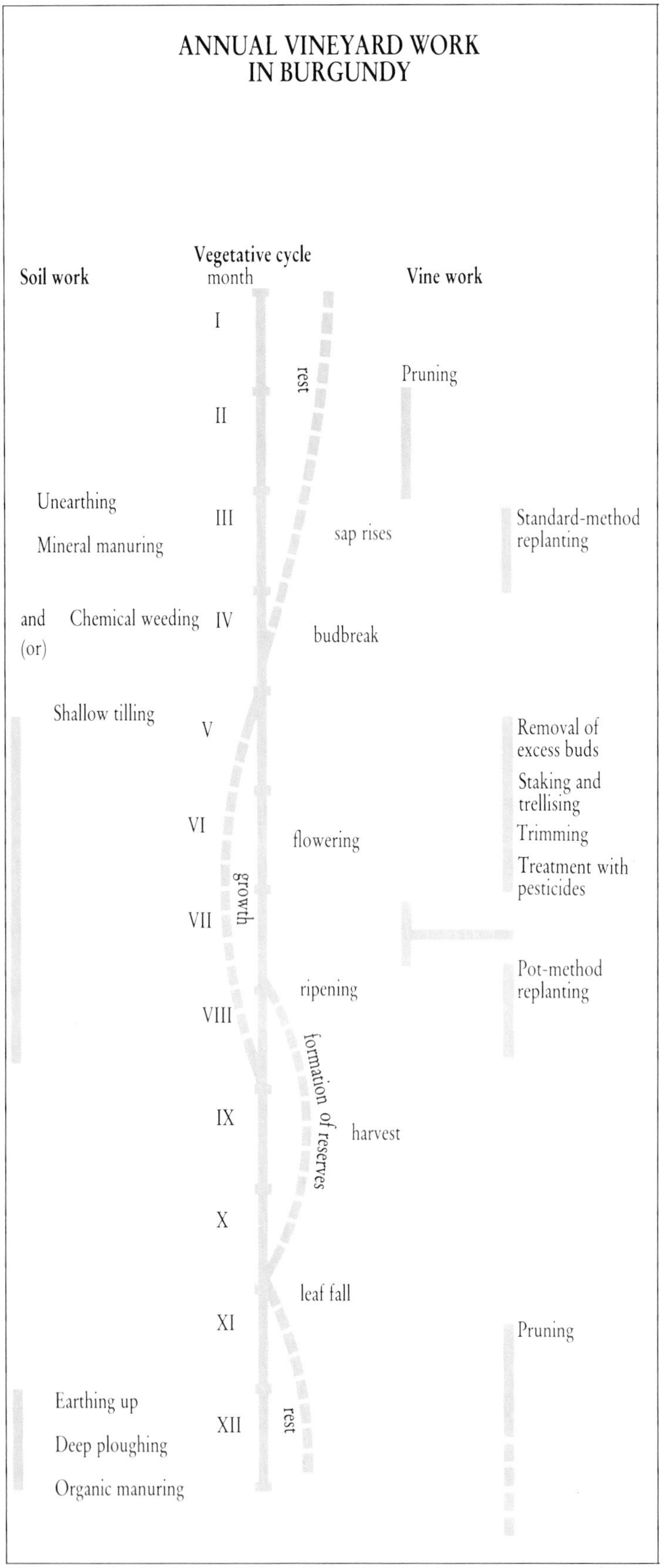

calendar on this information.

Since the average length of the harvest on a medium-sized property is two weeks, it is obvious that the grapes that go to make the first *cuvées* will not have reached the optimum stage of ripeness, and that those that go to make the last ones will perhaps have been attacked by parasites, grey rot (botrytis) or, indeed, hail ... it is impossible to win on all fronts. The weather always has its say. In Burgundy, very few harvests are completed in continuously hot and sunny conditions, as was the case in 1986.

Gathering the grapes

A manual harvest carried out by a team of 25 to 30 grape pickers can cover about one hectare per day. A grape-harvesting machine can carry out the same work in the same time, operated by two people in shifts. It can also work at night.

There are 82 grape-harvesting machines operating in Yonne, 73 in Côte-d'Or, 105 in Saône-et-Loire and 2 in Rhône. Most of them are self-propelled, but some are towed on a trailer chassis behind a tractor. Annual sales reached a peak in 1982 but have clearly fallen off since. It seems the market has, for the moment, reached saturation point.

Grape-harvesting machines are not used in the Beaujolais region for the sole reason that local vinification techniques require the fruit to be whole, with grapes still on the bunches ready to undergo carbonic maceration, and harvesting machines separate grapes from the stalks.

In certain respects, the advantages of the grape-harvesting machine are indisputable: reduction in the level of workers or pickers requiring feeding and lodging; rapidity and flexibility of picking when the plots are of a suitable size (a space of at least 5.5m must be allowed for turning at each end of the vineyard). But there are also disadvantages and constraints, varying according to the model used: greater or lesser losses of grapes on the bunches around the trellis posts, loss of juice, collection of rainwater containing the residue from pesticides and from wires, damage to the vine-training system, the need to replace galvanized wire with rustproof wire, damage to vine shoots and buds, weakening of the vine stocks, and more difficult pressing because of the absence of stalks.

Systematic studies undertaken over several years have not revealed any significant differences in the quality of wine obtained from mechanical harvesting or manual harvesting.

However, the juice from grapes picked mechanically must be vinified quickly, to avoid oxidization, and access to equipment and vats adapted to cope with a rapid delivery of grapes is also vital if the quality of the finished wine is to be maintained.

A grape-harvesting machine pays for itself

Some 70 wine growers share the Clos de Vougeot vineyard. The small surface area of each grower's plot explains the need for manual harvesting.

after an average of five years. The operating costs, including depreciation, are in the order of 5,000 francs/ha, which is slightly lower than the costs of manual harvesting.

Types of vinification

There have been significant developments in vinification equipment in Burgundy over the last 25 years. The following changes have occurred:

▷ The progressive replacement of wooden vats by vats made of cement with open or closed tops, and by metal containers made of enamelled sheet steel or stainless steel which can serve as storage vats;

▷ The use of self-emptying rotary vats, which cuts out the processes of shovelling the marc from the vat after vinification, and of pumping wine over the cap of grape skins, or of pushing the cap of skins down into the wine by foot, while ensuring that the must is fermented with correct skin contact;

▷ Modernization of the pressing equipment: semi-automatic or automatic programmed presses, which are very powerful and quick, saving manpower and time. Pneumatic presses are little used, and continuous presses are forbidden;

▷ Mechanization of operations of bringing the harvest to the place of vinification, crushing the grapes, destalking them, and emptying the marc from the vats;

▷ The use of efficient means of controlling fermentation temperatures.

Progress has also been facilitated by officials. providing technical information, especially on the following points: the use of selected dry yeast (or active dry yeast), the sensible use of sulphur dioxide, the maintenance of equipment, and cellar hygiene. Lectures and meetings are organized by the engineers and technicians of the INRA (Institut National de Recherche Agronomique) and by academics within the framework of local Interprofessional Committees.

White wine vinification

In all the subregions of Burgundy, the white grapes are treated in such a way that the sugars are totally fermented out, so as to obtain dry wines. Whether it be Chablis or Côte d'Or white wines, wines from the Mâconnais, Bourgogne Aligoté or Sauvignon Blanc wines from Yonne — all will be dry.

The grapes are crushed in the fermenting room, and are then pressed as quickly as possible. The two sets of juices produced by each process are run together into a single vat, with a dose of sulphur dioxide (8g to 15g per litre), and rest there for 24 hours. After this period, the juice is racked off the sediment that has formed. It is then aerated and yeast is added. Fermentation takes place either in a single large container or in oak barrels, for one to two weeks at the most, depending on the activity level of the yeast and the temperature of the premises. Malolactic fermentation may quickly follow the main fermentation, although this is not a rule.

Red wine vinification

The grapes are crushed and are then totally or partially removed from their stalks, depending

From 1971 to 1985, the number of grape-harvesting machines in France increased from 1 to 360.

Stainless steel storage vats on the premises of a large cooperative in the Hautes Côtes de Beaune.

on the healthiness of the crop and the characteristics of the vintage. The grape skins and pulp are macerated in the vat as fermentation proceeds over a period of 6 to 7 days. Sulphur dioxide and yeast are added at the start and then the must is both pumped up from the bottom of the vat and the cap of grape skins and pips is pushed down during fermentation in order to facilitate the diffusion of the colouring material and tannins contained in the grape skins. The temperature is checked during the entire period of vatting (*cuvaison*), as is the density of the fermenting must. The development of the latter provides information on the state of progress of fermentation and allows the right moment to be chosen for the running-off of new wine from the vat.

The *vin de goutte* (wine expressed by the grape matter without being pressed, or free-run wine) is run off from the vat; the solid sediment of marc is then pressed, giving the *vin de presse* (press wine). More often than not, both wines are combined to form the final *cuvée* (vintage blend).

As in the case of some white wines, malolactic fermentation may begin during the days that follow the alcoholic fermentation. The wine maker tries to encourage it to take place in every possible way — storing the wine at the favourable temperature of 18–20°C, culturing the wine with selected lees or starting agents. The consequences of the malolactic fermentation are beneficial to the quality of the wine, since it provokes the biological neutralization of acid in general, and the elimination of malic acid in particular, malic acid being hard on the palate. It is better if this fermentation takes place in barrel rather than in bottle.

Vinification by carbonic maceration is only practised in the Beaujolais region.

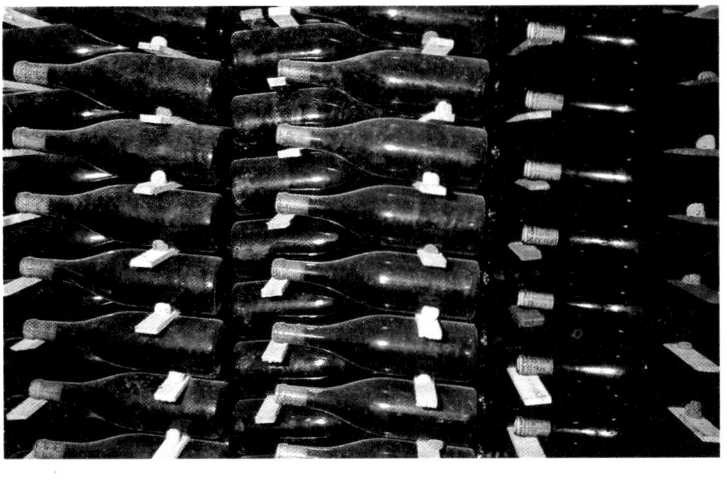

Bottled red wine maturing in a cellar in Nuits-Saint-Georges.

Vinification of rosé wine

In Burgundy, a few rosé wines from the Pinot Noir grape variety are sold as such under the Bourgogne *appellation*; Bourgogne Rosé de Marsannay is the most typical example. The three figures given below illustrate the fluctuations in production of rosé Burgundy wines made in the village of Marsannay:

1981: 491 hl; **1982:** 4,693 hl; **1983:** 1,420 hl

This pale rose-coloured wine is made by vinifying lightly pressed red grapes according to the method used for white wines. The practice of '*saignée*' vinification, in which a part of the must is macerated with the grape skins prior to fermentation, a method well known in the Côtes de Provence area, is not widely used in the Burgundy region.

Sparkling wine vinification

Crémant de Bourgogne sparkling wine, made by the *méthode champenoise*, is worthy of particular mention. The traditional red, white and rosé AOC Bourgogne Mousseux wines are now somewhat overshadowed by the white and rosé Crémant de Bourgogne AOC, created by the decree of 17 October 1975. This is a sparkling wine made by secondary fermentation in the bottle, following the *méthode champenoise* in every respect. The permitted grape varieties are Pinot Noir, Pinot Gris, Pinot Blanc and Chardonnay, with the Gamay Noir à Jus Blanc, Aligoté, Melon and Sacy as secondary varieties. Alcohol content should be no less than 8.5°, with a maximum yield per hectare of 7,000kg of grapes, giving 50 hl/ha of juice. The grapes can only be pressed using equipment that does not have a helicoidal screw or chains, and a 'wine press notebook' must be kept, containing full details of the origin, weight and variety of grapes pressed, the quantity and potential alcohol of the must, and the details of the pressing. These constraints are modelled exactly on those employed in the vinification of champagne, and are intended to produce only the highest quality results.

The *élevage* of the wine

The once-common French expressions '*conservation*' ('conservation') and '*vieillissement*' ('ageing') have now been replaced by '*élevage*', meaning 'raising' or 'nurturing', a term that signifies the art of bringing the basic, new wine to an optimum quality level at the moment when it is bottled.

Aligoté wines retain a pleasant freshness only if protected from oxidization; therefore they should not stay in cask for more than a few months. Chardonnay wines of the Mâcon or Petit Chablis type are often stored in large capacity vats, made of cement or metal, for less than a year. Chablis Premier Cru and Grand Cru wines, Pouilly-Fuissé wines, and wines from the villages of the Côte de Beaune (including Premier and Grand Cru wines) are kept in oak casks, partly new, partly used, for between one and one and a half years.

Pinot Noir wines, both *villages* and *crus*, are treated in the same way as their white Chardonnay counterparts. Gamay wines are either bottled and sold rapidly as Beaujolais Nouveau, or they are kept in wood for a few months. The wines are racked off their lees, fined and filtered before being bottled.

All wine producers rack their wines in order to separate clear wine from lees, and this is done initially in contact with the air, to eliminate the carbon dioxide which the wine contains in abundance, then in non-oxidizing conditions. Many wine producers continue to add finings to clarify their wines; these are clay-based, or are organic mineral substances based on nitrogen compounds, and have the ability to flocculate unwanted tannins or impurities by forming a fine film which, through a process of sedimentation, clarifies and stabilizes the wine. Large quantities of wine are stabilized by being filtered two or three times through cellulose plates combined with diatomaceous earth (kieselguhr), a very fine porous substance capable of retaining micro-organisms such as yeast. Membrane filters even hold back bacteria whose diameter is less than one thousandth of a millimetre. Fining and filtering operations are often combined.

Élevage in oak casks has been the subject of consistent study during the last few years. These studies have shown the beneficial effect of ageing in wooden casks, and how the exact character given the wine by the wood depends on the geographical origin of the trees and the treatment applied to the staves when the casks were made. The storage of wines in new casks always gives very positive results.

Buying new casks is an expensive investment: a Burgundy *pièce*, a cask with a capacity of 228 litres, costs between 1,700 and 2,000 francs today. In the 1930s, the wine was often sold to the trade in cask, and the cask cost as much as its contents. New barrels did not therefore stay very long in the wine maker's cellar. These days, it is very rare for wines to be sold in casks. It is up to the wine maker to plan the rotation of his barrels, and the acquisition of new ones as necessary.

The character of vintages in Burgundy

The quality of a harvest or a vintage is analysed by the professionals of the wine world as soon as the climatic and physiological evidence permits.

The first indications may come early, based on the taste of the wine while it is still hot in the vat, and the aroma given off by the marc on its removal from the vats.

The great cuverie *(cellar or vat room) of the Dukes of Burgundy, at Chenôve.*

The doors of the Exposition Générale des Vins de Bourgogne (General Exhibition of the Wines of Burgundy) open to lovers of wine, restaurateurs, traders and brokers at Beaune, on the day before the famous sale of wine from the Hospices de Beaune, in the middle of November. Thousands of samples are on show from the most recent harvest, as well as previous vintages, and from all over the Burgundy region. This event has been organized for more than a century by the Comité de Viticulture de la Côte d'Or (Wine-growing Committee of the Côte d'Or). A panel confers and reaches a judgment on the general quality of the harvest; this is circulated by the media. The vintage is launched . . .

As a general rule, the judgment made is objective and sound. It is obvious to anyone who has had the privilege to taste the last few remaining bottles of the 1865 harvest, which have been religiously conserved, that the then Committee's opinion that this was the vintage of the century was correct. The same is true of the 1929 vintage. What will be the destiny of 1985, which has also been described as a great vintage? The following points should be borne in mind when reading vintage reports of recent Burgundy harvests, in order to reach a correct and clear-headed judgment a few years later:

▷ 'Exceptional' years are much rarer for white wines than for red.

▷ The frequency of 'excellent' vintages is, on the other hand, much greater for white than for red, and this pattern is repeated in the 'good' vintage category. The quality of white burgundy is more consistent than that of red.

▷ A closer analysis of the subregions can reveal marked differences in the same year between, for example, the quality of a Chablis and that of a Pouilly-Fuissé; between a Pinot Noir from the

Côte d'Or and a Beaujolais; between the Côte de Nuits and the Côte de Beaune. These differences are due to individual mesoclimates and microclimates.

Quality is a whole: strength, subtlety of aroma, combined with a harmonious structure, balanced flavour, freshness (for white wines), correct levels and types of tannin, intensity of colour . . . It is obvious that more favourable elements need to be combined to obtain a distinguished red than are needed to place a white well up the quality scale. The bias in favour of the latter is particularly marked in years of average quality.

Marketing burgundy

The often minute division of properties and the impressive number of different *appellations* in Burgundy prevented, for many years, the marketing of wines direct from the producer to the consumer. It would have been a doubtful exercise for many wine producers to assume the burden not only of *élevage* of the wines, but also of their packaging for retail purposes. They lacked precise knowledge of the subject as well as the necessary equipment, and they had not been able to generate commercial interest in, and outlets for, small domain-bottled wines; the bureaucracy of exportation eluded them. The time at their disposal was limited, and so work on the vines remained their main preoccupation.

In the past, transactions concerning wine were exclusively in the hands of a few privileged people and were governed largely by habits and customs, without being subject to any sort of inspection, except when the tax man took an interest . . .

The 18th-century wine trade in Burgundy has furnished material for numerous studies, some of which have denounced the dishonesty of local merchants and purchasers foreign to the province who substituted second-rate wines for first-rate ones. During this period, Burgundian tradesmen wanted to satisfy the taste of 'foreign' consumers by presenting them with wines that were richer in body and colour, and of a darker appearance, than is natural in good burgundy, and this could only be achieved by increasing

BURGUNDY VINTAGES

year	Exceptional vintages		Excellent vintages		Good vintages	
	White	Red	White	Red	White	Red
1929		+				
1934				+		
1945				+		
1947				+		
1949		+				
1955				+	+	
1959		+			+	
1961			+	+		
1962					+	+
1964				+	+	
1966				+	+	
1967					+	+
1969			+	+		
1970	+					+
1971			+	+		
1972						+
1973			+			+
1974					+	
1975					+	
1976			+	+		
1978	+	+				
1979					+	+
1981			+			
1982			+			+
1983				+	+	
1984			+			
1985	+	+				
1986					+	+

the maceration time in the vat during vinification, sometimes to the detriment of quality of the wines.

Wine was advertised by distributing samples corresponding to selected blended lots stored in cellars managed by honest professionals — a precursor of the wine exhibitions and competitions of today.

The first commercial firm was founded in Beaune in 1720. It sold wine by correspondence, as well as offering its wines via salesmen who canvassed regional custom.

Today, the wines of Burgundy are largely sold in two ways: by *négociants-éleveurs*, and by direct sales from the producer to the consumer.

***The role of the* négociant-éleveur**

The *négociant-éleveurs* obtain 95 per cent of their requirements from individual properties in the form of bulk wine. They acquire the rest of their needs in the form of grapes, which they vinify themselves. They may also market the wines of their own estates, if they have vineyard holdings.

In 1984, there were 156 businesses registered as *négociant-éleveurs* in Burgundy, 5 of them in Yonne, 84 in Côte-d'Or, 32 in Saône-et-Loire and 35 in the Beaujolais region. They employed 4,100 workers. These firms market about 72 per cent of the region's wines, mostly of AOC status, and contribute greatly to exports, being responsible for 22 per cent of all AOC wine exported; among those red burgundies exported (Beaujolais excluded), 22 per cent goes to Switzerland, 15 per cent to the United States, 15 per cent to Belgium and Luxembourg, 15 per cent to Great Britain and 15 per cent to West Germany. The export figures for Beaujolais show that 28 per cent is exported to Switzerland, 16 per cent to West Germany, 15 per cent to Great Britain and 15 per cent to the United States.

It should, however, be noted that, over the last twenty years, the amount of trade undertaken by *négociant-éleveurs* has declined from more than 90 to 72 per cent, as a result of many wine producers starting to sell their produce directly. Balancing this, Burgundian traders are increasingly taking an interest in wines other than those produced in the region. They market branded wines, as well as buying and selling wines from other areas. In these other areas, they rarely deal directly with the wine producer; in general, they go through the intermediary of a local agricultural broker.

Direct sales to the consumer

Over the last two decades, the vineyard owners have considerably increased their direct sales, from a low percentage to about 30 per cent, both in the home market and on export markets. This has been made possible by the equipment that

Direct sales from the producer to the consumer have risen to 30 per cent in Burgundy.

THE WINE BROKER

The status of wine brokers (courtiers) *remained vague until specified by the law of 31 December 1949. The broker is the usual intermediary — almost indispensable but not obligatory — between the vendor and the purchaser. With experience gleaned from frequent visits to growers' cellars and from numerous tastings, the broker is the only person acquainted with the stocks of wine available by vintage, by type and by quality on the one hand, and with the needs of the trade on the other.*

He must be an excellent taster, capable of detecting faults in wine and wine-making equipment, and have all the practical qualities required of an oenologist. He has no storing facilities of his own and does not carry out business in his own name, unlike the wine agent (commissionnaire en vins)*, but he deals with every stage involved in a transaction — the taking of samples, the confirmation of purchases, racking, transport, paperwork . . . In exchange for his services, he receives a commission from both parties, calculated on the basis of the purchase price.*

The feast of St Vincent at Maligny in the Chablis region, with the traditional procession of the members of the Confrérie des Piliers de Chablis.

has become available to them, by the technical knowledge acquired by the younger generation, and by the commercial interest in their products they have been able to raise. Producers sell on their own premises, in shared *caveaux de dégustation* (tasting cellars), and through the intermediary of agents; they have been helped in this by the simplification of administrative formalities caused by the establishment of the authorization capsule or the *capsule-congé* (which contains a seal showing that the wine has been granted transport rights).

Wine events

There are numerous events connected with wine in Burgundy. They testify to the intense wine-producing activity of the region and the importance of wine in Burgundian society. The 'Trois Glorieuses' are a group of three events that follow one another almost without interruption, centred on the famous wine sale of the Hospices de Beaune, which takes place on the third Sunday of November. The first of the three events takes place the day before, with a chapter meeting of the Confrérie des Chevaliers du Tastevin. Two days later, on the Monday, the third event of the Trois Glorieuses takes place: a village feast in Meursault, called the Paulée de Meursault.

The Hospices de Beaune wine auction

The Hospices de Beaune, the Hôtel-Dieu and the Hospice de la Charité in combination put up for sale by public auction wines made from their own vineyard holdings, given to them over the years as gifts. The actual selling is conducted by candlelight, and it takes place under the presidency of top French and foreign personalities. The lots produce spectacular bids and the prices often reach dizzy heights. This is of course largely for the benefit of charity, but it is not without interest for the profession, because the fluctuation in prices from year to year provides an indication of the value of the vintage and market interest in it.

The most prestigious *cuvées* (vintage blends or lots) carry the names of the Hospices' major benefactors: in Beaune, Dames Hospitalières, Guigone de Salins, Nicolas Rolin, Rousseau Deslandes; in Corton, Docteur Peste, Charlotte Dumay, Françoise de Salins (Corton-Charlemagne); in Meursault, Bahèzre de Lanlay, Philippe le Bon (Meursault-Genevrières); in Gevrey, Madeleine Collignon (Mazis-Chambertin).

The Paulée de Meursault

On the Monday after the sales of wines from the Hospices, the growers and their guests take a meal together in Meursault, the former bringing their best bottles. This cheerful and good-natured meal is followed by the awarding of a literary prize, consisting of 100 bottles of finest Meursault.

The main courtyard of the Hôtel-Dieu at Beaune. Built in 1443, this magnificent example of the 'Burgundian-Flemish' style is crowned with a roof of glazed and coloured tiles.

The Saint-Vincent Tournante

This is the feast of the wine makers themselves. It is both a religious and secular ceremony, presided over by the Confrérie des Chevaliers du Tastevin. On St Vincent's day at the end of January, delegations from the villages of Burgundy gather together for a procession bearing

A PASSION FOR WINE

A passion for wine is an inherited trait. I have been careful not to rid myself of it. I owe my first memories of wine to my grandfather, who was a restaurateur and café owner in Roanne and a great lover of wine. Each year, he would put 27 barrels of Beaujolais in the cellar. My brother and I had to bottle them on Thursday mornings. I still retain the image of the 230 bottles, the smells and the atmosphere of the cellar and the wood.

Later, my father took me with him on his tours of the wine producers. We would always start at Chiroubles. Our preference was for the wines of Fleurie. At Fleurie, Mlle Chabert and her assistants ran the cooperative cellar with great masterliness. From seeing her working, I have retained a great admiration for women who are interested in wine.

From the age of 15, I accompanied my father to see his Burgundian friends. I knew all of them, from the youngest to the oldest. There I experienced some unforgettable, generous and colourful moments, such as only the soil of Burgundy can produce. But it wasn't until I was about 30, back in my father's restaurant, that I began to appreciate wine for itself. Like certain subtle arts, or like love, it can only be properly tasted with the benefit of age and maturity. Before this, the drinker only perceives the superficial aspect of wine, without feeling it from inside, without truly understanding it. Then, one day, something is triggered, click, and the wine stands revealed.

For a long time, my brother looked after our cellar with all his methodical sensitivity and I, being completely absorbed by my stoves, only rarely went to the vineyards. But wine played a full part in my cooking. I remember making five coqs au vin *on the same day with five different wines: one Chambertin, one Côte Rôtie, one Bordeaux, one Beaujolais and one Bandol.*

Beaujolais is my youth; some crus, *such as Moulin-à-Vent, are remarkable. But for me it is above all the wine for relaxing with, in the company of friends, over a game of* belote *or around a dinner table of happy guests. My fine wine preference is definitely for burgundy. With Richebourg and Chambertin, the summits are reached. Richebourg is the lord of Burgundy; a strong, balanced and noble wine. It is a long velvet drape to roll oneself up in. For me, it is Scheherazade. Chambertin is more of a warrior: I see it as a knight.*

Of course, these wines should be drunk with close friends who deserve them and understand them; not in great gulps, but almost in silence, with a sort of religious devotion. There are moments for these wines, as there are for all others. A given wine at a given moment. The same wine is not for drinking while playing boules, *or when going out with friends, or when one is in the company of a young lady.*

I also like Côte Rôtie greatly. Its vigour and vitality are akin to my cooking; both are spicy and characterful — a real infusion of ground pepper. As a young wine, it is an almost exotic delicacy. Afterwards it calms down for five, or six years, before becoming extrovert again. Some people are put off by its dense colour and its thickness. No wine, however, is more easily digestible. It should be drunk at a temperature of 19°C, or 21°C at the most. It does not gain from being served at a higher temperature; in fact, in my opinion, no wine gains from this.

Among other red wines, I can understand a Château Pétrus or Margaux being preferred to a burgundy, but among the dry white wines, I find those from Burgundy indisputably better — especially the three great ones: Meursault, Puligny and Chassagne. In the next rank, I put Corton, Chablis, Pouilly-Fuissé and Saint-Véran. However, discoveries can still be made elsewhere, such as the vin de voile *(wine covered with a 'veil' of yeast, as the Jura's* vin jaune *is) from Gaillac that I tasted recently . . . But my own cooking is best matched by the great classic wines:* oeufs en moeurette *with an Auxey, a Savigny or even a Côte Chalonnaise,* boeuf bourguignonne *with a Pommard or a Gevrey-Chambertin,* lièvre à la royale *with a Richebourg, Côte Rôtie with grills or rare meat, steak* au poivre *and roasts. I think that I will never grow tired of this game of combinations.*

Wine is part of my daily life. It is my greatest investment and my pleasure.

Pierre Troisgros

the statue of their patron saint, Vincent, who was a deacon in Saragossa and was put to death there in 303. He has always been venerated in the wine-producing areas of France and Spain.

The Hospices de Nuits-Saint-Georges

Each year in March, a charity auction takes place of wine from vineyards that have been donated to the Hospices. The sale is intended to form an integral part of a series of local events, others of which include the 'Carrefour de Dionysos' ('The Forum of Dionysus') at Morey-Saint-Denis, organized by the wine makers there, and the Tastevinage (see below) at the Clos de Vougeot.

The Tastevinage

The first Tastevinage took place on 28 June 1950. This event was established by the Confrérie des Chevaliers du Tastevin, which holds its meetings at the Château du Clos de Vougeot.

The Tastevinage is a learned gathering of professionals from the wine-producing world, government officials, consumer representatives and restaurateurs, assembled to pass judgment on wines that are tasted blind. This jury attempts to draw the public's attention to wines that are particularly representative of their *appellation* or vintage.

Wine makers and *négociants* are invited to submit samples of wines. (Stocks must be large enough for these wines to be marketed in commercial quantities.) The best 60–70 per cent of the wines are awarded the Tastevin label (*see* page 481). The remaining 30–40 per cent of the wines are not judged to be worthy of the *tastevinage*, though they need not be thought defective in any way, and can be submitted again at a later tasting.

The Foire Nationale des Vins (National Wine Fair) takes place every May in Mâcon. Created in 1948, it holds competitions open to all the AOC and VDQS wines of France, judged from representative samples from a consistent lot of at least several hectolitres. The judges award prizes that may take the form of stickers or neck labels to be affixed to the bottles.

Detail of one of the wrought-iron gates of the Clos de Vougeot.

THE CONFRÉRIE DES CHEVALIERS DU TASTEVIN

The Confrérie des Chevaliers du Tastevin (Brotherhood of the Knights of the Tasting Cup) was the first of the modern confréries *to be formed. Created in 1934 at Nuits-Saint-Georges in an attempt to assuage the crisis that was gripping Burgundy at the time, the Confrérie des Chevaliers du Tastevin put itself at the exclusive service of the wines of the region, transcending all private interests.*

Its headquarters are in the Château du Clos de Vougeot, its property, which it has restored and where it holds prestigious chapters throughout the year, when people gather from all horizons and all walks of life to celebrate Burgundy's wine.

Apart from its cheerful and effective publicity function, the confrérie *plays an active role in the economy of Burgundy, having instituted the Tastevinage, a literary prize, and numerous Commanderies (branches) abroad.*

The Tastevinage is the assembling of a strict jury to taste and designate, for the attention of the wine lover, bottles of burgundy of the highest quality and typicality. These bottles receive a special label (see page 481). The confrérie *has also created a magazine. A little after the publication of the first, luxurious number of* Tastevin en Main *('Tasting Cup in Hand'), the* confrérie *created a chamber of art and literature which, among other things, publishes works about wine and the vine, and awards an annual literary prize.*

Though the confrérie *only exceptionally travels within France, it has created numerous Commanderies in Africa, in America and in Australia which testify to a Burgundian presence and spirit abroad in the world.*

The Vine and Vineyard Work

A climbing plant which fruits meagrely, the wild vine can have shown our ancestors little sign of the spectacular future that lay in store for it. The patience of several civilizations was needed to make it productive, and the present-day art of wine growing combines this knowledge, accumulated over centuries, with the most modern scientific techniques. The once rampant and unruly vine has been tamed — so much so that thousands of ways of training it exist today.

A traveller visiting several different wine-producing areas cannot fail to be struck by the diversity in the shape of the vine stocks from one region to another. Yet there are similarities: all are formed by vines of different ages which have successively produced, during the course of the plant's development, a trunk and branches of extremely variable proportions. In their natural state, the great majority of *Vitaceae* are creepers. The shapes found in the vineyard are therefore, without exception, the result of annual pruning, often combined with a more or less sophisticated form of training. All varieties of fruit-producing vines, by whatever system they are trained, have component parts that are identical in their function and more or less similar in their shape.

The vegetative cycle

During this annual cycle, a certain number of plant organs, including the small, fruit-bearing shoots, develop on the pruned wood. These small shoots form as a succession of internodes (parts of plant stem between nodes or knots) called merithalli, separated by more or less bulbous knots. The knots are where the leaves, buds, tendrils and inflorescences (or flower-bearing stalks) grow from. During the summer, the small shoots ripen and change from green to brown, becoming woody as they do so. This is called *aoûtement* (from the French word for August, *août*) and, at this stage, the shoot has become a *sarment* (a lignified or woody vine cane).

VINE LEAF

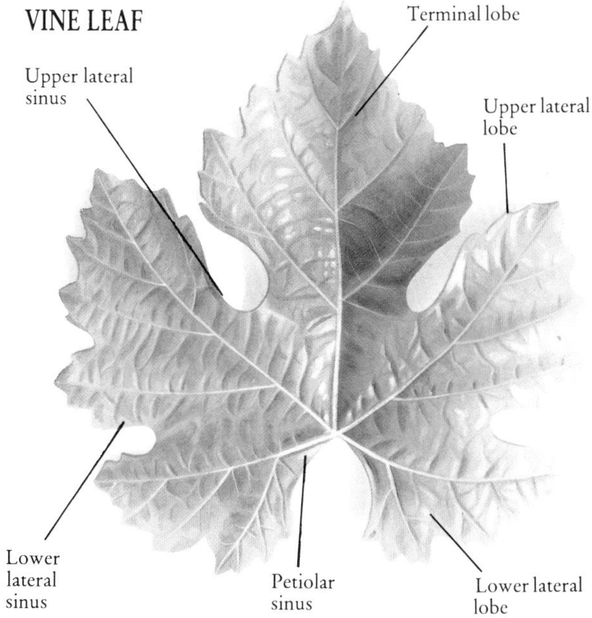

THE VINE

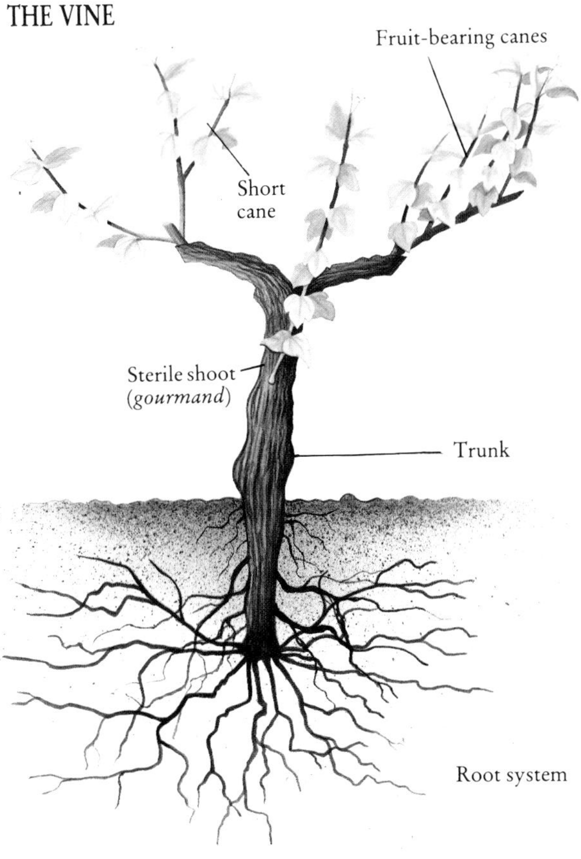

The leaves of the vine grow from the knots in alternating positions. Each leaf has five main veins, but the enormous potential for variation in other leaf characteristics — such as the lobes, teeth, villosity or hairiness, and pigmentation — means that the leaves are the main plant organs involved in the differentiation of vine varieties.

Two types of bud may be distinguished on vines: the prompt bud and the latent bud.

The prompt bud develops in the same year it is formed. It only produces small shoots, called *entre-coeurs*, that sometimes develop stunted bunches of grapes not usually able to reach full maturity. These underdeveloped bunches are almost never harvested.

The latent bud, which forms next to the prompt bud, does not develop into a fruit-bearing cane until the following year. Its developmental cycle is extremely complex. If it is examined under a microscope at the time of the *aoûtement*, it may be seen that a certain number of merithalli have already been formed, giving rise to microscopic leaves, tendrils and inflorescences. The number of the latter depends on the vine variety and on the conditions in which the shoot has grown, which means that the quantity of a harvest one year is partly

STAGES IN ANNUAL VINE GROWTH

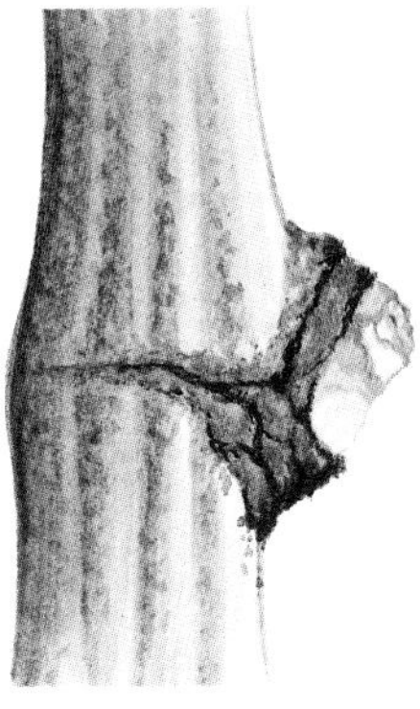
Winter bud

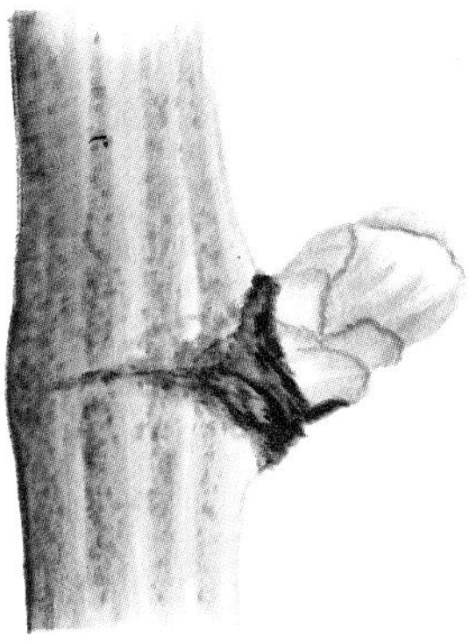
Early spring bud

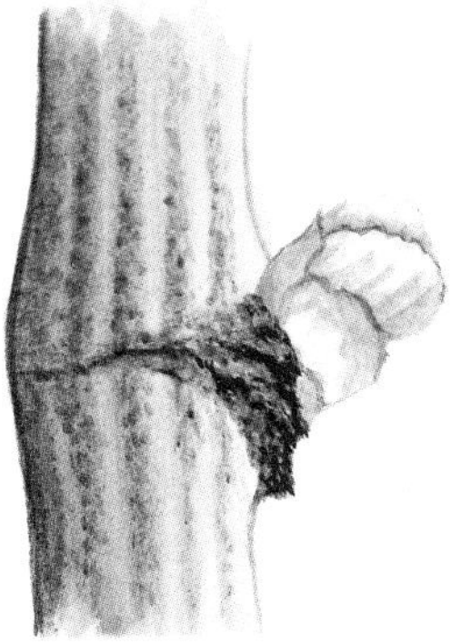
Spring bud

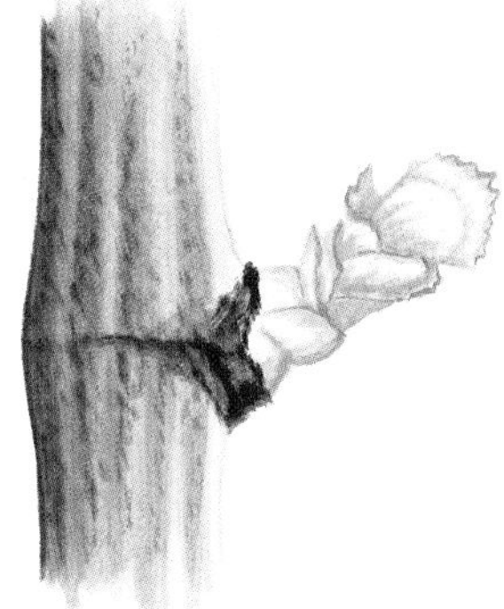
Budbreak

Appearance of leaves

Opening of leaves

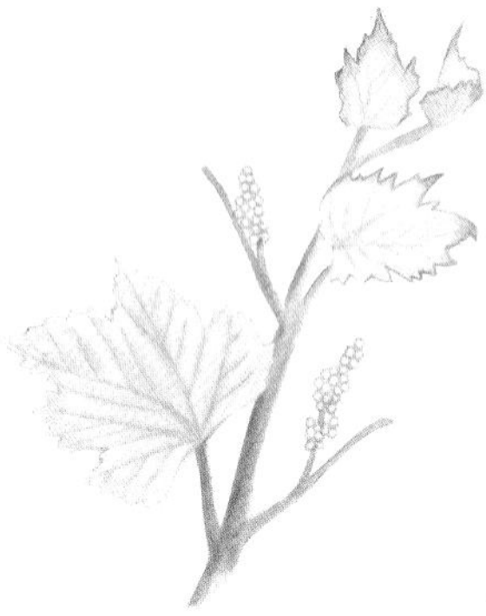
Appearance of embryo bunches

Separation of flower clusters

Flowering

Fruitset (transformation of flowers to berries)

Véraison (acquisition of colour by the grapes)

Maturity

dependent on the development of the plant during the previous year.

Budbreak occurs during the spring. The latent buds of the vine open much later than the buds of traditional fruit trees. The exact time of budbreak is an important variable characteristic of vine varieties, and it is imprudent to plant a variety with early budbreak in an area liable to late frosts.

The inflorescences, which will later become bunches of grapes, are located towards the base of the green shoots, on the opposite side to the leaves. Their number varies from none at all to four per shoot. The tendrils, situated on knots higher up the shoot, are simply potential inflorescences.

According to the vine variety and the growing conditions, the number of flowers that make up each inflorescence may vary from one hundred to several thousand. The great majority of vines have hermaphrodite flowers, i.e. ones that are both male and female. The corolla of each tiny flower is made up of five green petals, fused together, and these give the vine flower the shape of a hood or cap. During flowering, the corolla opens from the bottom and the hood thus released is pushed back by the distension of the stamens. The period of flowering depends both on the vine and, in particular, on the weather

A GRAPE

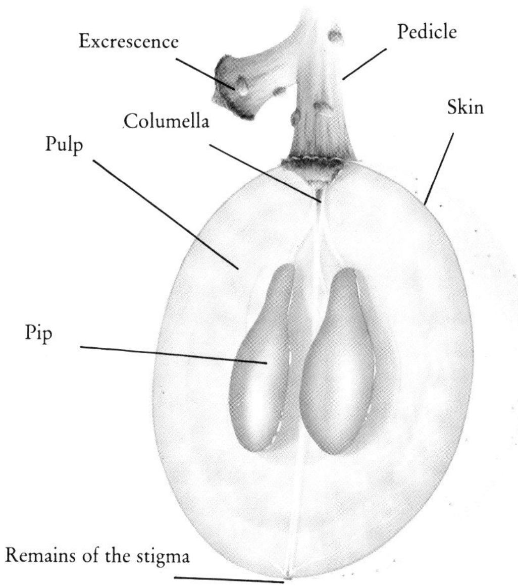

conditions at the time. It takes place five or six weeks after budbreak.

After *nouaison* (fruitset), a term which indicates that the ovaries of the fertilized flowers have changed into small grapes, the inflorescences become bunches of grapes. The size and shape of the bunches, and the composition of the grapes, are extremely variable. The number of pips per grape, for example, can vary from one to four. The shape and weight of the grapes vary considerably from vine to vine. For example, the Cabernet Sauvignon vine has grapes weighing about 1g each, the Carignan has grapes of about 4g, and some table grape varieties have grapes weighing up to 10g. *Nouaison* is the most critical part of the vegetative cycle of the vine because it largely determines the volume of the harvest.

A bunch of grapes always has considerably fewer berries than there were flowers on the corresponding inflorescence. The falling-off of unfertilized flowers and very small fertilized berries is quite normal, but sometimes the number of falling berries becomes excessive — this is called *coulure*, or flower abortion.

The reason for this phenomenon is well known: it is due to an insufficient flow of sugars to the flowers and the berries, caused either by a too-rapid growth of vegetation, or by unfavourable weather conditions preventing proper synthesis of the sugars in the leaves. *Coulure* particularly affects northern vineyards, where flowering takes place in conditions varying from excellent to atrocious. Annual yields consequently vary by 500 per cent or more. Some varieties are particularly susceptible to *coulure*, which is the vineyard calamity most feared by wine growers.

The growth of the grape takes place over four distinct phases. The first 20 days are slow, followed by a period of fast growth, after which the development slows down once more until the grapes start to ripen. The term 'ripening' designates a physiological process whereby sugar deposits in the grapes increase rapidly, while the structure of the grape changes little.

When the ripening process has begun, the weight and volume of the grapes increases considerably through accumulation of sugars until maturity is reached. The level of sugar accumulation depends partly on the number of grapes on the vine. If there are too many grapes, sugar is not accumulated as fully as it might be by each grape. Therefore excessive production is prejudicial to the various components that make up the quality of the fruit to be vinified. Sugars are the most important of these components, but acids, aroma constituents and phenolic compounds are also crucial.

The grape sugars take two forms: glucose and fructose. Grape acid, which is at its greatest at the start of the ripening process, is mainly (90 per cent) a mixture of tartaric acid and malic acid; citric acid is among the numerous acids making up

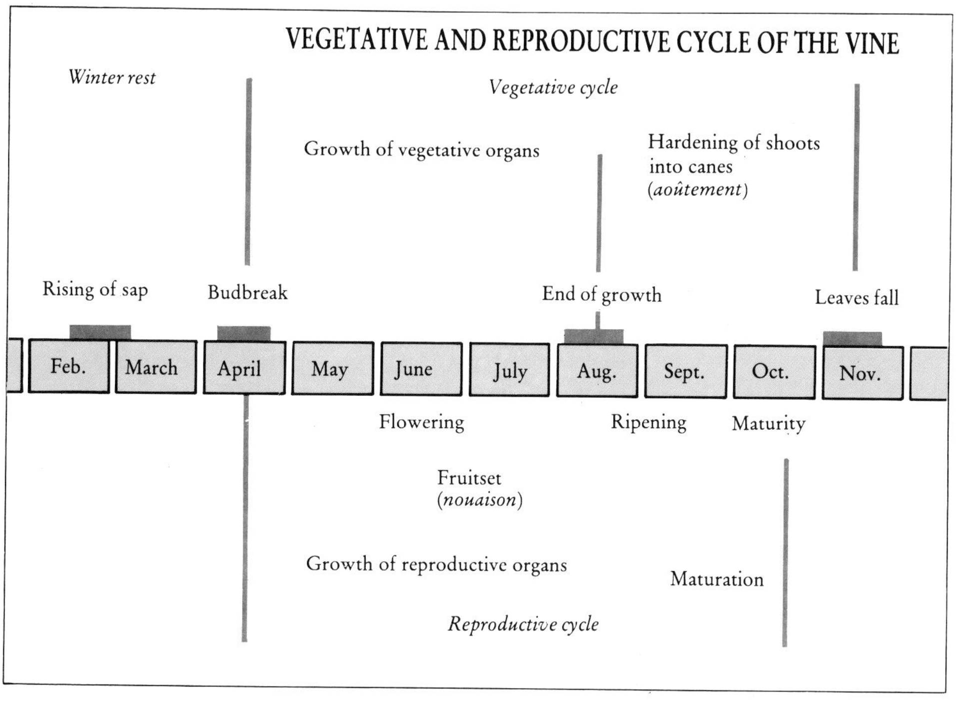

The two cycles influence the fruit quantity and quality of both the current year and the following year.

the remaining 10 per cent. The aromatic components, which play a large role in the organoleptic quality of the finished wine, are very numerous: more than five hundred substances, present in minute amounts, have now been isolated. The phenolic compounds, which have a beneficial effect on the colour of the wine and help point up and preserve the flavour and aroma of the fruit, are located in the grape skin cells. They consist mostly of anthocyanins and tannins.

Establishing a vineyard

Before the phylloxera disaster at the end of the nineteenth century, a plot of vines could be of extraordinary and often immeasurable longevity. Since the plants were not grafted on to alien rootstocks, a dead vine was simply replaced by *provignage* (layering), an operation consisting of placing a shoot from a live neighbouring plant in the soil. The shoot would form roots of its own in the earth, and would then be detached from the mother plant, forming a new and independent vine. The arrangement of vines in the plots was thus completely irregular, but this did not matter since all vineyard work in this period was done by hand.

A vineyard trained **en gobelet** *in the Châteauneuf-du-Pape area. This traditional method of vine training is very common in the South of France.*

Today, plots established with grafted plants have a lifespan of only 30–40 years, which means that several thousand hectares of French vineyards have to be replanted each year. Replanting with grafted vines presents the vineyard owner with a double choice: that of the vine variety, which will depend on the region and the type of wine produced; and that of the variety of grafting stock, which depends mainly on the nature of the soil and the climatic conditions of the area. These choices having been taken, two methods of planting are possible: by using ready-grafted plants produced by a nursery (bench grafting) or, in southern regions, by grafting on to rootstocks put in place the year before (field grafting).

Planting is, of course, preceded by such preparation of the soil as may be necessary: ploughing and levelling of the land, ensuring adequate drainage, fertilizing the soil, and disinfecting the soil to eliminate insect carriers of viral diseases. Before any vines are placed in the earth, an important decision must be taken: how densely to plant and how much space to leave between the rows. Vineyards were traditionally planted densely. Today, because harvesting is increasingly mechanized, the spaces between the rows of vines tend to be made wider, even if this means the actual vines within a row being planted more closely together. But, in vineyards with low-standing vines, such as in Burgundy, the use of *tracteurs enjambeurs* (tractors with a very high chassis that can drive over the rows) has enabled the density of planting to be maintained at about 10,000 vines per hectare. Planting always takes place in the spring, and care is taken to let only one or two green shoots grow on the young vine, one of which will form the trunk of the future vine stock.

Ways of training the vine

The term 'training' includes several operations carried out by the wine grower on the plant: shaping the vine stock, pruning, tying the shoots to a trellis; then various trimming tasks when the vine is in leaf, intended to adjust the balance between foliage and fruit.

The most critical operation is without doubt the winter pruning, which allows the required shape to be given to the vine, allows this shape to be maintained for years and thus allows production to be regularized. During the first two or three years, pruning is undertaken with the aim of creating a satisfactory shape for the vine. After the third year, this formative pruning is only used occasionally, on a corrective basis. It

CORDON DE ROYAT PRUNING

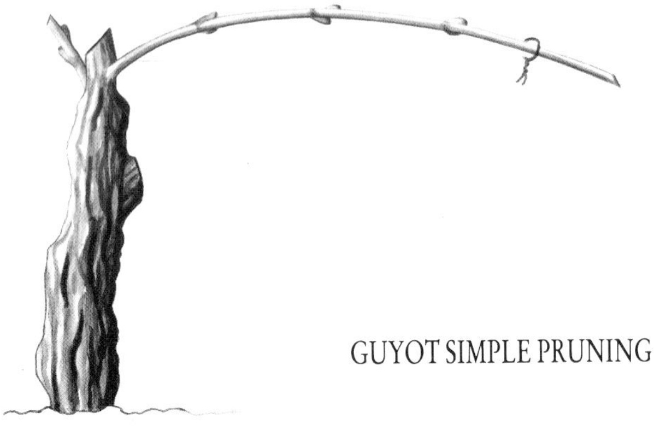

GUYOT SIMPLE PRUNING

Ploughing at Château d'Yquem. This, Sauternes' only Premier Cru Supérieur, no doubt owes some of its excellence to the fact that traditional techniques are still accorded great respect by its owners.

is replaced by pruning to perfect the fruit-bearing of the vine, the principle of which is to leave on the plant only the number of fruitful buds compatible with the desired or imposed level of production, and with the strength and age of the plants. This pruning is only concerned with the shoots and canes from the main trunk and spurs. It is called short pruning (*taille courte*) when only the bases of the canes, with a small number of buds, are left. These short canes have several names: for example, *court-bois, coursons, cots*. When fruit canes of medium length are left on the vine, this is referred to as long pruning (*taille longue*). The canes are then called *longs-bois, baguettes* or *astes*. The type of cut and the number of buds per vine vary from variety to variety, depending on the fertility of the buds, the weight of bunches of grapes, and so on.

Throughout the growing period, trimming and finishing operations complete the pruning done in the winter. In the spring, the wine grower removes the sterile shoots, known as *gourmands*, which have developed at the base of and along the trunk of the vines. During the summer, the ends of the spurs and canes are trimmed and the remaining foliage is raised and reattached to the trellis wires between the training stakes. These operations are vital if tractors and other machinery are to pass easily between the rows. Depending on whether it has been carried out in a moderate or over-rigorous manner, this trimming will have a beneficial or harmful effect on the quality of the harvest. In former days, this work was often completed by removing some of the leaves from around the bunches of grapes.

Winter pruning is the least mechanized of all the tasks in the vineyard. At present, conventional secateurs are generally used. Pneumatic secateurs, not yet common, will eventually allow this work to be done more quickly, and trimming, too, will be carried out mechanically with a clipper. Raising and attaching the foliage is done with limited mechanical help.

Traditionally, the vineyards of many French regions were trained *en gobelet*. The *gobelet* is a small bush with a fairly short, stout trunk, and with divergent branches or spurs, each ending with a short cane or *courson* that has been cut off to leave two buds. Each of these buds will produce a shoot in the spring, and will be fruit-bearing in the summer; one of them, generally the tallest, will then be cut off during the next winter pruning, and the other will be cut to leave two buds for the following year. Vines pruned *en gobelet* are still very common in the South of France.

In northern vineyards planted with vines that produce small bunches of grapes, in order to increase the overall number of buds per vineyard, the wine growers resort either to very dense planting or to long-pruning methods, resulting in many buds on each shoot.

In a hot and sunny climate, vines — like those trained *en gobelet* — do not necessarily have to be tied to stakes or a trellis system. But in vineyards where the climate is cooler, this operation is obligatory if normal maturation is to be achieved. Vines used to be tied only to stakes of wood. Today the stakes are joined by wires, and this development has led to various modifications in the shape of the vines and the pruning systems used. For example, training *en cordon* consists of bending the trunk and training it horizontally at the required height along a wire: this is achieved by formative pruning. The pruning to perfect the fruit-bearing of the vine is then carried out by creating short canes that grow vertically from the trunk and spur leader. *Guyot* training is the term applied to a vine stock pruned to leave a vertical trunk and one or two very short spurs. From these spurs, the wine grower trains a number of long fruit-bearing canes and single short cane, from which a shoot will be maintained to form the base of the following year's growth.

The innumerable other systems of vine pruning and training are often only variants of these three systems: *gobelet, cordon* and *Guyot*.

Since the Second World War, vineyard mechanization has led to a tendency towards taller trunks and greater distances between the rows, along with a simplification of the training systems used. This development has unfortunately given rise to a notable decrease in the quality of the harvests, especially when accompanied by a desire to increase yields. Researchers have recently perfected a method of training using a trellis system which, in cases where large distances between the rows are required, takes into account the imperative of quality. This consists of two trellises, constructed at a slight angle and each supporting one *long-bois* (thus two per vine). This system permits fruit quality at least equivalent to that of traditional training systems to be achieved.

Fertilization

The fertilization problems of the vine are much more difficult to resolve than those of ordinary crops because the volume of earth drawn into interaction with the root system is considerable, and the nature of this interaction varies with the type and depth of the soil and the subsoil.

The vine is one of the least demanding of all cultivated plants in terms of nutrition. For a yield of around 9 tonnes of grapes per hectare, the vine needs about 60g of nitrogen, 20g of phosphoric acid, 75g of potash, 80g of lime and 15g of magnesia. But a large proportion of these items (60 to 70 per cent) is returned to the soil by the fallen leaves, the shoot trimmings and vine shoot mulch after the pruning. Unfortunately, wine makers, especially in prosperous wine-producing regions, use too much fertilizer. The resulting excess of vine vigour often gives rise to *coulure* (flower abortion) and is one cause of grey rot (botrytis). Nevertheless, in most cases the vine does need a degree of balanced fertilizing, adapted to specific vineyard conditions and the type of fruit required.

For centuries, manure was the only source of nutrition for the vine. This is no longer the case today. Manure and other organic enriching agents contribute towards keeping the humus in the soil at a suitable level. Green manure (growing plant matter ploughed back into the soil) does not seem to have this property. Humus has a positive effect on the nourishment of vines and on the structural stability of the soil and its capacity to retain water. In the absence of any organic enriching agent and in a temperate climate, the rate of degradation of the soil is in the order of 2 per cent per annum.

Some experts consider that the improvement of the level of organic matter in wine-producing soil is superfluous, except in sandy or acidic soils. But the most widespread view is that the wine grower should see to it that a suitable level of organic matter is maintained in the soil.

Pruning allows the required shape to be given to the vine stock. Of all the tasks in the vineyard, this is the least mechanized.

Soil maintenance techniques

For thousands of years, hoeing and harrowing the soil between the vines was the only maintenance work carried out in the vineyards. This work was necessary to prevent the development of weeds, prejudicial to the growth of the vine.

To maintain the soil in a vineyard today, the wine grower can choose between mechanical, chemical or biological techniques, in the form of ploughing, chemical weeding or controlled planting of grass.

Ploughing is still widely used. It consists of earthing up the vine stocks before the winter, unearthing them in the spring and hoeing as many times as is needed to control the weeds.

Chemical weeding has been in use since 1958. A thorough application of this technique results in the total weeding of the soil, i.e. 'non-cultivation'. This process, which is more economical than ploughing, is becoming ever more widely used, especially since it seems not to have any negative repercussions on the quality of the soil. The herbicides used for this task are not persistent. This non-cultivation also makes it possible to maintain vineyards that cannot be treated mechanically, such as those on steep slopes which generally produce excellent wine, in good condition.

Another technique used for maintaining the soil is the

controlled planting of grass. This is popular at the present time because it is an excellent means of countering erosion — itself on the increase as a consequence of vineyard mechanization. In addition, it also allows the excessive vigour of vine stocks in moist climates to be reduced. It is also favourable to the organic content of the soil. In hot regions lacking a plentiful supply of water, it is obviously not possible to resort to this practice.

Diseases in the vineyard

Until the middle of the 19th century, the defence of the vineyard against the parasites so familiar today did not concern wine growers. Much, however, used to be written about the damage caused by snails, thrushes and badgers!

Among the diseases that affect vines today, we may first distinguish the cryptogamic ones — those that are caused by fungi. The first big attack of cryptogamic disease in French vineyards followed the introduction from America, via England, of oidium (powdery mildew). This fungus begins its development on the vine's new season's growth from budbreak onwards, and eventually attacks the skin of the grapes, which split, exposing the pips. The fungicide used against it is sulphur, either as a powder or as a spray. But to be effective, treatments for oidium and other cryptogamic diseases should be early and regular enough to assume a preventive function.

Systemic fungicides having a moderately curative effect have, however, recently become available. They are all effective against downy mildew (peronospora), which also originated in America, and which was found in France for the first time in 1878. This parasite is more difficult to eradicate than the preceding one and attacks the new season's growth, in particular the leaves and the young berries, through the stomata. The grapes turn brown and dry out, producing a poor quality harvest. The first fungicide used against downy mildew was bordeaux mixture (*bouillie bordelaise*), based on copper sulphate and slaked lime. Today, organic and organocupric fungicides and systemic products are used. The other major cryptogamic diseases of the vine are phomopsis (or dead arm) and *rougeau*, also known as *rougeot* or brenner (*Pseudopeziza tracheiphila*).

Grey rot, produced by the fungus *Botrytis cinerea*, is the most feared parasitic disease in Europe. It can affect all the green growth of the vine, but it is particularly harmful to bunches of grapes after they start to ripen. In hot and humid weather, it can quickly destroy a large part of the harvest. The development of grey rot (botrytis) is favoured by an excess of vine vigour, the crowding together of foliage, and damage caused by inclement climatic conditions or by insect parasites such as grape worms. It might be described as the plague of modern wine making, as phylloxera was of late 19th-century wine making. On the other hand, with favourable climatic conditions and on certain white grape varieties, late-season *pourriture grise* (grey rot) can improve the quality of the wine. It is then called *pourriture noble* (noble rot). When grapes thus affected are vinified, they produce strong, sweet wines of great subtlety, such as Sauternes, Monbazillac, Alsace Sélection de Grains Nobles, and the *moelleux* and *doux* wines of Anjou and Touraine.

Among animal parasites, apart from phylloxera — a gall-living and root-living aphid which has been successfully countered by the use of grafting stock — the caterpillars of small lepidopterous insects, or grape worms, must be mentioned. There are also minuscule ticks and mites like the erineum mite, and red and yellow spider mites.

Finally, viral diseases also attack the vine. These ailments are transmitted by the grafting process. By upsetting the various physiological functions of the vine, some of them, such as grape fan-leaf virus (*court-noué*) and grape leaf-roll virus (*enroulement*) can be very harmful to the yield and longevity of the vines, as well as to the sugar content of the grapes. Affected vines cannot be cured and the only way to curb such diseases is the preventive method, i.e. by selecting plant material that has been proved healthy by various virological tests. This is the reason why the marketing of vine plant material is subject to strict European regulations. The use of registered clones is the best guarantee against viral attacks of this sort.

Bunch of grapes attacked by oidium (powdery mildew). The grapes are covered with a grey mould, and dry out.

Downy mildew on a leaf. This fungus attacks the young grapes after the leaves.

Court-noué *(grape fan-leaf virus), a viral disease transmitted by grafting, causes the leaves to become discoloured.*

Under certain conditions and on certain varieties, grey rot (botrytis) can become pourriture noble *(noble rot).*

The Grape Harvest

The grape harvest marks the point of transition between vine work and wine work. It provides an opportunity for wine growers to see their efforts rewarded by the quality of the harvest. Each bunch holds within its grapes the memory of the year that has passed . . .

Manual grape harvest at Irancy. This very old vineyard area in Auxerre produces attractively coloured, full-bodied and generous red and rosé wines.

It is not easy to grow a quality grape, one that is rich in useful substances: sugars, extracts, aromatic components and colouring matter. A large number of factors come into play from the moment the vineyard is planted. In particular, the quality of the vine, the graft and grafting stock must be checked and care must be taken to train, manure, prune and trim the vine correctly. In addition, a patient, long-term struggle must be waged against pests likely to destroy the crop or the vines themselves. In order to obtain good grapes, the yield must almost always be limited. Finally, any rough or indifferent handling of the crop must be prevented, the aim being to obtain grapes that are in perfect condition on arrival at the cellar.

Split grapes have a doubly negative consequence for the quality of the wine. On the one hand, the must becomes oxidized and loses its freshness; on the other, the solid matter — stems, skins, pips — may begin to disintegrate, releasing stalky and bitter-tasting substances. Ideal harvesting is therefore that in which whole, sound grapes in a perfect state of maturity are gathered. The grape will then be able to offer all its quality potential, and an expert wine maker will be able to put this to good use throughout the vinification process.

The date of the start of the grape harvest

In order that the grape harvest should proceed as smoothly and swiftly as possible, it is important to be able to fix its starting date in advance. The number of harvesters and the period during which they will be required both have to be defined fairly early. This date can vary by more than a month from one year to another, depending on the precocity of the vintage.

The wine grower has several means at his disposal in order to determine this date. These are:

▷ the relative earliness or lateness of each of the phenological stages of the vine;

▷ grape maturity checks carried out by various regional laboratories;

▷ individual tests and measurements taken by the wine grower himself for each of his plots.

The phenological stages of the vine

The vine develops in successive, climate-related steps called phenological stages, beginning with flowering and proceeding to maturity by way of *nouaison* (transformation of flowers to berries) and *véraison* (when the grapes acquire colour, marking the beginning of ripening). Each stage may take place over a certain length of time. The flowers, for example, do not all appear at the same time. Samples are therefore taken throughout a plot of vines, and the flowering date is considered to be the day when 50 per cent of the bunches have flowered. (In certain cases, it may be necessary to harvest a plot in two sweeps rather than one. The circumstances provoking this are often linked with atmospheric conditions at the time of flowering.)

The point at which each of the phenological stages occurs depends on diverse factors such as the precocity of the vines, the local climate, the particular conditions of the year, and various factors involved in vineyard cultivation. The determination of each phenological stage is therefore a complex matter, requiring observations made in each individual vineyard plot. On the basis of the data thus obtained, the harvest date can be forecast, often by application of the 100-day rule. This may be expressed as follows: the grapes reach maturity 100 days after flowering. This 100-day rule permits the probable starting date of the harvest to be forecast in June, the period of flowering.

The date may be confirmed later when the grapes start to ripen. From half-ripeness (*demi-véraison*) to maturity, a period of 30 to 50 days elapses. In a large number of cases, it often turns out that 110, 120 or event more days are required between flowering and maturity. But the meticulous determination of the time of flowering, and then of the point of *demi-véraison*, allows the wine grower to fix for himself the dates of his harvests with a fairly high degree of accuracy.

Maturity checks

Public or agricultural union laboratories in the wine-producing regions conduct a maturity check each year. Representative samples of grapes are taken from certain plots. The sugar and acid content of the must obtained from them is measured. The various grape varieties grown in the region are checked in this way in several places. Averages are then established for each variety and these are converted into graphs called maturity curves. The probable evolution of maturity can then be extrapolated and the harvesting periods for the region can be fixed on the basis of this data.

For a particular grape variety, the trajectory of the maturity curve is the same every year. The only things to change, of course, are the date at which each maturity stage is reached, and the exact levels attained. The starting date of the curve is budbreak. This date is important because the earlier it occurs, the more rapidly will maturity be reached.

A 'maturity index' is defined by means of maturity curves. In order to establish this, the ratio of sugar to total acidity in the grape must be calculated. A high index figure is a sign of advanced maturity.

These figures are used by the wine growers' organizations and the INAO to establish the *ban des vendanges* (annual start of the grape harvest). In the past this expression used to refer to the date before which harvesting the grapes was forbidden. Nowadays it means the date from which chaptalization is allowed. Obviously, harvesting grapes earlier than this date is not forbidden, but it is not advisable since the level of natural grape sugar is then too low for quality wine to be made from them.

Individual measures

Wine growers can monitor the maturity of the grapes themselves. All they have to do is take some sample grapes from each vineyard, avoiding the ends of the rows, where samples are unrepresentative. The grapes should be taken from several vines and from several places in the row, from high and low bunches and from the interior and the exterior of the bunches. The grapes are reduced to must in a hand press, then pressed a second time (a process known as *rebêche*). The sugar content of the must is measured with a *mustimètre* or a refractometer. The wine grower can then refer to the statistics and advice provided by the local wine-growing authorities, and decide the dates and order of harvesting of the various vineyards in the property.

MATURITY CURVES FOR THE CHENIN BLANC IN TOURAINE

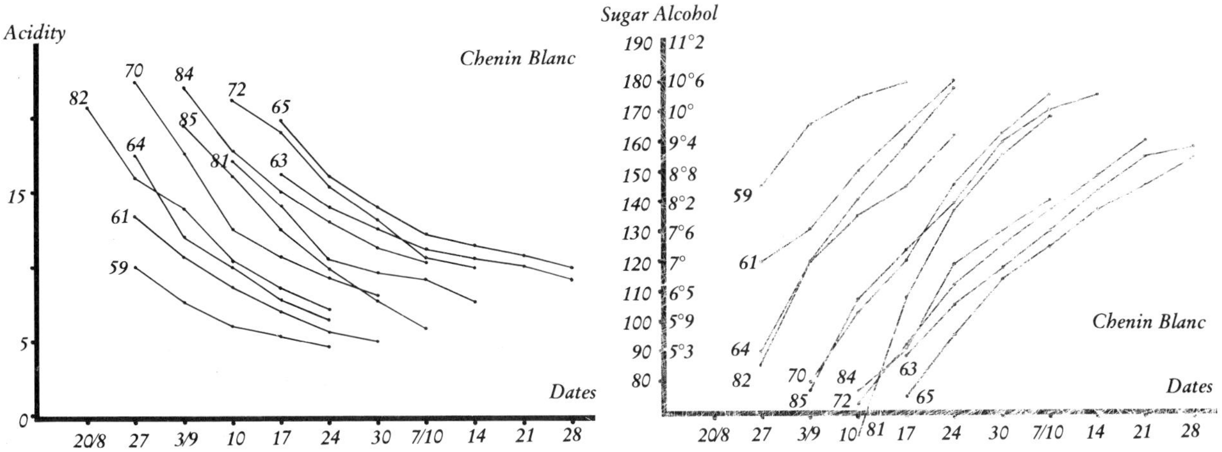

MANUAL HARVESTING

In the last few years, mechanical harvesting has been rapidly replacing manual harvesting. Unfortunately, this incontrovertible progress on the technical front does not always have a beneficial effect on the quality of the finished wine. For this reason manual harvesting is usually desirable wherever it is economically viable. It remains indispensable for plots that have to be harvested in several sweeps, for harvesting whole grapes, and for wines made by carbonic maceration.

Harvesting in sweeps

This is done for two different purposes:

▷ either to separate healthy grapes from spoiled grapes, whatever the type of wine to be made;

▷ or to select grapes that have reached a desired state of maturity or over-maturity in order to produce rich, sweet wines.

This second purpose can involve the harvesters going through the whole vineyard anything from two to six times. In straightforward cases, the first sweep allows the grapes that have been most completely affected by *pourriture noble* (noble rot) to be harvested, in order to produce a very rich must. The results of the second sweep will provide a wine of medium dry type. Sometimes, when only sweet wine is going to be produced, the sweeps are repeated at intervals until the first frosts in early winter, so that only grapes affected by *pourriture noble* will be harvested. This is the case for the best Sauternes, Monbazillac, Vouvray and Montlouis.

Harvesting whole grapes

The vinification rules for champagne require the grapes to be harvested whole. The pressing of white juice from red grapes — such as Pinot Noir and Meunier — for champagne means that any breaking of the skins and consequent maceration would result in stained must. This requirement has been extended to other sparkling wines, notably the Crémants of Alsace, Burgundy and the Loire.

A grape picker near Esclauzels in the Cahors area. Traditional wine-growing methods are deeply rooted in the South West of France.

A **hotteur** *at Riquewihr in Alsace. The small, often steep vineyards of this region are not suited to mechanical harvesting.*

Carbonic maceration

Complete, uncrushed bunches of grapes are essential for wines vinified by carbonic maceration as this process requires fermentation to take place within the grape itself in an anaerobic environment, to produce wines of fruit and aroma. This winemaking method is limited to the production of red wines for drinking young, such as Beaujolais Nouveau or Côtes du Rhône Primeur wines.

The logistics of manual harvesting

The harvest requires a large work force. Everyone involved in the harvest plays a specific role, and among those always required are:

▷ *vendangeurs* (grape harvesters), who pick the grapes;
▷ *porteurs* (carriers or porters), who carry the grapes to the end of the rows or to the collection point from where they will be taken to the cellar;
▷ people responsible for transporting the grapes to the place of vinification;
▷ a foreman to coordinate the work.

Picking the grapes

The harvesters, or *coupeurs* (cutters), generally work in pairs and take grapes from each side of a row. In former times, a *serpette* (pruning knife) — a short, sharp instrument with a crescent-shaped blade — was used for cutting the bunches. This had the disadvantage of causing the vine to shake as it was used, which could make the ripest and most sugar-charged grapes fall to the ground, leaving the harvester to gather bunches containing only those grapes firmly attached to their stalks, and therefore less completely ripe. Later, the *épinette* — secateurs with straight blades — was used; and then secateurs with curved blades, called a *vendangette*, much smaller than ordinary pruning secateurs. Nowadays robust scissors with rounded tips are also used.

The work of the grape picker. The vendangette, *secateurs with curved blades, has replaced the* serpette *or pruning knife of former days.*

Carrying the bénaton *— a traditional grape-harvesting basket — at Aloxe-Corton in Burgundy.*

The cut grapes are put in receptacles of varying shapes and capacities. Formerly, only wicker baskets (called *vendangerots* or *vendangeois*) and wooden baskets (called *baillots* or *bastiots*), which could hold 6kg to 10kg of grapes, were used. Buckets made of wood (*seilles*), and now metal or plastic, with a similar capacity to the baskets, are also used. Finally, some wine growers use wooden boxes or plastic crates, which can be used both for gathering and transporting the grapes. This technique reduces the physical handling of the bunches to a minimum and is therefore recommended if it is desirable to keep the grapes whole until they reach the place of vinification.

When the harvest is carried out with baskets or buckets, they must be emptied into larger receptacles to be transported back to the cellar. The harvested grapes are therefore collected by the *hotteurs* (also called *porte-hottes, hotteux* or *brantards*): men with large wooden or plastic hods strapped to their backs. Each man carries his *hotte* to the edge of the vineyard, where he pours its contents into the transport containers. Three to five *coupeurs* are allocated to one *hotteur*.

In Champagne, it was traditional to have *porteurs de petits paniers* (small-basket carriers) whose role was to carry the grape pickers' baskets to the end of the row where women sorted and cleaned the grapes on a wicker rack. In this way, the damaged grapes were removed and only the best quality grapes were put in large wicker baskets to be transported back to the press. In other regions, the bunches of grapes brought to the edge of the row are gently pressed into wooden transport containers with a pestle-like instrument. The crop thus takes up less room and more of it can be transported back to the cellar at one time. This method, though traditional, is not advisable, because many grapes will disintegrate, macerate and become oxidized if treated in this way.

Transport

Crates and boxes serve for both gathering and transporting the grapes. They are often carried on pallets and are handled by

Transporting the harvest in comportes *(wooden tubs) at Limoux in the Aude* département.

means of fork-lift trucks, or trailers that can pass over the vines. They keep to a minimum the amount of handling the grapes have to undergo between vine and cellar. A large number of detachable transport containers are also available. Their quality depends largely on their depth, as grapes piled to a height of more than about 50cm cause juice to be expressed prematurely. The choice of container depth depends also on how resistant the grapes are to being squashed and therefore on the grape variety and degree of maturity. These detachable receptacles can be divided into those that can be handled manually and those that require mechanical handling.

Those that can be handled manually have a capacity of no more than 100 litres. They are all traditional wicker or wooden receptacles, or modern equivalents made of plastic: *paniers mannequins* (Champagne), *banastes* or *banastons* (Midi), *bastes, comportes* (Gironde), *caques, bénatons, panusiaux, benesras, ballonges* (Burgundy), *ancets, gueule-bées, cuettes, cuettons* (Val de Loire), and so on.

Receptacles of a capacity of more than 100 litres must be handled by mechanized means — winches, hoists and lifts. Transportation is then provided by trailers. Sometimes the grapes are tipped directly into the trailer. This can be a simple tipper trailer lined with a canvas sheet, or it can be more elaborate, specialized equipment. Some tipper trailers exist, for example, that can pass over the rows of vines so that the harvesters can pour their grapes directly into them. Varieties of trailers and skips have been produced that enable the grapes to be gravity-fed or mechanically fed into the press, the crusher-stemmer or the reception container. Some models are raised by means of jacks, while others are equipped with a screw-feeding device and sometimes even with a pump, both of which greatly facilitate delivery at the cellar.

Grape harvest celebrations

The grape harvest begins and ends with all sorts of festivities, from a simple communal meal to great traditional *fêtes*. The custom of a communal meal or banquet used to be very widespread; the Paulée in Burgundy and the Gerbaude in the South West are survivors of the tradition. Some ceremonial *fêtes*, like the Accabailles in the Sauternes region, include a procession decked with flowers. Finally, it is traditional, on the last day of the harvest, for the grape pickers to accompany the final cartload of grapes back to the cellar or place of vinification. These festivities, which reward the hard work done by the pickers, take place in a particularly warm atmosphere and remain vivid in the memories of everyone who takes part in them.

The announcement of the start of the grape harvest at Champlitte in the Haute-Saône. At the beginning of September, the gourmet piqueur *(chief wine-taster) and his two* garde-vigniers *(vine wardens), in 18th-century costume, announce the start of the harvest.*

MECHANICAL HARVESTING

Machines at work in the vineyards of Bordeaux. From planting through to harvesting, modern vineyard work is more and more extensively mechanized.

Between the vines of ancient times, which were cultivated *en foule* ('in a crowd'), and those of today, which stand in battalions of perfect rows, many changes — even revolutions — have occurred. Among the latter one would have to include mechanization of harvesting . . .

For a long time, vineyard mechanization was mainly limited to the maintenance of the soil, to vine upkeep, and to grape transport. It is only since the 1960s that thought has been given to ways of attaining partial or total mechanization of grape gathering, with the ultimate aim of achieving a more complete, as well as more economical, harvest. A number of mechanical barriers had to be crossed before the grape-harvesting machine became a reality — as it now is.

The grape-harvesting machine

A grape-harvesting machine consists of:

▷ a self-propelling or towed chassis that can pass over the top of the vines;

▷ a mechanism, called the *tête de récolte* ('harvesting head'), which removes the grapes from the vines;

▷ a conveyor belt made of pliable plastic, pressed into the form of interlocking plates or cups, to collect the crop as it is gathered and to stop grapes falling around the vines;

▷ a mechanism to carry the grapes to collection hoppers;

▷ a system for sifting out leaves and pieces of vine (by centrifugal aspiration).

The grapes are usually detached from the vine by means of a system based on 'lateral shaking'. The bunches of grapes are subjected to a succession of alternating transverse movements, through the intermediary of 'shakers', thus causing them to fall from their stalks.

A large number of machines, of varying degrees of sophistication, are now available to vineyard owners. There are three main types: self-propelling, towed and semi-suspended models. The latest trend seems to be towards relatively small, simple and versatile machines. In fact, it is now possible to dismantle the chassis of a mechanical grape-harvester and to transform it into a machine for pruning or carrying out other treatments required by the vine.

Working the grape-harvesting machine

The arrival of the grape-harvesting machine has to a certain extent disrupted French wine-growing practices. It has often been necessary, for example, to replant or restructure a vineyard in order to suit the machine. But at the present moment practically all French vineyards are capable of being harvested mechanically. The machines can harvest bunches as low as 15 or 20cm from the ground, and their use poses no problems to the various high-wired training systems, which can be up to two metres high. In vineyards when the vines are grown *en gobelet*, however, mechanical harvesting is only satisfactory when the vines have well-defined and regular characteristics: a tall and solid trunk and widely spaced branches so that the shakers can explore them thoroughly.

Mechanical harvesting can also have an effect on the techniques of soil maintenance because, even in heavy rain, the machine must be able to operate smoothly. For this to be the case, chemical weeding must be practised between the rows.

The grape-harvesting machine is ill-suited to mediocre or sloppy vine growing. To mechanically harvest a good quality crop, the vineyard must be in a perfect state of upkeep. The development of grey rot (botrytis), for example, causes considerable problems because it results in the loss of large amounts of juice during the shaking process as the crop is picked. The foliage must also be in perfect condition so that it does not become detached during the harvest. If too many leaves get into the machine and become impregnated with must, then the aspirators have to rotate faster than is desirable in order to expel them, with the result that some of the grapes are expelled at the same time.

Mechanical harvesting in the Muscadet region. When the machine hopper is full, the grapes are poured into a waiting skip at the end of the row.

The quality of the wine

Wine makers have the obvious and fundamental task of maximizing the quality of their wines. From experiments conducted by oenologists over a 16-year period in various French regions, it seems that mechanical harvesting, when properly carried out, does not result in any qualitative or quantitative degradation of the crop, and it is practically impossible to detect any significant difference, on the basis of the means of harvesting, between two otherwise identical wines. This is mostly due to constant progress in the design of the machines.

For example, good quality stainless steel is always used today for the mechanical parts that come into contact with the crop. Similarly, reception and transport systems have been developed so as to minimize any physical damage to the grapes and to shorten the path travelled mechanically by the grapes. Some reception hoppers are equipped with a double bottom consisting of a perforated grille, so that such juice as is expressed can be separated as soon as possible from the rest of

SEMI-SUSPENDED GRAPE-HARVESTING MACHINE WITH ANTI-GRAPE-DROP PLATE SYSTEM

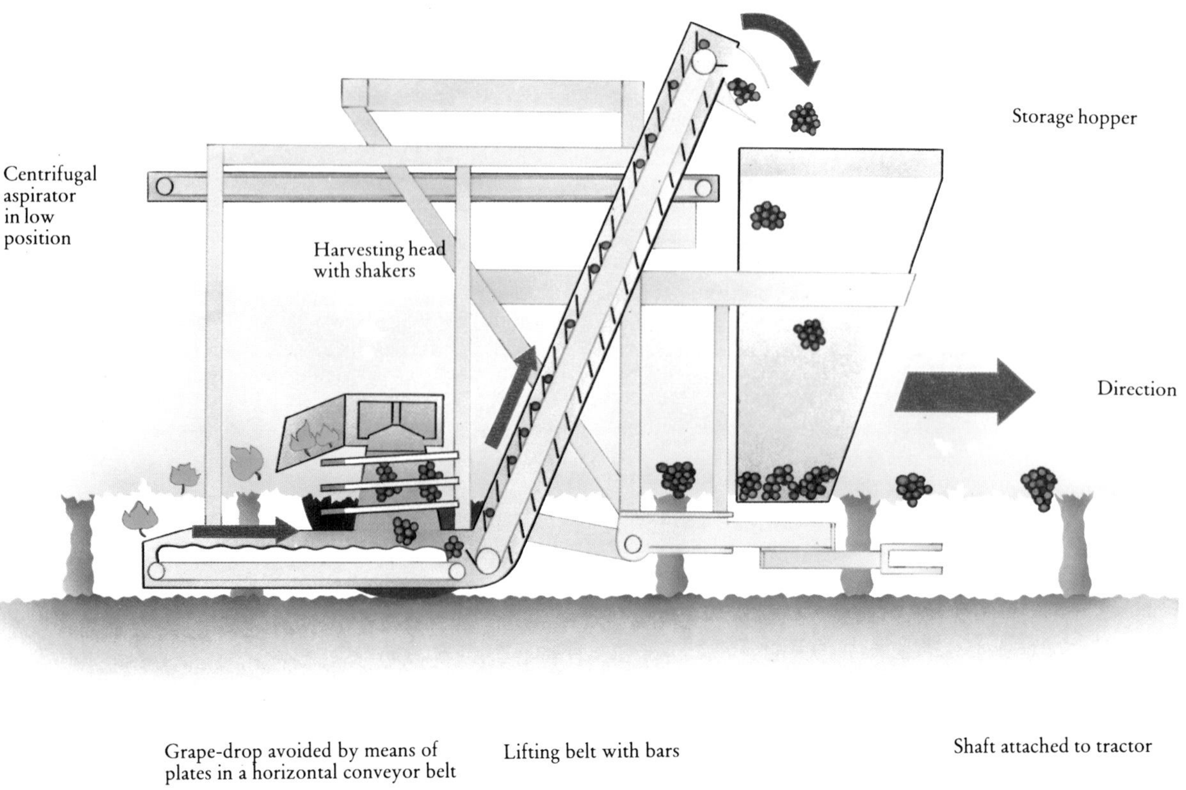

the crop. There are also detachable containers available in which the crop is stored, without having to be transferred to other containers, until it reaches the cellar.

In certain cases, in particular when white wine is to be produced, developments have been taken further, so as to initiate part of the vinification process on the machine. A draining rack and a press, arranged on the harvester, allow the must to be extracted minutes after harvesting.

Red wines made from mechanically harvested crops are generally more highly coloured than those from vineyards picked by hand. But from an organoleptic point of view, as already noted, it is very difficult to deduce the means of harvesting. Many red wines produced by mechanical harvesting have won prestigious medals in well-known competitions.

For white wines, the risks run in harvesting mechanically are greater, but by taking certain precautions in order to limit the effects of oxidation and maceration, quality should not suffer.

The development of mechanization

The mechanization of the grape harvest has developed very rapidly in France; between 1971, the year in which it first appeared, and 1986, more than 8,000 machines have been acquired by wine growers. Apart from Champagne and Beaujolais, where legislation and vinification practices require the harvesting of unbroken grapes, and the Sauternes region, where the harvesting of rot-affected grapes has to be done manually, practically all the wine-producing regions of France have been converted to this method of harvesting.

The Cognac region is definitely the most highly mechanized. It is followed by the Bordeaux region and the regions of the west of France (Val de Loire, Anjou, Muscadet), as well as the southeast region, notably the Côtes du Rhône. But the huge vineyard areas of Languedoc are not very highly mechanized yet, because of the prevalence of the *en gobelet* system of training, ill-suited to mechanical harvesting, and used in 75 to 80 per cent of this area. The great increase in mechanized harvesting elsewhere in France is no doubt linked to the financial savings it achieves.

The number of manual harvesters that can be replaced by a mechanical harvester depends on the category of the machine and the type of vineyard, but it is somewhere between 30 and 100 people. In other words, a machine can now do in one week what it used to take 50 people three weeks to accomplish.

Mechanized grape harvesting has thus cut operating costs greatly. This should not, however, obscure the fact that, for its use to be beneficial, certain fundamental wine-growing and oenological rules must be respected.

GRAPE-HARVESTING MACHINES SOLD IN FRANCE
from 1971 to 1985

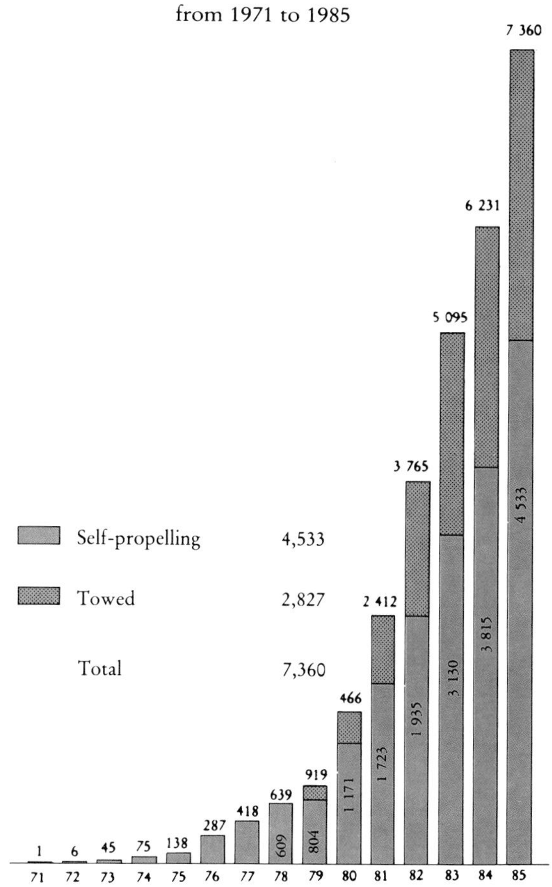

Towed harvesting machine.

Self-propelling harvesting machine.

Cabardès

See Côtes du Cabardès et de l'Orbiel.

Cabernet d'Anjou

This *appellation*, classed as an AOC by decree on 9 May 1964, covers a surface area of 3,000ha. Annual production approaches 135,000hl of rosé wine, made exclusively from the Cabernet Franc and Cabernet Sauvignon grape varieties. The production zone extends over all the areas designated for the *appellation d'origine contrôlée* Anjou.

These faintly amber-coloured rosé wines are medium sweet to sweet in type. Their alcohol level is between 11° and 12°, and they contain between 17g and 34g of unfermented sugar per litre. They are well balanced, with a good intensity of flavour, and fruity scents characteristic of the two Cabernet varieties. They mature well in bottle.

Cabernet de Saumur *See* the following page.

Cabernet Franc

Synonyms: *Breton* or *Plant Breton, Véron* or *Véronais* in the Loire valley, *Bouchy* at Madiran, *Bouchet* or *Gros Bouschet* in Saint-Émilion, *Gros Cabernet, Carmenet* and *Grosse Vidure* in the Médoc, *Carbouet* in the Bazas region, *Capbreton Rouge* and *Plant des Sables* in the Landes.

Growing tips felty white with carmine margins.

Young leaves downy with bronze patches, underside of blade felty, carmine.

Bunch of Cabernet Franc grapes. This variety is grown on 26,000ha in France.

Leaves orbicular, medium light green, glossy, smooth, deeply five-lobed, the lateral sinuses acute and narrow at bases, sometimes with a tooth at the base of the sinus; petiolar sinus narrowly lyrate; dentation narrow, convex; underside of blade arachnoid in tufts.

Green shoots ribbed, pale green, with light red striations on the side exposed to the sun; tendrils fleshy, fairly large. Bunches small, cylindrical-conical, loose, sometimes winged; grapes small, spherical, blue-black, thin skinned, with sweet, slightly astringent juice; ripening period: second epoch.

The Cabernet Franc is more robust than the Cabernet Sauvignon and, like it, requires long pruning because it is a small producer. When pruned long, it has produced good results in Languedoc (in Aude), proving itself to be both productive and providing wine of good quality, deep in colour and with an alcohol content of 11.5°. Its budbreak is midseason, preceding that of the Cabernet Sauvignon by about ten days. It is susceptible to downy mildew, oidium (powdery mildew), black rot and grey rot (botrytis); its leaves may carry (harmless) phylloxera galls.

Cabernet Franc wines are less highly coloured than those made from the Cabernet Sauvignon, and are less rich in tannin, so they therefore mature more rapidly. At Bourgueil in the Loire valley, highly perfumed wines reminiscent of raspberry fruit are obtained from this variety, while at nearby Chinon, this perfume is more discreet, recalling the scent of violets.

Thirty-four registered clones have been approved, the most widespread being numbers 331 (the most productive), 210 (aromatically pleasing but only modestly productive), and 393 (producing a full-bodied, very well-balanced and aromatic wine). Cabernet Franc has been classed as 'recommended' in several *départements* of the South West, including Gironde and Dordogne, and it is also grown in the Loire valley and in the Midi. It occupies a surface area of more than 26,000ha, winning it 9th place among French varieties.

Half of the vines are in the Bordeaux region and the surrounding *départements*: Gironde (10,000ha), Dordogne (1,080ha), Lot-et-Garonne, etc. Cabernet Franc is included in almost all the red AOCs of this area: Médoc, Graves, Saint-Émilion, Bergerac . . .

The Loire valley has almost 10,000ha of it, mainly in Maine-et-Loire and Indre-et-Loire for the AOCs of Bourgueil, Chinon, Saumur-Champigny and Touraine, and the Cabernet rosé wines.

Plantings of Cabernet Franc in the Mediterranean region are of recent date, but already exceed 500ha.

Cabernet Franc leaf, seen from below.

Cabernet Franc green shoot.

A Saumur vineyard.

Cabernet de Saumur

This *appellation*, classed by decree on 9 May 1964, covers an area of 40ha, planted with Cabernet Franc and Cabernet Sauvignon vines. Annual production is in the order of 2,000hl. The potential production zone covered by the AOC regulation is much larger than the actual area of present plantings. It stretches over Maine-et-Loire and Vienne, covering a total of 39 communes.

Cabernet de Saumur is slightly softer than Cabernet d'Anjou, but is otherwise similar in character.

Cabernet Sauvignon

Synonyms: *Bidure* (*bois dur*, meaning 'hard wood' in Occitan dialect), *Vidure*, *Petite Vidure*, *Bouchet* at Saint-Émilion, *Marchoupet* at Castillon-la-Bataille, *Carbouet* in the Bazas region, a name it shares with the Cabernet Franc there.

Growing tips crook-shaped, very downy white with dark carmine margins.

Young leaves downy, bullate, the edges of the blade having a wine-red or dark garnet tinge.

Leaves orbicular, medium sized, dark green, bullate, glossy, deeply five-lobed, with sinuses with concave bases, the upper sinuses having overlapping edges and the lower ones generally open; petiolar sinus lyrate, closed or with overlapping edges and often with a naked base (in which the bottom of the sinus is restricted by the junction of the veins); dentation wide, convex, not very plentiful; underside of blade downy in tufts, lightly pubescent; petiole purplish.

Green shoots ribbed, light green, slightly brownish at the base; tendrils small, thin.

Bunches small to medium sized, cylindrical-conical, winged; grapes spherical, small, black, very bloomy (the bloom is blue hued), skin thick, hard, with very firm, crisp flesh with a particular and characteristic flavour, reminiscent of both violets and wild fruit such as sorb apples, astringent taste; ripening period: second epoch, late.

The Cabernet Sauvignon has an upright habit and late budbreak; it is very susceptible to oidium (powdery mildew) and phomopsis, a little less susceptible to downy mildew, and fairly resistent to grey rot (botrytis), thanks to the thickness of the grape skins. Its leaves sometimes carry erineum mite galls and (harmless) phylloxera galls. It is the finest of all French

Leaf of the Cabernet Sauvignon vine, the main grape variety of the Médoc.

'noble' grape varieties. To obtain good quality, it is necessary to graft it on to a weak grafting stock: Riparia Gloire du Montpellier, 101–14, or 420A in slightly calcareous soils. The yield must be less than 40hl/ha and, in these conditions, highly coloured, very tannic wines are obtained, which need several years' cask ageing so as to allow the characteristic aromas of the variety to develop: these are a mixture of violet, blackcurrant and green pepper.

In the Médoc, Cabernet Sauvignon grapes are never vinified on their own, but they can make up 75 per cent of the total blend, the remainder being provided by the Cabernet Franc, the Merlot or the Petit Verdot.

Plantings of this vine are at present being greatly increased, with 20 million graft-cuttings in 1988, placing it in 4th position according to nursery demand. Twenty-four registered clones have been approved, two of which are very productive and are used in the Midi (numbers 15 and 169), and two more of which are of average production, but are rich in anthrocyanins and hence better suited to the Bordeaux region (numbers 337 and 341).

Like the Cabernet Franc, the Cabernet Sauvignon has been classed as 'recommended' in numerous *départements* of the South West, the Loire valley and the Midi. In 1980, it was grown on 23,000ha. Plantings are approaching 30,000ha today (putting it in 8th position among French varieties). In the South West it is grown on 20,000ha, with plantings highest in Gironde (17,500ha), followed by Dordogne, Lot-et-Garonne, Gers, Landes and the *départements* of the Pyrenees. Cabernet Sauvignon forms the basis of many AOC red wines of this region: Médoc, Graves, Bergerac, Côtes de Duras, etc.

Then there is a centre-west group of plantings in the *départements* of the Loire valley, contributing to the AOC red wines of Anjou, Bourgueil, Chinon, Saumur and Touraine, as well as to the AOC Cabernet d'Anjou and Cabernet de Saumur rosé wines (in combination with the Cabernet Franc).

The Cabernet Sauvignon has only recently been introduced to the Mediterranean region. There are therefore many new plantations in this area intended for regional Vin de Pays *appellations*, as well as for sale as varietal wines.

Cabrières *See* Coteaux du Languedoc.

Cacaboue

Synonyms: *Cacabois, Saint-Péray, Grosse Jacquère.*

This is a Savoy vine variety that is cultivated in vineyards beside the Lac du Bourget, but has not been classified.

Cadillac

The *appellation d'origine contrôlée* Cadillac, created by decree on 10 August 1973, can be used for white wines made from the grapes of delimited plots in 18 communes within the Premières Côtes de Bordeaux zone of the Bordeaux region. These white wines may only come from the Sémillon, Sauvignon Blanc and Muscadelle grape varieties. The grapes should be overripe, and they are harvested in several sweeps. The must should contain a minimum of 221g of sugar per litre and the wines should have a minimum potential alcohol content of 13°, with at least 12° of alcohol and 1° of potential further alcohol in unfermented sugar. The residual sugar content should be no less than 18g per litre.

Since 1980, sweet white wines from Cadillac must also obtain a certificate of quality from an official tasting panel before being marketed.

In 1985, only 80ha were devoted to the Cadillac *appellation*, and 3,279hl were produced, 404hl of which were made by a local cooperative. Though the wine makers of Cadillac consider that they produce the best wines of the Premières Côtes de Bordeaux, the *appellation* is not at present in great demand. It is always difficult to introduce a new name to the market, and for the moment most producers prefer to continue selling their wines under the broader regional *appellation* of Premières Côtes de Bordeaux.

Bunch of Cabernet Sauvignon grapes.

Cahors

The Cahors vineyards were established at the time of the Roman conquest. For a long time, the wine of Cahors was greatly appreciated by the English, who modified the course of the river Lot to allow it to be transported to Bordeaux.

Like other wines from the Haut Pays, Cahors competed with Bordeaux wine until the time of the French Revolution. It was exported throughout Europe as far east as Russia, but its production declined continuously until the beginning of the 20th century. The local wine growers then decided to devote themselves to the renovation of the vineyard, either individually or grouped in the Parnac cooperative. Their efforts were rewarded in 1951, when Cahors obtained the VDQS label. Even then, though, Cahors' struggle for survival was not over: the hard winter of 1956 came close to destroying all the vines. The area was finally classified as an AOC in 1971.

The vineyard area, situated in the south of the Quercy region, is equidistant from the Atlantic Ocean, the Mediterranean and the Pyrenees. It stretches over a length of about 50km on either side of the river Lot, at an altitude varying between 100 and 300m. This terrain is formed by a limestone plateau dating from the Mesozoic era, into which the Lot has cut many meanders and deposited large amounts of alluvium.

Two types of soil are found here: the type known as *causse*, and alluvial terraces. The *causse* is a stony, calcareous clay caused by the erosion of the limestone plateau. The arable layer it presents is not generally very deep (5cm to 20cm), but it is fertile, given adequate rainfall. Material from the *causse* and river-borne debris from the Massif Central have formed into terraces overhanging the Lot. When the *causse* is enriched with these ancient alluvial deposits, the soil is ideally suited to the cultivation of vines because of its extreme permeability.

The Cahors vineyards are situated in a climatic transition zone. The valley of the Lot opens up to the west into the plain surrounding Villeneuve-sur-Lot, and this sector is exposed to the influence of the Atlantic. The Mediterranean influence is caused mainly by the strong *autan* wind, which blows up from the southwest.

In this part of France, the rain gauge rarely records more than 800mm per year. In the early spring, as much rain as possible is beneficial to the development of the vine. A moderate amount of rain in the summer encourages the growth of the grapes; too much, though, can cause downy mildew to develop. As little rain as possible is hoped for in the early autumn, to encourage the development of sugar in the grapes.

The temperatures — 14°C on average — are generally favourable to the development of fruit on the vine. The insertion of the valley floor into the limestone plateau, and the meanders cut by the river, create a particularly sheltered environment, with cold air masses only reaching the *causse* uplands. However, frost in the spring can be devastating to the vines of the valley and the slopes. The difference in temperature between the *causse* and the terraces can also cause a discrepancy in the maturation of the grapes, with the valley frequently being one week ahead of the plateau. Finally, the *causse* is more often affected by hail than the valley and terraces.

The west wind brings rain. The north and east winds bring fine, dry weather. The southwest wind (the *autan*) is both dry and hot. It accelerates the evaporation of water contained in the grapes, and therefore encourages maturation. In some years it can compensate for lack of heat.

The AOC area has increased spectacularly over the last few decades. It has, in fact, grown from 208ha in 1962 to 2,600ha in 1984. But Cahors is still far from achieving the splendour and renown it knew in former times. Sixty-nine per cent of its surface area lies in the valley and on the terraces, and 31 per cent on the *causse*. The entire zone covers 45 communes, and 50 per cent of the vines meet AOC regulations.

The Côt grape variety (locally called the Auxerrois) is the essence of Cahors, since it is grown on 70 per cent of the area cultivated. Local conditions are very well suited to this vine. The only subsidiary varieties are the Tannat, the Jurançon Noir, the Merlot and the Syrah. The Tannat makes up about 10 per cent of the total harvest. Rich in tannins, it produces a wine that is hard when young, but which ages well.

The Jurançon Noir (locally called the Dame Noire) is susceptible to grey rot (botrytis) because of the compactness of the bunches. It has, though, found on the *causse* conditions dry enough to suit it. Since the wine it produces ages badly, it will be limited to 10 per cent of plantings from 1990.

The Merlot was introduced into the region in 1966 to compensate for the Côt's generally low alcohol levels. It lends a roundness and smoothness to Cahors blends, and adds bouquet.

The vineyard holdings producing AOC wines have an average surface area of 5.8ha. They total 600 of the 1,644 vineyard holdings in the region. Half the vine growers in the Cahors area belong to the Parnac cooperative, the 'Côtes d'Olt'. This cooperative collects grapes throughout the entire area of the *appellation*, and is responsible for 42 per cent of production. The rest of the wine makers are independent, and 95 of them carry out their own bottling. They are concentrated in the Puy-l'Évêque region. A slightly larger number of the independent wine makers do not do their own bottling. *Négociants* are particularly active in Cahors, and sell 43 per cent of the wine.

Most of the wine is sold in neighbouring *départements*, and in the Paris region. Only 10 per cent of production is exported.

Cahors has a deep and lively red colour, which from a good vintage can be almost black. It is a tannic wine, generous on the palate. It becomes finer and more velvety with age.

Depending on the vintage and its precise source, Cahors can be consumed young or after ageing. Wine made on the *causse* is generally more tannic and 'harder' when young than wine from the terraces and slopes of the valley.

Caladoc

This is a Grenache × Côt cross obtained by INRA (Institut National de la Recherche Agronomique) at Vassal, near Montpellier. Its foliage resembles that of the Grenache, and dentation that of the Côt.

Cahors, nestling on a turn of the river Lot, gives its name to an almost black, tannic wine, which keeps well.

Bunches medium sized, conical, not very compact; grapes fairly large, ellipsoidal; ripening period: third epoch.

It is not very susceptible to *coulure* (flower abortion) and adapts well to being trained either *en gobelet* (as a small, free-standing bush) or *en cordon* (trellis trained). Its wine is tannic, but smooth, well balanced and deeply coloured. Classed as 'authorized' in the Midi and Provence, with one clone approved: number 724.

Calitor

Synonyms: *Pécoui-Touar*, because of the characteristic shape of its peduncle, which assumes an almost right-angled bend — a deformation that is called *Touar* in Provence; *Ginoux d'Agasso*, a name taken from the similarity between the shape of a magpie's knee and that of the peduncle; *Canseron, Canseroun*, because it only produces bad wine; *Foirard, Fourial, Fouiraire* because of the laxative properties of its grapes; *Charge-Mulet, Cargo-Muou* because of its high productivity; *Rousset* because of the indistinct colour of its grapes.

Bunches, large, long, loose, cylindrical-conical, winged, with a sharply angled and bulbous peduncle; grapes spherical, medium to large, dark, with thin skin and juicy flesh; ripening period: third epoch, late.

This is a hardy vine, with midseason budbreak. It adapts to all types of soil and produces a *vin ordinaire* on the plains; when planted on the slopes, the Calitor produces a fine, light-bodied, alcoholic wine, though one without much colour. It is often attacked by downy mildew and grey rot (botrytis), but it is not often subject to oidium (powdery mildew). During the phylloxera crisis, it showed a moderate resistance to the insect. It has been classed as 'authorized' in Languedoc and Provence, where it is grown on 200ha at present.

The Calitor Gris or Saoule Bouvier exists in the form of isolated stocks in Hérault (where it is called the Fouirau) and in a small number of plots in Var.

The Calitor Blanc is found, but only rarely, in Gard, Ardèche and Vaucluse.

Calvi *See* Vin de Corse-Calvi.

Camaralet de Lasseube

Synonyms: *Camaralet Blanc, Camaralet à Fleurs Femelles, Petit Camarau.*

Young leaves downy, yellowish.

Leaves medium sized, truncate, thick, contorted, bullate, slightly crimped at the petiolar junction, five-lobed with medium deep lateral sinuses, acute at base, petiolar sinus lyrate; dentation narrow, convex; underside of blade downy in tufts. Flowers physiologically female with reflex stamens.

Bunches small, cylindrical-conical; grapes small, spherical, white; ripening period: third epoch.

This white Béarn grape variety has been classed as 'recommended' in Gers, Haute-Garonne and Pyrénées-Atlantiques, and has a role to play in the Béarn and Jurançon AOCs. Despite this, it is not widely cultivated in either region. It is said to produce a fine wine with a spicy taste, akin to those of pepper or cinnamon. Any supposed links with Riesling are mistaken.

The Camaralet Noir or Moustardet has been reported at Lasseube and in the Jurançon region.

Camaraou Blanc

Synonyms: *Camaraü Blanc, Camaroo, Camaralet.*

This vine differs from the Camaralet de Lasseube by virtue of its hermaphroditic flowers, its more deeply lobed leaves and also by the shape of its bunches.

Camaraou Noir

Synonyms: *Camaraü Rouge, Camaran, Camaras.*

Bunches large, conical, compact; grapes spherical, small, blue-black, juicy; ripening period: third epoch.

A grape variety from the Béarn and Jurançon areas, remarkable for its robustness; it is stake-trained, and produces *vin ordinaire*.

Canari

Synonyms: *Canaril, Canarill* in Ariège and Haute-Garonne, *Carcassès, Ugne Noire* at Mirepoix and Varilhes, *Belle Citat, le Bidan, Esquisse Braguette, Cargo Nalt* in Ariège, *Blanquette Rouge* at Caussens, *Caillaba* at Bigorre, *Chalosse Noire* in the South West, *Sainte Hélène* in the Madiran region, *Oeil de Chope, Ondenc Noir* in Tarn and the Toulouse area of Languedoc, *Grosse Négrette* at Lavilledieu, *Semis Rouge* in Landes, *Bourgogne, Balza, Cot à Queue Verte, Cot Vert du Saumurois* in the Cher region and in Anjou.

Leaves truncate, concave, thick, bullate, deeply lobed, closed upper sinuses with concave bases, open lower sinuses, petiolar sinus lyrate with overlapping edges; dentation wide, convex.

Bunches conical, medium sized, compact, sometimes winged; grapes spherical, medium sized, blue-black, juicy; ripening period: second epoch, late.

This is a very robust and productive vine, with blue-black grapes, producing a *vin ordinaire* that is not very highly coloured. It seems to have moderate resistance to black rot in the South West, but it is very susceptible to grey rot (botrytis). It is not classified, and can only be found on a few hectares now.

Canari Blanc and Canari Gris have been reported in Haute-Garonne; these differ from the above variety in colour only.

Canon-Fronsac and Côtes-Canon-Fronsac

The *appellation d'origine contrôlée* of Côtes-Canon-Fronsac was created by decree on 1 July 1939; to this, the decree of 28 July 1964 added the alternative name of Canon-Fronsac, practically the only one in use today.

The Canon-Fronsac *appellation* applies to red wines coming from delimited plots situated in part of the communes of Fronsac and Saint-Michel-de-Fronsac, in the Libourne region. To be entitled to the *appellation*, wines must be made from the Cabernet Sauvignon, Cabernet Franc, Merlot and Côt (Malbec) grape varieties. Since 1961, hybrid vines have been forbidden on properties claiming the Canon-Fronsac *appellation*. The minimum sugar content of the must has to be 162g per litre and the wines should have a minimum alcohol content of 10° and a maximum of 13°. The base yield is 47hl/ha. In 1985, the surface area was 299ha and the production was 17,298hl.

Château de la Rivière, in the Fronsac appellation *zone. Canon-Fronsac lies within Fronsac.*

The wines of Canon-Fronsac are very highly coloured and have good tannic and aromatic strength. They need several years in bottle to open out fully.

Carcajolo Blanc

Synonym: *Carcajolo.*

This is a secondary vine from the Sartène area of Corsica: it has been classified as 'authorized' there. Several clones exist, distinguished by the varying depths of their lateral sinuses.

Carcajolo Noir

Synonyms: *Carcajiola, Cacagliola, Bonifacienco, Bonifazino.*

Growing tips felty white. Young leaves downy, reddish. Leaves orbicular, contorted, concave, five-lobed, the upper sinuses deep with overlapping edges, the petiolar sinus lyrate, narrow; dentation narrow, pointed.

Bunches medium sized, conical, winged, compact; grapes ellipsoidal, medium sized, dark, bloomy; ripening period: third epoch.

A robust and fertile vine, which should be pruned long so as to avoid *coulure* (flower abortion). It produces a highly coloured, though not very alcoholic, wine. It is classed as 'authorized' in Corsica, but it is not widely planted.

Carignan

Synonyms: *Carignane, Carinena, Bois Dur, Bois de Fer, Plant d'Espagne, Roussillonen, Catalan* in Aude, *Plant de Lédenon* in Var, *Babounenc* or *Babonenc* in Alpes Maritimes, *Mataro* in Gard.

Growing tips open, flat, felty white with carmine margins.

Young leaves yellowish, felty, becoming glossy and thin as they grow.

Leaves very large, orbicular, contorted, markedly crimped around the petiolar junction, finely bullate, deeply five-lobed with narrow lateral sinuses, acute at base; petiolar sinus U-shaped and moderately open; dentation large, narrow, pointed; underside of blade arachnoid in tufts. In the autumn, the foliage reddens at the edges.

Green shoots vigorous, light green with light brown longitudinal striations, arachnoid at the tip; knots bulging, prominent; tendrils large, strong.

Bunches fairly large, cylindrical-conical, compact, winged, with a lignified peduncle; grapes spherical, medium sized, blue-black with thick and astringent skins; juice sweet, colourless, with a somewhat insipid taste; ripening period: third epoch, late.

A leaf of the Carignan vine — the most widely planted grape variety in France.

The Carignan has an upright habit, which is an advantage for vines trained, as it generally is, *en gobelet*; its budbreak is late. It is a vigorous vine, well adapted to vineyards on the slopes of hills, where it produces between 30 and 70hl/ha of wine high in alcohol, above 12°. The wines are full in colour, tannic, rather astringent and often with an unpleasant bitterness to them, which explains why the Carignan is limited to between 30 and 50 per cent of blends in many southern French AOCs, such as those of Côtes du Rhône, Coteaux du Languedoc, Corbières, Minervois, Côtes du Roussillon, Côtes de Provence and Coteaux d'Aix-en-Provence. On the other hand, on the plains, the yield can reach 200hl/ha, but the wines obtained are low in alcohol, lack character and are often acidic.

Carignan green shoot.

The Carignan is very susceptible to oidium (powdery mildew), downy mildew, grey rot (botrytis) and grape worms; in sandy coastal areas, though, its roots are fairly resistant to eel worms. It has been classed as 'recommended' in all the *départements* of the South of France, and 27 clones have been registered and approved, the most important of which are numbers 6, 7, 171 and 151.

At the present time, the Carignan is the most widely grown of all French wine vines, covering 210,000ha, 175,000 of them in Languedoc: 69,000ha in Aude, 60,500ha in Hérault, 23,000ha in Pyrénées-Orientales and 22,500ha in Gard. In Provence, relatively large areas are also devoted to it: 12,500ha in Var, 6,700ha in Vaucluse, 4,300ha in Bouches-du-Rhône and 5,400ha in Corsica.

The Carignan Blanc, which only differs from the Carignan in the colour of its grapes, takes up 2,300ha in Languedoc, half of it in Hérault for the production of white wine. Its wines are not very alcoholic.

The Carignan Gris is a mutation of the Carignan Noir discovered in Aude, where about 50ha of it are cultivated, the vine stocks often being mixed in with plots of Carignan Blanc.

Carignan Bouschet

A Petit Bouschet × Morrastel cross, whose foliage resembles the Morrastel but whose bunches resemble the Carignan. Cultivated in Languedoc on nearly 200 ha, it has not been classified. Its canes have the characteristic of achieving complete lignification and of therefore having '*bois de verre*' ('glass wood'), so-called because they break very easily. The fruit of this productive vine makes a *vin ordinaire*.

Carmenère

Synonyms: *Carmenelle, Cabernelle, Grande Vidure* in the Médoc, *Grand Carmenet, Carbonet, Carbouet* in the Graves, *Bouton Blanc*.

Leaves large, orbicular, shiny, contorted, concave with convex edges, deeply five-lobed with sinuses acute at base, often with a tooth at the base of each sinus; petiolar sinus lyrate, more or less closed and sometimes with a naked base; dentation medium sized, convex; underside of blade lightly arachnoid.

Bunches small, cylindrical-conical, loose; grapes spherical, medium sized, blue-black, with soft flesh; ripening period: second epoch.

The Carmenère is a vigorous vine, but not very fertile and it has to be pruned long. Its wine is highly coloured and is less astringent than that of the Cabernet Franc. Classed as 'recommended' in Gironde, this grape variety contributes to the Bordeaux, Médoc, Premières Côtes de Bordeaux and Saint-Émilion AOCs.

Cassis

Cassis is, first and foremost, a spectacular cliff that falls sheer into the sea. It is also a group of undulating hills and slopes, at the foot of which a beach and a series of rocky inlets make the area as attractive as it is to tourists.

But it is, too, a vineyard whose history dates back to the 11th century, to the time when ecclesiastical wine growers were already struggling to find the best *terroirs*.

In 1520, some members of the Albizzi family moved there from Arezzo for political reasons, replanted the vineyard, which had disappeared in the interim, and made white wine, having quickly realized that it had more character in this area than red wine.

But the importance the vineyard had even a century ago has greatly diminished under the constant pressure of urbanization. Cassis has become a sort of suburb of Marseille, and the harbour and the rocky inlets have become more important than the vineyards. The latter, however, have survived on the slopes.

The vines, planted on gravelly slopes and well-drained low terraces, cover 120ha, and produce on average 5,700hl per year. The AOC was ratified by decree on 15 May 1936.

The white wines make up most of the volume produced, not least because they accompany local seafood so well. Made from the Clairette, Marsanne, Ugni Blanc, Sauvignon Blanc and Bourboulenc grape varieties, their originality comes from their floral aromas, dominated by lime and narcissus.

The red and rosé wines are produced from the Grenache, Carignan, Cinsaut and Mourvèdre varieties, as well as from the good but little grown Barbaroux.

They are all wines which, by their nature as well as thanks to great local demand, are drunk and greatly enjoyed when young.

Castets

Synonyms: *Nicouleau* at Saint-Macaire, *Gros Verdot* (in error) at Gaillan, *Engrunat, Machouquet* or *Matiouquet* at Saint-Loubès.

This vine was found at Saint-Maixent in Deux-Sèvres. It is a vigorous vine of upright habit, with late budbreak. It is productive, and a good, highly coloured *vin ordinaire* can be made from its grapes. Classed as 'recommended' in Aveyron and in the Cantal area.

Cep Rouge

A vine of local origin grown in Vienne, but not classified.

Cérons

The Cérons *appellation d'origine contrôlée*, created by decree on 11 September 1936, is applicable to wines produced from grapes harvested in delimited plots in the communes of Cérons, Illats and Podensac, on the left bank of the Garonne. The Cérons *appellation* area forms an enclave within the Graves *appellation*.

To be entitled to the Cérons *appellation*, wines may only be made from the Sauvignon Blanc, Sémillon and Muscadelle grape varieties. The grapes must be overripened, and harvested in several sweeps. The must has to contain a minimum of 212g of sugar per litre and the wines have to have a total minimum alcohol content of 12.5°.

In 1985, the area given over to wine growing for the Cérons *appellation* was 125ha and production was 2,676hl, giving a yield of 21.4hl/ha.

The wines are fine and elegant, but they do not attain the concentration of those of Sauternes; they are lighter and defter. In recent years, because of the difficulties of selling sweet white wines, some of the production has been vinified into dry white wine and declared under the Graves *appellation*.

César

Synonyms: *Céear, Célar, Céelar* at Vermenton and in the Cure valley, *Romain* at Auxerre, *Ronçain, Picarniau, Picargneau, Picorneau, Picargniot* at Irancy, *Gros Monsieur, Gros Noir*.

This vine was brought into the Yonne by Caesar's Roman legionaries, who at the same time taught the inhabitants of this region to grow vines. It is a vigorous and productive variety, though it is susceptible to spring and winter frosts as well as to downy mildew and oidium (powdery mildew). It produces a hard, deeply coloured wine, somewhat acrid when young, but which keeps well. It is included among the approved varieties for the Bourgogne AOC in the Yonne *département*, where it has been classed as 'recommended'.

Chablis

The area of the Chablis *appellation d'origine contrôlée* includes 19 communes. It stretches from Ligny-le-Châtel in the north to Poilly-sur-Serein in the southeast; from Viviers in the east to Préhy in the west. The wines of Chablis are governed by the decree of 13 January 1938. This specifies in particular a base yield limited to 50hl/ha and a minimum alcohol content of 10°. The only authorized vine is the Chardonnay (locally known as the Beaunois). The full character of this vine emerges when grown in the Kimmeridgian limestone soils of the area, providing a clay-limestone-marl mixture in the best plots, where the oyster fossil *Exogyra virgula* is found. With an average annual production of about 70,000hl, the wines of Chablis are appreciated for their pale, bright colour, their dryness and their freshness. They are slightly acid, lively and elegant. Chablis improves by being kept for at least two years from the vintage date before being drunk.

Chablis Grand Cru

The conditions under which the Chablis Grand Cru *appellation d'origine contrôlée* is granted were fixed by the decree of 13 January 1938. Wines from the following *climats* (vineyard sites) are entitled to the *appellation*: Blanchot, Bougros, les Clos, Grenouilles, Preuses, Valmur and Vaudésir, all situated opposite the town of Chablis on Kimmeridgian marl soils. Each of these names designates an exceptional site on the slopes beside the river Serein.

In the Chablis region, vines are protected from spring frosts by **chaufferettes** *(small stoves).*

The site of the seven majestic plots is not enough alone to earn the *appellation*. The Chablis Grand Cru wines also have to come from must containing a minimum, before any additions are made, of 187g of natural sugar per litre and, after fermention, they should have a minimum alcohol content of 11°. Another constraint is that the yield per hectare should not exceed 45hl. Therefore, the average harvests of Chablis Grand Cru total no more than 6,000hl. This admirably smooth, full-bodied, direct and fruity wine develops rich aromas as it ages, in particular those of acacia and violet. Generally deeper in colour than other Chablis wines, it acquires wonderful golden and later amber hues. Depending on the vintage, Chablis Grand Cru is at its best between five and ten years old.

The main Premier Cru sites of Chablis are Beauroy, Côte de Lechet, Fourchaume, Les Fourneaux, Mélinots, Montée de Tonnerre, Montmains, Monts du Mileu, Vaillons, Vaucoupin, Vaudevey and Vosgros.

Chablis Premier Cru

The decree of 27 February 1978 states that wines from a number of delimited parcels in the Chablis AOC area may be sold as Chablis followed by the name of the *climat* of origin, or as Chablis Premier Cru, or as both. These parcels are situated on both sides of the Serein valley. Each year about 50,000hl of Premier Cru Chablis is produced; its alcohol content is fixed at 10.5° and the yield must not exceed 50hl/ha. Produced exclusively from the Chardonnay grape variety, these are white wines with a clear, light gold colour, sometimes with a green glint to them. In the mouth, they are dry and lively, light, fruity, and they sometimes acquire a delicate taste of violets. They should be drunk at cellar temperature, when they are at least three years old.

CHABLIS AND AUXERRE

The vineyards of the Yonne stretch from Chablis to Auxerre, with the vineyard area around Chablis being the largest and most famous part. Chablis has, in fact, made a worldwide reputation for itself, to the point where its name has become synonymous with the very best dry white wines.

Grape harvesting in the Chablis area. For the Chablis Grand Cru and Premier Cru appellations, *situated on steep slopes, the harvest is still carried out manually.*

Detail of carved wood in the church of Notre Dame at Noyers, dating from the 15th century.

No *appellation* has been as heavily plagiarized as that of Chablis. So-called generic 'chablis' wines are produced in California, Australia, South Africa and New Zealand. In contrast to the 100,000 to 150,000hl of authentic AOC Chablis produced annually, 3 to 4 million hl of wine bearing this name is sold throughout the world. This is the price of success no doubt, and Chablis has long been successful. In *Anna Karenina*, Tolstoy writes that, during the 19th century, the favourite wines of Russian society were Champagne and Chablis.

However, the Burgundians are striving to protect their vineyards. In 1982, to defend the honour and legal rights of the Chablis name, they obtained a ban on false 'chablis' from the supreme court of Bermuda. Similar proceedings have been instituted in Japan.

The history of wine growing in Chablis and Auxerre

The story of Chablis and its wine is intertwined with the history of the abbey of Pontigny. The second 'daughter' of the abbey of Cîteaux, Pontigny was founded at the beginning of the 12th century. From 1130 onwards, it has had vines at Chablis. The monks founded the Petit Pontigny, a magnificent 12th-century *cellier* (store for wine and food) contemporaneous with the one at the Clos de Vougeot. Their influence on the locality was decisive: the wine of Chablis quickly became more famous than that of Auxerre, the praises of which had been sung since the 7th century.

At the time of the sale of 'public property', after the French Revolution, more than one third of the vineyards of Chablis belonged to the abbey of Pontigny. Of these properties, only the memory of Moutonne has survived; this vineyard was situated in the *finage* (an administrative area of a commune or village) between the present areas of the Grands Crus Preuses and Vaudésir. Wines from this parcel of vines may still use the AOC Chablis Grand Cru Moutonne.

The wine-producing soils of the Chablis and Auxerre regions

This area lies on the southeast border of the Parisian basin. It consists essentially of Upper Jurassic series soils stretching towards the west, intersected by a number of valleys converging on the Seine and the Yonne. The valley of the Serein, between Tonnerre and Auxerre, waters the Chablis vineyards with its small tributaries.

CHABLIS: A CHALLENGE

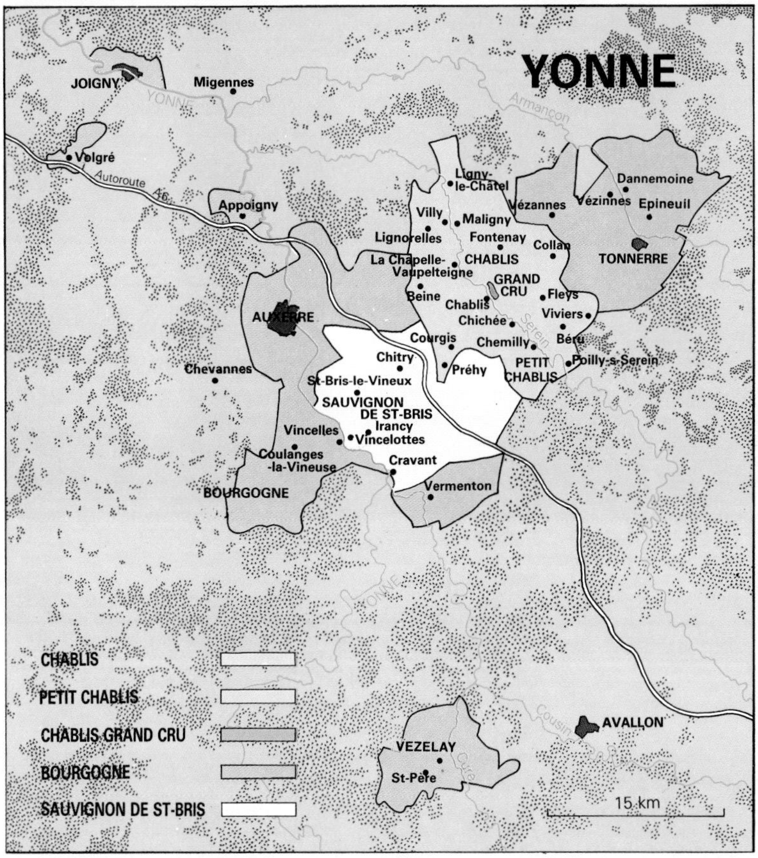

I was born at Saint-Père de Vézelay among the vineyards of the Yonne. These vineyards were almost annihilated by phylloxera, but the region remains deeply attached to viticulture, even today. From a very early age, my life was dominated by the vine and its cycles of pruning and harvesting, but without my being truly conscious of it. I had to reach adulthood before the wonderful secrets of wine revealed themselves to me. My vinous education took place in stages. I first discovered the 'riffraff' — Vins de Pays, Beaujolais — then I learnt to love the wines of the Loire with their rich perfumes; then the burgundies, white and red; and finally the wines of Chablis, of which I have remained enamoured. Chablis is the wine I prefer to all others — because of its qualities, not through chauvinism! My love for Chablis is spurred on by the perpetual challenge it presents me with. On this one terroir *there are 27* crus *to be found, each one different from every other; and yet the differences between them are so subtle! Simply being able to recognize them is something of an achievement. I love to struggle with them, without ever being able to master them completely. My preference is generally for virile, sober wines, which taste only of the earth — Chablis, but also the red wines of Auxerre such as Irancy or Coulanges. In my opinion, aroma serves only to add a touch of charm, and charm should always be discreet. Therefore, I find very characterful wines disagreeable. My approach to wine is reflected in my cooking, in which I try to achieve as pure a style as possible. I like it to be bare and devoid of all artifice — to use an artistic comparison, Romanesque rather than Gothic.*

For a long time I have been fighting the idea of combining very great wines with great dishes. For successful marriages between exceptional beings are just as rare in the gastronomic world as in life itself. This is why I recommend accompanying gastronomic meals with wines that are good but not outstandingly so. They provide a harmonious accompaniment to the dish without overwhelming it. On the other hand, if you want to appreciate a great wine, I advise you to drink it in the company of your greatest friends, but without eating, or only eating very little.

The temperature at which wines should be served is another of my favourite themes. I find that wine never provides so much of its characteristic pleasure as when it is cool and refreshing. As far as I am concerned, bringing wines to a warm room temperature is a heresy which, in any case, is no longer in keeping with current tastes. No wine has ever been ruined by being kept in a bucket of cold water for a while.

Everything surrounding wine and cooking should exalt them and bring happiness. As in love, the gradual and harmonious unfolding of delights, through the course of a meal, should be respected. This is why I recommend choosing wines that may have come from different terroirs *but that have been made from grape varieties of the same category. Mixtures are best avoided.*

I will willingly accompany my entrées, which are generally full of character, with Champagne or Chablis, but I also like to leave the well-trodden paths once in a while. Thus, for example, I have successfully served white wine from the Gard with oysters. Volnay can do wonders for foie gras. But the main thing, I repeat, is to continue the meal in the same spirit of harmony and continuity.

Like all feasts of the senses, a meal should leave room for fantasy. Therefore, I am naturally inclined to young or adolescent wines, which, more than the older ones, allow you to dream . . .

Marc Meneau

The vineyards classified as Premiers Crus and Grands Crus are situated on slopes with a southeast, south and southwest exposure, between 120m and 160m in altitude on average, though rising to 250m on slopes that can have a gradient as steep as 20 per cent. These are clay and limestone marls with a high proportion of pebbles, dating from the Kimmeridgian stage of the Upper Jurassic series, and they include a fossil mollusc, the *Exogyra virgula*, that is highly prized by wine makers, as its presence used to mark out the Chablis *appellation*. Today the *appellation* zone runs over in a few places on to soils from the more recent Portlandian stage, formed by a more compact form of limestone as plateaux lying between 200m and 250m. Much of the Petit Chablis *appellation* area lies on Portlandian limestone.

The percentage of pebbles in the soils of the Chablis vineyards varies from 25 to 58 per cent; the nitrogen content from 1.5 to 2.4 parts per thousand; the pH lies between 7.3 and 7.9; and the active lime level varies from 3 to 14 per cent.

The climate

The Chablis region is influenced by the continental climate of the Saône region. The prevailing winds are southerly and southwesterly. They bring rain on about 150 to 170 days per year, with a total annual precipitation of 700 to 850mm.

The average annual temperature is around 11°C. It is not uncommon for the region to experience minimum night-time temperatures of -20°C or -25°C in January, and night-time temperatures below 0°C at the end of April and the beginning of May, when the vine begins its vegetative growth. Favourable daytime temperatures of above 10°C begin in mid-April, and end around 1 October. All the main grape varieties of the Yonne — Chardonnay only in the Chablis region; Chardonnay, Pinot Noir and Gamay in the Auxerre region — ripen normally in this climate.

Irancy. This ancient vineyard in the Auxerre region was much esteemed until its destruction by the phylloxera louse at the end of the 19th century.

Protecting the vines from frost by spraying them with water in the Chablis region. The ice forms a protective sheath over the buds.

The Yonne vineyards are, though, subject to frequent destruction by winter and spring frosts, which explains why there are larger fluctuations in the harvest totals from year to year than anywhere else in Burgundy. Strenuous efforts have always been made to protect the vines against frosts where the danger is greatest — on both sides of the streams converging on the Serein, and especially along the Serein itself. This is done either by heating the lower levels of the atmosphere by means of braziers, or by releasing smoke to form a screen against the sun during the daytime thaw, or by spraying the vines with water so that the thick layer of ice protects the growing organs of the plant against the attacks of cold.

The regional AOCs

Outside the Chablis region, the most important vineyards are those of the Auxerre region, situated at Joigny and Coulanges-la-Vineuse; and those of the Tonnerre region, at Épineuil.

Chaillaud

A black grape variety from the Hautes-Alpes *département*. Unclassified.

Chambertin and Chambertin-Clos de Bèze

It is difficult to distinguish between these two adjoining Grands Crus, situated immediately to the south of Gevrey-Chambertin along the D122. Both cover about the same surface area (13ha and 15ha). Both are subject to the same conditions of production, according to the decree of 31 July 1937: minimum alcohol content is 11.5°; maximum yield is 35hl/ha. Chambertin and Chambertin-Clos de Bèze are both grown on gentle slopes at a moderate altitude and are appreciated for their richness, the strength and complexity of their aromas and their deep colour. These great lords of Burgundy — the favourite wines, so we are told, of Napoleon — present a happy combination of velvety smoothness, strength and subtlety. They are wines that may be cellared for a long period; they develop their remarkable qualities after ten to twenty years.

Chambolle-Musigny

Ratified by decree on 11 September 1936, this renowned 'village' *appellation d'origine contrôlée* from Burgundy is situated about half way between Chambertin and Romanée-Conti, and covers 128ha. The name of the *appellation* may be followed by 'Premier Cru' if the wine comes from one of the named Premier Cru vineyard sites, or by the name of the *climat* (or vineyard) itself. Red wine from Chambolle, produced from the Pinot Noir grape variety, must have a minimum alcohol content of 10.5° (11° for the Premiers Crus), with a maximum yield of 45hl/ha. Average production is about 5,000hl. Chambolle-Musigny also produces white wines, but only in very small quantities. They are therefore much sought-after for their bewitching scent, in which a fragrance of violets dominates. However, it is the red wines, with their beautiful ruby colour, that have won acclaim for this *appellation*. They are famous for their smoothness, their complexity and their richness. A subtlety and a feminine elegance distinguish them from their neighbours at Morey and Vougeot, which are more tannic and firm. The wines of Chambolle-Musigny reach their peak more quickly than the other red wines of Burgundy.

Chambolle-Musigny, on the Côte de Nuits, produces red wines of rare elegance.

The annual production total of Gevrey-Chambertin makes it the most important 'village' **appellation** *of the Côte de Nuits.*

Chambourcin

Synonym: *26.205 Joannès Seyve*.

Growing tips downy white. Young leaves arachnoid, copper coloured. Leaves orbicular-reniform, weakly five-lobed; petiolar sinus lyrate; base of veins pink; dentation very narrow, convex; underside of blade pubescent.

Green shoots ribbed, pale green, arachnoid at the tip, with red striations on the side exposed to the sun.

Bunches, compact, voluminous, often with *millerandage*; grapes medium sized, ovoid, blue-black with pulpy flesh; ripening period: first epoch, late.

This hybrid, with its spreading habit, is very vigorous and therefore susceptible to *coulure* (flower abortion); it has a good resistance to downy mildew and oidium (powdery mildew), but it does not thrive in dry conditions and calcareous soils. Its wine is ordinary, highly coloured, heavy and astringent with a grassy or leafy, and perfumed, taste. This variety has been classified as 'authorized' in numerous *départements* of the South West, the Loire valley and the Dauphiné (in southeastern France), covering a total of 3,369ha.

CHAMPAGNE

Champagne is a star that does not fade. When, at any hour of the day or night, anywhere in the world, a champagne cork pops in the joy of success or to celebrate a happy event, it does so thanks to the large houses and the small growers who use their skill to cultivate generous vineyards, rich in treasures.

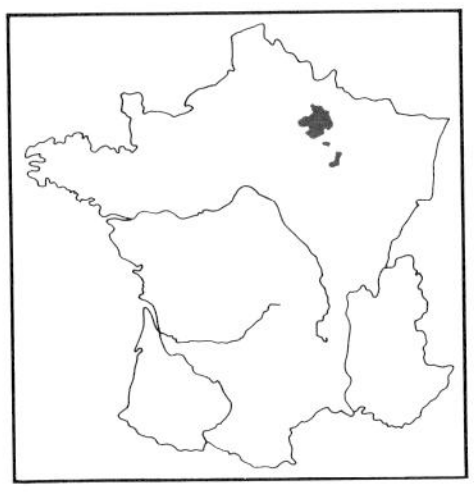

The Champagne vineyards occupy only two per cent of the French area devoted to vines, but they stretch over a large zone covering the *départements* of Marne, Aisne and Aube, as well as a few communes of Haute-Marne and Seine-et-Marne. As they are situated between the 48th and 49th parallels, the vineyards lie at the northern limit of wine growing in France. This means that the temperatures, the amount of sunshine and the rainfall in this region are exceptional in wine-growing terms. We may distinguish between two distinct climatic zones, one in the south and one in the north: the southerly Aube vineyards have a predominantly continental climate, while the northerly vineyards of the Marne and the Aisne have a more maritime climate.

The landmarks in the Champagne region are the Montagne de Reims, a vast plateau of about 20 km, situated southeast of Reims; the valley of the Marne — divided into the 'low valley' downstream from Hautvillers, and the 'high valley' from Hautvillers upstream to Tours-sur-Marne; the Côte des Blancs, to the south of the Montagne de Reims and south of Épernay; and, finally, the Aube vineyard area. Scattered about this huge tract of land, we find not only the Champagne *appellation*, but also those of Rosé des Riceys (in the Aube) and Coteaux Champenois.

Cross-section diagrams of the Champagne region are revealing. They always show the same outline: the river, a fluvial plain given over to agriculture, the wine-growing slopes at an altitude between 100m and 400m and, at the top, a forest. Champagne is therefore a vineyard area of slopes — of chalk, silica and marl.

The history of Champagne

Champagne is not, as legend would have us believe, the result of a sudden and miraculous monkish invention, but rather of a slow evolutionary process, the first stages of which date back 60 million years, as is attested by the prints of vine leaves found in travertine near Sézanne, dating from the Thanetian stage of the Paleocene epoch. Only at the time of the Roman conquest, though, can the presence of a

Saran, situated near the village of Cramant on the Côte des Blancs, in central Champagne. The vines of Champagne cover an area of 35,000ha, divided into four main parts: the Montagne de Reims, the Marne valley, the Côte des Blancs and the Aube vineyard area.

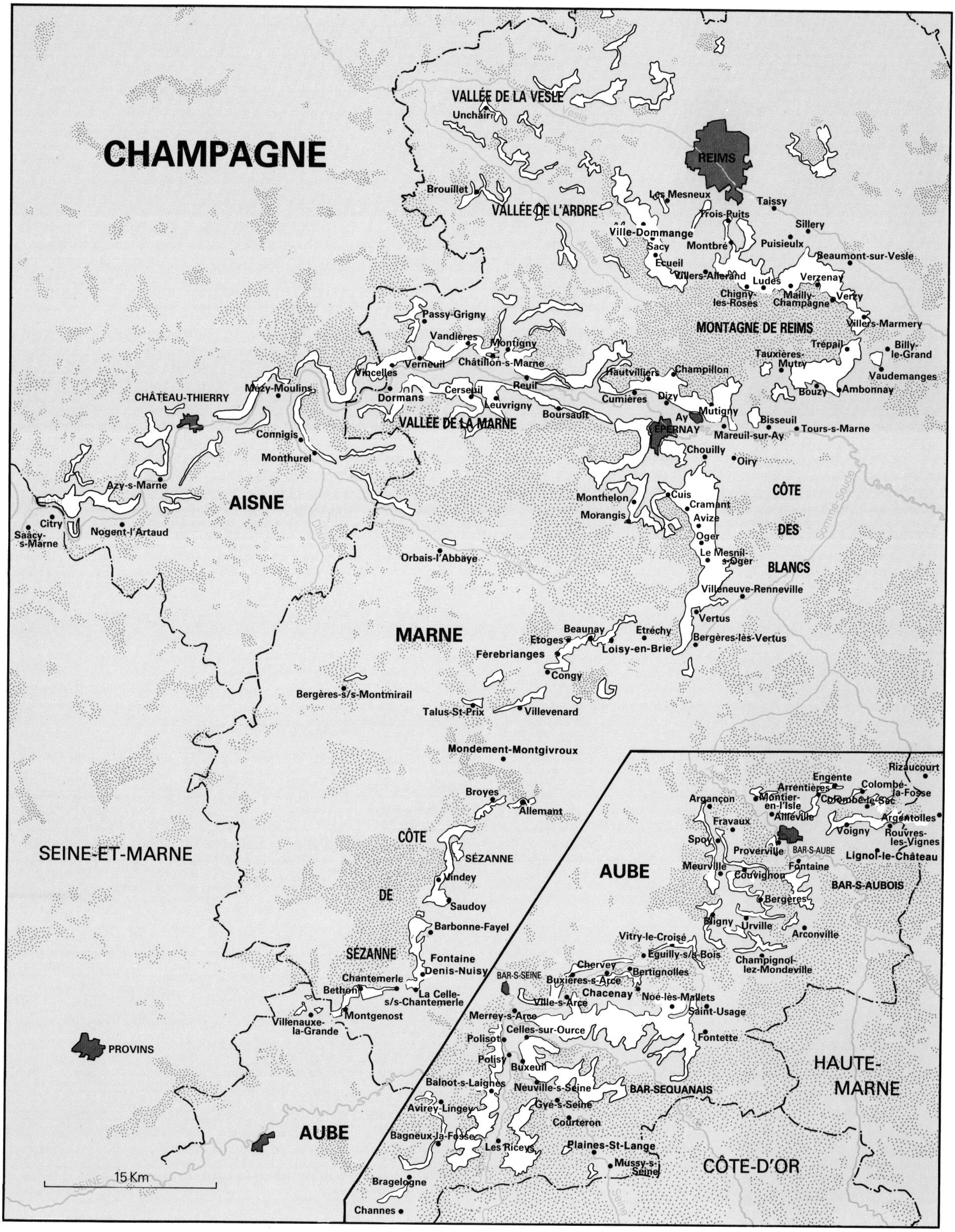
CHAMPAGNE
VALLÉE DE LA VESLE
Unchair
REIMS
Brouillet
VALLÉE DE L'ARDRE
Les Mesneux
Taissy
Trois-Puits
Sillery
Ville-Dommange
Sacy
Montbré
Puisieulx
Ecueil
Beaumont-sur-Vesle
Villers-Allerand
Ludes
Verzenay
Chigny-les-Roses
Mailly-Champagne
Verzy
Villers-Marmery
MONTAGNE DE REIMS
Passy-Grigny
Vandières
Montigny
Trépail
Billy-le-Grand
Tauxières-Mutry
Vaudemanges
Vincelles
Verneuil
Châtillon-s-Marne
Hautvilliers
Champillon
Bouzy
Ambonnay
Reuil
Mézy-Moulins
Cerseuil
Dormans
Cumières
Dizy
CHÂTEAU-THIERRY
Leuvrigny
Ay
Mutigny
Boursault
Bisseuil
VALLÉE DE LA MARNE
ÉPERNAY
Tours-s-Marne
Mareuil-sur-Ay
Connigis
Chouilly
Monthurel
Oiry
Azy-s-Marne
CÔTE
Monthelon
Cuis
Cramant
AISNE
Morangis
Avize
Citry
DES
Saacy-s-Marne
Nogent-l'Artaud
Oger
Le Mesnil-s-Oger
Orbais-l'Abbaye
BLANCS
Villeneuve-Renneville
Vertus
Beaunay
Etréchy
MARNE
Etoges
Bergères-lès-Vertus
Loisy-en-Brie
Fèrebrianges
Congy
Bergères-s/s-Montmirail
Talus-St-Prix
Villevenard
Mondement-Montgivroux
Rizaucourt
Engente
Broyes
Arrentières
Colombé-la-Fosse
Arganҫon
Montier-en-l'Isle
Colombé-le-Sec
Allemant
Fravaux
Ailleville
Argentolles
Voigny
CÔTE
Spoy
Rouvres-les-Vignes
Proverville
BAR-S-AUBE
SEINE-ET-MARNE
SÉZANNE
Lignol-le-Château
Meurville
Fontaine
AUBE
Vindey
Couvignon
BAR-S-AUBOIS
DE
Saudoy
Bergères
Bligny
Urville
Barbonne-Fayel
Arconville
Vitry-le-Croisé
SÉZANNE
Eguilly-s/s-Bois
Fontaine
Chervey
Champignol-lez-Mondeville
Denis-Nuisy
Chantemerle
BAR-S-SEINE
Buxières-s-Arce
Bertignolles
Bethon
La Celle-s/s-Chantemerle
Chacenay
Noé-lès-Mallets
Ville-s-Arce
Montgenost
Saint-Usage
Villenauxe-la-Grande
Merrey-s-Arce
Celles-sur-Ource
Fontette
Polisot
PROVINS
HAUTE-MARNE
Polisy
Buxeuil
Balnot-s-Laignes
Neuville-s-Seine
BAR-SEQUANAIS
Avirey-Lingey
Gyé-s-Seine
Courteron
AUBE
Bagneux-la-Fosse
Les Riceys
Plaines-St-Lange
Mussy-s-Seine
CÔTE-D'OR
15 Km
Bragelogne
Channes
Vesle
Ardre
Seine

A 16th-century carved wooden stall from the church of Rilly-la-Montagne, situated near Chigny-les-Roses, to the north of the Montagne de Reims.

vineyard be confirmed, since in AD 92 the Emperor Domitian forbade its cultivation. It was not until two centuries later that the Emperor Probus authorized the replanting of vines in Champagne. Production of wine (at that time red) continued as before. At the end of the 17th century, a monk from the abbey of Hautvillers makes his appearance: Dom Pérignon. He introduced spectacular improvements, so it is said, to the production of the wines of Champagne, including the use of the carbon dioxide produced by the reawakening of fermentation in wines containing residual sugar in the spring. He recommended the use of bottles and the manufacture of solid stoppers. (At the time, stoppers were made of cotton or cloth soaked with oil.) Whereas overproduction of red wine had previously brought destitution to the wine makers, the new white and sparkling champagne won favour at the court of Louis XV. This was the start of its great renown.

The Champagne terroir, *which is formed of chalky slopes, is situated at the northern limit of vine cultivation and is subject to severe frost in winter.*

The *terroir* of Champagne

One of the keys to an understanding of the *terroir* of Champagne lies in a grasp of the shape and substance of these vineyards, essentially composed of slopes. The chalky nature of the soils allows excess water to drain away, retaining just enough to nourish the vines. In fact, contrary to the classic rules of the French vineyard whereby the roots penetrate deep into the subsoil, the roots of Champagne vines are concentrated in the first layer of soil, which is improved by adding earth and enriching agents.

In dry weather, the water rises up through the limestone, while in a wet spell it rapidly sinks to the lower levels. If we also consider the role played by the white colour of these soils in reflecting the sun and accumulating heat, we can see how a wine-growing *terroir* can overcome some of the difficulties posed by a harsh climate.

The climate

The climate of Champagne is predominantly Atlantic in type, with continental influences from the east. The number of days of frost, often disastrous for the vineyards, and most severe in the valleys and depressions, is between 60 and 80 per year. The rain falls more on the higher plateaux and upland valleys than on the plain of Champagne — 700mm of annual precipitation on the plateaux and valleys compared with 600mm on the plain. Annual sunshine, over 288 days, is calculated at 1,750 – 1,850 hours. The prevailing winds are southwesterly in autumn and winter, and westerly in spring and summer.

The vineyard areas

Climatic factors are primordial in governing exactly where grapes can be grown in the Champagne region, and they are also referred to when calculating the relative merits of the *crus* and the internal classification of the wine-producing communes. Each commune is given a rating of between 80 and 100 per cent (the latter being reserved for the best communes or *grands crus*). This scale allows the annual price of grapes to be calculated for each of the 302 communes in the 35,000ha of the *appellation* area (specified by the law of 11 February 1951). However, of these 35,000ha, only 30,000 are cultivable, the remaining 5,000ha being sited on slopes too steep for mechanical cultivation.

At present, only 25,000ha of the cultivable area is under vines: 18,800 in Marne, 4,200 in Aube and 2,000 in the *départements* of Aisne and Seine-et-Marne. The additional 5,000ha is scheduled to be planted before 1990. This is in response to ever-increasing demand: annual production in 1910 was 40 million bottles; in 1970, it passed the 100 million mark; and it reached 200 million bottles during 1986.

ANNUAL CLIMATIC CONDITIONS								
YEAR	AVERAGE TEMPERATURE	SUNSHINE (hours/days)	RAIN (amount/days)	FLOWERING DATES	VOLUME HARVESTED in hl	WEATHER DURING THE HARVEST	HARVEST DATES (different zones)
1977	10°67	1 454/294	734mm/192	15/06–12/07	1 400 000	Mixed	6 and 10/10
1978	9°56	1 368/276	783mm/170	16/06–20/07	594 700	Dry	9 and 11/10
1979	9°87	1 517/298	830mm/177	16/06–13/07	1 750 000	Dry	3, 5 and 8/10
1980	9°78	1 549/298	704mm/162	15/06–20/07	848 500	Wet	9/10
1981	10°56	1 489/293	861mm/183	08/06–07/07	691 418	Dry	28/09
1982	11°35	1 763/292	724mm/158	06/06–30/06	2 211 537	Dry	17 and 20/09
1983	11°04	1 768/298	672mm/158	20/06–05/07	2 242 799	Dry	26 and 29/09
1984	10°44	1 518/280	760mm/175	20/06–14/07	1 486 250	Wet	6, 8, 9 and 10/10
1985	9°70	1 679/299	498mm/150	14/06–10/07	1 139 185	Dry	30/09
1986	9°90	1 603/299	720mm/208	18/06–02/07	1 956 000	Dry	28, 30/09 and 2/10

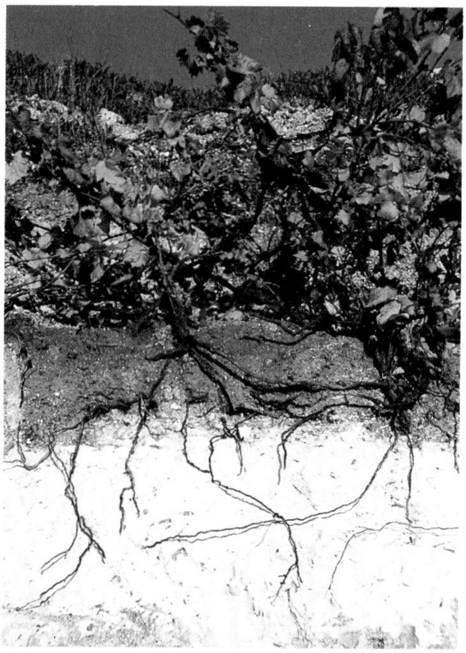

Cross-section of Champagne subsoil, which is fundamentally chalky, with a thin layer of arable topsoil where the roots concentrate.

The grape varieties

The *appellation d'origine contrôlée* for Champagne, as elsewhere, is governed by strict rules concerning the choice of grape varieties. The INAO authorizes the use of the Pinot Noir, whose grapes have dark skins and white juice, for its vigour, its high productivity and its ability to adapt to the various *terroirs* of the Champagne region. In 1986, the Pinot Noir occupied 36 per cent of plantings.

The second Champagne variety is the Meunier (36 per cent), which has dark grapes with white juice. Hardier than the Pinot Noir but not so fine, it has nevertheless achieved remarkable popularity in some *crus* because of its adaptability to the hazards of the local climate.

The third grape variety is the Chardonnay: this is confined to the Côte des Blancs, south of Épernay. It is planted on only 28 per cent of the vineyard area, because it has adapted less happily than the Pinot Noir to local conditions.

Finally, we must mention the Arbane and the Petit Meslier — both white grape varieties, though not very widely grown; and the Gamay, a black grape variety with white juice.

Though very definitely in the minority, these varieties are nevertheless a characteristic part of the Champagne vineyards. So too are the grafting stocks: 41B, used for its resistance to vine diseases; 161-49 and Teleki 8B used for their vigour, precocity and fruit-producing ability.

Clonal selection, the pruning system, the density of planting (8,000 plants per hectare) and the method of vine training (trellising by rows) all contribute to the quality of this northern vineyard area, where the sun is rare and the maximum temperatures are often barely sufficient to ripen the grapes.

The grape harvest

The quality of the vintage can be predicted well before the beginning of the grape harvest is announced. It can be foretold as early as the preceding autumn: the vine's inflorescences are usually of similar abundance and quality to the 'bunches' that appear on the local ivy in October of the previous year. But the quality of the flowering itself, which usually happens in the second fortnight of June, is now considered a more reliable guide.

Continued page 172

Grape harvest at Vertus on the Côte des Blancs. The grapes are still put in traditional wicker baskets to be transported.

The Méthode Champenoise

The production of champagne is characterized by five meticulous operations: careful harvesting, so as to bring the grapes whole to the press; gentle pressing, carried out as soon as possible after picking; blending of wines from different grape varieties and crus, *made between the first and second fermentations; the initiation of the second fermentation — called the* prise de mousse *— in bottle; and ageing* sur lie *(on the lees) in bottle for several years.*

Cultivation of the vine

The vine is trained low in Champagne and the great majority of the grapes develop very near to the ground, so that they can gain the maximum benefit of heat from the soil. In addition, the leaves are thinned out during the course of the summer to ventilate and dry the grapes and allow them to derive maximum benefit from the rays of the sun.

The grape harvest

The grape harvest takes place at the end of September or the beginning of October, and has to be carried out manually. The use of machine harvesting is forbidden for wines claiming the Champagne appellation.

Débourbage

The next operation, débourbage *(settling or purging of the must) is followed by racking, to remove impurities such as earth and pieces of leaf. A clear must is produced, allowing a wine rich in subtlety to be made, without an overpronounced* goût de terroir *(earthy smell and flavour).*

Pressing

Pressing is carried out very soon after the grape harvest so that the grapes do not become spoiled, and to prevent the skin of the grape from staining the juice. It is carried out very gently, usually with vertical presses of champenois *type, but also, more and more frequently today, with horizontal presses equipped with baskets or membranes. In either case, the volume of juice collected is 100 litres for every 150kg of whole grapes. The must is systematically divided up, because the quality of the juices differs according to whether they have been run from the beginning or the end of the pressing. Traditionally, ten* pièces *of 205 litres are pressed first* (vin de cuvée), *then two* pièces *from the second pressing* (première taille) *and one from the third* (deuxième taille), *giving a total of 2,665 litres for 4,000kg of grapes put through the press.*

The first fermentation

Fermentation takes place following the addition of selected yeast, either in wooden receptacles or, more commonly, in enamelled or glazed metal receptacles of differing capacities. In the most recent installations, stainless steel vats are used. Stainless steel allows the fermentation to take place at an ideal temperature — 18°C — by individual cooling of the vats. It also allows the equipment to be thoroughly disinfected before and after use. Since champagne is, in general, a relatively acid wine, it is often necessary to induce the malolactic fermentation in order to decrease acidity and avoid any unwanted secondary fermentation in the bottle.

Blending

When the alcoholic and malolactic fermentations are over, the wine from different varieties and different crus *are tasted and blended in order to form* cuvées *of different qualities. These blends are then subjected either to natural winter cold or else to artificial cooling, to precipitate tartrates and aid clarification of the wine. The latter technique is now more common than the former.*

Bottling

When all final impurities have been removed by filtering, the wine is bottled in the spring following the harvest. Selected yeast, sugar — 23g or 24g per litre — and fining agents are added.

The prise de mousse

The second fermentation, called the prise de mousse, *usually takes place in cellars dug in chalk in which the temperature is a constant 12°C to 13°C. It lasts for three to five weeks and its progress is checked frequently. At the end of the* prise de mousse, *the bottled wine contains less than 1g of sugar per litre and the pressure is between 5.5 and 6kg of carbon dioxide measured at 10°C.*

Ageing on lees

*The time required by law between the new wine being run off from the vats and the finished wine leaving the cellar is 12 months, but a longer period of storage is preferable for most champagne. This storage takes place with the bottles lying horizontally on strips of wood (*sur lattes*), still in contact with the secondary fermentation lees. Interactions between the sediment of dead yeast cells and the wine take place, and these continue to enhance the quality and maturity of the product. Vintage champagne must undergo at least three years' storage of this sort.*

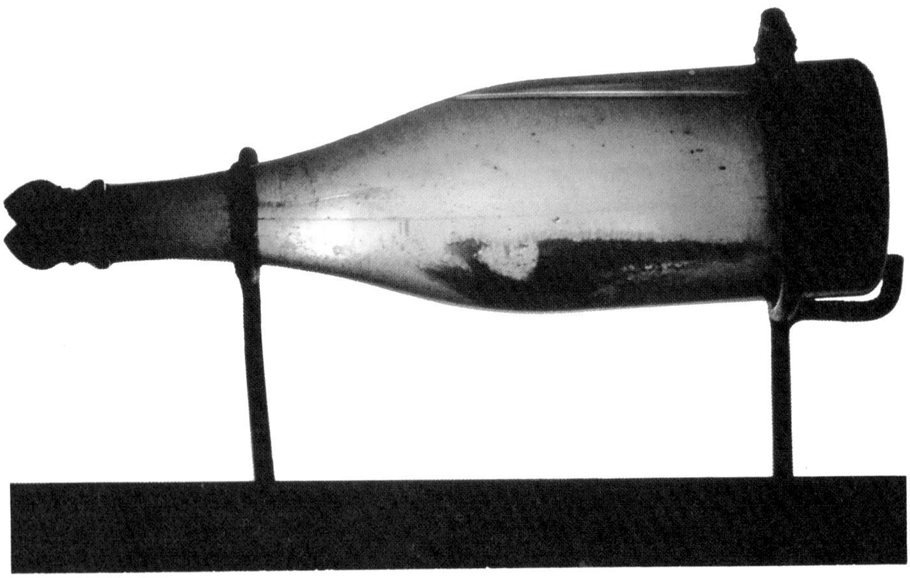

Remuage

When the ageing period in contact with the lees is completed, the wine has to be clarified. The traditional method of doing this is by remuage. *The bottles, which are initially placed in holes in an almost horizontal position, are turned by a* remueur *every day or every two days, first in one direction, then in another, inclining them gradually towards the vertical position. The deposit, which is formed of waste from dead yeast and fining matter, sinks into the neck of the bottle and, after four to six weeks'* remuage *(sometimes more), the wine becomes completely clear.*

Dégorgement

The deposit thus collected is trapped in a block of ice, formed by putting the neck of the bottle in a brine bath at −25°C for a few minutes. The deposit is expelled by opening the bottle; all that remains then is to add a small quantity of sweetened liqueur (the dosage). This operation is carried out immediately after disgorgement, so that the carbon dioxide does not escape from the bottle. The liqueur is made from a solution of cane sugar in champagne.

The dosage

The extent of sweetening varies according to the age, quality and destination of the champagne. Legislation requires less than 15g of sugar per litre for Brut, 12g to 20g for Extra Dry, 17g to 35g for Sec and up to 50g for Demi-Sec.

Corking and labelling

When the bottle has been corked, it is stored in the cellar for a further two or three months so that the recently added liqueur can blend with the wine and the cork settle into position. It is then time to label the bottle.

Champagne, like other wines, has two enemies: air and light. The cork, which is of very good quality, will keep air from the wine; it is up to the wine lover to keep his champagne away from light, preferably at a constant temperature of 12°C to 15°C, for a period of about one year, before drinking it.

A mosaic dating from 1898, decorating the front of the Champagnes Jacquart cellars in Reims.

Formerly, the date of the grape harvest was fixed by law, and wine growers who were too hasty and did not respect the orders were punished for picking too soon. Today, as well as the traditional announcement of the start of the grape harvest, the *ban des vendanges*, wine growers await the advice of the Comité Interprofessionel du Vin de Champagne (Interprofessional Committee of the Wines of Champagne) before taking this irreversible step.

The CIVC decides when the grapes are ripe enough to set the grape harvest in motion. This generally takes place from the beginning of the second or third week of September.

Champagne vinification

With a few exceptions — that of the Mailly cooperative, for example — the wine growers of Champagne do not vinify their harvest themselves. They deliver their grapes to the presses of those to whom the grapes have been sold, where the pressing, a fundamental stage of champagne vinification, takes place. This consists of extracting completely colourless juice from the grapes, most of which are black. In fact, champagne is the only quality white wine obtained largely by pressing black grapes. Only the skin of the grapes contains the coloured pigments, the juice expressed being colourless. In champagne, the quantity of grapes pressed at one time is a very specific one, called a *marc*: it amounts to 4 tonnes of grapes. The first pressing produces 2,000 litres of must, known as the *vin de cuvée*; the second pressing (known as the *première taille*) gives about two *pièces* (of 205 litres each) of must; and the third pressing (or *deuxième taille*) produces one further *pièce* of must. After the wine has received further treatment — sugar, for example, is added to raise alcohol levels and diminish acidity — the must ferments for two weeks. During the fermentation, yeast converts sugar into alcohol and carbon dioxide. When the fermentation is finished, the white wine (which, for the moment, is still) settles under the influence of naturally cold conditions or artificial refrigeration.

Bottling, which takes place in February or March, provides an opportunity to add yeast and a sugar cane solution, which causes a second

CHAMPAGNE SECRETS: BLENDING AND *CRUS*

Every bottle of champagne is a skilful blend of different cuvées, *which themselves come from distinct* terroirs, *grape varieties and plots. It is through such blends that each company 'signs' its name, and the exact composition of the blends is a very precious company possession, since there are sometimes fifty or sixty different* cuvées *in each.*

From the consumer's point of view, it is important to understand the classification of the crus *in the wine-producing communes, according to which the price of grapes is calculated. This is because a champagne made by blending wines from* cuvées *of Grands Crus (whose grapes achieve 100 per cent of the nominated annual grape price), left to mature on its secondary fermentation sediment for several years, will fetch a higher price than a more rudimentary champagne made from* crus *whose grapes only achieve 80 per cent of the nominated annual price. This percentage (100 per cent for the Grand Crus, 90 to 99 per cent for the Premiers Crus, and 80 to 89 per cent for the others) applies to the price per kilogram of grapes set yearly by a commission of traders and wine producers under the aegis of the Comité Interprofessionel du Vin de Champagne.*

▷ *Grands Crus (100 per cent): Ambonnay, Avize, Ay, Beaumont-sur-Vesle, Bouzy, Chouilly, Cramant, Louvois, Mailly-Champagne, le Mesnil-sur-Oger, Oger, Oiry, Puisieulx, Sillery, Tours-sur-Marne, Verzenay and Verzy.*

▷ *Premiers Crus (from 90 to 99 per cent): about forty communes.*

▷ *The lower* crus *are classified at 80 per cent and are produced in fewer than 100 communes.*

A champagne bottle dating from 1830. At that time, bottles were made individually, by glass blowers. Towards the end of the 19th century, with the invention of semi-automatic machines, the glass-blowing operation became mechanized and bottle shapes became regular.

CHAMPAGNE IN THE MORNING

I have lived in Champagne for a long time and I love it. I am happy here and well settled, with my feet 'in the earth'. This is probably why I am interested in matters concerning wine. Champagne is an extraordinary province — very secretive. You have to go out and look for it, to discover it in the spring and the autumn, at times when the sun is not at its zenith. You will find gently undulating landscapes, magnificent skies, full of nuances . . . like champagne.

Not everyone knows it, but there are several sorts of champagne: Blanc de Blancs, Blanc de Noirs, Rosé. Vintages play a role too, as does what I call the 'goût maison' *('house style'). Some champagne houses offer fresh, light wines; others produce more full-bodied, structured ones. The range of tastes in champagne is therefore very wide. It varies according to the different proportions of white grapes and dark grapes in the blend, the type of vinification, and the final addition of* liqueur d'expédition.

Just as there are several types of champagne, there are also several different occasions for drinking it. It may be drunk as an aperitif, at home at midnight, at a club with friends, or at the dining table. Each time, you must know how to choose your champagne — or else know how to leave it to the wine waiter.

In my opinion, the best time for champagne is eleven o'clock in the morning, when the palate is still fresh and clean! I also think that a particular context is necessary: a terrace on the Côte d'Azur, between ten and eleven; it is still not too hot. You are sitting down, relaxed, discussing life in general. I am convinced that wine, whatever it is, should be accompanied by a setting, a story, memories. It is too often forgotten these days that wine is made above all to be drunk and to give pleasure.

A meal may perfectly well be served with champagne throughout (le repas au champagne), *but delicate dishes should be chosen which are suited to it. In my opinion, people who serve champagne with game discredit themselves. In matters of cuisine, harmony is paramount.*

I use wine and, in particular, champagne in my cooking. The cook makes use of local raw materials with the same care and sometimes the same creative anguish as the painter chooses his colours. But I do not necessarily always combine it with fish. It is necessary to use champagne with imagination — but at the same time not to founder in the excess of baptizing everything in champagne. The main thing is to make people happy . . .

Gérard Boyer

fermentation in bottle, marking the *prise de mousse* (formation of foam) stage. After this, the wine begins a long period of rest in the darkness and silence of the cool, deep cellars dug out of the local chalk. This second fermentation produces a sediment which adheres to the sides of the bottles. This sediment has to be expelled. To achieve this, the bottles are placed in *pupitres* — racks with holes in which the bottles are positioned neck-first, pointing downwards.

The art of *remuage* — automatic or manual — consists of turning each bottle sharply over a period of several weeks. The sediment then moves down into the neck of the bottle, from where it is removed. The latter operation is called *dégorgement* (disgorgement). The little wine that is lost when this takes place is replaced by old champagne and old cognac or pure spirit, with a greater or lesser quantity of sugar added to it, depending on the style of champagne that is required — Brut, Sec or Demi-Sec.

Economic structures

Apart from the role played by brokers and agents, the economic activity of Champagne centres around the Comité Interprofessionel du Vin de Champagne. This harmonizes the relations between the many wine growers — there are around 18,000 harvest declarations each year — and the *négoce* — some 110 Champagne houses situated mostly in Reims and Épernay. It should be noted in this respect that, though the wine growers own about 22,000ha of vineyards, the *négoce*, with only 3,000ha of their own vineyards (in the best *crus*), carry out two thirds of all sales. The CIVC, as well as assuring good relations between the two main partners in Champagne, also strives to maintain the brand image of the product and to improve viticultural and oenological techniques in the region.

A prestige blend bottle designed by the French sculptor Arman.

Labels and styles

Blanc de Blancs: this is a champagne made only from (white) Chardonnay grapes.

Blanc de Noirs: a champagne produced exclusively from the black grapes of the Pinot Noir and Meunier grape varieties.

Brut Vintage: this wine is often more full-bodied than non-vintage champagne, and is made exclusively from the fruit of a single harvest. Not every harvest produces wines good enough to be marketed unblended, so vintage champagne is not released every year.

Crémant: this wine has 'creamier' or finer foam than champagne. This is because the pressure inside the bottle is lower than that of champagne: 3 atmospheres instead of 5 or 6.

Rosé Champagne: this is obtained by adding still red Coteaux Champenois to champagne.

Coteaux Champenois: this is a still red, white or rosé wine produced within the area of the Champagne *appellation*.

Bouzy: still red wine with a very characteristic fruitiness produced in and around the village of Bouzy, within the Coteaux Champenois.

Rosé de Riceys: a still rosé wine made from Pinot Noir grapes in and around the village of les Riceys in Aube.

Ratafia de Champagne: a *vin de liqueur* obtained by mixing two parts must (grape juice) with one part spirit. The spirit prevents the must from fermenting.

Marc de Champagne: a spirit produced by distilling the marc (the solid residue remaining after the grapes have been pressed, consisting of grape pips, skins and stalks).

Récemment dégorgé (recently disgorged): this is a vintage champagne that has matured on its sediment for 7–10 years. The late disgorging gives the champagne a youthful taste, though it has already reached complete maturity. A champagne that is *récemment dégorgé* should be drunk within a year of its disgorgement.

Also shown on the label is the registration number allocated by the CIVC, which is preceded by the following letters: RM for *récoltant-manipulant*: a small grower who makes and sells the wine from his own property; CM for *coopérative de manipulation*: champagne produced by a cooperative; NM for *négociant-manipulant*: a medium sized or large merchant house buying grapes or wines to assemble in house blends; and MA for *marque d'acheteur*: a champagne appearing under the name of the purchaser rather than the producer.

The relative sweetness of champagne is due to the variation in the amount of *liqueur d'expédition* (old champagne containing 625–650g of cane sugar per litre) added after disgorgement. This liqueur constitutes 0.5 to 1.5 per cent of Brut, 1.5 to 2 per cent of Extra Dry, 1.25 to 2.5 per cent of Sec, and 2.5 to 5 per cent of Demi-Sec champagne.

Wine celebrations in Champagne

Saint Vincent, the patron saint of wine makers, is honoured in every village of Champagne on the Sunday following 22 January. On this day, numerous bacchic *confréries*, in particular the Ordre des Coteaux de Champagne, the Commanderie du Saulte-Bouchon and the Échevins (aldermen) de Bouzy, get out their robes and diplomas to celebrate this symbolic moment with warmth and dignity.

THE ORDRE DES COTEAUX DE CHAMPAGNE

Inspired by an order that was more or less imaginary, but whose pedigree had been established by the pen of Boileau himself, the Ordre des Coteaux was founded in 1955 by a native of good Champagne stock, Rocher Gaucher. He had the idea of instituting the order so as to provide Champagne with an ambassador worthy of its name. The order set itself the task, in addition to advertising champagne, of cultivating ancient local traditions, of organizing celebrations — or participating at those which had sympathetic objectives, and of creating 'Relais de Champagne' *('Champagne Posts') throughout France and abroad.*

The success achieved by the founder and the first dignitaries exceeded the most optimistic expectations, and the order found immediate success both in France and abroad.

Receiving moral support from some of the great Champagne houses, the order prospered on the subscriptions of its members, who soon joined in their thousands. Following representations from the managers of several large houses, the order came under the aegis of the Comité Interprofessionel, which now allocates the resources necessary for permanent secretarial staff.

The Ordre des Coteaux de Champagne has nearly 8,000 members throughout the world and it is in that country where it is most active that champagne export sales are the largest!

Chapelle-Chambertin

This famous *appellation d'origine contrôlée* from the Côte de Nuits is in fact a combination of two *climats*: la Chapelle and les Gémeaux, both in the commune of Gevrey-Chambertin. They cover a total surface area of about 5ha.

This red Grand Cru, ratified by decree on 31 July 1937, is obliged, like its neighbouring Grands Crus, to have a minimum alcohol content of 11.5° and a maximum yield of 32hl/ha. With a production of 163hl in 1985, the wines of Chapelle-Chambertin are one of the most delicate creations of the commune of Gevrey-Chambertin. They are fruity, light wines of great and fascinating subtlety.

Chardonnay

Synonyms: *Pinot Blanc Chardonnay, Pinot Blanc* (but erroneously, as it is not the white form of the *Pinot Noir*), *Morillon Blanc, Auvernat Blanc* in Loiret, *Luisant* at Besançon, *Melon Blanc* or *Melon d'Arbois* in Jura, *Petite Sainte-Marie* in Savoie, *Rousseau* or *Roussot* in Yonne, *Noirien Blanc* in Côte-d'Or, *Beaunois* near Tonnerre, *Plant de Tonnerre* in Yonne, *Chablis* in Seine-et-Oise, *Épinette* in Marne, *Arnoison* in Touraine, *Romeret* in Aisne, *Auxois* in Moselle, *Petit Chatey* in Ain, *Weiss Klevner, Weiss Edler, Weiss Silber* in Alsace.

Growing tips downy white with carmine margins. Young leaves arachnoid, yellowish green, bronze coloured on the bulges.

Leaves medium sized, orbicular, contorted, bullate, fairly bright pale green, with convex edges, generally without lobes or slightly three-lobed, but leaves growing from sterile shoots can be deeply lobed; very characteristic lyrate petiolar sinus with naked base; dentation medium sized, convex; underside of blade glabrous with slightly pubescent veins.

Green shoots glabrous, finely ribbed, red-brown in the sun, pink nodes; tendrils thin, small.

Bunches small to medium, cylindrical, compact, sometimes with two shoulders; grapes spherical or sometimes slightly oblong, amber yellow in the sun, skin quite thin, lightly textured flesh with relatively small pips, flavour sweet, sugary; ripening period: first epoch, late.

The Chardonnay is the foremost quality white grape variety in the world, whose wines are distinguished by their finesse and great aromatic strength. This variety is dominant in all the great white AOCs of Burgundy: Montrachet, Meursault, Corton-Charlemagne, Chablis, Pouilly-Fuissé ...

It is also grown in Champagne, where it is the only white variety cultivated. In this area, the wines have a more discreet perfume and greater acidity than in Burgundy, and they readily acquire a *mousse* (sparkle).

The Chardonnay is fairly vigorous, and not very productive if pruned short, less than 30hl/ha producing wines of great quality. The present tendency is to train it by the *Guyot simple* or *Guyot double* methods (the latter with two main spurs rather than one) to obtain higher yields, which some years exceed 100hl/ha in Champagne; the quality of the wine, though, decreases with yields of above 80hl/ha.

Thirty-one registered clones have been approved: the most productive are numbers 78, 121, 124 and 125; while those that offer the best quality are numbers 75, 76, 95, 96, 277 and 548. The Chardonnay occupies third position in terms of nursery demand, with 21.5 million graft cuttings planted in 1986.

This vine has been classed as 'recommended' in most wine-producing *départements*, and the surface area devoted to its cultivation is constantly increasing, reaching 13,000ha in 1980 and exceeding 15,000ha today (putting it in 14th place among French varieties). Champagne leads plantings with 6,300ha, followed by Burgundy (6,000ha), then the eastern region of Jura, Ain, Savoie, the Loire valley (for sparkling wines) and the Languedoc region (either to improve Blanquette de Limoux or to produce dry white wines in Hérault and Ardèche).

A pink variety of Chardonnay has been found in the form of isolated stocks among plantings of ordinary Chardonnay.

A musky variety of Chardonnay may also be found in a number of vineyards, but its use changes the flavour of the wine produced and so is not considered desirable, especially not for sparkling wines. Only the wine producers of the Mâcon region wish to maintain a small percentage of this musky Chardonnay for their wines.

Bunch of Chardonnay grapes.

Chardonnay green shoot.

Leaf of the Chardonnay, the most distinguished of French white grape varieties.

Bunch of Chasselas grapes.

Chasselas leaf.

Charlemagne

The Emperor Charlemagne was indeed the owner of this vineyard in the Côte de Beaune, and he gave it as a gift to the abbey of Saulieu in 775. Its *appellation d'origine contrôlée* was ratified by decree on 31 July 1937, and is subject to the following conditions of production: minimum alcohol content 12°; maximum yield 30hl/ha. The area of the *appellation* merges with that of Corton-Charlemagne and stretches over the communes of Aloxe-Corton and Pernand-Vergelesses. The wine produced from these sandy and calcareous soils is a remarkable illustration of what white burgundy can be. It has a golden colour and a richly fruity bouquet, with a hint of cinnamon in it. It is often marketed under the Corton-Charlemagne AOC.

Charmes-Chambertin

This *climat* situated in the commune of Gevrey-Chambertin on the Côte de Nuits covers several hectares and produces a red Grand Cru whose average annual production is 700hl. The *appellation d'origine contrôlée* is governed by the decree of 30 July 1937, and some confusion exists between this *appellation* and that of the neighbouring Grand Cru of Mazoyères-Chambertin. The wines of both Charmes and of Mazoyères can be labelled under the name of Charmes, but Charmes does not have a right to the Mazoyères *appellation*. The AOC requirements are an alcohol content of 11.5°, and a maximum yield of 32hl/ha. The wines of Charmes-Chambertin are appreciated for their nuanced flavours and aromas, their finesse and their lightness. They therefore stand out from the other Chambertin Grands Crus, which are stronger, more austere and more virile.

Chasan

A Listan × Chardonnay cross made at INRA at Vassal, near Montpellier. Growing tips felty white, leaves orbicular, deeply five-lobed, petiolar sinus lyrate, sometimes naked at base. Bunches fairly large with two shoulders; grapes medium, spherical, golden white; ripening period: second epoch. The Chasan has a spreading habit and has to be trellis-trained; its productivity is average; the wine is slightly aromatic, not very acidic and of average alcoholic strength. It is classed as 'recommended' throughout France, with one approved clone: number 538.

Chassagne-Montrachet

The red and white wines of this famous *appellation d'origine contrôlée* are produced on various plots in the communes of Chassagne-Montrachet and Remigny, cited in the decree of 1 December 1977. Fifty-four vineyard sites or *climats* are enumerated as Premiers Crus, taking up 159ha; the rest of the *appellation* proper, for 'village' wines, covers 173ha. (Grand Cru *climats* are listed separately, under their individual names.) The *terroir* is characterized by siliceous and calcareous soils with magnesian subsoil. The Premiers Crus are situated to the south of the N6, and the Grands Crus to the north of it. The Chardonnay is the variety used for white wines, and is planted in the highest part of the *appellation* area; the Pinot Noir is used for the red wines. The average total annual production is 7,000hl of white wine and 6,400hl of red wine. The 'village' red wines of Chassagne-Montrachet have a minimum alcohol content of 10.5° and the Premiers Crus 11°, whereas 11° is required for the 'village' whites and 11.5° for the Premiers Crus. The maximum permitted yield is 35hl/ha for both types. Chassagne white wine is dry, firm, comparatively low in acidity, velvety, fruity, long on the palate. The red wines are sound, solid, occasionally powerful, with a subtle aroma of ripe plums or prunes. They are wines that keep well.

Chasselas

Synonyms: *Chasselas Doré, Chasselas de Fontainebleau, de Moissac, de Montauban, Abélione* in Ardèche, *Fendant* in Haute-Savoie, *Mornen Blanc* in Rhône.

Growing tips open, arachnoid, white.

Young leaves glossy, bullate, wavy, glabrous.

Leaves medium sized, truncate, smooth, light green, thin, slightly crimped at the petiolar junction, deeply five-lobed; upper lateral sinuses club shaped, acute at bases, lower lateral sinuses open; petiolar sinus lyrate and more or less closed; dentation medium sized, convex.

Green shoots striated, reddish green with purple hues, glabrous; tendrils large, fleshy.

Bunches medium sized, cylindrical, loose; grapes spherical, medium sized, light green to amber yellow in colour, speckled russet in the sun; skin thin but strong; flesh juicy, easily expressed; ripening period: first epoch.

This is a vigorous grape variety with early budbreak, making it susceptible during flowering to variations in temperature and to rain, which can sometimes lead to extensive *coulure* (flower abortion) in northern vineyard areas. It performs well when grafted on to Riparia and 3309, rootstocks that favour its precocity, as well as 41B in dry and calcareous soils.

The Chasselas is sensitive to a number of diseases: downy mildew, oidium (powdery mildew), and grape worms; it is also sensitive to hail and winter frosts. It is often trained *en gobelet*, but it also responds well to Guyot and Cordon de Royat pruning and training.

Yields are variable: the best eating grapes are obtained in poor earth on slopes with a production of 1–2kg per vine stock, whereas on the plain, the bunches are more compact and tightly packed and the yields are higher.

The Chasselas is grown for two purposes. It is still the most common French vine for the production of table grapes, with nearly 10,000ha of plantings, despite a significant decrease in its cultivation (21,400ha in 1958) due to difficulties in selling its grapes for export. There is a table grape *appellation d'origine protégée* 'Chasselas de Moissac' in Tarn-et-Garonne, which is the *département* that produces the most (3,300ha), followed by Hérault, Gard, Vaucluse and Lot-et-Garonne.

As a wine variety, the Chasselas is grown on 1,040ha, mainly to meet the needs of the AOCs of Alsace (585ha), Haute-Savoie (Crépy, Vin de Savoie) and Nièvre (Pouilly-sur-Loire).

The wine of the Chasselas is pleasant when drunk young. It is generally not very alcoholic or acidic, with a lightly aromatic character, depending on the *terroir*. In Alsace, a *vin de paille* dessert wine called *Strohwein* used to be made with very ripe Chasselas grapes placed on rye straw in order to make the berries wither and the sugars become concentrated.

Numerous varieties of Chasselas exist and are scattered throughout the vineyards: Chasselas Rose, Chasselas Rose de Falloux, Chasselas Violet, Chasselas Musqué, a seedless Chasselas (Chasselas sans Pépins), and Chasselas Cioutat with palmatisect or parsley-like foliage.

Château-Chalon

This *appellation*, ratified by decree on 29 May 1936, is reserved for *vins jaunes* (*see* the Jura regional entry) produced around the small village of this name northeast of Lons-le-Saunier. It includes the communes of Château-Chalon, Menétru-le-Vignoble, Domblans and Nevy-sur-Seille. The other wines produced in this area are classed as Côtes du Jura. The 30 or so hectares in production are divided between numerous owners. As well as being limited to one single wine type, the *appellation* rules are equally unique in the way in which they are applied: it is the only case in France where, on the day before the harvest, a commission fixes the yield — about 20hl/ha — vineyard by vineyard. In bad years, the wine makers refuse the AOC and no *vin jaune* is produced, as happened in 1974, 1980 and 1984.

The vines grow on the steep slopes of the Premier Plateau on grey, blue or black marl, well exposed to the sun and protected from the wind by the cliffs of the Baume blind valley. This position makes Château-Chalon the greatest of all *vins jaunes*; it keeps exceptionally well, sometimes for more than a century. These wines often need to age for a few years in the bottle, after which they acquire a remarkable suppleness, distinguished structure, and a powerful aroma of almonds and hazelnuts which win them appreciation on their own as an aperitif, or as an accompaniment to rich food.

Chassagne-Montrachet on the Côte de Beaune produces the Grands Crus Montrachet, Bâtard-Montrachet and Criots-Bâtard-Montrachet: dry white wines with a worldwide reputation.

Château Grillet

This *appellation d'origine contrôlée* from the Côtes du Rhône presents an almost unique case in French wine legislation, since it applies to only one property.

The vineyard has probably existed since ancient times, like its neighbours Côte Rôtie and Condrieu. It has not, though, been widely described down the centuries, possibly because its smallness meant that it was confused with the surrounding vineyards. Some vines are mentioned here in 1683, but the reputation of the name only became well established at the beginning of the 19th century.

Around the château building, which was constructed between the 16th and 18th centuries, 2.5ha of vines grow on terraces of granitic sandstone with a south-facing exposure. The annual production of the estate is under 90hl. The AOC was ratified on 8 December 1936.

This is, therefore, a rare wine. Made from the Viognier grape variety, its organoleptic characteristics are similar to those of Condrieu, whose wines are also made from the Viognier. With its peach and apricot perfume and its oily, almost unctuous texture, it may be drunk in all its freshness when very young, but it also ages remarkably well.

Châteaumeillant

On 18 February 1965, this *appellation* was classified as a VDQS for red and rosé wines. The area of the *appellation* covers four communes in Cher: Châteaumeillant, Reigny, Saint-Maur and Vestun, and four communes in Indre: Champillet, Feusines, Néret and Urciers.

The wines are made from the Gamay, Pinot Gris and Pinot Noir grape varieties. Average production is 4,500hl per year, 60 per cent of this figure being red wine and 40 per cent rosé. The red wines are light and fruity and the rosés are dry and lively. They are best drunk young.

Châteauneuf-du-Pape

This prestigious *appellation d'origine contrôlée* has had so much written about it, and so much importance has been attributed to the papal role in the extension of the vineyard area, that it is advisable to establish facts at the outset.

The development of the vineyards was very slow initially. This was because the large boulders scattered about the terraces that covered most of the area were an obstacle to cultivation, and there were no sufficiently strong steel implements to work with at the time.

The first vines were probably planted by the Templars in the 13th century. They disappeared soon afterwards, but were replanted thanks to the Avignon Pope John XXII. The vineyard was, for a while, cultivated by shepherds who drank its wine, whereas the popes drank wine sent south from Beaune. This local wine was not known by its present name; the place was in fact called Châteauneuf-Calcernier at the time, because of the numerous lime kilns that operated there. It was only later that the wine and the town became called Châteauneuf-du-Pape, not because Pope Innocent VI drank its white wine, but because a castle had been built there by the popes, and because there was a small vineyard within the castle enclosure. During the 18th century, the vineyard area increased and the wine ceased to be of merely local interest. From 500ha or 600ha in 1873, it has expanded to 3,050ha in 1985. Present-day production is around 100,000hl.

The wine makers of Châteauneuf, led by one of their number, Baron Charnay, were the first to ask the courts for a precise production and zonal statute. In doing so they sowed the seeds of the entire French *appellation contrôlee* system. The *appellation* was recognized by a judicial judgement in 1929, then classified as an AOC by decree on 18 May 1936, for five communes of the Côtes du Rhône.

The soils of the *appellation* consist of four layers of clay terraces containing a large number of sizeable boulders. There is also sand and clay terrain, and slopes of limestone from the Barremian stage of the Cretaceous period.

There is a complex mixture of permitted grape varieties: no less than 13 of them, both red and white. Each grower's wine is made from those varieties that are best adapted to such-and-such a part of the *terroir*, without changing the general character of the *appellation* product. The commonest variety — the Grenache — is generally combined with a number of other varieties that complement it perfectly. In the hot and dry climate of the region, the vines are trained *en gobelet* and very rarely staked or trellised.

Thanks to modern vinification methods, the wine makers have been able to reintroduce to the market, over the last thirty years or so, the local white wines. These were already known in 1370, but had practically disappeared over the course of the centuries. Some 5,000hl of white wines are now produced annually. They have a fairly strong floral bouquet; the high alcohol content is disguised by an appealing aromatic freshness. The wine is not heavy on the palate, but is firm and boldly flavoured, and not without a certain elegance.

But it is above all the red wines that have created the reputation this *terroir* enjoys. Generally vinified with long vatting periods, they are very tannic and need to age for several years in order to express themselves fully. They have a bouquet dominated by the aroma of fruit kernels, aniseed, liquorice and other spices, with an ample, full, round, smooth body.

Châtillon-en-Diois

This is a very small vineyard area northeast of the Côtes du Rhône, the antiquity of which is not precisely known. Some seventy years ago, however, there was a vineyard on a local estate, planted with the white Burgundy varieties of Melon and Chardonnay; the estate produced, thanks to vinification technology in advance of its time, excellent white wines. This vineyard was probably the origin of today's Châtillon-en-Diois wines.

The *appellation d'origine contrôlée*, ratified by decree on 3 March 1975, today covers the area between Luc-en-Diois and Pont-de-Quart in the Drôme *département*, at a sufficiently high altitude to limit production. Fifty hectares produce up to 2,500hl of red and white wines.

The white wines, made today from the Aligoté and Chardonnay varieties, have a pleasant floral perfume. They are light and lively, and have a marked level of acidity, which distinguishes them from Rhône valley whites.

The red wines, produced from the Gamay,

the Syrah and the Pinot Noir have a very fresh, fruity bouquet. Light and with little tannin, they are at their best when young.

Chatus

Synonyms: *Corbel* or *Corbeil* in Drôme, *Corbesse* in Isère, *Gros Chenu, Chanu* or *Vert Chenu* at Roussillon and Hyerieux, *Persagne-Gamay* in Rhône, *Ouron* or *Houron* at Saint-Péray, *Mourre, Mouret, Mouraud.*

Bunches conical, narrow, medium sized or fairly large, compact; grapes spherical, small, blue-black, juicy, with slightly harsh juice; ripening period: first epoch.

This is a fertile grape variety, often stake-trained in Isère and Savoie, producing a wine that is rich in colour but flat and ordinary to taste. It is unclassified, but was grown on 157ha in Ardèche and 2ha in Savoie in 1958.

Cheilly-lès-Maranges, Sampigny-lès-Maranges and Dezize-lès-Maranges

Red and white wines are produced in these three communes of Saône-et-Loire on an area of 230ha, forming a continuation of the Côte de Beaune. The decree of 21 May 1970 stipulates that the wines from these three *appellations d'origine contrôlée* should have a minimum alcohol content of 10° for reds and 10.5° for whites. The maximum yield is 35hl/ha.

An average of 9,000hl of red and white wine is produced here annually. These wines can also be marketed under the Côte de Beaune-Villages *appellation*, or that of Côte de Beaune followed by the name of the relevant village.

Chenanson

A Grenache × Jurançon Noir cross obtained at the INRA at Vassal, near Montpellier.

Bunches large, winged, fairly compact; grapes medium sized, spherical, black; ripening period: third epoch, early.

A productive grape variety, with early bud-break, it produces a highly coloured, fairly distinctive wine, with a quality similar to that of the Grenache. It is classed as 'recommended' and a clone, number 602, has been approved.

Chénas

The *appellation d'origine contrôlée* Chénas, ratified by decree on 11 September 1936, is the smallest of all the Beaujolais *crus*. Covering only just over 100ha, it produces 14,000hl (1,800,000 bottles) of red wine per year. This *appellation* is also the least homogeneous of the Beaujolais *crus*, since there are many differences between the terrain found near Moulin-à-Vent and that of the area closer to Juliénas. Overall, the soil is shallow and consists of a mixture of manganese and decomposed granite.

The village of Chénas owes its name to the forest of oak trees (*chênes* in French) that covered the region at the dawn of the Christian era, well before the expansion of the vineyards.

The best bottles of Chénas can be kept for five to six years. They are warm, voluptuous and tender, and have an attractive bouquet. 'Chénas is a spray of flowers in a velvet basket,' say the locals. A frequently encountered aroma is reminiscent of peony.

The growers of this complicated and much-debated *appellation* may also produce Moulin-à-Vent within the commune of Chénas.

Chenin Blanc

Synonyms: *Plant d'Anjou, Blanc d'Anjou, Plant de Brézé, Pinet d'Anjou, Pinot de la Loire, Gros Pineau, Pineau de la Loire, Pineau de Savennières, Pineau de Vouvray, Pineau Vert, Pineau Blanc* in Cheverny, *Pointu de Savennières, Petit Verdet* or *Arbois* in Touraine, *Blanc d'Aunis* in Charente, *Franc Blanc* in Vendée, *Franche* on the Île de Ré, *Confort* in Vienne, *Ronchalin* in Gironde, *Péra* in Indre, *Verdurant* in Allier, *Rajoulin* in Corrèze, *Gamay Blanc* in Aveyron, *Capbreton* in Landes, *Couéfort* or *Quéfort* in Gers, *Tête de Crabe* or *Tite de Crabe* ('goat's udder' in Gascon), *Plant de Salcès.*

Growing tips open, felty white with pink margins.

Young leaves downy with bronze patches, underside of blade felty.

Leaves orbicular, dark green, bullate, contorted, five-lobed with lateral sinuses more or

Chénas, in the Beaujolais region, whose wine is a 'spray of flowers'.

less closed, acute at base; petiolar sinus lyrate with the base of the veins red on the upper side (in some clones the veins are green); dentation narrow, convex; underside of blade downy in tufts. Green shoots glabrous, mahogany-red on the side exposed to the sun, with longitudinal brown striations beneath; tendrils long, red, fleshy.

Bunches medium sized, conical with one or two wings, fairly compact; grapes ovoid, medium sized, golden yellow, with thin skin, crisp flesh and dense pulp; ripening period: second epoch.

The Chenin Blanc is a vigorous grape variety, with early budbreak, and therefore susceptible to late frosts; it is also affected to a moderate degree by grey rot (botrytis) and grape worms.

Six registered clones have been approved — numbers 220, 278, 416, 417, 550 and 624 — and the most precocious clones are selected in Anjou so as to gain about ten days. The Chenin Blanc has been classed as 'recommended' in the Loire valley, in the South West and in Languedoc.

Wine from the Chenin Blanc is very fruity, with a generous aroma, and it may be kept for a long time. It is generally vinified as a sweet wine, which is characteristic of the best white wines of Anjou — Coteaux du Layon, Savennières, Vouvray. It is said to be less well suited to making dry white wines; but it is capable of acquiring a fine *mousse* (sparkle), and is used to make a number of AOC sparkling wines, like those of Saumur, Vouvray, Montlouis and Touraine.

It is the 6th most important white grape variety in France, and is grown on an area of about 10,000ha, a decrease since 1958 (16,500ha) as a result of the drop in sales of sweet white wines. Apart from a few small plantations in Aude for Blanquette de Limoux, cultivation of the Chenin Blanc is concentrated in the Loire.

Chevalier-Montrachet

This Grand Cru from the Côte de Beaune covers 7.15ha, and is situated in the commune of Puligny-Montrachet. It lies at a higher altitude than the Montrachet vineyard, which makes it a lighter wine. The vineyard is on barren and arid land, well suited to the cultivation of the Chardonnay. This no doubt explains — with its east-southeast exposure — the sumptuousness of this great white wine. The decree of 31 July 1937, which ratified the *appellation*, fixed the minimum alcohol content at 12°, the maximum yield at only 30hl/ha, and authorized the Chardonnay as the only grape variety. Very similar to Montrachet, apart from being slightly lighter, Chevalier-Montrachet is rightly considered to be one of the greatest dry white wines of France and of the whole world. It is strong, lively, very fruity, with a fine aromatic presence suggesting hazelnuts, almonds and honey. Its delicate, very pale colour, full of reflections and glints, is equally fine. It is advisable not to drink it over-chilled, since its aroma is most splendid at around 12°C or 13°C.

Cheverny

The vineyard area, classed as a VDQS by the decree of 17 July 1973, covers about 300ha. Numerous grape varieties are grown in it. The white varieties are Chenin Blanc, Arbois, Chardonnay, Romorantin and Sauvignon Blanc; the reds are Gamay, Cabernet Franc, Cabernet Sauvignon, Pinot Noir, Côt and Gamay de Chaudenay (to a maximum of 15 per cent); the same varieties are used for the rosés, with the addition of Pineau d'Aunis and Pinot Gris; while for the sparkling wines the varieties used are Chenin Blanc, Arbois, Chardonnay, Meslier Saint-François, Pineau d'Aunis, Cabernet Franc and Cabernet Sauvignon.

Annual production over the last few years has approached 6,000hl of white wine, with 5 to 10 per cent of this figure vinified as sparkling wine; and 6,000hl of red wine, with 10 per cent of this figure vinified as rosé wine. The area of production lies in the *département* of Loir-et-Cher, and covers 23 communes.

Chiroubles, in the Beaujolais region, with its characteristic onion-shaped church tower.

The siliceous soils give these well-balanced, pleasant wines lightness and subtlety. They are best drunk young.

Chichaud

Synonyms: *Tsintsao* (in Ardèche dialect) at Aubenas, *Brunet* at Privas, *Chicaud*.

Bunches large, winged, cylindrical-conical, compact; grapes spherical to ovoid, medium sized, dark, juicy; ripening period: second epoch.

This grape variety has late budbreak, is not very productive and gives wines that are weakly coloured, but that are nevertheless attractive and aromatic. Its grapes may also be eaten. Unclassified.

Chinon

The vineyard zone, classed as an AOC by decree on 31 July 1937, covers about 1,550ha. The varieties used for the red and rosé wines are the Cabernet Franc (locally called the Breton) and up to 10 per cent of the Cabernet Sauvignon if necessary; for the white wines, only the Chenin Blanc is used.

The annual production of red wine is 47,000hl. The volume of rosé wine produced varies from year to year, but is usually somewhere between 2 and 5 per cent of the red wine total. The production of white wines is tiny; no more than 210hl per year. The zone stretches over 19 communes or parts of communes.

The colour of the red wines can be light or deep, depending on the terrain on which they are grown. Gravelly, warm soil brings the wine garnet hints; calcareous soil, a purple shade. With age, the wines acquire an amber hue. The aroma develops a vegetal, then an animal character, finally becoming mineral, fruity and floral. Chinon is velvety, and has a lively tannic structure, but one in complete harmony with the wine's fine, supple body.

The white wines of Chinon have an astonishing longevity. One vineyard has been entered in the land *cadastre* as 'Champ Chenin', which indicates the importance of the Chenin Blanc in Chinon. The wines, which are dry or off-dry depending on the amount of sunshine each year, are well structured and elegant.

Chiroubles

Chiroubles nestles in a recess in the Beaujolais hills. Its granite and sandy soils have nourished vines since the 11th century. In an area of 260ha, an average of 18,000hl, or 2,400,000 bottles, are produced annually. This *cru*, which was classed as an AOC by the decree of 11 September 1936, is greatly admired in France, but still not very widely appreciated abroad. It is commonly considered to be the most typically 'beaujolais' of all the Beaujolais wines. It is generally the lightest of the *crus*: of great delicacy and charm, with its bright red colour and its aroma of violets, its impulsive quality encourages people to drink it before any of the other *crus*. A few Chiroubles wines, though, have a distinctive solidity, recalling that of the small, dry-stone walls found locally, called *rases*.

An aerial view of vineyards near Chinon, in Touraine.

Chorey-lès-Beaune

Unlike neighbouring *appellations*, Chorey-lès-Beaune does not possess any Premiers Crus. This is because the *terroir*, which is mostly situated on the plain, is composed of earth that is too rich, luxuriant and well irrigated to produce wine of the highest quality. The 150ha of the *appellation d'origine contrôlée* are almost all, apart from the plot called les Beaumonts, situated on the east side of the N74. The decree of 21 May 1970, under which the *appellation* was classed, specifies a minimum alcohol content of 10.5° for red wines and 11° for white, and a maximum yield of 35hl/ha. Average annual production is nearly 1,500hl of red wine with only 10hl of white.

Though little known because of the proximity of other, more highly prized *crus* such as Savigny-lès-Beaune, the red wines of Chorey are nevertheless firm and supple in the mouth, with a bouquet and good keeping qualities. They are often sold under the Côte de Beaune-Villages *appellation*.

Chouchillon

Leaves orbicular, contorted, bullate, five-lobed with lateral sinuses club shaped, acute at base, petiolar sinus closed or with overlapping edges; dentation medium sized, convex; underside of blade weakly arachnoid, practically glabrous.

Bunches short, cylindrical, fairly loose; grapes spherical or slightly ovoid, medium sized, white or slightly pink, skin veined, soft flesh; ripening period: second epoch, late.

This vine used to be included in the Chagnon vineyard area of the Loire and produced a good quality white wine. Unclassified.

Leaf of the Cinsaut, a variety classed as 'recommended' in the Midi and South West France.

Cinsaut

Synonyms: *Cinsault, Cinqsaut, Cinq-saou* in Languedoc, *Piquepoul d'Uzés* at Béziers, *Plant d'Arles* in Bouches-du-Rhône, *Boudalès* or *Bourdalès* in Pyrénées-Orientales, *Milhau* or *Milhaud du Pradel* in Tarn-et-Garonne, *Morterille* or *Morterille Noire* in Haute-Garonne, *Prunella* or *Prunelas* and *Espagnol* in Gers, *Bourdelas* in Hautes-Pyrénées, *Prunaley* and *Gros de Lacaze* in Gironde, *Gros Marocain* in Charente, *Marroquin, Marrouquin, Picardin Noir* in Var, *Espagnen* in Vaucluse, *Salerne* at Nice, *Cuvillier* at Grenoble, *Pétaïre* and *Plant de Broqui* in Aveyron.

Bunch of Cinsaut grapes.

Growing tips open, felty white with carmine margins. Young leaves downy, bullate, reddish yellow, five-lobed.

Leaves orbicular, medium sized, soft, contorted, light green, deeply five-lobed with lateral sinuses acute at base, sometimes with a single tooth at the base of the sinus, more or less closed; petiolar sinus lyrate, narrow or closed; dentation pointed, very narrow; underside of blade arachnoid in tufts or pubescent, depending on the clone. In the autumn, the foliage turns partly red.

Green shoots ribbed, light green, glabrous with large tendrils. Bunches large, cylindrical-conical, compact; grapes ellipsoidal, large, a fine blue-black colour with bloom, firm skin, crisp to the bite, juicy but fairly firm flesh; ripening period: second epoch.

The Cinsaut is of average vigour and has a spreading habit, hence its name, Cinsaut Couché (Lying Cinsaut), in Vaucluse. There is, however, also an upright Cinsaut, called Cinsaut Droit. The budbreak of Cinsaut is fairly late, in mid-April, and the variety is susceptible to downy mildew, oidium (powdery mildew), grape worms and yellow spider mites. The fertility of the Cinsaut is regular, requiring vigorous grafting stock when grown on plains, where its production can reach 100hl/ha. On the slopes, where quality fruit and early ripening are desiderata, grafting stock is of average strength, numbers 3309 or 4453 being used. When harvested from vineyards on favourable slopes, Cinsaut's wine has a fine red colour, is soft and rich, and has a pleasant perfume.

Broadly speaking, the Cinsaut is grown for two purposes. In the Midi, it is used to give suppleness and balance to wines made primarily from the Carignan and Grenache grape varieties. It is also grown to provide table grapes, sold under the name of 'Oeillade' (an ancient vine that it resembles, but one that is no longer grown), mainly for the French market. It is not much exported because its grapes are considered too small by international traders. The Cinsaut is specified for the AOCs of Châteauneuf-du-Pape, Côtes du Rhône, Côtes de Provence and Coteaux du Languedoc among others. It has been classed as 'recommended' in all the *départements* of the Midi and the South West. Twenty-one registered clones have been approved, the most useful of which appear to be numbers 5, 3, 4, 103 and 252. In the last few years, the surface area devoted to plantings of Cinsaut has risen from 11,000ha to more than 51,000ha, which puts it in 5th place among French varieties. It occupies an important position in Languedoc with 35,000ha, as well as in Provence and Corsica with 16,000ha.

Ciréné de Romans

Synonyms: *Siranié, Sérené, Ciranė, Cérigné, Céréné, Sérénèze de la Tronche.*

Leaves orbicular, smooth, slightly concave, weakly three-lobed with shallow lateral sinuses, petiolar sinus lyrate, open; dentation medium sized, convex; underside of blade arachnoid, fluffy. Foliage turns partly red in the autumn.

Bunches cylindrical, small, compact; grapes spherical, medium sized, blue-black; ripening period: second epoch, late.

The Ciréné de Romans is a grape variety orginating in Drôme, where it is grown in the Romans-sur-Isère and Bourg-de-Péage region. It is also grown in Isère at la Tronche, near Grenoble. Its wine is said to be delicate, and to keep well. This fertile variety is fairly resistant to downy mildew and grey rot (botrytis), but is susceptible to oidium (powdery mildew). Unclassified.

Clairette

Synonyms: *Clérette, Clairette Blanche, Petite Clairette, Clairette Pounchudo* in the lower Rhône basin, *Clairette Verte* at Bandol, *Petit Blanc* at Aubenas, *Blanquette* in Aude and Gard, *Cotticour* in Tarn-et-Garonne, *Malvoisie* (erroneously) in Gironde and Lot-et-Garonne, *Muscade* at Loupiac, *Colle-Musquette* at Sainte-Croix-du-Mont.

Growing tips open, felty white with carmine margins.

Leaf of the Clairette.

Young leaves downy, yellow, with felty underside.

Leaves orbicular, medium sized, dark green with a slightly blue hue, thick, contorted, bullate, five-lobed with lateral sinuses narrow, acute at base; petiolar sinus closed, with overlapping edges; dentation small, narrow, convex, pointed; underside of blade felty-pubescent.

Green shoots ribbed, light green, downy at the tips and weakly striated with red; tendrils small, thin.

Bunches medium sized to large, cylindrical-conical, winged, generally not very compact; grapes ellipsoidal or olive shaped, pointed, medium sized, white, speckled with brown dots; flesh firm, juicy; ripening period: third epoch.

This is a very vigorous vine with an upright habit, which adapts well to poor soils and which must be grafted on to weak grafting stocks, otherwise its excessive vigour makes it susceptible to *coulure* (flower abortion), Its green shoots are susceptible to high winds. It suffers more from downy mildew and grape worms than from oidium (powdery mildew) and phomopsis. With low yields — below 50hl/ha — very strong wines can be produced (from 12° to 14°). However, they do not have much bouquet, and they oxidize easily — a property that was once much sought after for the blending and manufacture of wine-based aperitifs. The Clairette is vinified on its own today for two AOC white wines: Clairette de Bellegarde in Gard, and Clairette du Languedoc in Hérault. The regulations concerning this last *appellation* permit three types of wine to be produced: *vins de liqueur*, dry wines, and *rancio* wines made from grapes harvested when overripe, and given a natural ageing process lasting three years to produce an oxidized wine.

It is also combined with Muscat Blanc à Petits Grains to make a sparkling wine, Clairette de Die, and it is mixed with other white grape varieties to produce a number of southern French AOC white wines: Châteauneuf-du-Pape, Côtes du Rhône, Côtes de Provence, Cassis, Bellet, Palette and others.

Ten registered clones have been approved, the most useful being numbers 68, 69, 97 and 175. The cultivation of Clairette is in decline, falling from 14,000ha in 1958 to only 5,400ha in 1980, as a result of a slump in the sales of the very strong, oxidized white wines that Clairette was previously chiefly used for. The main plantations of it are in Languedoc (Gard, Hérault, Ardèche and Aude), in Provence (Vaucluse, Var and Bouches-du-Rhône), as well as in the Drôme. A few small plantations still exist in the South West (Gers, Gironde, Tarn-et-Garonne, Pyrénées-Atlantiques).

Bunch of Clairette grapes, which are used to make still and sparkling white wines in Languedoc and elsewhere.

Clairette green shoot.

The Clairette Rose is grown to a small extent in Gard, Hérault, Var and Vaucluse. Clairettes have been classed as 'recommended' for wine making in all the *départements* of the Midi and South West; they have also been classed as an approved variety for table grapes.

Clairette de Bellegarde

The vineyard area, classed as an AOC by the decree of 28 June 1949, is situated to the south of Nîmes, within the Costières du Gard AOC zone. Only one grape variety — the Clairette — is grown in the stony local soils and it produces a dry white wine with a characteristic bouquet. Production is 2,000hl, 80 per cent of it from the cooperative at Bellegarde.

Clairette de Die and Clairette de Die Mousseux

The vineyard area for these still and sparkling wine AOCs is situated on the well-exposed slopes that border the river Drôme between Aouste-sur-Sye and Luc-en-Diois.

It was originally a shepherds' vineyard. The Romans developed it, mostly by planting the Clairette vine, which they probably brought from the shores of the Mediterranean. Pliny speaks with great admiration of the 'Clarette de Dea Augusta'.

Religious orders, particularly the Cistercians, took an interest in the vineyards and the reputation of Clairette from Die spread for centuries thanks to ecclesiastical viticulture.

The *appellation d'origine contrôlée* was ratified by the decrees of April 1942 and May 1971 for 32 communes of the Côtes du Rhône. The vineyard area, sited on slopes, covers 1,000ha and produces 55,000hl, 35,000hl of which are vinified by the cooperative at Die. Two grape varieties are used: the Muscat à Petits Grains, grown on marly soils; and the Clairette, better suited to calcareous scree.

Still, dry white Clairette-based wines account for only a small amount — 20,000 bottles.

The sparkling wines are made following two different methods. The *méthode traditionelle* (traditional method) wines are vinified from a minimum of 50 per cent of the Muscat, the balance being made up by the Clairette. The method consists of allowing the natural sugars of the grapes to ferment in bottle, without any syrup-based enrichment, so that the maximum amount of Muscat grape perfume is retained. This method produces sparkling dessert wine, which should be drunk young. The other method by which sparkling wines are obtained is the *méthode champenoise*, vinified from at least 75 per cent Clairette. This method produces light, dry white wines, which are excellent for an aperitif or for refreshment at any time.

Clairette du Languedoc

This AOC, ratified by decree on 12 April 1965, is one of the three *crus* situated within the regional Coteaux du Languedoc *appellation*. The vineyard area lies in the central valley of Hérault on calcareous and clay soils. It is planted with the Clairette grape variety, and produces annually some 10,000hl of white wine that is light gold in colour, with an aroma reminiscent of apples, fruity, full on the tongue, and leaving a slightly bitter taste typical of the Clairette. It may be dry or sweet. When vinified from late-harvested grapes, the wine is very rich, and can be aged to acquire a *rancio* (oxidized) taste.

Clape (La) *See* Coteaux du Languedoc.

Clarin

An Ugni Blanc × Clairette cross, this vine is vigorous, well adapted to *gobelet* training and less sensitive to wind damage than the Ugni Blanc; its production is consistent and its wine, lightly aromatic, may be used to improve the quality of other white table wines. Classed as 'authorized' with clone number 761 approved.

Claverie

Synonyms: *Clabarien, Clabérieu, Clabérien, Clabéria, Chalosse Blanche* or *Chaloussenc, Bourguieu* in the Tursan area, *Galia Zuria* in the Basque country.

Bunches long, 20 to 30cm, cylindrical, compact, with two distinct shoulders; grapes medium sized, ovoid, yellowish white, speckled with brown in the sun, thin skin, juicy flesh; ripening period: third epoch.

A grape variety from the Chalosse area in the Landes, and from the Vic-Bilh and Jurançon *appellations* in Pyrénées-Atlantiques. Its strong wine was for a long time highly prized by Dutch wine traders for sale in either dry or sweet form. This variety is very susceptible to oidium (powdery mildew). It is classed as 'recommended' in Pyrénées-Atlantiques and Landes.

Clos des Lambrays

This 8.7ha *clos* (enclosed vineyard) lies in the commune of Morey-Saint-Denis on the Côte de Nuits. It was not until April 1981 that the Clos des Lambrays received official recognition as a fully fledged Grand Cru, even though it had been labelled 'Grand Cru' by its owner before that time. Average annual production is 246hl; minimum alcohol content is 11.5°; and maximum yield is 35hl/ha. This excellent red wine is often described as the most typical of Morey-Saint-Denis: it has robustness, structure, subtlety and strength.

Clos de la Roche

This Grand Cru AOC, situated in the commune of Morey-Saint-Denis on the Côte de Nuits, was ratified by decree on 8 December 1936. The vineyard, with its 16.9ha, is one of the largest in Morey. Minimum alcohol content is fixed at 11.5° and base yield at 35hl/ha. Average annual production approaches 400hl. The combination of calcareous clay soils and favourable microclimatic conditions is responsible for the quality of this robust, sprightly red wine with its dark, glinting colour. It has a strong aroma of strawberries and violets. It ages well.

Clos Saint-Denis

This *clos*, in the commune of Morey-Saint-Denis on the Côte de Nuits, covers a surface area of 6.5ha. Its well-reputed red wine has a long pedigree, having been the property of the collegiate church of Saint-Denis in the 13th century. It was not, though, until 1936 that the offical rank of Grand Cru was granted to the Clos Saint-Denis, with the decree of 8 December. This wine has to have a minimum alcohol content of 11.5°. Maximum yield is 30hl/ha, and the annual harvest is about 210hl.

It is said to be more elegant than the other *crus* of Morey, and lighter and less structured than the *crus* of the Clos de Tart and the Clos de la Roche. It nevertheless ranks among the foremost red Grands Crus of Burgundy.

Clos de Tart

A long history preceded the decree of 4 January 1939, which ratified this Côte de Nuits Grand Cru *appellation*. The vineyard was even the subject of a papal bull, confirming its sale by the Bernardine Sisters; at that time the *clos* was called the Climat de la Forge. Situated to the north of Morey-Saint-Denis, between Bonnes Mares and the Clos des Lambrays, the 7.2ha vineyard lies half way up the slope and is completely enclosed by a wall. Minimum alcohol content is 11.5°, and maximum yield is 35hl/ha.

Clos de Tart is a paradoxical wine: it has a dark colour, while on the palate it is both robust and nuanced, graceful and vigorous. Its bouquet combines the scents of strawberries and violets in a harmonious whole.

Clos de Vougeot

This Grand Cru AOC should not be confused with the Vougeot AOC (for 'village' and Premier Cru wines), which covers only 16.49ha. The famous *clos*, completely surrounded by walls, has an extent of some 50ha on both the plain and the slopes, divided up into about 70 properties! Each year, 1,600hl of red Grand Cru wine is provided, whose minimum alcohol content and maximum yield per hectare are fixed at 11.5° and 30hl respectively. It is difficult to accurately describe this *appellation* because of its many variations in terms of site and grower, and it is useful to remember the judicious classification established by the monks of Cîteaux, who used to divide the *clos* into three *cuvées*: the Cuvée des Papes (or 'Popes' blend', from the highest part of the slope), the Cuvée des Rois (or 'Kings' blend', from the vines half way down the slope) and the Cuvée des Moines (or 'Monks' blend', from the richer soils of the plain).

This luxurious red wine enjoys a worldwide reputation because of its dark colour, its vigour and its firm texture. It is solidly structured, but is fleshy, round and full on the palate. Its complex aromas mingle the scents of violets, truffles and wild herbs; some detect violets and mint in it. It can be profitably cellared for a long time. The division of the *clos* into 70 properties (and thus 70 different wine makers) explains why Clos de Vougeot wines do not always live up to their great reputation.

The old Clos de Tart press at Morey-Saint-Denis, dating from the 16th century.

COGNAC

Four hundred years old and the result of a chance combination of natural features (suitable soils, favourable climatic conditions and the proximity of the sea), cognac rests on a long tradition, a tradition which guarantees its future. Both product and art, cognac travels from France around the globe, participating fully in the genial world of wine and wine's great distillates.

Delimited region of Cognac.

The creation of vineyards in the Charentes area probably dates from the 3rd century, when Emperor Probus extended to the Saintonge, Poitou and Angoumois provinces the privilege of growing vines. But it was the marriage of Eleanor of Aquitaine to the future king of England, Henry II Plantagenet, in 1152 which opened up the lucrative Anglo-Saxon and Scandinavian markets to the large vineyard area that had formed around la Rochelle, under the impetus given by Eleanor's father Guillaume X (1099–1137), Duke of Aquitaine and Gascony.

This opening to international trade was not new to the Charente basin. Since the 5th century, Dutch fishermen would go there for the local sea salt, famous for the preservation of fish, produced on the Île de Ré, the Île d'Oléron and along the Atlantic coast.

Thanks to the proximity of the ocean and the Charente, which was navigable at that time, the vineyard area gradually increased, and soon the sailors who came to stock up with salt also started to buy wine. In this period, the white wines from the slopes of the Champagne subregion within Cognac became famous.

The Tiffon *chais at Jarnac, built on the banks of the Charente to maximize humidity levels. Humid conditions are ideal for ageing cognac.*

Distillation in Cognac

Wine began to be distilled in the Aunis and Saintonge provinces about 1600, after a number of surplus harvests, at a time when methods of preserving wine were unknown, and under pressure from Dutch traders whose wine purchases deteriorated during long journeys by sea.

It is not necessary, as some have done, to find a legend for cognac and attribute the discovery, at the end of the 16th century, of the art of distilling '*à repasse*' (by pot still) to a certain knight of the Croix-Marron to whom the method was revealed in a fantastic dream. This process was in fact simply copied from the ancient model of the Greeks and Arabs, and it rapidly became widespread in the area. Sales of *eau-de-vie* soon overtook those of wine.

The first *eaux-de-vie* had been distilled from Charentes wines by the Dutch in Holland, under the name of *brandewijn* (literally 'burnt wine'). This word became 'brandy' in England, and thus synonymous with the French term *eau-de-vie de vin*.

It is understandable that this work was quickly transferred from Holland to the place of production, in Cognac. The brandies produced here soon showed themselves to be remarkable, and it was discovered that they improved still further after a period of preservation in oak casks. Thus a great *eau-de-vie*, later to be called cognac, came into being.

Cognac

Being an important river port, Cognac had both a political and an economic role to play; from the 12th century onwards, it became the '*port Saulnier*', endowed by the French king with a monopoly of all the saltworks of the Atlantic coast. Via salt commerce, the name of Cognac quickly became known throughout Europe and in particular in the three great Hanseatic ports of Hamburg, Bremen and Lübeck, later to play a large role in the cognac spirit trade.

The revocation of the Edict of Nantes in 1685 increased foreign commerical contacts still further. Members of the Protestant families of the Aunis province and of la Rochelle, now forced into exile in England or Holland, kept in close touch with the peasants who remained on their land. At the same time, *négociants* (shippers or merchants) began to establish sales syndicates for brandy. In the 18th century, exports spread to North America and to the islands of the Indian Ocean. Cognac soon acquired worldwide fame, especially since the brandy was bottled at source to facilitate its transport. This development went hand-in-hand with the development of marques and brands, so fundamental to the cognac trade.

The vineyard area was almost totally destroyed by phylloxera. It wasn't until the early years of the 20th century that it began to recover. Since then, lasting prosperity has come to the region via viticulture and the brandy trade.

The climate

The climate of this region formed by the two Charentes *départements* is favourable to the cultivation of the vine. It is a moderate Atlantic climate, mild and humid, with hours of sunlight similar to those of Mediterranean districts, but with mists on hot summer days which filter the sun's rays and slow the ripening process, thus preserving a subtlety of aroma in the wines.

The soils

The large majority of the soils in the Cognac region are calcareous. These calcareous soils are of two types: one is called '*groie*' and is a thin pebbly decalcified clay of reddish brown colour, dating from the Jurassic period. This predominates in the area to the north of the river Charente. To the south, the soil type is known as '*champagne*', and is a friable, grey, chalky soil, very sticky in wet weather. The highly calcareous subsoils allow excess water to drain quickly away, permitting good vegetative growth.

The vineyards

The situation of the vineyards — on slopes, or in areas easy to reach by water transport — meant that their initial planting and development were comparatively straightforward. This area of gently undulating hills, peneplains and wide horizons is easily cultivable, and in recent years has adapted to developments in viticultural techniques and mechanization without difficulty. Furthermore, Limousin oak conveniently offered itself as a neighbour to the wine makers of the Charente. According to specialists, the quality of this oak wood is ideal for ageing brandies. Without it, cognac would not be the fine spirit we know today.

The grape varieties

The Folle Blanche, introduced to this region by the Dutch in the 18th century, was largely replaced during the period of replanting that has followed the phylloxera crisis by the Ugni Blanc. This is the variety that makes up 97 per cent of the vines today. The Ugni Blanc is grown in the Cognac region at the northern limit of its zone of cultivation. The wine it produces has a high level of acidity and great aromatic finesse, both qualities which are required for the production of fine brandies to be aged in wood.

The Colombard, a local grape variety, is still grown to a small extent. As must (unfermented grape juice), it plays an important role in the production of Pineau des Charentes. The decrees of 15 May 1936, 13 January 1938 and 3 February 1955 also permit the use of the following varieties: Meslier Saint-François, Jurançon Blanc, Sémillon, Sauvignon Blanc and Sélect.

The production zones

In the 1870s, the Cognac vineyards covered nearly 300,000ha and produced up to 15 million hl of wine annually. It was the largest white wine vineyard area in the world. Devastated by the phylloxera at the end of the 19th century, it now covers 90,000ha — still enough to retain its title of the largest white wine vineyard area in the world. Thirty thousand wine growers tend the vines, many of them in small plots, almost on a gardening basis, and often as part of a mixed farming concern. Only 2,500 properties have more than 10ha of vines.

The decrees of 1 August 1909, 13 January 1938 and 16 February 1978 delimited the area of production and brought cognac into the fold of *appellations d'origine contrôlées*.

The area of production, which groups together the west part of Charente, most of Charente-Maritime, and two small enclaves in Dordogne and in Deux-Sèvres, is itself divided into six *crus*. A map of these *crus* bears a striking

Juillac-le-Coq. This vineyard lies in the heart of the Grande Champagne zone.

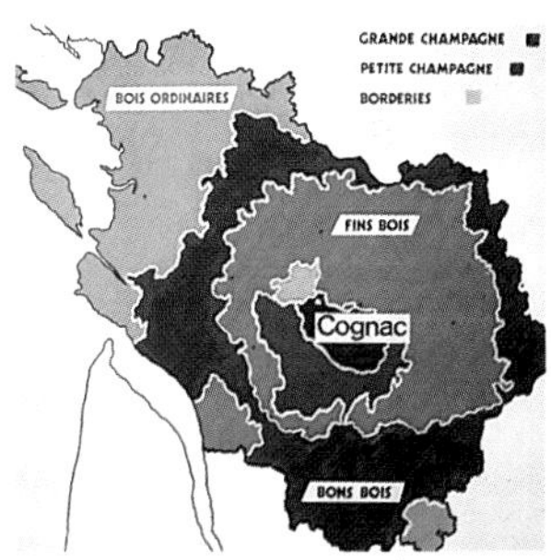

Map showing the different cognac-growing zones.

THE COGNAC TRADE

This important trade has doubled in size every 15 years since the end of the Second World War.

COUNTRY	1977	1979	1980	1981	1982	1983	1984	1985	Equivalent in millions of bottles (1985)
1 United States	26 998	56 919	67 652	71 442	70 234	72 318	82 544	87 993	31,4
2 United Kingdom	46 148	57 491	44 785	40 546	41 406	44 195	41 632	44 257	15,8
3 France	44 745	48 224	47 095	44 587	40 852	34 641	31 010	33 792	12,1
4 West Germany	24 968	33 326	32 108	33 432	28 909	26 903	30 594	29 546	10,6
5 Japan	8 991	14 275	16 926	19 857	21 213	27 850	27 364	28 582	10,2

resemblance to a target, in which the bull's-eye is the Grande Champagne zone, with the Petite Champagne, Borderies (in an enclave), Fins Bois, Bons Bois and Bois Ordinaires zones placed concentrically around Grande Champagne. This classification is based on geological factors, and on the influence of sea winds, which are more active in the west part of the region. It also fully respects ancient traditions.

The system of vinification

The white grapes are vinified into white wine and, probably uniquely in France, the vinification takes place without the addition of antioxidants or of sulphur. As soon as the must emerges from the press, it is run into vats. Natural fermentation quickly develops. The wine is then kept on its sediment until it is time to distil it. Everything happens much as it did 400 years ago, apart from the fact that the vats are bigger today, up to 200hl in capacity.

The decree of 15 May 1936 imposed two strict rules: it forbade both chaptalization (the addition of sugar to the must to increase the alcohol level of the wine) and the use of continuous presses, which have Archimedes' screws and press the grapes so powerfully that the result is detrimental to the quality of the wines and brandies. The wines of Cognac are low in alcohol — only 7°–9°. They are high in acid, with 5–8g of sulphuric acid per litre and a low pH of 3 to 3.1. Volatile acidity is very low (less than 0.2g per litre), and the wines are very dry: less than 1g per litre of residual sugar. Finally, malolactic fermentation generally starts when alcoholic fermentation finishes, the wines being kept on their sediment without any suphur being added.

The cellarmaster checks a first coupe *(blend).*

Distillation

This may not be undertaken outside the delimited zone, or all rights to the AOC are forfeited. Distillation may start as soon as the harvest is declared in November, and must finish by 31 March following, so that the wines are stored for no more than five months: an important factor if quality is to be maintained.

The ageing of cognac in wood

Oak, which is astringent and bitter when it is young, acquires a softness and an aroma of

INDICATIONS OF QUALITY

▷ ***Three stars:*** *no cognac less than thirty months old; older cognac five to nine years old may be included.*

▷ ***VSOP*** *(Very Superior Old Pale),* ***VO, Réserve:*** *the minimum age for cognacs thus designated is four and a half years. Réserve cognacs may contain some brandies which have been aged in cask for between ten and twenty years.*

▷ ***Napoléon*** *and other similar names signifying long ageing: these can only include cognacs that are at least six years old and have been aged in wood.*

▷ *The word* ***'Fine'*** *can only be used for cognac coming from a recognized AOC zone area, for example 'Fine Cognac', 'Grande Fine Champagne', 'Fine Bons Bois'.*

▷ ***Fine Champagne:*** *may only be used for cognac coming from the two Champagne areas (Grande and Petite), with at least 50% from Grande Champagne.*

The minimum strength of cognac for sale to the consumer in France and abroad is 40 per cent alcohol by volume.

COGNAC DISTILLATION

Distillation is carried out with a traditional Charente pot still, made entirely of copper and heated over an open fire. A double distillation method is used. The first heating and vaporization (premier chauffe) *concentrates the wine into an initial distillate called the* 'brouillis'. *The second heating and vaporization* (deuxième *or* bonne chauffe) *concentrates the* brouillis *into a young* eau-de-vie *which, when aged, will become cognac.*

The Charente still takes the form of a large copper pot or boiler, set in a brick base and placed over a firebox. It is surmounted by a smaller chamber or chapiteau *(head), which acts as an anti-foaming device and filtering system: some of the vapours condense on its sides, cooled by the air outside, thereby keeping back any heavier, undesirable materials swept up with them. The swan-neck pipe* (col de cygne) *continues this process, taking the purest vapours towards the final condensing system. This is formed by a simple copper condenser coil submerged in water. At the end of the chain, an alcoholometer permits the alcohol content of the distillate flowing from the system to be monitored. A wine-heater* (réchauffe-vin) *may be installed between the swan-neck pipe and the condenser coil. This is a heat-recuperating device which makes it possible to preheat the wine or the* brouillis.

The process is very slow: eight to ten hours for the first distillation of the wine to obtain a milky brouillis, *which is still imperfect, with a strength of 25° to 30°. Ten or twelve hours are required for the second distillation from which the spirit emerges at a strength of 70° to 71°.*

Throughout this time, the wine, and later the brouillis, *are genuinely 'cooked', with naked flames heating the bottom of the boiler directly. The separation and concentration of the volatile elements of the wine released by the heating process take place very gently so as to obtain a final distillate that is harmonious, rich and subtle.*

The Charente still is a very demanding one. It requires wholesome wine, with a clean taste, as its base material. The distiller must have a great deal of experience so as to regulate the rhythm of his fire to the ideal pace of distillation, and to make the correct separations between the different parts of the distillate. Both the first and second distillations are divided into three portions: the tête *(head), followed by the* coeur *(heart) and the* queue *(tail). Only the* coeur *is of adequate quality, and the second distillation takes place using the* coeur *of the first distillation as its base material. It is the* coeur *of the second distillation that forms the finished spirit, ready to begin the ageing process.*

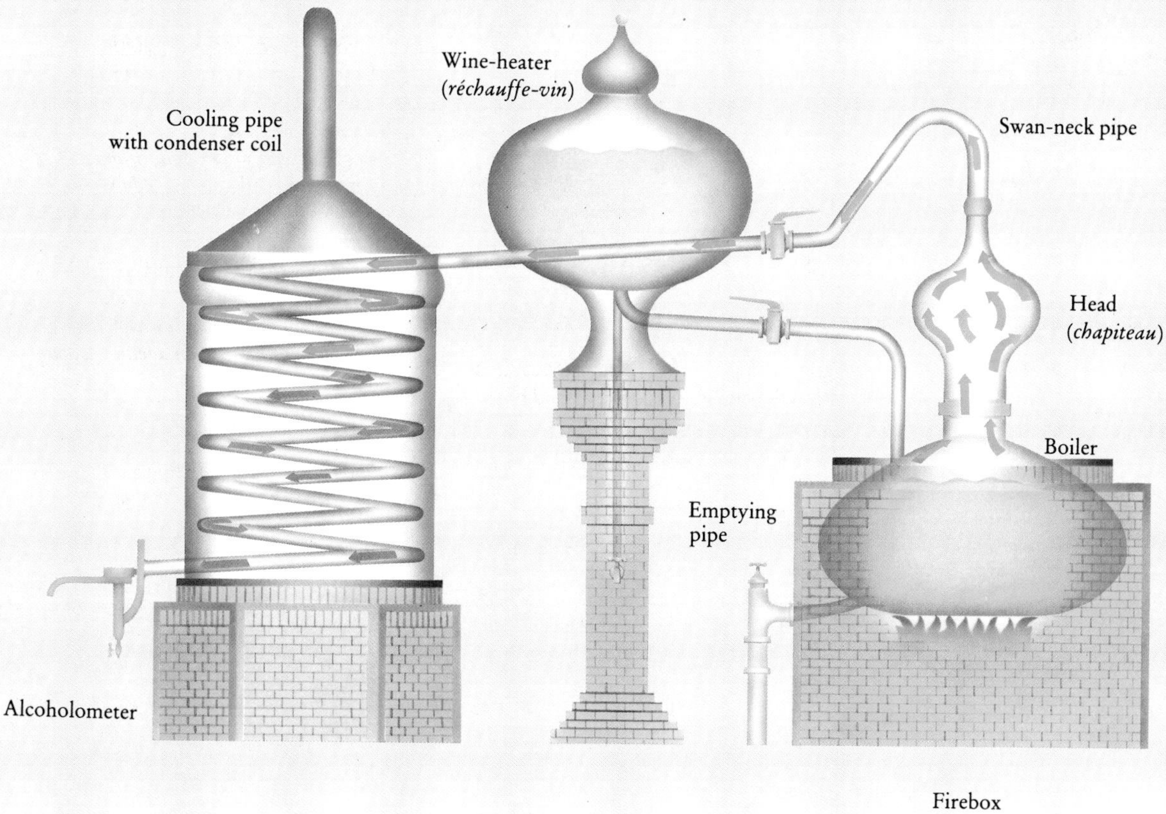

The **Paradis**, *a* **chai** *where brandy that has already been in cask for more than forty years continues to age.*

vanilla as it dries out by natural methods. Artificial methods of drying the wood by a process of steaming block the timber's enzymatic mechanisms, and cognac kept in contact with this type of wood acquires an unpleasant astringency and bitterness. Cognac should therefore only be stored in naturally dried wood.

The role of the cask

Though watertight, wood is permeable in that it permits an exchange of gases between the air and the brandy. Alcohol can thus evaporate — in fact 3 per cent of the contents of every cask evaporate during the first years of storage in wood. In the Cognac cellars, it is estimated that 50,000hl of pure alcohol go to form 'the angels' share' (*la part des anges*).

The wood also adds various constituents to the brandy, extracted by the action of the spirit. These are hemicelluloses (which provide sweet flavours), tannins, lignins, polyphenols, colouring substances and aromatic organic acids.

Complex reactions take place between the components of the wood and the brandy: oxidization, and hydrolysis catalyzed by enzymes in the wood or enzymes secreted by mould on the surface.

A cellar of recent design where cognac, stored in **barriques**, *acquires its amber colour and its fine aroma.*

The *maître des chais* (cellarmaster)

The *maître des chais* has before him a whole palette of different brandies, *crus*, ages and qualities. His art consists of blending them in such a way as to provide the best balance between length of flavour, perfume, wood-related flavours, richness, sweetness and the structure lent by tannin. With each blending or *assemblage*, he effects a slight reduction in strength by adding distilled water. These blendings are carried out in large barrels: the result is a first selection (or *coupe*), then a second selection, and a third, each put back into casks to age once more until the final selection (*coupe finale*) is made. This is then bottled. In view of the conditions under which blending takes place, Cognac has forbidden itself the use of vintage dates.

The storing and ageing of cognac in *chais*

Scattered throughout the area of cognac production, these *chais* (or cellars) are built at ground level. They have little thermal insulation and a floor of beaten earth is preferable to concrete or stone floors for good levels of humidity.

Nearly 3 million hl of pure alcohol lie dormant in this way, in 1.5 million oak casks. After 50 years in cask, the brandy will have lost more than half its volume and, from an initial strength of 70°, will have weakened through evaporation to only 40°. It is then kept in a special cellar called 'le Paradis'.

The cognac trade

The 18th century marked the beginning of cognac's international success. Between 1718 and 1736, the port of la Rochelle alone exported nearly 500,000 casks of cognac, which had first travelled along the Charente via Châteauneuf-sur-Charente, Jarnac, Cognac, Saintes and Saint-Savinien in *gabarres* or flat-bottomed boats. During this period, the first cognac companies, which have survived to this day, came into being: Augier in 1643, Guillet-Gautier in 1680, Martell in 1715, Rémy-Martin in 1724.

Cognac can be found in all the countries of the world, and in 1985, more than 90 per cent of its sales were exports, consisting of nearly 120 million bottles with a value of more than 5.5 thousand million francs. The countries of Europe, Asia and America take a more or less equal share of exports. Asia takes first place in terms of the value of trade (44 per cent), as it buys the oldest quality cognacs.

The French market for cognac has remained more or less steady for the last 20 years. Including duty-free sales, it oscillates between 40,000 and 50,000hl of pure alcohol annually, having reached this level through a series of steady progressions between 1945 and 1965.

Since 1945, trade has become concentrated in the hands of a few very large groups. Among the 200 or so *négociants* (shippers or merchants) dealing in cognac, the four top firms represent 60 per cent of the global market, and the largest firms between them enjoy 90 per cent of the market. The wine growers and small-scale distillers (*bouilleurs de cru*) are hardly concerned with the marketing of cognac. They only represent 5 per cent of the French market and a tiny percentage of exports: 0.3 per cent.

Collioure

This *appellation* from the Roussillon area, classified as an AOC by the decree of 3 December 1971, occupies 50ha lying within the Banyuls *appellation* zone. The vineyards are planted with the Grenache, Carignan and Mourvèdre grape varieties, and produce some 2,000hl annually of a characterful, strong and full-bodied red wine that keeps well.

Colobel

A 6150 Seibel × 5455 Seibel cross, the Colobel is also called 8357 Seibel.

Growing tips arachnoid.

Young leaves green with reddish edges.

Leaves orbicular, glossy, grooved, bullate, crimped at the petiolar junction, without lobes, petiolar sinus V-shaped; dentation pointed, narrow; blade glabrous on both sides; the foliage turns completely red in the autumn.

Bunches large, narrow, cylindrical, compact; grapes spherical, blue-black, with soft pulp; ripening period: second epoch.

This hybrid achieved by Seibel has plenty of colouring material in its skin and, thanks to this fact, has been classed as 'authorized' in France, up to a limit of 5 per cent on each holding. In fact, less than 1,000ha of it are grown. Its wine is strongly coloured, thick, astringent and bitter. This vine has good resistance to downy mildew, but is susceptible to anthracnose.

Colombard

Synonyms: *Colombar, Colombier* in Gironde, *Colombié* at Jonzac, *Queue Tendre* at Saint-Palais, *Chabrier Vert, Donne Verte et Rousse, Gros Blanc Roux, Pied Tendre* in the Blaye region, *Queue Verte* or *Guenille, Bon Blanc* in Vendée, *Blanc Emery* at Thouarcé (Maine-et-Loire), *Blanquette* in Tarn-et-Garonne.

Growing tips open, felty white with carmine margins.

Young leaves downy, yellowish.

Leaves orbicular-reniform, thick, with edge of blade concave, without lobes or weakly three-lobed, petiolar sinus open, V-shaped; dentation convex, medium sized; underside of blade downy, as are the veins.

Green shoots ribbed, arachnoid at the tip, green-brown with partially pink nodes; tendrils medium sized, pale yellow, thin.

Bunches medium sized, cylindrical, winged; grapes medium sized, ovoid, golden white, with juicy pulp; ripening period: second epoch.

The Colombard has a semi-erect posture and its budbreak occurs at the same time as that of the Folle Blanche; it is of average vigour, but is improved by grafting. This vine is extremely susceptible to oidium (powdery mildew), grey rot (botrytis) and stalk dehydration. It is fertile, easily producing 100hl/ha and sometimes more with certain productive clones.

Its wine is reputed to be better than that of the Folle Blanche, stronger in alcohol, less tart and less harsh; this is true of average yields, but with higher yields, the quality decreases considerably and the wines become more acid and less strong in alcohol. Its *eau-de-vie*, on the other hand, is slightly inferior to that of the Folle Blanche and the Ugni Blanc.

Classed as 'recommended' in the *départements* of the South West and the Charentes, the Colombard is included in both the Cognac and Armagnac *appellation* plantings; it is also used in the preparation of Pineau des Charentes and it is a supplementary grape variety in certain Bordeaux AOCs: Bordeaux, Blaye, Bourg, Entre-Deux-Mers, Sainte-Foy-Bordeaux.

Ten registered clones have been approved, the most useful being numbers 551, 552, 553 and 626.

Plantings of Colombard are in decline: 5,800ha only remain, compared with 13,100ha in 1958, because of the uprooting of several plantations in Gironde and Charente-Maritime. More than 1,000ha of Colombard are planted in Armagnac.

Condrieu

Situated adjacent to Côte Rôtie, the Condrieu vineyard area lies at the crossroads of the Lyon,

Condrieu, downstream of Vienne on the river Rhône, is well known for its striking white wine, made from the Viognier grape variety.

Vienne and Forez regions, a fact of no small economic importance for it.

Condrieu is an ancient town. Its riverbank, consisting of creeks and gentle slopes, provided easy access for the loading and unloading of boats. The Romans made a port here from where the *Nautae Rhodanici* left for the south. Later, these boatmen of the Rhône made Condrieu a very important trading centre, until the advent of railway transport robbed them of their work.

Many Condrillots (as the inhabitants of Condrieu are known) had been Rhône boatmen, and plied the river singing the praises of their home town, and reminding people that the shepherds of the Grésivaudan valley (between Grenoble and Albertville) created vineyards in the area at the same time as they did the local *rigotte* cheese.

The vineyards of Condrieu have a correspondingly long history. First planted nearly 2,000 years ago and developed by the canons of Saint-Jean, they were reduced to a very small area by the end of the 19th century because the effort required to cultivate their steep slopes led to a drift of population away from the land.

The *appellation d'origine contrôlée*, which groups together seven communes, was ratified by decree on 27 April 1940. There are now only 16ha under vines, producing an average harvest of 400hl, vinified by a small number of wine growers in the Condrieu region.

A sunlit vine in a Corbières vineyard.

Though the nature of the grape variety, the Viognier, and the southerly exposure of the vineyard both result in a high-alcohol wine, Condrieu nevertheless presents the drinker with a subtle bouquet, dominated by scents of apricot and violet. This rich, silky, almost unctuous wine should be drunk when still young.

Russet autumn vine foliage at Thézan-des-Corbières.

Corbières

This *appellation d'origine contrôlée* is one of the best known in Languedoc-Roussillon. It covers 87 communes of the *département* of Aude, and lies between the valley of the Aude in the north, a mountainous chain in the west, a line of hills marking the border with Roussillon in the south and the Mediterranean in the east. It produces 600,000hl annually, from an area of 23,000ha. The *appellation* was ratified by decree on 24 December 1985. The main grape variety used is Carignan (85 per cent at present, but this proportion must be reduced to 60 per cent by 1990, or 70 per cent if Syrah and Mourvèdre plantings exceed 10 per cent), with smaller proportions of Grenache, Syrah, Mourvèdre and Cinsaut for the red and rosé wines; Bourboulenc, Macabeu and Grenache Blanc are used for the whites. The density of vines per hectare, the method of pruning and the yield of the vineyard are all regulated. Carbonic maceration is a com-

On the right bank of the Rhône, opposite Valence, Cornas produces dark, muscular red wines for long keeping.

monly used vinification technique in Corbières, especially for Carignan wines. The red wines, which make up 90 per cent of the production, have a deep ruby colour and are strong in alcohol, well structured, fleshy and rounded. They are wines with character, and they keep well.

The vineyard lies in a picturesque region of irregular relief. The marked topographical variations and large size of the Corbières zone results in a wide diversity of climatic conditions, in which the influence of the Mediterranean nevertheless predominates. The soils are composed of schist, terraces of water-borne boulders, calcareous piedmont scree and basins formed of sandstone or calcareous clay with an admixture of pebbly colluvium. Four subregions may be distinguished on the basis of these different soils: the Hautes Corbières, the Corbières de l'Alaric, Corbières Centrales and Corbières Maritimes.

The Corbières region is characterized by sun, wind and arid earth. The visitor is struck by the mineral austerity of the countryside, dotted with silhouettes of the ruined castles of the Marches d'Espagne, in which persecuted Cathars took refuge during the 13th century.

Cornas

The wines of Cornas, mentioned by the French agronomist Olivier de Serres (1539–1619), were already well known in the 10th century. But at that time they were white wines. This is not surprising; it must be remembered that, a long time ago, many *crus* famous today for the quality of their red wines used to produce white wines for religious reasons. In 886, the village of Cornas in the Côtes du Rhône was a trusty supplier of communion wine to the ecclesiastical authorities of Tournon.

The *appellation d'origine contrôlée* was ratified, for one commune only, by the decree of 5 August 1938. The vineyard, which is unfortunately very small, only covers 53ha, producing some 2,000hl of red wine annually, made by individual wine growers and by the cooperative cellar of Tain-l'Hermitage. The Syrah is the only grape variety permitted, and it is grown in soils of granitic sand.

It has unjustly been said that Cornas has little bouquet. In fact, its tannic red wine simply remains 'closed' for several years; it is very firm, tightly structured, and serious. But with time — after four or five years — the wine starts to open up. A fruity and spicy fragrance is released and the wine becomes more accessible and supple on the palate, while the firm structure remains intact. Cornas ages well, keeping all its qualities for ten years or more.

Cornet

Synonyms: *Baude, Parverot* at Crest (Drôme).

Bunches small, cylindrical-conical, compact; grapes small, spherical, with juicy pulp; ripening period: first epoch, late.

The Cornet is very susceptible to downy mildew. In the Die region, it is mostly used for table grapes; when vinified, it produces a light, pleasant wine. Unclassified.

CORSICA

Wine growing on Corsica owes its singularity as much to geography as to history. Situated 300km from the continental coast of France, at the same latitude as Rome and Barcelona, Corsica, the fourth largest Mediterranean island (8,722km²), bathes in the Ligurian Sea, which takes the form of a huge bay and is as deep as an ocean. It is at sea that the main part of Corsica's history has taken place. On the island itself, the vine has played a cultural and symbolic role, producing rugged, characterful wines resembling Corsica's irregular and rocky landscape.

Corsica's geographical position places it on some of history's most important maritime routes. Fernand Braudel has defined the Mediterranean as a 'movement-space'; and indeed even in neolithic times Corsica was visited by the Shardanes, seafarers from the eastern Mediterranean. In 564 BC, 35 years after the founding of Marseille, the Phocaean Greeks settled at Aléria (anciently known as Alalia). They thus brought Corsica into the civilization symbolized by the olive tree, dedicated to Athena, and the wine vine, dedicated to Dionysus. Like the islands of Crete, Samos and Thera (Santorin), Corsica offered ideal conditions for the cultivation of the vine — the Greeks were not mistaken in their choice of site.

Corsica's relief and geology

Corsica is nothing more than a mountainous massif. In fact, 55 per cent of the surface area is above 400m, and 20 per cent above 1,000m. The main mountain chain, 140km long, has more than ninety peaks over 2,000m and eight over 2,500m, with Monte Cinto marking the highest point at 2,710m.

Ridges have given this central chain a fishbone pattern, partitioning the island and creating small isolated regions which were independent for a long time, each with its own particular economic, political, cultural and linguistic systems. There were no vast spaces here, but a great number of small valleys and minuscule *terroirs* favourable to individualized products, often of a high standard.

To this great subregional variety should be added an extreme geological diversity. The western two thirds of the island date from the Hercynian mountain-building orogeny, like the Maures or the Esterel Massifs, from which Corsica is thought to have detached itself in the Oligocene or Miocene epochs of the Tertiary period, 15 million years ago at the most. The

A vineyard at Morsiglia on Cap Corse. Cap Corse produces red and rosé wines but its reputation is based largely on its fruity white wines and its Muscats.

island drifted off from the mainland together with Sardinia, opening up the Provençal land basin by this action.

Gneiss, granite, granulite, porphyry, diorite and gabbro are the principal constituents of Corsica's granitic rock. The soil is generally rich in potash but lacks phosphorus, and the high carbon/nitrogen ratio it contains underlines the slowness of the mineralization of organic matter. The granitic sandy soil is sometimes very thick and rich in clay, sometimes shallow and lacking in alluvium. In the latter case, the ground is porous and susceptible to erosion. The wine-producing areas of Calvi, Ajaccio, Sartène, Figari and Porto-Vecchio are situated in this granitic zone.

The east of the island is schistous, with gentler hills and less elevated mountain ridges. The soil is lacking in potash and phosphorus, but the cycle of minerals and water is favoured by a good carbon/nitrogen ratio. In places, the presence of limestone produces a high pH.

Elsewhere, there are regions of sedimentary deposits. This is the case in the central depression betwen granitic (western) Corsica and schistous (eastern) Corsica; in the coastal zones; and, above all, along the Tyrrhenian Sea, from Bastia to Solenzara, where the sedimentary plain stretches for more than 100km.

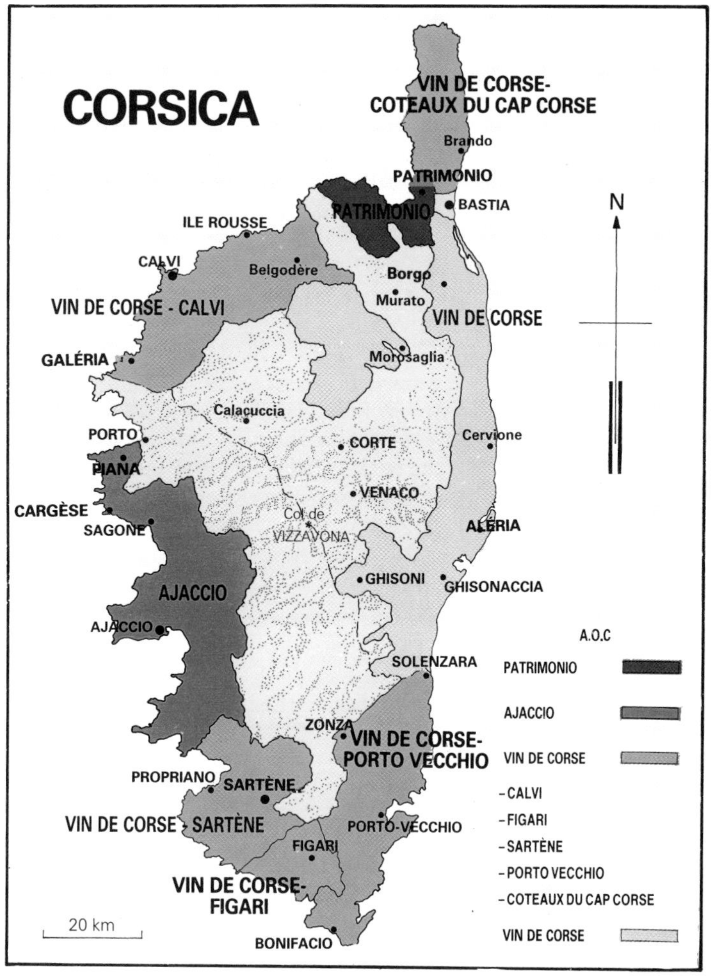

The island climate

The Gulf of Genoa has its own climatic regime, which passes from Mediterranean to subtropical or temperate, according to the seasons. Corsica follows this general pattern, but the sea, the mountains and the complex configuration of relief create an original climatic entity.

The sea plays two important roles: it is a powerful thermal regulator which mitigates summer heat and prevents winter frosts; it also acts as a reservoir of humidity which encourages both the swelling of the grapes and slow maturation, the latter being beneficial to the development of the wine's bouquet.

The mountains also exercise a strong thermal influence, but this is less important than their influence on rainfall. They serve as a condensation screen and are responsible for the comparatively high level of precipitation on Corsica.

Finally, the complex relief creates a number of small subregions, each with its own microclimate. To summarize, then, there are four main characteristics to Corsica's climate:

Mildness

The coastal zone enjoys an annual isotherm of 17°C. Average annual temperatures are 14.4°C at Ajaccio and 16.1°C at Bastia.

Long hours of sunshine

Cap Corse benefits from 2,475 hours of sunshine per year, Bonifacio from 2,531 hours, Calvi from 2,704 hours, and Ajaccio from 2,885 hours — more than anywhere else in France.

High rainfall

Corsica has some of the highest rainfall figures for any French region: it receives $10{,}560m^3$ of rain per hectare per year, compared with an average of $8{,}910m^3$ for mainland France. But this rainfall, as throughout the Mediterranean area, is not evenly distributed during the year.

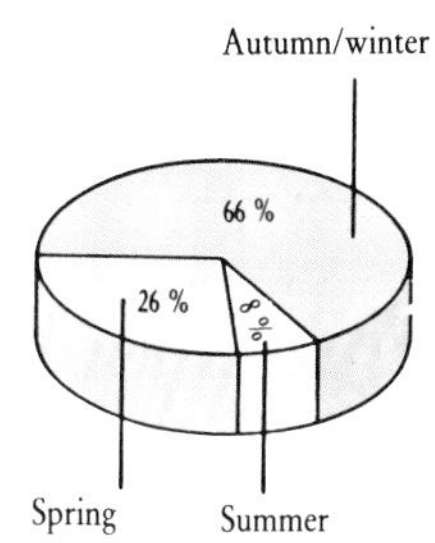

RAINFALL

The importance of winds

Winds are frequent and violent in some parts of the island, such as Cap Corse or Bonifacio. There are also local, thermal winds, created by variations in temperature between the land and the sea. Thus there is a sea breeze from nine in the morning till seven at night, and a land breeze from seven at night till four in the morning. These breezes play an important role because they stir up the lower layers of the atmosphere and disperse the morning mists.

The relation between the climate and the vine is an important one. It is possible to establish a correlation between the quality of the harvests and the climatic conditions, defined by the sum of the temperatures between April and Septem-

Sartène gives its name to red, white and rosé wines. The vineyards, sited on small terraced plots, are in decline.

ber, inclusive, from which the rainfall level is subtracted. The higher the resulting figure, the better the quality of the harvest will be.

The climatic conditions at Ajaccio from April to September over the last decade are shown in the table below. The example of Ajaccio applies, with a few small differences, to most of the main wine-growing areas of the island. These high values mean that the climatic conditions of Corsica are favourable to good and even excellent quality wine.

Year	Sum of temperatures in degrees Celsius	Rainfall in millimetres	Temperature minus rainfall	Sunshine hours
1976	3 334	281	3 053	1 689
1977	3 295	273	3 022	1 678
1978	3 217	229	2 988	1 637
1979	3 346	188	3 158	1 779
1980	3 187	235	2 952	1 702
1981	3 362	163	3 199	1 742
1982	3 548	126	3 422	1 760
1983	3 582	249	3 333	1 655
1984	3 227	315	2 912	1 532
1985	3 561	88	3 473	1 838
1986	3 524	241	3 283	1 773

The Corsican vineyards

The course of wine-producing history since the Greeks settled at Aléria is not easy to follow. Before the Roman conquest, Ptolemy mentions about thirty small harbour settlements around which vines were cultivated. From 160 BC, Rome began to place some army veterans on the eastern coast to form an agricultural colony there. In 35 BC, Virgil remembered a Corsican wine that was 'ruby, so pleasant to the palate'. We next pick up the trail of the vine much later, in 1092, with the monks of the island of Gorgona off the Tuscan coastline who kept vineyards on Cap Corse and traded wine with Pisa. However, it was under the domination of Genoa, particularly after 1560, that the surface area of vines started to expand. Until 1768, the Corsican wine economy progressed within the Mediterranean trading spheres of the great Italian cities, Pisa and Genoa, which were centres of great commercial power at the time. Wine growing was just one of the agricultural projects encouraged. The type of plantation and production, as well as the commercialization of produce, were determined by the Italian occupiers. Genoa was mainly concerned with exploiting the island's resources, but also undertook the task of organizing the countryside, obliging the Corsicans to make land enclosures, and combating the nomadism of the livestock keepers.

At the end of the 17th century, 9,000ha of the island were covered by vines. This area probably doubled in the 19th century (though estimates of the exact extent vary greatly) because of the proliferation of small vineyards for the growers' own consumption.

The phylloxera pest reduced the vineyard extent to 6,000ha. The First World War then reaped its bloody harvest: 30,000 Corsicans were killed in the conflict, leaving the island

Bas-relief in wood, depicting the grape harvest. Ajaccio.

chronically short of manpower. Agriculture became fossilized for a number of years.

A plan for economic recovery was finally drawn up in 1957, and this process accelerated quickly in 1960 with the arrival of 17,000 repatriated settlers from North Africa. The vineyard area grew from 9,000ha in 1960 to 32,000ha in 1976. However, this growth in plantings was largely opportunist, geared to the production of so-called '*vins médecins*' (deeply coloured table wines, designed to bolster those of the Midi), and it has been almost entirely grubbed up since 1976. By 1987, the area devoted to viticulture was less than 12,000ha.

The grape varieties

The geographical situation of the island, its natural internal barriers, and its remarkable history have favoured the development of Mediterranean and native grape varieties.

Old local grape varieties can still be found in the island's vineyards: the Codivarte at Cap Corse; the Aleatico Noir at Cap Corse, Patrimonio and Ajaccio; the Barbarossa at Ajaccio and Sartène; the Carcajolo Noir at Sartène and Figari; the Biancu Gentile and the Mariscola at Sartène. Many local vines have disappeared, but more than 20 still exist, wisely gathered together several decades ago in ampelographical collections, and subject today to clonal selection.

In fact, only three varieties are truly well known and widespread in the region: one white, the Vermentino, which produces an aromatic wine of great delicacy; and two reds: the Nielluccio, the main variety at Patrimonio and in eastern Corsica, which produces wine with a strong colour, round and well balanced; and the Sciaccarello, a variety from the granitic soils of Corsica, unrelated to any known Mediterranean vine and the main variety used in the Ajaccio area. It produces a very elegant wine with a light colour, but which keeps well.

This authentically Corsican mixture of grape varieties is progressively winning the esteem of wine producers and a place in their vineyards.

The grape harvest

This generally begins in the middle of September, though in some years it can begin at the end of September or even the beginning of October.

The phenological stages of vine development on Corsica have not been systematically studied over a long period. The first observations only date from 1984 and do not yet allow any conclusions regarding the relative earliness or tardiness of the grape harvest to be drawn.

Corsica is well equipped with grape harvesting machines, and these are chiefly used on the east coast. Most of the other *appellation* zones continue to harvest manually.

Vinification

Apart from certain *primeur* wines made by carbonic maceration, the vinification processes used on Corsica are relatively standard.

For Blanc de Blancs wines vinified from free-run juice, *débourbage* (racking of the must after a period of settling) is often carried out and the temperature of the fermentation is regulated between 17°C and 19°C.

Vinification of rosé wines is generally carried out by the *saignée* method, in which a part of the must is macerated with the grape skins prior to fermentation. Fermentation then proceeds at a controlled temperature of 18°C to 22°C, with a relatively brief period in vat of four to six days.

For red wines, the grapes are generally removed from the bunch, and the fermentation temperature is between 28°C and 30°C. Vatting periods vary considerably, depending on the type of wine required. These can be anything from four to five days for supple wines, intended to be drunk young, to twenty days or even longer for wines that are to be laid down.

Corsican cellars are practically all above ground, which can pose temperature problems for the *élevage* and ageing of the wine.

The use of wooden vats for *élevage* is confined mainly to traditional wine producers who both vinify and store the wine in casks of 10hl to 50hl, usually made by local coopers from oak or chestnut; or to modern wine producers who are rediscovering the virtues of wood and keep the wine in *barriques* for about six months.

MEANS OF PRODUCTION

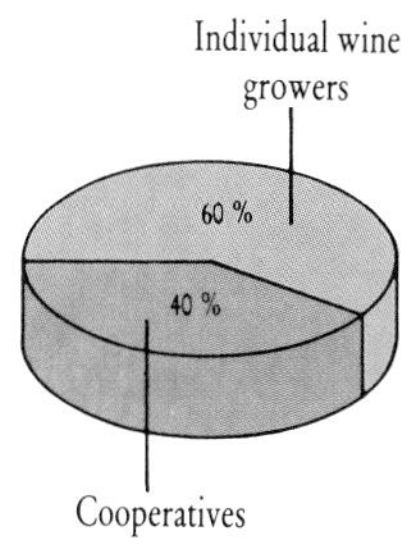

Grape harvest in the Calvi area. Traditional, manual harvesting methods are still used in most of the appellation *zones.*

Vineyard near Galéria, southwest of Calvi. The granitic sands of this area produce red wines that keep well.

WINE PRODUCTION

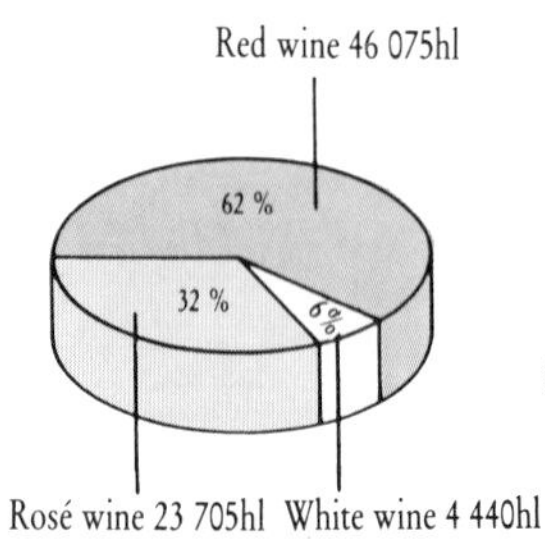

Corsican *appellation* wines

Certain *clos* or *domaine* wines have had a good reputation in Corsica for, in some cases, more than a century. These wines have collected medals and diplomas in France and abroad, thereby contributing towards creating the image of wines of high standard and decided character for the island. Thus it was not by way of encouragement, but as recognition of their incontestable quality, that the INAO agreed to grant the wines of certain regions of the island the benefit of *appellation contrôlée* status. Overall, in recent years, the total volume of *appellation* wines has declined a little. The degree of change varies, though, from region to region.

▷ Patrimonio, Calvi, Ajaccio have maintained constant production.

▷ The production of the east-coast vineyards fluctuates greatly.

▷ Figari and Porto-Vecchio have experienced considerable falls in production due to a high percentage of uprooting. The Sartène area is in marked viticultural decline.

The precise delimitation of the *appellation* zones has recently been completed. The combined area covers 77,386ha. The extent of the wine-producing potential of Corsica can be gauged by comparing this figure to that of the vineyards of the great wine-producing regions on the mainland. The Bordeaux vineyard area covered 100,000ha in 1983; the Burgundy vineyard area, spread over four *départements* and including Beaujolais, covers 40,000ha. In 1983, however, the AOC vineyard area on Corsica actually planted with vines amounted to between 2,000 and 2,500ha. Corsica is thus a long way from taking full advantage of its rich potential in terms of *terroirs* and grape varieties.

Wine's role in Corsican life

As in all Mediterranean countries, wine and the vine have always occupied a special place in Corsican life, playing a cultural and symbolic role as well as a nutritive one. Wine is a fundamental reference point for the Corsican. Numerous local proverbs, sayings and maxims

THE *APPELLATIONS* OF CORSICA

Corsican AOCs have a three-level structure, with increasingly rigorous requirements for each stage.

▷ **Wines with the *appellation régionale* 'Vin de Corse'** *(decree of 2 April 1976):*
The appellation *applies to all land on the island, and in particular to those areas not enjoying an* appellation village *(such as the Golo valley and the east coast).*

▷ **Five *appellations village*** *(decree of 2 April 1976):*
Vin de Corse-Calvi;
Vin de Corse-Coteaux du Cap Corse;
Vin de Corse-Figari;
Vin de Corse-Porto-Vecchio;
Vin de Corse-Sartène.

▷ **Two *appellations de cru*:**
Ajaccio (decree of 21 April 1971 and of 3 April 1984);
Patrimonio (decree of 13 March 1968 and of 23 October 1984).

A rule shared by all three levels of appellation *forbids any enrichment of the must of non-fortified wines by chaptalization or concentration. The yields specified vary according to the* appellation *level:*

— Régionale *50hl/ha*
— Village *and* Cru *45hl/ha*

Finally, the different grape varieties and the proportions in which they are used varies from appellation *to* appellation.

assess life, work, happiness, women, love, vanity or modesty and many other qualities and faults in relation to wine and the vine.

At a more practical level, wine has dictated the structure of many rural houses, which have small windowless cellars on the ground floor with the residential floor situated above, accessible via a front door placed at the top of a flight of steps.

Today, the vine seems almost lost amid vast stretches of scrub. For anyone keeping only to the main roads, Corsican viticulture might seem to be a myth. In fact, to drink at the source, you have to follow sunken lanes, climb up and down, wander this way and that. The reward is found at the end of the path: small, cool cellars, wines that surprise, and wine makers who are proud of their products.

Vintages

The best Corsican vintages do not always correspond to those of the wine-producing regions of the mainland. In general terms, the white and rosé wines age at most for three to five years, and the red wines for up to ten or fifteen years, from the finest vintages. The call for aged Corsican wines is slight at best, and the operation is usually onerous for the wine maker. It is therefore more out of love and respect for their wines than with any commercial benefit in view that some wine makers age them in bottle.

Country dwelling at San Lorenzo. Under the steps is the entrance to the windowless cellar.

THE ISLAND OF VINES

It was Corsican cooking, the cooking of my childhood, that led me to make my life among saucepans and stoves.

After many years spent in the greatest restaurants of the French mainland and abroad, I could not resist the temptation of returning to my homeland. This is why I settled in Guagno-les-Bains, a mountain village east of Vico, with the sole ambition of helping the local cuisine and wines, neglected for too long, to establish their pedigree. Far from being insignificant and of passing interest, this cuisine and these wines are worthy of leisurely inspection and thoughtful tasting.

The real Corsican cuisine has kept all its originality, its diversity, its authentically flavoured dishes, its succulent patisseries; and this cuisine remains to be discovered. The trout in our mountain streams, the eels and fish in our lakes, the sea fish — probably the best in the Mediterranean! — the crayfish and crustaceans, the oysters, the unrivalled sheep's and goat's milk cheeses, these will not fail to attract gastronomes. But they should know that Corsican food only opens its soul and reveals its secrets when accompanied by a glass of local wine.

Our red, white and rosé wines are as varied as our traditional dishes. It is important to know the best ways of combining them with food. If you want to drink the same wine throughout a meal, I suggest a rosé from the slopes of Ajaccio, served very cool. For hors d'oeuvres, local charcuterie and fish, a young white wine made from the Vermentino grape variety will be perfect. With grills and sauced meats, a red wine from Sartène, with its easy fruitiness, is ideal. With game and dishes in spicy sauces, I always serve a four- or five-year-old red wine from Patrimonio. This fleshy, supple wine with its spicy aroma will not pass unappreciated.

Corsican goat's milk cheese should be eaten with a rosé or white Vermentino wine from the east coast. Sheep's milk cheese, on the other hand, can only be accompanied by a red wine from Figari. Finally, sweet vins doux naturels *from Cap Corse, or the* vin de liqueur *Rappu, based on the Muscat and other white grape varieties, go very well with desserts and other sweetmeats.*

There are many other combinations I could suggest to you, so wide is the choice of wines and dishes in my native Corsica.

Guy Bartoli

The Patrimonio area produces a distinctive red wine that is supple, full-bodied and characterful with a spicy aroma.

Corton

Covering nearly 120ha and more than 15 *climats*, Corton, on the Côte de Beaune, is not only famous for its red Grands Crus, but also for three white Grands Crus, Corton, Corton-Charlemagne and Charlemagne.

The decree of 31 July 1937 ratifying this *appellation d'origine contrôlée* requires that the white wines should have a minimum alcohol content of 12° and the reds 11.5°. The base yield for both is fixed at 30hl/ha.

Established in the communes of Aloxe-Corton and Ladoix-Serrigny, with a few plots in Pernand-Vergelesses, the Corton *appellation* produces an annual average of 32,000hl of red wines and 59hl of white wines.

The red wines, which were greatly appreciated by Voltaire, have a certain similarity to the wines of the Côte de Nuits, with their generosity of flavour, their powerful structure and their vigour, which, in their early years, can also include a certain astringency. This is why it is necessary to be patient before drinking them, allowing them the time to become supple. They are extremely well suited to cellaring. A rest of twenty or thirty years in a dark, cool cellar does not in any way attenuate their remarkable bouquet, dominated by the aromas of blackcurrants, violets and peaches.

Only a very small amount of white Corton is produced but it is greatly appreciated for its vivacity and perfume.

Harvesting the white Grand Cru Corton-Charlemagne, at Aloxe-Corton.

Corton-Charlemagne

This Grand Cru from the Côte de Beaune is produced from a *terroir* of about 75ha situated in the area of the Corton *appellation d'origine contrôlée*, i.e. in the communes of Aloxe-Corton, Ladoix-Serrigny and Pernand-Vergelesses. Nearly 1,200hl of white wine is produced here each year. The wine has to have a minimum alcohol content of 12°. The base yield is fixed at 30hl/ha. The exceptional quality of this wine of worldwide reputation is no doubt due to its apparently barren soil, which is poor and difficult to cultivate, but from which the vine produces a unique quality of fruit.

This wine has an undisputed position among the best white wines in the world because of its breed, its firmness, its power and its vigour. With its sunny golden colour, it releases complex and delicate aromas, dominated by cinnamon. The best Corton-Charlemagne comes from the highest sites.

Costières du Gard

This AOC, ratified by decree on 4 July 1986, is the most recent of the Gard *appellations d'origine contrôlée*. It occupies an area stretching to the southeast of Nîmes and north of the Camargue, between the valleys of the Gardon and the Vidourle on the one hand and the valley of the Vistre on the other. Twenty-six communes fall within the zone, from which 25,000ha have been accepted as AOC, with a present production of 200,000hl (5 per cent white, 15 per cent rosé and 80 per cent red). The combination of grape varieties used is typical of Languedoc, but a recent trend indicates that the Carignan is giving way to the Grenache, which is the dominant vine in the neighbouring Côtes du Rhône; the Syrah, Mourvèdre and Cinsaut varieties are also used. Before the outbreak of phylloxera, the Mourvèdre (locally known as the Plant de Saint-Gilles) had an important place in the vineyards. The Macabeu, Clairette, Marsanne and Grenache Blanc are the main varieties used for white wines. The soils are formed of the water-borne boulders that provide such favourable conditions for vine growth, and the vineyards are generally sited on gentle slopes falling away to the south. The wines are generous, tasty and fruity in character.

Côt

Synonyms: *Malbec* or *Malbeck*, *Pressac*, *Lutkens*, *Estrangey* or *Étranger*, *Côte Rouge*, *Cot de Bordeaux*, *Cot de Pays* in Touraine, *Auxerrois*, *Cahors* in Lot, *Vesparol* in Gers, *Gourdoux* in the Blaye region, *Grifforin* on the Île de Ré,

Jacobin or *Jacobain* in Vienne, *Noir Doux* or *Nègre Doux* in Gironde, *Oeil de Perdrix*, *Pied Rouge*, *Pied Noir* in Lot-et-Garonne, *Queue Rouge* in Dordogne, *Teinturier* or *Tinturin* in the Blaye region, *Claverie Noire* in the Landes, *Pruinéral* in Corrèze, *Gros Noir* in the Aube, *Grosse Mérille* in Haute-Garonne, *Hourcat*, *Saint-Émilion*.

Growing tips open, felty white with lightly carmine margins.

Young leaves downy with bronze patches.

Leaves orbicular, soft, contorted, wavy, with the edges of the blade convex, without lobes or weakly three-lobed with a very wide central lobe, petiolar sinus U-shaped or open V-shaped; dentation narrow, pointed; underside of blade arachnoid in tufts. The foliage turns partly red in the autumn. Green shoots large, ribbed, with prominent nodes, reddish on both sides.

Bunches medium sized or large, fairly loose, conical, with one or two shoulders; grapes spherical, small, black, not very juicy; ripening period: first epoch, late.

The Côt has early budbreak and is often said to be susceptible to *coulure* (flower abortion), which has led to a decrease in its use: 4,800ha in 1985 compared with 10,752 in 1958. This vine is generally pruned long and grafted on to weak grafting stock so as to limit the effects of *coulure*. Its yield can reach 80 to 100hl/ha in the Midi, producing wine between 11° and 12°. These wines are used, in a 20 per cent to 80 per cent proportion, to make Carignan wines more supple. When grown on slopes, the yields hardly exceed 40 to 50hl/ha and wines from the Côt are highly coloured, rich in tannin, less perfumed and more delicate than wines from either of the Cabernet grapes, which enables them to be drunk more quickly. The Côt brings colour and mellowness to wines made from a blend of grape varieties. In the Loire valley, it is used in blends with the Cabernet Franc and the Gamay to produce very fruity rosé wines. The Côt is susceptible to downy mildew, grey rot (botrytis), phomopsis and winter frosts, which destroyed many vines in the South West in 1956; it does, though, have some more resistance to oidium (powdery mildew). Fifteen registered clones have been approved, the most useful being number 46, followed by numbers 279, 353 and 419.

The Côt is classed as 'recommended' in many *départements* in the South West, the Centre West and the Midi. In fact, its cultivation is concentrated in the South West: Gironde (2,148 ha), Lot (1,765 ha), and a little in Dordogne, Lot-et-Garonne, Tarn-et-Garonne, Haute-Garonne and Gers, making a total of 4,310ha. In these *départements*, it forms one of the approved varieties for the red AOCs of Bordeaux, Médoc, Graves, Saint-Émilion, Pomerol, Premières Côtes de Bordeaux, Sainte-Foy-Bordeaux, Fronsac, Bourg, Bergerac, Pécharmant, Côtes de Duras, Côtes de Buzet, Cahors (where it makes up 70 per cent of the blend), and Côtes du Frontonnais. In the Loire valley it is not very widespread at present (358ha) and it forms one of the approved varieties for the Touraine and Rosé d'Anjou AOCs.

The small village of Gamay, on the Côte de Beaune. Its wines are sold under the Saint-Aubin or Côte de Beaune-Villages names.

Côte Chalonnaise

See the following page.

Côte de Beaune

See the Côte d'Or regional entry.

Côte de Beaune

Harvested on the territory of the commune of Beaune itself, these red and white wines, whose *appellation d'origine contrôlée* was ratified by decree on 5 December 1972, should have a minimum alcohol content of 10.5° for the reds and 11° for the whites, with a maximum yield of 35hl/ha. The area of production occupies 547ha, and is more or less identical to that of the Beaune AOC.

These quality wines, which are honest and often very successful, were produced in the following amounts in 1985: 171hl of white wine, 2,447hl of red wine. The Côte de Beaune wines should not be confused with those of the Côte de Beaune-Villages, which are red wines produced from 17 communes on the geographical stretch of land known as the Côte de Beaune, between Ladoix and Chagny. The words 'Côte de Beaune' can also accompany little-known *appellations* of communes such as Saint-Romain (as in Saint-Romain-Côte de Beaune), for example.

Côte Chalonnaise

Between the Côte de Beaune and the Mâcon region, the countryside changes. The monotonous Côte suddenly assumes new forms: hills and valleys with less uniform slopes. Meadows, fields and vineyards become mixed together. The palette of colours acquires warmer tones. Tournus heralds the Midi.

Mercurey: a gate decorated for the feast of St Vincent.

The vineyards of the Côte Chalonnaise begin at Chagny and continue as far as the outskirts of Saint-Gengoux-le-National, between the valleys of the Dheune and the Grosne. The wine route passes through Bouzeron, Rully, Mercurey, Givry, Buxy and Saint-Vallerin, covering an area about 25km long and 7km wide.

The wines of the Côte Chalonnaise were for a long time sold under borrowed names: Chablis, or Villages de la Côte de Beaune. Happily, thanks to the AOC system, these wines have now managed to make names for themselves.

The story of the vine in these parts is a very old one. The wines of Givry were well known in the Middle Ages and Henri IV courted them by exempting them from transport taxes to Paris. The wines of Montagny, meanwhile, flourished thanks to the abbey of Cluny.

But it is the Clos de Germolles, 3km from Givry and one of the most illustrious of its kind in Burgundy, which testifies to the solid reputation of the Côte Chalonnaise. The wife of Philip the Bold, Margaret of Flanders, created an admirable agricultural estate and vineyard at Germolles consisting of a *clos* of 380 *ouvrées* (about 14ha) whose wine was offered to all the nobility at the court of Burgundy.

The vine-growing soils of the Côte Chalonnaise, from the valley of the Dheune near Chagny in the north to Saint-Gengoux-le-National in the south, are formed of materials from the Triassic period (sandstone in certain places) and the Jurassic period (calcareous clay); these are planted with Chardonnay and produce white wines of great delicacy — Montagny and Rully, for example. In other places, brown calcareous soils are planted with the Pinot Noir, and produce red wines that are much sought after, such as Mercurey.

Wine production on the Côte Chalonnaise

On the Côte Chalonnaise, Pinot Noir (67 per cent), Chardonnay (10 per cent), Gamay and Aligoté are cultivated within a delimited area of 3,300ha, yielding an average production of 14,000hl.

White wines, appreciated for their freshness and bouquet, are mainly produced at Bouzeron (Aligoté), Montagny and Buxy, and red wines, which are tannic and keep well, at Mercurey and Givry. The commune of Rully produces both white and red wines.

The Château de Rully looks out over a vineyard that dates back to the earliest period of Burgundian viticulture. Red and white wines of subtlety are produced here. Rully is also an important producer of sparkling Crémant de Bourgogne.

Côte de Beaune-Villages

Regulated by the decree of 21 May 1970, the wines of the Côte de Beaune-Villages have a minimum alcohol content of 11° and a maximum yield of 35hl/ha.

The wines produced are all red and come from any of 17 communes of the Côte de Beaune, or are composed of a mixture of wines from several of these communes. The production fluctuates between 2,000hl and 3,000hl from year to year, according to the policy of the traders who make these blends, and according to the quality of the annual harvest. Average production is 2,500hl.

Some communes of the Côte de Beaune that produce little of their own wine or whose village name is not very well known, often abandon their own *appellation* and simply use that of the Côte de Beaune-Villages. This applies in particular to Chorey-lès-Beaune, Dezize-lès-Maranges, Sampigny-lès-Maranges and Cheilly-lès-Maranges.

Côte de Beaune-Villages wines are honest and generally typical burgundies, but they do not always have the breadth found in wines from Beaune itself.

Côte de Brouilly

A sister *appellation* to that of Brouilly, Côte de Brouilly was classed as an AOC by decree on 19 October 1938.

The vineyard area is situated on the slopes of Mont Brouilly, which is topped by a chapel, Notre-Dame-du-Raisin. The *appellation* terrain is formed of blue granite.

From an area of 200ha, average production is 16,000hl (2,100,000 bottles) of a wine whose aroma recalls bilberries, raspberries, violets and peonies. The wine may be made from the grapes of the Gamay Noir à Jus Blanc, Pinot Noir and Pinot Gris varieties, though in practice the Gamay is used almost exclusively.

The alcohol content of Côte de Brouilly wines is higher than that of any other Beaujolais *cru*: a minimum of 10.5° instead of 10°, and it is often higher still because of the strong sunshine the fruit enjoys, thanks to its position on the slopes of Mont Brouilly.

Côte de Nuits

See the Côte d'Or regional entry.

Côte de Nuits-Villages

This *appellation* can only be claimed by plots sited on the territories of the communes of Brochon, Comblanchien, Corgoloin, Prissey and part of Fixin, on the Côte d'Or. The AOC area of Côte de Nuits-Villages is regulated by the decree of 20 August 1964, and stretches over about 320ha. The production consists almost exclusively of red wines, whose minimum alcohol content is fixed at 10.5°, with a maximum yield of 35hl/ha.

Though production is limited — 20hl of white wines and 6,000hl of reds — it also varies a great deal in quality. One reason for this is that the nature of the soils and the microclimates changes constantly between Fixin and Corgoloin, a distance of about 20 km. But it can, in general, be said that these pleasant wines are well structured, firmly textured, and aromatic.

***F**ixin has several red Premiers Crus as well as a 'village' AOC. Some of its wines are also sold under the Côte de Nuits-Villages denomination.*

Côte d'Or

See the following page.

Côte Roannaise

This vineyard zone, classified VDQS by the decree of 18 May 1955, covers an area of 100ha. The Gamay Noir à Jus Blanc annually produces some 3,800hl of red wine and 200hl of rosé. The area of production extends over 24 communes or parts of communes.

The red wines have a light cherry or garnet colour. They are well balanced and solid, with the fine, light aromas characteristic of wines grown in regions of high altitude.

The rosé wines are dry and well balanced. (*See* the Vins du Centre regional entry.)

The Côte d'Or

Thanks to the extraordinary potential of this* terroir *for wine growing, men have — since earliest times — made the Côte d'Or into a temple of the wine world. The name of each village is, justly, known across five continents: Gevrey-Chambertin, Vosne-Romanée, Chambolle-Musigny, Richebourg, Vougeot, Aloxe-Corton, Meursault, Puligny-Montrachet . . . A wonderful peal of names, and a wonderful route of wines.

The origins of Burgundian viticulture are unknown. It is probable, however, that the Aedui (or *Éduens* in French: a Gaulish Celtic tribe), having settled in northern Italy, took up viticulture there around 400 BC and later brought it back to their Burgundian homelands. The oldest local text to mention vines is the 'Panegyric to Constantine' of Eumenius, composed in the year 312. In the 6th century, Gregory of Tours described the Côte as 'covered with vines'; by the Middle Ages, the distinctive Burgundian *clos* (enclosed vineyards) had started to appear.

The Côte de Nuits and the Côte de Beaune

The development of wine growing on the Côte de Nuits and the Côte de Beaune owed a great deal to local religious communities, particularly the abbey of Cîteaux, which built *celliers* (wine stores) at Meursault, Aloxe and Vougeot at the beginning of the 12th century. The court of the Dukes of Burgundy — one of the main cultural centres of western civilization in the 14th and 15th centuries — ensured a lasting foreign appreciation of Burgundian *crus*, particularly in what are today Belgium and the Netherlands. Under the *ancien régime* of pre-Revolutionary France, the Burgundian bourgeoisie paid great attention to improving the quality of their wines.

The Revolution broke up property ownership patterns and favoured the advancement of small, individual wine growers. Later, the commercial expansion of France under the Second Empire proved to be very profitable for the vineyard areas of the Côte d'Or.

Two further events occurred that improved the quality of Burgundy's wines still further: the phylloxera crisis, which, by the time it had been overcome, had helped to eliminate most of the mediocre vineyards of the region; and a reaction against the 'democratization' of the vineyard, which led to the establishment of a hierarchy of *crus* and *climats*.

The 20th century has overseen many dark years for burgundy, and it was not until the beginning of the 1960s that, thanks to worldwide demand for fine wine, the region's production became a luxury item with a similar market profile to that of French perfume or *couture*.

Santenay, on the Côte de Beaune, produces well-balanced, richly flavoured yet delicate red wines with an alluring bouquet.

The Hautes Côtes

In the Middle Ages, the powerful House of Vergy, an ally of the Dukes of Burgundy, dominated this part of the province from the Château de Vergy (*see* photograph on page 289). The first donations of parts of the Clos de Vougeot to the abbey of Cîteaux came from the Vergy family. The Clos Saint-Denis (Morey-Saint-Denis) and Romanée-Saint-Vivant (Vosne-Romanée) vineyards also owe their origin to religious communities established by the Vergy family.

The Hautes Côtes used to be known simply as the Arrière-Côte (the 'Côte behind'). 'We are in fact the Avant-Côte' (the 'Côte in front') would be a reasonable reply from the wine growers of this plateau, which is bordered to the north by the valley of the Ouche and blends with the southern Côtes de Nuits and the Côte de Beaune to the west and south, as far as the Côte Chalonnaise. In keeping with the geology and the wine-growing traditions of this region, the names Hautes Côtes de Nuits and Hautes Côtes de Beaune have been used for the last sixty years. These were authorized by the granting of AOCs to each zone in 1961.

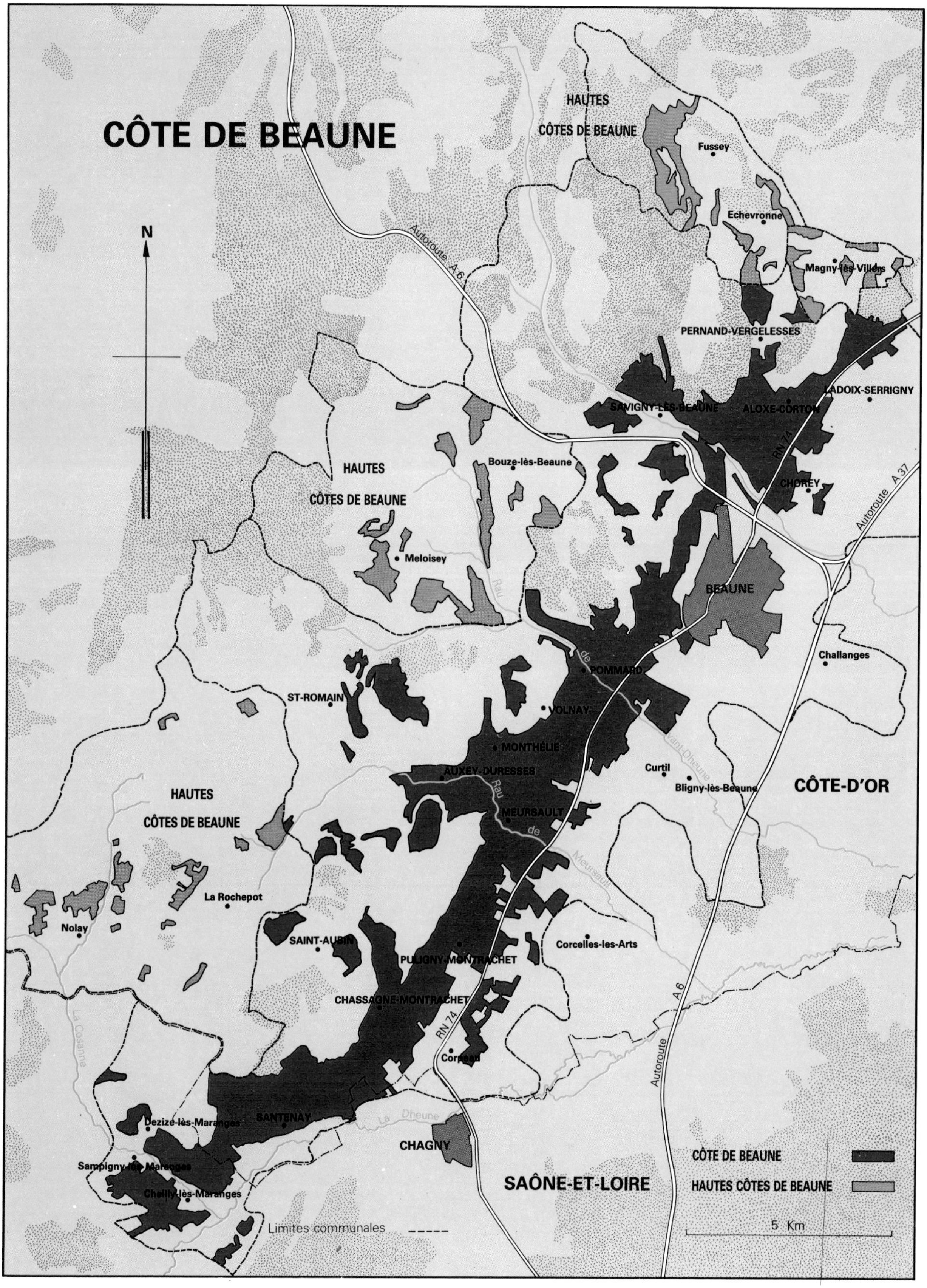
CÔTE DE BEAUNE
N
HAUTES
CÔTES DE BEAUNE
Fussey
Echevronne
Magny-lès-Villers
PERNAND-VERGELESSES
LADOIX-SERRIGNY
SAVIGNY-LES-BEAUNE
ALOXE-CORTON
Autoroute A 6
Bouze-lès-Beaune
HAUTES
CÔTES DE BEAUNE
Meloisey
CHOREY
Autoroute A 37
RN 74
Rau
BEAUNE
Challanges
POMMARD
de
ST-ROMAIN
VOLNAY
MONTHELIE
AUXEY-DURESSES
Curtil
Bligny-lès-Beaune
CÔTE-D'OR
HAUTES
CÔTES DE BEAUNE
MEURSAULT
La Rochepot
Nolay
SAINT-AUBIN
Corcelles-les-Arts
PULIGNY-MONTRACHET
CHASSAGNE-MONTRACHET
La Cosanne
RN 74
Corpeau
Autoroute A 6
SANTENAY
Dezize-lès-Maranges
La Dheune
CHAGNY
Sampigny-lès-Maranges
Cheilly-lès-Maranges
SAÔNE-ET-LOIRE
CÔTE DE BEAUNE
HAUTES CÔTES DE BEAUNE
Limites communales
5 Km

THE WINES OF THE CÔTE D'OR

REGIONAL *APPELLATIONS*		
AOC	**Type**	**Main Grape Varieties**
Bourgogne Grand Ordinaire	red or rosé	Gamay, Pinot Noir
Bourgogne Grand Ordinaire	white	Chardonnay, Pinot Blanc, Melon, Aligoté
Bourgogne Aligoté	white	Aligoté
Bourgogne Passetoutgrains	red or rosé	⅓ Pinot Noir, ⅔ Gamay
Bourgogne	white	Chardonnay
Bourgogne	red or rosé	Pinot Noir
Bourgogne-Hautes Côtes de Beaune Bourgogne-Hautes Côtes de Nuits	red, rosé, white	Pinot Noir, Chardonnay

'VILLAGE', PREMIER CRU AND GRAND CRU *APPELLATIONS*			
Communes	'Village' AOCs (AOC *Communales*)	Premiers Crus	Grands Crus
CÔTE DE NUITS			
Fixin	Fixin Côte de Nuits-Villages	Clos de la Perrière Le Clos du Chapitre - Les Arvelets Clos Napoléon - Les Hervelets.	
Brochon	Gevrey-Chambertin Côte de Nuits-Villages	Clos de la Perrière.	
Gevrey-Chambertin	Gevrey-Chambertin	La Boissière - Clos des Varoilles - Bel Air - Aux Combottes - Le Clos Saint-Jacques - Issart - Cazetiers - Les Petits Cazetiers - Champeaux - Combe aux Moines - Estournelles - Poissenot - Lavaut Saint-Jacques - Les Goulots - Les Corbeaux - Cherbaude - La Perrière - Clos Prieur - Champonnet - Au Closeau - Le Fonteny - En Ergot - Petite Chapelle - Craipillot - Clos du Chapitre - La Romanée.	Chambertin Chambertin-Clos de Bèze Chapelle-Chambertin Charmes-Chambertin Griotte-Chambertin Mazis-Chambertin Mazoyères-Chambertin Latricières-Chambertin Ruchottes-Chambertin
Morey-Saint-Denis	Morey-Saint-Denis	Les Genevrières - Monts Luisants - Les Chaffots - Le Clos Baulet - Les Blanchards - Les Gruenchers - La Riotte - Les Millandes - Les Faconnières - Les Charrières - Clos des Ormes - Aux Charmes - Aux Cheseaux - Les Chénevery - Les Sorbés - Clos Sorbé - La Bussière - Les Ruchots - Côte Rôtie - Le Village.	Clos de Tart Clos Saint-Denis Bonnes Mares Clos de la Roche Clos des Lambrays
Chambolle-Musigny	Chambolle-Musigny	Les Sentiers - Les Baudes - Les Noirots - Les Fuées - Les Lavrottes - Aux Beaux Bruns - Aux Echanges - Les Charmes - Les Plantes - Aux	Musigny Bonnes-Mares

Communes	'Village' AOCs	Premiers Crus	Grands Crus
Chambolle-Musigny (continued)		Combottes - Derrière la Grange - Les Gruenchers - Les Cras - Les Groseilles - Les Combottes - Les Fousselottes - Les Chatelots - Les Carrières - Les Chabiots - Les Amoureuses - Les Borniques - Les Hauts Doix - La Combe d'Orveaux.	
Vougeot	Vougeot	Les Cras - Clos Blanc - Clos de la Perrière - Les Petits Vougeots.	Clos de Vougeot
Flagey-Echézeaux	Vosne-Romanée	Les Beaux Monts - Les Rouges - En Orveaux.	Echézeaux Grands Echézeaux
Vosne-Romanée	Vosne-Romanée	Les Suchots - Les Beaux Monts - Aux Brûlées - Les Chaumes - Aux Raignots - La Combe Brûlée - La Clos des Réas - La Grande Rue - Les Gaudichots - Aux Malconsorts - Les Petits Monts - La Croix Rameau - Cros Parentoux.	Romanée-Saint-Vivant Richebourg La Romanée La Tâche La Romanée-Conti
Nuits-Saint-Georges	Nuits-Saint-Georges	Aux Champs Perdrix - Aux Damodes - Aux Cras - En la Perrière Noblet - Aux Boudots - Aux Murgers - Aux Vignes Rondes - Aux Chaignots - Au Thorey - Aux Argillats - Aux Bousselots - Les Perrières - Aux Crots - Les Hauts Pruliers - Les Procès - Rue de Chaux - Les Pruliers - Roncière - Les Saint-Georges - Les Cailles - Les Vallerots - Les Porrets Saint-Georges - Les Poulettes - Les Chabœufs - Les Vaucrains - Chaînes Cartaux - Clos des Porrets Saint-Georges - La Richemone - Château Gris.	
Premeaux-Prissey	Nuits-Saint-Georges (in Premeaux) Côte de Nuits-Villages (in Prissey)	Clos de la Maréchale - Clos Arlot - Les Argillières - Clos des Corvées - Aux Perdrix - Clos des Forêts Saint-Georges - Les Didiers - Clos des Grandes Vignes - Clos Saint-Marc - Clos des Corvées Paget - Clos des Argillières - Les Terres Blanches.	
Comblanchien	Côte de Nuits-Villages		
Corgoloin	Côte de Nuits-Villages		
CÔTE DE BEAUNE			
Serrigny	Ladoix (*)	La Micaude - La Corvée - Le Clou d'Orge - Les Joyeuses - Bois Roussot - Basses Mourottes - Hautes Mourottes - Les Mourottes - La Coutière - La Maréchaude - Les Petites Lolières - La Toppe au Vert - Clos des Maréchaudes.	Corton Corton-Charlemagne
Aloxe-Corton	Aloxe-Corton	Les Maréchaudes - Les Paulands - Les Valozières - Les Chaillots - Les Fournières - Les Guérets - Les Vercots - Clos du Chapitre.	Corton Corton-Charlemagne Charlemagne

Communes	'Village' AOCs	Premiers Crus	Grands Crus
Pernand-Vergelesses	Pernand-Vergelesses (*)	En Caradeaux - Creux de la Net - Les Fichots - Ile des Vergelesses - Vergelesses.	Corton Corton-Charlemagne Charlemagne
Savigny-lès-Beaune	Savigny-lès-Beaune (*)	Les Charnières - Les Talmettes - Les Vergelesses - Basses Vergelesses - Les Lavières - Aux Gravains - Petits Godeaux - Aux Serpentières - Aux Guettes - Aux Clous - Les Rouvrettes - les Narbantons - Les Peuillets - Les Marconnets - Bataillière - Les Hauts Marconnets - Les Jarrons - Redrescul - Hauts Jarrons - Aux Fourneaux - La Dominode - Champ Chevrey.	
Chorey-lès-Beaune	Chorey-lès-Beaune (*)		
Beaune	Beaune	Les Marconnets - En l'Orme - En Genêt - Les Perrières - Les Cent Vignes - Clos de l'Ecu - Les Bressandes - Les Fèves - Les Toussaints - Les Grèves - Les Bas des Teurons - Les Teurons - Sur les Grèves - Aux Cras - Aux Coucherias - Clos du Roi - Le Clos de la Mousse - Les Reversées - Les Epenottes - Les Chouacheux - Les Aigrots - Les Boucherottes - Les Vignes Franches - Les Sizies - Le Clos des Mouches - Pertuisots - Les Tuvilains - Belissand - Les Avaux - Les Seurey - Montée Rouge - Champs Pimont - La Mignotte - Les Montrévenots - Clos des Ursules - Clos Saint-Landry - A l'Ecu - Sur les Grèves - Clos Sainte-Anne - Clos des Avaux - Blanches Fleurs - Les Sceaux.	
Pommard	Pommard	La Chanière - Les Charmonts - La Platière - La Refène - Les Arvelets - Les Sausilles - Les Pezerolles - En l'Argillère - Les Boucherottes - Clos Blanc - Les Grands Epenots - Le Clos Micot - Les Poutures - Les Petits Epenots - Clos des Epeneaux - Les Bertins - Les Combes Dessus - Clos des Vergers - Le Village - Clos de la Commaraine - Derrière Saint-Jean - Les Rugiens Bas - Les Chaponnières - Les Jarolières - Les Croix Noires - Les Fremiers - Les Rugiens Hauts - Les Chanlins Bas.	
Volnay	Volnay	Pitures Dessus - Chanlin - Clos des Ducs - Village - Clos de la Cave des Ducs - Lassolle - Les Brouillards - Les Mitans - En l'Ormeau - Les Angles - La Gigotte - Pointes d'Angles - Fremiets - Chevret - Les Grands Champs - Robardelle - Les Lurets - Caillerets - Carelles - Ronceret - Les Aussy - Clos des Chênes - Taille Pieds - Champans - Les Caillerets - Clos des 60 Ouvrées - Clos de l'Audignac - Clos de la Chapelle - Clos du Château des Ducs - Fremiets - Clos de la Rougeotte - Clos du Verseuil -	

Communes	'Village' AOCs	Premiers Crus	Grands Crus
Volnay (continued)		Carelles sous la Chapelle - Clos de la Bousse d'Or - Clos de la Barre.	
Monthélie	Monthélie (*)	Les Riottes - Sur la Velle - Le Meix Bataille - Le Clos Gauthey - Le Cas Rougeot - Le Village - Les Vignes Rondes - Les Champs Fulliot - La Taupine - Les Duresses - Le Château Gaillard.	
Auxey-Duresses	Auxey-Duresses (*)	Les Breterins - La Chapelle - Reugne - Les Duresses - Bas des Duresses - Les Ecusseaux - Les Grands Champs - Climat du Val - Clos du Val.	
Saint-Romain	Saint-Romain (*)		
Saint-Aubin	Saint-Aubin (*)	Derrière la Tour - Les Créots - Les Champlots - Bas de Vermarain à l'Est - Sur Gamay - La Chatenière - Les Murgers des Dents de Chien - Les Combes - Village - Les Castets - Le Charmois - Les Puits - En Remilly - Les Frionnes - Sur le Sentier du Clou - Derrière chez Edouard - En Montceau.	
Meursault	Meursault (*) Blagny (*)	Les Caillerets - Les Cras - La Jeunelotte - Perrières - La Pièce sous le Bois - Sous le Dos d'Âne - Charmes - Genevrières - Les Bouchères - Poruzots - Les Plures - Les Santenots Blancs - Les Santenots du Milieu - Clos des Perrières - Santenots - Sous Blagny - Les Gouttes d'Or.	
Puligny-Montrachet	Puligny-Montrachet (*) Blagny (*)	Sous le Puits - La Garenne - Hameau de Blagny - Les Chalumeaux - Champ Canet - Les Folatières - Le Cailleret - Les Pucelles - Clavoillon - Les Referts - Les Perrières - Les Combettes - La Truffière - Champ Gain - Les Demoiselles - Clos de la Garenne -- Clos de la Mouchère.	Chevalier-Montrachet Bâtard-Montrachet Montrachet Bienvenues-Bâtard-Montrachet
Chassagne-Montrachet	Chassagne-Montrachet (*)	Les Blanchots Dessus - En Remilly - Les Vergers - Dents de Chien - Les Chaumées - Les Macherelles - Les Chenevottes - Clos Saint-Jean - Les Champs Gain - La Maltroie - Cailleret - Morgeot - Abbaye de Morgeot - Bois de Chassagne - Vide Bourse - La Grande Montagne - Les Brussonnes - Boudriottes - Tonton Marcel.	Montrachet Bâtard-Montrachet Criots-Bâtard-Montrachet
Santenay	Santenay (*)	La Comme - Les Gravières - Beauregard - La Maladière - Clos des Mouches - Beaurepaire - Passetemps - Grand Clos Rousseau - Clos Rousseau - Clos Faubard - Clos de Tavannes - Les Gravières.	

(*) plus 'Côte de Beaune', or 'Côte de Beaune-Villages', if wished.

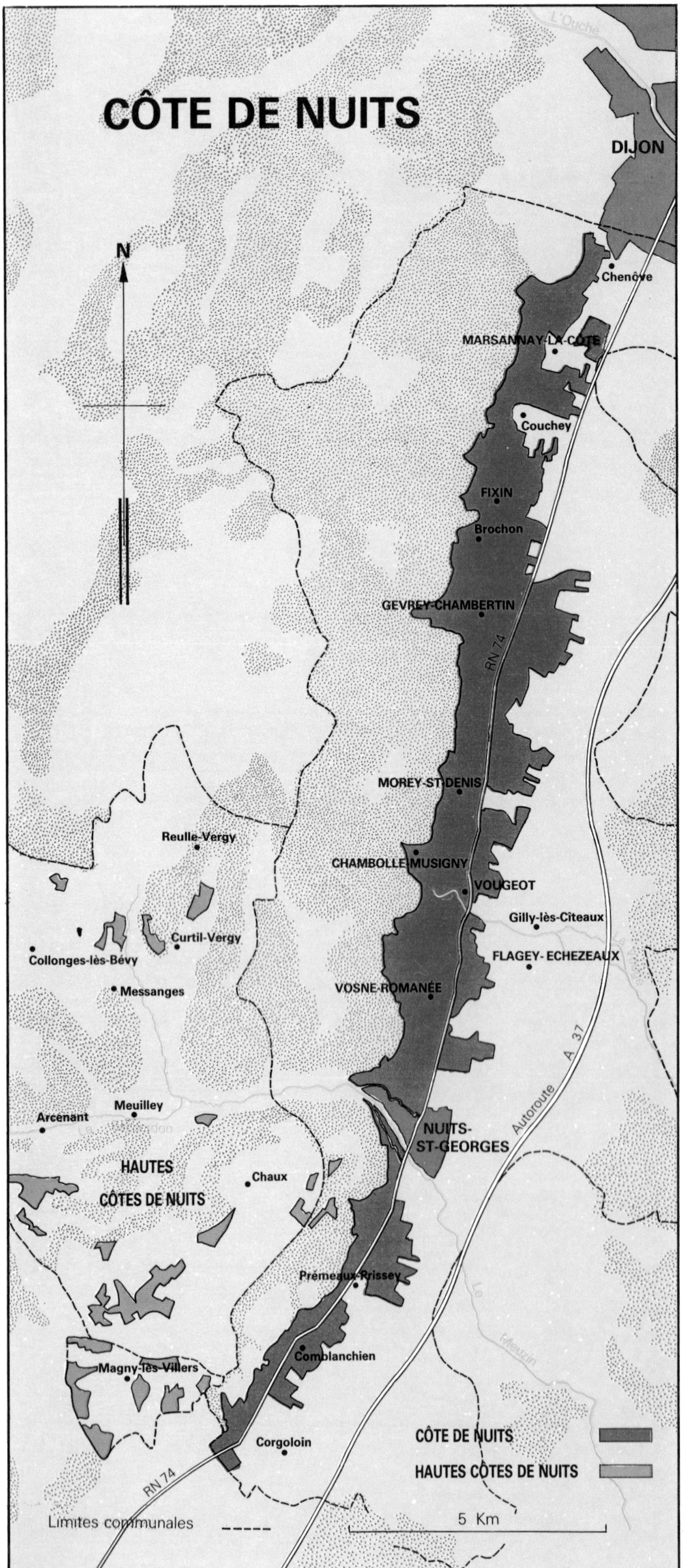

A very distinctive part of Burgundy, the Hautes Côtes can now tell the story of a viticultural rebirth. There were 3,000ha of vines here in 1914, but only 770ha in 1963, at a time when local rural depopulation was continuous. With support from the whole of Burgundy, this subregion has managed to turn the tide: vines now cover 1,200ha in the Hautes Côtes, and the wines produced are of excellent quality.

The wine-producing soils of the Côte

The arable layer given over to vines has different orientations consequent on the presence of small valleys or combes, which are mostly dry, and around which villages have developed.

Vineyard aspects are generally east or southeast, and sometimes south, as at Corton-Charlemagne. They are more rarely northeast, though this is the case at Savigny-lès-Beaune, for the Marconnets and Dominodes Premiers Crus.

The altitude of the vineyards varies between 220m and 300m. Along the edge of the plain, the N74 forms, with a few exceptions, the boundary of the 'village' AOC area. To the east of this, the vineyards are for AOC Bourgogne only. Mounting west up the slope, first the 'village' AOC areas are found, then the Premiers Crus, followed by the Grands Crus and finally the 'village' *appellation* areas once more, as far as the edge of the forest. At this point the rocks break through the topsoil.

The Côte is a Jurassic period massif with numerous longitudinal faults, forming important breaks covered with deposits of colluvium. Another feature of the massif is the undulation of its structural layers, forming an anticline on the Côte de Nuits, from Dijon to Corgoloin (the Gevrey anticline), and a syncline from that point as far south as Santenay, on the Côte de Beaune (the Volnay syncline). This arrangement causes different rock layers to come to the surface, and these condition the characteristics of many of the wines of the Côte.

The southern end of the Gevrey anticline, beyond Nuits-Saint-Georges, tapers to a narrow strip of vines several hundred metres in width. On the side of the hill there is an opencast quarry for the extraction of a high-quality, compact limestone named after the nearby village of Comblanchien. Here it is stone, rather than wine, that is prized.

The wine-producing area of the ***Côte de Nuits*** is situated on entrochal limestone and marl from the Bajocian stage of the Jurassic period, covered with a greater or lesser amount of stony scree from the later Bathonian stage. No great white wines are produced here.

The ***Côte de Beaune*** is formed of limestone from the still later Oxfordian stage of the Jurassic period, and this permits the production of both great red and white wines, often side by side. This is particularly true of the hill of Corton, whose eastern side yields red Corton and whose southern side produces white Corton-Charlemagne.

Aspect, slope, stoniness and soil permeability are the decisive factors in the delimitation of the *terroirs* or *climats* (vineyard sites) that are the object of so many different *appellations* in the Côte d'Or.

The soils at the foot of the Côte, with little or no gradient, few stones, a high clay content and poor permeability are only eligible for the regional AOC Bourgogne. It is the steeper slopes, sometimes with a gradient of 20 per cent, and containing 5 to 40 per cent of permeable stone, that support the 'village', Premier Cru and Grand Cru AOC vineyards.

The ***Hautes Côtes de Nuits*** and the ***Hautes Côtes de Beaune*** are situated to the west of the Côte d'Or itself, at an altitude of between 300m and 400m in an undulating region on hillsides of generally good aspect. This difference in height in relation to the main Côte is reflected in the vegetative cycle of the vine. The vines of the Hautes Côtes are, on average, ten to fifteen days later in budbreak, flowering and fruit maturing than those of the Côte. The wines are consequently more acid and less rich in alcohol and colour than those of the Côte, though with a pleasant bouquet. The risk of spring frosts in the Hautes Côtes is greater than on the main Côte.

The climate of the Côte d'Or

Rainfall

The average annual rainfall total is between 650 and 700mm, over 161 days, with rare extremes of as little as 450mm or as much as 900mm. February is the month with the least precipitation, followed by September and sometimes October. June is the wettest month, and this rain falls at the critical period during which the vine flowers, bringing a consequent risk of *coulure* (flower abortion) and *millerandage* (failed grape development). Late summer and early autumn are generally sunny, which favours good fruit maturation. Short periods of torrential rain sometimes occur (20 to 50mm per hour); these periods are often associated with hail storms and can sometimes destroy the promised harvest in May, or the actual harvest on the bunch in August and September.

Temperature

The annual average temperature lies between 10.7°C and 10.9°C. The average temperature during the vegetative cycle is around 16°C.

Extremely low temperatures, between −17°C and −22°C, can occur in January and February, causing the vine stocks to die, particularly in damp microclimates where the vines have not been earthed up for the winter.

Sunshine

There is an average of 2,000 hours of sunshine per year, of which 1,400 occur in the all-important April to September period.

Aloxe-Corton on the Côte de Beaune. Both Premiers and Grands Crus are sited among its vineyards. The red wines of Aloxe-Corton are appreciated for their solidity and their pronounced aroma of peaches.

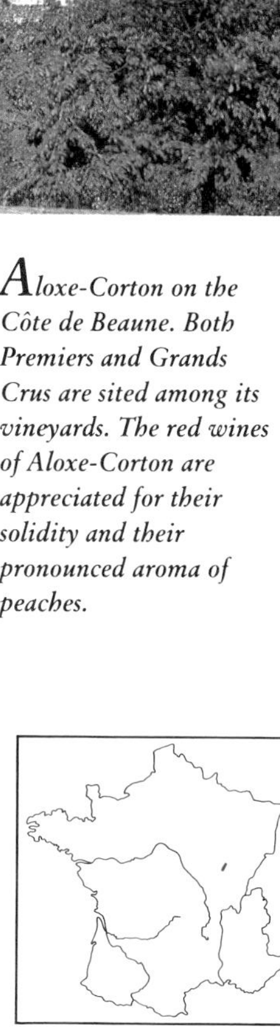

The *appellations*

In the Côte d'Or, it is necessary to distinguish between four levels of *appellation*. There are the regional AOCs; then the 'village' AOCs, known in French as *appellations communales*; then the Premiers Crus; and finally the Grand Cru *appellations*.

The regional appellations

Most of the Bourgogne, Bourgogne Aligoté, Bourgogne Passetoutgrains, Bourgogne Ordinaire and Bourgogne Grand Ordinaire *appellations* are produced in the area of the Hautes Côtes de Nuits and the Hautes Côtes de Beaune.

The appellations communales

All the red and rosé 'village' AOC wines are made from one grape variety only, the Pinot Noir. The white wines are produced from the Chardonnay, which may, if wished, be combined with the Pinot Blanc and the Pinot Gris varieties. The minimum alcohol content required for *appellation communale* or 'village' wines is 11° for the whites and 10° for the reds. In the case of the Premiers Crus (which will also carry the 'village' or commune name on the label) it is 11.5° for the whites and 11° for the reds. The base yield is 40hl/ha for reds and 45hl/ha for whites. The yields can, however, be modified after an exceptional harvest on the request of the wine growers' unions and following recommendation by the regional committee of the INAO.

WHAT IS A *CLIMAT*?

French wine legislators, in drawing up AOC regulations, have wisely respected local usage in different provinces: the name of the property is still paramount in the Bordeaux region, the grape variety in Alsace, the marque in Champagne.

In Burgundy, the cru *(literally 'growth', meaning a 'vineyard plot') has been chosen, as this has always been the main unit of reference in this area. The word* climat *is also used: this is a specifically Burgundian term meaning a smaller parcel of land than a* cru. *But by extension, this expression has become synonymous with* cru.

So we might describe a climat *as a small sub-area whose exact name and form have been lost in the mists of time, and which now simply means a vineyard plot or* cru. *This plot has its own peculiar characteristics: soil and subsoil, exposure to the sun and wind, frost-risk. To this may be added the fact that only one grape variety is usually used — the Chardonnay being more successful in one place, the Pinot Noir in another — and a number of historical factors: age and reputation of the name, whether or not the* climat *is in single ownership, quality of its vinification, commercial renown.*

Some climats *are minute — la Romanée is only 0.85ha — while others are much larger — Corton-Charlemagne stretches over nearly 74ha. Since the beginning of the 19th century, with vineyard legislation playing an increasingly important role, the notion of the* cru *has often attenuated that of the original* climat. *The Clos de Vougeot, for example, used to include, in its 51ha, about 15* climats: *Musigny, Plante-l'Abbé, Petit-Maupertuis . . . names which have all but disappeared today.*

A commune like Gevrey-Chambertin, with 400ha of vines, includes about 40 present-day climats. *Is this unnecessarily complex? This minute tapestry reflects the fine nuances of Burgundy's prodigious* terroirs. *And a good taster will recognize each* climat, *and will often be able to specify the vintage and the name of the producer.*

Chambolle-Musigny, nestled in a small valley on the Côte de Nuits, boasts two red Grands Crus: Bonnes-Mares and Musigny.

The Grands Crus

In the case of the Grands Crus, the name of the *climat* is the only one allowed to appear on the harvest declaration and on the labels.

All the red wines in this category must come from the Pinot Noir grape variety, and all the white wines from the Chardonnay, with the Pinot Blanc as a secondary white variety. The base yield is 35hl/ha or 37hl/ha for the reds and 40hl/ha for the whites. The minimum alcohol content is 11.5° for red wine and 12° for white.

On the Côte de Nuits, a concentration of red Grands Crus in the villages of Gevrey-Chambertin, Morey-Saint-Denis, Chambolle-Musigny and Vosne-Romanée will be noted. This is the prestigious heart of the Côte de Nuits, where wines are produced with a sumptuous colour, rich in aromas that are sometimes floral, sometimes fruity, with remarkable concentration and length on the palate and the potential for improvement in bottle over a long period — up to 20 or 30 years and more.

There are two islands of Grands Crus in the Côte de Beaune. Puligny-Montrachet and Chassagne-Montrachet at the southern end of the Côte produce great white wines possessing exquisite qualities of flavour and bouquet that only the Chardonnay vine can combine. Aloxe-Corton and Pernand-Vergelesses, further north, produce both red and white Grands Crus, with the whites providing the greatest bottles.

Côte Rôtie

This is probably the oldest vineyard area in the Rhône valley. Its development is attributed by some to the Greeks, but in fact Côte Rôtie was created by the Romans during the 1st century BC. They quickly realized that the steep slopes overlooking the Rhône here made an ideal site for vine cultivation. The vineyards they established have obviously been subject to many vicissitudes over the centuries, but man's faithfulness to this barren land has never faltered, and Côte Rôtie has enjoyed a fine reputation from as early as the end of the 18th century.

The *appellation d'origine contrôlée*, which today covers three communes, was ratified by decree on 18 October 1940. The vines now occupy 106ha and produce an average of 3,500hl of exclusively red wine. Grown on small terraces, sometimes containing only a few vines tied to stakes, they have to be tended by hand, never by machine. The principal grape variety used is the Syrah; however, the white grape variety Viognier can also be used — in a proportion of less than 20 per cent, and in soils to which it is well suited.

A characteristic of the Côte Rôtie *appellation* zone is that it includes, along with other slopes, two hillsides called the Côte Brune and the Côte Blonde; these names are said to be derived from the colour of the hair of two sisters who inherited the hillsides. They are easy to distinguish from each other in tasting, perhaps because of differing soils, but more clearly because the Viognier is used less extensively on the Côte Brune. The wines of this Côte are very expressive, with a severe quality that means that they take a long time to reach maturity; the wines of the Côte Blonde are more tender and evolve more quickly. They are sometimes vinified and sold separately (one producer, for example, makes a noted wine from the 'La Mouline' locality of the Côte Blonde), but are more generally blended together in a subtle manner.

Harvesters carrying wicker baskets at Cumières in the Coteaux Champenois.

The Côte Rôtie vineyards, on steep slopes in the commune of Ampuis, produce red wines only.

In general, the wines of the Côte Rôtie have a fine, intense aroma, dominated by the scents of violets, resin, spices and — with age — truffles and kirsch. They are full and ample on the palate, and become very elegant with age; they can be happily cellared for ten, fifteen or twenty years. They are fine wines.

Coteaux Champenois

The Coteaux Champenois wines are harvested in the wine-producing parts of Champagne. The area of production covers the following communes: Bouzy, Ambonnay, Ay, Mareuil, Tours-sur-Marne, Chigny-les-Roses, Rilly-la-Montagne, Jouy-lès-Reims, Cumières and Vertus, whose names may follow that of the *appellation*, which was ratified by decree on 21 August 1974. The best commune is indisputably Bouzy, which produces an average of 200,000 bottles every year.

These are still red, white and rosé wines, produced from the Champagne grape varieties: Meunier, Pinot Noir and Chardonnay. The white wines are both supple and elegant. The red wines have an aroma of red summer fruits, and of raspberries in particular.

Coteaux d'Aix-en-Provence and Coteaux d'Aix-en-Provence-les Baux

These *appellations d'origine contrôlée* were ratified by decree on 24 December 1985, and cover 49 communes.

The Coteaux d'Aix-en-Provence occupies a vast region, beginning at the western limit of the Var with the commune of Rians, then following the left bank of the Durance eastwards, and continuing along the Alpilles to les Baux-de-Provence, to the south of Avignon. The *appella-*

tion area then returns southwards and eastwards via the edge of the Étang de Berre, taking in the slopes of the Chaîne de l'Estaque on the coast, and ending at the edge of the Côtes de Provence zone, near Mimet.

The vine has been installed here for as long as anywhere in the Mediterranean; it seems likely that it was the Romans who first cultivated it. The vineyard zone, which extends over some 3,000ha and produces an average of 120,000hl (20 per cent of this total from cooperatives) is in fact composed of several subregions. The subregion of the Coteaux des Baux, because it harboured the area's first commercial vineyards of quality, earned the VDQS *appellation* just after the Second World War. In addition, the vine was a complement to, or ornament of, the châteaux, *mas* and *bastides* that surrounded the town of Aix-en-Provence.

The climate, as in the Rhône valley and the northern part of the Côtes de Provence, is dominated by a long dry period in the summer. But the large dimensions of the growing zone and its variegated pattern of relief create differing mesoclimates: continental and relatively cool at Rians and along the Durance, but much warmer in the area of les Baux and around the Étang de Berre.

The soils are all derived from limestone massifs of the Cretaceous period, among which the impressive peaks of the Montagne Sainte Victoire and of les Baux stand out. The bedrock, made of a mixture of marlacious limestone, calcareous molasse, clay and sandstone, has produced very poor, thin topsoils, including red soils which are pebbly or gravelly in varying degrees, covering terraces or fan deltas. There is therefore a certain heterogeneity about the terrain, and this results in a large variety of wine types and styles.

The red grape varieties are mostly those that are grown in other areas of the Rhône and the Mediterranean: Cinsaut, Counoise, Mourvèdre and Syrah. The Cabernet Sauvignon, a noble visitor from the Bordeaux region, is used to improve the potential quality of the vineyards in the northern part of the zone.

White wines are made from local grape varieties, such as the Bourboulenc and Clairette, with additional aromatic qualities provided by the Sauvignon Blanc and Sémillon vines. But two new rules have been instituted with the AOC: for red wines, none of the constituent grape varieties may exceed 40 per cent of the whole; and for white wines, no single variety may exceed 20 per cent of the whole.

White wines make up the smaller part of production at the moment. The mixture of grape varieties used, and modern wine-making technology, have given them a very elegant floral and vegetal aroma and a fresh taste, with a pleasantly acid finish. The rosé wines are very aromatic, and firm on the palate.

The red wines, though they share an Aixois family resemblance, vary in specific nuance according to the predominant grape variety used. The Mourvèdre gives an aroma that is animal in character; wine made with the Syrah is characterized by fruity and floral aromas, while the Cabernet Sauvignon, here as elsewhere, produces vegetal and balsamic aromas. These wines are full-bodied, and become elegant, warm and well balanced after a maturation period of several years in bottle.

The Moulin de Brissac looks out over vines in the Coteaux de l'Aubance, in Anjou.

Coteaux d'Ancenis

This *appellation*, classed VDQS by decree on 27 August 1973, may be followed by the name of the grape variety used: Chenin Blanc (known locally as the Pineau de la Loire) or Pinot Gris (locally called the Malvoisie) for the whites, and Gamay or Cabernet Franc for the reds and rosés. An average of 17,000hl of red, white and rosé wines are produced in an area of about 300 ha, covering 27 communes in Loire-Atlantique and Maine-et-Loire.

The red wine has a carmine hue. It is pleasant, lively, and is without astringency. It is best drunk young. The white and rosé wines are fresh and fruity.

Coteaux de l'Aubance

This vineyard area, classed AOC by decree on 18 February 1950, covers an area of around 80 ha, with the Chenin Blanc as sole grape variety.

The production of white wines has been around 2,000hl for the last 10 years. The area of production covers the communes or parts of communes of Brissac, Denée, Juigné-sur-Loire, Mozé-sur-Louet, Mûrs, Saint-Jean-des-Mauvrets, Saint-Melaine-sur-Aubance, Saint-Saturnin-sur-Loire, Soulaines and Vauchrétien.

The must has to contain 187g of sugar per litre, vinified to produce dry or medium dry wines. These are yellow in colour, with green glints. On the palate they are fruity and well structured, with aromas of verbena.

Coteaux de la Méjanelle *See* Coteaux du Languedoc.

Coteaux de Pierrevert

This large VDQS area, created by decree on 10 August 1959, covers 42 communes and 400ha, producing on average 18,000hl of red, white and rosé wines annually. In practice, the wines of Coteaux de Pierrevert come from about ten communes only, the most important of which lie on the right bank of the Durance in the Alpes de Haute-Provence *département*.

Before becoming the tourist wines they are today, the wines of Pierrevert refreshed the shepherds who went up to the mountain pastures with their sheep in the spring. At that time they were mountain wines, slender and lively. Many of today's wines have kept this delicacy and charm, especially those grown around Sainte-Tulle, Manosque and Les Mées, thanks to a climate that is much cooler than in Vaucluse. The mixture of grape varieties includes Clairette, Ugni Blanc and Marsanne for the white wines; and Grenache, Carignan, Cinsaut, Mourvèdre and Syrah for the reds. Both red and white wines are appealingly light in alcohol, with a fresh, delicately tart taste.

Coteaux de Saint-Christol *See* Coteaux de Languedoc.

Coteaux de Saumur

The volumes shown in harvest declarations for this *appellation* are very low, and do not correspond at all to the potential of the production area, classed AOC by decree on 21 April 1962. Only 100hl to 200hl of this wine, produced exclusively from the Chenin Blanc, are marketed each year. The area of production covers 12 communes in Maine-et-Loire, plus one — Saix — in Vienne.

The wines are off-dry in character, and have a minimum alcohol content of 12° with a residual sugar level of 10g or more per litre. The wines are fine and persistent on the palate, harmonious, and age well in bottle.

Coteaux de Vérargues *See* Coteaux de Languedoc.

Coteaux du Cap Corse *See* Vin de Corse-Coteaux du Cap Corse.

Coteaux du Giennois *See* Côtes de Gien.

Coteaux du Languedoc

The area of this *appellation*, classed as an AOC by decree on 24 December 1985, is vast, covering 50,000ha over 121 communes in Aude, Gard and Hérault, with a production of about 400,000hl. Within the overall *appellation* zone lie three *crus*: Clairette du Languedoc, Faugères and Saint-Chinian; and 12 *terroirs*: Cabrières, La Clape, Coteaux de la Méjanelle, Montpeyroux, Picpoul de Pinet, Pic-Saint-Loup, Quatourze, Coteaux de Saint-Christol, Saint-Drézery, Saint-Georges-d'Orques, Saint-Saturnin, Coteaux de Vérargues. The *cru* wines are labelled with their *cru* name alone; the other wines are labelled with the Coteaux du Languedoc name, either on its own or followed by the name of one of the *terroirs*, if applicable. The area classed as Coteaux du Languedoc without any additional indication of geographical origin covers part of the vineyards of the Ceressou valley, Aspiran, Lodève and Saint-Félix de Lodez in Hérault, and Langlade in the Gard.

Together with Roussillon, Corbières and Minervois, the vineyards of the Coteaux du Languedoc are among the oldest in France. Developed and cultivated by the Romans, the vine flourished in the Languedoc region before spreading to the rest of France and Europe.

Cabrières

The grape varieties planted here are the same as those found throughout the Coteaux du Languedoc. For red wines, the Carignan, Cinsaut, Grenache, Syrah and Mourvèdre are used, no one variety being permitted to form more than 50 per cent of the AOC blend. For white wines, the Bourboulenc, Carignan Blanc, Clairette, Macabeu, Ugni Blanc and Piquepoul Blanc are planted, again with no one variety forming more than 50 per cent of the finished blend. The vines should not be planted at a greater density than 3,300/ha, and all except the Syrah are pruned short, with a maximum of 6–8 short canes of 2 buds each per stock. Yields are limited to 50hl/ha.

The Cabrières vineyard area is sited on schistous soil and yields red, white and rosé wines of great finesse. Some 7,000hl are produced annually.

Coteaux de la Méjanelle

The zone of production occupies four communes surrounding, and to the east of, Montpellier, sited on a terrace of sea-deposited pebbles very similar to those that form the *terrior* of Costières du Gard. The vineyard area covers 600ha and produces 15,000hl annually of red, white and rosé wines. Numerous 18th-century manor houses and farmhouses, surrounded by attractive pine groves, dot the countryside.

Some of the first French vines grew in the Languedoc region.

Coteaux de Saint-Christol

The area of production occupies one commune only, and covers 400ha of excellent wine-growing soils formed by water-borne pebbles. Annual production is tiny. The vineyards are cooled by sea breezes. The red and rosé wines of this area are supple, fruity and fine. They have a long history, and were already well known at the time of Louis IX (1214–1270), known as Saint Louis.

Coteaux de Vérargues

The area of production, which overlaps part of the Muscat de Lunel *appellation* zone, covers 2,200ha in nine communes, and yields 18,000hl annually. The calcareous clay soil is scattered with pebbles and colluvium. The red, white and rosé wines produced here are supple with a delicate bouquet.

La Clape

The area of production occupies five communes to the southeast of Narbonne, situated on the limestone massif from which the *appellation* takes its name. The calcareous soil is a good medium for quality wine growing. The extent of the *appellation* is 50,000ha, with an annual production of 45,000hl of red, white and rosé wines. The mixture of grape varieties used for the red and white wines is the same as that of the other Coteaux du Languedoc *terroirs*; the white wines, though, also make use of the Malvoisie and Terret Blanc. They are fresh, fruity and supple, with yeasty, varietal aromas. The red and rosé wines are fruity and full.

Montpeyroux

The area of production is sited in two communes to the northwest of Montpellier, at the foot of the Causse du Larzac, situated on frost-created piedmont gravels. The vineyards cover an area of 900ha, with an annual production of 15,000hl of red and rosé wine. The red wine of Montpeyroux, rich in colour, has a firm structure well suited to ageing.

Picpoul de Pinet

The production zone of Picpoul de Pinet covers six communes near the Bassin de Thau, between Sète and Pézenas. The zone occupies 2,200ha, and annual production of white wine only is around 13,000hl. The wine is made from a minimum of 70 per cent Piquepoul Blanc, with up to 25 per cent Terret Blanc and 5 per cent Clairette. It is a very dry wine, fruity, fresh and vital, with a beautiful green-gold colour.

Pic-Saint-Loup

The vineyard area is sited in 13 communes to the north of Montpellier. It covers 5,000ha, and has an annual production of 37,000hl. The best *terroirs* within the zone occur on gravel and scree at the bottom of slopes found at the edge of small limestone massifs — the '*gravettes*' of Corconne are a good example of this. The major part of production is of red wines, which are light in colour, fresh and pleasant, with aromas of summer fruits. Small amounts of white and rosé wines are also produced.

Quatourze

The wine-growing area covers 500ha to the south of Narbonne and has an annual production of 15,000hl of mainly red wine. The *terroir* is formed by a plateau of water-borne stones that slopes down to the coastal lakes. The red wines of Quatourze are warm and robust and keep well. A little fresh and aromatic white wine is also produced.

The silhouette of the Pic Saint-Loup rises above the vineyards of this sub-*appellation *within the Coteaux du Languedoc.

Saint-Saturnin, in the Coteaux du Languedoc, enjoys a reputation for its light and fruity red 'vin d'une nuit'.

Saint-Drézery

The 500ha area of production covers a single commune to the northeast of Montpellier, and yields 4,500hl of red and rosé wines annually from calcareous clay and sandstone soils. These wines are pleasant, fruity and light.

Saint-Georges-d'Orques

The 2,200ha area covers five communes to the west of Montpellier and has an annual production of 14,000hl of red and rosé wines. The *terroir* is essentially calcareous clay. Saint-Georges-d'Orques is the oldest and best known of the Coteaux du Languedoc *appellations*. Its wines were already famous in the Middle Ages.

Saint-Saturnin

The 750ha area of production covers four communes between Gignac and Lodève, next to the Causse du Larzac; annual production is around 22,000hl. The calcareous clays and pebbly screes of this *terroir*, sited at the bottom of well-exposed slopes, produce round, full red wines, rich in aromas. The zone specializes in the production of a very light red or deep rosé *vin d'une nuit* (wine given a 12-hour maceration period only), and it is this that has made the reputation of Saint-Saturnin.

Coteaux du Layon

This vineyard area, classed as an AOC by decree on 18 February 1950, covers 1,200ha. The Chenin Blanc is the only grape variety used. Annual production over the last ten years has approached 45,500hl. Production of Coteaux du Layon-Chaume (produced from certain plots in the commune of Rochefort-sur-Loire) is about 1,500hl per year. The Coteaux du Layon area of production covers 25 communes or parts of communes.

The wine makers can, if they wish, claim the Coteaux du Layon-Val de Loire *appellation*, provided they meet the same conditions of production and use the same grape variety as for the Coteaux du Layon *appellation*.

The grapes may benefit from the action of *Botrytis cinerea* (*pourriture noble* or 'noble rot'), and must contain 204g of sugar per litre of must at the time of harvesting. In six favourable *terroirs*, 221g per litre is required and, in this case, the name of the commune may be combined with that of Coteaux du Layon. This applies to Beaulieu-sur-Layon, Faye-d'Anjou, Rablay-sur-Layon, Rochefort-sur-Loire, Saint-Aubin-de-Luigné, Saint-Lambert-du-Lattay.

The colour of the wines is a pronounced yellow, becoming golden yellow as the wines acquire age. The level of sweetness is perfectly balanced by the acidity and severity of the Chenin Blanc. The aromatic qualities of the wines — characteristic scents are of quince or dried fruit — improve with age.

Coteaux du Loir

From an area of about 30 ha, the vineyards of this *appellation*, classed as an AOC by decree on

The following Coteaux du Layon communes may attach their names to that of the appellation: *Beaulieu-sur-Layon, Faye-d'Anjou, Rablay-sur-Layon, Rochefort-sur-Loire, Saint-Aubin-de-Luigné or Saint-Lambert-du-Lattay.*

The Coteaux du Layon-Val de Loire name is an alternative to the Coteaux du Layon name.

Wines sold under the Coteaux du Layon-Chaume appellation *are produced on plots in the commune of Rochefort-sur-Loire.*

12 May 1948, produce red, white and rosé wines. The red wines are based on the Pineau d'Aunis, Cabernet Franc, Gamay and Côt grape varieties, and annual production is about 800hl. The rosé wines contain a maximum of 25 per cent of the Grolleau variety, with the balance made up by the Pineau d'Aunis, Cabernet Franc, Gamay and Côt varieties; annual production is 200hl. The white wines are made from the Chenin Blanc, and 300hl are produced annually.

The area of production covers 23 communes or parts of communes in Sarthe and Indre-et-Loire. The wine makers can also use the Coteaux du Loir-Val de Loire *appellation* for their wines if wished.

The white wine is straw-yellow in colour; it is full and lively, and off-dry after sunny years. The reds are refreshing, full and supple, with a slight astringency and often spicy aromas.

Coteaux du Lyonnais

The area of this AOC, governed by the decree of 9 May 1984, covers 50 communes in the *département* of the Rhône.

Only red and rosé wines made from the Gamay Noir à Jus Blanc, and white wines made from the Chardonnay, the Aligoté and the Melon grape varieties are entitled to the *appellation*.

From a surface area of some 400 ha, the wine makers produce about 10,000hl of mostly red and rosé wine each year. The white wine production is tiny. These are pleasant wines to drink young.

Coteaux du Tricastin

This AOC, classed for 22 communes by decree on 27 July 1973, produces red, white and rosé wines.

Vines existed here in Roman times, but for many centuries they were only a subsidiary crop. As in many areas near the Rhône, the vine shared its soil with mulberry trees, cereal crops, nut trees, and oak trees for truffle production.

The vineyard zone stretches between Montélimar, Saint-Paul-Trois-Châteaux, Taulignan and Dieulefit. It is a tortured landscape, consisting of barren summits and deep valleys. Between these two extremes, the large clay and pebble terraces near the river Rhône form privileged sites for the vine. The climate across most of this zone is harsher and less predictable than in the Côtes du Rhône, with the result that clear differences emerge in wines from different parts of the *appellation*.

The grape varieties used are the same as those found elsewhere in the Côtes du Rhône. The Grenache is the main variety. Because of the climate, the Carignan is rarely at home in this region, whereas the Syrah is well suited to it.

The vineyard area covers 2,000 ha; an average of 100,000hl of wine are produced each year, more than half of which is made by the cooperative of Suze-la-Rousse.

White wines are only made in small amounts. Because of the fickle climate, they are fresh, light and keen-edged. The rosé wines are similar to many of those produced in the surrounding areas. They are, however, fresher than most, and slightly less strong in alcohol.

The red wines vary according to the precise area they come from. In the north and east of the zone, where the soil is sandy and the aspects predominantly south-facing, the wines are fruity and elegant. These are, in principle, carafe wines or *primeurs*, best drunk within the first year of their existence. In the pebbly clay terraces of the west, near Roussas and les Granges-Gontardes, the red wines have a more complex bouquet and a full and well-balanced form, without excessive strength. They remain at a peak for two to three years.

Coteaux du Vendômois

This vineyard area, classed VDQS by decree on 21 June 1968, covers about 100 ha. The grape varieties used are the Chenin Blanc and the Chardonnay (20 per cent maximum) for white wines; the Pineau d'Aunis and the Gamay (30 per cent maximum) for rosé wines; and the Pineau d'Aunis (30 per cent minimum) with the Gamay, the Pinot Noir and the Cabernet Franc for red wines. About 4,000hl, two thirds rosé and one third red, is produced annually. The production of white wine is about 500hl per year. The area of production stretches over 35 communes or parts of communes in Loir-et-Cher.

The dry rosé wine is given character by the Pineau d'Aunis variety: it is a light rosé with spicy aromas. The red wines are pleasant and lively. The white wine is fresh and dry. These are wines to enjoy young.

Coteaux Varois

This VDQS, classed in 1984, is formed of 28 communes in Var, which lie fairly near those of the Côtes de Provence AOC zone. From north to south, the area of the *appellation* stretches from near the border with the Alpes-de-Haute-Provence *département* — Villecroze, Tavernes — to la Roquebrussanne and Signes. At present, some 100,000hl are produced annually. It is too soon to say exactly what the future of the *appellation* will be.

Both soils and climatic conditions vary within this large zone. Red and rosé wines are produced from the Carignan, Cinsaut, Grenache, Mourvèdre, and Syrah grape varieties (with no one variety present at more than 70 per cent of the final blend) and from the Cabernet Sauvignon and Tibouren varieties (not present at more than 30 per cent of the blend). Quality is thus ensured without jeopardizing local character.

The rosé wines are fresh, with good acidity and lightness, while the red wines are tasty, with a fruity aroma. They are best drunk as young as possible.

In the Vendôme region, cave cellars are dug into the calcareous tufa rock.

Côtes Canon-Fronsac

See Canon-Fronsac.

Côtes d'Auvergne

This vineyard area, classed VDQS by decree on 14 March 1977, covers an area of 600ha. The grape varieties used are Chardonnay for white wines, and Gamay and Pinot Noir for red and rosé wines. Production is small.

Five of the best communes have the right to add their name to the *appellation* name: Côtes d'Auvergne-Boudes, Côtes d'Auvergne-Chanturgue, Côtes d'Auvergne-Châteaugay, Côtes d'Auvergne-Corent and Côtes d'Auvergne-Madargues. A further 61 communes are included in the basic Côtes d'Auvergne appellation zone.

The colour of the red wine is a light carmine or amber. Its aroma is fruity and well developed, with a characteristic scent of wild mountain cherries. It is pleasant and well structured on the palate. Both the white and rosé are dry and full.

The vines of Châteaugay in the Côtes d'Auvergne produce light red wines as well as dry rosé and white wines.

Côtes de Bergerac

See Bergerac.

Côtes de Bergerac Moelleux

See Bergerac.

Côtes de Blaye

See Blaye.

Côtes de Bordeaux-Saint-Macaire

This vineyard area is situated on the right bank of the Garonne. It forms a southerly continuation of the Premières Côtes de Bordeaux, extending almost as far as the point at which a small tributary of the Garonne, the Dropt, joins the river.

The *appellation d'origine contrôlée* Côtes de Bordeaux-Saint-Macaire, created by decree on 31 July 1937, only applies to white wines made from grapes harvested in delimited parcels in 11 communes situated in the southeasterly part of the Bordeaux region.

To be entitled to the *appellation*, the wine must be made from the following grape varieties: Sémillon, Sauvignon Blanc and Muscadelle. The minimum sugar content of the must has to be 178g per litre. The white wines must have a minimum alcohol content of 11.5° and a maximum of 13°.

In 1985, the surface area declared was 58ha and the production 2,298l; one third of this figure was produced by the Gironde and Saint-Pierre-d'Aurillac cooperatives.

Côtes de Bourg *See* Bourg.

Côtes de Buzet

The AOC Côtes de Buzet, ratified by decree on 19 April 1973, is the oldest and the most famous of the *appellations* of the Garonne. The vineyard area covers about 1,300ha and produces 70,000hl of red wines, 1,800hl of rosé and 1,000hl of white wine.

The red wines are produced in large part by the growers' cooperative at Buzet-sur-Baïse. The grape varieties used are the Merlot, Cabernet Franc and Cabernet Sauvignon. The vinification is carried out by the cooperative with great care, and includes the practice of using selected fruit only, and long maceration periods. Fermentation temperatures are kept as near as possible to 32°C, thanks to an automatic cooling system. The cooperative, called Les Vignerons Réunis des Côtes de Buzet, is unusual in that it has its own cooperage. The wines are kept in new oak *barriques* for between six and twelve months.

The high proportion of gravelly soils found in the region means that the wines have considerable finesse. They are tasty, rich and rounded, with a subtle tannic structure. They reach maturity after five to eight years in bottle, and remain at a peak for about fifteen years. Since the vineyards have largely been planted in recent times, Côtes de Buzet has only been able to reveal its full potential with vintages released since the late 1970s.

Côtes de Duras

The name Côtes de Duras is an old one, granted *appellation d'origine contrôlée* status by the decree of 16 February 1937 for the production of red, white and rosé wines. It covers the best wine-growing *terroirs* of the canton of Duras, situated at the far northeastern end of the *département* of Lot-et-Garonne.

The town of Nérac, in the heart of the Côtes de Buzet.

The region is formed of hills threaded with numerous valleys; this topography does not permit the unbroken cultivation of vines and they are only to be found on the summits of hills and on south-facing slopes. The soil is clay or calcareous clay. There are few gravel soils.

The vines cover a surface area of about 2,000ha, with an average production of 100,000hl. White wines dominate, making up about two thirds of production. Many of the 350 producers are independent, but the cooperative sector, with 40 per cent of total production, is important in volume terms.

The quality of the wines is excellent, but they are insufficiently appreciated by consumers. The dry white wines are light, fresh and fruity, with Sauvignon Blanc varietal character and a very pale colour with green glints. The sweet white wines have a perfume of ripe fruit, with Sémillon varietal character and a light amber colour.

The rosé wines make up a very small percentage of production. They are fresh and fruity, with the stamp of the two Cabernet varieties on them.

The red wines differ in character according to the method of production used. If they have been made by carbonic maceration, they are light, supple, elegant and very aromatic, best served cool and drunk young. If the grapes are vinified in the classic and traditional way, then the wines are more highly coloured and full bodied; these wines should be allowed to age for two or three years before being drunk.

The varieties permitted for the *appellation* are Sauvignon Blanc, Sémillon, Muscadelle, Mauzac, Chenin Blanc, Ondenc and Ugni Blanc for the whites; and Merlot, Cabernet Franc, Cabernet Sauvignon and Côt for the reds and rosés.

Côtes de Fronsac *See* Fronsac.

Côtes de Gien or Coteaux du Giennois

This vineyard zone, classed VDQS by decree on 26 November 1954, covers a surface area of 75ha.

For red wines, the Pinot Noir and Gamay varieties are grown, and for white wines, the Sauvignon Blanc and Chenin Blanc.

Annual production is in the order of 400hl for white, 3,000hl for red and 500hl for rosé. The area of production is found mainly within the Loiret *département* and covers 16 communes or parts of communes. The name Côtes de Gien may be followed by the name Cosne-sur-Loire, if the wines are produced in a small part of the nearby Nièvre *département*.

The red wines have a light ruby colour and a fruity aroma. They are slender but soundly structured, and keep well in the bottle. The rosé wines are dry, light and lively. The white wines are dry, firm and fresh.

Côtes de la Malepère

The *appellation*, classed VDQS by decree on 27 January 1983, is situated to the southwest of Carcassonne, on the slopes of the Coteaux du Razès, and is itself bordered on the southeast by the Blanquette de Limoux vineyard area. The *appellation* stretches over 31 communes and has a surface area of 6,000ha, with a production of 10,000hl, mainly of red and rosé wine. Its position at the western limit of the Mediterranean climatic zone is reflected in the grape varieties used: a typical Languedoc range, supplemented by the Merlot, Cabernet Sauvignon and Cabernet Franc varieties more characteristic of western France.

Côtes de Montravel *See* Montravel.

Côtes de Provence

The *appellation d'origine contrôlée* Côtes de Provence, ratified by decree on 24 October 1977 for 68 communes, is, in terms of quantity, the largest in the Mediterranean area: 19,000ha produce an annual average of 800,000 to 900,000hl of white, rosé and red wine.

Its climate is that of Provence as a whole: warm, but tempered in the southern part by sea breezes, and by colder and wetter continental influences in the north.

The soil varies greatly within the *appellation*. Near the coast lies the Massif des Maures, whose granite slopes yield about 20 per cent of the total production.

To the north of the N7, around Draguignan, is an undulating plateau of calcareous origin, whose red soil is sometimes covered with white limestone gravel. The vineyards of this part again provide some 20 per cent of production.

Between these two extremes lies a depression zone, in which erosion elements from the Massif des Maures and from the limestone plateau have both accumulated. Above the lowest parts of this, consisting of alluvial silt of little interest for wine growing, the vines are planted on gentle slopes and terraces of red clay and sandstone. It is in this central area that the most important vineyard plantings are to be found — some 50 per cent of the total. Here, too, a number of cooperatives produce a large proportion of the *appellation contrôlée* wines.

Finally, to the west of this area, there are slopes consisting of red gravelly or pebbly clay soil, on which vines grow to an altitude of 400m. Here, under the influence of the Massif de la Sainte Baume, the climate is markedly less warm than in the coastal regions of Provence. This last part of the Côtes de Provence vineyard area does not produce more than 10 per cent of the total.

Thus, taking into account both soil and climatic factors, the Côtes de Provence can be seen to be formed of four more or less distinct subregions. Each of the wine types — white, rosé, red for drinking young, and red for keeping — are at their best in different subregions within the AOC zone.

The white wines have recently changed greatly in character. The rules of production, and above all the increasing use of the Rolle and Sémillon grape varieties, now provide wines with elegant floral and vegetal perfumes. Their structure is relatively light. At present, they account for no more than 6 per cent of overall production.

Rosé is the dominant wine type, with 60 per cent of the total production. There are historical reasons for this. For a long time, the wine growers of the Côtes de Provence have been, so to speak, the victims of their geographical position, lying at the gates of a region that had become the winter and summer residence of an initially privileged clientele, and then of tourists of all sorts. In conditions dominated by the demands of tourism, production was obviously geared towards the type of wine most appreciated in the summer: rosé. It may thus be said that this type of wine has become a Provençal speciality. It is primarily appreciated for its colour, which is enhanced by sunshine. But it is more than simply pretty: since the practice of vinification by the *saignée* method, in which a part of the must is macerated with the grape skins prior to fermentation, has become widespread, the rosé wines have acquired a richer aromatic character, while remaining supple, fresh and thus very attractive.

The red wines can be extremely good, especially when grown on the edges of the Massif des Maures, in the sandstone soils between le Muy and Hyères, and on some of the slopes of the limestone plateau north of Draguignan. These are wines with a complex aroma and fine balance. They are full-bodied, and seem to fill out further after several years of maturation. Their peak is generally reached at four or five years.

Vines at Eygalières in the Côtes de Provence production area.

Côtes de Saint-Mont

The vineyard area of Côtes de Saint-Mont is situated in the heart of Gascony, in southwest Gers. Its origin probably dates back to the time of the Roman conquest of Gaul, as is the case with many of the vineyards of the South West. The Romans began wine growing in this region at a very early stage on the hillsides near the river Adour.

From 1050, the Benedictine monks of the abbey of Saint-Mont applied themselves to vineyard development. They did so with such success that in the 16th and 17th centuries the wines of Côtes de Saint-Mont, like many others from the Pyrenean area, were transported along the Adour to Bayonne and then shipped to England and Holland, where they were greatly appreciated. After the French Revolution, the vineyard area diminished constantly until dealt a final blow by the phylloxera invasion at the end of the 19th century.

But, thanks to the creative genius of a handful of new 'musketeers' who combined cooperative principles of organization with modern oenological techniques, this vineyard area has now been reborn, and has the first VDQS *appellation* ever awarded in Gers. Red, rosé and white wines are produced.

The 700ha of vineyards are sited on a vast collection of hills, mostly about 250m in height and south and southeast facing. They benefit from both the maritime climate of Aquitaine and the mountain climate of the Pyrenees: average temperatures are around 13°C, spring is wet, summer is hot with periods of drought, and autumns are long, mild and sunny, conditions favourable to the full and satisfactory maturing of the grapes. Average rainfall is around 950mm per year.

The wine-growing slopes are mainly composed of calcareous marl. There are some gravelly soils that produce elegant, light wines to be drunk young, while other, 'stronger'

A vineyard in the neighbourhood of Collobrières, in the Côtes de Provence appellation *zone.*

clay soils yield tannic red wines suitable for ageing. Finally, the calcareous clay soil of the western slopes is favourable to the production of aromatic dry white wines.

The vines grown are a combination of Aquitaine and Pyrenean varieties. For reds and rosés, those used include the Tannat, which is characterized by the ripeness and richness of its tannins; Cabernet Franc, Cabernet Sauvignon, Fer and Merlot, the last named being employed to add aromatic roundness. The varieties used for white wines are: Arrufiac, Clairette, Petit Manseng, Gros Manseng and Courbu Blanc. Present production is 15,000hl per year, and this figure is growing continually. Ninety per cent of this total is red and rosé wine, and 10 per cent is white wine.

Three cooperatives undertake most of the harvesting and vinification of the grapes, with independent, small growers only accounting for 10 per cent of production. Exports are in the region of 35 per cent of production.

The red wines have a strong crimson colour. They are firmly structured, but not at the expense of delicacy and aroma. They should be drunk when still fairly young. The rosé wines are firm and lively, with a bright, attractive colour and a fruity aroma provided by the two Cabernet varieties. The dry white wines are remarkably aromatic and elegant.

Côtes de Toul

This vineyard just outside Toul, not far from the two big Lorraine towns of Nancy and Metz, produces a very distinctive wine from the Gamay Noir à Jus Blanc variety. This grape has coloured skin and colourless juice, and the wine produced is a *vin gris* (a very pale rosé) with a lively taste, pleasant fruitiness and satisfying length. Made according to the principles of white wine vinification, it has been entitled to a VDQS *appellation* since 1951. Red wines can also be made, from the Meunier and Pinot Noir varieties, and white wines from the Aligoté, Aubin Blanc and Auxerrois.

The small vineyard area, which covers about 60ha, includes the communes of Lucey, Bruley, Pagney-derrière-Barine, Bulligny, Blénod-lès-Toul, Charmes-la-Côte and Mont-le-Vignoble. Before 1880, the vineyard area was much larger: it covered 16,000ha in 1865. The great reduction in plantings was the consequence of the phylloxera blight and the First World War. The small scale of production, which on average is between 3,000 and 4,000hl, means that consumption is mostly regional. But, thanks to efforts made by the local wine growers, its reputation has now grown beyond the geographical limits of Lorraine.

Côtes du Brulhois

This vineyard area adjacent to the river Garonne obtained a VDQS *appellation* on 21 November 1984 for its red and rosé wines.

About 120ha are planted, producing 7,000hl annually of mainly red wines. Production is divided between two cooperatives: one at Donzac in Tarn-et-Garonne and one at Goulens in Lot-et-Garonne. The latter vinifies grapes grown in the part of the *appellation* adjacent to the Côtes de Buzet, but these vineyards are in decline and most of the production here is *vin de pays* rather than VDQS wine. The Donzac cooperative produces both red and rosé Côtes du Brulhois.

The Fer grape variety, combined with the Merlot and Cabernet Franc, produces light, lively wines with an aroma of raspberries and redcurrants. These should be drunk young, within two to four years of the vintage date shown on the bottle.

Côtes du Cabardès et de l'Orbiel

This wine-producing zone, classed VDQS by decree on 21 September 1973, has a potential area of 3,600ha, spread over 14 communes. Production at present stands at 15,000hl of red and rosé wines.

The *appellation* zone is situated to the north of Carcassonne, on the slopes of the Montagne Noire; it is bordered in the east by the vineyard of Minervois. The permitted grape varieties include the Cabernet Franc, Cabernet Sauvignon and Merlot, as well as the customary varieties of Languedoc and the South West. The picturesque Orbiel valley, dominated by the four châteaux of Lastours, forms the spine of the *appellation*.

Côtes du Forez

The vineyard, classed VDQS by decree on 23 January 1956, covers a surface area of 150ha, and is planted with Gamay. Annual production is in the order of 4,000hl of red wine and 2,000hl of rosé wine. The area of production stretches along the upper Loire and covers 21 communes or parts of communes.

The red wines are light garnet in colour, with fruity aromas. They are easy to drink, lively, finely structured wines. The rosés are dry and light. Both are best drunk young. (*See* Vins du Centre.)

Côtes du Frontonnais

The reputation of wines from the Fronton area dates from the 12th century, a time when this small town was both a bishopric and a seigneurial residence. For several centuries, the vineyards were administered by the order of Knights Hospitallers.

Despite the rigorous protectionism of the Bordeaux trade, who controlled shipments from further down the Garonne, these wines reached a peak of popularity in the 18th and 19th centuries. Then came the phylloxera crisis: the Frontonnais vineyards were practically annihilated. Their recovery has been slow and difficult. On 30 July 1945, Fronton wine obtained its VDQS *appellation*; an AOC for the areas of Fronton and Villaudric followed on 19 October 1974.

The Fronton-Villaudric vineyard zone is situated to the north of Toulouse, in Tarn-et-Garonne (11 communes) and Haute-Garonne (9 communes).

The vines grow on three alluvial terraces on the left-hand bank of the river Tarn. The area of the *appellation* is bordered to the west by the Canal Latéral à la Garonne and to the northeast by the Tarn. Numerous winding, deeply entrenched streams cut through these terraces before flowing into the Tarn.

The topsoil is formed of white, siliceous *boulbènes*: a finely textured soil poor in clay and iron. Underneath this layer, which may be up to 30cm thick, is a clay sediment, rich in ferruginous and magnesium elements, called '*rouget*' ('red') because of its colour. All of this lies on a bed of more or less compressed stones, pebbles and gravel. These three layers, each of which may come to the surface in various places, have been thoroughly washed by rain over a long period and are poor in nutrients. They are therefore ideally suited for vines and produce good quality wine.

The climate is basically maritime, as in Aquitaine, though it is drier in the summer. Rainfall and sunshine figures are comparable to those of Toulouse. The prevailing winds come from the west or the northwest and are wet. The easterly wind, called the *autan*, is an incursion of the Mediterranean climate. A distinction is drawn between the *autan blanc*, which is dry, strong and dehydrating, and can often be beneficial to the maturing grapes in the autumn; and the *autan noir*, which comes from the southeast and brings storms that are sometimes violent.

The diversity of grape varieties found in the region is a consequence of the phylloxera crisis. In order to rebuild the vineyard, the wine growers resorted to a wide range of different varieties and grafting stocks. The main traditional variety is the Négrette, which produces wines that are of good quality, but lack acidity. Additional varieties used are the Côt, Mérille, Fer, Cabernet Sauvignon, Cabernet Franc, Syrah, Gamay Noir à Jus Blanc, Mauzac and Cinsaut.

Of the 3,500ha under vines in this region, only 1,200ha yield wines meeting *appellation* requirements. The base yield is fixed at 50hl/ha, and alcoholic strength at 10.5°.

At the centre of the *appellation* area are nine communes in which 86 per cent of the vineyards are concentrated. With its 800ha, the commune of Fronton alone represents 47.5 per cent of the *appellation's* wine-growing area.

Production consists almost exclusively of red wines (90 per cent), with a very little rosé (10 per cent). The red wines owe their very pronounced bouquet to the Négrette variety, while their strength and body comes from the Cabernet Sauvignon and Syrah varieties. The rosé wines, which are generally light, fruity and aromatic, should be drunk young.

Côtes du Jura and Côtes du Jura Mousseux

The decree of 31 July 1937 defined this as the largest *appellation* area in the Jura region, since it covers the whole wine-producing zone, apart from the individual commune *appellations*. However, only 560ha have been planted, with an average annual production over a 20-year period of 19,000hl, amounting to a 34hl/ha yield.

The red wines are made principally from the Pinot Noir; the whites from the Chardonnay alone, or a blend of Chardonnay and Savagnin; and the rosés from the Poulsard. But it is impossible to isolate the differing characteristics of wines from the Côtes du Jura in terms of variety alone, because each has become adapted to and changed by its *terroir*, with its particular aspect and climate (*see* the Jura regional entry). Certain areas have gradually turned towards production dominated by red or white wine, *vin jaune*, or sparkling wine. However, the harvest declarations point to a clear predominance of white wine from the Chardonnay and Savagnin varieties, which alone represent nearly 85 per cent of the overall production of this *appellation*, compared with 45 per cent in Arbois.

Every year on the first Sunday of September, the festival of the 'Biou' takes place. This is the local name given to an enormous bunch of grapes made of hundreds of bunches of grapes, carried as a thanksgiving offering to the church of Saint-Just, patron of Arbois. The size of the bunch varies annually, and represents the volume of the harvest. It is blessed at mass, then offered to the local hospice.

Ploughing in a Côtes du Jura vineyard. The major part of production in this area is of white wines based on Chardonnay and Savagnin.

Côtes du Lubéron

The vineyards of this *appellation* stretch between Cavaillon, Bonnieux and Mirabeau, on both sides of the Montagne du Lubéron, east of Avignon — an enchanting region where, amid a forest of cedars, the valleys of the Calavon and the Durance are to be found. Vines were already being grown here in Virgil's time and, as in other places, wine was used as currency for the payment of taxes and dues.

By 1876, communes such as Cucuron, Lourmarin, Oppède, Pertuis and Saignon already had large plantations of vines. But by the end of the 19th century and during the first half of the 20th century, most of the production was of table grapes. It is only in the last 20 years that the wine vine has been restored to its former pre-eminence.

Côtes du Lubéron was classed VDQS by decree on 20 December 1951, for 35 communes. The vineyard area today covers some 2,900ha and produces an annual average of 120,000hl, a large part of which is made by cooperatives.

The climate and soils are very similar to those of the eastern part of the Côtes du Ventoux. The red soils, and especially the arid calcareous rubble of the slopes, are complemented by a relatively harsh climate in the winter and spring, particularly near Pertuis.

The mixture of grape varieties is similar to that of the Côtes du Rhône and the Côtes du Ventoux: the main ones are Grenache, Syrah and Cinsaut for red and rosé wines, and Clairette and Ugni Blanc for white wines.

Thanks to the efforts of a dynamic growers' union and the technological developments undertaken by individual growers and cooperatives, the Côtes du Lubéron is trying to make up in wine terms for the time lost in the past producing dessert grapes, which are unable to make commercial headway today in the face of competition from inexpensive Italian, Spanish and Greek fruit.

The harsh climate and soil characteristics of the region favour the production of fresh, elegant and charming white wines. The red wines, grown on well-exposed slopes, have a delicate fruitiness. Both are best drunk young.

Côtes du Marmandais

Covering 900ha, these vineyards situated on either side of the Garonne obtained their VDQS *appellation* on 18 June 1975. Annual production of 55,000hl of red wines, 1,500hl of white wines and 500hl of rosé wines is in the hands of two cooperatives: that of Beaupuy, on the north side of the river, and that of Cocumont on the south side.

The red wines are made from the Bordeaux group of varieties with the addition of a local one, the Abouriou Noir, which gives the wines a characteristic spiciness. The white wines are similar in some respects to those of the Côtes de Duras, and are produced mainly from the Sauvignon Blanc variety. These light and fruity wines should be drunk young, within three to five years of their vintage.

CÔTES DU RHÔNE

From the steeply terraced vineyards of Côte Rôtie to the flat boulder-fields of Châteauneuf-du-Pape, only rich and full-bodied wines are made, wines as warm and stately as the Rhône that feeds them, but each with a character of its own.

The vineyards of the valley of the Rhône, and especially those of the northern Rhône, are among the oldest in France. The Greeks, who arrived on the Mediterranean coast of France some 600 years before the birth of Christ, founded Marseille and planted vines around the town, thereby creating the first French vineyards. They then travelled upriver, established trading posts far to the north and imposed their commercial activities on the indigenous population.

The first vineyards of the Côtes du Rhône

It has often been said that the vineyards of the Lyon region were first planted with Greek vines. This has, however, never been proved.

The first attestable vineyards were created some centuries before the birth of Christ by the Romans. Arriving at the gates of Lyon after several victorious battles, they founded Vienne, and soon made it into a prestigious city. Then, initially on their own thanks to the manpower provided by their armies, who were idle after the conquest, and later with the help of the local Allobroge population, they set about planting the first vineyards of the Rhône valley, on both sides of the river. From these came what were called the 'wines of Vienne' — sumptuous additions to banquets and symposia given by the occupying class in Vienne, and later exported to the tables of the nobility of Rome.

Barbarians coming from both north and south drove the Romans from their possessions, and this led to the total disappearance of the cultivated vine. Several centuries went by before vineyards were planted and tended again, this time thanks to the impetus given by the Church and the royal court. Wine was rediscovered as part of the pleasures of life, and it returned once more to its privileged position in the agriculture of the Vienne region.

The inhabitants of the southern Rhône valley did not take an interest in growing vines until later, however. Being continually invaded and occupied, they had other worries. Through obligation or personal need, they concerned themselves primarily with producing the provisions necessary for daily sustenance, especially in the regions on the left bank of the river. The very rich alluvial plain of the former province and papal possession of the Comtat Venaissin was a providential cereal granary, and the peasants who worked it had no desire to cultivate arid slopes and terraces. They reserved those for the grazing of livestock.

It was on the right bank of the Rhône that the first great vineyard of the southern part of the valley was to appear. From the end of the 17th century, vines gradually began to cover the land of this part of the kingdom of France. Encouraged by consuls, provosts and the royal court, the cultivation of vines and the quality of the resulting wines led to an area being delimited which was given the name of the Côte du Rhône Gardoise. The villages of Pont-Saint-Esprit and Tavel marked its northern and southern limits.

The reputation of these wines soon spread to other French wine-producing regions, creating strong feelings of jealousy that led to counterfeit wines being sold under this name. Early regulations to ensure respect for the place of origin were subsequently created, including both verification of the quality of the exports and inspection of the volumes marketed. No wine could be transported without the barrels containing it being branded CDR (Côte du Rhône).

This regulation was spelt out in every point by a royal edict of 1729, and confirmed by a number of voluntary local measures which fol-

Treading the grapes. A mosaic from Saint-Romain-en-Gall, dating from the 3rd century AD.

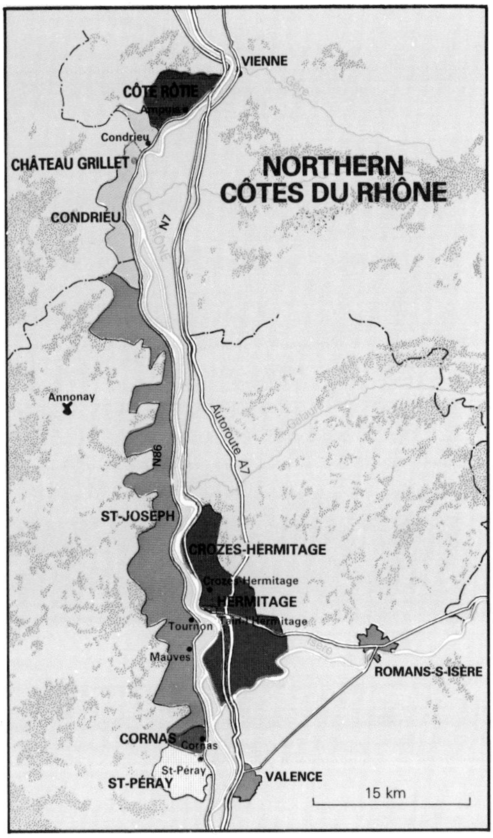
NORTHERN CÔTES DU RHÔNE
VIENNE
CÔTE RÔTIE
Ampuis
Condrieu
CHÂTEAU GRILLET
CONDRIEU
LE RHÔNE
N7
Annonay
N86
Autoroute A7
ST-JOSEPH
CROZES-HERMITAGE
Crozes-Hermitage
HERMITAGE
Tain-l'Hermitage
Tournon
Mauves
ROMANS-S-ISÈRE
CORNAS
Cornas
St-Péray
ST-PÉRAY
VALENCE
15 km

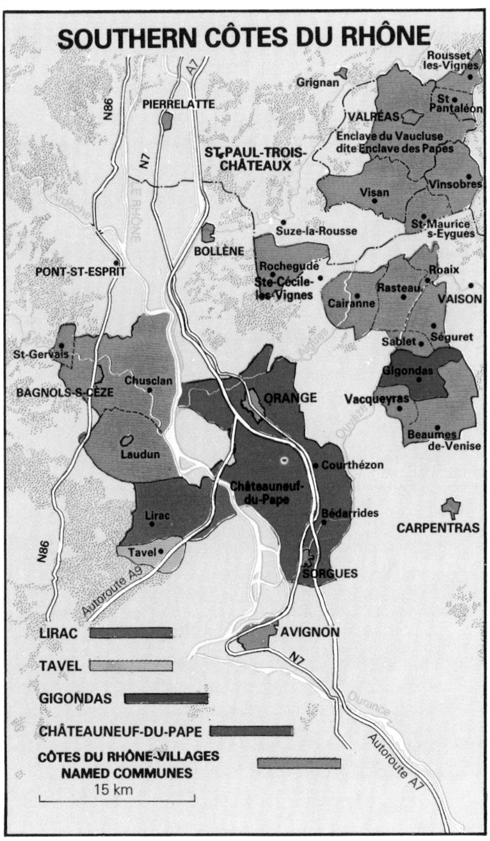
SOUTHERN CÔTES DU RHÔNE
Rousset les-Vignes
Grignan
N86
PIERRELATTE
St Pantaléon
VALRÉAS
Enclave du Vaucluse dite Enclave des Papes
ST-PAUL-TROIS-CHÂTEAUX
N7
Vinsobres
Visan
LE RHÔNE
St-Maurice s-Eygues
Suze-la-Rousse
BOLLÈNE
Roaix
Rochegude
PONT-ST-ESPRIT
Ste-Cécile-les-Vignes
Rasteau
VAISON
Cairanne
Séguret
Sablet
St-Gervais
Gigondas
Chusclan
BAGNOLS-S-CÈZE
ORANGE
Vacqueyras
Beaumes de-Venise
Laudun
Courthézon
Châteauneuf-du-Pape
Lirac
Bédarrides
CARPENTRAS
N86
Tavel
Autoroute A9
SORGUES
AVIGNON
N7
Durance
Autoroute A7
LIRAC
TAVEL
GIGONDAS
CHÂTEAUNEUF-DU-PAPE
CÔTES DU RHÔNE-VILLAGES NAMED COMMUNES
15 km

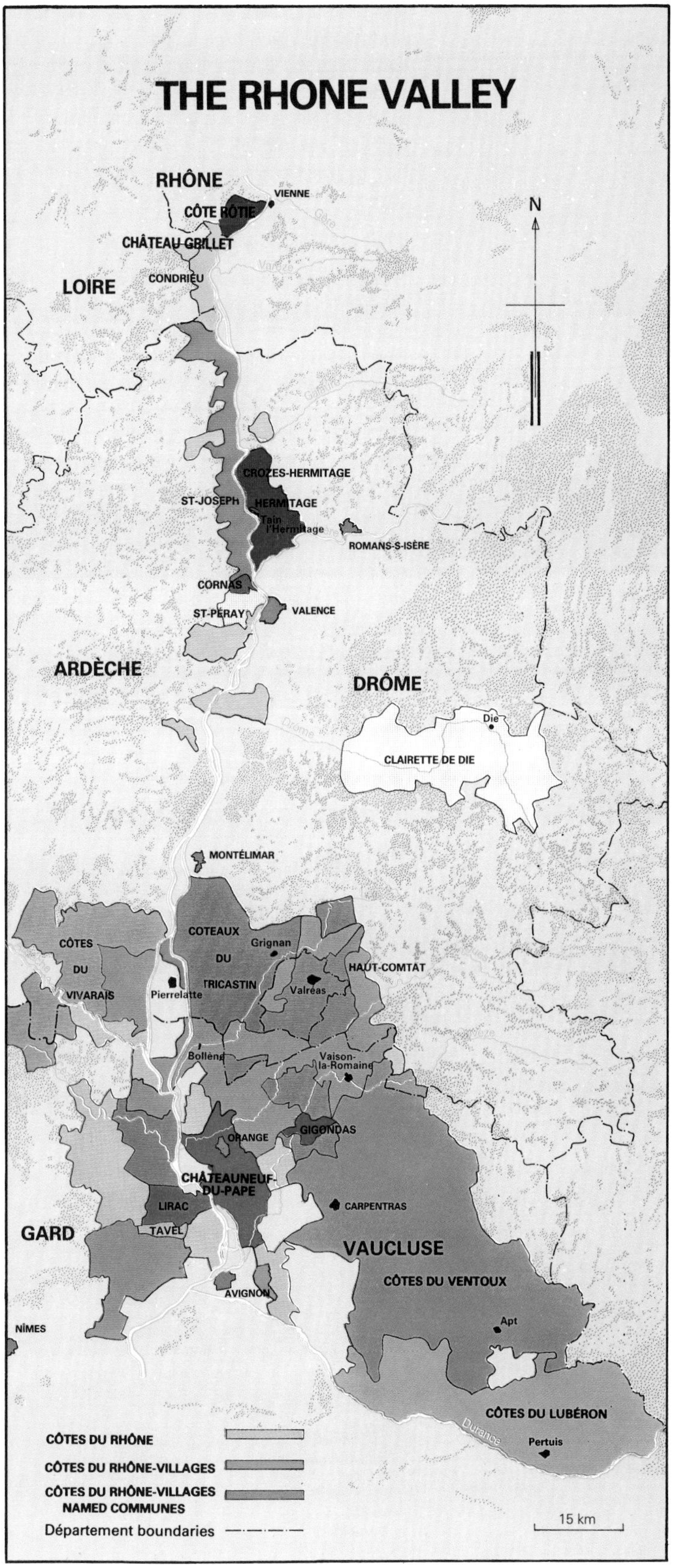
THE RHONE VALLEY
RHÔNE
VIENNE
CÔTE RÔTIE
N
CHÂTEAU GRILLET
LOIRE
CONDRIEU
CROZES-HERMITAGE
ST-JOSEPH
HERMITAGE
Tain l'Hermitage
ROMANS-S-ISÈRE
CORNAS
ST-PÉRAY
VALENCE
ARDÈCHE
DRÔME
Die
CLAIRETTE DE DIE
MONTÉLIMAR
COTEAUX DU TRICASTIN
Grignan
CÔTES DU VIVARAIS
Pierrelatte
Valréas
HAUT-COMTAT
Bollène
Vaison-la-Romaine
ORANGE
GIGONDAS
CHÂTEAUNEUF-DU-PAPE
LIRAC
TAVEL
CARPENTRAS
GARD
VAUCLUSE
CÔTES DU VENTOUX
AVIGNON
NÎMES
Apt
CÔTES DU LUBÉRON
Durance
Pertuis
CÔTES DU RHÔNE
CÔTES DU RHÔNE-VILLAGES
CÔTES DU RHÔNE-VILLAGES NAMED COMMUNES
Département boundaries
15 km

lowed it. It is thus possible to say that quality commercial viticulture in the Côte du Rhône dates from the 18th century, and that this early start was a decisive element in both the establishment and the actual delimitation of the regional *appellation*. The *appellation* was ratified by the decree of 19 November 1937 and covers 163 communes.

The position of the vineyards

Six *départements* are included in the *appellations* of the Rhône valley: Rhône, Loire, Ardèche, Gard, Drôme and Vaucluse. The main groups of vineyards, running between Lyon and Avignon over a distance of some 200km, can, in fact, be divided into two distinct wine-producing zones.

The first, which stretches from Vienne to Valence, is known in French as the *Côtes du Rhône septentrionales* (the northern Côtes du Rhône). Here the Rhône has cut deeply into the landscape, leaving the vineyards on two very steeply sloping strips, facing south, southeast and south-southwest. In this very hilly region, no Rhône tributary exists to produce alluvial deposits that could significantly change the structure of the local soils.

Beyond Valence, as far as the Donzère gorge, the vines disappear and, apart from a few small and isolated vineyard zones, this subregion has never produced high-quality wine.

The vineyards of Tain-l'Hermitage are among the oldest in the Rhône valley. They profit from the beneficial influence of the river Rhône.

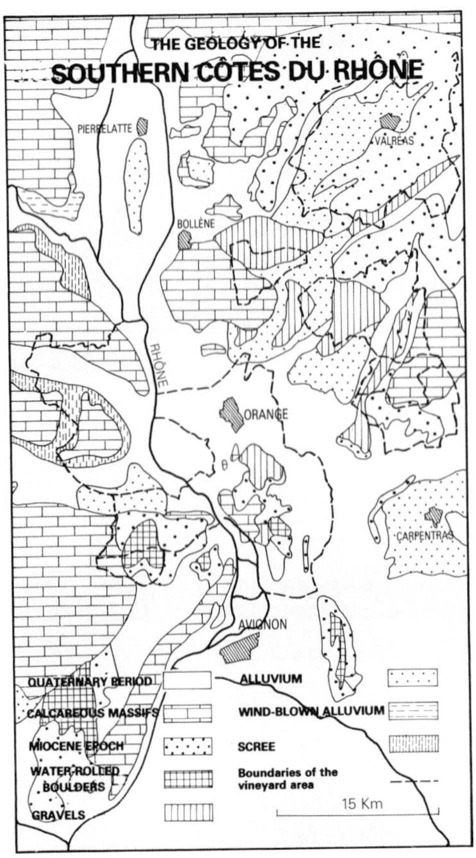

Pierrelatte marks the start of what is called in French the *Côtes du Rhône méridionales* (the southern Côtes du Rhône). The river valley, which until this point has been very narrow, opens out suddenly and the slopes of the hills become progressively more distant from the river itself. This is especially apparent to the east, between Orange and Cavaillon, where the plain of the former Comtat Venaissin is situated, and where Avignon lies today. Geologists call this the Durance isthmus. Here, both to the east and the west, lie a succession of vast terraces and gentle slopes where vines have been growing happily for several centuries.

But the vineyard has also spread higher. Over about the last 25 years, and particularly in the *départements* of Drôme and Vaucluse, modern earth-moving machines have made possible the planting of vineyards on arid summits of hard rock covered with little or no earth, which beforehand had supported only evergreen trees or scrub bushes.

It may seem paradoxical that two regions that are so geologically and geographically different as the northern and southern Côtes du Rhône should have received the same *appellation d'origine*. The explanation for this is a traditional principle, given legal backing.

The basic law of 6 May 1919 required, as a condition of recognition of an *appellation d'origine*, that ancient local customs should be res-

Châteauneuf-du-Pape. The prestigious wine grown here has developed its full character on water-rolled boulders overlying clay soils.

pected. In compliance with this principle, all vineyard areas producing wines sold in the past under the Côtes du Rhône name were integrated into the same *appellation*. Much the same thing has happened elsewhere. The Beaujolais region includes both granitic and calcareous soils; the Burgundy region is made up of very different *climats*, based on both calcareous soils and schistous soils; and Champagne combines the different soils and climates of the Marne and the Aube. It is therefore not surprising that the climates, soils and grape varieties of the northern and southern Rhône valley should create two distinct subregions within a single *appellation*.

The climate

The northern part of the Côtes du Rhône is subject to the same climatic pattern as Lyon. The rain regime is regular, the heat moderate and the risks of drought are less than elsewhere. Among other criteria, the role of aspect is very important in this part of the Rhône.

The southern part presents three specific characteristics: very irregular distribution of rainfall, resulting in a long period of mostly dry weather from April to September, preceded and followed by violent storms with torrential downpours; a propensity for periods of intense heat and various degrees of drought which, in certain cases, has a profound influence on the composition and ripening of the grapes; finally, a regime of violent winds, from both the north and the south, dominated by the *mistral*. This cold, dry wind which blows from the north is beneficial when it follows rainy days, but it can also sometimes have the disadvantage of increasing the effects of heat and drought. These southern climatic characteristics obviously vary in intensity depending on whether a vineyard is sited near the Rhône itself, or on the edge of the hills, which are sometimes far from the river. The *mistral*, for example, is not so strong at the base of these hills as it is near the river. In general, this wind is responsible for a number of strongly localized microclimates, producing wines that do not differ fundamentally from the general type, but that have a clearly defined character of their own.

The soils

Between Vienne and Valence, the soil is almost entirely composed of granitic sands originating in the Massif Central, which the Rhône, in former times, cut into in order to make itself a channel, leaving soil of the same type on both banks as it did so. Only a few traces of soils of calcareous origin are to be found on the left bank, at the bottom of the Hermitage hill and in the soil along the Isère; these are ancient alluvial deposits from the Alps.

To the south of the gorge of Donzère, on the other hand, the soil on both banks is mostly of calcareous origin. The traveller will soon notice that he or she is in an area of red earth. This is scree from the tributaries of the Rhône. In ancient times, the Cèze, the Tave and the Gardon to the west, and the Isère, the Drôme, the Aigues and the Ouvèze to the east flowed with a sufficient force to remove material from the sides of the mountains and form it into shelves and terraces, which were then reshaped and re-formed during the course of several millennia. We are thus faced with a great variety of soils and soil structures: sands; sandstone; red sandy clay soils, with pebbles or without; thin calcareous clay soils with pebbles; and quartziferous river-borne pebble terraces.

These extremely varied soils, combined with subregional or local climatic factors, mean that different parts of the region each have their own specializations. One vineyard area is best suited to the production of wines for laying down, another to *primeur* wines, a third to rosé wines. It is nature, finally, that rules out the possibility of being able to make Châteauneuf-du-Pape in Ardèche or in northeast Vaucluse.

A wine merchant's sign in the Côtes du Rhône-Villages, at Séguret.

The grape varieties

The creation and development of different types of cultivated grape variety from the wild vine that lived in the forests took place under the

Leading white Côtes du Rhône grape varieties: Bourboulenc, Clairette, Grenache Blanc, Marsanne, Piquepoul Blanc, Roussanne, Ugni Blanc, Viognier.

Leading red Côtes du Rhône grape varieties: Brun Argenté (Vaccarèse), Carignan, Cinsaut, Grenache, Mourvèdre, Muscardin, Piquepoul Noir, Syrah.

The Grenache is the main variety used in Châteauneuf-du-Pape.

influence of local climate factors. Certain grape varieties came into being in northern France, others in the west, and still others in the south and southeast, or in the countries bordering France. Man transported grape varieties away from their area of origin with the aim of improving what nature permitted him to do with local resources. This is how vines from Spain came to the Rhône valley, via Roussillon and Languedoc, and how others went from Burgundy to the Loire valley.

This human interference sometimes produced good results, but on other occasions innovators were disappointed, because a vine transported to a different soil and a different climate does not always produce the high quality obtained in its region of origin.

In the northern Côtes du Rhône, as in the Beaujolais region or in Burgundy, red wines are made from a single grape variety, in this case the Syrah. White wines come from three varieties: the Roussanne, Marsanne and Viognier.

By contrast, several different types of grape variety are used in the southern Côtes du Rhône. These come from three different sources. Some varieties originate on the French coast of the Mediterranean, a few come from Italy, but most have been imported from Spain.

This contrast has much to do with climate. In the northern Côtes du Rhône, just one red variety and one or two white varieties are enough to produce the best wines under the prevailing natural conditions. This is not so in the south. Here the excesses of the climate push the ripeness of the grapes to levels often close to disequilibrium. The subregion's first winegrowers therefore considered it a fundamental rule to use several different grape varieties to make one type of wine. In this way, they tried to hide or lessen the shortcomings of one variety by bringing the qualities of another into the equation. It is still difficult under such variable climatic conditions to obtain striking, original and well-balanced wines with a good bouquet and keeping qualities. Success in this respect is thus very commendable.

INCREASED PRODUCTION

The vineyards of the Rhône valley are among those French vineyards that have enjoyed the greatest expansion in the shortest time. The figures given below are in hectolitres.

Year	Rhône *crus**	Côtes du Rhône
1950	65,000	255,000
1960	110,000	840,000
1970	300,000	1,200,000
1980	400,000	1,700,000
1985	280,000	2,120,000

** Châteauneuf-du-Pape, Condrieu, Cornas, Côte Rôtie, Crozes-Hermitage, Gigondas, Château Grillet, Hermitage, Lirac, Saint-Joseph, Saint-Péray, Tavel.*

Production developments

Between 1945 and 1950, wines declared with the Côtes du Rhône *appellation* or under the name of one of the Côtes du Rhône *crus* represented some 25,000hl, produced on 6,000ha of land.

In the 40 years that have followed, the compulsory improvement in the grape varieties used, new plantings, the abandonment of the cultivation of fruit trees that were no longer profitable, the big decline in the number of olive groves, and the increase in vineyard yields thanks to more efficient parasite control have resulted in a large and rapid expansion of the vineyard area. This has not been without consequent economic problems.

The surface area of the northern Rhône *crus* is now 1,500ha, that of the southern Rhône *crus* 5,500ha, and the Côtes du Rhône and Côtes du Rhône-Villages area extends over 59,000ha.

Harvesting and vinification

At a time when many of man's activities have been given over to machines, mechanized harvesting has not taken over the vineyard to the extent that some would like. The use of this new method of harvesting runs into significant problems in this region, because of the fragility of the grape skins of many of the varieties grown here, and the consequent harmful aeration and oxidization of the juice during harvesting.

Though manual harvesting has lost part of its charm and intimacy with the disappearance of family and village collaboration, it nevertheless remains the most common harvesting method in the Rhône valley, particularly in the *crus*, where great attention is paid to preserving fruit quality.

Most of the varieties used in the southern Côtes du Rhône have a longer vegetative cycle than those used farther north. In the same climate, they would need more time for their fruit to ripen. But, since it is much hotter in the southern part of the valley than in the north, the ripening process of these varieties is accelerated and most of the vines are harvested at the same time as in the northern Côtes du Rhône. The harvesting period takes place over a month or so, beginning around 10 September and ending on about 15 October.

Classic vinification processes are used for the whites and rosé wines. The white wines owe their new qualities to two modifications of the old method: temperatures are now controlled during the alcoholic fermentation, and great pains are taken to minimize oxidization and aeration of the must and wine.

The rosé wines are produced from red grape varieties whose grapes are pressed directly. To obtain the required colour of must, the grapes are macerated for several hours. This procedure allows just the right depth of colour to be extracted from the grape skins, and produces the maximum amount of aroma, also from contact with the skins.

The red wines obtain most of their characteristic aroma and flavour from the relatively long maceration of the bunches in the juice, which has been partly squeezed out of the grapes during crushing. As a consequence of this, the wines are often very tannic and are only drinkable after several years' ageing.

It has, however, been established that the crushing and subsequent vatting times were often excessive. The traditional techniques were therefore modified; the grapes are now very lightly crushed or vinified whole. If vinified whole, a process of carbonic maceration takes place inside each grape, and this aromatic fermentation gives the wines more bouquet, while preserving their traditionally full flavour and their ability to age.

The character of Rhône wines

It is always difficult to pass general judgments on wines that have been produced in very different conditions of climate and soil. A very good year in the northern Côtes du Rhône is not necessarily mirrored in the southern Côtes du Rhône, and vice versa.

It would also be imprudent to consider wines from the regional *appellation* as being in any way great. They are less rich than the Côtes du Rhône *crus*, and so they evolve more quickly, generally reaching full maturity within three or four years of the vintage.

Finally, it should be stressed here that the white wines of the southern Côtes du Rhône, and all of the rosé wines, are best drunk young.

White wines

Apart from well-known *crus* such as Hermitage or Saint-Joseph, the white wines of the Rhône were for many years produced in tiny quantities only. The warm climate and widespread lack of knowledge of the best vinification methods for this type of wine meant that what was produced did not always have the desired quality. But, over the last ten to fifteen years,

Manual harvesting is still the most commonly used method in the Côtes du Rhône.

new techniques have finally allowed classic white wines to be made from local grape varieties. These appeared first at Châteauneuf-du-Pape, then at Laudun, and finally throughout the Côtes du Rhône: wines of a yellow-green colour, perfumed, fresh and often elegant. These qualities are especially evident during the first year after the wines have been produced.

Rosé wines

No rosé wines are produced in the northern Côtes du Rhône, where the local red and white wines are of a sufficient quality to make the production of this wine type unnecessary.

It is in the southern Côtes du Rhône that rosé wines have acquired a deserved reputation, as is testified by the admirable quality of the *cru* rosé wines of Tavel and Lirac, the Chusclan region and numerous other smaller *terroirs* of the Côtes du Rhône.

Faced with growing competition from rosé wines produced on the shores of the Mediterranean, formerly VDQS, now mostly AOC, the production of rosé wines in the Rhône valley has greatly diminished in recent years. In one sense, this development is fortunate, because certain soils allow red wines more expressive than their rosé forebears to be made. However, Tavel, Lirac and several other places in the Rhône valley, mostly in the Gard region, remain fine production zones for rosé wines.

Vine interlacing motif in stone from the Merovingian period at Fontaine-de-Vaucluse.

The charm of the Rhône rosés comes first of all from their colour, which is pink or pink tinged with gold. Their aromatic presence is fairly complex, while the wines are relatively light in body. They are very refreshing and make perfect drinking.

Red wines

The aptitudes of different soils and consequent variations in vinification techniques mean that three distinct types of red wine exist:

▷ Red wines made from grapes grown on certain gravel terraces are given a brief maceration period only; they have an aroma characterized by the scents of berries and currants and by a delicate structure, low in tannins and therefore very supple. They used to be marketed under the name of *vins de café* (café wines) because they were the delight of drinkers in the cafés of Lyon and nearby mining regions. Today they are called *primeur* or *nouveau* wines, or *vins de carafe* (carafe wines). They should be drunk within one year.

▷ Red wines made from grapes that undergo a much longer period of maceration are strong in alcohol and heady, with rich, tangy aromas. Though they are often elegant, medium-bodied wines, their tannin levels are higher than those of the preceding wines and they can therefore be advantageously kept for two or three years.

▷ Red wines that, for reasons of climate or soil, are still more assertive and characterful than wines in the previous category may be kept for three, four or five years. They are round, full, ample and rich wines.

Economic and commercial organization

The economic system of the Rhône valley *appellations* is peculiar in that medium-sized or small regional *négociants* (merchants or traders) do not have the same importance as in other regions of France. The commercial structure has been shrinking for the last 30 years to such a point that today only 42 traders of this sort remain in business.

After the Second World War, there were many small businessmen here making a living dealing in large amounts of table wine and greater or lesser amounts of *appellation* wines. This small-scale trade was unable to withstand the modern law of mergers.

Coinciding with this is a recent trend whereby large purchasing companies from outside the region are increasingly making direct contacts with growers and cooperatives, which means that local brokers, through lack of business, no longer have an incentive to find successors when they come to retire. The figures speak for themselves. The distribution of transactions during the 1985–1986 campaign was as follows: out of 1,500,000hl of wine marketed, 770,000hl passed through the hands of local traders and agents, 510,000hl were bought direct by outside traders, and 220,000hl were sold direct by producers' groupings, consisting mostly of cooperatives.

This situation has developed rapidly. If the 1980–1981, 1984–1985 and 1985–1986 campaigns are examined, it can be seen that the percentage purchased by outside traders has increased from 19 to 27 and then to 34 per cent, and the quantity that passed through the hands of local traders has been reduced from 72 to 62 and then to 53 per cent. There is a clear increase in the volume sold by cooperatives, which is hardly surprising since more than 60 per cent of all Côtes du Rhône AOC wine is now produced by cooperatives.

Wine's importance in the Rhône valley

The Rhône valley is fortunate in having an exceptional centre of studies in its midst: the wine university of Suze-la-Rousse, in Drôme. It was established in 1978 and is the first of its kind

The wine university at Suze-la-Rousse, the first of its kind in France and in the world.

CHÂTEAUNEUF-DU-PAPE

When I think of the Côtes du Rhône, I think first of all of Châteauneuf-du-Pape, and Châteauneuf-du-Pape always reminds me of something that happened 35 years ago when I was starting with my father at our restaurant (Hiély) in Avignon.

I met Raymond Baudoin, the secretary-general of the Académie des Vins de France (French Wine Academy), a colourful person whose knowledge of wines was equalled only by his bad temper. While passing through our region, he tasted a Châteauneuf-du-Pape of which we were very proud, but he found it much too heavy. This was the shortcoming of the Côtes du Rhône wines of that time; 'wine for carters,' as he put it.

Then my father, together with Monsieur Raymond Fabre from the estate of Mont-Redon, tried to 'manufacture' a Châteauneuf Nouveau — a young wine to be drunk the same year. It was a revolution.

At the first attempt, it was put into a demi-john and exploded like champagne.

But gradually, Monsieur Fabre perfected its vinification and gave us in the end a light and fruity young wine, a little like Beaujolais, which we have served ever since in a carafe, for the greater pleasure of our customers.

Pierre Hiély

in the world. It is installed in a 12th-century château, built in the rock that dominates the town. This château was extended during the Renaissance, and restored during the 1970s. The university's founder, Jacques Mesnier, has managed to turn an ancient monument into a completely functional teaching centre.

The wine university

This establishment is, above all, a centre of higher education. For the last three years, it has been teaching courses leading to the conferment of a Diplôme d'Études Supérieures Spécialisées. It also provides further training for practising wine growers and makers. All the problems of vine growing and wine production are studied and taught there, as well as matters relating to the development and tasting of wines, and to their packaging, marketing and consumption.

The Suze-la-Rousse wine university is also a meeting place for all those interested in wine. Thanks to the provision of a wide range of up-to-date facilities — library, sound archives, photographic collection, museum, wine library — everyone who is keen to get to know the world of wine may find, alone or in groups, the facilities he or she may require.

The wine routes

Following initiatives taken by the interprofessional wine committee of the Côtes du Rhône, this great region of AOC vineyards may now be visited by means of several itineraries or 'wine routes'. These will help the traveller to get to know all the types of wine produced, as well as show him or her something of the Rhône valley's rich history, as revealed by a number of archeological sites. These wine routes are marked with signs made by the painter Georges, and the different itineraries are identified by a system of colours.

The 'ruby route' covers the northern Côtes du Rhône, and runs from Vienne to Valence. In the southern Côtes du Rhône, the 'red route' goes from Bollène to Nyons; the 'mauve route' from Beaumes-de-Venise to Bollène; the 'orange route' from Orange to Nyons; the 'gold route' from Vaison-la-Romaine to Avignon; the 'emerald route' from Pont-Saint-Esprit to Comps; and the 'blue route' from Bourg-Saint-Andéol to Montfrin.

Fairs, museums and various wine events

There are two important regional wine fairs, at Ampuis and Orange; both of these take place in January.

There is no public wine museum in the region, but the wine-producing world of the Rhône is memorably evoked by two private collections: the Musée des Établissements Jean-Pierre Brotte at Châteauneuf-du-Pape, and the Musée de Paul Coulon at Rasteau.

For several years, many Rhône villages have been holding their own local festivals between 1 July and 30 August. Of particular note are the Côtes du Rhône-Villages festival at Vacqueyras, the Côtes du Rhône 'travelling' festival and the Rhône valley events organized by the 'Vins en Fêtes' association.

Côtes du Rhône *See* the regional article on pages 226–233.

Côtes du Rhône-Villages

The southern Côtes du Rhône stretches over a territory of some 4,000 sq. km. In such a vast area, where soils and climatic conditions vary between extremes, it is to be expected that differences in the intensity and quality of the wines should result.

In the years following the end of the Second World War, centres of wine production with distinguished viticultural traditions began to try to distinguish themselves from the crowd. It was in 1953, via a series of ministerial decrees, that some communes of the Côtes du Rhône were granted the right to give a little more personality to their wines by using their commune name on the label, on condition that they followed stricter rules of production than those of the basic Côtes du Rhône *appellation*. Since 1966, 17 communes embracing 27 localities have been able to benefit from this privilege (see box).

However, since the wines of several of the better communes were traditionally blended to ensure consistent quality, the decree of 16 November 1967 created the *appellation* Côtes du Rhône-Villages, for 74 communes. Wines from a single commune can now be called Côtes du Rhône followed by the name of the commune, or else Côtes du Rhône-Villages. Wines that have been blended and that come from several communes, though, may only be called Côtes du Rhône-Villages.

To this series of 74 communes another 47 have been added, which, though not sharing the production traditions of the preceding ones, nevertheless had land whose value corresponded to what was required for the 'Villages' *appellation*. The wines of these 47 additional communes are only entitled to be called Côtes du Rhône-Villages.

THE NAMED COMMUNES OF THE CÔTES DU RHÔNE-VILLAGES *APPELLATION*

Drôme: *Rochegude, Rousset-les-Vignes, Saint-Pantaléon-les-Vignes, Saint-Maurice-sur-Eygues, Vinsobres.*

Vaucluse: *Beaumes-de-Venise (4 localities), Cairanne, Rasteau, Roaix, Sablet, Séguret, Vacqueyras (2 localities), Valréas, Visan.*

Gard: *Chusclan (5 localities), Laudun (3 localities), Saint-Gervais.*

The vineyards are generally sited on well-drained slopes and stony terraces with poor soils; yields are limited to 42hl/ha. Of the grape varieties used for Côtes du Rhône wines, some are limited to 10 per cent for the Côtes du Rhône-Villages AOC. Others, which provide wines of high quality, have to be used in variable minimum proportions: these are the Roussanne for white wines, and the Cinsaut, Syrah and Mourvèdre for rosé and red wines.

The nature of the soils and, above all, the climate, pushes the white grapes to levels of maturity that are too high for the classic characteristics of white wine to be obtained. However, there are villages, such as Laudun or Saint-Gervais, that produce white wines which are characterized by an attractive floral bouquet and general aromatic freshness, an elegant body, and not too high or intrusive a level of alcohol.

For the same soil and climatic reasons, rosé wine does not occupy a large volume of production either. However, some of the vineyards in the Gard produce noteworthy rosés, especially Chusclan, where the wines have a light, fruity bouquet and a freshness and delicacy on the palate that masks the alcohol content.

The red wines provide the most vivid expression of the wine-producing aptitudes of this *appellation*. They are definitely more distinguished than those of the Côtes du Rhône, and may be differentiated from them by their bouquet, which is dominated by the scents of raspberries, redcurrants and spice, and by their greater levels of tannin and acidity, which do

Guilherand, near Valence, at the southernmost limit of the northern Côtes du Rhône.

A country house or bastide *hidden among the vines in Roussillon.*

not, however, prevent the wines from being elegant. They may, in general, be kept for four to five years, sometimes longer.

Côtes du Roussillon

Roussillon occupies the southernmost part of the Languedoc-Roussillon area. It is bordered by the Corbières massif to the north, and is separated from Spain by the eastern end of the Pyrenees to the south and west; to the east lies the Mediterranean. The vines of this, the warmest and sunniest region in the south of France, enjoy an environment that is very favourable to the production of strong wines that keep well. Sweet, fortified *vins doux naturels* form a large part of its production, together with the red, white and rosé AOC Côtes du Roussillon wines.

The vineyards were classed AOC by the decree of 28 March 1977. The *appellation*, which covers the whole of the Roussillon area from the Albères massif in the south to the foothills of the Corbières massif to the north, occupies 6,500ha, with a production of 300,000hl, 95 per cent of this red and rosé wines, and 5 per cent white wines. The vines are planted in a variety of soils, including calcareous clay, schist, granitic sands and terraces of water-borne pebbles.

The grape varieties used include the Carignan (to a maximum of 70 per cent), the Grenache, the Lledoner Pelut, the Syrah and the Mourvèdre. The Cinsaut is authorized, but is not at present planted in the region. The Tourbat, the Grenache Blanc and the Macabeu are the main vines used for white wines. The *saignée* method (in which a part of the must is macerated with the grape skins prior to fermentation) is compulsory for the vinification of the rosé wines. Carbonic maceration is widely used for the red wines.

The red wines, which have a fine ruby colour, are strong in alcohol, well structured and have complex aromas of berries and spice. The rosés are fruity and vigorous. The whites are aromatic, delicate and fine.

Côtes du Roussillon-Villages

The Côtes du Roussillon-Villages AOC was instituted by the decree of 28 March 1977.

Only two communes are entitled to this *appellation*: Caramany and Latour-de-France. The former is singled out because its vinification technique (carbonic maceration) lends its wines distinction; the latter thanks to the schistous soils on which its vineyards are situated, which produce excellent wines. The *appellation* name may, if wished, be followed by the name of one of the two communes.

The AOC is only available for red wines, which must have a minimum alcohol content of 12° and a maximum yield of 45hl/ha.

Côtes du Roussillon-Caramany *See* Côtes du Roussillon-Villages.

Côtes du Roussillon-Latour-de-France *See* Côtes du Roussillon-Villages.

Mormoiron and its vines, at the foot of Mont Ventoux.

Côtes du Ventoux

The *terroir* of this *appellation d'origine contrôlée*, wedged between the Côtes du Rhône and the massif of Mont Ventoux, forms a sort of crescent running from the edge of the Baronnies south of Nyons to the countryside around Apt.

Vines have been cultivated here since the 9th century by the monks of Notre-Dame-du-Grozeaux, but it was not until the 18th century that they spread on to the sides of Mont Ventoux, the 'giant of Provence', especially around Carpentras. The villages of Caromb, Bédoin, Mazan and Mormoiron were such great producers of wine that local municipalities arranged for roads to be built to these villages so that the wine the inhabitants themselves could not drink could be transported to Sault and elsewhere.

The climate is of Mediterranean type, but the presence of Mont Ventoux (1,909m) creates cold airstreams, especially to the east of the zone; springs are later and autumns are earlier than in the Rhône valley, and this influences the type of wine produced.

Geologically, the whole Côtes du Ventoux region is a limestone transition zone, where red Mediterranean soils, calcareous brown soils and rendzina soils are juxtaposed on the slopes. Most of these soils are poor and arid.

Above the alluvial plains reserved for arboriculture and market gardening, the vineyards of the *appellation* are planted with the same grape varieties as the Côtes du Rhône: predominantly the Grenache vine, combined with the Cinsaut, the Syrah and a little Carignan for the red wines; with the Clairette, Bourboulenc and Ugni Blanc varieties forming the basis of the white wines.

The decree of 27 July 1973 gave 51 communes the right to this *appellation*, for red, white and rosé wines.

The white wines only represent a small proportion of total production. They are fresh, relatively light and slightly sharp, which is far from being a failing in southern French white wines.

The rosé wines are very pleasant: a floral and fruity bouquet, with elegance and good balancing acidity on the palate.

The red wines are more susceptible than the white or rosé wines to climatic variations, and they differ according to whether they are produced in the east or the west of the zone. In the west, around Carpentras, their solid structure makes them similar to some Côtes du Rhône wines. In the east, they are lighter. The former consequently keep better, but only up to a limit of three or four years.

Côtes du Vivarais

The Côtes du Vivarais vineyards in the Côtes du Rhône provide further proof of the continuity that exists everywhere in southern France between the viticulture of antiquity and that of today. Its permanency in this small area is confirmed by numerous written texts. Here the vine has found a choice position in a climate and on soils too severe and harsh for other crops, and in doing so it has brought local workers a livelihood they might not otherwise have had.

The vineyard area covers 740ha, and produces an average of 36,000hl of red, white and rosé wine. Classed as VDQS by the decree of 8 September 1962 for 12 communes, the *appellation* name may also be followed by that of one of three *crus*: Orgnac (a well-known potholing region), Saint-Montan and Saint-Remèze. It should be remembered that throughout France great importance is attached to the word *cru*, and that considerable legal difficulties are involved in obtaining the authorization to use it. It is an indication of the merit of the Côtes du Vivarais that it has been able to do so.

In a climate that is hot and dry in the summer and fairly cold in spring, and on red, terraced soils, loess soils and rendzina soils derived from compacted limestone, the usual Rhône grape varieties are grown. The Grenache dominates rosé- and red-wine plantings, but the Cinsaut and Syrah make valuable contributions to blends. The Marsanne, Piquepoul and Ugni Blanc dominate white-wine plantings.

The red and rosé wines are fresh and fruity. Their light, lively flavours mean they make excellent summer drinking. The white wines are fresh and firm.

Couderc Noir

A hybrid of 70 Jaeger (*Rupestris lincecumii*) × *vinifera*, this variety also goes by the name of *7120 Couderc*.

Green shoots angular, glabrous, green, glossy. Bunches medium sized, cylindrical, compact; grapes spherical, black, with soft, not very juicy flesh; ripening period: third epoch.

This is a vigorous, productive and hardy vine, and it can be cultivated almost without the use of fungicides. Since it is susceptible to phylloxera and to high levels of active lime, it is best to graft it (although it is a direct producer). Its wine has a peculiar taste reminiscent of blackcurrants and tar, and it is quite highly coloured; it is best vinified as a rosé. The Couderc Noir has been classed as 'authorized' in the Midi and the South West.

Counoise

Synonyms: *Counoïso, Quennoise, Guénoise.*

This grape variety has often been confused with the Aubun, from which it may be distinguished by the following differences: a slightly more upright habit; more open felty white growing tips with carmine points; more widely spreading and more felty young leaves; adult leaves generally larger, thick, markedly bullate and sometimes even crimped around the petiolar junction — they are often convex, whereas the leaves of the Aubun are concave; the lobes are less deeply cut, which gives a bulkier appearance to the leaves; the petiolar sinus is lyrate, closed, sometimes with a naked base; the teeth are convex, wide; the underside of the blade is very downy or felty, whereas, during the period leading to full maturity, that of the Aubun becomes downy in tufts; the shoots are light yellow with violet nodes, those of the Aubun being light brown; finally, the bunches of the Counoise are situated lower down the fruiting canes than those of the Aubun and the grapes are a little larger, with a more highly coloured skin.

The Counoise has its budbreak one week later than the Aubun, around 15 April in Vaucluse, and its whole vegetative cycle — flowering, ripening and eventual maturity — continues with a week's delay on the Aubun. The wines are said to have an average of 1° more alcohol than those provided by the Aubun, and are certainly able to reach 12° when quality is good, the wine being fine, with a dark, lustrous colour. The yields are lower than those of the Aubun, between 40 and 50hl/ha only. The Counoise is said to be more resistant to downy mildew than the Aubun. Two registered clones have been approved: numbers 508 and 725. This grape variety has been classed as 'recommended' in Languedoc. In Provence, it is one of the varieties used in the Châteauneuf-du-Pape, Côtes du Rhône, Coteaux d'Aix-en-Provence and Coteaux du Languedoc AOCs.

Courbu Blanc

Synonyms: *Courbi Blanc, Courbis, Coubiès, Courbut, Courtoisie* at Portet (Pyrénées-Atlantiques, *Cougnet* at Vic-Bilh, *Vieux Pacherenc* at Lembeye.

Bunches small, cylindrical, sometimes winged; grapes small, spherical, golden yellow; ripening period: third epoch.

The Courbu Blanc is a vine group. Two registered clones have been approved: numbers 726 and 727. It is a vigorous plant, producing regular quantities of a good-quality wine, strong in alcohol, with a certain degree of finesse. It is generally stake-trained and pruned long. It is fairly resistant to downy mildew and to oidium (powdery mildew) and not very susceptible to grey rot (botrytis). It is classed as 'recommended' in Gers, Landes and the two *départements* of the Pyrenees and is used in the Jurançon, Pacherenc du Vic-Bilh, Béarn and Irouléguy AOCs. It occupies about 30ha at present.

Courbu Noir

Said to be the black form of the Courbu Blanc. About 10ha of it exist and are used for the red wines of the Béarn AOC. It is classed as 'recommended' in the Pyrenean region and two clones have been approved: numbers 728 and 729.

Crémant d'Alsace

This *appellation d'origine contrôlée,* regulated by the decree of 24 August 1976, is for the production of quality sparkling wines using the technique of fermentation in bottle (*méthode champenoise*).

Crémant d'Alsace has only become an important product for the region in the last ten years. It can be made from the Pinot Blanc, Auxerrois, Pinot Gris, Pinot Noir, Riesling or Chardonnay grape varieties. The essential quality striven for is lightness and elegance, combined with a full and fruity flavour.

Crémant de Bourgogne

These sparkling white or rosé wines are governed by the decree of 17 October 1975. This decree describes in detail all the conditions necessary to obtain a quality sparkling wine. The area of the *appellation d'origine contrôlée* stretches over all of greater wine-producing Burgundy. The choice of grape varieties is largely regional: Pinot Noir, Pinot Gris, Pinot Blanc, Chardonnay, Gamay Noir à Jus Blanc (20 per cent maximum), Aligoté, Melon and

Sacy can all be used. A requirement of the *appellation* is that each pressing of the grapes should be limited to 100 litres of juice per 150kg of grapes, any further must expressed not being entitled to the *appellation*. Bottling may only take place after 1 January in the year following the harvest and the bottles must be stored with their sediment for at least nine months. Finally, the pressure inside the bottle should be at a minimum of 3.5 atmospheres, measured at a temperature of 20°C. This sparkling wine, of which an average of 7,000hl is made each year, possesses remarkable finesse, and when the grapes have been grown on limestone soils the results can be outstanding. Regrettably, its quality is under-appreciated.

Crémant de Loire

This *appellation*, governed by the decree of 17 October 1975, is only available for wines produced within the areas of the Anjou, Saumur and Touraine *appellations*.

Some 10,000hl of sparkling white wines and 500hl of sparkling rosé wines are produced by a process of secondary fermentation in bottle.

Crépy

Two varieties of Chasselas (Chasselas Vert and Chasselas Roux) are grown near Lake Geneva, on a calcareous clay moraine slope with a west-southwest aspect (altitude below 500m), for the wines of Crépy. The main production centres are Douvaine, Loisin and Ballaison on the south-eastern corner of the lake.

Taking advantage of a climate that is tempered by the influence of the water, some 75ha of vines produce 4,000hl annually of a dry, *perlant* (containing a prickle of gas) Savoyard white wine. The *appellation d'origine contrôlée* was ratified by the decrees of 29 April 1948 and 27 August 1986.

This pale yellow wine is always bottled off its fine lees and is soon ready to drink, though aroma and flavour may improve further for two to three years, or longer after a fine vintage. The diuretic qualities of Crépy are thought to be considerable, and the wine is always sold in *flûtes* (slender green bottles).

Criots-Bâtard-Montrachet

This white Grand Cru from the Côte de Beaune is found in the territory of Chassagne-Montrachet. The site known as Les Criots is very small in extent — only 1.5ha — and is directly exposed to the south, which explains its comparatively rich character. The decree of 31 July 1937 specified a minimum alcohol content of 11.5° and a maximum yield of 30hl/ha. The low annual production — around 40hl — means there is always great demand for this superb wine, slightly less dry than Montrachet, with an exuberant but well-balanced bouquet.

Crouchen

Synonyms: *Cruchen Blanc, Crouchen* (meaning 'crunchy'), *Cruchenton Blanc* and *Messanges Blanc* in Landes, *Trouchet Blanc* at Monein, in Pyrénées-Atlantiques, *Grand Blanc, Sable Blanc, Navarre Blanc* in Landes.

Bunches small to medium sized, cylindrical, compact, winged; grapes slightly ovoid, medium sized, white, with easily expressed juice; ripening period: second epoch, late.

The Crouchen is a Pyrenean wine that is classed as 'recommended' in the *départements* of that region, but it is not very widespread and mostly exists as isolated stocks in plantations. It is very sensitive to downy mildew, oidium (powdery mildew), grey rot (botrytis) and grape fan-leaf virus. It has late budbreak and its somewhat acidic wine has a scented quality.

Crozes-Hermitage

Originally, this *appellation* only covered vineyards within the commune of Crozes-Hermitage, whose quality had been recognized by the classing of a small part of its *terroir* for the prestigious Hermitage AOC.

The low areas and some of the terraces of the communes bordering on Crozes were at that time taken up by profitable orchards. There were only a few vines on the tops of slopes and, thanks to a lack of local interest, these potentially good wine-growing localities were only classified in the basic Côtes du Rhône AOC. The quality of the wines soon became evident, however, and the *appellation* area was extended to a number of surrounding communes by the decree of 4 March 1937. The vineyards today cover 822ha, stretching over 11 communes.

About 43,000hl is produced annually, half of it by the cooperative at Tain-l'Hermitage.

The white wines, made from a combination of the Roussanne and Marsanne grape varieties, with a larger proportion of the latter, have a light, fine and very pleasant floral bouquet. They may not be kept as long as the white wines of Hermitage, and indeed are best drunk young.

The red wines, produced from the Syrah grape variety, are distinguished by the scents of raspberries and blackcurrants. They are full, but are less dense and concentrated than those of Hermitage. Their evolution is more rapid, and it is best to drink them within three or four years of their vintage date.

WINE TECHNOLOGY

The fermenting of grapes and grape juice into wine is a perfectly natural process which has been practised by man for nourishment and pleasure since earliest times. However, wine production today is no longer a series of empirical actions dictated by instinct and tradition. The foot-treading of grapes, screw pressing, and racking from one barrel to another using the simplest of siphons have given way to a series of mechanized and scientifically controlled operations. Wine making may appear to have lost its romance, but the wines themselves have certainly improved in quality.

It is generally agreed that the state of maturity of the grapes at harvest time is the most important factor in determining the quality of a wine. Any factor having an influence on the maturation of the fruit can thus increase or diminish this quality. Among these factors, the climate, microclimate and soil composition are those that are most difficult to alter. On the other hand, the wine maker can improve the results obtained through choice of grape varieties and, especially, choice of cultivation methods. But to make good wine, it is not simply enough to achieve a good harvest; the producer must also know how to make the best possible use of the fruit gathered in. This is why the skills of the wine grower and those of the wine maker must complement each other perfectly, for the quality of the final product depends on this relationship.

Wine is produced from fresh grapes by vinification, a term signifying all the processes brought into play during this transformation. The composition of the grape, and in particular the presence or absence of colouring matter, and the length of the maceration period (the contact between the must and the solid matter, particularly the skins) are the determining factors governing the type of vinification: white, red or rosé. Maceration intensifies the colouring effect. The vinification type depends on the nature of the grape. Three different variants are encountered:

The Pinot Noir, Burgundy's leading grape variety, has a black skin and colourless pulp and is vinified as a red wine in this region.

▷ The grapes are coloured, while the skin is coloured and the pulp is colourless. All three systems of vinification may be used for this type of grape, and these are defined by the length of maceration. Thus, if no maceration takes place, the vinification produces white wine. If the maceration period is long, the result is red wine. If a short maceration period is used, rosé is produced.

The Sylvaner, a white grape with colourless skin and pulp, has given its name to the most commonly drunk white wine in Alsace.

▷ The grapes are white but the skin and pulp are colourless. Grapes of this type are always vinified into white wine and it is important that only the juice from the grapes, with all the solid parts of the bunch and berry removed, should be fermented. Maceration and oxidization of grapes and must should also be avoided for this type of vinification.

▷ Both the skin and the pulp of the grapes are coloured. These are called Teinturier (literally 'dyeing') grapes. Whether or not they are macerated, red wine will always be obtained. In fact, this type of grape is rarely used alone but is generally combined with grapes from other red grape varieties to intensify the colour of a blended wine.

The Alicante Bouschet is one of the few red-fleshed (Teinturier) grape varieties authorized for use in France.

White and Rosé Wine Vinification

White wines vary greatly in taste and structure. They may be dry, medium dry, sweet or lusciously sweet, very aromatic or modestly aromatic, and they may be kept for a long time or should be drunk young. Their final nature depends on the vine plant and the type of grape produced as well as its relative maturity when harvested, but it also depends on the various processes of vinification and the treatment of the wine after vinification. One factor of constant importance for the manufacture of all white wines is that only the juice of the grape — with all solid matter from the bunches and berries removed — should be fermented.

The maturity of the grape

If the wine's alcohol-sugar-acidity equilibrium is to be as harmonious as possible, an optimum sugar/total acidity ratio has to be obtained at harvest time. This is why, in regions where acidity levels tend to diminish rapidly during the course of maturation, it is sometimes necessary to harvest the grapes before they are completely ripe. In regions where acidity levels are sufficiently high, but where sugar levels are insufficient — in many northern vineyards, for example — it is advisable, and indeed necessary, to wait until the grapes are as ripe as possible, or even overripe, before harvesting them.

Wines made from aromatic grape varieties, and those to be used to make lively, fresh white wines, often need to be harvested a few days before optimum maturity. This applies, notably, to the dry Muscat wines of Alsace. Other wines require grapes in as mature a state as possible, and sometimes overripe. Sweet and dessert wines are always obtained by overripening. The greatest wines of this type are harvested by selecting only overripe bunches or individual grapes.

Pre-fermentation operations

In the manufacture of white wine, the operations carried out before fermentation begins are very important. It is advisable above all to avoid maceration and oxidization during this period. The most certain way to achieve this is to harvest the grapes intact and to keep them intact until the must is extracted from them.

Manual harvesting is still the only means of obtaining whole grapes in perfect condition for white wine vinification. But mechanical harvesting has made great progress in the last few years and gives fairly good results today, if the optimum conditions for using the harvesting machine are respected. When grapes can be collected whole by the machine, the harvest should consist of individual berries that have been neatly shaken from the bunch. Problems occur if the structure of the grape is not sufficiently strong, as the grapes will partially burst and some of the juice will escape. Rapid transport from the vineyard to the wine-making centre, and the immediate extraction of the rest of the juice, may then limit the effects of this maceration.

Whatever the method of harvesting, it is important that the fruit should be transported in such a way that the structure of the bunches or grapes is not damaged. In most cases, methods that allow the grapes not to be heaped in too deep a layer should be chosen.

A traditional vertical press in Alsace. The grapes are first destalked, to avoid astringency in the must.

The extraction of the must

The must is generally extracted by means of presses. The grapes can be pressed whole in them, as is the case in Champagne, but they can also first be subjected to the processes of *foulage* (crushing) and *égrappage* (destalking). These two operations are carried out in order to facilitate the extraction of the must during the pressing, and to allow the harvest to be transferred to the press by pump.

The *foulage* consists of tearing open the grapes without damaging the stalks and skins or crushing the pips. This is accomplished with a *fouloir*, made of two fluted rollers that turn in opposite directions to one another. When the grapes have been put through this, they are removed by means of a piston pump — with a vertical or oval piston — and are transferred to the press.

Égrappage (also known as *éraflage*) consists in separating the grapes from the stalks in order to avoid contact between the stalks and the must. This technique is mostly used when, as in the case of white wines, large quantities of tannin are not required in the final product. After *éraflage* the grape pulp is — as above — transferred to the press by means of a pump.

The pressing operation extracts all the juice from the grapes. It is one of the most delicate operations of vinification, because the quality of the must largely depends on it. The press should therefore satisfy a certain number of requirements. It should respect the physical structure of the bunches, avoid maceration and oxidization of the juice and flesh, and produce a must that is largely free of debris from the grapes. The pressing should not take too long.

Many different kinds of presses exist. Formerly, vertical presses with wide baskets, producing very good must, were much used. This type of press is still in use in Champagne. Completely automatic presses are now, however, being used by many wine producers. Three types of automatic, mechanical presses may be distinguished:

▷ discontinuous mechanical presses;
▷ continuous mechanical presses;
▷ discontinuous pneumatic presses.

They vary in capacity from a few hundred kilograms to several tonnes.

Discontinuous presses are essentially formed of a horizontal basket turning around a central axle at each end of which two mobile plates are fixed. These plates gradually move towards each other, pressing the juice from the grapes as they do so. Discontinuous pneumatic presses consist of a perforated cylinder moving around a central axle surrounded by a diaphragm. This diaphragm is slowly inflated by compressed air, pressing the juice from the grapes and out of the cylinder perforations. Continuous presses work with a continuous screw, and provide uninterrupted pressure for as long as they are supplied with fruit.

These are all machines of great potential, and the way they are used affects the quality of the must as much as their own design does. Good and bad results can be obtained with each type of press.

Débourbage and sulphurization

The juice extracted from the grapes is known as must, and it is always cloudy to some extent. It is therefore advisable to subject it to the process of *débourbage* (settling or purging), which consists in removing the foreign matter suspended in the must, which can spoil the taste of the wine. *Débourbage* can be static or dynamic. Static *débourbage* consists in leaving the must to stand for a certain length of time and then siphoning or racking off the clear must from the settled sediment. Dynamic *débourbage* is carried out by continuous centrifugation of the must as it comes out of the press.

In both cases, the addition of sulphur dioxide, in solid, liquid or gaseous form, is necessary to protect the must against oxidization: this is sulphurization. Sulphur dioxide also plays an important antiseptic role by destroying the microorganisms in the must whose presence is undesirable at this stage in the vinification. The amount of sulphur dioxide added depends mainly on the state of health of the grapes, and on the ambient temperature at the time. The clarified must is then ready for fermentation.

Alcoholic fermentation

It is by means of alcoholic fermentation that must is transformed into wine. This phenomenon, which because of its intriguing appearance and sound (a noisy bubbling) has always intrigued man, was not understood until the 19th century, when the work of Lavoisier, Gay-Lussac, Buchner and especially Pasteur revealed its mechanisms. The principle of fermentation is that under the action of yeasts — microscopic fungi that secrete enzymes — the following chemical reaction occurs:

sugar + action of yeast → alcohol + carbon dioxide + by-products + calories.

This exothermic reaction causes such an increase in heat (calories) that it is advisable to cool the must artificially, sometimes even before fermentation. For the production of quality white wines, the advice given today is that fermentation should take place at a temperature of around 20°C. Depending on the exact type of white wine to be made, this temperature can vary slightly.

Alcoholic fermentation may be induced spontaneously by the yeast attached to the bloom on the grapes — that waxy substance that covers their skin. But active dry yeast may also be added to the must.

The by-products of alcoholic fermentation contribute greatly to the taste of the wine and play a part in the so-called 'secondary' or 'fermentation' aromas.

Alcoholic fermentation generally ends after two to four weeks. The young wine is then very cloudy because it is full of lees kept in suspension by the carbon dioxide. Depending on the type of wine to be made, it is then subjected to malolactic fermentation to lower overall acidity levels, or stabilized to preserve the initial fruitiness of the young wine.

Malolactic fermentation

This secondary fermentation is not, even today, completely mastered, and whether or not it will begin is always a matter of uncertainty. It causes the total acidity of the wine to be reduced through the action of lactic bacteria. The reaction is as follows:

malic acid + action of lactic bacteria → lactic acid + carbon dioxide + by-products − calories.

This reaction is endothermic and, in order for it to take place, it is advisable to keep the wine at a temperature of around 18°C. It is usually induced a little after the alcoholic fermentation. It is used especially to produce white wines in which secondary or fermentation aromas are preferred to primary aromas of fruit — as is the case with some great white burgundies, for example — and also for wines that have to be microbiologically stable to avoid unwanted developments during the later stages of vinification.

A discontinuous horizontal press. It works by rotation, and the gradual closing of two plates from either end.

Stabilizing the wine

After malolactic fermentation, the wine can no longer be spoiled by microorganisms. It is then racked in order to separate it from its fermentation lees. This may be done in the presence of air to reoxygenate the wine and, above all, to get rid of certain undesirable odours produced by the malolactic fermentation. Sulphurization follows immediately, and allows the wine to be stabilized definitively until it is bottled.

If the wine has not undergone malolactic fermentation, it is unstable and can still be attacked by lactic bacteria. Any loss or diminution of the malic acid, which gives the wine its freshness, must therefore be avoided. When the alcoholic fermentation is complete — at the point at which no more carbon dioxide is being given off — the wine is racked off its fermentation lees. Sulphurization allows it to be immediately protected against microorganisms. Then, about two months after the end of fermentation, preclarification takes place. This is generally carried out by means of filtration with a solid fining agent, by centrifugation or by a combination of both these techniques. An optional additional dose of sulphur dioxide allows the wine to be kept until bottling.

Sometimes preclarification is replaced by storage at a sufficiently low temperature (10°C to 12°C) to prevent the development of any bacteria. Spontaneous clarification follows and the wine may thus be kept without risk of it spoiling until bottling.

Pad filtering apparatus. Filtering precedes bottling and gives the wine brilliancy.

Manual bottling at Vouvray. This process is now only used by small-scale wine makers.

Treatment of the wine for bottling

Bottling is generally carried out during the year that follows the harvest. Further maturation and ageing takes place in bottle. The wine may sometimes become cloudy and leave deposits while in bottle. These deposits are usually due to precipitations of tartaric acid crystals, or proteins, which take the form of fluffy greyish white flakes.

These deposits do not usually spoil the taste of the wine. They can even improve it by making it more supple. However, preventive treatments do exist. To eliminate the proteins, the must or the wine are fined, i.e. a specific product is added to them which is intended to precipitate the constituent that could be the cause of the fault. The wine can also be treated against tartaric precipitations by being stored for 4 to 5 days at a temperature of around − 4°C.

Before being bottled, the wine is subjected to a finishing filtration, which gives it a brilliant clarity. This is carried out either with fine pad filters, or with membranes with pores of a diameter of only 0.65 microns. In the first case, the pressure under which the wine is forced through the pad influences the end result. It must be regular and not excessive.

It is essential that bottling equipment should always be scrupulously clean.

Bottling can be done manually, but there now exists a whole range of appliances that can perform, separately or as a single unit, the various operations of filling, corking, capsuling and labelling.

Wood-matured white wines

Certain white wines may be both fermented and aged in wooden casks. Wines of this sort generally undergo malolactic fermentation. The wood gives these wines a characteristic and very pleasant flavour. They are bottled later than most white wines, having first been clarified by fining and then filtered — not very finely — so that the aromatic and flavour components they contain are not endangered or lost.

WHITE WINE VINIFICATION

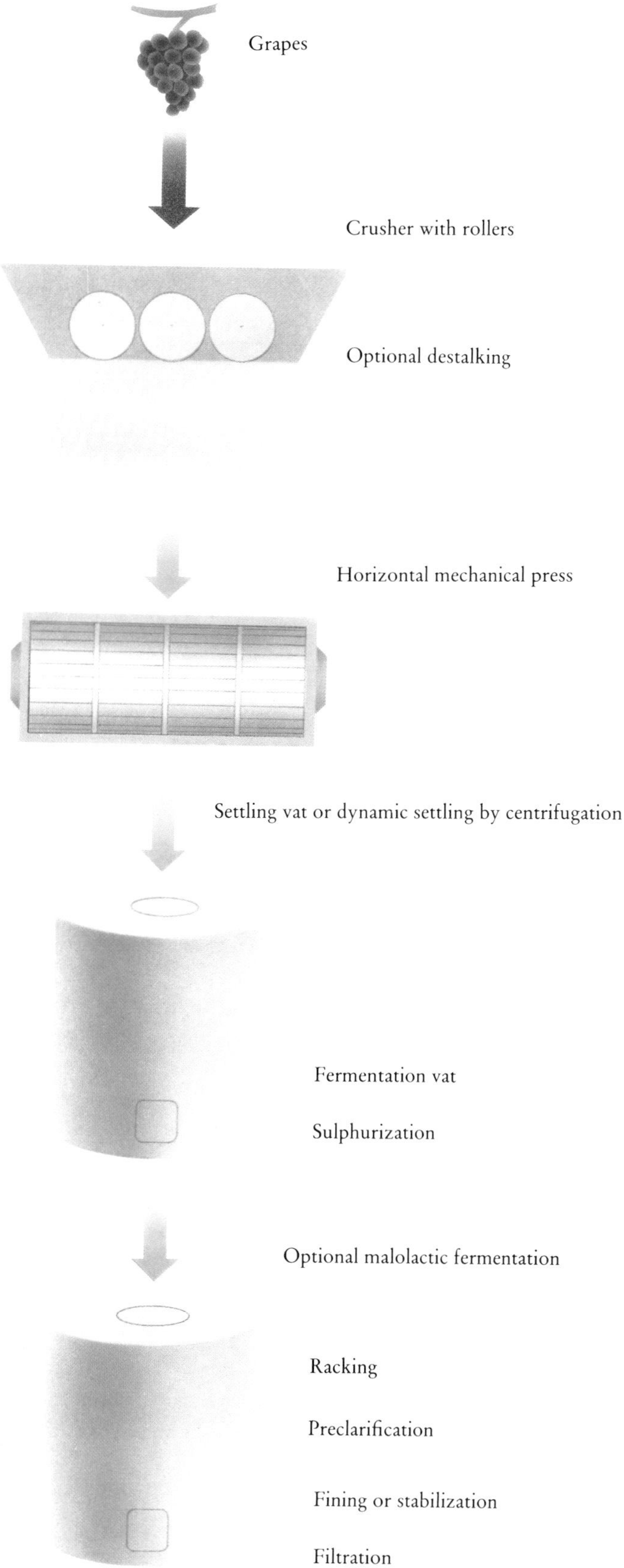

The vinification of rosé wine

Rosé wines generally have a bright but very light red colour. On the other hand, they usually have the olfactory and gustative characteristics of white wine. They are wines with an agreeable fruitiness, backed up by freshness and, at best, by an appealing vivaciousness. Malolactic fermentation is generally not induced so that the primary fruit aroma of the grape remains predominant.

Rosé wine is generally made from grapes with a coloured skin and colourless pulp which have been macerated for a short time. Some rosés, though, when prepared from grapes that are very rich in colouring matter and sufficiently ripe, can be made simply by pressing red grapes; this is the case of rosés from Anjou and Touraine (a typical example is shown above). The techniques of white wine vinification are then used on the must produced, but a little maceration is often necessary to give the wine a pleasingly distinct colour. The second method of making rosé is called the '*saignée*' (which means 'bleeding') method, made by macerating a part of the must with the skins for several hours (a maximum of 24 hours' contact). Most of the rosés from Provence are made in this way (a typical example is shown below). This must, which has not yet started to ferment, is then vinified according to the principles of white wine vinification. These *saignée* wines are supple, fresh and fruity. There also exist rosés made following a longer maceration period of two to three days. These may, depending on the circumstances, be obtained by macerating a free-run must that has not yet started to ferment, or a free-run must that is in the early stages of fermentation. The rest of the must is then extracted by pressing the marc, and the free-run must and the press must are blended for final fermentation, according to the techniques of white wine vinification. To avoid obtaining too highly tinted a juice, it is necessary to take precautions during the pressing, so that not too much of the colouring matter is released. This type of rosé has a slightly tougher structure than the *saignée* wines, because it is richer in tannins. A longer stay in vat or bottle helps it to reach its full potential.

RED WINE VINIFICATION

This type of vinification has as its aim the conversion of red grapes into red wine by alcoholic fermentation. The characteristic feature of red wine vinification is maceration. In fact, unlike white wine vinification, in which only the juice from the grapes is fermented, red wines are obtained by fermenting the juice together with the solid parts of the grape, after the *foulage* or crushing. A process of infusion takes place and the colouring matter, the tannins and numerous aromatic compounds contained in the skin of the grapes are dissolved, giving the red wine its colour and its character. Since the composition of the grape skin depends greatly on external conditions (soil, situation of the vineyard) and climatic conditions, the *terroir* exerts considerable influence on the manufacture and final quality of red wines.

Modern oenology has provided perfect descriptions of the ideal method and conditions for red wine vinification. It has also incorporated the lessons of traditional wine-making practices, established by trial and error, by flashes of inspiration and by the sensitivity of wine makers, which sometimes led in the past to sublime results.

The wine maker first used the theoretical insights given by oenology to understand the mechanisms of fermentation and maceration. He was then able to correct the accidents and unwanted developments that could occur during these processes, which led to imbalances or even spoilage of the wine. Now, as the 20th century nears its close, oenology has advanced far beyond its initial corrective brief. It now provides the wine maker with a body of knowledge and battery of techniques that enable him or her, from the fruit of a given grape variety and *terroir*, and with a known pattern of consumption in view, to achieve the finest possible result.

The conditions of vinification

There is a general pattern to red wine vinification that applies universally. But it is obvious that this scheme must include an infinite number of variables, allowing it to be adapted to every possible individual case. Vinification thus means realizing these various universal stages on the basis of a number of local factors. Among these variables are the following:

▷ the grape variety;
▷ the *terroir*;
▷ the type of *élevage* and market requirements: the wine may be either a *primeur* for drinking young or a *vin de garde* to be kept for a long time in cask and then in bottle;
▷ the method of harvesting (manual or mechanical);
▷ the vintage conditions: degree of maturity of the grapes, condition of the grapes when harvested;
▷ the vinification equipment used.

Minimizing the negative aspects of the harvest and extracting the full potential from the positive factors is the major role of the wine maker. Of course, this does not mean that an identical wine should be produced each year. Quite the opposite: the characteristics of each vintage should be preserved and enhanced by striving to produce the best possible result from the given raw material.

The grape harvest. This tapestry, from the end of the 15th century, provides a valuable account of vinification methods of the period. The grapes were harvested with a pruning knife, transported in wicker baskets, trodden by foot, pressed in a screw press, then stored in casks. A tapestry in the mille fleurs *style. Musée de Cluny, Paris.*

The process of vinification

The vinification of red wine involves carrying out a certain number of basic operations. These are:

▷ checking and examining the crop;
▷ *foulage* (crushing), by which juice is released from the grapes;
▷ *égrappage* (destalking), by which the grapes are separated from the stalk (the vegetal part of the bunch). Only the berries are used for vinification;
▷ pre-fermentation treatment;
▷ transfer of the grapes to the fermentation vat;
▷ maceration and fermentation, which occur simultaneously;
▷ *écoulage*, which is the running off from the fermentation vat of the *vin de goutte* (free-run wine);
▷ *décuvage*, which consists in removing the marc, formed by the solid residues of the grapes, from the fermentation vat;
▷ pressing, in order to extract the juice still contained in the marc, which is known as the *vin de presse* (press wine);
▷ running the wine into the finishing vat;
▷ malolactic fermentation, in which lactic bacteria are used to transform the malic acid in the wine into lactic acid and carbon dioxide;
▷ *débourbage*, which, after the wine has been left to stand for a while, consists in separating the clear part from the lees, and from the other impurities it may contain, which will have been deposited on the bottom of the vat.

The red wine's vinification is now finished and it may begin its period of ageing and its *élevage* ('raising' or maturing of the wine in cask).

Each of the operations described above calls for various pieces of equipment, checks and techniques which are peculiar to that stage. Some of these will now be examined in detail.

Checking and examining the crop

So as to be best able to direct the vinification, the wine maker must be well acquainted with the raw material he is going to use. A series of inspections is therefore carried out, among which the most important are checking the type and origin of the grapes and checking their maturity and condition.

The type and origin of the grapes is defined particularly by the grape variety, the age of the vines, the yield, and the position of the vineyard. The state of maturity is determined by visual observation and analytic inspection of the following factors:

▷ average weight of the grapes;
▷ sugar content of the grapes;
▷ total acidity of the grapes.

The condition of the crop must also be inspected, since it may have been negatively affected by poor leaf canopy on the vines, by vine disease or by unfavourable climatic conditions. Finally, the physical condition of the grapes is another very important variable. If the harvest has been carried out manually and transported carefully, then the grapes should be intact. But grapes are often split, to a greater or lesser extent, because of mechanical harvesting or bad transport conditions.

These observations are extremely important and allow the wine maker to form a plan for vinification and to proceed with another essential operation: selection. This consists in sorting out the crop according to the categories revealed by the inspection; each group will then be vinified separately.

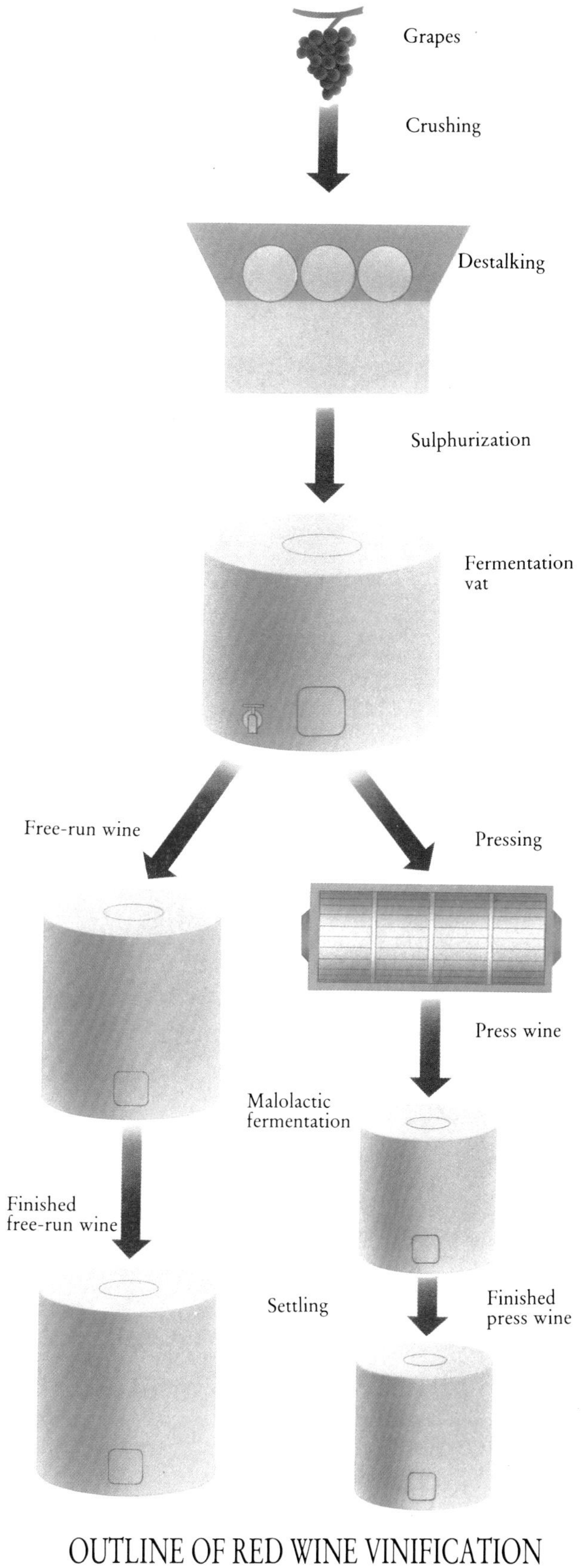

OUTLINE OF RED WINE VINIFICATION

Foulage

As mentioned above, when grapes have been carefully harvested and transported to the wine-making centre, they will be whole. To release the juice and allow fermentation and maceration to proceed, they must be split and crushed. This process of *foulage*, which used to be done by foot in open vats, is now completely mechanized.

The equipment most commonly used consists of two fluted rollers that turn in opposite directions and crush the grapes between them as they do so. Many different degrees of *foulage* are possible, depending on the type of *fouloir*, the distance between the rollers, etc. The juice can therefore be extracted to a greater or lesser extent, resulting in different maceration conditions. The use of a greater or lesser intensity of *foulage* gives the wine maker a direct influence on the quality of the wine to be made.

It is generally agreed that maceration and the extraction of solid matter from the grape will be facilitated by a more complete *foulage*. On the other hand the technique of carbonic maceration requires whole grapes, which have been subjected to neither *foulage* nor *égrappage*, to be put in the fermentation vat.

Égrappage

The separation of the stalk from the grape is optional. It is done if the maceration is to be fairly long and if there is a risk that substances present in the stalks — which can spoil the wine by giving it a bitter, astringent taste — may dissolve into the wine.

During a short maceration period, the dissolution of the components of the grapes' skin always occurs more quickly than that of the components of the stalks. The latter do not therefore have time to be absorbed into the must and *égrappage* becomes unnecessary.

Égrappage, which used to be manual, is now mechanized. It may, in certain cases, be carried out before *foulage*.

Pre-fermentation treatment

This can take place before or during the filling of the vinification vat. Few treatments are necessary for red wine vinification. The main ones are sulphurization and the addition of yeasts.

Sulphurization

The addition of sulphur dioxide (SO_2) to the grapes has two effects: an antioxidant effect and an antibacterial effect. The antioxidant effect is brought about by the sulphur dioxide inhibiting the action of the grape oxidases, which are responsible for the oxidization of the phenolic compounds — tannins and colouring matter. The sulphur dioxide also inhibits the activity of lactic bacteria in the must, whose action is undesirable until the transformation of the sugars is complete. Exactly the right amount of sulphur dioxide must be used. An insufficient dose brings the risk of oxidization or the premature intervention of lactic bacteria. An excessive dose causes the total destruction of these bacteria, making malolactic fermentation impossible. In addition, from the beginning of fermentation, the yeasts produce acetaldehyde in a quantity proportionate to the sulphur dioxide present, and an excessive dose of acetaldehyde in a wine limits its ageing potential and its hygienic qualities. The minimum amount of sulphur dioxide should therefore always be used.

Another essential is that the sulphur dioxide should be evenly distributed throughout the crop. The best way to achieve this is to use a dosing pump during the transfer of the grapes after crushing to the fermentation vat. This starts automatically at the same time as the grape pump.

The addition of yeast

All grapes have yeasts on the surface of their skin and, when these are in contact with the juice, they multiply and initiate

CARBONIC MACERATION

This vinification technique, which is widespread in the Beaujolais region for the production of wines intended to be drunk young, consists in putting whole bunches of grapes in a vat which has first been filled with carbon dioxide. Under the effect of this gas, a particular phenomenon called 'intracellular fermentation' takes place. A small quantity of alcohol is produced inside each of the whole grapes, together with a lowering of acidity levels, through the autolysis of malic acid. This fermentation is accompanied by the production of characteristic fruit aromas.

A short period of fermentation in vat — four to six days — produces very supple, floral wines. Carbonic maceration is now often also practised in Mediterranean areas, producing wines suitable for longer keeping. The length of maceration is in this case extended — from ten to twenty days — and the tannic structure of the wine, as well as its suitability for ageing, are identical to those obtained by traditional vinification. But the wines are more highly perfumed, rich and rounded, and their individual characteristics are more fully developed, than is the case with traditionally vinified wines.

Stainless steel vats at Château Loudenne, in the Médoc.

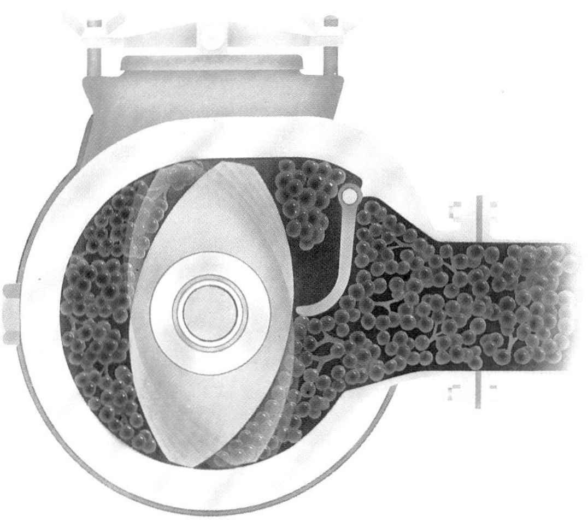

Olive pump. This new type of pump is gentle with the grapes, and does not grind or crush them.

fermentation. The addition of yeasts intended to accomplish this task in place of those found on grape skins is by no means a standard practice. However, it is justified in certain cases by the mediocre quality of the natural yeasts, or when it is necessary to start fermentation quickly. The dry yeasts added are the result of a rigorous selection of natural yeasts chosen for their fermentative powers and their aromatic neutrality.

The transfer of the grape crop to the vat

This operation may seem mundane, but it is in fact vital, and if it goes badly, the quality of the wine may suffer. In general, the grapes must be transported from the reception area to the vat room and this trip should, as a rule, be as short as possible. The ideal arrangement is for the grapes to be received directly over the vats. The *fouloir* is then placed on top of the vat to be filled. Unfortunately, the reception area and the vat room are usually separated, and the situation is made worse if the vat room is at a higher level than the reception area. The greater the distance and height to be covered, the more handling and working the grapes will require and the more this will spoil the wine. Transport is generally provided by large-diameter piston pumps connected to pipes. During the late 1970s, a new generation of pumps became available: these take greater care of the grapes and do not require them to have been previously crushed. They are called olive pumps and are now coming into widespread use.

The layout of the vat room, the shape and size of the vats and the material they are made from also play an important role, because they influence the conditions of fermentation and maceration, as well as the working conditions of those involved in making the wine.

The materials used for fermentation vats are wood, cement, enamelled steel and stainless steel. Wood, which was once the only material used, is now employed less and less frequently because of the difficulty of making large-volume wooden vats and the lack of guaranteed hygiene. Furthermore, only new wood can make a real contribution to improving the quality of the wine. The use of wood is thus limited to great wines, which are vinified in small-capacity barrels made of new oak. Since the beginning of the century, cement vats have gradually replaced wooden receptacles. This material, which is inexpensive and easy to use, is suitably inert and hygienic, once it has been covered by a layer of tartar. The problems of cement vats are that, once built, they cannot be moved, and that it is very hard to restore them once they become dilapidated.

Sheet steel vats are covered on the inside with a thin layer of alimentary epoxy resin, which is perfectly neutral, forms a smooth surface and provides perfect hygiene. These vats, apart from the largest ones, are easy to move. Their only drawback is the relative fragility of the interior coating to the blows it may receive when the vat is being emptied.

The clean surface and almost total inertia of stainless steel mean that it is often preferred to all other materials, despite its purchase price, which is high.

A vat intended for the vinification of red wine will include:

▷ a top hatch with a diameter of at least 40cm for filling;

▷ an inspection hatch. This allows access to the vat for maintenance operations and for removing the marc after the wine has been run off. The position of the hatch relative to the bottom of the vat must correspond to the average depth of the marc remaining after the wine has been run off;

▷ at least two taps, one of them at the bottom of the vat to provide total drainage. This tap should have an interior grill behind it to filter out solid matter;

▷ a *remontage* system, to enable must to be poured over the floating cap of grape skins during fermentation;

▷ a tasting tap, for taking the samples necessary for gauging the progress of fermentation;

▷ a thermometer, showing the temperature of the must.

Self-emptying vats are available. Some of them have a taper-

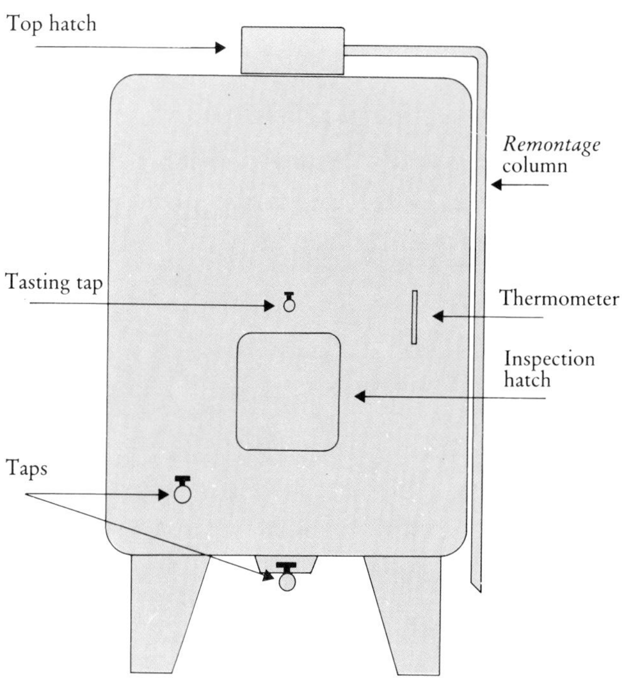

A VINIFICATION VAT

ing base and a large hatch activated by a jack. The marc is then extracted by gravity alone.

Others contain mechanical equipment consisting of a rake on the bottom of the vat which drags the marc, with a turning movement, into a shoot equipped with a continuous screw. This type of self-emptying vat is not very widespread because of its high price, despite the manpower savings it makes possible, and the elimination of the tedious work involved in emptying the marc from the vat.

Fermentation and maceration

These two operations cannot be usefully distinguished because they occur simultaneously, and interact in numerous ways.

When the fermentation vat has been filled with grapes, and the sulphurization and optional addition of yeast have been carried out, fermentation begins. This is the most spectacular phase of vinification because of the vigorous bubbling caused by the escaping carbon dioxide. As soon as this bubbling starts, the wine maker must ensure that fermentation and maceration are proceeding properly by carrying out checks. The first way of doing this is by tasting.

Tasting is the most important check, the one that provides the most information and, unfortunately, the one that is most neglected. Being able to taste a fermenting must while disregarding masking elements such as the dissolved sugar and carbon dioxide, and the suspended solid matter, is an essential skill for a wine maker, allowing him to assess simultaneously the progress of fermentation, the development of maceration, the quality of the future wine and, possibly, the appearance of abnormalities.

As the sugar is transformed into alcohol by the action of the yeast, the relative density of the must decreases. The wine maker thus monitors the progress of fermentation by measuring the changes in relative density, assessing the speed of these, and watching for any abnormal deceleration or cessation.

The transformation of sugar into alcohol is also accompanied by the production of calories. The temperature of the fermenting must will therefore tend to increase. It is important to measure it as often as checking the density. Depending on the type of wine being made, there is in fact an ideal vinification temperature which should be maintained in order to ensure that the fermentation and maceration proceed properly. This temperature varies according to the stage of vinification reached. In general, the process of fermentation is initially encouraged by heating the grapes a little. The grapes arrive at the wine-making plant at a temperature of between 15°C and 20°C and this is raised to 23-24°C, after which it increases naturally. It is then advisable to maintain it at between 27°C and 30°C by cooling the must or the vat. After the free-run wine has been drained off, the end of fermentation — a particularly delicate phase — is carried out at 23-25°C. When alcoholic fermentation is complete, the wine is maintained at between 16°C and 20°C to induce rapid malolactic fermentation.

The fermentation and maceration temperature must be checked regularly. The higher the temperature, the more complete and rapid will be the maceration. However, the yeast starts to die above 30°C so if this point is passed, there is a risk that fermentation will cease. Temperature control is therefore an essential part of vinification. These days, heat exchange systems allow calories or negative calories to be manipulated in the must or the wine so as to maintain an ideal temperature.

Other checks, generally requiring the help of a laboratory, may be carried out during fermentation, such as the determination of volatile acidity, the relative presence of sugars, the

Fermenting must. This spectacular phase of vinification is notable for the production of bubbles caused by carbon dioxide. It results in the transformation of sugar into alcohol and the production of heat.

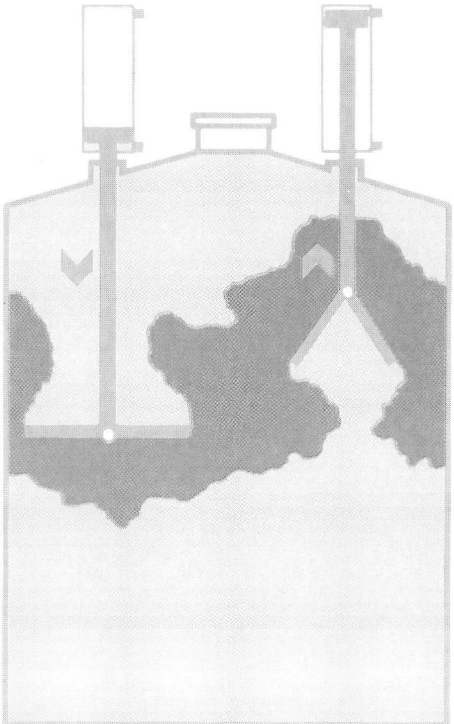

*A*utomatic **pigeage** *vat.* **Pigeage** *is a technique for the extraction of compounds from the solid grape matter, achieved by pushing the marc down into the fermenting juice.*

yeast count, and the activity of lactic bacteria.

The wine maker must also regulate the maceration time. In some cases, the maximum extraction of compounds from the solid grape matter is required. This is obtained by increasing maceration time beyond the period of alcoholic fermentation. At Chinon, for example, the grape crop is left in the vat for one month and sometimes longer. This extraction is sometimes artificially aided by *remontage*, which consists in pumping the must from the bottom of the vat up over the solid cap of marc on top of the must. Another technique—*pigeage*—is used to break up the marc on top of the must and push it down into the fermenting juice. *Pigeage*, which used to be carried out by foot, is now achieved automatically with jack arms. The wines obtained by these methods are rich in tannins and require both cask and bottle ageing before being drunk.

If the composition of the grapes used is naturally very rich in extracts, the wine maker only requires the partial extraction of substances from the solid matter. This applies notably to the Mediterranean vineyards, where vatting times rarely exceed ten days, apart from in those areas, like Châteauneuf-du-Pape, where wines for long keeping are being made.

When red wines intended to be drunk young are being produced, little extraction of solid matter is required, since the primary aromatic characteristics of these wines are their most important feature.

'CORRECTION' OF A GRAPE HARVEST

If the meteorological conditions during a vintage cycle are not favourable, grape maturity may not be normal. Either it is incomplete, and the sugar content of the grapes is too low while acidity is too high; or it is too far advanced and the wines produced lack acidity. The wine maker can then resort to adjustment techniques enabling him to deacidify the must or, on the contrary, to increase acidity by adding tartaric acid, the main natural acid in grapes. The best-known correction, introduced by Jean Antoine Chaptal (1756–1832) and named chaptalization after him, consists in adding sugar to the must in order to increase its potential alcohol level. All these practices, which are subject to strict legislation and verification procedures, are carried out under the supervision of oenologists.

Écoulage

When the wine maker considers that maceration has gone on for long enough, whether the fermentation is finished or not, he starts the process of *écoulage* (running off). From the beginning of fermentation, all the solid matter in the grapes will have risen to the top of the vat to form the '*gâteau de marc*' ('cake of marc'). Opening one of the taps at the bottom of the vat allows the liquid part, which has been naturally separated from the solid elements, to be drained off. This operation puts an end to the maceration phase. The juice that has been run off forms the finest and noblest part of the wine: the *vin de goutte* (free-run wine).

Décuvage

Extracting the marc remaining in the vat after *écoulage* is a tedious job, which is still all too rarely automated. When accomplished manually, it is carried out with forks or, more often nowadays, with a portable marc extractor that uses a continuous screw mechanism.

Pressing

After the *vin de goutte* has been run off, the marc still contains some wine (8 to 15 per cent of the total), which must be extracted by pressing.

Various types of press are used. At the present time, excluding the old systems using screws, jacks and hydraulic pressure, three sorts of press are used: the discontinuous horizontal press with moving plates, the pneumatic press and the continuous press. In the horizontal press with plates, the grapes are placed in a horizontal basket and pressed by two plates coming together from each end. After the first application of pressure, the plates separate, causing the marc to crumble. This is called the *rebêche*, and it is followed by another application of pressure. After three to five applications, the marc is completely dry. The pneumatic press works with a horizontal bladder that is slowly filled with air, causing the marc to be pressed on to the sides of a perforated cylinder. When the air is released, the marc crumbles as before.

Unlike the two other types of press, the continuous press is supplied continuously. A large-diameter continuous screw

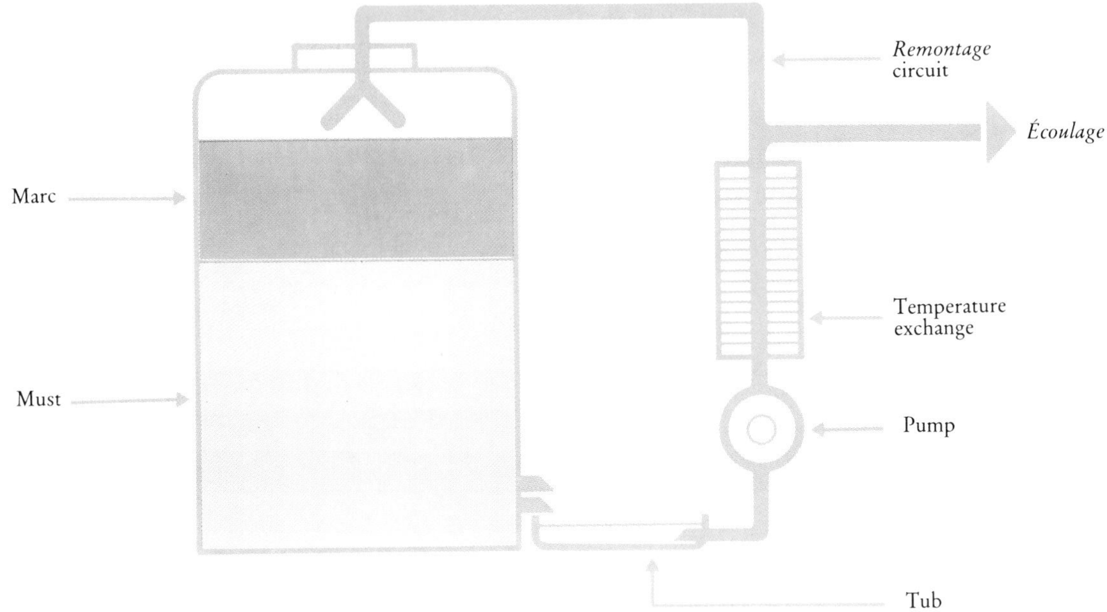

INSTALLATION FOR *REMONTAGE* (PUMPING OVER) AND *ÉCOULAGE* (RUNNING OFF)

transports the grapes and pushes them through a horizontal grill, which is partially blocked by a jack-controlled door. Though it works faster than the other systems, the continuous press has the disadvantage of mishandling the marc and extracting more astringent substances and tannins from it. It therefore produces press wines of lower quality than the two other systems.

Press wine always contains more extracts from the solid parts of the grape than free-run wine does. It is also more deeply coloured and more tannic, though often with a lower alcohol content and lower total acidity. Though it is rougher, if produced with a good-quality press and if adequately treated after extraction, it can profitably be used for blending with the free-run wine.

Putting the wine into the finishing vat

The free-run wine and the press wine are then put in vats where, if the fermentation was not complete at the time of running-off, this may be allowed to finish. The end of fermentation is carefully supervised by the wine maker. At this point, the residual sugar content of the wine is carefully determined in the laboratory. This should not exceed 2g per litre. A complete analysis of the wine, revealing its exact chemical composition, may also be made at this point.

Malolactic fermentation

Some time after the end of the alcoholic fermentation, the wine is said to 'move'. When this activity is observed, the wine is undergoing a second fermentation caused not only by the yeast but by lactic bacteria; this fermentation converts malic acid into lactic acid and carbon dioxide. The results of the process are a partial deacidification of the wine and a considerable improvement in its organoleptic qualities. This is why malolactic fermentation is systematically encouraged in red wines. Since it is difficult to induce, the wine maker has to ensure favourable conditions for it: a temperature above 17°C and the moderate application of sulphur dioxide to the new wine.

Débourbage

This should take place as soon as possible after malolactic fermentation. *Débourbage* (settling or purging of the wine) consists in separating, after a period of rest, the clear wine from the *bourbes* (literally 'mud') formed by the yeast, the dead lactic bacteria and the last solid particles from the grapes that were still in suspension in the wine at the time of the running off. This racking operation is usually accompanied by aeration of the wine and the addition of sulphur dioxide to protect the wine as it ages.

Continuous press. This is faster than other systems of pressing, but it produces press wine of inferior quality because it maltreats the marc.

The Production of *Vins Doux Naturels*

During the 13th century, when Roussillon was part of the Kingdom of Majorca (in existence between 1276 and 1343), a scholar from Roussillon, Armand (or Arnaud) de Villeneuve, is said to have achieved the 'miraculous marriage of the spirit and the juice of the grape'. *Mutage* (fortification) was born and *vins doux naturels* (sweet fortified wines) were made possible, as a large part of the sugar from the grapes could now be preserved in the wine by the action of the spirit.

The *vin doux naturel* vineyard areas, soils, and grape varieties

The AOC *vins doux naturels* are made in a number of different production areas in the south of France: Rivesaltes, Banyuls and Maury, with the Muscat de Rivesaltes AOC covering all of these three areas; and Muscat de Frontignan, Mireval, Lunel, Saint-Jean-de-Minervois and Beaumes-de-Venise.

Soils that are poor in organic matter and a climate that is hot, sunny (2,600 hours of sunshine per year) and dry are the characteristics of these vineyards, producing low yields of grapes rich in sugar.

Five main grape varieties are used to make *vins doux naturels:* the red, white and rosé Grenache varieties, the Macabeu, the Tourbat, the Muscat à Petit Grains Blancs and the Muscat d'Alexandrie. The grapes are harvested when they are very ripe; they should contain more than 252g of sugar per litre of must.

Methods of vinification

The production of *vins doux naturels* is characterized by *mutage* (fortification), an operation which consists in adding alcohol to the must during fermentation. This additional alcohol is in a proportion of about 5 to 10 per cent of the volume of the fermenting must. In order to ensure trouble-free fortification, the wine makers can denature this alcohol with an equal quantity of non-fermented *vin doux naturel* must before use. The sweetness of the finished wine will depend on the density of the must at the moment of fortification.

Several different types of *vin doux naturel* may be made, depending on the method of vinification used.

The white wines are vinified according to usual white wine vinification methods, sometimes including a short period of maceration.

The red wines are subjected to a short maceration of two to three days and are then run off, so that fortification can take place in the liquid phase of vinification. However, in some cases, and notably at Banyuls and Maury, fortification of the solid marc is practised. It is accompanied by a long maceration in the presence of this alcohol for ten to fifteen days. Wines obtained in this way are richer in colouring matter, tannins and aromas.

The Muscat wines are vinified according to white wine vinification methods, often with the addition of a short maceration period, because the aromatic elements typical of this variety are found on the skin. It is important to monitor the temperature of fermentation carefully, as too warm a fermentation could cause significant loss of aroma.

The *élevage* of *vins doux naturels*

The specific characteristics of *vins doux naturels* are defined during the period of *élevage* ('raising' or maturing of the wine). It is important to distinguish between two categories of wine in this respect: the Muscats, which must be protected from oxidization to preserve their aroma; and the Rivesaltes, Maury and Banyuls wines, which only reach maturity after a period of *élevage* in which oxidization plays an important role.

The Muscats are generally kept for some time in vats, then quickly bottled. Great care is necessary to avoid exposure to the air, as this might spoil their primary aromas of flowers and fruit, especially ripe grapes and citrus fruit.

White AOC Rivesaltes wines undergo slight oxidization in part-empty vats or in wooden casks. The wines then assume a light amber colour and acquire characteristic aromas reminiscent of fruit and honey.

Red AOC Rivesaltes wines, and the AOC wines of Maury and Banyuls, can if wished be bottled relatively early. They then preserve their ruby colour, and the aromas of fruit such as blackcurrants, cherries and blackberries. But in most cases they are aged in part-empty vats or in wooden casks. (Banyuls Grand Cru must age for at least thirty months in wood.) Slow oxidization changes their character completely. They acquire a tile-red colour, and their aromas take on hints of cocoa, prunes and coffee.

These processes of oxidization are sometimes accelerated by putting the wines outside in *bonbonnes* (demijohns) exposed to the elements. This method of ageing is used for the most tannic and firmly structured wines. The skill of the *maître de chais* (cellarmaster) is applied to combine these aged wines to make a single *cuvée*.

When the wines have aged for a long time under oxidizing conditions, they acquire a *'rancio'* character; *'ranci'* means 'slightly rancid' in Catalan. They are aged in a part-filled *demi-muid*, and each year some younger *vin doux naturel* is added. These wines have an amber colour with greenish tinges and a distinctive aroma of nuts and nut shells.

Vins doux naturels *(sweet fortified wines) from Maury ageing in* **bonbonnes** *(demijohns).*

BRANDY AND MARC

Full-bodied and aromatic, or elegant and refined, French brandies and marcs present, like French wines, a complete range of different characters, depending on the soils and grape varieties from which they come.

The terms '*eau-de-vie de marc*' or '*marc*' are reserved for a spirit produced exclusively by distillation of the marc of grapes, with or without added water. 'Marc' here means the residues of wine making: the skins, pips and stalks impregnated with the dregs of the red wine that has just been run off from the vat, pressed after fermentation; or what is left over after the grapes have been pressed prior to fermentation in the case of white wine vinification. This material has always been used to make brandy.

'*Eau-de-vie de vin*' is a denomination reserved for brandy exclusively produced by the distillation of wine. The origin of this type of spirit was later than that of marc, and would have depended on the economic conditions of the moment, as it would generally have been an outlet for over-production of wine. In only two areas — Armagnac and Cognac — did it become the main reason for growing vines.

The reputation acquired by these two great brandies, already granted *appellation d'origine contrôlée* status before the Second World War, meant that they were exempted from the law of 13 January 1941, which required all alcohol and *eaux-de-vie* to be given over to the state for the needs of war. In reaction to this, the wine-producing regions that were then making brandy demanded the advantage of an *appellation contrôlée*. A new category was therefore created for these brandies, that of '*eau-de-vie à appellation réglementée*' (brandy of regulated *appellation*). The first decrees granting this *appellation* were published in 1942.

Today, sixteen wine-producing regions and subregions benefit from the use of this *appellation* for the production of brandy or marc (see table on opposite page). It should be noted that the terms 'Eau-de-Vie de Marc de . . .' and 'Marc de . . .' are synonymous.

The decrees

The regulations governing these brandies or marcs cover various geographical, viticultural, technical and administrative points.

The geographical area of production

The regulated areas of production of *eaux-de-vie* are either the *département*, the canton or the commune.

The grape varieties

Only wine or marc from grape varieties authorized in the local area of production may be used. In certain cases, only some of these varieties may be used.

In Burgundy, Champagne, and the Côtes du Rhône, only the products of grape varieties used for AOC wines are authorized. In Alsace, only the marc from Gewürztraminer is allowed to be distilled.

For Fine Bordeaux ('Fine' is used here and elsewhere as an accepted French term for brandy), only white grape varieties are authorized, with at least 70 per cent of Ugni Blanc or Colombard, and no more than 30 per cent of the Merlot Blanc, Mauzac and Ondenc varieties.

The quality of the raw material

Wine for brandy must be sound and good, with a volatile acidity of no more than 1.2g per litre (1g per litre in the case of Eau-de-Vie de Savoie and Fine Bordeaux). Eau-de-Vie de Vin de la Marne can be distilled from the wine ejected in the 'disgorgement' part of the Champagne process.

Marc for distilling should be wholesome, well preserved and sealed from the air so that it does not oxidize before distillation. In most cases, it can be used unwashed, as it is raked from the press; in some cases, though, it should be washed, (i.e. 'rinsed' with water) before being distilled.

The distiller, an allegorical engraving dating from 1735.

Special measures apply to Marc d'Alsace Gewürztraminer. The grapes should have been destalked and pressed lightly, as 4.5 litres of pure alcohol per 100kg of grapes used are required. These regulations are advantageous, as regards both the quality of the wine and that of the marc. Marc de Lorraine must be the result of a distillation that yields 4 litres of alcohol per 100kg of grapes.

If marc is stored before being distilled, it is kept in wooden, metal or concrete tanks and sealed with a loosely airtight cover such as clay. When marc from white wine vinification presses is stored in this way, some fermentation of the residual sugars left in the fresh grape matter will take place. In both cases — marc from white wine vinification or from the vats in which red wine has been fermented — wild and strong aromas develop during this storage period. Some people find these a little abrasive, but they are an authentic characteristic of marc.

The processes of distillation

Pot stills heated by a naked flame are authorized for all regulated brandies and marcs. These are the most difficult to operate successfully but they are also the ones that give the best results. They are the only stills authorized for the Faugères and Fine Bordeaux *appellations*, for Marc d'Alsace Gewürztraminer and for Marc de Lorraine.

BRANDY AND MARC *APPELLATIONS RÉGLEMENTÉES*

Region	Zones of Production and Denomination	Decree
ALSACE	Marc d'Alsace Gewürztraminer	22 July 1966
LORRAINE	Marc de Lorraine	28 November 1979
BURGUNDY	Eau-de-Vie de Marc de Bourgogne Marc de Bourgogne Eau-de-Vie de Vin de Bourgogne	23 February 1942 11 April 1946
	Eau-de-Vie de Vin & Eau-de-Vie de Marc du Centre-Est	24 July 1950
	Eau-de-Vie de Vin & Eau-de-Vie de Marc du Bugey	17 August 1950
	Eau-de-Vie de Vin & Eau-de-Vie de Marc de Franche-Comté	23 February 1942
	Eau-de-Vie de Savoie Eau-de-Vie de Marc de Savoie Marc de Savoie	27 October 1967
CHAMPAGNE	Eau-de-Vie de Vin de la Marne Eau-de-Vie de Marc de Champagne Marc de Champagne	23 February 1942
CÔTES DU RHÔNE	Eau-de-Vie de Vin & Eau-de-Vie de Marc des Côtes du Rhône	19 March 1948
LANGUEDOC	Eau-de-Vie de Vin & Eau-de-Vie de Marc du Languedoc	23 February 1942
ROUSSILLON	Eau-de-Vie de Faugères	19 March 1948
PROVENCE CORSICA	Eau-de-Vie de Vin & Eau-de-Vie de Marc de Provence	23 February 1942
SOUTH WEST	Eau-de-Vie de Vin & Eau-de-Vie de Marc d'Aquitaine	23 February 1942
	Fine Bordeaux	5 August 1974
LOIRE VALLEY	Eau-de-Vie de Vin & Eau-de-Vie de Marc des Coteaux de la Loire	23 February 1942
	Marc d'Auvergne	26 October 1949

PRODUCTION OF REGULATED BRANDIES AND MARCS

BRANDY		
REGIONS	1968/69	1985/86
Aquitaine	26	4 856
Bourgogne	411	285
Bugey	—	8
Coteaux de la Loire	231	20
Franche-Comté	7	27
Languedoc	994	139
Marne	507	1 025
Fine Bordeaux	—	42
Côtes du Rhône	7	—
Faugères	—	—
Provence	43	—
Central & Eastern France	4	—
Savoie	—	—
TOTAL (in hectolitres)	**2 230**	**6 402**

MARC		
REGIONS	1968/69	1985/86
Aquitaine	7 492	214
Bourgogne	6 820	5 130
Bugey	251	32
Coteaux de la Loire	3 857	56
Champagne	1 215	1 915
Franche-Comté	313	167
Languedoc	41 150	761
Provence	14 154	1 525
Lorraine	—	15
Auvergne	8	45
Central & Eastern France	475	50
Savoie	642	136
Alsace Gewürztraminer	119	169
Côtes du Rhône	61	—
TOTAL (in hectolitres)	**76 557**	**10 215**

In the case of marcs, these stills have to be double-walled, and the naked flame heats the outer wall. The pot still itself is positioned inside, in a sort of water- or steam-filled *bain-marie*. As the base matter for distillation is solid, it is obviously not possible, as in Cognac, to heat the still directly, because the marc would then stick to the bottom of the still and caramelize.

Another method of double-walled pot-still distillation involves directing a jet of pressurized steam (at about 110°C) between the two walls of the still.

In both of the above cases, a certain amount of water will have been put in the bottom of the inner still as a security measure before loading the marc.

As well as pot stills, *alambics au premier jet*, either continuous or discontinuous and steam-heated, are used to produce most of the regulated brandies and marcs. The maximum amount that can be distilled daily is 200hl of base matter or wine, which increases to 400hl for Marc de Champagne and Eau-de-Vie de Vin de la Marne.

For brandies or marcs from Provence, Languedoc, Aquitaine and the Loire valley, the *colonne à distiller à premier jet*, steam-heated and able to process up to 400hl of base matter or wine every 24 hours, is also authorized.

The characteristics of the brandies and marcs

Legislation regulates the alcohol content of brandy and marc both on its exit from the still and at sale.

Alcohol content on exit from still

A maximum of 71 per cent alcohol by volume is fixed as the manufacturing strength for the majority of regulated brandies. This is justified by the desire not to produce a spirit of very pure or 'rectified' character, which would fail to reflect the authentic base matter used. This maximum is even lowered to 68 per cent alcohol by volume for the Gewürztraminer and Lorraine marcs, and to 63 per cent alcohol by volume for the *eaux-de-vie* produced in Savoie and at Bugey. Fine Bordeaux is distilled to a strength of between 65 per cent by volume and 72 per cent by volume.

Alcohol content at sale

After ageing and dilution, an almost universal minimum alcohol content of 40 per cent by volume has been fixed, with the exception of Marc d'Alsace Gewürztraminer, which has a minimum of 45 per cent by volume. Brandies and marcs may be sold at a higher alcoholic strength than these minima.

The 'non-alcohol' content

This term, which is not ideal and is only slightly better than the alternative term 'impurities', refers to all the volatile elements in the base matter subject to distillation, apart from ethyl alcohol, methyl alcohol and water. These congeners include aldehydes, esters, volatile acids and higher alcohols, and they are responsible for providing much of the flavour of brandy and marc.

Marc, in fact, always contains more 'non-alcohol' than brandy does on its exit from the still. It also contains much more methyl alcohol. The greater degree of roughness and lesser degree of organoleptic refinement of marc compared with brandy is due, among other things, to its 'non-alcohol' content, fixed by law at between 350g and 500g per hectolitre of pure alcohol. The minimum non-alcohol content of brandy is fixed at 300g, with the exception of Fine Bordeaux, which has a minimum of 350g. By way of contrast, it is worth noting that very high levels of non-alcohol elements, up to 1,100g per hectolitre of pure alcohol, exist in old cognacs and armagnacs that have been aged for 30 to 50 years.

The certificate of approval and the transport pass
All brandies and marcs are tasted by a commission of tasters appointed by the INAO. If they are judged to be suitable, a certificate of approval is granted and is required by the tax office before a transport pass is issued. This documentation cites the name of the *appellation* to which the brandy or marc is entitled.

Labelling
The rules for brandies and marcs are the same as those laid down in the general French regulations for drinks labelling. The regulated *appellation* has to be shown clearly, and no item of information given on the label should be ambiguous or lead to confusion in the mind of the consumer.

The ageing of brandies and marc

The decrees concerning brandy and marc of regulated *appellation*, which are more precise than those concerning cognac and armagnac on certain points (volatile acidity of the base wine or marc, and minimum quantities of non-alcohol elements), do not say anything about ageing. The absence of age controls and regulations for brandy and marc is therefore a key area in which they are distinguished from the great *appellations contrôlées* of Cognac and Armagnac, both of which specify certain age requirements.

Ageing conditions vary according to where the brandy or marc is produced. For example, Marc d'Alsace Gewürztraminer must be aged for a short time in casks of ash wood, so as to mellow in flavour but without acquiring colour. Marc de Bourgogne, on the other hand, is aged in oak casks. Most brandies are also aged in oak. When marc or brandy is aged in wood, it is generally for a shorter period than the ageing undergone by cognac and armagnac.

Marc

The raw material used for marc is, as already stated, a by-product of vinification. The finished spirit will therefore have a very strong *'goût de terroir'* (an earthy, rugged taste caused by very high levels of aldehydes, esters and methyl alcohol), and is greatly appreciated by local enthusiasts who have grown used to it. Ageing in wood eventually brings refinement to marc.

Brandy

The raw material in this case is wine, but it is often wine originally made to be drunk as such, and not specifically to be distilled, as is the case in Cognac and Armagnac. A higher level of aldehyde, a less rich spectrum of esters, and a reinforced presence of methyl alcohol and higher alcohols mean that these brandies cannot achieve the quality levels of cognac and armagnac. The best among them are those made with white wines and distilled in a pot still over a naked flame.

The production of brandy and marc

The production of regulated brandies is increasing, but with a very strong regional bias in favour of the South West and the vineyards to the north of the Loire.

On the other hand, a clear decrease in the total production of marc may be noted. Only the marcs of Burgundy, Champagne and Alsace (Gewürztraminer) are maintaining their rate of production.

These by-products of the vine reflect very closely the economic conditions of the time, and the year-to-year volume of the grape harvest. The evolution in production of and demand for these regulated *appellation* marcs and brandies also corresponds to changing tastes on the part of consumers.

A travelling still, such as is found in various regions of France.

DE

Dameron ~ Etraire de la Dui   257–259

Dameron

Synonyms: *Valais Noir de Poligny, Foirard Noir d'Arbois, Pinot Rouge* at Fontaine (Aube), *Dameret Noir* at les Riceys and at Polisot, *Luisant Noir, Noir de Lorraine, Verdun, Verdunais, Valdenois* in the Vosges.

This very old grape variety from Aube, Haute-Marne, the Vosges mountains and Jura has now almost disappeared. It is susceptible to disease and only produces *vin ordinaire*.

Dezize-lès-Maranges.

See Cheilly-lès-Maranges.

Douce Noire

Synonyms: *Corbeau* in Isère, *Charbonneau* or *Charbono, Turino, Turin, Plant de Turin, Bi, Picot Rouge, Plant de Calarin, Gros Plant, Plant de Moirans, Gros Noir de Montélimar, Bathiolin* or *Batialin, Oçanette, Plant de Montmélian, Montmélian, Crête de Coq, Plant de Savoie, Plant de Provence, Noirin d'Espagne, Mauvais Noir, Chasselas Noir, Plant du Roi, Cot Rouge, Cot Rouge Mérillé* in Lot-et-Garonne.

Bunches medium sized, cylindrical, compact; grapes medium sized, spherical, blue-black, juicy; ripening period: second epoch.

This grape variety of Italian origin used to be fairly widespread in Savoie and in the neighbouring *départements*, which explains why it has so many synonyms. In 1958, it was grown on nearly 1,000ha, mainly in Savoie, in Ain and in Isère. It has not been classified and is therefore disappearing. The Douce Noire is productive and gives a highly coloured, not very alcoholic wine, best drunk within a year of its production. It is susceptible to untimely frosts and vine diseases.

Duras

See Côtes de Duras.

Duras

Synonyms: *Duras Mâle, Duras Femelle, Duras Rouge* in Tarn, *Durazé* in Ariège, *Durade*.

Growing tips open, felty white with carmine margins.

Young leaves downy, yellowish with slightly bronze-coloured patches.

Leaves orbicular, medium sized, contorted with convex lobes, deeply five-lobed with sinuses concave and open at base; petiolar sinus narrowly lyrate or with slightly overlapping edges; dentation pointed, narrow; underside of blade pubescent; petioles red.

Green shoots ribbed, pale green with longitudinal brown striations, pink nodes; brown tendrils.

Bunches large, conical, compact, with two well-developed shoulders; grapes small, ovoid, blue-black and not very juicy; ripening period: second epoch.

This grape variety from the Tarn is only modestly productive, and is used in blends with the Fer and Gamay vines to produce the red wines of AOC Gaillac. Its very highly coloured, strong, full-bodied wine is hard when young, but becomes more supple with age. It has been classed as 'recommended' in Tarn (441ha), Tarn-et-Garonne, Haute-Garonne, Aveyron (VDQS Vins d'Estaing) and Ariège. Four registered clones have been approved: numbers 554, 555, 627 and 654.

Dureza

Synonyms: *Durezza, Dué, Petit Duret*.

Bunches medium sized, cylindrical, compact; grapes spherical, small, blue-black, not very juicy; ripening period: second epoch.

This is a grape variety from Drôme and Ardèche, where 11ha of it are still grown; it is productive and gives a lightly coloured *vin ordinaire*. Unclassified.

Durif

Synonyms: *Dure, Duret, Plant Durif* (from the name of its selector), *Pinot de Romans, Pinot de l'Ermitage, Plant Fourchu, Sirane Fourchue, Nérin, Bas Plant*.

Bunches medium sized, cylindrical, fairly compact; grapes spherical or slightly ovoid, small, dark; ripening period: first epoch, late.

This variety is said to be a seedling or selection of the Peloursin, propagated around 1880 by a Dr Durif because it was considered to show a certain resistance to downy mildew. It produces an indifferent, highly coloured wine. Its cultivation (530ha in 1958) is in regression because it has not been classified and it is only at present included in the range of varieties used for the Palette AOC (Bouches-du-Rhône).

Echézeaux

This red Grand Cru burgundy from the Côte de Nuits, produced in the commune of Flagey-Echézeaux, is linked with the family of great *climats* found in Vosne-Romanée: Romanée-Conti, Richebourg, Romanée, La Tâche, Romanée-Saint-Vivant and Grands Echézeaux. However, this *appellation d'origine contrôlée* of 31ha, divided into 11 parcels and ratified by the decree of 31 July 1937, does not benefit from the

The village of Vosne-Romanée contains five of Burgundy's red Grands Crus. Echézeaux is a further red Grand Cru, sited in the adjacent commune of Flagey-Echézeaux (pictured above). Its wines are often declassified to Vosne-Romanée Premier Cru.

same fame as its glorious neighbours, and with good reason: most of the vines are planted on the wrong side of the road, i.e. in the plain, where the fertile soils provide too rich a medium for the very best wines. This is why the 1,000hl produced are often sold by the better-known *appellation d'origine contrôlée* of Vosne-Romanée Premier Cru.

The wines have to have an alcohol content of 11.5°, or only 11° if they are to be sold as *premiers crus*. The base yield is fixed at 30hl/ha. Echézeaux wines, when they have been carefully made and stored, are fine, with good vinosity and an attractive bouquet.

Éderena

A Merlot × Abouriou Noir cross obtained at INRA at Bordeaux, this productive vine has fine bunches of loosely packed, black grapes that ripen in the second epoch.

Wine from the Éderena has an average depth of colour; it is aromatic, light and supple, and is best vinified and drunk as a young red wine or a rosé. This vine is classed as 'authorized' and one clone has been approved.

Egiodola

This vine comes from a Fer × Abouriou Noir cross, obtained at INRA at Bordeaux. It has large, semi-compact bunches and its dark grapes ripen early in the second epoch.

This vine is very productive and gives a deeply coloured, quality wine. It is useful because of its precocity, its low susceptibility to *coulure* (flower abortion) and its regular production. It was classed as 'recommended' in 1983 and one clone has been approved: number 600.

Elbling

Synonyms: *Elbe, Elben, Alben, Elwena, Burger Blanc, Burgyre, Burgauer, Rheinelbe, Hartalbe* in Alsace, *Gros Blanc, Gouais Blanc, Facun, Faucun* in Rhône, *Allemand Blanc* in Franche-Comté, *Albuelis, Albuelin, Blesec, Blesez, Kurzstingel, Marmot, Plant Madame* in Marne and Aisne.

Growing tips open, felty white, with pink tips.

Young leaves yellowish, bronzed on bulges, undersides felty white.

Leaves large, orbicular, thick, bullate, crimped, without lobes or two-lobed, petiolar sinus closed or with overlapping edges; dentation pointed, narrow; underside of blade arachnoid, pubescent, rough; petioles pubescent.

Green shoots mahogany red on both sides; tendrils small, thin and brown.

Bunches medium sized, cylindrical, compact; grapes spherical or slightly ovoid, medium sized, white with fibrous pulp; ripening period: second epoch, late.

This German vine is said to be the *Aubuelis* mentioned by Pliny and Columella and therefore to be of Roman origin. It was introduced into Alsace after 1870 for the production of indifferent, acidic *vins ordinaires* for the German market. It is sensitive to grey rot (botrytis) and to grape worms, but remains 'authorized' in Alsace and Moselle. There is also an Elbling Rose or Elbling Rother.

Enfariné

Synonyms: *Gouais Noir, Goix Noir, Gouët, Gouât, Gau, Petit Goix* in Aisne, Marne and Seine-et-Marne, *Lombard* in Yonne, *Gaillard, Chaigneau, Chagnot, Urion, Saint-Martin* in Côte-d'Or, *Grisard, Encendré* in Haute-Marne and Côte-d'Or, *Chamoisien* in Aisne, *Nerre* in Haute-Marne, *Mureau* at Vitteau (Côte-d'Or), *Brégin Bleu* or *Brézin de Pampan* at Gy (Haute-Saône), *Grison* at Dole.

Bunches small, cylindrical, compact.

The grapes are spherical or slightly ovoid, coloured black or blue-grey and pruinose (giving it its name of *enfariné*, which in French means 'covered in flour').

This variety is related to the Gueuche Noir, but its dentation is more pointed and its leaf blade is not downy. It is productive, yielding large amounts of very acidic, astringent and acrid wine. It has not been classified, but there are still some hectares of it remaining in Jura.

Entre-Deux-Mers and Entre-Deux-Mers-Haut-Benauge

The Entre-Deux-Mers region is situated between the rivers Garonne and Dordogne. It is shaped like a triangle, with the two rivers forming two sides, and the boundary between the *département* of Gironde and the *départements* of the Dordogne and Lot-et-Garonne forming the third. With its numerous valleys scattered with abbeys and farmhouses, it is a very pleasant region to travel through.

The *appellation d'origine contrôlée* Entre-Deux-Mers, created by decree on 31 July 1937, is reserved for dry white wines made from grapes harvested on the territories of the following *appellations*: Premières Côtes de Bordeaux, Loupiac, Sainte-Croix-du-Mont, Côtes de Bordeaux-Saint-Macaire, Sainte-Foy-Bordeaux and Graves de Vayres. Following the decree of 15 July 1955, the name of Haut-Benauge may be added to that of Entre-Deux-Mers for dry white wines made in the delimited territory of the communes of Arbis, Cantois, Escoussans, Gornac, Ladaux, Mourens, Saint-Pierre-de-Bat, Soulignac and Targon.

To be entitled to either of these *appellations*, the wines should be made from the following grape varieties: the Sémillon, Sauvignon Blanc and Muscadelle varieties, for 70 per cent of the blend; and as secondary vines the Merlot Blanc (up to 30 per cent), and the Colombard, Mauzac and Ugni Blanc varieties (up to 10 per cent).

The minimum sugar content of the must has to be 144g per litre and the wines should have a minimum alcohol content of 10° and a maximum of 13°. The residual sugar content in the wine has to be less than 4g per litre, following the decree of 14 December 1977. The base yield is 60hl/ha.

In 1985, the extent of the Entre-Deux-Mers *appellation* was 2,339ha and 118,740hl were produced, more than a quarter of this figure by cooperatives. The Entre-Deux-Mers-Haut-Benauge *appellation* produced 11,255hl.

The white wines of the Entre-Deux-Mers generally have more secondary, fermentation aromas than primary, fruit aromas. They are light and lively in the mouth; their acidity, which was very high in the 1960s, has greatly diminished in the 1980s, making them more palatable, but without removing their freshness. These are wines to drink young.

Espanenc Noir

This grape variety, classed as 'recommended' in Hautes-Alpes and as 'authorized' in Alpes-Maritimes and Alpes-de-Haute-Provence, is said to be the same as the Marocain Noir, a table grape variety grown on about 100ha in these three *départements*. In the Nice area, another table grape, the Danugue, is known by a similar name: Espagnin.

A wine-producing estate near Guillac, in the heart of the Entre-Deux-Mers region. Every little valley in this area of gentle hills conceals an abbey or a small château.

Étoile *See* L'Étoile.

Etraire de la Dui

Synonyms: *Etraire de l'Adui, Etraire de la Dot, Etraire de l'Adu, Grosse Etraire, Betu, Beccu de l'Adui.*

Growing tips open, felty white with carmine margins.

Young leaves downy with bronze patches.

Leaves medium sized, orbicular, dark green, slightly concave, thick, crimped at the petiolar junction, usually five-lobed with narrow and often closed lateral sinuses, petiolar sinus lyrate, closed, base of the veins red; dentation narrow, ogival; underside of blade arachnoid in tufts, lightly pubescent, rough. The foliage reddens slightly in the autumn.

Green shoots soft, ribbed, arachnoid with longitudinal brown striations; tendrils long, fleshy and green.

Bunches small, cylindrical, compact; grapes ellipsoidal to olive-shaped, blue-black and juicy; ripening period: second epoch, late.

This variety is said to be a seedling of the Persan, found at the Mas de l'Adui, at Saint-Ismier in Isère. It became popular during the phylloxera crisis, because it was thought to have resistance to the insect. In fact, the Etraire is simply a very vigorous vine that nevertheless succumbs in the end. It must be pruned long in order to obtain a satisfactory product. Its wine is very acid, deeply coloured (three times more deeply coloured than that of the Aramon), but relatively weak in alcohol. It is classed as 'recommended' in Isère, and is grown on 50ha.

THE MICROBIOLOGY OF WINE

The microbes that exist on grapes, in must or in wine are responsible for various types of beneficial fermentation, but they are also responsible for activities that are damaging to the vinification process and to the preservation of wines. It is therefore necessary to encourage the development of some microbes and counteract the growth of others.

Grapes are not very favourable media for the development of microbes, because they contain few nitrogenous substances and have a low pH. Wine, with its alcohol component, is still less favourable to microbe development. These factors mean that no pathogenic germs are to be found in wine.

Three types of microbe take part in the making of wine. These are moulds, in particular *Botrytis cinerea*; yeasts; and lactic bacteria. Depending on the circumstances, they may have a positive or a negative effect.

Botrytis cinerea

This mould, which develops on the skin of the grape, has a positive value when it affects certain ripe white grape varieties as *pourriture noble* (noble rot). The production of fine sweet white wines such as Sauternes or Coteaux du Layon is then possible. More frequently, however, this mould has negative effects.

As *pourriture grise* (grey rot, or botrytis), it produces glucans, polymers of glucose which impede the clarification of the wine. It also generates laccase, a soluble enzyme that oxidizes polyphenolic compounds, modifies the colour of the wine and can give it an unpleasant taste.

Yeasts and alcoholic fermentation

Yeasts, whether indigenous or exogenous, play an important role in alcoholic fermentation. Very many species and strains of yeast are present on the vine and the grape, as well as in the must, in wine and in wine cellars. They may be differentiated notably by their morphology, their means of reproduction and their metabolism, in particular with respect to sugars. Moreover, within a given species there are numerous strains that may be distinguished by one or several characteristics that may have an influence on vinification, such as resistance to alcohol, a potential for flocculation or the production of sulphur dioxide.

Yeast cells vary in dimension from 2 to 10 thousandths of a millimetre. They also vary in shape: spherical, elliptical, apiculate... They reproduce by budding, fission, or the formation of spores, which, after germination, form new yeast cells.

No yeast is present inside the grape itself, but only on its surface. As soon as the grapes have been crushed or pressed into must, a rapid multiplication of two types of yeast takes place: apiculate yeasts of the *Hanseniaspora* genus, which are very numerous but have a low resistance to alcohol; and elliptical yeasts called *Saccharomyces cerevisiae*, which permit the transformation of sugar into alcohol.

It is therefore strains of *Saccharomyces cerevisiae* that are responsible for alcoholic fermentation, the main process by which grapes are transformed into wine. These yeasts multiply thanks to a fermentative metabolism and fairly quickly reach a population of 10 to 100 million cells per millilitre of must.

The two main grape sugars, glucose and fructose, are essentially transformed by the yeasts into ethanol (alcohol) and carbon dioxide. This transformation is accompanied by the release of 25.4 kilocalories of heat per 180g of sugar. Glycerol, esters, and the higher alcohols of ethyl aldehyde, acetic acid and succinic acid are other by-products of this process. Some of these products are sometimes particularly desirable in the production of certain wines. This is the case, for example, of acetaldehyde, which is essential for the manufacture of wines that are to age under a veil of yeast, such as the *vin jaune* of the Jura.

Saccharomyces cerevisiae also metabolizes up to 40 per cent of the malic acid present in the grapes to produce ethanol (alcohol), and this has the effect of diminishing the overall acidity of the wine. Some other species of yeast, such as *Schizosaccharomyces*, are capable of metabolizing all of the malic acid, and are used in certain cases to obtain wines devoid of malic acid.

When the yeast has completed alcoholic fermentation, it is able to diffuse amino acids and nucleotides into the medium of

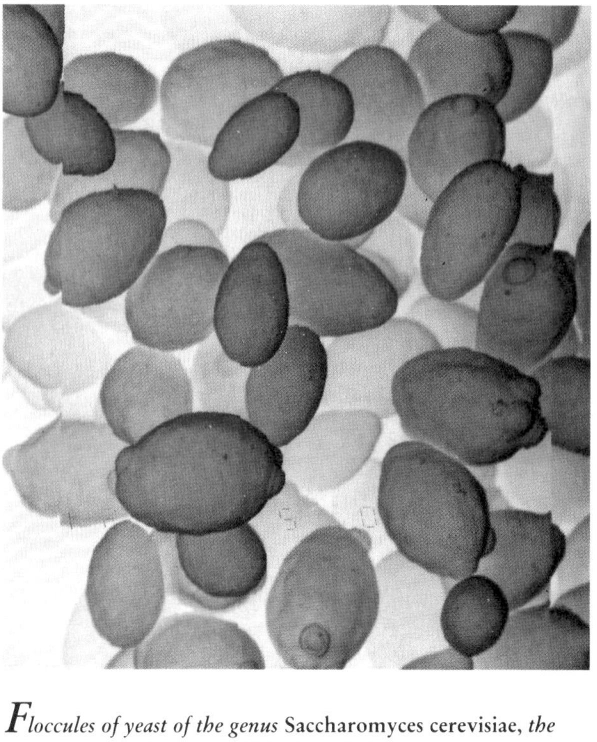

Floccules of yeast of the genus **Saccharomyces cerevisiae**, *the yeast strain used to accomplish alcoholic fermentation.*

the wine. The wine's amino acid composition is thus different from the amino acid composition of the must. In addition to this, when the yeast has stopped developing, it autolyses, i.e. it destroys itself, breaking up its own cell structure. The length of this operation depends on the strains of yeast involved and the type of wine medium. It may take place after a delay of several months and last several years. The slow autolysis of yeast is desirable in the production of sparkling wines by the *méthode champenoise*.

The yeasts also absorb sulphates and the sulphurated amino acids present in the must and, from these substrates, produce sulphur dioxide, which has the advantage of protecting the wine against oxidization, but the disadvantage of hindering the secondary fermentation in bottle of sparkling wines made according to the *méthode champenoise*. Other yeast products — hydrogen sulphide and the thiols (mercaptans) — may give the wine undesirable odours.

Finally, some strains of yeast attack certain polyphenolic compounds, causing the appearance of volatile phenols that have a very weak aromatic threshold, which is sometimes useful and sometimes harmful, depending on whether the phenols are a desired aromatic component or not of the wine.

A halt in alcoholic fermentation can have several causes: insufficient *remontage* (pumping over of the must) with a consequent lack of aeration, too high a fermentation temperature, the presence of fungicidal products in the must, or the inhibitory action of ethanol (alcohol) itself. But it has also been demonstrated that, while it is growing, yeast secretes inhibitory substances of its own, mainly fatty acids, which act in synergy with the ethanol. This is why yeast preparations called *écorces de levures* are added to fermenting musts. These absorb a number of the inhibitory fatty acids and stimulate alcoholic fermentation, or at least prevent halts in fermentation.

The 'killer mechanism' in yeasts also plays an important role in vinification. A killer yeast is one that secretes a toxin that kills strains of sensitive yeasts. Neutral strains also exist that do not produce toxins, and are resistant to them. This mechanism is of fundamental importance in the competition between strains of yeast. It is therefore better to use neutral or killer strains exclusively for yeasting so as to avoid selected yeasts being quickly eliminated by indigenous killers.

Factors such as temperature encourage or inhibit the development of the yeasts, which multiply between 13°C and 38°C. As the alcohol content increases, yeasts become more temperature-sensitive. It is therefore often necessary to heat the must in order to facilitate the onset of alcoholic fermentation, but equally necessary to cool it during fermentation, because the heat is more and more likely to stop the activity of the yeasts as the alcohol level rises.

The presence of oxygen is also necessary for the development of yeasts, particularly at the start of fermentation. It plays an important role in the production of sterols, constituents of the cytoplasmic membrane in yeasts. The sterols increase the membrane's permeability to the ethanol (alcohol) formed inside the cell and thus avert an accumulation of this substance which would soon become toxic for the yeast and would lead to a halt in fermentation.

The resistance of yeasts to ethanol (alcohol) is very variable, depending on the strains. Some grow sensitive to its presence at around 4 to 5 per cent, some at 11 to 12 per cent and some at as much as 18 to 20 per cent. This is a factor that should be taken into account in yeast selection, according to the type of wine to be produced.

Impurities formed of yeasts, and crystals of cream of tartar and calcium tartrate.

The pH of the must and the wine does not harm the development of the yeasts. Yeasts are, though, sensitive to inhibitors that may be contributed by the grape, such as fungicides, or to inhibitors added in the process of vinification, and particularly when the termination of fermentation is required for sweet wines, such as sorbic acid and sulphur dioxide.

Today, the alcoholic fermentation of grapes is never carried out by means of a pure strain of yeast. Instead, a number of selected yeasts are chosen according to the type of wine to be made. The criteria used are partly technical (rapid onset of fermentation, resistance to alcohol, good production of alcohol, adaptation to extremes of temperature, high production of glycerol, low production of acetic acid, metabolism of malic acid, resistance to the killer mechanism, ease of preparation in dry form, ease of use), and partly organoleptic (production of particular aromas, absence of production of unpleasant or inappropriate tastes).

In order to be effective, selected strains of yeast should be added after the maximum possible elimination of indigenous yeasts from the grape skins or wine-making equipment. This elimination is achieved by the addition of sulphur dioxide, by centrifugation or by filtration. It is advisable to use a comparatively large quantity of yeast (about 3 to 5 per cent of vat capacity). The yeasting is carried out either by using a *pied de cuve* (a yeast starter, prepared in a small quantity of must beforehand: this is the method employed when wild yeasts are to be used for fermentation), or by adding commercial yeast

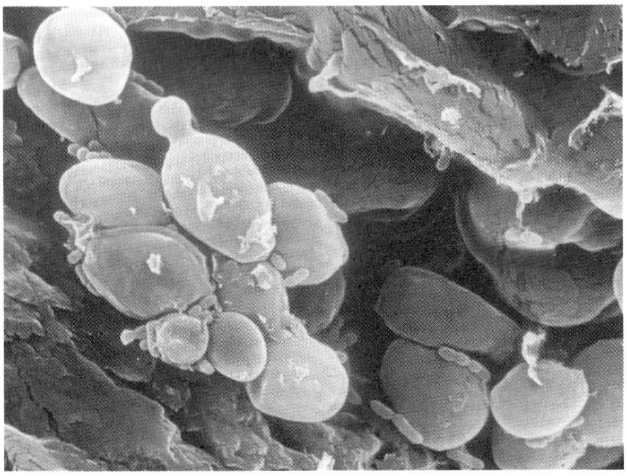

Yeasts and lactic bacteria.

starters in either liquid or powder form. Yeasts in powder form are called active dry yeasts. They first became available in 1973, and are now the most commonly used type. They have many advantages: a high density of living yeasts (30,000 million per gram), good preservation, good speed of rehydration, great ease of use.

The aim of alcoholic fermentation is generally to obtain good levels of ethanol (alcohol) and by-products, and to ensure the complete conversion of sugars. This result is obtained by adequate preparation of the must, and by adding selected yeasts according to the type of wine required.

Lactic bacteria and malolactic fermentation

Lactic bacteria are characterized by the production of lactic acid from various substrates. These bacteria, which are of still smaller dimensions that yeasts, reproduce by fission and can achieve population levels of 10^9 cells per millilitre. They do not, though, produce spores, and are thus less resistant than yeasts, particularly to heat. They exist in wine in spherical form (cocci) or rod-shaped form (bacilli).

Four main species of lactic bacteria are found on the vine and in grapes, must, wines and wine-making cellars. These are the leuconostoc, heterolactic and pediococcus bacteria, and lactobacilli (homolactic and heterolactic).

These bacteria attack sugars, producing mainly lactic acid, acetic acid, carbon dioxide and ethanol (alcohol). But they are capable of attacking numerous substrates other than sugars, in particular malic acid. This acid is then transformed into lactic acid and carbon dioxide. The fermentation produced by lactic bacteria, which is called malolactic fermentation, is desirable in the production of almost all red wines, because it helps to stabilize them and to improve their organoleptic qualities, by removing the sharpness of the malic acid and helping aromatic development.

Malolactic fermentation is not always wanted for the vinification of white wine, because the disappearance of malic acid is not necessarily an advantage, particularly in so far as taste is concerned. Some white wines, like those of Alsace, are better able to preserve fruit aroma without malolactic fermentation taking place.

Four factors play an important role in the development of these bacteria: temperature; pH; the presence of amino acids and growth factors in the medium; and the presence of inhibitors, in particular sulphur dioxide, which is used to avoid oxidization, but which also limits fermentation, in particular lactic fermentation. It should be noted that some strains of lactic bacteria are not greatly affected by high alcohol levels, and can develop in dessert wines.

In practice, in order to encourage malolactic fermentation, the following three conditions are important: the temperature should be above 18°C; total acidity should not be too high (some chemical deacidification may be necessary in order to achieve this); and the addition of sulphur dioxide should be done in moderation.

Lactic bacterial starters do exist. They are usually formed of leuconostoc bacteria or lactobacilli, and have to be reactivated before use, preferably in a wine medium. A certain number of oenologists also use wines in the process of malolactic fermentation as starters for other wines, or they obtain the lactic bacteria from these wines by centrifugation. But, despite progress made in recent research, malolactic fermentation remains a stage of vinification that has yet to be fully understood and mastered.

Microbiological analyses

Microbiological analyses have several purposes in oenology: to check the yeast starters used; to check the indigenous yeast populations in a must before culturing; to check the rate of yeast cell proliferation in the wine; and to check on the presence or absence of small microbiological populations in the wine before it is marketed.

The techniques used are traditional laboratory culture methods in a liquid or solid medium. They require between three and eight days to produce results.

In practice, the development of yeasts is checked by measuring the rate of sugar consumption in fermenting must. The multiplication of lactic bacteria is checked by enzymatic measurement of the transformation of malic acid into lactic acid in the must. The small populations of living germs in finished wines are evaluated by fine filtration methods, which enable exact microbiological populations to be determined per 500ml or 1 litre units of wine.

Several avenues of research are being pursued today with the aim of improving the process of fermentation. They follow three main directions.

The first of these is an improvement in the choice of yeast strains available, achieved by selection or by genetic engineering. Researchers are also working on ways of improving the process of alcoholic fermentation, in particular as far as the roles played by temperature and oxygen are concerned. The results of this research would be an organoleptic improvement in the wine, the disappearance of breaks in fermentation, and savings in investment and operation of equipment. Finally, researchers are trying to control populations of chosen microbial strains — yeasts or lactic bacteria — particularly by using the technique of germs fixed in or included in a gel. This last avenue of research is of particular relevance to the control of malolactic fermentation and the *prise de mousse* stage (secondary fermentation in bottle) in the manufacture of sparkling wines.

THE *ÉLEVAGE* AND MATURATION OF WINE

Like all living beings, wine is sensitive . . . sensitive to microbes, to epidemics, to indifferent treatment. Its health, and the balance of its tastes, can be spoiled or even destroyed. It is therefore essential to give careful attention to wine, at every stage from vinification to bottling, to ensure that it develops as satisfactorily as possible.

After fermentation, wine is rough, cloudy, full of carbon dioxide and lees. In the mouth, it is green and astringent. Its true character will not emerge until after a period of *élevage*, consisting of a series of meticulously overseen stages to help it towards its final resting place — the bottle — where it will enjoy the peaceful years of maturation.

The length of *élevage* depends on the type of wine required. *Primeur* wines, for example, are bottled soon after the completion of vinification; while red wines that require a period of ageing before achieving maturity are given an *élevage* of six to eighteen months.

Premises and equipment

At the end of fermentation, the wine is put in a vat or a cask, depending on regional customs, the quantities of wine involved, the quality desired and the final destination of the wine. The greatest wines are generally given an *élevage* in oak barrels, because the wood, especially when it is young and air-dried, gives them fine and desirable aromas. This expensive and laborious method of *élevage* is only worthwhile for wines of reputation.

Whatever the method chosen, it is essential to ensure that the premises, *cuveries* (fermenting rooms) and *chais* (storage areas) are clean. The best type of fermenting room, suitable for the vinification of a large quantity of wine, will be spacious, well ventilated, protected from variations in temperature and above all easy to wash down and clean.

As for *chais*, they should meet the same standards of hygiene: well-ventilated premises with clean, washable walls. Too great a circulation of air, and large variations in temperature, should be avoided.

The hygiene that is indispensable in the premises should, of course, also be extended to the equipment used in the *élevage* of the wine. All vats have to be cleaned and scaled of tartrates periodically, regardless of the material they are made of (wood, cement or stainless steel). Tartar, a compound of bitartrate, can in fact form pockets that provide ideal hiding places for the bacteria that may contaminate wine. These pockets are also responsible for unpleasant tastes in wine due to the spoilage of the organic matter and lees that get caught in them.

Scaling is carried out by brushing, scraping or, if the layer is very thick, by applying a solvent solution. Empty wooden vats should always be kept dry. Very regular sulphuring is necessary to keep them aseptic.

Barrels or casks should also be kept clean, especially if they have already been used. Low standards of barrel maintenance and hygiene will increase the risk of microbial contamination, unpleasant odours and high volatile acidity in the wine. The barrels should be systematically washed with a pressurized hose, then drained and completely dried, before being fumigated with sterilizing sulphur. They should then be hermetically sealed. The fumigation should be repeated about every two months. The best solution of all is never to leave a barrel empty. This is why wine is traditionally bottled shortly before the grape harvest. The barrels are then filled with wine from the previous year, until that point stored in vats, and the vats themselves are filled with new wine.

Depending on their original quality, new barrels may also need to be '*affranchi*' ('freed'), i.e. the wood is cleaned with cold sulphured water, with boiling water or with steam, to reduce the sawdust and other 'new wood' elements that could otherwise dominate the wine.

The stages of *élevage*

Young wine is characterized by varying degrees of cloudiness and a certain viscosity, attributable to particles of grape matter, yeasts and bacteria still in suspension in it.

The first stage of a wine's *élevage* consists in clarifying it by racking (siphoning of the wine from one container to another). This operation is particularly important and its success conditions the quality of the wine to come, because if the wine was left in contact with the sediment, it would encourage the development of microorganisms and would soon give the wine an unpleasant smell.

In addition, racking releases the carbon dioxide remaining in the wine after fermentation. This gas is only discernible to the taste when it is present in the proportion of 500mg per litre. Though it is normal to find it in *primeur* wines, its presence is not satisfactory in older wines, apart from Muscadet *sur lie* (bottled directly from its lees) or sparkling wines.

Racking also aerates young wine. This process begins the wine's maturation, gives it its first refinements, and enables it to get rid of its very youthful character. In the case of red wines, this contact with the air makes the wines more supple.

The number of rackings a wine receives varies according to the character of the wines and the average temperature of the *chai* or *cuverie*, but the first one is always carried out after the malolactic fermentation is complete. If the wine is being stored in cask, it generally receives three or four rackings during the first year — in November, March, June and September — and two or three rackings in the second year. Wines kept in vats are treated in more or less the same way.

Racking casks or barrels is carried out by means of bellows, taps or siphons. The wine is drained off from the first cask or barrel into the new one by gravity until the lees appear. The operation is then stopped.

Vats are racked by means of a tap. The first racking takes place with exposure of the wine to the air, while during subsequent ones the wine is protected from the air. A light filtering may accompany the third racking, if there is still a considerable quantity of grape matter and yeast in the wine.

To avoid *piqûre acétique* (acescence or souring of wine) connected with microbial proliferation and other forms of spoilage, it is advisable to protect the wine from oxidization by filling up wine-containing vessels regularly: this is called ullaging (as, paradoxically, is its opposite: leaving casks part-empty). The frequency of ullaging depends on various factors, including the level of humidity and ventilation in the storage area, and the nature of the containers themselves.

If the wine is kept in a cask or barrel, the wine maker takes his *noyau* (a wine grower's tool used in cellar work) and removes the bung from the cask using this. He then fills up the barrel with an *ouillette*, a small receptacle with a curved spout, and restops it. This is done weekly. Vats are equipped with hatches made of cement, cast iron or plastic, finished with a bung through which the same filling operation may be carried out. Completely airtight installations also exist, should these be required.

The quality of the wine used for ullaging must always be equal to the quality of the wine in the cask or vat.

Towards the end of the period of *élevage*, fining takes place: this is a clarifying and stabilizing operation carried out by adding a protein product that flocculates in the wine and slowly sinks down through it, taking all suspended impurities with it. Among the authorized fining agents, gelatine and egg white are both widely used, especially for fining red wines.

In most cases, the wine is finally filtered through a plate or membrane filter before being bottled.

Bottling

At this stage in its evolution, the wine, which is perfectly clear and stable, should be bottled. Care and cleanliness are once again all-important, because sloppy bottling can compromise the maturing of the wine. The risks of contamination from equipment and glass are great. Damage can also occur if the wine is given too much exposure to the air. Finally, precautions should be taken to ensure that airtight corking takes place.

The colour of the bottles is another factor of importance. It varies from region to region and from wine to wine, but it should always be dark enough to protect the wine from the light. It has, in fact, been established that wine always ages more quickly in transparent bottles than it does in coloured ones, even if the cellar is dark.

It is essential that the bottles should be absolutely clean. The process most often used for new bottles is a mechanical hot water wash. The re-use of old bottles is risky, even if they are thoroughly cleaned by immersion in hot water containing detergent, and with brushing and rinsing under pressure. The main difficulty in the bottling process lies in filling the bottle with the precise volume of wine required by the regulations, while leaving room for the cork, and for an increase in volume of the wine caused by changes in its temperature.

In some very small properties, bottles are still filled directly from the cask tap, but the rate and quality of this sort of bottling are far from ideal. This is why bottling machines have become widespread.

The stopping of the bottle with a cork is carried out by a corking machine. A new, good-quality cork is compressed by mechanical 'jaws' so that it is smaller than the neck of the bottle, into which it is then pushed by a vertical piston.

The maturing of wine

A distinction should be drawn between two types of maturation: reductive and oxidative. The first type is that maturation that keeps the wine more or less protected from the oxygen in the air; this is the type undergone by classic wines, both red and white, which do not develop properly until they have spent some time in airtight bottles. The second method consists in keeping the wine under the constant influence of the oxygen in the air; this is the method applied to most of the French *vins doux naturels* (sweet fortified wines) and *vin jaunes* (wines aged under a veil of yeast).

Red wine maturation

After it has completed alcoholic and malolactic fermentation, red wine is characterized by fruity smells, a tannic astringency on the palate that is sometimes rough, bitter and reinforced by the presence of carbon dioxide from the fermentations, a lack of clarity, and a dark red colour with tinges of violet. In some cases the fruity character is more marked and pleasant, and the tannic character is weaker. But the richness in phenolic compounds, particularly tannins, is the main factor governing the longevity of red wine.

By gauging the level of tannins, red wine may be divided into three categories: fruity wines, with little tannic structure, which are best drunk young and which cannot age for more than three years; very tannic wines, in youth bitter and astringent, but capable of great longevity and of developing suppleness with time; and balanced wines that combine the smell and attraction of fruit with a tannic richness that allows them to age for up to twenty years.

During ageing, which begins with *élevage*, the colour of red wine develops, because the substances responsible for colour change. Red wine loses its vivacity: the violet hue gradually gives way to a more yellow shade of red, often called brick-red or tile-red. In a young wine, 40 per cent of the colour is due to free anthocyanins, 50 per cent to tannin-anthocyanin combinations and about 10 per cent to condensed tannins. During the first three years, the free anthocyanins diminish by 80 per cent; they disappear altogether at the end of five to ten years. The red tannin-anthocyanin combinations vary little, but diminish slowly. On the other hand, the tannins condensed with polysaccharides, salts or acids, increase regularly.

At the beginning of *élevage*, red wines require a certain amount of aeration. This is achieved either by the gradual diffusion of air through the wood of a cask, or, if the wine is undergoing *élevage* in vat, by periodic aeration when racking takes place. Racking allows the wine to become saturated with oxygen (about 8mg per litre). Aeration encourages the polymerization of the anthocyanins and their combination with the tannins: the result is an increase in the intensity of colour.

For this reason wine stored in airtight conditions is always less highly coloured than wine stored in a vat and racked regularly, or wine stored in cask. Organoleptic characteristics evolve along a similar path. Wines that are stored in airtight conditions have an unpleasant, stuffy smell; they are thin, short and often bitter, and they develop little. Wines that have been judiciously aerated are more complex. They may have

ÉLEVAGE IN CASK

After malolactic fermentation, the great red wines of Bordeaux and Burgundy are traditionally given an élevage *in oak casks. This enables the wine to receive a slow aeration through the wood and the bung, and to rid itself of its carbon dioxide. The colour becomes intensified and the wine clears and settles more quickly than in a vat, because the wood fibres retain solid microparticles from the wine.*

Oak wood modifies the character of wine to such a point that it can become — as people often confuse the smell of oak with bouquet in general — the only criterion for recognizing old wine. However, far from hiding the typical qualities of the wine, the wood should in fact remain discreetly in the background and should do no more than increase the complexity of the aroma.

Oak adds tannins that are different from those of the grape to the wine: coumarins, acids and odorous substances. These substances may come from the wood itself, from its pyrolysis during the heating required for cask manufacture, or from reactions produced on contact with the wine. They are mostly phenolic compounds. The most characteristic of them are vanillin, syringaldehyde and scopoletin. Apart from the dominant vanilla perfume, a coconut scent may very often be detected and other phenolic smells include those of carnations, cloves, leather, smoke, burning, liquorice and coffee.

The wood also adds ellagic tannins to the wine which can reinforce its astringency and bitterness, but can also contribute to the structure and the volume of wine in the mouth.

The wood's contribution decreases as it ages. The younger and smaller the cask and the longer the stay in it, the more the wine will be affected by it. However, keeping wine in cask causes a loss of 0.3° of alcohol per year, and wood also transfers a little acetic acid to the wine. To avoid any loss of quality due to these factors, the wine should not be kept in cask for more than two years; indeed élevage *in general is best limited to a period of between 3 and 24 months.*

lost intensity and fruit, but they are fleshier, rounder, and last longer in the mouth than wines that have not undergone aeration. Five rackings with aeration, one month apart from each other, are enough to produce the best result. Further aeration should then be avoided, and the wine should be protected from excess oxidization by the addition of a sufficient quantity of sulphur dioxide. Thanks to these successive rackings, the wine becomes clear and loses carbon dioxide from the fermentations. Part of its acidity disappears through the precipitation of tartrates. The reduced astringency of the tannins, the loss of carbon dioxide and the decrease in acidity all work together. The wine seems to be more and more fleshy and fat. As soon as it is judged sufficiently supple to the taste, it is bottled to preserve maximum fruitiness.

The wine continues to age in the bottle, isolated from the air. Bottles should be stored on their sides to ensure that the corks are completely airtight. The temperature should remain constant and should be lower than 15°C. Variations in temperature cause the wine to expand and to ooze past the cork and out of the bottle, or to push out the cork. Air then enters the bottle, causing an undesirable oxidization of the wine. Wines that do not undergo *élevage* in cask should in fact have a bouquet that is purely reductive.

After bottling, the smells of fruit and oak gradually become blurred, as the polysaccharides, salts and tannins continue to combine. The concentration of tannins, and consequently the astringency of the wine, diminishes. After two to three years, red wines can lose their initial smell (primary and secondary aromas). But the development of a bouquet (tertiary aroma) takes time and, in some great red wines, a tannic dumbness dominates completely during this middle period. The wine seems disappointing. It is necessary to wait for the bouquet to develop. The notion of 'bouquet' is, in any case, difficult to define. The chemical nature of the substances that appear at this later stage is unknown. Among those scents that seem to develop with time are violet, blackcurrant, cigar, liquorice, faded rose, black cherry, Morello cherry, crystallized cherry, coffee, cocoa, bay leaf, cinnamon, pepper, resin, cloves, truffles, musk, leather, fur, venison, and finally the scents of tea, hay, dry leaves and humus.

White wine maturation

Most white wines are appreciated for their floral and fruity scents that come from the grape (primary aroma) or from fermentation (secondary aroma). But some are appreciated for their tertiary aroma or bouquet: the scents they acquire with age. They are often among the most famous (white wines from Burgundy or Bordeaux, the Grands Crus of Alsace . . .).

Bottling is carried out relatively speedily: three to eight months after the harvest, to preserve as much of the wine's fruitiness as possible. Any period of *élevage* in cask should be short — eight months at most. The wine acquires the smell of hazelnuts, grilled almonds or crusty bread from the oak.

Development in bottle can take place over anything from two to ten years. The colour changes and becomes darker. The wine loses its hardness and becomes more balanced, complex and rich in aromatic nuances.

During the ageing process, floral smells of rose, lemon balm and elder flower decline, as do the fruity smells of banana and apple. The esters responsible for these smells are reduced by hydrolysis, which occurs more quickly the more acid a wine is, and the higher the temperature it is kept at. Though less floral and fruity, aged white wine acquires the smell of crystallized fruit, of 'petrol' in the case of the Riesling grape variety, and of truffles. With more age still, it may develop hints of Reinette apples, lemon, apricot, plums and cinnamon.

At the same time, overall acidity decreases. This development, like the aromatic changes described above, accelerates if the wine is stored at a warm temperature. The wine becomes more mellow, more harmonious and more balanced.

WINE DISEASES

MICROBIAL SPOILAGE

During its vinification and maturation, wine may lose its qualities or even become unfit for consumption because of spoilage caused by the development of microorganisms. To combat these, it is necessary to understand and control every stage of the fermentation of grapes, and above all to maintain the highest standards of hygiene in harvest and vinification practices.

Microbial spoilage is characterized by a cloudiness, a scum or a deposit in wines, by the release of gas, or by a modification in the structure of a wine, its viscosity, its composition or its flavour. Three types of microorganisms are responsible for these diseases. These are yeasts, lactic bacteria and acetic bacteria.

Spoilage of wine caused by yeasts

All yeasts may, depending on the time and place of their development, behave like germs and spoil wines. For example, the *Saccharomyces cerevisiae* responsible for alcoholic fermentation can also be the cause of unwanted refermentation of sweet wines in the bottle, producing gas, cloudiness, flakes or deposits. A bad choice of yeast, or badly selected yeasts, may cause various other problems: the production of an unwanted sparkle in the wine, the production of sulphur dioxide, or the appearance of a phenolic (carbolic) taste, of unpleasant higher alcohols, esters or smells. These latter problems could also be due to the development of undesirable indigenous yeasts, or the presence of fungicidal products, in the must. Some species of yeast, the *Zygosaccharomyces*, are responsible for spoilage resulting from refermentation of the sugars. Others, such as the *Schizosaccharomyces*, act as spoiling germs when they develop spontaneously. They provoke exaggerated deacidification, particularly in continuous vinificators and in wines vinified under temperature-controlled conditions.

However, the most frequent form of spoilage is the work of yeasts that form a scum or 'veil' on the surface of the wine. The development of such yeasts is encouraged in certain types of wine, such as fino sherry or the *vin jaune* of the Jura, but most of the time it is considered to be an unwanted phenomenon, the work of strains belonging to the *Candida, Pichia, Hansenula, Debaryomyces* or *Brettanomyces* genera. The most frequent form of this type of spoilage is known in France as the *maladie de la fleur* (flower disease). The strains responsible belong to the *Candida* genus. They break alcohol up into carbon dioxide and water. Acetaldehyde may simultaneously appear in large quantities. In addition to the scum on the surface, the wine takes on an unpleasant aroma and a yellow tinge, due to the combination of alcohol and polyphenols.

Aeration is necessary for the development and aggravation of this disease. Its symptoms are often slight, limited to the formation of a thin scum on the surface of young wines, low in alcohol and stored in bottles kept upright and plastic capped, without corks.

More serious symptoms, characterized by the presence of volatile acidity and, in particular, of ethyl acetate, may occur if certain other strains of yeast develop, notably the *Brettanomyces*. These are responsible for a mousy taste in the wine, due to the production of acetylpyridine.

Spoilage caused by lactic bacteria

This sort of spoilage is generally much more serious than that caused by yeasts. It can occur during breaks in alcoholic fermentation, while the wine is being stored in cask, or even sometimes in bottle.

It is characterized by a modification in the gustative balance of the wine, as well as by the presence of volatile acidity, of gas and of cloudiness followed by a deposit, generally on a smaller scale than in the case of yeast-based diseases.

A distinction is made between various types of spoilage by lactic bacteria, depending on the medium from which they develop. Some develop from sugars, some from organic acids and some from glycerol.

Spoilage caused by sugars

Piqûre lactique (lactic acescence) mainly affects musts that still contain sugar after a break in fermentation has occurred, or sweet wines. It can also take place in fortified wines that are rich in sugars and alcohol. The lactic bacterium transforms part of the sugars into lactic acid, carbon dioxide and acetic acid. The production of acetic acid per unit of sugar broken up varies greatly, depending on the bacterial strain involved, the nature of the sugars broken up and the presence of acceptors of hydrogen such as dissolved oxygen.

Mannitol, a substance responsible for the spoilage of mannite, may be formed from levulose in the must. In this case, relatively large amounts of acetic acid may appear. In addition, if they are not consumed by the yeasts, pentose sugars will, under such circumstances, inevitably be transformed into acetic acid, expressed as sulphuric acid. This disease, which is closely linked to the pH of the wine, is encouraged by malolactic fermentation and all other forms of deacidification. It is liable to occur if alcoholic fermentation flags or halts, if untimely additions of sugar are made to the must, or if musts have large residual sugar contents.

In cases where part-fermented musts are affected, the disease may be combated by using technology that allows the alcoholic fermentation to be carried out completely and rapidly. In other cases, if the spoilage is slight and involves small quantities of residual sugar or of pentose, stabilization treatment should be carried out as quickly as possible: racking, sulphurization and clarification.

La graisse ('ropiness') is a disease caused by certain strains of leuconostoc bacteria. These surround themselves with sheaths formed of polysaccharides from the sugars. The wine then starts to look oily and ropy.

This is not a serious problem, and it occurs mostly in the more northern French wine-growing regions. It is treated by beating and aerating the wine, then treating it with sulphur and finally filtering it.

Spoilage caused by organic acids

Lactic bacteria can attack malic, tartaric and citric acid in wine. The first two, when attacked, are normally changed into lactic acid. This is the phenomenon of malolactic fermentation, so often encouraged. However, if it occurs after bottling, this fermentation produces carbon dioxide in the wine, as well as volatile acidity and a slight cloudiness. Citric acid, which only exists in very small quantities in wine but is sometimes added to it, breaks up when attacked by lactic bacteria to form lactic acid, acetic acid and, above all, diacetyl, which gives the wine an unpleasant buttery taste.

The most serious spoilage due to the effect of lactic bacteria on wine acids is *la tourne* (tartaric fermentation). In this case, tartaric acid is attacked in an abnormal way. The result is a release of gas, a decrease in fixed acidity, an increase in volatile acidity and the development of a peculiar visual appearance. However, few lactic bacteria possess the enzymatic equipment necessary to attack tartaric acid in this way. For this reason, tartaric fermentation only occurs in wines with a high pH (above 3.4) which have been subject to a miscalculated or mishandled process of deacidification.

Spoilage caused by glycerol

The *maladie de l'amer* (bitter fermentation) is characterized by the fact that glycerol, a by-product of alcoholic fermentation, is transformed into lactic acid, acetic acid and carbon dioxide. Sometimes acrolein is formed during this process and this substance, by combining with polyphenols in the wine, makes it taste bitter. It is, unfortunately, easily distilled and so, if the disease occurs in base wines for distilling, acrolein can give brandies a tart smell. The disease develops mostly in wines with a high pH.

Various other types of spoilage

Lactic bacteria are also responsible for the formation of more or less temporary 'off' odours produced from the sugars or from citric acid. In some wines, they are also able to produce histamine. This product can be moderately toxic, which might explain the undesirable effects certain wines have on their drinkers.

Finally, sorbic acid, a yeast-inhibiting substance which is authorized for the stabilization of some sweet wines, can — when attacked by lactic bacteria — give wines an unpleasant taste of geranium.

Diseases due to lactic bacteria are often brought on by a hesitant progress of alcoholic fermentation. The use of appropriate fermentation controls and correct storage after fermentation allows the great majority of unpleasant developments to be avoided.

Spoilage caused by acetic acid bacteria

Acetic bacteria, or vinegar ferments, provoke *piqûre acétique* (acescence). This is a very serious, though rare, spoilage, occurring only in badly maintained cellars.

It manifests itself as an increase in volatile acidity, a decrease in alcohol content, a weakening of colour and an increase in ethyl acetate. Undesirable at any stage of vinification, acetic bacteria belong to the *Bluconobacter* and *Acetobacter* genera. Some of them form a cellulose-based scum or 'veil' on the surface of the wine, which is sometimes white and thin, sometimes oily and thick, or even very thick. This scum is the vinegar mother. These bacteria sometimes develop in *chais* (or vinification plants) as slimy clusters at points where wine has been allowed to leak, and in pipes that have been left containing a certain quantity of wine. Acetic bacteria are present at all stages of vinification: on the grapes, in the must, in the wine, on the marc left after the vinification of red wine, in receptacles that are not fully filled or are badly protected against oxygen, on floors, walls and equipment. It is therefore always advisable to begin alcoholic fermentation as soon as possible to prevent them from developing. The main substance attacked is alcohol, which, in the presence of oxygen, is transformed into acetic acid and water. Some bacteria, the *Acetobacters*, are even capable of transforming acetic acid into carbon dioxide and water. Others also oxidize lactic acid and glucose, producing aldehydes, ketones, acids and carbon dioxide.

Acescence is always accompanied by the production of ethyl acetate. It is this acetate that is the substance responsible for the characteristic 'vinegar' smell of the wines affected. As little as 150mg of ethyl acetate per litre of wine is enough to produce a noticeably vinegary smell, whereas as much as 0.8g of acetic acid per litre of wine may go undetected by the consumer. Ethyl acetate is, however, a volatile substance that evaporates easily.

Numerous factors play a role in the development of acetic bacteria in wines, the most important of which are oxygen and a warm fermentation temperature. Acetic fermentation is, in fact, twice as rapid at 30°C as it is at 25°C. Acetic bacteria are less sensitive to pH than are lactic bacteria, developing mainly in environments with a pH above 3.2 and with low alcohol levels of less than 10 per cent.

The prevention of microbial spoilage

During the vinification, storage and bottling of wines, a certain number of principles make it possible to guard against or avoid microbial spoilage, whether this be caused by yeast or bacteria. In the first place, the cellar and cellar equipment, which can harbour germs, should be kept in a state of perfect hygiene. Secondly, the number of germs present in the must or wine should be reduced by fining, filtration, centrifugation, thermolysis or pasteurization. When the germ level of the wine has been reduced, and it has been protected from recontamination, sulphur dioxide and sorbic acid may be added, especially to sweet wines. Finally, the wine should be protected from the air by storage in a fully filled container, or by being kept under a blanket of inert gas.

It is always best to carry out a series of microbiological, biochemical and chemical checks on wine to guard against contamination, particularly when the wine is undergoing *élevage* or when it is being bottled. These checks reveal the effectiveness of preventive measures, or a need for further measures and adjustments.

PHYSICOCHEMICAL SPOILAGE AND UNPLEASANT TASTES

Apart from microbial accidents, wines can be spoiled by the appearance of deposits or cloudiness, or by the acquisition of unpleasant tastes. This spoilage is generally caused by the phenomena of oxidization, chemical or enzymatic reduction, or precipitation by crystallization or polymerization, these last two occurrences often being linked.

Significant oxidization of wine may result in a change of colour, a browning, particularly noticeable in the case of white wine, sometimes followed by a precipitation of polyphenolic compounds, especially in the case of red wine, or by a precipitation of iron compounds.

Spoilage linked to oxidization

As wines age, their colour changes. This phenomenon is entirely natural and is often used as a guide to maturity and quality in great wine. On the other hand, young wines can sometimes acquire an amber or brown colour. This change in colour is often accelerated if the wine is being preserved at a high temperature, and in the presence of oxygen. It may be a chemical or an enzymatic change.

If the change is chemical, an oxidization of certain polyphenolic compounds has occurred, generally catalyzed by the presence of metals and a consequent polymerization resulting in precipitation of colouring matter.

If the change is enzymatic, it is often more serious, as the wine may be affected by brown *casse*. This form of spoilage often occurs in wines made from botrytis-affected grapes which are rich in laccase. This enzyme is responsible for a significant oxidization of the polyphenolic compounds, resulting in precipitation of colouring matter.

Excess oxidization can also result in maderization, particularly in the case of white wines: the colour of the wine becomes slightly brown and the smell and taste take on some of the characteristics of madeira, owing to the appearance of acetaldehyde in the wine.

These changes in colour in white wines may be avoided or mitigated by fining with casein, a milk protein, and by the addition of a suitable amount of sulphur dioxide. The problem of brown *casse* is more difficult to solve in red wines, but the techniques of thermovinification allow the enzyme responsible to be destroyed.

The two iron *casses*, further types of spoilage caused by oxidization, are less likely to occur if modern equipment, or equipment finished with a neutral coating, is used in vinification and storage. These iron *casses* in fact only occur when the iron content of the wines is relatively high (more than 10mg per litre). Substances that make the wine cloudy may then form. White *casse*, which occurs mainly in white wines, is caused by a precipitation of iron phosphate. Blue *casse* is caused by the formation of a tannin-iron complex in the wine. This results in a bluish precipitate, and affected white wines will often turn a brownish colour.

These types of spoilage may be prevented by avoiding iron contamination, from agricultural machinery or vinification equipment, at any stage of processing of the grapes or wine. If iron has found its way into the must or wine, citric acid, which forms a soluble complex with the iron, may be added, or a treatment of calcium phytate or potassium ferrocyanide may be applied. This treatment must be carried out by a qualified oenologist.

Spoilage linked to reduction

Unlike the iron *casses*, copper *casse* occurs in reductive (non-oxidizing or airtight) conditions, often some time after bottling, particularly when the bottles are exposed to light and kept at a high temperature. The signs of this *casse* are a cloudiness in the wine, followed by the production of a reddish brown deposit. The cloudiness is caused by the presence of copper sulphide. It occurs in wines that contain large quantities of copper (more than 0.5mg per litre) and hydrogen sulphide, produced by the metabolism of sulphur from sulphur dioxide.

To avoid this type of spoilage, it is necessary to avoid excessive contamination by copper, which may occur as a result of the too-frequent repetition of vine treatments, or be caused by joints in piping at the vinification plant. Affected wine may be treated by potassium ferrocyanide, as in the case of iron *casses*.

Another type of spoilage occurring in reductive conditions is the appearance of a sulphurous taste, caused by the formation of sulphur dioxide or thiols (mercaptans) as a result of metabolism of the yeasts and insufficient aeration of the affected wine during racking.

Spoilage caused by precipitations

Precipitations found in wine fall into two categories, depending on whether they are the result of crystallization or of flocculation.

Precipitation of crystals of tartar

Precipitation of tartar crystals, although completely harmless, is one of the hazards most feared by wine makers, as this phenomenon is not understood by consumers. The crystals formed consist mainly of salts from tartaric acid: cream of tartar and calcium tartrate. The higher the ambient temperature and the lower the alcohol content of the wine, the more soluble the cream of tartar is.

To avoid this crystallization in finished wines, it is advisable to subject the wine to refrigeration so as to facilitate the crystallization of the tartar, it being possible to accelerate the latter by adding crystals of cream of tartar. The wine is then filtered before bottling to remove the crystals. In the case of wines that are to be drunk quickly, an alternative procedure is to add a product that delays precipitation such as metatartaric acid.

Precipitation of proteins

Some large molecules in the wine may flocculate and cause turbidity: this applies notably to proteins and, less commonly, to pectin.

Protein *casse*, a precipitation of polyphenols, may be due to the presence of proteins in the grape matter, but also to proteins that have been added when the wine was fined. This is particularly likely to occur when wines have been over-fined, and excessive quantities of proteins have been used for clarification. These proteins may be precipitated by a variation in the pH, or by heating in cases where the wine is pasteurized to stabilize it.

To avoid this type of spoilage, bentonite may be added to the must, in the case of white wine, or the wines may be heat-treated before receiving a final clarification. Heat-treating the wine may also help with the elimination of copper and the formation of protective colloids, which delay the crystallization and deposit of certain substances.

Precipitation of proteins is also sometimes linked to the precipitation of tannin-protein complexes.

The presence of proteins or crystalline deposits, particularly of crystals of tartar, in bottles of sparkling wine causes the wine to gush out in a fountain when the bottles are opened: bubbles of carbon dioxide are rapidly produced as a result of the drop in pressure, and this can lead to a significant loss of wine.

Unpleasant tastes

Among the unpleasant tastes that occur in wine because of physicochemical spoilage, we may note a number of well-defined tastes repeatedly identified by wine tasters. They are as follows:

▷ *goût de bouchon* ('corky taste'), caused by the poor quality of a cork, or by certain processes the cork has been subject to, either when it was made, during its storage or just before its insertion into the bottle;

▷ *goût de lumière* (literally 'taste of light'), caused by the production of volatile sulphur compounds in the wine because of the chemical break-up of sulphurized amino acids in the wine under the influence of light;

▷ *goût de filtre* ('filter taste'), caused by inadequate maintenance of the items of equipment used for filtering the wine, or of filtration additives kept in inappropriate or undesirable conditions;

▷ *goût de fût* ('cask taste'), caused by storing the wine in badly maintained casks;

▷ *goût d'amande amère* ('bitter almond taste'), found in certain wines containing a significant quantity of benzaldehyde (more than 0.4mg per litre). This excess is probably caused by the transformation of benzyl alcohol, a product that migrates from some coatings used to protect the wine-making equipment, and in particular from coated vinification and storage vats.

Spoilage of bottled wines

Leaky bottles are sometimes found, resulting from damage to the neck of the bottles, or from poor quality corks or corking equipment. The wine in these bottles may slowly seep between the cork and the glass when the bottle is stored horizontally, causing mould to appear between the cork and the capsule. Most of the moulds appearing on top of corks in this way are harmless, but sometimes undesirable moulds appear and contaminate the wine.

Most types of physicochemical spoilage or unpleasant tastes in wine can be avoided by using an adequate programme of preventive checks throughout the wine-making, storing and bottling cycle, by using equipment and vats that have been properly maintained, by well thought-out protection against excessive aeration and oxidization, by the use of appropriate techniques for stabilizing wine (fining, refrigeration, centrifugation, filtration, etc.) and, in some cases, by the use of appropriate additives in doses strictly limited by legislation (citric acid, sulphur dioxide, gum arabic, etc.) In addition, once alcoholic and malolactic fermentations have been completed, it is advisable to keep the wine at a low temperature of no more than 13°C at all times.

THE MAIN TYPES OF CLOUDINESS AND DEPOSITS AFFECTING WINE

Name	Cause
Microbial cloudiness	Yeast — Lactic bacteria — Acetic bacteria
Brown *casse*	Action of enzymes on polyphenols
Iron *casse*	Precipitation of iron in the form of phosphates or with tannins
Copper *casse*	Precipitation of copper salts
Protein *casse*	Precipitation of polyphenols
Precipitation of colouring matter	Polymerization of polyphenols
Tartar crystals	Precipitation of cream of tartar Precipitation of neutral calcium tartrate

F

Faugères

With Clairette du Languedoc and Saint-Chinian, this is one of the three *crus* of the Coteaux du Languedoc regional *appellation*, officially classified as an AOC on 5 May 1982.

Lying to the north of Béziers and not far from Saint-Chinian, the *appellation* area covers a potential 5,600ha of vineyards dispersed over seven communes. The vineyards, planted on schistous hills below the peak of la Coquillade at an average altitude of some 250m, produce about 50,000hl of red and rosé wine annually.

The grape varieties planted are the same as those of the Coteaux du Languedoc: Carignan, Cinsaut, Grenache, Mourvèdre and Syrah, with the Lledoner Pelut as a subsidiary variety. The red wines have a fine ruby colour, suppleness and fruit, with the elegance and finesse typical of wines grown on schists. The wines can, if wished, also be marketed under the regional *appellation* Coteaux du Languedoc.

Fer

Synonyms: *Fer Noir, Fer Servadou* (meaning 'keeps well' in local dialect), *Ferre, Hère, Herre, Petit-Hère, Couahort* in the Madiran district, *Bordelais, Petit Bordelais* in the Pyrenees, *Bois Droit* in Entre-Deux-Mers, *Braucol* in Tarn, *Camirouch* in Ariège, *Pinenc* in Madiran and Béarn, *Estronc* in Lot, *Mouraa* or *Mourach* in Pyrénées-Atlantiques, *Panereuil* in Gabarnac, *Salebourg* in Landes, *Véron* in Deux-Sèvres, *Mansois* or *Saumansois* in Aveyron, *Saumancès* or *Soumancès* in Tarn-et-Garonne. It appears to have derived its main name (which means 'iron') from the hardness of its wood and the toughness of its stalks.

Leaves medium sized, orbicular, thick, finely bullate with concave edges, sometimes crimped at the petiolar junction, generally three-lobed but can be deeply five-lobed, petiolar sinus narrow or closed; dentation convex, medium sized; underside of blade arachnoid with a tuft of hairs around the petiolar junction.

Bunches medium sized, conical, compact; grapes medium sized, ovoid, blue-black, skin thick, pulp expresses juice easily, taste recalling that of the Cabernet Franc; ripening period: second epoch.

This low-producing variety is one of the grape varieties used for the AOCs of Madiran, Béarn, Gaillac and Côtes du Frontonnais, as well as of the Vins de Lavilledieu, de Marcillac, d'Estaing, and d'Entraygues et du Fel in the VDQS category. Eleven registered clones have been approved, the most useful being numbers 420, 421 and 730. The Fer is classed as 'recommended' for all the *départements* of the South West and the Mediterranean. It grows at present on nearly 300ha, in Aveyron, Tarn and Lot-et-Garonne.

The village of Caussiniojouls in the heart of the Faugères AOC, not far from Saint-Chinian. The vineyards are sited on schistous hills.

Feunate

Synonyms: *Fleuna, Flona, Fumate.*

Bunches medium sized, cylindrical, winged; grapes ovoid, medium sized, black, juicy; ripening period: second epoch, late.

Authorized in Drôme, this grape is grown in the vineyards of the Die area, where it gives a deeply coloured wine, astringent and low in alcohol. The Feunate is productive but susceptible to grey rot (botrytis).

Fiefs Vendéens

Wines from the Fiefs Vendéens were granted VDQS status by decree on 24 October 1984.

The area covered by this *appellation*, some 370ha, extends over the Vendée *département* and includes 19 communes.

The coastal region around les Sables-d'Olonne produces mainly white wines, with Chenin Blanc as the principal grape variety. Red and rosé wines, chiefly made from the Gamay Noir à Jus Blanc, are produced in the Mareuil-sur-Lay and Dissais areas.

The Fiefs Vendéens produce an annual total of 15,000hl of light, agreeable wines that are suitable for drinking young.

Figari *See* Vin de Corse-Figari.

Fitou

This is the oldest red-wine *appellation d'origine contrôlée* of Languedoc-Roussillon, its decree of establishment dating from 28 April 1948.

Fitou, an appellation *formed by two enclaves within the Corbières district, is the oldest red-wine AOC in Languedoc-Roussillon.*

Covering nine communes, it forms two enclaves within the Mediterranean zone of the Corbières *appellation*. It is also entitled to produce sweet fortified wines (*vins doux naturels*) under two AOCs, those of Rivesaltes and Muscat de Rivesaltes. The Grenache and the Carignan between them account for 90 per cent of total vine plantings, with the latter variety occupying up to a maximum of 75 per cent. The balance is made up by the Mourvèdre, Syrah, Terret Noir and Macabeu varieties. The vineyards are on two kinds of soils, one clay and limestone, the other schistous, and each produces a different type of wine. Those from the clay and limestone soil of the Tuchan area are full, rich, robust and strongly constituted. They contrast with the finesse and silky suppleness of wines from the schistous soils; those of Villeneuve-les-Corbières provide a good example of this character.

The Fleurie vineyards in Beaujolais cover 700ha, and yield about 44,000hl annually of a fine, charming red wine for drinking young.

Fixin

Premier Cru vineyards occupy 21ha of the 200ha covered by the Fixin *appellation d'origine contrôlée*, defined by decree on 8 October 1938. These are found mostly on the higher parts of the commune. The rest of the area is entitled only to the 'village' or 'commune' *appellation*. As is the case nearly everywhere in Burgundy, the minimum alcohol content is set at 10.5° for red wines and 11° for red Premiers Crus, with 11.5° for white Premiers Crus (though very little white wine is made here). Maximum yield is 35hl/ha, and average annual production of mainly red wine is 3,500hl. It is to be regretted that the wines of Fixin do not enjoy the reputation they deserve, for they have character, a deep colour, strength and suppleness. They also have the merit of keeping well and acquiring, with age, a pronounced aroma of blackcurrant.

Fleurie

The Fleurie vineyard area, officially classed as an AOC on 11 September 1936, is adjacent to that of Chiroubles, and is sited on granite soils. From its 700ha, it produces an average of 44,000hl (5,850,000 bottles) annually. Lively and fruity, this pleasant wine is often said to be the most 'feminine' of all the Beaujolais *crus*. Its charm lies in an elegant taste that quite soon reaches a peak, usually after two years. Fleurie lives up to the floral promise of its name: its delicate scents suggest irises and violets, as well as blackcurrant, peach, and sometimes a touch of cocoa.

Florental

Synonym: *7705 Burdin*.

A hybrid, resulting from a crossing of 8365 Seibel × Gamay. This black variety ripens in the first epoch. It is classed as 'authorized' in Burgundy and the Loire valley, and is grown on 17ha.

Folle Blanche

Synonyms: *Gros Plant* in the Nantes area, *Enrageat* or *Enrageade* in Gironde, *Enragé, Fol* or *Fou* at Montpont, *Plant de Dame* or *Plant de Madame* at Nérac and Condom, *Piquepoul, Picpoul, Picpout* or *Picquepouille* in Gers, *Dame Blanche* in Lot-et-Garonne, *Bouillon* in Bas-Limousin, *Chalosse Blanche, Grosse Chalosse* or *Chalot* in Gers, *Mendik* or *Mondic* in the north of Aveyron, *Amounédat, Camobraque*.

Young leaves downy.

Leaves medium sized, orbicular, thick, bullate, contorted, with base of veins red, quite deeply five-lobed, the upper lateral sinuses resembling the spaces between glove fingers, the lower lateral sinuses open; petiolar sinus in a closed V-shape, with overlapping edges on some leaves; dentation convex, wide; underside of blade downy-pubescent. Green shoots ribbed, reddish brown with red nodes; tendrils brown, medium sized, fleshy.

Bunches medium sized, compact, conical, sometimes winged; grapes spherical or slightly ovoid, medium sized, greenish white; ripening period: second epoch.

The Folle Blanche is a Charente variety, mainly grown to provide acid wines for distilling into cognac and armagnac. The wines are thin and low in alcohol: ideal for the production of fine brandy. Unfortunately grafting has increased the vigour of the shoots and the susceptibility of the variety to grey rot (botrytis), which has meant that the Folle Blanche has been largely replaced in Charente by the Ugni Blanc. In the Armagnac area, nearly 200ha of it are still grown. The largest plantings of the vine, however, are in Loire-Atlantique (2,800ha), for making white VDQS Gros Plant du Pays Nantais; and in Vienne (600ha), where it is used for producing wine and *mistelle* mixtures for export to Germany.

Franc Noir de la Haute-Saône

Synonyms: *Franc Noir de Vénère, de Gy, de Gendrecourt* or *de Jussey, Gougenot.*

Bunches small, conical, compact; grapes ovoid, small, blue-black; ripening period: first epoch.

This little-grown variety, classed as 'recommended' in Aube, is vigorous and productive. It ripens some 10 days before the Gamay.

Fronsac

The Fronsac *appellation d'origine contrôlée*, ratified by decree on 21 September 1976, replaced that of Côtes de Fronsac, which had been established on 4 March 1937. It is reserved for red wines from grapes harvested in an area that covers the communes of Fronsac, la Rivière, Saint-Germain-de-la-Rivière, Saint-Michel-de-Fronsac, Saint-Aignan, Saillans and certain sites in the commune of Galgon in the Libourne district.

To be entitled to the Fronsac *appellation*, wines have to be made from the Cabernet Sauvignon, Cabernet Franc, Merlot and Côt grapes. Since 1961, hybrid vines have been banned from properties laying claim to a Fronsac *appellation*. Minimum sugar content of the musts has to be 162g per litre and the alcoholic strength of the wines should be a minimum of 10° and a maximum of 13°. The base yield is 47hl/ha.

In 1985 the area occupied by the *appellation* was 735ha and production amounted to 45,759hl, of which 4,936hl was vinified by the cooperative at Ludon. The wines of Fronsac are rich and well structured and often require ageing for five years or more before revealing all their qualities.

Frontignan *See* Muscat de Frontignan.

Fuella Nera

Synonyms: *Folle Noire, Fuola, Beletto Nero, Folle de Nice, Grassenc.*

Bunches medium to fairly large, many branched, conical; grapes spherical, small, black; ripening period: third epoch.

An old Provençal grape from the area of Grasse, Antibes, la Gaude and Bellet. It has late budbreak and its yield is rather low, around 30hl/ha. Its wine is deep in colour, without much acid but with a good bouquet; usually, however, it is blended with other varieties for vinification. It is classed as 'recommended' in Alpes-Maritimes, where it forms part of the Bellet AOC plantings.

Furmint

A white grape variety from the Hungarian Tokay vineyards, used together with the Hárslevelü (meaning 'lime leaf') there to make the famous sweet white wine. It was introduced into France at the beginning of the 19th century and planted in Gard, Hérault and Aude, where some owners produced a highly perfumed, very alcoholic sweet white wine from it. Unclassified, it is nevertheless included among the grape varieties used for the Palette AOC in Bouches-du-Rhône.

Aerial view of the Fronsac vineyards, in the area of Libourne, watered by the Dordogne. This AOC produces full-bodied red wines that require ageing to show at their best.

Leaf of the Folle Blanche.

A bunch of Folle Blanche grapes. VDQS Gros Plant du Pays Nantais is produced from this variety.

Coopers and Casks

Connaître son métier de tonnelier,
Faire le bon ouvrage, tout est là.
Faire dire à la matière ce qu'elle a de divin,
Faire dire par quoi l'homme
Fait son métier de tonnelier,
Et le fait comme il faut.

Cooper know your craft,
Doing work well is all.
Make matter speak of its divinity,
Speak of how a man
Does a cooper's work,
And does it as it should be done.

The cooper's craft seems to have been overlooked by the march of technology. Unless, of course, it is the cooper who, wisely and fittingly, has chosen to ignore the advance of technology and preserve his craft, out of a deep respect for wine, the commodity to be stored in his casks.

Of the numerous ancient crafts that are still practised today, most have evolved along with modern technology: electricity, machinery, and now electronics and information technology. These developments, it should be acknowledged, have often brought great benefits. But wherever standardization, prefabrication and technological advances have replaced ancient methods, the old crafts of times past, so dear to popular imagination, have disappeared or become unrecognizable.

At the end of the 20th century, cooperage (the craft of barrel making) remains astonishingly similar in its practice to what it was in the time of our distant predecessors, long before the beginning of the present era. The cooper practises a traditional craft, an artist's craft, an irreplaceable craft. And yet is not even cooperage threatened by industrial methods and procedures that would have the time-honoured oak cask replaced with a commonplace container made of metal, cement or plastic, for the sake of lower costs?

The exhibition piece of the craftsman known as 'Angoumois-l'Amie-des-Arts', a Compagnon-Tonnelier-Doleur-Du-Devoir (guild cooper). Amphora-shaped cask in wood formed by heating; height 1.30m. It has two handles and can be used. The tapered bottom rests in a supporting stand and the chime at the top is unusual in being realized externally, not internally.

Storing wine

All the great wines described in this book call for tradition, respect, quality, wisdom and continuity in the matter of their storage and will always, let us hope, be kept in oak, the guarantee of their future.

For many centuries, and at the same time as terracotta amphoras and bottles made of animal skins were utilized, the wooden cask was employed for containing and storing all kinds of liquids. Time and experience showed that in wood — and especially in oak — wines were transformed, developed and improved; they achieved a fullness there that was never reached in other containers. Oak does much more than just contain. In fact, it takes an active part in the processes of maturing, of *élevage* and of preservation of the wine — although this was not scientifically confirmed until well after the First World War. Thus down the years the tradition of storing great French wines in French oak, a living, noble and natural material, has gone hand-in-hand with the remarkable craft of cooperage.

In the period 1930–40, when a large quantity of oak was imported to France from central Europe, the suspicion was confirmed that only oaks grown in French soil and, further, in certain well-defined areas, had the required powers of resistance and impermeability, and above all the capacity to improve the wines stored in them.

Oak wood is a living material; it lives and breathes in coexistence with the wine it contains. It favours chemical exchanges, especially oxidization, oxygenation and a slight oxidization-reduction, that preserve and enhance the fundamental and particular qualities of each wine. The tannins that are slowly released by the wood in contact with the wine bestow on it distinguishing aromatic elements. Tannins are the indispensable complement to the making and keeping of wines for long ageing.

Origins

It would be tempting to fall back on the legend according to which the barrel was a Gallic invention. It has to be admitted, however, that the origins of this marvellous receptacle are much hazier than this, and lie much further back in time.

For a long time, wherever the local clay was suitable for the purpose, liquids — wine, oil, water, milk, alcoholic drinks — were kept in terracotta jars. At the same time, men also used leather bottles made from the skins of cattle, pigs or goats for this purpose. These leather bottles were excellent containers: light, but by no means fragile and, it seemed, the wine in them was good so long as the skin had been used a number of times, and was 'well seasoned'.

Later, amphoras were widely used for transporting wine over long distances, but due to their fragility this was a rather primitive and transitory method. Wooden vessels were the true ancestors of the modern barrel. They had been initially devised, long before the time of the Gauls, for transporting solid produce, then a good deal later used for transporting liquids.

During the 3rd and 2nd centuries BC the need to transport

Boat-hauling scene from a Gallo-Roman bas-relief from Cabrières d'Aygues in Vaucluse, with barrels clearly visible.

solid items such as gold, tin, amber, bronze or pottery, commodities that could not be moved around loose without obvious risk, would have led to the development of methods of packing. The qualities of wood, in particular its flexibility, meant that it would have played an important part in these. The very nature of some of the items transported would have given their packaging a form approaching that of the barrel as we know it, and it was this shape that the Gauls were eventually to exploit.

Ancestors of the barrel

Crude containers of this kind could have been made up from fir or larch, or any other resinous wood found locally, the timber being cut in straight, narrow slats and then fashioned in much the same way as the staves of modern barrels are, i.e. wider at the centre than at the ends.

Very long, convex in profile with a slight bulge in the middle, these ancestors of the barrel were devised so as to be joined by thongs of animal or vegetable fibre at either end. They were not bent into shape by heating, as was eventually to be the case for containers used for transporting liquids. These early containers did not have a base or bottom as such, and their strength and solidity was given them by the thongs that pulled all the pieces of wood together into a close fit. It is very likely that there were quite a number of these thongs encircling the wooden slats, and the whole container would have been given a coating of tar or a resinous substance on the outside to make it waterproof.

Later, containers for storing and transporting liquids, based on the same construction principles, were developed. All that was necessary was to refine the pieces of wood into staves planed on each side, and to finish them a little more widely at each end, instead of cutting them to very fine ends as was done for the containers for solid items. All the pieces of wood were then fitted together; the whole container was stopped by a cork plug at each end, and bound tightly together with numerous thongs. Such a container must have been very slender if the wood was to be bent into shape, as it was, without the use of fire. (The technique of heating staves to shape them was a subsequent development.) The widest part of the cask (the *bouge* or central bulge) was still barely prominent, and the staves must have been very long to have provided a worthwhile cask of such narrow diameter. A resinous substance was used to coat the inside of the cask, providing a perfect seal.

The barrel in Roman times

As is commonly the case with everyday objects, logic led quickly to a definitive way of making these containers assembled from a number of pieces of wood. From having been secured by rather rudimentary ties, they were soon bound by wooden or iron hoops — or more often a judicious combination of the two. The addition of a base and a top, also of wood, fitting neatly into the two ends, produced a watertight container that did not need sealing or coating, was resistant to shocks and convenient to handle: a barrel, in fact. It was relatively light, and could be rolled rather than carried. The Romans called it a *vascellum*, the word being derived from *vas*, jar or receptacle; this word gave birth to the Old French word *vaissel*, which in turn has given the English language 'vessel', meaning a container, especially for liquid. The cooper's craft had, by Roman times, reached a comparable stage of perfection to that which we know today. The exact period during which this happened, however, cannot be precisely specified.

The medieval cask

Among the 5th-century mosaics in the magnificently decorated basilica of Theodoric the Great (454–526) in Ravenna, one scene from the life of Christ shows the woman of Samaria about to give Christ water from a bucket she has just drawn from the well. The bucket could have been made in this century, for it is in no way different from the modern product. It is made of wood and the staves can readily be made out through the different shades they are given in the mosaic. It is narrow in diameter, deep and conical. One iron and three wooden hoops hold it together.

Charlemagne (742–814) had his own cooper's workshop on his Burgundian estates. Towards the end of the Middle Ages, the Guild of Coopers presented Chartres cathedral with a stained-glass window showing a cooper at work. He is in the process of tapping wooden hoops down over a very tall cask that would probably hold about 500 litres and would stand 1.5m high; it is very similar to the Cognac *tierçon*. To one side is a journeyman, adze in hand. The work is entitled, significantly, 'Noah's cooper'.

Making a barrel

The series of precise movements and actions the cooper makes in building a barrel has hardly changed down through the ages.

Making a barrel begins with the shaping of staves.

Through his skill a barrel, made up of pieces of wood termed staves, and a top and a base, takes on a form that is round, pleasing, elegant and useful.

The cooper is guided only by his practical knowledge, based on experience, of the forms and details of the cask of which he is the sole creator. He does not have plans, descriptions or technical specifications to guide him in his work. He has to gather and class according to their dimensions and with respect to their future use the various pieces which he will cut and shape for the type of cask required.

The staves are placed one at a time in a hoop and fitted together.

The staves are usually bent into shape by heat from a wood fire placed in a small burner inside the barrel.

Making a cask requires a number of coordinated, but distinct, operations: measuring up, shaping the staves, fitting them together, heating and bending the staves, trimming to size, making the top and bottom and fitting them, putting on the iron and wooden hoops, finishing off and testing for strength and solidity.

The first stage begins with shaping the wood into staves — 28 to 32 per barrel, on average — and the tops and bottoms, which are made up from 12 to 16 slats.

The cooper then carries out the initial assembly of the barrel, positioning the staves one at a time within a hoop. He then tightens up and balances the whole assembly before applying heat.

This phase in the making of a barrel is very important, for to a great extent it conditions the quality and durability of the container. If the barrel is incorrectly heated, it may prove faulty: the staves, being continually in contraction, would reach the point where they snapped at the cask's widest part. If correctly heated, however, the same barrel can be used for decades without risk or problem.

The next task, trimming, consists of getting the ends of the barrel ready for the top and bottom to be fitted in them. After positioning the top and bottom, the finish of the cask is all that remains to be done. This task requires a good deal of attention, for the general look of the cask depends on it. Each barrel, each capacity, each destination and each region or country has its own particular trim and finish, to which the cooper has to conform.

The finished barrel is then signed top and bottom by its maker. The purpose of this signature is first of all to enable the maker to be traced, even after some years. This simple gesture is also an expression of the workman's pride, and a pledge of his integrity and skill. It is an action that gives him an incentive to pursue his craft, to enjoy it and to be justly proud of it.

The cooper's signature testifies to the precision and craftsmanship of the work.

OAK

The wood of the oak tree — of which France has the biggest reserves in Europe — is a hard, compact material made up of fibres and vessels transporting sap. It takes an oak tree 150 to 200 years to reach maturity and to be ready for commercial use.

Wood from two species of oak is used in making casks for the storage and ageing of wine.

Pedunculate oak (Quercus robur *or* pedunculata) *This, the* chêne pédonculé, *is the oak of the open countryside of France.*

It needs plenty of light; its wood, which is very similar to that of the sessile oak, is of considerable denseness and is very strong. This coarse-grained wood, or Limousin oak as it is called, is very hard and often irregular in its growth, but it can add 10mm to the thickness of its trunk in one year. It grows outward more than upward and its wood provides wine with powerful, fast-acting tannin.

Sessile oak (Quercus petraea *or* sessilis)

This is pre-eminently a tree of the forest and the coppice. It is seldom found growing by itself. It is dominant in central France, where it prefers damp soils.

The sessile oak produces fine-grained wood. Also known as Tronçais oak, or as the chêne du Centre, *its timber is slightly less hard than that of the pedunculate oak.*

Its small annual increase in girth — sometimes no more than 1mm in a year — is nevertheless regular. As this is a forest oak it seeks the light, pushing upwards. Its tannin is released more slowly into wine stored in its casks than is the case with Limousin oak, and the tannin is gentler and more supple than is that of Limousin.

In order to stabilize it, season it and rid it of impurities, oak wood for barrel staves is dried out of doors, in rain, snow, frost and sunshine, for a period of about three years.

CASKS AND THEIR CAPACITIES

By putting an appropriate area of wood in contact with the wine being stored, the size and capacity of a cask conditions effective and beneficial ageing. This size and capacity have evolved over the course of centuries as a result of usage and practical experience. It is for this reason that in every region of France, and quite independently, the average cask volume has generally evolved to between 200 and 230 litres.

The two main cask capacities in use today are the 225 litres of the Bordeaux *barrique* and the 228 litres of its Burgundy counterpart. It should be pointed out here that the latter cask is known as a *tonneau* when it is empty and a *pièce* when it is full.

The capacity of all types of casks, while variable , is always bound up with the same limiting factors: the land, the vine, the harvest and the storage of wine. In the harvesting of grapes, the unit of measure used, in so far as it was related to cask capacity, was what the grower could produce from one plot of land planted with vines, and the area a labourer could work by hand in one day of 10 to 14 hours.

The Burgundy cask

The 228 litres that a Burgundian *barrique* must hold corresponds to the amount of wine the grower can get from one *ouvrée* (plot) of land planted with vines. The *ouvrée*, a unit of measure still in use, equals 4,828m^2 (slightly more than 1 acre). Formerly, in the 16th, 17th and 18th centuries, it corresponded to the amount of land a labourer could work in a day. During these centuries, the average volume of wine produced was 228 litres to the *ouvrée*, and so a cask was devised that would hold the result of one day's work by one labourer.

This Burgundian cask or *pièce* has a length of 0.885m and is the shortest of all the traditional French barrels. The diameter at each end is 0.595m, the circumference around the central bulge is 2.305m; it is made from wood 27mm to 30mm thick. Unlike the other traditional casks, it has no reinforcing bars or slats inside the top and bottom.

Burgundy wine casks.

Two wooden hoops are always placed at the top and the bottom of the cask to protect the ends of the staves from any impact in the course of handling. Formerly the wooden hoops were tied with rather fragile, expensive willow twigs (wicker) but today they are secured by rings or clips of iron.

The Burgundy cask is functional, strong, durable and easy to handle. It is to be found in all the cellars and wine vaults of the region. It is queen in its home territory, but rarely leaves it. In this it is unlike the other types of casks — particularly the 225-litre Bordeaux cask, which is widespread throughout all the French regions and, indeed, all the countries of the world.

The Bordeaux cask

The classic Bordeaux *barrique*, which holds 225 litres, is the epitome of the world's wine casks. It has been copied in every country and in nearly every kind of wood. As with its Burgundy equivalent, a possible hypothesis is that it corresponded to the yield of wine from one measure of land planted with vines — a measure termed a *sadon*, though this is hardly ever used today.

A *sadon* was a unit equal to about 833m^2. It formerly provided the basis for the wages of a day labourer, who was paid the *sadon* rate for pruning or staking 900 vine plants. Today, the amount has been adjusted to a nominal 1,000 plants and the term *sadon* is no longer used; but the wages (220 francs in 1981 for a nominal 1,000 plants pruned or tied) are still paid per measured area — the area is now 1,000m^2. There used to be 4 *sadons* to the *journal* and 12 *sadons* to the hectare. Yield was 450 litres to the *sadon*. A cask was therefore devised that corresponded to this particular volume then, for ease of handling, was divided into two. The volume of wine yielded was thus two 225-litre casks to the *sadon*, eight casks to the *journal* and 24 to the hectare. As in Burgundy, this gave a total of about 54hl/ha — in good years and for wines that were not classified in any way in those days. It has to be assumed that it was a maximum yield that was provided for. Grape harvests are not always of the same volume and yield must have been lower in many years.

Putting forward such hypotheses on these relationships inevitably suggests an alternative possibility based on the same line of reasoning: that the Burgundian yield was 228 litres from 2 *ouvrées*, not 1; and that it might have been 225 litres to the *sadon* in Bordeaux, relating to one cask rather than two. In these two quality wine regions a — perfectly respectable — yield of around 27hl/ha would be quite conceivable. Whatever the explanation, a comparison of the two capacities, all but identical, linked to factors of soil and yield, leads inevitably to the idea that the capacity of these casks fashioned in wood by a cooper's hand has a direct relationship with the area planted with vines, the work of a day labourer and the volume of wine produced.

The Bordeaux transport cask

This is the most commonly seen and most familiar of the casks. It is 0.94 to 0.945m long, 0.55 to 0.555m in diameter at the ends and the diameter at the central point is 0.69 to 0.695m.

The Bordeaux château cask

This *barrique* is certainly the most beautiful of all wine casks. It is functional, and is noble and elegant in appearance. It is, though, relatively light and thus rather fragile. Its dimensions are: length 0.95m; diameter at the ends 0.565m; circumference around the central point 2.20m; thickness of wood 22mm. A fairly wide reinforcing bar or slat is placed inside each end.

It is bound with eight iron hoops and four chestnut wood hoops bound with wicker and placed in pairs at each end of the cask.

In February 1908, the Bordeaux Chamber of Commerce laid down specifications for the local cask. The length was to be 0.93m, the circumference at the two ends 1.81m (0.575m being the diameter at these points), the circumference around the middle 2.17m, the length of the chime (the protecting rim at each end) 75mm and, finally, the thickness of the staves at the joints should not be less than 12mm, and not less that 13mm at the top and bottom.

The hoops were as follows: at the top, two wooden hoops with a binding of wicker, then an iron hoop, 27mm by 13mm, around the neck; then another iron hoop, 27mm by 13mm, around the central part, with two wooden hoops to either side of it; then a further iron hoop at the bottom, with two more wooden hoops with a binding of wicker below it. Capacity of the cask was set at 226 litres, or as close to this as possible, with a tolerance of 2 per cent either way.

A Bordeaux château cask.

A Bordeaux transport cask.

A second, variant cask, referred to as the *façon Médoc* (the Médoc type), became accepted. The two wooden hoops around the central section were dropped and replaced by an extra iron hoop, so that there were now two iron hoops to either side of the central bulge: this is the Bordeaux cask of today. The coopers, though, often used to go out to the wine growers' *chais* one year after making the casks to fit protective wooden hoops around the middles of the casks, *in situ*.

It was stipulated that if the capacity of a Bordeaux cask exceeded the 2 per cent tolerance, the buyer should either refuse to accept it, or demand alterations at the cooper's expense, even if he only noticed the defect some years later.

It is to be noted how thin the wood was (12mm staves, 13mm at top and bottom), which meant a rather fragile cask. Even today, with the thickness of the wood slightly increased, the Bordeaux type remains the lightest of all the French wine casks.

On the Bordeaux cask, the ends of the staves, forming the chime, are very long: 70mm to 75mm. There are two reasons for this. The first is that growers, to prevent evaporation of their wines, sometimes apply one or two centimetres of plaster mixed with jute sacking to the cask ends. The second reason is that when the wines were transported in cask by ship, as they used to be in the past, the dockers rolled the casks down wooden planks from deck level. The full casks were therefore travelling at speed when they reached the quayside. The worker at the receiving end had to position himself so that as the cask passed him he could deliver a light kick in the chime with the toe of his boot. The cask, checked on one side, spun like a top. As it slowed down the unloader had simply to realign it and roll it to where it was to be stacked. It was therefore to make this unloading easier and safer that the ends of the staves on Bordeaux casks were left long; and, in addition, that wooden hoops were placed there to protect the *barriques* by acting as shock absorbers.

If each of the regional types of cask listed below has what might seem to be a whimsically arrived-at capacity, it should be remembered that this does, in reality, relate to the hard facts of daily work in the vineyard, the area of vineyard plots under cultivation, the wine produced and maximum storage requirements after the harvest.

CASKS OF YESTERDAY AND TODAY

Name	Capacity in litres
Anée, Isère	72–76
Anée, Mâcon	300
Anée, Rhône	93
Bar, Champagne (small)	205
Bar, Champagne (large)	228
Barbantane	560–565
Baril, Alicante	38
Baril, Madeira	15
Baril, Málaga	30
Barillo, Corsica	150
Barral (Baril), Carpentras	26
Barral, Gard	45
Barral, Hautes-Alpes	32–34
Barrica, Porto	250–260
Barrique, Ardèche	214
Barrique, Basse-Pyrénées	270
Barrique, Beaune	228
Barrique, Bordeaux	220–225
Barrique, Brittany	228
Barrique, Cahors	224
Barrique, Chalosse	304
Barrique, Champagne	200
Barrique, Charente	205–215
Barrique, Châtellerault	300
Barrique, Cher	259
Barrique, Cognac (earlier form)	205
Barrique, Cognac (around 1900)	275
Barrique, Cognac (1970)	350
Barrique, Deux-Sèvres	295
Barrique, Drôme	210
Barrique, Frontignan	228
Barrique, Hautes-Alpes	80
Barrique, Hérault	214
Barrique, Landes	304
Barrique, Lot	228
Barrique, Lot-et-Garonne	228
Barrique, Paris	402
Barrique, Rhône	220
Barrique, la Rochelle	225
Barrique, Saumur	232
Barrique, Tarn	214
Barrique, Tours	232
Barrique, Vienne	252
Botte, Provence	520
Botte, Saône-et-Loire	430
Bussard	350
Busse, Anjou	230
Busse, Mayenne	225–232
Busse, Sarthe	240–250
Charge, Castelnaudary	135–140
Charge, Hautes-Alpes	110
Charge, Isère	100
Charge, Lorraine	40
Charge, Meurthe	40
Charge, Meuse	40
Charge, Narbonne	94
Charge, Pyrénées-Orientales	118
Charge, Toul	39
Comporte, Midi	43
Cruche, Béarn	23
Demi-bordelaise	110–112
Demi-botte	221
Demi-feuillette	68
Demi-mâconnais	106
Demi-muid, Gard	560
Demi-muid, Paris (large)	152
Demi-muid, Paris (very large)	167
Demi-pièce, Côte-d'Or	128
Demi-pièce, Paris	112–115
Demi-pièce, Reims	200
Demi-queue	108
Demi-queue, Anjou	243
Demi-queue, Aube (called *jauge gros bar*)	228
Demi-queue, Auvergne	280–297
Demi-queue bâtarde	236
Demi-queue, Blois	236
Demi-queue, Cahors	221
Demi-queue, Chalon	214
Demi-queue chalonnaise	224
Demi-queue, Champagne	183
Demi-queue, Château-Thierry	185
Demi-queue, Cher	243
Demi-queue, Chinon	243
Demi-queue, Condrieu	251
Demi-queue, Garonne	217
Demi-queue, Gâtinais	221
Demi-queue, Languedoc	274
Demi-queue, Mâcon	213
Demi-queue, Montigny	213
Demi-queue, Montlouis	243
Demi-queue, Nantes	243–248
Demi-queue, Saint-Gilles	289
Demi-queue, Sancerre	221
Demi-queue, Sologne	232
Demi-queue, Vaucluse	275
Demi-queue, Villenouve	175
Demi-queue, Vouvray	255
Émine, Hautes-Alpes	22–30
Feuille ordinaire	130
Feuille, Paris	133
Feuille, Yonne	136
Feuillette, Burgundy	136
Feuillette, Côte-d'Or	112–114
Feuillette, Mâcon	112–114
Héralde, Béarn	23
Hotte, Lorraine	40
Mannée, Anjou	40
Mesure, Lorraine	44
Mesure, Vosges	42
Muid, Aisne	250
Muid, Burgundy	297
Muid, Burgundy (very large)	350
Muid, Cahors	297
Muid, Chaumont	230
Muid commun	300
Muid français	274
Muid français (large)	320
Muid, Hérault	685
Muid, Langres	241
Muid, Languedoc (small)	365
Muid, Montpellier	510
Muid, Orléans	289
Muid, Paris	268
Muid, Rhône	288
Muid, Roussillon	472
Muid, Yonne	272
Pièce, Burgundy	228
Pièce, Champagne	182
Pièce, Lorraine	180
Pièce, Saône-et-Loire	142
Pièce, Villenox (Aube)	181
Pipe	410
Pipe, Anjou	480
Pipe, Cognac	600
Pipe, Languedoc (small)	533
Pipe, Languedoc (large)	650
Pipe, Paris	620
Pipe, la Rochelle	533
Poinçon, Touraine	230–258
Pot, Auvergne	40
Quart-bordelaise, Bordeaux	54–55
Quart-botte	104–106
Quart de muid	68
Quart, Paris	67
Quartaut	94
Quartaut, Auvergne	137
Quartaut, Beaune	114
Quartaut, Burgundy	57
Quartaut, Chalonnais	114
Quartaut, Orléans	114
Quartaut, Vouvray	125
Queue, Paris	897–900
Sétier, Doubs	50
Sixain	60
Tiercerolle, Gard	230
Tierçon, Champagne	91
Tierçon, Cognac	530–560
Tierçon or demi-coque	53
Tinne, Doubs	53
Tonneau, Bordeaux	900

CORKS

Cork stoppers were used by the Greeks and Romans to seal their amphoras. However, after the decline of the Roman empire, and throughout the Middle Ages, cork ceased to be common. It did not reappear until around 1680, when Dom Pérignon came across it, in use to seal the gourds of Spanish pilgrims visiting his abbey of Hautvillers. Wooden plugs wrapped in oiled hemp were what he was using at the time, and he was immediately interested in the elastic qualities of this new material.

Growth in the trunks and branches of the cork oak comes about through the proliferation of cells in two concentric areas of generative tissue, one producing wood and bast, the other, a layer containing suberin (a fatty, protective substance), producing bark, or cork.

The nature of cork

Quercus suber, the cork oak, has the characteristic unique among trees of producing abundant, durable cork. In this type of oak, the cells formed from generative tissue die one by one, emptying themselves of their contents, and the cell walls then become impregnated with suberin, in other words converted into cork. Annual increase in girth can be from 1mm to 10mm, depending on the particular tree, the care taken of it, and the climate.

The first cork, produced after 15 years of growth, is hard, cracked and cannot be used for stopping bottles. It is termed the 'male' cork. What is produced subsequently, called 'reproduction' cork, improves in quality until it reaches an ideal level of fineness and elasticity around the time of the fifth or sixth harvest. A commercially exploited cork oak can live from 150 to 200 years.

Area of production

The cork oak thrives only in a fairly limited geographical area: the Iberian peninsula, the south of France, southern Italy, Corsica, Sardinia and North Africa. Its thick bark means that it can withstand extremes of heat and cold better than other species. As it is sustained by a strong root system, it can also adapt to windswept or to dry areas. It is thus better equipped than other trees of spreading habit to resist the pressures of natural selection within its environment. However, attempts at acclimatizing the tree in the southern hemisphere, in America or in Asia have never produced positive results, a fact of considerable economic importance for the various cork-producing countries.

Structure and properties of cork

Cork is a vegetable tissue made up of polyhedral cells varying in size from 10 to 40 microns, according to the speed of growth. The thickness of the cell walls varies from 1 to 3 microns. Cork grows by means of cells formed between spring and autumn. These cells include successive layers of suberin and wax, as well as other substances such as lignin, cellulose, tannins, mineral salts and water. They are connected by very fine ducts called plasmodesmata. The interior of the cells is filled with a gas that is close to air in its composition.

Harvesting cork. By the fifth or sixth harvest after the **démasclage** *(the first stripping of the cork from the tree at the end of 15 years' growth), the material will have reached its optimum quality.*

CORKS/PANELS

The rate of growth of cork varies according to the country in which it is grown and so, therefore, do the intervals between harvesting:
Portugal: 9 years
Spain: 9 to 15 years
North Africa: 11 to 15 years
Italy: 10 to 12 years
France: 11 to 15 years

Distribution of cork oak trees	Production per country
Portugal: 32.8%	Portugal: 50.8%
Spain: 21.8%	Spain: 22.5%
Algeria: 17.9%	Algeria: 10.6%
Morocco: 14.8%	Morocco: 3.8%
France: 4.4%	France: 3.8%
Tunisia: 4.3%	Tunisia: 2.6%
Italy: 3.9%	Italy: 4.4%

Also found within the structure of cork are pores called lenticels. These pores are arranged perpendicularly to the bark and allow the ligneous organs of the tree to breathe and transpire. The number and fineness of these lenticels are important factors determining the quality of cork intended for stopping bottles.

Boiled cork has a low density — an average of 0.20 (mass to volume). The best corks are those with the lowest densities: 0.13 to 0.20.

Cork is impervious to liquids, but very small quantities of gas can pass through its plasmodesmata. It is compressible and elastic, springing back into its original shape after being pressed. The presence of micro-suckers, formed from cells bisected when the cork is cut, enables it to stick to smooth surfaces. In addition it is incorruptible and chemically neutral. It has other uses besides providing stoppers for bottles: its low thermal and electrical conductivity, and its low combustion point, are utilized to advantage in other industries. A material offering all these properties simultaneously is unique; even today there is no synthetic product that can take the place of cork.

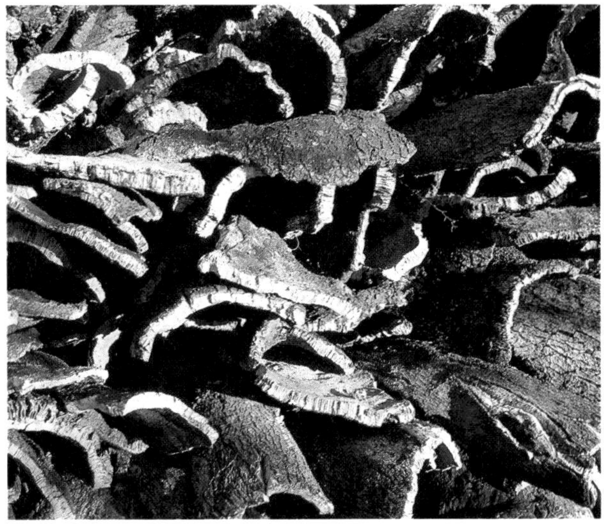

Cork lengths left to weather, in Var. After harvesting, the cork has to dry out for more than two years in the open air before it can be processed.

As a natural product, cork is not absolutely uniform in its characteristics. It differs according to its place of origin, the individual tree it comes from, and even from one part of a tree to another. To achieve homogeneity of quality in the finished corks, a number of thorough selection procedures have to be carried out.

Cork processing

The sheets of cork pulled from the trees are stacked in the open air to dry. They must be exposed to sun, rain and cold for two

The lengths of cork are immersed in boiling water for 30 to 60 minutes.

winters and one summer before they can be used. While drying out, the cork loses its sap and its tissues shrink.

After this period of drying the cork sheets are boiled in water at 100°C for 30 to 60 minutes. The cork swells, increasing its volume by about 20 per cent and acquiring maximum elasticity. The sheets are sterile when they come out of this bath and can be planed smooth. They are then left to rest for two to three weeks so as to become moist enough for cutting and punching. A first selection takes place at this stage, on the basis of two criteria: thickness and quality. This selection is facilitated by squaring off the four edges of the cork sheets.

Making the corks

When the cork sheets have attained maximum moistness they are cut into strips whose width is equal to the length of the future corks. The unit of measure for the length of corks is the *ligne*, which equals 2.256mm. For a cork with a diameter of 24mm — the most common size — the cork strips must have a depth of 28mm to 30mm. The strips of cork then go to the cutting machine. This machine has to be fed manually so that the numerous natural faults in the material can be spotted and a good percentage of quality corks achieved. The final yield is between 15kg and 25kg of finished corks per 100kg of the raw material.

When they leave the cutting machine the corks are milled with emery, to obtain a smooth, even surface. They are then washed to remove dust and waste matter present in the lenticels. Their appearance is often improved by passing them through a bath of dye.

There now comes a second stage of selection, which may be partly automated using machines that are able to count the number of lenticels on the surface of the corks. However, the operation is largely done by hand as green or dry patches, or cracks, might otherwise pass unnoticed.

Certain finishing processes may be applied. The pores of the lenticels, for example, may be filled with a paste made of powdered cork. This process can be used with any grade of cork, and it improves its mechanical properties without harming its intrinsic quality. The practice, however, has sometimes allowed important defects to be concealed. Regrettable abuses have occurred, and these have bred a certain mistrust on the part of consumers towards this type of cork finish.

Punching corks by machine.

Champagne corks are largely made up of compacted particles of cork. The part in contact with the wine, however, is of solid cork.

The surfaces of corks can be treated to make them slide more easily into place. Applying paraffin to cork is an ancient and widespread practice which can be helpful if corks are to be used dry. The natural adhesion of the cork, derived from the suction effect of the bisected lenticels, is largely neutralized and replaced by adhesion due to the paraffin. But if the wrong quantity of paraffin is applied, it can sometimes prove ineffective, with corks that pop out, or go too far in and become difficult to extract again. Nowadays paraffin is often replaced by silicon-based products or synthetic resins.

Composite corks also exist. These are made of particles of cork compacted together with a special gum. The shafts of champagne corks are often made of this substance. The end of the cork that is in contact with the champagne is then made up of one or more discs of solid cork.

Corks for still wines are selected according to the expected length of the ageing period: wines for long ageing require the finest category of cork.

Corks are generally sold in lengths of 15 *lignes* (34mm), 17 *lignes* (38mm), 20 *lignes* (45mm), 22 *lignes* (50mm) and 24 *lignes* (54mm).

The standard diameter for a cork is 24mm, which suits the standard bottleneck diameter of 18.5mm. For sparkling wines, the length is 47mm, while the diameter may vary from 30 to 48mm. Some corks are supplied in a sterile state, having been processed in hermetically sealed bags filled with an antiseptic gas.

G

Gaillac, Gaillac Doux and Gaillac Mousseux

Roman remains bear witness to wine growing in the Gaillac area from the 2nd century BC onwards. However, the real impetus for extensive viticulture here did not come until the 10th century AD, and was provided by Benedictine monks. The wines made by the monks were sold in France, and also in England and Holland up to the 18th century, but then their sales suffered from France's wars with these two countries. Periods of good fortune but also of difficulty followed, marked by overproduction and by confrontations with the Bordeaux growers, anxious to protect their own trade against competition from wines from this part of the Haut Pays.

The first half of the 19th century saw a revival in the popularity of the red and white wines of Gaillac, appreciated for their body, colour, and their frank and full flavour. But here, as elsewhere, the second half of the century was marked by the triple catastrophe of outbreaks of oidium (powdery mildew), of phylloxera and of downy mildew. The reconstruction of this wine-growing region after these setbacks favoured white wines rather than reds. The latter, from high-yielding, hybrid, direct-producing (ungrafted) varieties were of middling quality at best.

The choice of these 'safe' varieties was of doubtful wisdom, for it lost Gaillac its reputation. Nevertheless, the white wines were given the right to an *appellation d'origine contrôlée* in 1938; and in 1970 this right was also granted to the red wines, grown in 73 communes.

Structurally, Tarn is a transitional area between the last spurs of the Massif Central and the low-lying Aquitaine basin. It takes the form of a semicircle turned towards the west and made up of a mosaic of different geological terrains. The Gaillac vineyards stretch out on both sides of the river Tarn, between Albi and Saint-Sulpice. The climate is maritime and semi-continental, subject to both Mediterranean and mountain influences.

The Gaillac wine-growing area is one of the most extensive in southwest France. But although 10,733ha are planted with vines, only 1,400ha of these are of AOC status. Eighty per cent of the vines qualifying for the AOC are planted in 14 communes around the town of Gaillac. The rest grow in the Rabastens and Florentin areas.

White grape varieties account for 47.2 per cent of the vineyard area. They comprise three traditional varieties: the Mauzac, the Len de l'El, and the Ondenc, together with the Sauvignon Blanc, Sémillon and Muscadelle.

The Mauzac is the most commonly grown grape in the Gaillac vineyards. It is picked over-ripe to make white dessert wines. Very aromatic, it gives white wines of 12° to 12.5°, with low acidity. It is also picked before it is fully ripe to make *moustillant* (slightly sparkling) and *mousseux* (sparkling) wines. When picked ripe, it produces dry white and *perlé* (very slightly sparkling) white wines.

The Len de l'El is often used in association with the Mauzac to heighten the latter's acidity and add finesse. On its own, it generally produces wines low in alcohol.

The Ondenc is planted less and less widely because of its poor fertility and its sensitivity to *coulure* (flower abortion). Appreciated for its clear yellow wines, it is often used as a supplement to the Sauvignon Blanc or the Len de l'El.

Plantings of Sauvignon Blanc here are of recent date. This variety gives fine, perfumed wines that run true to their type. Sometimes, however, it can mask the more discreet aromas of the other grapes it is used with. The Muscadelle grape produces light, fruity wines with a musky perfume.

There are numerous red grape varieties. The Duras, a typical Gaillac grape, with moderate yields, gives fine wines with good colour and acidity.

The Fer (locally known as the Braucol) is limited and irregular in its production. The wine from its grapes, though, is well structured and characterful.

It is the Syrah, however, that is the most widely planted variety for the red AOC wines of this district. Besides a good colour, the wines of the Syrah have a firm structure.

Using a pipette to take a sample of Gaillac wine from a cask.

The Gamay is a variety that lends itself well to the *macération carbonique* system of vinification of whole bunches of grapes, producing *primeur* wines that are fruity, light, lively — but that sometimes lack colour.

The Cabernet Sauvignon and Cabernet Franc yield modestly, but produce wines of quality, suitable for ageing. Wines from the Merlot grape variety are of good quality, with suppleness and colour. The Jurançon Noir and Portugairs Bleu varieties are reserved for use in *vins de pays* only.

The wine growers of the Gaillac area practise mixed farming. Of the 3,000 farmers who cultivate vines, 2,780 sell grapes or wine; only 1,300 of them, though, grow varieties suitable for making AOC wines, and a little less than half of this number claim any form of AOC. There are four large cooperatives in the region.

The Gaillac area has a wide range of products to offer the consumer. Its red wines include a Gaillac *primeur*, light and lively; a young Gaillac, generally made by blending the Duras for lightness and acidity with the Syrah for tannin, colour and aroma; and a Gaillac for laying down and ageing for an average of four years. This wine is based on one of the local varieties that lends itself to a period of extended ageing, such as the Fer (which some consider the Gaillac hallmark), blended with smaller quantities of the Syrah or the Duras.

The white wines of Gaillac are differentiated from each other by the amount of residual sugar and carbon dioxide they contain. Dry white Gaillac, often quite high in alcohol, has fruit but little acid. It is made from the Mauzac and a minimum of 15 per cent Len de l'El. Gaillac Perlé is a dry white wine given a very slight sparkle by the start of malolactic fermentation; this reinforces its freshness and its scent. Gaillac Doux, made from the Mauzac grape variety, is sweet and rich. The fermentation of this wine is checked by successive rackings, lowered must temperatures and the use of sulphur dioxide. In producing Gaillac Mousseux by the *méthode rurale*, the fermentation is first slowed by the means described above for Gaillac Doux, then it is continued in bottle, where the wine becomes sparkling due to the production of carbon dioxide by this fermentation. However, this traditional technique is being increasingly abandoned in favour of the *méthode champenoise*. Gaillac Moustillant, an incompletely fermented, slightly sparkling wine without an AOC, is made from Mauzac grapes picked before they are fully ripe. The must ferments until it reaches an alcoholic strength of 6° and contains low levels of carbon dioxide. It is then bottled and, after bottling, pasteurized to ensure no further unwanted fermentation takes place.

Gaillac Premières Côtes

This recently created AOC, governed by legislation of 11 September 1984, is for white wines produced from the Len de l'El, Mauzac, Muscadelle, Ondenc, Sauvignon Blanc and Sémillon grape varieties.

The area of production is different from that of the Gaillac AOC. It covers the communes of Bernac, Broze, Cahuzac-sur-Vère, Castanet, Cestayrols, Fayssac, Gaillac, Labastide-de-Lévis, Lisle-sur-Tarn, Montels and Senouillac. The wines have similar characteristics to those of the Gaillac Doux *appellation*, being rich in sugar and with a pronounced bouquet. They are very suitable for bottle ageing.

Gamay de Bouze

Synonyms: *Rouge de Bouze, Plant Rouge de Bouze, Rouge de Couchey, Gamay Teinturier de Bouze.*

Bunches medium, cylindrical; grapes small, ovoid, blue-black with pink juice, pale colour; ripening period: first epoch.

Of unknown origin, this variety is chiefly grown in Saône-et-Loire. A good producer, giving a moderately deeply coloured Teinturier wine. ('Teinturier' signals red grapes with red juice. The deeply coloured wines made from Teinturier grapes are usually used for blending and adding colour to other wines — hence the name 'Teinturier', which means 'dyer'.) Classed as 'authorized' for all of France, though not much of it is grown. There are three approved clones: numbers 223, 360 and 431.

Gamay de Chaudenay

Synonyms: *Gamay Teinturier de Chaudenay, Plant Rouge de Chaudenay, Teinturier de Chaudenay, Gamay Six-Pièces, Plant Gris.*

Growing tips downy with carmine margins.

Young leaves arachnoid, light green, slightly coppery.

Leaves cuneiform-truncate, five-lobed with lateral sinuses medium open and quite deep; petiolar sinus lyrate; dentation pointed, medium; underside of blade and veins pubescent. Foliage reddens completely in autumn.

Green shoots ribbed with pink nodes; tendrils small, thin.

Bunches medium to large, often winged; grapes ovoid, medium, blue-black with coloured juice; ripening period: first epoch.

This grape is a mutation of the Gamay de Bouze, observed at Chaudenay in Saône-et-Loire, and propagated initially under the name of Gros Mourot or, sometimes, Plant Gris, because of the greyish colour of its verjuice; and also known as Gamay Six-Pièces to indicate its enormous fertility (six casks or *pièces* to the *ouvrée*, in other words 300hl/ha). Its growth is not very vigorous and it has to be pruned *en gobelet*, in free-standing low bushes. It ripens a little later than the Gamay Fréaux and its wine is less strongly coloured, though its quality is better. Two registered clones have been approved: numbers 567 and 568. Classed as 'authorized' for all of France, a few hectares are planted with it in the Loire valley.

Gamay Fréaux

Synonyms: *Gamay Fréau, Gamay Teinturier Fréaux, Violet de Saint-Denis* on the Côte Chalonnaise, *Teinturier Supérieur, Teinturier de Couchey, Teinturier le Roy* near Dijon.

Young leaves arachnoid, glossy, entirely red.

Leaves medium, orbicular, smooth, thin with convex edges, fully or slightly three-lobed, petiolar sinus in open V-shape; dentation pointed, narrow; underside of blade slightly pubescent; from the beginning of ripening (*véraison*) the foliage turns an intense purplish-blue.

Green shoots ribbed, smooth, bloomy, mahogany red with pink nodes; tendrils medium sized, fleshy.

Bunches small, winged, conical; grapes small, ovoid, blue-black (grey at *véraison*), juice strongly coloured; ripening period: first epoch.

This variety is another mutation of the Gamay de Bouze, discovered by Fréaux at Couchey in 1841. It is fertile, readily producing 80–100hl/ha of a wine that is low in alcohol but very deeply coloured and therefore useful in blending. Classed as 'authorized' in all of France, with one registered clone being approved, number 361, it is grown on a few hundred hectares in the Loire valley, Haute-Garonne and Saône-et-Loire.

A bunch of Gamay Noir à Jus Blanc grapes. This early-ripening variety is at its best when planted in the granite soils of Beaujolais or the Auvergne.

Gamay Noir à Jus Blanc

Synonyms: *Gamay Beaujolais, Gamay d'Auvergne, Petit Gamay, Bourguignon Noir, Petit Bourguignon, Lyonnaise* in Allier. There are also many selected clones that generally bear the names of their breeders: *Gamay Picard, Gamay Nicolas, Gamay Labronde, Gamay Geoffray, Gamay Magny, Gamay d'Arcenant*, etc.

Growing tips downy white with pink points.

Young leaves arachnoid, glossy, with bronze areas. Leaves medium sized, orbicular, smooth, thin, glossy, light green, slightly three-lobed; petiolar sinus in a fairly open V-shape; dentation pointed, narrow; underside of blade almost glabrous or slightly pubescent, according to the clone. Some leaves on sterile shoots are deeply five-lobed. In autumn, the foliage reddens substantially, though not totally.

Green shoots light green, smooth, glossy; tendrils small, thin, green.

Bunches medium sized, cylindrical, compact, slightly winged; berries medium sized, slightly ovoid, a fine violet-black in colour, with a plentiful whitish-blue bloom, fine skin, abundant juice of straightforward taste; ripening period: first epoch, late.

The Gamay has early budbreak, at the beginning of April, and so is vulnerable to spring frosts; however, it has the advantage of producing a small crop on its secondary buds, should the main buds be frost-bitten.

As its grapes ripen early, the Gamay is widely distributed in northern and mountain wine districts. It is a vine of average vigour and needs to be trained low and pruned short, otherwise it soon exhausts its strength, its buds being very prolific. Its yield is abundant: up to 60 to 70hl/ha on the slopes and more than 100hl/ha on plain sites with certain clones. It is on the granite soils of Auvergne or Beaujolais, grafted on to Vialla or 3309 Couderc, that the best results are achieved: fine, aromatic wines.

Thirty-four registered clones have been approved, the most important being numbers 284, 222, 509, 282 and 358. By nature, wine made from the Gamay is not high in alcohol, since the vine is such a prolific producer. Its red colour is shaded with violet and it keeps a measure of acidity, desirable in a *primeur* wine. Unfortunately, Beaujolais growers often over-chaptalize their musts to produce very alcoholic wines, exceeding 13°. Such wines are too heavy and unbalanced, with an alcohol to dry extract ratio of more than 6 or 7, whereas by law red wines should not have a ratio higher than 4.6. The wines are less heavily chaptalized in Auvergne and the Loire valley.

The Gamay has been classed as 'recommended' in the many *départements* found in the

Gamay Noir à Jus Blanc leaf.

Gamay Noir à Jus Blanc green shoot.

wine regions of Auvergne, Beaujolais, the Loire valley, Savoie, southeastern France, Languedoc and the South West. It forms a greater or lesser part of the plantings in numerous AOCs: Beaujolais, Touraine, Coteaux du Loir, Anjou, Rosé de Loire, Châtillon-en-Diois and Vin de Savoie among others; and also in many a VDQS: Côtes de Gien, Valençay, Châteaumeillant, Coteaux d'Ancenis, Saint-Pourçain, Côtes d'Auvergne, Côtes du Forez, Côte Roannaise, Vin du Bugey. Rosé wines are produced in many of these *appellations* using the Gamay alone.

The Gamay Noir à Jus Blanc is in 7th place among French red varieties, and is grown on 34,000ha divided among four large zones:

▷ Burgundy-Beaujolais, with more than 23,600ha: Rhône, Saône-et-Loire, Côte-d'Or and Yonne.

▷ The Auvergne, with 1,700ha: Puy-de-Dôme, Allier and Loire.

▷ The Loire valley, with nearly 5,500ha: Loir-et-Cher, Maine-et-Loire, Indre-et-Loire, Loire-Atlantique, Indre, Cher, Loiret and Nièvre.

▷ Savoie-Dauphiné, with 800ha: Savoie, Ain, Drôme, Isère and Haute-Savoie.

Ganson

A Grenache × Jurançon Noir cross obtained at the INRA at Vassal, near Montpellier. Well adapted to *en gobelet* training (as a small, free-standing bush), its black grapes can be picked two weeks earlier than those of the Carignan. They are not very susceptible to grey rot (botrytis).

More productive than the Carignan, the Ganson provides a wine of less marked characteristics, lower in alcohol and colour, but of rather better overall quality.

Garbesso

Synonym: *Garbès* in the Calvi area, Corsica.

This grape, classed as 'authorized' in Corsica, is very close to the Vermentino and is probably simply a clone of the latter.

Garonnet

Synonym: *18.283 Seyve-Villard*, obtained by crossing 7053 with 6905 Seibel.

Growing tips arachnoid, white.

Young leaves green, smooth.

Leaves orbicular-reniform, crimped, contorted, deeply five-lobed with lateral sinuses acute at base and narrow, the lobes concave, petiolar sinus lyrate and practically closed; dentation pointed, medium; blade smooth on both surfaces.

Green shoots smooth, finely ribbed.

Bunches voluminous, conical, compact; grapes ovoid, black, medium sized; ripening period: first epoch.

This is a vigorous hybrid that produces well, giving a *vin ordinaire* without much depth of colour. It cannot tolerate drought and is susceptible to downy mildew, requiring frequent preventative treatments against this disease. Classed as 'authorized' in the Midi, the South West and the Loire valley, where several hundred hectares of it are grown.

Gascon

Synonyms: *Franc Noir de l'Yonne, Franc Noir du Gâtinais* in Loiret, *Arribet* or *Larrivet* in Gironde, *Rochelle Noire, Plant de Moret, Morineau, Plant de Villeneuve* at Coulanges-la-Vineuse, *Doyen* in Yonne.

Growing tips open, felty white, with carmine margins.

Young leaves downy, greenish.

Leaves orbicular, medium sized, whole or slightly three-lobed, petiolar sinus lyrate with slightly overlapping edges; dentation convex, narrow; underside of blade slightly pubescent with woolly hairs, fluffy. The foliage reddens fully in the autumn.

Green shoots finely ribbed, light green, glabrous; tendrils small, thin.

Bunches small to medium, winged, cylindrical, compact; grapes spherical, medium sized, blue-black; ripening period: second epoch.

This old Yonne variety was grown to a considerable extent before phylloxera; its wine was not very strong, but it was valued by the Paris wine trade for its ability to freshen certain Midi wines. Its budbreak is late, which means that it is not threatened by spring frosts.

It is classed as 'recommended' in Indre, Loiret and Loir-et-Cher, where it is grown on a few hectares.

Genouillet

Synonyms: *Genouillet Noir* in Aube, *Genouillat, Genouillé, Genouilleret* in Indre, *Genoillet, Genoilleret, Moret Noir* or *Gros Moret* around Bourges, *Plant Mercier* in Yonne.

Bunches cylindrical, medium sized, compact; grapes spherical, medium sized; ripening period: second epoch.

This grape variety used to be more widely grown than any other in the vineyards of Issoudun and la Châtre in Indre, and Châteaumeillant in Cher, as well as the Coteaux de la Vanne in Aube. Its wine is light, fresh, rather hard initially, but it softens and mellows with age. It has not been classified and therefore has only a limited future.

Genovese

Synonyms: *Raisin Génois, Genove, Genevose, Genovesilla, Bianchetta Genovese, Uva Albarola* (erroneously), *Calcatella.*

Growing tips felty white with carmine margins.

Young leaves downy, with bronze patches.

Leaves deeply five-lobed, with narrow lateral sinuses, petiolar sinus lyrate, narrow. Dentation convex, wide; underside of blade downy, with main veins pubescent.

Bunches medium sized, cylindrical-conical, compact, winged; grapes medium sized, spherical to ovoid, greenish white, skin thick; ripening period: third epoch, early.

Classed as 'authorized' in Corsica, this vine originated from the Italian Cinqueterre wine district in Liguria, where it is known as Bosco and is used to make DOC Cinqueterre. In Corsica it gives wines that have plenty of alcohol, are golden yellow in colour and have a pronounced perfume. Despite these apparently attractive qualities, the variety is little grown.

Gevrey-Chambertin

The 446ha of Gevrey-Chambertin are responsible for the most relaxed, leisurely, silky smooth style of red burgundy. Confronted with the complexity of *climats*, microclimates and *terroirs* that make up this large *appellation d'origine contrôlée*, the legislators of 11 September 1936 distinguished both Grands Crus and Premiers Crus from the remainder of the *appellation* ('village' or 'commune' wines). The Grands Crus Chambertin, Chambertin-Clos de Bèze, Latricières-Chambertin, Mazis-Chambertin, Mazoyères-Chambertin, Charmes-Chambertin, Griotte-Chambertin, Chapelle-Chambertin and Ruchottes-Chambertin are, of course, the flower of this *appellation*; there are also 25 fine Premiers Crus. The general rules governing the labelling of Premiers Crus throughout Burgundy apply here: the name of the *appellation* can be followed by that of the particular holding, the *climat*, if it is classified as a Premier Cru, or by the words 'Premier Cru', or by both. The wines must have a minimum alcohol content of 10.5°, with 11° for the Premiers Crus, and 11.5° for the Grands Crus. The maximum yield varies between 35hl/ha for the 'village' or 'commune' *appellation* to 32hl/ha for most of the Grands Crus, and 30hl/ha for Chambertin-Clos de Bèze.

This wonderful area of hills and slopes produces splendidly distinguished wines of an intense ruby red, with powerful, almost violent bouquets. They are full, mellow and soft, and age well.

Gevrey-Chambertin. The château of the lords of Vergy, dating from the 10th century, looks down over a remarkable wine district.

Gewürztraminer

Synonym: *Gentil Rose Aromatique* formerly in Alsace.

Growing tips felty white with carmine margins. Young leaves felty, yellowish, those growing lower on the vine having bronze patches.

Leaves large, orbicular, markedly bullate, crimped, with convex edges, base of veins red, five-lobed, the upper lateral sinuses deep but the lower lateral sinuses shallow; petiolar sinus wholly closed with edges largely overlapping; dentation convex, wide; underside of blade downy white.

Green shoots ribbed, light green, with some brown longitudinal striations, arachnoid at the tip; tendrils small, thin.

Bunches small, conical, rather loose; grapes small, ovoid, pink to light red, skins thick, juice perfumed with a slightly musky taste; ripening period: second epoch, late.

This is a vigorous vine, budding early and susceptible to frost and to oidium (powdery mildew). The grapes, especially when picked overripe and with *pourriture noble* (noble rot) affecting them, have a sweet spiciness and a powerful perfume, often floral in character (hence the vine's former synonym). The wines made from them are very distinctive and can be drunk between meals, for example as 'conversation wines' in the afternoon, as well as with rich foods such as foie gras. Yields are low, barely exceeding 50hl/ha.

Classed as 'recommended' in Alsace and Moselle, Gewürztraminer forms part of the Alsace AOC. Three registered clones have been approved: numbers 47, 48 and 643.

Gewürztraminer leaf. The only French plantings of this vigorous, strongly aromatic variety are in Alsace.

Gewürztraminer green shoot.

Gigondas, at the foot of the Dentelles de Montmirail in the Côtes du Rhône. The Grenache is the leading grape variety of this region.

Gigondas

This *appellation* does not have the venerable traditions that some ascribe to it. If the vine was grown here before the 16th century, then it was as part of a pattern of subsistence cultivation on small plots of land surrounding this market town. For several centuries it was primarily a sheep-rearing and olive-growing area. However, the fall in the price of wool, brought about by Australian imports, meant that olives became the main crop. After the disastrous frosts of 1956 and 1957, the vine replaced the olive tree on the terraces and slopes, so the reputation of Gigondas as a wine-growing area dates very much from the 20th century. The *appellation d'origine contrôlée*, for one commune, was ratified on 6 January 1971.

The present wine-growing area is 1,000ha. Average annual production is 35,000hl. Of this, 6,000hl is produced by the Gigondas cooperative. The Vacqueyras cooperative also produces a small volume of Gigondas wine.

The terrain is mainly composed of red clay terraces, gravelly or pebbly, lying at the foot of, or on the slopes of, the imposing Dentelles de Montmirail mountains.

There are no white wines produced in Gigondas. The growers considered that the soil here would not be able to produce white wines of true Rhône character and so they were officially excluded from the *appellation* regulations. There is, however, a small production of heady and powerful rosé wine, with a bouquet suggesting soft fruits such as peaches or apricots.

As at Châteauneuf-du-Pape, it is red wines that are pre-eminent here. They are made mainly from the Grenache grape, which is particularly well suited to the local soil and climate, and they benefit from a small admixture of Cinsaut and Syrah, which improves their balance.

There is something almost savage in their bouquet, suggested by a combination of spice, peach, apricot, and liquorice. The wines are powerful, tannic, hard during their early years. Five years of ageing are often needed to reveal their deeper qualities.

Givry

The mainly red wines of Givry occupy a special position on the Côte Chalonnaise. They have been renowned since the Middle Ages for their particular character, combining lightness with a chewy, mouth-filling quality. Henri IV, who liked them, had numerous casks of Givry delivered to his château at Saint-Germain.

The legislation of 8 February 1936, which ratified the *appellation d'origine contrôlée*, stipulates that the wines must have a minimum alcohol content of 10.5° for the reds, and 11° for the whites. Maximum yield is 40hl/ha. Production conditions for the Givry Premiers Crus require 11° for the red wines and 11.5° for the white wines.

The 140ha of the *appellation* produce about 9,000hl of red wine a year, made from the Pinot Noir grape variety, and 750hl of white wine from the Chardonnay and the Pinot Blanc.

Goldriesling

Synonym: *Riesling Doré*. This is a cross of Riesling × Muscat Précoce de Courtiller.

Growing tips downy white.

Young leaves arachnoid, lobed.

Leaves truncate, deeply five-lobed, upper lateral sinuses with overlapping edges, petiolar sinus lyrate with overlapping edges; dentation medium sized, convex; underside of blade pubescent, rough.

This white variety has late budbreak but ripens early, in the first epoch. It is fertile and gives a wine with plenty of alcohol, best drunk young. It is susceptible to grey rot (botrytis). It is classed as 'authorized' in Alsace, where ten or so hectares of it are grown.

Gouais Blanc

Synonyms: *Gueuche Blanc, Foirard Blanc du Jura, Gouge Blanc* at Montluçon and Gannat, *Gros Blanc* at Chantelle, *Gouai, Goix, Got, Gau, Gouest, Gouet* in Nièvre, *Gouge* in Loir-et-Cher.

Bunches medium sized, cylindrical-conical, loose; grapes spherical, golden yellow, small, not very juicy, acid, astringent; ripening period: second epoch.

This grape, grown in central France (Allier, Cher and Indre) produces acidic *vins ordinaires*. Unclassified.

Gouget Noir

Synonyms: *Gouge Noir, Gauget Noir* in Allier and Nièvre, *Lyonnais* in Indre.

Bunches small to medium sized, cylindrical, compact, often winged; grapes spherical or ovoid, medium sized, black; ripening period: second epoch.

This is a grape variety grown in the Montluçon area, with vines also found in Cher at Châteaumeillant, and on the banks of the river Indre. Vigorous and productive, it gives a *vin ordinaire* of acidity but not much colour. It is very vulnerable to spring frosts and susceptible to grey rot (botrytis). It is classed as 'authorized' in Allier.

Graisse

Synonyms: *Plant de Graisse,* a name that arose from the almost 'oily' flesh of its grapes and is rendered in Gascon dialect as *Grecho* or *Plant de Grecho*, which has mistakenly been interpreted as *Plant de Grèce* (from Greece); other names are *Gras* in Hautes-Pyrénées, and *Chalosse* and *Ramassou Blanc* in Landes.

Growing tips felty white with carmine margins.

Young leaves downy, yellowish.

Leaves large, orbicular, thick, contorted, crimped at the petiolar junction, with concave lobes, generally five-lobed with the lateral sinuses narrow and acute at base, petiolar sinus lyrate, closed, or with overlapping edges; dentation convex, narrow; underside of blade pubescent; petioles red, pubescent.

Green shoots finely ribbed, reddish-brown on the side exposed to sun, nodes pink, tendrils thin and small.

Bunches large, winged, conical, voluminous, compact; grapes medium, ovoid, yellowish-white; ripening period: third epoch.

This is a vigorous, productive vine that forms a small part of the Armagnac AOC plantings. Its wine is acidic and of average quality. The Graisse is susceptible to oidium (powdery mildew), but less susceptible than the Folle Blanche to grey rot (botrytis). It is classed as 'recommended' in Gers, Haute-Garonne and Tarn-et-Garonne, where it is grown on nearly 500ha.

Gramon

This crossing of Grenache × Aramon has its budbreak a few days before the Carignan, and ripens in the third epoch. Its bunches are medium sized, not very compact, with blue-black, spherical grapes. Its productivity and the alcoholic strength of its wines are superior to those of the Grenache or Carignan. It makes a good table wine, though not very deeply coloured. Classed as 'recommended' in the southern half of France, it has one approved clone: number 539.

Grand Noir de la Calmette

Synonym: *Grand Noir.*

Bunches large, pyramidal, winged, loose, with wine-red stalks; grapes small, spherical, black, thick-skinned, with deeply coloured juice; ripening period: second epoch.

A crossing of Petit Bouschet × Aramon. It has late budbreak, enabling it to escape untimely frosts; its habit is erect. This variety is vigorous, fertile, readily producing 100hl/ha of rather dull wine, low in alcohol but moderately rich in colour, thanks to the Alicante Bouschet element of its parentage. It is more susceptible to oidium (powdery mildew) than to downy mildew.

Grand Roussillon and Grand Roussillon Rancio

This *appellation d'origine contrôlée,* governed by legislation of 19 May 1972, is available for the combined area of production of all *vins doux naturels* (sweet fortified wines) of AOC status in the *départements* of Pyrénées-Orientales (90 communes) and Aude (9 communes). The *appellation* area thus extends over 29,000ha, and takes in the Rivesaltes and Banyuls zones.

The principal grape varieties used to make the wines of this AOC are the Muscat à Petits Grains Blancs, the Muscat d'Alexandrie, Grenache, Macabeu and Tourbat. Subsidiary varieties are the Carignan, Cinsaut, Syrah and Listan, which may not exceed 10 per cent of the vines planted in any single plot.

To be entitled to the Grand Roussillon Rancio *appellation,* the Grand Roussillon *vins doux naturels* have to be vinified and aged in the conditions that bestow on them the special *rancio* (oxidized) taste, which comes about through storage with exposure to the elements.

Grands Echézeaux

Only a few plots of vines within the commune of Flagey-Echézeaux, in the Côte de Nuits, can lay claim to the Grands Echézeaux AOC, defined by legislation of 31 July 1937. The wines of this red Grand Cru can also make use of the Vosne-Romanée Premier Cru *appellation* if wished — an *appellation* that ranks lower in the hierarchy, but enjoys greater fame.

Pool at Château La Mission-Haut-Brion, a Graves Cru Classé, in the Bordeaux region.

The alcohol content has been set at 11.5° for both Grands Echézeaux and Vosne-Romanée Premier Cru. The maximum yield is 30hl/ha for Grands Echézeaux, and 35hl/ha for Vosne-Romanée Premier Cru.

The vineyard plots, which cover around 9ha between Vougeot and Vosne-Romanée, produce about 260hl a year on average of a great wine with the structured vigour of the Vougeots and the finesse and elegance of the Vosne-Romanées. The delicate bouquet of Grands Echézeaux is often described as being a blend of violet and hawthorne.

Graves and Graves Supérieures

The Graves district lies along the left bank of the Garonne from the Jalle de Blanquefort stream, which marks the boundary with the Médoc, as far as Langon, on the edge of the Landes forest. The Graves *appellation d'origine contrôlée*, for red and white wines, was created by decree on 4 March 1937, and covers 43 communes.

To be entitled to the Graves *appellation*, red wines have to be made from Merlot, Cabernet Sauvignon, Cabernet Franc, Petit Verdot and Côt grapes. The minimum sugar content of the musts is set at 162g per litre and the alcoholic strength of the wines has to be between 10° and 13°. The base yield is restricted to 50hl/ha.

Since 1959, wines of the Graves *appellation* have to have a certificate of quality from a tasting panel before being allowed on sale.

To benefit from the Graves *appellation*, white wines have to have been made from Sémillon, Sauvignon Blanc and Muscadelle grapes. The musts have to have a minimum sugar content of 144g per litre. The alcoholic strength of the wines must be between 10° and 13°. White wines with a minimum strength after fermentation of 12°, and made from musts containing a minimum 187g per litre of sugar, can claim the Graves Supérieures *appellation*. There has been a steadily increasing trend in recent years for Graves white wines to be dry, and Graves Supérieures to be sweet. It should be emphasized, however, that sources and references are less than precise on this subject. The base yield for all wines is 50hl/ha. In 1985, the area given over to red Graves was 1,617ha, and production was 98,585hl. There were 844ha given over to dry white Graves and production was 48,814hl. Production of Graves Supérieures was 14,516hl from an area of 440ha.

Just one Graves *cru* figured in the 1855 classification: the red wine from Château Haut-Brion in Pessac. A recent classification of all the Graves *crus* was officially endorsed in 1959.

There is no cooperative within the *appellation* area; but in 1985 the Langoiran cooperative, on the right bank of the Garonne, made 341hl of Graves dry white and 403hl of Graves Supérieures sweet white wines.

Graves reds are supple, full-bodied wines with very pronounced bouquets, and are suitable for ageing. The dry white wines are always fine and elegant, but their exact character varies according to how large a percentage of Sauvignon Blanc they contain, and whether they have been cask-fermented and given *élevage* in new oak or not. They can either be drunk within the first two or three years, or they can be aged for a longer period in bottle to acquire complexity and depth.

The sweet wines, which generally come from areas surrounding the Barsac, Cérons or Sauternes *appellations*, are at their best after a few years' bottle ageing.

Graves de Vayres

This *appellation d'origine contrôlée*, established by decree on 31 July 1937, is reserved for white and red wines made from grapes picked within the boundaries of the Vayres and Arveyres communes, on the left bank of the Dordogne opposite Libourne.

To be entitled to the Graves de Vayres *appellation*, the red wines have to be made from the same grapes as those stipulated for the Bordeaux *appellation*. Minimum sugar content of the musts is set at 162g per litre and the wines should have a minimum alcoholic strength of 10° and a maximum of 13°. Base yield is 50hl/ha.

The white wines can only be made from the Sémillon, Sauvignon Blanc and Merlot Blanc grape varieties, and the proportion of the last-named variety should not exceed 30 per cent of plantings. The minimum sugar content of the musts has to be 161g per litre. The wines are required to have a minimum alcoholic strength of 10.5° and a maximum of 14.5°. Base yield is 60hl/ha.

Since 1966, both the red and the white wines have to have a certificate of quality awarded by an official tasting panel before they can be sold.

In 1985, the area given over to red wines was 264ha, with a production of 14,579hl, of which 1,784hl was vinified by the Arveyres cooperative. The area given over to white wines was 170ha and production 9,370hl, with 2,217hl made by this cooperative.

For a number of years, there has been a decrease in the area planted with white grape varieties in favour of red varieties. There has also been a clear reduction in the production of sweet white wines, which were predominant in this area until the 1960s; dry white wines, fresh and fruity in style, and for drinking young, have taken their place. The red wines are supple and aromatic, and achieve maturity quickly.

Grenache

Synonyms: *Alicante, Roussillon, Rivesaltes, Rivos-Altos, Bois Jaune* in Languedoc, *Redondal* in Haute-Garonne, *Tinto* in Vaucluse, *Sans-Pareil* in Alpes-de-Haute-Provence.

Growing tips flattened, open, downy white with faintly carmine margins.

Young leaves arachnoid, very shiny, green or with slightly bronze patches.

Leaves medium sized, cuneiform, smooth, light green, very shiny, thick, contorted, glabrous on both surfaces, usually five-lobed with upper lateral sinuses very narrow, acute at base; petiolar sinus lyrate and more or less open, veins light yellow; dentation pointed, small, narrow.

Green shoots finely ribbed, light green all over, shiny with swollen nodes; tendrils small.

Bunches medium sized to large with woody peduncles, conical, winged, compact; grapes medium sized, spherical or slightly ovoid, black, with fairly thick skins, juice quite abundant, colourless; ripening period: third epoch.

The Grenache has slightly later budbreak than the Aramon. Its upright habit and its vigorous shoots enable it to stand up to drought and to high winds. It is a vine that gives its best results on dry, pebbly slopes, such as those of Rivesaltes or Châteauneuf-du-Pape. Its wine is strong in alcohol, very heady, with a fine russet-red colour, but it ages rapidly, its colour fades and it tends to acquire oxidized, *rancio* flavours. This characteristic is sometimes valued and accentuated by exposing the wine to the sun in part-filled casks or demijohns in the courtyards of wine-making establishments, or on flat roofs. To obtain good wines for ageing, therefore, it is necessary to add grapes of other varieties with more body than the Grenache (the Syrah, Mourvèdre or Morrastel); or more suppleness and mellowness (the Cinsaut, Aspiran or Piquepoul Noir). When grown on the fertile plains of the Midi, the Grenache loses all its character.

The Grenache is little affected by oidium (powdery mildew) but it is very susceptible to downy mildew, to grey rot (botrytis) and to bacterial infection. Yields are therefore very variable: from 20hl/ha to 80hl/ha, and even over 100hl when the vines are pruned long. Twenty-one registered clones have been approved, the most important of which are numbers 70 (productive), 224 and 362. The last-named clone is susceptible to *coulure* (flower abortion), but gives high alcohol levels, useful in the making of *vins doux naturels* (sweet fortified wines). Classed as 'recommended' in all the southern French *départements*, the Grenache figures among the varieties used in most of the Mediterranean AOCs: Châteauneuf-du-Pape, Côtes du Rhône, Tavel, Côtes de Provence, Coteaux du Languedoc. It is used for *vins doux naturels* in Banyuls, Maury and Rasteau. The area planted

Grapes, leaves and green shoots of the Grenache. This vine performs best in the dry, pebbly soil of the Rhône valley, at Châteauneuf-du-Pape and Gigondas.

with Grenache now exceeds 80,000ha, making it the third most grown variety in France after the Carignan and the Ugni Blanc.

Two groups of Grenache plantings can be distinguished. One is the Provençal group, with 42,000ha, of which 25,000ha are in Vaucluse and the rest divided among Drôme, Var and Bouches-du-Rhône; and the Languedoc group, with 38,000ha in Gard, Pyrénées-Orientales, Hérault, Aude and Ardèche.

The Grenache Blanc, grown on more than 16,000ha, differs from the Grenache only in the colour of its grapes. It is mainly used in the Roussillon area for making white *vins doux naturels*, as at Rivesaltes. Its cultivation, though, is declining. Its approved clones are numbers 141 and 143.

The Grenache Rose and Grenache Gris are grown on 3,600ha devoted to the production of *vins doux naturels*. The four approved clones are numbers 147, 148, 149 and 150.

Gringet

This vine is chiefly found in the Arve valley in Haute-Savoie and sparkling wines are made from it at Ayse. It appears to be identical to the Savagnin. It is classed as 'recommended' in Haute-Savoie and is included in the Vin de Savoie AOC. It is grown on 10ha.

Griottes-Chambertin

The site of this red-wine Grand Cru lies in the commune of Gevrey-Chambertin, on the Côte de Nuits, opposite the famed Clos de Bèze. It is a worthy member of the celebrated local group of Grands Crus, in particular because of the subtle, fruity aromas that the name Griotte (a variety of cherry) implies.

The *appellation d'origine contrôlée*, governed by the decree of 31 July 1937, requires the wines to be made exclusively from the Pinot Noir grape variety, have a minimum alcoholic strength of 11.5° and a maximum yield of 32hl/ha. The 5.5ha of Griottes-Chambertin produce some 47hl a year of a wine that is alluringly full of vigour, body and taste, and possesses a rich colour.

Vine tender's stone hut in Côte-d'Or.

Grolleau

Synonyms: *Groleau, Groslot, Gros Lot* (names derived from the old French word *grolle*, meaning the raven, a bird with plumage as black as the grapes of this vine), *Groslot de Cinq-Mars, Groslot de Vallères, Gamay de Châtillon*, at Savennières, *Pineau de Saumur, Plant Mini, Plant de Boisnard*.

Growing tips downy white with carmine margins.

Young leaves arachnoid, bullate, dull, bronze in colour.

Leaves orbicular, flat, finely bullate, wide central lobe, without other lobes, with the edges of the blade slightly concave; petiolar junction and base of veins red; petiolar sinus lyrate, narrow, sometimes closed; dentation convex, medium sized; underside of blade slightly pubescent, as are the main veins. Foliage reddens partially in autumn.

Green shoots ribbed, reddish brown; tendrils strong.

Bunches quite large, conical, winged, compact; grapes medium sized, spherical, blue-black, abundant juice; ripening period: second epoch.

The Grolleau has midseason budbreak; it is a productive vine with yields of 80 to 120hl/ha. Its wine is light, with a low alcohol content, often used for vinifying as rosé. The Grolleau is classed as 'recommended' in the Loire valley *départements*, as well as in the South West. Six registered clones have been approved: numbers 226, 288, 364, 365, 366 and 437. This variety is one of those specified for the AOCs of Anjou, Rosé d'Anjou, Rosé de Loire, Crémant de Loire, Anjou Mousseux, Saumur Mousseux and Touraine. It is in decline: only 5,855ha were given over to this variety in 1980 compared with no less than 11,400 in 1958. Its cultivation is concentrated in the vineyards of the Loire valley: Maine-et-Loire (4,000ha), Indre-et-Loire (1,000ha), Loire-et-Cher, Loire-Atlantique, Deux-Sèvres and Vienne.

A little Grolleau Gris is grown in Maine-et-

Loire and Loire-Atlantique, on 225ha. It has been classed as 'recommended' in the Loire *départements* listed above. A Grolleau Blanc, with white grapes, has been recorded in the Coteaux du Layon area.

Gros Manseng

Classed as 'recommended' in Gers, Landes, Lot-et-Garonne and the two Pyrenean *départements*, this variety is very close to the Petit Manseng.

It forms part of the plantings of the AOCs of Jurançon, Pacherenc du Vic-Bilh and Béarn, and grows on about 100ha.

Gros Plant du Pays Nantais

The vineyard area given over to this VDQS, classed by legislation of 26 November 1954, covers 1,500ha.

The grape variety used is the Folle Blanche, known locally as the Gros Plant. Average annual production during the first half of 1980 was around 220,000hl. The vineyards extend over 87 communes in Loire-Atlantique, Maine-et-Loire and Vendée.

Gros Plant du Pays Nantais is a dry white wine, pale greenish yellow in colour; its predominantly acidic character is compensated by its appealingly fruity taste. It is supple and pleasant, especially with the seafood of the Nantes coastline; it should be drunk young.

Gros Verdot

Synonyms: *Verdot Colon, Colon, Mancin-Colon* in Entre-Deux-Mers, *Verdau-Colon* around Saint-André-de-Cubzac and *Pruéra* at Saint-Pierre-d'Aurillac.

Growing tips felty white.

Young leaves rapidly become arachnoid, green with an orange hue and bronze glints.

Leaves large, orbicular, crimped with convex edges, deeply five-lobed, the upper lateral sinuses closed and acute at the base, the lower sinuses open, the petiolar sinus narrow or closed; dentation pointed, narrow; underside of blade weakly arachnoid. In autumn the foliage reddens very slightly.

Green shoots ribbed, pale green with nodes partly pink; tendrils long, fleshy.

Bunches small, conical, loose; grapes spherical, small, black; ripening period: third epoch.

This Bordeaux grape variety of secondary importance was previously planted in the *palus*, the low-lying marshy area alongside the Gironde estuary, where it gave a large quantity of deeply coloured *vin ordinaire*, acid and astringent. Unclassified.

The Nantes wine-growing district supplies some lively wines, among them Gros Plant du Pays Nantais, made from the Folle Blanche grape.

Gueuche Noire

Synonyms: *Gros Plant, Plant de Treffort* in Ain, *Foirard* at Poligny, *Plant d'Arlay* at Salins-les-Bains, *Guat* or *Gouais* at Saint-Amour (Jura), *Plant d'Anjou Noir* and *Plant de Saint-Rémi* at Saint-Génis, in Rhône.

Bunches medium sized, cylindrical, compact; grapes medium sized, spherical or slightly ovoid, blue-black; ripening period: third epoch.

The Gueuche is a productive variety, but its wine is hard, rough, generally too high in acidity as the grapes ripen too late for the Jura region, where it is mainly grown. This vine is very susceptible to disease, and has a limited future. It has not been classified.

Guillemot

Synonyms: *Bougaou, Gouboil, Coé de Baque* or *Coué de Bacho* ('cowhide') in Landes, *Mourejalès* in Gers, at Condom.

Bunches medium sized, winged, cylindrical, compact; grapes golden yellow, ovoid, fairly large; ripening period: second epoch, late.

This Béarnais grape, unclassified and not now very widespread, was in former times grown high up in the mountain valleys of the Pau region. Very fertile and vigorous, it gives an acidic, rather rough wine.

BOTTLES

It is impossible to talk about wine without thinking of its inseparable companion, the glass bottle. For in the minds of professionals, be they wine growers, oenologists or wine merchants, as well as wine drinkers, wine and its glass cell are indissolubly linked.

Wine and glass have gone hand-in-hand for centuries, and it is evident that the two are necessary to each other. Wine needs glass bottles for its transport, sale, and service at table. No other material could fulfil these functions so efficiently and so glamorously. And the reverse is also true: what looks better in glass than wine?

The marriage of wine and glass is a perfect one, since it unites wine, the living and mysterious fruit of the earth, sun and man's labour, with glass, which is another product of the earth, of fire and man's labour. This noble union has been consecrated by tradition and by the satisfaction of customers through several centuries.

The legend of glass

The origins of glass are a mystery. They stretch back so far that it would be almost impossible to trace them historically with any certainty. The information we have on the subject is hazy, and sometimes even contradictory. In the absence of real and tangible evidence, only legend can help us to imagine and visualize the discovery of glass.

For thousands of years, this legend was handed down orally. It was at last written down by the naturalist Pliny in the 1st century AD. The story is that, about 3,500 to 4,000 years before the birth of Christ, some sailors landed on a beach in Asia Minor to spend the night there. They lit a fire to cook their meal, and as they could not find a stone on which to rest their cooking pot, they used a few pieces of soda (sodium carbonate) from the cargo they were carrying. Next morning, in the remains of the fire, they found a shiny, solid deposit. The sand from the beach and the soda had fused in the heat of the fire and produced this strange substance. Glass had been born.

The glass blower; a 19th-century coloured print. The ancient techniques of glass blowing have lasted to our own times.

The history of glass

Glass, like wine, is therefore several thousand years old. For the period between 4000 BC and 1600 BC, finds of glass are limited to vitreous coatings on stones such as quartz. Then came Egyptian pottery. Until the time of the Egyptians, glass had been of very minor importance; it was mainly used to make beads and other ornaments.

The first glass objects

Between 1600 and 50 BC, important developments took place in the process of glassmaking, and the first glass vessels came into being.

The technique used to make them was to apply a coating of glass paste to a clay mould. The mould could be broken up and removed, leaving the glass object intact. This method spread throughout the Middle East, and the Egyptians in particular were masters of it. The latter part of their era saw the emergence of glass objects shaped by abrasion and by the moulding of fused sticks or beads of glass.

By this time, vases, goblets and flasks of glass were being made. However, they were small, and appear to have been used only for ointments, make-up, perfumes, oils and toilet waters.

Technical advances

At the beginning of the Christian era, an anonymous glass maker had the ingenious idea of taking a little melted glass with one end of an iron tube, and then blowing at the other end. A useful glass container was the result. In this way, glass blowing was invented. This technique has lasted two thousand years, and will no doubt exist for a long time yet in various mechanized and automated forms.

The discovery of the technique was an exceptionally important one, giving impetus to the use of glass under many guises in every sphere of the arts, industry and science; and it was thanks to this technique, too, that wine and glass were eventually to become associated with one another several centuries later.

The technique of glass blowing changed very little from the time it came into being until the late 19th century. Certain improvements within glass manufacture in general were, of course, introduced, such as open, and later closed, moulds, first in one piece, then in two pieces; and the invention of ring moulds. However, glass making remained basically a manual task.

The invention of semi-automatic glass-blowing machines towards the end of the 19th century made the bottle worker's task less laborious and very much quicker. But the work of feeding the machine and removing the finished bottles still had to be done by hand.

Automation

The third stage in the development of glass-making technology brought the complete automation that we know today, by enabling the machines to be fed and discharged mechanically.

Throughout most of this long period of development, there had been little contact between wine and glass, or glass in bottle form, at least. Such contact as there was between the two came about because wine had become readily associated with the glass goblet, and then the drinking glass.

The birth of the bottle

There are numerous illustrations proving that glass bottles, flasks and carafes have been used since antiquity. For a long time, however, these vessels were essentially ornamental or, as far as wine was concerned, they were simply used for serving it at table. Until the end of the 17th century, the standard practice was to store and transport wine in barrels then draw it off for serving, and even at table it was generally served in earthenware or pewter jugs or in carafes, depending on the period and the circumstances.

However, glass bottles existed as early as the 14th and 15th centuries, although they were not very widely used at that time, nor were they used in the way they are today. It is likely, though, that the storage of great wines in glass bottles dates from about this time. According to historians, blown bottles were then very fragile, and often had to be protected by a wicker covering.

The relationship between wine and the glass bottle began in earnest in France about 1700. This came about thanks to two things: firstly, the introduction of thick glass bottles from England, which were very much stronger than those made in France at the time; and secondly, the use of cork to seal the bottles, an innovation which seems to have been pioneered in France by Dom Pérignon, who is said to have used this advance in his 'invention' of champagne. Sealed bottles meant that vintage wines could be matured without the addition of wines from subsequent vintages.

Although the sources are sometimes contradictory, it does

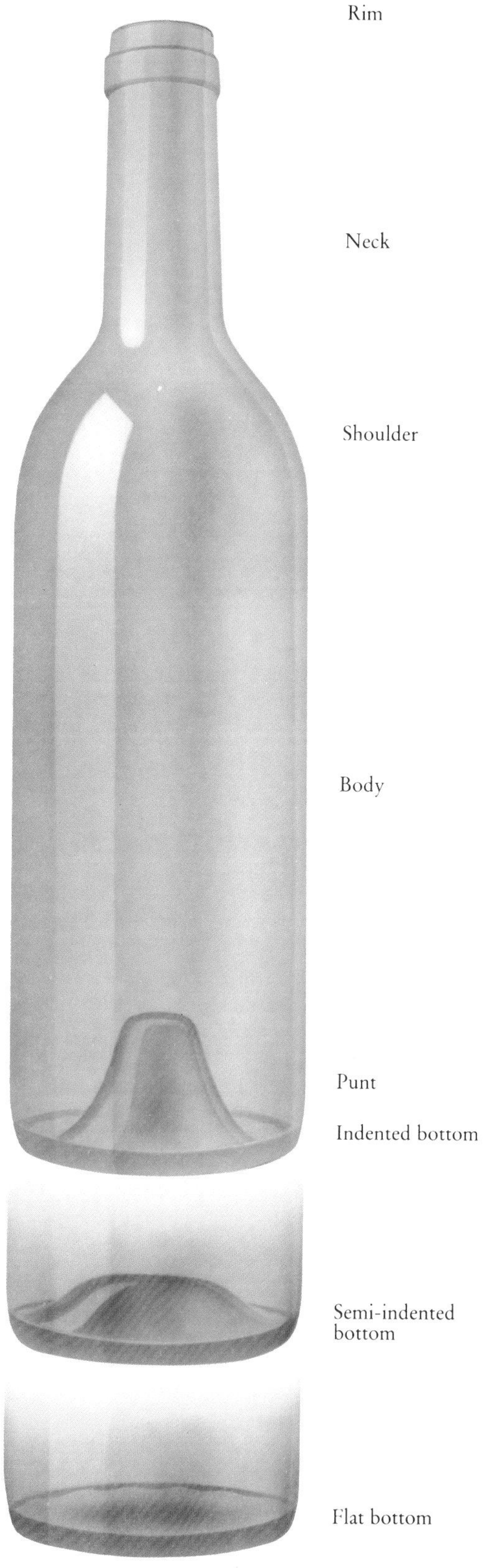

ANATOMY OF A BOTTLE

seem that until this time not only were bottles fragile, but their stoppers were made of wood, hemp or oiled linen, and were therefore not very reliable. They were far from watertight or airtight, and this obviously did not aid the keeping qualities of wine.

Later on, the invention of the ring mould made it possible to produce bottles with slimmer, more suitably sized necks, easily stopped with cork. From then on, wine could safely be kept in bottles. The storage and transport of wine in glass began to develop.

The evolution of shapes

For a long time the shape of bottles was inspired by the forms of the Gallo-Roman flask, in that the base was usually a flattened sphere, to give stability, and the neck was very long in proportion to the base, to make the vessel easy to grasp and to pour from. This was the shape in use at the beginning of the 18th century.

Then the shape began to evolve, bottles tending to get longer and more cylindrical. This was because wine was increasingly being stored, aged and transported in bottles, and a longer, slimmer bottle was not only easier to transport, but it also could be laid down and stacked horizontally without difficulty. The squat bottles of previous times could not be stacked horizontally.

In the 19th century, some regions added their own local touch by creating bottles that were felt to be representative of their *terroir* and their wine. First came the *bourguignonne*, or Burgundy bottle, then the *champenoise* from Champagne, and the Alsace *flûte*.

The bottles of today

It seems strange that, with the exception of this Alsace *flûte*, bottles have now lost their individuality to some extent. However, although the bottle market is now dominated by traditional Bordeaux and Burgundy shapes, moves are afoot to promote new designs that reflect a particular *appellation* or region. The impetus for this has come in some cases from merchants, but more often from local growers' groupings and interprofessional committees.

The Alsace *flûte*

This tall, slender bottle is famous and is protected by the decree of 20 May 1955, which sets out its dimensions and conditions of use. The name Alsace is embossed on the bottom, and the bottle is used for most of the region's wines. Since 1972, all Alsace wines have had to be bottled within the regional production area, and this regulation has promoted a still more extensive use of the *flûte*.

The capacities have varied according to the intended destination: 37.5cl, mainly for use in restaurants; 70cl for the French market (until 1989); and from 1 January 1989 75cl for export and domestic purposes.

The tint used for these bottles is always green, of the shade known to glass manufacturers as Champagne green. Some clear or lightly tinted glass bottles are used for certain wines, such as Pinot Noir d'Alsace.

GLASS

Glass is a hard, homogeneous, isotropic, resistant substance. It is normally transparent, but can be made opaque. It is made by the fusion of a basic mixture of silica, soda and lime, at a temperature of about 1,500°C.

This mixture is fused gradually by the effects of the heat, and turns into a paste which can be shaped at about 1,000°C.

Typical composition:

Silica	*72 per cent*
Soda	*13 per cent*
Lime	*12 per cent*
Various stabilizers and colorants	*3 per cent*

The Bordeaux bottle (*bordelaise*)

This bottle evolved over a period of centuries, particularly in its shape, which changed from roughly conical to cylindrical. In the Bordeaux area, it is known as the *Frontignan*; it seems that the shape originated in this Hérault village in the 18th century.

In the mid-1980s, in order to have a bottle for the use of Bordeaux wines only, the Comité Interprofessionnel des Vins de Bordeaux (Bordeaux Interprofessional Wine Committee) created a new 75cl *bordelaise* known as the *CIVB*, which has the inscription 'Bordeaux' embossed on the shoulder three times, and bears a motif of interlaced crescents from the city coat of arms. Much Bordeaux wine is now marketed in bottles of this type.

In Gironde, green *bordelaises* are used for both red and dry white wines, and clear ones for sweet white wines. There are also a few special bottles in circulation used by certain châteaux, whose name or coat of arms is usually embossed on the shoulder.

From quarter bottle to imperial, the Bordeaux family, with its characteristically abrupt shoulder and dark green colour, is an important range.

Each bottle in the Burgundy range is characterized by a slope-shouldered profile. This range is widely used in France and around the world.

The Burgundy bottle (*bourguignonne*)

This is the bottle used in greater Burgundy, the area stretching from the vineyards of Chablis to the gates of Lyon, and including the whole of the wine-producing area of Beaujolais.

The predominant bottle colour is the shade of green known as *feuille morte* (autumn leaf). This is the colour used for almost all the red wines of Burgundy and for many of the great white wines, too. Bottles of a more lively green are also used for some of the white wines.

The most common capacity of Burgundy bottles is 75cl, but there are also magnums (1.5 litres) and a few bottles of 3 litres and more. There are also some bottles of special design on the market, usually inspired by bottle shapes of the past. For the most part, these are used by Burgundian growers or merchants for wines from the finest domains or vineyards.

Provence and Corsica

This region makes use of Bordeaux and Burgundy bottles for the most part. However, there are two special designs both used for the AOC wines of Côtes de Provence.

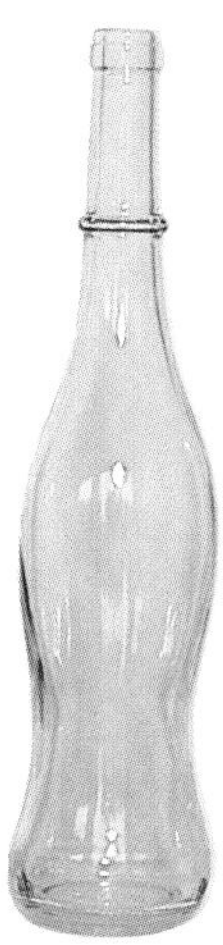

The *flûte à corset*, with its striking, wasp-waisted shape (shown left) is used by growers for bottling their own wines within the production area. Its most usual capacity is 75cl, and it is generally clear.

The other type is known as the *Côte de Provence*, and it is slightly differently shaped from the *flûte à corset*. This type is used by *négociants* (shippers or merchants). Its capacity is also 75cl and it is generally clear. There are in fact quite a number of special bottle designs in Provence belonging to either growers or merchants, who use them to personalize their products.

Corsica has a bottle of its own known as the *corse*, which has the famous 'head with headband' — the island's emblem — embossed on the shoulder.

Jura and Savoie

Bottle designs in these two regions are standardized. Basically, they are of the 75cl *bourguignonne* type for red wines, and the flute type known as *Véronique* for white wines.

However, there are two bottle types peculiar to Jura. These are the *Jura*, a bottle (shown left) which sometimes has 'Jura' embossed on it, and the dumpy *clavelin*, which has kept its ancient form and is used for the bottling of *vin jaune* (see page 327). It has a legally permitted capacity of 62cl.

The Loire valley

The 75cl *bourguignonne*, usually green in colour, is widely used in the Loire. But there are also other bottles, representing particular areas and *appellations*, designed to emphasize the originality of the wines grown there.

The *Muscadet* for example, a slim and elegant bottle (shown left), bears the *appellation* name at its base. Green in colour, it comes in two capacities, 37.5 and 75cl. The shape of the *Anjou* bottle differs in that it is squatter. It is either plain or embossed with three fleurs-de-lys, a crown, a star, two laurel branches and the name 'Anjou'. Again, further bottle types are found in the Loire belonging to individual growers or merchants.

Côtes du Rhone

There are a number of standard bottle types in use in the Côtes du Rhône, notably the *bourguignonne*, but Rhône wines are also bottled in the *normande*, the *hollandaise* and the *Véronique* types.

The Côtes du Rhône range of bottles in characteristic feuille morte *(autumn leaf) colour.*

However, for a few years now, there has been a special Côtes du Rhône bottle, developed at the instigation of the local wine-trade Comité Interprofessionnel. This is the *rhodanienne* (shown on page 299); it has 'Côtes du Rhône' embossed on its shoulder to show its origins. Most of the bottles in this region are *feuille morte* in colour; some are clear.

In the 1980s, the Syndicat des Vignerons de Tavel (Tavel Wine Growers Association) created a bottle specifically for that *appellation*.

The Châteauneuf-du-Pape bottle, embossed with the papal arms, is used by the growers for wines bottled within the *appellation* production area.

Finally, there is also a Côtes du Lubéron bottle, exclusive to this particular *appellation*.

The South West

The wines of this vast region are mostly offered for sale in Bordeaux bottles. There are also *flûtes* in use in Irouléguy and Jurançon, and the *gaillacoise* is a specially designed bottle used for Gaillac wines.

Languedoc-Roussillon

The *bordelaise* bottle is widespread in this area, but *bourguignonnes*, *hollandaises*, *normandes* and *Véroniques* are also used, especially for certain dry white wines. Some of the wines or *appellations*, however, have their own bottles, three examples being the *occitane*, the *minervoise* and the *tuccitane*.

There are also some individual designs used by wine growers or merchants. The choice is therefore wide in this area, and colours range from clear to bright green and include *feuille morte*.

Champagne

The overwhelming majority of the bottles used for champagne are of the *champenoise* type, traditionally of 75cl. A few firms, however, have their own special bottles for their prestige blends: the most famous example is Moët et Chandon's Dom Pérignon, which reproduces an 18th-century design.

Champagne bottles: a range of remarkable elegance.

THE RANGE OF CHAMPAGNE BOTTLES

Quarter bottle	*20cl*
Half bottle	*37.5cl*
Bottle	*75cl*
Magnum	*1.5l*
Jeroboam	*3l*
Methuselah	*6l*
Salmanazar	*9l*
Balthasar	*12l*
Nebuchadnezzar	*15l*

Champagne bottles come either in the shade of green known as *vert Champagne* (Champagne green) or in clear glass. The clear bottles are used for white or pink champagnes, especially prestige blends, an example being Roederer's Cristal.

With a few rare exceptions, champagne's second fermentation takes place in the bottle, and the larger the container, the more harmonious the result. Consequently, smaller champagne bottles (under 75cl) do not come into use until vinification is complete. The champagne is then decanted into them.

Regulations governing bottles

The glass bottle has acquired its present form in accordance with the technical and commercial needs of the wine market. Thanks to better quality raw materials and improvements in the manufacturing process, the bottle is today more practical and reliable than at any previous moment.

The official regulations governing bottles apply to several aspects of their manufacture, of which one of the most important is capacity . This has, logically, always been a preoccupation of legislators. A decree of 1735 stipulated that a bottle should contain 1 Parisian pint, a measure equal to 93cl. However, the wording of the decree also sanctioned the existence of quarter, half and double-size bottles. Louis XV fixed the capacity of the Champagne bottle at 80cl, and this regulation remained in force in 1974–5.

For many decades, the most widely used capacities in France have been 100cl, 75cl and 37.5cl. New capacities have now been specified by the European Community. These are, for French wines: 10, 25, 37.5, 50, 62 (for *vins jaunes*), 75, 100, 150, 200, 300, 500, 600, 900 and 1000cl. Bottles with a capacity of 24, 35, 70, 73, 99 and 125cl will no longer be permitted by Community legislation. This ruling came into full effect from 31 December 1988.

H I

Haut-Comtat

This VDQS *appellation* in the Côtes du Rhône has not been used for some years now.

Haut-Médoc *See* Médoc.

Haut-Montravel *See* Montravel.

Haut Pays *See* the Haut Pays regional entry on page 304.

Hautes Côtes de Beaune *See* the Côte d'Or regional entry on page 204.

Hautes Côtes de Nuits *See* the Côte d'Or regional entry on page 204.

Hermitage

Hermitage and Côte Rôtie are certainly among the oldest wine-growing areas in the Rhône valley. We know that Hermitage was important to the Romans as it was cited in documentation concerning the wines of Vienne. Much later, but still long before other wines known today as outstanding *appellations*, Hermitage appeared on the Dutch and English markets. This was due to the fact that it could be transported by road and then by river, and exported via Bordeaux.

At first, the wines of this area were called 'Vins du Coteau de Saint-Christophe', then the name changed to 'Vins de Tournon'. It was in the 14th century that the hill and its vines took the name of Hermitage, in honour of the chapel built there by the Chevalier de Sterimberg.

The vineyards of Hermitage cover 125ha. The area has hardly changed in centuries, nor will it, for all the valuable soils have long been planted.

Average annual production is 4,700hl, 1,500hl of which is made by the cooperative at Tain-l'Hermitage. The decree of 4 March 1937 specifies that the *appellation d'origine contrôlée* covers one commune and a few plots in Crozes-Hermitage.

The soils are mainly granitic sands suited to the production of red wines. Certain plots have been famous since the 14th century — Bessards, Méal and Greffieux, for example. However, there are also a few bands of alpine alluvial deposits brought down by a previous course of the river Isère. These are to be found in the plots of Roucoule and Muret, and they produce white wines of great repute.

Like all the other *appellations* of the northern Côtes du Rhône, the red wines of Hermitage are made entirely from the Syrah grape variety. The white wines are made from the Roussanne and the Marsanne, and the grapes are picked and vinified every year in such a way as to ensure high quality and guarantee long life.

The white wines are pleasing and characterful right from the start. They have floral and vegetal aromas suggesting orris root and mown hay, unroasted coffee and almonds. Although they are low in acidity, they stand the test of time very well, and are still at their peak after ten years in bottle.

The red wines are so structured that they combine a full, perfectly balanced form with an

The vineyards and small chapel of Hermitage overlook the Rhône valley and the town of Tain-l'Hermitage.

exceedingly expressive aroma, rich in the scents of violet, leather and blackcurrant. They are often fleshier, more succulent wines than those of Côte Rôtie, and they develop very slowly, retaining their quality for decades.

Hibou Blanc

This vine from Savoie used to be planted at the foot of trees. Its powerful shoots would then climb upwards and twine around the trees for support. It used to produce considerable quantities of a light wine of local interest only. It is unclassified, and a few isolated stocks still exist in Haute-Savoie.

Hibou Noir

Synonyms: *Hibou* at Chambéry, *Hivernais* in the upper Isère valley, *Palofrais* or *Polofrais* in the Arc valley, *Pomêtre* in Aime, *Promèche* in Chautagne, *Promère* in Seyssel, *Bibou, Guibou, Luisant* and *Raisin Cerise* in the Grésivaudan valley, between Grenoble and Albertville.

Bunches large, cylindrical-conical, quite loose; grapes spherical, large, black and juicy; ripening period: second epoch.

This is an old Savoie variety. It is productive, with early budbreak, and it used to be stake-trained or grown on cherry trees, hence one of its synonyms, Raisin Cerise (cherry grape). It gives a wine with a bouquet of violets and raspberries, and was much appreciated in the Maurienne and Tarentaise areas. Unclassified.

Irouléguy

This small wine-growing area occupies about 100ha in the heart of the Basque country, 50km from Biarritz, between Saint-Jean-de-Luz and Saint-Jean-Pied-de-Port. The vineyards are tucked away on the hillsides around Saint-Étienne-de-Baïgorry and five neighbouring communes. The area was given its *appellation d'origine contrôlée* on 23 October 1970.

The religious houses of the Basque country, established by the abbey at Roncevaux (Spanish Roncevalles), laid the foundations of the modern wine district. And it was the monks of St James of Compostella who were the ambassadors for this wine, spreading news of its sacramental virtues and invigorating properties.

Of all the wine-growing areas in the Pyrenees, Irouléguy benefits more than any other from a gentle maritime climate. This means evenly distributed rainfall of 1,500mm per annum; an average temperature of 12.8°C; the influence of warm winds from Spain, such as the *haice-egoa* ('maddening wind' in Basque), which favours overripening; and finally, bright, warm autumns permitting late harvesting.

Irouléguy, the only **appellation** *in the Basque country, produces fleshy red and rosé wines with plenty of character.*

The schists, sandstones and marine limestones of these hills are permeable and rich in iron oxide. They particularly favour the luxuriant vegetation of the local grape varieties, which are generally late ripening, aromatic and low yielding. They are stake-trained.

Two grape varieties are used for the red wines of Irouléguy: the Tannat (a variety characteristic of the Pyrenean vineyards), for the richness and unusual nature of its tannins; and the Cabernet Franc (locally known as the Acheria) to temper the coarseness of the Tannat.

For white wines, the delicately flavoured Courbu Blanc (locally known as the Xiuri Cerratia) is used, together with the Petit Manseng (locally known as the Ixipiota Xuri).

The merit of the wines of Irouléguy lies in their authenticity, their originality and their imposing character.

A third of the wines produced are rosés. These are appreciated for their vivid raspberry colour and their refreshing and harmonious bouquet of blackcurrant, raspberry and wild flowers from the Basque mountains. They are dry, silky wines, both lively and supple. On the whole, they should be drunk young, but they can also age happily for two or three years, this time allowing the wines to show their fine qualities. Very little white wine is produced.

The other two thirds of the wines are red. These are a beautiful deep purple in colour, with an aroma of red berries. They are muscular and fleshy, with a powerful, ripe tannin content and a characteristic length of flavour. After three or four years in bottle, they achieve a remarkable level of quality. When young, they are wines of vigorous, rustic honesty.

The Haut Pays

History has not yet said its last word concerning the wine districts of the Haut Pays. The wines of this area have been cherished in the past by abbots, monks, kings and generations of wine growers; now the area is beginning to show signs of justifiable ambition. It is beginning to make a name for itself once again.

The region described in French as the Haut Pays (the High Country) is situated around the rivers Lot, Garonne, Tarn and Aveyron. It includes the wines of Toulouse, Agen, Gascony, Périgord, Quercy, Rouergue and Tarn. A transitional area between the Massif Central and the Pyrenees on the one hand, and between Aquitaine and Languedoc on the other, it is a very varied region, containing a mosaic of differing wine districts.

The vineyards of Château de Hauteserre lie within the Cahors **appellation contrôlée.**

Regional history

Since this region includes the wines of both Cahors and Gaillac, each with a long and distinguished past, historians have quite a task on their hands. Let us begin with Gaillac. Here, the cultivation of vines was already widespread in the Gallo-Roman era. A charter of 1271 has no difficulty in describing its wines as 'of exceptional and striking quality'. The wines of Cahors have enjoyed an equally celebrated history; among other distinctions, they are recorded as being served at the wedding of Eleanor of Aquitaine and Henry II of England. However, the wines of Bordeaux began to establish their supremacy in the South West as early as 1205.

The Bordeaux merchants blocked sales of wines from the Haut Pays upstream of Saint-Macaire, so that their own wines would enjoy pride of place in export markets. Sales and shipments of wines from the Haut Pays were only allowed after Martinmas on November 11—too late for foreign winter fleets. This privilege was eventually abolished in 1776, but the vineyards were already in decline. In the 19th century, as they were beginning to recover, the plagues of oidium (powdery mildew), downy mildew and phylloxera struck in succession, wiping out the good work of reconstruction.

After these catastrophes, hybrid vines were planted in place of the native French varieties, but these produced only mediocre wines. A genuine revival of these wine districts had to wait until the early 1950s.

Regional climate

The climate governing the vineyards of the Haut Pays is, on the whole, similar to that of Aquitaine. The winters are cold and wet and the summers are hot and dry. Hail, fog and late frosts are all threats in certain areas. This is why it is often vital to choose hardy species of vine, with late budbreak. The various local mesoclimates and relief play a most important role in this respect, for these factors can greatly modify the fundamental characteristics of the maritime climate. For example, the Buzet district benefits from a favourable mesoclimate, as its vineyards are protected by the forests of the Landes, and enjoy more sunshine and slightly lower rainfall than surrounding areas in consequence.

The Tarn-et-Garonne *département* comes under two climatic influences. The predominant one is that of the Atlantic, and the second is that of the Mediterranean. The latter makes itself felt to a greater or lesser extent depending on the season and the year. The winter is usually mild, and sometimes wet. Spring frosts are rare, and they affect the vines little.

The Quercy area has a hot, dry climate during the summer, influenced by the dry, warm wind from the south known as the *autan*, which speeds the ripening process and ensures a healthy harvest. Climatically speaking, the Cahors wine district to the north of the Quercy area is in a transitional zone. The Lot valley, which opens out to the southwest of Cahors on the plain of Villeneuve-sur-Lot, comes under Atlantic influences.

Regional soils

The soils of this large region vary greatly. East of Caussade in the Tarn-et-Garonne *département* there are Jurassic period limestones. In the river valleys of the area, the soils tend to be recent alluvial deposits, and these are very easy to work. The best soils for wine growing are the clay and calcareous slopes of molassic origin found in the southeast of the Tarn-et-Garonne *département*; and the *boulbènes* (fine sands and clays) found in the southern half of the Tarn-et-Garonne *département* on the terraces formed by previous courses of the Garonne, Tarn and Aveyron rivers.

Wine growers and professional bodies seek out the best plots in each area, even going so far as to redesign the slopes, as at Marcillac, north of Rodez in Aveyron, where large terraces have been constructed by mechanical means, following the contours of the hillsides.

In the Lot, Tarn and Garonne valleys, the vineyards are arranged on slopes in the classic manner, with the best plots facing southeast. Nonetheless, each *appellation* in this area has its own specific characteristics: Fronton, for example, has terraced slopes of pebbles and sand carried down by the Tarn. Then there is Cahors, where the wine district is divided into two distinct zones: the valley, with its infertile soils of pebbles, quartz, siliceous gravels and limestone; and the rugged plateaux of the Causse, at an altitude of between 250m and 300m, with its soft, friable limestones interspersed with marls, and its terrain cut by small valleys and escarpments. The Buzet *appellation* produces its best wines on the pebbly and sandy gravels of the terraces on the left bank of the Garonne.

The grape varieties

The INAO and other experts in the field have taken the greatest care in selecting sound grape varieties for the Haut Pays. This was necessary partly because of the widespread plantings of hybrids here in the early part of the century, and partly because of the tragic frosts of 1956. Thus, when new regulations governing the wines of the Côtes du Marmandais came into effect, the permitted percentage of Merlot and Négrette rose from 50 to 75 per cent, while varieties such as the Côt, the Abouriou Noir, the Fer and the Gamay were limited to 50 per cent. It was thanks to a similar stimulus that research into grafting Négrette vines in the Côtes du Frontonnais area was carried out. After a long process of trial and error, the rootstock was found that would best take this hardy, vigorous vine, which is most at home in light, pebbly soils. The Négrette has also been the main variety used in the replanting programme undertaken by the Lavilledieu cooperative since 1970, for the Vins de Lavilledieu VDQS.

Situated in the heart of Gascony, the Côtes de Buzet wine-growing area produces red wines with brilliant colour and a delicate perfume, suitable for ageing.

Apart from the Négrette, the other leading grape of the region is the Côt, known locally as the Auxerrois, and as Malbec in Bordeaux. This grape is particularly associated with the Cahors *appellation*, as it covers 70 per cent of the area cultivated there. It is well suited to the Quercy region's soils and slopes, where it produces wines rich in tannins and the anthocyanins which make up the colouring matter of red wines. After a warm, sunny year the wine produced by the Côt is superb. Better results still can be obtained by adding Merlot for extra fullness, and Tannat to help the wine age. Continuing with red wines, those of the Côtes de Buzet are made from a Bordeaux-style combination of grape varieties: 50 per cent Merlot, with the balance contributed by Cabernet Franc and Cabernet Sauvignon, and a little Côt.

The Tarn *appellation* of Gaillac provides in itself an illustration of the richness and diversity of the wines of the South West because, as well as red *primeur* wines, ordinary red wines and rosé wines, a wide range of white wines is produced: dry, sweet, *perlé*, *moustillant* and two further types of sparkling wine, one made by the Champagne method, and the other by the Gaillac method, in which the *mousse* is obtained by fermentation of residual sugar in the bottle. This surprising display of versatility is due to six white grape varieties: the Muscadelle, the Ondenc, the Sauvignon Blanc, the Sémillon, the Mauzac and the Len de l'El.

The *appellations* and production

This vast region has four *appellations d'origine contrôlée*: Côtes de Buzet, Gaillac, Côtes du Frontonnais and Cahors. In addition to these, there are seven VDQS: Côtes de Saint-Mont, Côtes du Brulhois, Côtes du Marmandais, Vins de Lavilledieu, Vins de Marcillac, Vins d'Entraygues et du Fel, and Vins d'Estaing; as well as a number of *vins de pays*.

The region is in the process of profound change, especially with regard to Cahors, the Côtes du Frontonnais and Gaillac. The *appellations* vary from a comfortable size, like Gaillac with its 1,400ha, down to those of Lilliputian dimensions, such as the Vins d'Estaing, which covers an area of about 10ha. Some *appellation* areas are increasing in size, for example, Vins de Lavilledieu, which now covers 25ha as opposed to only 2ha in 1977. The production is equally varied, with a balance struck between reds and whites, and a smaller quantity of rosés. It should be noted, however, that thanks to the joint efforts of the wine growers and professional organizations (i.e. the cooperatives and trade associations), all of the *appellations* have seen their production increase considerably since 1970. In 1971, for example, the amount of wine produced within the Cahors *appellation* was 23,000hl; by 1983, it was over 130,000, and the forecast for 1990 is in the order of 220,000hl.

Professional organizations

It is no exaggeration to say that this region has been both saved and shaped by cooperatives. It is hardly surprising, therefore, that many parts of the Haut Pays are still under the influence of such organizations—particularly Buzet, which is 96 per cent cooperative-run; Vins de Lavilledieu, which is 100 per cent cooperative-run; and Côtes du Frontonnais, 80 per cent cooperative-run. In other places, though, there is a tendency for growers to undertake their own vinification and join together in an association for marketing purposes, as at Entraygues and Estaing.

Those who enjoy the wines of the South West can derive great pleasure from journeying through this pleasant countryside. The cooperatives are as welcoming as they are numerous, and much can be learned from a visit to them and particularly to the spectacular cellars at Buzet. Armagnac enthusiasts will find much of interest at Lavardac in the Marmande area, where barrels for armagnac were once made. Finally, there is the famous *fête de Gaillac* in the first weekend in August with its 'Cocagne des Vins' ('Feast of Wines').

Vineyards at Entraygues. This tiny wine-growing area in Aveyron is sited on very steep hillsides, so the grapes cannot be harvested mechanically.

THE WINE COOPERATIVE MOVEMENT

Cooperatives have played an important part in the growing and making of wine since the beginning of the 20th century. Their rôle seems set to increase in both these spheres, as well as in the marketing of wines, in the future.

The true beginning of the cooperative movement came early in the 20th century. The very first cooperatives in France appeared in 1901, in Hérault and in the Bergerac region. The Ribeauvillé cooperative in Alsace had been established six years earlier, but Alsace was at that time part of the German Empire.

By 1914 there were already 76 cooperatives in existence, and the number had increased to 827 by 1939. In the 1960s there were some 1,200 cooperatives in France, and the number has stayed at about this level since.

The philosophy and role of cooperatives

The original idea of the cooperative movement was that of a mutual benefit society. It was an attempt to ensure the survival of the small and medium-sized family concern in the face of the successive crises suffered by the French wine regions.

Like all such agricultural groupings, wine cooperatives are companies with a special statute based on equality and solidarity among the members, and the absence of the profit motive. The cooperatives are prohibited, by their very nature, from paying out dividends or disbursing their financial reserves to members. On the other hand, they benefit from certain fiscal advantages and special loan terms.

At first, the main function of the cooperative movement was a purely technical one. It enabled members to take advantage of collective facilities for vinification and cellarage, something they would not have been able to undertake on their own.

Once this had been achieved, the cooperatives were able to take on an economic role for themselves in the organization of the market before the Second World War. This activity took the form of progressively eliminating inferior quality vines and wines, restructuring vineyards and wine districts, financing maturing wine stocks and stimulating sales.

Now that the movement has reached maturity, it is channelling its activities in four main directions: quality winemaking, a healthy organization of the market, finance, and providing material and moral support for family wine-growing businesses.

A policy of quality

It was once the case that many cooperatives were run by retired civil servants who were punctilious managers but lacked knowledge of vineyards and wine. However, this era has long since passed. The cooperatives are now in the forefront of the general movement to promote quality in French wine growing which began after the Second World War and intensified in the 1970s.

In 1946, a group of cooperatives in the South of France established the Institut Coopératif du Vin (Cooperative Wine Institute), an organization dedicated to technical progress in exactly the same way as the Institut Technique du Vin (Technical Wine Institute) is, and the 1,500 or so practising oenologists in France are. Evidence of their efforts can be seen, for example, in the increased production of *vins de pays* on the part of the cooperatives. The same goes for the strengthening of the cooperative movement in *appellation d'origine contrôlée* areas.

The organization of the market

An effective and sound organization of the market has always

The Fête des Ménétriers (Festival of the Strolling Fiddlers) at Ribeauvillé, where the cooperative dates back to 1895.

The cooperative at Crouseilles in Madiran produces red AOC Béarn and Madiran as well as vins de pays, *all of them generous and fleshy in character.*

been an imperative for the cooperative movement, particularly as regards table wines governed by EC regulations. Cooperatives play a determining role in the process of self-regulation, by undertaking voluntary stockholding after large harvests. Thanks to this kind of discipline and the large storage capacity of their cellars, it is possible to delay the sale of considerable quantities of wine, and thus maintain minimum prices.

The economic role

Although at first the cooperatives functioned purely in the sphere of wine growing and making, they gradually took on a sales function, moving from a passive position in which they provided little more than cellar and production facilities, to an active role that involved them in the marketing of wines both at home and abroad. To help themselves achieve these goals, 150 or so *unions économiques de caves coopératives* (economic associations of wine cooperatives) have been formed, and these fulfil this financial function, sharing production, storage and bottling facilities, as well as, of course, pooling marketing knowledge and resources.

The social role of the wine cooperatives

The quest for quality and influence over the structure of the market do not constitute an end in themselves, but are simply a means of ensuring that family wine-growing businesses flourish materially and morally to the greatest possible extent.

The cooperative formula involves not only professional wine growers, but also small producers for whom the cultivation of vines is not a main activity. Furthermore, cooperatives contribute towards sustaining the life of the countryside, to the correct management of agricultural land and the maintenance of demographic balance in rural areas. They ensure jobs in communities and regions where social conditions are often difficult.

The place of cooperatives in the French wine industry

Cultivating vineyards, harvesting grapes and making wine are activities carried out by cooperative members, by growers with their own private cellars and by *négociants-éleveurs* (merchants with wine-growing concerns). The part played by cooperatives is tending to increase in each of these sectors of wine production.

The vineyards

In the 1960s, the total vineyard area in France rose to over 1.2 million ha. A third of this was cultivated by cooperatives. Over the last 30 years, however, the total wine-growing area has decreased by about 20 per cent. There are now 1 million ha, with cooperatives involved in the cultivation of half of this. The exact proportions vary greatly from one region to another (see diagram below).

Relatively as well as absolutely speaking, the area worked by wine cooperatives has been increasing steadily for a number of years.

Percentage of cooperative members in French wine-growing regions

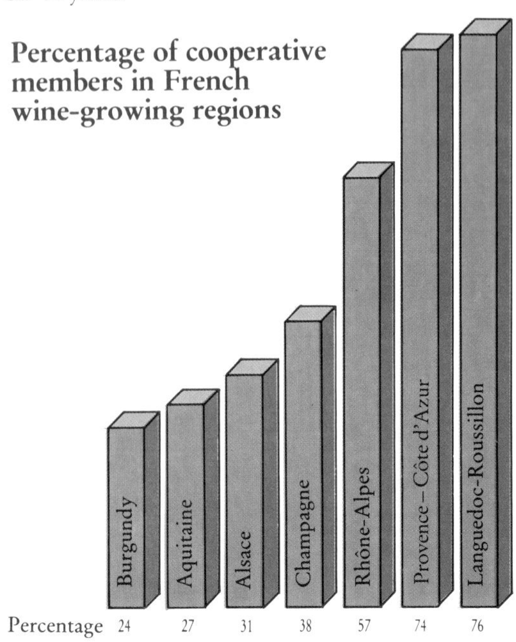

The growers

The number of individual harvest declarations has fallen by half in less than 20 years, while the average amount of wine produced has remained stable at about 60 to 70 million hl. At the beginning of the 1960s there were 1,300,000 separate harvest declarations (20 per cent of these being declarations from cooperative members). Now, however, there are fewer than 650,000, and this number is decreasing constantly. On the other hand, the number of cooperative members has remained at about 250,000, and thus the proportion of cooperative members to non-members throughout France as a whole is rising steadily.

These facts and figures regarding size and personnel show that, within France, each cooperative member works a larger average area than that cultivated by an independent grower.

Increase in number of cooperative members

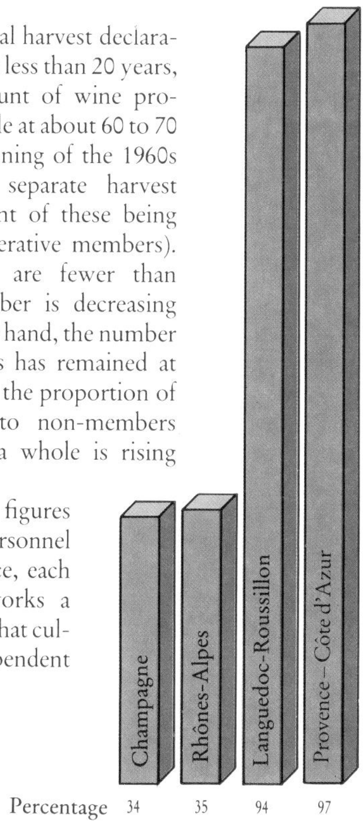

Wine production

The average amount of wine produced in France is about 70 million hl per year. About 10 million hl of this consists of base wines suitable for distilling into cognac. Over 50 per cent of the 60 million hl of wine for consumption as such is now produced by cooperatives, as opposed to only 35 to 40 per cent in the 1960s (see chart below). The average yields per ha are about the same for cooperative members and non-cooperative members, i.e. about 60 to 70hl/ha.

PROPORTION OF FRENCH WINE PRODUCED BY COOPERATIVES		
Type of wine	Production in millions of hectolitres	Percentage produced by cooperatives
AOC	18	Over 40 per cent
VDQS	2	Over 50 per cent
VINS DE PAYS	40	Over 60 per cent
TOTAL	70	Over 50 per cent

The future

Ensuring the survival and well-being of small wine growers is a noble aim, and entirely justifies both the protection and the financial assistance given to the cooperatives during the course of their development. Gradually a collaborative outlook has been established among all those involved in every stage of production — in the best interests of wine itself.

This interprofessional cohesion, aimed at safeguarding the worth and authenticity of French wine, is now established on a firm basis, and this is reassuring for consumers and French taxpayers alike.

The remarkably well-equipped wine-making cooperative at Beaumes-de-Venise. It demonstrates the efforts and expenditure cooperatives are prepared to make to produce quality wines.

The Role of the *Négociant*

Wine, for all its antiquity and nobility, is nonetheless a consumer item which has to be made, packaged and marketed. The 3,000 or so French négociants *(shippers and merchants) carrying out the complex and often little-appreciated tasks required for this process bear the considerable responsibility of providing an increasingly well-informed clientele with quality wines.*

The principal role of the wine *négociant* is that of an intermediary between the producer and the customer. His three main functions are the purchase of wine or grapes, the *élevage* and ageing of the wine he has bought, and the marketing process.

For the wine grower, the advantage of using a *négociant* as an outlet for his wines is that he can ensure the sale of all or a large part of the harvest, thus guaranteeing himself an income and relieving himself of some of his less welcome responsibilities. Rather than having to go out and look for prospective buyers, he can dedicate himself totally to the work of the vineyard and cellar.

From the consumer's point of view (and, outside France, the consumer will probably be a wine merchant or importer), the *négociant* provides a complete range of wines selected with great care by a professional team. If a *négociant* prints his name on the labels of the bottles he distributes, this is a further guarantee of quality, because he is staking his reputation on those bottles.

Wine businesses of this type are often regional in origin, and therefore specially geared to the areas where they are situated. So a *négociant* in Champagne will differ from one in Bordeaux or Burgundy, and both will differ from a large cooperative grouping handling a range of wines from the Côtes du Rhône. But all have the same aim: to buy, age and sell quality products.

Buying wines

Négociants rarely possess their own vineyards. Most of them acquire their 'raw materials' in three ways: by buying grapes after they have been harvested; by buying wine in bulk after the initial fermentation process is complete; or by purchasing it after it has been bottled.

In the first case, the *négociant* has to make the wine himself. This requires considerable investment in wine-making equipment. In Champagne, most *négociants* work in this way, as do most Champagne cooperatives. The volumes handled are usually very large, and make it worthwhile installing the most up-to-date equipment.

In the second case, too, a considerable amount of investment in equipment is involved. It is necessary to have vats to store wines in until they are ready to be bottled, and also a stock of wooden casks for wines requiring *élevage* in wood. These casks have to be renewed regularly. Finally, a bottling line will also be needed. This is usually fully automatic. If the wine is for immediate dispatch, the bottles must have their capsules fitted, be labelled and placed in cardboard cases. If not, they should be stacked on wooden pallets and left to mature in a cool, dark environment.

Professional buyers often have to taste hundreds of samples before making a purchase.

In the third instance, the *négociant* buys wine already bottled. Sometimes this wine has been labelled by the estate owner (as is the case with Bordeaux *crus classés*, for example), and sometimes it is unlabelled, in which case the *négociant* will label it himself.

The choice of wines

Whatever the type of wine required, purchases are only made after a rigorous selection process. The *négociant* who assumes his responsibilities and cares about his reputation owes it to himself to choose impeccable wines. For this purpose, he employs professional buyers, true wine technicians, who scour the wine-growing regions in constant search of the best samples. Although there is no substitute for tasting before buying, this has to be supplemented by laboratory analysis, which will reveal characteristics that would otherwise be impossible to detect. Some merchants have their own laboratories for this purpose.

The fact that a *négociant* has access to a large number of products enables him to judge their relative quality and value and then make a wise choice based on these factors. He often needs to taste several hundred samples before proceeding to a purchase.

The range of products

The number and range of wines on offer varies from one *négociant* to another, depending on the region where he is established and the type of wine he has chosen to handle. A merchant situated in Champagne, for example, may offer only sparkling wines. In order to supplement this limited range, he will often add other drinks to his portfolio, such as ports, whiskies and brandies, on an agency basis.

Other *négociants*, however, offer a range largely representative of the wines produced in France as a whole, selling branded table wines along with wines and spirits from the most prestigious *appellations* in the country. In this way, the *négociant*'s customers are offered the widest possible choice in terms of both price and *appellation*, the wines or spirits in the range being sold either under the producer's or the *négociant*'s name.

Wines sold under the producer's name are generally market-ready products, and all that remains to be done is distribute them. This is what happens to most of the *crus classés* of Bordeaux. They leave the estate, already bottled, labelled and packed in wooden cases, and go to the *négociant*'s cellar to age. Sometimes a small label bearing the name of the *négociant* is added to each bottle. Some highly prestigious wines are sold only on allocation and are hence very difficult to obtain; if a *négociant* is able to persuade an estate owner to sell him part of his harvest, then this is a mark of the *négociant*'s respectability and standing.

In many cases, wines only show the *négociant*'s name on the bottle, and this will generally signify that the *négociant* has undertaken all or part of the process of *élevage*, and that he stakes his name and reputation on every bottle. It would be fatal for a merchant to put his signature to poor-quality products. The increased interest in wine evident everywhere today means that the customer is more fastidious in his or her choice, and better able to judge what is available on the market. Recourse to a *négociant*'s wines should therefore be a guarantee of quality.

Élevage and ageing

The *négociant* is, or should be, preoccupied with the quality of his products. Consequently, throughout the processes of vinification, if he undertakes this, and *élevage*, he will make use of the most up-to-date techniques and the most efficient equipment available.

Technical aspects

Wine is a delicate substance, and vinification is not always easy. The use of modern materials such as stainless steel enables many of the failures and pitfalls involved in this stage of wine making to be avoided. However, stainless steel equipment is expensive, and it can only be used by firms with sufficient means to afford it. The same principle applies to *élevage*. Some wines need to be kept in new wood for several months, and since this involves great expense, only firms with a sound financial basis can afford this investment.

Stainless steel vat for ageing wine.

Quality control

Every process that the wine is subjected to is rigorously checked, first by tasting, then by means of laboratory analyses. Experience and practical knowledge are by no means to be despised when it comes to this checking process, but they must go hand-in-hand with a sound scientific basis. This presupposes a team of technicians and oenologists, wine lovers all, who will follow every step of the wine-making process, and use the most careful techniques to ensure the best possible result.

The development of a wine is monitored by means of technical analyses.

The cellars of the French Savour Club mail-order company house some 400 Burgundy pièces, *in which the club's buyers mature their bulk purchases.*

Bottle ageing
Ideally, a *négociant* should be able to sell wines when they are fully mature and at their peak in terms of development. This is easy in the case of wines that do not need to spend a long period in bottle. It is more difficult, however, in the case of prestigious *crus*, because it involves tying up large amounts of capital for a long period. When the cost of borrowing money is taken into account it becomes clear how difficult it is to offer great wines at their peak. Therefore, when deciding to allow the great wines he has purchased to age, a *négociant* must take into account his own financial resources and whether or not there will be a market for these wines at the price they will fetch when mature. And, of course, the longer the ageing process, the larger the overall stock must be in order to cope with sales. For example, if you wish to offer five-year-old wines, you must have five years' worth of sales in stock, in order to have something to sell during the waiting period.

To be able to leave wines to mature, no matter how long or short the period, it is necessary to have large amounts of storage space offering ideal conditions for the development of wine, in other words, darkness, ventilation and a constant temperature. Cellarage expenses form an important element in the final sale prices *négociants* charge.

Marketing

The third function of the *négociant* follows logically on the first two, namely the marketing of his wines.

Presentation of the wines
A *négociant* sells a large proportion of his wines under his own name. He must therefore present them in such a way as to make himself readily identifiable to the consumer. He does this primarily by means of the label and capsule. This aspect of marketing should not be neglected, for it suggests to the customer the worth of what is in the bottle.

The labelling of bottles is carried out at the last minute so that they will reach the customer in impeccable condition.

Distribution channels

Sales take place at several levels. *Négociants* in France can either offer their products direct to wholesalers, foreign merchants or agents, cafés, hotels and restaurants, or else to French private customers. In the first instance, the *négociant* will use a network of distributors, each one situated in a different geographical zone within France or abroad. Some of these distributors handle the products of a single *négociant*, others represent several.

A number of possibilities are open to *négociants*, or merchants in general, wishing to reach individual clients directly, such as door-to-door canvassing, trade fairs and mail-order sales. The first two methods have their supporters, one advantage being that the customer is able to taste the wine. However, mail-order selling spread rapidly throughout France in the 1970s owing to the efforts of the three main French companies who use the method: the Savour Club, the Club Français du Vin and Métairie.

The principle is a simple one, and makes it possible to reach large numbers of people rapidly. Each customer is sent a list of available wines at regular intervals. The price list gives the dates for which each price is valid, thus ruling out untimely price fluctuations. As a rule, copious information about the wines is also supplied to help customers make a fully informed choice.

The Savour Club dispatches about 50,000 bottles to its clients every day.

SELLING WINE BY MAIL ORDER

One of the leading companies in France selling wine by mail order is the Savour Club, an organization with customers both in France and in various other European countries. As well as its mail-order business, it has numerous retail wine shops in France, called Les Caves du Savour Club.

A company such as this combines the two functions of négociant *and retailer. Wines are bought as soon as possible after the harvest in order to benefit from the widest choice and the best possible prices. Purchases are made by two buyers, who are constantly tasting wines and taking samples in most of the wine-growing areas of France. The wines are given their* élevage *and are bottled either on the estate in question or in the company's cellars, depending on their type. When these operations take place on the estate of origin, they are carried out under the responsibility of the Savour Club and in cooperation with the wine grower.*

Every aspect of élevage, *bottling and packaging can, if required, be carried out by the company, thanks to a storage capacity of 12,000hl, two bottling lines with a capacity of 5,000 and 6,000 bottles an hour respectively, and equipment for the mechanical packing of bottles into cases. All bottles are packed horizontally in Savour Club cases, thereby ensuring that the cork is in constant contact with the wine, and that there is consequently little danger of coming across imperfectly sealed bottles. Once they have been bottled, the wines are stored in the company's cellars, which can hold about nine million bottles.*

Members of the club are regularly offered, by magazine listing, about 120 recommended wines, from branded table wines to examples of the most prestigious appellations, *including champagnes and brandies.*

Orders can be sent by post or by the French Minitel phone-line PC system. Deliveries are carried out by SERNAM (Service National des Messageries, a branch of SNCF, the French national railway company), or by independent transport companies, and take about two weeks. Refunds are guaranteed on any defective bottles.

VERIFICATION OF WINE QUALITY

Wine is subject to a large number of constraints and controls at every stage, from vineyards to cellars and sales networks. Its purity and quality are effectively guaranteed by the fact that all the French appellations *have to adhere to strict production conditions.*

In France, the government pays great attention to wines, partly because of the fiscal system these products are subject to, and partly because of their economic importance to the nation. They are the direct concern of the tax authorities, and those departments dealing with wine quality control in the general food and agriculture context. Two offices connected with the Ministry of Finance are involved, namely the Director General of Taxes and the Department for the Prevention of Fraud, as well as the Ministry of Agriculture. There are two other public bodies responsible for supervising the quality and correct economic management of the wine trade. They are the Office National Interprofessional des Vins (ONIVINS) and, in the case of *appellation d'origine contrôlée* wines, the Institut National des Appellations d'Origine des Vins et Eaux-de-Vie (INAO).

The wine producers themselves are organized into professional associations, and play a direct part in controlling the quality of *vins de pays, vins délimités de qualité supérieure* (VDQS) and *appellation d'origine contrôlée* wines (AOC).

There are two types of regulatory control: checking the product itself, by means of chemical and sensory analysis; and checking the documents and declarations required of producers and merchants.

Quite apart from the official controls exercised by the government and professional bodies, attention should also be drawn to those carried out by the growers, who make the wines, and the *négociants*, who select and sell them. The role played by these professionals is a crucial one. It is part and parcel of the French wine-growing and wine-making tradition, but it also reflects and reinforces the rigorous laws in operation. French wine, then, is subject to a combination of checks and constraints that effectively guarantee quality and purity.

Controls in operation affecting vineyards

Wine growers are not free to choose which grape varieties they use for their wines. They are allowed to grow only the officially listed varieties, those that have been chosen by agricultural experts, professional associations and the appropriate government departments for a particular region. These lists are published in an official EC document. They have been drawn up bearing in mind local climate factors, *terroir* and traditions.

Each vineyard unit is obliged to make a declaration to the local office of the Director General of Taxes, which knows its wine-growing area and can carry out inspections to check the truth of the declarations made. These declarations and inspections make it possible to keep a register of wine growers and vineyard plots (*le cadastre viticole*). The register was drawn up in 1953, and has been revised on a regular basis since; it is the only real means of maintaining ordered and disciplined production on a national scale.

Although the choice of the *terroir* itself has long been left to the grower's own judgment, plantings of vines — subject to prior authorization — could only be made in officially recognized 'viticultural areas'. In 1980, the EC classified *terroirs* into three categories, with the aim of gradually phasing out those vineyards in areas that do not produce wines of sufficiently high quality. Furthermore, as there is an excess of table wines, the policy now is to discourage the planting of new vineyards or the replanting of old ones for table-wine production except in *terroirs* that are particularly suited to this wine type rather than any other form of cultivation.

Controls in operation affecting wine cellars

Government officials have extensive powers in respect of cellar supervision. They are authorized to go into wine growers' cellars and check the quantity and category of the wines there. They can also take samples of the wine and carry out sensory analyses, and inspect all documents concerning wine growing and production.

Every year, once the harvest is in, grape growers must make a declaration, stating precisely the amounts of wine produced, or the quantities of grapes sent to market or for vinification, and either the name of the *appellation d'origine* or, in the case of *vins de pays*, the place of origin, the grape varieties used and the location of the vineyard.

In this way, officials can check details against the register of wine growers and vineyard plots, so that it is impossible for a wine producer to increase by illegal means the stock of wine he holds, or declare a greater quantity of *appellation d'origine contrôlée* wines or *vins de pays* than have actually been produced on the specified sites. At the end of the wine-growing year, that is to say before September, growers make out a detailed declaration of their present stocks, stating the holdings of *appellation d'origine contrôlée* wines or *vins de pays* they have in their cellars.

The distribution of harvested grapes, musts (i.e. grape juice intended for vinification) and wines is dependent on the issue of an accompanying document of authorization, variously called an *acquit à caution, congé, laisser passer, passavant* or *capsule congé*, depending on the destination. This document is issued under the direct and strict supervision of officials of the office of the Director General of Taxes, and is an important one, since it is by means of this documentation that the taxes on the wine are levied.

As wines are dispatched from the cellars, each firm's stock-holding sheet must be debited and made available for checking. It is therefore impossible to send out more wine than has been declared at the time of harvest or declared as being in storage. By checking outgoing stocks against stocks held at the beginning of the wine-making year, the quantities harvested and the quantities currently in stock, stocks can be verified

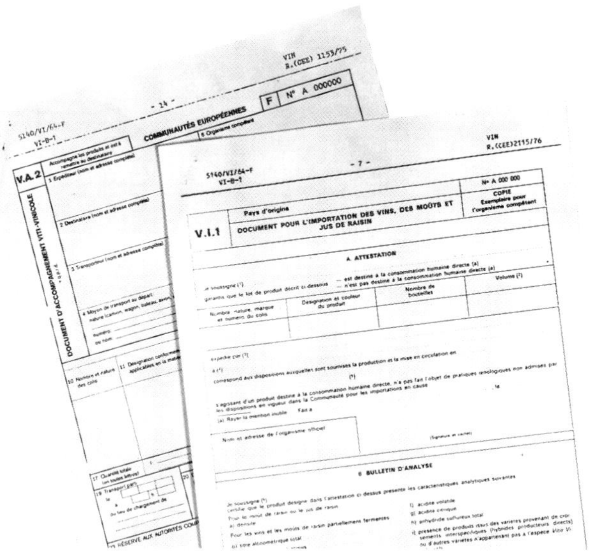

The documents that accompany a wine on its every journey guarantee that it meets the required quality standards.

estate by estate. If more stock is missing than is normal (a 'normal' amount being understood to include wine for family consumption and wastage — in other words evaporation and spillage during racking operations) then the producer is liable to answer for wines dispatched without an accompanying document. If it is a case of excess outgoing stock in relation to stocks held, the producer will be asked to account for an apparently fraudulent increase of the quantities actually produced, or for having under-declared the grape harvest or existing stocks of wine. The latter possibility might have extremely grave consequences for the producer, for strict limits are imposed on grape yields and excess quantities are refused access to the market. This restriction on quantity has a direct bearing on quality: excessive yields are detrimental to the quality of the wine. The maximum penalties imposed on anyone concealing excess yields are extremely high, involving both a fine and a prison sentence.

Appellations d'origine controls

The grape varieties used to produce all *appellation* wines are clearly specified by a committee of experts, which includes a geologist, an oenologist and representatives from the wine trade.

Appellations controlées *(AOC)*
A map of the plots producing AOC wines is kept in local town halls, and can be consulted by all who are interested.

The list of authorized grape varieties is established with reference to local traditions, while the conditions of production for each *appellation* are laid down by decree. A special declaration of grape varieties is always submitted along with the harvest declaration. In this way, the various supervisory bodies concerned, particularly the Institut National des Appellations d'Origine, can check that production controls are being adhered to.

Before the wines can be marketed, they must be analysed in a laboratory approved by the Department for the Prevention of Fraud and submitted to a tasting panel chosen by the wine-growers' association and supervised by a technical adviser from the INAO. All wine-making properties, no matter how large or small, must submit their products for scientific and sensory inspection in this way.

Vins délimités de qualité supérieure *(VDQS)*
Areas growing VDQS wines are delimited on the basis of communes, not sites. These wines are nevertheless subject to the same kind of controls as AOC wines are. These include analytical and organoleptic testing of the wines before their dispatch from the producers' cellars.

Control of *vins de pays*

The conditions of production of this category of wine are more general than for *appellation d'origine contrôlée* wines. *Vins de pays* are submitted for scientific and sensory tests carried out under the supervision of a professional organization, which is in turn approved and watched over by ONIVINS.

Distribution

Wines may not be distributed without the relevant documents issued by the Director General of Taxes. These documents must show the quantity of wine dispatched, the number and type of the containers and the *appellation* — particularly the *appellation d'origine* — claimed, or carry the words '*Vin de pays*' followed by the geographical name of the wine. In the case of wines dispatched under a bond note (*acquit à caution*), the alcohol content is shown and, if appropriate, the grape variety and the vintage are given. The name of the estate does not appear in the description of the wine. It can, however, feature in the company name of the consigner, and must be shown on the invoice in the description of the product. These documents accompany the wine on its every journey, and must be presented on request to police, tax and customs officers or officials of the Department for the Prevention of Fraud.

Bottled wines must also have a label, or there must be some form of identification on the container itself (if it is a cask, for example), corresponding exactly to the information shown on the accompanying documents. This is so that inspectors can check the two sets of information against each other and make sure that the merchandise transported is what it claims to be.

Capsules-congés, which are printed seals appearing at the top of capsules of bottled French wines for sale in France, are legally recognized tax documents specifying the capacity of the bottle, the user's licence number and mention of whether the user is a *négociant* or wine grower. Green *capsules-congés* are used for AOC and VDQS wines, and blue for *vins de pays* and table wines.

Controls in operation affecting wholesale wine merchants

Wholesale wine merchants are those merchants who have a 'wholesale account' with the tax office. This account permits them to receive wines and suspend payment of distribution and purchase tax. The account is kept by the tax office.

The wholesale merchant himself also keeps an account book showing incoming and outgoing stock, and a special account book for *appellation d'origine* wines (AOC and VDQS), imported wines and *vins de pays*. A record is also kept of any processing and bottling of wines undertaken by the merchant. This obligatory book-keeping is supplementary to that prescribed by general legislation on commercial book keeping. It would be no exaggeration to say that this particular commercial activity is the most closely supervised of all activities in the agricultural and food sector, perhaps even in French commerce as a whole.

Every year, the tax authorities carry out an inventory of wine lots held by wholesale wine merchants. This can be done without warning at any time during the year. The task is made easier by the fact that each lot stored must, by law, be identified by an exact description of it, especially its *appellation d'origine*.

Controls in operation affecting retail sales

A retailer in France is not allowed to accept wines without accompanying documentation or, in the case of bottled wines, without a *capsule-congé*. The full title and description of the wine must be marked on the containers during transportation, as well as when they are put on sale to the consumer. Restaurant and hotel wine lists and café tariffs must include the full name of the wine, its selling price and the price unit. In order to avoid any confusion, wines are grouped into categories on such lists.

Inspections can be carried out, day or night, whenever the establishments in question are open. Tax documents, sales documents, labels and prices are all checked against one another, in order to establish the legitimacy of the *appellations d'origine*. The checking process is thus a continuous one, from the producer right through to the consumer.

Analytical and organoleptic testing of wines

Checks on the physical and sensory qualities of wine are carried out in two ways: firstly by tasting, and secondly by the scientific analysis of samples.

Sensory analysis

The most traditional method of checking quality is by means of tasting: this is sensory analysis. It is an extremely old practice and is prescribed under article 487 of the Civil Code for commercial transactions. Under the *ancien régime* in France, tasting was one of the basic duties of wine brokers. The rules by which these merchants were governed are reflected today in the regulations of the Compagnie des Courtiers, Jurés, Piqueurs de Vins de Paris (the Paris Guild of Wine Brokers, Agents, Tasters).

Wines are sometimes actually tasted on the premises of wine growers, wholesale merchants and retailers. More often, though, samples are sent to official laboratories and to professional tasting panels.

Sensory analysis is an art, but it is also becoming a science; it is developing and spreading throughout the whole of the French agricultural and food sector. It is now subject to particularly precise rules laid down by scientists based at the Office International de la Vigne et du Vin (OIV), which is an international, intergovernmental organization uniting 33 countries situated throughout the five continents.

The rules state that any wine with an obviously bad taste must be considered unfit for consumption. The courts accept sensory analysis as proof of adulteration or falsification, but this method of proof is less secure than is proof by chemical or physico-chemical analysis. In certain cases, however, sensory analysis is the only checking process applied in the evaluation of wines. In the case of *vins de pays* or *vins d'appellation d'origine*, sensory analysis is extremely important, for it is the only way of checking whether or not a wine is a true example of its *appellation*. A wine that has undergone changes after it has been approved can be pronounced no longer good on the basis of re-tasting carried out by experts.

Chemical and physico-chemical analysis

Inspectors can take samples of wines for analysis at any time. When they do this, they follow procedures laid down in legislation that states that three identical samples should be taken, and then analysed according to a process that involves cross-checking results.

Analysis is carried out in official laboratories, in accordance with methods worked out and perfected by the OIV's subcommittee on analysis and evaluation of wines. The methods are those published in EC regulations or those developed by the OIV. Traditional analytical methods employed by EC countries may also be used.

These strict rules derive from the need to ensure the sound administration of justice, and from the need to prevent any kind of fraudulent practice. It is important to ensure that, in national and international dealing alike, buyers, sellers and experts conform to the same standards.

Chemical and physico-chemical analysis does not always reveal the exact composition of the wine. In fact there is a limit to these testing methods, of which the OIV has codified 67. Some factors cannot be established by this type of checking. For instance, the grape variety used cannot be revealed by laboratory means, but only by checking the documents accompanying the wine.

Official analyses are generally limited to establishing the basic constituents of wine and to checking for the presence of common disorders. To try to carry out all the available tests would hardly be possible in practice. The OIV proposes 23 tests for a basic analysis and 41 for an in-depth one. The limits on laboratory testing mean that the overall process of control rests as much on the examination of documents and sensory evaluation as it does on laboratory testing.

The efficacy of controls

This combination of control and test procedures gives the consumer an ample guarantee of the quality and authenticity of French wines.

According to European Community rules, wines imported to France from abroad must be accompanied by two documents: a certificate from the government of the country of origin stating that the wine is in accordance with national regulations and with those of the EC; and a certificate of analysis issued by an EC-approved laboratory in the country of origin, including eight obligatory tests.

The rules governing the control of wines are of little use unless they are effectively applied. Effective application depends on the number and calibre of the officials assigned to the sector. The number of disciplines involved and the nature of the product means that these officials need to be independent, specialized and mobile. France is lucky enough to have officials with these qualifications, and the quality of French wines in circulation can be considered reliable.

J K

Jacquère

Synonyms: *Jacquerre*, *Jacquière*, *Plant des Abymes de Myans*, *Cugnette* and *Cugniette* in the Grésivaudan area, *Buisserate* at Saint-Marcellin, *Martin-Cot Blanc* in Savoie, *Robinet* at Conflans, *Roussette de Montmélian* around Annecy, *Molette de Montmélian* at Chessenaz, *Cherché* and *Coufe-chien* in Ain, *Redin* at Saint-Jean-de-la-Porte.

Bunches medium sized, winged, cylindrical-conical, very compact; grapes spherical or slightly elongated, medium sized, pale green to golden yellow, becoming pink when fully ripe; skin thick, flesh not very juicy, astringent; ripening period: second epoch, late.

The Jacquère is a productive vine, easily yielding 100hl/ha in favourable soils. Its white wine is acidic, low in alcohol and has diuretic properties. However, when grown in the rugged landscape of Abymes de Myans, it acquires a flavour of gunflint, and is very pleasant if drunk within a year of its harvest.

The Jacquère has late budbreak, and its fruit is prone to grey rot (botrytis). Five registered clones have been approved: numbers 569, 629, 658, 769 and 788.

Classed as 'recommended' in Savoie, Ain, Loire and Isère, it is one of the grape varieties used in the Vin de Savoie AOC and the Vin du Bugey VDQS. It is grown on a total area of about 900ha: 660ha in Savoie, 150ha in Isère and 30ha in Ain.

Jasnières

This wine-growing area was classified as an AOC by the decree of 31 July 1937. It covers about 20ha and the grape variety used is the Chenin Blanc. The average annual production is about 900hl. The production area extends over the communes, or part of the communes, of Lhomme and Ruillé-sur-Loir.

The wine is straw yellow to golden yellow in colour, and has a well-developed aroma. It is full, delicate and lively, with a firm finish. It keeps very well in bottle.

Joubertin

Synonyms: *Plant de la Claye*, *Jaubertin* in Isère, *Plant d'Aix* in Savoie, *Pinot Joubertin* in Côte-d'Or, *Plant de la Mure*.

Bunches medium sized, cylindrical with two shoulders, quite loose; grapes medium sized, ovoid, blue-black; ripening period: first epoch.

This vine is the result of a chance mutation noted by a wine grower from Claix, called Joubert. It is very vigorous and is pruned very long. It is a fertile vine and gives a deep-coloured wine. Classed as 'authorized' in Isère, it covers 7ha there.

Juliénas

This wine-growing area, situated between Saint-Amour and Chénas, is the oldest in Beaujolais. Its clay soils are covered by alluvial deposits. The *appellation* covers an area of 560ha, situated for the most part in the commune of Juliénas, with some vineyards in Jullié, Pruzilly and Emeringes; annual production is some 32,000hl (4,250,000 bottles) of red wine.

Juliénas became an AOC on 11 March 1938. Made popular by Parisian journalists and gastronomes from Lyon, it sometimes suffers as a result of this flamboyant reputation. People think it is a one-dimensional wine. In reality, however, it possesses all the attributes of Julius Caesar, after whom the village is said to be named, i.e. firmness, vigour, character and a purple toga.

It matures well. It can be left quite happily for five or six years, but it attains perfect balance after two or three years, acquiring an ample bouquet, yet retaining its characteristic freshness. It has aromas of raspberry and cherry.

Juliénas, the oldest Beaujolais cru, *produces a firm, fresh wine with fruity aromas which ages well.*

Jura *See* the regional article on the next page.

Jurançon and Jurançon Sec

Jurançon is one of the family of wine districts to be found at the foot of the Pyrenees, in Béarn and in the Basque country, and it has much in common with those areas in terms of soil and climate. However, as a wine, Jurançon has exceptional character, and a personality very much of its own.

All the history books tell us that Jurançon is the only wine in France to have had the honour of being used to baptize a royal child, namely Henri IV.

The Jurançon wine district is situated on sunny, rolling slopes just below the Château de Pau, between the Gave de Pau and the Gave d'Oloron (*gaves* are mountain streams or rivers) and facing the imposing Pyrenean massif that leads to Aragon in Spain. These are the highest vineyards in the Pyrenean area, rising from 300m up to 400m and covering an area of 550ha.

The soils are based on disrupted strata of clay-chalk or clay-silica marls known as the '*poudings de Jurançon*' (Jurançon puddings).

The vineyards are directly affected by the cold air, late spring frosts and early snowfalls of the Pyrenean climatic regime. But, at the same time, they enjoy the benefits brought by maritime influences, namely, good distribution of rainfall and light, warm autumns. As a wine-growing area, Jurançon is full of contrasts, with plots of vineyards huddled in the hollows between steep slopes, or cultivated in terraces on these slopes. They are sheltered from the north wind and generally face due south or southwest, forming natural greenhouses where the grapes bask in the sun.

Throughout the course of the centuries, local growers have chosen particularly aromatic varieties of grape, able to thrive in this climate of extremes: the Gros Manseng, the Petit Manseng and the Courbu Blanc. These varieties are normally grown high and trained to three wires.

The Gros Manseng gives musts with an average alcohol content of 12.5° to 13°. These form the basis of the dry white wines of Jurançon. The Petit Manseng produces fine sweet white wines. Both grape varieties communicate remarkable and characteristic aromas to Jurançon's wines.

The sugar-rich and acid-rich musts are often vinified during the very cold weather of a Pyrenean winter. Elaborate oenological techniques and temperature-controlled vinification apparatus are needed to combat the cold and ensure that malolactic fermentation takes place if required. The average annual production over the last ten years has been about 25,000hl, two thirds of which is handled by the cooperatives based in Gan.

The Jurançon terroir *yields both dry and sweet white wines of great breeding.*

Jurançon became an AOC on 17 October 1975. The decree covers 25 communes in Pyrénées-Atlantiques. Jurançon is a sweet white wine made from the Petit Manseng. The grapes are harvested late and selectively in a series of pickings up to late November or early December. A young Jurançon, with its glinting amber-yellow and bright gold lights, is rare among the great sweet wines of France in that it is full, lively and fresh at the same time. It is fragrant with the unforgettable aromas of Pyrenean honey, toasted hazelnuts and acacia blossom, enhanced by a touch of guava or vanilla, depending on its exact area of origin. It is a most alluring wine. It also ages remarkably well. The great sweet wines of Jurançon may be kept for 20 or 25 years or even more.

Jurançon Sec was decreed an AOC on 17 October 1975. Growers produce about 14,000hl of dry white wine every year, within the same 25 communes as are specified for sweet Jurançon. It is a fine white wine, elegant, with breeding, its luminous pale green colour tinged with light gold. It has a fresh, delicate bouquet with aromas of acacia blossom and broom enhanced by slightly exotic notes (guava) and, sometimes, a hint of white truffle seasoned with pepper. Beeswax and balsamic (resinous) aromas may also be present, depending on local soil structures. These aromas are agreeably counterpointed by the flavour of Jurançon Sec. It is a lively, light, very dry, slightly *perlant* wine, but it also has a full-bodied, fleshy side to it. When aged, it acquires a luminous, golden amber colour and a spicy, peppery bouquet. Its fleshiness and structure are then most apparent.

JURA

The Jura wine region consists of an 80km strip of French countryside stretching from Saint-Amour to Salins. This small territory, however, contains such a great diversity of relief, of exposures and aspects, of* terroirs *and of grape varieties that a whole palette of wines and spirits, uniquely varied, can be offered: red, rosé,* vin jaune, vin de paille, *sparkling,* macvin, *marc and brandy.

Statue of St Vernier, pruning knife in hand.

To discover the origins of the Jura wine region it is necessary to go right back to Roman antiquity: Pliny the Elder mentions the wine of the Jura in his *Historia Naturalis.* Its fame in those days brought Phocaean mariners sailing up the Saône to load their ships with it and take it to Italy. None-too-scrupulous merchants in Ostia and Naples used to steep indeterminate local wines with resin in goatskins in order to endow them with something resembling the very special flavour prized in the Jura's wines.

In AD 92, however, the Emperor Domitian ordered the Jura vineyards to be grubbed up, leaving a bigger area for the growing of cereals to ensure bread supplies to the Roman legions.

Two centuries later, the Emperor Probus gave the local Sequani tribe, in common with other Gaulish tribes, an 'authorization to replant the vines formerly uprooted'. This is the earliest known text concerning the Jura wine district. At a small locality known as Proby, in the commune of Arlay, there is a very fine Roman wine cellar remaining from the imperial residence of Castellum Probi. Another indication of the ancient roots of this wine region is the similarity of a pruning hook held by the figure of a Gallic god, found at Bourbonne, with one seen on the statue of St Vernier at Conliège, near Lons-le-Saunier.

The development of the wine region

It is quite certain that at the time of replanting that followed Probus' decree, the wine-growing region would have clung to the banks of the river Seille, where its product served as currency in bartering with the peasants of the uplands; the little hill at Arlay is often quoted as the first of Jura's modern vineyards. That is where, in 650, the lord of Arlay, Patrice Donat — who became St Donat — built the first Christian church in the area and dedicated it to St Vincent, the patron of wine growers. His gift of the Domblans vineyards to the church at Besançon in 654 underlines the importance and vitality of wine growing in this part of the Jura.

Château-Chalon vineyards. The vines in early autumn acquire the colour of the vins jaunes *produced in this splendid* appellation.

At the end of the 7th century his brother Norbert went to Château-Chalon and founded an abbey there — and planted its vineyard, indispensable for the religious life, but also a source of revenue for the canonesses. Did they perhaps introduce the 'Swiss Sylvaner' to the region towards the end of the 9th century, the celebrated grape now known as the Savagnin, from which *vin jaune* is made? Or does it perhaps come from vines brought in to the region at the beginning of the 14th century by the Granvelle family and the counts of Chalon-Arlay, who grew Savagnin on their own lands before propagating the vine in the neighbourhood? Others state that the Savagnin is distantly related to the Andalusian sherry grape Palomino (known in France as the Listan), due to the fact that Franche-Comté was for a long time a Spanish province, or to a wild form of the Gewürztraminer. A recent theory, apparently corroborated by etymology (Savagnin = 'savage'), suggests it is the noble successor of the very earliest wild vines of the Jura region itself. The Savagnin keeps its secret, but there is no doubt that the latter thesis would be the most popular one locally. By the 14th century, the Savagnin had acquired its name: reference is made to it by a Lons landowner in a document of the time.

Many other early texts illustrate the importance of wine growing in the medieval Jura economy. John I, count of Chalon and the powerful lord of Arlay, decreed in 1276 that, 'Those who sell false measure shall incur a penalty of 60 sous ... once in every month the lord shall be shown ... all wine measures. Those who have bought wine with a large measure and used a small one to sell it shall be left to my mercy.' This is the oldest known by-law in Jura. Among the 65 articles in the exemptions granted to the town of Lons in 1293 by Hugues de Vienne, six deal with vineyards and wine and show a remarkable concern for quality: 'The announcement of the grape harvest shall be made by men of skill and judgment ... whoever harvests outside of the allotted time shall pay a 20 sous fine.'

It was in about 1460 that the abbey of Château-Chalon began the production of *vin jaune*; the abbess had the vineyards guarded by armed men so that the harvest could safely be delayed and the grapes reach perfect maturity.

In the 16th century, Philip II, King of Spain (among whose possessions was Franche-Comté), forbade the planting of 'The Gamay, the Melon' and other grape varieties thought too productive in an edict of 1 December 1576. By this time the wine-growing area covered the whole of the region, from Sainte-Agnès in the south to Dole and Besançon in the north.

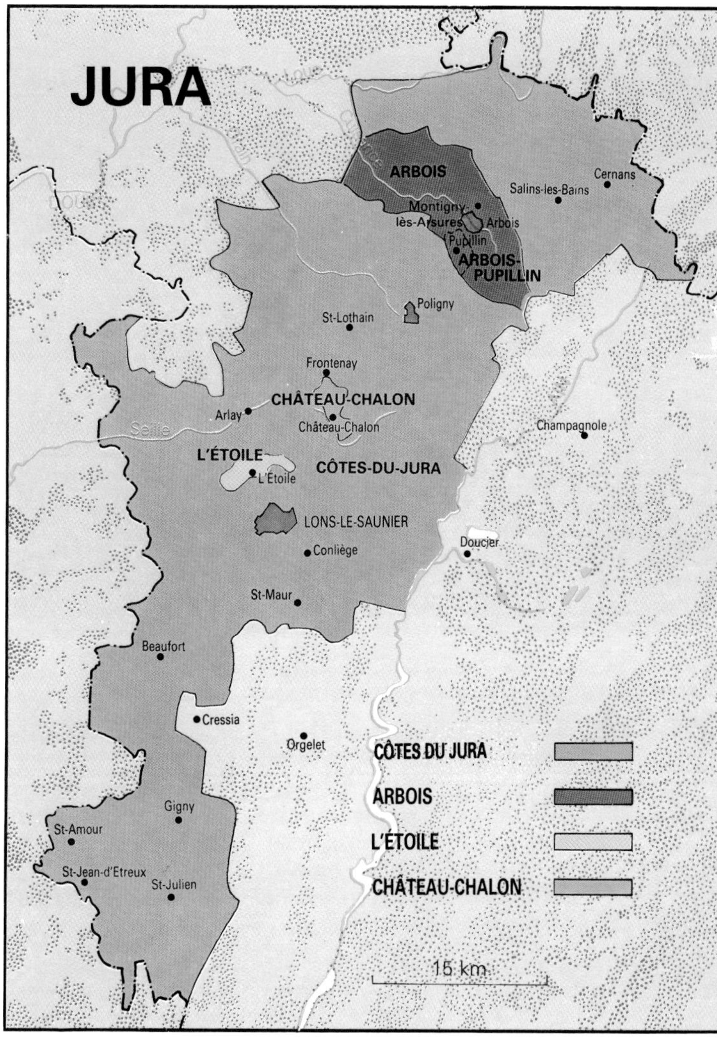

Royal families and heads of state throughout the world have long given the wines of Jura a place of honour on their tables. Henri IV, who had a great liking for them, made gifts of them when being reconciled with his enemies, while the Duc de Sully, one of Henri IV's ministers, served them to the queen's ladies; Prince Metternich was their ardent defender before Napoleon, putting *vin jaune* above the greatest Rheingau Johannisberg; Charles V, Tsar Nicolas II, kings and queens of the Netherlands, the French lawyer and statesman Alexandre Millerand, Edward VII ... Many are those who have enjoyed these peerless wines, so full of character.

In the 19th century the wine region was marked out by a series of small towns — Salins-les-Bains, Voiteur, Arbois, Poligny, Lons-le-Saunier, Beaufort, Cousance, Saint-Amour — that owed a great deal of their prosperity to flourishing local vineyards. Each of these little 'wine capitals' of Jura had its own wine growers' quarter.

Arbois, the best known of the Jura **appellations.**

A native of Dole, Louis Pasteur did important work on fermentation in Arbois; the house and personal vineyard of this father of modern oenology can still be visited there.

European wine growing owes much to another native of Jura, the little-known Alexis Millardet. He was the first to graft French vines on to American rootstocks to counter the phylloxera scourge, the presence of which was officially verified in Montfleur, in the extreme south of Jura, in 1879.

The 19th century also brought a thorough study of the extent of the Jura wine-growing area. The first such statistics ever recorded are those given by Jullien in his survey of 1816, *Topographie de tous les vignobles connus*, where he cites the following assessments of areas: Lons *arrondissement*, 8,652ha; Dole *arrondissement*, 3,798ha; and 3,610ha for that of Poligny.

In the early 19th century, wine growing in the Jura enjoyed a period of prosperity as a result of the development of the road system. Land registry returns in 1838 indicate a wine-growing area of 18,550ha. In 1888, when the phylloxera had already destroyed many vineyards in the Midi, the Jura was as yet little affected and demand for its wines was high. It was then that the wine-growing area reached its greatest extent: 19,384ha. But thereafter it declined rapidly with the swift spread of phylloxera during the warm, dry years of 1892 to 1895.

By 1900, the wine-growing area had been reduced to 7,915ha, with barely 500ha of vineyards as yet replanted with grafted vines. However, it grew between this point and the eve of the First World War, when it reached about 11,000ha. The war was the second great blow sustained by the Jura wine region; it took away its manpower and put it into a new decline.

The Jura region was cultivated by a very large number of wine growers; after the First World War it was basically an area of smallholdings, with 16,770 owners working 6,272ha for which harvest returns were required, which gave them an average of only 37 ares each. The rest of the area, about 2,000ha, belonged to thousands of growers producing wine for family consumption only, and thus exempted from making harvest returns.

The exodus from the countryside has been the last shock for this splendid wine region. No more than 1,450ha are used for the production of AOC wines today, to which should be added the 7ha or so of the vineyards around Offlanges, last trace of the Dole wine district.

The geographical setting

The Jura wine-growing region, as mentioned above, consists essentially of a strip of country 80km long stretching from Saint-Amour in the south to the area around Salins-les-Bains in the north, near the border of the Jura *département*. In the east, it reaches the slopes of the Premier Plateau (the plateau of Champagnole), and in the west it borders on the Bresse region.

A detailed study of this zone, called the Revermont by geologists, reveals many internal differences in relief, in exposure and in the make-up of the subsoils. These differences are the cause of the variety of wines produced in the Jura.

From Saint-Amour to Lons-le-Saunier, the vineyards mostly occupy the lower slopes, lying at a height between 200m and 400m. They generally face west, sometimes southwest or south in certain valleys. The many fractures in the Jurassic period strata — belonging to the Lias series of the Jurassic system, or the Triassic system — are particularly favourable for vineyards. Limestone debris is mixed with clay in those fractures to form stony, warm soils (at, for example, Rotalier, Grusse or Maynal), where ripening the grapes is easy, and where harvesting often takes place a week earlier than in the part of the region that lies north of Lons-le-Saunier.

From Lons to Poligny, the wine-growing area stretches from the edge of the western slopes of the Premier Plateau for about 10km, as far as the boundaries of Bresse. The altitude ranges from 200m to 500m. The centre of the wine-growing region is crossed by the N83, flanked on either side by gentle hills or isolated knolls. These benefit from long hours of sunshine that greatly favour the vines planted on them, while the slopes of the Premier Plateau, also planted with vines, have a favourable west-facing aspect. Certain of the deep, high valleys cut into the Plateau, such as the Cirque de Baume, which shelters the Château-Chalon vineyards, protect the vines from cold winds and at the same time enable them to benefit from extra sunlight reflected from the rocky surfaces.

This varied landscape has an equally varied subsoil: grey, blue or black marls of the middle or upper Lias series, sometimes mixed with limestone beds with *Gryphaea* fossils of the lower Lias series; these soils offer rich, deep, well-watered earth favourable to the growing of wines of repute.

The semi-continental climate, common to the whole of the wine-growing area, is responsible for very agreeable weather conditions here. The luxuriant vegetation of the Jura is in distinct contrast to the austerity of the Bresse region and the Premier Plateau; this formerly earned it the name *Bon Pays*, the good country.

North of Lons-le-Saunier, towards Arbois, the vineyards cover a more extensive area, at heights of 200m to 400m, occupying both the slopes of the Premier Plateau and the range of hills to the west. Here, too, the terrain is far from homogeneous. It is made up of marls of various hues, often wine-coloured thanks to a high iron content, forming compact soils that are hard to work. Dolomitic and limestone beds are intermixed with these marls. High up, on Lias series marls, are grown the celebrated wines of Arbois, at Arbois itself, at Montigny-lès-Arsures and at Mesnay.

Northeast of Arbois, around Salins and Mouchard, the vineyards found in the valley of the Furieuse have the same varied terrains, from Lias series marls to Bajocian stage soils. The vineyards sited on the slopes of Mont Poupet,

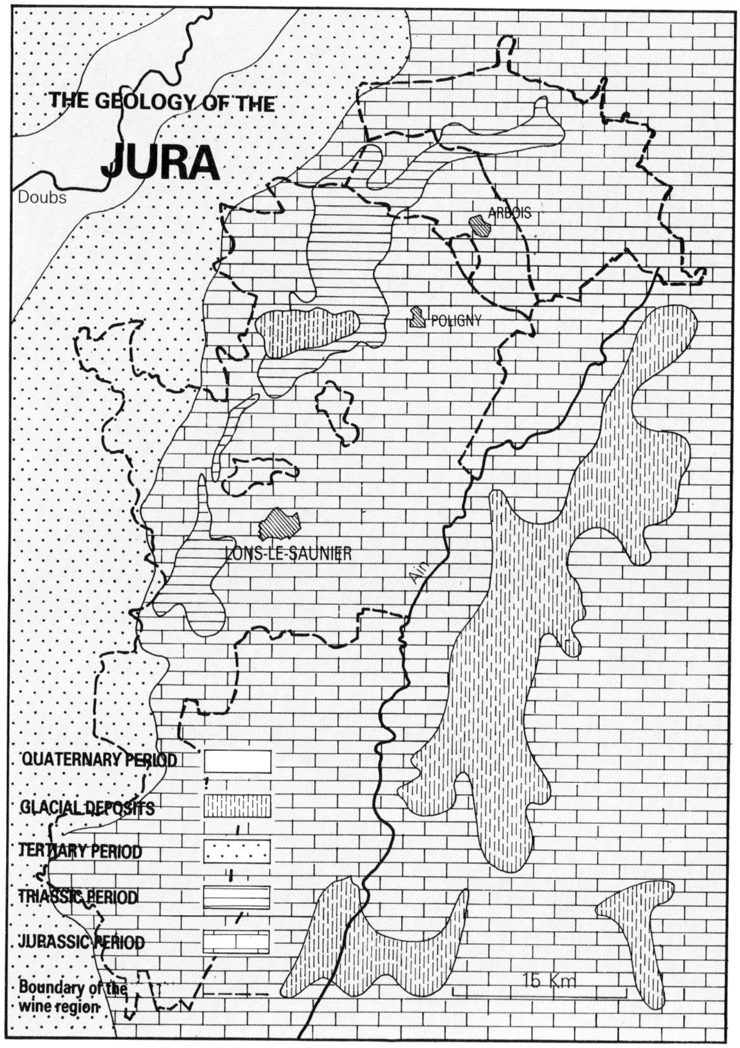

Château d'Arlay is the oldest castle in France to give its name to a vineyard site. It lies in the Côtes du Jura.

with plenty of sunlight but sheltered from north winds, yield wines of quality. The Mouchard vineyards were the first in Jura to be replanted after the phylloxera scourge.

Finally mention should be made of the granitic sands and fine gravels that make up the soil of the small wine district of Offlanges, some kilometres to the north of Dole.

Climate

This is of semi-continental type. Winters are long and rigorous, but snowfalls in the wine-growing areas are not very heavy. This can be a disadvantage, as it sometimes makes the vines vulnerable to January frosts. Springs are short, cold and damp and can bring hard, destructive May frosts. Summers, though, are warm, dry and sunny, conditions that frequently continue into autumn. The Jura vines are generally late ripening and so benefit from this fine end-of-season weather. It is said, locally, that 'September makes the wine'.

The figures given in the table below complete this description of the climate of the Jura wine-growing area. It sets out the climatic statistics relating to the vegetative period of the vine

Montigny-lès-Arsures. This wine district endures rigorous winter conditions.

Years	Heat summation (above 0°C threshold)	Hours of sunshine	Rainfall	Flowering period (1)	Volume of grape harvest (2)	Weather during grape harvest (3)
1972	2 928°	1 539	525 mm	4	N−	D
1973	3 161°	1 447	606 mm	3	N+	D
1974	2 991°	1 287	752 mm	3	N−	W
1975	3 156°	1 256	648 mm	3	N	M
1976	3 428°	1 549	514 mm	1	N+	M
1977	3 069°	1 169	806 mm	1	N−	M
1978	2 989°	1 356	568 mm	4	N	W
1979	3 207°	1 412	638 mm	3	N+	D
1980	3 019°	1 258	795 mm	5	N−	W
1981	3 217°	1 213	869 mm	3	N−	D
1982	3 346°	1 510	773 mm	2	N+	D
1983	3 434°	2 818	811 mm	3	N+	D
1984	3 051°	1 411	654 mm	3	N	W
1985	3 287°	1 688	663 mm	3	N−	D
1986	3 252°	1 419	687 mm	3	N+	D

(1) Flowering period: 1 = early June
2 = mid-June
3 = end of June
4 = early July
5 = mid-July

(2) Volume of grape harvest:
N− = below normal
N = normal
N+ = above normal

(3) Weather during grape harvest:
D = dry
W = wet
M = mixed

(1 April to 1 November) for the period 1972–1986.

Grape varieties

Like all ancient wine-growing areas, Jura has numerous local grape varieties. About 40 were counted in 1897: Foirard Blanc, Melon, Sacy, Chasselas, Pourrisseux, Meslier Saint-François, Gueuche Noir, Mondeuse, Enfariné, Gamay Noir à Jus Blanc, Béclan, Valais Noir, Meunier, Corbeau, Argant, and so on. In addition there are the five quality grape varieties recommended by the INAO, all of which were widespread in the region before the onset of phylloxera: Savagnin, Chardonnay, Trousseau, Poulsard and Pinot Noir. Each of these, separately or in combination, plays a part in the local range of wines and spirits: red, rosé, white, *vin jaune*, *vin de paille*, sparkling, *macvin*, marc and *fine* (brandy).

The Savagnin

This vine is specific to Jura and requires the deep marl or argillaceous limestone soils of the Lias series if it is to flourish. Although found in all parts of the region it remains modestly planted: its particular soil requirements, its need for sunny situations and its slow growth discourage many growers.

The Savagnin is picked when it is very ripe: its thick skin enables it to resist mould attacks. Nowadays it can attain up to 300g of sugar per litre of must, which corresponds to a potential alcohol level of 15°. Used by itself it produces the region's finest wine, *vin jaune*, as well as characterful ordinary white wine. When combined with other grapes, it brings an element of quality and longevity.

The Chardonnay

The great white variety of the Burgundy and Champagne vineyards grows more vigorously here than in either of these other regions. Its strong, spreading roots enable it to adapt to the most difficult stony or gravelly soils. It plays a part in the fame of the local white wines, either by itself or with the Savagnin, to which it contributes subtlety and finesse.

The Trousseau

This red-wine variety is particularly well suited to the marls and argillaceous soils of the high ground around Arbois. Although it is susceptible to anthracnose in the mist-prone upland valleys, and to winter frosts, it regrows vigorously on old wood. Its must has a high sugar content, and gives a wine with plenty of body that keeps well, though it is sometimes a little hard in its youth. It acquires a beautiful colour with age. It is often the sole grape variety used for Arbois reds, but it is also to be found in the rest of Jura, and is used in combination with other grapes to make red, rosé or sparkling wines.

The Poulsard

The special affection of the Jura wine growers for this grape is due to its long presence in the region — from the 13th century — and to its exceptional delicacy. It performs well in rich soils on well-exposed sites, in years when a sunny early summer provides good conditions for flowering, and with a mild, warm autumn for good ripening. Its early budbreak makes it susceptible to late spring frosts, and it also suffers from *coulure* (flower abortion). It gives a delicate red wine, high in alcohol and with a good colour — but this disappears with age, and the wine acquires a pleasing onionskin tint and a particularly fine bouquet.

The Poulsard is found throughout Jura. In Arbois it is often vinified and bottled on its own, but elsewhere in the region it is mostly combined with other grapes for the making of red and rosé wines.

Pinot Noir

There can be no doubt that the introduction of this famous Burgundy red grape variety, known locally as the Noirien, Savagnin Noir or Salvagnin, came early in Jura's viticultural history. It is generally attributed to the counts of Chalon-Arlay, a cadet branch of the family of the dukes of Burgundy; they planted it in their vineyards at Arlay and it subsequently spread to other areas. It should be noted that, even today, it is the favoured variety for red wines in the neighbourhood of Arlay.

The characteristics of the Pinot Noir are the same in the Jura as they are in Burgundy. Deep, well-drained soils of clay and limestone type, ferruginous and stony, allow the Pinot Noir to yield perfect grapes and great wines, comparable in good years to those of the Côte d'Or. When combined with the Poulsard and vinified without maceration (*en blanc*), it produces a sparkling wine of great class.

The characteristics of Jura wines

The variety of soils and grape varieties found here present the consumer with a wide choice of brandies and wines. Such diversity may sometimes confuse the uninitiated, but for those who like making discoveries, the Jura offers a storehouse of treasures, with the renowned *vin jaune* in pride of place.

Vin jaune

This wine comes exclusively from the Savagnin grape. The grapes are picked late and taken to the press. The musts are extracted by a series of different pressings, then settled and cleared by *débourbage*. The wine begins a slow fermentation, which sometimes lasts into the spring. When this has been completed, the wine is taken down into a cool cellar and run into small casks, called *pièces*, of 228-litre capacity.

***A cellar of 228-litre casks for ageing* vin jaune.**

A slow ageing process now begins which transforms this liquid into *vin jaune*, via the action of a film of yeast that appears on the surface of the wine. This phenomenon takes place thanks to the special qualities of the grape variety and the particularities of the Jura climate. *Élevage* proceeds from this point on without handling, racking or topping up of the casks. Natural evaporation or cask absorption produces an empty space above the wine. A film of *Mycoderma vini* (wine yeast) then forms on the liquid surface, and this aids the formation of aldehyde. The cells in this film, mainly of *Saccharomyces bayanus*, protect the wine from violent oxidization. The wine changes colour and acquires its special aromas. It is said that, during this process, it 'eats its lees'.

There is a wait of at least six years while this result is attained — with no human intervention, solely at the whim and behest of nature. After these six years, just 65 per cent of the original wine remains. The *vin jaune* then goes into special bottles: the famous 62cl *clavelins*. Their invention is attributed to the Vieille Loye glassworks, around 1506.

Vin jaune has a powerful, complex aroma, composed of the scents of nuts and spices. On the palate, nuts are again present in this dry wine, whose flavours open up in a 'peacock's tail', powerful, but also elegant. The finish and aftertaste of *vin jaune* is said to be the longest in the world, the flavour of the wine sometimes lingering in the mouth for more than a minute. It is a strong, heady wine, especially when pro-

THE SPARKLING JEWELS OF JURA

One of my friends, a great shot when it came to woodcock, had some fine two-barrelled successes in the year 1949. Thus it was that five brace or so of these birds were to be found hanging in his cellar, not far from his cigars. They waited there, with a string through their beaks, until they were 'ripe' enough to take down. Unfortunately my friend's wife could not stand the high, gamy odours of these trophies, and so one day he came to me, rather sheepishly, bringing the little beauties wrapped in newspaper. 'My wife can't cook them for me,' he said. 'Do what you like with them!'

He did not need to say it twice. I invited him and two of my wine-growing friends and turned to the stove. It was a real joy gently cooking these plump birds, wrapped in bacon, in a cast-iron casserole.

When we lifted the lid off the casserole in the restaurant the aroma released thrilled our nostrils and those of the customers round about. But this aroma was but a discreet hint of the flavour of the woodcock, which, in combination with a 1947 red Arbois from Montigny-lès-Arsures and some 1942 vin jaune, *became a real firework display of flavours . . .*

The gastronomy of the Jura is very much in the image of this multi-faceted region, rich in forests that teem with game, in lakes and rivers full of fish, and in lush pastures. The gastronomy also reflects the diversity of regional produce, both vegetable and animal.

The vineyards offer a thousand sparkling jewels. How beautifully these wines — whether red, rosé, white, jaune *or* de paille *— partner the produce of this land!*

The cuisine of the Jura is simple and unpretentious; it is what our grandmothers cooked on Sundays. Charcuterie and cochonailles *(pork products) have an important place, and still today in small villages it is not unusual to see a pig slaughtered. To accompany* Jésus de Morteau, pâté en croûte, boudin *and black pudding, various hams, and terrines with mushrooms I generally serve red wines made from the Poulsard grape variety: Arbois-Pupillin or Côtes du Jura.*

Fish from our rivers or lakes, crayfish and frogs call for white wines from the Savagnin or Chardonnay grapes.

Game from our lovely forests of Joux, Chaux or Tresse — roe deer, wild boar, hare, thrush, teal, mallard, woodcock — gain by being seasoned with aromatic mountain herbs and marinated in some good red Arbois, such as that from Montigny-lès-Arsures. Red meats, too, demand red wines — braised meat or a rib of beef with the same wine.

White meats, poultry and calves' sweetbreads go well with Château-Chalon vin jaune, *or a white wine from Arbois or Étoile. An astonishingly good partnership is that of cockerel,* vin jaune *and morels.*

Then there are our magnificent cheeses, mellow and rich — the delicate Comté with its nutty taste, Vacherin scented with pine bark, Septmoncel from the Saint-Claude area, the runny Cancoillotte — they go equally well with an Arbois red or with a vin jaune *with its flavour of nuts.*

Jura has a wine that one might think was expressly created for desserts: vin de paille. *In an enchanting way, its sweetness balances perfectly that of* pain aux œufs, *apple charlotte, or tarts made with the fruits of our forests.*

Finally there is macvin, *the characteristic* vin de liqueur *of our region, which can be drunk equally happily as an aperitif or with sweet dishes.*

André Jeunet

duced from a good site and a fine vintage. Without any doubt, *vin jaune* ranks among the greatest *crus* of the French vineyards; the more so as its length of life is remarkable — 50, even 100 years and more!

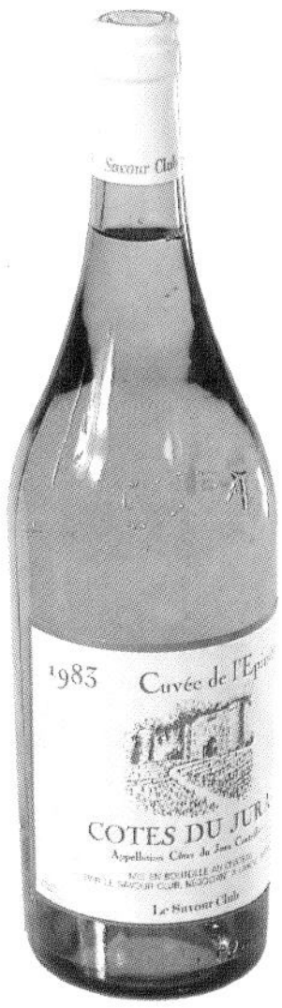

Jura's white wines

These are dry, fruity, fine wines, whether from the Chardonnay or the Savagnin individually, or from a combination of the two. They often need to be kept for two to three years in order to acquire their characteristic bouquet of nuts and roast almonds. From the qualities of the local *terroir*, the Chardonnay can also acquire in Jura a '*goût de jaune*' (a taste of *vin jaune*). To reinforce this, Chardonnay wine often spends some time in *vin jaune* casks, impregnated as they are with *vin jaune* yeasts. Jura's white wines have good keeping qualities, and can continue to improve for 10 or even 20 years.

Jura's red and rosé wines

The colour of these two categories is sometimes so close that it is hard to distinguish them. This phenomenon arises from the grape varieties, which are the same, and from similar methods of vinification, with skin-maceration in both cases. Thus there are very lightly coloured red wines as well as very deeply coloured rosé wines.

The Trousseau grape gives a wine that is rich in colour and tannin. It is often used with the Poulsard, which gives paler and less tannic, but much stronger wine. The Pinot Noir produces wine of pale colour, but with attractive glints; it is delicate, of moderate longevity (six to ten years) and recognizable by its scents of currants and berries. The hardier Trousseau requires several years' ageing to acquire finesse, and its length of life is excellent: 15 to 20 years.

When vinified into a rosé style, all three varieties offer balanced wines with a great range of colour nuances. Their powerful, rich, vinous aromas can astonish: these are without doubt great wines, but unfortunately they suffer from the fact that consumers have lost their liking for rosé wines in general.

Vin de paille

Often mistakenly confused with *vin jaune*, *vin de paille* is a sweet wine. This traditional Jura product is made on the basis of a selection of the very best grapes harvested. These bunches are then hung up on wooden slats, or sometimes still laid out on straw as in days gone by, whence the descriptive term *vin de paille* (straw wine). The grapes lose some of their moisture through evaporation. After two to three months, the wizened grapes are pressed with a view to a slow fermentation of two to three years in oak casks.

Desiccating grapes to be used for making **vin de paille**. *The grapes are hung on slats, or laid out on straw, then pressed two or three months later.*

Today *vin de paille* has become very hard to find, even in Jura itself; this is because it demands a great sacrifice on the part of the grower. The grapes have to be well ripened and free of any rot. The drying of the grapes has to be carefully watched and their degree of desiccation monitored: if they are vinified too soon then the must will be over-acid with too little sugar; too late and the grapes will be lacking in juice. Long periods of time and large quantities of the best fruit are needed in order to obtain a very small amount of *vin de paille*. It has been estimated that it takes about 100kg of grapes to produce some 25 litres of this wine.

Served cool, at 8°C, it makes a heady, perfumed and subtle aperitif. It has an alcoholic strength of 16°. It is also much appreciated with foie gras or with a dessert. It used to be recommended as a tonic for convalescents or young mothers.

Jura's white and rosé sparkling wines

The fame of these wines goes back a long way: sparkling wine production in the Jura seems to have started at the end of the 18th century, the same period as in Champagne. The varieties generally used for this purpose are the Pinot Noir and the Chardonnay. Sparkling wines

Vin jaune *goes into a* **clavelin**, *a 62cl bottle, which is sometimes sealed with wax.*

have become the main production in certain parts of the region, as at Voiteur.

Macvin

This very singular 'wine' is made by mixing unfermented grape must and local marc in the proportion of two to one, whence the name *macvin* (*marc* + *vin*). This method, although close to that used for Pineau des Charentes and the Ratafia of the Champagne district, nevertheless produces a very original fortified wine with the perfumes characteristic of the Jura *terroir*. Served cool, it makes a pleasant aperitif. It can also be enjoyed as a delicate dessert wine. Its alcoholic strength is around 17°.

Year	Arbois	Côtes du Jura	L'Étoile	Château-Chalon
1945	17	17	18	16
1946	12	10	12	13
1947	19	20	20	19
1948	11	10	13	10
1949	18	18	17	17
1950	11	11	12	14
1951	12	10	13	10
1952	12	14	14	16
1953	13	15	14	12
1954	11	12	10	14
1955	13	11	15	14
1956	11	10	10	10
1957	15	15	13	16
1958	12	14	13	11
1959	18	20	19	18
1960	11	10	10	12
1961	14	14	15	15
1962	13	16	16	14
1963	13	10	15	12
1964	19	18	14	17
1965	13	12	13	11
1966	14	16	10	14
1967	15	17	16	16
1968	12	11	11	13
1969	17	19	18	17
1970	12	13	10	12
1971	18	16	15	16
1972	13	10	13	14
1973	17	17	15	14
1974	10	10	11	no *appellation* wines made
1975	14	15	14	14
1976	17	18	17	16
1977	13	10	13	14
1978	12	14	15	17
1979	17	20	17	19
1980	11	11	10	no *appellation* wines made
1981	15	16	14	quality not yet decided
1982	14	15	15	”
1983	16	17	17	”
1984	13	12	13	no *appellation* wines made
1985	17	17	17	quality not yet decided

Source: Société de Viticulture du Jura

***Marc and* fine**

These grape- and wine-based spirits, produced under the Franche-Comté *appellation*, are regarded with favour by connoisseurs. Often very strong (45° to 50°), they embody the potency and elegance of a noble *terroir* and are considered to be among the best in France.

The remains left after grapes have been pressed are distilled to make marc. This distillation is sometimes repeated to improve the quality. *Fine* is obtained by distilling base wines not intended for bottling. It is done after they have matured for a period of between two to ten years, contributing delicacy and a beautiful straw-yellow colour to the final brandy.

Economic structures of Jura wine production

Today the economic structure of the Jura wine region is still dominated by the family character of its wine-producing units; and there are very many growers who are also engaged in some other agricultural activity, such as stock rearing. Production of AOC wines is provided by 1,000 growers with about 1,450ha between them. Growers who produce less than 30hl a year number 800.

There are only 200 agricultural units engaged solely in wine growing. If the few large holdings are left out of the reckoning — one of 250ha, ten or so from 15 to 20ha — this means an average of 2.5ha per wine-growing unit.

In 1970, a renewal programme was able to establish that there were about 13,500ha of land suitable for vines in the region. The action taken under this programme has been able to check the slow erosion of the Jura wine region: every year young wine growers are replanting about 50ha in AOC areas.

Production is divided among three roughly equal groupings, namely the *négociants*, the cooperatives and the private growers. This tripartite structure derives partly from the small size of the wine-growing units, and partly from the early founding of both dairy and winemaking cooperatives in the Jura.

The Jura wine *appellations* are organized under the patronage of the Société de Viticulture du Jura, the body that applies the directives issued by the INAO; it also promotes the profession of wine growing generally, both within the region and outside. There are also five local wine associations, and the Confrérie des Nobles Vins du Jura et Comté, involved in the promotion of the Jura's *appellations* and wines.

Jurançon Blanc

Synonyms: *Quillat, Quillard, Plant Dressé* (on account of its upright habit), *Plant Debout* at Sables-d'Olonne, *Braquet* in Landes, *Dame Blanc* in Lot-et-Garonne.

Growing tips open, felty white with carmine margins.

Young leaves downy, bullate.

Leaves orbicular, bullate with pink petiolar junction, deeply five-lobed, concave at base, often with overlapping edges; petiolar sinus lyrate with overlapping edges; dentation convex, medium; underside of blade downy-pubescent.

Green shoots upright, reddish green on both sides, without bloom, nodes pink; tendrils small, thin.

Bunches medium sized, conical, compact, shouldered; grapes small, spherical, yellowish white; ripening period: second epoch.

Despite its name, this vine does not appear in the Jurançon plantings but rather in those of the Cognac and Armagnac AOCs, where it is distilled to give an *eau-de-vie* with a not very pronounced or persistent bouquet. It is a hardy, but not very vigorous plant that has to be pruned and trained short. It is less susceptible to oidium (powdery mildew) than the Colombard. Classed as 'authorized' in Charente, Gers, Gironde and the two Pyrenean *départements*, in practice it is little grown except on 650ha in Gers, with a little in Lot-et-Garonne.

Jurançon Noir

Synonyms: *Jurançon Rouge, Folle Noire, Fola Belcha* in the Basque country, *Folle Rouge* in Lot-et-Garonne, *Enrageat Noir* in Dordogne, *Petit Noir, Saintongeais, Dégoûtant* in Charente, *Giranson, Nanot, Nochant, Gros Grappu, Cahors, Arrivet, Pousse-en-l'Air* in Gironde, *Dame Noire* in Lot, *Cannut de Lauzun* in Agen, *Gamay-Moutot* in Ardèche, *Piquepout Rouge, Quillard Rouge* at Port-Sainte-Marie, *Plant Quillat* in Lot, *Sans Pareil Précoce* in Lot-et-Garonne, *Gouni* in Hautes-Alpes, *Chalosse Noire* or *Jalosse* in the Montauban region.

Growing tips open, felty white with carmine margins.

Young leaves downy, yellowish, with bronze patches.

Leaves medium sized, orbicular, thick, contorted, bullate, crimped at the petiolar junction, deeply five-lobed with wide lateral sinuses, concave at the base; petiolar sinus lyrate and virtually closed or with overlapping edges, sometimes naked at base; dentation convex, small; underside of blade arachnoid with pubescent veins. Foliage reddens slightly in autumn.

A bunch of Jurançon Noir grapes, a variety grown in the South West, and in the Mediterranean region.

Green shoots ribbed with mahogany brown longitudinal striations; tendrils small, thin.

Bunches large, conical, compact; grapes medium, spherical, blue-black; ripening period: second epoch.

The Jurançon Noir is a vine that originated in the Agen area, but is widely distributed nowadays through the wine districts of the South West, which explains its large number of synonyms. It produces abundant amounts of *vin ordinaire*, light in colour; the variety is the regional counterpart of the Aramon. It is rather susceptible to grey rot (botrytis), but more resistant to downy mildew and oidium (powdery mildew). Four registered clones have been approved, the most useful being number 438. This variety has been classed as 'recommended' in all the *départements* of the South West, and as 'authorized' in the Mediterranean region. However, less and less of it is being grown: no more than 500ha today, compared with 12,300ha in 1958. The main *départements* in which it is found are Tarn (3,254ha), Gers (1,070ha), Haute-Garonne, Lot and Tarn-et-Garonne. It is disappearing from Charentes, Gironde and Dordogne.

Leaf of the Jurançon Noir vine.

Underside of Jurançon Noir leaf.

Knipperle

Bunches small, cylindrical, sometimes winged; grapes medium, spherical, white; ripening period: second epoch. This variety became very widespread at the end of the 18th century, thanks to publicity given it by the nurseryman Ortlieb, who extolled its productivity and its early ripening. However, it is very susceptible to grey rot (botrytis) and to the cochylis moth and has now been abandoned. Although it is still classed as 'recommended' in Alsace, it no longer features in plantings there. Its wine is low in acidity, and is pleasant for drinking *en primeur*.

BUYING WINE

With the elevation of the finest wines to the status of works of art, buying wine has ceased to be simply a matter of impulse, but is also now a question of investment. The pleasures of purchase have become complex ones, in which a quest for the object of desire needs to be tempered by the calculations of financial management ...

The French, in common with other European nations, are currently taking an unprecedented interest in wine. Quality wines (*vins de pays*, VDQS and AOC wines) are favoured to an ever-increasing extent. French interest in the country's viticultural riches is growing each day, and the traditional and almost automatic alternation of burgundy and bordeaux when quality wines are required is now a thing of the past.

The specialist press and leading restaurateurs have contributed greatly to this increased awareness on the part of the French public; so have new developments, such as courses in wine tasting, wine fairs, exhibitions, clubs, societies, tasting groups and wine bars.

Another notable change is that women are found more and more often in vineyards and cellars. They make, taste, buy and choose wines with ease, and with great sureness of judgment. Clearly, wine buying and drinking patterns have been influenced by this welcome stimulus.

The current infatuation with wine has also had significant consequences for wine makers. At a time when French people move readily from place to place, and live in smaller homes without or with poor cellars, and in an age when keeping in shape has become a priority, the trend towards lighter wines that do not need to mature for a long period of time is marked. What should be the wine maker's attitude to this? Should he conform to the demands of the consumer, or should he continue to make wines according to his own tastes, tastes often shaped by ancestral traditions? The best solution, no doubt, lies halfway between the two extremes. The wine maker should remain faithful to his *terroir* and respect its wine-making requirements, while at the same time adopting commercial practices that will encourage customers to buy. Different *terroirs* imply different wines. France, with its ten great wine-growing regions, can offer the consumer unmatched variety without fidelity to *terroir* being compromised.

Wine tasting in a grower's cellar.

The pleasure of discovering a wine for yourself can be intense. Just as there are numerous ways of getting to know wine, so there are numerous ways of buying it. Within France, it can be bought direct from an estate. In France or abroad, it can be bought from a wine grower's stand at a wine fair, by mail order, or via specialized wine-selling clubs. You can also buy from specialist, wholesale or retail wine merchants.

Whichever way you choose, only one thing is certain: quality has its price. A good bottle of wine is the outcome of a number of costly operations: vineyard upkeep, harvesting, making and ageing the wine, preparation of bottles, distribution, etc. All these operations have to be paid for. To arrive at the true value of a bottle of wine, three things must be taken into account: quality, price and the pleasure it gives when it is drunk.

Buying direct

Anyone travelling to or living in France can buy direct from a wine-growing estate. You might like to do so out of a spirit of curiosity, or on the advice of friends, or after having consulted specialist books and magazines. It is an excellent way of discovering a *terroir* or an estate; of acquiring a better knowledge of wine; or simply of absorbing local atmosphere. It is often the best way to buy wine at a reasonable price, as no intermediary is involved in the transaction.

When buying direct from an estate, it is best to arrange by prior appointment to meet the grower or the cellarmaster in person, so that you can properly taste what is on offer. When tasting, do not allow yourself to be carried away by the enthusiasm that the surroundings may arouse.

If the cellar is clean and well maintained, this is generally a good sign. The temperature in the cellar may be low, about 12°C, so remember that the flavour of any wine you taste there will be radically transformed when you drink it at room temperature at home. It is therefore a good idea to spread your purchases over a number of wines or estates rather than making a large impulse buy, to avoid expensive mistakes. Finally, it is better to concentrate on the wine or wines on which the estate's name has been built, rather than on its less well-known products. For example, if you are visiting a grower in Sancerre, explore the range of white wines on offer first, before allowing yourself to be diverted by the grower's rosé and red wines.

One of the more advantageous possibilities of buying wine direct from an estate is that you can purchase it in bulk, in plastic containers with a capacity of between 5 and 35 litres, or even in barrels or casks holding 100 to 250 litres.

The cheapest way to buy is in plastic containers, and this method of purchase is particularly suitable for wines for immediate drinking. If you buy by the cask or barrel, it is best to obtain bottles and corks, and bottle the wine yourself in hygienic and technically correct conditions. Remember that the finest French wines, though, are never sold in bulk, but only in bottle.

When buying more than 15 litres of wine direct from an estate, you must obtain a transport permit (*congé*) and a *document d'accompagnement communautaire*. These documents are issued by the French tax office and are given to the client by the wine grower at the time of sale. The name of the seller and purchaser, the *appellation*, the quantity being transported and the method and duration of transport will all be shown. The transportation of wine without a permit is a fiscal offence. Finally, if you return to France and buy regularly from the same producer, remember that most growers will not hesitate to give their best customers preferential treatment.

Buying direct from French cooperatives

France has 1,200 cooperatives, with a total of 280,000 members. Many of these cooperatives operate under the direction of very talented oenologists, and they are therefore in the vanguard of wine-making developments in their regions. Cooperative customers can taste a range of wines from different *terroirs* — this range will often be wider than that offered by the individual grower — and buy them in bulk or in bottle at a very reasonable price.

In the last ten years, cooperatives have improved the quality of their wines considerably, by making a selection of members' grapes, and by vinifying grapes from various *terroirs* separately, with the help of greatly improved equipment, to maximize individual character.

Cooperatives are an excellent solution for the grower whose small vineyard holding, even if well situated, cannot justify the expense of buying elaborate equipment for making or bottling wine, nor the cost of searching for appropriate commercial outlets. Thanks to the quality of the wine on offer, cooperatives are doing much to establish the reputation of their regions. *Appellations* and wine-growing zones struggling to assert their identity have, in turn, much to gain from the presence of a dynamic cooperative.

Buying by mail order

There are a number of different ways of purchasing wine by mail order: it may be from merchants, wine clubs, wine magazines or special offers arranged by or advertised in newspapers and journals. Remember always to confirm the conditions of sale before proceeding with any purchase.

Firstly, check the price per bottle carefully. Bottles are sold either inclusive or exclusive of tax (VAT on wine in Britain is 15 per cent). Then check the minimum quantity to be purchased. Is the price inclusive or exclusive of delivery charges? How much do you have to spend before delivery is free? This is worth looking into, because transport costs can be high. In order to minimize costs, it may be a good idea to get together with friends and make group purchases. Finally, always check the merchandise when you receive it, so that you can lodge an immediate complaint in the event of any errors or breakages having occurred in transit.

Buying from wine clubs

Wine clubs have sprung up as the purchase and enjoyment of wine have come to assume greater importance in society. They strive to guarantee their clients an interesting and substantial range of wines chosen for quality and reasonable price. The larger French wine clubs offer a complete service: they seek out *crus*, store their stock in the best conditions, sell by mail order, provide a home delivery service and supply regular information on, and access to, wines selected by great restaurateurs, oenologists, tasters and *sommeliers*. These clubs are able to offer very good value for money, as they buy in large quantities, have well-designed, labour-saving depots and employ a small, specialized staff.

Buying *en primeur* (pre-arrival)

At one time, this method of buying was limited to the purchase of wines from Bordeaux by professionals. It has now spread to other regions, however, and is being used more and more often by the general public.

The principle is that wine is bought in the spring of the year following the harvest, but not delivered until after it has been bottled, some 18 months later. At the time of sale, the merchant concerned gives the customer a title deed. By the time the vintage actually reaches ordinary retail shops, two or more years later, the price will have risen and the wine may be scarce, so this is a way in which the wine enthusiast can both make a saving and guarantee himself a supply that may not be easy to come by on the market later. In the case of modest vintages, however, the saving is very small. For example, the 1984 Bordeaux vintage scarcely increased in value between the time it was offered *en primeur* and the time it appeared in retail shops.

In response to their customers' wishes, wine merchants are selling wine *en primeur* to an ever-increasing extent. This brings in a considerable amount of money for the growers, and is an excellent way of financing the ageing of their wine stocks. Choose your supplier with care, though, as integrity and a firm business base are more than usually important when money is to change hands well in advance of the delivery of goods.

Buying from wine warehouses

This type of retail outlet came into being in the late 1970s and is now tending to become more widespread, especially on the outskirts of large towns. In France, local wine makers deliver their wines on pallets to a warehouse, where they are left on a sale or return basis. It is a way for the wine maker of ensuring new outlets for his wines and enabling them to reach a wider clientele. It is also a way of cutting out the middleman, and thus reducing storage, maintenance and transport charges, and making it possible to sell at a lower price. Abroad, the principle is much the same, though the range of wines on offer is much wider, and the warehouse owner has made an initial selection and purchase of wines, and must make his or her profit on this.

Selling from a warehouse cuts out all the tricks and devices of display and thus appeals simply to the curiosity of the wine enthusiast, obliging him to pick his way through a labyrinth of cases and bottles. Great attention must be paid to the origin, condition and vintage of the wines on offer, and remember that in some countries, such as Britain, a purchase of at least 12 bottles is generally necessary, for legal reasons, from such establishments.

Buying from wine merchants

A good wine merchant is a true specialist. He tastes his wines before purchasing them, and will take the time to advise his customers on their requirements. Knowledge, intuition and psychology are essential elements of his trade. Each choice he makes will be based on, and build a reputation for, his own personal taste. There is a sense in which, being in a position to recommend a wine to a customer to go with a particular menu, he actually enters the customer's home; a relationship of mutual trust is established in this way. The better he knows his clientele, the wiser and more valuable his advice will be.

His list then, should contain examples of the most illustrious *crus*; wines that, although less expensive, are a faithful expression of their *terroir*; and simpler wines. The prices he charges, which will not be the very cheapest, can be justified in terms of the quality of his advice and service, free local delivery, special offers of bin ends, tasting opportunities and so on ... Many wine merchants will also offer wines for buying *en primeur*.

Buying from supermarkets

A few years ago, this was a rather dubious method of purchasing wines, on account of the bad storage and display conditions found in many supermarkets. Today, however, the position is different. There are still a number of small and medium-sized shops where wine is displayed in unfavourable temperature and lighting conditions, but most large supermarkets and hypermarkets do now understand the requirements of quality wines, and have made praiseworthy efforts to accommodate them. Special corners have been set aside, away from the brightest lights, where both temperature and humidity are regulated.

The supermarkets offer a wide range of wines: table wines, *vins de pays*, *appellation contrôlée* wines and even *crus classés*. Occasionally excellent bargains are to be had in supermarkets, in which case it is best to take advantage of them straight away, as the best bottles are usually snapped up by wine enthusiasts within a matter of days.

Occasionally lesser vintages of the finest wines are offered in promotion drives, and this enables people to buy 'great label' wines at an affordable price. However, you do not usually find wines from very small estates, no matter how prestigious, on sale in supermarkets, because they are unable to supply in large enough quantities. Prices are usually attractive, because supermarkets aim to sell large quantities at low profit margins.

Sales between private individuals

A new type of small advertisement has begun to appear in specialized wine magazines, placed there by enthusiasts looking for vintages they do not yet possess, or seeking to improve their cellars in general; or by collectors who find they have stocks of a particular wine surplus to their requirements. This type of transaction can be a good idea, provided the wine has been stored in good conditions by its original owner. Once again, prudence is in order and tasting before purchase is desirable.

Sale by auction

This type of sale is primarily of interest to specialists who know the exact value of a given wine from a given vintage. In fact, auctions are sometimes the only opportunity a collector has to find the old or rare vintage that he lacks. For other buyers, it is a way of being able to enjoy wines that are fully mature and ready to drink, without having to age them in their own cellars. Lastly, these sales are a joy to lovers of excitement, who greatly appreciate the heightened and rarefied atmosphere that prevails at auctions.

They are held in major cities like London, Paris and Chicago, as well as in the provinces, and their dates are advertised in the press and on the news sheets of the auction rooms themselves. Bottles are usually put up for auction by institutions following a takeover, a reorganization of cellars or a bankruptcy, and by private individuals for all manner of reasons. If you wish to buy at auction, it is best to seek information from the auctioneers beforehand regarding the origins, storage conditions and state of the bottles (labels, corks and wine level). A reputable auction house should, in any case, supply this information in the sales catalogue. It is best to enquire about the market price of the wines on offer, if you do not know this already, so as not to be carried away by the auction-room euphoria and end up paying too high a price. You should also remember that, after having made a successful bid, you still have to pay a buyer's premium (usually ten per cent of the hammer price), plus VAT on the complete purchase (including the buyer's premium). These costs can add considerably to the total purchase price.

Wine auction at the Hospices de Beaune. This auction takes place by candlelight on the third Sunday in November. The bidding ends when the candle is snuffed.

LABELLING

STILL, SPARKLING AND FORTIFIED WINES

The label on a bottle of wine or brandy is the identity card of a product with thousands of different potential identities. It must inform the customer, and communicate to him or her all the information needed in order to make an enlightened choice. It is also a document of legal standing, guaranteeing the authenticity of the wine inside the bottle.

At a time when wines are increasingly being sold in supermarkets — the proportion of AOC wines bought by French families in supermarkets rose from 40 per cent in 1975 to 60 per cent in 1985 — the label has become the customer's privileged informant. It must act as a silent salesman, answering all the buyer's questions. It is therefore not surprising that the authorities, concerned that the consumer should be given objective information, have laid down precise and detailed rules on the subject. These have the sole aim of ensuring that the minimum of essential information is provided.

EC regulations

In addition to the above-mentioned rules, there are also EC regulations. These apply to every member country of the Community, and have been drawn up in an effort to bring each individual nation's regulations into harmony and establish a free, unrestricted market in wine within the EC. These inter-Community labelling regulations apply to still and sparkling wines. *Vins doux naturels* and *vins de liqueur* (sweet, fortified wines), and *eaux-de-vie* (brandies and spirits) are still governed by national regulations.

The table on the following pages shows what information is likely to be shown on the labels of French still, sparkling and fortified wines.

Obligatory and optional information

The principle ruling on labelling specified by French national law remains in force for fortified wines and *eaux-de-vie*; this states that any information may be shown, provided it is not expressly forbidden and does not lead to confusion or contain claims that could mislead the buyer. This principle is not in force, however, under the EC regulations for the labelling of still wines. These forbid the presentation of any information that is not provided for in the obligatory and optional categories.

The Community regulations governing sparkling wines are less clear cut. They set out a restricted list of obligatory and optional items of information, which should be stated in clearly defined terms. But they also permit the further free use of all other types of information, with the usual proviso that these should not confuse the buyer. In their concern to cover everything that might relate to the presentation of the product, the EC regulations are complex and often difficult to understand.

Informing the consumer

Obligatory information is concerned with giving the consumer certain essential facts: the category to which the wine belongs, the name of the country or region of origin, the alcohol content, the name of the producer and, finally, the capacity of the bottle.

These items must all be shown on the same label (though its size and shape are unimportant), and this label should be stuck to the bottle. The printing should be clear, legible, indelible, and sufficiently large to contrast with any other writing or illustrations appearing on the label. The optional information may appear on the same label as the obligatory information, or on one or several complementary labels around the neck of the bottle.

The label must attract the customer, while reflecting the true nature of the wine contained in the bottle, and respecting the regulations that govern its description and sale.

OBLIGATORY INFORMATION	STILL WINES			SPARKLING WINE
	TABLE WINES		APPELLATION WINES	
	Table wines with no indication of origin	**Vins de pays**	**Vins délimités de qualité supérieure**	**Appellation contrôlée wines**
Product description	Vin de table de France or Vin de table français Wine from different countries of the European Community	Vin de table de France or Vin de table français + Vins de pays de ... (name of département or zone of production)	Appellation name + Appellation d'origine Vin délimité de qualité supérieure + Special seal issued by the Fédération des VDQS	Appellation name + Appellation contrôlée or Appellation d'origine contrôlée In the case of champa omission of one or othe these details from the lab allowed. When a brand name, a grov name, or a grape variety n is shown prominently c label, the appellation n must be shown twice: firstl itself, and secondly betv 'appellation' and 'contrôlé
Alcoholic strength	OBLIGATORY	OPTIONAL		
	Obligatory for all from 1 May			
Product qualification	Optional information		'Extra brut', 'brut', 'extra dry', 'sec', 'demi-sec', '	
Volume	In litres, centilitres or millilitres followed by the symbol for the unit of measurement used. The			
Name or company name and address of the bottler, wine maker or seller	'Mis en bouteilles par' ('bottled by') or 'mis en bouteilles pour' ('bottled for') or 'embouteilleur' ('bottler') + Name and address of the bottler + Name of the commune where the wine was bottled, if different from the commune where the bottler has his main headquarters. The name, company name or address must be coded if they include all or part of an appellation name.			'Élaborateur' (maker) or 'élabo (made by) unless the maker's cc name shows that the manufac sparkling wines is his main activi + Name or company name of the n + Name of the commune or EC c where the wine was made. Or 'd teur' or 'distribué par' (or any equivalent term) + Name or company name distributor + Name of the commune or EC c where the distributor is based.
Name of the country of production	For French wines to be sold in France, see 'Product description'.	For French wines for export, the name of the country of origin (e.g. 'Produce of France').		

		VINS DOUX NATURELS		VINS DE LIQUEUR
SPARK- VINES	SPARKLING WINES	NON-APPELLATION VINS DOUX NATURELS	APPELLATION WINES	NON-APPELLATION VINS DE LIQUEUR
usseux té	Vin mousseux	Vin doux naturel	Vin doux naturel / Vin de liqueur Name of appellation + Appellation contrôlée	Vin de liqueur
			OBLIGATORY	
ure is followed by the symbol '% vol.'				
ing on the residual sugar content.				
ch can be placed before or after the measurement, denotes that the capacity of the container has been checked.				
The name, company name or address must be coded if they include all or part of an appellation name.	Name and address of the wine grower, maker or seller.			
	OPTIONAL			

OPTIONAL INFORMATION	STILL WINES — TABLE WINES: Table wines with no indication of origin	STILL WINES — TABLE WINES: Vins de pays	STILL WINES — APPELLATION W: Vins délimités de qualité supérieure	
	The optional items of information set out below are subject to prescribed conditions of use, and are the only authorized terms to the exclusion of all others.			
Colour of the wine. Special production details. Type of wine.	**Colour of the wine:** 'blanc', 'rouge', 'rosé', 'vin tuilé', 'pelure d'oignon', 'vin gris', 'gris de gris', 'ambré', 'doré'.		**Special production details:** 'vendange tardive', 'vin primeur', 'vin nouveau', 'blanc de blancs', 'sur lie'.	
Traditional extra information	NONE			
Residual sugar content	'doux', 'moelleux', 'demi-sec', 'sec'			
Name of a geographical entity other than that of the appellation.	NO		YES	
Grape variety	NO	YES		
Vintage date	NO	YES, if the wine is made 100 per cent from the vintage indicate		
Consumer advice	Recommendations concerning the storage and serving of the wine.			
Brand names	These should in no case lead to confusion as to the quali			
Name of country of production	See Product description, page 334.		YES	
Name of wine-growing concern	NO	Domaine, mas, château, abbaye, clos, moulin or any other similar term in so far as the wine comes from a wine-growing estate that actually exists and where the grapes have been grown and the wine made.		
Bottling information	NO	'Mis en bouteilles dans la région de production', 'mis en bouteilles à la propriété', 'mis en bouteilles par les producteurs réunis', 'mis en bouteilles au domaine' or 'au mas', 'mise d'origine', 'mise en bouteilles au château'.		
Bottler's qualification	The bottler may be described as: 'viticulteur', 'négociant', 'importateur' etc.			
Name and address of persons who have played a role in the wine's commercialization	The name and address of any persons who have played a physical or moral part in the commercialization of the wine may be shown, together with their profession or the nature of the part played (for example: 'viticulteur-négociant', 'sélectionné par ...')			
Numbered bottles	NO		YES	
Information regarding superior quality	NO			
Official distinctions awarded to the wine	NO	YES		
Information citing the persons responsible for the wine	YES			
History of the vineyard, the wine and the wine-growing concern	NO	YES		
Other information	NO			

	SPARKLING WINES		VINS DOUX NATURELS	VINS DE LIQUEUR	
	QUALITY SPARKLING WINES	SPARKLING WINES	NON-APPELLATION VINS DOUX NATURELS	APPELLATION WINES	NON-APPELLATION VINS DE LIQUEUR
ellation contrôlée wines					
	Optional information other than that set out below may be used, provided that it is subject to prescribed conditions of use and is not likely to confuse those to whom it is addressed, and provided that it is accurate.		Information other than the obligatory sort may be used, provided that it is accurate and not likely to confuse those to whom it is addressed.		
f wine: ne', 'vin de paille', on de grains nobles', , 'roussette', 'clairet', e', 'vin de café', 'vin	The only authorized terms that may be used to state the manufacturing method are: 'fermentation en bouteille', 'méthode traditionnelle' or 'fermentation en bouteille selon la méthode traditionnelle', 'méthode + name of the appellation (or its derivative adjective)', 'méthode champenoise' (for wines other than champagne until 31 December 1988)				
, 'Premier re)', 'Cru', 'Premier rand Cru', Grand Cru 'Grand Vin', 'Cru is', 'Vin Fin', ', 'Ordinaire', Grand Ordinaire', 'Supérieur(e)', icker', wein', 'Cru Classé', ', 'Premier Cru 'Passetoutgrains', ne Cru Classé' etc., ble', 'Grand Cru 'Petit', 'Haut'.		The terms 'Réserve' and 'Premium' are reserved for appellation contrôlée and quality sparkling wines only.			
	See Product qualification, page 334.				
	NO	NO			NO
	YES				
		NO			
ents of the product,	the appellation name or the geographical origin.				
	NO			YES	NO
	YES	NO			
	YES				

THE CELLAR

In the 1st century AD, the Roman farmer and writer Columella said of the cellar: 'It should face north, and be situated well away from the bathrooms, the oven, the cesspit and the water cisterns.' These requirements are still valid today, in principle if not in detail, for wine is as fragile as a human being and requires a considerable amount of care while it is maturing.

The cellar began as a simple hole dug in rock. This is how the magnificent and irreplaceable cellars of Champagne and Touraine were created. If there is no rock, a cellar can be dug underground, in which case it will already have a number of the qualities required in order to be able to keep wine and mature it well.

Unfortunately, today's urban way of life and the modern building methods resulting from it have meant that the cellar is often no more than the overheated concrete basement of a block of flats, while it is generally left out of new houses altogether. Yet wine, which is a living thing, needs a suitable place and appropriate conditions if it is to improve with keeping. It is therefore quite difficult to create a good cellar in a modern flat or house. It can be done, though, if you really want to, even if the space at your disposal is limited.

The ideal cellar

The best cellars are those that have been dug in rock. However, a modern cellar will also be ideally suited for keeping wine if it has the following features:

- a north-facing position;
- ventilation via a north- or east-facing door, basement window or air bricks;
- high humidity levels (of between 75 to 80 per cent relative humidity);
- constant temperature of between 10°C and 15°C;
- darkness;
- cleanliness and absence of strong smells;
- absence of vibration;
- moist sand or gravel floor;
- walls of stone, limestone or brick.

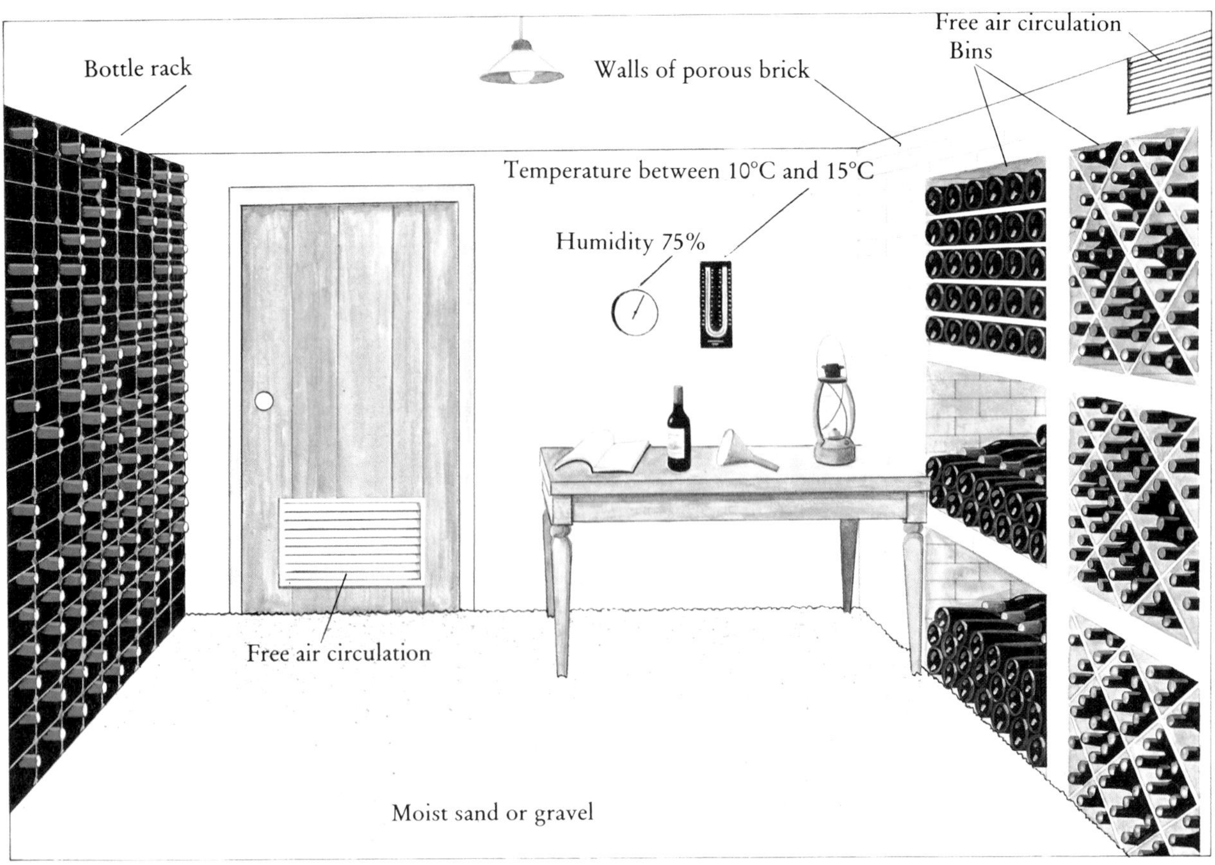

A good cellar should be airy, dark, clean, quiet, cool and with some humidity.

This cellar in Champagne has been dug in the local chalk, a natural material that forms the ideal environment in which to store wine.

How to improve your cellar

The orientation is the only factor over which you generally have no control when setting up a cellar. You can control ventilation, and this is indispensable if you do not wish your wine to taste and smell musty. You can also control humidity, the floor material, the temperature, the insulation, the light levels and protect the cellar from vibrations.

Ventilation

When a cellar has to be kept shut and perhaps even locked, it can still 'breathe' naturally if its basic fabric is an appropriate material. Stone or limestone conglomerates are the best, while porous brick is also suitable. If the walls are concrete or mortared brick, however, you will have to drill holes in them, or position airbricks in them, in order to allow air to circulate between the cellar and the outside walls.

Internal ventilation is also necessary, and this can be achieved by placing a low air-intake to the north and a high air-outlet to the south. Do not place these directly opposite one another, as this might cause a cold draught. If the cellar space is completely enclosed or very large, you may have to resort to artificial ventilation. In the former case, place an air-conditioning unit over the door, with the warm part of the unit facing outwards. In the latter case, install a number of extractor fans at the cellar's extremities.

Humidity

You should pay considerable attention to trying to achieve the correct level of humidity in your cellar. If humidity is excessive, it will encourage the growth of mould which will eventually damage the corks. However if humidity is insufficient, the corks may dry out in the long term, even though the bottles are stored on their sides. In both these cases, you will run the risk of the bottles having their contents spoiled. Try to ensure a level of 75 to 80 per cent relative humidity. In order to check this, you simply need to install a hygrometer.

A cellar in Burgundy. The bottles are arranged in metal racks, and each batch is labelled. The floor (not visible) is covered with gravel, which permits ideal humidity levels to be maintained.

Cellar at the Château de Monbazillac. The stone walls allow free movement of air.

THE MODERN CELLAR

Prefabricated cellars are now available to those who do not at present have the good fortune to own a traditional cellar. Firstly, there are models designed for individual houses. These consist of a cylindrical unit made of fibre-glass, with a capacity of 480 to 1,920 bottles. This module is installed in a hole dug beneath a house, or in the garden. Access is via a trapdoor, and inside is a spiral staircase. These units combine most of the characteristics of an ideal cellar: quiet, appropriate temperature and humidity levels, and ventilation.

Ready-made cellars for use in flats are essentially air-conditioned store cupboards divided into compartments. The temperature of each compartment can be regulated independently, and therefore each type of wine can be kept in the conditions that will enable it to develop perfectly. Unfortunately, these cellar-store cupboards have a limited capacity of between 50 and 360 bottles.

The floor

The nature of the floor is of particular significance for the problems of dryness or excessive humidity mentioned above. If the cellar is too dry, cover the floor with sand or gravel and sprinkle this with water from time to time, especially in summer. You could also install a sand tray or bin and moisten this, or even a large bowl of water. In order to combat excessive humidity cover the floor with a thicker layer of dry gravel or sand, about 4 to 5 cm deep. Any water seeping up from below will be neutralized by this medium. If excessive humidity is still causing problems, you can cover the walls with cork tiles, fixing them so as to leave a space between the cork and the walls to allow the air to circulate.

Temperature

The temperature of a cellar should be between 5°C and 18°C, and seasonal variations should be slight. The best temperatures are between 10°C and 15°C. Heat is more harmful to wines than cold. Any temperature above 20°C speeds up the maturation process and hastens the wine towards its decline. Furthermore, if wine develops too quickly, its organoleptic qualities are less satisfying than when it is allowed to age in cool tranquillity. It should be noted that old wines are particularly fragile and do not keep well at temperatures above 15°C. White wines are more sensitive to warm storage conditions than red ones and they should therefore be kept in the coolest part of the cellar, near the floor, for example. The worst that cold can do to white wine is cause crystallization of its tartrates, and this does not affect the quality of the wine.

A prefabricated cellar for an individual house. The cylindrical unit is installed in a hole dug underneath the house or in the garden.

Insulation

If necessary, you should insulate your cellar against temperature extremes caused either by external weather conditions or by heating systems inside the house. This is normally done by lining the walls with expanded polystyrene or fibreglass tiles. You could also wrap these materials around any hot water or central-heating pipes that pass through the cellar. If the cellar has any sort of air vent, you may need to cover it partly or completely when weather conditions outside are extreme.

Light levels

Wine needs to mature in the dark. Exposure to bright light may encourage the development of certain diseases such as protein *casse* in the wine, or it may cause the wine to oxidize. So do not be careless about the light levels in your cellar. It is best to avoid high-wattage bulbs or neon lighting. A dim bulb, an inspection lamp, or even a simple table lamp will do. If too much daylight is penetrating into the cellar, block it out.

Noise and vibration

The cellar should be a quiet place. Wines should not be subject to vibration, as this fatigues them and causes premature deterioration of their quality. Wine growers, who know these phenomena well, avoid storing their wines in cellars situated near main roads or railways. The effect of minor vibrations will not be too damaging, however, if you cushion the bottles against this by the use of wine racks, rather than putting them directly on the floor or against the walls.

The cellar, a single-purpose room

The cellar should be clean and free from all foreign objects and substances. Banish any product likely to give off an odour, as this may penetrate the cork and get into the wine: cans of fuel oil, pots of paint, chemical products, fruit, vegetables and cheeses, etc. If the walls are not clean and dry, they should be whitewashed (two measures of lime to three of water).

The arrangement of the cellar

When you have created all the ambient conditions necessary for a good cellar, you should give some thought to how best to arrange your wine in it. Storage in cardboard boxes or cases is not recommended. In order to separate the different categories of wine from each other, you should use appropriately sized bins. For smaller quantities, you can use individual wine racks, made of plastic or metal. It is best to avoid wooden racks, as these can deteriorate with age and damp conditions. Plastic does not suffer in this way, but it is sometimes fragile and unattractive. The best choice is iron. For large quantities of wine, you will need huge bins made of breeze-blocks or reinforced concrete. Each unit will hold 24, 36, or 48 bottles, sometimes even more.

Stocking the cellar

Whatever method of storage you choose, the bottles must be placed on their sides, so that the cork is in contact with the wine. However, aperitif wines, brandies and spirits, and liqueurs should be stored vertically, and kept separate from the main wine area. A storage system based on a large number of wine racks means that you can remove each bottle without disturbing the others. In bins, the bottles should be stacked in rows not more than six deep, with the bottle necks visible so that the corks can be checked from time to time. Wines of the same type should be kept in the same bin. Each batch of wine should be clearly marked, and the labels on the bottles will keep longer if they are positioned face downwards. If the cellar is very damp and the wines are to be stored for a long period, mark each bin with a plastic label and indelible ink.

Finally, it is useful to keep a cellar book and note down each purchase, as this will enable your stock to be correctly managed. You should enter the name of the wine, the vintage, the date of purchase, where you bought it from, and the price. It is also worthwhile noting the date on which it was tasted, and jotting down a few comments on its qualities.

WHAT TO PUT IN YOUR CELLAR

Creating a cellar means putting bottles full of promise in a quiet, dark place where they can mature in cool secrecy. In this way, they will more fully reveal themselves and express themselves when the time comes to drink them.

The cellar, though, must also be able to satisfy present requirements, whatever they may be. Here are three suggestions for different approaches to cellar building, depending on whether you are drinking wine informally with your family, with close friends or on special occasions.

THE RUSTIC CELLAR							
WINTER				SUMMER			
WHITE		RED		WHITE		RED	
Jurançon Moelleux	24	Beaujolais Nouveau	36	Vin de Savoie	24	Touraine	24
Muscadet	48	Touraine Primeur	24	Sancerre	24	Beaujolais-Villages	24
Touraine Mousseux	36	Cahors	24	Pouilly-Fumé	24	Collioure	24
		Minervois	24	Sylvaner	24	Côtes du Roussillon	24
		Gigondas	24	Jasnières	6	Côtes du Rhône	24
		Corbières	24	Vin de Corse-Patrimonio	12	Saumur-Champigny	24
		Madiran	12			Saint-Pourçain	12
		Bergerac	12			Bandol	24
						Coteaux Champenois	24
Number of bottles	**108**	**Number of bottles**	**180**	**Number of bottles**	**114**	**Number of bottles**	**204**

THE CONVIVIAL CELLAR				THE CONNOISSEUR'S CELLAR			
WHITE		RED		WHITE		RED	
Châteauneuf-du-Pape	12	Médoc	36	Chassagne-Montrachet	24	Pommard	18
Montlouis	24	Graves	36	Montrachet	6	Pomerol	18
Graves	24	Premiers and Deuxièmes Crus Classés de Bordeaux	18	Vouvray	24	Saint-Émilion	24
Alsace Riesling	36	Châteauneuf-du-Pape	24	Savennières	12	Various Côtes de Nuits wines	36
Corton	12	Côte Rôtie	12	Alsace Gewürztraminer	24	Côte de Nuits Grands Crus	18
Champagne	48	Chinon	24	Vintage Champagne	36	Volnay	24
Loupiac	12	Bourgueil	24	Condrieu	12		
Cérons	12	Corton	12	Sauternes	36		
Monbazillac	12	Various Côte de Beaune wines	36	Bonnezeaux	12		
Vouvray Pétillant	36	Côte de Beaune Grands Crus	18	Vin Jaune (Jura)	12		
Hermitage	12	Hermitage	24				
Chablis	24	Cornas	12				
Number of bottles	**264**	**Number of bottles**	**276**	**Number of bottles**	**204**	**Number of bottles**	**138**

L

La Clape *See* Coteaux du Languedoc.

Ladoix

The commune of Ladoix-Serrigny is situated in the northernmost part of the Côte de Beaune, northwest of Beaune itself and adjacent to Aloxe-Corton.

The *appellation d'origine contrôlée* covers an area of about 165ha, 15ha of which are Premier Cru. The average production is 1,500hl of red wine and 150hl of white. The *appellation* decree of 21 May 1970 set the minimum alcohol level at 10.5° for red wine and 11° for white. The base yield was fixed at 35hl/ha.

This *appellation* has a peculiar characteristic in that the best wines of Ladoix are permitted use of the *appellation* Aloxe-Corton. The vineyards of Vergennes and Rognet, for example, which are adjacent to Aloxe-Corton, officially have the right to use the Grand Cru *appellations* Corton and Corton-Charlemagne. This auspicious geographical position explains the discreet success of these sturdy, straightforward wines with their charming bouquet and their capacity for long keeping.

Lalande-de-Pomerol

The *appellation d'origine contrôlée* Lalande-de-Pomerol was created by decree on 8 December 1936, and applies only to red wines made from grapes harvested on specified plots of land within the communes of Lalande-de-Pomerol and Néac in Libourne. The latter commune was attached to the *appellation* zone by decree, on 2 September 1954.

The *appellation* requirements — grape variety, minimum sugar content of the musts, alcohol level of the finished wines — are the same as for Pomerol. The base yield is 42hl/ha. It has been obligatory for this wine to be submitted to a tasting panel before receiving its AOC certificate since 1974.

In 1985, this *appellation* covered an area of 910ha, and the amount of wine produced was 29,461hl.

The wines of Lalande-de-Pomerol are similar to those of Pomerol, particularly with respect to the way in which they mature, though they are less well known. With age, they acquire a velvety quality and a spicy bouquet reminiscent of the wines of Pomerol.

La Méjanelle

See Coteaux du Languedoc.

Landal

Synonym: *244 Landot*, originating from a cross between Seibel 5455×8216.

Growing tips white, arachnoid.

Young leaves glabrous, bronze-coloured.

Leaves orbicular-reniform, contorted with concave lobes, five-lobed with narrow lateral sinuses, acute at base; petiolar sinus lyrate with pink veins; dentation pointed, tapering and very narrow. The leaves redden in autumn.

Green shoots ribbed, glabrous, reddish.

Bunches medium sized, cylindrical, loose; grapes ovoid, small, blue-black, with little juice; ripening period: first epoch, late.

This hybrid vine grows vigorously and is fertile, but is not very resistant to disease. It gives an attractively coloured wine with a satisfactory alcohol level and a raspberry-like flavour. Although classed as 'authorized' in a number of *départements*, it is not widely grown (350ha only in France).

The long-lived, tannic, 'village' wines of Ladoix-Serrigny on the Côte de Beaune are often sold under the appellation *Côte de Beaune-Villages.*

Languedoc *See* overleaf for the Languedoc-Roussillon regional entry.

La Romanée *See* Romanée.

La Tâche *See* Tâche (La).

Latricières-Chambertin

This great Burgundian *climat*, belonging to the world-famous Grand Cru Chambertin family on the Côte de Nuits, covers about 7ha. The wines of Latricières-Chambertin are subject to the decree of 31 July 1937, which specifies a minimum alcohol content of 10° and a base yield of 35hl/ha; annual average production is about 200hl. The Latricières vineyards are situated on top of the slope of the Côte, surrounded by an ancient wall and bordered by a thick wood. The wines of Latricières do not have the same finesse as those of Clos de Bèze, for example, but they have power and nobility, accompanied by a remarkably refined aroma very close to that of Chambertin.

Lauzet

Synonyms: *Lauzet Blanc*, *Laouset*.

Bunches medium to large, conical, compact; grapes small, spherical, amber-green to pink when ripe, with little juice; ripening period: third epoch.

The Lauzet is a very minor vine grown in the vineyards of Jurançon. It is classed as 'recommended' in Pyrénées-Atlantiques and Hautes-Pyrénées, where it is one of the grapes grown for the AOCs of Jurançon and Béarn. One registered clone has been approved: number 732.

Len de l'El

Synonyms: *Len de l'Elh* (meaning 'far from the eye' in Tarn dialect), *Len de Lel*, *Lenc de l'El*, *Lendelet*, *Cavaillès*, *Cavalié*, *Cavalier* in the Castres region.

Bunches medium sized, conical, narrow, loose; grapes medium sized, ovoid, yellow, very juicy; ripening period: second epoch.

This vine from Tarn is one of the grape varieties specified for the AOC of Gaillac. It makes a very fine wine, and one which can acquire an extremely high alcohol level — as much as 17° — when left to overripen. The Len de l'El ripens two weeks before the other main grape of the Tarn region, the Mauzac. It buds early in the year and is not very productive; it is also susceptible to grey rot (botrytis). One registered clone has been approved, number 733, and the variety

Grape harvest at Lalande-de-Pomerol, an appellation *that produces full, deeply coloured wines with a spicy bouquet.*

has been classed as 'recommended' in Lot, Tarn and Lot-et-Garonne — though in fact it is only grown on 457ha in Tarn.

Léon-Millot

A cross between seedlings of 101-14 Mgt × Goldriesling, also known as 194-2 Kuhlmann.

Bunches small, cylindrical, winged, loose; grapes small, spherical, blue-black and very juicy; ripening period: first epoch.

This is a vigorous hybrid which must be pruned long if it is to produce sufficient fruit. It is resistant to disease, and requires little treatment in rainy years. The wine it produces has a high alcohol level, and is of passable quality, although somewhat flat. It is classed as 'authorized' in the *départements* of Central France, where it occupies 112ha.

Latricières-Chambertin. This climat, *situated at the top of the Côte, yields fine wines, similar to those of Chambertin.*

LANGUEDOC-ROUSSILLON

The vineyards of Languedoc-Roussillon constitute the most extensive wine-growing region in the world, spread over mountain slopes, hillsides,* garrigue *(scrubland), terraces, plains and coastline. The vine, certainly the most widely grown plant here, yields generously, and from it man has been able to create wines to satisfy the tastes of all wine lovers, whether simple or sophisticated.

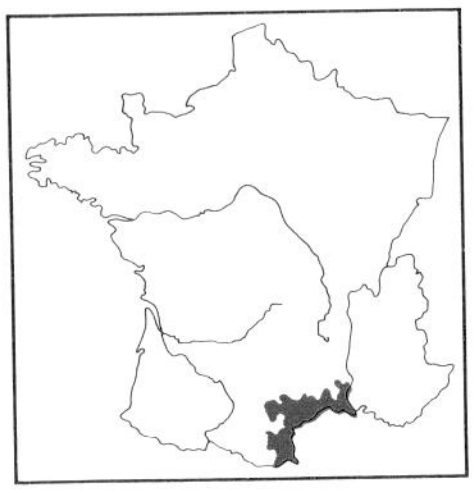

The wine-growing area of Languedoc-Roussillon is enormous, stretching from Nîmes in the east to Carcassonne in the west, with the edge of the Massif Central lying to its north. Most of the southern part of the region spreads on to the shores of the Mediterranean, and it is separated from Spain only by the eastern slopes of the Pyrenees. It takes the form of a vast, crescent-shaped amphitheatre, facing the sea.

Two corridors link the area to the rest of France: the Rhône valley; and the Naurouze shelf that runs between the Montagne Noir, north of Carcassonne, and the Pyrenees, and on which the vineyards of Corbières are to be found. A main road runs right through from east to west, from the Rhône to Narbonne and then on, both in the direction of Carcassonne and Toulouse, and southwards towards the Spanish border.

From the high plateaux and mountainous ridges down to the river and coastal plains, it is possible to distinguish four successive zones, all at different levels. The highest zone consists of ancient uplands such as the Cévennes (north of Lodève and St-Martin-de-Londres) and the Montagne Noir, marking the edge of the Massif Central. The second zone hugs the contours of the first, but lies one step lower down. Next comes the undulating scrublands known as *garrigue*, based on limestone folds that follow one another downwards until they lose themselves in the alluvial plains; finally, there is the coastal zone itself, which consists of offshore bars and salt-water lakes linked to the sea by channels known as *graus*. These four zones of Languedoc have all been colonized by the vine.

Vineyards cover almost 400,000ha, which is more than 50 per cent of the cultivable agricultural area of the region's four *départements*: Aude, Gard, Hérault and Pyrénées-Orientales. These vineyards make up the largest wine-growing area in the world. Districts classed as having a high quality potential on account of their climatic regime and soils can be estimated at more than 100,000ha, representing a notional annual production of AOC wines of some 5 million hl.

Roussillon shoreline east of Bages. This wine district produces sweet fortified wines sold under the Rivesaltes or Muscat de Rivesaltes appellations.

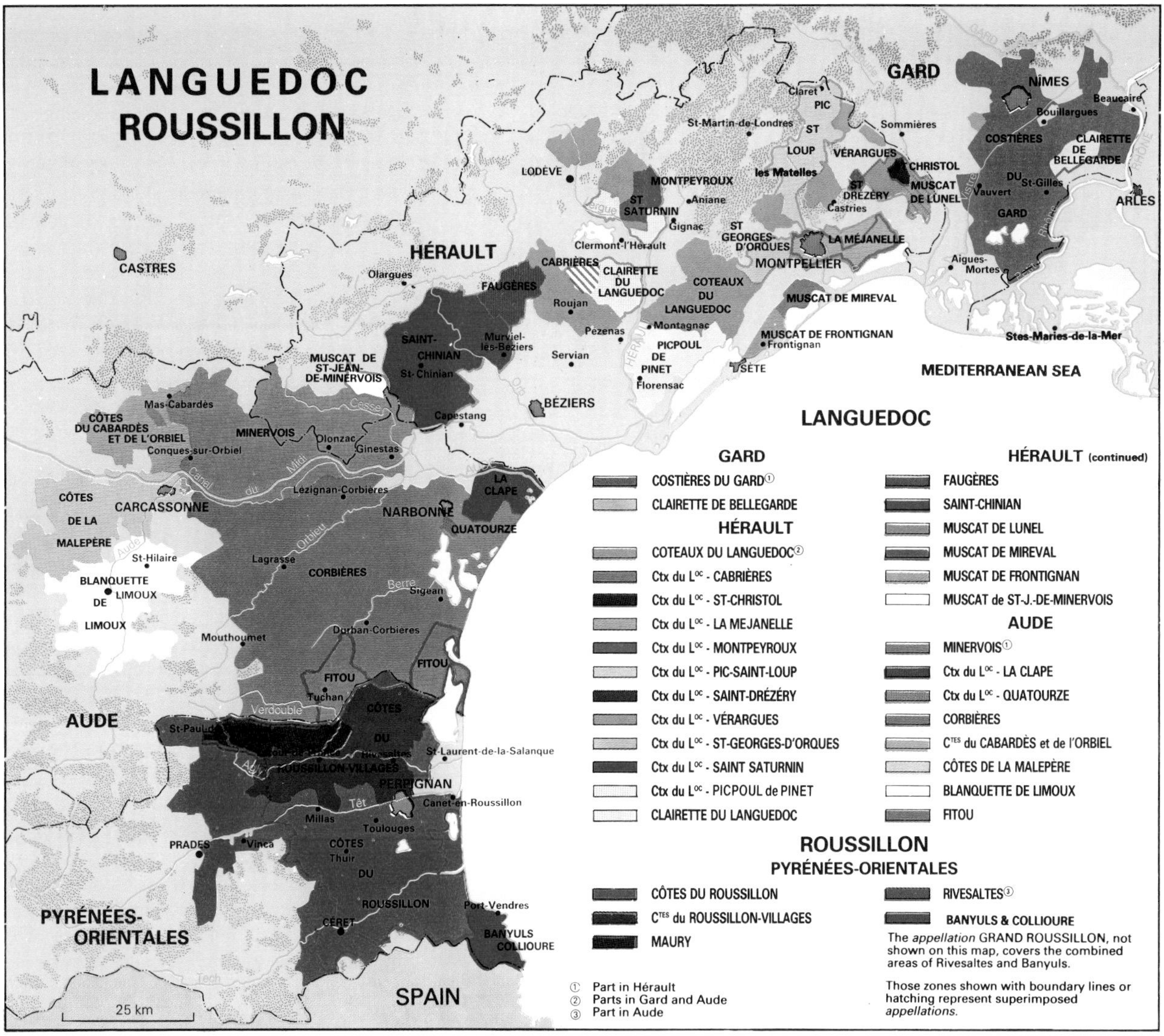

Twenty-five centuries of wine growing

The history of the vine in Languedoc-Roussillon goes back more than 2,500 years, and Greek amphoras, richly ornate Etruscan and Ionian drinking vessels, and Roman wine goblets unearthed at numerous archeological sites bear witness to this. The two most famous sites are at Ensérune, situated between Narbonne and Béziers, and at the port of Agde at the mouth of the river Hérault.

As the historian Roger Dion says, 'This was the first region in France to be touched by the Graeco-Roman wine-growing civilization. It was a point of access and of exchange. Viticulture flourished on account of the climate: here, vines received sufficient warmth and light to be able to furnish more or less consistent amounts of wine every year.'

The vineyards so quickly became prosperous that Rome was forced to take protectionist measures, and in AD 92, the Emperor Domitian issued a decree ordering half of all the provincial vineyards of the Roman empire to be grubbed up. Wine growing remained the speciality of the Narbonne area only, until the Emperor Probus lifted the ban in 280 and permitted all Gauls to grow vines and make wines again, also allowing the vineyards to spread west as far as Aquitaine and north along the Rhône valley and as far as the Moselle.

In the period after the fall of the Western Roman Empire in 412, when the southern French region of Septimania was occupied by the Visigoths, vine growing continued to flourish. The Visigoths were in turn driven out by the Arabs, who occupied the territory until 759. There then came a long period of decline for this wine region, with no revival until the 9th century. At this time, it was the Church that played a large part in replanting and cultivating the vineyards: Lagrasse abbey in Corbières, the abbey at Caunes-Minervois, and the Aniane and

Attic wine cup, 4th century BC, known as 'The Spinner'. It comes from the Ensérune site in Hérault.

Saint-Chinian abbeys in Hérault were jointly responsible for the return of the vine to Languedoc. Vines during this period were grown on the slopes rather than the plains, primarily because that was where they grew best and gave the best wine, but also because the richest lands had to be reserved for those cereal crops that would provide local people with their daily bread. This balance was maintained almost until the end of the 18th century.

During the 14th and 15th centuries, the wine trade in Languedoc continued to develop. Wines began to be exported to Italy, the Eastern Mediterranean, Flanders and England, and these markets became one of the prime motives for wine growing in the region. The wine trade profited from the revival brought about by the creation of the port of Sète during the 17th century, from the construction of the Deux-Mers canal linking the Mediterranean to the Atlantic (now called the Canal du Midi), and from the creation of royal cloth mills in Languedoc. In the 18th century, public works continued in the region, and an edict issued in 1776 by Louis XVI's comptroller general, Anne-Robert-Jacques Turgot, declared the free circulation of wines throughout the entire kingdom of France, making certain inland markets more accessible to the wines of Languedoc, and also creating new ones.

Cellar of the Cistercian abbey of Valmagne in Minervois, founded in 1155. This abbey is the only one in Languedoc still producing wine.

The 18th century also saw progress in the making and marketing of local brandy, and this was accelerated in the 19th century. By the eve of the French Revolution, in 1788, the vineyards covered an area of 170,000ha, and were producing 3 million hl of wine annually, a large part of which was exported. It was bought particularly by the English, the Dutch and the Hanseatic Free Towns, and enjoyed an excellent reputation in foreign courts as well as throughout the entire kingdom of France. The remainder was consumed locally, or made into brandy.

At the beginning of the 19th century, the growing demand for brandy and the modernization of distilling equipment by Édouard Adam, in 1801, brought about the emergence of new vineyards, stretching out over the plain. They were mainly planted with high-yielding vines, such as the Terret Gris and the Aramon.

With the building of the French railway system and 19th-century industrialization, large new markets opened up, and after the phylloxera crisis (1868-78) had passed, the bulk-producing vineyards of Languedoc-Roussillon came into being. By 1900, they covered 465,000ha, and a considerable portion of the wine produced was soon being blended with Algerian wine for table wine brands. Meanwhile, up on the slopes, the traditional vineyards continued to exist. Heirs to the former glory of Languedoc-Roussillon, they now provide the backbone of the present-day regional *appellations*.

A long geological adventure

The *terroirs* of Languedoc-Roussillon are the result of a long geological adventure that has left the region with a richly varied heritage. The highly complex and mountainous terrain of the hinterland descends swiftly to the sea, which borders most of the region, and adjacent to which are found the wine districts of Roussillon, Corbières, La Clape and Frontignan.

There is an exceptionally dense network of rivers in this area. Between the Rhône and the Têt, which flows down from the Lac des Bouillouses in the eastern Pyrenees, there are some 20 water courses. During the Quaternary period, these rivers deposited extensive, thick layers of pebbles in the area, a fact that has directly contributed towards the formation of high-quality wine-growing *terroirs*. Of particular importance in this respect have been the Rhône in the eastern part of Languedoc as far as Montpellier, the Orbiel and the Argent-Double in Miner-

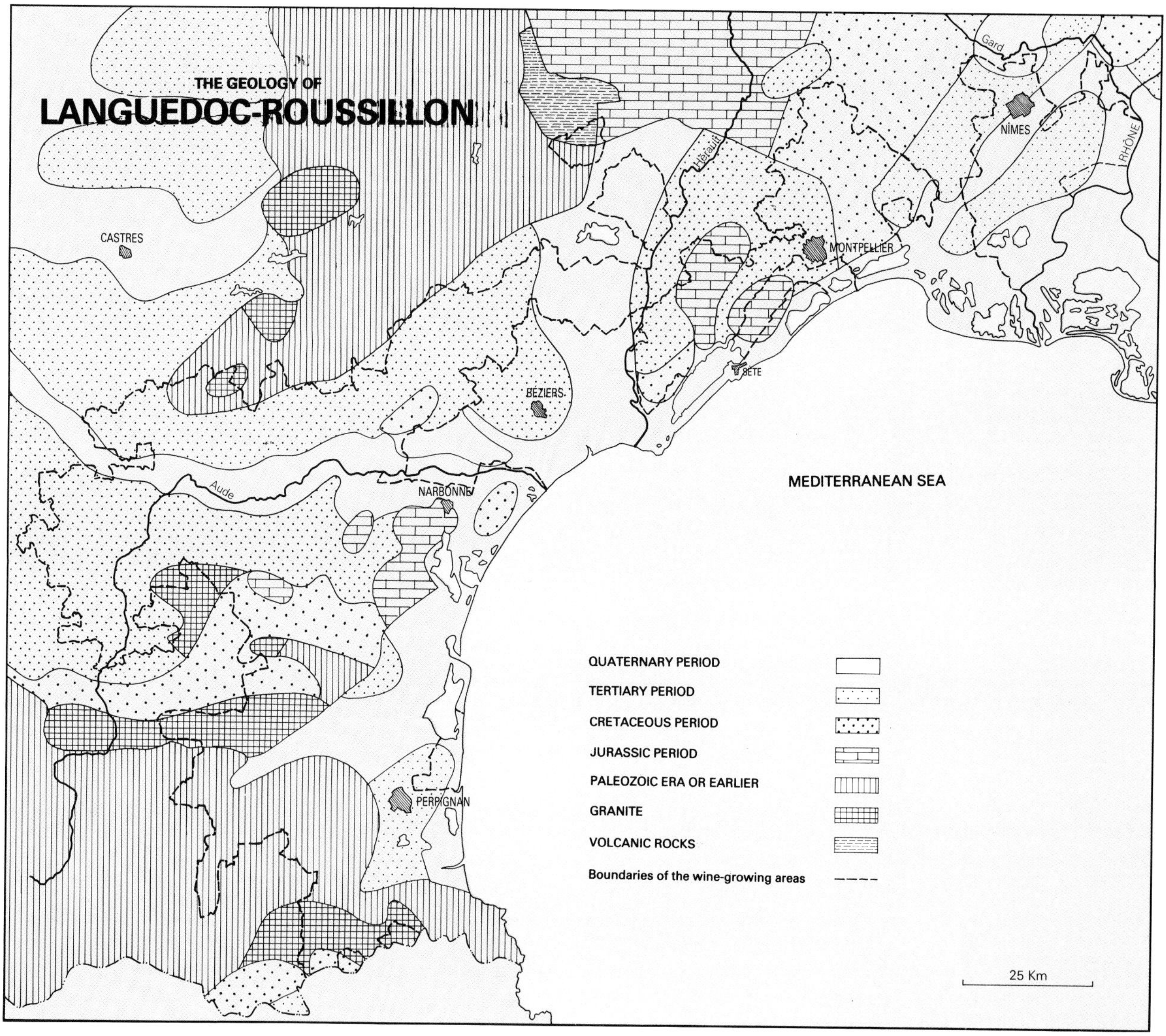

vois, the Orbieu in Corbières and the Agly in Roussillon. The different production zones vary greatly, then, in altitude and proximity to the sea, in whether they are sited on river terraces or on hillsides, and in the precise types of soil and *terroir*.

Soils are sometimes schistous, as in Banyuls, Maury, Corbières, Minervois, Saint-Chinian, Faugères, and Cabrières in the Coteaux du Languedoc; more rarely, granitic sands or volcanic soils are found, as in the Agde region; there are also Triassic and Jurassic (Lias) sandstones, often alternating with variegated marls, which, thanks to their mineral colouring, give the landscapes and villages a distinctive and very beautiful appearance, as in Corbières and Saint-Chinian. You will also find other sandstone formations, such as the Mourrels in Minervois and the Ruffes of the Lodève area; terraces of river-borne pebbles from the Quaternary period, which form excellent wine-growing *terroirs* at Rivesaltes, Val d'Orbieu, Caunes-Minervois, in the La Méjanelle zone of Coteaux du Languedoc and in Costières du Gard; and calcareous, stony terrains created by glacial and frost action on limestone massifs during the Quaternary period. These last types of soil are usually found on slopes or plateaux, and are the most common geological feature of Roussillon, Corbières, the Minervois and most of the *appellations* of Coteaux du Languedoc. Between the coastline and the *garrigue* inland lie alluvial terrains of recent origin, based on gentle coastal river valleys. These are the zones devoted to the production of huge quantities of table wine, and they are also areas of mixed farming. Finally, there is the *garrigue* itself, which occupies an important place in the landscape of Languedoc and in the heart of the French southerner.

Detail of a tapestry from the Château de Flaugergues in the Coteaux du Languedoc area.

Vineyard in the Fitou area. This kind of limestone terrain, known as grèzes, *is common in Corbières; it was created by the action of frost during the Quaternary period.*

*Some 20,000hl of non-*appellation vins doux naturels *(sweet fortified wines) are produced every year in the* départements *of Aude, Gard, Hérault, Pyrénées-Orientales and Vaucluse.*

The climate, a unifying factor

The climate is the factor that unifies the diversity of Languedoc-Roussillon. It is a Mediterranean climate, with mild winters, dry summers, and occasional violent contrasts. There are sometimes harsh cold spells in spring and torrential rains in autumn that damage the grape harvest.

The fact that Languedoc-Roussillon is situated in the far south of France, between latitudes 43° 7′ and 42° 5′, makes it the hottest region in the country. The average annual temperature is 14°C. In July and August, temperatures sometimes exceed 30°C. However, considerable local variations are observed, depending on proximity to the sea, which brings freshness to the dog days of summer; or on local topography.

Rainfall is infrequent, irregular and unevenly distributed. In summer, the period between 15 May and 15 August, there is always prolonged drought. The bulk of the rain comes in two short periods, one in autumn and the other at the beginning of spring. Consequently, seemingly high annual totals, 766mm in Montpellier for example, are really the result of violent rains concentrated over a short period of time. These tend to break down the soils rather than encourage the growth of vegetation. Sometimes it rains on less than 50 days a year. Throughout the whole of the wine-growing territory of Hérault, rain falls on fewer than 80 days. Barcarès, the driest village in France, has a bare 350mm of rain per year. However, the amount of rainfall increases progressively the farther one travels inland (400mm on the coast, 1,200mm in the Cévennes).

The third important factor in this region's climate is that of wind. When winds blow from inland (the *mistral*, the *cers* and the *tramontane*) they make the climate even drier. These dry winds dominate in Roussillon, Corbières and Minervois, particularly in spring, when they can cause devastating damage to young vine shoots. The winds from the sea, on the other hand, moderate the adverse effects of the heat and bring a beneficial humidity to the vines.

In the light of these climatic facts, bioclimatologists have been able to distinguish 11 Mediterranean subclimates within the wine-growing area of the Aude alone. This diversity of mesoclimates and microclimates, and the great variety of soils, are two important features of the Languedoc-Roussillon region. They explain both its rich agricultural potential and the reason why wine growing is its prime vocation. Unlike any other region of France, vines grow well everywhere in Languedoc-Roussillon, and so it is not surprising that more than 40 per cent of the country's wine is produced here. The region has almost 400,000ha of vineyards and produces 25 to 30 million hl of wine a year. Almost 3 million hl of this total is made up by AOC wines. These AOC wines consist of 600,000hl of *vins doux naturels* produced mainly in Roussillon and Corbières, the remainder being Muscat wines from Hérault; 80,000hl of sparkling wines from Blanquette de Limoux in Aude; 1,700,000hl of AOC red wines; and 60,000hl of AOC white wines.

The grape varieties

Of the table wines not qualifying for AOC or VDQS status, 95 per cent are red or rosé. Among these, *vins de pays* and varietal wines are assuming greater and greater importance. The districts that grow grapes for table wines have been changing and developing for almost 20 years now; plantings of the Aramon variety have declined significantly and hybrids have practically disappeared, giving way to the better quality, traditional varieties of Languedoc-Roussillon: Carignan, Cinsaut, Alicante Bouschet, Grenache, Ugni Blanc, Carignan Blanc and Terret Gris. Varieties new to the region, such as the Cabernet Franc, Cabernet Sauvignon, Merlot, Syrah, Mourvèdre, Sauvignon Blanc and Chardonnay, are also being planted.

In the AOC vineyards, plantings are strictly regulated, with the Carignan, Grenache, Cinsaut, Syrah and Mourvèdre varieties being used in proportions clearly specified for each red-wine *appellation*.

Among the white grapes to be found in the *appellation* areas are the Macabeu, Grenache Blanc, Carignan Blanc, Clairette, Bourboulenc, Piquepoul Blanc, Muscat à Petits Grains Blancs and Muscat d'Alexandrie; finally, in Blanquette

VINS DOUX NATURELS

The vins doux naturels *(sweet fortified wines) of Languedoc-Roussillon are produced in accordance with precise rules which codify very old local traditions. It was in the 13th century that Armand (or Arnaud) de Villeneuve discovered that it was possible to retain the sweetness in a wine to some extent by adding alcohol to the must during fermentation. This inhibits the action of the yeast, thus stopping the fermentation process so that the must retains some of the sugar from the grapes. The quantity of alcohol added, and the point at which it is added during fermentation, determine the final alcohol level and sugar content. This operation, known as* mutage, *is carried out on red and white wines whose initial vinification has been traditional. In this way, it is possible to obtain a very wide range of wines that vary in colour, aroma and organoleptic characteristics, as well as in richness of tannins and extracts.*

Another, less common, practice is to carry out mutage *not on wines, but on the* marc, *following the draining off of the free-run wine after vinification* (mutage sur grains). *This technique is used in Banyuls, Maury, and to some extent in Rivesaltes. The wines it produces are rich in aromas and tannins, and are particularly suitable for ageing.*

Sweet fortified wines are aged for a length of time that varies according to the appellation: *one year for Banyuls and Rivesaltes, two years for Maury and 30 months for Banyuls Grand Cru. The maturation process takes place in part-empty vats, wooden casks or, in the case of the best wines, in* bonbonnes *(demijohns) known as* 'touries', *which are kept outside the cellars, exposed to the sun and to the elements. During this time, oxidation-reduction plays a large part in forming the bouquet and developing the colour of these wines, which tends towards tile red or amber. Colour is particularly important in the case of the Rancios, a special* appellation *of sweet fortified wines from Banyuls, Grand-Roussillon, Maury and Rasteau, which have to be matured in wood.*

Muscats, on the other hand, have a delicate aroma, which comes from the grape variety itself, and this aroma is particularly sensitive to oxidation. Consequently, they are protected from air at every stage of vinification, and are sold for drinking young as they do not benefit from ageing. Muscat grapes give vins doux naturels *a powerful, characteristic aroma of lime blossom, with hints of rose, honey, pollen and beeswax, these last four elements becoming more pronounced as the wine matures. The must has to contain at least 252g of sugar per litre at harvest. The quantity of added alcohol (at 96°GL) should be between 5 per cent and 10 per cent of the volume of the must. The finished wine should have a total alcohol content (actual alcohol plus potential alcohol in the form of unfermented sugar) of 21.5°, with 15° actual alcohol.*

Sweet fortified appellation d'origine contrôlée *wines come from quality grape varieties only: Grenache, Macabeu, Tourbat, Muscat à Petits Grains Blancs and Muscat d'Alexandrie, with a permitted 10 per cent of Carignan.*

The South of France as a whole produces 600,000hl of these AOC wines annually. They are, however, the particular speciality of Roussillon, on account of its southerly geographical position, meaning that the vines always benefit from a remarkably dry, hot, sunny environment. The AOC vins doux naturels *of Roussillon are Banyuls Grand Cru, Grand Roussillon, Maury, Muscat de Rivesaltes and Rivesaltes. Languedoc's AOC* vins doux naturels *are Muscat de Frontignan, Muscat de Lunel, Muscat de Mireval and Muscat de Saint-Jean-de-Minervois; and in Vaucluse are found the AOC* vins doux naturels *of Muscat de Beaumes-de-Venise and Rasteau. Muscat wines account for 25 per cent of the annual production of* vins doux naturels *(150,000hl).*

A vineyard in Banyuls. The schist hillsides, which stretch down as far as the Golfe du Lion, are characterized by these low-walled terraces. They are known as* 'péons de galls' *('cock's feet').

A STROLL IN LANGUEDOC-ROUSSILLON

One day, without knowing what it was, I tasted an irresistible wine. It made me think of boats on a wild sea and of the landscape of the Cévennes, once so overcrowded, now completely deserted; the schist and its wine told their story, bringing forth from arid terraces visions of battles and men. Then I cheated, and discovered that the phantom bottle was in fact a 1969 Banyuls 'Vieille Vigne'. This revelation further intensified an emotional moment by transporting me, in my mind's eye, to the vineyards, with their walls seemingly piled one on top of the other, leading up to a dry stone house at the top, like a pyramid! . . .

I saw the whole of humanity there — Graeco-Roman civilization, international markets, the moon and its astronauts, the Grenache grape variety as well as the Clinton grape variety . . .

Not far away is Fitou, the first red-wine AOC of Languedoc-Roussillon. The wine produced there is alluring and robust. It calls for good honest cooking to go with it. Half helpings and a paucity of aromas would be disastrous! This Cathar cuisine implies vitality.

The wines of Corbières are more complex in their disparity. There are the authentic Corbières . . . and the others. But even if the bees nuzzle their way into the Grenache or the Cinsaut in springtime, and end by producing Cabernet, this serves only to give us greater pleasure. Those wonderful alchemists, the master wine-growers, know in the same way how to mix and marshal the grape varieties to perfection.

Next, let us take a look at Saint-Chinian, with its smaller, though elder, sister-appellation Faugères. Man has played just as big a part here as the terroir, having dared to subject the grapes to carbonic maceration, and having proved that the more 'minor' the grape variety, the greater the need to bring out its aromatic potential.

Then there is La Clape, a triumph of iodine and know-how, the first AOC white wine in Languedoc-Roussillon and a brilliant success. Pale yellow in colour, it is made by a slow process of vinification that brings out all the subtle aromas of the grape variety used. It was once straw-coloured and oxidized; now it is delicate and fresh as a result of the serious thought and hard work that has gone into it. Seriousness and hard work could easily be the motto of Coteaux du Languedoc, a region that has always striven to be at the forefront in terms of quality. Do you know Langlade, a village west of Nîmes? Now in Coteaux du Languedoc, it was once part of Costières du Gard. But what does this matter? It produces good wine that is easy to drink, delicate, fine and feminine in character. Enjoy it slightly chilled through a meal and it will delight!

Closer to home as far as I am concerned, in the Gard where I was born, lies Costières du Gard. This area once produced vin de café, a minor red wine nearer to rosé that took no pride at all in its origin. It has now, though, become an AOC wine, the happy event taking place on 4 July 1986. The efforts that went into this! In the past Nîmes has been famous for Villaret biscuits, Cuisinier Durant's brandade (salt cod pounded with oil and cream), and for its historic past. Tomorrow, its authentic wines will surprise and delight all those who practise the art of good drinking.

However, I must not let this make me forget to pay homage to those wines of the Côte du Rhône situated in Gard, from the most famous to the most obscure. As an honorary companion of its young and dynamic confrérie, I could not fail to keep my oath to defend and promote these racy wines with their strong bouquet and their flavour that, in some indefinable way, makes you want to come back for more. The wines of Tavel and its neighbour Lirac, celebrated locally and nationally, stand apart from the rest in their originality. Tavel lays claim to being France's finest rosé, while Lirac surprises by being so different from its neighbour.

In the midst of this multitude of changing terroirs, there is room for an authentic gastronomy. Through their delicacy and complexity, the wines of this region harmonize closely with local cuisine. Discord is unthinkable; there is no point playing 'sorcerer's apprentice' here, as few dishes will allow this. Thanks to new vinification techniques and new grape varieties, however, some of the Vins de Pays are able to bring a touch of imagination to the proceedings. Take Merlot, for example, with its aromas of passion fruit and mango . . .

Languedoc-Roussillon is, more than anything else, a wine-growing region of France. Compare it with no other! It is searching for an actual, not an apparent identity. Soon, the locals will take charge of their region, and the less they project their problems on to politicians, and the more they take upon themselves, the better their products, and their savings accounts, will be. Politics cannot protect bad wine. Many of my wine-growing friends have realized this, and have been wise enough to react with discipline and hard work. Thanks to the actions and examples of such pioneers, Languedoc-Roussillon will find and keep its own authenticity.

Travellers from afar, such as the Americans and Japanese, will discover our culture, our way of doing business and our vineyards, and only then will we become the 'French Florida'. Then people will appreciate more than ever before our accent steeped in the honey of Muscat grapes, and our pétanque balls, which, viewed from the sky, seem like little Muscat d'Alexandrie grapes.

A page of history is being written in Languedoc . . .

Patrick Pagès

Vineyards on schistous soils in the Saint-Chinian wine district. This part of the Saint-Chinian AOC area is characterized by distinctively soft-edged ridges covered with garrigue *(scrub) and vines.*

de Limoux, the Mauzac, Chenin Blanc and Chardonnay are also found.

Today, the Languedoc-Roussillon wine region is characterized by a shift towards the production of high-quality wines, and away from table-wine production. This shift has been brought about by the energy of local growers and the economic and social importance of cooperatives. The region has a very high concentration of cooperatives: 550 of them, making wine from the grapes of almost 60,000 growers. This represents 60 per cent of the total regional production, and 90 per cent of the production of all harvest declarers. There are about 6,000 individual growers in the region.

The character of the wines

The shift towards quality wine production in this region is in fact a real revolution. Until 1962, the wines of Languedoc-Roussillon were no more than a shadow of their former selves; puny little wines only gaining a modest palatability after being blended with Algerian wines.

Then the INAO and the regional and local bodies began to rethink the whole concept and image of wine in Languedoc-Roussillon. They had to take into account the potential of the grape varieties, while respecting the nature of *terroirs*. Within a few years, some of the Languedoc-Roussillon *appellations* became real research centres, with small-scale wine-making experiments being carried out site by site. Today, if one wishes to describe the character of the different wines of this region, generalizations have to be forgotten and each individual *terroir* must be scrutinized. Nor should the vinification methods and wine-making styles of individual growers be overlooked.

One way that the different styles of wines can be distinguished one from another in Languedoc is according to the proportion of Carignan they contain. This grape is most at home in Fitou, where it expresses itself fully in wines that have a powerful bouquet, and are harsh and tannic to taste. It is also found in Minervois, where it can lend violet flavours to blends. The best way, though, to understand the Minervois *appellation* is by analysing its *terroirs* — the Mouvèdre grape predominates in the east, Syrah in the centre, Carignan in the west and Carignan-Syrah in the limestone upland areas; and its wine-making methods: carbonic maceration for fruity, Beaujolais-type wines, and traditional maceration and vinification for wines for ageing. This same Carignan grape is present in all Corbières wines, but is nowadays rounded with Grenache, Cinsaut and Syrah.

Other *appellations* stand out, each in their own way: Costières du Gard is quite close stylistically as well as geographically to Côtes du Rhône, and is dominated by Syrah and Grenache. It is a full-bodied, pleasantly spicy wine, distinguishable from a Faugères, which is more robust; from a Saint-Chinian, which is more delicate; and from a La Clape from the Coteaux du Languedoc, which is more solidly structured.

In Roussillon, the wines of Collioure are easily recognizable: they are heady, rich and deep. A Côtes du Roussillon will reveal itself by its firmness and fruitiness and its spicy bouquet.

Among white wines, Blanquette de Limoux, the ancestor of all French *bruts*, charms with its creamy bubbles, as do the still Clairettes of Languedoc and Bellegarde, both dry and sweet, each with a rich, subtle bouquet.

Languedoc-Roussillon has nine different confréries *(wine fraternities). That of Banyuls and Collioure, 'Als templeres de la Serra', draws its origins from a guild dating back to 1350, which had the task of choosing wines for the kings of Aragon.*

Lirac is a wine-growing area in Gard, on the right bank of the Rhône. The soils are stony and siliceous.

L'Étoile and l'Étoile Mousseux

This, the third communal *appellation* of the Jura wine-growing area, was ratified by decree on 31 July 1937. It embraces the production of the villages of l'Étoile, Plainoiseau and Saint-Didier.

Some 64ha of vineyards produce white and sparkling wines, as well as *vin jaune* and *vin de paille*, all renowned for their typicality and authenticity.

The name *Étoile* (star) is said to derive from the star-shaped fossils found in the marly subsoil of this *terroir*. The vineyards are divided among a small number of owners, and there is also a cooperative active in the district.

Lignage

Synonyms: *Lignage Noir* in Loir-et-Cher, *Maće Doux* or *Massé Doux* in Indre-et-Loire, *Sucrin*.

Bunches medium sized, conical, compact; grapes medium sized, ovoid, black; ripening period: first epoch.

A grape variety formerly grown in the vineyards of Blois, alongside the Pinot Noir. It is of average vigour and not very productive, producing a wine with little colour. It has not been classified.

Liliorila

This is a Baroque × Chardonnay cross obtained by INRA at Bordeaux.

Its white grapes ripen in the second epoch. It is a fertile variety, producing a wine that is aromatic, high in alcohol and low in acidity. It can be pruned long, and stake-trained.

It is classed as 'authorized' throughout France and has one approved clone: number 374.

Limberger

Bunches large, cylindrical, winged, compact; grapes quite large, spherical, blue-black, juicy; ripening period: second epoch, normally a week before the Gamay.

This Central European vine was introduced to France by Count Odart, and grown in the Auvergne under the erroneous name of Portugais, or Portugais Bleu, at the time of the phylloxera crisis. It proved very productive on the fertile plain of Limagne, giving up to 200hl/ha of a wine that was deeply coloured, with a pronounced bouquet and low in acidity. It is unclassified and is now disappearing from the vineyards.

Limoux

The still, sweet wines of this AOC were ratified by decree on 13 April 1981. They are the product of grapes harvested in the area of the Blanquette de Limoux AOC (*see* page 71). Only 60 to 70hl of this wine are made each year.

Lirac

No doubt vines have always existed here, as in other places, but it was not until the 17th century that they were systematically cultivated and covered the hillsides, contributing greatly to the success of Côtes du Rhône wines from Gard. Commercial documents of the time place Lirac and Saint-Laurent-des-Arbres on a level with Tavel and Chusclan. The *appellation d'origine contrôlée* was ratified by decree on 14 October 1947; it covers four communes.

Today, the vineyards cover 500ha. The average annual production is 20,000hl, 5,000hl of which are made by the Saint-Laurent-des-Arbres cooperative.

In the main, the soils are the same as those at Tavel. In addition, however, there are well-drained clay slopes with a dense covering of gravel.

Lirac's originality lies in its being the only local *appellation* to produce each of the three main types of wine.

The white wines of Lirac have an attractive perfume, and are typical of the southern Rhône. The rosé wines are very similar to those of Tavel, but are less dry, broader and easier in style. The red wines are powerful and well balanced.

Listan

Bunches large, many branched, conical, loose; grapes spherical, medium sized, golden yellow, juicy; ripening period: second epoch.

This is the French synonym of the Spanish Palomino grape variety, used to make sherry at Jerez in Andalusia. In order to produce good-quality wine, the Listan must be planted in a dry, very sunny spot; it will then give musts rich in sugar, with over 15° of potential alcohol. When the wine is first made, it is neutral and has little character, but it improves greatly with maturation in cask and under yeast, as practised in Jerez. One registered clone has been approved: number 367. Listan is classified as 'recommended' in all the *départements* of the South West and South of France; 900ha of it are grown, with 360ha in Gers, 275ha in Aude and 135ha in Hérault.

It is classed as 'recommended' in the Midi, for all *départements* south of Haute-Garonne and Drôme. It is grown at present on slightly more than 200ha, mainly in Aude and Pyrénées-Orientales.

Listrac

The *appellation d'origine contrôlée* of Listrac, in Médoc, was created by decree on 8 June 1957. It is reserved for red wines made from grapes picked on specified sites in the commune of Listrac.

The number of vines per hectare has to be between 6,500 and 10,000, and there are rules governing pruning. Since 1962, hybrid vines have been forbidden on estates wishing to use the *appellation*.

To be entitled to the Listrac *appellation*, the wines must be made from the same grape varieties as specified for AOC Médoc. The minimum sugar content of the must should be at least 162g per litre, and the wines must have an alcoholic strength of between 10° and 13°. Base yield is set at 45hl/ha.

Since the creation of the *appellation*, all wines have had to pass a tasting panel before they can be marketed, in order to check quality.

In 1985, the *appellation* covered 555ha and total production was 23,669hl, of which 5,855hl was made in the cellars of the Listrac cooperative.

The best of the châteaux of Listrac fall into the Cru Bourgeois category (*see* page 100 ff.). There are no Crus Classés in Listrac. Wines of this *appellation* require seven to ten years in bottle before they reach full maturity.

Lledoner Pelut

Synonyms: *Grenache Velu* or *Grenache Poilu* in the Midi.

The bunches of this red-wine vine are usually a little longer and less compact than those of the Grenache. The Lledoner Pelut produces more regularly than the Grenache does, because it is a healthier vine, and it is also said to be less susceptible to grey rot (botrytis). Its wine does not have much colour and is comparable in quality to that of the Grenache.

Loire

See the regional entry on the next page.

Loupiac

The *appellation d'origine contrôlée* of Loupiac, which was created by decree on 11 November 1936, is reserved for white wines made from grapes harvested on specified sites in the commune of Loupiac, which is situated on the right bank of the Garonne, south of Bordeaux and adjoining the commune of Sainte-Croix-du-Mont.

The regulations governing production are exactly the same as those for AOC Sauternes.

In 1985, the *appellation* covered 215ha and produced 6,230hl of mainly sweet white wine. The base yield is 30hl/ha.

Although, geographically speaking, Loupiac is part of the Premières Côtes de Bordeaux, it forms a distinct area with a character of its own. Its wines are quite close to those of the Sainte-Croix-du-Mont *appellation*, in style as in geographical proximity. The sweet white wines of good, sunny vintages keep well. The remainder of the wine grown here is vinified as dry white wine, and sold under the generic AOC Bordeaux.

Lussac-Saint-Émilion

The *appellation d'origine contrôlée* Lussac-Saint-Émilion, lying northeast of Libourne, was created by decree on 14 November 1936, and is reserved for red wines made from grapes picked on specified sites within the commune of Lussac.

The grape varieties specified are the same as for the Saint-Émilion *appellation*. Hybrid vines have been forbidden since 1961. Minimum sugar content of the must should be 162g per litre, and the wines have to have an alcoholic strength of between 10° and 13°. The base yield is 45hl/ha. The wines of this *appellation* can only be marketed when they have received a certificate of quality, issued by a tasting panel.

In 1985, the area covered by the *appellation* was 1,113ha and production was 64, 212hl, of which 24,683hl was made by the Puisseguin cooperative.

The wines of Lussac-Saint-Émilion have a similar taste and lifespan to those of the other 'satellite' *appellations* of Saint-Émilion.

THE LOIRE VALLEY

The largest vineyard area of France lies scattered about the course the river Loire has carved for itself through the centuries, from Languedoc to Brittany. There are dozens of wines, of the most diverse aspects, adorning the length of the river, offering a great efflorescence of bouquets and styles, and united only in charm and allure.

Looking at the map of France, the course of the Loire comes as something of a surprise. After Gien, one would expect it to become a tributary of the Seine, but this did not happen. It refused to cross the limestone plain of Beauce, and thus the lovely region of the Pays de Loire was born.

The Loire, France's 'royal river', crosses 10 of the 33 provinces that once made up the country. This area corresponds to about one fifth of French territory. The former provinces that have profited from the Loire and its wines are Brittany, Anjou, Touraine, Orléanais, Nivernais, Berry, Bourbonnais, Burgundy, Lyonnais and even Languedoc, since it is here that the river has its source. The fact that the Loire is a link between the Mediterranean and the Atlantic has encouraged trade the whole length of its course; and it was this that laid the foundations of viticulture throughout this vast region.

The vineyards of the Loire

The river flows for about 1,000km across extremely varied geological terrains, and these have a major influence on the character of the wines.

The Loire begins at Mont Gerbier-de-Jonc, at a point 1,375m up on the mountainside. First it flows through the granite mass of Central France, then across the Tertiary period plains to the southern edge of the Parisian basin. Finally, it reaches the crystalline rock terrains of the Breton peninsula. In topographic terms, it initially pursues a winding course among ancient volcanoes. It then goes through the gorges of Velay, and around le Puy, before more granite-walled gorges and the Chamalières defiles. After this it flows past the hills of the Lyonnais on its right bank and those of Forez on its left bank. Forez is the first wine-growing region to feel its influence, and the river slows through the plain of Forez.

Next, to the west, come the vineyards of Côtes d'Auvergne, situated along the river Allier. This is the Loire's second wine-growing area. The Loire at this point flows through gorges once again, until it finally leaves the Massif Central and begins a calmer journey across Tertiary period plains. It approaches the region of Roanne and its third wine-growing enclave, Côte Roannaise. Before reaching Moulins, it passes the wine district of Saint-Pourçain. A little farther to the west, in the Cher valley, lies Châteaumeillant and, to its north, the vineyards of Reuilly and Quincy, with those of Valençay to the west again. The altitude of the Loire at

Montlouis, on the right bank of the Loire, lies in the heart of the appellation of that name.

In these 13th-century cellars at Montreuil-Bellay, the wines are first left to clarify and deposit their sediment before being matured in bottle.

Roanne is 255m, and between Bourg-le-Comte and Lamenay-sur-Loire it forms a border between the *départements* of Allier and Sâone-et-Loire.

By the time the river reaches the *département* of Nièvre, it has come down to an altitude of 200m and is flowing slightly northwest. When it reaches the Menetou-Salon area and the foot of the hill at Sancerre, with the Pouilly wine district on the opposite bank, its altitude is only 140m. As it approaches Gien and the vineyards of Côtes de Gien, it turns westwards and from then on takes a definite westerly direction. Next, it skirts the forest of Orléans. From the town of Orléans until it reaches the sea, the river is dyked to a width of 150m to 300m. By the time it reaches Beaugency, two thirds of the way between its source and the sea, it has come down to an altitude of 80m. On either side are hills. After Blois, it makes its way through tufa — a calcareous rock — to beyond Saumur.

When it reaches the vineyards of Touraine, its altitude is a mere 50m. In Touraine, the Loire is joined by the Cher, the Indre and the Vienne, all of which are flanked by vine-covered slopes. It then passes the Saumur and Anjou vineyards.

At Ancenis, the river enters the Atlantic corridor, favouring wine growing in the area around Nantes. From Nantes onwards, it widens progressively.

So the Loire might be summarized by enumerating the names of a string of towns, each one associated with renowned wine districts: le Puy, Clermont-Ferrand, Roanne, Moulins, Saint-Pourçain (on the left bank of the Allier), Nevers, Bourges, Gien, Orléans, Blois, Tours, Saumur, Angers and Nantes.

The wine districts

The wine-growing districts of the Loire valley offer a wide range of wines. Dry, medium dry and sweet white wines, and even the sweetest dessert wines after sunny summers and autumns; dry or off-dry rosés; light red wines such as those of Touraine and Sancerre, or deeper, richer red wines such as those of Bourgueil or Chinon; and numerous sparkling and slightly sparkling wines.

The closer to the river's source, the lighter and drier the white wines become. This is the case with Sancerre, Pouilly-Fumé, Reuilly, Quincy and Saint-Pourçain. A similar principle operates towards the river mouth, in the Muscadet area.

In the central Loire, on the other hand, the tannic wines of Bourgueil, Chinon, Saumur-Champigny and Saint-Nicolas-de-Bourgueil are to be found, together with the great sweet wines of Vouvray and Coteaux du Layon.

Climatic conditions mark out four zones of production.

Loire-Atlantique

This first zone has a maritime climate. The local *appellations* are Muscadet des Coteaux de la Loire and Muscadet de Sèvre-et-Maine. A third *appellation*, Muscadet with no further qualification, is also produced in small quantities in the areas of the *départements* of Maine-et-Loire and Vendée that border on Loire-Atlantique.

This zone produces the VDQS wines Gros Plant du Pays Nantais and Coteaux d'Ancenis, and the production areas for these also extend into Vendée and Maine-et-Loire. Since 1984, Vendée has been producing a VDQS Fiefs Vendéens.

The wines of the Loire are renowned for their sometimes impressive longevity in bottle.

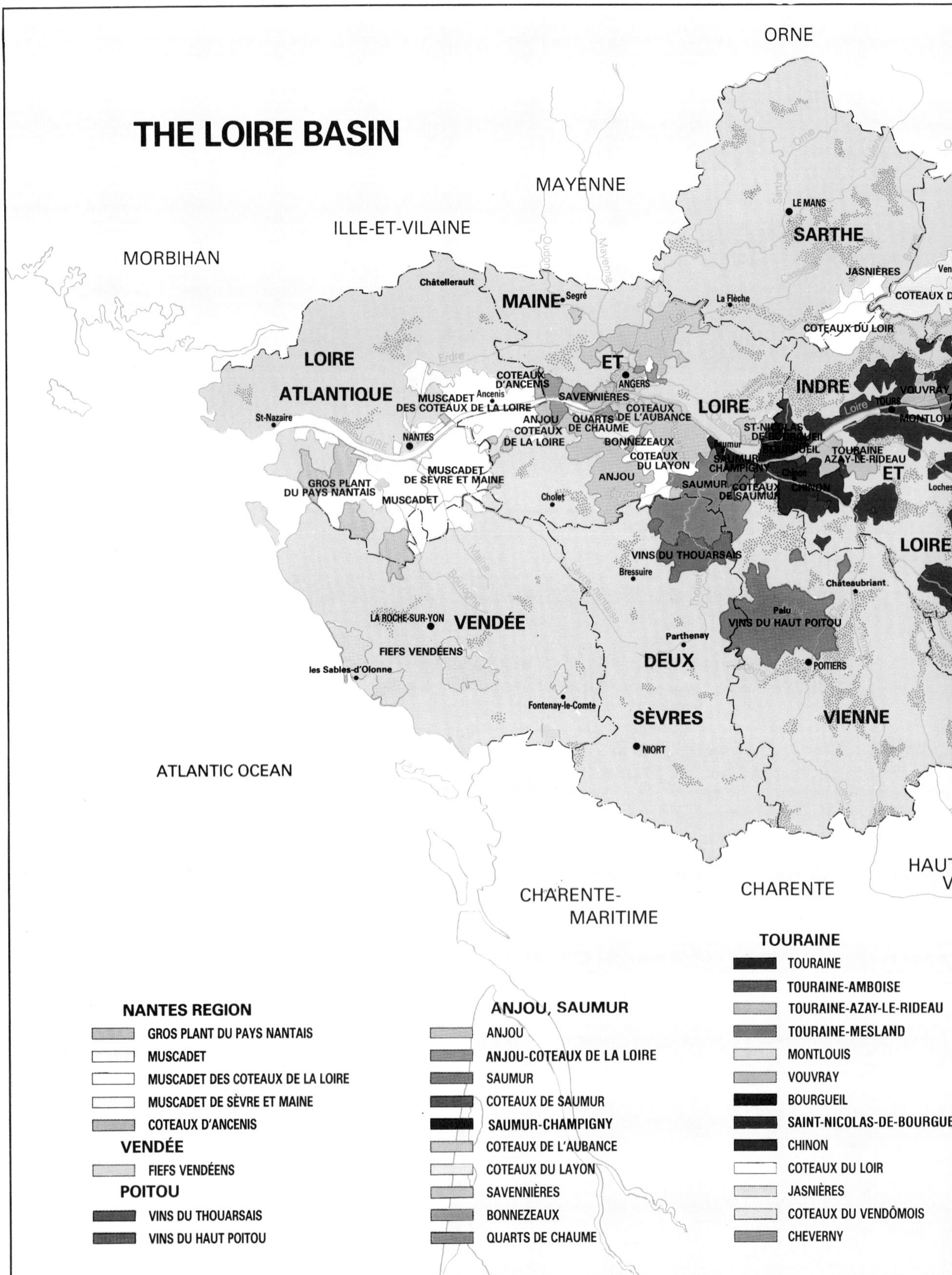
THE LOIRE BASIN
ORNE
MAYENNE
ILLE-ET-VILAINE
MORBIHAN
LE MANS
SARTHE
JASNIÈRES
COTEAUX DU LOIR
La Flèche
Châtellerault
MAINE
Segré
ET
LOIRE
LOIRE
ATLANTIQUE
ANGERS
COTEAUX D'ANCENIS
SAVENNIÈRES
MUSCADET DES COTEAUX DE LA LOIRE
Ancenis
St-Nazaire
ANJOU COTEAUX DE LA LOIRE
QUARTS DE CHAUME
COTEAUX DE L'AUBANCE
BONNEZEAUX
COTEAUX DU LAYON
ANJOU
NANTES
MUSCADET DE SÈVRE ET MAINE
GROS PLANT DU PAYS NANTAIS
MUSCADET
Cholet
SAUMUR
SAUMUR CHAMPIGNY
COTEAUX DE SAUMUR
CHINON
INDRE
VOUVRAY
TOURS
MONTLOUIS
TOURAINE AZAY-LE-RIDEAU
ET
Loches
LOIRE
VINS DU THOUARSAIS
Bressuire
Châteaubriant
VINS DU HAUT POITOU
LA ROCHE-SUR-YON
VENDÉE
FIEFS VENDÉENS
les Sables-d'Olonne
Parthenay
DEUX
SÈVRES
POITIERS
VIENNE
Fontenay-le-Comte
NIORT
ATLANTIC OCEAN
CHARENTE-MARITIME
CHARENTE
NANTES REGION
GROS PLANT DU PAYS NANTAIS
MUSCADET
MUSCADET DES COTEAUX DE LA LOIRE
MUSCADET DE SÈVRE ET MAINE
COTEAUX D'ANCENIS
VENDÉE
FIEFS VENDÉENS
POITOU
VINS DU THOUARSAIS
VINS DU HAUT POITOU
ANJOU, SAUMUR
ANJOU
ANJOU-COTEAUX DE LA LOIRE
SAUMUR
COTEAUX DE SAUMUR
SAUMUR-CHAMPIGNY
COTEAUX DE L'AUBANCE
COTEAUX DU LAYON
SAVENNIÈRES
BONNEZEAUX
QUARTS DE CHAUME
TOURAINE
TOURAINE
TOURAINE-AMBOISE
TOURAINE-AZAY-LE-RIDEAU
TOURAINE-MESLAND
MONTLOUIS
VOUVRAY
BOURGUEIL
SAINT-NICOLAS-DE-BOURGUE
CHINON
COTEAUX DU LOIR
JASNIÈRES
COTEAUX DU VENDÔMOIS
CHEVERNY

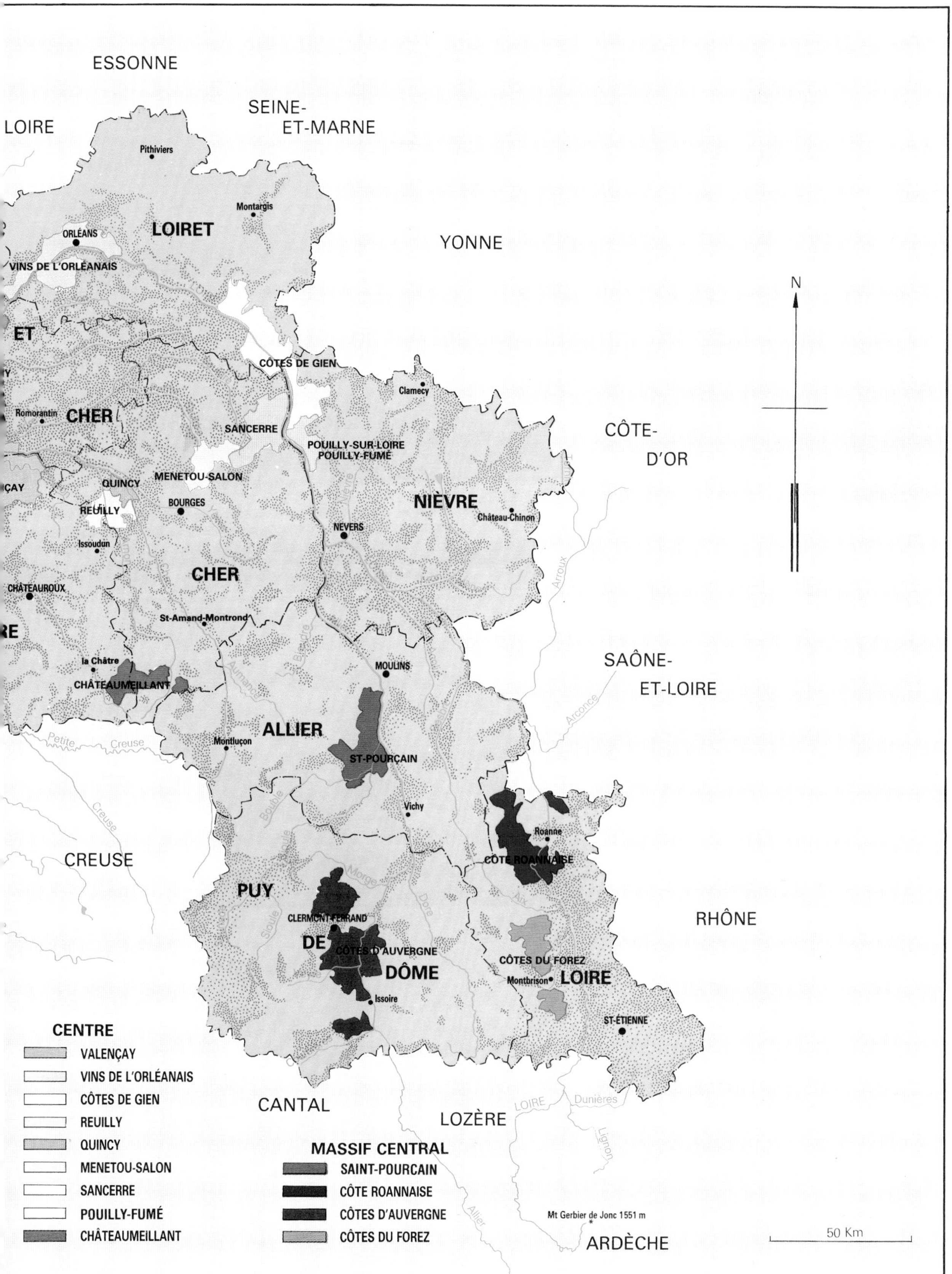
ESSONNE
SEINE-ET-MARNE
LOIRE
Pithiviers
Montargis
ORLÉANS
LOIRET
YONNE
VINS DE L'ORLÉANAIS
N
ET
CÔTES DE GIEN
Clamecy
Romorantin
CHER
SANCERRE
POUILLY-SUR-LOIRE
POUILLY-FUMÉ
CÔTE-D'OR
QUINCY
MENETOU-SALON
BOURGES
REUILLY
NIÈVRE
Château-Chinon
NEVERS
Issoudun
CHER
CHÂTEAUROUX
St-Amand-Montrond
SAÔNE-ET-LOIRE
MOULINS
la Châtre
CHÂTEAUMEILLANT
ALLIER
Montluçon
ST-POURÇAIN
Vichy
Roanne
CREUSE
CÔTE ROANNAISE
PUY
CLERMONT-FERRAND
RHÔNE
DE
CÔTES D'AUVERGNE
CÔTES DU FOREZ
DÔME
Montbrison
LOIRE
Issoire
ST-ÉTIENNE
CENTRE
VALENÇAY
VINS DE L'ORLÉANAIS
CÔTES DE GIEN
REUILLY
QUINCY
MENETOU-SALON
SANCERRE
POUILLY-FUMÉ
CHÂTEAUMEILLANT
CANTAL
LOZÈRE
MASSIF CENTRAL
SAINT-POURCAIN
CÔTE ROANNAISE
CÔTES D'AUVERGNE
CÔTES DU FOREZ
Mt Gerbier de Jonc 1551 m
ARDÈCHE
50 Km

Anjou and Saumur

There are many AOCs in this second major Loire production zone: Anjou, Anjou-Coteaux de la Loire, Anjou Gamay, Anjou Pétillant, Anjou Mousseux, Bonnezeaux, Cabernet d'Anjou, Cabernet de Saumur, Coteaux de l'Aubance, Coteaux du Layon, sometimes followed by -Val de Loire, -Chaume, or the name of the commune of origin, Coteaux de Saumur, Quarts de Chaume, Rosé d'Anjou, Rosé d'Anjou Pétillant, Saumur, Saumur-Champigny, Saumur Pétillant, Saumur Mousseux, Savennières, Savennières-Coulée-de-Serrant, Savennières-Roche-aux-Moines and Crémant de Loire. Also associated with this area of climatic influence is the VDQS Vins du Thouarsais from Deux-Sèvres.

Vineyard of Chenin Blanc grapes in the Chalonnes-sur-Loire area. Here, the great sweet wines of the Coteaux du Layon are grown.

Touraine

This third zone contains the following *appellations d'origine contrôlée*: Bourgueil, Chinon, Montlouis Pétillant, Montlouis Mousseux, Rosé de Loire, Saint-Nicolas-de-Bourgueil, Touraine, Touraine-Azay-le-Rideau, Touraine-Mesland, Touraine-Amboise, Touraine Pétillant, Touraine Mousseux, Vouvray, Vouvray Pétillant, Vouvray Mousseux and Crémant de Loire, to which should be added Coteaux du Loir and Jasnières, as well as the VDQS wines Cheverny, Coteaux du Vendômois and Valençay. The VDQS Vins du Haut-Poitou can also be included in this zone.

The Vins du Centre

In this zone are AOC Pouilly-Fumé, Pouilly-sur-Loire, Menetou-Salon, Quincy, Reuilly and Sancerre, as well as VDQS Châteaumeillant, Côtes de Gien, Saint-Pourçain, Côte Roannaise, Côtes d'Auvergne, Côtes du Forez and Vins de l'Orléanais.

The roots of a vineyard region

It is easy to recover traces of the past in the Loire, and to see how faithfully this wine-growing region has maintained the widely differing styles that are traditional there. The many historic centres to be found throughout the Loire provide a key to understanding the characteristics of the area as a whole.

A *terroir* must be capable of producing at least 30 successive vintages in order to define its own identity and, most importantly, prove the qualities of the wines that have made its reputation. To taste an 1858 Vouvray and discover in it all the style of today's Vouvray authenticates the *terroir* more convincingly than any written text could do.

An *appellation* wine, however, exists because it has a history. The history of the Loire is rich and fertile and has left many tokens of the close relationship that has bound men and wine together.

There are texts showing the existence of vineyards in Sauvignon, Berry and Niverne before Roman times. By the time of the barbarian invasions, there was already a long history of vine growing in Gaul. A 2nd-century Gallo-Roman wine press can be seen in the Musée du Vin in Tours. In about 371, St Martin encouraged the growing of vines in Touraine, to provide wine for religious and medicinal purposes. Around 580, Gregory of Tours wrote a description of the vineyards of the Nantes area. In 990, when Bourgueil abbey was founded, Countess Emma gave some vineyards to the Benedictine monks. They planted Cabernet Franc vines, and this variety has given the area its means of viticultural expression for almost a thousand years.

By the 11th century, the Loire wine districts were already renowned. The local poet Appolinus sang the praises of Anjou wines, and the vineyards of Bonnezeaux in Coteaux du Layon also enjoyed a high reputation.

Subsequently, the vineyards continued to develop, thanks in particular to monastic viticulture; trade with England, especially during the Plantagenet period, from 1154 to 1485; and to the various moves of the French court along this 'royal river'. As a result of these developments, growers were able to improve their wines by selecting better grape varieties and refining their methods of cultivation. Thus, the history and development of the vine in the Loire valley are closely linked to the other events that took place along the banks of the river and its tributaries.

The particular character of these wines, then, is rooted in a thousand-year-old tradition. And these roots are stronger thanks to the fact that they draw their sustenance from small

The historic wine district of Chinon, in the heart of Touraine, stretches along the left bank of the Loire and both banks of the Vienne.

vineyards, a feature that has always characterized these districts. The growers of the Loire are sturdy and tenacious; each of them feels it is his responsibility to produce wine that clearly expresses its surroundings.

The châteaux of the Loire were built in the 15th and 16th centuries. Most of them are in the area of Blois and Touraine, but they are also found in Berry and Anjou. Had this region not been blessed with such fine food and wine, the Italian artists and craftsmen that worked on them might not have exercised their talents with such harmonious results. As it is, the exquisite architecture of these châteaux blends well with the Loire, with the countryside around and with the character of its wines.

The geographical setting

The wine-growing districts are situated along the banks of the Loire and its main tributaries. The vines grow in stony alluvial deposits on the lower slopes of the hills, and in areas adjacent to such terrains. Therefore, although the soil is dry, it absorbs air and moisture easily, and the slope sites mean that the vineyards are above all well exposed. The individual character of the wines depends on the varying clay, silica or limestone content of the soils. Generally speaking, the wine districts are on dry, shallow land, as it is on this that the best results are obtained.

In former times, the wines of the *Côtes d'Auvergne* were dispatched to the Paris area via the waterways of the Allier and the Loire, and then the Orléans, Briare and Loing canals, leading to the Seine. The Côtes d'Auvergne vineyards are situated in the area around Madargues, Châteaugay and Chanturgue, most of them at an altitude of less than 500m. Other stretches of vineyard are to be found near the *puys* (hills) of Gergovie and Corent. All these vineyards are situated on slopes crowned with ancient basalt formations.

From Moulins, the terraces of *Saint-Pourçain* are visible to the south, with plateaux and hills above them to the west. It is on these slopes near Chemilly that the vineyards are planted, on soils consisting of colluvial deposits that slid from the plateau.

The wine-growing districts of *Pouilly* and *Sancerre* are situated at an altitude of about 350m. In Pouilly, the vineyards are on well-exposed west- and southwest-facing slopes. Those of Sancerre are set in a harmonious landscape of gently contoured hills dominated by the picturesque medieval town of Sancerre.

The vineyards of *Châteaumeillant* and *Menetou-Salon* are both planted on prolongations of the limestone hills of Sancerre.

Quincy, *Reuilly* and *Valençay* are situated on fairly flat land, in the Cher valley, upstream from Vierzon.

Côtes de Gien lies on both banks of the Loire. At Gien, the vines grow in siliceous soils.

The vineyards of the ***Vins de l'Orléanais*** share land with orchards and market gardens, from Bou to Tavers, downstream from Orléans.

Most of the Touraine vineyards are to be found on the edge of the plateaux that lie between the Loire, the Cher, the Indre and the Vienne. The vines grow in the side valleys,

Fountain of Bacchus at Veretz in Cher.

where the slopes are well exposed to the sun. The valley floors are never used to grow grapes for fine wines. To explore the vineyards, you have to go up into the hills, following delightful pathways lined with troglodytic dwellings and cellars dug in the limestone rock. A string of vineyards succeed each other here: *Touraine-Mesland* then *Touraine-Amboise* on either side of the Loire, followed by *Montlouis*, which is situated on the left bank of the river and stretches west as far as the hills on the right bank of the Cher.

The commune of *Vouvray* is the capital of the wine area of this name. The hillside vineyards follow the right bank of the Loire. The wine district of *Touraine-Azay-le-Rideau* in the Indre valley begins at Saché and continues down the Indre. The vineyards of *Bourgueil* and *Saint-Nicolas-de-Bourgueil* bring us back to the right bank of the Loire. They are situated on a vast alluvial terrace about 20km long, 2km wide and nearly 15m above river level. There are also vineyards on the north bank of this terrace, sited on areas of tufa, rising as high as 50m in some places. The commune of Benais includes one *terroir* that is renowned for its '*vins de tuf*' (tufa wines). On ancient gravel terrain on the left bank of the Loire is *Chinon*, an important *appellation*. This covers a vast area of differing soils and relief, including gravel terraces and steep-sided limestone plateaux that drop down, vine covered, to the left bank of the Loire and the right bank of the Vienne. On the left bank of the Vienne, the vineyards are often hidden away in wooded uplands. The Chinon wine district stretches along both sides of the Vienne, on terraces 5m to 10m high, formed of ancient alluvial deposits.

Further on towards Saumur is the wine district of *Saumur-Champigny*, situated on a plateau between the Thouet and the Loire valleys.

The wines of *Coteaux du Layon* are produced in the region of Thouarcé, on either side of the Layon, a small tributary lying south of the Loire. The Layon vineyards are planted on sunny slopes with schist outcrops; they extend to Rochefort, where this river flows into the Loire.

Anjou-Coteaux de la Loire, an *appellation* situated on steeply sloping terrain between Angers and Ingrandes, contains within its boundaries the famous *crus* of *Savennières* (Roche-aux-Moines and Coulée-de-Serrant).

The vineyards of *Coteaux de l'Aubance* border a small river of this name that flows between the Loire and the Layon. The slopes here are gentler than in Coteaux du Layon.

Finally there is the *Pays Nantais*, home to *Muscadet* and *Gros Plant*, a tranquil landscape in which vineyards swathe low hills.

The many watercourses that cover this region have been the major influence on the wine-growing districts of the Loire, providing lines of communication as well as dictating the position

A vineyard in Muscadet, underneath a rain-heavy sky typical of the Atlantic climatic zone.

of the vineyards. The present-day boundaries of the *appellation* zones have become clearly defined over the centuries. They testify to the ceaseless work of the wine growers — as well as to the soils found in the zones, as it is these that give the wines their basic character.

The soils

The soils of the Loire valley are, in general, varied. In the Muscadet area, the soils are predominantly stony, with silica lending finesse to the wines. A greater range of soil types is found in Anjou: in the Layon region, and in Savennières and Aubance, schist predominates, while in the Saumur region, there is a calcareous layer covering gravel, silica or clay.

In Touraine, the main constituent of the *terroirs* is tufa. On top of this are clay or siliceous soils of varying depth. In the inland area around Orléans, the soils are siliceous and gravelly, sometimes with a little clay. The chief characteristics of Sancerre are limestone and the famous Kimmeridgian soils, as found also in Chablis. In Pouilly, the soils are a mixture of marl, Kimmeridgian limestone, clay-silica and silica. They bring out the full potential of the Chasselas grape, used for AOC Pouilly-sur-Loire. Côtes de Gien has siliceous, gravelly soils. In Menetou-Salon, clay and chalk mixtures and siliceous soils are both found.

At Quincy, the soils are siliceous and more or less gravelly. At Reuilly, there are various soils,

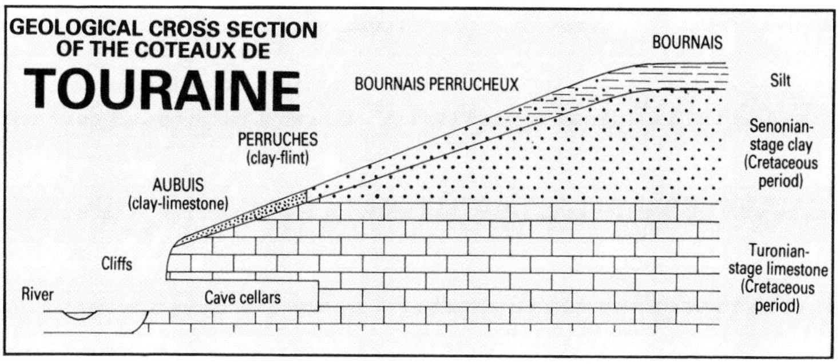

but Kimmeridgian marls predominate.

At Châteaumeillant, the soils are siliceous and more or less clayey. In Côtes d'Auvergne and Côtes du Forez, the dry, well-drained soils include sands, limestones, marls and volcanic rocks.

The great variety of soils found in Saint-Pourçain explains the diversity of white and red grape varieties used there.

The life of the vine

A vine plant grows in the same ground for half a century, sometimes more. During the course of this long period, the vines have to be trained and adapted to fluctuations in the climate.

The age of a vine and annually varying climatic conditions alter the character of a wine; this is a phenomenon very much in evidence in the more northerly wine regions. Those who

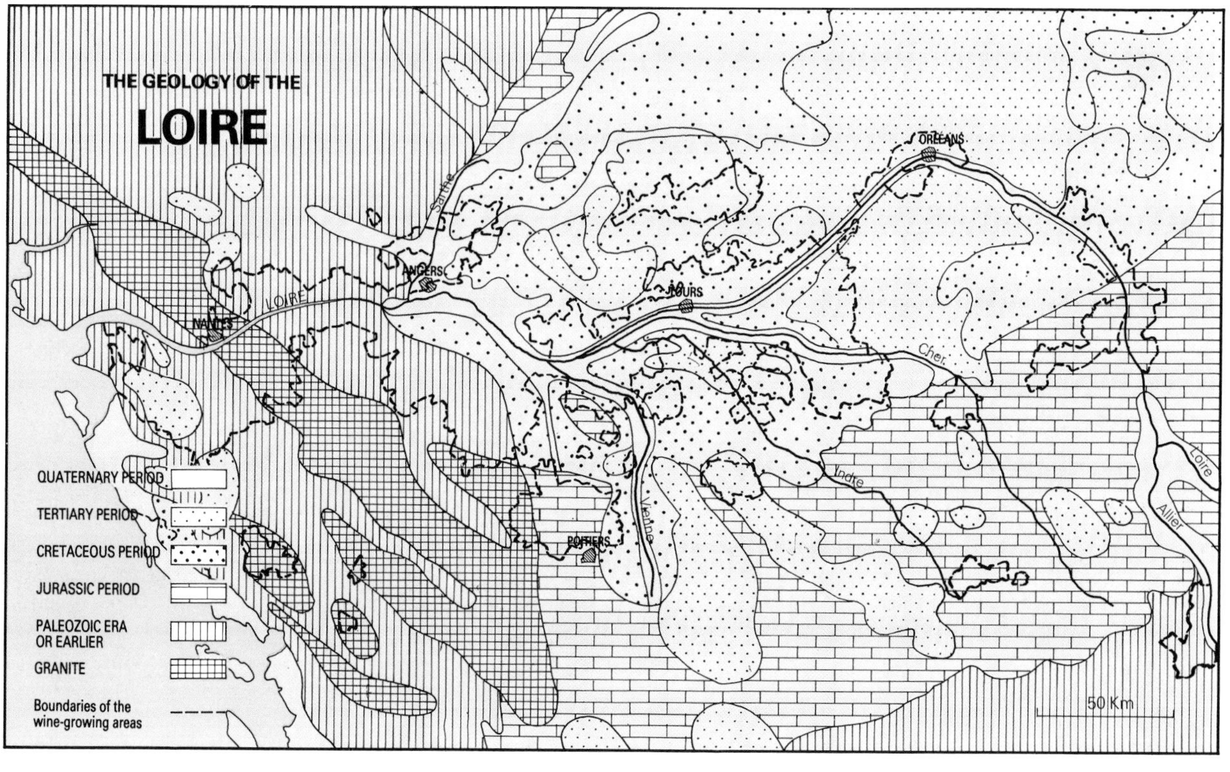

wish to use the name of their *appellation* for their wine must therefore tend their vineyards with great skill. The concept of vineyard environment (microecology) takes on an extremely important dimension in such regions, much more so than in those where the climate is more constant.

In the Loire region, the slightest error in cultivation can have grave consequences. The type of soil in which vines are planted, the amount of exposure to sunlight the vines receive, the way in which the ground is worked and in which the vine plants are pruned have a profound effect on the composition of the wine.

The northern French wine-growing regions are a single college of applied vine-growing; here, the wines are much more obviously moulded by man than in other parts of the country. They bear his stamp and his every gesture. The saying that 'God makes vines, man makes wines' is never more apt than when applied to the Loire valley.

The vegetative cycle of the vine is a series of stages, the timing of which is variable. When the weather begins to turn cold around All Saints' Day (1 November), the leaves fall to the ground. The rest period for the vine begins on about 15 November, although this varies by up to two weeks. This stage comes to a close at the end of March, when the buds break. At the beginning of April, the buds swell and open, and their opening is judged to be either '*belle*' (good) or '*modeste*' (not so good). At this time of year, the risk of spring frosts is an ever-present threat.

Flowering occurs in the period of the year when the days are longest. The vines usually come into flower around St John's Day, 24 June. They can, however, flower up to 20 days before or after this, depending on the exact climatic conditions of the year. The point at which flowering occurs is crucial to the vineyards of the Loire region, because the period between the flowering and grape ripening is 100 days. Consequently, in years when the vines blossom before the summer solstice (around 21 June), the grapes will receive a greater amount of beneficial sun and light. The reverse is true when flowering occurs late. When this happens, the grapes will come under the 'influence of the night', and the wine will have a more sober, unobtrusive character.

The wines of the Loire vary in character from one district to another, thanks to the different climatic zones they grow in. However, they also have certain common characteristics: the ability to harmonize with their surroundings, vivacity, elegance, a great aptitude for ageing in bottle, and the colours of purple or gold.

The general climate picture

The tables on the opposite page show the general climatic divisions of the different wine-growing areas of the Loire. The figures are cumulative, and represent averages for the last 30 years.

It is possible to establish a relationship between these climatic divisions and the types of wine produced. The sum of the temperatures in zones 1 and 2 during the rest period gives a good indication of the warming effect of the Atlantic. This can be felt as far inland as Touraine. The Allier, on the other hand, in zone 4, has the lowest temperatures during this period, but in July and August temperatures there are higher than anywhere else. This points clearly to a continental climate. Thus the valley can be described in the following general way: Muscadet has an Atlantic climate and Anjou a near-Atlantic one. Touraine has a near-continental climate, though maritime influences can still make themselves felt there. From Sancerre to Côtes d'Auvergne, the climate is continental.

Anjou and Touraine have the highest temperatures in September and October, which explains why sweet white wines are produced in these two zones. It is impossible to grow these wines in Loire-Atlantique, as the rainfall is higher in the same period, and this reduces the total temperature to 746°C, as opposed to 864° in Anjou and 840° in Touraine. This reduction in temperature occurs despite the fact that Loire-Atlantique enjoys considerable amounts of sunlight during this period. These factors explain why Muscadet, a wine made from grapes that ripen early, before the rainy period, is produced in Loire-Atlantique. This wine very clearly reflects climatic conditions.

In Loiret, Loir-et-Cher, Nièvre and Allier,

LIFE OF A VINE IN THE LOIRE VALLEY

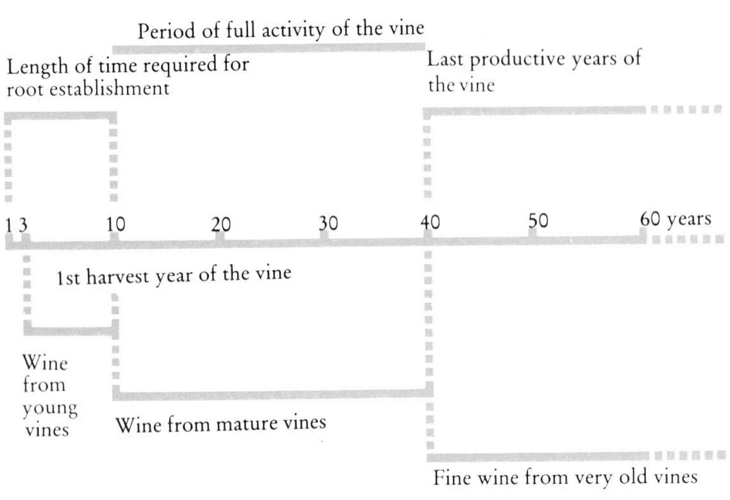

AVERAGE TEMPERATURES						
Zones	**Départements**	**Nov. Dec. Jan. Feb.**	**March April May**	**June**	**July August**	**Sept. Oct.**
Zone 1	Loire-Atlantique	732	941	495	1 110	746
Zone 2	Maine-et-Loire	702	987	522	1 155	864
	Indre-et-Loire	621	987	525	1 154	840
Zone 3	Loir-et-Cher	573	945	510	1 140	988
	Loiret	549	915	495	1 107	807
	Cher	573	972	525	1 161	840
Zone 4	Nièvre	515	939	516	1 122	792
	Allier	495	936	528	1 170	813

All the figures are in degrees Celsius.

AVERAGE RAINFALL					
Zones	**Nov. to February**	**March April May**	**June**	**July August**	**Sept. Oct.**
1 Loire-Atlantique	314	176	53	98	144
2 Maine-et-Loire	224	149	50	83	115
3 Indre-et-Loire	239	165	56	95	115
Loir-et-Cher	238	170	51	97	116
Loiret	209	156	58	101	112
4 Cher	215	166	63	115	113
Nièvre	260	183	74	132	136
Allier	201	202	85	158	153

All the figures are in millimetres.

AVERAGE HOURS OF SUNSHINE					
Zones	**Nov. to February**	**March April May**	**June**	**July August**	**Sept. Oct.**
1 Loire-Atlantique	345	619	277	536	348
2 Maine-et-Loire	330	566	240	463	307
3 Indre-et-Loire	276	518	244	476	298
Loir-et-Cher	271	570	240	472	304
Loiret	264	530	230	454	306
4 Cher	264	526	230	452	302
Nièvre	330	468	251	490	312
Allier	348	510	271	528	318

All the figures are in hours.

Climatic factors have to be taken into account before a wine can be fully understood and appreciated.

the total temperatures are not high enough to permit the regular production of wines containing residual sugar. Consequently, the white wines of these regions are dry. For the same reason, the red wines in these parts are made from non-tannic grapes such as Gamay or Pinot Noir. By contrast, Cabernet Franc, which is a tannic grape, is grown in Touraine and Saumur, where the total temperatures are sufficiently high to avoid producing excessively astringent, harsh wines.

The climatic divisions explain the diversity in the grape varieties and the character of the wines produced. All of this is in keeping with the spirit of the *appellation contrôlée* system, according to which a wine should reflect its surroundings. In these areas, though, this idea is carried further than elsewhere, because annual variations in climate intensify the natural differences between the character of the wines.

The higher the total temperature, the more full-bodied a wine will be. On the other hand, low total temperatures can increase the wine's vivacity and subtlety. High levels of sunshine result in a strong colour, and are also responsible for developing the aromas of fully ripe grapes. If it rains while the vines are flowering, this can cause a decrease in the harvest volume. If rain falls at harvest time, it can dilute the sugars in the grapes, increasing the yields of must but at the expense of quality.

The table below clearly shows the effect of annual climatic variations. These climatic statistics, for the cultivation of the Cabernet Franc in Touraine over the last 22 years, also reveal the general climatic outline of all the wines of the Loire region for the years in question. Note that flowering dates for the other *appellations* are as follows: Muscadet 15 days earlier, Sancerre and Pouilly 12 days earlier, Anjou and Vouvray 10 to 20 days later, depending on the microclimate. When the total temperatures are high, the wines are more suitable for maturing over a long period of time, as in 1964, 1976 and 1982. In 1972 and 1984 the vines flowered unusually late, therefore the wines of those years were somewhat subdued in character, but the lack of rain, particularly at harvest time, gave them a great cleanness and directness of flavour.

The wind

The last of the climatic factors affecting vine growth is the wind. In the Loire, the north and east winds have a drying effect, the west wind is humid, while the south wind provokes vine diseases.

TOURAINE CLIMATIC STATISTICS (CABERNET FRANC)

	Total temperatures in degrees Celsius	Hours of sunshine	Rainfall in millimetres	(1) Flowering period	(2) Volume of harvest	(3) Weather during harvest
1964	3 461	1 350	379	3	N	
1965	3 122	1 352	525	5	N	W
1966	3 277	1 433	499	4	N−	M
1967	3 300	1 420	407	4	N	W
1968	3 329	1 406	438	4	N−	M
1969	3 366	1 455	277	4	N−	M
1970	3 273	1 400	351		N+	D
1971	3 414	1 602	403		N−	M
1972	3 017	1 353	238	5	N	D
1973	3 164	1 549	338	4	N	M
1974	3 012	1 803	354	4	N	W
1975	3 223	1 487	385	2	N−	D
1976	3 610	1 790	274	1	N	D
1977	3 156	1 348	421	4	N−	M
1978	3 135	1 409	337	3	N−	M
1979	3 294	1 344	444	4	N	M
1980	3 274	1 365	443	5	N	M
1981	3 527	1 192	410	2	N−	D
1982	3 430	1 441	433	1	N	D
1983	3 410	1 408	601	2	N	M
1984	3 183	1 465	518	4	N	D
1985	3 294	1 633	396	2	N+	D
1986	3 203	1 480	447	3	N+	M to W

(1) Flowering period:
1 - early June
2 - mid-June
3 - 24 June
4 - early July
5 - 10 July

(2) Volume of harvest:
less than normal: −N
normal: N
above normal: +N

(3) Weather during harvest:
dry weather during harvest: D
wet weather during harvest: W
mixed weather during harvest: M

The wind can also limit the action of damaging physical agents such as hail. The development of cryptogamic diseases like grey rot (botrytis) and downy mildew are slowed by the wind. On a well-aired plateau, a moderate wind reduces the level of humidity in the air by 15 per cent. In 1969, the northeast wind that was blowing at harvest time checked the rotting process and dried out the grapes, thus giving the wine a raisin-like quality. The same phenomenon was noted in 1962. In 1985, the wind blew hard all year, producing grapes with a lower water content than normal. Consequently, the wines that year were dense and particularly fruity.

In the Allier *département*, winds are regular and veer from south to north, with westerlies tending to prevail, particularly in June. In Nièvre, the west wind prevails all year round — and the same goes for Cher, the two *départements* facing one another on either side of the Loire. In September and October the west wind does not blow quite so hard in Cher as it does in Nièvre.

In Loiret and Loir-et-Cher, a southwest wind blows all year round. Indre-et-Loire, however, because of its crossroads position, has a greater variety of winds: they veer from southwest to northeast. In September and October, the northeast wind ensures a fine late autumn, and this permits overripening of the grapes on the vines. Although westerlies tend to prevail in Maine-et-Loire, the overall wind pattern is very similar to that of Indre-et-Loire except in September and October, when the influence of the west wind is stronger. Loire-Atlantique has a more pronounced tendency towards west wind; and when the west winds freshen up in the autumn, it signifies that the grape harvest must be gathered in.

The wine-growing potential of the Loire valley

The climatic conditions governing the wine districts of the Loire suggest a division into four large zones. These conditions have been responsible for shaping the whole wine-growing economy of the Loire valley, and they dictate the kinds of wine produced there (*see* adjacent diagrams).

The Atlantic zone is a region of dry white wines. It produces the three Muscadet AOCs, and the Gros Plant du Pays Nantais and Coteaux d'Ancenis VDQS wines. The area has about 13,000ha of vineyards producing *appellation* wines. The average annual production of white AOC wine is 450,000hl, and that of VDQS is about 170,000hl.

The near-Atlantic zone of Anjou and Saumur is mostly known for the production of medium-dry or sweet white and rosé wines. Today, however, there is a noticeable swing towards red wines, at the expense of rosé and even white wines. The vineyards occupy an area of about 15,000ha, and annual production is around 820,000hl.

The third zone is that of Touraine, which produces red AOC wines, a few dry rosés and some dry, sweet, and sparkling white wines. The area has about 10,500ha of vineyards producing around 450,000hl of AOC wine annually.

The fourth zone, the Centre, has a continental climate. It produces a number of AOC and VDQS wines. The bulk of the production consists of dry white wines, with some rosés and reds. The vineyards cover about 4,000ha, and produce about 220,000hl of wine a year (*see* diagram overleaf).

The total present potential area of the whole of the Loire valley for the production of *appellation* wines is about 42,000ha, providing:

- *1,098,000hl of white wine;*
- *390,000hl of rosé wine;*
- *450,000hl of red wine.*

The grape varieties

In each of these four zones the climate is the guiding factor in the choice of grape varieties.

In the Nantes area, two white grape varieties are used: the Melon, locally known as the Muscadet, and the Folle Blanche, locally known as the Gros Plant; the Gamay is also used for red and rosé wines in the Coteaux d'Ancenis.

The predominant white grape variety in Anjou and Saumur is the Chenin Blanc. The Grolleau is also to be found in areas where large amounts of rosé are produced, as is the Cabernet Franc. The latter, in combination with varying

This Loire red-wine producer is checking the cask development of his wine before deciding whether or not to bottle it.

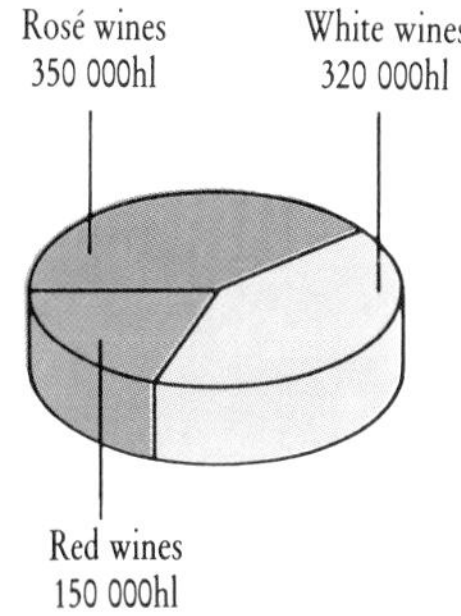

ANJOU AND SAUMUR

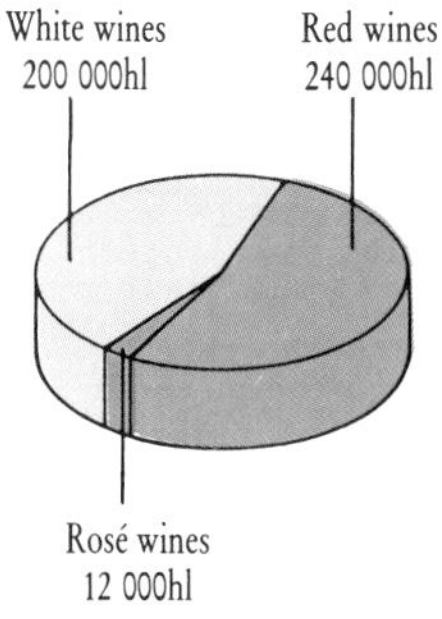

TOURAINE

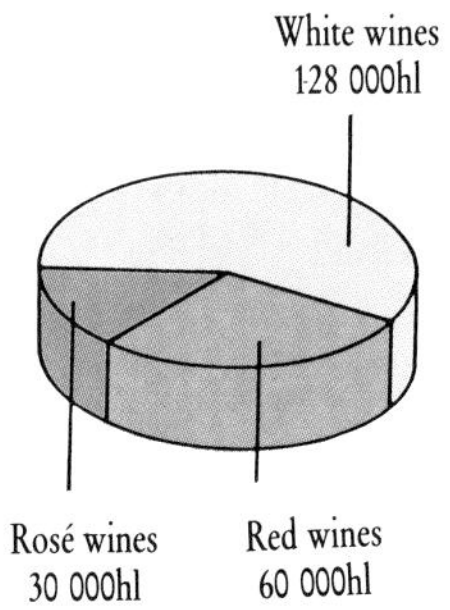

WINES OF CENTRAL FRANCE

proportions of Cabernet Sauvignon and Pineau d'Aunis, is used to make red wines. The Chardonnay and the Sauvignon Blanc are used as secondary grape varieties for white winemaking.

In Touraine, the white grape varieties used are the Chenin Blanc and the Sauvignon Blanc. Red wines are made from the Cabernet Franc and the Gamay, while the Grolleau, Gamay de Chaudenay, Côt, Cabernet Sauvignon, Pinot Noir, Meunier, Pinot Gris and Pineau d'Aunis are all used as secondary or complementary red wine varieties.

The grape varieties used in the Centre are the Sauvignon Blanc for white wines, with the Chenin Blanc, the Chardonnay and the Chasselas as subsidiary varieties; while the Pinot Noir is used for red and rosé wines, with the Meunier, Pinot Gris and Cabernet Franc as subsidiary varieties.

The grape harvest

Harvest time, as already stated, depends on exactly when the vines flower. Grapes need an average of 100 days from this time in order to ripen sufficiently. The flowering period is brief if the weather is hot and dry, but flowering can sometimes take as long as eight or ten days if the weather is cold. If it rains during flowering this hinders fertilization and the harvest will be significantly smaller than normal.

As the vineyards of the Loire lie in a northerly zone, and as varieties such as the Chenin have a late growing cycle, flowering dates are important for the consumer as well as the producer if the character of the wines is to be thoroughly appreciated. If flowering occurs early, for example at the beginning of June, the grapes receive more light as their growth will take place during the longest summer days. Powerful, long-lived wines can therefore be the result of early flowering. In 1980, though, the opposite happened; flowering did not take place until about 14 July and, consequently, the climatic conditions and daylight hours were not so favourable, making the wines livelier, but less powerful and with less potential for bottle-ageing.

The flowering times and harvest dates shown in the table below are those of the Cabernet Franc in Touraine. By making the following adjustments, the dates for other wine-growing areas can be worked out:

▷ Muscadet: Melon grape variety, 15 days earlier.
▷ Sancerre: Sauvignon Blanc grape variety, 12 days earlier.
▷ Sancerre and Touraine: Gamay grape variety, 10 days earlier.
▷ Anjou and Touraine: Chenin Blanc grape variety, 10 to 20 days later.

These charts and dates only suggest tendencies, but the annual variations are important ones, and they demonstrate the necessity of giving bottles of wine a vintage date. When the growing cycle and ripening is late, few sweet wines can be made, or possibly none at all. But when full ripening is achieved early, and some overripening is possible, as in 1976, sweet wines can be made in large quantities. Furthermore, sunny years herald a long life for the wine in bottle, as the grapes have been able to absorb plenty of 'solar energy'.

Most important, too, in obtaining fine sweet wines is the practice of selective picking of the overripened grapes by making a number of sweeps through the vineyards (*récolte par tries*). Leaving the grapes on the vine encourages the

***B**unches of Melon grapes, used for producing Muscadet, one of the simplest and happiest of French white wines.*

Years	Flowering date	Harvest date
1976	8 June	15 September
1977	15 July	25 October
1978	10 July	20 October
1979	8 July	17 October
1980	14 July	21 October
1981	13 July	21 October
1982	14 June	27 September
1983	15 June	6 October
1984	1 July	18 October
1985	21 June	12 October
1986	24 June	13 October

Traditional grape harvest in the Nantes area.

development of *Botrytis cinerea* on them, and allows them to dry out and concentrate their sugars. Grapes and bunches affected in this way are those that are picked selectively.

Methods of harvesting have developed considerably over the last few years. The harvest time has been shortened so that grapes can be picked at a later stage of ripeness. On many estates nowadays — except in the case of the great sweet white wines — the harvest lasts from eight to ten days, about half the time it took previously. Furthermore, mechanization has been introduced on some estates. This does not always lead to better results qualitatively speaking, but it can satisfy financial needs. Mechanization is out of the question in the case of some wines, though, particularly sweet white wines, *vins de primeur* and sparkling wines.

Vinification

The region as a whole uses traditional vinification methods, and fermentation and *élevage* proceeds much as it has always done.

There have been some developments, however, in the choice of equipment, casks and vats. The most successful advance is the ability to control fermentation temperatures. This means that vinification progresses entirely normally every year, thus giving the wines freedom to develop both their *appellation* and their vintage characteristics.

Élevage of the wines

There are two principal stages in this operation; firstly the process of *dépouillement* (the post-fermentation equivalent of *débourbage*: allowing suspended particles present during fermentation to settle), which takes place in large casks or vats, and secondly the period of maturation in bottle. The white wines of the Loire are bottled early, at the end of March. The period of *élevage* ('raising' or maturing of the wine in cask) is therefore a brief one in the Loire. The whole development process of fine Loire white wines takes place in bottle. The *élevage* of the light red wines of the Loire is also very rapid — sometimes nonexistent, as some wines are sold *en primeur*. On the other hand, in the case of wines made from the Cabernet Franc, *élevage* lasts for a period of between one and two years. It is carried out in large wooden vats or casks, stored in cellars dug in the tufa bedrock.

Characteristics of the wines

The white wines of the Nantes region are dry and have a perfume reminiscent of fresh almonds and sea spray. They are lively but not acid, easy to drink and yet firm, with a satisfactory length and finish.

Anjou and Saumur produce dry, sweet and sparkling white wines. These are well constructed and have an excellent length of life in bottle, especially the sweet wines. The red wines are tannic and full bodied, with those from Saumur being particularly fruity. The rosés are off-dry.

Touraine also produces dry, sweet and sparkling white wines. These have a solid structure and, like Touraine's red wines produced at Bourgueil and Chinon, they last extremely well. In general the red wines of Touraine are tasty, lively and firmly structured. The rosés are dry to off-dry, depending on the vintage.

In the Centre, the white wines are dry, with well-developed aromas reminiscent of blackcurrant leaves. They are full bodied and characterful. The red wines are lightly coloured and delicate, with aromas that are floral or spicy in varying measure: very typical 'mountain' wines, in fact.

Economic and commercial structures

Economically speaking, the wine trade here, as elsewhere in France, is divided into three classic sectors: *négociants*, cooperatives and private growers. Exports form an important part of sales. The most widely exported wines are Muscadets — 40 per cent of total production leaves France — followed by Rosé d'Anjou, Saumur Mousseux, Bourgueil, Chinon, Saumur-Champigny, Vouvray, Sancerre and, finally, Pouilly-Fumé.

Region	Négociants	Cooperatives	Private growers
Muscadet	70	—	25
Anjou-Saumur	45	25	30
Touraine	50	12/15	35/38
Centre	20	40	40

Cellars for maturing wine, dug out in the rock at Dampierre-sur-Loire.

Wine and the community

The growers of the Loire wine districts have always felt a need to exhibit their wines in the first few months after the harvest. Thus, each *appellation* has a calendar of local wine fairs. Today, these fairs give consumers the opportunity to see all the wines produced in a particular *appellation*, and meet the growers, together, in one place. A visit to one of them is also a good way of getting to know all about the latest vintage.

The great years

The commonly used term 'great' deserves an explanation here. What is meant by 'a great wine' ('*un grand vin*')? A great wine is one which, from the first, possesses a density and a consistency that marks it out from others. Such wines generally have a history, an ancestry, and are not simply the consequence of favourable weather conditions. It is continuing and unvarying excellence from year to year that merits the use of the term 'great'. In order to be great, a wine must be capable of maturing in bottle; it must have a life ahead of it. You often hear people refer to 'a minor vintage' or 'a great vintage', when they simply mean a good or less good year. But the adjectives 'minor' and 'great' should not be used in this way. A wine can be either modest or great, and if it is great, this is by virtue of its breeding alone. On the other hand, the lifespan of a great wine can be longer or shorter, depending on the climatic conditions of the vintage. The table below shows the lifespan of a number of Loire wines. It should be clearly understood, however, that this life expectancy can be modified in either direction, depending on the quality of the wine making and the origin of the wine — its potential greatness, or lack of it. Finally, it should be noted that once a wine reaches this optimal stage, it may remain there without deterioration for a number of years.

AVERAGE LENGTH OF LIFE OF FINE LOIRE WINES (in years)

Vintages	Muscadet	Anjou Moelleux	Champigny Bourgueil Chinon	Vouvray	Sancerre Pouilly-Fumé
1959	20	50	40	50	20
1960	—	—	—	—	—
1961	—	30	30	30	—
1962	—	25	25	25	—
1963	—	—	—	—	—
1964	—	30	30	30	—
1965	—	—	—	—	—
1966	—	25	25	25	—
1967	—	20	20	20	—
1968	—	—	—	—	—
1969	—	25	25	25	—
1970	—	25	25	25	—
1971	—	25	25	25	—
1972	—	15	15	15	—
1973	—	15	15	15	—
1974	—	10	10	10	—
1975	15	25	25	15	—
1976	20	50	40	50	20
1977	—	15	10	15	10
1978	15	25	20	25	15
1979	10	15	15	15	10
1980	—	10	10	10	—
1981	15	40	30	40	20
1982	15	40	30	40	15
1983	10	20	20	20	10
1984	5	10	10	10	5
1985	15	30	30	30	15
1986	10	20	20	20	10

Among the distinguished years prior to those shown in the chart are 1893, 1921, 1933, 1945 and 1947.

GLASSES AND WINE

A glass is a beautiful object — a graceful, transparent bubble. When the table is laid, it adds a vertical dimension, setting off the silverware and reflecting the light of the candles, the sun or the chandeliers! The magical qualities of a glass can lead to a forgetfulness as to its purpose, that of a drinking vessel, and its function, that of a vehicle giving wine its freedom of expression. If you serve the same wine in different glasses, it will speak different languages.

The glass as an everyday object

In its original form, the glass was inspired by already existing objects, such as Gallic drinking horns supported on tripods. Over the centuries, a gradual transformation took place, until the glass became the transparent vessel we use today.

A glass is basically a goblet intended to hold liquid. It may have a stem, a vertical support that widens out just below the bowl, and a base to give it stability.

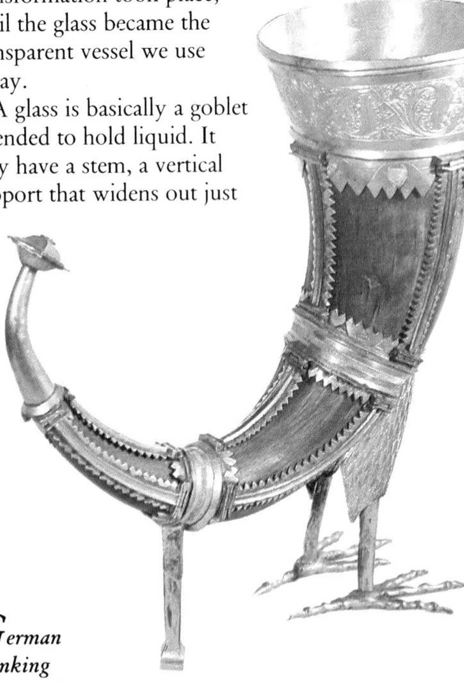

German drinking horn, 15th century. ***The decoration on this vessel, an ancestor of the wine glass, is extremely refined. It is made of bull's horn in a setting of finely engraved gold.***

These elements vary considerably from one era and from one region to another, and sometimes reach such a degree of refinement that the glass becomes a real work of art, not just an everyday object designed to contain a drink.

This should not obscure the fact, though, that the material, decoration and form, every parameter of this container known as the glass, serves ultimately to enhance the contents, and never more so than when a glass contains wine.

The glass as a tool of wine tasting

In order to be suitable for wine tasting, a glass must satisfy the eye, the nose and the mouth.

It should be transparent, smooth and unexceptional in itself, showing the wine to advantage, reflecting and displaying its colour and its visual nuances. It should not be so large as to modify the bouquet of the wine in any way, although some burgundies are at their best in a very big glass.

The bowl should be oval or egg shaped, with a slight narrowing at the top to concentrate the aromas. The rim should be narrow, to aid mouth contact. The glass must have an extended base for the taster to grip, so that he or she will not transfer hand heat to the wine. With these requirements in mind, the experts of the Institut National des Appellations d'Origine have created a glass intended to be ideal for tasting. It is known as the AFNOR (Association Française du Normalisation) or INAO glass. It is smooth, completely transparent and semi-ovoid, stemmed and with a solid base. The material is crystal glass, that is to say, glass that contains a certain percentage of lead (about 9 per cent). The capacity of this glass is about 210ml to 225ml, but it should not be filled more than a third full (70ml to 80ml). In this way, a ratio of 1 is established between the total area of the liquid and its volume. Furthermore, if the glass is only a third full, it is possible to swirl the wine in it, thus releasing the

The AFNOR wine-tasting glass.

Flûte for sparkling wine.

Loire red-wine glass.

Burgundy wine glass.

Claret (Bordeaux) glass.

Alsace wine glass.

aromas progressively, without the risk of spillage. This volume of wine in the glass also creates the most pleasing visual effect. Although the AFNOR glass is widely used by professionals, it is not the only glass to possess the characteristics necessary for good tasting. The Baccarat and Sèvres glassworks offer several models of glasses that conform to these criteria.

To each wine its glass

These standardized AFNOR glasses should not make us overlook or despise the traditional glass styles of France. These are,

DECORATED GLASSES

The transparent drinking glass first appeared at the end of the 17th century, and from the beginning, the glasses were made to a high level of refinement. Decorated glasses abounded, from the coloured crystal of Bohemia and Venice to the luxuriously engraved work of the Baccarat and Saint-Louis glass works.

***Cemetery glass* (verre chrétien):** with a double-layered base enclosing thin gold leaf.

***Chased glass* (verre ciselé):** etched with acid.

***Crackle glass* (verre craquelé):** this type is made by covering the ready-shaped vessel with splinters of glass while still hot, and finishing it off by reheating, blowing and other processes.

***Enamelled glass* (verre émaillé):** glass covered with a vitreous opaque or transparent glaze.

***Filament glass* (verre filigrané):** the basic paste contains threads of coloured glass that form patterns.

***Engraved glass* (verre gravé):** engraved by wheel.

***Beaded glass* (verre perlé):** decorated with glass beads.

***Reticulated glass* (verre réticulé):** glass made of two layers, with openwork cut into the outer layer.

***Cut glass* (verre taillé):** cut to produce facets.

Venetian crystal glass, 17th century.

Drinking vessel found at Hendebouville in Eure, dating from the Gallo-Roman era.

in fact, deeply rooted in regional customs, and each has its own good reason for existing.

So it is that red or dry white Bordeaux wines, which are naturally dense and astringent, require a tall, slender glass that narrows slightly at the top and has a delicate base. On the other hand, the more open, earthy wines of Pomerol, Saint-Émilion, Chinon and Bourgueil call for squatter, wider-rimmed glasses.

Vouvray, like all the white wines of the Loire, is best served in a glass of basically conical shape.

Burgundies, dessert wines and *vins doux naturels*, all of which are rich, generous, dense and heady, require wide-bowled glasses that will allow their aromas to blossom.

The wines of Alsace are served in a small balloon glass with a tall, slender green stem; in a more sophisticated Rhine wine glass; or even in a thick, squat *Römer*; or a *Rütscherle*, which is a small fluted tumbler.

A tall tulip glass or *flûte* shows the effervescence and elegance of champagne at its best. It is preferable to a wide-bowled champagne *coupe*, which allows both bubbles and aroma to escape.

Finally, as a general rule, care should be taken to match types of wine with suitable glasses. The more rustic and honest the wine, the simpler the glass should be. The more generous and full it is, the larger and more elegant the glass.

The success of wine tasting, part celebration and part devotion, depends on the harmony possessed by wine's components being realized in the glass.

A LITTLE GLOSSARY OF DRINKING VESSELS

Balloon glass: *spherical glass.*

Chalice: *originally a Roman drinking vessel; now used particularly for Holy Communion.*

Canthare: *cup with vertical handles.*

Ciborium: *originally a cup made from the seed vessel of the Egyptian water lily, it then became a drinking vessel of the same shape.*

Cotyle: *a bowl-shaped natural object that can be used as a vessel.*

Coupole: *small vessel for wine tasting, also known as a* tastevin.

Flûte: *tall, narrow glass with a base, used for serving sparkling wines.*

Goblet: *cylindrical, slightly bell-shaped vessel generally with a base and stem but without handles.*

Godet: *small drinking cup without a stem.*

Hanap: *large drinking vessel or goblet with a base but no handles.*

Mazarin: *glass goblet of very ordinary quality.*

This 'Hunting' patera comes from Ugarit, an ancient Canaanite city whose ruins lie in present-day Syria. Fourteenth century BC.

Patera: *shallow, dish-shaped vessel used for libations.*

Pinton: *small drinking vessel to hold the measure of wine served to each monk with his meal.*

Pivette: *a greenish-coloured drinking glass.*

Quart: *metal goblet to hold a quarter of a litre.*

Rhyton: *drinking vessel made of cow's horn, or in the shape of a horn or an animal's head.*

Tasse: *small vessel with handle; a cup.*

Tastevin: *small, wide, shallow pewter or silver vessel with no stem and a handle surmounted by a thumb rest. This vessel is used for wine tasting.*

Timballe: *small silver or silver-plated goblet.*

Trinquette: *drinking vessel with no base which must be emptied before it can be put down.*

Tulip glass: *glass shaped like a tulip.*

Oenology

At the beginning of the 19th century, oenology was considered to be the art of making wine. Although something of this idea has been retained, oenology has since acquired the status of a science, one that covers the preparation and storage of wine and the raw materials from which it is made, as well as vinification itself.

It is very difficult to say when wine first came into being, although we know it was over 6,000 years ago because a wine press dating back to that time has been discovered near Damascus. However, it is easy to say when oenology was born. It dates back to the work of Pasteur.

Louis Pasteur (1822–1895) dedicated several years of his scientific work to the study of wine. He discovered the role of yeasts and bacteria, and also the secondary products of fermentation. His fundamental work in this area, entitled *Études sur le vin, ses maladies, causes qui les provoquent, procédés nouveaux pour le conserver et pour le vieillir (A Study of Wine, Diseases of Wine and their Causes and New Procedures for Keeping and Maturing Wine)*, provides ample proof that Pasteur was the creator of scientific oenology.

Since the time of the Second Empire in France (1852–1870), oenology has developed progressively, thanks to research carried out in various university and agricultural laboratories established in wine-growing areas, as well as to the creation of Stations Oenologiques (Oenological Research Centres), Instituts Techniques du Vin (Technical Institutes for the Study of Wine), Centres Interprofessionnels (Wine Profession Study Centres) and various other professional establishments.

At first, scientific oenology applied itself to providing a knowledge of wine by means of analysis, and to theoretical and practical problems concerning the vinification and conservation of wines. But it soon came up against the problem of the mediocrity of many grape varieties and wines, and a lack of knowledge on the part of those responsible for transforming grapes into wine. It is in these areas that recent developments have been concentrated.

It is an indisputable fact that the quality of a grape, the basic ingredient of wine, depends upon there being a good balance between its acids and its sugars. This balance is created by climatic factors such as temperature, rainfall and amount of sunshine, and by other aspects of the ripening process.

So far, progress in this field has been made on the basis of deciding the correct degree of ripeness in relation to the wine in question — red, white or rosé — and a judicious choice of grape variety. This should lead to raw materials of excellent quality being obtained.

The second stage of wine making, i.e. the transformation of the grapes into wine, has benefited greatly from oenological expertise and from progress made in the techniques and materials used in vinification. In order to be able to carry out vinification of red, white or rosé wine in the best possible manner, a wine technician must be able to apply both theoretical and practical knowledge, being able, for example, to control temperatures satisfactorily during fermentation.

No wine, however grand or humble, is consumed in its crude state. First, it is subjected to physico-chemical and physical treatments, most of which are aimed at giving it perfect stability.

Sensory analysis is one of the principal means by which oenologists check the quality of wines, and it is therefore an important element in oenological training.

THE WORK OF THE OENOLOGIST

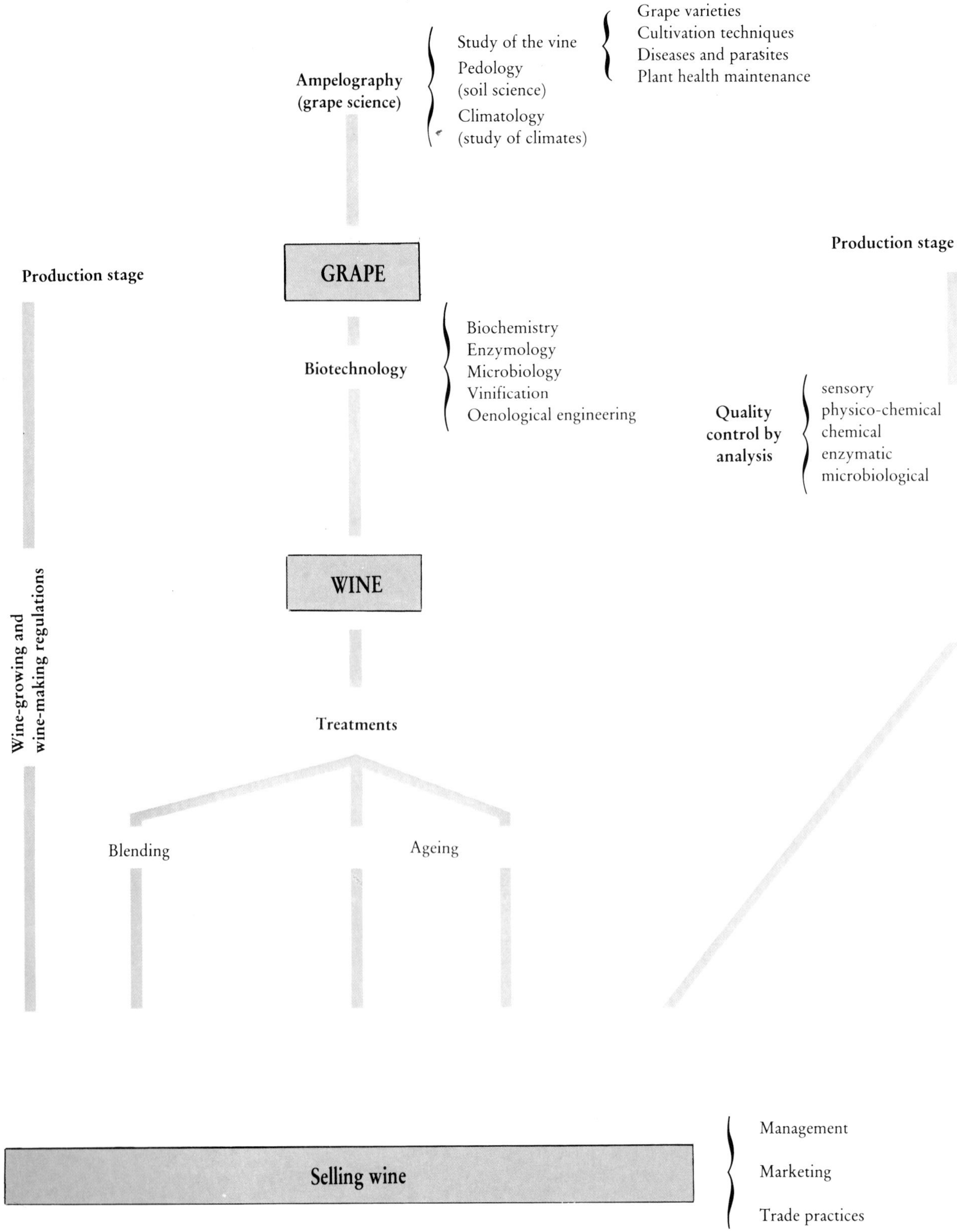

Following these treatments, the trade has been prompted by circumstances to blend wines, in order to be able to offer the consumer a very wide range of products. Until recent years, the quality of these wines was all too often founded simply on alcohol content, which is only one of the several hundred constituents of wine. As most wine is not consumed on the spot, it has then to undergo transportation before reaching the consumer's table, and it must not lose any of its intrinsic qualities in the process.

In order to achieve this, the notion of quality has to be adhered to at every stage of production, and this should be supported by systematic sensory analysis as well as by chemical, physico-chemical and microbiological tests.

Finally, implicitly or explicitly, consciously or subconsciously, the consumer relates his appreciation of quality in wine to the price paid. What he is really trying to do is work out whether the wine is good value for money, and this consideration has now become vital to the competitiveness of any wine-making concern.

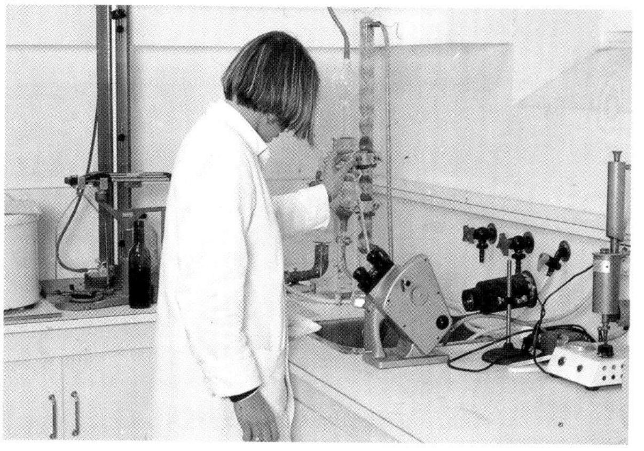

The oenologist studies the composition of wine by means of physical, chemical and microbiological analyses.

The oenologist

A winery, whether cooperative or private, must have someone in charge who has a thorough knowledge of every stage of wine making, from vine growing to marketing. This is the role of the oenologist, whose title and functions were laid down by French law on 9 March 1955.

Wine making is not the oenologist's only task. He or she is concerned with all the products of the vine, for example, grape juice, musts, brandies and even secondary products such as tartar, grape seeds and anthocyanic dyes.

From the time of Pasteur until 1955, there were often numerous wine technicians, agronomic engineers, chemical engineers, pharmacists and *maîtres de chais* responsible for various stages of production, but there was little or no contact between them.

The decree of 1955 marked the beginning of a new profession, which was then built up within the Union Française des Oenologues (French Union of Oenologists), a body that enables oenologists to promote their profession, further their knowledge and help newly qualified members to establish themselves. Consequently, for 30 years now, oenologists have been carrying out their duties in a wide range of posts, as managers of private cellars or cooperatives, of blending and bottling plants, of state-owned or private laboratories, and for firms that make and sell wines and spirits. They also act as technical and commercial agents for oenological materials and products, agents for professional and administrative bodies, researchers and teachers. This wide range of activities gives a good idea of the place of the oenologist in the world of wine.

The profession has now gone beyond the borders of France and is practised in all wine-growing countries. The majority of oenologists belong to the Office International de la Vigne et du Vin (OIV). In 1976, in Ljubljana, this body adopted an international definition of the title and function of the oenologist, and approved a training programme.

The Office International de la Vigne et du Vin

One of the OIV's 1976 resolutions is that the oenologist must exercise full responsibility in the preparation of wine, grape juice and grape derivatives, and must ensure that they are properly stored until the moment of consumption. In order to achieve this the oenologist should carry out numerous physical, chemical, microbiological and sensory tests and check that current procedures for the growing and making of wine are applied. He or she should also help to promote knowledge of wine among consumers.

In addition to these basic functions, the oenologist will be called upon to collaborate in the setting up and cultivation of vineyards, and in the design of technical equipment. He or she may also be asked to carry out research in various oenological fields.

The training of the oenologist

In order to be able to fulfil all these aims, an oenologist must have a comprehensive scientific training in the different disciplines touching wine studies, i.e. botany, physics, chemistry, biology and biochemistry.

At first, in France, it only took two years' study to obtain an oenologist's diploma, but because of considerable developments in basic and applied sciences, the introduction of the computer and the need to educate the oenologist in management and marketing techniques, the period of study was lengthened in 1982 to two years' general training and two years' specialized oenological training. Those in charge of the French oenological centres, which are situated in Bordeaux, Dijon, Montpellier, Toulouse and Reims, have established a new programme of disciplines that the trainee oenologist will have to master in order to be able to carry out all the tasks expected of him or her. To round off oenological studies, students must also acquire an extensive knowledge of connected subjects such as packaging, bottling, labelling, storage and transport, although none of these 'fringe' areas is shown on the table opposite.

A viti- and vinicultural jack of all trades, the oenologist most understand every aspect of vineyard functioning and wine-making practice. He or she places this knowledge at the disposal of the consumer, and of wine itself.

M

Macabeu

Synonyms: *Maccabeu*, *Maccabéo*, *Malvoisie* in Aude, *Perpignan* at Beaucaire, *Lardot* in Drôme.

Growing tips open and crook shaped, felty white with carmine margins.

Young leaves downy and yellowish, markedly bullate, with underside felty and pink.

Leaves large, soft, contorted, orbicular, deeply five-lobed with sinuses acute at base and sometimes with a single tooth at the base of the sinus; petiolar sinus lyrate with the edges more or less overlapping; dentation medium sized, convex; underside of blade downy-pubescent, yellowing in late autumn.

Bunches very large, pyramidal, many branched, often winged, loose; grapes spherical, medium sized, golden yellow, juicy; ripening period: third epoch.

This is a very vigorous vine, of erect habit, with shoots that are easily torn off the plant by the wind. It has late budbreak. The Macabeu is a sensitive vine: it cannot withstand too dry a soil, and yet it is subject to rot if planted in the fertile soil of the plains. Therefore it must be very carefully sited and requires a dry autumn if the grapes are to ripen healthily. It produces a large crop of grapes and gives a fine, fruity, straw-yellow wine with a high alcohol content and low acidity.

In France, it is mainly grown in Banyuls, Maury and Rivesaltes, and used for the production of AOC fortified sweet wines. It is also used for the white wines of the Côtes du Roussillon. It is sometimes vinified by itself to make sparkling wines, which are a little less fine than those made from the Mauzac.

Eight registered clones have been approved: numbers 630 to 633, 706, and 735 to 737. The Macabeu is classed as 'recommended' in all Mediterranean areas. Its cultivation is increasing. It occupies 7,075ha, 6,200ha in the eastern Pyrenees, 680ha in Aude and a few plantings in Hérault, Gard, Bouches-du-Rhône and Var.

Mâcon Blanc

Following the decree of 31 July 1937, wines produced within the *arrondissement* of Mâcon (*see* Mâcon Rouge and Rosé) have the right to be classed AOC under the names of Mâcon or Pinot-Chardonnay-Mâcon. The wines are chiefly made from the Chardonnay and Pinot Blanc grape varieties, and are supple and fruity. They should be drunk young.

Mâconnais *See* the following page for the Mâcon regional entry.

Traditional wine grower's house in the Mâconnais.

Mâcon Rouge and Rosé

This *appellation d'origine contrôlée*, governed by the decree of 31 July 1937, covers a vast area almost 50 km long, situated between Sennecey-le-Grand and Romanèche-Thorins. It includes the communes of Boyer, Bresses-sur-Grosne, Champagny-sous-Uxelles, Champlieu, Trigny, Jugy, Laives, Mancey, Montceaux-Ragny, Nanton, Sennecey-le-Grand and Vers, all west or northwest of Tournus.

Wines produced within the area of the *appellation d'origine* must have an alcohol content of at least 9°. The maximum yield is 50hl/ha.

These red and rosé wines, made from the Gamay Noir à Jus Blanc, Pinot Noir and Pinot Gris, vary greatly in character because they are grown over such a vast area. It is generally agreed, however, that at their best (when the village name may be included in the *appellation*, with a 45hl/ha yield and 10° alcohol), the red wines have an attractive firmness. They gain by being drunk young.

Both red and rosé Mâcon, and white Mâcon-Villages, may — if they have been produced in a single, approved commune — be followed by the name of their commune of origin.

Mâcon Supérieur

Ratified by the decree of 31 July 1937, the *appellation* Mâcon Supérieur is basically the same as that of Mâcon Blanc, Rouge and Rosé, except that the minimum alcohol content is fixed at 11° (instead of 10°) for white wines, and 10° (instead of 9°) for the red wines; the base yield is 45hl/ha instead of 50hl/ha. The wines of this *appellation* are light, fresh and straightforward. They have all the advantages of AOC Mâcon wines, but with greater refinement.

The white wines are full of rustic charm, while the reds and rosés are brisk, full bodied and have a pronounced fruitiness.

Wines of the Mâcon Supérieur appellation *may be white, red or rosé.*

THE MÂCON REGION

The Mâcon region is a transition zone, gently opening the door that links northern France with the Midi. It once marked the border between the langue d'oïl *region (to the north) and the* langue d'oc *region (to the south). There is a chain of hills running across the landscape, and two of the villages sited in them have given their names to illustrious grape varieties: Chasselas and Chardonnay.*

The wine-growing area around Chasselas overlooks the Saône valley. This village produces white wines with a floral or fruity bouquet, generally sold under the appellations *Mâcon or Mâcon-Villages.*

About 50km long and 15km wide, the wine-growing region of the Mâconnais culminates at Pouilly-Fuissé, at the foot of the rock of Solutré, a spot famed for its prehistoric past. Early hunters drove animals off it, and many of their bones have been found beneath the rock.

History of the Mâconnais

Founded in 910, the abbey at Cluny expanded considerably throughout the Christian world, and soon found itself at the head of 1,200 monasteries or priories. A proverb in Burgundy ran: '*Partout ou le vent vente, l'abbé de Cluny prend ses rentes*' ('Wherever the wind blows, the abbot of Cluny takes his tithes'). This abbey played an important part in the development of wine in the Mâconnais during the 11th and 12th centuries.

History has also preserved the memory of Claude Brosse, a wine grower of Charnay-lès-Mâcon and Chasselas, who loaded his casks on to an oxcart in about 1660, and trundled it all the way to the court at Versailles, so 'launching' Mâconnais wines in the capital.

Soils and grape varieties

The wine-growing soils of the Mâcon region form two belts west of the Saône, one lying in the northeast of the region, and the other in the southwest. Bordering them to the south is the granite of Beaujolais. Moving from west to east across the Mâconnais, Triassic period sandstones, limestone from the upper and middle Jurassic period and Oxfordian-stage marls (upper Jurassic) succeed each other.

The Mâconnais has a varied selection of grape varieties (Chardonnay, Pinot Noir and Gamay), so that it is possible to select a variety in accordance with the nature of the *terroir*. Chardonnay, for instance, is the most suitable vine for the dun-coloured, calcic soils of Pouilly-Fuissé. There it gives wines with a remarkable bouquet and excellent keeping qualities. The more acid, siliceous and sandy soils give *vins primeurs*, such as red and white Mâcon, and Bourgogne Grand Ordinaire. The 'active lime' level of the different soils in the Mâconnais varies greatly, but in most of the terrains that give good and very good quality white wines it is between 6 per cent and 11 per cent.

Statue of grape harvesters, Place de la Barre, Mâcon.

The climate

The wine-growing areas of Mâcon are subject to both Atlantic and continental influences. These influences are tempered, however, by quite long spells of frost in the north of the region, and by Mediterranean influences in the south. The Mâconnais receives plenty of sunshine, a factor that contributes to the quality of its wine.

The total rainfall between April and October for two different years — 1980, which was considered a mediocre vintage, and 1983, an exceptionally good one — was 475mm in 1980 and 627mm in 1983. On the face of it, this seems perplexing and contradictory, but it can be explained by looking at the distribution of rainfall. In 1983, April and May were the wettest months. August was also wetter than normal, but September was very dry, which meant that any tendency to rot was halted abruptly, and the fruit was harvested in an excellent state of maturity.

In temperature terms, there are considerable differences between the two years we have taken as our example. Using the system of seasonal heat summation (*see* page 48), the 1980 total was 1,110°C, with only five days in June, July and August when the temperature reached 30°C. In 1983, however, the summation figure was 1,425°C, with 26 days at 30°C during the same period. Finally, there were 1,250 hours of sunshine in 1980, as opposed to 1,331 hours in 1983.

Detail of the façade of the Palais Jacques Amboise, in Cluny.

The *appellations*

The *appellations* of the Mâcon region are divided into two types: AOC *'sous régionales'* (subregional AOCs, the main region being Burgundy) and AOC *communales.*

AOC *'sous régionales'*

The wines of these *appellations* (Mâcon Blanc, Rouge, Rosé and Supérieur) are produced on about 4,500ha of land, planted at 67 per cent Chardonnay, 25 per cent Gamay and 8 per cent Pinot Noir. They account for 45 per cent of Saône-et-Loire's total production.

White Mâcon wines have a refined bouquet. The floral aromas of the Chardonnay grape variety emerge to the maximum here (local wines acquiring such aromas are said to *'chardonner'*: to 'chardonnize'). These are *vins de primeur*, for drinking young.

The Gamay give pleasantly coloured, full-bodied, fruity red wines. These are, though, different from the red wines that come from the granite soil in the heart of Beaujolais, and less true to type.

AOC *communales*

The wines of these *appellations* (Mâcon-Villages, Mâcon-Villages + village name, Mâcon + village name, Pouilly-Fuissé, -Loché and -Vinzelles, and Saint-Véran) possess marked and intense Chardonnay characteristics; they have nutty and toasted almond flavours not found in other Mâconnais *appellations.* They are golden green in colour and have good keeping qualities.

The finest wine of the Mâcon region is Pouilly-Fuissé, in which the Chardonnay grape variety finds its greatest range of local expression.

Mâcon-Villages

It is an undisputed fact that the wines of Mâcon find their best expression within this *appellation d'origine contrôlée*, ratified by decree on 31 July 1937, and covering 43 communes (which may be named if the wine comes from a single commune). Made from at least 80 per cent Chardonnay with up to 20 per cent Pinot Blanc, these exclusively white wines vary according to the exact composition of the soils they are grown in, which can include chalk and slate, limestone and slate and oolitic limestone. The minimum alcohol content is 11°, and base yield is fixed at 45hl/ha. The Mâcon-Villages *appellation* produces fresh, graceful, charming wines, with clean, fruit-acid and vanilla aromas, sometimes recalling hot brioche. They are excellent value for money.

Madiran

The wine-growing area of Madiran was owned successively by François I, and Charles d'Alençon and his wife Marguerite d'Angoulême, figures who contributed greatly to the fame of these 'lordly wines, powerful, richly flavoured, purple in colour, which age most happily!'

Rarely has a *terroir* been so coveted. The inhabitants of Gers claim it is Gascon, those of the Hautes-Pyrénées describe it as Bigourdan, those of the Landes wish to annexe it for themselves, while even Burgundians make a claim to its paternity. It is nothing but Béarnais though, since of the 310 wine growers producing *appellation* wines, 205 are situated in Pyrénées-Atlantiques.

The creation of the Crouseilles-Madiran cooperative in 1950 marked the beginnings of a spectacular revival within this wine-growing district, for the vineyards had rather fallen into disuse over the course of the centuries.

The vines flourish today on natural terraces facing directly south towards the Pyrenees. The soils are glacial in origin, and very varied. In those areas best suited to wine growing, clay, clay-silica and clay-limestone mixtures predominate. The infertile, gravelly soil of the ridges near Crouseilles also produce quality wines.

The Madiran *appellation d'origine contrôlée*, which was ratified by decree on 28 August 1975, is applicable to red wines produced in the same zone as for Pacherenc du Vic-Bilh, in the north-east of Pyrénées-Atlantiques. These vineyards cover 1,300ha and 28 communes, 6 of which share a border with the Bigorre area of Hautes-Pyrénées, and 3 with Gers.

These wines are a deep purple in colour, and are characterized by their weight in the mouth and by their harmonious blend of aromas. The strongest primary aroma is that of berries and red fruits. Next comes a toasty odour, an odour of wheat, and finally a bouquet of spices and cinnamon.

The best years here are those when there is very plentiful sunshine, enabling the Tannat grape to achieve its full potential ripeness. The bouquet is developed chiefly from the fourth year onwards. If drunk young, Madiran is astonishingly balanced, muscular, frank and vigorous. But it is also very suitable for ageing. The area under vines has increased considerably in the last 35 years, and production has risen from 1,380hl in 1950 to 54,000hl in 1986.

The Paradis area in Madiran, one of the best sites for the Tannat grape.

Malbec *See* Côt.

Malpé

Synonyms: *Malpied Fin* and *Barrat* in Lot, *Plant Fort* in Averyron.

Bunches large, conical, winged, narrow at base; grapes medium sized, ovoid, blue-black, juicy; ripening period: second epoch.

This grape variety was once very widespread throughout the *arrondissement* of Figeac (Lot), where it produced a quality wine. It was also to be found in the areas of Brétenoux (Lot) and Beaulieu (Corréze). There was also a more vigorous and productive version of the Malpé, known as the Peldur, but the wine it produced was of lower quality. The Malpé has not been classified.

The bunches of the Barras are very similar to those of the Malpé, but this Tarn variety differs in that its growing tips are downy, its young leaves reddish, and its leaf blade is more deeply lobed.

Mancin

Synonyms: *Maussein*, *Coulant* in Médoc, *Tarnay-Coulant* at Macau, *Coulon-Tilbré*, *Petit Fou* in the Libourne area, *Pousse-Debout* in the area around Saint-André-de-Cubzac, *Mourtau* or *Mourtaou* at Caudrot.

Bunches medium sized, cylindrical, narrow, loose; grapes small, spherical or slightly ovoid, black; ripening period: second epoch, late.

This is an old, productive Bordeaux vine. It is grown in the marshlands of Médoc and Libourne. It gives a full-bodied, highly coloured, astringent wine with a very distinctive flavour, chiefly used in blending. The grapes do not rot.

The vine is classed as 'recommended' in Corrèze and 'authorized' in Gironde, and is planted on about 15ha.

Mansenc Noir

Synonyms: *Manseng Noir*, *Petit Mansenc*, *Gros Mansenc*, *Arrouya* in parts of Jurançon, *Mancep* at Brétenoux (Lot).

Bunches cylindrical, small to medium sized, compact; grapes spherical, small, black; ripening period: third epoch, late.

This is a productive vine originally from the Pyrenees. It is pruned long, and gives a highly coloured, astringent wine that needs to be aged before it becomes palatable.

It is classed as 'recommended' in Gers, Hautes-Pyrénées and Pyrénées-Atlantiques, and it plays a part in the Béarn AOC, where it is grown on about 790ha.

Mansonnet

Synonym: *Gros Ribier*. A black grape with spherical berries, cultivated to a small extent in Ardèche. Not classified.

Maréchal-Foch

This vine is also known as 188-2 Kuhlmann, and is a product of the same hybridization as the Léon-Millot.

Bunches small, cylindrical, winged, loose; grapes small, spherical, blue-black; ripening period: first epoch, early.

A very vigorous vine, it needs to be pruned long in most soils in order to produce an acceptable yield of 500g to 2kg per stock. Because the grapes ripen early, they are rich in sugars when the vines are favourably situated.

The wine produced is violet in colour and has a stalky flavour. Its quality is inferior to that of the Léon-Millot. The Maréchal-Foch is quite resistant to disease.

It has been classed as 'authorized' in Burgundy and Central France, but it is little grown and is found on only 27ha.

Grape picking at Château Margaux, one of the five Premiers Crus Classés of the Médoc.

Margaux

Created by decree on 10 August 1954, the *appellation d'origine contrôlée* of Margaux is reserved for red wines made from grapes picked in delimited areas of the communes of Margaux, Cantenac, Soussans, Arsac and Labarde.

The grape varieties are the same as those specified for the Médoc regional *appellation*. The number of stocks per hectare must be between 6,500 and 10,000, and there are regulations governing pruning.

Hybrid vines have been forbidden since 1959 on estates wishing to use the *appellation* Margaux. The must should contain at least 162g of sugar per litre and the alcohol content of the wine should be at least 10° and no more than 13°. The base yield has been fixed at 45hl/ha. Since 1955, these wines may not be marketed without a certificate of quality issued by a tasting panel. In 1985, the total area under vines was 1,001ha and the amount of wine produced was 53,375hl.

The Margaux *appellation* boasts 21 of Médoc's 60 Crus Classés, including the prestigious first-growth Château Margaux; and no less than 35 Crus Bourgeois. There is no cooperative involved in making Margaux.

The wines of Margaux enjoy a worldwide reputation. They are very rich, and need several years to reach their peak, at which they remain for a very long time.

THE CRUS CLASSÉS OF MARGAUX

Premier Cru
Château Margaux

Deuxièmes Crus
Château Brane-Cantenac
Château Durfort-Vivens
Château Lascombes
Château Rausan-Ségla
Château Rauzan-Gassies

Troisièmes Crus
Château Boyd-Cantenac
Château Cantenac-Brown
Château Desmirail
Château Ferrière
Château Giscours
Château d'Issan
Château Kirwan
Château Malescot-Saint-Exupéry
Château Marquis-d'Alesme-Becker
Château Palmer

Quatrièmes Crus
Château Marquis-de-Terme
Château Pouget
Château Prieuré-Lichine

Cinquièmes Crus
Château Dauzac
Château du Tertre

Marsannay

Following the decree of 19 May 1987, the *appellations* Bourgogne-Marsannay-la-Côte and Bourgogne Rosé de Marsannay were replaced by the *appellation communale* or 'village' *appellation* of Marsannay. This AOC is applicable to red, rosé and white wines of the 1987 and subsequent harvests, as well as to earlier harvests meeting the approval of a tasting panel. Maximum yield is 40hl/ha for red wines, and 45hl/ha for white and rosé wines, with a minimum alcoholic strength of 10.5° for red and rosé wines and 11° for white wines.

The *appellation* zone includes parcels from the three communes of Marsannay-la-Côte, Couchey and Chenôve. Red and white wines are produced in increasing quantities, whereas the rosé wines that have been traditionally produced in Marsannay are decreasing in importance: annual production is around 9,000hl of red wine, 3,000hl of rosé wine and 1,000hl of white wine. The red wines of Marsannay are appreciated for their balance and their typicality, while the whites may readily be compared to a number of Côte de Beaune counterparts.

Marsanne

Synonyms: *Grosse Roussette* in Savoy, *Rousette de Saint-Péray*, *Roussanne*, erroneously, in Saint-Péray, *Avilleran* in Isère, *Metternich* in Barsac.

Bunches medium to large, conical, winged, not very compact; grapes small to medium sized, spherical, golden white, juicy; ripening period: second epoch, late.

The Marsanne is a vigorous vine, with late budbreak; it is pruned short, and yields abundantly. At one time, it grew together with the Roussanne in the vineyards of the Rhône valley, and although not equal to the Roussanne in terms of quality, in the end it took over the vineyards completely because of its greater productivity. The wine it gives is lighter than that of the Roussanne, less refined and with a less pronounced bouquet. It has low acid levels, and ages quickly.

***The arid wine-growing district of Maury, where the Grenache yields a powerful, virile* vin doux naturel.**

One registered clone has been approved: number 574. The Marsanne has been classed as 'recommended' in all *départements* bordering the Rhône, and as far south as Languedoc and Provence. It is used in a number of AOCs.

Maury

The Maury wine district lies on schistous soils, and covers the communes of Lequerde, Maury, Rasiguères, Saint-Paul-de-Fenouillet and Tautavel. Classed as a *vin doux naturel* (sweet fortified wine) AOC by the decree of 19 May 1972, it produces about 50,000hl per year. Plantings have to be at least 50 per cent Grenache. Although not obligatory, maceration is traditional. About a third of production is fortified

Leaf of the Mauzac variety, classed as 'recommended' in the Mediterranean areas of the Midi and in the South West.

sur grains (on the marc, after the wine has been run off). This practice is most common when the Carignan grape variety is used, and it is to this variety that the wines of Maury owe their virility. The ageing process takes two years. The wines are powerful yet well-bred, with complex and varied aromas of cooked fruits and cocoa, and sometimes with hints of venison.

Maury Rancio

The sweet fortified wines of Maury may have 'Rancio' added to their name if they have acquired this very particular flavour during the ageing process.

Mauzac

Synonyms: *Moissac, Moisac, Moysac, Mozac, Meauzac, Mauza, Maousac, Manzac, Blanquette, Blanquette de Limoux, Blanquette Sucrée, Blanquette Aventice* (i.e. early), *Feuille Ronde, Primard, Bekin, Bécquin.*

Leaves small, truncate, thick, bullate, dark green with a bluish tinge, contorted, without lobes or weakly three-lobed with the central lobe wide and elongated; petiolar sinus closed or with overlapping edges; dentation convex, wide; underside of blade downy in tufts.

Green shoots ribbed, pale green and bloomy; tendrils green, rather slender.

Bunches medium sized, conical, compact, often winged, with lignified peduncles; grapes medium sized, spherical, golden yellow, thick skinned, hard, with large, thick pips; ripening period: second epoch, late.

This vine has late budbreak. Although not susceptible to oidium (powdery mildew) and downy mildew, it is prone to grey rot (botrytis). It is of average vigour, and is normally pruned *en gobelet* (as a small, free-standing bush). Yields vary from 25-40hl/ha on the slopes to over 100hl/ha on the plain. In Limoux and Gaillac the variety used to be harvested late, in order to obtain the high sugar content required for sparkling wines made by the *méthode traditionnelle*. Today, however, the champagne method is preferred for sparkling wine manufacture in these areas, so the grapes are gathered early to ensure a higher acid content in the musts, as this means the wine is better able to retain its sparkle.

Five registered clones have been approved: numbers 575 and 738 to 741. Mauzac has been classed as 'recommended' in the Mediterranean areas of the Midi and in the South West. Its cultivation is now in decline: it only covered 6,422ha in 1985 as opposed to 8,512ha in 1958. It is mainly grown in Tarn (4,177ha), for the Gaillac AOC, and in Aude (675ha), for the Blanquette de Limoux AOC. It is used as a secondary grape variety in the AOCs of Entre-Deux-Mers, Sainte-Foy-Bordeaux, and Côtes de Duras, and for the VDQS wines of Vins de Lavilledieu (Tarn-et-Garonne), and Vins d'Estaing and Vins d'Entraygues et du Fel in Aveyron.

Mayorquin Blanc

Synonyms: *Mayorcain, Majorquen, Mayorquen Blanc, Plant de Marseille, Plant de Languedoc, Pansal de Majorque, Bormenc, Damas Blanc, Espagnol* in Bellet.

Leaves large, soft, orbicular, thick, smooth, with convex edges; usually five-lobed with lateral sinuses narrow, acute at base, petiolar sinus lyrate; dentation convex, medium sized; underside of blade downy in tufts.

Bunches very big, cylindrical-conical, winged, many branched, compact; grapes large, spherical, pale yellow, juicy; ripening period: third epoch.

This vine is probably Spanish in origin. It has become very widespread throughout North Africa, where it has many synonyms, largely because the fruit can be eaten as table grapes and even used to make sultanas, as well as vinified. It was once used to make the famous white wines of Mascara (a wine-growing district near Algiers). It is a vigorous plant, although sometimes subject to *coulure* (flower abortion) when grown on plains, and always to grey rot (botrytis). It is classed as 'recommended' in Alpes-Maritimes.

Mazis-Chambertin

This Grand Cru *climat*, a neighbour of the celebrated Clos de Bèze, is situated to the south of

Gevrey-Chamberin on the Côte de Nuits, where it covers 12.5ha. The *appellation d'origine contrôlée* was ratified by decree on 31 July 1937. The minimum alcohol content was set at 11.5° and the maximum yield at 32hl/ha. The vineyards, which are planted entirely with Pinot Noir, are divided between Mazis-Bas and Mazis-Haut, and each produces an average of 200hl of wine annually.

This well-balanced, delicate wine is considered to be lighter and more finely structured than its two glorious neighbours: Latricières-Chambertin and Clos de Bèze.

Mazoyères-Chambertin

This Grand Cru AOC, found on the Côte de Nuits, is governed by the decree of 31 July 1937. It is little seen because its wines can also be sold as Charmes-Chambertin, and this name is generally preferred by growers.

Médoc and Haut-Médoc

Médoc is a roughly triangular region in the northwest of Bordeaux, lying between the Atlantic to the west and Gironde to the east.

The wine-growing area stretches along the Gironde estuary for about 80km, and is generally around 10km wide. Pine forests shelter it from the Atlantic.

The area is divided into two regional *appellations d'origine contrôlee*, Médoc and Haut-Médoc, and includes, from south to north, six communal *appellations*: Margaux, Listrac, Moulis, Saint-Julien, Pauillac and Saint-Estèphe. To be entitled to either of the Médoc *appellations*, wines must be made from the following grape varieties: Cabernet Sauvignon, Cabernet Franc, Merlot, Carmenère, Petit Verdot and Côt.

The minimum sugar content of the must should be 162g per litre, and the wines must have an alcohol content of at least 9.5° but not more than 13°.

The Médoc and Haut-Médoc *appellations* were created by decree on 14 November 1936. In 1985, the Médoc *appellation*, which stretches from Saint-Seurin-de-Cadourne northwards to Saint-Vivien-de-Médoc, covered an area of 3,074ha, and produced 208,725hl of wine. Of this, 79,853hl was vinified by five cooperatives: those of Bégadan, Ordonnac, Prignac-en-Médoc, Queyrac and Saint-Yzans-de-Médoc.

The Haut-Médoc *appellation*, which covers an area of 3,174ha, is spread out over 16 communes, stretching from Blanquefort outside Bordeaux northwards to Saint-Seurin-de-Cadourne. The total amount of wine produced in 1985 was 172,376hl, of which 20,138hl was made by the cooperatives of Arcins, Cissac-Médoc, Saint-Sauveur, Saint-Seurin-de-Cadourne and Vertheuil.

Since 1955, these wines have been marketed only after they have received a certificate of quality from a tasting panel.

The red wines of these two *appellations* have a very long life, and develop a powerful and refined bouquet over the years, thanks to their Cabernet Sauvignon content. Wines with the Médoc *appellation* are generally of lesser quality than those from Haut-Médoc.

A small amount of white wine is produced in both areas, and is sold under the AOC Bordeaux. The most famous of these white wines is undoubtedly the Pavillon Blanc produced at Château Margaux.

Château Latour, a Premier Cru Classé sited in Pauillac in the Haut-Médoc, on the left bank of the Gironde.

Melon

Synonyms: *Melon de Bourgogne*, *Muscadet* in the Nantes area, *Gamay Blanc à Feuilles Rondes*, *Petite Bourgogne*, *Bourgignon Blanche* in Anjou, *Grosse Sainte-Marie*, *Perry* in Savoy, *Pourrisseux* in the Saône valley, *Pétouin* or *Pétoin* in Loiret, *Biaune* or *Petite Biaune* at la Châtre in Indre, *Blanc de Nantes* in Gironde, *Lyonnaise Blanche* in Allier, *Gros Auxerrois Blanc* in Moselle.

Growing tips felty white with carmine margins.

Leaves orbicular, bullate with convex edges giving them a characteristic appearance; without lobes, petiolar sinus lyrate; dentation pointed, medium sized; underside of blade arachnoid in tufts.

Green shoots ribbed with longitudinal red

striations on the side exposed to the sun; tendrils small, thin.

Bunches medium sized, cylindrical, compact; grapes spherical, small, golden yellow, thick skinned; ripening period: first epoch.

The Melon is an old Burgundian grape variety. It is used there in small quantities only, in the making of the Mâcon Blanc and Crémant de Bourgogne AOC wines. It is used very extensively, on the other hand, in Loire-Atlantique, having suddenly increased in popularity in the Nantes region, under the name of Muscadet, after the terrible winter of 1709. It is an early budding vine and fairly vigorous, with an average production of 40 to 50hl/ha. The white wine

Bunch of Melon grapes. This variety is known as the Muscadet in the Nantes region, and gives a pleasant white often bottled sur lie, *for drinking young.*

it gives is pleasant and low in acidity. It is often bottled *sur lie*. The wine is left on its lees all winter, and is then bottled before 15 February of the year following the harvest. In this way, it acquires an extremely pale colour and a bouquet and suppleness that are much appreciated by enthusiasts, especially when drunk young.

Ten registered clones have been approved, the most useful being number 443. In France, this variety is grown on around 10,000ha, 9,700ha of which are in the AOC areas of Muscadet, Muscadet de Sèvre-et-Maine and Muscadet des Coteaux de la Loire; the rest is used to make AOC wines in Burgundy, or table wines.

Menetou-Salon

This wine-growing area, classified as an AOC on 23 January 1953, covers an area of 500ha. The grape variety used for white wine is the Sauvignon Blanc, and the Pinot Noir is used for red and rosé wines. The amount of wine produced is about 2,600hl of white 1,200hl of red and 200hl of rosé, and the production area covers the communes or parts of communes of Aubinges, Menetou-Salon, Morogues, Parassy, Pigny, Quantilly, Saint-Céols, Soulangis, Vignoux-sous-les-Aix and Humbligny.

The white wines are straw yellow and have a distinctive vegetal aroma. They are full and quite lively to taste. Most are best drunk young, though the finest examples will also age well. The red wines are rustic in style and light, sometimes cherry red in colour. The rosés are dry, fresh and easy to drink. (*See* Vins du Centre.)

Mercurey

The wines of the *appellation d'origine controlée* of Mercurey are produced on specific sites around Mercurey and Saint-Martin-sous-Montaigu in Saône-et-Loire. The 560ha of the *appellation* are sited on ferruginous clay and limestone soils. This is the largest wine-growing area of the Côte Chalonnaise; the AOC was created by the decree of 11 September 1936. The white wines, from the Chardonnay grape variety, have to have a minimum alcohol content of 11°. The red wines, made exclusively from the Pinot Noir, have a minimum of 10.5°

Mercurey on the Côte Chalonnaise produces fine, elegant red wines plus a very small amount of charming white wine.

alcohol. Maximum yield is 35hl/ha.

The Mercurey Premiers Crus must have a minimum 11° alcohol for red wines and 11.5° for whites. The white wines are delicate and distinguished, but since only 20hl is produced each year, they are little known. On the other hand, 20,000hl of rich, supple and tannic red wine is produced annually in Mercurey. These wines are characterized by aromas of blackcurrant, violet and raspberry, and keep well.

Mérille

Synonyms: *Grosse Mérille* in Lavilledieu (Tarn-et-Garonne), *Bordelais* or *Boudoulès* in Tarn, *Périgord*, *Plant de Bordeaux* in Dordogne, *Pica*,

Picard or *Picardie* in Premières Côtes de Bordeaux, *Piquat* in Corrèze, *Pouchou* or *Pouchon* at Périgueux, *Saint-Rabier* in Charente, *Plant de Gibert*.

Bunches long, conical, compact; grapes medium sized, slightly ovoid, blue-black, juicy; ripening period: third epoch.

This is a vigorous vine, but rather prone to disease. It produces a light *vin ordinaire* with no particular finesse. Three registered clones have been approved: numbers 444, 445 and 790. Classed as 'recommended' in most of the *départements* of the South West, and 'authorized' in Gers, Gironde, the two Charente *départements* and Landes, this variety is grown on 662ha, mainly in Tarn-et-Garonne, Lot, Tarn, Haute-Garonne and Gers.

Green shoot of the Merlot.

Merlot

Synonyms: *Merlot Noir*, *Merlau Rouge*, *Vitraille*, *Bigney Rouge*, *Crabutet Noir* or *Plant Médoc* around Bazas, *Alicante* at Podensac, *Sème dou Flube* (Plant du Fleuve) in the south of the Graves, *Sème de la Canau* at Portes, *Semilhoun Rouge* in Médoc.

Growing tips open, felty white with carmine margins.

Young leaves downy, white, five-lobed.

Leaves medium sized, cuneiform, dark green, bullate, grooved, crimped at the petiolar junction; deeply five-lobed, concave and sometimes dentate at the base of the sinuses; petiolar sinus U-shaped, more or less open; dentation pointed, narrow; underside of blade arachnoid in tufts. The foliage reddens partially in autumn.

Green shoots angular, reddish brown, mahogany or brown-green with longitudinal red striations; tendrils fleshy, medium sized.

Leaf of the Merlot.

Bunches medium sized, cylindrical, loose, sometimes winged; grapes spherical, small to medium, blue-black, with medium-thick skins and juicy pulp; ripening period: second epoch.

The Merlot is a vigorous vine from the Bordeaux region, where it existed but was little used before the phylloxera crisis. It has early budbreak and is therefore vulnerable to spring frosts; it also suffers greatly from hard winter frosts. In the Bordeaux area it is prone to *coulure* (flower abortion), which can reduce yields to only 20 or 30hl/ha. By contrast, in the Mediterranean area of the Midi, yields of about 80hl/ha are obtained, and even at this level of yield the wines can still be aromatically interesting. However, if the yield exceeds 100hl/ha, the quality deteriorates rapidly.

Merlot wines are supple, and they rapidly become drinkable after two to three years' ageing. When mixed with wine from the Cabernet Sauvignon, the Merlot lends suppleness to the blend, which explains why it is so fashionable at present. Although rarely attacked by oidium (powdery mildew), the Merlot is susceptible to downy mildew and grey rot (botrytis). Fifteen registered clones have been approved, and the most useful for Bordeaux purposes are numbers 181, 182, 342 and 343, all of which have a medium level of productivity. In the Midi, on the other hand, productive clones, such as numbers 348, 346 and 184, are preferred. The Merlot is, at present, the second most common vine in the nurseries — 22 million cuttings were grafted in 1986.

After the Pinot Noir, the Merlot is today's most fashionable black grape. The area devoted to it has increased from 17,000ha in 1985 to over 40,000ha today, making it the fifth most planted vine in France. It is mainly grown in the South West, the largest area being in Gironde (32,000ha) and the next largest in Dordogne (2,000ha), followed by Lot-et-Garonne and Lot. Its appearance in the Midi is more recent and on a smaller scale, the largest plantings so far being in Aude, followed by Hérault and Gard.

Merlot Blanc

Despite its name, this is not a white variety of the Merlot. It seems that a vineyard owner at Lalande-de-Fronsac called Guinaudie brought it back from a trip to the South West in 1891, and was responsible for spreading it under the name of Merlot Blanc.

Young leaves at tips of shoots downy, pale green-yellow, with felty undersides; young leaves at base of shoots glossy, pale green with downy undersides.

Leaves orbicular, dark green, coarsely bullate with concave lobes, deeply five-lobed with lateral sinuses of average size, acute at base; petiolar sinus lyrate and more or less closed; dentation convex, narrow; underside of blade arachnoid with pubescent veins.

Green shoots ribbed, pale green with a few longitudinal brown striations; tendrils long, fleshy and entangled at the base.

Bunches medium sized, cylindrical, compact; grapes spherical, medium sized, white, juicy; ripening period: second epoch, early.

The Merlot Blanc has early budbreak, and is therefore susceptible to spring frosts. In Bordeaux and the neighbouring *départements*, its use has increased greatly of late on account of its fertility. Its grapes are very sensitive to grey rot (botrytis) and, in sandy soils, it is subject to attack by eelworms, which diminish its vigour. The wines it produces are usually low in alcohol and of poor quality.

The Merlot Blanc is a secondary grape variety used in the white-wine vineyards of Gironde for the Bordeaux, Entre-Deux-Mers, Graves de Vayres, Sainte-Foy-Bordeaux, Blaye and Bourg AOCs. However, its cultivation is declining: present plantings cover 1,900ha, as opposed to 5,277ha in 1958. The bulk of it is grown in Gironde (1,776ha). It is classed as 'recommended' in Gironde, as well as in the two Charentes *départements*, Dordogne, Landes, Lot-et-Garonne and Tarn-et-Garonne.

Meslier Saint-François

Synonyms: *Gros Meslier*, *Meslier Blanc*, *Meslier d'Orléans*, *Meslier du Gâtinais*, *Blanc Ramé* in Charente; *François Blanc*, *Co* (vine) *de France* in l'Aube, *Pot de Vin* in Loiret.

Leaves orbicular, medium sized, coarsely bullate, contorted, five-lobed with deep, narrow lateral sinuses, acute at base; petiolar sinus lyrate, closed or overlapping at the edges, with pink petiolar junction; dentation convex, medium sized; underside of blade downy-pubescent.

Bunches medium to large, conical, quite compact; grapes ovoid, medium sized, white to golden yellow; ripening period: second epoch.

Originally from the Gâtinais area southeast of Paris, where this grape formed the basis of plantings, the Meslier Saint-François has now spread throughout the Loire valley, the Charentes districts and the South West, thanks to its productivity and relative resistance to black rot. It has very early budbreak, but its *contre-bourgeons* are usually fertile and will produce a small crop if the main buds have been nipped by spring frosts. It is highly susceptible to oidium (powdery mildew) and grey rot (botrytis).

This is an abundantly productive variety, and can easily yield over 100hl/ha. The wine it gives is a fresh, neutral *vin ordinaire*, sometimes with a high alcohol content. When distilled, it produces a fine brandy with a plentiful bouquet, which harmonizes well with those distilled from other varieties grown in the Charentes area.

This vine is classed as 'recommended' in Gers, Indre, Indre-et-Loire, Loir-et-Cher, Vienne and Haute-Vienne; and as 'authorized' in Charentes, Corrèze, Dordogne, Gironde, Deux-Sèvres, Loiret, Lot-et-Garonne, Hautes-Pyrénées and Pyrénées-Atlantiques. It is one of the grape varieties used in the Cognac and Armagnac AOCs. Its area of cultivation is decreasing: it has dropped to between 800ha and 600ha, compared with 2,300ha in 1958. It is mainly found today in Gers (178ha) and Loir-et-Cher.

Meunier

Synonyms: *Pinot Meunier*, *Gris Meunier* or *Auvernat Gris* in Loiret, *Blanche Feuille*, *Farineux*, *Morillon Taconé* in Marne, *Plant de Brie* in the Paris area, *Fernaise* in Lorraine, *Noirin Enfariné* in Doubs, *Frésillon* in Alsace.

Growing tips open, felty white.

Leaves medium sized, orbicular, finely bullate; deeply five-lobed with concave and sometimes dentate lateral sinuses; petiolar sinus lyrate, more or less closed; dentation convex, medium sized; underside of blade downy. The foliage reddens partially in autumn.

Green shoots ribbed, downy at the tip, mahogany red in sunlight; tendrils thin, medium sized.

Bunches small to medium sized, cylindrical-conical, compact; grapes small, spherical, blue-black, thick skinned, with soft, very juicy flesh; ripening period: first epoch.

The Meunier is of average vigour. It has late budbreak, and this is a valuable feature; in Champagne, for example, it can be grown on badly situated north-facing slopes and in chilly, frost-prone hollows. The average yield varies from 50 to 80hl/ha, but with reduced pruning, as much as 100hl/ha can be obtained. Its wine does not have much colour, and is less fine and lower in alcohol than that of the Pinot Noir. Consequently, in Champagne, its grapes fetch a lower price than do those of the Pinot Noir. It is susceptible to oidium (powdery mildew) and to grey rot (botrytis), but its frost resistance makes up for these weaknesses.

Two registered clones have been approved: numbers 458 and 791. The Meunier is classed as 'recommended' in Champagne, the Loire valley and Burgundy. Plantings of it are increasing, and it is now grown on more than 10,500ha. It is one of the specified grape varieties for the Champagne and Touraine AOCs, and for the Vins de l'Orléanais VDQS.

Bunch of Meunier grapes. Also known as the Pinot Meunier, this variety is popular in Champagne for its ability to withstand frosts.

The Château de Meursault. This Côte de Beaune village is famous for its dry white wines, which have delicate aromas of hazelnuts and wild mousseron *mushrooms.*

Meursault

In this prestigious Côte de Beaune commune, dry white burgundy, made from the Chardonnay and the Pinot Blanc grape varieties, finds its fullest expression. The 439ha of this *appellation d'origine contrôlée* is characterized by soil rich in ferruginous magnesian limestone. Legislation of 21 May 1970 set the base yield at 35hl/ha; minimum alcohol content at 10.5° for red wines and 11° for Premiers Crus, with 11° for white wines and 11.5° for Premiers Crus. These mainly white wines are dry, yet their richness conveys an impression of sweetness. Their colour is delightful: a limpid pale gold, sometimes tending towards green. The best of them have a delicate hazelnut flavour. Premier Crus of good vintages will keep for 20 years. An average 12,000hl of white wines are produced per year, compared with only 800hl of red. The latter may use the Volnay-Santenots *appellation* if they come from the Santenots vineyard. The red wines of Meursault are light and delicate, with an aroma of raspberries.

Milgranet

Synonym: *Petite Mérille* in Lavilledieu.

Bunches small to medium, conical, compact, with two shoulders; grapes spherical, medium sized, blue-black, not very juicy; ripening period: second epoch.

This vine has been classed as 'recommended' in the *départements* of Tarn-et-Garonne, Tarn and Haute-Garonne, where it is planted on less than 300ha for the Côtes du Frontonnais AOC and the Vins de Lavilledieu VDQS.

Minervois

This *appellation* was ratified as an AOC on 15 February 1985. It covers 61 communes, 45 of which are in Aude and 16 in Hérault. Minervois is situated north of Corbières, and the vineyard zone stretches from Narbonne to Carcassonne. It begins beneath the Montagne Noir, north of Carcassonne, and descends gradually southwards as far as Aude. The landscape is one of gentle hills and hillocks covered in holm oaks and Aleppo pines. Minervois takes its name from the village of Minerve, historically one of the most important places in Languedoc. The soils are composed of flat stretches of water-borne pebbles; rounded slopes and hill tops of sandy marls, and stony slopes at the foot of the Montagne Noir. The climate of the region is typically Mediterranean, but with subtle variations between the eastern and western sectors. The grape varieties grown there are typical of those in Languedoc, and it is traditional to use a smaller proportion of Carignan and a larger proportion of Cinsaut in Minervois than in Corbières. Specified white grape varieties include the Grenache Blanc, the Bourboulenc, the Macabeu, the Piquepoul Blanc, the Clairette and the Terret Blanc. A few well-made dry rosés and some dry white wines are produced here, but this is basically a land of red wines. These are softer than the red wines of Corbières. They are garnet red in colour, delicate and pleasant to drink with complex aromas reminiscent of redcurrants and raspberries, with a touch of spice. The AOC covers an area of 18,000ha and produces 200,000hl annually.

Molette

Synonyms: *Molette Blanche*, *Molette de Seyssel*.

Bunches large, cylindrical-conical, attached to the cane by a long peduncle, compact, often with two shoulders; grapes spherical, sometimes ovoid or oblate, greenish white, soft (hence the name Molette, derived from the French word *mou* or *mol*, meaning 'soft'); ripening period: second epoch, late.

The Molette is a highly productive vine, able to yield 60 to 80hl/ha, and even more than that in well-manured soil in the Seyssel area. It gives a rather ordinary wine, low in alcohol, with a stalky flavour and an unpleasant, slightly acrid aftertaste. Classed as 'recommended' in Ain and 'authorized' in Savoy, the Molette is one of the vines grown for the Vin de Savoie and Seyssel Mousseux AOCs and the Vin du Bugey VDQS. It is planted on about 40ha altogether.

Mollard

Synonyms: *Molar*, *Mollar Noir*, *Molard*, *Tallardier*, *Chaliant*, *Cholion*, *Plant de Veynes*, *Boissier* or *Beissier*.

Bunches medium sized, cylindrical-conical,

The village and vineyards of la Caunette in the Cathar country of Minervois, an area that produces hard, fruity red wines with a bouquet of wild berries and flowers.

quite compact; grapes spherical or slightly ovoid, medium sized, blue-black; ripening period: second epoch.

The Mollard has late budbreak. A vigorous, hardy vine, it is nevertheless susceptible to downy mildew. It gives a fresh, pleasantly garnet-coloured wine with an average alcohol content, capable of ageing for a number of years. Classed as 'recommended' in Hautes-Alpes, this vine is planted on about 90ha situated between Tallard and Embrun in the upper Durance valley.

Monbadon

Synonyms: *Frontignan* or *Frontignan des Charentes* in Charente, *Gros Montils* on the Île d'Oléron, *Castillonne* in Charente-Maritime, *Grand Blanc* and *Blanc de Cadillac* in Gironde, *Ugni* around Montpellier, *Aramon Blanc* (erroneously) in Var.

Leaves truncate, finely bullate with concave lobes; deeply five-lobed, sometimes seven-lobed with lateral sinuses wide, open, concave at base; petiolar sinus lyrate, narrow or with slightly overlapping edges; dentation convex, wide; underside of blade pubescent.

Bunches large, conical, compact, with a small shoulder; grapes medium sized, spherical, yellowish white, very juicy; ripening period: third epoch.

This is a highly productive vine grown in Charente, where it gives thin wines because of its late ripening. It is susceptible to diseases, particularly grey rot (botrytis). Although not classified, it is one of the grapes used in the Blaye AOC. Its cultivation is decreasing, and it is now grown on only 130ha, as opposed to 1,731ha in 1958.

Monbazillac

Monbazillac, classed as an AOC by the decree of 31 July 1937, occupies a choice place in the heart of the Bergerac region. The Monbazillac vineyards, which are dominated by the Château de Monbazillac, are situated in the south of Bergerac, on a north-facing slope. They cover 2,500ha spread over five communes: Monbazillac, Pomport, Saint-Laurent-des-Vignes, Colombier and Rouffignac-de-Sigoulès. The clay and limestone soils and the local autumn weather conditions — mist in the mornings and hot sun during the day — create a mesoclimate that greatly favours the overripening of grapes and the onset of *pourriture noble* (noble rot). The production of Monbazillac, like that of all the greatest white dessert wines, is governed by these climatic and soil conditions.

It is small, family units that are responsible for producing many of the wines of the area. The grapes are harvested late, the must is very delicate and vinification has to be carried out with great and watchful care.

Éraflage — stripping the grapes from the bunches — during harvesting means that the grapes can be macerated with their skins for a number of weeks, giving wines that are particularly rich in tannins. These white wines often undergo maturation and *élevage* in barrel, as do most fine red wines. Bottling is not carried out until at least 18 months after the harvest.

Annual production of Monbazillac is in the region of 50,000hl, and there is normally two years' worth of wine maturing in the cellars.

The Château de Monbazillac, a solid and elegant 16th-century building, houses a small wine museum.

The Château de Monbazillac cooperative is a dynamic force in the production of Monbazillac, vinifying between 25 and 30 per cent of the total AOC production.

Monbazillac may be drunk young, but it also gains by being aged. It can be kept for 15 years, or even longer in the case of the best vintages. Monbazillac is the *vin de garde par excellence* of Périgord and was praised very highly as long ago as 1850, by Victor Rendu, in a work entitled *Ampélographie française*.

Mondeuse

Synonyms: *Mouteuse*, *Mondouse*, *Mandouze*, *Molette Noire* in Savoie, *Persagne*, *Persaigne*, *Prossaigne* in Ain, *Savoyard*, *Savoyanche*, *Savoyange*, *Savoyanne*, *Savoyet* in Isère, *Maldoux*, *Maudoux* in Jura, *Grosse Syrah* in Drôme, *Vache* or *Pinot Vache* around Vichy, *Grand Chétuan*, *Gros Chétuan* in the Revermont area, *Salanaise* at Givors, *Persanne* around Lyon, *Tournerin* at Tour-du-Pin, *Gueyne* in Morestel, *Marsanne Ronde* in Saint-Marcellin, *Angélique* at Gy, *Gros Rouge du Pays* in Switzerland, *Grand Picot* or *Grand Picou*.

Bunches large, conical, elongated, quite compact; grapes small, spherical or slightly ovoid, blue-black, juicy; ripening period: second epoch.

The Mondeuse is one of the vines of Savoie. It may have been the 'vine of the Allobroges' referred to by Columella. It is a vigorous plant, usually pruned short and trained *en gobelet* (as a small, free-standing bush). The grapes, when ripened on a sunny slope and subject to yields of no more than 40 to 60hl/ha, give a deep-coloured, firm, chewy wine with a high alcohol content, one which ages well and has a perfume reminiscent of the Côt. When grown on alluvial plains, however, yields exceed 100hl/ha, and this results in a more ordinary wine, low in alcohol.

One registered clone has been approved: number 368. The Mondeuse is classed as 'recommended' in Savoie, Ain and Isère. It is among the vines planted for the Vin de Savoie AOC and the Vin du Bugey VDQS, and it occupies about 200ha.

Mondeuse Blanche

Synonyms: *Blanche*, *Blanchette*, *Donjin*, *Aigre Blanc*, *Jongin* in Savoie; *Couilleri* in Jura, *Dongine* in Ain.

Growing tips downy white with carmine margins.

Bunches medium sized, winged, cylindrical, compact; grapes spherical or slightly ovoid, medium sized, golden green, with a somewhat rough skin; ripening period: second epoch.

This grape, despite its name, is not the white version of the Mondeuse. It differs in that the growing tips are less hairy and the leaves rounder and more deeply lobed. It is a less productive vine, but it gives a quality wine that will keep well. Classed as 'recommended' in Savoie and Ain, and included in plantings for Vin de Savoie AOC and the Vin du Bugey VDQS, the Mondeuse Blanche is grown on about 21ha.

Monerac

A Grenache × Aramon cross, this vine was produced by INRA at Vassal, near Montpellier. It has early budbreak, while its ripening period is during the third epoch. Its productivity comes midway between that of the Grenache and the Carignan. Its wine is high in alcohol, but does not have much colour.

The Monerac has been classed as 'recommended' throughout France and it has one approved clone, number 536. As it has a spreading habit, it is sometimes cordon-trained.

Montagne-Saint-Émilion

The Montagne-Saint-Émilion *appellation d'origine contrôlée*, created by decree on 14 November 1936, was originally reserved for red wines made from grapes picked on designated plots in the communes of Montagne and Saint-Georges in the Libourne district. However, the decree of 5 December 1972 extended the *appellation* to the Parsac commune.

To be entitled to the Montagne-Saint-Émilion *appellation*, wine must be made from the same grape varieties as specified for the Saint-Émilion AOC. The minimum sugar content of the must is fixed at 162g per litre and the wines must have an alcohol content of at least 10° and no more than 13°. The base yield is 45hl/ha. Since 1958, wines of this *appellation* have had to be submitted to a tasting panel before being marketed.

In 1985, the area covered was 1,388ha and the amount of wine produced 70,802hl, 6,367hl of which were vinified by the Montagne cooperative.

Montagny

The *appellation d'origine controlée* area surrounding this village on the Côte Chalonnaise was ratified by the decree of 11 September 1936, and covers nearly 306ha spread over the communes of Montagny, Buxy, Saint-Vallerin and Jully-lès-Buxy.

These white wines must have a minimum alcohol content of 11.5°. The maximum yield is set at 55hl/ha. The grape variety used is the Chardonnay, and it is grown in clay and limestone soils. An average of 5,500 to 6,000hl are produced annually. The wines of Montagny are distinguished by their lightness, grace and finesse, qualities that are evident in the wines from the very first.

Monthélie

A neighbour of Meursault and Volnay, the commune of Monthélie on the Côte de Beaune produces mainly red wines on about 135ha, of which 31ha are Premiers Crus. These wines were once very fashionable and are still highly esteemed. The soils are made up of clay, silica and iron oxide, and the best plots face south. The decree of 21 May 1970, by which this AOC was ratified, fixed the minimum alcohol content for red wines at 10.5°, and 11.5° for Premiers Crus; and for white wines at 11° with 11.5° for Premiers Crus. The base yield is 35hl/ha. Average annual production is 3,500hl of red wine and only 70hl of white. The red wines, with their light and handsome colour, are considered to be firmer than those of neighbouring Volnay, while being more delicate than those of Pommard.

Montils

Synonyms: *Blanc de Montils, Chalosse.*

The Montils is a Charente region grape variety, approved for the Cognac AOC. Little is grown today, however (less than 10ha). It is a fairly productive vine, giving a thin, acid wine. It is classed as 'authorized' in the two Charentes *départements*, Dordogne and Gironde.

Montlouis

This wine-growing area, classed AOC on 6 December 1938, covers some 200ha, planted exclusively with the Chenin Blanc grape variety.

The average annual production is about 8,400hl, though this can vary greatly: there was an exceptionally high yield in 1986 of 15,700hl, and an exceptionally low one in 1981 of 6,100hl. The production area covers the following communes or parts of communes: Montlouis, Saint-Martin-le-Beau and Lussault-sur-Loire.

Montlouis is a lightly coloured wine, with just a hint of yellow, acquiring a golden hue with age. It is fine, delicate and lively, with the firm finish typical of the Chenin Blanc. It matures well. (*See* Touraine.)

Montlouis Mousseux

This AOC received its classification on 6 December 1938, and was modified by the decree of 14 October 1974. The *appellation* covers an area of 81ha, planted exclusively with Chenin Blanc.

The average annual production is about 4,800hl and it is often vinified from grapes not required for still Montlouis. In 1976, for example, an exceptionally good year for still wines, only 2,104hl of Montlouis Mousseux were produced, as opposed to 10,500hl of still Montlouis. The harvest of Montlouis Mousseux therefore varies in both quantity and quality according to annual weather conditions, which determine the richness of the grapes, and therefore the best use for them. The area of production is the same as that of Montlouis.

Montlouis Mousseux is a lightly sparkling wine. It is fruity, full and lively, and has the firmness typical of the Chenin Blanc.

Perched on a hill overlooking Meursault, Monthélie produces elegant red wines which are, however, somewhat eclipsed by those of neighbouring Volnay.

The wine-growing district of Montlouis, situated between Tours and Amboise, produces a white wine of finesse, reminiscent of Vouvray.

Montlouis Pétillant

Up to 30 per cent of the total sparkling wine production of Montlouis is vinified in slightly sparkling (*pétillant*) form. The *appellation* was classed by decree on 6 December 1938, with the Chenin Blanc as the sole grape variety used. The production area is the same as for Montlouis.

Montlouis Pétillant is full, rounded, firm and yet delicate, with a very slight sparkle. It matures well.

Montpeyroux

This AOC, one of the 12 *terroirs* of the AOC Coteaux du Languedoc, was ratified by decree on 24 December 1985. It is situated in two communes to the north of Montpellier, at the foot of the Causse du Larzac, where the terrain is one of piedmont scree produced by the action of frost. The wine district, planted with the same grape varieties as throughout the Coteaux du Languedoc *appellation* (*see* page 215), covers an area of 900ha, and yields 15,000hl of red and rosé wine. The red wines of Montpeyroux are richly coloured and firmly structured, and they age well.

Montrachet

One of the world's most prestigious white wines is undoubtedly Montrachet, a Grand Cru from the Côte de Beaune produced in the communes of Puligny-Montrachet and Chassagne-Montrachet. In this *appellation d'origine contrôlée*, which covers 7.5ha, the Chardonnay grape variety achieves one of its most successful manifestations. The soil, comprised of siliceous sands, lime, clay and iron oxide, with a magnesian subsoil, interacts with the microclimate in an astonishing manner. Ratified by the decree of 31 July 1937, this AOC is subject to strict conditions with regard to production. Montrachet must have an alcohol content of at least 12°. The maximum yield is 30hl/ha. Every year, some 250hl of this superb dry white wine are produced, a brilliant pale yellow in colour, and bottles are immediately snapped up by enthusiasts from all over the world. Its glory lies in its magnificent and complex aromas of hazelnut, almond and honey, aromas which can be violent, subtle or harmonious by turns, but which are never facile. Montrachet is at its best within 5 to 6 years of the harvest.

Chassagne-Montrachet (shown above) and Puligny-Montrachet share the Montrachet appellation. *It is in this white Grand Cru that the Chardonnay grape finds its most successful expression.*

Montravel, Côtes de Montravel, Haut-Montravel

The Montravel wine-growing area is situated in the hills on the right bank of the Dordogne, on the border of the Gironde *département* and in the extreme west of the Dordogne *département*. It is an area with a historical and geographical entity very much of its own, although it looks as if it has been snatched from Bordeaux; it occupies the canton of Vélines. Montaigne was born there in 1533, in the château that bears his name.

The vineyards cover about 1,000ha, and the soils are mainly clay-limestone mixtures derived from Agenais molasse. Because of maritime influences, the grapes tend to ripen more fully than in the rest of the Bergerac region.

About 25,000hl to 30,000hl of wine are produced each year, and this total is made up of the dry white wines of Montravel and the sweet white wines of Côtes de Montravel and Haut-Montravel. Both of the latter have a sugar content of between 17g and 54g per litre.

All the Montravel wines, whether dry or sweet, are distinguished by their rich structure, delicacy and length. They may be drunk young, after 9 to 18 months, or after several years' maturation in bottle.

Morey-Saint-Denis

Like many of the other Burgundy *appellations*, Morey-Saint-Denis has three types of *cru*. These are clearly described in the decree of 8 December 1936, by which the *appellation* was ratified. There is the 'commune' or 'village' *appellation* itself, covering 109ha, then the Morey-Saint-Denis Premier Cru *appellation*, and finally the Grands Crus, which appear under their own and not the village name. The red wines must have an alcohol content of at least 10.5°, with 11° for Premiers Crus; while the white Premiers Crus must contain at least 11.5° of alcohol. The maximum yield is fixed at 40hl/ha for red wines and 45hl/ha for white. The latter are produced in small quantities only: 70hl per year as against about 3,000hl of red.

The clay and limestone soils and classic grape varieties — Pinot Noir for red wines and Chardonnay for white — make for subtle, delicate, supple wines, which are nevertheless vigorous and lively. There is an alluring quality about the rich, dark colour of the red wines, and their powerful bouquet of strawberries and violets.

Morgon

Facing the Côte de Brouilly and situated in the communes of Morgon and Villié-Morgon, this is the most important wine-growing community in Beaujolais. The wine district was classified as an AOC by decree on 11 September 1936. The soils, known locally as '*morgnons*' are composed of pyritic schists, broken up and impregnated with iron oxide. These decomposed soils give a wine that is sometimes almost on a par with the great red wines of the Côte d'Or: a deep garnet colour, firm-bodied and powerful with a light bouquet. But the qualities of Morgon could be discussed for ever; the local growers have invented the verb '*morgonner*', which means to enjoy a glass of Morgon and talk about it . . .

There are abundant aromas and flavours of red fruits — redcurrants, raspberries, etc. — in Morgon, conveying a range of supple and warm sensations to the drinker. Perhaps the most characteristic aroma is the Kirsch-like scent of wild cherries.

In general, Morgon ages well, although recently wines for drinking young have also been made.

The vineyards cover an area of 850ha and produce an annual average of 58,000hl.

Mornen

Synonym: *Mornerain* in the Loire area.

Bunches medium sized, conical, compact; grapes spherical, small, blue-black, not very juicy; ripening period: first epoch, late.

This grape variety is peculiar to certain areas in the *départements* of Loire (canton of Rive-de-Gier) and Rhône (cantons of Mornant and Givors). In spring, its green shoots look somewhat like those of the Chasselas. Later in the year, however, the differences can be clearly seen and the Mornen could not be mistaken even for the black variety of Chasselas. The wine it gives is deeply coloured and not very alcoholic. It was chiefly intended to be drunk locally by the working people of the Gier valley. It has not been classified, and less than 50ha of it remain today.

Morey-Saint-Denis on the Côte de Nuits has five Grands Crus. The village is known for its full, dark red wines.

Morrastel

Synonyms: *Mourastel*, *Morestel*, *Marastel*, *Monastel*, *Monastrell*, *Couthurier* or *Couturier* in Dordogne and Lot-et-Garonne, *Plant de Lédenon* in Provence, *Courouillade* and *Grosse Négrette* in Tarn-et-Garonne, *Perpignan* at Fronton, *Cargo-muol* in Landes.

Young leaves arachnoid, markedly bronze-coloured or even orange, underside of blade downy, carmine.

Bunches medium to long, conical, winged, compact, with red stalks; grapes spherical, small, blue-black, fairly thick-skinned, flesh soft, juice with little colour; ripening period: third epoch.

This vine originated in the Rioja Alta region in Spain, where it is known as Graciano. Once introduced to France, it spread all over the Midi, and consequently has many synonyms. Before the outbreak of phylloxera, it grew in sizeable areas of Languedoc, contributing to the wines of the Coteaux de Langlade and de Villeveyrac, and of Costières du Gard, and spreading as far east as Provence. It has a small yield, and gives a dry, somewhat coarse wine with plenty of colour and extract. It is of upright habit and it has very late budbreak. Although able to withstand drought, and not very susceptible to oidium (powdery mildew), it is prone to downy mildew. With the post-phylloxera replanting and reorganization of the vineyards, it gave way to the hybrids Bouschet and Morrastel-Bouschet, the latter being a particularly productive vine. Classed today as 'recommended' in Tarn, Aveyron, Haute-Garonne and Tarn-et-Garonne, only a few hundred hectares of it remain.

Morrastel-Bouschet

Synonyms: *Morrastel Bouschet à Gros Grains, Gros Mourrastel Bouschet.*

Bunches large, conical, compact; grapes large, spherical or slightly ovoid, black with a dark purplish tinge, thick skinned, juice quite deeply coloured; ripening period: first epoch, late.

This vine is a Morrastel × Petit Bouschet cross, obtained in 1885 by Henri Bouschet. It has a spreading habit and is very susceptible to downy mildew. It is highly fertile, and will yield as much as 6kg per vine when planted in rich, plain soils. The wine it gives is deeply coloured and not very alcoholic, although it can sometimes exceed 10°. Not classified.

Moulin-à-Vent

Moulin-à-Vent was declared an AOC on 11th September 1936. Of all the 'nine apostles' of Beaujolais, it is almost unanimously agreed to be the one nearest the heavenly throne. Situated northeast of Romanèche-Thorins and Chénas, between the wine districts of Chénas and Fleurie, it takes its name from a 300-year-old windmill that has lost its sails. A fine subject for allegory: wine paying homage to corn.

The vineyards, which are planted in shallow granite soils containing manganese, cover 600ha and produce some 35,000hl (4,600,000 bottles) of a heady, concentrated, deep ruby-coloured wine that does the Gamay great honour. The influence of the manganese gives structured, full-bodied wines with a powerful flavour. Their aroma is harmonious, with hints of raspberry, cherry, redcurrant, iris and rose.

Moulin-à-Vent can be enjoyed in its youth, but it often benefits from being matured for five years, and sometimes even longer. With 'the charm of Beaujolais and the prestige of Burgundy', this *appellation* marks something of a transition point between the two.

The village of Moulis in Haut Médoc, with its gravel and limestone soils, produces delicate, supple and charming red wines.

Moulin-à-Vent, a Beaujolais cru *of high repute, grows on granite soils overlooked by an old windmill.*

Moulis or Moulis-en-Médoc

The *appellation d'origine contrôlée* Moulis or Moulis-en-Médoc, created by decree on 14 May 1938, is reserved for red wines made from grapes picked within the Moulis commune and in parts of the neighbouring communes of Listrac-Médoc, Lamarque, Arcins, Avensan, Castelnau-de-Médoc and Cussac.

The prescribed grape varieties are the same as for the regional *appellation*, Médoc. Hybrid grapes have been forbidden since 1961 on estates wishing to use the Moulis or Moulis-en-Médoc *appellation*. The minimum sugar content in the must is 162g per litre, and the wines should have at least 10° and no more than 13° alcohol. The base yield is 45hl/ha.

Since 1955, it has been compulsory for wines of this *appellation* to obtain a certificate of quality issued by a tasting panel before being marketed. In 1985, the *appellation* covered 603ha and produced 21,339hl of wine, 474hl of which were vinified by the cooperative of Listrac-Médoc.

There are no Crus Classés in Moulis, though there are a number of Crus Bourgeois.

Wines of the Moulis *appellation* combine great aromatic finesse with a supple, fleshy structure in their early years. After further ageing, they acquire great complexity.

Mourvaison

Synonyms: *Mourveson, Mourvesoun, Mourvedoun, Mourvezon, Raisin des Maures, Mouenc, Négrau.*

Leaves medium sized, orbicular-reniform, thick, flat with rippling edges, without lobes or weakly three-lobed, petiolar sinus lyrate, more or less closed; dentation convex, narrow; underside of blade markedly arachnoid or downy.

Bunches very big, conical, quite bulky, winged, very compact; grapes small to medium sized, ovoid, black, juicy; ripening period: third epoch.

This variety of unknown origin was formerly grown around Grasse and on the right bank of the river Var, from where it spread to a number of wine districts in Var.

It is a productive vine and quite resistant to disease. The wine it gives is deeply coloured and quite astringent. Classed as 'authorized' in Provence, about 20ha of it remain.

Mourvèdre

Synonyms: In Provence *Mourvède, Mourvès, Morvède, Mourvégué, Mourvézé, Négron* and *Négre Trinchiera* or *Trinchiera*, all names derived from the dark colour of the grapes; also *Estrangle-chien* ('dog strangler') on account of the harsh, rough flavour of the fruit, *Buona Vise* ('good cane'), which has been turned into *Bon Avis* in Drôme, *Tire-Droit* in Drôme, a name reflecting the upright growth of the shoots, *Espar* or *Spar* in Hérault, *Plant de Saint-Gilles* in Gard, *Catalan* in Bouches-du-Rhône, *Balthazar* in Gironde, *Piémontais* in Vaucluse, *Flouron* or *Flouroux*, indicating the copious bloom on the fruit, *Maneschaou* in Ardèche, *Balzac, Balzar* and *Balzac Noir* in Charente and Vienne, *Damas Noir* in Puy-de-Dôme, *Espagne* or *Espagnen* in Ardèche, *Rossola Nera* in Corsica, *Clairette Noire* in Drôme, *Mataro* in Pyrénées-Orientales, *Beni Carlo*, erroneously, in Dordogne. The name Mourvèdre is thought to be derived from the name of the town of Murviedro in Valencia.

Growing tips open, felty white with carmine margins.

Young leaves downy yellow, with the petiole and underside of the blade felty.

Leaves cuneiform-truncate, flat, finely bullate, without lobes; petiolar sinus lyrate; dentation pointed, medium sized, saw-like; underside of blade downy-pubescent.

Green shoots ribbed, purplish, downy at tips; tendrils medium sized, violet in colour.

Bunches medium sized, conical, narrow, sometimes winged, compact; grapes small, spherical, black, abundantly covered in bloom, thick skinned, with easily expressed, harshly flavoured flesh; ripening period: third epoch.

The Mourvèdre has late budbreak, which makes it invaluable in sites that are prone to frost. Of upright habit, it is well suited to being trained *en gobelet* (as a small, free-standing bush) without needing to be staked. It is quite susceptible to downy mildew and oidium (powdery mildew), but is resistant to phomopsis and grey rot (botrytis).

Its wine is very alcoholic, deeply coloured, rough at first, very firm and needing several years to mature and become accessible. The grapes are sometimes destalked prior to vinification in order to obtain more supple wines that can be sold and drunk earlier. Clonal selection has enabled the yield to be increased from 25–30hl/ha to 50–70hl/ha, but beyond that the quality deteriorates rapidly. The vine is not suited to all sites, as it matures late.

Sixteen registered clones have been approved. Some of these are productive but give wines low in alcohol: numbers 244, 245, 246 and 250. Others are not very productive but give wines with a much higher level of alcohol: numbers 247, 248 and 450. Others have medium productivity and alcoholic potential: numbers 249, 251, 369 and 370.

The Mourvèdre is classed as 'recommended' in Provence and Languedoc, where it occupied a total area of 3,145ha in 1980. In Provence, it is used in the preparation of a number of AOC wines: Bandol, Cassis, Côtes de Provence, Coteaux d'Aix-en-Provence, Palette, Châteauneuf-du-Pape, Côtes du Rhône and Côtes du Ventoux, and in the VDQS areas of Coteaux de Pierrevert, Coteaux Varois and Côtes du Lubéron, to give total Provence plantings of 2,500ha. Although less widely grown in Languedoc, it is used for the AOC wines of Tavel, Lirac, Costières du Gard, Faugères, Saint-Chinian, Coteaux du Languedoc, Fitou, Corbières, Minervois, Collioure and Côtes du Roussillon, and for the Côtes du Cabardès et de l'Orbiel VDQS.

Bunch of Mourvèdre grapes. This variety, classed as 'recommended' in Provence and Languedoc, gives strong, very deeply coloured wines that need ageing.

Mousseux du Bugey *See* Vin du Bugey Mousseux.

Mousseux de Savoie and Mousseux de Savoie-Ayze *See* Vin de Savoie Mousseux.

Mouyssaguès

Synonyms: *Négret* or *Plant du Pauvre* in the Lot valley, *Rouge Menu* at Aubin, *Farineux* at Maleville in Aveyron, *Peyregord* (pronounced 'Pey de Gor') and *Pey de Gorp*.

Bunches medium sized, conical, winged, compact; grapes medium sized, spherical or slightly ovoid, blue-black; ripening period: second epoch, late.

This is an old Aveyron vine that originated in Moissac (hence its name). It could once be seen all over the Lot valley. It is an abundantly productive vine, and gives a weak, astringent wine that is usually blended with wine from the Fer. It is said to graft badly, with a high level of failed graftings. It is classed as 'recommended' in Aveyron and Cantal, but it is grown on a few hectares only, and used for the VDQS Vins d'Estaing, Vins de Marcillac and Vins d'Entraygues et du Fel.

Müller-Thurgau

Bunches medium to large, cylindrical or pyramidal; grapes medium sized, ovoid, green to greyish, becoming golden yellow when fully ripe; skin fine, flesh juicy, perfumed with a slight taste of Muscat; ripening period: second epoch, early, 10–15 days earlier than the Riesling.

This vine is said to be a Sylvaner × Riesling crossing achieved by a Swiss called Dr Müller, who worked at Geisenheim research station in Germany (and who was born in the Swiss canton of Thurgau). Some present-day German researchers, however, think that it was simply a seedling of the Riesling, or that it originated from self-fertilization of the Riesling. The Müller-Thurgau is moderately vigorous. It has late budbreak, and is prone to diseases, especially grey rot (botrytis). A consistent producer, it readily yields 100hl/ha or more. The wine has a medium alcohol content, low acidity and a characteristic perfume reminiscent of Muscat. Seven registered clones have been approved: numbers 644 to 650. The variety is classed as 'authorized' in Alsace and Moselle. However, it is little used, and is planted on less than 40ha in all, not being one of the specified varieties for the Alsace AOC.

Muscadelle

Synonyms: *Muscat Fou*, *Blanche Douce* in Bergerac, *Muscade* in Sauternes, *Musquette*, *Colle-Musquette* at Sainte-Croix-du-Mont, *Muscadet Doux* and *Angelico* in Gironde, *Guilan-Muscat* or *Guillan Musqué* in Lot, *Raisimotte* or *Raisinotte* in Barsac, *Douçanelle* in Lot-et-Garonne, *Guépié* at Sainte-Foy-la-Grande.

Growing tips felty white.

Young leaves downy, bullate, bronze-coloured on bulges.

Leaves large, orbicular-reniform, bullate, contorted, three-lobed with lobes of average size and definition, narrow sinuses; petiolar sinus lyrate, normally closed; petiolar junction pink; dentation pointed, medium sized; underside of blade lightly arachnoid; petioles and veins pubescent, rough.

Green shoots ribbed, dark mahogany red on the side exposed to the sun, but only partly red and with pink nodes on the other side; tendrils long, red, thin.

Bunches large, conical, loose; grapes medium sized, spherical, white to pinkish grey, speckled when fully ripe, slightly musky flavour; ripening period: second epoch.

This variety has late budbreak and is fairly vigorous. It produces 50–80hl/ha, rarely more. It is susceptible to diseases, particularly grey rot (botrytis) and grape worms. Its wine is often very sweet and has a marked perfume, reminiscent of the Muscat.

Two registered clones have been approved: numbers 451 and 610. The Muscadelle is classed as 'recommended' in the whole of the South West and in the two Charentes *départements*. It is used for numerous AOCs in Gironde (Sauternes, Barsac, Entre-Deux-Mers), Dordogne (Bergerac, Monbazillac), Tarn (Gaillac) and Lot-et-Garonne (Côtes de Buzet). It is not, though, vinified by itself in any of these *appellations*. The area on which it is grown has dropped to 3,710ha from 6,258ha in 1958. The distribu-

Leaf of the Muscadelle, a white variety that gives a very sweet wine with a pronounced perfume reminiscent of that of the Muscat.

tion of principal areas of planting is as follows: Gironde (2,370ha), Dordogne (733ha) and Tarn (458ha).

Muscadet

See the regional entry on the next page.

Muscadet

This wine-growing district, classed AOC on 23 September 1937, covers an area of 1,000ha and is planted with the Melon grape variety (locally known as the Muscadet). The amount of wine produced annually from this *appellation d'origine contrôlée* over the last ten years has been about 40,000hl.

The production area spans 14 communes, or parts of communes, in Loire-Atlantique. The communes, or parts of communes, of Montfaucon in Maine-et-Loire, and Montaigu and Rocheservière in Vendée, are also included in the *appellation*.

Muscadet is a dry and vivacious wine with a good length of flavour. Its aromas are reminiscent of sea spray and fresh almonds. It should be drunk young, but is capable of developing in bottle for a few years.

Muscadet des Coteaux de la Loire

This wine-growing area, classed AOC on 14 November 1936, covers about 410ha and is planted with the Melon grape variety. The average amount of wine produced annually over the last ten years has been about 16,000hl. The production area spans 24 communes or parts of communes.

Muscadet des Coteaux de la Loire is a dry, medium-bodied, firm wine with mineral aromas. It matures well in bottle.

Muscadet de Sèvre-et-Maine

This wine-growing district, classed AOC by decree on 14 November 1936, covers an area of 8,700ha, and is planted with the Melon grape variety. The average annual production over the last ten years has been about 415,000hl. The production area spans 23 communes or parts of communes.

Muscadet de Sevre-et-Maine is a dry wine, easy to drink and yet not without finesse.

It represents 85 per cent of all the wine produced in this region. Wines that have *sur lie* printed on the label have been bottled 'off the lees', i.e. straight from the fermentation vat, without racking. They have a very fresh taste and sometimes a small prickle of gas.

Passage lined with large casks at the Domaine de la Galissonière in Muscadet.

Muscardin

Growing tips downy white with carmine margins.

Young leaves arachnoid, green, glossy.

Leaves truncate, glossy, coarsely bullate, with convex edges; three-lobed with narrow V-shaped upper lateral sinuses; petiolar sinus lyrate, narrow; dentation convex; underside of blade arachnoid.

Bunches medium sized, cylindrical, very compact; grapes medium sized, ovoid blue-black; ripening period: second epoch.

This is one of the grape varieties of Châteauneuf-du-Pape, where it grows on about 20ha. The wine it gives has little colour, and an average alcohol content. It is classed as 'recommended' in Gard, Hérault, Vaucluse, Drôme and Ardèche.

The name 'Val de Loire' may, if wished, be added to any of the three Muscadet appellations.

At work in the vineyards near Machecoul. Traditional ploughing methods are still widely used in the Nantes region.

MUSCADET AND THE NANTES REGION

In this region, the appellation ***names have been inspired by local names for the main grape varieties cultivated. The Folle Blanche — under its local name Gros Plant — provides the VDQS Gros Plant du Pays Nantais, while the Melon or Melon de Bourgogne, known locally as the Muscadet, gives its name to the most famous of the region's wines.***

This wine-growing area starts below Ingrandes, and stretches along both banks of the Loire. To the north of the river, the vineyards form a narrow band. To the south, however, they spread out into a vast area, surrounding the Lac de Grand-Lieu southwest of Nantes.

The vine spread as far as Brittany during the Middle Ages. In 1639, the red-wine vines were replaced by white varieties from Burgundy, and from then on, leases made out between landowners and tenant growers referred to 'Muscadet de Bourgogne'.

Until the phylloxera outbreak, the region was planted exclusively with Muscadet (Melon) and Gros Plant (Folle Blanche). The latter was dominant, with two thirds of plantings given over to its cultivation.

There was already a market for these wines outside the region before the First World War. But it was not until between 1920 and 1930 that they became known in Paris and the fashionable seaside resorts of the north and west coasts.

The vineyards

Vineyards separate Brittany from the hills of Poitou. The vines are planted in crystalline schist soils with scarcely any limestone content. There are also a few strips of metamorphic and volcanic soils belonging to the Armorican massif, and these are made up of granite, gneiss, mica-schist and even gravels. The vineyards cover gentle hills a few dozen metres high, and these form a tranquil, soothing landscape. The soil is pebbly. Most of the slopes face southwest, and this aspect enables the vines to enjoy maximum benefit from the sun. The plateaux come under maritime influences, and are therefore breezier than the hill locations. In the Gros Plant zone, near the Lac de Grand-Lieu, the soil

Saint-Fiacre-sur-Maine, in the Muscadet de Sèvre-et-Maine zone, is surrounded by vineyards.

Grape picking beneath the cloud-laden skies so characteristic of the Muscadet region at harvest time.

is siliceous with varying amounts of gravel. In the VDQS area of Fiefs Vendéens to the south, the vineyards are focused around four centres: the Brem area, north of les Sables-d'Olonne; Mareuil-sur-Lay; Vix; and Pissotte.

The grape varieties

It is easy to understand why the Muscadet (Melon) has become so widely used in comparison with the Gros Plant (Folle Blanche) when one considers its vegetative cycle. It flowers early, and the grapes also ripen early. In this maritime region, the growers fear the rainy conditions that prevail around the time of the equinoctial tides in September, hence the need for a grape variety that will ripen before this period. It has taken years of observation to ensure the correct orientation of the vines, a factor that is all the more important because the Melon produces small bunches of tightly packed grapes that lie concealed beneath its small round leaves. Fortunately the soils are well drained, which limits the length of time the vines are damp after rains.

The climate

The prevailing maritime influence brings plenty of sunshine to the region, with moderate temperatures, regular rainfall and quite strong winds. Although the winds pose a threat to young vine shoots, they also help the quick evaporation of moisture after rain. During the growing and fruiting period, the prevailing wind blows from the west, keeping the vines dry and healthy.

The style of the wines

A knowledge of the environment, i.e. the soil and the climate, makes it easier to understand the style of the wines. Their principal characteristic is finesse, and this is the result of pebbly, siliceous terrains. The pebbles store up heat during the day, and transfer it to the vines during the night, bringing strength to the wines.

The plentiful sunlight provides the grape varieties with considerable aromatic potential. The humid atmosphere prevents the fruit from drying out and the wind keeps the vines healthy. These factors explain why Muscadet is a dry, finely balanced, moderately strong wine, smoothly structured, without excessive acidity and with the aroma of ripe but not overripe grapes.

Gros Plant du Pays Nantais

This VDQS zone, planted with the Folle Blanche variety, has a siliceous soil and a markedly maritime climate. These conditions give white wine with a supple, lively character, and very positive aromas. It is a dry, straightforward wine.

Coteaux d'Ancenis

This VDQS produces mainly red wines, the principal grape variety being the Gamay. Their chief characteristic is lightness. They are fruity and need to be drunk young.

Fiefs Vendéens

These VDQS wines vary in style according to different local climates and soils. Around Mareuil-sur-Lay the production is of mostly red wines, made with at least 50 per cent Pinot Noir plus Gamay. They are light, tasty wines,

Official Gros Plant sticker. It reads 'Gros Plant — the wine of my holidays'.

influenced by siliceous soils. In the coastal area of Brem, north of les Sables-d'Olonne, the principal grape variety is the Chenin Blanc, and the mainly white wines are dry. Vix and Pissotte, north of Fontenay-le-Comte, are sited on schistous soils and produce mostly dry white wines, which may contain up to 20 per cent of the Melon variety.

The lie (lees) is a yellowish deposit that forms during fermentation. It is chiefly made of dead yeast cells.

White wine vinification

The fermentation of the white wines takes place in cellars, traditionally in 220- or 600-litre casks. Nowadays larger vats are used, and the temperature is regulated between 15°C and 20°C. It has always been local practice to try and ferment the wine slowly, in order to ensure prolonged contact between the lees (the deposit produced during fermentation) and the new wine. This slow fermentation encourages the process of autolysis in the yeast and permits optimum aromatic development. Malolactic fermentation is avoided. In fact, the presence of malic acid is desirable, as it gives the wine a characteristic liveliness.

Bottling wine *sur lie*

Muscadet is the chief example of an *appellation d'origine contrôlée* wine bearing the description '*sur lie*' ('on the lees'). The regulations governing the use of this phrase state that the wine must pass one winter only in cask, and must remain on the lees formed during fermentation throughout this period to the moment when it is bottled, which should be no later than the 30 June following the harvest.

After pressing, the must is left to settle carefully (*débourbage*), and fermented at a low temperature. The new wine is then kept on the lees. The latter consist mainly of dead yeast cells, and these are said to 'nourish' the wine. However, this process is not necessarily beneficial to the quality of the wine, for if the lees come from a tainted or otherwise damaged harvest, the wines produced will be heavy. In this case, it is to be avoided.

We know today that dead yeast cells, the principal constituent of the lees, release amino acids into the wine during the process of autolysis. So when, in a purely empirical way, the growers use the term 'nourish', they are in fact using exactly the right word. When the term '*sur lie*' is seen on the label of a bottle of Muscadet or Gros Plant du Pays Nantais, it should indicate a lively, full white wine, perhaps with a very slight prickle of gas. It should have a good length of flavour, while the aroma should recall fresh almonds, with a touch of sea spray in the case of Muscadet.

Chéreau. A panoramic view of part of the Gros Plant du Pays Nantais zone, where the Folle Blanche grape variety is planted in siliceous soils.

Château de Haute Goulaine, a meeting place for the wine-growing world of the lower Loire valley.

The *élevage* of the wines

The ordinary white wines of the Nantes region are generally racked two or three times. Like the *sur lie* wines, they are bottled very early. These wines are appreciated for their fresh character, a feature of their youth. But some vintages will mature perfectly well in bottle for two or three years, and even more if they have been made in the best parts of the region.

Economic and commercial structure of the Nantes wine trade

The wines of this region come mainly from individual producers. The only cooperative, which is in Ancenis, vinifies about 2 per cent of AOC Muscadet and 30 per cent of VDQS Coteaux d'Ancenis.

According to the statistics of the Comité Interprofessionnel des Vins d'Origine du Pays Nantais (Interprofessional Committee of the Wines of the Nantes Region), there are about 1,500 wine growers in Loire-Atlantique. The table opposite shows the production figures for the last five years.

In 1986, the Nantes region sold a record 500,000hl of Muscadet (all *appellations*) and 500,000hl of Gros Plant du Pays Nantais.

Négociants-éleveurs (shippers or merchants, some of whom have their own wine-making facilities) play an important part in selling the wines. Their share of the market in this region is estimated at 70 per cent. The remainder is sold by the growers themselves. There are 28 large *négociants-éleveurs* in the region. A third of these are also wine producers, a double role that gives them an understanding of the problems of both production and marketing.

PRODUCTION IN HECTOLITRES OF THE NANTES REGION

	Muscadet (all appellations)	Gros Plant du Pays Nantais	Coteaux d'Ancenis
1981	236 770	135 223	6 760
1982	689 521	247 006	25 893
1983	571 544	235 517	17 878
1984	462 838	223 534	14 500
1985	769 000	296 000	20 414

The region is very active in export terms: 40 per cent of the wine produced goes to over 15 different countries. The main overseas customers are the United Kingdom and the Netherlands. This increase in exports is a consequence of the international demand for dry, fresh, fruity white wines.

Wine's role in the community

Muscadet is sold in France as a '*vin de vacances*' ('holiday wine'). It is to white wines what Beaujolais is to red wines. It is the subject of local festivals, fairs and numerous other events; for example, the Saint-Viacre festival, normally held on the second Sunday of October; and the Vallet wine fair, which takes place on the second Monday in March.

The Ordre des Chevaliers Bretrins, which is based at the Château de Haute Goulaine, holds numerous chapter meetings. Finally, there is a small regional wine museum, the Musée Pierre Abélard, found in the village of le Pallet, dedicated to the arts and popular traditions of wine growing.

Muscat à Petits Grains Blancs

Synonyms: *Muscat Blanc, Muscat de Frontignan, Muscat de Lunel, Muscat de Die* in Drôme, *Muscat d'Alsace* in Alsace.

Leaves orbicular, thick, finely bullate, crimped, five-lobed with deep, very narrow upper lateral sinuses, petiolar sinus closed with parallel edges; dentation pointed, in two lines, very narrow; underside of blade smooth with pubescent veins.

Green shoots ribbed, with flattened nodes towards the tip, with longitudinal brown stripes; tendrils large, green.

Bunches medium sized, cylindrical, long, narrow and compact, rarely winged; grapes medium sized, spherical, thick skinned, amber yellow, becoming speckled with red when fully ripe; flesh firm, juicy, very sweet with an aromatic, musky flavour; ripening period: second epoch.

The Muscat à Petits Grains Blanc has early budbreak, is of average vigour and of upright habit.

It is very susceptible to grape fan-leaf virus, oidium (powdery mildew), downy mildew, grey rot (botrytis), grape worms, bees and wasps. The last-named can damage the fruit to the point of emptying the grape of its flesh completely, leaving just the skin and the pips.

In stony and barren soils, the yield of the Muscat à Petits Grains Blancs is low, but in any case, the maximum yield for *vins doux naturels* (the sweet fortified wines for which most Muscat grapes are used) is limited to 28hl/ha, with a minimum potential alcohol content of 14°.

Twelve registered clones have been approved: number 154, which is the most widespread on account of its aroma; number 455, a good clone selected in Roussillon; number 579, worthwhile on account of its aroma; number 452, a productive plant with large berries, and 8 others. Classed as 'recommended' in the coastal zone of the Midi, in Drôme and Alsace, this vine is grown on a total area of 4,600ha. The largest plantings are in Hérault (1,280ha), Pyrénées-Orientales (1,240ha), Vaucluse (240ha) and Aude.

In the Midi, Muscat à Petits Grains Blancs grapes are used in the preparation of Muscat *vins doux naturels*. They are used alone, as at Frontignan, Lunel, Mireval, Beaumes-de-Venise and Saint-Jean-de-Minervois; or together with the Muscat d'Alexandrie for making Muscat de Rivesaltes. In Drôme, the Muscat à Petits Grains Blancs is used to make Clairette de Die, a sparkling wine. In Alsace, this grape variety is vinified together with the Muscat Ottonel to give a dry white wine — Muscat d'Alsace.

Muscat à Petits Grains Roses

This vine is the same as the Muscat à Petits Grains Blancs, except for the colour of the berries, which are pink. Classed as 'recommended' in Alsace, it is grown on 30ha there.

Muscat à Petits Grains Rouges

This is a red variety of the Muscat à Petits Grains Blancs. It is classed as 'recommended' in the Mediterranean region.

Muscat d'Alexandrie

Synonyms: *Muscat Romain, Panse Musquée, Muscat d'Espagne, Muscat à Gros Grains, Raisin de Malaga, Augibi Muscat.*

Leaves medium sized, orbicular, glossy, finely bullate, contorted, fairly deeply five-lobed with very narrow lateral sinuses, acute at base; petiolar sinus lyrate, narrow, petiolar junction red; dentation pointed, very narrow.

Bunches medium sized, cylindrical-conical, winged, loose; grapes ellipsoidal, large to very large, yellowish white; skin quite thin; pulp fleshy with a musky flavour; ripening period: third epoch, late, to fourth epoch.

The Muscat d'Alexandrie is said, as its name suggests, to have originated in the town of Alexandria in Egypt. From there, it would have spread to all the wine regions around the Mediterranean, and wherever it found suitable conditions for its late-ripening grapes. A vigorous vine of upright habit, it requires high temperatures during flowering or it can fall prey to *coulure* (flower abortion) or *millerandage*

Leaf of the Muscat d'Alexandrie, a grape variety used to produce sweet wine with a characteristic bouquet of dried figs.

(failed grape development). It is also susceptible to downy mildew, oidium (powdery mildew), winter frosts and spider mites. However, it is remarkably resistant to drought, and this means it is popular in hot dry regions. Its aromatic structure is different from that of the Muscat à Petits Grains Blancs, as its grapes contain a larger proportion of geraniol and less nerol. During the course of maturation, wines made from the Muscat d'Alexandrie develop characteristic aromas of dried figs and raisins.

Two registered clones have been approved: numbers 308 and 635. The former is the more useful, on account of its aromatic potential. The Muscat d'Alexandrie is classed as 'recommended' in the Mediterranean area. It is grown on a total of 3,341ha in France.

Bunch of Muscat d'Alexandrie grapes.

Muscat de Beaumes-de-Venise

Even though vineyards covered 70 per cent of the agricultural land of Beaume-de-Venise as early as the 14th century, there is no record of the Muscat grape being planted here until the 18th century.

For a long time, this area was the domain of the table grape and of fruit trees such as the apricot. The warm climate and the attenuated influence of the *mistral* produced extremely high-quality fruit. However, foreign competition made table grape production a difficult matter, and the soils tired of fruit trees; so wine growing, and especially the cultivation of Muscat grapes for *vins doux naturels*, became increasingly important.

Beaumes-de-Venise as a specialized wine-growing area dates back some 40 years. The *appellation d'origine contrôlée*, ratified by the decree of 1 May 1945, includes two communes. Today it covers 220ha and produces an annual average of 9,000hl.

Grown in the greyish limestone soils, red marls, sands and sandstones here, the Muscat à Petits Grains Blancs produces sweet fortified wines with a high degree of sensory expressiveness. They have an intense bouquet with aromas of flowers, citrus fruits and sometimes honey. Due to the fact that there is a minimum sugar content of 110g per litre in the finished wines, the sensation in the mouth is sweet, lush, oily, and long.

Beaumes-de-Venise in the southern part of the Côtes du Rhône produces a vin doux naturel *of great finesse.*

Frontignan. This dry, rocky area in Hérault produces honey-sweet Muscat vins doux naturels *and* vins de liqueur.

Muscat de Frontignan

This is both a *vin doux naturel* and *vin de liqueur* AOC, ratified by the decree of 31 May 1986. Along with Muscat de Lunel and Muscat de Mireval, this *appellation* is one of the glories of Languedoc-Roussillon. The sweet wines of this area were praised by Rabelais and prized by Louis XIV and Voltaire.

Situated in the heart of the Midi, not far from the sea on the slopes of the Montagne de la Gardiole near Montpellier, the vineyards cover almost 800ha and produce over 20,000hl of wine a year. The powerful, characteristic aroma of the wine comes from a single grape, the Muscat à Petits Grains Blancs. The unusual thing about Muscat de Frontignan is that it can be made either as a *vin doux naturel* or a *vin de liqueur*. For the latter, the must is subjected to fortification (*mutage*) before any fermentation has taken place, rather than when partially fermented, as for the former. Consequently, the wine produced has an even higher sugar content — at least 185g per litre. The sugar content of the *vin doux naturel* is 125g per litre, and the minimum alcohol content of both is 15°.

Muscat de Lunel

This *vin doux naturel* AOC was ratified by the decree of 28 October 1943, and its zone is situated around Lunel, in the communes of Lunel, Lunel-Viel, Vérargues and Saturargues. It covers an area of 250ha and produces 7,000hl of sweet fortified wine annually, made exclusively from the Muscat à Petits Grains Blancs. The finished wine must contain at least 125g of sugar per litre and have a minimum alcohol content of 15°. Like Muscat de Frontignan and Muscat de Mireval, Muscat de Lunel is known for its pronounced aromatic qualities.

Muscat de Mireval

This wine-growing district, which covers 250ha, lies next door to Frontignan, in the communes of Mireval and Vic-la-Gardiole. It produces about 8,000hl of wine a year from a single grape

Muscat de Rivesaltes, a suave vin doux naturel *with a flowery bouquet, comes from schistous soils baked dry by the Roussillon sunshine.*

variety, the Muscat à Petits Grains Blancs, which gives its wines characteristic suggestions of lime flower, rose, honey and beeswax. This *vin doux naturel* AOC was ratified by the decree of 28 December 1959.

Muscat Ottonel

This vine was the result of a crossing made by the Loire wine breeder Moreau-Robert. Its parentage is not known for sure, although it seems that one parent may have been the Chasselas, as suggested by the characteristics of its buds, leaves and tendrils. The other parent may be the Muscat de Saumur and, if so, it has handed down its musky perfume.

Leaves small, orbicular, smooth, deeply five-lobed with lateral sinuses club shaped, acute at base, petiolar sinus lyrate, sometimes with overlapping edges; dentation convex, medium sized; underside of blade slightly pubescent, rough.

Bunches small, cylindrical, fairly loose; grapes medium sized, spherical, pale yellow, with a delicately musky flavour; ripening period: first epoch.

Propagated from 1852 onwards, Muscat Ottonel was originally grown as a table grape. It became a wine-making grape in Alsace, and is now one of the varieties used in the Alsace AOC, often instead of the Muscat à Petits Grains Blancs, which ripens later. It is susceptible to downy mildew, oidium (powdery mildew) and grey rot (botrytis), and is also prone to *coulure* (flower abortion), which means that its yields vary greatly. Its wine, although quite musky, is low in alcohol and of fairly poor quality. One registered clone has been approved: number 59. The variety is classed as 'recommended' in Alsace, where 435ha of it are grown.

Muscat de Rivesaltes

This *appellation d'origine contrôlée*, ratified by decree on 19 May 1972, is applicable to the entire 24,000ha of the Rivesaltes *appellation* area. In fact 4,500ha are given over to Muscat de Rivesaltes, and annual production is 100,000hl. The *appellation* is reserved for *vins doux naturels* made from the Muscat à Petits Grains Blancs and the Muscat d'Alexandrie. These two grape varieties pass on their characteristic and powerful floral aromas to the wines.

Muscat de Saint-Jean-de-Minervois

This *vin doux naturel* AOC, ratified by the decree of 19 May 1972, lies west of Béziers, covers 100ha, and produces 2,500hl of wine a year made exclusively from the Muscat à Petits Grains Blancs. This wine district is situated far from the sea, 200m up on the limestone plateau of Minervois. Consequently, the aroma of the wines has great finesse, a quality also to be found in the Muscats of Beaumes-de-Venise.

Chambolle-Musigny on the Côte de Nuits is the home of Musigny, a Grand Cru red wine that is rounded, fruity, floral, and infinitely delicate.

Musigny

This red- and white-wine Grand Cru is situated on the Côte de Nuits and lies in the commune of Chambolle-Musigny. The vineyard covers 10.6ha, producing an average of 300hl of red wines and 20hl of white wines annually. The decree of 11 September 1936, ratifying the *appellation d'origine contrôlée*, states that Musigny red wines must have a minimum alcohol content of 11° and the whites 12°; the maximum yield is set at 30hl/ha.

The vineyards are situated on the slopes above the plateau where the Château du Clos de Vougeot stands. They are planted with the classic Burgundy grape varieties: Pinot Noir for red wines and Pinot Blanc and Chardonnay for white wines.

The red wines, often described as 'feminine' in character, are appreciated the world over for their rounded delicacy, allied to a subtle and fruity aroma that suggests raspberry and wild berries.

The white wines, produced in tiny quantities only, keep well and are delicately aromatic, suggesting violets and almonds.

WINE TASTING

Any mention of wine tasting conjures up ideas of an extraordinary skill acquired by certain individuals, who are able to recognize subtle qualities in wines that supposedly escape the perception of ordinary mortals. However, all that is required to become a good taster is an open, willing mind, and sufficient love of wine to enable you to develop your senses in this direction through diligent practice.

There are two routes by which an individual can become a qualified wine taster: the first is that of the professional, the second that of the amateur.

As far as the professional approach is concerned, tasting is simply one of the principal tools of wine growing, making and buying. From the vineyard to the shop shelf, tasting is the chief way of checking the quality and authenticity of a wine. The wine grower, the merchant and the restaurateur are all obliged by their calling to be able to taste wine; and in most cases such aptitude as they possess for this comes purely from the practical experience accumulated over a long period of time. They are able to judge the quality of the products and spot faults, if necessary. Due to lack of training, they are not always able to transform their sense impressions into objective language. Nowadays, however, thorough, purposeful and communicative tasting is slowly penetrating every professional sphere connected with wine growing and making, thanks to those oenologists and other wine professionals who have mastered every aspect of it.

Jean-Claude Jambon, world champion **sommelier** *of 1986.*

The amateur approach to wine tasting follows the same sort of pattern as development in any artistic sphere. It begins with simple enjoyment, which may later become a strong attraction and then, suddenly, an obsession, the day the taster comes across an unforgettable bottle of wine. It is at this moment that the newly converted wine lover realizes that he or she knows nothing of the art of drinking and will have to learn . . . learn what though? Not how to use flowery language, but how to recognize authentic sense impressions, identify them and qualify them exactly, so as to be able to construct an objective outline or picture of the wine tasted. This is the long process of development by which a wine lover becomes a connoisseur.

The development of wine tasting

The learning process for the amateur has been assisted of late by the publication of a number of works by top oenologists, revealing the sensory mechanisms of tasting, and their practical applications, to the public, with a view to making the process of wine tasting objective, methodical and rational.

The father of modern wine tasting is Jules Chauvet. He published an article on the aromas of wine in 1950, and then, in 1951, a work entitled *La dégustation des vins, son mécanisme et ses lois* (*Wine Tasting, its Mechanism and its Laws*). Everything written on the subject since has taken its basis and methodology from this original work.

Interest in wine tasting developed during the 1960s, alongside a more general type of research into the tasting of food products, carried out by Magnien and Depledt, and called sensory analysis. After a conference in Dijon in 1966, André Vedel and his associates compiled a work entitled *Essai sur la dégustation des vins (Essay on Wine Tasting)*, the aim of which was to gather together all the facts on the subject and coordinate tasting terminology.

Since the early 1970s, schools and courses dedicated to methodical wine tasting have flourished; and Émile Peynaud's work *Le goût du vin (The Taste of Wine)*, which appeared in 1983 (English translation Macdonald Orbis 1987), is in a way the crowning achievement of this interest.

So, gradually throughout French-speaking Europe and in neighbouring Flemish- and German-speaking regions, wine tasting has become the expression of a type of sensibility, a level of culture and, in fact, a true phenomenon of civilization.

In everyday terms, the practice of wine tasting remains divided between the professionals on one hand and the individual consumer and enthusiast on the other; but this separation is only apparent, for the first group is permanently at the service of the second, paving the way for it with all the means at its disposal.

Professional tasting

Professional wine tasting has recently acquired very great significance, since all EC wines have now to be tasted by a qualified panel before they can be released for sale. For many years, of course, there have been fairs and competitions, during which quality wines are tasted and awarded diplomas and medals. There are also tasting panels of top professionals who publish their own choice of wines in gastronomic magazines. Furthermore, groups of technicians from viticultural research establishments meet periodically in order to assess the quality of wines.

When the job of a jury is to decide whether a wine is fit for consumption, or to grant awards or subsidies to wines, then a simple yes or no vote is taken by a small panel of three to five people.

When tasting is carried out by large panels, with the aim of assessing the differences between wines in respect of experimental testing, or working out scales of preference on the part of consumers, it is necessary to mark in order to make a hierarchical classification. Various points-based classification systems have been adopted, but experience seems to indicate that, generally speaking, wine tasting does not lend itself well to statistical analysis carried out by groups.

Individual tasting

Individual tasting is, of course, the basis of group tasting, and the quality and competence of any tasting panel depends on the training of those that compose it.

It is training, too, that provides the connoisseur with the analytical principles he needs in order to identify his perceptions and enhance his pleasure. For it is, finally, pleasure that is involved here.

Pleasure is not simply the product of enjoyable sensations; less tangible aspects of psychology and memory also play an important part. The basic sensations aroused by the elements contained in wine are not in themselves particularly pleasant. When tasted in isolation, the acidity of the wine is sharp and aggressive, the tannin astringent, the alcohol fiery, the glycerine viscous and the water, which binds them all together, flat and insipid. However, if mixed in the right proportions, these ingredients render the wine as a whole homogenous, balanced and pleasing, since one ingredient offsets, or complements, the others.

So it is this architecture of the wine that the taster must appreciate, and not just the building bricks, which are, as often as not, simply forgotten in the end, unless they are particularly unpleasant. Once the tasting is over, the taster passes an aesthetic judgment, explicit or otherwise, which may vary from a long commentary to a simple expression of satisfaction or disapproval. In order to express this verdict, the taster must first understand all the elements that go to make up the sensations he or she feels, as well as understanding his or her own sensory apparatus. From such an analysis comes an objective apprehension of the sensory characteristics of the wine, often referred to as its organoleptic qualities. The means of understanding these characteristics are vision, smell and taste.

THE TASTING CARD

At each tasting session, tasters fill in numbered tasting cards headed by details of the appellation, *the vintage, and the supplier of the wine or wine grower. Their impressions concerning the wine follow. When the cards are filled out in detail, they are called in French* commentaires de dégustation approfondie *(in-depth tasting notes). Here is an example:*

No 8 Bourgogne Pinot Noir 1983

The colour of 1983 burgundy in 1987 surprised all those who saw the intense, dark hue these wines had while in cask; in bottle, this wine has only a scant, light colour with an orange tinge. This is the result of the rapid development of an overripened, concentrated crop with unstable colloids. Here, the beautiful luminosity of the wine compensates for this loss of intensity. Limpid and transparent, then, this wine bodes well for tasting purposes.

The 'nose' surrenders the usual basketful of fruity aromas typical of burgundy: blackcurrant, peach, cherry, combined in classic fashion with vanilla and oak, soot and pepper. All this with an intensity that offers itself readily to the nostrils, without undue searching.

The aromas in the mouth reinforce this first impression. Vanilla and pepper emerge particularly strongly, encircling the basket of soft fruit. The final, closing impression is a subtle aroma of bitter almonds.

This is the normal and habitual aromatic level present in an AOC Bourgogne, in which the character of the Pinot Noir is intense, but is less nuanced and less individualized than a 'village' or 'commune' *appellation* wine.

The flavours, on the other hand, present a more unusual balance sheet:

▷ The *tannin*, which was extremely high at the time of harvest, has softened considerably, and if it is still there at all, it manifests itself in the 'shrivelled' flavour of grapes that have been dried on the vine. This gives a form of astringency that defies all our normal classifications.

▷ The *richness (moelleux)*, very much in evidence, is divided between alcohol and glycerine. Its intensity helps to balance that of the tannin described above.

▷ The *acidity* seems to be somewhat lost in the overall make-up of the wine, but it is still lively and is recognizable by the salivation it stimulates.

The result of these three tendencies is a very substantial, unctuous, yet firm, almost lively, wine that avoids any heaviness. Its length of flavour is good, lingering in the mouth for as long as 6 or 7 seconds.

The future development of this wine will probably be like that of wines of the 1964 vintage, which were also 'burned' and 'shrivelled', and which lost their colour very early, to the extent of becoming pale orange within a few years. However, the wines stabilized at this point, and remained stable for the next 20 years, acquiring wonderful aromas.

In the meantime, the impatient and the unaware will drink it, as will, of course, those prudent persons who take care to monitor the development of the bottles in their cellar. They should, however, avoid serving it with common, everyday entrecôte steaks and grills, and at least keep it for rich, substantial dishes with highly seasoned sauces, for example, coq au vin, stews, duck salmis and breasts, venison and also cheeses such as Cantal, Saint-Nectaire, the various 'Fourme' cheeses and even — why not? — a good Swiss Appenzeller.

(Tasting carried out at 16°C in the late afternoon.)

HOW TO TASTE

Firstly, it is best to position yourself in daylight, so as to be able to appreciate the colour of the wine, its subtle shades and reflections. The place should be quiet and peaceful, between 19°C and 20°C in temperature. There should be no other smells, in order to avoid distorting the aromas of the wine.

The glass should be smooth, transparent, colourless and hemispherical at the bottom. It should be possible to observe the mass of liquid in horizontal, oblique and vertical positions. Furthermore, the glass should preferably be semi-elliptical, and the top should be narrower than the bulge of the bowl, so as to concentrate the aromas and channel them towards the nose. The AFNOR glass (see page 372) has been specially designed for this purpose, but any tulip-shaped glass should also be suitable. Hold the glass by the foot or the stem, never by the bowl. Next, proceed with the three stages of tasting: the visual examination (eye), smelling the wine (nose) and tasting the wine (mouth).

When first practising tasting, it is advisable to taste only one wine a day, in order to be able to maintain good powers of discrimination. Taste the wine once on an empty stomach, then half an hour before a meal and once again during the meal, making sure to serve it with a dish that will bring out its best qualities. In time, you will find you can accurately taste up to five or six wines at a time, although you must take care to go from the lightest to the most full-bodied, from the firmest to the most supple, from the youngest to the oldest. This will sometimes necessitate a summary pre-tasting. You should order your wines in the following way:

1) *Sparkling wines:* crémants *or champagnes;*
2) *light, vivacious white or rosé wines;*
3) *dry, supple white and rosé wines;*
4) *young red wines or red* vins nouveaux*;*
5) *mature, full white wines;*
6) *mature red wines or young red wines for laying down;*
7) *fortified dry or sweet wines.*

The sensory apparatus of tasting

The role of the three senses employed in tasting, and the way in which they function, are not yet properly understood by most people. In fact, there is a very close underlying relationship between the activities of the different senses for the wine taster. As an example of the close connection between sight and taste, an experienced taster can tell at a glance the general state, age and condition of a wine before he has even tasted it. But a still greater gulf of comprehension surrounds the relationship between smell and taste. Even for many professionals, 'smell' is still limited to the direct perception of smells by means of breathing them in through the nose, and 'taste' to the perception of flavours by the specialized papillae on the surface of the tongue. Today, we have to modify this idea. Wine tasting has made us discover a much wider range of taste–smell functions, involving the salivary glands, the mucous membranes inside the mouth and also the passage inside the nasal cavity that links the oral cavity with the back of the nose.

We should stress two phenomena in this respect:

▷ today, people rarely perceive smells by breathing them in through the nose, partly for reasons of propriety, partly through indifference;

▷ what we normally refer to as the 'taste' of something is really the smell, which is perceived by the inside of the mouth, made volatile by chewing and carried to the olfactory area of the nose via the passage in the nasal cavity. Thus it is usually the smell of a food that gives it a distinctive character, without which it would be completely anonymous.

Numerous specific reactions do take place in the mouth, but they are not adequate on their own to identify the substances absorbed, and many experiments have proved that the olfactory sense is the means by which we identify food, even though this process takes place inside the mouth.

Since Baudelaire, it has generally been understood in France that, symbolically speaking, wine has a 'soul' — an identity and an individual personality. We should look for this in the bouquet, i.e. in the aromatic properties of the wine. But if we

THE SENSORY APPARATUS OF TASTING

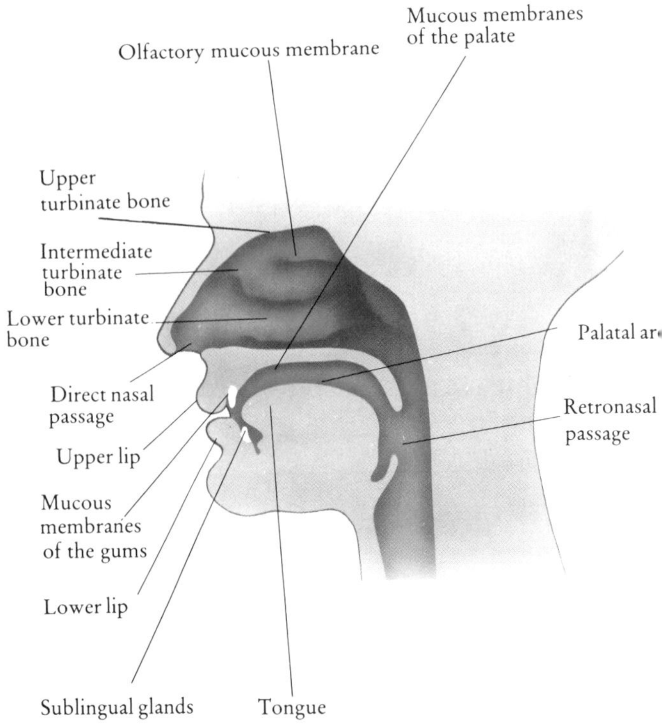

searched too much through this sense alone, in the end we would reduce the wine to 'pure soul', forgetting that it also has a solid presence, a 'body'. This body can be perceived by means of a combination of contact reactions including taste, in its strict sense; touch and salivation. This process, although complex, can be analysed perfectly well, provided it has been inventoried first.

Inside the oral cavity, even when no intentional tasting is going on, the muscles of the tongue, the papillae, the mucous membranes, the gums and the salivary glands are all reacting constantly to the slightest stimulation.

There are four areas of papillae on the tongue, and these apprehend (or produce) the four principal tastes: salty, sweet, sour and bitter. The role played by these four flavours in wine tasting has been greatly exaggerated. In reality, there is hardly ever any saltiness in wine, except for the tiniest hint in those produced close to the sea. Bitterness is an anomaly or a spoilage flavour in wine and is always unacceptable. Sweetness, and in its narrowest sense sugariness, exists only in a minority of sweet wines, although diluted alcohol provides a related flavour. Tannin, which is a specific ingredient of red wines, cannot be perceived as a flavour in the real sense of the word. It is a tactile experience according to some, and a chemical sensation according to others. The only true, permanent and universal flavour in wine, then, is acidity, which is present in all wines, in perceptibly varying degrees and shades.

Salivary secretions play an important role. The parotid glands, which are situated underneath the ear, at the hinge of the jaw, emit a serous, alkaline and very fluid saliva that becomes more abundant on contact with acid, because its function is specifically to neutralize acids. This reaction is a way of isolating acidity in complex wines in which its presence may be eclipsed or counterbalanced by other substances. The sublingual glands underneath the tongue are able to detect sweetness and other related sensations (diluted alcohol, glycerine). When brought into contact with sweet substances, they secrete a mucous, viscous saliva.

The third organic system to come into action during tasting is that of the mucous membranes of the palate, the inside of the cheeks and the gums. These mucous membranes give extra information on acidity, perceiving its corrosive, irritant nature, and also the 'metallic' tinge of tartaric acid, the slightly 'acidulous' nature of citric acid and the 'tartness' of malic acid. The mucous membranes around the inside of the lips are good at picking up the stickiness left behind by sugary solutions, or the 'warm' sensation generated by any drink containing alcohol. However, the main function of the mucous membranes is to detect astringency, in other words, tannin. Astringency is a term signifying the effects of tightening and constriction of the mucous membranes of the mouth in response to substances such as the flesh of the sloe, copper salts, quince juice and the numerous tannins: oak, chestnut, walnut, grape, etc.

In the case of grapes, most of the tannin is contained in the pips and is transferred to red wine when it undergoes maceration. White wine, on the other hand, is not macerated and therefore has much lower tannin levels. When tasting wines produced within a single region, there is a tendency to evaluate the tannin only in terms of quantity and intensity. But if red wines of very different origins and different grape varieties are compared, this quantitative evaluation is no longer sufficient, for qualitative differences and variations in type of tannin then became apparent.

PERCEPTION ZONES OF THE TONGUE

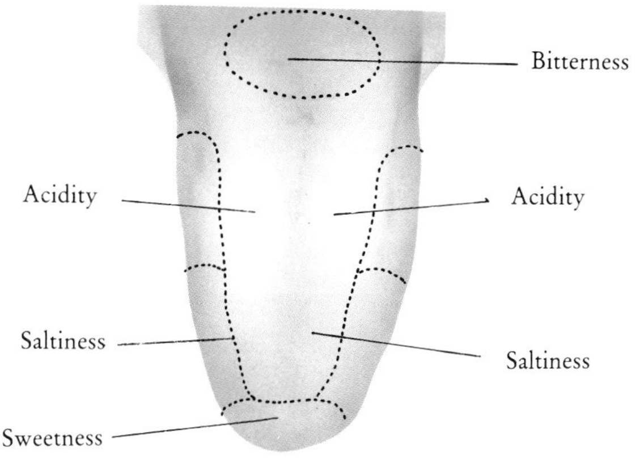

Astringency is not a simple phenomenon. It can be appreciated according to two qualitative parameters, one of which is expressed in time, in terms of persistence and impact; and the other spatially, in terms of localized harshness and aggressivity. Some tannins produce a barely perceptible constriction, but then give place to a kind of incrustation or impregnation of the mucous membranes in the cheeks, which is sometimes more persistent than others. If present in excess, this characteristic gives the wine a kind of thickness or a heavy quality. Its absence is felt as an element of finesse. This first level of astringency, then, can be translated into a scale of tannic consistency, the points of which, in descending order, might be: dense, chewy, sticky, persistent, clinging and light.

The second parameter, which is perceived more instantaneously, has to do with corrosiveness and aggressivity, as in rhubarb, or the tannin from oak wine casks. It can be translated into a scale of harshness, the degrees of which are far more clear cut than in the above scale, i.e. harsh, moderate or attenuated, and soft.

If we add the basic notion of quantity to these two parameters, it can be seen that the tannin content of every wine can be defined in the following three terms: quantity, consistency and harshness. This means that subtle differences in the perception of tannin in wine can be expressed.

The mucous membranes of the mouth are also good at sensing the temperature of the wine, and other far less well-defined sensations such as the pressure and nature of carbonated bubbles in a sparkling wine. It is possible to perceive a slight acidity in carbon dioxide, which is natural, since it is an acid gas, but differences in texture are also perceived, linked to the physical nature and size of the bubbles, and the rate at which they are released.

In fact, the collective sensations that any wine produces on contact with the mouth can be expressed in terms of texture. In French, the term used to signify this is the '*grain*' (grain) of the wine, and to speak of this aspect is to qualify the impressions of finesse or coarseness experienced while the wine is in the mouth.

Traditionally and methodically speaking, the taster senses and analyses wine by means of his own natural perceptions, and the scientific terminology of the laboratory chemist does not interest him much. He or she will describe perceptions in terms of the appropriate sensory faculty, chiefly the sense of smell and the sense of taste. This will be preceded by a visual examination.

The appearance of wine

For many people, the visual aspect of wine (when they take the time to look at it at all) is confined to its immediate attractiveness, for it is an iridescent, mobile substance with many fleeting shades of colour, and it is further enhanced by the glass in which it is served. Wine has the twin attributes of beauty and nobility, a combination of qualities not to be found in any other food or drink. These attributes are evident in the appearance of wine; in studying them, numerous other small attractions catch the eye, such as the 'legs' or 'tears' that form on the side of the glass; the reflections given to wine by light from chandeliers, ceiling lights and windows; and the fact that the crystalline hemisphere of liquid lying in the bottom of the glass is like a large precious stone.

'Legs' or 'tears' result from the difference in speed of evaporation of water and alcohol in a thin film of wine.

'Legs' were long equated with an abundance of sweet substances or glycerine in the wine. It is now known, however, that these veils of liquid result from the different speeds of evaporation of water and of alcohol within the thin layer of wine.

The surface of the wine in the glass, which some call the 'disc', has a fluctuating, fleeting quality. It varies in nature and intensity according to the lighting, the colours of the surroundings and the tablecloth, the diameter of the glass, the density of the wine, and the angle and distance from which you look at it — in fact, you can read as much into it as a fortune-teller can read in coffee grounds. In order to have a sound point of reference, the visual examination of wines should always take place under the same conditions and in the same surroundings.

More serious and significant than a general appreciation of colour is the work that can be carried out using a *tastevin*. The *tastevin* has been perfected and refined as a tool by centuries of experience. Being shallow and wide, it does not allow the taster to 'sniff at' the wine. It is, first and foremost, a vessel in which the wine can be scrutinized in terms of clarity, colour and intensity. In this way, the professional taster can judge the general state of a wine, its stage of development and how it will develop in the future.

Visual evaluation is not the only reason for taking a look at the wine in this way. It also prepares the mind and sensory organs for the tasting process that is to come. A white, red or rosé wine with a decided and positive colour is always a wine rich in substance. Lightness of colour goes with lightness of body, at least in the case of young wines. There is an exception to this rule, in that some red wines lose their colour, but not their power and body, with age.

A brilliant or luminous colour means that the wine is lively or high in acidity. There are three categories of tonality of colour: brilliant, satiny or matt. A matt colour is a sign of very low acidity; brilliance increases in proportion to acidity content. But the most significant aspect of the colour of a wine is, without doubt, its underlying shade. This shade develops continously with the wine's age and condition. Young white wines have a greenish hue that goes with their fresh aroma. As the aromas lose freshness, the colour turns to straw yellow. If a wine is left to mature for a very long time, it turns a shade of amber or gold, often intensely so. (When this happens, the colour is referred to as golden, not yellow.) Brilliance of colour in general denotes quality. Dull wine with brownish or greyish edges suggests a product that has deteriorated.

Rosé wines follow a similar pattern of development to white wines. Initially, they are intensely fruity and this is generally indicated by a raspberry-like colour. Later, the colour changes to a strawberry hue, indicating a more settled bouquet. In their final stage of development, they turn apricot coloured and develop aromas of new-mown hay, cooked peaches and dried almonds.

The range of colours is particularly spectacular in red wines, and variations in intensity provide further nuances. The anthocyanins that make up the colouring matter in red wine are the same as those in fruit, flowers and coloured vegetable produce, and so follow the same development process. Just as a rose in a vase loses its brilliance and yellows, then browns, so a red wine goes from red to brown. At first, most grape varieties will give a beautiful purplish red wine. The purple shade disappears little by little, leaving only the red. The red is then progressively invaded by yellow, acquiring an orange or ochre tone. Finally, a hint of brown appears, and some very old red wines turn completely brown.

This process of colour development does not have the same significance and importance for all wines. The purplish hue and bright red colour are right for *vins de primeur* and wines

The tastevin *permits detailed examination of the limpidity, shade and intensity of the wine's colour.*

A visual examination enables you to judge the colour, depth, brilliance and transparency of the wine.

that are to be drunk young. When these deep colours begin to attenuate, the wines will have lost their freshness. Orange and ochre tones go with the well-developed bouquet and harmonious, homogenous flavours of wines capable of lasting into middle age. Browns are only acceptable in wines capable of maturing over a long period of time. In wines with only modest levels of extract and aromatic potential, such a colour is a sign of decrepitude.

The smell of wine

A taster smells a wine to examine what is termed the wine's bouquet — or its aroma, *fumet*, aromatic complex, the exact choice of phrase depending on your training and inclination. This means, quite simply, the volatile substances present in the wine. These are always numerous, complex and variable. Even their origin is mysterious, except in the case of naturally aromatic varieties such as the Muscat or other white grapes from the Rhinelands of Alsace or Germany; most wine-making grapes have no real perceptible odour at the time of harvest. The aromas first begin to emerge during vinification. The combination of smells that eventually becomes the 'bouquet' goes on changing as the wine ages. Nowadays, researchers believe that these aromatic substances are already present in the grape, in an odourless, dormant form, and are brought into odoriferousness by the processes of fermentation and ageing.

DIFFERENT COLOURS OF SWEET WHITE WINES

Green-gold

Gold

Amber

THE COLOUR OF WINE

The colour of a wine is made up of a great many different shades. This colour develops constantly in accordance with the wine's age, and the conditions under which it has been kept. When tasting a wine, a knowledge of these colours is of prime importance if an accurate appraisal of the wine is to be made.

White wines are predominantly green when young, turning to straw yellow, then, as time goes on, to gold and amber.

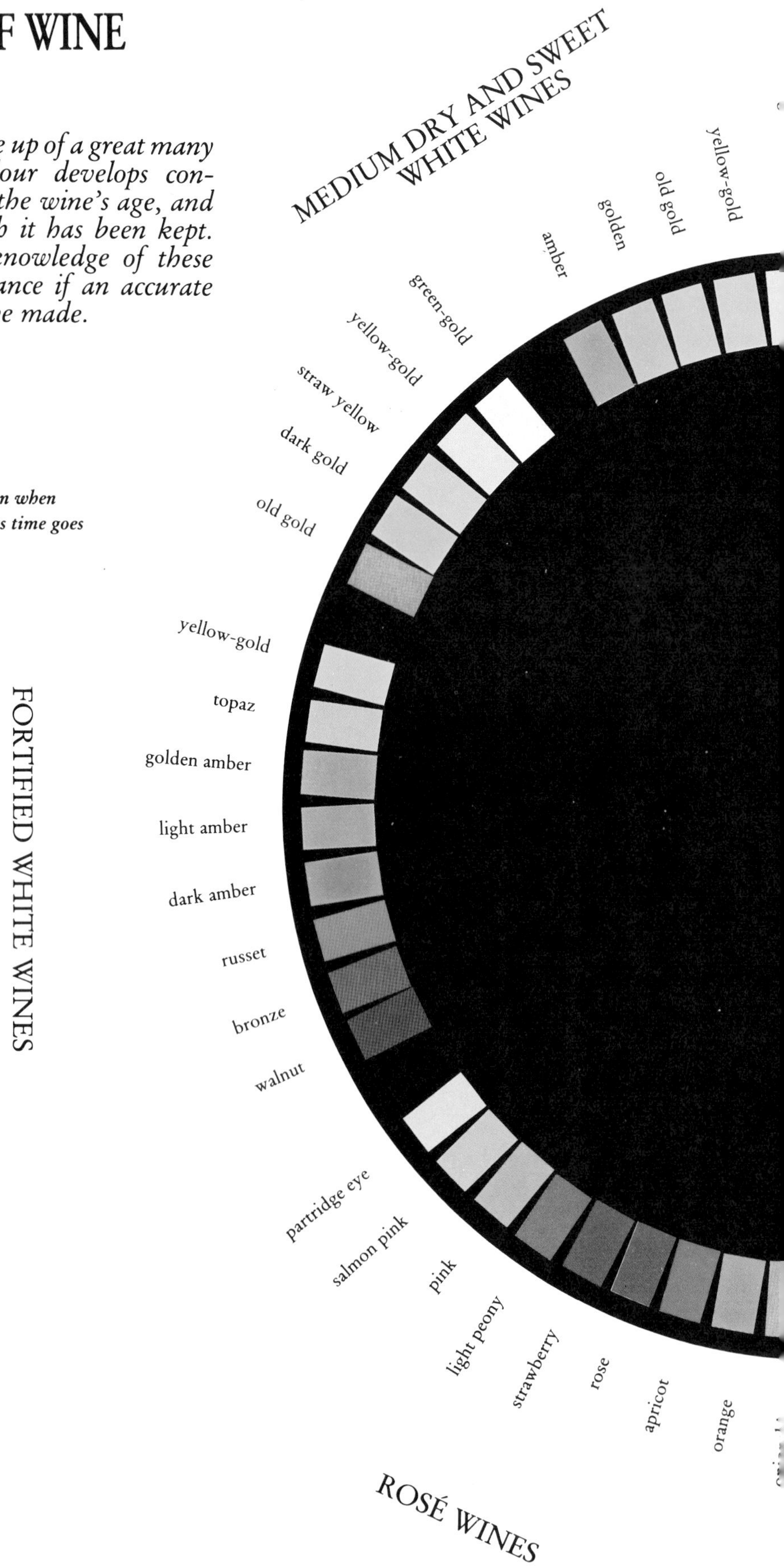

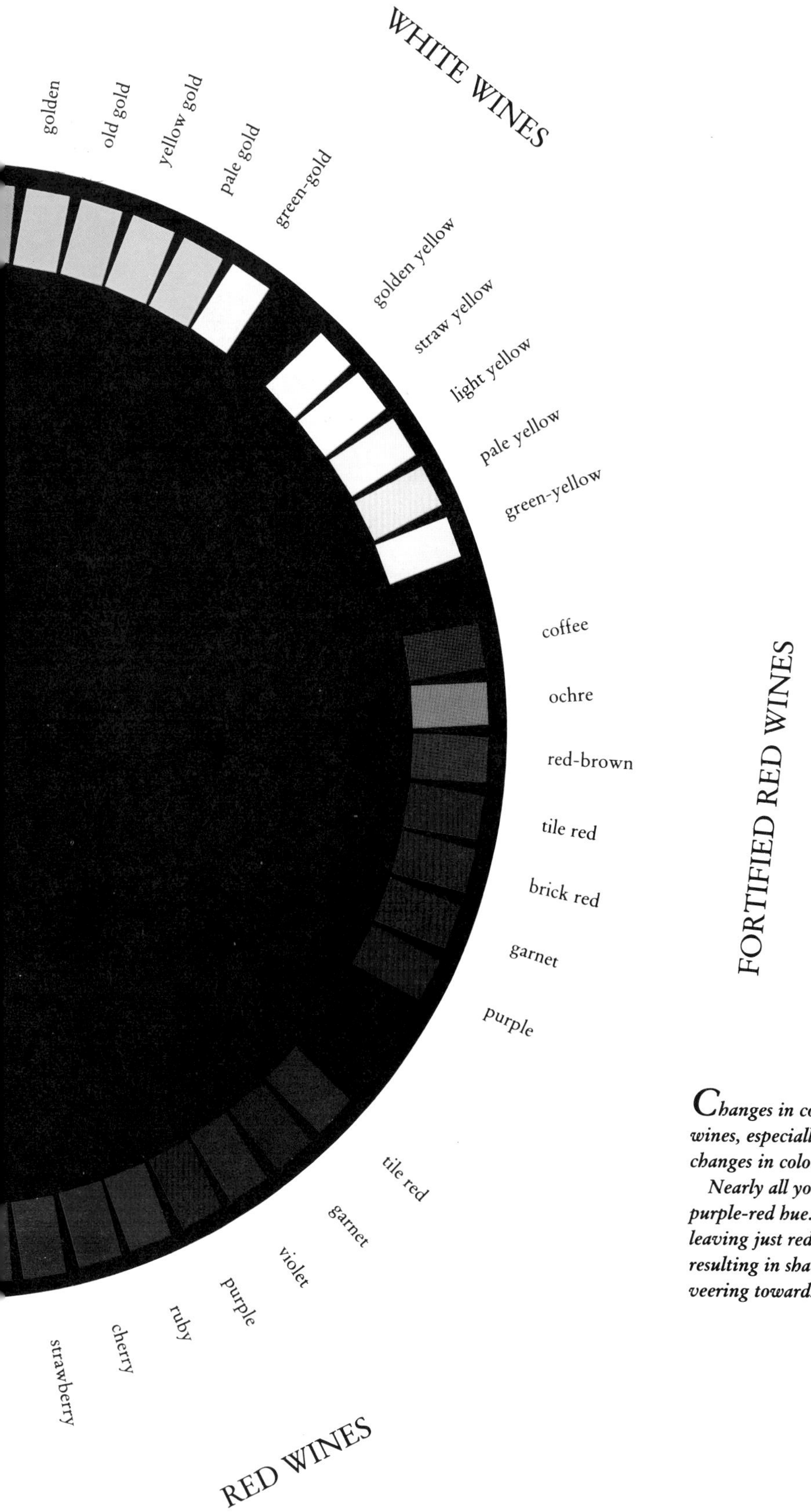

Changes in colour are extremely important in red wines, especially when they are accompanied by changes in colour intensity.

Nearly all young red wines have a beautiful purple-red hue. The purple disappears slowly, leaving just red, which is soon infiltrated by yellow, resulting in shades of orange and ochre, and finally veering towards brown in old wines.

The novice taster finds it particularly surprising that wine, apart from Muscats and the like, has no distinctive 'grape' smell, but rather takes its aromas from all aspects of nature, and that these are described in terms of natural analogies. Such analogies are actual, not merely imitative: a list of some 200 possible aromatic notations has been established. It is useful to practise recognizing aromas from time to time, for a taster must have practical experience as well as a thorough background knowledge. The practical aspect of training is all the more difficult since the taster has to deal with the wine just as nature hands it to him, with its light, fleeting, fluctuating bouquet. So the list of aromas shown on the right is only a simple means of notation, for the bouquet of a wine is never the same twice. It varies according to the length of time the wine has been exposed to the air, any movement or journey the bottle has undergone, the glass, the time of tasting, the humidity, air pressure, and the mood of the taster, not to mention other imponderables.

For the purposes of teaching, the external phase of examination of a wine's odour, known as direct olfaction, has been separated from the internal phase, the examination of the wine's 'retronasal' aroma, sometimes described as 'retro-olfaction'. This takes place after the wine has been taken into the mouth, via the retronasal passage to the olfactory mucous membrane. In reality, the two phases are almost continuous, but they vary in importance depending on the wine and on regional traditions of appreciation. The appearance, volume and structure of regional wine glasses reveals everything about the old customs and methods of tasting employed in these various areas. The small balloon-shaped glass used for Rhine wines shows that direct olfaction was never practised here, only internal olfaction. The same is true of the old-fashioned wide-mouthed white wine glass of the Loire region (especially Vouvray). With the great red wines of Bordeaux, where aromatic subtleties often intermingle with delicate flavours, the internal phase of aromatic perception is more enjoyable, more enriching and longer lasting than the phase of direct external olfaction. An elliptical glass that narrows slightly at the top suits the Bordeaux balance between external and internal olfaction. In order to capture the whole aromatic range of the finest burgundies and the neighbouring wines of the Rhône valley, where external olfaction is of more consequence, a bulging tulip-shaped glass is the best possible aid.

A common practice is to swirl the glass as soon as the wine has been poured into it, in order to release the aromas in greater amounts and with greater intensity. However, this movement can harm the very light or delicate aromas such as peppermint, cigar leaf and violets, and you may not then be able to recognize them. They can only be smelled in isolation if the glass is held still. In the case of wines with a rich, expansive bouquet, this initial still, delicate, exquisite phase can lift the taster into an aromatic reverie. Only when you have carried out this still, aromatic examination is it permissible to swirl the glass from time to time in order to capture the 'medium-density' aromas, such as flowers, fresh fruit, delicate spices, roasted food and animal smells. At this point, you will notice that these aromas do not reveal themselves as an overall mixture, but often in series, almost as if they have been arranged in an exit order. This order is not invariable, however, for it can result from any change in the environment, such as the temperature of the room, the temperature of the bottle, atmospheric conditions and humidity, as well as from the shape of the wine glass. Glass shapes are, of course, a determining factor in the search for aromas. The same wine tasted in three differently shaped glasses will present three distinctly different aromatic profiles.

Finally, a constant and energetic swirling of the glass will enable you to detect the 'heavy' aromas, if any; for example, dried and crystallized fruits, burned aromas and heady, pungent spices.

When the wine reaches the mouth, the process of aromatic perception changes. It also undergoes a dramatic change in intensity. Instead of the aromas being received successively, at a distance, they are received directly, all at once, by means of

SOME OF THE AROMAS DETECTABLE IN WINE

FLOWERS: acacia, almond blossom, honeysuckle, broom, wallflower, bluebell, carnation, peach blossom, geranium, peony, rose, elderflower, lime blossom, privet, violet.

FRESH FRUITS: apricot, pineapple, banana, various sweet and bitter cherries, lemon, blackcurrant, strawberry, raspberry, passion fruit, redcurrant, melon, blackberry, bilberry, peach, pear, various kinds of apple and plum, grapefruit.

DRIED OR PRESERVED FRUITS: almond, glacé cherry, quince, dried fig, cooked strawberries, hazelnut, prune, raisin.

SPICES: cinnamon, ginger, cloves, bay, nutmeg, pepper.

LEAVES, GRASSES and other vegetal aromas: pine needles, sandalwood, amber, incense, blackcurrant leaves, fern, cigar leaf, lemon balm, oak moss, undergrowth, mushroom stalks, capsicum (sweet pepper).

CONFECTIONERY: aniseed, bergamot, acid drop, mint, liquorice, vanilla.

ROAST OR BURNED AROMAS: burned wood, cocoa, coffee, caramel, wood tar, tea.

Other FOOD SUBSTANCES: garlic, butter, beer, cabbage*, silage*, dairy produce*, onion*, vinegar*.*

ANIMAL SMELLS: civet, leather, marinaded game, musk, wildfowl, hare entrails.

* = abnormal smells

Examination of the smell of wine enables you to identify aromas. Those detected initially belong to the direct phase of olfaction, and those detected after sipping belong to the phase of retro-olfaction.

direct oral contact. Furthermore, they immediately mingle with the underlying flavours, which either bring the aromas into greater prominence, or distract attention from them. This effect is particularly striking when a wine seems to lack expansiveness under external olfaction, but the internal phase, by contrast, proves rich and intensive. For the true enthusiast and connoisseur, tasting can never be limited to the search for a few aromatic components. Such a taster will judge the simplicity or complexity of the aromas as a whole, together with their degree of rusticity or refinement, their coherence or dispersion, their youth or age, and try to draw one or two worthwhile conclusions. Tasting also leads the taster to realize that everything to do with the sense of smell is closely linked with feelings and emotions. Even if you sniff a wine very lightly, the aromas it releases evoke the whole natural and domestic environment of its region of origin: the fruits, the plant life, the woods and forests, the smell of the country cottages, the cuisine and the pastimes, the gaity or austerity of the inhabitants, even the climate . . .

The taste of wine

When sufficient attention has been given to the enjoyment of the aromatic character of a wine, it is time to apply yourself to recognizing the other sensations it has to offer: those that reveal themselves on the tongue and in the mouth. Three groups of substances correspond to three different taste reactions. They are acidity, richness and tannin.

▷ Acidity includes all the organic acids to be found in wine — tartaric, malic, citric, succinic, lactic and acetic — most of which come from the grape flesh.

▷ Richness (*moelleux*) means the unctuousness provided by the sweet substances such as sugar, and also by the alcohol and glycerine produced during fermentation.

▷ The tannin and the other phenolic substances, which have varying degrees of astringency, are all products of the pips, skins and stalks of the grapes, and are released by the process of maceration in the vat.

The appreciation of these groups of sensations is carried out in two stages. Firstly, the nature and intensity of each one is ascertained. Secondly, its relationship to the other two groups is analysed. This results in an evaluation of the consistency and structure of the wine variously called the silhouette, form, body, volume, or substance of the wine. These terms refer to the corporeal aspects of the wine, as opposed to the more subtle and intangible aspects provided by the aromas.

Acidity is detected by the appropriate specialized zones of the tongue as well as by irritation of the mucous membranes in the mouth; but above all, by copious fluid salivation from the parotid glands.

Richness is sensed by movements of the tongue, and by thickening of the sublingual saliva. It has been noted many times that diluted alcohol has a definitely sweet taste and is one of the group of sweet flavours. Alcohol, in fact, is the principal sweetening agent in dry wines. However, tasters of traditional sweet white wines and dessert wines, in which most of the richness comes from residues of unfermented sugar, believe that a more analytical method of tasting is needed in this respect. In fact, they try to separate the taste of alcohol from the perception of richness and relate it separately to the other two groups, acidity and tannin.

The tannin, in red wines, is perceived by means of its action on the mucuous membranes of the mouth. It is defined in terms of quantity, harshness and consistency (or persistence). The quantity is linked to the grape variety and the method of vinification. The harshness also depends on the grape variety. It is especially noticeable in the Pinot Noir of Burgundy, the Nebbiolo of Piedmont in northern Italy and the Mourvèdre. The Gamay, on the other hand, produces a mild tannin. The consistency–persistency factor changes with time, and is decisive when it comes to the delicacy and overall quality of the wine. A fine wine cannot have a coarse tannin content. In this case, however, there is no direct connection with the *terroir* or the grape variety, because the same top-quality *cru* can give a very rough or a very supple wine, depending on the year, the ripeness of the grapes, the vinification and the age and development of the wine. Tannin always decreases in amount and harshnesss, and its consistency becomes less heavy and more refined as the wine ages in bottle. The reverse is never true.

ABNORMAL FLAVOURS

Wine can be spoiled, acetic, reduced, oxidized, musty, maderized or undergoing an undesirable refermentation. It may also have alien or unpleasant flavours, such as a stalky taste, a corky taste, a woody taste, or a taste of sulphur, mercaptan, lees, glue, phenol, tar or mould. It can be putrid, rancid, or fetid. These flavours and defects may be due to a number of factors, one of the most important of which is microbial spoilage (see The Microbiology of Wine, Glossary of French Tasting Terms and Technical Glossary).

Analysing sensations

Those who have had no training in wine tasting perceive sensations as a whole, and are unable to analyse their impressions because the sensations are so complex.

When a professional carries out sensory analysis, he or she receives the same overall impression as the layman, as well as being able, at the same time, to perceive individual sensations of acidity, richness and tannin. From the overall impression, the professional first extracts what may be termed the salient or predominant characteristics of the wine. These predominant characteristics act as a background for the more detailed ones. White wines and red wines must be treated differently in this respect, however, as they have different structures.

The fact that white wines and non-macerated rosé wines have no tannin means that the tasting profile is reduced to a balance between richness and acidity groupings. The different positive and negative combinations of these two categories are still numerous, of course, and certainly enable the taster to analyse the style of any white wine in the world.

It is generally believed that richness and acidity neutralize or attenuate the effect of one another, but this is only true in very limited circumstances.

As a general rule, it is quite difficult to evaluate acidity and richness or sweetness separately in white wine. If you take a number of wines with the same level of acidity, the least sweet will always seem to be the most acid and vice versa. The salivary secretions of the parotid glands are a good aid to sensitivity in this respect, for the secretions will be the same for different wines with the same degree of acidity, regardless of the level of sweetness.

Gradations of acidity in wines with no notable degrees of sweetness can be expressed as follows. A slight acidity makes the wine lively; a palpable excess is called acidity. A deficiency of acidity, on the other hand, is experienced as softness.

Gradations of richness or sweetness in wines with a normal degree of acidity gives fatness to the wine if the presence is marked, while the wine will have a honey-like quality where there is an abundance. A calculated reduction of richness or sweetness is a characteristic of dry wines.

If both sweetness and acidity are strongly present, the wine will be rich in substance, with pronounced flavours. But if there is an excess of both, and the wine in question is simultaneously very sweet and very acid, then it is descibed as *nerveux*, literally 'tense', meaning vigorous and vital, due to the oppositions it contains within itself. In contrast to this, if there is a deficiency of both elements, the wine will be small and flat.

The most common combination is a normal or positive level of acidity and a moderate to low level of sweetness. This is typical of the freshness and suppleness of most dry wines. The combination can turn to tartness, however, if the acidity increases and the sweetness decreases still further.

On the other hand, an abundance of sweetness and low acidity results in the unctuousness and generosity of *vins de liqueur* and *vins doux naturels*.

THE ACIDITY-RICHNESS SPECTRUM IN WHITE WINES AND UNMACERATED ROSÉ WINES

1 aggressive
2 acid
3 thin
4 slender
5 hollow
6 green
7 fresh
8 dry
9 flat
10 small
11 sharp
12 lively
13 balanced
14 soft
15 flabby
16 hard
17 firm
18 fat
19 cloying
20 unctuous
21 nervy
22 full
23 honeyed
24 luscious
25 heavy

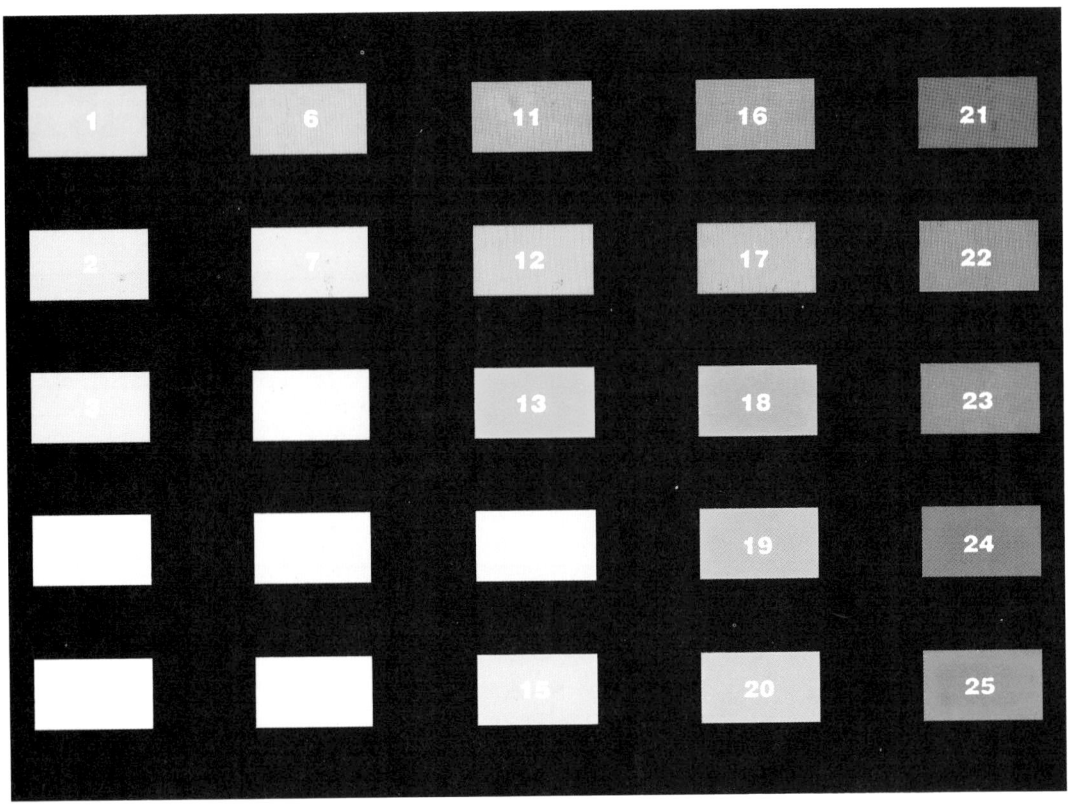

Besides the acidic and sweet elements of taste, red wines have the further important factor of their tannin. The introduction of this third base factor makes the permutations still more numerous and difficult to express. It is necessary to determine the predominant characteristics in the same way, but it is also necessary to note that when a dominant feature should be 'evident', i.e. just tannin, or acidity, or sweetness, it in fact emerges against a background of the other two sensations mixed together, and this factor can make the 'evident' feature quite difficult for the taster to discern. The other two sensations confuse the picture.

A predominance of tannin is expressed according to the following ascending scale: well structured, tannic, rough, harsh. For acidity, the ascending scale is: fresh, lively, *nerveux*, acid. For richness, the scale is the following: *fondu* (literally 'melted', and by extension 'supple' or 'succulent'), fat, unctuous, thick. These terms are not such as to be able to describe a great wine to full advantage, and a fine wine of any sort will rarely have a single pronounced characteristic.

If there are two predominant characteristics, such as tannin + richness, tannin + acidity or acidity + richness, then all kinds of nuances and distinctions are possible. These are expressed in anthropomorphic terms. Thus, tannin is the skeleton, richness is the musculature and flesh, and acidity is the nervous system.

For example, the combination of tannin and richness expresses, in varying degrees, the substance, corpulence and breadth of the wine. Two parts tannin to one of richness suggests solidity, while two parts richness to one part tannin would identify a wine as having a fleshy character.

A combination of tannin and acidity produces firmness and hardness in wine. When very acute, this hardness can be described as stiffness. Two parts tannin to one part acidity produces severity; two parts acidity to one part tannin gives the wine an angular, bony character.

Within these pairs of sensations, it is still necessary to be able to distinguish between a genuinely predominant feature and a relatively dominant one, i.e. a dominance that in fact results from the lack of a third component. For example, side by side with a true predominance of tannin + richness, a combination that gives rise to corpulence, there will be cases where such a combination is suggested by a lack of acidity. Here, the sensation is no longer akin to corpulence, but rather to softness or flabbiness.

In the same way, the combination of tannin + acidity can be enhanced, without creating firmness or hardness, by a slight decrease in richness that lends delicacy, finesse and elegance. The ambivalence of pairs of dominant characteristics is even more evident in the case of the combination of acidity and richness. In principle, such a combination should not exist in a red wine. But this is how the best red *vins de primeur* are made. A little extra richness makes them supple, a little more acidity makes them delicate. Here, however, the balance is a subtle one. When there is a true predominance of acidity + richness in a red wine with a normal level of tannin, this gives rise to an overloaded, even disharmonious character, which is unpleasant. Only when the combination of acidity and richness is brought out by a reduction of tannin do you achieve the fresh, 'easy to drink' character of *vins de primeur*. This is why they are given such short vatting times during vinification.

DOMINANT CHARACTERISTICS OF RED WINES

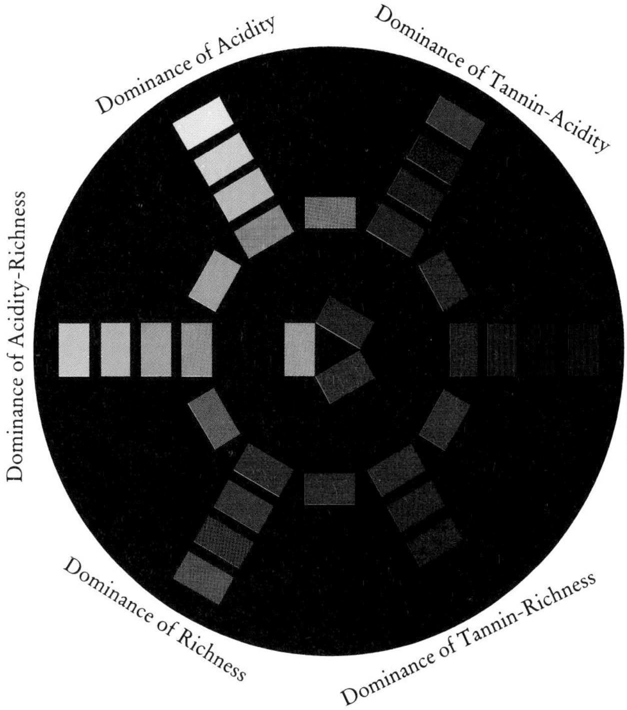

A true mixture of the three dominants — tannin + acidity + richness — is normally only present at the earliest, undeveloped stage of a wine's life, and it is rarely met with in wines ready for drinking.

To all these purely qualitative evaluations, many tasters add an evaluation of the length of the wine. Length means the impression left in the mouth and the degree of persistence of the aromas there after the wine has been swallowed or spat out. It is expressed in *caudalies*, one *caudalie* being equal to one second of persistence. Length is connected with the degree of quality of the wine: the greater the persistence, the higher the quality. However, this is not an infallible or universal rule. It should only be applied within a restricted sphere, to compare successive vintages, or to neighbouring *cuvées* of wine under consideration for blending.

The length of white wines is quite easy to grasp. In the case of red wines, it is important not to confuse it with the persistence of the tannin. After the aromatic persistence has finished, there is a last, attenuated sensation known as the aftertaste. This is separate from the length of the wine.

There are no grounds for thinking that these sensory analyses can only be achieved by a minority of specialists. Amateur enthusiasts who have developed their sensitivity and broadened their knowledge of wine and wines have succeeded in becoming connoisseurs, and are as competent as the professionals. Such connoisseurs sometimes chair important tasting panels in France.

Besides heightened sensory awareness, tasting demands an open, ready disposition, an absence of preconceived ideas and, most important of all, great prudence, for of all skills, it is the one in which the worst mistakes are possible. Even the most experienced tasters make such mistakes.

N O

Néac

The *appellation d'origine contrôlée* of Néac, situated in the Libourne area, was created by the decree of 8 December 1936. It was reserved for red wines made from grapes gathered in the commune of Néac.

However, this commune became linked to the Lalande-de-Pomerol *appellation* by the decree of 2 September 1954, and the growers have subsequently stopped using the Néac name, preferring to sell their wines as Lalande-de-Pomerol.

Négrette

Synonyms: *Négret, Négret de Gaillac, Négret du Tarn, Négrette de Villemur, Négralet* at Auvillars, *Morillon, Morelet, Mourelet* in Tarn-et-Garonne, *Villemur* at Cazères (Haute-Garonne), *Cap-de-More, Chalosse Noire* and *Vesparo Noir* in Gers, *Noirien* in Ariège, *Petit Noir, Dégoûtant* in Charente, *Folle Noire* on the islands of Ré and Oléron, *Ragoûtant* or *Bourgogne* in Vendée, *Saintongeais* in Touraine, *Couporel* in Aveyron.

Young leaves downy, yellowish, bullate, underside felty white.

Leaves cuneiform, finely bullate, red petiolar junction, five-lobed, lobes of average size, lateral sinuses narrow, acute at base, petiolar sinus V-shaped, more or less narrow; dentation pointed, underside of blade downy with pubescent veins.

Bunches small, cylindrical, compact, winged; grapes small, spherical to slightly ovoid, black with very pulpy flesh; ripening period: second epoch.

The Négrette is a fertile vine. It gives a deeply coloured, well-structured, quality wine and is the reason behind the reputation enjoyed by the red wines of the Côtes du Frontonnais; it was also grown to make the best red wine of Charentes. Unfortunately, it is prone to oidium (powdery mildew) and grey rot (botrytis), and its plantings have consequently decreased in recent years. Five registered clones have been approved: numbers 456, 580, 581, 582 and 663. Classed as 'recommended' in the South West, Charentes and Languedoc, this vine is grown on 1,125ha, mainly situated in Haute-Garonne (718ha) and Tarn-et-Garonne (378ha). It features in plantings for the Côtes du Frontonnais AOC and the Vins de Lavilledieu VDQS.

Nielluccio

Synonyms: *Niella* around Bastia, *Nielluccia* at Cervione, *Negretta* at San Martino.

Grown on Corsica, this vine is of Italian origin. It is related to Tuscany's famous Sangiovese, on which the reputations of Chianti and Brunello di Montalcino have been built.

Bunches cylindrical, loose, with two shoulders; grapes ovoid, blue-black, juicy; ripening period: third epoch.

This vine buds early, and is of average productivity. The wine it gives is high in alcohol, but without much depth of colour; it has a certain finesse and matures well. Classed as 'recommended' in Corsica, the Nielluccio is one of the grape varieties used in the Vin de Corse and Ajaccio AOC wines. It is grown on an area of 2,552ha.

Noir Fleurien

Bunches conical, winged, compact; grapes spherical, black, with very pulpy flesh; ripening period: second epoch.

An old grape variety from the Auvergne, the Noir Fleurien is cultivated in the commune of Mirefleurs, south of Clermont-Ferrand, where it came to the attention of Girard-Col at the time of the first outbreak of downy mildew in the Auvergne. Having shown a certain resistance to this disease, it enjoyed some popularity for a while, all the more so because it is suited to the arid, limestone soils found in the Auvergne. A productive vine, the wine it gives is deeply coloured, but low in alcohol, flat, lacking in acidity and tannin. It is classed as 'recommended' in Puy-de-Dôme, where some few hectares of it are still grown.

Burning the vine trimmings in Nuits-Saint-Georges. This operation takes place in winter, just after pruning.

Noual

Synonyms: *Noubal* in the Cahors area, *Nouval* or *Loubal* in Tarn-et-Garonne, *Noual* at Prayssac (Lot).

Quite a productive vine, the Noual is grown in a few districts of Lot and Tarn-et-Garonne, as well as a few hectares in Aveyron and Tarn. It has not been classified.

Nuits-Saint-Georges

This *appellation d'origine contrôlée* was ratified by decree on 5 November 1972. There are no Grands Crus in Nuits-Saint-Georges, but there are some great Premiers Crus. The vineyards of this *appellation* reflect the complexity of the *terroir* in their richness. The traditional Burgundy grape varieties of Pinot Noir for red wines and Chardonnay for white are used. Red wines must contain at least 10.5° alcohol, with 11° in the case of Premiers Crus; and white wines must have at least 11°, 11.5° in the case of Premiers Crus. The maximum yield allowed is 35hl/ha. In 1985, the amount of wine produced was 1,022hl of red and 26hl of white. The red wines of Nuits-Saint-Georges are a beautiful ruby colour; they are fine and frank, combining and balancing finesse, firmness and structure. Their bouquets are rich and forthcoming, some of them suggesting raspberries, strawberries and even game, depending on the degree of maturity. These wines are slow to reveal themselves, and age remarkably well. The white wines, which are very rarely seen, as they are made in such small quantities, are also excellent.

Oberlin Noir

A Gamay × *riparia* cross, also known as *595 Oberlin*.

Leaves cuneiform, dark green, finely bullate, crimped at the petiolar junction, five-lobed with deep, narrow lateral sinuses; petiolar sinus lyrate; dentation very large, pointed; underside of blade pubescent.

Green shoots ribbed, red on the side exposed to the sun. Bunches small, cylindrical, loose; grapes spherical, small, black, with coloured juice; ripening period: first epoch.

This hybrid has the advantage of being early and vigorous, with the long canes possessed by *riparia* varieties. If it is to be sufficiently productive, it must be pruned long, as the bunches weigh less than 100g each. It has a good resistance to disease and requires few or no preventative treatments.

Oberlin Noir wine is deeply coloured, alcoholic and rich in dry extracts. It has a resinous flavour. It is classed as 'authorized' in northeastern France, where it grows on less than 1,000ha.

Odola

This is a Baroque × Côt cross achieved at INRA at Bordeaux. It is of erect habit, its fertility is good and it is very vigorous — which sometimes makes its growth capricious. The bunches are semi-compact with black grapes, ripening early in the second epoch. This vine has good resistance to grey rot (botrytis). Its wine is deeply coloured, with an excellent flavour, more delicate than that of, for example, the Tannat. The Odola is classed as 'authorized' throughout France and one registered clone has been approved: number 601.

Œillade Blanche

Synonyms: *Picardan, Picardan Blanc, Araignan* or *Aragnan* in Var, *Gallet* in Gard in the Costières region, *Milhaud Blanc* in Tarn.

Bunches medium sized, conical, compact; grapes ellipsoidal, medium sized, white, speckled with brown spots when fully ripe, not very juicy; ripening period: third epoch.

This variety is little cultivated today, and has not been included in the EC's classified list. However, under the name of Picardan it is one of the grapes permitted for the Châteauneuf-du-Pape, Côtes du Rhône and Palette AOCs. It is grown on 60ha, divided between Var and Bouches-du-Rhône.

Œillade Noire

Synonyms: *Œillade, Ouillade, Uliade, Ouillard, Ouliade, Aragnan Noir, Araignan* in Vaucluse, *La Croque* at Cambon in Tarn.

Bunches medium sized, conical, winged, loose; grapes ellipsoidal, large, a lovely blue-black colour, bloomy, with crisp flesh; ripening period: second epoch.

This vine is often confused with the Cinsaut, from which it differs in that its leaf blade is downy-pubescent, and its fruit-bearing is more capricious due to a susceptibility to *coulure* (flower abortion). Consequently, it is planted much less widely than in the past.

Ondenc

Synonyms: *Blanc* or *Plant de Gaillac, Piquepoul de Moissac, Blanc Sélection Carrière* in Gers, *Blanquette* or *Blanquette Sucrée* in Gironde and in the Bergerac region, *Béquin* in Entre-Deux-Mers, *Primaic* at Fronton, *Primard, Dourec* or *Dourech* in Jurançon on account of its early growth cycle, *Œil de Tour* at Beaupuy (Lot-et-Garonne), *Oustenc* at Marcillac, *Prendiou* or *Prentiou* at Oloron (Pyrénées-Atlantiques), *Sable Blanc, Sensit Blanc, Semis Blanc* in Landes, *Chalosse* or *Chaloche* in Charente-Maritime.

Bunches medium sized, conical, compact; grapes ellipsoidal, medium sized, yellowish white, with juicy flesh; ripening period: second epoch.

This grape variety has early budbreak, and produces only modestly. It is of spreading habit, with bushy growth, and it is often weak, being prone to attack by a number of different viral diseases. It is also susceptible to grey rot (botrytis). Although it gives a pleasantly flavoured wine with a medium degree of alcohol, it is rarely vinified by itself.

Three registered clones have been approved: numbers 674 to 676. The Ondenc is classed as 'recommended' in all the *départements* of the South West. It now grows on a mere 160ha, as opposed to 1,600ha in 1958. Of these, 110ha are in Gironde and 32ha in Gers. It is included among the approved varieties for the Bordeaux, Côtes de Duras and Gaillac AOCs.

THE WINE LIST

The wine list is both image and announcement, a promise, an act of faith in the land, the vine and the work of man. It is a diamond with a thousand facets, each one representing a wine.

How many people know that the blonde Isabella of Portugal, wife of Philip the Good of Burgundy, the third 'Grand Duke of the West', invented the written menu at the brilliant Burgundian court in the 15th century? The purpose of the menu is simply to show which dishes are available to satisfy the appetites and desires of the guests. In aim and format it is similar to the wine list; indeed it often lists both food and wines together.

The wine list is a faithful reflection, modest or luxurious, but always attractive, of the actual restaurant cellar containing bottles of wine and spirits. They lie below, in darkness and calm, waiting for someone to rouse them and hurry them out into the daylight, sometimes spruce, smooth and clean, but more often hoary, dressed in the *Penicilium glaucum* that covers the cellar walls like black velvet.

The characteristics of the wine list

A wine list must be clear and accurate, true to each of the drinks it describes and offers. It must be comprehensive and attractive, so as to catch the customer's eye and arouse his or her interest in and desire to try the wines listed.

Furthermore, it is an act of faith on the part of the restaurateur, a contract between this skilled artist of the table and his cellar. This bond between host and wine is tenuous at first, but soon becomes much firmer and will rarely disappoint.

If a wine list has been lovingly composed, it is more likely to arouse curiosity and even passion in the customer than if it is a businesslike list. A wine list should be much more than just an inventory drawn up of the contents of the cellar; it should be a catalogue of the many beauties, simple or luxurious, young or mature, that reside there; and the restaurateur, often a craftsman but always an artist, will be proud of them. There are instances where a wine list fails to keep its promise, and proves disappointing or even misleading, but these are the exception rather than the rule.

The accuracy of the wine list

A wine list must be accurate. It should not contain alterations, erasures or deletions; the latter, in particular, are a hideous disfigurement of its charms. Yet at the same time the list must always be revised and kept up to date if customers are not to be disappointed. Listing a wine that is no longer in stock is unfortunate and can harm the reputation of the establishment, suggesting at best a want of taste, at worst a lack of honesty.

One of the most important ways in which a wine list displays its accuracy is by not unduly embellishing or adjusting the names of the wines listed. Thus a Gevrey-Chambertin, no matter how good, is not a Chambertin-Gevrey (a Chambertin from Gevrey) nor a Chambertin. To say so would be illegal, since misuse and direct or indirect usurpation of a name, position or function are all legally classed as fraud. So a wine list should be subject to an appropriate ethical code of practice, arising out of a spirit of fair competition, and respecting the laws of the land.

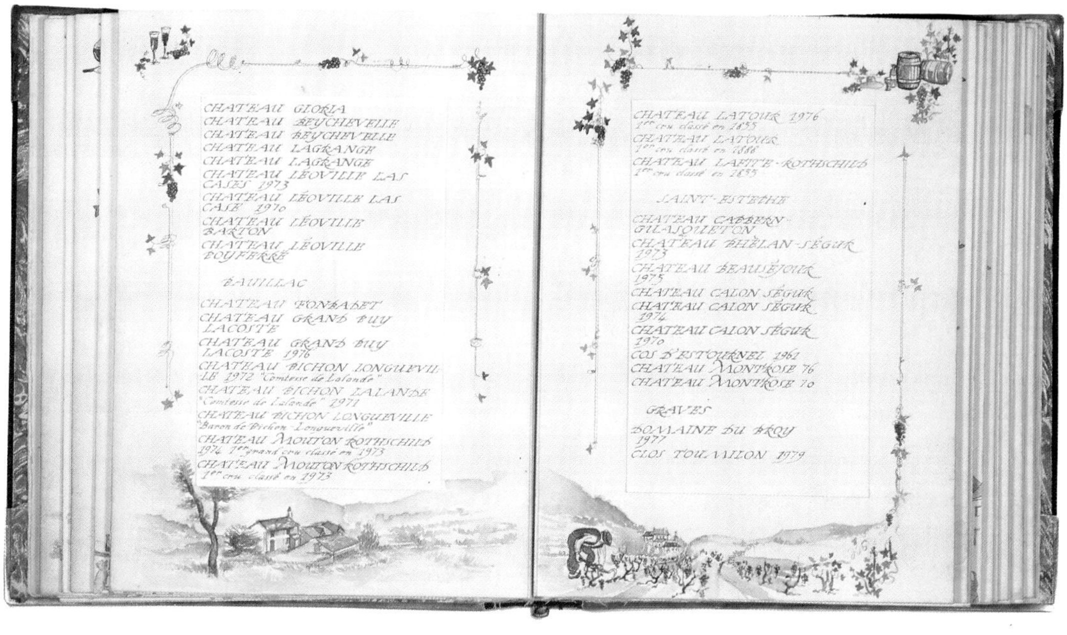

***M**arc Meneau's cellar book, offering a harmonious combination of pleasant reading and pleasant tasting.*

The wine list and the wine waiter

A wine list has the wine waiter (the *sommelier*) as its ambassador. He or she is the one who offers it to the wine-loving client and comments upon it, bearing in mind the age, sex, state of health, degree of tiredness, tastes and means of the client, as well as the dishes being taken. The wine waiter's role is to reveal the mysteries of the wine list with wisdom, skill, patience and courtesy. He or she is the adoptive parent of the wines in the cellar, rarely owning them, yet often having chosen them, even sometimes having taken the trouble to go straight to the grower or the *négociant* to do so. He or she has cherished them from the moment of their arrival, ascertained their vigour and classified them precisely according to their potential for future development. He or she knows them both intellectually and physically, having noted any minor ailments they may have suffered, and cured them. This, then, is the wine list that is offered in the restaurant at the beginning of the meal.

The wine list and the restaurateur

Great restaurateurs are often honoured with awards and indications of merit by private organizations and publications. These indications take the form of stars, chef's hats, forks, etc., and their number generally indicates the standard of the restaurant in terms of gastronomy, wines (the quantity, variety and worth), aesthetic merit, the cleanliness of the kitchens and dining area, welcome, service and price. These gradings are reviewed annually. The scope and presentation of the wine list is a vital element when it comes to awarding these much sought-after distinctions.

There is a tendency nowadays for some restaurateurs in France to specialize more and more in regional and foreign foods and wines (or other drinks). Breton, Basque, Languedocien, Provençale, Alsatian, Burgundian, Angevin, Tourangeaux, Nantais, Scandinavian, Flemish and Béarnais restaurants mainly prepare the dishes of their home or chosen territory, accompanied by the appropriate wines and beverages.

The wines listed

Wines can be divided into red, white, rosé, *gris, vin jaune* or *vin de paille*. Another fundamental division is between still (non-sparkling) wines — although even some of these, especially *vins de primeur* meant for immediate consumption, can be very slightly sparkling (*perlant*), which enhances their freshness and fruitiness — and sparkling wines proper. The less effervescent sparkling wines are described as *'pétillant'*, the rest are termed *'mousseux'*. Sparkling wines are mostly white, sometimes rosé, but rarely red.

France offers the following types of still wine:

▷ Table wines (*vins de table*), which are mostly wines of the same colour (red, white or rosé) but of different geographical origins, blended together. The designation of such wines is national but never geographical, and consists of the words *'vin de table'*, followed by the alcoholic strength and the trade mark, if any.

▷ *Vin de pays* ('country wines'), which are superior table wines. These can also be red, white or rosé, and carry the words *'vin de table'*, followed by *'vin de pays de . . . '*, the *pays* (region or district) in question being either the *département* where the wine was produced (Vin de Pays de l'Aude); or in some cases a more restricted area, as in Vin de Pays des Coteaux du Pont du Gard; or sometimes a larger area than a *département*, as in Vin de Pays du Jardin de la France, or Vin de Pays de l'Île de Beauté. It is no longer obligatory to state the alcoholic strength. The name of the grape variety used may be specified.

▷ Quality wines, or VQPRD (an EC term), produced in specific areas. In French terms, this means all *appellation d'origine contrôlée* wines (AOCs), examples being Pommard, Médoc, Touraine, Côtes du Rhône, etc., and the same EC category covers the *vins délimités de qualité supérieure* (VDQS), such as Sauvignon de Saint-Bris, Gros Plant du Pays Nantais, Coteaux Varois, Saint-Pourçain or Côtes de Toul. The labels of these wines bear the geographical name in question, followed by *'appellation contrôlée'* or *'vin délimité de qualité supérieure'*.

Although not wines in the very strictest sense of the term, the following are also products of the vine:

▷ *Vins doux naturels* (VDNs, or sweet fortified wines), almost all of which are also *appellation contrôlée* wines. These result from the process of *mutage* (fortification), carried out part-way through fermentation. They are made from high-class grape varieties grown in some of the best soils and most favourable climates in France: Banyuls, Maury, and various Muscats, such as Muscat de Rivesaltes and Muscat de Frontignan.

▷ *Vins de liqueur* (VDLs or *mistelles*, also sweet fortified wines, but this time fortified before fermentation has begun): Pineau des Charentes is an example.

▷ Wine-based aperitifs (*apéritifs à base de vin*), for example famous branded aperitif drinks such as Byrrh, Dubonnet, Cinzano, etc.

▷ Vermouths, such as Vermouth de Chambéry.

The spirits listed

The best-known spirits (*eaux-de-vie*) are those that bear the name of the region in which they were produced. For example:

▷ Brandies such as Cognac and Armagnac, both of which are AOCs.

▷ Spirits based on apples or pears, such as the apple-based Calvados from Normandy.

▷ Wine-based spirits or marcs, such as Marc de Bourgogne, Marc de Champagne or Marc d'Alsace Gewürztraminer, all of which are *'appellations réglementées'*, giving them a similar status to AOC spirits.

The structure of the wine list

In order that the customer may be fully informed, there are certain items that a wine list should make clear.

Obligatory information

▷ The name of the drink, if it is the product of an *appellation d'origine*, plus any vineyard information attached to the name, must be quoted exactly and in full; in practice this should be more or less as it would read on the label: Nuits-Saint-Georges les Pruliers, for example, or Châteauneuf-du-Pape Clos des Papes, Champagne Clos des Goisses, Fine Champagne (Cognac), Armagnac, Banyuls Grand Cru . . .

▷ The volume of drink served, for example bottle or half

bottle. If a wine or spirit is served by the glass, the capacity of the glass should be given in centilitres.

▷ The price, stating whether service is included or not.

Optional information

Provision of the following information is desirable, although not compulsory:

▷ The vintage and, in the case of spirits and brandies, an indication of the age or quality level (Napoléon, 'three star').

▷ The name of the grower or merchant, for example: Château X for a wine from one of the Bordeaux AOCs; the name of the producing house in the case of a champagne; or the name of the *négociant* in the case of certain burgundies.

▷ Information such as '*blanc de blancs*' for a white wine made only from white grapes, especially a sparkling wine; or the name of the grape varieties used for any wine if specified and if not already implied by the *appellation* name.

Presentation

According to the rules of fair trading, *appellation contrôlée* wines and spirits should be listed separately from other wines to avoid any confusion. This is particularly important when the list is arranged according to regions of origin. A wine, technically a table wine, prepared by a Beaune *négociant*, that consists of a blend of wines of different origins and which therefore has no AOC or VDQS (though it may be an excellent wine) cannot be entered on the wine list under the heading 'Burgundy', despite the Beaune address on the bottle. It is the *appellation* that counts.

The most common arrangement of the wine list, and certainly the most convenient for the customer, is by region. Thus, under the headings Bordeaux Blancs and Bordeaux Rouges would be grouped all the red and white AOC wines from the Gironde area sold by the restaurant.

THE CLASSIFICATION OF WINES AND SPIRITS ON WINE LISTS

A number of specialist publishers in France and elsewhere supply handy, and in some cases elegant, printed wine lists on which restaurateurs can enter the drinks they are offering for sale. Here is an example of how French wines and spirits may be classified. The order may be varied at will:

- *Bordeaux — AOC (Gironde* département*);*
- *The South West — AOC (from the Spanish border to Bordeaux: Dordogne, Haute-Garonne, Lot-et-Garonne, Tarn-et-Garonne, Tarn, Lot, Pyrénées-Atlantiques, Hautes-Pyrénées);*
- *The South West — VDQS (the above-mentioned* départements *plus Gard, Landes, Aveyron, Cantal);*
- *Burgundy — AOC (Yonne, Côte-d'Or, Saône-et-Loire, Rhône), including the districts of Chablis, Auxerre and Tonnerre, Côte de Nuits, Côte de Beaune, Côte Chalonnaise, the Mâcon district and Beaujolais;*
- *Franche-Comté and the Lyon district — AOC (Jura and Rhône);*
- *The Bugey district — VDQS (Ain);*
- *The Lyon district — VDQS (Loire);*
- *The Rhône valley — AOC;*
- *Provence and Corsica — AOC;*
- *The Rhône valley, Provence, Corsica — VDQS;*
- *Languedoc and Roussillon — AOC;*
- *Languedoc and Roussillon — VDQS;*
- *The Loire valley — AOC, including the Nantes area, Anjou, Saumur and Touraine;*
- *Other parts of the Loire valley — AOC (Maine-et-Loire, Sarthe, Indre-et-Loire, Loir-et-Cher and Indre);*
- *Other parts of the Loire valley — VDQS (Cher, Indre, Loir-et-Cher, Loire-Atlantique, Maine-et-Loire, Vendée, Allier, Puy-de-Dôme, Loiret, Vienne and Deux-Sèvres);*
- *Alsace — AOC;*
- *Lorraine and the Toul district — VDQS;*
- *Champagne — AOC. This heading also includes the still wines of Coteaux Champenois and Rosé des Riceys;*
- *Other sparkling wines — AOC;*
- *Vins Doux Naturels and Vins de Liqueur — AOC;*
- *Non-*appellation d'origine *sparkling wines;*
- *Vins de Pays;*
- *Wine- or cider-based aperitifs;*
- Appellation d'origine *brandies and spirits;*
- *Non-*appellation d'origine *brandies and spirits;*
- *Liqueurs;*
- *Other drinks (beers, ciders, fruit and vegetable juices, waters and sodas).*

The wine list should be a permanent inventory of those drinks in the cellar that are ready for consumption. Drinks are not included if the person in charge of the cellar decides they have not yet reached maturity.

The wine list should, in broader terms, be a necessary and valuable part of a restaurant's appeal to its customers. It is the means by which a customer composes and orders a pleasurable meal, with the help of the head waiter and wine waiter if necessary. This choice is determined by the customer's tastes and state of health, the time of day and occasion for the meal, and the available dishes.

The customer should be presented with the wine list as soon as he has sat down, in order to help him make a decision. The wine list should precede the menu, or, at the very least, be brought at the same time. This will facilitate the task of the wine waiter in giving advice, particularly concerning compatibility between the wines and dishes on offer.

THE WINE WAITER AND WINE SERVICE

Technician, psychologist, oenophile, jurist and gastronomical fanatic, the wine waiter oversees the grand ceremony of wine, as well as offering tactful guidance on the subtle connections between wines and dishes.

In a hotel or restaurant, the wine waiter is an important person, partly on account of his or her management responsibilities, but also because alcoholic drinks represent about 30 per cent of turnover. A wine waiter is therefore indispensable, both in commercial terms and in terms of the reputation of an establishment.

The role of the wine waiter

The wine waiter carries out his duties both in the dining room and in the cellar. In the dining room he serves drinks, therefore his job is to serve each wine as it reaches maturity, making sure that it goes with the dish or menu in question, that it is served at the correct temperature, given the correct amount of exposure to air and not handled to an unnecessary degree. His worth lies in the quality of the advice he gives concerning the wines, spirits and liqueurs on the wine list.

In the cellar, he takes care of the maintenance, control and management of stocks. He is also involved in the ordering of wines and spirits; the normal situation is for him to advise the restaurateur or hotel buyer in this respect.

An efficient wine waiter must:

▷ know as much about vines, wine and wine making as possible, and be familiar with the geography of the wine-growing regions and their different *crus*. To this end, he should visit these regions as often as his work permits;

▷ taste wines analytically at frequent intervals;

▷ keep up with developments in wine making and growing by reading wine and wine trade magazines, so that he can advise his clients satisfactorily;

▷ take his clients' remarks into consideration, and pass them on to the wine producers in question, or their agents.

The cellar

In the cellar, the wine waiter's main task is to take care of stocks. First and foremost, he must make sure the wines are properly kept. If they are to mature well, the cellar must have the following characteristics:

▷ it should face north or east;

▷ it should have a constant temperature of about 11°C;

▷ the relative humidity should be constant at around 70 per cent;

▷ it should be dark;

▷ ventilators should be installed, so that air enters the cellar close to ground level on the north side, and leaves high in the wall on the south side;

▷ the floor should be of beaten earth;

▷ cleanliness should be observed;

▷ nothing but wine should be kept there.

The wine waiter should be able to explain the origin and characteristics of a wine and its vintage.

The bottles should be arranged in numbered, stable bins, according to region. New arrivals should not be stored among old stock of the same origin.

The development of the wines should be checked by regular tasting and by reading specialized wine magazines.

The wine waiter's secondary cellar task is to keep stock records up to date. This can only be done by daily checks, using stock cards or a cellar book containing all the necessary information on stock levels, and incoming and outgoing stock.

Buying

Building an appropriately sized cellar in a restaurant depends on the numbers and nature of the clientele, as well as on the traditions of the establishment. Purchases are also linked to important financial decisions, such as investment and the tying-up of capital.

Once the cellar is established, wines are bought in accordance with the turnover of stocks. It is important to know how to strike a balance between stocking old wines, stocking wines to be bought and sold quite young, and stocking those that are bought young but must be left to mature.

The wine list

A wine list has to respond to both legal and commercial requirements. The different categories of wine must, above all, be indicated very clearly. Wines are therefore grouped as follows:

▷ table wines produced within the EC, including French *vins de table* (table wines) and *vins de pays* (country wines);
▷ quality wines produced in specific regions (VQPRD), including French *appellations d'origine contrôlée* (AOC), champagne (whose name is so protected that it need not cite its AOC), *vins délimités de qualité supérieure* (VDQS), and wines imported from other EC countries;
▷ wines from other countries of the world;
▷ sparkling wines;
▷ dessert wines.

The degree of alcohol should be shown, and so must the quantity, i.e. half bottle, bottle, magnum, carafe, glass, etc. The final piece of obligatory information is the price.

The wine list must only show wines that have reached full maturity, and are available in quantities adequate to last until the list is next produced. It must be up to date, easy to consult, thorough and attractive to handle and read.

At the beginning, as suggested above, should be placed a selection of table, carafe or 'country' wines, wines that are particularly good value for money, and any regional wines given special prominence.

The other wines will then be listed according to their different categories: VQPRDs distinguished by region and country of origin, sparkling wines and dessert wines. Within each category, the wines will be grouped according to type: red, white, rosé, *gris, vin jaune, vin de paille,* and so on. Each type will come, first, under the main regional heading, e.g. Burgundy, Bordeaux, Alsace, etc., and then under the various subdivisions of the main regional grouping. For example, in the case of red burgundies, the subdivisions might be: Côte de Nuits, Côte de Beaune, Côte Chalonnaise, Mâcon and Beaujolais.

The wine list should be precise and show, in addition to the exact wording of each *appellation,* pertinent information, such as the name of the château and place of bottling in the case of Bordeaux wines, or the name of the estate owner and/or *négociant* in the case of burgundies. Vintages should be shown in order of age, with the youngest listed first.

The *cave du jour*

The *cave du jour* is restocked daily. It is an air-conditioned 'mini-cellar' situated close to the service area, its function being to have wines ready and acclimatized for service. Red wines are stored there on their sides, the quantity depending on the available space and ambient temperature. White and rosé wines and champagnes are stored in small amounts in air-conditioned wine cabinets with separate compartments maintained at different temperatures, so that each type can be kept in conditions appropriate to its age and structure (temperatures vary from 9°C to 13°C).

This system enables the wine waiter to ensure a quick and efficient service, as wines will be arranged at his disposal, close to the service area, at a temperature between that of the main cellar (11°C) and the restaurant (22°C).

Glasses

Glasses should be clear, transparent and as thin as possible, so that the colour of the wine can be appreciated. They should be tulip-shaped, to permit the aromas of wines to be enjoyed to the full, and have a stem, so that they are easy to hold.

It is best to wash them in a detergent that does not have too strong a smell, then rinse them thoroughly and wipe them dry immediately with a clean, washed cloth made of fine linen. Finally, glasses should be hung upside down when not in use, so as to keep dust out.

Serving wine

The wine waiter knows his wine list and all it has to offer perfectly. He presents it to his clients, having first acquainted himself with the kitchen order, which has been taken by the head waiter.

Taking the wine order

The wine waiter must be unassuming and have a measure of psychological acuity, as well as being a good adviser and salesman. He should be able to draw on reserves of initiative and confidence.

He also needs to take an interest in cuisine, its ingredients and the origins of the produce used. A sound knowledge of cuisine will enable him to create harmonious partnerships between the dishes and the wines to accompany them. He must have an excellent relationship with the head waiter and the chef, since all three should work in close cooperation.

When choosing a wine, he takes into account local tastes and preferences, the time of year, the number of people in a party, the type of meal, and also the states of mind of his clients: they may not all wish for the same combinations, and especially not when clients are of different ages.

If asked, the wine waiter should be able to explain the origins and characteristics of a wine and its vintage.

Presenting the bottle

Once the order has been taken, the wine waiter sets out the glasses appropriate to the chosen wine. He then brings the bottle, at the correct temperature, ready to be served.

The wine waiter shows the bottle to the person who has ordered it, pointing out to him the main points of information given on the label.

Opening the bottle is carried out in front of the customer's table. The capsule is cut below the rim of the bottle neck to avoid any contact with the wine.

The wine waiter removes the capsule to see the wine in the bottle neck.

He removes the cork carefully to avoid disturbing the sediment.

He wipes the neck of the bottle, inside and out, with a clean cloth.

With the carafe held at a slight angle, away from the neck, he pours in the wine.

The candlelight enables him to follow the movement of the sediment.

He pours some wine from the carafe, tastes it, then places the carafe on the table.

Opening the bottle

The wine waiter stands before the table when opening the bottle. He cuts the capsule below the rim of the neck, so that the wine never comes into contact with it. During this operation, the bottle must be held firmly. He then wipes the neck with a table napkin.

Next, the cork is removed prior to serving the wine. This should be done in the following manner:

▷ Use a good, lever-operated corkscrew, of the 'waiter's friend' type, with a slender thread with five spirals.
▷ Check that the length of the thread is adequate to penetrate the length of the cork.
▷ Place the tip of the corkscrew carefully in the middle of the cork; give the corkscrew a single turn, then pull gently so as to loosen the cork.
▷ Screw the corkscrew in fully, taking care not to go through the bottom of the cork. Draw the cork. When the cork is three-quarters out, remove the corkscrew and pull the cork out by hand, gently, so as not to break it, and also in order to prevent the air from rushing into the neck of the bottle, as this makes an unseemly noise.
▷ Wipe the neck of the bottle, inside and out, with a clean cloth.
▷ Smell the bottom and then the top end of the cork, to make sure that the wine is not 'corked'. If the cork smells particularly insalubrious and unpleasant, the bottle should be rejected immediately.
▷ If the cork is of fine quality, and bears stamped details of its origins, present it to the host on a saucer.
▷ Turn away slightly from the client and discreetly take a sip of the wine to verify its quality.

Lastly the wine waiter pours some wine for the person who has ordered it to taste and give his or her approval.

Serving the wine

The proper way to serve wine is as follows:

▷ Allow the person who has ordered the wine to taste it.
▷ Ask him or her if the temperature of the wine is as wished.
▷ If the wine meets with approval, serve the guests in customary order of precedence, reminding them discreetly of the name of the wine. Finish by serving the host.
▷ While serving, do not hide the label of the bottle, and be careful not to knock the glasses, which should be half- or three-quarters filled.

▷ Serve the guests regularly with wine during the course of the meal, tactfully enquiring what the host's wishes are (a further bottle of the same wine, or else a change of wine).
▷ In either case, the glasses must be changed, for the new bottle will not have the same aromatic profile or structure as the previous one, due to its different temperature and length of exposure to air.

When the wine has been served, the wine waiter slips away discreetly, having made sure that everything is arranged so that the meal will be as pleasurable as it can be.

Decanting

This is a delicate operation. It has three effects: separation of the sediment from the wine, oxidization of the wine and, finally, a change in the wine's temperature.

Oxidization develops the bouquet of the wine, but if it occurs to too great an extent, the wine loses its subtlety, nuance, finesse and freshness. Thus decanting should only be carried out if you are sure of the wine's structure, its ability to withstand exposure to air, and the persistence of the bouquet. Only experience and common sense can guide you in this respect. The time of exposure to air is very important. It can vary from a brief instant to about an hour; although some fortified wines, such as tawny port and madeira, which have to undergo a long process of maturation in wooden casks, hold up excellently under the effects of exposure to air. If a wine is very old, it should be opened at the last moment and should not be decanted.

Finally, if a wine is to be served in bottle, it does not matter if it is opened three hours before it is served, or at the last moment. There can be no evaporation, and oxidization is minimal. The quantity of oxygen that penetrates the wine after it has been uncorked is very small: it absorbs twice as much while being poured into the glass and three times as much after it has stood in the glass for 15 minutes.

Apart from oxidization, there is also the fact that the temperature of the wine changes in accordance with that of the room. The carafe into which the wine is decanted should be at the same temperature as the *cave du jour.*

The temperature of a wine served in bottle rises more slowly than does that of a decanted wine. In a room of 22°C it takes about three hours to rise from 11°C to 18°C.

SERVING TEMPERATURES FOR WINES

The temperature at which a wine should be served depends on its age, structure and character, on the season of the year, and on the temperature of the surroundings in which it is to be served.

If the temperature is too low, this makes most red and even white wines seem hard and thin and destroys the finesse of their bouquets. If the temperature is higher than 20°C, this destroys the balance of wine, making it seem coarse and lacklustre.

As a general rule, dry white wines are served at between 7°C, and 13°C, depending on their breadth and character.

Sweet white wines need to be served at between 6°C and 10°C depending on age: young sweet wines from 6°C to 8°C and older wines from 8°C to 10°C.

White vins doux naturels *and* vins de liqueur *are served at 6°C or 7°C, while red wines in these categories are served at between 10°C and 15°C, depending on their age and tannin content.*

Champagne should be drunk at 8°C or 9°C; vin jaune *at 15°C or 16°C.*

Vins gris, *rosés and* clairets *require a serving temperature of between 8°C and 12°C.*

Fruity, thirst-quenching red wines with exuberant aromas are drunk at between 11°C and 14°C. Red wines from the Côtes du Rhône are served at 13°C to 18°C, depending on their structure and method of vinification.

Red burgundies require a serving temperature of between 14°C and 17°C. In the case of red wines from Bordeaux, which have a higher tannin content, the temperature should be between 16°C and 19°C.

The general rule is that the greater the tannin content of the wine, the higher the serving temperature should be.

Serving champagne

The bottle should be placed in a bucket containing water and a little ice, in such a way that it will reach a temperature of 8° or 9°C in ten minutes. The bucket is then placed in a bucket-holder (called a *stand* in French) or on an occasional table covered with a table napkin. It should always be close to the dining table.

The wine waiter places the bottle of champagne in the ice bucket at an angle.

He removes the capsule and wire muzzle while holding the cork with one hand to keep it in place.

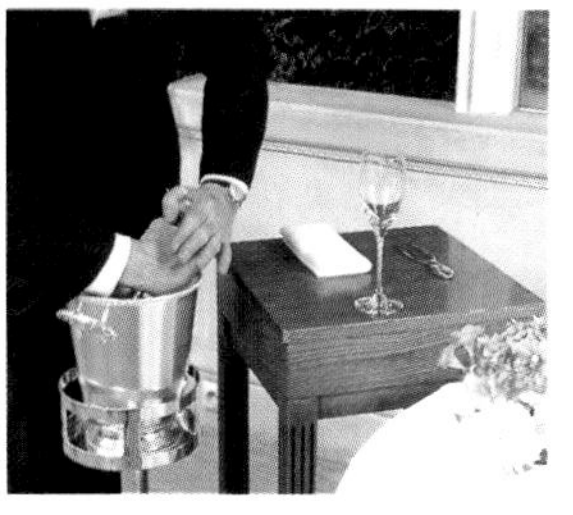

Grasping the cork firmly, he rotates the bottle.

He serves the champagne, filling the glasses no more than two-thirds full.

AVERAGE AGEING PERIODS FOR FRENCH WINES

To ensure that a wine develops soundly to maturity, it should be stored in a cellar for an optimum length of time. This time varies according to the temperature of the cellar and the structure and character of the wine. These two last factors are linked to the wine's origin and vintage, the vinification method employed and the type of élevage *it underwent before bottling.*

Wines	Average age at maturity	Lifespan
BURGUNDY WINES		
• ***White wines***		
Light, dry, fruity white wines (Chablis, Mâcon Blanc, St-Véran, Rully Blanc, Montagny, etc.)	1 to 3 years	Best drunk young
Pouilly-Fuissé, Chablis Premier Cru, Mercurey Blanc, Côte de Beaune-Villages (and 'village' AOCs)	2 to 4 years	5 to 10 years
Premiers Crus and Grands Crus of Côte de Beaune and Côte de Nuits	4 to 8 years	6 to 15 years
• ***Red wines***		
Beaujolais, Beaujolais-Villages	3 to 18 months	Best drunk young
Beaujolais crus	1 to 4 years	4 to 10 years
Côte de Beaune 'village' AOCs	4 to 6 years	12 years
Côte de Nuits 'village' AOCs	5 to 8 years	15 years
Côte de Beaune Premiers Crus, Grands Crus	6 to 10 years	15 to 20 years or more
Côte de Nuits Premiers Crus, Grands Crus	8 to 12 years	20 to 30 years or more
CÔTES DU RHÔNE WINES		
• ***White wines***	1 to 2 years	Best drunk young
Hermitage Blanc, Château Grillet	2 to 3 years	10 years or more
• ***Rosé wines***	1 to 2 years	Best drunk young
• ***Red wines***		
Côtes du Rhône-Villages	1 to 2 years	3 to 5 years
Cornas, Châteauneuf-du-Pape	3 to 8 years	10 to 15 years
Côte Rôtie, Hermitage	5 to 10 years	20 to 30 years
BORDEAUX WINES		
Entre-Deux-Mers	1 to 2 years	3 years
Graves Blanc	3 to 6 years	10 years
• ***Sweet white wines***		
Ste-Croix-du-Mont, Loupiac	6 to 15 years	20 years
Sauternes and Barsac	8 to 20 years	Several decades
• ***Red wines***		
Bordeaux, Bordeaux Supérieur	2 to 5 years	6 to 8 years
Médoc	4 to 10 years	15 years
Haut-Médoc	5 to 15 years	20 years
St-Julien, St-Estèphe	8 to 20 years	Several decades
Pauillac, Margaux	8 to 30 years	Several decades
Graves Rouge	5 to 15 years	Several decades
St-Émilion	7 to 15 years	Several decades
Pomerol	6 to 15 years	Several decades
LOIRE VALLEY WINES		
• ***Dry white wines***		
Light and fruity: Muscadet, Sancerre, Pouilly-Fumé, etc.	6 months to 1 year	2 to 4 years
Savennières crus	4 to 6 years	10 years or more

• ***Sweet white wines***		
Anjou: Coteaux du Layon, Bonnezeaux, Quarts de Chaume, Coteaux de l'Aubance Touraine: Vouvray, Montlouis	4 to 10 years	10 to 30 years or more
• ***Red wines***		
Light and thirst-quenching: Touraine, Anjou, Sancerre Rouge, etc.	4 to 18 months	2 to 5 years
Saumur-Champigny	1 to 2 years	3 to 10 years
Chinon, Bourgueil	2 to 4 years	5 to 25 years
ALSACE WINES		
Muscat, Pinot Blanc, Sylvaner	6 months to 1 year	3 to 4 years
Gewürztraminer, Riesling, Tokay	1 to 5 years	10 years or more
Gewürztraminer, Riesling, Tokay Vendange Tardive and Sélection de Grains Nobles wines	10 years or more	20 to 30 years or more
CHAMPAGNE		
• ***Non-vintage***	2 to 3 years	Best drunk young
Blanc de Blancs	2 years	Best drunk young
Richly structured champagnes	3 to 5 years	6 to 8 years
• ***Vintage***	4 to 6 years	8 to 10 years
Blanc de Blancs	4 to 5 years	6 to 8 years
• ***Recently disgorged***	Ready to drink	Ready to drink
• ***Non-vintage rosés***	2 to 4 years	Best drunk young
• ***Vintage rosés***	4 to 6 years	Best drunk young
JURA AND SAVOIE WINES		
• ***Dry white wines***	2 to 3 years	10 to 15 years
• ***Vins jaunes***	6 to 10 years	100 years or more
• ***Vins de paille***	3 to 5 years	Several decades
• ***Rosé wines***	2 to 3 years	5 to 6 years
• ***Red wines***	5 to 10 years	20 to 30 years
• ***Savoie white wines***	1 year to 18 months	3 years
Roussette (or Altesse)	2 to 3 years	5 years
MEDITERRANEAN REGION WINES		
• ***White wines***		
Provence, Cassis, Corsican white wines	1 to 2 years	Best drunk young
• ***Rosé wines***	1 to 2 years	3 to 4 years
• ***Red wines***		
Côtes de Provence, Corbières, Minervois, Fitou, Corsican red wines, Côtes du Roussillon	2 to 3 years	5 to 10 years
Bandol	3 to 5 years or more	20 years or more
• ***White Vins Doux Naturels***		
Muscat	2 to 3 years	5 years
• ***Red Vins Doux Naturels***	3 to 5 years	10 years or more
Maury, Banyuls	5 to 10 years	20 to 30 years
WINES OF THE SOUTH WEST		
• ***Dry white wines***		
Jurançon, Gaillac, etc.	1 to 2 years	3 to 5 years
• ***Sweet white wines***		
Jurançon, Pacherenc du Vic-Bilh, Monbazillac	3 to 5 years	15 to 20 years or more
• ***Red wines***		
Madiran, Cahors	5 to 8 years	15 years
Gaillac Rouge	6 to 12 months	3 years
Pécharmant	2 to 8 years	15 years
Côtes de Buzet	3 to 10 years	20 years

VINTAGES

Each year brings new wines of great or humble birth, always different, though always reflecting the same conditioning factors: a terroir, *man's work and, most of all, the climate. It is this last element that will shape the wine and decide its longevity.*

Wine is the product of three variously changeable factors that have combined to produce it: the *terroir,* which never varies; the wine growers, some of whom practise their art with greater care than others; and the climate, which is essentially changeable and unpredictable.

The influence of the climate is preponderant in France. As a result of the air masses that push along the Garonne corridor on their way to the Mediterranean basin, France has the greatest fluctuations of climate in Europe. Consequently, French wine can only be understood by considering its style (the result of its *terroir*) in conjunction with its form (or *silhouette*), which depends upon the prevailing weather during a particular year. Since the effects of climate and of *terroir* are interlinked, it is impossible to discuss an *appellation* wine with any surety without also having some knowledge of its vintage.

The climate factor

The idea of a 'vintage' implies the climatic conditions surrounding each of the different vegetative phases of the vine, and especially flowering and ripening. To fully understand a particular vintage, then, certain questions need to be asked relating to a number of different factors:

▷ The climate in April and May. If these two months are hot, the vegetative cycle of the vine will be advanced and flowering will be early.

▷ The exact flowering date of the vine. The later this comes after the summer solstice, the less the vine will benefit from the length of daylight in the 100 days separating this occurrence from the maturity of the grapes. Full, rich wines cannot be expected from a year when the vine flowers late.

▷ Rainfall. If rain is plentiful during the harvest, it will not be possible for the grapes to dry out and consequently the wines will be thinner and more diluted than normal.

▷ Sunshine. An important factor, conditioning both temperature and light levels.

▷ Temperature summations. A high total favours full grape ripening, or even overripening. In this case, the grapes will be rich in sugar, and therefore with high potential alcohol levels, and low in acidity. If there is a cold summer, the resulting wines will not be as 'warm', that is to say, they will be lower in alcohol and more acid.

▷ Length of daylight. The more light there is, the more intensely coloured the grape skin will be, and the greater will be its aromatic potential.

▷ The wind. In drying out the grapes, the wind speeds the whole ripening process, giving the resulting wines greater expressive density.

A consideration of these factors leads to the conclusion that there are no great or poor vintages. The notion of 'great' or 'poor' can only really be applied to wine-growing *terroirs* and *crus.* All that can be said is that in some years the weather pattern shapes the vegetative material differently, giving the grapes, and ultimately the wine, a greater or lesser degree of 'energy', that is to say, a longer or shorter life.

It is true, however, to say that the reputation of the great wines came about through a tendency towards longevity. The simpler wines have a short life. The renown of all vineyards is based on the length of life of the wines they produce, and it is this factor, too, that provides the framework for the French *appellation contrôlée* system.

The longevity of wines

A *terroir* gives wines of greater or lesser birth and hence greater or lesser longevity, but their precise lifespan, and the form that this will take in terms of vivacity, fullness, tannin and aroma, will be decided by the climatic conditions of the year in question. It is for this reason essential to know about prevailing weather patterns if one is to understand the developmental trajectory a vintage wine will take.

We can, to some extent, make a sympathetic identification with the grape. The wine enthusiast can say to himself: 'My French holidays were not very sunny that year, so of course the wine will be lighter and livelier.' The vine has no overcoat or umbrella to cover its shoulders; it offers us the weather it has been exposed to throughout a whole year in a single mouthful of wine. It has then to be left to mature in the shelter of an appropriate container, taking into account the precise lifespan the weather has bestowed upon it.

The diagram opposite shows two possible lifespans for a great wine, governed by the weather conditions of a vintage. For a wine of medium potential, the probable lifespan is shorter by one quarter, and in the case of a simple wine, by three quarters.

The table, and the two further tables on page 434, show the general lifespan of wines from the principal AOCs. This lifespan is a consequence of *terroir,* but in each case it will be modified by climatic factors. You can gauge the longevity of a wine by looking at its origin, to check the longevity of which it is capable, and its vintage, to see how the climatic factors of the year have modified this potential. It should be remembered that the longevity specified in the tables applies to the best growths of an *appellation* only.

The concept of vintage

Rather than speaking of a great vintage, then, it would be better to speak of 'a long-lived vintage'.

In 1947 and 1959, the weather was generous in France and consequently the grapes were packed with energy. This does not mean that the wine was great or poor, good or bad. It simply means it was born with a potential for long life. On the other hand, the wines of 1984 will have a short life because the weather was inclement.

Wine is known to pass through three main stages during the course of its evolution in bottle: a primary or adolescent phase, a secondary or adult phase and, finally, a tertiary or mature phase, when it reaches its optimum stage of development. It may remain at this stage for a number of years.

In a fine wine with a lifespan of 40 years, the stages of development will be as shown by the left-hand paths in the diagram on the right. Yet the same wine, produced in a year when the weather is unkind, will have an estimated lifespan of 10 years only, as shown by the right-hand paths in the diagram. Thus, a wine from a 'poor' vintage will be more developed after 10 years than one from a 'great' year. 1976 for example, might be considered a 'great' vintage in some parts of France, and 1980 a 'poor' one. Yet the difference is not, contrary to popular belief, absolute, but relative. In 1987, a wine lover might have derived more pleasure from drinking the wine of the so-called 'poor' vintage of 1980 than from that of 1976. The latter needs a longer period of time in which to demonstrate its greatness.

Wines interact in a most interesting way, then, if the short-lived or normal vintages can meet demand, allowing their siblings born during more generous years to mature quietly in bottle and so derive the fullest possible degree of individuality from their raw materials.

These surprising observations should encourage every wine enthusiast to set up his or her own cellar. Besides the fact that it is possible to watch the wines mature there, it will also be a worthwhile investment, because wines double in value every five years.

The notion of vintage enables us to appreciate better the language wines speak. It demonstrates the need to refrain from drinking wines too young when they have so much to offer in the future, and shows the importance of allowing them to develop at their own pace. Only those who have taken the trouble to study the hierarchy of longevity that exists among wines and vintages can profit from it, and pay wine the respect it deserves.

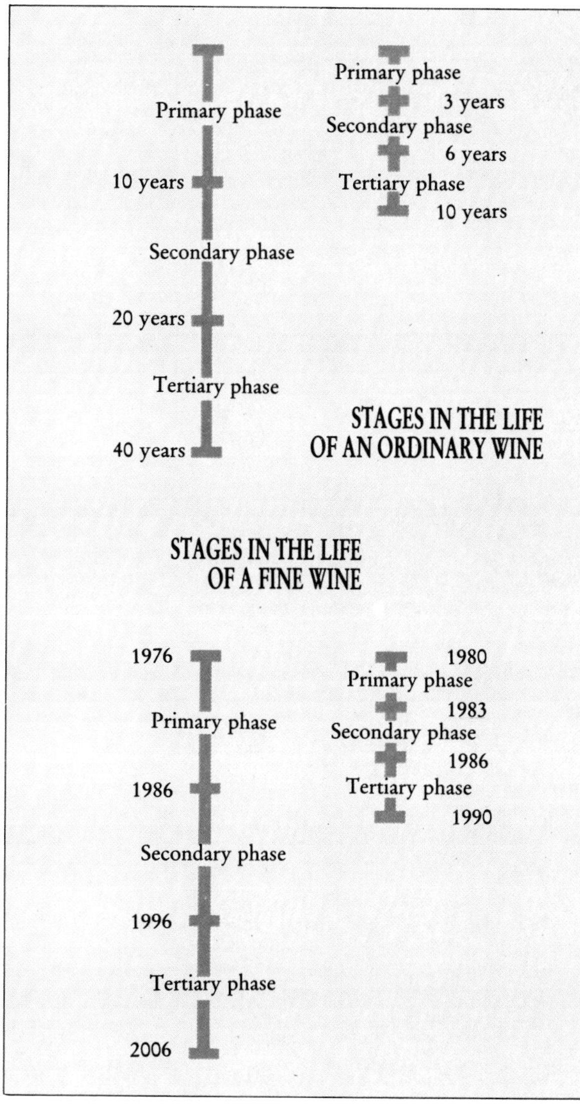

LIFESPAN OF THE BEST WINES OF SOME FRENCH APPELLATIONS			
AOC	Lifespan in years	AOC	Lifespan in years
Alsace	30	Côtes du Roussillon	10
Bandol	30	Gaillac	10
Banyuls Grand Cru	40	Hermitage	35
Bonnezeaux	40	Jurançon	30
Bourgueil	30	Madiran	30
Chablis Grand Cru	30	Margaux	40
Chambertin-Clos de Bèze	40	Monbazillac	40
Château-Chalon	50	Montrachet	30
Châteauneuf-du-Pape	40	Morgon	10
Collioure	10	Muscadet	10
Corton-Charlemagne	30	Pomerol	40
Coteaux du Languedoc	10	Saint-Chinian	10
Côtes de Duras	15	Sancerre	20
Côtes de Provence Rosé	5	Sauternes	50

LIFESPAN OF THE BEST WINES OF FRENCH REGIONS

E=	40 years	40 years	10 years	40 years	50 years	40/20 years		10 years
Appellation	Burgundy		Beaujolais	Bordeaux	Bordeaux	South West		Côtes du Rhône
	red	white	red	red	sweet white	Monbazillac	red	
years								
1964	E	E	M	L	B	L	L	L
1965	B	B	B	B	B	B	B	B
1966	L	L	L	L	L	L	L	L
1967	M	L	L	L	L	L	L	M
1968	B	B	B	M	M	M	M	B
1969	L	L	L	L	L	L	L	L
1970	L	L	M	E	E	E	E	L
1971	M	M	M	L	L	L	L	L
1972	M	M	M	M	M	M	M	M
1973	M	M	M	M	M	M	M	M
1974	M	B	M	B	M	M	B	B
1975	B	B	B	E	L	E	E	B
1976	E	E	L	L	M	B	L	M
1977	M	L	B	M	M	M	M	L
1978	L	L	M	L	M	L	L	E
1979	M	B	M	M	M	M	M	M
1980	B	B	B	B	B	B	B	B
1981	B	M	M	L	L	L	L	L
1982	M	M	L	L	L	L	L	B
1983	E	E	E	L	L	L	L	L
1984	B	B	B	B	B	B	B	B
1985	L	L	L	L	L	L	L	L
1986	L	L	L	L	L	L	L	L

E = year with exceptionally good weather: full lifespan.
L = year when weather guarantees a fairly long life: ¾ of E lifespan.
M = mixed year in terms of weather: ½ of E lifespan.
B = bad year in terms of weather: ¼ of E lifespan.

E=	40 years	30 years	20 years	20 years	30 years	20 years	40 years
Appellation	Anjou-Touraine white	Anjou-Touraine red	Vins du Centre white	Jura vin jaune	Alsace	Savoie white	Banyuls VDN
years							
1964	E	E	L	E	M	—	E
1965	B	B	B	B	B	—	M
1966	M	M	L	M	L	—	L
1967	M	M	M	L	M	—	L
1968	B	B	B	B	B	—	B
1969	L	L	L	E	L	—	M
1970	M	M	M	B	M	—	M
1971	L	L	L	L	E	—	M
1972	B	B	M	M	B	—	B
1973	M	M	M	L	M	—	B
1974	M	M	L	B	B	—	B
1975	L	L	M	M	M	—	M
1976	E	E	E	L	L	—	B
1977	B	B	M	M	M	B	B
1978	M	M	L	L	B	M	M
1979	B	B	B	E	M	L	M
1980	B	B	B	B	B	B	M
1981	L	L	M	L	M	L	B
1982	L	L	M	L	M	M	L
1983	L	L	L	L	E	L	M
1984	B	B	B	B	B	B	M
1985	L	L	L	L	L	L	E
1986	L	L	L	M	M	M	M

P

Pacherenc du Vic-Bilh

The wine-growing area of Vic-Bilh, in the northeast of the Pyrénées-Atlantiques *département*, was declared an *appellation d'origine contrôlée* on 28 August 1975. Production is small (about 2,500hl per year) and most of the wine is drunk locally. It is chiefly produced by family concerns rather than cooperatives.

Pacherenc du Vic-Bilh comes from a variety of grapes, among them the Gros Manseng, the Petit Manseng, the Courbu Blanc, the Lauzet, the Arrufiac and the Camaralet de Lasseube.

Dry or sweet, depending on the amount of sunshine the summer has brought, this wine is always lively and agreeable, with a many-faceted charm. When it is dry, it is a brilliant pale yellow shaded with green. It has a delicate, floral aroma, sometimes with a whiff of gunflint brought it by the Arrufiac. It has a pronounced retronasal aroma (aroma in the mouth), and is both fresh and fleshy, delicate and long, with hints of hazelnut and almond.

When it is sweet, the colour is a full pale yellow, and the floral aromas are combined with those of tropical fruit, such as pineapple or banana. Pacherenc du Vic-Bilh is then an elegant, full, yet fresh wine.

Paga Debiti

Synonyms: *Paga Debito*, *Pagadebidu* ('pays its debts').

Growing tips open, felty white.

Bunches very large, conical, quite compact; grapes large, white, spherical; ripening period: third epoch.

This vine, grown on Corsica, is not the same as the Italian Pagadebito: the two vines have differences of leaf lobing and of dentation. The Paga Debiti seems to be closely related to the Biancone di Portoferraio, grown on the nearby island of Elba, and known on Corsica as the Biancone. It is classed as 'authorized' in Corsica, and one registered clone has been approved: number 768.

Palette

The small wine-growing area of Palette officially became an AOC, covering three communes, on 21 April 1948. It has stood up well to the rapid urbanization that has spread out from Aix-en-Provence. Situated at the eastern entry to Aix, most of the vineyards face north and look on to the *route de Cézanne*, the D17, which links Aix and Puyloubier.

The vineyards were planted about 500 years ago by the Carmelites of Aix on gravelly slopes and pebbly terraces — very difficult terrain to cultivate. The entire *appellation* zone covers barely 20ha, and produces 600hl annually.

The combination of grape varieties is very complex, and has been carefully and devotedly adapted to the *terroir*: classic Mediterranean varieties identical to those found in neighbouring regions have been used: Clairette, Bourboulenc, Grenache, Cinsaut, Syrah and Mourvèdre, but the *appellation's* originality lies in the use of other varieties, such as the Aramon, Colombard, Durif, Brun Fourca, Téoulier and others.

The floral bouquet and light, fresh style of the white wines is the result of the favourable aspects enjoyed by the vineyards.

Parsac-Saint-Émilion is a satellite appellation *of Saint-Émilion. It is sited on gravelly soils and produces full-bodied red wines, generally sold under the Montagne-Saint-Émilion* appellation.

The rosé wines have a depth of colour rare in this type of wine, and a fruity bouquet. They also have a slight trace of tannin, and this ensures them a long life.

The red wines, which are dense and austere at first, have a predominantly vegetal aroma. They are full bodied, but not heavy. All three styles of wine — white, rosé and red — keep astonishingly well. They are still very good after six to ten years.

Palougué

Synonyms: *Cruchinette* in Landes, *Pédauque*, *Coer de Baco*, *Blancard* in Pyrénées-Atlantiques.

Bunches large, conical, compact, with very pronounced shoulders; grapes large, spherical, white, juicy; ripening period: second epoch, late.

The Palougué produces fine bunches of grapes. Unfortunately, however, these tend to rot easily because they are so compact. The vines are vigorous, with fine, well-developed shoots and canes. This variety is unclassified, and gives an ordinary wine.

Panéa Nero

Synonyms: *Panéa*, *Négroun*, *Négrot*, *Pornéa*.

The Panéa or Panée was once the principal vine of the wine-growing area of la Gaude (Alpes-Maritimes). However, it has now completely disappeared. It gave a deep-coloured, quality wine with a good bouquet.

Pardotte

Synonyms: *Petite Parde* in Graves, *Gros Pignon*, *Petit Pignon* in Médoc, *Boutignon* in the Blaye district, *Sauvignon Rouge* at Saint-Macaire, *Sauvignon Noir Pigue* at Ludon, *Machouquet*, *Petit Machouquet*, *Gros Machouquet* in Entre-Deux-Mers, *Matiouquet* at Saint-Loubès, *Courbinotte* at Budos, *Chaussin* at Tonneins.

Bunches medium sized, conical, compact; grapes small, spherical or slightly ovoid, blue-black, not very juicy, with a leafy or stalky flavour; ripening period: second epoch.

The Pardotte is an old variety from the Bordeaux area, once grown on the *palus* (the low-lying, marshy land by the Gironde estuary). It gives a flat, ordinary wine. It is unclassified, with only a few hectares remaining.

Parsac-Saint-Émilion

The *appellation d'origine contrôlée* of Parsac-Saint-Émilion in the Libourne area was created by the decree of 14 November 1936. It was then reserved for red wines made from grapes gathered within the commune of Parsac. On 5 December 1972, the Montagne-Saint-Émilion *appellation* was officially extended to cover the commune of Parsac, and since then the latter *appellation* has been used in preference to the former.

Patrimonio. This wine-growing area, set in an amphitheatre near Saint-Florent and its bay, is mainly planted with local grape varieties, which give the wines a particularly Corsican character.

Pascal Blanc

Synonyms: *Pascaou Blanc* around Aix-en-Provence, *Brun-Blanc* at Draguignan.

Bunches medium to large, conical, compact; grapes medium sized, spherical, green-white, becoming dark yellow or reddish brown when completely ripe, hence the name Brun-Blanc; ripening period: third epoch.

The Pascal Blanc is a grape variety from Provence, classed as 'recommended' in Bouches-du-Rhône, Vaucluse, Drôme, Ardèche, Gard and Hérault. But it is hardly grown at all nowadays (less than a hectare), despite the fact that it features among the permitted varieties for the AOCs of Cassis, Palette and Côtes du Rhône. It is a hardy vine, very well suited to dry, arid soils. However, it is highly susceptible to oidium (powdery mildew) and grey rot (botrytis), and this is why it has declined in popularity.

Patrimonio

The red, white and rosé wines of this Corsican *appellation d'origine contrôlée* were defined by the decree of 13 March 1968. The decree was modified in 1972 and 1976, then reverted to its original form in 1984. The vineyards cover 483ha out of a potential growing area of 760ha. The amount of wine produced fluctuates around 10,000hl a year.

Harvest time at Château Lafite-Rothschild, one of Pauillac's three Premiers Crus Classés. The wine produced here is well structured, refined and full of vitality and breeding, in some ways the quintessence of the great wines of the Médoc.

The wine district of Patrimonio is situated in the amphitheatre surrounding the port and bay of Saint-Florent. The vines flourish on schistous bedrock, covered with limestone deposits. The vineyards are sheltered from winds and frosts, but are often shrouded in fog.

The varieties used for the wines of Patrimonio are 28.77 per cent Nielluccio, 11.90 per cent Vermentino, 15.31 per cent Carignan and 13.18 per cent Ugni Blanc.

This is an old wine-growing region, whose wines used to be shipped around Cap Corse, tasted in Bastia, and then sold in Genoa as *vini navigati* (wines that had stood the test of the sea), provided their quality had remained unchanged. Patrimonio today produces fresh, aromatic white wines and full, fruity rosés. The red wines, which are dark ruby in colour, are full and warm. Plum and apricot scents mingle in their bouquet. The area also produces some very fine Muscat *vins doux naturels*, and Rappu (a *mistelle*).

Pauillac

The *appellation d'origine contrôlée* of Pauillac, in the Médoc, was created by decree on 14 November 1936. It is reserved for red wines made from grapes gathered within the Pauillac commune, and on certain sites in the communes of Cissac, Saint-Julien, Saint-Estèphe and Saint-Sauveur.

The grape varieties specified are the same as those for the Médoc regional *appellation*. The use of hybrid vines has been forbidden since 1961 on estates laying claim to the Pauillac *appellation*. The minimum permitted sugar content of the musts is 162g per litre. The wines must have an alcohol content of between 10° and 13°. The base yield is 45hl/ha.

Since 1955, wines of this *appellation* have had to obtain a certificate of quality from a tasting panel before being marketed.

In 1985, the total vineyard area was 890ha, and annual production was 60,944hl, of which 5,478hl was made by the local cooperative.

The Pauillac *appellation* includes 18 of the 60 Médoc Crus Classés of 1855. Three of these

PAULLAC CRUS CLASSÉS

Premiers Crus
Château Lafite-Rothschild
Château Latour
Château Mouton-Rothschild

Deuxièmes Crus
Château Pichon-Longueville-Baron
Château Pichon-Longueville-Comtesse-de-Lalande

Quatrième Cru
Château Duhart-Milon-Rothschild

Cinquièmes Crus
Château Batailley
Château Clerc-Milon
Château Croizet-Bages
Château Grand-Puy-Ducasse
Château Grand-Puy-Lacoste
Château Haut-Bages-Libéral
Château Haut-Batailley
Château Lynch-Bages
Château Lynch-Moussas
Château Mouton-Baronne-Philippe
Château Pédesclaux
Château Pontet-Canet

are Premiers Crus: Châteaux Lafite-Rothschild, Latour and Mouton-Rothschild. The wines of Pauillac are famous for their capacity for ageing. After they have been in bottle for a number of years they acquire a matchless bouquet.

Pécharmant

The Pécharmant wine district (the name *pech-charmant* means 'delightful hilltop') is situated on the right bank of the Dordogne, on south-facing slopes of Périgord sands and gravels which lie in a half-circle around Bergerac.

The soil here, made up of various modified granite materials brought down from the Massif Central, has undergone a process of rain-washing resulting in the formation of an impermeable clay and iron substratum known as *tran*. It is this that gives Pécharmant its incomparable character.

The AOC area takes in the communes of Bergerac, Creysse, Lembras and Saint-Sauveur, where it occupies about 200ha, planted with Cabernet Sauvignon, Cabernet Franc, Merlot and Côt (Malbec).

The base yield is limited to 40hl/ha. This may vary by a few hectolitres each year, depending on the circumstances and on the ruling of the INAO. Such strict controls ensure exceptional quality. Average annual production is between 7,000hl and 8,000hl of a deeply coloured red wine, which needs time to blossom and mature.

Peloursin

Synonyms: *Pelossard*, *Pellourcin*, *Pellorcin* at Morestel, *Mal Noir*, *Mauvais Noir* at Bourgoin, *Gondran* at Saint-Savin, *Parlousseau* at Moirans, *Salis* at Voreppe, *Sella*, *Saler*, *Soler* at la Mure, *Treillin* at Saint-Marcellin, *Gros Noir*, *Pourrot*, *Gros Béclan* in Jura, *Gros Nat* in Haute-Saône, *Famette*, *Fumette*, *Feunette*, *Vert Noir* in Savoie.

This is an old variety from the Grésivaudan valley, between Grenoble and Albertville, which subsequently spread throughout Savoie and Franche-Comté. It is similar to the Durif, but the underside of its leaves are completely glabrous, while those of the Durif are arachnoid. The name Peloursin derives from the blue-black colour of its grapes, which recall the fruit of the wild blackthorn, called *pelosse* in the local dialect.

The Peloursin is an unclassified vine, and has a limited future. There is a Peloursin Gris, which has grey berries, but it is not in cultivation.

Penouille

Synonyms: *Pelouille*, *Pédouille*, *Pétouille*.

Bunches medium sized, conical, loose; grapes medium sized, black, ovoid, the skin having a slightly grassy or leafy taste; ripening period: second epoch, late.

This is an old Bordeaux variety. It is unclassified and no longer planted. It produced a flat, ordinary wine.

Perdea

This is a Raffiat de Moncade × Chardonnay crossing, achieved by INRA at Bordeaux. It is an early budding vine, producing white grapes that ripen early in the second epoch. It is highly fertile, but is susceptible to *millerandage* (failed grape development) in certain years. Yields vary from 70hl/ha to 220hl/ha, and alcoholic strength ranges from 9° to 12.6°. The wine it gives is fine, with a delicate bouquet; its quality is good when grown in the vineyards of the South West. It is classed as 'authorized', and one clone has been approved: number 742.

Pernand-Vergelesses

Governed by the decree of 21 May 1970, the *appellation d'origine contrôlée* area of Pernand-Vergelesses is situated between Aloxe-Corton and Savigny-lès-Beaune, and includes parts of the famous Grands Crus of Corton, Corton-Charlemagne and Charlemagne. The prestige of these *appellations* has no doubt inspired local growers to improve their wines, and some of these enjoy Premier Cru status. The *appellation* covers 116ha, 56ha of which are occupied by Premier Cru sites. The bulk of the production — an average of 2,876hl per

Pernand-Vergelesses, set back in a small valley on the Côte de Beaune, produces long-lasting red wines with aromas of raspberry.

annum — is red, with a much smaller quantity of white wine being produced (about 776hl). The minimum alcohol content is 10.5° for red wines, 11° in the case of Premiers Crus; and 11° for white wines, 11.5° in the case of Premiers Crus. The maximum yield per hectare is fixed at 35hl. The red wines are grown in ferruginous clay and limestone soils, and have great charm. They are characterized by a fine depth of colour and a certain firmness, and they develop quickly. The white wines are grown on siliceous limestone and sandy soils, and are attractive. They have something of the fruitiness of the white wines of Meursault, but cannot match them in subtlety.

Persan

Synonyms: *Étraire* or *Étrière* in the Isère valley, *Batarde* at Voiron, *Aguzelle* or *Aguyzelle* at Voreppe, *Guzelle* at Saint-Marcellin, *Batarde Longue* at Bourgoin, *Cul-de-Poule* at Saint-Savin, *Siranne Pointue* at Monestier-de-Clermont, *Pousse de Chèvre* at la Mure, *Bégu* at Valbonnais, *Beccu*, *Becuette*, *Étris*, *Princens* in Savoie, *Serinne Pointue*, *Petit Becquet*.

Bunches small to medium, cylindrical, compact; grapes small, ovoid to ellipsoidal, blue-black, flesh soft, not very juicy; ripening period: second epoch.

The Persan is a vine from the Grésivaudan valley, northeast of Grenoble. It has early budbreak, is extremely vigorous, and is trellis-trained. The red wine it gives is of a high quality and ages well. Classed as 'recommended' in Savoie and Isère, it is little grown today (20ha).

Pessac-Léognan

The AOC of Pessac-Léognan in the Graves region was created by decree on 9 September 1987. It is reserved for red and white wines made within the communes of Cadaujac, Canéjan, Gradignan, Léognan, Martillac, Mérignac, Pessac, Saint-Médard-d'Eyrans, Talence and Villenave-d'Ornon. The grape varieties used for white wines are the Sémillon, Sauvignon Blanc (minimum of 25 per cent) and Muscadelle; while for the red wines the Merlot, Cabernet Franc, Cabernet Sauvignon, Côt (Malbec), Petit Verdot and Carmenère are used. Both red and white wines have a minimum alcohol content of 10°; base yield is 45hl/ha for the red wines and 48hl/ha for the whites.

Petit Bouschet

Synonyms: *Aramon-Teinturier*, *Le Bouschet*.

Growing tips felty white with carmine margins, red stipules.

Bunches fairly large, conical, loose; grapes medium sized, spherical, dark black with abundant bloom, deep red juice; ripening period: first epoch, late.

The Petit Bouschet is an Aramon × Teinturier du Cher cross, produced in 1824 by Louis Bouschet. This new Teinturier (red-fleshed) variety rapidly gained considerable popularity, not just in France, where it was used to give colour to weak, Aramon-type wines, but in new wine districts all over the world. The Petit Bouschet has later budbreak than the Aramon. It is of only average vigour, and has the defect of growing numerous *gourmands* (sterile shoots) along the trunk and spurs, and these have to be nipped off carefully. Its habit is erect, and it is very fertile. On lowland sites it will easily yield 4 to 5kg per stock. The wine it gives is deeply coloured, flat and generally low in alcohol. Since it ripens earlier than the other southern French vines, it has to be harvested first, otherwise the grapes wither and fall prey to grey rot (botrytis). An unclassified vine, it has now completely disappeared from France.

Petit Chablis

The decree of 5 January 1944, granting Petit Chablis an *appellation d'origine contrôlée*, was

A vineyard near Préby, in the Chablis district. Certain plots in this commune produce wines with the Petit Chablis appellation.

intended to distinguish the area from the rest of Chablis, especially in terms of its *terroir*. Many of the plots that make up Petit Chablis are situated in the communes of Maligny, Lignorelles, la Chapelle-Vaupelteigne and Villy, mainly on plateaux with Cretaceous period soils. Most of the other Chablis wines come from Kimmeridgian marls from the Jurassic period. The minimum alcohol content of these wines is 9.5°, and the yield is fixed at 40hl/ha. Petit Chablis is made from the Chardonnay (known locally as the Beaunois). It is a wine for drinking fresh and young.

Petit Manseng

Synonyms: *Petit Mansenc*, *Manseng Blanc*, *Mansengou*, *Ixipiota Xuri* in Pays Basque.

Bunches small to medium sized, conical, winged; grapes small, white, spherical; ripening period: third epoch.

The Petit Manseng is a grape variety of quality, chiefly responsible for the fame of the white wines of Jurançon. It is a modest producer that, when *pourriture noble* (noble rot) has affected the grapes, can give a must with a very high sugar content, from which dessert wines of great refinement can be made. Classed as 'recommended' in the Gascony area, it is one of the white grapes used in the Jurançon, Béarn and Pacherenc du Vic-Bilh AOCs. Two registered clones have been approved: numbers 440 and 573.

Petit Meslier

Synonyms: *Meslier Doré*, *Petit Meslier Doré*, *Petit Meslier à Queue Rouge*, *Mélié Blanc* in Aube, *Maillé*, *Mayé*, *Melier* in Franche-Comté, *Arbonne* in Haute-Marne, *Feuille d'Ozerolle* at Selongey (Côte-d'Or), *Bernet*, *Bernais*, *Barnau* in the Troyes area, *Hennequin*, *Meslier de Champagne*.

Bunches small to medium sized, cylindrical-conical, loose; grapes spherical or slightly ovoid, medium sized, golden yellow; ripening period: first epoch.

The Petit Meslier comes from the area of northeast France that lies between Champagne and Franche-Comté. It is not a very vigorous vine, and has to be pruned short. Yields are quite low: 30 to 40hl/ha on average, rarely more. It is a quality grape variety, and the wine it gives is high in alcohol, slightly acid and fruity; it is very suitable for vinification as a sparkling wine. The Petit Meslier has early budbreak, is susceptible to downy mildew, but less affected by grey rot (botrytis) than is the Meslier Saint-François. It is classed as 'recommended' in Champagne.

Petit Paugayen

Synonyms: *Paugayen*, *Pogayen*, *Pogaï*.

Bunches medium sized, cylindrical, quite compact; grapes medium sized, ellipsoidal, black; ripening period: second epoch.

This vine comes from the region of Die in Drôme. It gives a medium-quality, lively red wine, with the ability to age. It has late budbreak, and is quite susceptible to oidium (powdery mildew). It has not been classified.

Petit Verdot

Synonyms: *Petit Verdot Noir*, *Petit Verdau*, *Verdot Rouge*, *Carmelin* at Bergerac, *Heran* at Roquefort in Landes, *Lambrusquet* at Gan (Pyrénées-Atlantiques), *Bouton Blanc*.

Bunches medium sized, loose, cylindrical; grapes small, blue-black, spherical; ripening period: third epoch.

This Bordeaux variety was once thought to be suited only to the plains and low-lying *palus* sites. Now it is grown throughout the region. Since it does not rot, it is the last of the grape varieties to be harvested each year in the Médoc. Its wine is deeply coloured, rich in tannin and improves with age.

One registered clone has been approved: number 400. Classed as 'recommended' in Gironde, Dordogne, Lot-et-Garonne, Landes and both the Pyrenean *départements*, it is one of the specified grape varieties for the Bordeaux, Médoc and Graves AOCs. There are about 420ha of it in Gironde.

The Gros Verdot or Verdot Colon is another Bordeaux variety, highly productive, but producing a poor wine. Unclassified, the Gros Verdot has a limited future.

Peurion

Synonyms: *Pourrisseux*, *Pourriette* in Jura, *Purion*, *Peurichon* in Aube, *Menu Blanc* in Haute-Saône, *Meslier Vert* in Allier, *Lyonnais* at Champlitte, *Milleron* in Bar-sur-Aube.

Bunches small to medium sized, cylindrical; grapes small, spherical, orange-yellow; ripening period: second epoch.

The Peurion is a consistent producer, giving wines of generally good quality, though sometimes acid. It was much grown in Aube and Franche-Comté before phylloxera.

Picardan *See* Œillade Blanche.

Picpoul de Pinet *See* Coteaux du Languedoc.

Pic-Saint-Loup *See* Coteaux du Languedoc.

Juillac-le-Coq in the Grande Champagne zone of Cognac, where Pineau des Charentes is made. This is not a wine, but a mistelle *— a drink made from must fortified with alcohol.*

Pineau d'Aunis

Synonyms: *Plant d'Aunis, Pineau Rouge, Plant de Mayet* in Sarthe, *Gros Véronais, Chenin Noir* in the Loire valley, *Côt à Queue Rouge, Côt à Bourgeons Blancs* (erroneously).

Bunches medium sized, compact, cylindrical-conical; grapes medium sized, ovoid, black; ripening period: second epoch.

This is a vigorous, fertile vine, but it exhausts itself quickly, and is susceptible to grey rot (botrytis). Its average yield varies between 40hl/ha and 80hl/ha. The wine it produces has between 9° and 11° of alcohol.

Two registered clones have been approved: numbers 289 and 235. Classed as 'recommended' throughout the whole of west central France, the Pineau d'Aunis is one of the specified varieties for the AOCs of Touraine, Coteaux du Loir, Anjou, Rosé de Loire, Crémant de Loire and Saumur, and for the VDQS regions of Coteaux du Vendômois and Valençay. Its main area of cultivation is in the Loir valley, especially around Vendôme, and in Sarthe. Out of a total of 1,500ha, Loir-et-Cher has the largest area, 861ha, followed by Maine-et-Loire (163ha) and Sarthe (105ha).

Pineau des Charentes

Pineau des Charentes is an AOC *vin de liqueur* or *mistelle* (a sweet fortified wine, with fortification taking place before the start of fermentation). Its *appellation* was granted by decree on 12 October 1945, for the same area as the Cognac AOC.

White Pineau des Charentes is made from the Ugni Blanc, Folle Blanche, Colombard, Meslier Saint-François, Montils, Jurançon Blanc, Sémillon, Sauvignon Blanc and Merlot Blanc grape varieties. It is a discreet, stylish blend of white grape juices with cognac.

Pineau des Charentes can also be rosé, in which case it is made from the Cabernet Sauvignon, Cabernet Franc, Côt (Malbec) and Merlot grape varieties. In this guise, it reveals the virtues of the Merlot and the two Cabernets, with well-constituted aromas of blackcurrant, raspberry, cherry and strawberry.

Pineau des Charentes is produced by both *bouilleurs de cru* (who may only distil their own wine) and *bouilleurs professionnels* (who may buy wine for distillation), as well as by cooperatives. It should be made from must and brandy both produced on the same estate. The musts are required to have a minimum sugar content of 170g per litre. Fortification is carried out by adding one part cognac to every three of must.

Ageing takes place exclusively in wood and continues until the Pineau is to be sold — no earlier than 1 October following the date of manufacture. It is first approved by a tasting panel appointed by the INAO, and then put on sale, with no indication of age or vintage.

For a long time, Pineau des Charentes existed in the shadow of cognac, and was produced almost entirely on a local and family basis. Between 1965 and 1985, however, sales greatly improved under the direction of the Comité National du Pineau des Charentes, reaching 75,000hl for the year 1985-6.

Pinot Blanc

This is the white form of the Pinot Noir, and therefore very different from the Chardonnay (which is sometimes erroneously called Pinot Blanc or Pinot Blanc Chardonnay).

Two registered clones have been approved: numbers 54 and 55. The Pinot Blanc has been classed as 'recommended' in every part of France except the South West, and it is grown on 1,500ha: 900ha in Alsace, and the remainder in the Loire valley (500ha) and Burgundy (100ha).

Pinot-Chardonnay-Mâcon *See* Mâcon Blanc.

Pinot Gris

Synonyms: *Pinot Beurot* or *Burot* (a comparison with the rough cloth — *la bure* — of a monk's habit), *Gris Cordelier* in Allier, *Fauvet* in Haute-Saône, *Fromentot* in Champagne, *Malvoisie* in Savoie and the Loire valley, *Auvernat Gris* in Loiret, *Tokay* in Alsace.

This is a pinkish-grey form of the Pinot Noir, the two vines differing only in the colour of the grapes. Sometimes, plants bearing both black and pink berries can be seen, and occasionally all three colours (black, pink and white) appear on the same berry, arranged like slices of melon. Vinified on its own in Alsace, this grape gives extremely fine wines. Three recommended clones have been approved: numbers 52, 53 and 457. Classed as 'recommended' in most *départements* except those of the South West, the Pinot Gris is grown on 620ha, of which 550ha are in Alsace and 20ha in the Loire valley.

Pinot Meunier *See* Meunier.

Pinot Noir

Synonyms: *Franc Pinot* or *Pineau*, *Pynoz*, *Noirien*, *Petit Vérot* in Yonne, *Auvernat Noir* at Orléans, *Morillon Noir* in Loir-et-Cher, *Noble* or *Noble Joué* in Touraine, *Berligout* in Loire-Atlantique, *Plant Doré*, *Vert Doré* or *Petit Plant Doré* in Champagne, *Bourguignon Noir* in Beaujolais, *Savagnin Noir* or *Salvagnin* in Jura.

Growing tips almost felty white in the early spring, later becoming downy white.

Young leaves downy at first, then becoming arachnoid or smooth, the underneath of the blade remaining downy.

Leaves medium sized, dark green, thick, orbicular, concave, very coarsely bullate, usually either without lobes or with three very shallow lobes; the petiolar sinus is narrowly lyrate, with overlapping edges on markedly concave leaves; dentation medium sized, convex; underside of blade weakly arachnoid. In autumn, the foliage turns an attractive yellow, spotted with red to varying degrees.

Green shoots ribbed, green with a few longitudinal brown striations, pink nodes; tendrils medium sized, fleshy.

Bunches small, cylindrical, rarely winged, compact, with very hard, lignified peduncles; grapes small, spherical or slightly ovoid, blue-black or deep violet, covered with an abundant bloom, skin thick, rich in colouring matter, flesh scanty but expressing its juice easily; ripening period: first epoch.

A leaf of the Pinot Noir, one of the 'noblest' of France's grape varieties, used for all of Burgundy's red Grands Crus.

The Pinot Noir has early budbreak and is vulnerable to spring frosts, so in northern wine districts it must always be grown on slopes exposed to plenty of sunlight. It is not a very fertile vine, and is pruned *en gobelet* (as a small, free-standing bush) with three or four short canes (*coursons*); by the Cordon de Royat system; or by the single or double Guyot system, depending on the region.

Extensive clonal selection has been undertaken in Burgundy and Champagne, and this work has showed that clones with leaves without lobes produce the best yields, while clones with deeply lobed leaves only bear very small bunches of grapes. Some clones yield three times as much as others (figures vary from 26hl/ha to 90hl/ha), while the alcohol content ranges from 8.8° to 11.7°. Clones also differ with regard to susceptibility to grey rot (botrytis). Of the registered clones, 46 have been approved. Number 459 is the best of these in terms of quality, followed by numbers 111, 114 and 292, all of which are used in Burgundy. The most productive, numbers 386, 388 and 389, are used in Champagne.

Pinot Noir green shoot.

Wines from the Pinot Noir have an attractive but not very intense colour, and a natural 10° to 12° alcohol. They have a very pleasant bouquet, lingering in the mouth for a long time. They mature well, but the red colour gradually fades towards onionskin and, in the end, deposits itself on the sides of the bottle.

The Pinot Noir is classed as 'recommended' in most *départements*, excluding those of the South West. In Burgundy it is vinified in isolation in the region's various red-wine AOCs, although it is vinified with the Gamay for Bourgogne Passetoutgrains. In Champagne, it is used in conjunction with the Chardonnay and the Meunier. In the Loire valley, it is one of the specified varieties for the red and rosé AOCs of Sancerre, Menetou-Salon, Touraine, Rosé de Loire and Crémant de Loire. It is also used for the Alsace AOC.

Today, the Pinot Noir is the most popular vine in France in terms of nursery propagation, and its area of cultivation is constantly on the increase: 8,500ha in 1958, 17,300ha in 1979 and now, probably, close to 19,000ha. It is the 12th most widely grown wine-making grape in France, and is distributed as follows: 9,000ha in Burgundy, 8,000ha in Champagne, 600ha in Alsace, 500ha in the Loire valley and 300ha in Jura and Savoie.

Piquepoul Blanc

A white version of the Piquepoul Noir, grown on 600ha in France. Half of this area is in Hérault, where the grape is used for the Picpoul de Pinet AOC, a dry white wine from vines grown near the Bassin de Thau. Four registered clones have been approved: numbers 176, 237, 238 and 463.

Piquepoul Gris

This vine is the grey (or pink) version of the Piquepoul Noir. It is classed as 'recommended' in the Midi, but is little grown nowadays, on less than 50ha. Three registered clones have been approved, the most useful of which is number 71.

The underside of a Plantet leaf.

Piquepoul Noir

Synonyms: *Picquepoul, Picpouille, Picapoule.*

Growing tips open, felty white with carmine-coloured patches.

Young leaves downy, bullate, bronze coloured.

Leaves orbicular, contorted, finely bullate with slightly concave lobes, deeply five-lobed, lower lateral sinuses acute at base, upper lateral sinuses closed, club shaped, petiolar sinus lyrate, slightly open, base of veins red around the petiolar junction; dentation convex, narrow; underside of blade arachnoid or arachnoid-pubescent, depending on the clone. In autumn, the foliage reddens at the edges, on the leaf dentation.

Green shoots ribbed, pale green with red longitudinal striations; tendrils large, brown.

Bunches medium sized, cylindrical-conical, winged, compact; grapes medium sized, ovoid to ellipsoidal, blue-black, with a thin skin and juicy flesh; ripening period: third epoch.

The Piquepoul is a vine of the Midi, with a spreading habit, and late budbreak. It is susceptible to oidium (powdery mildew), grey rot (botrytis) and erineum mites. Average production varies from 50 to 80hl/ha. The wine it gives has little colour, but has a high alcohol content and quite a rich bouquet; its grapes are usually vinified with those of other varieties. Four registered clones have been approved: numbers 239 and 294 seem to be the best. Classed as 'recommended' in Provence and Languedoc, the Piquepoul Noir is one of the specified varieties for the AOCs of Châteauneuf-du-Pape, Côtes du Rhône and Palette. It is grown on 350ha in Gard, Vaucluse, Var, Aude and Hérault.

Plant Droit

Synonyms: *Cinsaut Droit, Plant Dressé.*

Bunches medium to large, cylindrical, compact; grapes ovoid to ellipsoidal, a little like those of the Cinsaut, medium sized, black, with a thick skin; ripening period: second epoch.

The Plant Droit was first named and described by Marès. Later, it was given the name Cinsaut Droit so that it could be introduced to the Côtes du Rhône, for it is more productive than the real Cinsaut. However, the wine it gives is ordinary and without character. Susceptible to grey rot (botrytis), it is on the decline and is now grown on less than 200ha. It is classed as 'authorized' in the Midi.

Plantet

Synonym: *5455 Seibel.*

Growing tips felty white, with felty white stems.

Young leaves felty.

Leaves orbicular, contorted, slightly crimped at the petiolar junction, slightly

A bunch of Plantet grapes. This hybrid variety is hardy and produces consistently.

three-lobed, petiolar sinus lyrate; dentation pointed, medium sized; underside of blade arachnoid-pubescent; petioles short, squat, felty white and pubescent.

Green shoots ribbed, downy, easy to detach; tendrils downy.

Bunches large, cylindrical or conical with two shoulders, compact; grapes small, spherical, black, difficult to crush, foxy taste; ripening period: first epoch.

The Plantet has been the most widely grown Seibel hybrid since vine classification eliminated number 7053. It is classed as 'authorized' in all western French *départements*, and 4,000ha of it still exist.

It has attractive cultivation qualities: the grapes need little or no anti-disease treatments; it has a very consistent rate of production, sometimes yielding as much as 100hl/ha; and it has late budbreak.

The disadvantages are the fragility of its branches, which break easily in a strong wind, and, more importantly still, the poor quality of its wine, which has a repellent raspberry-like flavour when fully mature.

Plant Vert

Synonyms: *Verdet, Servagnien.*

Bunches small, cylindrical, compact, sometimes winged; grapes medium sized, spherical, yellowish white with a harsh flavour; ripening period: second epoch.

This is an old variety from Yonne, from the areas around Irancy and Lignorelles. It was once used in conjunction with the Pinot Blanc and the Roublot to make table wines. A vigorous variety with late budbreak, the Plant Vert is prone to grey rot (botrytis). It is not classified.

Pointu

Synonyms: *Gros Plant* in the Loire region.

Bunches medium sized, cylindrical, tightly packed, with two shoulders; grapes black, ovoid and pointed (hence the name), flesh not very juicy, with a grassy or leafy flavour; ripening period: second epoch, late.

This is a highly productive though disease-prone vine once grown, together with the Mornen, in the Gier valley. It is unclassified, and is thought to be identical to the Pointu that was once grown in the Drôme valley, but has now completely disappeared there.

Pomerol

The *appellation d'origine contrôlée* Pomerol, created by decree on 8 December 1936, is reserved for red wines made from grapes picked within the commune of Pomerol, and on a few sites in the Libourne commune.

The Pomerol vineyards are composed of ferruginous soils with a top layer of sand or gravelly clay. The wines produced here are rich and long-lasting.

Red wines laying claim to the Pomerol *appellation* must be made from the following grape varieties: Cabernet Franc, Cabernet Sauvignon, Merlot and Côt. Hybrid vines have been forbidden since 1961 on estates wishing to market AOC Pomerol wines. The minimum permitted sugar content in the must is 171g per litre, and the wines must have an alcohol content of at least 10.5° and no more than 13.5°. The base yield is 42hl/ha. Tasting of the wines in order to verify quality before sale has been obligatory since 1974.

In 1985, the vineyard area totalled 751ha, and the amount of wine produced was 35,565hl.

Experts say that the wine of Pomerol has the finesse of the great wines of the Médoc allied with the vigour and firmness of those of Saint-Émilion. It is usually fine, deeply coloured, with an ample bouquet, and full-bodied and rich on the palate. It is a good wine for laying down and the best wines of the *appellation* will improve over a number of decades.

Pommard

This Côte de Beaune *appellation d'origine contrôlée* was ratified by decree on 11 September 1936. Its exclusively red wines enjoy great fame. Minimum alcohol content is 10.5°, with 11° for the Premiers Crus; maximum yield is 35hl/ha; the only permitted grape variety is the Pinot Noir. The village boasts 28 Premiers Crus, which cover 125ha, and are situated for the most part on sites west of the D973. The entire *appellation* area covers 337ha. One of the leading lights of Burgundy, this commune produces an average of 10,000hl of red wine

The Château de Pommard and surrounding vineyards. This village on the Côte de Beaune is famous for its generous, fine and vigorous red wines, which are some of the longest-lived in Burgundy.

Detail of an embroidered banner carried at the festival of St Vincent in Pommard. St Vincent, a Spanish deacon martyred in 304, is the patron saint of wine growers. He is honoured every year on 29 January in most French wine-growing communes.

each year. It is a wine that faithfully reflects the clay and limestone *terroir* with its rich iron content.

Wines from Pommard are dark red in colour, with a warm, powerful aroma and body. They are appreciated both for their generosity and for their fruity, spicy flavour. Somewhat astringent when young, they are best left to mature for a few years. They are, in fact, the longest-lived wines of the Côte de Beaune. Although their precise character varies appreciably from one *climat* to another, they are always impressive.

Portan

This is a Grenache × Portugais Bleu cross, achieved by INRA at Vassal.

The Portan has early budbreak, and its grapes ripen during the second epoch. It is therefore well suited to the coolest areas of the Midi. Its bunches are quite large, winged, with black, almost spherical grapes.

The wine it gives is deeply coloured and high in alcohol. Classed as 'recommended', the vine has a single approved clone: number 537.

Porto-Vecchio

See Vin de Corse-Porto-Vecchio.

Portugais Bleu

Synonym: *Raisin des Roses.*

Bunches medium sized, winged, cylindrical, compact; grapes large, spherical, blue-black, with easily expressed juice; ripening period: first epoch, early.

Despite its name, this vine is Austrian in origin, and has been grown there, and in Hungary, for a long time. It is an early variety, very productive, giving a light but deeply coloured wine. Its fruit is eaten as table grapes in the Rhinelands, as was also the case at one time in the Paris area.

The Portugais Bleu is very susceptible to downy mildew, to oidium (powdery mildew) and to grey rot (botrytis). It is classed as 'recommended' in Tarn, where it covers 1,150ha.

Pougnet

Synonyms: *Pouquet* or *Quercy* at Aubenas and Largentière, *Négrou* in Ardèche.

Bunches medium sized, conical, compact; grapes spherical, medium sized, blue-black, not very juicy; ripening period: second epoch, late.

This unclassified vine from Ardèche is very little grown today. It once produced large quantities of hard, astringent, quite deeply coloured wine that was, however, low in alcohol. This vine has a moderate resistance to oidium (powdery mildew).

Pouilly-Fuissé

The wines of Pouilly-Fuissé are made exclusively from the Chardonnay variety, and are produced in the communes of Fuissé, Solutré, Pouilly, Vergisson and Chaintré in the Mâcon region. Governed by the decree of 11 July 1936, these white wines must have a minimum alcohol content of 11°, and 12° if a vineyard name is specified on the label. The maximum yield is 45hl/ha.

The *appellation d'origine contrôlée* of Pouilly-Fuissé covers about 640ha, and produces an annual average of 40,000hl of high-quality wine, grown on propitious limestone and slate soils.

A superb dry white wine, with a golden colour tinged with emerald green, Pouilly-Fuissé is universally appreciated for its aromas of acacia and violet, and its soft, pleasantly almond-like flavour.

Pouilly-Fumé

This wine-growing district, declared an AOC on 31 July 1937, covers an area of 540ha, and has the Sauvignon Blanc, also known as the Blanc Fumé, as its only grape variety. The vineyards extend over the same communes or parts of communes as for Pouilly-sur-Loire (see below). About 30,000hl of Pouilly-Fumé are produced each year.

The colour of Pouilly-Fumé is light straw-yellow. It has an elegantly varietal aroma. It is simultaneously full and light, and is fresh and long on the palate. It matures well in bottle. (*See* the Vins du Centre regional entry.)

Pouilly-Loché

This white wine is made from Chardonnay grapes harvested in the commune of Loché, near Fuissé, in the Mâcon district. The *appellation d'origine contrôlée* was granted on 27 April 1940, and the wines are subject to the same conditions of production, and grown on the same soils, as those of Pouilly-Fuissé and Pouilly-Vinzelles. Average annual production is 1,300hl. Pouilly-Loché is a pleasant white wine, with a yellow colour highlighted with green. It has an agreeably floral bouquet with a touch of hazelnut: similar characteristics to Pouilly-Fuissé, though more modestly realized.

Pouilly-sur-Loire

This wine-growing district was declared an AOC on 31 July 1937. It covers an area of 65ha, planted with the Chasselas variety, with or without a Sauvignon Blanc admixture. The vineyards extend over the communes, or parts of communes, of Pouilly-sur-Loire, Saint-Andelain, Tracy-sur-Loire, Saint-Laurent, Saint-Martin-sur-Nohain, Garchy and Mesves-sur-Loire; Pouilly-Fumé is grown on the same area.

This wine is best when it is made from the Chasselas alone, as is the larger part of production. Pale yellow in colour, it is a light, supple, lively and very delicate wine. It ages satisfactorily. (*See* the Vins du Centre regional entry.)

Pouilly-Vinzelles

The *appellation d'origine contrôlée* of Pouilly-Vinzelles is produced in the commune of Vinzelles, surrounded by the communes of Loché, Fuissé and Chaintré, in the Mâcon region. It is subject to the same conditions of production as Pouilly-Fuissé, even though ratified by a different decree, on 27 April 1940. The grape variety used is the Chardonnay, the minimum alcohol content is 11°, and the base yield is 45hl/ha. There is an appreciable similarity in the pattern of soils and vineyard sites, but the wines of Pouilly-Vinzelles do not have the same class as those of Pouilly-Fuissé. Nevertheless, they are excellent white wines, typical of the Mâconnais. The 2,800hl produced every year finds enthusiastic customers, who appreciate the wines' freshness, their floral aromas and their pale golden colour.

The commune of Pouilly-sur-Loire in Nièvre has been producing fine white wines, made from the Chasselas grape variety, since the Middle Ages.

Poulsard

Synonyms: *Pelossard*, *Ploussard*, *Pleusart*, *Plussart*, *Pulceau*, all these names being derived from the colour of the grape, which resembles that of wild blackthorn, known as *pelosse* in local dialect, *Mescle*, *Miècle*, *Méthie*, *Meikkle* in the Revermont area: in the Ain dialect, all these names mean 'mixture', indicating the mixed colour of the berries, *Drille de Coq* or *Quille de Coq* (an allusion to a supposed resemblance between the grapes and cocks' testicles), *Cornelle* or *Cougnelle* in Lorraine, *Plant d'Arbois* in Doubs, *Pendoulot*, *Pandouleau* or *Raisin Perle*.

Growing tips arachnoid white with carmine margins. Young leaves glabrous, deeply lobed, with bronze patches.

Leaves cuneiform-truncate, contorted, blue-green, smooth with convex lobes, deeply five-lobed with wide sinuses and concave bases, petiolar sinus in a wide, open U-shape; dentation pointed, very narrow; underside of blade smooth with pubescent veins.

Green shoots ribbed, glabrous, glossy, pale green with some longitudinal brown striations; tendrils long, fleshy.

Bunches small to medium sized, cylindrical,

winged, not very compact; grapes medium sized, ellipsoidal, blue-black, fleshy, with a thin skin that splits easily; ripening period: second epoch.

The Poulsard is a delicate vine, with early budbreak. It is susceptible to *coulure* (flower abortion) during cold, rainy weather, and prone to diseases. It is a modest producer, rarely yielding more than 40 to 50hl/ha. The wine it gives is pale in colour, acquiring an onionskin hue as it ages. It has a delicate aroma, and a rich flavour. This variety is responsible for the fame of the red wines of Jura, and it features prominently among the specified grape varieties for the AOCs of Arbois and Côtes du Jura. Three registered clones have been approved, the best of which is number 296. Classed as 'recommended' in Jura, Ain and Doubs, it is grown on 300ha, mainly in Jura (283ha). The Poulsard Blanc and the Poulsard Rouge differ from the Poulsard Noir only in the colour of the berries.

Précoce Bousquet

This is a white grape variety from Tarn. Achieved by T. Bousquet in 1898, it is a Chasselas × Ondenc cross. It ripens during the first epoch. Classed as 'recommended' in Tarn, it covers 23ha there.

Précoce de Malingre

Synonyms: *Blanc Précoce de Malingre*, *Madeleine Blanche de Malingre*.

Bunches medium sized, cylindrical-conical, loose; grapes ellipsoidal, yellowish white, with soft flesh and easily expressed juice, simple flavour; an early ripening grape.

This is a table grape, created in about 1840 by a gardener from the Paris area called Malingre. It is not very widely grown, owing to its numerous defects: the stocks are stunted, it is highly susceptible to downy mildew and grey rot (botrytis), and the grapes do not stand up well to transportation or market and shop storage. For the purposes of vinification, however, it is of interest in northern districts because its grapes ripen so early.

Premières Côtes de Blaye *See* Blaye.

Premières Côtes de Bordeaux

The wine-growing area of the Premières Côtes, situated on the right bank of the Garonne, begins a few kilometres east of Bordeaux and ends just north of Langon. It includes two *appellations communales*, namely Loupiac and Sainte-Croix-du-Mont. The AOC of Premières Côtes de Bordeaux, which was created by the decree of 10 August 1973, covers 37 communes in all.

For red wines, the required grape varieties are the same as for the Bordeaux *appellation*. The minimum sugar content in the must is 162g per litre, and the wines have to have between 10° and 13° alcohol. The base yield is 50hl/ha. If a red wine has an alcohol content of not less than 11.5°, the name of the commune of origin may be added to the Premières Côtes de Bordeaux *appellation*.

Since 1974, wines have required a certificate of quality issued by an official tasting panel before being allowed on the market.

White wines appearing under the Premières Côtes de Bordeaux name may only be made from the Muscadelle, Sauvignon Blanc and Sémillon grape varieties. The minimum sugar content in the must is 200g per litre, and the wines have to have a total alcohol content (actual alcohol plus potential alcohol in the form of unfermented sugar) of at least 11.5°, with a minimum of 10.5° of actual alcohol. The residual sugar content must be more than 4g per litre, following the decree of 18 December 1980. The base yield is 50hl/ha.

In 1985, the total area of vineyards producing white wines was 728ha, and the amount of wine produced was 24,343hl, of which 3,703hl was made by a cooperative. The total area of vineyards producing red wines was 1,562ha, and the amount of wine produced 78,242hl, one fifth of this by three cooperatives.

Tabanac, in the Premières Côtes de Bordeaux, produces well-structured red wines and medium-dry or sweet white wines.

The red wines are usually powerful and well structured; they mature very well. The white wines vary from a rich medium-dry style to sweet dessert wines.

Provareau

Synonyms: *Pourvareau*, *Proveral*, *Prouveyraou*, *Proveraut*, *Parverau*, *Mastellet*.

Bunches small, cylindrical, narrow, quite compact; grapes spherical, small, blue-black; ripening period: third epoch.

This vine comes from the area around Vif, just south of Grenoble. It has early budbreak, is very productive, and gives a harsh, astringent wine. It is unclassified, and is now only cultivated on 15ha in Isère.

Prueras

Synonyms: *Chalosse Blanche* in Gironde and Dordogne, *Prunelat* in Gironde, *Blanc Pic* at Saint-Bazeille, *Œil de Tour* or *Œil de Sour* at Clairac, *Menu Blanc*, *Annereau* in the Charente region.

Bunches small, cylindrical, loose; grapes spherical, medium sized, yellowish white; ripening period: second epoch.

The Prueras is an old variety from Bordeaux. It is unclassified. Its main fault is that the grapes fall from the bunch easily when ripe. Furthermore, the wine it gives is light, flabby and of mediocre quality. It was once used for distillation purposes.

Prunelard

Bunches small, cylindrical, compact; grapes medium sized, spherical, black; ripening period: second epoch, late.

A vine from the Gaillac region in Tarn, where it is classed as 'recommended'. However, it is not widely grown, being prone to grey rot (botrytis).

Puisseguin-Saint-Émilion

The *appellation d'origine contrôlée* of Puisseguin-Saint-Émilion, created by decree on 14 November 1936, is reserved for red wines made from grapes picked on specific sites in the Puisseguin-Saint-Émilion commune in the Libourne district.

The grape varieties used are the same as those for the Saint-Émilion *appellation*. Hybrid vines have been banned since 1961.

The minimum permitted sugar content in the must is 162g per litre, and the wines must have an alcohol content of at least 10° and not more than 13°. Since 1956, these wines have had to meet with the approval of a tasting panel before being allowed on sale.

In 1985, this *appellation* covered 636ha, and the amount of wine produced was 36,540hl, of which 8,404hl was vinified by the cooperatives of Puisseguin and Gardegan.

Puligny-Montrachet

The white wines of this village on the Côte de Beaune are probably the most famous and most widely acclaimed in the world. This is undoubtedly due to the local microclimates, and the clay, siliceous sand and lime content of the soils. The following requirements are laid down by the decree of 21 May 1970, by which the Puligny-Montrachet AOC was granted: only Chardonnay grapes may be used for the white wines, and the minimum alcohol content is fixed at 11°, or 11.5° in the case of Premiers Crus; the base yield is 35hl/ha. The *appellation* covers 243ha, of which 121ha are Premiers Crus. The summit of the village's viticultural potential is to be found in the four Grands Crus, which cover an area of 21ha. These are Montrachet, Chevalier-Montrachet, Bâtard-Montrachet and Bienvenues-Bâtard-Montrachet.

The white wines of Puligny-Montrachet are lively, dry and very fruity. Although not as unctuous as the wines of Meursault, they are distinguished by their aromatic finesse, characterized by the scents of hazelnut, almond and honey. The brilliancy of their colour adds to their charm. There is also a small amount of red wine produced within this *appellation*: about 350hl annually, as opposed to 11,000hl of white wine. The red wines are considered to be well structured and expressive.

Putzscheere

Synonyms: *Putchir* in Armagnac, *Weisser Tokayer* and *Sauerlamper* in Alsace.

Bunches medium to large, cylindrical-conical, long, narrow; grapes medium sized, spherical, golden white; ripening period: second epoch, late.

This vine is Hungarian in origin, and it has been identified with the Gyöngyszöllö (by Goethe among others). Propagated in the second half of the 18th century, it reached Alsace, and finally Armagnac, having made its way there via Baden and Württemberg.

It is a highly productive vine giving a wine of mediocre quality. It has not been classified.

Pyrénées *See* the regional entry on the Pyrenees on page 456.

PROVENCE

The vineyards of Provence are certainly the oldest in France. This great tradition of wine growing, combined with many favourable sites, carefully chosen grape varieties, technological progress and, of course, the famous Provençal sunshine means that this region offers an excellent variety of wines today.

Given the antiquity of the vineyards of Provence, it is difficult to establish a precise relationship between the existence of wild vines in forests and their separate, early cultivation by the indigenous population. Documents which might make this possible are almost nonexistent.

The Greeks were certainly the first to cultivate the vine systematically along coastal Provence. Originally, this seafaring race was engaged in trading its own products with the local people: pottery, luxury goods, olive oil and ceramics, many remains of which were found along the Mediterranean coast long before similar discoveries were made in the Seine and Doubs valleys.

Nothing in the research which has been carried out points to a general cultivation of the vine in inland Provence at this stage. By contrast, there was an important vineyard on the slopes around the ancient town of Massilia, later to become Marseille. Wine existed; numerous amphoras found on the seabed near Marseille and Antibes prove there was at least an import trade of wines from Greece and Italy. There may also have been an export trade from the first Provençal vineyards.

Over the centuries, the vine in Provence developed in its own way, undergoing as elsewhere the vicissitudes of time and man's early, rather haphazard attempts at cultivation. It was planted on well-exposed hillsides and plateaux, but it remained a secondary and comparatively unimportant crop, just one element in a family's subsistence cultivation. Grown with other fruits and vegetables in the same plot, for a long time the vine and its wines had no role other than that of being a part of everyday nourishment. During this period there were no commercial vineyards in Provence.

The wines produced then included both white wines and pale red wines, *clairets*, like rosé wines with a deeper colour. The area later gave sound, robust red wines made from a Spanish vine, Mourvèdre, which was introduced into Provence during the 12th century, at a time of Aragonese expansion in the Mediterranean. These wines must have enjoyed a modest reputation because they were exported from Bandol, Antibes and sometimes Marseille.

The consequences of phylloxera

In the second half of the 19th century, the

A wine-growing estate in the Bandol AOC zone. The vines are planted on **restanques***: walled, dry-stone terraces typical of Provence.*

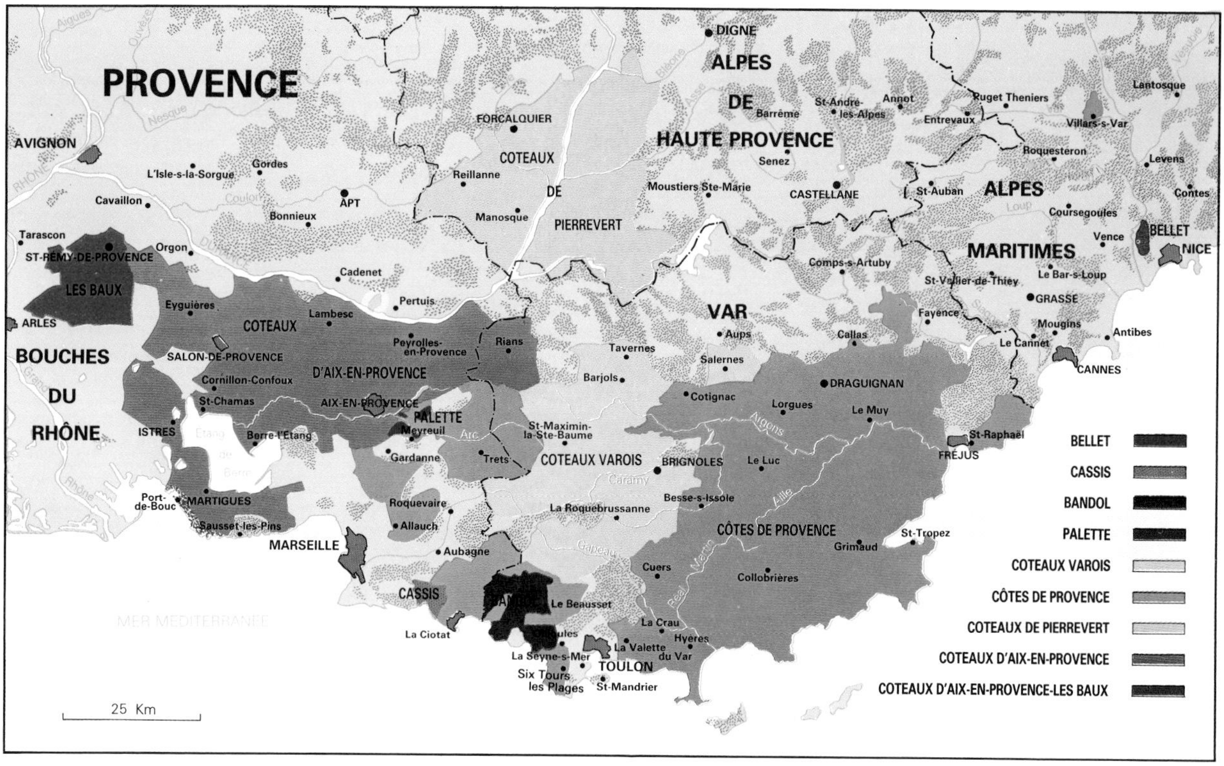

phylloxera crisis occurred. The Provençal vine had a great deal of trouble recovering from this terrible catastrophe.

To replace the old, dead vinestocks, new vineyards were planted that were exclusively given over to vines, no longer on the hillsides but on the richer, more fertile plains. The grape varieties chosen were poor ones, though productive; and indifferent wines came on the market, sought after by a certain type of commercial buyer. An old evil thus returned to viticulture in Provence which, according to historians, had already affected it before the French Revolution: quantity before quality.

By one of those accidents which mark out the course of history, this trend was favoured by the creation of wine cooperatives. In a region of very small properties such as Provence was, phylloxera caused terrible hardship and the collective production of wine seemed the only way to prevent this happening again. But if the cooperatives initially saved the wine growers from financial ruin, they also reinforced the errors made in choosing over-fertile soils and over-productive grape varieties.

Happily, things have changed since then and the mediocrity of the wines of that period is now no more than a bad memory.

Quality wine-growing has made a gradual recovery since the First World War, thanks to the efforts of a few pioneers. Grape varieties of authenticity and style have been planted and the wines have improved considerably.

The birth of VDQS wines

It was not until the end of the Second World War that the best wines of Provence made any commercial impact outside the region itself. Between 1940 and 1945 table wines were taxed, whereas prices of AOC wines were exempt from tax. Many Provençal table wines were superior in quality to their rivals, and so they had a higher price set on them. Because of the tax structure, though, these wines were uncompetitive in price, and their existence came under threat. In order to preserve and encourage their quality, and that of other wines like them, a special class of *appellations d'origine contrôlée* was created, known as *vins délimités de qualité supérieure* (VDQS).

The Count of Rohan-Chabot, president of the Syndicat des Vins de Provence, realized very quickly that the high quality of the local product gave him and his fellow growers a trump card. Supported by a handful of wine growers and *négociants*, he succeeded in gaining recognition for the VDQS Côtes de Provence in 1953. This large area of vineyards, lying between Fréjus, Draguignan and Toulon, quickly established its name as being synonymous with an original and authentic quality which, 24 years later, earned it elevation to the rank of an AOC.

Earlier, smaller subregions within Provence, already noted for the high quality of their production — Cassis, Palette and Bandol — had been awarded their AOCs between

1936 and 1948. Recognition of Coteaux d'Aix-en-Provence and other regional *appellations* came later.

The climate

In this large area extending from Nice to Avignon and Marseille, the climate varies distinctly according to the latitude. While the south, between Nice and Marseille, enjoys a temperate climate conditioned by maritime influences, the climate of the north of Provence has a more continental character, with two zonal differences. The vineyards of the northeast are sensitive to cold air currents from the Alpes-de-Haute-Provence, which the relief of the sub-region accentuates; and the western area around les Baux-de-Provence is subject to long, dry summers and great heat. Autumn rain is common in the northeast, while it is usually dry until well after the harvest in the west, where it can become very cold in winter. The coastal region is mild in both winter and summer.

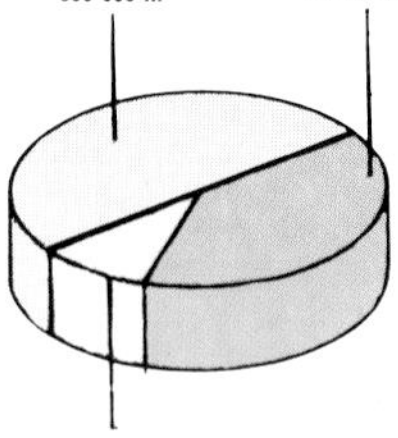

WINE PRODUCTION IN PROVENCE

The soils

Like many regions in France, Provence has no geological unity. Its large size explains the considerable variation in its soils. As is the case with the Côtes du Rhône, an overall similarity in production methods and a measure of commercially sound regional identification have been legally enshrined in the *appellation* names, despite many soil differences.

In all, there are three main soil groups. One area in the south, near the sea, includes the crystalline rock mountains of the Massif des Maures and the limestone rocks of the Massif de la Sainte-Beaume, le Beausset and Cassis.

A sandstone depression stretches inland from Fréjus to Hyères and continues, as red clay, from the foot of the Montagne Sainte-Victoire, east of Aix-en-Provence, to the edge of the Étang de Berre, west of Marseille.

In the north, a series of limestone hills beginning near Draguignan runs as far west as the river Durance and the slopes of les Baux.

Déchaussage — *exposing the base of the vine and its roots to spring rains — at Carcès in the Argens valley.*

Types of wine

White wines

With long decades of tradition behind them, the white wines of Provence have maintained, on the whole, a steady, small production of average quality. It is only since the arrival of new technology, such as cold fermentation methods, that the potential of certain vineyards for producing fresh and memorable white wines has been realized.

Rosé wines

Sneered at for a long time, the rosé wines of Provence are still considered by many to be of invariably mediocre quality. This is not so. If basic and traditional vinification methods produce correct but rather bland wine, the developments of the last 15 years have produced aromatic wines, full of fruit scents, which prove to be elegant, well balanced and remarkably fresh on the palate. They must be drunk within 18 months of production, though.

Red wines

The summer visitor's search for vinous satisfaction — nearly always focused on white and rosé wines — has held back the production of red wines to some extent throughout the region. Of course, red wines are produced, and have been for many years, particularly by the more innovative private growers. The cooperatives were not involved in red wine production to such an extent, because of a lack of equipment and the always buoyant consumer interest in rosé wines.

The improvement in the choice of grape varieties and a more rigorously technical approach over the last 20 years have led to the discovery that certain parts of the region are perfectly suited to red-wine production. Today there are some red Provençal wines worthy of being included among the greatest of Mediterranean wines, and both private growers and cooperatives are producing good red wines regularly.

The grape varieties

The grape varieties used to produce the wines of the different *appellations* of Provence have been selected over the years to complement each other in a blend, just as they are in the Côtes du Rhône, white wines excepted. But choices between varieties are still made, and the proportions in which each variety is used is varied, in order to respect the climatic characteristics of the various Provençal *terroirs*.

WINES WHICH CHARM US

On arriving in Provence, I probably had no more knowledge of the region's wines than most tourists, whose infatuation with rosés — readily associated with the sun — explains some of their current vogue. They are also, of course, dry, fruity, with a generous bouquet and a lightly spicy flavour, of remarkable quality in all the appellations *of Provence, with the advantage of accompanying nearly every dish without rendering it splendid but without clashing with it either.*

Gradually I began to sniff around in books . . . and glasses, and I was soon taken by a passionate interest in the wines of Provence.

'The genius of a wine lies in its grape variety,' Olivier de Serres has said. Here it is the genius of the Provençal wine grower, who has selected the numerous main and subsidiary grape varieties and blended them harmoniously together (within the appellation *regulations), that lies behind the success of the wines. Thus the Mourvèdre, one of the oldest grape varieties cultivated in Provence, gives its remarkable velvety quality, its deep red colour and its exquisite perfume of violets to the splendid red wine of* ***Bandol****, which is completed by the addition of Cinsaut for finesse and Grenache for strength and vigour.*

Bellet *is noted for its red, rosé and white wines, all of them excellent, because each has its origin in grape varieties peculiar to this* appellation*. In the case of the red, for example, it is the Folle Noire (or Fuella Nera), in combination with the Braquet (or Brachet) and Cinsaut, which gives the wines their originality and character.*

Cassis *is especially famous for its dry white wine, very low in acidity and with great delicacy, personality and freshness, but its red wine is warm and velvety, its rosé supple and fruity . . . Cassis is the only commune in France where the entire territory is classed as AOC, so that 'you could just as well grow your vines on beaches as on rocky hillsides', as the doyen of Cassis's wine growers so nicely puts it.*

Palette *produces exceptional wines: white, red or rosé, they all have finesse, elegance and an original distinction that never fails to strike connoisseurs. The reds have the nuanced smoothness which is one of the hallmarks of very good wines, while the whites are pure, fragrant, complex, but never heavy or coarse, which is surprising given the southerly latitude at which they are grown.*

The ***Coteaux d'Aix-en-Provence*** *and the* ***Coteaux d'Aix-en-Provence-les Baux*** *red, rosé and white wines all have elegance and breed; the reds are particularly warm and enticing and the rosés notably fragrant.*

The ***Côtes de Provence*** appellation *evokes, by its name alone, the memory of holidays in the sun. The regional standard-bearer is the popular rosé (let us thank the good Roi René of Aix-en-Provence, 1409-80, for encouraging Provençal wine growers to make wine in this way!). It is a pity, nevertheless, that its popularity eclipses the red wines of the Côtes de Provence, whose exact character depends on the sub-region of origin within the AOC zone, but which have in common a fine glowing appearance, a pleasant bouquet and a robust, tangy flavour. The dry, full-bodied white wines oxidize rather quickly — so why wait to taste them? Try them as young as possible.*

As a chef, I am grateful for the possibilities offered by the range of Provençal wines in the kitchen. The dry but full-bodied white wines go very well with hot entrées served with a well-flavoured sauce, with fish and shellfish, with smoked and marinated fish, with poultry, with foods served with cream sauces and even with foie gras.

Rosé wines, always in demand by my summer customers, never jar with regional dishes and are, if anything, even better with exotic, highly seasoned preparations . . . and they quench the great August thirsts so agreeably!

The heady red wines (those from the north side of the Massif des Maures in the Côtes de Provence zone, for example; or Bandol) are marvellous with foie gras, dishes flavoured with truffles, furred game and duck. Lighter red wines (Palette, Bellet or Côtes de Provence from the Argens valley) marry well with young lamb, ceps, morels and feathered game.

Provence is beautiful, and its wines delight body and soul!

Louis Outhier

A Mourvèdre vine.

The Coteaux d'Aix-en-Provence-les Baux area is subject to long drought and great heat during the summer period.

The white wines are generally based on the Clairette and Ugni Blanc varieties, but extra dimensions are added by the use of Rolle, Sémillon and Sauvignon Blanc. Rosé wines are made from a blend of Grenache and Carignan grapes. In southern Provence, the best red wines are based on the Cinsaut, Syrah and Mourvèdre, while in the north of Provence, Cabernet Sauvignon is more frequently used.

The commercialization of Provençal wine

As in the Rhône valley, one major change has come to the way wine is sold in Provence in recent years. The local specialized trade has declined and today it is traders from outside who are the principal buyers, both in terms of quality and quantity.

Estate bottling and direct selling to consumers have also developed very rapidly over the last 15 years. A major reason for this is the growth in the consumption of quality wines from AOC and VDQS areas. Many private growers now bottle their own wines, and bottling is also done by producers' associations.

Finally, it should be said that the low price which consumers still expect of all Provençal wines makes the development of the best AOC wines of the region more difficult than it might otherwise be.

Tourism and publicity

There is a wine route in the Côtes de Provence *appellation* with many attractive twists, turns and detours, reflecting the topography of this large AOC zone. There is also a very beautiful tourist route in the wine-growing region of Bandol.

The most important *confréries* in the region are the Chevaliers de Méduse, based at les Arcs (see above right), and the *confrérie* of the Échansons du Roi René, at Aix-en-Provence.

Diploma of the Chevaliers de Méduse, a **confrérie** *whose aim is to promote and publicize the quality of the best wines of Provence.*

THE ORDRE ILLUSTRE DES CHEVALIERS DE MÉDUSE

As soon as the grape harvest was over on 30 September 1951, the first solemn chapter of the Ordre Illustre des Chevaliers de Méduse was held in the castle of Sainte-Roseline at les Arcs. Its object, announced on that day, is 'to promote the quality of the great crus of Provence, to distinguish the best among them, to honour their prestige and to confer on them the mission of acting as ambassador for Provençal wines both in France and abroad'.

To attain this objective, the founders chose to revive an order created in 1690 whose statutes were found to have been published at the time under the title 'Pleasant Amusements at Table, or the Rule-Book of the Society of the Frères de Méduse'.

This esoteric order counted among its ranks the cream of the Provençal nobility and haute bourgeoisie, *who were delighted to serve the cause of Provence so pleasantly by celebrating the virtues of its wines and food, and all the produce of its sea, earth and sun.*

The Ordre de Méduse draws its name from two symbols connected with Medusa: Pegasus, the winged horse which sprang from the blood of the slain Medusa, and a symbol of poetic inspiration; and coral, Medusa's petrified blood. The former evokes the creative exaltation induced by good wine, and the latter that 'liquid coral' which lies, bottled, in the dark recesses of cool cellars, and symbolizes the treasure that may lie at the bottom of every abyss.

The Ordre, as proud of its past as it is of the labour of its wine growers today, encourages the struggle for quality in the wines of Provence. It has contributed to the achievement of AOC status for many wines. Its prestigious celebrations encourage and show the way to local producers in their fight for quality, and lend an image of distinction and high quality to the wines of the region.

This vineyard near Puyloubier in the appellation *Côtes de Provence is pictured after winter pruning.*

THE PYRENEES

The Pyrenean wine region is sited on an unusual* terroir*, one that is both southern and mountainous in type. Its history, its landscape, and above all its wines, put it in a most enviable position.

All the literature written on the region halts in the beautiful setting of Pau to salute the event that did so much for the renown of Pyrenean wine: the baptism of Henri IV in 1553. On that day, according to history and legend, garlic and the wine of Jurançon were used to baptize the future king. The region has known hard and difficult times, like those of the Visigothic and Moorish invasions and the Hundred Years War, as well as great glory and success, as witnessed by the vogue for Pyrenean wine in England, Holland and Scandinavia in the 16th and 17th centuries. Modern interest is intense, too, in these wines of charm and character.

Appellations and production

The river Adour, with the wide loop it describes between Tarbes and Bayonne, acts as a boundary to the Pyrenean wine region, which corresponds to the northern part of the former kingdom of Navarre. The region has five *appellations d'origine contrôlée*: Jurançon, Madiran, Béarn, Irouléguy and Pacherenc du Vic-Bilh; as well as VDQS Tursan (extending over 41 communes in the *département* of Landes) and Vin de Pays de Bigorre, created in 1984 and situated in the Hautes-Pyrénées. Red and white wines are both well represented, the former by Madiran, Béarn and Irouléguy, and the latter by gems such as Pacherenc du Vic-Bilh, Béarn and especially Jurançon, which produces 25,000hl a year of dry white wine (some 66 per cent of production), as well as a famous sweet white wine. The rosés of Béarn and Irouléguy also deserve mention.

Henri IV baptized at Jurançon. Illustration by Job, around 1900.

The soils

The Pyrenean wine region has uniformity neither of soil type nor of relief.

The Irouléguy district

This *appellation* is composed of a large number of small vineyard parcels sited on hill slopes between 200m and 400m above sea level, lying north of the massifs of Ursuya, which date from the Paleozoic era. The vineyard zone itself extends over Jurassic and Tertiary period limestones, Triassic period sandy clays, and Permian period sandstones with alluvial zones near Sainte-Étienne-de-Baïgorry.

The Béarn district

Spread over south- and east-facing slopes, this wine district has the richest soils of the Pyrenees. These are very varied, the most common kinds being clays, marls, grits, sands and gravels. In other respects this landscape is typical of the region, with its slopes ranging in gradient from 8 per cent to 15 per cent, and generally stony earth.

The Chalosse and Tursan districts

The clay-limestone hillsides that characterize this zone have outcrops of limestone and molasse. The Tursan area is known for its limestone scree slopes, while Haute Chalosse (in the south of Landes) has many small vineyard plots on alluvial and sandy soils.

The Jurançon district

The vineyards here are situated on heavier hillside soils (puddingstone and sandy gravels), and are interspersed with woodland.

The Madiran district

The soils here are, for the most part, clayey and siliceous, mixed with pebbles and fine gravel. The vineyards often occupy enclosed hillside plots lining the sides of wooded valleys.

The climate

There is something paradoxical about the Pyrenees as a wine-growing region in that it

The Jurançon area. The vineyards are situated at high altitude, and the vines are stake-trained.

has both a southerly and a mountainous character. Rainfall decreases from west to east; low temperatures often occur on the upper slopes, while high summer temperatures are a feature in other parts. Spring is generally wet and cold, with frosts in April and May. There are violent thunderstorms in summer, and warm early autumns, which are excellent for the production of sweet wines. But all these factors are, of course, modified by local microclimates, which play an important role.

The grape varieties

For red wines, the Tannat is in its element here. This grape variety, which gives a strong, robust and rich wine, likes clayey or stony soils, such as those found in the Irouléguy wine district. It also performs well in hot conditions, and shows at its best in the wines of Madiran. Nevertheless, to round out a character that is sometimes too exuberant, Tannat needs to be complemented by the Cabernet Franc, which adapts very well to acid and schistous soils, also found in the Irouléguy zone. The Fer (called the Pinenc in the Béarn area) is grown for the fullness and delicacy it can bring to blends.

The grape varieties used for the white wines of Jurançon are the Gros Manseng and the Petit Manseng. The Petit Manseng, which is the more fragrant of the two, produces the famous sweet white wines. It should be remembered that these are not affected by *pourriture noble* (noble rot), but are simply overripe. The grapes remain on the vine until the bunches acquire a golden brown colour. When the overripe grapes have dried out on the vine, harvesting takes place. The more productive Gros Manseng is used exclusively for the dry white Jurançon Sec.

The Raffiat de Moncade — the white grape variety of Pacherenc du Vic-Bilh — likes the well-drained, dry slopes of the Madiran area. It combines well with the Courbu Blanc and Sauvignon Blanc, much-remarked new arrivals in the Pyrenees, though some think their presence detrimental to the orginality and authenticity of the region's white wines.

Professional organization

Cooperatives have played a decisive role in the development of the Pyrenean wine region; they still account for 100 per cent of Irouléguy wine production, while 93 per cent of the Béarn growers are cooperative members. There is, nevertheless, a slight decline on their part, which benefits growers making, bottling and selling their own wines.

The Pyrenean wine region is like its products — lavish and warm. This character trait, and the importance of cooperatives here, explains the large number of tasting cellars (*caveaux de dégustation*) in the region. There is also very great pleasure to be found in travelling in the Pyrenees. The already splendid scenery becomes truly magnificent along the lesser roads of Jurançon, most notably with the outstanding panorama that unfolds beyond the Chapelle de Rousse, southwest of Pau, on the D217 near Artiguelouve.

THE ORIGINS AND HISTORY OF WINE

Wine in the broadest sense is a drink made from fermented fruit, and more specifically from the fermented juice of the grape. It was one of man's earliest companions and to a large extent has been a source of inspiration to him. Without it, Western civilization would not be what it is.

The first wine was a phenomenon of nature, fermented by wild yeast into alcohol in a rock niche or in the hollow of a mammoth's footprint. During the autumn, sloes, sorb apples and elderberries would have ripened on branches and fallen beneath trees and bushes. Bubbles would have burst from them in the sunlight. A man passed, sat down, took his fill of the fallen fruit. He had some difficulty in getting up, and felt strangely transported beyond himself . . . We can hardly doubt the truth of this story. At the time of Christ, the use of a large earthenware jar, placed in the middle of a field for the collection and fermentation of fruit, was widespread in Palestine, and is mentioned in the Song of Songs and in Isaiah. This jar, which is never given a name, is possibly the oldest utensil in the world, since it appeared before flint tools and survived after they had been discarded.

The dawn of viticulture

Although some people agree on a period in historic times for dating wine, it seems likely that it came into being long before that. Fossilized leaves dating from the Eocene and Pliocene epochs bear witness to the existence of vines climbing and spreading through trees towards the beginning of the Tertiary period. But the first attempts to use its fruit for food date to the Neolithic age (circa 5000-2500BC). Piles of pips from wild vines have been found dating from this time, particularly near lakeside dwellings. At that time the grapes were so tiny they were probably pressed rather than eaten. The cultural level permitting the development of wine was possible from the Palaeolithic age onwards (before the Neolithic age), and there may have been wine in the cave at Lascaux, whose occupation dates from the Palaeolithic age (a warmer period than the Neolithic). If this is confirmed, one day there will be a great battle between the experts, as the birth of wine appears to be no less precious to the faithful than the Holy Sepulchre!

The forests of Transcaucasia

A more classical theory gives Transcaucasia (corresponding to present-day Georgia, Azerbaijan and Armenia) as the birthplace of wine. Wild vines are creepers, and they would have found an ideal natural environment there, as this region was once richly forested.

Such vines still grow in Transcaucasia, but it is certain that they also existed in many other parts of the world. In Transcaucasia, however, they flourished to a greater degree than elsewhere, thanks to the many natural advantages of the region. The vines produced real grapes — and not the tiny berries that they produced in other locations. One of the best navigable networks in the world had its source in Transcaucasia; finally and most importantly, it was home to a man who had, as likely as not, already tasted wine: Noah's ancestor, the goatherd.

That the goatherd should have encountered the vine in the forest is not at all surprising as he spent his life there. At that time, there was no other pasture. The meadow was an 18th-century English invention. Herds previously lived off branches and leaves, and used their teeth to chew through

Standard from Ur, with banqueting scene. Sumerian art, 2800-2500BC. British Museum.

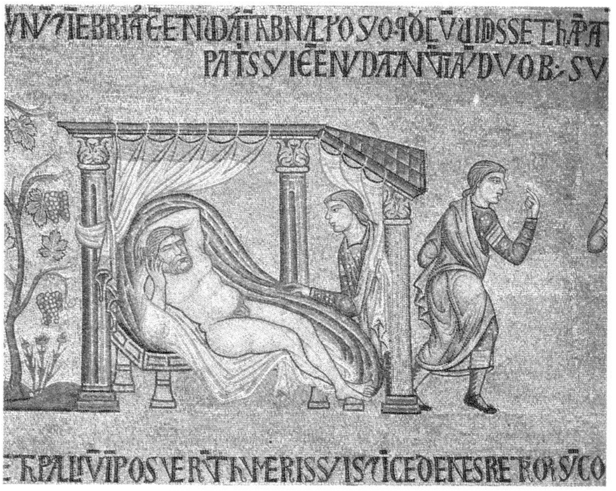

The intoxication of Noah. Detail of mosaic from St Mark's Basilica, Venice. 13th century.

and prune the vine!

Contrary to legend, then, the inventor of wine would not have been Bacchus, but a Transcaucasian shepherd, or rather a long succession of men from this pastoral land, dedicated to the same task and handing down their knowledge from century to century.

Towards the Near East

Wine had stagnated for a long time in bark, in skins, in clay sealed with straw, and for a long time it was of poor quality. In fact, it had to wait for solid containers that were waterproof and rotproof, which man had never tried to make because he had never had any need to. Wine provided such a need, so ceramics were created. Soon there were jars, amphoras, jugs and pitchers . . . In particular, they were made throughout the Tigris basin, from its source near Mount Ararat to its entry into the Persian Gulf, passing through the ancient lands of Assyria, Sumer and Babylonia in Mesopotamia (present-day Iraq).

So perhaps it was the birth of wine, around 6000BC, that led to the creation of the beautiful vessels of terracotta and wood which it has used for so long. If definite proof is still lacking, it can at least be assumed that from this era, man had mastered the materials he needed to make and store wine.

That wine had a long, secret life before being given a name seems almost obvious. In fact, when writing, invented in Sumer some time before 3000BC, first cites the vine it was already being systematically cultivated. Rudimentary *crus* existed: there was mountain wine and the other kind. In the famous *Royal Standard of Ur*, which represents the activities of the king and court during war and peace, the monarch and his retinue are described drinking wine at a peace banquet, some 2,700 years before our era. Twelve hundred kilometres separated the great *crus* — the source of this wine — from the royal table. This wine route was not only the most luxurious and the most ancient, it was also the one that lasted the longest. Pioneered before Noah's time, it was finally closed during the 17th century when Persian wine-lovers bowed to the Islamic ban on alcohol.

Noah — wine grower and merchant

Wine gradually became an object of competitive trading, and its transport, even over long distances, commonplace. It was carried by *keleks* on the Tigris and Euphrates; these were rafts kept afloat by the same goatskins which had been used to bring the wine down from the mountains.

Noah was perhaps one of the merchants who travelled between Mount Ararat and Sumer. During one of these trips, around 2200BC, he was surprised by a flood which pushed his *kelek* on to a flattened knoll not far from the ancient city of Assur, about 10m or 20m above the level of the plain. According to the archaeologist André Parrot, it was Mount Nizir. Much wine therefore flowed into the river before Noah was able to plant his first vine shoot. The climate and soils of this region lead us to believe that the wine he made would have been a rather coarse red.

Table wine and funeral wine

Trade led to the expansion of wine growing from the Persian Gulf to the Mediterranean region, and especially to Egypt and Greece.

From the pre-dynastic period onwards (3000BC), funeral wine was made in Egypt. Preserved in sealed amphoras, it accompanied dead kings to their last abode. There was also table wine, probably reserved for kings and important personages in the kingdom, while the populace made do with other drinks, such as barley beer.

Egyptian wines were generally white, sweet, very aromatic and sometimes resinated; they lasted well.

Funerary paintings show vivid scenes of Egyptian viticulture. Grape harvesters can be seen, men and women, using sickles and wicker baskets, as some Western wine growers still do today. The grapes were then crushed by foot and put to ferment in vats of robinia (locust tree) wood. Vine growing in Egypt was localized around the Nile delta for reasons of irrigation.

A wine as sweet as honey

Wine probably appeared in Greece during the third millennium before our era. At the time of Homer, about 800BC, the Greeks drank it in quantity, as the poet mentions many times in his verse. But it must not be forgotten that the cupbearers who served the wine in the *Iliad* and the *Odyssey* always added three or four parts of water to it. This was not for reasons of either virtue or thrift, but because the liquid in the amphoras had the consistency of syrup. This is partly explained by the fact that the grapes were often vinified like some of our modern dessert wines, that is, dried in the sun, then hung up or placed on raised frames. Furthermore, they nearly always had honey added to them, and this thickened during storage. These wines were considered choice. However, kept in pottery containers coated with pitch, diluted on occasion with sea water, and with resin and herbs added to them, they must have tasted very different to our wines.

The Greeks were gifted with a spirit of adventure which led them to travel widely and to colonize other lands. 'In 532BC,' Paul Faure has written, 'a Greek who wanted to flourish and be creative had to emigrate. It was not the poorest but the best, the most active, the most enterprising

The treading of grapes. Tomb of Nakht, astronomer of the god Amon under Thutmose IV (reigned 1425-1417BC). Valley of the Nobles, Thebes, Egypt.

who left the old land of Greece. Samos, at the peak of its economic power and maritime supremacy, had several colonies . . . Its vats of sweet wine . . . were found in all the towns of eastern Sicily, in the Gulf of Taranto, in Campania.'

The Greek settler therefore planted his vines all over the Mediterranean coasts, creating an almost continuous wine-growing region from the Crimea to Andalusia.

Vinum indigena et transmarina

It is likely that the early inhabitants of Italy had long made wine. Besides the wild vines that flourished in this country, there were, well before the arrival of Greek settlers, local cultivated varieties that produced fairly good wine.

Pliny the Elder (AD23-79), in the 14th book of his *Historia Naturalis*, talks about the vine and the different wines produced in his time. He knew no fewer than 80 'native wines' (*vinum indigena*) made from indigenous vines. The best came from grapes from the Aminea region, near Naples. He also cites, among the reputable varieties, those of Tuscany and numerous varieties of Muscat.

The Greek settlers did not fail to bring their own grape varieties with them to Italy. Among the vines imported from Greece was one known as the Graecula — fairly close, it seems, to those grown in Aminea. Furthermore, the *vinum transmarina* — imported wine — was held in high regard. It was brought in from Greece and the islands of Lesbos, Chios and Thasos, but also from Rhaetia to the north, and the country of the Allobroges, in Gaul.

The Romans perfected viticulture. Well-spaced rows of vines trained on high trellises, with sundry vegetables growing between them, were succeeded by vineyards planted quincuncially (with four vines positioned around a single central vine), which the Roman writer Varro regarded as progress. They knew how to prune the vine and even to graft it, as recounted by Pliny and Columella. They had a range of wine-growing techniques. The press, which was already used for olives, consisted of a huge wooden beam on a vertical axle, lowered by ropes, by means of a winch.

They produced black (i.e. dark red) wine, light red, amber and white. Kept for one or two years in *dolia*, enormous amphoras with a capacity to 500 to 2,000 litres, lined inside with pitch, the wine was later decanted into much smaller amphoras of about 26 litres. Thanks to the practice of covering corks with pozzolana — a volcanic material — these amphoras could preserve wine for about 20 years, and probably longer. Wine was named after consuls in office at the time it was put into amphoras. The vintage of 121BC, the year of the consulship of Opimius, was particularly fine, if Cicero and Pliny are to be believed.

The greatest consumers of Italian wine seem to have been the Gauls. This is attested by the many amphoras found at certain sites in Gaul, and in shipwrecks, notably that at la Madrague in the Golfe de Giens, east of Toulon, where the wreck of a ship that could have held 7,000 to 8,000 amphoras has been found.

The origins of French wine-growing

The conviction that French wine-growing began around 600BC, with vines planted by Greek sailors in the Canebière reedbeds of Marseille, is not easy to eradicate. There are, however, two objections to this theory. Wherever access was possible, people on foot, and especially shepherds, would have gone ahead of the sailors, for the ancestors of the French had a deep fear of the sea.

Secondly, vines imported from regions with mild winters could only have been planted in the rest of the country after a very long period of acclimatization, and there is no evidence that this occurred. The famous vineyards of Marseille might only have been a small island, as it were, sufficiently well situated to attract the light needed by Greek vines. In any case, the Greeks could well have set foot in the Basque country some 500 years earlier! They were certainly living in Andalusia around 1000BC and had gradually proceeded along one of the oldest prehistoric routes in the world, the *Camino de la Plata* (the Silver Way) which, via Cáceres, Salamanca and Oviedo, led to the mines of the Cantabrian mountains in northern Spain. This was the route used by flocks, and shepherds were the first miners. Coming on the Bay of Biscay, these pioneers then turned towards France. They established a section of the future pilgrim route to Compostela, and may have planted the first vines of the vineyards of San Sebastián in Spain, and of Irouléguy and Capbreton in France. This may explain how, from Roman times, Bordeaux seems to have enjoyed excellent grape varieties that were resistant to the cooler, damper climate of the Atlantic seaboard.

Whatever the role played by these two access routes, it can only be regarded as modest when compared to the importance of the route that led into France from the Danube and Central and Eastern Europe via the Belfort Gap. Pushed west by the exhaustion of their pastures and the population explosion caused by new agricultural progress, Caucasian shepherds arrived in France, driving their sheep and goats before them and carrying their vines on their backs. Geographers say, unsurprisingly, that Switzerland then played a pivotal role in European viticulture, just as it still does. In Switzerland, and in the surrounding lands, the first northern vines began to fan out — in Bavaria, along the banks of the Rhine, in Alsace and in Franche-

Comté. It is also remarkable to see the Romans, from the moment of their arrival in northern Europe, valuing the wine of Trier most highly and being enthusiastic about the wines of Rhaetia (which included parts of present-day Tyrol and east Switzerland) to the point of placing them above their own.

French wine, shepherds' wine

All French wines, as likely as not, were originally made by shepherds. The vine is the natural complement of the sheep. Both are happy with poor, stony soil, softened only by humus and the ashes of the forest that once stood above the stones. The best manure for the vine, and for a long time regarded as the only acceptable one, is provided by sheep.

The great pasture lands usually lie fairly high up, in sunny spots on valley slopes. The Vosges grasslands come down to the Alsace wine-growing districts, those of the Jura to Arbois, those of Morvan to the Côte d'Or . . . That great French water tower and cheese store, the Massif Central, is bounded by vine slopes: the Mâconnais, Beaujolais, Côte Rôtie, Côtes du Rhône, Tavel, Lirac, Marcillac, Gaillac, Bergerac, Touraine, Sancerre, Chablis, and inland as far as Saint-Pourçain, Côtes d'Auvergne, Côte Roannaise. The same pattern can be observed in the Pyrenees, where the vineyards are found along the axis of seasonal flock movements (transhumance): Limoux, Madiran, Pacherenc du Vic-Bilh, Irouléguy and Tursan. Also of pastoral origin are two of France's most famous wine regions: Champagne, where sheep have only been eliminated by the artificial grain cultivation of the 19th century; and Médoc, where Pauillac lamb is still famous.

The narrow bottlenecks where travellers and beasts used to pass each other were found to be the most suitable for the vine. Once won for wine growing, very few have reverted to previous vocations. Opening out from valleys, transverse valleys and mountain passes, they offered, in a small area, the best conditions for viticulture. In addition, there was usually a stream there. If so, a prolonged halt soon became the rule and then there was all the more occasion to drink or work: this was the case at Château-Chalon, Beaune, Mâcon, Hermitage, Saint-Péray, Châteauneuf-du-Pape, Jurançon, Cahors, Monbazillac, Chinon, Bourgueil . . .

A wine in every port

Besides the shepherd, the sailor played his part. What did he do on first setting foot on virgin creekside? He planted it with vines. For thousands of years, wine and maritime navigation shared a common history — and it is not by chance that shipping capacity is still measured in tons (derived from 'tun' — a cask). Although it has suffered many losses, such as the succulent *vin de sable* (wine made from vines grown in sand) of Capbreton, near Bayonne, the roll call of sea wines remains impressive: Samos, Marsala, Málaga, Jerez and its sherry, Oporto and its port; and, in France, Nice and Bellet, Toulon and Bandol, Cassis, Sète and Frontignan, Narbonne and Fitou, Port-Vendres and Banyuls, Bordeaux, Nantes . . .

Nothing has done so much for wine as water, fresh as well as salt. The great rivers of France and their tributaries all water great wine regions: there are Rhine, Saône and Rhône wines, as well as wines of the Garonne and Gironde, the Dordogne, the Loire and Maine, even the Seine and the Marne. Inland ports have grown up under the vine's influence, such as Beaune, Mâcon, Lyon, Avignon, Narbonne, Agen, Bordeaux, Libourne, Orléans, Bar-sur-Aube and Reims . . .

View of the old harbour of Toulon seen from the provisions stores. Claude Vernet, 1756. Musée de la Marine, Paris.

The Roman influence

Many historians ascribe the decisive influence in the development of French wine growing to the Romans, simply because they are the authors of the first written documents about wine in France. It must be remembered, though, that the Gaulish Celts had a very advanced civilization — and a primarily oral tradition. Their unwritten records leave a considerable margin of doubt as to the extent of Roman influence in this matter. Present knowledge is sufficient, however, to render unto Rome the due which is Rome's. Two distinct periods can be distinguished.

From the beginning of the Roman conquest in 120BC through until AD313, the 'wild' viticulture of the shepherds gave way to an enlightened amateurism on the part of large landowners and high-ranking officials. Some of them made a specialization of viticulture, particularly in the Béziers and Narbonne regions, and exports from France to Rome competed seriously with the famous wines of Campania. This pressure explains the action of the Emperor Domitian, who, in AD92, banned the planting of new vines in Gaul, and ordered the uprooting of half the existing vineyards.

In 313, a great event in the history of wine occurred. In gratitude for victory at the Battle of Milvian Bridge, Constantine proclaimed Christianity the only and official religion of the Roman Empire. Wine, a fundamental element of Holy Communion, was thereby given considerable impetus, and its use in both religious and secular life spread quickly to all levels of the population.

The wine of Christ

The transformation of Roman wine to Christian wine came about gently. As happens with many revolutions, those in power remained in place. Generals became bishops, centurions abbots, legionaries priests. Hermits, who were numerous at the time, began cultivating the vine. They became less solitary, formed themselves into groups. The hermitage became a monastery; small vineyards became famous *crus*. Popes, bishops and canons soon administered vast wine-growing estates. The religious orders mastered the techniques of viticulture and participated on a large scale in the development of new wine districts, with the exception of the Bordeaux region, which was the work of merchants. The wines of the Côte Chalonnaise and of the Mâconnais, and some of the best *crus* of Burgundy, owe their fame to the Benedictines of Cluny. The spread of Burgundian wine-growing in general is largely the work of the abbey of Cîteaux.

The king's wine

The clergy, however, were not alone in contributing to the glory of wine. The other representative of God on earth, the king, also played his part — from earliest times. In Sumer, as in Egypt, king and high priest were one and the same person. The temple was the first great wine cellar, just as it had been the first granary. When the king, secularized, left the temple, he took his wine with him. From Cyrus the Great to Henri IV and Louis XIV, the glory of wine has always seemed to be indispensable to monarchies. The kings of France even owned vineyards on the hills of Paris and the Île-de-France. Henri IV owned Jurançon.

Press at the Clos de Vougeot, formerly the estate of the abbey of Cîteaux. 12th century.

In a reflection of royal taste, the wine estates of noblemen brought to the far reaches of the French provinces the justification of a taste that lay outside material necessity. Dukes and marquises reminded the public that wine is different to food. It can be appreciated for itself, like a work of art, and can destroy a person. Vineyards were fought over. One of the most famous of such squabbles took place in the 18th century, when a royal favourite found herself outbid by the Prince of Conti for the purchase of a small vineyard of less than two hectares — Romanée-Conti.

The development of France's wine-growing regions

Sited at one of the great crossroads of Europe, but in an area where the local population was neither numerous nor rich, the Burgundian wine region has to live off a select and distant clientele. The estates are therefore small. It can happen that a single family there owns a single site planted with a single grape variety. The region, however, was able to develop as it did between 1100 and 1500 thanks to the religious orders, and also thanks to the 'publicity campaigns' run by the great estate owners. The Dukes of Burgundy, in all modesty, proclaimed themselves 'lords of the best wines of Christendom'. Another touch of genius, at a time when wines were still pale in colour, was when an unknown person fermented Pinot Noir grapes with their skins and stalks, and launched the result as 'ruby' wine. From then on, great drinkers wished only to see red.

The growth of the Bordeaux wine region has taken place between 1200 and the present day. Spurred on by important customers in Holland, England and Germany, the Bordeaux landowners saw themselves obliged to invest in large estates. So large, in fact, that the nature of the soil varied greatly, and different grape varieties were required. The crop from each site was vinified separately, and in spring blended to maintain the same character from year to year and so avoid confusing the consumer's palate. But because the boats carrying away wine needed to have cargo to deliver in exchange, the Bordeaux wine growers had to abandon local cheese-making. Bordeaux is the only region in France that has agreed to such a sacrifice at the altar of wine — its great *crus* for Edam and Gouda!

The history of the vine in Languedoc-Roussillon is more than 25 centuries old, as it dates from Greek colonization in the 11th century BC. Viticulture had become so widespread in this region that the Emperor Domitian was obliged to limit production with his famous decree of AD92, referred to above. The vine was confined to the Narbonne region until the Emperor Probus, in 280, allowed all the Gauls to produce wine once again.

After the collapse of the western Roman empire in 412, the Languedoc wine region went into a long decline, which only ended in the 9th century when the abbeys of Lagrasse, Caunes-Minervois, Aniane and Saint-Chinian took up viticulture again. The economic expansion of the 17th century encouraged the planting of new vineyards in Languedoc, and the edict of Turgot, in 1776, declaring the free circulation of wines throughout the French kingdom, opened up new markets for the region's wines. So successful was this trade that on the eve of the French Revolution the wine-growing area of Languedoc-Roussillon covered 170,000ha and produced 2-3 million hl a year.

New wines

From the 17th century onwards, and throughout the 18th century, the development of the French wine regions was linked with that of Paris. The capital increased its consumption of wine, and to satisfy it, wines from Orléans were given precedence. They were greeted sympathetically, but their success was far from equalling that of champagne, which first appeared in 1650.

Chalky and miserable, the soil of Champagne only tolerates a few grape varieties, sharing the Pinot Noir and Chardonnay with Burgundy; high yields, though, are possible there. The district's wines were already valued by the Romans, and perhaps earlier, but stagnation set in until the 16th century. What was the problem? — their bubbles! Acceptable and controllable locally, the bubbles, or *mousse*, did not travel long distances. They made the barrels explode, and these were the only wine containers authorized under the rules of the monarchy. Wine growers of all countries saw an enemy when they saw a delicate pattern of bubbles in their wine. In districts with mild winters, such as in Limoux, Saint-Péray, Die or Gaillac, the wine could be cajoled and hectored into stillness. Such efforts would have been a waste of time in Épernay and Reims, where the early and severe winter soon halted fermentation, only to set it going again in spring. The bottle, invented by the English, made its appearance, and with the help of Portuguese cork the unruly bubbles could be tamed. The other piece of luck for Champagne was Dom Pérignon. Appointed chief cellarer of the abbey of Hautvillers in 1668, he knew all the moods of the *mousse* and understood the subtle demands of blending. Soon the new science of wine making was complemented by new purchasing trends. From 1726 on, champagne was no longer delivered in barrels but in bottles — it was in this form that Mme de Pompadour, champagne's most famous admirer, lodged her orders. Following tremendous demand from two of the richest customers of the 18th century, England and Paris, the *négociants* were soon led into selling more than was being produced. But rather than purchasing estates, they bought grapes from growers. Thus a new type of producer appeared: one without vines. This producer

Dom Pérignon (1638-1715). Chief cellarer of the abbey of Hautvillers. Painting by Frappa. Collection Moët et Chandon.

Louis Pasteur carried out his studies on alcoholic fermentation at Arbois, in the Jura.

blended, bottled, twisted, disgorged, recorked and finally delivered a type of wine as new as he was: a *vin de marque* (branded wine).

It was also thanks to the Paris market that Beaujolais production was developed, towards the end of the 18th century; this is the newest French wine district.

The 19th century was a time when the 'little' men were trying to catch up with the grander ones, and their route, too, passed through the vineyards. The clerk of the court as well as the great parliamentarian would have his *vin bourgeois*: good wine which, especially in Bordeaux, was not ashamed to appear for what it was, even at the best tables. This was the great age of merchants, who perfected selling methods, and invented estate bottling.

At this time, wine became one of France's main products, particularly because of industrialization and the arrival of the railways. The Languedoc-Roussillon wine region in particular produced large quantities of table wine from its new, high-yielding grape varieties.

Phylloxera

Mediocre grape varieties, excessive yields and slapdash production methods — viticulture was in a poor state at the end of the 19th century. Nature decided to take a hand, by welcoming an immigrant from America — phylloxera. Vines had already known epidemics and parasites, but phylloxera was the ultimate evil. There has been no comparable disaster in the history of French agriculture. Appearing in Gard in 1864 and active until 1900, it ravaged every wine-growing region. Its effects continued to be felt even after it had retreated, and this retreat was in any case only conditional. When these regions took stock after the scourge, they were unrecognizable. Whole areas had been wiped out, while others had fallen into an irreversible decline, even those that had clung to a policy of quality.

The plague had come from America; so did the cure. The vineyards were first repopulated by crossing French vines with American varieties resistant to the parasite, then later by using these varieties as rootstocks. But the French viticultural landscape had changed permanently.

The science of wine

Based for a long time on practical knowledge and age-old tradition, vinification was the object of little scientific study until comparatively recently. It was not until Pasteur's research into the fermentation of beer that the foundations of a scientific understanding of these phenomena were laid.

Unfortunately this research was not applied until the 20th century. It did not penetrate wineries and cellars until 1945 or even later. Oenology had existed for many years before there were oenologists. Eventually, university and laboratory training programmes were established, and oenologists were entrusted with directing private as well as cooperative wine making. While no one would suggest that wine can be an exact science, there has at least been great progress in its technology, and this is largely thanks to Pasteur.

The *appellations d'origine*

At the end of the 19th century, the reputation of French regions was in serious decline. Baron Leroy de Boiseaumarié arrived in time to halt this. The baron could simply have gone on running his vineyard at Châteauneuf-du-Pape, which already enjoyed a fine reputation, but he was consumed by a passion for wine, and the state of decay of the French wine regions grieved him.

To achieve the rescue operation that was so important to him, Baron Leroy advocated only the highest standards. He proposed that the easy options of the late 19th century — mediocre, high-yielding grape varieties, unsuitable *terroirs*, ill-considered manuring, limitless watering — should be abandoned. He recommended the use of certain varieties of grapes and the banning of others, as well as fixing the alcohol content and the maximum yield per hectare. His fight lasted for nearly ten years. Finally, this baron, no less a general, was victorious. In 1930, the law on *appellation d'origine contrôlée* became the charter of the wine growers of Châteauneuf-du-Pape. Champagne adopted it in 1935; Arbois, the Loire valley, Bordeaux and Burgundy in 1936. All the other regions followed. A government decree of 30 July 1935 created the Institut National des Appellations d'Origine (INAO), uniting the different administrative bodies concerned with wine: agriculture, taxation, justice and the anti-fraud department, as well as the wine growers and the *négociants*. Its first task was to codify all the operations connected with the manufacture of wine, from vine planting to vinification. The second object was to protect wines that had been granted an *appellation*. This legislation has provided a true moral code for wine. It is one of the great achievements of 20th-century France.

TRADITIONS AND PROHIBITIONS

There is a much greater danger for wine than an outbreak of phylloxera: prohibition. Throughout history, prohibition has acted as a brake on the galloping progress of the vine, perhaps to show that wine plays just as important a role when absent as when present . . .

The wine of China

Wine does not exist in China. Rice wine, made as it is from rice and soya, is not strictly speaking a wine. However, wine made from grapes had its chance in that country, as a number of travellers who tackled the silk route witnessed. It is probable, in fact, that at the time vines were becoming established in Sumer, the Caucasian vine launched its offensive on the east. These vines have lasted three or four thousand years and William of Rubrouck, the envoy of St Louis (Louis IX) to the Great Khan of the Mongol Empire, found traces of them in 1255. They were at that time concentrated in areas towards Europe, wherever a predominantly pastoral way of life was maintained. But wine soon found itself in competition with a very popular Asian drink, kumiss, *made from fermented mare's milk.*

The main factor responsible for the elimination of the vine from China was that such care and cultivation as it was given there came to an end. There were very special reasons why these activities ceased. First of all, there was overpopulation. When Chinese land is fertile, it very quickly becomes rich in people. This proliferation leads inevitably to continual subdivision of plots and to very intensive exploitation of the soil. When it became impossible to get yields comparable to those of other agricultural products while using the same manpower, the tending of vines ceased. There was no longer any chance of achieving the usual shepherd-wine grower partnership.

There was worse to come: the cultivation of new cereals, rice and soya, which were also capable of producing wine. In China, wine was therefore faced with what amounted to a ban, imposed by economic factors. Since 1981, however, a vineyard has been established in Tianjin (Tientsin), south-east of Beijing (Peking), on French initiative. The vineyard's production is 20,000hl a year.

Kosher wine

The Jewish religion permits wine provided that it is kosher. This stringent requirement effectively limits the consumption of other, non-kosher wines. Rabbinic supervision is also required throughout the wine-making process, and these controls have limited the historical expansion of Jewish wine growing. The origin of kosher wine legislation perhaps lies in the hardship of desert shepherd life, the lot of the early Hebrews. Vine growing did not satisfy their economic needs, so they were forced to favour the more profitable cultivation of wheat.

The bacchic poets of Islam

In the Muslim world, there was a complete tolerance of wine until the 17th century. Tolerance, moreover, is a euphemism. Arab poetic exuberance before Mohammed's founding of Islam in the 7th century was shared equally between three sources of inspiration: war, riding and women, with wine a prominent feature in the celebration of each. The greatest bacchic poets of all time, indeed, were Muslims. The most famous of them, the Persian Hafez (1325–1390), was an Islamic religious commentator and lecturer.

The ban on alcohol, so widely followed today, only dates from two or three hundred years ago at the most. This difficult task was ostensibly carried out in the name of sunnah *or religious correctness, based on the behaviour of the Companions of Mohammed. In fact the Sunni Muslims, the majority group of Islam (Sunni meaning 'one who follows the* sunnah*') decided to ban wine because Islam was threatened with famine. After a series of conquests, of which history has no equivalent, Islam lived for a long while on the trophies of these wars. Gradually its resources became depleted, while at the same time the number of mouths to feed increased. There was not enough land to do this. The vine at that time took up a great deal of cultivable land, and required considerable labour. Wheat and rice soon nodded where the grape used to ripen. This measure, which may seem draconian to us, has enabled the Islamic world to maintain a standard of living for its peoples above that of other countries at a similar stage of development.*

Abu Zayd at Anah, in a tavern. Manuscript of the councils of Hariri, decorated with paintings by al-Wasiti, 1237. Bibliothèque Nationale, Paris.

Q R

The vineyards along the Angevin ridge near Rochefort-sur-Loire include those of the Quarts de Chaume **appellation**, *and they produce an unctuous, sweet white wine of great finesse.*

Quarts de Chaume

The Chenin Blanc grape variety produces 700hl of white wine annually here, from about 20ha. The area of production, classed as *appellation d'origine contrôlée* by the decree of 10 August 1954, extends over the commune of Rochefort-sur-Loire in the *département* of Maine-et-Loire, particularly the vineyard parcels of Les Quarts, Les Rouères and Le Veau.

The wines are made from grapes affected by *Botrytis cinerea* (*pourriture noble* or noble rot). They are rich and deep yellow to golden yellow in colour. They have a perfect balance of sweetness and acidity, with good length and excellent ageing potential.

Quatourze *See* Coteaux du Languedoc.

Quincy

This area, designated an *appellation d'origine contrôlée* on 6 August 1936, covers 100ha. Wine growers produce an average of 3,500hl of white wine here each year from the Sauvignon Blanc grape variety. The area of production covers the communes, or parts of communes, of Quincy and Brinay in Cher.

The wine of Quincy has a light, distinctive, straw-yellow colour, and its aroma is very characteristic of the Sauvignon Blanc. The wine is dry, delicate, supple and lively, and ages well. (*See* the Vins du Centre regional entry.)

Raffiat de Moncade

Synonyms: *Raffiat* or *Arréfiat* in Béarn, *Rousselet* in Saliès-de-Béarn.

Growing tips open, felty white.

Young leaves downy, with bronze patches.

Leaves orbicular-reniform, smooth, flat, thick, with concave edges; slightly three-lobed, petiolar sinus lyrate, open; dentation medium sized, convex; underside of blade arachnoid with pubescent veins.

Green shoots ribbed, lightly arachnoid at the tip, with longitudinal red striations.

Bunches large, winged, conical, loose; grapes medium sized, spherical, white, juicy; ripening period: second epoch, late.

This Béarnais grape variety is fertile, sometimes prone to *coulure* (flower abortion), giving a fine, strong wine. Classed as 'recommended' in Béarn, Landes and the Basque country, it is grown on 85ha. One registered clone has been approved: number 465.

Raisaine

Synonym: *Durasaine* at Aubenas.

Bunches medium sized, cylindrical-conical, sometimes winged; grapes ovoid, white; ripening period: second epoch, late.

This white Ardèche variety is vigorous, and is grown in the Aubenas, Joyeuse and Privas wine districts. Never vinified on its own, it used to be blended with red varieties, and was sometimes served as a table grape locally. Not classified.

Rasteau and Rasteau Rancio

The village of Rasteau is known for its rosé wines and more particularly for its reds, which are of such good quality that they are included within the Côtes du Rhône-Villages *appellation* under the name Côtes du Rhône-Rasteau. However, it is less widely known that there is also a *vin doux naturel* (sweet fortified wine) produced here, almost exclusively from the Grenache (and Grenache Blanc) grape variety.

In sandy, marly and pebbly soils, well sheltered from cold winds, the best sites of the village are reserved for VDN production, or *vin spéciale*, as it is called locally.

Some 80ha produce an annual average of 3,200hl of Rasteau VDN. This is far below the *terroir*'s potential, but Rasteau, like many Grenache VDNs, suffers from the economic problems consequent on lack of demand. Production tends more towards red-wine production at present.

The *appellation*, ratified on 19 May 1952 for three communes, produces two kinds of wine: one is golden white in colour, with an aroma of cooked fruit; the other is red, with aromas of prunes and, sometimes, *rancio* (oxidized or maderized) aromas.

Ravat Blanc

Synonym: *Ravat 6.*

Growing tips arachnoid, light pink.

Young leaves glossy, almost glabrous.

Leaves orbicular-reniform, bluish green, thick, glossy, three-lobed, upper sinuses acute and narrow at base, petiolar sinus in an open V-shape, petiolar junction red; dentation pointed, narrow; underside of blade glabrous with slightly pubescent veins.

Green shoots ribbed, slightly arachnoid and pubescent at the nodes.

Bunches small to medium sized, cylindrical, elongated, winged; grapes spherical, small, pink-white, with an aromatic, pomade-like flavour; ripening period: first epoch.

The vine is a Seibel 5474 × Chardonnay hybrid; it is not very vigorous and its productivity is average; it gives a strong, perfumed wine. It is very susceptible to oidium (powdery mildew) and grey rot (botrytis), but it is little affected by downy mildew. As it has low resistance to phylloxera, it has to be grafted. Classed as 'authorized' in Burgundy, nearly 300ha of it are still grown there.

In addition to the wines of the Côtes du Rhône-Villages **appellation**, *Rasteau produces two* **vins doux naturels** *under its own name, one golden white and the other red, and both made from the Grenache grape variety.*

Rayon d'Or

Synonym: *4986 Seibel.*

Growing tips downy white, with carmine margins.

Young leaves arachnoid, green.

Leaves truncate, dark green, glossy, contorted, deeply five-lobed with concave lobes, lateral sinuses acute and narrow at base, upper lateral sinuses often with overlapping edges, petiolar sinus lyrate, narrow, with overlapping edges; dentation convex, wide, large; underside of blade pubescent.

Green shoots finely ribbed, pale green, glabrous.

Bunches medium sized, cylindrical, compact; grapes small, spherical, golden yellow, with mauve bloom, not very juicy and with a sickening, pomade-like flavour; ripening period: first epoch.

Rayon d'Or is a 405 × 2007 Seibel hybrid, very fashionable at one time; only 368ha are grown now, however, as it has been classified as 'authorized' for Loiret and Loir-et-Cher alone.

The white wine of the Rayon d'Or has a delicate smell, a wild flavour and a light taste of strawberries, diminished a little when the grapes are affected by rot. The plant has late budbreak, and produces good results in frost-prone areas. It has good resistance to disease and can be grown without grafting in many different types of soil.

Reuilly

This area, classed as an *appellation d'origine contrôlée* by the decree of 24 August 1961, covers 30ha, with the Pinot Noir and Pinot Gris as the specified grape varieties for red and rosé wines, and the Sauvignon Blanc for white wine. Production is about 400hl a year, two thirds of this figure as rosé. The production area covers the following communes or parts of communes: Reuilly and Diou in Indre, and Cerbois, Lury-sur-Arnon, Preuilly, Chéry and Lazenay in Cher.

The colour of the white wines is a moderately deep straw-yellow. They are delicate in flavour, and very well balanced; they are dry, fleshy and very fresh, with good length.

The red wines are a light redcurrant-red in colour. They have a fruity bouquet, and are supple and easy to drink.

The rosé wine is dry and smooth.

These wines, especially the whites, last well in bottle, their breed emerging with time. (See the Vins du Centre regional entry.)

Ribier

Synonyms: *Petit Ribier* at Aubenas, *Rivier* at Saint-Péray, *Petit Rouvier* at Privas.

Bunches small to medium sized, cylindrical-conical, sometimes winged; grapes spherical, medium sized, black; ripening period: second epoch, late.

This is an old Ardèche variety, vigorous, fertile, producing a robust, pleasant wine, but less fine than that of the Syrah. Not classified.

Ribier Gris differs from the Ribier only in the colour of its grapes. The Ribier Gris is grown in Drôme, at Espenel.

Richebourg

In the famous commune of Vosne-Romanée on Burgundy's Côte de Nuits, the red Grand Cru of Richebourg covers 8ha lying high on the hillside, north of Romanée and Romanée-Conti and bordering Romanée-Saint-Vivant.

The Pinot Noir vines are situated on a clay-limestone subsoil here, and it is this that gives the wine of Richebourg its very firmly structured character. The decree of 11 September 1936 states that Richebourg must have a minimum alcohol content of 11°, and a 30hl/ha maximum yield.

Richebourg, which is second in importance in Vosne-Romanée after Romanée-Saint-Vivant, produces an annual average of 125hl of fine wine, much sought-after for its deep colour and its splendid constitution. These qualities mark it out as a wine for long ageing.

Riesling

Synonyms: *Raisin du Rhin, Petit Riesling*.

Growing tips flattened, downy, greenish white with carmine margins.

Young leaves arachnoid, yellowish with bronze glints; underside of blade downy white.

Leaves orbicular, thick, coarsely bullate and crimped around the petiolar junction; the base of the veins is often pink; deeply five-lobed; the upper lateral sinuses club shaped, closed, the lower sinuses open, the petiolar sinus with parallel edges, often overlapping; dentation medium sized, convex; underside of blade arachnoid-pubescent, veins pubescent.

Green shoots ribbed, red-brown with light pink nodes; tendrils thin, small, green.

Bunches small, cylindrical or cylindrical-conical, compact, with short, lignified peduncles; grapes small, spherical, light green to golden yellow, speckled with red-brown spots when fully ripe, skin thick, fine, aromatic flavour; ripening period: second epoch.

The Riesling has late budbreak. In northern wine districts, because it ripens late, it has to be planted on well-exposed slopes to permit a harvesting date towards mid-October.

Wine made from the Riesling has a characteristic bouquet which develops very intensely in the German Mosel and Rheingau regions (on soils of slaty schist and clay). In Alsace, Riesling wines are among those produced in Vendange Tardive (late harvest) form, with grapes yielding 220g of sugar per litre (potential alcohol of 12.4°) or in Sélection de Grains Nobles (selected grapes with 'noble rot') form, with grapes yielding 256g of sugar per litre (potential alcohol of 14°).

This variety, which is susceptible to oidium (powdery mildew) and to grey rot (botrytis), provides yields of 40hl/ha to 80hl/ha. Classed as 'recommended' in Alsace and Moselle, it is grown on an area of 2,500ha and is included in the plantings of the Alsace and Alsace Grand Cru AOCs. One registered clone has been approved: number 49.

Riminese

Synonyms: *Criminese*, *Creminese* at Bastia.

Bunches large, long, cylindrical, narrow, compact, winged; grapes small, spherical, white with thick skin, juicy; ripening period: second epoch, late.

This variety is grown on Corsica and must have originated in Italy, probably in the Rimini area. It could be the Albana, but this has not yet been verified.

It is a vigorous vine, pruned long and providing a good white wine which can be aged, and is both alcoholic and delicate. It is classed as 'recommended' in Corsica and is one of the specified varieties for the Vin de Pays de l'Île de Beauté.

A bunch of Riesling grapes. This aromatic grape variety is grown in the northern French vineyards of the Moselle and Alsace.

Riesling green shoot.

Riesling leaf.

Rivesaltes and Rivesaltes Rancio

This vineyard zone, covering a wide area, received its *vin doux naturel* AOC by decree on 19 May 1972. Its *terroir* extends over 86 communes in Roussillon and 9 in Corbières, and covers 24,000ha. Annual production is about 350,000hl. Five grape varieties are authorized: Grenache, Macabeu, Tourbat, Muscat à Petits Grains Blancs and Muscat d'Alexandrie.

The range of Rivesaltes wines is varied. They are vinified as white, rosé or red wines, and may be fortified in different ways. As they mature — for at least one year — they acquire an amber or tile red colour, and develop aromas of cooked cherries, honey, cocoa and vanilla. Rivesaltes wines, therefore, offer devotees a great variety of styles, from the youngest — just over a year old — to the oldest, the Rivesaltes Rancios, which are sometimes 25 years old.

Rolle

Synonyms: *Rollé, Rôle.*

This variety is grown in the Nice area for the Bellet AOC, and elsewhere in Provence for the AOC Côtes de Provence. It is probably the Rollo of Liguria. Its wine is of good quality, high in alcohol, delicate, superior to that of the Ugni Blanc. It can be eaten as a table grape and was even used in the past to make into raisins.

Rolle is similar to the Vermentino, grown in Corsica and Sardinia, and also to the Valentin or Sauvaget, but there are small differences between the three varieties in the morphology of their leaves and the characteristics of their green shoots. Unclassified.

The Catalan wine district of Rivesaltes, overlooked by Mont Canigou (2,785m), produces warm red and white **vins doux naturels**, *including some very sweet, rich* **rancios**, *which develop fine cooked-fruit aromas.*

Romanée, La

With an area of less than a hectare (84 ares, or 8,400m^2), the Côte de Nuits Grand Cru of La Romanée, adjoining the Grands Crus of Romanée-Conti and Richebourg, is one of the smallest vineyards in Vosne-Romanée. A single path separates La Romanée from Romanée-Conti, and yet the two wines are quite distinct.

The soils have the same characteristics, but the interaction of the soil and subsoil, the effect of microclimate and the art of wine making sometimes does make all the difference, as in this case, for La Romanée is thought rarely to match Romanée-Conti. The decree of 11 September 1936 laid down the usual conditions of production for red Grands Crus: a minimum alcohol content of 11.5°, a maximum yield of 30hl/ha. Thus there can be vintages when the total harvest of the vineyard is around 20hl (as in 1983). The red wine of La Romanée, made from the Pinot Noir grape variety, has the customary qualities of Côte de Nuits Grands Crus — longevity, power and breeding.

Romanée-Conti

This red Grand Cru of the Côte de Nuits, sited in the commune of Vosne-Romanée, continues to inspire the unanimous approbation that it has always done down the centuries. The monks of Cîteaux were able to draw such expressiveness from these wines that their reputation very quickly extended beyond the borders of the region. A kind doctor had the excellent idea of prescribing some for Louis XIV; Mme de Pompadour pursed her lips with anger when she learned that the Prince de Conti had outbid her for the vineyard at a sale in 1760. The area of the *appellation d'origine contrôlée*, ratified by decree on 11 September 1936, covers less than 2ha (1 hectare 80 ares 50 centares, to be precise).

The wine of Romanée-Conti, made from Pinot Noir grapes, must have a minimum alcohol content of 11.5°. Maximum yield is 30hl/ha.

Each year, the whole world awaits the release of the new vintage of this wonderful wine, which never ceases to astonish with its perfect balance and thoroughbred distinction. It is perhaps the most complete of all Burgundy's great wines.

Romanée-Saint-Vivant

Bordering on Richebourg and Romanée-Conti, the Romanée-Saint-Vivant site covers an area of 9.5ha. This Côte de Nuits red Grand Cru was long cherished by the monks of the abbey of Saint-Vivant.

Today the vineyard is split between four owners. Although the wine recalls that of La Romanée, it has its own distinct character — a difference probably due to the soil and subsoil. On the eastern side, adjacent to the village of Vosne-Romanée, the soil is dominated by clay and limestone. On the western and southern sides, adjacent to Richebourg and Romanée-Conti, the land is poorer. The highest part, near La Romanée, has more calcareous soils. The lowest parts of Romanée-Saint-Vivant, nearest the Vosne road to the south, are the least esteemed because the soil is both rich and well watered. The decree of 11 September 1936, ratifying this *appellation d'origine contrôlée*, requires that Romanée-Saint-Vivant wines should have a minimum alcohol content of 11.5° and a maximum yield of 30hl/ha. Each year this *cru* produces about 160hl of elegant, smooth and velvety wine, with all the class expected of great burgundy.

Romorantin

Synonyms: *Petit Dannezy*, *Dannery* in Allier and Cher, *Petit Mâconnais* and *Lyonnaise Blanche* around Moulins, *Framboise* at Gien, *Gros Blanc de Villefranche* in Loir-et-Cher.

Bunches medium sized, cylindrical, compact, winged; grapes small, spherical, white, turning pink when fully ripe, not very juicy; ripening period: first epoch.

This variety has early budbreak and gives a fairly strong, aromatic, yet tart wine. One registered clone has been approved: number 466. The variety has been classed as 'recommended' throughout the Loire valley, but in fact is hardly grown outside Loir-et-Cher (258ha), where it features in the VDQS Cheverny plantings.

Rosé d'Anjou and Rosé d'Anjou Pétillant

See Anjou and Anjou Pétillant.

Rosé de Loire

The wine-growing potential of this *appellation*, classed by decree on 4 September 1974, is considerable, but it is not as widely used as it might be. Production borders on 20,000hl per year, with the Cabernet Franc and Cabernet Sauvignon grape varieties accounting for at least 30 per cent of the blend, the balance being made up by the Pineau d'Aunis, Pinot Noir, Gamay and Grolleau varieties.

Rosé de Loire is dry: it should not contain more than 3g of sugar per litre. The wine is smooth, lively and easy to drink.

Vineyards in Vosne-Romanée. This Côte de Nuits commune produces only red wines of great breeding, and includes the prestigious crus *of La Romanée and Romanée-Conti within its boundaries.*

Rosé des Riceys

This *appellation*, with a tiny production of only 50hl to 100hl a year from its 300ha, is for rosé wine made from the Pinot Noir variety, grown in the commune of les Riceys in the Aube part of the Champagne area. The AOC was ratified by decree on 8 December 1947 and 2 February 1971. The wine has to be made by maceration with the grape skins, and it has a distinctive aroma of hazelnuts.

Rosette

This *appellation d'origine contrôlée*, ratified on 12 March 1946, is for sweet white wines from an area of production largely congruent with that of Pécharmant in the Bergerac region. Production is tiny: less than 500hl a year.

Roublot

Synonyms: *Roubleau*, *Roblot*, *Plant de Vaux* at Coulanges-la-Vineuse, *Plant Paule* at Irancy, *Aubanne*, *Haubanne* at Vaux, *César Blanc* or *César Femelle*.

This variety is peculiar to the Yonne, the *département* for which it has been classed as 'recommended'. A good producer of table wine, and often used by growers to blend with wines from the Chardonnay and Plant Vert in the past, it has almost disappeared now because of its vulnerability to oidium (powdery mildew) and grey rot (botrytis).

Roussanne

Synonyms: *Bardin* in the Gélon valley and on the left bank of the Isère, *Bergeron*, *Greffou* at Chignin, *Rebolot*, *Rabellot*, *Ramoulette* in the Grésivaudan area, *Picotin Blanc* at Vienne, *Roussette* at Saint-Chef and in the Bugey area, *Fromental* or *Fromenteau* in Isère.

Growing tips felty white with carmine margins.

Young leaves deeply lobed, downy, bullate.

Leaves large, orbicular, bullate, crimped, thick, contorted, markedly concave, deeply five-lobed, with bases concave and wide, upper lateral sinuses sometimes closed, petiolar sinus lyrate with overlapping edges; dentation convex, wide, large; underside of blade pubescent, rough.

Green shoots finely ribbed, hard, glabrous, light green; tendrils long, entangled.

Bunches small, cylindrical, compact; grapes small, spherical, golden white, almost russet in colour when fully ripe, not very juicy; ripening period: second epoch, late.

The Roussanne is a 'noble' grape variety, capable of producing high-quality, fine, aromatic wines; it is the variety that has made the reputation of the white wines of Hermitage. Unfortunately it is a very modest producer, ripening rather late for the Rhône valley, and is susceptible to oidium (powdery mildew) and grey rot (botrytis).

At present it is in Savoie and in the Chignin area that the best Roussanne wines are to be found, with a lovely straw-yellow colour, a remarkable bouquet, and with good ageing potential.

Four registered clones have been approved: numbers 467 to 469 and 522. Roussanne has been classified as 'recommended' in Savoie, Drôme, Provence and Languedoc, and is grown on 120ha for the Savoie, Hermitage, Crozes-Hermitage, Saint-Péray, Saint-Joseph, Côtes du Rhône and Châteauneuf-du-Pape AOCs.

The six crus of Roussette du Bugey come from the Anglefort, Arbignieu, Chanay, Lagnieu, Montagnieu and Virieu-le-Grand vineyards.

Roussanne du Var

Synonyms: *Rosé du Var*, *Barbaroux* at les Arcs.

Bunches medium sized, conical, compact; grapes spherical or slightly ellipsoidal, large, pink, juicy; ripening period: third epoch.

This variety, often known in Var by the names Grec Rose or Barbaroux, has qualities very similar to these (different) varieties. It is a productive vine, giving wines of low alcohol content. It has early budbreak, and its grapes are susceptible to grey rot (botrytis). This variety, classed as 'recommended' in Provence but banned from 1986 for the Côtes de Provence AOC, covers about 1,000ha, but this area is likely to be reduced in the future as a consequence of this prohibition.

Rousse

Synonyms: *Rousse de Lyonnais*, *Rousse de la Vallée du Gier*, *Roussette*.

Bunches small, cylindrical, loose, sometimes winged; grapes medium sized, ellipsoidal, yellowish-white, becoming russet (*rousse*) when fully ripe, skin thick; ripening period: second epoch.

This is a secondary variety from the Loire *département*, previously grown in the Gier valley on poor soils, sometimes in combination with the Mornen. It is productive, but gives a wine of poorer quality than, for example, that of the Viognier. Not classified.

Roussette d'Ayse

A variety peculiar to the Ayse wine district in Haute-Savoie, the *département* where it is classed as 'recommended', and where it is used to make a light, sharp, sparkling white wine.

Roussette du Bugey

With the decree of 27 September 1963, wines produced from a blend of Altesse (locally called the Roussette) and Chardonnay grapes, grown in the Vin du Bugey *appellation* area, acquired VDQS status. An annual average of 600hl of fine, aromatic, light white wines are produced.

Roussette du Bugey followed by a *cru* name

Growers producing wines meeting the Roussette du Bugey criteria may add a *cru* name to that of the *appellation* if their wine comes exclusively from a designated site (see the margin list).

Roussette de Savoie

On 4 September 1973 this *appellation d'origine contrôlée* was granted to 29 communes in Savoie, 22 in Haute-Savoie and 2 in Isère.

The basic grape variety used is the Altesse (locally called the Roussette), in conjunction with the Chardonnay. Wines from the communes of Brison Saint-Innocent, Billième, Cruet, Freterive, Saint-Pierre-d'Albigny and Yenne are among the most distinguished of the *appellation*. Some 3,000hl of a dry, keen-edged white wine, very delicate and fruity, are produced here annually.

Roussette de Savoie followed by a *cru* name

As a result of the decrees of 27 August and 4 September 1986, Roussette de Savoie, based on the Altesse (Roussette) grape variety, can be followed by the name of one of four *crus*. In 1986, 1,200hl of Roussette de Savoie *cru* wine was produced.

Frangy: This *cru* name is available to 11 communes within the overall *appellation* area, sited about 10km northeast of Seyssel. The south-facing slopes of glacial alluvium above the river Usses are particularly propitious for wine growing.

Marestel: This *cru* is restricted to the very steep, west-facing slopes on the Mont de la Charvaz, lying to the west of the Lac du Bourget, in the communes of Jongieux and Lucey. The more or less stony soils consist of limestone debris.

Monthoux: This *cru* covers the single commune of Saint-Jean-de-Chevelu, and is sited on similar slopes and soils to those of the adjacent *cru* of Marestel.

Monterminod: This *cru* is sited close to Chambéry, in the commune of Saint-Alban-Leysse. The Altesse is grown here on the marl and limestone soils found on the very steep south-west-facing slopes of the right bank of the river Leysse, in the southern part of the Massif des Bouges.

These four *crus* rival each other in elegance and delicacy. Harmonious and flowery when young, the wines acquire a bouquet full of the scents of hazelnut and walnut after three or four years.

Rubilande

Synonym: *11803 Seibel*.

Bunches medium sized, cylindrical, compact, winged; grapes ovoid, medium sized, pink tinged with purple, not very juicy; ripening period: second epoch.

This variety has early budbreak, thanks to its parentage of 2859 × 4643 Seibel; it is prone to *coulure* (flower abortion), and this means that it has an irregular production. Rubilande is susceptible to grey rot (botrytis) and drought conditions. It gives a bitter rosé wine which turns yellow with age. Classed as 'authorized' in the Loire valley, it is still grown on 40ha there.

Ruchottes-Chambertin

The vineyard parcels of the Ruchottes-Chambertin *appellation d'origine contrôlée* adjoin those of Clos de Bèze, but the altitude at which they are sited gives them a special character which distinguishes them from the other famous red Grands Crus of Gevrey-Chambertin on the Côte de Nuits. The decree of 31 July 1937, ratifying this *appellation*, specifies that the wines of Ruchottes-Chambertin must have a minimum alcohol content of 11° and a maximum yield of 32hl/ha, which means that the 3ha of the *appellation* provide an average of 90hl a year. Ruchottes-Chambertin wines are known for their delicacy and their breeding, but never quite reach the summits attained by some of the other red Grands Crus of Gevrey-Chambertin.

Rully

Pinot Noir and Chardonnay are both planted on the limestone and clay soils of the 260ha Rully *appellation d'origine contrôlée*, applicable to red and white wines produced from designated sites within the communes of Rully and Chagny, in Saône-et-Loire. The decree of 13 June 1939 specifies that both the red and white wines of Rully must have a minimum alcohol content of 11°. Wine growers here produce 10,000hl of red wine and 5,000hl of white per year. The red wines have a lovely ruby colour, with a taste of raspberries, whereas the more sought-after whites are valued for their finesse and vivacity.

The Château de Rully overlooks a vineyard largely planted with Chardonnay, whose firm, vigorous white wine benefits from being aged for several years in bottle.

THE SIGNIFICANCE OF WINE

It may come as a surprise to the uninitiated to discover that the birth of modern oenology is due to Pasteur. By studying the fermentation of the grape, this scientist discovered microbes: a double benefit for mankind. In revealing the action of yeasts in fermentation, some of the magic of wine was exorcized. But the way was prepared for wine's future, a future both royal and democratic.

From being, in earliest times, a thirst-quenching drink, uplifting but fragile because of its instability, a drink that could have remained commonplace, wine has assumed a perennial nobility, thanks to its new qualities of stability, clarity, and the potential to age for long periods and acquire aromatic sublimity as it does so. More than a science, the production of wine for long ageing has become an art, like the act of tasting that makes it possible to explain, to understand and to experience such a wine completely.

Dionysus has gained in glory what he has lost in mystery . Wine has come far since the time of the early shepherds' drinks — when it did not even have a name — to today, when it is a specific product, identified and identifiable, the issue of *crus* and *terroirs*.

This naming of wine by its place of origin goes back a long time. Hermitage, Côte Rôtie and Gaillac are all names that were already in use during the Gallo-Roman period. As for dating wine, this was also practised by the Romans, who used the name of the consul in power to indicate the year of vintage. This was probably a first attempt at organization and reference of the still infant world of wine, a world that was already complex, babbling in many tongues, and full of the significance felt, but rarely understood, by every wine drinker. A charismatic world, then as now, today like yesterday: Beaujolais, for example, is always *nouveau* and always renews our joy in life. From Greek *symposia* and Periclean banquets to present-day wine societies and *confréries*, the link is unbroken, even if the ritual has changed a little . . .

Conviviality

Whatever the occasion, men and women like to meet to drink wine and talk about it — and about themselves. Alcibiades could arrive late for dinner today and say with no less truth: 'You have had your fill of philosophy and intoxication' to fellow city guests, arguing points with geometrical precision, or debating, not the latest rumours circulating in the agora, but the movement of the dollar, or the likely fate of an arrested terrorist. For centuries, man has celebrated the wine that celebrates mankind.

What product other than wine contains such a humanitarian charge? Wine is a living body where diverse elements are held in balance, volatile elements and weighted elements, 'the meeting place of a heaven and a *terroir*', as the philosopher Gaston Bachelard has said. To drink wine is to drink time and space as well. The person who drinks this unique beverage enters into a dialectic meditation. A dispute is engendered between the maker of the product, the wine grower, and its drinker, the wine lover. One questions the other and vice versa. The artisan of the vine offers the drinker, whether he is a king or a commoner, worker or captain of industry, his humility but also his taste for adventure. A fearful lesson. He offers him a resumé of his life. His offering enters the drinker's body with the strength of soil, the colour of skies, through the medium of ancient recipes which the wine grower possesses in his memory, and thanks to the devotedly stubborn efforts necessary to realize such recipes . . . who is the more philosophical, then, the drinker of wine or the maker of wine?

The ancient Greeks loved to gather together and drink wine at festive banquets, like that depicted in this Greek tomb painting, called 'The Tomb of the Diver', near Paestum (southern Italy, southeast of Salerno), 480BC.

The art of the wine grower

The wine grower does not make a wine, but a *cru*; he does not receive you at home, but firstly in his cellar. He does not ask you to visit it; he simply welcomes you there. He does not give you wine, but offers it as a token of friendship. In Colmar, Nantes, Beaune, Mâcon, Bordeaux, Cahors, Reims and Avignon the ritual is the same — proof, if proof were necessary, that wine governs identical behaviour.

To be a wine grower is to be careful, observant, curious, enthusiastic in meditation, fiery but patient, artistic but methodical, bold but thoughtful, obstinate but imaginative. For the wine grower the vine is a battleground between matter, the elements, biology and craft. The matter is rock, earth. The elements are air, sunlight, wind, water and cold. Biology is the vine, its wine.

The wine grower's craft begins in a reverie of will. Wine growing is a school of adversity, and in practising his craft the grower's faith is nourished, his resolution strengthened, his wisdom deepened.

It takes five years to build a productive vine and twelve to give it intelligence; any mistake on the wine grower's part will be paid for over forty years. Furthermore, a year is needed to get a good crop, three years to get wine that will stand the test of time into a bottle, and ten years, sometimes twenty, for that wine to achieve a state of grace. When the wine grower prunes the vine, the snip of his secateurs conditions not only next year's crop, but also the one after that.

The wine grower lives in fear, fear of the hard winter frost that can destroy his vineyard, fear of the storms that can cut swathes through his vines, fear of the hail that destroys grapes, fear of the spring frosts that nip vine buds . . . and when he has overcome all these fears, he sits down at the roulette wheel to decide when to begin harvesting, and stakes his annual income on the result.

Living constantly in the future, the wine grower is therefore a craftsman of meditation — the virtues of which have universal value — doubling as a formidable technician. Nourished by the long experience accumulated by his predecessors, his is a virtuoso performance with the elements of chance and of necessity. He works for wine, but wine works for him . . . before working for us.

At the great festival in the vat, among the millions of yeasts working at the invention of wine, each yeast has its place. Its duty is to open the link of a molecular chain, to exchange such a link with another, according to a plan inscribed in its protoplasmic memory. Nothing distracts it from its task! Does it not know the three hundred or so substances in the must and the means of breaking them up or uniting them to satisfy its tastes as an alchemist of the infinitesimal? Does it not have its master plan, its 'sixth sense', its creative will? It has its secrets, its moments of illumination and epiphany. It repeats nothing.

The variety of bouquets

From this great work are born the perfumes of wine. Corresponding to the lacework of molecules imagined by the yeast is the lacework of aroma, the true breath of the cellar, always sweet but never the same as any previous aroma. And man has taken it into his head to tame it! Oenology is the science of phenomena that are never the same twice . . .

The wine grower's art is notably evident in pruning: one snip of the secateurs conditions the future of the vine.

Look at it, that yeast, drifting on the sea of must that its task is to sublimate. Thousands of years have armed it for this eternal struggle. It holds all the keys to turn the mechanism of nature. But what road will it take to lead it to its goal of disintegration? Ten, a hundred directions beckon it . . . The wine lover will not be surprised, learning this, by the variety of bouquets he or she will encounter from one year to the next. Remember the yeast, committed to pursue its laborious cleaving to the secret heart of the must-matter, ready finally to die for it, suffocated by what it has so magisterially created.

Such is the destiny of a great wine, a kind of patient mastery of the universe, capturing and taming the underlying, disorganized creative forces. A unique destiny. Wine, a substance of hierarchies, confident of its benefits, is the only 'intelligent' drink; and it never ceases to allow itself to be explored by a still more intelligent being: the drinker who understands its meaning and pleasures.

An intermediary of passion, wine is also a magnifying glass for our sensitivity. It puts light in the mouth. Through wine, our intimate emotions can reach the matter in which the soul of things, singular as it must be, may be read.

THE TRADITIONS OF WINE

Wine is born, it grows, sings, grows sad, takes shape, ages ... Then it reveals its name. It is a living creature that speaks and whose language expresses — in the same way as the languages of men and women — its joy and sorrow, the vocation to grow to its full potential, the desire to become its own name.

It is commonly said that wine has body, but also that it has spirit. These everyday, figurative expressions are the remains of traditions that are several thousand years old; they are the traces of ancestral rites connected with wine and the vine, which were, and still are, expressed by the legends and rituals of the people from the lands around the Mediterranean.

Their origin may no doubt be traced back to the analogy between wine and blood, the symbol of life, but also to the phenomenon of intoxication, which represented an unfathomable mystery for the peoples of antiquity. This transformation of grape juice into a drink capable of changing man's behaviour or speech, of making him happy, sad or angry, is indeed an astonishing process. It no doubt explains why wine has, since ancient times, had an initiatory value, in so far as it marked the transition from a state of nature to that of culture.

Thanks to wine, men are able to apprehend the inexpressible. It is a route of access to a universal, symbolic language, of which the most obvious day-to-day translations are the raising of one's glass to the health of another or to the success of one's friends and, at a different level, the religious celebration of the Eucharist.

A theatre mask representing Bacchus. Mosaic from Hadrian's villa, 2nd century AD. Capitoline Palace Museum, Rome.

Wine — an expression of divinity

Before monotheistic traditions attributed the origin of wine to Noah — at the moment, in other words, when the new humanity was purified by the waters of the flood — wine had been ascribed virtues linked to the supernatural. Thus, in the civilizations of ancient Greece and Rome, intoxication was not a simple matter of cause and effect, but a supernatural process by which a divinity took possession of the senses. The Etruscan, Roman or Greek did not consider himself intoxicated by wine, but by a deity, Fufluns, Bacchus and Dionysus, who used the wine as a vehicle.

The celebration of Roman Bacchic mysteries was the expression of Bacchus himself. These ceremonies, a representation of which has come down to us thanks to one of the most famous wall paintings of Pompeii, were not at all orgiastic. They were privileged moments during which man could communicate with the beyond. The same was true of the mysteries of Nithra, where wine, as well as bread, were thought to confer strength, wisdom and immortality on those being initiated.

Wine — an expression of humanity

With the Semitic peoples' development of the myth of Noah planting the first vine at the foot of Mount Ararat after the flood, a greater spiritualization of wine seems to have been reached. Certainly, the legend that the patriarch sprinkled the first vine with the blood of a lion to give it strength and spirit and with the blood of a lamb to remove its wildness is still connected to pagan myths. Similarly, the tradition that Noah had the idea of extracting the juice from the vine when he saw a goat intoxicated by the grapes is the expression of a mythology connecting the sexual symbolism of the goat with Bacchic potency. But the fact that Noah discovered how to make wine after the flood introduces a notion of transcendence that is foreign to the pagan tradition. For it was after the work of the waters and after the inner turmoil to which Noah's soul was subject for forty days and forty nights that the miracle of transformation was performed. God allowed Noah to come out of the waters, and Noah in his turn made the vine come out of the earth, to produce the wine which allowed him access to the Creator's consciousness. The transformation of water into wine, a symbol of man's transition to consciousness, has become the symbol of the transition from bestiality to humanity. Sanctified wine could, from that time, serve as a means of expression for a symbolic system imbued with mysticism and spirituality. It could now be celebrated for its own sake, no longer as the expression of God, but as a gift from God and as one of the signs of his presence in the world.

Wine and the Jewish tradition

For Jews, wine, like oil and bread, is a benediction: 'He bringeth forth grass for the cattle and green herb for the service of men; that he may bring food out of the earth and wine that maketh glad the heart of man and oil to make him a cheerful countenance and bread to strengthen man's heart.' This passage from Psalm 104 signifies, according to the Jewish tradition, that bread should be blessed at each meal, whereas wine should only be blessed on the Sabbath and on feast days. In fact, the text only alludes to wine once, whereas it makes two references to bread. For wine, the blessing is as follows: 'Praise be to you, our eternal God, king of the Universe who hast created the fruit of the vine.' This sanctification of wine by the transcendant act of prayer assumes a precise meaning during the Seder, a Passover meal celebrating the Israelites' departure from Egypt. The participants at the meal have to drink wine four times in succession to symbolize the departure from Egypt, salvation, atonement and adoption. In this ritual, wine is associated with the happiness of man, whose heart is fortified by manifestations of divine mercy.

It is perhaps through the symbolic system of wine and the vine that Christianity most clearly reveals its attachment to Jewish traditions and sensibility. But, whereas in the Jewish religion, wine and the vine serve as reminders of the goodness of the Almighty towards his people, with Christianity, a further level of abstraction is reached. For Christians, wine is neither God himself, as it was for the pagans, nor a manifestation of the divine will, as it is for the Jews. It takes on an allegorical form and serves as a symbolic medium for the teaching of Christ and the Church. Allegorical use of

Vine branches with grapes. Church of Saint-Germain de Mièges, 15th century.

Two Israelites carrying the giant bunch of grapes that symbolized the Promised Land.
L'automne. La grappe de la Terre Promise.
(Autumn. The Bunch of Grapes of the Promised Land). Nicolas Poussin (1594-1665). Musée du Louvre.

wine and the vine was already present in the Old Testament, notably in the Song of Songs, a mystical celebration where love and wine make the poet sing: 'Thy navel is like a round goblet that wanteth not liquor ... Thy breasts shall be as clusters of the vine ... And the roof of thy mouth like the best wine for my beloved.'

Metaphors based on wine and the vine abound in the Scriptures. Thus Christ said: 'I am the true vine and my Father is the husbandman' (John 15, 1). For Jesus of Nazareth, each being is a vine heavy with the potential of his fruit. This vine is his spouse, carrying the messianic promise, a spouse that is sometimes veiled or sterile, as the prophets lamented.

The blood of Christ

The symbolism of wine and the vine was used by Christian mystics from the early days of the Church. This tradition rests on the Church Fathers identifying the tree of life planted in the Garden of Eden with the vine. This interpretation is based on the idea that the water preceding life changes gradually into blood — the source of life and love — as is proved by the fact that blood and water flowed out of the side of the crucified Christ. Thus, the vine is considered to be the tree of life that draws its strength from the water needed to produce wine, the blood of the earth.

The story of the Round Table: 'How the Holy Grail appeared to the knights of the Round Table.' 15th-century miniature.

The New Testament tells us that Christ's first miracle was to change water into wine at the Cana wedding, and that his final miracle, at the Last Supper, was to change wine into blood, anticipating the spilt blood of the crucifixion. At Cana, Christ had six jars filled with water and changed them into wine. The seventh jar was filled with his wine, his blood, and all mankind was then invited to a new feast where the life of Christ was sublimated in the wine. This wine was formed by life-giving water, which symbolizes God the Father, but also by impalpable elements related to the spirit, the Holy Spirit. In this episode in the life of Christ, the mystery of the Trinity is thus completely symbolized by wine.

But access to knowledge, far from being acquired simply, requires long and hard work — a quest. It is this quest that is related in the adventures of the Holy Grail, according to legend an emerald goblet in which Joseph of Arimathea collected the blood and water that flowed from Christ's side, which had been pierced by a spear. In the Middle Ages, believers thirsted all the more for the wine of the Eucharist because, from the 11th century, the Church had denied this to the faithful, reserving it for the priest alone. It should also be noted that, from this time onwards, the wine used for the Eucharist was no longer red, but white, as if the Church had wanted to make the signs of knowledge still more inaccessible to the faithful. Thirsting for lost knowledge and for a transcendence whose meaning was beyond them, the Christians of the Middle Ages expressed their mystical aspirations by means of art. Desiring also to place their harvests — the source of life — under God's protection, the artists of the Middle Ages produced a growing number of allegories concerning wine and the vine. Some of these representations — vine leaves, vine branches — are purely decorative. Others are more directly symbolic, like sculptures showing birds drinking from a chalice — a symbol of the happiness of Eden — or the Mystic Winepress shown in the stained-glass window in the cloister of Saint-Étienne-du-Mont in Paris.

The theme of the Mystic Winepress comes from the phrase *Torcular calcavi solus* ('I have trodden the winepress alone': Isaiah 63, 3), interpreted by St Augustine: 'Jesus is the grape of the Promised Land, the bunch of grapes in the press.' The press is therefore the cross itself. In the Saint-Étienne-du-Mont window (above right), the Patriarchs dig the vines over and the Apostles gather the grapes, while Christ lies in the press. The barrel containing the divine blood is pulled by animals representing the Evangelists — ox, lion and eagle — driven by the angel symbolizing St Matthew. The Church Fathers put the wine into barrels. This wine is then distributed to the faithful at Holy Communion.

Similarly, the vine symbolizes the Church, as can be seen in the chapel of Saint-Quentin at Vaison-la-Romaine in Vaucluse, where an early Christian relief represents a chalice with two vines flowing from it. According to an interpretation of Jewish origin, the Church is indeed the Lord's plantation. For Isaiah, the vine symbolized the people of Israel. God has transplanted this vine from Egypt to the Promised Land and he tends it:

Stained-glass window called Le pressoir mystique *(The Mystic Winepress). 16th century. Church of Saint-Étienne-du-Mont, Paris.*

'... My well-beloved hath a vineyard
in a very fruitful hill.
And he fenced it, and gathered out the stones thereof,
and planted it with the choicest vine,
and built a tower in the midst of it,
and also made a winepress therein:
and he looked that it should bring forth grapes,
and it brought forth wild grapes.' (Isaiah 5, 1–7)

The metaphors of Islam

Whereas, in the Middle Ages, Christianity was striving to produce both a naïve and realistic representation of the vine and of the symbols of wine, in the same period, Islam was illustrating them in a much more spiritual and abstract way. Within Islam, there developed a tradition, particularly strong among the Sufis, which consisted in singing the praises of divine love by making systematic use of metaphors based on wine, the vine and intoxication. The Sufis, those wise mystics who took their name from the white woollen coats they wore (*suf* means wool in Arabic), gave a mystical interpretation of verse 76 of the Koran, which says: 'The Lord will make them drink a pure drink'; verse 83, 25: 'They will be given a perfumed and sealed wine to drink'; and verses 47, 16; 37, 44-46; 56, 18; 77, 34; 76, 5 ff., which speak of drink, wine, goblets and springs.

In the 12th century, the great mystical poem by Ibn al-Farid, *Khamriyah* ('Wine Ode'), is completely based on the metaphor of wine, the vine and intoxication as the expression of God and of his love for men. For mystical Sufi poets, wine symbolizes divine grace, the intoxication of spiritual love and esotericism. 'Wine, the torch and beauty are the epiphanies of Truth' — or God, says the 13th-century Persian poet Sa'di in the *Golestan* ('The Rose Garden'). He also says: 'Drink great draughts of the wine of annihilation ... Drink the wine which will deliver you from yourself and will make the being of the drop of water fall into the ocean. Drink wine, for its goblet is the face of a friend; the goblet is his eye that is spinning with intoxication. Seek the wine with neither goblet nor cup; the wine is the drinker, the cupbearer is the cup.' The poet signifies that, through intoxication, wine (as substance and symbol) annihilates the individual and makes him become absorbed into divine unity. Another Persian poet, from the 9th century, Abu Yazid al-Bistami, writes: 'I am the drinker, the wine is the cupbearer. In the world of Unification, all are one.' In the world of Islam, thirst is also a mystical symbol of the desire for knowledge and for love, as is illustrated by this text by al-Bistami: 'Another drank the seas of the sky and of the land and his thirst is still not quenched. He sticks out his tongue and asks whether there is more.'

The allegory of thirst

The first words which François Rabelais (*c.* 1494–1553) made Gargantua say when he was born were: 'Drink! Drink! Drink!' Pantagruel is so called because he was born during a drought, when even the dew was saltier than the sea. 'And because Pantagruel was born on that very day, his father gave him the name he did: for *Panta* in Greek is equivalent to *all*, and *Gruel*, in the Hagarene language, is as much as to say *thirsty*; by this meaning to infer that at the hour of the child's nativity the world was all thirsty, and also seeing, in a spirit of prophecy, that one day his son would be ruler over the thirsty . . .' (trans. here and below J.M. Cohen). The last phrase of the fourth book is '*buvons*' ('let's have a drink') and the fifth book finishes with the Oracle of the Holy Bottle, which pronounces the word '*Trinch*' ('*Trink* ... To us it signifies: Drink'). For Rabelais, drinking obviously meant the acquisition of knowledge, absorbing the juice and essence of things, and to drink without restraint meant to accede to unlimited knowledge.

When the Oracle of the Holy Bottle uttered '*Trinch*', the Priestess Bacbuc made Panurge drink a flask full of Falernian wine, meaning that it is within things themselves that their real significance is to be found, and that it is perhaps not necessary to go to great lengths to find the truth. The words of Frère Jean at the end of the first book make a similar point: 'You can read all the allegorical and serious meanings into it that you like, and dream on about it, you and all the world, as much as ever you will. For my part, I don't think there is any other sense concealed in it ...'

These words could also be applied to wine, because, charged with symbols and mysteries as it is, it perhaps finds its fundamental significance in the pleasure it gives us, its prime truth being to gladden our hearts.

CONFRÉRIES

There is no doubt that wine has long been a symbol, but it has also been, and primarily so, a vehicle of enjoyment and companionship. Little by little, a close complicity has been woven between men and wine, leading to a kind of doctrine of pleasure, and an art of living. In France, the wine confréries *(fraternities) have naturally cast themselves in the role of priests and apostles of this doctrine of human pleasure.*

The pleasures of good eating and drinking, so magisterially extolled by François Rabelais, constitute a tradition that has been magnificently upheld in France. It has survived political turmoil, wars, epidemics, even famine! It seems that charitable and convival *confréries* have always abounded, from the knights bachelors, clerks and adventurers of all kinds who met in the taverns of the Middle Ages for an evening of drinking and singing, down to the gourmet societies and drinking clubs of our time.

Confréries and guilds

Originally, the *confréries* existed alongside each of the craft associations that later became known as guilds or as corporations. The latter had the sole aim of protecting and defending the material and social interests of their members, while the *confréries* looked after their spiritual interests.

This organization into guilds was only able to gather momentum as the towns became enfranchised, in other words from the 11th century onwards. However, it is reasonable to take the real starting point for the large-scale formation of guilds as being the beginning of the 13th century, for more is known about the urban middle class from that time, especially in Paris. It was about this time, in fact, that the Provost of Paris, appointed by Louis IX, had the idea of compiling a register of the regulations of all such trade organizations.

It was the task of the *confrérie* to appoint representatives to attend the numerous religious offices of the time, or the festivities of other guilds. It administered the workings of mutual aid, finding a replacement if a master craftsman was sick or had died, for example, so that work in hand could be carried through. Each *confrérie* had a patron saint, usually St Vincent for the wine growers and St Nicholas for the coopers. Although these fraternities often served as a model for various societies with pious aims and objects, they also inspired other groups that were frankly secular, bacchic and often bawdy!

There were light-hearted drinking and literary fraternities. One of the most famous, the Confrérie des Montuzets, was founded in Bordeaux. It began with pious aims, but these gradually became blurred, and in the end its meetings were nothing but an excuse for merriment. While passing through Bordeaux, Louis XI was happy to accept the title of *Premier confrère*! By letters patent, he bestowed certain benefits and privileges on the Confrérie, including a permanent annual rent of three casks of wine from the office of the High Constable.

In the 19th century, Arthur Dinaux, head of the French Archives du Nord and author of a number of scholarly works, gathered most of the material together for a book that was not published until after his death, in 1867, under the title of *Les Sociétés badines, bachiques, littéraires et chantantes, leur histoire et leurs travaux* (The Jocular Bacchanalian, Literary and Singing Societies [of France], their History and Works). Among the 490 societies recorded in this book are a number quite similar to the *confréries* of today — for example, the Ordre de la Méduse (of Medusa — *see* page 455), de la Grappe (of the Bunch), de la Boisson de L'Étroite Observance (of the Drink of Strict Observance) or de la Treille (of the Vine Arbour). The rules of these societies inspired a number of modern *confréries*, some of which even revived the former names, insignia and rituals.

Others, such as the Jurade de Saint-Émilion or the Confrérie Saint-Étienne d'Alsace, which watched over the quality of wines leaving their area of production, drew inspiration from the old system of trade guilds. These guilds and their associated *confréries* were sustained by the wish to see work well done, and their members enjoying a certain quality of life. It is eternal values such as these that today's *confréries* wish to stand for, in placing themselves at the service of all, for the happiness of all.

The first *confrérie*

The interest aroused by wine today is one of the most remarkable phenomena of modern Western society, both in commercial terms and for the civilized values such an interest engenders. Some time ago, in the heart of Burgundy, poverty was rife. The cellars were full of excellent wines, but they didn't sell. The wine growers were so desperate that they feared good harvests, as these made their situation worse — they had to get deeper into debt in order to purchase the casks necessary to store the new wine. It was during the 1930s that this happened. A handful of energetic, far-sighted men, stimulated by adversity, refused to give in without a fight. They knew how good their wine was; they also knew that since the vine was perennial, the crisis could only be temporary. The problem was that they could not dispose of their wine because no one was ordering it, so they decided to invite friends and potential customers to come and inspect and taste it. Thus the first modern-day brotherhood, the Confrérie des Chevaliers du Tastevin, came into being on 16 November 1934 in the municipal wine cellar at Nuits-Saint-Georges. Next day, there was a memorable meeting at the nearby Château du Clos de Vougeot, during which the founding dignitaries, headed by two local growers, dubbed the first 30 Chevaliers.

The stroke of genius here lay in celebrating the *terroir* in its entirety, extolling its human virtues as well as those of the wines, the two merging appreciably: Burgundian wine growers make wine in a Burgundian image, just as God is said to have created man in a Godlike image. The Confrérie des Chevaliers du Tastevin had the success it did by going right back to the wellspring of the French spirit, drawing inspiration from sources such as Rabelais and Molière in a striking demonstration of physical and moral robustness. This in turn led to joy, good humour and the most unshakeable confidence in the future, thereby exorcizing the gloom of the times. Not only did it restore the courage of all the wine makers, but it also turned its newly dubbed Chevaliers into active ambassadors for the great wines of Burgundy. Its success was immediate and lasting.

The Chevaliers du Tastevin

Today no one would dream of disputing the decisive role

The **tastevinage** *is an annual tasting designed to draw the attention of wine enthusiasts, via the awarding of this label, to burgundy of outstanding quality within its category, and of appropriate maturity.*

The Confrérie des Chevaliers du Tastevin, the first of France's modern-day **confréries**, *was founded in 1934.*

the Confrérie des Chevaliers du Tastevin has played, and continues to play, all over the world on behalf of the wines of Burgundy in particular, and of France in general. As an institution, it soon set a trend. One of the most enthusiastic of the early Chevaliers du Tastevin was Charles Vavasseur, mayor of Vouvray (in the Loire valley), and also a distinguished wine grower. In 1937, under the patronage of the Burgundian fraternity, he set up the Confrérie des Chevaliers de la Chantepleure, a society dedicated to the promotion of the wines of Vouvray.

This new fraternity adopted the same rules as the Chevaliers du Tastevin, and it even assumed a similar costume. However, it took its name not from the *tastevin*, but from the *chantepleure*, which is a local term for a cask tap that 'sings' when you turn it, and 'weeps' as the wine flows out. The Second World War then put a stop to the activities of the two societies. The Château du Clos de Vougeot suffered considerable damage in successive military occupations. After 1945, the owner handed it over, for a token sum, to the Society of Friends of the Château du Clos de Vougeot so that it would become, for all legal and practical purposes, the property of the Chevaliers du Tastevin.

Within the Château walls, surrounded by vines, the fraternity has continued to exert a powerful influence on the world of wine in France and internationally. Its meetings, both ordinary and extraordinary, arouse lasting enthusiasm in the participants, and these now run into hundreds of thousands.

The fraternity does not merely undertake a representative role. It has played an active part in the Burgundian and the national economy by instituting an important wine tasting — the *tastevinage* — as well as a literary prize, and *commanderies* or lodges abroad.

It is not surprising, then, that such a successful venture has given rise to other similar bodies throughout France, each with its own regional style.

The Herrenstubengesellschaft

The movement for the establishment of *confréries* gathered momentum in the years following 1945, with wine fraternities often established before any real prosperity had returned to their regions. The first, and also one of the most important of the postwar fraternities, the Confrérie Saint-Étienne d'Alsace, was established in 1947. The credit for this is due to a grower from Ammerschwihr called Joseph Dreyer. A mathematics teacher at the *lycée* in Colmar, he also owned a small area of vineyard. The little town where he was born, for centuries a showpiece of medieval architecture, was completely destroyed in 1945. He resolved to restore its shattered spirit by reviving the ancient association of important citizens that had been known as the Herrenstubengesellschaft. The chief function of this association had been to check the quality of wines before they were allowed to leave Ammerschwihr.

The present *confrérie* owes its new name simply to the fact that it holds its grand annual meeting, followed by an extraordinary banquet, on 26 December, the Feast of Saint Stephen (Étienne).

Gaiety, good humour and optimism went hand-in-hand with the serious work carried out by this fraternity. Its influence was such that, in 1951, it was asked to place itself at the service of the whole of Alsace. It had, consequently, to take on a number of new duties, most notably providing representation at private and official functions.

In 1976, the headquarters of the fraternity moved to the Château de Kientzheim. This had formerly been the property of Lazare de Schwendi, a high-ranking officer of the Imperial Army of the Austro-Hungarian Empire who is reputed to have brought the famous Tokay (Pinot Gris) grape with him from Hungary in the 16th century. This legend has never been proved, however, despite the statue by Bartholdi in the Place de l'Ancienne-Douane in Kientzheim, showing Schwendi flourishing a handful of vine shoots.

The Jurade de Saint-Émilion

The Jurade de Saint-Émilion is a very similar organization to the Confrérie Saint-Étienne d'Alsace. It was founded on 13 September 1948, by members of the Syndicat Viticole et Agricole de Saint-Émilion who wished to revive the old Jurade that had for many years protected the extremely high quality of the wines of Saint-Émilion. The *jurats* (magistrates) who carried out their functions in the nine parishes that now form the *appellation* area were not only magistrates, but also military chiefs, tax collectors and controllers of the quality of all wines leaving their jurisdiction. The *marque* (seal of quality) — a stamp bearing the arms of the town — was held by them, and they controlled its use. They proclaimed the date of the grape harvest, and held back any wines that were felt to be 'of inadequate fineness'.

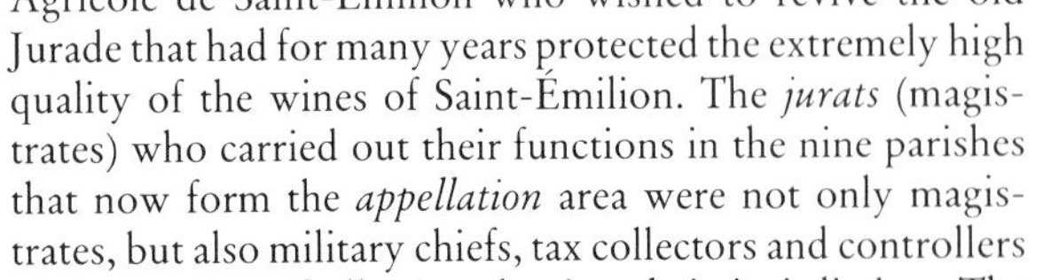

In 1957, the Confrérie Saint-Étienne d'Alsace instituted this seal, guaranteeing the quality of the wine in the bottles on which it appears.

The modern Jurade has made many good friends in France and around the world on account of the prestigious events and initiatives it organizes. All through the year, visitors flock to the ancient and historic town of Saint-Émilion, with its many traces of a great past. In this evocative setting, traditional rituals come to life again quite naturally: the proclamation of the start of the grape harvest, the judging of the new wine, the affixing of the seal, and the solemn enthronement of *pairs* ('peers'), *prud'hommes* ('elders'), and *vignerons d'honneur* (honorary wine growers). This prayer by a 14th-century troubadour, 'Dear Lord God, bless Thou these hills, and give us wine, joy and peace', expresses perfectly the wise philosophy of the man who knows his task, is careful to fulfil it well and happy to live in peace.

Beaujolais

Although Beaujolais was certainly a well-known wine in 1947, it was mainly celebrated in the Lyon area, and Beaujolais Nouveau was still something enjoyed principally by the guests of wine growers. The ideals of the old guilds were brotherhood, the love of work well done and respect for traditions, and this was especially true in the case of the Compagnons du Tour de France, the memory of which remains very much alive in Beaujolais; so much so that in Romanèche-Thorins there is a fascinating Musée du Compagnonnage, a trade guilds museum. The spirit, as well as the costume, of this old fraternity has of course been preserved by the new Beaujolais *confrérie*, the Compagnons du Beaujolais, which has been active for 40 years now, in cooperation with branches in Paris (the Devoir Parisien), and elsewhere, imparting a passion and taste for this incomparable wine.

The Commanderie du Bontemps

The Commanderie du Bontemps was born in a very different setting to that of Beaujolais. Its first grand event was held underneath the cedars of Château Lafite-Rothschild. The founders called the organization a *commanderie* (lodge, commandery) in memory of that of Ars, which once owned and worked vineyards in Margaux, Soussans, Avensan, Moulis and Cussac.

Besides its year-round programme of events, the Commanderie invites its friends to three annual meetings: the festival of Saint Vincent in January, the Fête de la Fleur (a celebration at around the time of the vine's flowering in June), and the proclamation of the start of the grape harvest.

The chapters, which normally take place in one of the distinguished châteaux of Médoc or Graves, are always invested with great solemnity, and never fail to make a strong impression on those gathered there. Participants, whether from France or from abroad, inevitably succumb to the charm of the place and of the wines, taking away with them a fairytale image of the French countryside.

The growth of wine fraternities

The rebirth of the two major modern *confréries*, and the institution of the first ten or so others, dates from the period immediately after the Second World War. The success of these organizations stimulated similar initiatives all over

A Jurat de Saint-Émilion during the ceremony of the proclamation of the grape harvest.

France, and the 1950s saw the creation of over 20 new *confréries*, *commanderies*, *vigueries* and other orders, such as the Ordre Illustre des Chevaliers de Méduse of Provence, which goes back to an association of the same name created in the late 17th century. The spirit and aims of these new wine fraternities may not be identical to those of the old guilds, but there was a sufficient harmony of interest to warrant such a revival. Today's goal is generally the fraternal celebration of the gastronomic delights, wine chief among them, of a *terroir* and a region.

Despite extraordinarily positive results, the principle of the fraternity as a sound instrument of collective public relations above and beyond individual private interests was not immediately accepted by all. There were many stern critics of the costumes, rituals and ceremonies, and of the quality of the banquets.

Some of these criticisms were fair; most, though, arose from a spirit of contrariness rather than through objective reasoning. They did not prevent fraternities from multiplying, not just in France, but in Italy, Germany, Switzerland and other countries with a wine-growing tradition.

In every case, the success of the *confréries* far surpassed the predictions of the most optimistic founders; and they were sustained by the public, who supported and wholeheartedly encouraged even the most diffident initiatives.

The reception accorded the Ordre des Coteaux de Champagne during the first 20 years after its foundation in 1956 is a typical example. It took all of this time for the French wine trade as a whole, and its official bodies, to realize that Champagne had at its disposal a powerful means of publicity in the Ordre.

The Ordre now has more than 7,000 members all over the world, and it has been shown that the sale of champagne flourishes especially well in those countries where the Ordre des Coteaux is most active. Similar cases exist; consequently the idea of the fraternity is now widely accepted not only in the wine-growing areas of France but also abroad.

The work of the Fédération Internationale

Given the rapid proliferation of wine fraternities, it soon became desirable to coordinate their efforts with a view to holding joint events in the interests of the wines of France and of the world. Most French and non-French wine fraternities belong to the Fédération Internationale des Confréries. This body holds an annual meeting, which takes place in a different regional or national capital each year; it has, for example, been held in Reims, Nice, Paris, Sacramento, Barcelona and Budapest.

All the *confréries*, prestigious and light-hearted alike, have in their different ways made a great contribution towards furthering the understanding of viticultural endeavour and of wines themselves. They have been, and still are, privileged meeting places, not just for producers and consumers but, above all, for wine growers!

Never before have wine growers been able to go and taste their neighbour's wine as freely as they do today. Links and friendships have been forged between wine growers from different regions, enabling them to exchange ideas and compare methods. Growers' wives, who undertake book keeping and sales duties to an ever-increasing extent, have benefited greatly from this contact, taking an active part in the social and professional life of the wine world.

The unfailing success of the wine fraternities has only been made possible by the full and committed support of a loyal and ever-growing public. Historically speaking, the first modern fraternity, the Chevaliers du Tastevin, was born of necessity. The rest were formed to a greater or lesser extent as a result of pressure from wine lovers, who refused to accept the passive role of being mere customers, and who wished to understand more profoundly the human and cultural values, including those of the *terroir*, that are so faithfully and magnificently reflected in wine.

It is this message that the *confréries* are proclaiming loudly and clearly, and they are now as firmly rooted as vines on the slopes. Furthermore, the folkloric aspects of their solemn and lavish ceremonies, and especially their colourful costumes, endow all their gatherings with a touch of fairytale glamour that cannot be found anywhere else. It is in this conjunction of the significant and the colourful, no doubt, that the real basis of the tremendous success of the fraternities, both great and small, lies. With good humour and frank enjoyment, they celebrate the virtues and mysteries of wine, of the vine, and of their own particular *terroir*.

Between Solutré and Saint-Amour, Gamay vines grow in soils of granite, schist and pebbles. The result is a light ruby-red wine with great charm, especially when young.

Sacy

Synonyms: *Plant de Sacy, Sassy, Plant d'Essert, Peut Blanc, Gros Blanc, Blanc Vert, Fariné, Farinier Blanc, Fairené, Ferné, Fernet* in Doubs and Haute-Saône; the Sacy is the same as the *Tressallier*, which has the synonyms *Tresallier, Trézali, Trézari* in Allier, *Blanc de Pays* in Saint-Pourçain, *Aligoté Vert* in Côte-d'Or, *Pivoine, Peau Verte.*

Leaves thick, orbicular, bullate, five-lobed, with lobes of average size and definition, lateral sinuses concave at base, petiolar sinus narrow, V-shaped; dentation convex, medium.

Bunches conical, small, winged; grapes spherical, small, white, juicy; ripening period: second epoch, late.

According to tradition, the Sacy was brought over from Italy in the 13th century by the monks of the abbey of Reigny, near Vermenton. It spread from Yonne to Franche-Comté and Allier. A vigorous, fertile vine, it is, however, susceptible to vine diseases. It gives an ordinary wine with low alcohol content and such a high level of acidity that the Parliament of Besançon prohibited its planting for this reason in 1732. At the beginning of the 18th century, A. Berget proved that the Sacy and the Tresallier were identical vines. However, the leaves of the Tresallier at Saint-Pourçain are slightly more deeply lobed than those of the Sacy, and the underside of the blade is downier; these may just be clonal differences. The Sacy is classed as 'recommended' in Yonne and Allier, and is used for the Saint-Pourçain VDQS. One registered clone has been approved, number 637. Currently, Sacy is grown on 210ha, with 120ha in Yonne and 90ha in Allier.

Saint-Amour

This village is named after a Roman legionary called Amore who was converted to Christianity and martyred here in the 4th century. The Saint-Amour AOC, ratified by the decree of 8 February 1946, is situated northeast of Juliénas, on the borders between the calcareous area of Mâcon and the granite of Beaujolais. It has 240ha of vineyards, and these produce an annual average of 13,000hl of wine, some 1,800,000 bottles.

The granitic, schistous and pebbly soil is wonderfully suited to vine growing. Saint-Amour is, unsurprisingly, reputed to have aphrodisiac qualities. The truth is that it is supple and finely balanced, halfway between solidity and finesse, with a bouquet of raspberries. Its bright red colour is its only direct concession to passion. It should preferably be drunk quite young, at about two years old.

Saint-Amour is the nearest of the Beaujolais *crus* to the Mâcon region, and at one time, the canons of Mâcon took as much interest in this wine as they did in their most precious relics.

Saint-Aubin

Situated on the Côte de Beaune, west of Puligny-Montrachet and Chassagne-Montra-

GRANDS CRUS CLASSÉS OF SAINT-ÉMILION

Ch. L'ANGELUS
Ch. L'ARROSEE
Ch. BALESTARD-LA-TONNELLE
Ch. BEAU-SEJOUR-BECOT
Ch. BELLEVUE
Ch. BERGAT
Ch. BERLIQUET
Ch. CADET-PIOLA
Ch. CANON-LA-GAFFELIERE
Ch. CAP-DE-MOURLIN
Ch. LE CHATELET
Ch. CHAUVIN
Ch. CLOS DES JACOBINS
CLOS LA MADELEINE
CLOS DE L'ORATOIRE
CLOS SAINT-MARTIN
Ch. LA CLOTTE
Ch. LA CLUSIERE
Ch. CORBIN
Ch. CORBIN-MICHOTTE
COUVENT DES JACOBINS
Ch. CROQUE-MICHOTTE
Ch. CURE-BON-LA-MADELEINE
Ch. DASSAULT
Ch. LA DOMINIQUE
Ch. FAURIE-DE-SOUCHARD
Ch. FONPLEGADE
Ch. FONROQUE
Ch. FRANC-MAYNE
Ch. GRAND BARRAIL LAMARZELLE-FIGEAC
Ch. GRAND CORBIN
Ch. GRAND CORBIN-DESPAGNE
Ch. GRAND MAYNE
Ch. GRAND PONTET
Ch. GUADET-SAINT-JULIEN
Ch. HAUT-CORBIN
Ch. HAUT-SARPE
Ch. LANIOTE
Ch. LARCIS-DUCASSE
Ch. LAMARZELLE
Ch. LARMANDE
Ch. LAROZE
Ch. MATRAS
Ch. MAUVEZIN
Ch. MOULIN DU CADET
Ch. PAVIE-DECESSE
Ch. PAVIE-MACQUIN
Ch. PAVILLON-CADET
Ch. PETIT-FAURIE-DE-SOUTARD
Ch. LE PRIEURE
Ch. RIPEAU
Ch. SAINT-GEORGES-CÔTE-PAVIE
Ch. SANSONNET
Ch. LA SERRE
Ch. SOUTARD
Ch. TERTRE DAUGAY
Ch. TOUR DU PIN-FIGEAC
Ch. LA TOUR-FIGEAC
Ch. TRIMOULET
Ch. TROPLONG-MONDOT
Ch. VILLEMAURINE
Ch. YON-FIGEAC

chet, the AOC of Saint-Aubin was ratified by the decree of 21 May 1970. Although Saint-Aubin does not enjoy the same reputation as its glorious neighbours, it does produce some very pleasant wines, both red and white. There are 30ha of vineyards producing AOC 'village' wines, and 80ha of Premiers Crus. The red wines must have an alcoholic strength of at least 10.5°, and 11° in the case of the Premiers Crus; for white wines the minimum is 11° and 11.5°. The maximum yield for all wines is 35hl/ha. The fact that the vines are planted right at the top of the Côte, almost into the Hautes Côtes area in fact, explains why the red wines are relatively light compared with other red burgundies. Their reputation is modest, but this should not obscure their best features: freshness and fullness. These are wines to drink young. The white wines also have a great deal of charm.

Saint-Chinian

Saint-Chinian, lying to the northwest of Béziers, was classed as an AOC by decree on 24 December 1985. It covers an area of about 20,500ha spread over 20 communes, and produces 60,000hl of wine. The soils are based on sandstone or calcareous gravels in the south and schists in the north. The vineyards benefit from an exceptionally good mesoclimate, being well sheltered in the north by the Mont de Somail and le Caroux massifs. The grape varieties used are the same as in the Coteaux du Languedoc. The wine of Saint-Chinian is well rounded, structured and full bodied when grown on calcareous soils; on schist, it is elegant, delicate and velvety.

Saint-Drézery *See* Coteaux du Languedoc.

Saint-Émilion and Saint-Émilion Grand Cru

When this *appellation d'origine contrôlée* was created, its area corresponded to that of the former Saint-Émilion administrative area, which consisted of Saint-Émilion itself and the seven neighbouring communes of Saint-Christophe-des-Bardes, Saint-Laurent-des-Combes, Saint-Hippolyte, Saint-Étienne-de-Lisse, Saint-Pey-d'Armens, Vignonet and Saint-Sulpice-de-Faleyrens. The former *appellation* area of Sables-Saint-Émilion, which covers part of the commune of Libourne, was added to this list, by decree, on 14 December 1977. The *appellation* is now subject to new rules, laid down by the decree of 11 January 1984. The most notable change is that the hierarchy of the four *appellations*, namely Saint-Émilion, Saint-Émilion Grand Cru, Saint-Émilion Grand Cru Classé and Saint-Émilion Premier Grand Cru Classé, created by the decree of 7 October 1954, no

Old-style grape harvest on the schist slopes of Saint-Chinian in the lower foothills of the Cévennes. The red wine produced here is dark in colour, elegant and velvety.

PREMIERS GRANDS CRUS CLASSÉS OF SAINT-ÉMILION

Château Ausone (A)
Château Cheval-Blanc (A)
Château Beauséjour (B)
Château Belair (B)
Château Canon (B)
Château Figeac (B)
Clos Fourtet (B)
Château La Gaffelière (B)
Château Magdelaine (B)
Château Pavie (B)
Château Trottevieille (B)

longer exists in *appellation* form (though the Crus Classés continue to exist as subdivisions of the Saint-Émilion Grand Cru AOC: see below). There are now only two *appellations*: Saint-Émilion and Saint-Émilion Grand Cru.

Use of the terms 'Grand Cru Classé' or 'Premier Grand Cru Classé' is permitted for wines that meet certain production conditions and whose classification as a Grand Cru Classé or Premier Grand Cru Classé has been officially confirmed (see the lists left and above). All the wines of Saint-Émilion must be made from the following grape varieties: Cabernet Franc, Cabernet Sauvignon, Merlot, Carmenère and Côt.

The minimum permitted sugar content in the must is 171g per litre and the wines, which are all red, have to have an alcohol content of at least 10.5° in the case of Saint-Émilion, and 11° in the case of Saint-Émilion Grand Cru.

Medieval street in Saint-Émilion.

The maximum alcohol content for both *appellations* is 13°.

In the case of the *appellation* Saint-Émilion Grand Cru, any damaged or diseased grapes have to be removed from the harvest; and the wines may not go on sale until 1 July in the year after the harvest.

Since 1966, the wines of both *appellations* have had to obtain a certificate of quality from a tasting panel before they may be marketed.

In 1985, the *appellation* Saint-Émilion covered an area of 2,038ha, and the *appellation* Saint-Émilion Grand Cru, 3,090ha. Their respective production totals were 114,221hl and 164,000hl. The cooperative in Saint-Émilion vinified almost 48,000hl, of which 18,000hl was Saint-Émilion Grand Cru.

The character of the wines varies greatly, depending on the nature of the soil or subsoil (*see* page 83). Some of them are quickly at their best; others need to mature much longer to reach their peak in terms of quality.

CRUS CLASSÉS OF SAINT-ESTÈPHE

Deuxièmes Crus
Château Cos-d'Estournel
Château Montrose

Troisième Cru
Château Calon-Ségur

Quatrième Cru
Château Lafon-Rochet

Cinquième Cru
Château Cos-Labory

Saint-Estèphe

The *appellation contrôlée* of Saint-Estèphe in Médoc, created by decree on 11 September 1936, is reserved for red wines made from grapes gathered within the commune of Saint-Estèphe.

The authorized grape varieties are the same as those for the regional *appellation* of Médoc. Hybrid varieties have been banned since 1961 on estates wishing to use the Saint-Estèphe *appellation*. The minimum permitted sugar content in the must is 162g per litre, and the wines have to have a minimum alcohol content of 10° and a maximum of 13°. The base yield is 45hl/ha.

Since 1959, these wines have had to obtain a certificate of quality issued by a tasting panel before being marketed.

In 1985, the total area under vines was 1,127ha and the amount of wine produced was

The Premier Grand Cru Classé Château Ausone is, together with Château Cheval-Blanc, one of the two 'Class A' properties of the Saint-Émilion Premier Grand Cru Classé category. The wines of Saint-Émilion are generous, robust and beautifully rounded, with a very long lifespan.

71,525hl. The cooperative in Saint-Estèphe made 18,466hl of this.

The *appellation* of Saint-Estèphe has five Crus Classés and about 40 Crus Bourgeois.

The wines of Saint-Estèphe require ageing. After a few years in bottle, they develop a highly complex and distinguished bouquet.

Saint-Georges-d'Orques *See* Coteaux du Languedoc.

Saint-Georges-Saint-Émilion

The *appellation d'origine contrôlée* of Saint-Georges-Saint-Émilion, situated in the Libourne district, was created by decree on 14 November 1936, and is reserved for red wines made from grapes picked on specified sites within the Saint-Georges-Saint-Émilion commune. As this commune is situated within the *appellation* area of Montagne-Saint-Émilion, wine producers may use either of the AOC names.

The grape varieties used are the same as for the *appellation* of Saint-Émilion. Hybrid varieties have been forbidden since 1961.

The minimum permitted sugar content in the must is 162g per litre, and the wines have to have a minimum alcohol content of 10° and a maximum of 13°. The base yield is 45hl/ha. Since 1958, the marketing of these wines has been subject to approval by a tasting panel.

The granite slopes of the hill of Saint-Joseph, between Mauves and Tournon, is a fine site for the Syrah grape variety, which produces an elegant, fruity red wine there.

In 1985, the total area covered was 135ha and the amount of wine produced was 8,022hl.

Wines of this *appellation* have a similar profile and lifespan to those of Saint-Émilion.

Saint-Joseph

Although the Saint-Joseph AOC is a relatively recent one, the wine-growing area itself has a very long history. Like Côte Rôtie and Condrieu, most of the present vineyards already existed in Roman times.

It took many years for the wine of Saint-Joseph to make a name for itself, one reason being that anything produced on the right bank of the Rhône was difficult to distribute and reached its markets only slowly. However, thanks to a handful of ecclesiastical and later secular wine growers, this wine became known at the court of France, and even as far away as Moscow, at first under the name of Vin de Mauves, then as Vin de Tournon.

Even though the actual hill of Saint-Joseph, situated between Tournon and Mauves just to its south, possessed all the necessary characteristics of a *cru*, it was not accorded any particular status at first. In 1937, all the communes that now form the Saint-Joseph AOC were classed as AOC Côtes du Rhône. It was not until 1954 that it was awarded its individual status, in the light of the quality of its wines and the fact that placing it within Côtes du Rhône was economically anomalous. It finally became an AOC on 15 June 1986.

Although this is a large area geographically, there are only 298ha of vineyards within it. The average amount of wine produced annually is 12,000hl, of which 3,500hl is made by the cooperatives of Saint-Désirat and Tain-l'Hermitage.

The white wines are made from the Marsanne grape variety. They have a floral and honeyed aroma. They are supple, develop quickly, and should be drunk young.

The red wines are, on the whole, marked by aromas of strawberry, blackcurrant and spices. They can be solid and tannic, but most of them are charming, elegant and quite delicate. They are best drunk within three or four years.

Saint-Julien

The *appellation d'origine contrôlée* of Saint-Julien, sited in the Médoc, was created by decree on 14 November 1936. It is reserved for red wines made from grapes picked within the commune of Saint-Julien-Beychevelle and on a few sites in those of Cussac and Saint-Laurent-Médoc, since at the time of the decree these sites formed part of a number of estates within Saint-Julien.

The grape varieties used are the same as those laid down for the Médoc regional *appellation*. Hybrid varieties have been forbidden since 1961 on estates claiming the *appellation*. The minimum permitted sugar content in the must is 162g per litre, and the wines have to have a minimum alcohol content of 10° and a maximum of 13°. The base yield is 45hl/ha.

Since 1955, the wines of this *appellation* have required a certificate of quality from a tasting panel before they can be marketed.

In 1985, the *appellation* covered 773ha and produced 42,444hl of wine.

The Saint-Julien *appellation* has 11 *crus classés* (see box above). None of the wine is made by cooperatives.

The wines of the Saint-Julien *appellation* have a rare complexity, founded on a tannic base of great quality. They belong to those fine wines that only reach their peak of quality after ageing for a number of years.

CRUS CLASSÉS OF SAINT-JULIEN

Deuxièmes Crus
Château Ducru-Beaucaillou
Château Gruaud-Larose
Château Léoville-Barton
Château Léoville-Las Cases
Château Léoville-Poyferré

Troisièmes Crus
Château Lagrange
Château Langoa-Barton

Quatrièmes Crus
Château Beychevelle
Château Branaire-Ducru
Château Saint-Pierre
Château Talbot

Saint-Laurent

Synonyms: *Saint-Laurent Noir*, *Saint-Lorentz*, *Pinot Saint-Laurent*.

Bunches medium sized, cylindrical; grapes medium sized, blue-black, ovoid, thick-skinned; ripening period: first epoch.

This vine originally came from the south of Alsace; it reached Baden in Germany, and was propagated in that area. It gives full-bodied wine of an attractive, dark-red colour. An unclassified variety, it is very little grown in France.

Saint-Macaire

Synonyms: *Moustère*, *Moustouzère* in Gironde, *Bouton Blanc* in the Ludon *palus* (marsh) area, *Macau*, *Margaux*.

Bunches small to medium, conical, winged, loose; grapes medium sized, black, spherical, rather pulpy with a harsh, tart flavour; ripening period: second epoch, late.

This is one of the secondary varieties of Bordeaux, where it is grown on 25ha. Classed as 'authorized' in Gironde, it is a vigorous vine, generally planted in the low-lying, marshy areas of the Médoc and of Saint-Macaire. It gives an ordinary though deeply coloured wine, less astringent than that of the Petit Verdot.

Saint-Nicolas-de-Bourgueil

This wine-growing area, decreed an AOC on 31 July 1937, covers some 675ha, planted with the Cabernet Franc variety (locally known as the Breton). Up to 10 per cent of Cabernet Sauvignon can also be included. Average annual production is around 24,500hl. The vineyard area covers only part of the commune of Saint-Nicolas-de-Bourgueil.

The wine has a light, lively colour, taking on greater depth when the wine has been grown on calcareous tufa soils. Depending on vineyard site and age, the aromas can be animal, mineral, fruity or floral. This is a wine of breeding, succulent, finely balanced, lively, tannic but not harsh or hard. It ages very well in bottle. (*See* Touraine.)

The commune of Saint-Julien in Haut-Médoc is famous for its well-balanced, tannic, velvety, vigorous red wines.

The Château de Crussol overlooks the Rhône valley and the Saint-Péray wine district, which produces an unusual white wine, golden in colour, vigorous, with a floral bouquet.

Saint-Péray and Saint-Péray Mousseux

The first unusual thing about this *appellation* is its surroundings. It is situated at the foot of a very steep hill crowned by the ruins of the Château de Crussol. Even the splendid view from the top of the hill cannot remove the memory of the tragic military and religious events that befell this eagle's nest over several centuries.

There have been vineyards in Saint-Péray for at least ten centuries. Their development took an opposite course to that noted in Cornas, for light red wines were produced here at first. These were, no doubt, thought insufficiently original, and so the growers turned to white wines instead. This was a fortunate move, and the white wines of Saint-Péray were praised by Pope Pius VII, Wagner and Baudelaire, among others.

The soils here are richer than those further north in Cornas, while the climate is less hot, as the amount of exposure to the sun varies from one side of the hill to the other. These conditions favour white wine growing.

The *appellation d'origine contrôlée*, created by decree on 9 December 1936, is for one commune only. Vines are grown on an area of only 35ha. This area used to be much bigger, but a number of houses have been built in part of the commune, and Saint-Péray has become a suburb of Valence.

The average amount of wine produced is 2,000hl per year, most of it made in local growers' cellars or by the cooperative of Tain-l'Hermitage.

The still white wines have floral and vegetal aromas. They are dry, full and fresh in style. Since the beginning of the 19th century, sparkling wines have also been produced, and the *méthode champenoise* is stipulated for these.

Saint-Pierre Doré

Synonyms: *Saint-Pierre de l'Allier*, *Épinette Blanche* in Allier, *Cerceau* in Loiret, *Lucane* in Deux-Sèvres.

Bunches quite large, conical, winged, compact; grapes small, spherical, golden white; ripening period: second epoch.

This is a very vigorous, productive variety that can yield over 200hl/ha, but the resulting wine is low in both acidity and alcohol. It is susceptible to grey rot (botrytis) and spring frosts. Classed as 'recommended' in Allier, and 'authorized' in Cher and Loiret, it is one of the varieties grown for the VDQS Saint-Pourçain, on an area of 80ha. There are a further 20ha in Cher and Loiret.

Saint-Pourçain

Classed VDQS on 20 December 1951, this wine-growing area covers 450ha. Gamay and Pinot Noir are grown for red, *gris* (very pale rosé) and rosé wines; Tresallier (a maximum of 50 per cent), Saint-Pierre Doré (a maximum of 10 per cent), Aligoté, Chardonnay and Sauvignon Blanc for white wines.

The average amounts of wine produced annually are 5,000hl of white, a small amount of which is sparkling; 14,000hl of red; and 7,000hl of rosé. The production area is spread over 20 communes.

The white wines are straw yellow in colour, and have a characteristically vegetal aroma. They are dry, supple, lively and delicate.

The rosé wines are dry and elegant.

The red wines are a beautiful ruby-garnet colour. They have a mineral and fruity aroma (of cherries and dried fruits), and are light and delicate, yet full. They keep well in bottle.

The sparkling wines are pleasant and characterful, especially when the Tresallier is dominant.

Saint-Romain

On the edge of the Hautes Côtes de Beaune lies Saint-Romain, tucked away in an excellent site in the hills west of Meursault and Auxey-Duresses. Both red and white wines are produced from this honest *terroir*. The *appellation d'origine contrôlée*, which covers 130ha, was ratified by the decree of 21 May 1970. Red wines must have a minimum alcohol content of 10.5° and white wines a minimum of 11°. The maximum yield is 45hl/ha. There are no Premiers Crus in Saint-Romain. Red wines are made from the Pinot Noir grape variety, and white wines from the Chardonnay variety. In 1985, the harvest declarations were 1,234hl of white wine and 1,100hl of red wine. Both types are pleasant, fresh and quite lively, with a characteristic bouquet of violets.

Saint-Saturnin *See* Coteaux du Languedoc.

Saint-Véran

The following eight communes in the far south of the Mâcon region are authorized to produce white wines under the AOC of Saint-Véran: Saint-Vérand, Chânes, Chasselas, Davayé, Leynes, Prissé, Saint-Amour and a few sites in Solutré. The decree of 6 January 1977 set a minimum alcohol content of 11° and a maximum yield of 45hl/ha.

The wines of Saint-Véran are an excellent expression of the characteristics of the Chardonnay grape variety. Distinctive and subtle, these are among the best of the simpler white burgundies.

Sainte-Croix-du-Mont

The *appellation d'origine contrôlée* of Sainte-Croix-du-Mont was created by the decree of 11 September 1936, and is reserved for white wines made from grapes picked on sites within the commune of Sainte-Croix-du-Mont, situated on the right bank of the Garonne about 45km southeast of Bordeaux. The undulating terrain of the *appellation* area is dominated by a medieval church and castle. The wine-growing area is situated on plateaux and slopes of clay and limestone soils, surrounding the village and stretching down towards the river.

The production requirements for Sainte-Croix-du-Mont are exactly the same as for Sauternes. They are among the best of the dessert wines from the right bank of the Garonne. They are matured for 18 months before being bottled, and do not blossom until they are three or four years old. Great vintages can age and improve for several decades.

A certain proportion of the harvest is vinified as dry white wine and sold under the *appellation* Bordeaux Sec.

In 1985, the vineyard area of Sainte-Croix-du-Mont was 446ha, and the amount of wine produced was 16,021hl, the yield being 35.9hl/ha.

Sainte-Foy-Bordeaux

Wines of this *appellation d'origine contrôlée*, created by the decree of 31 July 1937, must come from the canton of Sainte-Foy-la-Grande, and the communes of Gensac, Pessac-sur-Dordogne, Pellegrue and Massugas. The Sainte-Foy-Bordeaux wine district is an easterly extension of Entre-Deux-Mers. The red wines produced here are made from the Cabernet Sauvignon, Cabernet Franc, Merlot, Côt (Malbec) and Petit Verdot, and the white wines from the Sémillon, Sauvignon Blanc and Muscadelle varieties.

The red wines are deeply coloured and suitable for ageing. Traditionally the white wines have been sweet and supple. For the last few years, however, growers have been producing a very pleasant dry white wine.

Sampigny-lès-Maranges *See* Cheilly-lès-Maranges.

San Antoni

Synonyms: *Saint-Antoine*, *Arimtalou*.

Bunches small, cylindrical, compact; grapes ellipsoidal, large, blue-black, crisp, fleshy, with elongated seeds; ripening period: second epoch.

The hills of Sancerre, once given over to the cultivation of red-wine vines, are now a favoured **terroir** *for the Sauvignon Blanc grape variety. It gives a dry, full-bodied white wine of great finesse here.*

This is an old grape variety from the Roussillon area. It was greatly appreciated in the past both as a table grape and for wine making. It gave a delicate wine that improved with age. It has not been classified.

Sancerre

This wine-growing area, classed as an AOC by the decree of 22 January 1959, produces mainly white wines. The largest part of the vineyard area, 1,600ha, is planted with Sauvignon Blanc, producing an average 75,000hl of white wines per year. There are also 300ha of vineyards planted with Pinot Noir, producing about 15,000hl annually, two thirds of this total as rosé and the remainder as red wine. The production area includes 15 communes or parts of communes.

The white wines are green to straw yellow. They have a characteristic and highly developed smell close to that of blackcurrant leaf. They are full, dry and fleshy, and are suitable for ageing in bottle. The rosé wines have a delicate colour. They are dry, fine and full.

The red wines are an attractive cherry colour, and have a floral retronasal aroma (aroma in the mouth). Red Sancerre is well balanced, with both power and finesse resulting from its generous aromatic profile, which assumes an animal character as the wine ages. (*See* the Vins du Centre regional entry.)

Santenay

Santenay is the southernmost commune on the Côte de Beaune. The siliceous and calcareous soils and magnesian subsoils found there are particularly suitable for vine growing. The *appellation d'origine contrôlée*, ratified by decree on 21 May 1970, covers some 330ha, of which 130ha are occupied by Premier Cru sites. The wines of Santenay are subject to Burgundy's usual regulations: a minimum alcohol content of 10.5° for red wines, and 11° for Premiers Crus; and 11° for white wines, with 11.5° in the case of Premiers Crus. The base yield is 35hl/ha. The grape varieties are Pinot Noir for red wines and Chardonnay for white wines. In 1985, the harvest figures showed that 12,241hl of red wine had been produced, but only 228hl of white. The *terroir* of Santenay is sufficiently complex for several styles of wine to be distinguishable within the *appellation*. The supplest wines, most characteristic of the Côte de Beaune, come from the western end of the village, near the commune of Remigny; while the fullest wines come from the eastern end of the village. In general, the wines of Santenay are fine and aromatic, but also pleasantly firm.

The 15th-century Château de Montreuil-Bellay is an important historical site in the Saumur region, an area in which still and sparkling red and white wines are produced.

Sartène

Sartène *See* Vin de Corse-Sartène.

Saumur

This wine-growing area, decreed an AOC on 31 December 1957, produces an annual average of 39,000hl of white wines and 11,000hl of red. The production area is spread over 28 communes or parts of communes in Maine-et-Loire, Deux-Sèvres and Vienne. The white wines must be at least 80 per cent Chenin Blanc, supplemented by a maximum of 20 per cent Chardonnay and Sauvignon Blanc. The Cabernet Franc, Cabernet Sauvignon and Pineau d'Aunis are used for red wines.

The white wines are aromatic, dry, lively, delicate and supple, reflecting the calcareous soils they are grown in.

The red wines have lightness and freshness, within a firm tannic structure.

Saumur-Champigny

This wine-growing district, declared an AOC on 31 December 1957, covers 500ha and is planted with the Cabernet Franc, Cabernet Sauvignon and Pineau d'Aunis varieties. Average annual production is around 40,000hl. The production area takes in 38 communes in Maine-et-Loire and part of Deux-Sèvres.

The wine normally has a good depth of colour, the shade being that of ripe redcurrants. It is a light, lively wine, very easy to drink, though not at the expense of structure or tannin. Wines from the best sites of the *appellation* age well in bottle.

Saumur Mousseux

This wine district, decreed an AOC on 24 August 1976, covers a potential area of about 1,200ha. Present production is about 100,000hl of white and 6,000hl of rosé wines per year. The production area is spread over 92 communes in Maine-et-Loire, Vienne and Deux-Sèvres.

The white grape varieties used are the Chenin Blanc, together with a maximum of 20 per cent Chardonnay and Sauvignon Blanc.

The black grape varieties used are the Cabernet Franc, Cabernet Sauvignon, Côt, Gamay Noir à Jus Blanc, Grolleau, Pineau d'Aunis and Pinot Noir. Black grape varieties may not represent more than 60 per cent of the blend.

The white wines have a green to straw yellow colour and a highly developed vegetal bouquet. They are full, delicate, lively, with a good sparkle. They age well. The rosé wines are also full and lively.

Saumur Pétillant

Saumur Pétillant was classed AOC by the decree of 31 December 1957. The amount of wine produced is small. The grape varieties used are the same as for AOC Saumur, and the production area extends over the same communes as for the Saumur *appellation*.

The wine is pleasant, firm, delicate, lively and of course *pétillant* (very slightly sparkling, with a pressure of 2.5kg at 10° C). It has a good bottle life.

Saussignac

This is a small *appellation* zone to the west of the wine-growing area of Monbazillac. It was decreed an AOC on 28 April 1982, and produces about 2,500hl of wine a year. In character, this wine is midway between Côtes de Bergerac Moelleux and Monbazillac. While often richer than the former, it is less lusciously sweet than the latter. The total alcohol content (actual alcohol plus potential alcohol in the form of unfermented sugar) must be between 12.5° and 15°.

Sauternes

The *appellation d'origine contrôlée* of Sauternes, which was created by the decree of 11 September 1936, is reserved for white wines made from grapes picked within the communes of Sauternes, Bommes, Fargues, Preignac and Barsac. These are all situated on the left bank of the Garonne, on either side of a small river called the Ciron, about 40km southeast of Bordeaux. To be entitled to this *appellation*, the wines must be made from the Sémillon, Sauvignon Blanc and Muscadelle grape varieties. The grapes have to be overripe, and then picked selectively, the workers going through the vineyards several times. The minimum sugar content of the must is 221g per litre. The wines have to have a minimum total alcohol content (actual alcohol plus potential alcohol in the form of unfermented sugar) of 13°, with a minimum of 12.5° actual alcohol.

In 1985, Sauternes was grown on 1,364ha, and production was 30,363hl, giving a yield of 22.3hl/ha.

Sauternes, in its youth, is a pleasing wine with fruity and floral aromas. However, it

Setting out to pick grapes in the vineyards of Château d'Yquem, in Sauternes.

CRUS CLASSÉS OF SAUTERNES

Premier Cru Supérieure
Château d'Yquem

Premiers Crus
Château Clos-Haut-Peyraguey
Château Guiraud
Château Lafaurie-Peyraguey
Château Rabaud-Promis
Château de Rayne-Vigneau
Château Rieussec
Château Sigalas-Rabaud
Château de Suduiraut
Château La Tour Blanche

Deuxièmes Crus
Château d'Arche
Château Filhot
Château Lamothe-Despujols
Château Lamothe-Guignard
Château de Malle
Château Romer
Château Romer du Hayot

quickly loses these characteristics and acquires, with age, a very special aroma and flavour, derived from *pourriture noble* ('noble rot'). Sauternes ages better than even the greatest red wines. As time passes, it acquires a breeding and vitality that makes it unique among the wines of the world.

Sauvignon Blanc

A bunch of Sauvignon Blanc grapes. This variety produces firm, dry white wines, and sweet white wines when used in combination with other varieties.

Synonyms: *Blanc Fumé* or *Fumé* in Nièvre, *Surin* in Loir-et-Cher, *Fié* in Vienne, *Sauternes* in parts of Indre and of Cher.

Leaves small, orbicular, contorted, rippling and coarsely bullate, deeply five-lobed, lateral sinuses narrow, acute at base, petiolar sinus lyrate, more or less open; dentation convex, narrow, pointed; underside of blade downy.

Bunches small, conical, compact, sometimes winged; grapes small, ovoid, an attractive golden yellow when fully ripe, thick skinned with easily expressed juice that has a very special flavour recalling that of the Muscat; ripening period: second epoch.

This is a vigorous Bordeaux vine with mid-season budbreak. It is not very fertile, as it often suffers from *coulure* (flower abortion), either through its excess vigour or on account of poor vine health. There are now, though, high-quality, productive clones available that yield between 50 and 100hl/ha, and these have encouraged new plantings. Twenty-one registered clones have been approved, the best in terms of quality being numbers 297 and 316. In the Sauternes district, the Sauvignon Blanc is grown, with other varieties, to produce white dessert wines with a minimum alcohol content of 13°; it has a maximum yield there of 25hl/ha, often less because of the onset of *pourriture noble* ('noble rot') and the need for pickers to go through the vineyards several times to select the overripe grapes. In the Loire valley, on the other hand, this grape produces dry, highly perfumed white wines with lower levels of alcohol: 11° for Pouilly-Fumé, and 10.5° for Sancerre, Quincy, Reuilly and Menetou-Salon, with a greater yield of 45hl/ha.

The cultivation of the Sauvignon Blanc is on the increase, and it is now grown on over 7,000ha, having been classed as 'recommended' in most of the *départements* of the South West, the Loire valley, Languedoc, Provence and Burgundy. In Gironde (2,400ha) and Dordogne (800ha) it is used, in a 25 or 30 per cent proportion, with Sémillon and a little Muscadelle, in the production of the great sweet wines of Sauternes, Barsac, Loupiac, Sainte-Croix-du-Mont and Monbazillac. In the Loire valley, the Sauvignon Blanc is vinified alone to produce the AOC wines of Pouilly-sur-Loire (Blanc Fumé or Pouilly-Fumé), Sancerre, Menetou-Salon, Quincy and Reuilly, on a total of 3,300ha. In Yonne it is used to make the VDQS Sauvignon de Saint-Bris (63ha). In Provence there are about 30ha. A Sauvignon Rose and a Sauvignon Rouge (with reddish-black fruit) are sometimes found growing among the white vines.

A Sauvignon Blanc leaf.

Sauvignon de Saint-Bris, a fresh white VDQS wine with a slightly smoky flavour, is produced in the Irancy area.

Sauvignon de Saint-Bris

This white wine made from the Sauvignon Blanc variety is produced to the southeast of Auxerre, in the seven communes of Saint-Bris-le-Vineux, Chitry, Irancy, Vincelottes, Quenne, Saint-Cyr-les-Colons and Cravant (Yonne). It received its VDQS on 20 August 1974. This large territory of some 450ha has a great variety of soils including gravels, clays and hard limestones. The yield is limited to 50hl/ha and the minimum alcohol content is 9.5°. Sauvignon de Saint-Bris is fresh and thirst-quenching, with a slightly smoky flavour. Aromatically, it is not unlike Sancerre and Pouilly-Fumé, though the strength of its aroma varies according to the soil type, and the vivacity of the wine in question.

Sauvignonasse

Synonyms: *Sauvignon de la Corrèze*, *Sauvignon à Gros Grains*, *Sauvignon Vert* in Allier, *Blanc Doux* in Gironde, *Cinquien* in Jura.

Bunches medium sized, cylindrical, fairly compact; grapes spherical, golden white, juicy; ripening period: second epoch.

This variety is related to the Sauvignon Blanc, but it produces a common wine lacking the perfume of the Sauvignon. The grapes are susceptible to downy mildew and grey rot (botrytis). The variety is unclassified.

Savagnin

Synonyms: *Savagnin Jaune*, *Savagnin Blanc*, *Sauvagnin*, *Salvagnin*, *Naturé* or *Naturel* in Arbois, *Fromenté*, *Fromenteau*, *Fromentais* (by analogy with the colour of wheat grains, *froment*), *Gringet* in Haute-Savoie, *Gentil Blanc* at Besançon, *Bon Blanc* at Misery, *Blanc Brun* at Salins, *Traminer* in Alsace.

Growing tips felty white with carmine margins. Young leaves downy, yellowish.

Leaves small, orbicular, very bullate, crimped at the petiolar junction, generally without lobes, though sometimes fairly deeply five-lobed, petiolar sinus narrowly lyrate, almost closed; dentation convex, medium sized; underside of blade downy.

Green shoots arachnoid at the tip, light green with slightly pink nodes; tendrils medium sized, fleshy. Bunches small, cylindrical, compact; grapes small, spherical, white, juicy; ripening period: second epoch.

The Savagnin came originally from the town of Tramin in the Italian Tyrol. From there it spread to Switzerland, Germany, Central Europe and France. It has midseason budbreak and needs to be pruned long, as the eyes at the base of the shoots are not very fertile. It is something of a vine-group rather than a clearly defined variety, with varying degrees of leaf lobing, veins either green or red, and shoots sometimes green, sometimes red or brown. Four registered clones have been approved: numbers 611 to 614. This grape variety is used to make the famous long-lived *vins jaunes* of the Jura (and especially Château-Châlon); it also gives some full, pleasantly perfumed white wines that keep well. It can, too, be used in making sparkling wines.

Savagnin Rose

Synonyms: *Fromenteau Rouge* and *Fromenté Rose* in Doubs, *Savagnin Rose non-musqué*, *Heiligensteiner Klevner* or *Clevner d'Heiligenstein* in Alsace.

Bunches small, cylindrical-conical, compact; grapes small, ellipsoidal, golden white, turning pink when fully ripe; ripening period: second epoch.

The Savagnin Rose is the non-musky pink form of the Savagnin. There is a slight difference between the Savagnin Rose and the Savagnin: the latter has longer leaves with pointed dentation and an open petiolar sinus. One registered clone has been approved: number 763. This variety has been classed as 'recommended' in Alsace, but is not very widely grown.

Savennières

This wine-growing area, granted its AOC on 8 December 1952, covers 50ha, planted exclusively with Chenin Blanc. Production between 1975 and 1985 averaged about 1,800hl. The production area is spread over the commune of Savennières and parts of the communes of la Possonnière and Bouchemaine.

The wines may be labelled with the additional names of Coulée-de-Serrant and Roche-aux-Moines if they come from these two *lieux-dits* (vineyard sites).

Savennières must be made from musts with a minimum sugar content of 212g per litre, and this explains why these dry wines are so richly flavoured. They are full bodied, well structured and powerfully aromatic, though not without delicacy. They age very well in bottle and have great breed. (*See* the Anjou and Saumur regional entry.)

Savigny-lès-Beaune

Savigny-lès-Beaune is a village on the Côte de Beaune. Its *appellation* area, ratified by the decree of 21 May 1970, lies between Beaune and Pernand-Vergelesses, stretched out on the hillsides on either side of the Rhoin valley. It is here that the best sites (*climats*) of the village are to be found, and a number of these have been awarded Premier Cru status — 141ha in all. The alcohol content has been specified as 10.5° for 'village' red wines, and 11° for red Premiers Crus; with 11° for white wines and 11.5° for white Premiers Crus. The maximum yield is 35hl/ha in all cases. The *appellation d'origine contrôlée* area covers 378ha in total and produces an annual average of 540hl of white wines and 10,700hl of red.

It is generally agreed that the red wines of Savigny-lès-Beaune have finesse, distinction and a well-developed floral bouquet, especially the Premiers Crus. They are quite light, and are at their best in years when there is plenty of sunshine.

Savoie

That there are vines at all in Savoie has always been a source of amazement. Yet, among glaciers and year-round snow fields, the vineyards of Savoie have found excellent pockets of land for themselves, by scaling steep slopes, hugging hillsides and putting down roots in the sunnier spots. There they produce wine as keen-edged and fresh as the air of the Alpine pastures.

There are many documents to show that vineyards have flourished in Savoie throughout the centuries. The Roman agricultural author Columella wrote of the vineyards of Allobrogia, which later became Savoie. Pliny the Elder described the resinous flavour of these Allobrogican wines, transported to Rome in goatskin bottles sealed with a coating of resin. There is no doubt that the Allobroges were successful wine growers.

There are some 11th-century documents preserved today that prove the existence of vineyards in Seyssel, and a charter of 1050 mentions the vineyards of Monterminod. In 1180, the abbot of Hautecombe, Ganfried, paid tribute to the quality of the Montmélian vineyards, which were probably planted in Roman times. The cartularies of the abbey of Notre-Dame-de-Filly (in Haute-Savoie) refer to vineyards on the hillsides of Crépy and Marignan in the 13th century.

The account books of the Chaumont castellany show the existence, in 1356, of a vineyard belonging to the lord or governor of Frangy. They state that 25 *sammées* (an old measure varying from 115 litres to 194 litres, depending on the commune) of Chaumont wine were delivered to the Countess of Geneva in 1367.

St Francis of Sales (1567-1622) reported the creation of a parish called Mère d'Eglise sur les Vignes, in the Arve valley in Haute-Savoie.

From 1628 onwards, the concept of the *cru* began to be applied to the wines of Montmélian, Chignin and Cruet.

It was in 1768 that the term 'Vins de Savoie' made its first written appearance in a report by M. Devoize, a French deputy, and in a survey by the head of the École Impériale de la Saulnaie. This name is still in use in today's AOC legislation.

A book by the Comte de Résie, entitled *Voyage à Chambéry et aux eaux d'Aix* ('Journey to Chambéry and the Waters of Aix'), published in 1847, relates the story of the landslide that occurred on Mont Granier on 24 November 1248, which later became the

The vineyards of Chignin near Chambéry are planted with Jacquère, one of the most important grape varieties of the Vin de Savoie AOC.

site of vineyards — the present-day *crus* of Abymes and Apremont.

In 1942, the district of Seyssel became an *appellation d'origine contrôlée*, followed by Crépy in 1948. The Vins de Savoie had been classed VDQS from 1945 onwards, and acquired AOC status in 1973.

Vineyards and soils

The vineyards are generally found in the lower valleys of the region, around the Lac du Bourget and the shores of Lac Léman (Lake Geneva), and on the banks of the rivers Rhône and Isère. There are around 1,550ha of AOC vineyards, sometimes climbing high up on the mountainsides, as high as 500m.

Most of these south- and southwest-facing vineyards are situated in the *départements* of Savoie (1,200ha) and Haute-Savoie (161ha); Isère has 95ha and Ain 80ha.

The types of soil here — calcareous scree, marlacious limestone or clay-limestone in Savoie, and glacial moraines in Haute-Savoie — generally favour white grape varieties. The red-wine variety Mondeuse also flourishes in these soils. White and red wines from the predominantly calcareous *terroirs* are generally full bodied and well defined. Those from clay soils, and river and glacial alluvium, are less firmly structured and deeply coloured; but such conditions benefit certain dry white wines.

The climate

The climate is continental, but tempered by strong maritime influences. The south and southwest winds bring rain; the north wind, known as the *bise noire*, brings fine, but dry and cold spring weather, with the danger of frost. Spring is often cool and rainy, and the vine remains dormant until mid-April. Flowering usually occurs in mid-June, generally during the second week of this month.

Summer begins without excessive heat, and generally continues with good weather, although August tends to be stormy. By contrast, September is often mild, dry and sunny, which underlines the truth of the wine growers' saying: '*C'est Septembre qui fait le vin*' ('It's September that makes the wine'). These weather conditions are enhanced by the beneficial effects of microclimates resulting from the presence of large lakes, or from the mountain slopes that shelter the vineyards.

The grape varieties

This region has no fewer than 23 different grape varieties, giving a wide number of highly individual wines. There are six main white varieties.

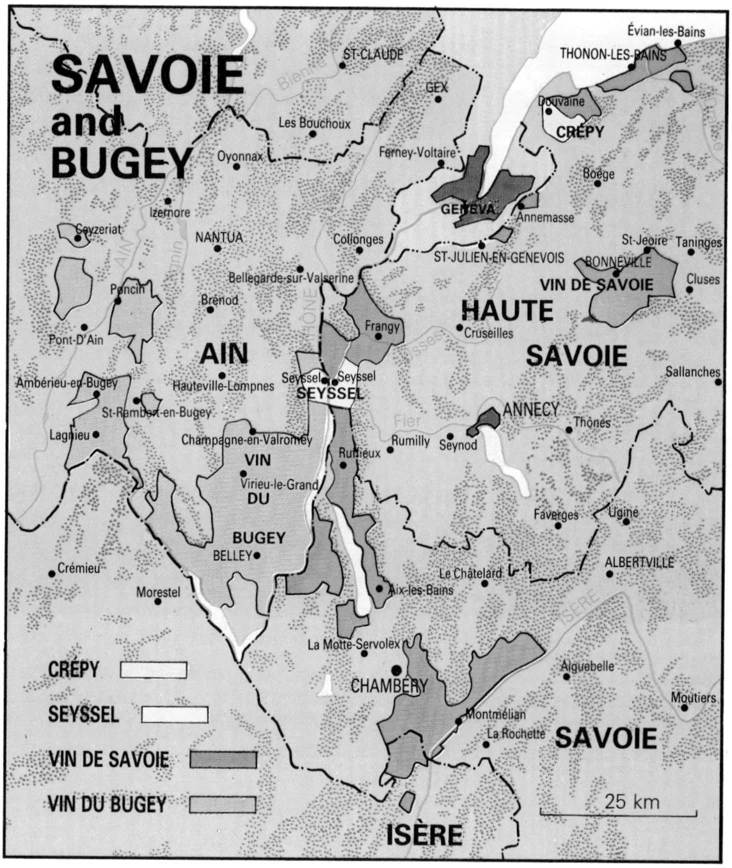

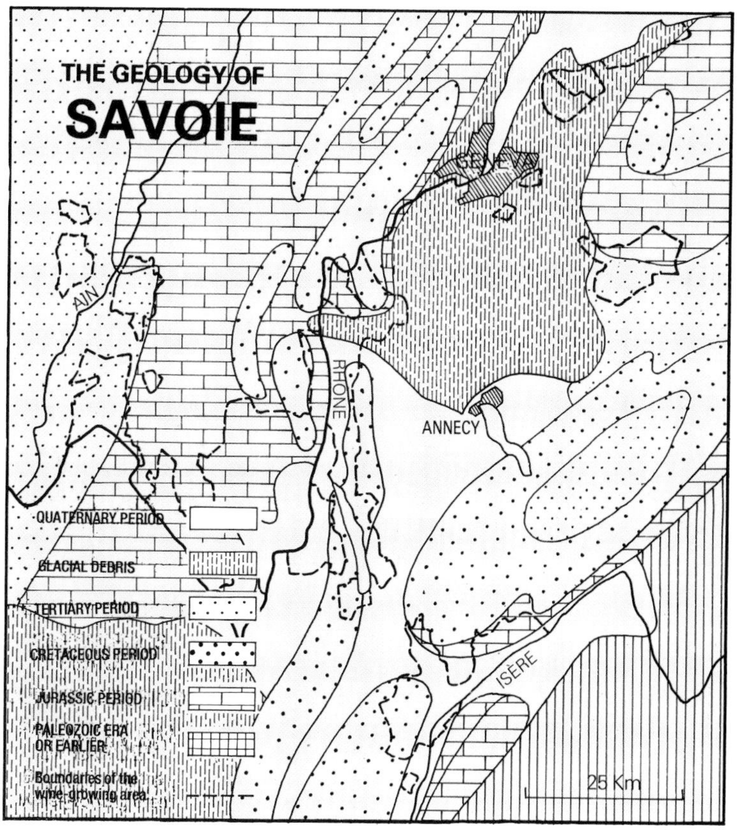

The **Jacquère**, the most widely grown variety, is a hardy vine that forms the basis of the dry white wines of Savoie. It is at its best in the Vin de Savoie *crus* of Abymes, Apremont, Chignin, Cruet, Montmélian and Saint-Jeoire-Prieuré. These wines have the barest hint of colour. They are fresh, light wines with a floral bouquet, often *perlant* (very slightly sparkling), with diuretic properties. They are very good as aperitif wines, and should be drunk as young as possible.

The **Altesse**, locally known as the **Roussette**, is a variety rich in sugars and aromatic potential; with a low yield, it produces wines of great class, such as Seyssel and Roussette de Savoie from the *crus* of Frangy, Marestel, Monterminod and Monthoux. These are harmonious, aromatic wines of great breed, suitable for ageing. A blend of Altesse and a maximum of 50 per cent of Chardonnay is used for Roussette de Savoie not followed by a *cru* name.

The **Chasselas** used in Savoie is the **Chasselas Roux** or the **Chasselas Vert**, from Switzerland. It is grown around Lac Léman (Lake Geneva), and is the only grape used in Crépy and for the Vin de Savoie *crus* of Ripaille, Marignan and Marin.

It gives white wines that are dry, fruity, light, delicate and *perlant*, also with diuretic properties; they can be drunk from the first year after their harvest, but they also age well.

The **Gringet**, a variety found only in the Arve valley in Haute-Savoie, is the real secret behind the character of the Vin de Savoie Mousseux or Pétillant *cru* of Ayze. It is sometimes used together with the Roussette d'Ayse. These are dry sparkling wines made by a local method.

The **Roussanne**, locally called the **Bergeron**, is grown in three communes in Savoie and is often picked slightly overripe, to bring out the qualities necessary to make the high-class white Vin de Savoie *cru* of Chignin-Bergeron.

The **Molette**, together with a little Altesse, is used to produce Seyssel-Mousseux.

The **Chardonnay** (locally called the **Petite Sainte-Marie**), the **Aligoté**, and the **Velteliner Rose** and the **Pinot Gris** (locally known as the **Malvoisie**) are all much less widely grown, and give aromatic, delicate wines of marked Savoie character.

For red wines, four main varieties are grown.

The **Mondeuse**, native to Savoie, is a late-ripening variety rich in the aromas, colouring matter and tannins that characterize the region's finest red wines. It finds its best expression in the Vin de Savoie *crus* of Arbin, Saint-Jean-de-la-Porte, Jongieux and Chignin: deep-coloured wines with berry aromas, soundly constituted and long lived.

The **Gamay Noir à Jus Blanc** is grown on numerous *terroirs* on account of the popularity of its light, pleasant and easy-to-drink wines. It is the grape variety that is used for the most sought-after Vin de Savoie *cru*: Chautagne.

The **Pinot Noir**, if planted in a sunny site, gives memorably subtle wines.

The **Persan** has the latest growth cycle of all the red varieties of Savoie, and for this reason has virtually been abandoned.

A traditional harvest

Most of the vines in Savoie are trained low and staked to wires, with a density of plantation of about 6,000 to 8,000 stocks per ha. The grapes are picked in the traditional way, by hand, usually in the first fortnight of October.

Vinification

Savoie produces mainly white wines for drinking young. Consequently, the growers strive to bring out the youthful characteristics of the wines as much as possible, and preserve them by means of early bottling.

The traditional **hotte** *grape-picking basket (shown above left) has been replaced by more practical tubs such as the ones carried by these workers in the Abymes vineyards.*

WHITE WINES OF SAVOIE

CHARACTERISTICS OF HARVESTS AND VINTAGES 1977-86

Period from April to September	Total temperature in degrees Celsius	Hours of sunshine	Rainfall in mm	(1) Flowering period	(2) Volume of harvest	Weather during the harvest
1977	2 801	1 136	603.2	4	N	W to M
1978	2 846	1 217	536.0	4	N	D
1979	2 911	1 347	556.6	2	N	D
1980	2 853	1 211	768.7	4	N	W
1981	2 963	1 271	478.3	2	N	D
1982	3 054	1 390	568.6	1	N+	W
1983	3 117	1 251	811.2	2	N+	M
1984	2 832	1 319	520.3	3	N+	M
1985	3 183	1 424	631.7	2	N+	D
1986	3 029	1 435	583.3	2	N+	M

CHARACTERISTICS OF THE WINES

Terroir, *grapes and methods of vinification aside, the character of wines is also influenced by climatic factors. The development and ripeness of the fruit, as well as the volume of the harvest, are conditioned by the total annual temperatures, the number of hours of sunshine, the total rainfall recorded and the weather during the harvest. The ultimate characteristics of the wines of any given vintage will be a reflection of all these factors.*

1977— Late harvest; light, lively wines.
1978— Slow, late ripening; quality of the wines comparable to 1977.
1979— Grapes fully ripe; good vintage, wines true to type.
1980— Rainy year, ripening disrupted and delayed; wines very light and lacking in structure, best for early drinking.
1981— Good ripening; balanced wines.
1982— Satisfactory ripening, early harvest; wines moderately true to type.
1983— Perfect ripeness achieved; wines very true to type and well balanced, very good vintage.
1984— Middling ripeness; wines quite light with lively, youthful characteristics.
1985— Good ripening; good-quality wines with highly developed aromas.
1986— Satisfactory ripeness; wines modestly aromatic, very pleasant in the mouth.

KEY

1. *Flowering period:*
   1 — beginning of June
   2 — mid-June
   3 — 24 June
   4 — beginning of July
2. *Volume of harvest:*
   normal .... *N*
   higher than normal: .... *N +*
3. *Dry weather during the harvest* .... *D*
   Wet weather during the harvest .... *W*
   Mixed weather during the harvest ...... *M*

WINES WITH PERSONALITY

Some sixty years before the birth of Christ, the Roman general Lucius Licinius Lucullus was serving wine made by the Allobroges at his celebrated table. By AD1000, the good monks of Savoie had succeeded perfectly in acclimatizing a number of robust grape varieties to the harsh winters around the Lac du Bourget. These are just two pieces of evidence to show how ancient the origins of the Savoie vineyards are.

The wine growers of Savoie produce wines full of character and charm, that are easy to digest. The old people of Savoie used to say, furthermore, that they don't 'overheat the spirit'; they are light wines, and make for good company . . . though even they can be treacherous in excess.

The wines of Savoie are really a single entity, and sometimes the distinctions drawn between them are too subtle. However, each wine does have its own personality. The Mondeuse, for example, a local grape variety, gives a red wine that ages extremely well, retaining its aromas of wild fruits, bilberries and blackcurrants.

I also like certain wines from the Vin de Savoie cru *of Ayze with their perfume of flint and gunpowder, but my favourite wine is the* cru *of Cruet. In years when its grapes have been soaked in sunshine, it is fragrant with the delicate aroma of raspberries.*

The pétillant *or sparkling wines of Savoie have a certain allure, but they tend to take the legs from under you, so it is best to drink them after your walk in the mountains, not before — or else as an aperitif.*

Savoie wines are an ideal accompaniment for the fish from our streams and our lakes. The two blend in perfect harmony.

But this is all I want to say on the matter. A wine deserves and expects patience and a very open mind. You have to discover a wine for yourself. Remember that, in Savoie as elsewhere, the most famous wines are not necessarily the best or the most authentic.

Françoise Bise

Discovered at Cruet, this copper door plaque is engraved with a papal mitre and two bunches of grapes.

The Château de Ripaille, situated in the Vin de Savoie cru *of the same name, produces a supple white wine with a bouquet of sweet almonds.*

Production

The average annual amounts of wine produced are 81,868hl in Savoie, 8,410hl in Haute-Savoie, 7,217hl in Isère and 3,759hl in Ain, making a yearly total of some 100,000hl. Thirty per cent of this is red and rosé, and 70 per cent white. Ninety per cent is sold under the *appellations* Vin de Savoie, Roussette de Savoie, Vin de Savoie Pétillant and Vin de Savoie Mousseux. The remainder is sold under the *appellations* Crépy (4,450hl), Seyssel and Seyssel Mousseux (3,220hl).

Sales and tourism

The marketing of Savoie's wines is divided almost equally among the growers, the cooperatives, and wholesale wine merchants. Most of the wine is sold to tourists visiting the Alps. Very little is exported. Nevertheless, the Savoie wine region is developing and in 1986 the Comité Interprofessionnel des Vins de Savoie was set up, based in Chambéry.

There are several itineraries that enable the visitor to explore a wine region that remains one of the least known in France, no doubt because it is so fragmented. Signposted routes take the tourist through magnificent landscapes, and there are many stopping places where typical wines can be tasted.

Sciaccarello

Synonyms: *Sciuchitajolo* (crispy), *Schiucheta-diuru* at Sartène, *Barbera*, erroneously.

Leaves medium sized, truncate, finely bullate with concave edges, five-lobed, with lobes of average size and definition, narrow lateral sinuses, petiolar sinus lyrate, more or less closed; dentation pointed, medium sized; underside of blade arachnoid.

Green shoots ribbed, vigorous, arachnoid at the tip, light green with pink nodes; long, large tendrils, more or less entangled.

Bunches large, conical, compact, sometimes winged; grapes ovoid, purplish black, crisp, juicy; ripening period: third epoch.

This is a Corsican vine, possibly of Italian origin, and mainly found in the Sartène region. It has late budbreak and an upright habit, and has to be pruned long as it otherwise tends to produce more wood than fruit. It is not very susceptible to diseases and gives one of the best red wines in Corsica, one that is well structured, subtle, with a special flavour of its own, although a little lacking in colour. One registered clone has been approved: number 744. Classed as 'recommended' in Corsica, this variety occupies 730ha there, and is used in the AOCs of Vin de Corse and Ajaccio.

Segalin

This is a Jurançon Noir × Portugais Bleu cross, made by INRA at Vassal. This black grape produces a deeply coloured, quite tannic wine with plenty of body and a good bouquet. It can also be eaten as a table grape. Classed as 'authorized' in the South West, with one approved clone, number 745.

Seinoir

Synonym: *8754 Seibel.*

Growing tips white, arachnoid.

Young leaves glabrous, bronze-coloured.

Leaves truncate, concave, dull, slightly five-lobed with narrow, pointed lateral sinuses, petiolar sinus narrowly V-shaped or with overlapping edges; dentation pointed, very narrow, underside of blade and veins pubescent. Green shoots arachnoid, purplish. Bunches small, compact, conical; grapes small, slightly ovoid, black, with coloured juice and soft flesh; ripening period: first epoch, late.

The Seinoir is a 5163 × 880 Seibel hybrid, classed as 'authorized' in the *départements* of western Central France to provide the family wine of the farmers there. It is somewhat prone to downy mildew and grey rot (botrytis), but it is more resistant to oidium (powdery mildew). It gives a deeply coloured, purplish-red, bitter wine. The vines, which are of average vigour, need to be grafted on to strong rootstocks. The Seinoir is grown on about 1,000ha.

Sélect

Synonym: *100 T Vidal.*

Bunches medium sized, cylindrical; grapes white, spherical, quite tightly packed; ripening period: second epoch, late.

This vine is an Ugni Blanc × Jurançon Blanc cross, with late budbreak, ten days after that of the Ugni Blanc. The wine it gives is quite delicate, with a good bouquet. The Sélect is one of the secondary grape varieties of the Cognac AOC. Its brandy is classed slightly below that of the Ugni Blanc.

Semebat

A Baroque × Côt cross, created by INRA at Bordeaux. This is a vigorous variety with consistent fertility. Its black grapes ripen during the second epoch and give a deeply coloured, well-structured quality wine. Yields vary from 68hl/ha to 127hl/ha, with alcohol content ranging from 9.8° to 12.5°. The Semebat is classed as 'authorized' in the South West, and one clone has been approved, number 746.

Sémillon

Synonyms: *Sémillon Muscat* in Sauternes, *Sémillon Roux* and *Gros Sémillon* in Gironde, *Blanc Sémillon* in Bergerac, *Malaga* in Lot, *Chevrier* in Dordogne, *Blanc Doux* in Montpon, *Mansois Blanc* or *Mancès Blanc* in Aveyron, *Colombier* in Gironde, *Sauternes* sometimes in Indre and in Cher.

Growing tips open, felty white with carmine margins.

Young leaves downy, yellowish, with bronze bulges.

Leaves orbicular, contorted, finely bullate, crimped at the petiolar junction, thick, deeply five-lobed with lateral sinuses narrow, acute at base, petiolar sinus lyrate, usually open; dentation medium sized, convex; underside of blade arachnoid, slightly pubescent.

Green shoots ribbed, very thick, green with pinkish nodes; tendrils small, thin.

Bunches medium sized, cylindrical, winged, compact; grapes medium sized, spherical, golden white, sometimes even turning pink when fully ripe, skin thick, juice plentiful with a slightly musky flavour; ripening period: second epoch.

This is a vigorous, productive vine from the Bordeaux region. It has midseason budbreak, but budding is staggered from vine to vine, which is an advantage if there are late frosts. The Sémillon is not very susceptible to downy mildew or oidium (powdery mildew), but it is prone to grey rot (botrytis), grape fan-leaf virus and grape leaf-roll virus.

In Sauternes, yields are low, in order to obtain top-quality dessert wine musts. On low-lying sites, however, yields are sometimes as high as 80hl/ha to 100hl/ha, with alcoholic strength ranging from 10° to 11°. If yields are high, dessert wines can only be made with large quantities of sulphur dioxide, a process that makes for poor-quality wine. A recent tendency is to produce dry white wines from the Sémillon, but these often lack bouquet and freshness. Four registered clones have been approved, the most useful being numbers 173 and 315.

The Sémillon is the second most widely grown white grape in France, after the Ugni Blanc, but its plantings are on the decrease: 23,400ha in 1980, compared with 36,000ha in 1958. This decline is due to a slump in the sales of sweet white wines.

Classed as 'recommended' in western Central France, the South West, Languedoc and Provence, it is included in plantings for a number of *appellations d'origine contrôlée* in Gironde (16,662ha), for example, Sauternes, Loupiac, Cérons and Entre-Deux-Mers; in Dordogne (5,800ha), for Bergerac, Monbazillac and Montravel; in Lot-et-Garonne (700ha) for Côtes de Duras and Côtes de Buzet; and for Côtes de Provence in Var and Coteaux d'Aix-en-Provence in Bouches-du-Rhône.

Sérénèze de Voreppe

Synonyms: *Sérénèze*, *Sérène de Voreppe*, *Serine*, *Sereine*, *Cérénèse*.

Bunches small, conical, narrow; grapes medium sized, black, spherical or slightly oblate; ripening period: second epoch.

A black variety giving a wine of good quality, found in the vineyards of the Grésivaudan, between Grenoble and Albertville in Savoie. The variety is unclassified.

Serrigny *See* Ladoix.

Servanin

Synonyms: *Servanien*, *Servagnien*, *Servagnin des Avenières* in the north of Isère, *Servagnie* or *Servanit* at Saint-Ismier, *Salagnin* at Saint-Savin, *Martelet* at Bourgoin, *Petite Mondeuse*.

Bunches small to medium, cylindrical-conical, compact; grapes small, ellipsoidal, black; ripening period: second epoch, late.

This is an old variety from Isère. It has late budbreak, and gives a deeply coloured, highly astringent wine. A vigorous variety, it is usually trellis-trained at Saint-Ismier and les Avenières. It adapts well to the soils known locally as *marcs* (glacial silts mixed with stones).

The Servanin is classed as 'authorized' in Isère, where there are 10ha of it, with a little more grown in Ain and Drôme.

Seyssel

This is the premier *appellation d'origine contrôlée* of the Savoie region, situated in the *départements* of Ain and Haute-Savoie, which are separated by the Rhône at Seyssel itself. The AOC was ratified by the decrees of 11 February 1942 and 27 August 1986.

The brown, glacial alluvium of the gentle, east-facing slopes on either side of the Rhône was once used for the commercial cultivation of irises. The Altesse now grows there, acquiring a very pleasant odour of violets.

Annual production of 2,400hl of white wine comes from 70ha in the communes of Corbonod and Seyssel. Often locally called Roussette de Seyssel, this velvety wine, with its characteristic flavour of bergamot, ages well for three or four years in bottle.

Seyssel Mousseux

Together with the Altesse, grown in sandy molasse soils, the Molette grape variety forms the basis of Seyssel Mousseux.

Under the rules governing the AOC this sparkling wine, made by the *méthode champenoise*, must contain at least 10 per cent Altesse, in order to give it its slight but characteristic hint of violets. Production in 1986 was 800hl. Both the Brut and Demi-Sec versions are best drunk in the third year after secondary fermentation in bottle has taken place.

Seyval

Synonyms: *5 276 Seyve-Villard*.

Growing tips downy white with carmine margins.

Young leaves arachnoid, slightly bronze-coloured.

Leaves small, orbicular, smooth, concave, thick, glossy, contorted, slightly three-lobed, petiolar sinus narrow with overlapping edges; dentation convex, medium sized; blade glabrous with slightly arachnoid veins.

Bunches small, cylindrical; grapes small, spherical, golden yellow, dulled by a grey bloom; ripening period: first epoch.

This is a vigorous, productive 5656 × 4986 Seibel cross. The wine it gives is light yellow with an aroma that recalls ether and pomade, as does that of the 4986 Seibel. Although quite resistant to downy mildew, it is susceptible to grey rot (botrytis) and spring frosts, because of its early budbreak. Classed as 'authorized', it is not now widely grown (65ha).

Sylvaner

Synonym: *Sylvaner Vert.*

Bunches medium sized, cylindrical or cylindrical-conical, not usually winged; grapes medium sized, spherical, fairly thick skinned, green with brown spots, becoming golden yellow when exposed to plenty of sunlight, flesh juicy, with a neutral, slightly acid flavour; ripening period: second epoch, early.

The Sylvaner buds a few days before the Riesling. It is a vigorous vine, consistently fertile with yields of 60hl/ha to 80hl/ha on hillside sites, but up to 150hl/ha and sometimes even more on the low-lying sites if pruned long. It has only average resistance to spring frosts, and it is also susceptible to severe winter frosts. The Sylvaner is vulnerable to downy mildew, oidium (powdery mildew) and grey rot (botrytis).

It gives a medium-quality wine with a low alcohol content, a light bouquet and sustained though not dominant acidity.

Two registered clones have been approved: numbers 50 and 487. Classed as 'recommended' in Alsace and Moselle, it occupies 2,650ha in Alsace.

Syrah

Synonyms: *Schiras*, *Sirac*, *Sirah*, *Petite Sirah*, *Hignin Noir* at Crémieu, *Candive* at Bourgoin, *Entournerein* at la Tour-du-Pin, *Marsanne Noire* at Saint-Marcellin, *Plant de la Biaune* at Montbrison, *Serenne* or *Séreine* in the Isère valley, *Serine* at Côte Rôtie.

Leaves medium sized, orbicular, bullate, crimped at the petiolar junction, contorted, often wavy, five-lobed with lobes of average size and definition, lateral sinuses narrow and acute at base, petiolar sinus lyrate, more or less closed; dentation medium sized, convex; underside of blade finely pubescent and downy in tufts. The edges of the leaves redden partially in autumn.

Green shoots markedly ribbed, quadrangular (a most distinctive feature), green with red nodes, downy at tip; tendrils long and thin.

Bunches medium sized, cylindrical, sometimes winged, compact, with peduncles that quickly become woody; grapes small, ovoid, a beautiful blue-black with abundant bloom, skin thin but quite strong, soft flesh, juicy with a pleasant flavour; ripening period: second epoch.

No one knows the exact origins of this vine. Some say it came from the town of Shiraz in Iran, and was brought to France from Iran or Cyprus by the Chevalier de Sterimberg, who planted it around his hilltop dwelling at Hermitage. Others say the Syrah was introduced even earlier to France, in the 3rd century AD, when the Emperor Probus permitted vines to be planted once again in Gaul. Finally, some historians think the Syrah came from the town of Syracuse in Sicily.

The Syrah has quite late budbreak. It is of average vigour and is often not very fertile, yielding only about 30hl/ha if pruned short. If pruned long, using the single or double Guyot systems, and with productive clones, better yields can be obtained. Sixteen registered clones have been approved: number 383 is the best in terms of quality; number 100 is the most widely used, being the most productive. The Syrah is susceptible to drought, grey rot (botrytis) and grape worms; in addition, its branches break in high winds.

The Syrah gives a deeply coloured, astringent wine with a high alcohol content and a very pleasant perfume, reminiscent of violets.

Its cultivation is very much on the increase, growing from 1,603ha in 1958 to 12,300 in 1980, and it has now probably reached 15,000ha. Classed as 'recommended' in the South West, Languedoc, Provence and the Rhône valley, this variety is included among the specified grape varieties of numerous AOCs in the northern Rhône: Côte Rôtie, Cornas, Saint-Joseph and Hermitage, with plantings in Rhône (100ha), Loire (85ha), Ardèche (1,236ha) and Drôme (2,075ha). The Syrah is also widespread in the southern Rhône, for the AOCs of the Côtes du Rhône and Châteauneuf-du-Pape, in Vaucluse (2,109ha) and Gard (2,584ha); also for the AOCs of Palette, Côtes de Provence and Coteaux d'Aix-en-Provence in Var (658ha) and Bouches-du-Rhône (360ha). Its cultivation in Languedoc is more recent. It is grown there for the AOCs of Coteaux du Languedoc, Saint-Chinian, Faugères, Minervois, Fitou, Corbières, Collioure, Côtes du Roussillon, Costières du Gard, Banyuls, Maury, and Rivesaltes, in Hérault (651ha), Aude (530ha) and Pyrénées-Orientales (265ha). Finally, there are a few plantings of Syrah in the South West, in Tarn and Tarn-et-Garonne.

A leaf of the Syrah, a variety that is very widespread in the Côtes du Rhône, with plantings increasing throughout southern France.

The underside of a Syrah leaf.

Green shoot of the Syrah.

THE SOUTH WEST

For long cast into shadow by the giant of Bordeaux on one side and the colossus of Languedoc on the other, the South West cherishes hopes today of finally emerging into the sunlight. This elusive region is made up of greatly varying soils and abruptly changing climatic patterns: a disconcerting mixture, but wine growers hope to succeed in building a regional identity through the common cause of quality in diversity.

The wine-growing area of the South West embraces no fewer than ten *départements*: Aveyron, Dordogne, Gers, Haute-Garonne, Lot, Lot-et-Garonne, Tarn, Tarn-et-Garonne, Pyrénées-Atlantiques and Landes, these forming parts of the traditional regions of Guyenne, Gascony, Béarn, Aquitaine and the Pays Basque.

The INAO has distinguished three categories of wine in this vast area: 16 AOCs (including most notably Cahors, Jurançon and Madiran), 9 VDQS and about 10 Vins de Pays.

The shadow of Bordeaux

The wines of the South West have been in the shadow of those of Bordeaux throughout the region's viticultural history — a clear reflection of its geographical position. Some scholars have stressed the importance of the Gallo-Roman origins of viticulture in the South West, notably at Gaillac, but the reputation and marketing of these wines has always been closely linked to the Bordeaux wine trade. Bordeaux and its merchants once enjoyed numerous privileges giving them a commercial stranglehold on the South West, and this situation lasted for nearly five centuries.

Some events did, however, bring joy to the hearts of South Western wine growers. Firstly, in 1553, the future Henri IV had his lips rubbed with garlic and Jurançon wine at his baptism. Later, Turgot's edict of 1776 finally removed Bordeaux's privileges (*see* page 348). The South West subsequently experienced a period of prosperity, but prospects again darkened with the decrease in the export of Gascon wines to the north, due to wars, blockades, new trends in consumption, and, most seriously of all, the phylloxera crisis, which reached the South West in 1875. It was not until the 1950s that the first signs of revival in the region could be sensed.

The soils and climates

The wine growers of the South West have been able to realize their aspirations to quality via a huge range of soils and subsoils. The region has a spectacular geological inventory, which varies from one *appellation* and even from one site to another, chief among the soil types

The rustic red and white wines of VDQS Vins d'Estaing are grown on vineyards situated to the northeast of Rodez, in Aveyron.

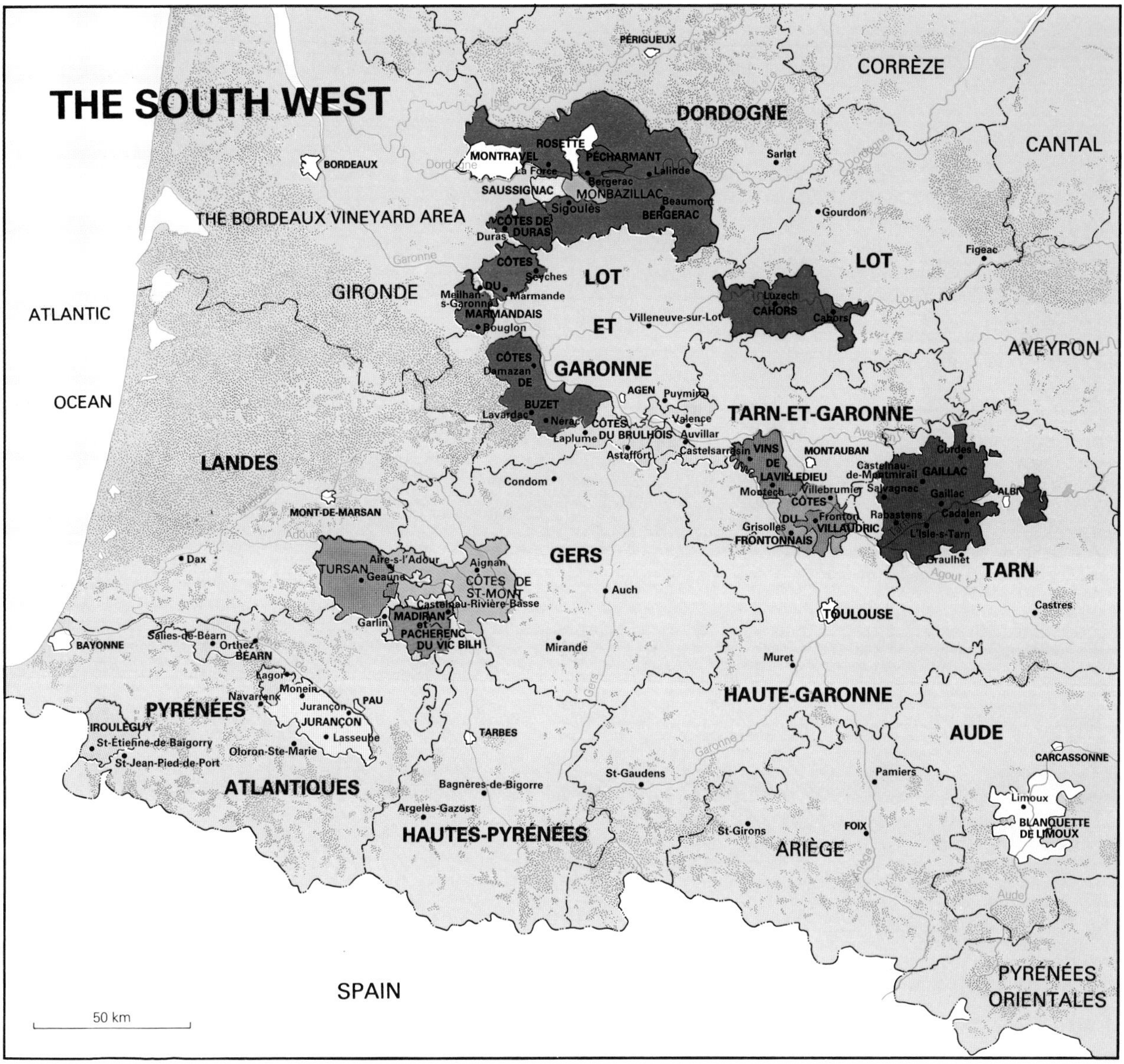

being limestones, molasse, alluvial or lacustrine deposits, sands and clays.

The climate, too, changes from one district to another, but the generally recognized pattern of the South West is one of variable temperatures and sudden changes in weather conditions: a hot spell, for example, followed by heavy showers.

Production

The vineyards of the South West have been in the throes of significant changes for some years now. Throughout the region's 100,000ha, there has been a spectacular decline in the amount of wine produced for everyday consumption, and a large increase in quality vineyards.

Appellations d'origine contrôlée now account for 23,700ha. The AOC Côtes de Duras, for example, has increased from 565ha in 1951 to 1,750ha in 1984, and is scheduled to reach 2,000ha in the 1990s. Other *appellations* vary enormously in area, from the few hectares of the VDQS Vins d'Estaing, to the few dozen of AOC Irouléguy, to the 11,500ha of AOC Bergerac. This spectacular difference in size is reflected in annual production figures: 170,000hl for Bergerac and about 600hl for Estaing. If we add to this the varying yields from one *appellation* to another — only 40hl/ha for the sweet wines of Jurançon, for example — this gives us a more complete picture of the wines of the South West, whose great strength continues to lie in their exceptional variety. Between them the various districts produce about 31 different red wines, 21 rosés, 19 dry white wines, 9 sweet white wines and 2 sparkling wines.

PEARLS OF THE SOUTH WEST

I discovered my love of wine thanks to an old négociant *from Langon who taught me everything he knew, nearly 30 years ago. What is more, my wife and I spent our wedding night at his house, with a pile of bottles underneath the bed!*

Wine makes me dream. I often go down into my cellar simply to gaze at the bottles there. They tell me stories and anecdotes, and evoke memories and images . . .

My favourite wine is Haut-Brion. I love the taste of this Graves, and I have long associated it with events concerning my family life, such as marriage, birth and birthdays. However, it also plays a part in my cooking, because to my mind wine and food complement one another. The main thing is to have imagination and know how to break away from convention.

For example, I often cook fish in red wine — salmon or sea bass, for example. And what sometimes happens is that I am presumptuous enough to go up to my customer's table and ask him for a few drops of his wine to finish the sauce, for there must be harmony and continuity between what you eat and what you drink. The success of a sauce depends on the quality of the wine you put in it.

A few years ago, for a 'dinner of the century' which brought together the 12 greatest chefs in France, I ordered a whole case of white Haut-Brion, which was something of a rarity in those days, simply to deglaze the duck!

I also think, as I have suggested above, that it is very important to serve the wine that has been used for the sauce with the dish, in order to achieve the harmony that must prevail in cooking, as in every art.

The first pleasure you derive from a dish is a visual one. Every day I am comforted by the thought that to cook well, you must have the soul of an artist. If I did not paint, how would I be able to match colours? Others compare cooking with music or architecture, and why not? The same kind of sensibility applies in all these fields. The only difference is the raw material.

Bordeaux wines inspire me; but Biarritz is only 200km away, and I also like to experiment with the wines of the South West. There are some treasures to be found there, such as the white wines of Jurançon, which have been improving greatly for some time now, thanks to the younger generation of wine growers. The trend in Jurançon nowadays is to return to the tradition of dry white wine making, after years of nothing but the sweet wines preferred by the English, and I think this is a good thing. As far as red wines are concerned, I love the wines of Madiran, especially those that are given an ageing period in new oak. They are sturdy wines, like the area they come from, but they are often drunk too young.

In my opinion, however, the true pearl of the South West is armagnac. A well-chosen armagnac is always guaranteed to give people a pleasant surprise; some are exceptionally good. However, price does not always reflect quality, and the best plan is to discover armagnac for yourself, on the spot.

The Armagnac region, once so poor that, as one of my wine-growing friends says, the crows used to fly upside down so as not to have to look at the human misery found there, is, even today, a land bathed in an atmosphere of secrecy. Everything is whispered from ear to ear, and there has to be a feeling of complicity between buyer and seller. If you find something very fine there one day, grab it, for the wine growers of Armagnac, in this respect very much in the Gascon mould, are always happy to acquaint you with their product, but they do not always want you to take it away, and they invariably regret having to sell it!

There you have the essence of the wine-growing spirit of the South West, that of craftsmen who love their work, and know the true value of the wine they produce.

Pierre Laporte

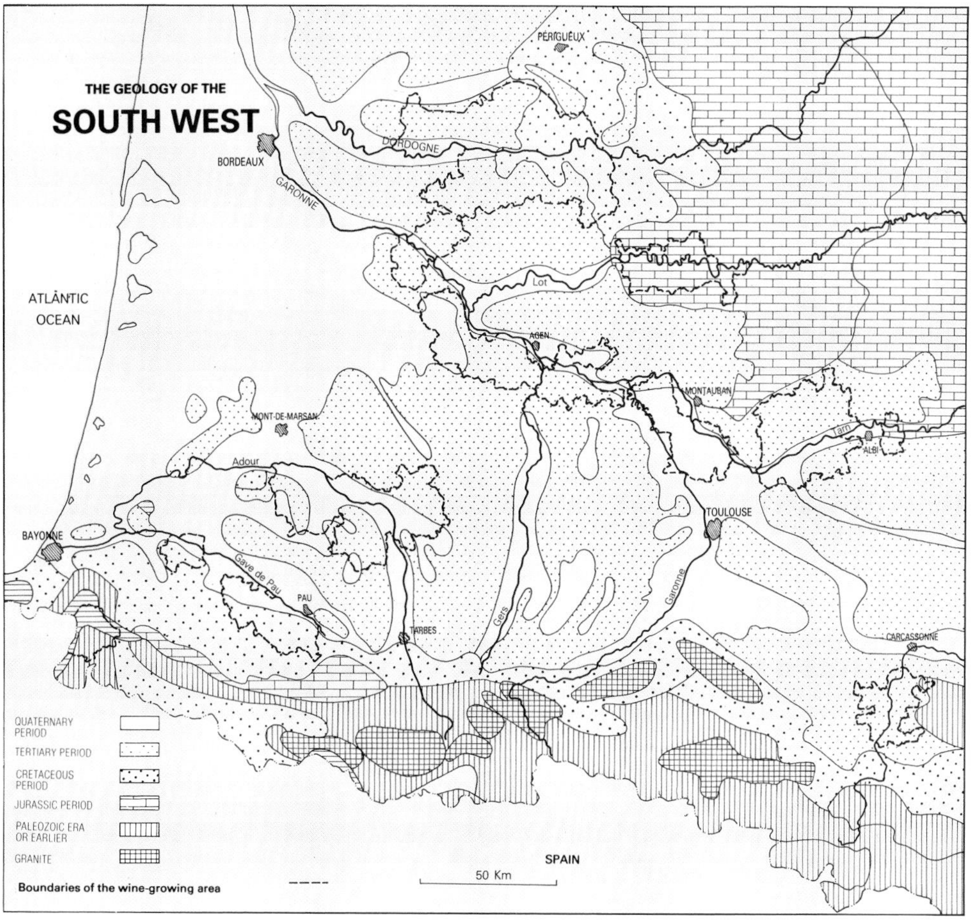

Grape varieties and viticulture

This wide range of wines in the South West would not be possible without an equally splendid range of grape varieties. Some of these are from Bordeaux, notably those used for the wines of the Côtes de Buzet, with the Merlot, Cabernet Franc and Cabernet Sauvignon for red wines, and the Sémillon, Sauvignon Blanc and Muscadelle for whites. However, there are also many local varieties used, notably the Tannat (Béarn wines), Négrette (in the Côtes du Frontonnais), the Côt and the Fer for red wines; and for the whites the Baroque (in Tursan), Petit and Gros Manseng, Camaralet de Lasseube and Lauzet (all in Jurançon), the Mauzac and Len de l'El (in Gaillac).

In the service of this great range of varieties, considerable progress has been made in growing methods during the last few years. Not only is mechanization greatly on the increase, but great efforts are also going into the search for the right grape varieties and clones for particular *terroirs*. Also important is the prodigious work that has gone into improving vinification methods, and in this respect the region has learned greatly from the Bordeaux oenological institutions.

The process of change in the South West is in full swing. The role of the cooperatives, formerly decisive — without them, many of the *appellations* would not exist today — is now tending to diminish. Certainly they vinify and sell more than half the quality wines of the region, but the number of private growers, many of them ex-cooperative members, increases every year. Also worthy of note is the increase in regional *négociants* and the appearance of business partners from outside the South West who have now seen the considerable potential offered by this evolving wine region.

The regional *appellations*

The regional subdivisions of the South West's wine districts are not as clear-cut as in other regions. The *appellations* pay scant attention to the boundary lines of *départements* and provinces. Each of the following regional entries contains information on the wine and spirit production of the South West: the ***Bergerac Region***, the ***Haut Pays***, the ***Pyrenees*** and ***Armagnac***. These entries are to be found in the appropriate alphabetical position.

WINE AND ART

A theme and source of inspiration for artists of all kinds, the vine and wine find expression in every artistic medium: painting, sculpture, engraving, tapestry, miniatures, gold- and silverware, cabinet work, opera, music and poetry. Naturally so, for they have always been man's companions and have been present with him throughout history.

The first examples of art inspired by the vine and wine come from early Egyptian and Mesopotamian civilizations. At that time, however, there was no clear boundary between aesthetic and religious expression. The arts were a part of the worship of the gods, and so when vines, vine leaves and branches were depicted, it was perhaps not so much out of a love of their decorative beauty, but rather as a means of expressing the mystery surrounding the gods of wine.

Egypt: wine venerated

From pre-dynastic times onwards the Egyptian people carved their veneration of wine in stone. But the task of the engravers was not to produce a work of aesthetic worth, but to create something imperishable in order to ensure their subjects' eternal life. Egyptian narrative reliefs and drawings must be seen, above all, as elements of a grander work, not just as a decorative evocation, because the artist was in fact obeying conventions imposed by religion. This is not, of course, to suggest that such frescos are devoid of aesthetic intentions; the contrary is true, as is demonstrated by the emotional response they can still arouse in us today.

The viticultural themes that Egyptian artists drew on down the centuries show countless scenes of vine growing and grape harvesting, giving us a faithful picture of everyday wine-related activity in this civilization. These illustrations, in some ways the forebears of today's cartoons, laid the foundations of popular art — though neither consciously nor intentionally. You would search in vain for these illustrations on obelisks, or on the façades of palaces dedicated to the glorification of heroes and conquests. On the other hand, they appear in great numbers on sarcophagi, in the crypts leading to funerary monuments, on bas-reliefs, and most of all on everyday objects such as pitchers and caskets. Bunches of grapes and vine leaves occur frequently as motifs in burial places throughout the Valley of the Kings.

Mesopotamia: wine enjoyed

The Assyrian civilization, one of several Mesopotamian cultures, also paid fervent homage to vines and wine. Unencumbered by the religious constraints imposed on Egyptian practitioners, sculptors and other kinds of artists gave free rein to their creative verve.

The bas-relief in the British Museum entitled *Royal Banquet after Victory* is a good example. It depicts Ashurbanipal drinking in the shade of a trellis in the company of the queen, while servants fan them. There is no pantheistic symbolism here; the love of beauty alone justifies the work of art. The way in which the royal throne is shown adorned with vine leaves stretched between two trees is wonderfully successful in sculptural terms. It is an early example of the spirit of conviviality mixed with a certain solemnity that is a fitting homage to wine. In Persia, the skill of the goldsmiths showed itself in vessels for drinking wine: for example, a golden rhyton in the form of a gazelle's head, dating back to the Achaemenian dynasty (668-330BC).

Royal Banquet after Victory. *Bas-relief showing Ashurbanipal and his queen drinking in their palace, after the battle of Til Tuba. 653BC.*

Sileni grape harvesters. Amphora attributed to the Amasis Painter. About 530BC.

Ancient Greece: wine deified

Great civilizations, like constellations, can die, and the dazzling cultures of Egypt and Mesopotamia were soon eclipsed by the immense influence of Ancient Greece, which was founded to a not inconsiderable extent on wine growing. After all, does the legend not say that the wine cup was designed from the imprint of Aphrodite's breast?

The mystery of fermentation captured the imagination of the Greeks. Here, as with other civilizations, man's answer to the mystery was to create a god. So Dionysus was born from the thigh of Zeus, and as he was the god of vegetation, he watched over the cultivation of vines and of fig trees. In this capacity, he is often associated with the demi-gods and other nature spirits. It is therefore not surprising to see him in the middle of a joyous troop of satyrs, sileni and nymphs. He is escorted by Pan, Priapus, the maenads, the thyads and the bacchantes: plenty of material there to stimulate the imagination of the artists of the time.

Dionysian festivals, whether rustic or orgiastic (like the mysteries), played an important part in everyday life. It was during these festivals that artists, particularly poets, appeared in public, and dithyrambic contests and theatrical events were organized.

These Dionysians abandoned themselves to wild dances, for wine always inspired people to dance. It seems, in fact, that wine was not unconnected with the development of dance in general.

The cult of Dionysus had far-reaching repercussions in various artistic disciplines. In particular, it contributed towards introducing a feeling for nature into lyric poetry, and passionate movement into sculpture.

The decorative arts of Greece — ceramics (vases and amphoras), mosaics and, above all, statuary — also served to extol the vine and wine. It would be difficult to find a temple or theatre that does not evoke some Dionysian scene or bear some motif of interlaced vines.

Ancient Rome: the triumph of Bacchus

Besides Greece, Italy and Sicily were also colonized by vines. The Etruscans paid great homage to Fufluns, the spirit of wine and protector of the town of Populonia (anciently known as Pupluna or Fufluna).

It would be no exaggeration to say that vine growing played a part in the spread of Roman civilization. The vineyards early became the objects of great care and attention. Different methods of pruning were used, and the choice of grape varieties was by no means haphazard; some were even imported from Greece. The Roman emperors were won over to viticulture to such an extent that it became their habit to abandon all other activities in order to go and harvest their own grapes.

Dionysus became Bacchus. He was endowed with the same characteristics: a staff tipped with a pine cone and garlanded with vine tendrils and strands of ivy, and a crown of vine tendrils. His chariot was drawn by panthers. He, too, was the object of an enthusiastic cult, marked by wild, sumptuous feasts that were perhaps even more frenzied than anything that had gone before.

Innumerable remains bear witness to the cult of Bacchus. The most beautiful examples are unquestionably to be found in the frescos at Pompeii and Herculaneum. At Pompeii, in particular, some superb examples can be seen in the Villa of the Mysteries, depicting an initiation rite into the mysteries of Bacchus. The towns of Pompeii and Herculaneum were, in fact, major wine-growing centres, as we are told in this epigram by Martial (40-104): 'Behold Vesuvius, once crowned with green vines whose generous fruit flooded our presses with its juice! Behold these slopes that Bacchus preferred to the hills of Nysa! But a short time ago, satyrs danced on this mountainside. It was the abode of the goddess Venus, and more dear to her than Sparta! Hercules, too, made it famous with his name. The flames have destroyed it all, engulfed it all in piles of cinders! The gods

WINE – A SOURCE OF LITERARY INSPIRATION

'It's wine that arouses me, that mad creature that makes the staidest man sing, dance and laugh until he cries, and makes us say words that would be better left unsaid.'

There is nothing surprising about these lines from Homer's Odyssey. *They are part of the Bacchic tradition that has inspired writers and poets since pagan times. It is rare to find a writer who has not, at some time, praised the vine and its fruit, and the wonderful drink that it gives us.*

'I broke a roll made of barley and honey for my breakfast, and having downed my jug of wine, I can now relax and make my beloved lyre resound.' Thus, in his poems, the Asian-Greek Anacreon (c.582-c.485BC) sang of the pleasure the company of wine can bring. Two thousand years later, François Rabelais (c.1494-1553) dedicated much of his work to singing the praises of wine. He too wrote a comically lyrical poem, at the end of Gargantua and Pantagruel, *in which Panurge dances before the Holy Bottle, the ultimate goal of his journey of initiation.*

O bouteille
Pleine toute
De mystères,
D'une oreille
Je t'écoute:
Ne diffères,
Et le mot profères
Auquel pend mon cœur.
En la tant divine liqueur,
Qui est dedans tes flancs reclose
Vin tant divin, loin de toi est forclose
Toute mensonge et toute tromperie ...

'O Bottle brimful of mysteries, I am listening to you with a single ear. Don't delay, proffer the word for which my heart longs. In the liquor so divine, enclosed within your flanks, wine so divine, from which all lies and trickery are excluded ...' It seems that, for Rabelais, wine was a bearer of truth as well as a source of pleasure; in the words of the famous saying, In vino veritas *(In wine, truth). But, surely, this much-sought-after truth is also a matter of oblivion and renunciation, the keys of real wisdom! For the 11th-century Persian poet Omar Khayyám, author of the collection of Bacchanalian poems known as the* Rubáiyát, *the mystery of wine did indeed lie here.*

'Renounce, renounce everything in this world: fortune, power, honours. Step aside from your path if it does not lead to the tavern. Ask nothing, desire nothing but wine, songs, music and love.'

Wine is the drink of oblivion, the mysterious liquid that pushes back the barriers of reality and reason and makes us lose our heads. Under its influence, Paul Valéry (1871-1945) threw his bottle into the sea, addressing an enigmatic message to the vastness of the ocean.

J'ai quelque jour, dans l'océan
(Mais je ne sais plus sous quels cieux)
Jeté, comme offrande au néant
Tout un peu de vin précieux ...
Qui voulut ta perte, ô liqueur?
J'obéis peut-être au devin?
Peut-être au souci de mon cœur,
Songeant au sang, versant le vin?

'Once (I can't remember under what skies) I threw more than a drop of precious wine into the ocean, an offering to emptiness. Who wanted your loss, O liqueur? Was I obeying some divine? Or was it a concern of my heart's, dreaming of blood, spilling wine?'

Wine is life itself, and the thirst that Molière (1622-1673) describes in Le Bourgeois Gentilhomme *is surely none other than an insatiable thirst for life!*

Buvons, mes chers amis, buvons,
Le temps qui fuit nous y convie;
Profitons de la vie
Autant que nous pouvons.
Quand on a passé l'onde noire
Adieu le bon vin, nos amours;
Dépêchons-nous de boire,
On ne boit pas toujours.
Laissons déraisonner les sots
Sur le vrai bonheur de la vie;
Notre philosophie
Se permet les pots.
Les biens, le savoir et la gloire
N'ôtent point les soucis fâcheux;
Et ce n'est qu'à bien boire
Que l'on peut être heureux!

'Drink, dear friends, drink, for the time that slips away invites us to it; let us gain as much as we can from life. When we have crossed the dark waters, there'll be no more wine, no more love; let's make haste and drink while we can, for we shall not drink forever. Fools can rave on about life's true happiness; our philosophy has room for a jug of wine. Fortune, learning and glory do not take away life's troublesome cares; only in drinking well can we be happy!'

Wine indeed exists to gladden the heart. So Scarron (1610-1660) claims, in his loose burlesque style:

Que j'aime le cabaret,
Tout y rit, personne n'y querelle ...
Jetons nos chapeaux et nous coiffons de nos serviettes,
Et tambourinons de nos couteaux sur nos assiettes,
Que je sois fourbu, châtré, bègue, tondu, cornu,
Que je sois perclus, alors je ne boirai plus.

'How I love the tavern, where all is laughter and no one quarrels ... Let's throw away our hats and wear our napkins on our heads, let's beat a tattoo on our plates with our knives, only if I were worn out, neutered, a stammerer, cropped, horned, only if I were crippled, would I drink no more.'

In human eyes, the virtues of wine are so great that the fear of being without it is very easy to understand. A century earlier than Scarron, Ronsard (1524-1585) expressed this anxiety in one of his odelettes *(little odes):*

La terre les eaux va boivant,
L'arbre la boit par sa racine,
La mer éparse boit le vent,
Et le soleil boit la marine;
Le soleil est bleu de la lune,
Tout boit, soit en haut, soit en bas;
Pourquoy donc ne boirons-nous pas?

'The earth goes drinking the waters, the tree drinks water through its roots, the scattered sea drinks the wind, and the

sun drinks the sea; the sun is blue from the moon, everything drinks, above and below; so why, then, don't we drink?'

If we must drink, we might as well drink the best: champagne, which sparkles as brilliantly as the wit of Voltaire (1694-1778), who greatly appreciated it.

Allons souper. Que ces brillants services,
Que ces ragoûts ont pour moi de délices!
Qu'un cuisinier est un mortel divin!
Chloris, Églé, me versant de leur main
Qu'un vin d'Aï dont la mousse pressée,
De la bouteille avec la force élancée
Comme un éclair fait voler le bouchon;
Il part, il rit; il frappe le plafond.
De ce vin frais l'écume pétillante
De nos Français est l'image brillante . . .

'Let's go and sup. How this gleaming tableware and these ragouts delight me! What a divine being a cook is! Chloris, Églé, pouring out for me with their own hands a wine from Ay with its fine bubbles, that make the cork shoot out of the bottle and fly through the air like lightning; it takes off, it laughs; it hits the ceiling. The sparkling foam of this fresh wine is the bright image of the French people . . .' (Le Mondain, satires, 1736.) Thus wine, the blood of the land of France, has always been sung by French poets. For example, Joachim du Bellay (c.1522-c.1560) makes an Angevin wine grower recite this pagan prayer:

Ces vigne tant utile
Vigne de raysins fertile,
Toujours coustumière d'être
Fidèle aux vœux de son maistre,
Ores, qu'elle est bien fleurie,
Te la consacre et dédie,
Thenot, vigneron et d'icelle,
Fay donc, Bacchus, que par elle
Ne soit trompé de l'attente
Qu'il a d'une telle plante:
Et mon Anjou foissonne
Partout en vigne aussi bonne!

'So serviceable and fruitful are these vines, and always faithful to the wishes of their master, and now that they are in full bloom, Thenot the wine grower dedicates them to you; please Bacchus, don't let him be disappointed in what he awaits from such plants, and make vines as good as these flourish all over my homeland of Anjou!'

But vines do not only flourish in Anjou. All, or almost all, of France is covered with them, and their origin has been called the 'French mystery', as described by Georges Duhamel (1884-1966) in his Civilisation française (French Civilization). Colette (1873-1954), whose work sings the praises of the wealth of the land, also sees the alchemy of wine as an astonishing mystery: 'The vine and wine are two great mysteries. Of all the plant kingdom, the vine alone can help us understand what the good earth is . . .' Equally mysterious is the secret ageing process undergone by wine, which François Coppée (1842-1908) compares to the cycle of life itself:

Longtemps, dans l'atmosphère humide des caveaux,
Sous la voûte profonde et de nitre imprégnée,
Sous la poussière et sous les toiles d'araignée,
Le jeune vin veillit dans les flacons nouveaux.

'In the damp air of the cellars, beneath the tall vaults steeped in nitre, beneath the dust and the spiders' webs, the young wine ages slowly in its new flasks' (Poésies diverses).

Finally, a more astonishing phenomenon still is wine's power to break down barriers between people, and to transcend everyday values, as Baudelaire (1821-1867) emphasizes in his poem le Vin des chiffoniers (The Ragpickers' Wine):

C'est ainsi qu'à travers l'humanité frivole
Le vin roule de l'or, éblouissant pactole;
Par le gosier de l'homme il chante ses exploits
Et règne par ses dons ainsi que les vrais rois.

'Thus, wine rolls its rich, dazzling gold seam across frivolous humanity, singing out its deeds from men's throats, and through its bounty, reigning as true kings do.' (Les Fleurs du mal.)

Detail from a poster by Robida from the end of the 19th century, illustrating the war with King Picrochole described in the first book of **Gargantua and Pantagruel.** *Gargantua quenches his thirst at the height of battle, probably with a jug of the same Bourgueil that Rabelais himself so appreciated.*

themselves wish their power had not gone thus far!' At least the tragedy of the year AD79 had the merit of preserving for us, almost in its entirety, the type of artistic environment with which the Romans liked to surround themselves: paintings on domestic altars, bathroom mosaics, sculptures. Everywhere, both in private buildings and in those intended for public worship, vine leaves and branches, and bunches of grapes, hold pride of place as a decorative element. Sometimes the theme of wine and drunkenness gave the artist an opportunity to depict realistic scenes, such as the statue of drunken Hercules urinating, which was discovered among the excavations at Herculaneum. Latin literature also contains numerous references to vines and wine. Pliny the Elder and Columella, in particular, are well known for their writings on wine growing and vinification. The poets were not slow to take up this theme either. Virgil sings of the joys of rural life, and gives the following advice to wine growers, in a verse from the *Aeneid*: 'Vines love an open hillside.'

The Gallo-Roman period perpetuated this tradition. Thus, in the 4th century AD, Ausonius was the first to extol the virtues of the wine of Bordeaux.

We now know that long before the Roman conquest, the Gauls, and probably the Celts among them, were growing vines. However, it is also an undisputed fact that the presence of the Romans encouraged the spread of vineyards in France, especially in the South. In fact, from the 1st century BC, the Roman provinces of Transalpine Gaul quickly took to wine growing. The regions of Arles, Vaison-la-Romaine, Bordeaux and Narbonne became covered with vineyards. Everywhere in these conquered provinces, wine growing became the established symbol of the fertility of the land and of public wealth. Bunches of grapes and ears of corn spill from the horns of plenty that painters and sculptors placed in the hands of their heroes. All the remains that have come down to us from this period abound in such images, from Marseille to Orange, from Aix to Bordeaux.

Christian images of the vine

The mythologies of Greece and Rome were progressively forgotten in the light of the triumph of Christianity. The vine could have suffered because of this, but it did not. Secular literature assigned an important role to the vine, but it became equally important in religious writings. In fact, it is impossible to open the Old or New Testaments without coming across images of the vineyard or of wine on almost every page. The grape, fruit of the Christian faith, represents the sweetness of Paradise, just as in paganism it represented the sweetness of the Elysian fields.

The mosaics of the early Christian era show naïve images of bunches of grapes and drinking vessels. Then, as the Church became stronger, it took artistic expression in hand. At the second Nicene Council, the Church Fathers decreed the following: 'The composition of pictures is not to be left to the artist. It should call attention to the principles laid down by the Catholic Church, and to religious tradition. The artistic execution alone rests with the artist, the content and its arrangement rests with the Fathers.' Although seemingly rigid, these provisions did not prevent Christian artists from giving free rein to their aesthetic sensibilities.

Romanesque art blossomed at the meeting point between two civilizations. It was in some way a synthesis between two different orders: the material order of Rome, and the spiritual order of Christianity. The Christian religion, to which it is almost exclusively dedicated, still carried traces

Detail from a fresco showing an initiation rite into the cult of Dionysus. Villa of the Mysteries, Pompeii. Late 2nd century BC.

of oriental paganism, but it delved deeper than ever before into the mysteries of man.

The Christians of that period seemed to sense that their time of trouble and insecurity was coming to an end, and began building churches. They went about this task with the utmost zeal and dedication.

This was the beginning of an artistic adventure that was as tremendous as the spiritual force behind it. Sculptures, paintings, reliquaries, gold- and silverware and manuscripts were in demand as never before. Vines and wine, now rendered sacred by the words of the Bible, flourished under the sculptor's chisel, the brush of the fresco painter and the pen of the illuminator. They also featured in craftsman's work, as we know from certain Coptic textiles from Abyssinia (Ethiopia), which have a design of grapes and vine leaves.

Sculpture disappeared with the Roman Empire. But in France at least, the Romanesque period produced the first sculptures to be allowed in church. Satan, his minions and evil itself were depicted by the stone carver as demons, and were contrasted with the vine, symbol of the Eucharist and the forces of good. The vine appeared on façades, tympanums, lintels, wall surfaces and projections. It could be found in ambulatories, on the porticoes of cloisters and the capitals of columns.

Painting also experienced a splendid revival during this period (10th to 12th centuries). This manifested itself in the anonymous frescos in churches, depicting the life of Christ and of the saints. Vines and wine, of course, feature in these. The Last Supper is illustrated over and over again. Notable French examples can be found in the churches of Vicq-sur-Saint-Chartrier and Nohant-Vic, and on the cornice of the Basilique Sainte-Madeleine at Vézelay (12th century). The churches are also filled with illustrations of tools and instruments used in wine growing: pruning knives, tubs, hatchets, knives, crushing pestles, baskets, barrels and casks.

Romanesque art took up some of the early Christian symbols, such as that of the birds drinking from a chalice, an allegory of the joys of Paradise inherited from Roman paganism. This particular symbol can be seen in the apse of the church at Aulnay-de-Saintonge in Charente-Maritime, and in the nave of the cathedral of Saint-Sauveur in Aix-en-Provence. The latter example shows griffins face to face drinking from a cup.

The art of illumination also flourished during the Romanesque period. Never before had writing been so widely practised and so honoured, for the book was a sacred object that received and transmitted the word of God. During worship, it was placed next to the cup of wine and the host. This was why it could never be too beautiful. The vine and wine, symbols of the Eucharist, were a constant source of inspiration for its illuminators. It is therefore not surprising that the sacred books of the time were often illustrated with a decorative motif of interlaced vines. The strong symbolic significance of the vine explains why it was so widely depicted in Romanesque art, which was an expression of the mysterious and the symbolic, and which always suggested more than it stated.

From the 13th century onwards, the artist acquired a greater freedom with regard both to religion and to the strictly didactic representation of scenes from everyday life.

Capital in the church of Moutiers-Saint-Jean, about 1125.

This trend became firmly established during the Gothic period. Iconographical sculpture became closely associated with the architecture of church façades. The idea now was to move the faithful by direct means, and present the Scriptures in a dramatic way. The Gothic sculptor was concerned with representing things realistically. Vines and wine therefore lost some of their symbolic significance. There is a harvest scene on the west front of the cathedral of Saint-Étienne at Bourges, and a grape-pressing scene over the main door of the cathedral of Notre-Dame at Amiens. A capital from Moutiers-Saint-Jean in Côte-d'Or, on display in the Louvre, depicts the harvested grapes being tipped into a tub. This same theme also appears on the front of the abbey church of Saint-Denis in Seine-Saint-Denis. A medallion in the Sainte-Chapelle in Paris shows Noah planting the vine. Finally, one of the choirstalls in Rouen cathedral has a carving of two Hebrews carrying a vine plant and an enormous bunch of grapes symbolizing the wealth of the land of Canaan, the Promised Land. Wine as a symbol of Christ's blood is also a favourite theme. The most famous example is the altarpiece known as *The Adoration of the Lamb* (shown overleaf), in Ghent cathedral in Belgium, attributed to Jan van Eyck (1390-1441). The art of stained glass, which is closely linked to architecture, also experienced a unique period of growth. All the great French cathedrals have decorative

*A*ltarpiece **The Adoration of the Lamb,** ***attributed to Jan van Eyck (1390-1441). Cathedral of Saint Bavon, Ghent.***

stained-glass windows: Bourges, Poitiers, Rouen, Lens, Reims, Chartres, Notre-Dame in Paris, Troyes and Metz. The vineyards, by now, had spread to the Île-de-France and the Loire valley, and vines adorned many of the most luxurious stained-glass compositions. One of the most famous wine allegories bequeathed to us in stained glass is the theme of the *pressoir mystique* (the Mystic Winepress) in the cloister of the church of Saint-Étienne-du-Mont in Paris (see page 479). The figure of Christ is positioned in the winepress itself, while the Patriarchs dig the vines and the Apostles gather the grapes.

The Renaissance: the paganization of wine

The Roman Catholic church became weakened by schisms and the spread of heresies. The Renaissance came at the right time to revive the formal and intellectual values of antiquity. It brought with it the emergence of a free and critical spirit of individualism which, in many cases, had pagan roots. It was also a time of revival for France. A national unity was beginning to take shape. The feudal tyrannies became tempered to some extent. Agriculture was developing at an astounding rate, a process that had begun in the Middle Ages. The vine, already a religious symbol, soon became one of economic prosperity.

During this period, tapestries were full of references to vines and wine. The most notable example of this is the group of floral tapestries of which there are some beautiful specimens in the Musée de Cluny. Grape harvesting scenes are also depicted in two 16th-century Flemish tapestries, one from Tournai and the other from Brussels. Wine appears in paintings depicting festive scenes, such as *La Table du Roi* (The King's Table) by Niklaus Manuel (1484-1530) or the *Marriage at Cana* by Veronese (1528-1588). Its only significance at this time, though, seems to be as a drink to quench thirst. No glasses are seen on the table; the cupbearers pour wine directly from amphoras into cups when asked to by the guests. Wine tasting had not yet come into being, but wine was the most important feature of any festivity just the same. This is also evident, too, in the *Très Riches Heures du duc de Berry* by the Limbourg brothers (early 15th century).

Now that classical antiquity had been restored to a place of honour, the greatest artists, Leonardo da Vinci, Michelangelo and Caravaggio, were able to celebrate the virtues of wine in the person of Dionysus or Bacchus. Feasts in honour of the god of wine form the subject of some very famous paintings, for example the *Bacchanal of the Andrians* by Titian (1489-1576) shown below, in which a

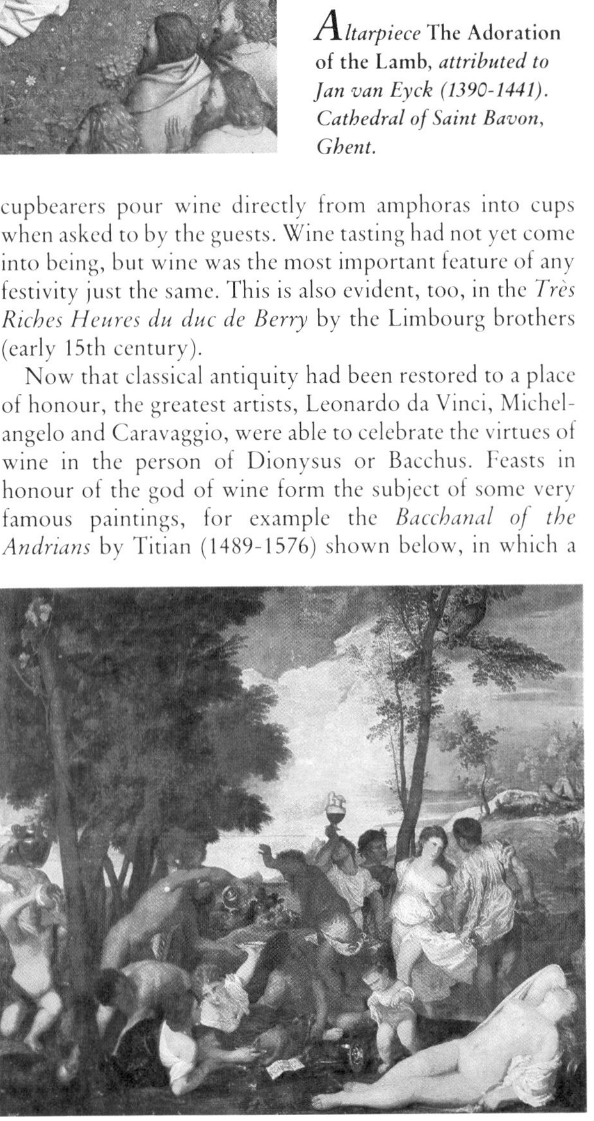

Bacchanal of the Andrians, ***by Titian (1489-1576).***

WINE — A SOURCE OF MUSICAL INSPIRATION

It is difficult for us to envisage accurately the musical events of antiquity. No doubt people sang the praises of old Silenus, foster father of Dionysus, very early on! Odes and dining songs, accompanied by flute or lyre, were inspired to a great extent by wine, as we know from those written by Anacreon (6th century BC); these in turn inspired the Renaissance genre known as Anacreontic poetry, and also much light verse of the 18th century. Playwrights were also well aware of the myth of Dionysus. In 407BC Euripides wrote a lyric tragedy called the Bacchae, *the theme of which was the punishment and death of the king of Thebes, for having opposed the introduction of the cult of Dionysus.*

Throughout Greek civilization, the cavorting, fantastic figures of satyrs and fauns inspired all kinds of airs and refrains for singing and dancing. Traces of these popular songs may well have come down through the centuries; for example, it is claimed that in the 19th century, wine growers from the Marseille area still used to sing fragments in Greek from an ode by Pindar, at harvest time.

In the Middle Ages, classical odes were adapted to suit the tastes of the day by the troubadours and trouvères. *We may also assume that urban and street songs from that time praised the vine and its fruit, but unfortunately none of them has survived. The earliest examples of such songs we have are from the 15th century, like this anonymous piece:*

Bon vin, je ne te puis laisser
Je t'ay m'amour donnée
Je t'ay m'amour donnée
Souvent m'as faict la soif passer,
Bon vin, je ne te puis laisser.

'Good wine, I cannot leave you/I have given you my love/I have given you my love/You have often quenched my thirst,/Good wine, I cannot leave you.'

All the signs point to the fact that this tradition continued throughout the Renaissance. The laborious work of tending the vineyards certainly gave rise to folk songs:

Chantons la serpette!
Tous vignerons ont en elle recours,
C'est le secours
Pour tailler la vignette,
Ô serpillette, Ô serpillonnette!

'Let us sing of the pruning knife!/All wine growers use it/To help them/Prune the vines,/O little pruning knife, sweet little pruning knife!'

Drinking songs are of urban origin. They are generally literary works, and it is not unusual to find in them mythological allusions to Dionysus and Bacchus. Some of them date back as far as the 15th century, like those in a manuscript kept in Bayeux. The work of 16th-century polyphonic song-writers is full of such allusions.

This genre flourished above all in the 17th and 18th centuries. For example, the famous French song of the Knights of the Round Table is from this period:

Chevaliers de la Table ronde
Goûtons voir si le vin est bon (. . .)
Si j'en meurs, je veux qu'on m'enterre
Dans une cave où y a du bon vin.

'Knights of the Round Table/Let's taste the wine and see if it's good . . ./If I die of it, please bury me/In a cellar full of good wine.'

Musicians drew much inspiration from this inexhaustible source. The theme of wine, merrymaking and dance eventually reached its peak of expression in the operetta. Johann Strauss immortalized champagne in Acts II and III of Die Fledermaus. *The theme of wine is often present in the work of Jacques Offenbach, especially in* la Périchole *and* Tales of Hoffmann, *both of which have a drinking chorus in the prologue and the finale.*

However, it would be wrong to say that the theme of wine is confined to what is generally considered to be a minor musical genre. Wine soon featured in any libretto that included popular festivities. Thus Jean-Philippe Rameau ended his comic opera Platée *with a ballet honouring Bacchus. A few years later, wine provided the inspiration for Christoph Willibald Gluck when he composed the scenes of rejoicing in* Alceste. *In the chorus of Act II of* The Abduction from the Seraglio, *Mozart celebrated the joys of drink in brilliant fashion. Wagner, who took his subjects from mythology and legend, was no exception to the rule; in* Parsifal, *the motif around which the plot revolves is the Holy Grail, the cup from which Christ is supposed to have drunk during the Last Supper. Closer to our times, in 1929, Alban Berg composed a song for soprano and orchestra entitled 'Wine', based on poems from* Les Fleurs du Mal *by Baudelaire.*

Italian musicians have also exalted wine, giving free rein to their generous musical vitality. Antonio Rossini, for example, did so in the drinking chorus of Act II of Count Ory, *as did Giuseppe Verdi in the Garter Inn aria from that masterpiece of comic opera,* Falstaff. *This particular aria sings the praises of wine as a cure for gloominess. Verdi had already extolled the virtues of wine in the aria 'Let's drink from the joyous chalice' from* La Traviata. *Finally, Gaetano Donizetti's love potion in* L'Elisir d'Amore *was none other than a flask of Bordeaux!*

It was easy, of course, for French composers to take wine as a theme of musical inspiration. In Act II of Béatrice et Bénedicte, *Hector Berlioz places a drinking song on the lips of Somarone. In Charles Gounod's* Faust, *the King of Thule sings of the virtues of the fruit of the vine. In Georges Bizet's* Carmen, *the toreador sings 'Votre toast je peux vous le rendre' ('I can return your toast'). The glory of wine is also emphasized in* Werther *and in* Le Jongleur de Notre-Dame *by Jules Massenet. Finally,* Samson et Dalila *by Camille Saint-Saëns is a theatrical* danse bacchanale *in the purest tradition of antiquity.*

central figure is seen admiring the colour of the red wine contained in the carafe he holds; *The Young Bacchus* by Caravaggio (1573-1610); *Bacchus* by Leonardo da Vinci (1452-1519); and the *Triumph of Bacchus and Ariadne* by Annibale Carracci (1560-1609).

The late Renaissance abounds with examples of art inspired by the legend of Bacchus. The Dutch artist Abraham Bloemaert (1564-1651) painted a scene of the gods at a banquet, in which drunkenness was portrayed in a realistic manner. Jacob Jordaens (1593-1678) used this same theme in his famous painting *The King Drinks*. Grapes feature many times in his work, as in the painting that shows his family with one of his daughters holding a basket of grapes. The bunch of grapes was a very common theme in religious paintings of the time, especially the Virgin offering grapes or a bunch of grapes to the Infant Jesus. It can be seen in a painting by the German painter Hans Memling (*c.*1433-1494); in the work of Martin Schongauer (*c.*1445-1491), also German; and of the Italian painter, Masaccio (1401-1428).

At the same time, the decorative arts of the Renaissance, and gold- or silversmith's work in particular, were almost entirely given over to the cult of wine drinking. Princes and rich bourgeois gentlemen drank the best *crus* of their day from richly decorated chalices or goblets. German metalworkers were particularly good at making these. One fashion was for shells set in silverware, and an example of these ingenious vessels features in *Queen Artemis* by Rembrandt (1606-1669). Such articles of gold- and silverware were popular all over Europe throughout the 16th century.

From the 18th century to modern times: wine in festive mood

The end of the Renaissance also saw the end of the great era of mysticism and religious fervour. The monumental fabric of cathedrals and monasteries had been completed; the allegiance of artists to the imperatives of religion came to an end. It was now the dawn of the 18th century, and monarchs were in the process of establishing the unity of their kingdoms. They assumed the role of artistic patronage previously played by the Church, and employed artists to decorate their castles and châteaux. Painting benefited more than other arts from this change of direction and, of course, wine had its place in this new pictorial world. During this period, wine became a powerful stimulus to the imagination of artists, and ever since then, its representation has mainly found expression through painting. The great themes connected with wine were still exploited, but in a more lighthearted way. An illustration of this is the treatment given to the legend of Bacchus and his attendants in paintings such as *Los Borrachos* (The Topers) by Velázquez (1599-1660), in which Bacchus is depicted surrounded by a group of merry drinkers; *Drunken Silenus* by José Ribera (1591-1652); *l'Enfance de Bacchus* (The Childhood of Bacchus) by Nicolas Poussin (1594-1665); and *The Two Satyrs* and *Drunken Silenus* by Rubens (1577-1640).

The influence of Dutch painting placed wine firmly in the realm of everyday life, in the intimate surroundings of people's homes. This influence gave rise to paintings of mealtime scenes, showing the opulence of bourgeois life at the time. But the Dutch and Flemish painters were not the only ones to bring back the gentle atmosphere of interior scenes. French artists such as Jean-Baptiste Chardin (1699-1779) and the Le Nain brothers (early 17th century) also painted them. In the Le Nain brothers' *le Repas des paysans* (The Peasants' Meal) the characters are sharing their wine with a certain solemnity. It was during this era that still-life painting, which had never managed to find its place in an artistic world fashioned by religious constraints, established itself as a discipline in its own right. Glasses and casks were an important element of still-life paintings, as can be seen in *The Large Glass* and *Large Glass of White Wine, with Crabs* by Pieter Claesz (1597-1661); *la Nappe* (The Tablecloth) by Chardin; and in a still life by Georg Flegel (1563-1638) showing a pitcher and goblet.

Ovid wrote, 'wine inclines the soul towards love'. This truth has given birth to a number of works that feature scenes of love with wine much in evidence, such as those painted by Jean-Marc Nattier (1685-1766), a rival of Watteau. Rembrandt, who did not come from a wine-growing country at all, was tempted by this subject in *Saskia and Rembrandt Drinking a Glass of Wine*. Wine even appeared in the context of sinful love, as in *The Procuress* by Vermeer (1632-1675).

The euphoria engendered by wine is similar in every way to that which can be aroused by love, and this may have been

Double Portrait with a Glass of Wine, *sometimes also called* **Lovers with a Glass of Wine,** *by Marc Chagall (1887-1985).*

WINE AND CONTEMPORARY ART

There are close links and analogies between wine and painting, and these have long been emphasized by specialists in both fields. Lately, a certain amount of experimental research has been carried out in this area. It has taken two directions. Firstly, there is the artist who tastes a wine, and then paints a picture in which he strives to reproduce the sensations he has felt. Secondly, there is the taster who tries to make an association between an already existing painting and a wine that he or she feels arouses the same emotion.

The painting shown below left is by Didier Michel, an artist from Touraine, and represents a 1976 Arbois vin jaune. *This wine is characterized by a range of sustained and powerfully contrasting tones which are reflected by the colour contrasts within the painting.*

Serge Dubs, sommelier *at the Auberge de l'Ill at Illhaeusern, Alsace, immediately associated a 1979 Savigny-lès-Beaune Premier Cru with the painting shown below* Was bleibt? *(What is left?), by Günter Scholz. Serge Dubs' notes on the analogy, made in 1985, are given below.*

'The viewer instantly feels in harmony with this picture. It has great charm, and at the same time great force of expression. The same goes for the bouquet of Valentin Bouchotte's 1979 Savigny-lès-Beaune Hauts-Jarrons. This red burgundy does not have the colour of an old wine, rather, it is reminiscent of freshly picked strawberries or raspberries. Furthermore, the colour is not dense. That is not to say it is attenuated, but it has a certain limpidity, which is also a surprising characteristic of the painting in that the background shines through and reveals itself brightly to the eye.

'The best quality of this wine is its perfume. Its charm lies entirely in its well-developed bouquet. You can tell straight away that the wine is fresh and pleasant to drink. You want to taste it immediately. It is delicate and fine in the mouth, but only for a brief moment, which is typical of this type of cru. *It always has an abundant bouquet. It is a wine that one does not forget and that one takes pleasure in remembering. The same goes for the painting.'*

Günter Scholz, 'Was bleibt?' 1983, 84 × 105cm.

Didier Michel, 'Vin jaune d'Arbois Savagnin 1976.'

Jacques Puisais's notes: 'A chromatic scale of powerfully contrasting perfumes. With its deep, muted harmonies, it conjures up visions of proteinaceous undergrowth rich with black fungi, root stocks, the oiliness of fertile soil. The brilliance of moist fluorescent moss shines out in these half-muted surroundings, while the general harmony suggests the passion and violence of mutually fertilizing extremes.'

Le déjeuner champêtre *(The Country Picnic), by Maurice de Vlaminck (1876-1958).*

the message Marc Chagall (1887-1985) wished to convey to us in the painting *Double portrait au verre de vin* (Double Portrait with a Glass of Wine, shown on page 516), in which the male figure, who is holding a glass of wine, seems to be flying away above his female companion.

Finally, and above all, wine expresses the festive spirit of celebratory gatherings, such as the paintings of village feasts by Bruegel the Elder (1525-1569); the somewhat less exuberant gathering in *Officers of the Militia Company of Saint Hadrian* by Frans Hals (1581-1666); and the *fêtes galantes* of Antoine Watteau (1684-1721) and of his imitator, Nicolas Lancret (1690-1743) in *la Danse à la campagne* (Country Dance).

The 17th and 18th centuries can also take pride in the fact that they left a magnificent collection of portraits of drinkers, including *The Merry Toper* by Frans Hals, *Man with a Glass of Wine* by Velázquez and *The Drinkers* by Goya (1746-1828).

Far from repelling painters, drunkenness inspired them. As a theme, it is depicted in *The Allegory of Taste* by Bruegel; *The Drinker* by Adriaen van Ostade (1610-1685); *Le déjeuner de jambon* (The Ham Lunch, shown on page 545) by Lancret; and *The Country Outing* by Goya.

However, wine also came to be represented in a completely negative way, as a symbol of degradation and debauchery, for example in *le Retour de l'ivrogne* (The Return of the Drunkard) by J.-B. Greuze (1725-1805); or earlier in *The Corruption of the World* by Cornelis van Haarlem (1562-1637) and *Loth et ses filles* (Lot and his Daughters) by Jan Massys (1509-1575).

The development of large-scale wine production and the coming of the railways in the 19th century contributed greatly to the spread of wine drinking. Typical social gatherings of the time were immortalized in paintings of remarkable freshness and gaiety, such as *le Déjeuner des canotiers* (River Picnic, shown on page 576) by Renoir (1841-1919), *Bal au Moulin de la galette* (Dance at the Moulin de la Galette) by Dufy (1877-1953), and *le Déjeuner sur l'herbe* (Picnic on the Grass) by Manet (1832-1883), in which the wine placed on the tablecloth constitutes the organic and tonal nub of the composition.

It is also during this period that places for drinking wine, such as cafés, restaurants and clubs, multiplied, thus providing a new and very productive source of inspiration. Examples are Manet's *Un bar aux Folies Bergères*; *le Café de nuit* by Vincent van Gogh (1853-1890); and *Au café*, by Gustave Caillebotte (1848-1894). Toulouse Lautrec (1864-1901), who was a pillar of these establishments, has given us some famous portraits of drunkards.

This immense body of work has contributed at least as much as literature has towards providing us with enthralling evidence of the manners, customs, dress and history of generations that have gone before. It has, equally, helped us to understand the place of wine in the many societies of the past.

Nowadays, wine is no longer a symbol, as in the Middle Ages, nor yet simply an invitation to a feast of the senses, as in the 17th, 18th and 19th centuries. It is often no more than a trigger for artistic improvisation, as shown by the still-life paintings of Cézanne, Braque, Gauguin, Matisse, de Vlaminck, de Staël and Juan Gris.

Even today, though, the myth of Dionysus is not dead, as is testified by the painting of Salvador Dali (1904-1989) entitled *Dionysus Spitting out the Complete Image of Cadaqués on the end of the Tongue of a Woman with Three Shelves*. With a picture like *Buveurs* (The Drinkers) by André Dunoyer de Segonzac (1884-1974), the artist gives us a painter's translation of the world of the wine *terroir*. Artistic inspiration continues to come from wine, even though the development of modern oenology has apparently sounded the death knell of wine's symbolic role. It is now appreciated for its own sake. No doubt it will continue to be present in art, but perhaps in a different form, with a new symbolic status.

Les vignes rouges *(Red Vines), Vincent van Gogh (1853-1890).*

WINE MUSEUMS

Wine, vineyards and wine growing are given a place of importance in some thirty museums in France. This is thoroughly justified by the rich history of French wine, its economic importance, and the cultural significance it possesses.

Wine cannot but enjoy a favoured position in French museums. There are many museums devoted to it, and these constitute a testament to the work of the dedicated men and women down the ages who have given their lives to the vine and to wine.

Wine within Western civilization

From the times of antiquity, wine has been celebrated by poets, writers and artists, whether Greek or Roman, pagan or Christian. The place of wine in the art of our civilization was thus established, and this has lasted and been enriched down the centuries. To be convinced of this, you have only to think of Titian, Veronese, Michelangelo, Velázquez, Goya, Rubens, Rembrandt, the Le Nain brothers, Poussin, Watteau, Delacroix, Cézanne, Corot and Van Gogh, all of whose works were inspired by wine and the vine. And such a list contains only painters ...

But the museums echo equally vividly the work and the traditions of the wine growers whose activity was such an intimate and perennial part of daily life in the vineyards and countryside of France. Tools and machinery recalling times past are shown, and many of these have today become invaluable *objets d'art.* Vine cultivation, the tools used for this, the history of the vineyards and their social organization all differ from one wine-growing region to another. Each regional institution has taken pains to reflect this, in its own way. This is why the wine museums, scattered about France, are complementary to one another. Many different museums are necessary to show the richness and the diversity of this heritage to its full extent.

Today the production of wine is an extremely important economic activity in many of the regions of France. French wine museums provide an essential link between traditional and modern wine growing. They are the living showcase of a dynamic activity rooted in the everyday life of an epoch.

The first museum of wine

In 1927, in the cellars of the Musée Unterlinden, sited in a 17th-century monastery in Colmar, the first serious attempt was made to provide exhibition space devoted to wine. Among the superb objects put on view there were showpieces of the guild cooper's craft dating from the 17th and 18th centuries. In this way, the vineyards of Alsace came to have their own museum. So, later, would all the other wine-growing regions of France, in a movement which gathered momentum after the Second World War.

After Beaune's Musée du Vin was opened in the *hôtel* of the Dukes of Burgundy, in 1947, every founder of such a museum was at pains to choose an outstanding location and building for it: here a 13th-century château, there a Dominican convent, an episcopal palace, a Benedictine abbey, a monastery or simply a wine grower's house.

A typical, traditional Alsace cellar, with decoratively carved casks. Musée Unterlinden, Colmar.

SMALLER FRENCH WINE MUSEUMS

Angers *Since 1937, the Musée de Vin at Angers has occupied the 12th-century cellars of the Greniers-Saint-Jean. Wine-presses, vats, baskets, growers' tools, local edicts and the insignias of guilds can be seen there.*

Arbois *The town hall cellars, excavated between the 14th and the 18th centuries, house a museum which shows the history of the vine and of wine, the work of the wine grower through the seasons, and the work of associated craftsmen such as the cooper, the carpenter and the basket maker.*

Bergerac *The Cloître des Récollets, built between the 12th and 18th centuries, contains the Maison du Vin and the Musée du Vin et de la Tonnellerie (Museum of Wine and Cooperage).*

Béziers *Since 1935, a 14th-century Dominican monastery has contained the Musée du Vieux Biterrois (Museum of Old Béziers). One of the collections there is devoted to the history of wine growing.*

Cloître des Récollets, Bergerac.

Le Chambon-sur-Lignon *Wine growing is recalled by the ancient winepresses exhibited in the Musée des Arts et Métiers du Massif Central (Museum of Arts and Crafts of the Massif Central).*

Chinon *A museum with wax figures recounts the life of the wine grower and cooper.*

Cognac *Six rooms and the central hall of the Musée de Cognac are devoted to vine cultivation, wine production, distilling, cooperage and the* négociants' *role in cognac production and marketing.*

Condom *The Musée de l'Armagnac occupies outhouses of the old episcopal palace, dating from the 18th century. Its collections concern armagnac production within the wider context of wine growing's place in society.*

Hautvillers *A museum is housed in the buildings of the old Benedictine abbey of Hautvillers. It recalls the life and work of Dom Pérignon, whose cell and laboratory have been re-created there. The casks and tools which were used in making champagne in earlier times can also be seen in the museum.*

Kientzheim *The Musée du Vignoble et Vins d'Alsace (Museum of the Vineyards and Wines of Alsace) is housed in the Château de Kientzheim, belonging to the Confrérie Saint-Étienne d'Alsace. A wine grower's cellar has been re-created there, and all the tools formerly used for cultivating the vine, as well as a collection of glasses, bottles, decanters and stone jugs from the 15th century to the present day, are on exhibition in a series of the Château's rooms.*

Narbonne *The Maison Vigneronne in Narbonne shows the history of vineyards in Aude via the evolution of wine-growing and wine-making tools.*

Le Pallet *Collections devoted to the arts and popular traditions of the vineyards of the Nantes area can be seen at the Musée Pierre Abélard, sited in the former Chapelle Saint-Michel of le Pallet.*

Paris *The Paris Musée du Vin is housed in the vaulted cellars of the old wine store of the Couvent de la Visitation. There you can see tools used in wine growing, cooperage and vinification, and thousands of bottles. Wax figures show the art of wine making via a series of tableaux.*

Saint-Pourçain-sur-Sioule *The former Prison de la Justice Seigneuriale (Prison of Feudal Justice), dating from the 11th century, contains a Musée de la Vigne et du Vin (Museum of the Vine and of Wine).*

Saint-Yzans-de-Médoc *The Musée des Outils de la Vigne et du Vin (Museum of Wine-growing and Wine-making Tools) is housed in a former* chai *at Saint-Yzans-de-Médoc. On display are tools once used in the vineyards and cellars of the South West, and of the Bordeaux region.*

Salles-d'Angles *One room of the museum sited in the stables of the presbytery of Salles-d'Angles is devoted to vine cultivation.*

Selles-sur-Cher *The Musée Municipale d'Histoire et de Traditions Locales (Municipal Museum of Local History and Traditions), housed in a royal abbey dating from the 17th century, contains a collection of exhibits on the subject of vine cultivation.*

Sigean *The Musée des Corbières occupies an 18th-century house at Sigean. One room contains numerous documents relating to wine, and to the life of wine growers in Corbières.*

Suresnes *The Musée Municipale René-Sordes at Suresnes has on exhibition a number of tools and works of art connected with vines, wine growing and the life of wine growers in the 19th century.*

The Musée de l'Armagnac, Condom.

Beaune's Musée du Vin

The location of this museum is superb. The *hôtel* of the Dukes of Burgundy, with the Gallo-Roman town walls at its rear, contains buildings of the 13th, 15th, 16th and 18th centuries in a perfect state of preservation. The exhibits have been collected with great care and patience by André Lagrange, the author of a book called *Moi, je suis vigneron* ('I am a wine grower') — a true love poem about his profession and the vine. André Lagrange researched some 600 wine-growing communes of Burgundy, from the Côte d'Or itself to all the other vineyards of the region. He questioned and photographed old wine growers. He looked through their cellars and their storerooms and found forgotten tools there, discarded but precious, and salvaged them, thus carrying out the work both of a historian and an ethnologist.

To visit the museum at Beaune is to follow the development of wine growing from the shores of the Mediterranean up to Burgundy, and from Roman times up to the present day. It is to learn about wine production down the centuries and through the seasons: the grape harvest, treading and pressing the grapes, the vinification and *élevage* of the wine, tools used before industrialization, early machines . . . Two superb tapestries exhibited in the great hall of honour, *Le Vigneron* (The Wine Grower) by Michel Tourlière and *Le Vin, source de triomphe de la mort* (Wine, the Source of Death's Triumph) by Jean Lurçat testify to wine's role as a source of artistic inspiration. The museum also contains much of ethnological interest in its documentation of the social relationships of those associated with the vine. It is worth pausing in front of the faithfully reconstructed interior of a wine grower's house in Savigny-lès-Beaune around 1875, in order to enter into the atmosphere of the 'wine-growing community of Burgundy' with its traditional celebrations, its wine tasting and its commercial activities.

The Musée d'Épernay

The Musée du Vin et du Champagne in Épernay transports us back to the beginning of the 19th century, to times before the devastation wrought by the phylloxera louse.

In glass cases, wax models, faithfully dressed in the clothes of the time, repeat the unchanging movements of a century when all work was done by hand. The actions of the growers surrounded by their traditional implements, the actions of the grape sorter seated behind an osier tray resting on two *mannequin* baskets, the actions of the cellarman transferring wine from vat to cask, filling the bottles, storing them horizontally (*sur latte*) and then in *pupitres*, disgorgement, the adding of the *liqueur d'expédition*, the final corking, and the muzzling of the corks can all be seen by visitors.

In the press room, a press 7m high can be seen. It is called a 'squirrel press' (*pressoir à écureuil*) because, to tighten the screw, the vineyard workers used to clamber up the spokes of a big wheel like squirrels in a cage. There is also a full collection of old bottles, glasses, labels, and posters.

The Musée de Tours

At Tours, the great 13th-century vaulted Gothic wine stores of the abbey of Saint-Julien have housed the Musée des Vins de Touraine since 1975. This museum forms part of the even larger Musée de Compagnonnage (Museum of Trades and Crafts). It is here, in Tours, that Roger Lecotté has created the most comprehensive wine museum of France, with a collection of historical objects from antiquity to the present day. The museum's very attractive visual approach highlights the role that wine has played in daily social life.

To visit this museum is therefore to experience traditional French family rituals — meals celebrating a first communion, betrothal, marriage, a golden wedding, a hundredth birthday; as well as traditional social rituals — local religious celebrations, a patron saint's day, commercial festivities or the festivities of the Touraine *confréries*. Wine's broader religious significance is examined, via the iconography of the Mystic Winepress (*see* page 478), the Marriage at Cana, and much of the imagery of St John's Gospel. This museum tells of the gastronomy of Touraine too — the *miot* (red wine and bread soup), mulled wine; and it also documents the dangers and ravages wrought by wine.

Museums in the Bordeaux region

The wines of Bordeaux are featured in several museums. One of the most remarkable is at Château Mouton-Rothschild in Pauillac, taking as its theme 'Wine and the vine in art'. Baron Philippe de Rothschild created a museum which is unique for the quality of its exhibited works — pictures, tapestries, sculptures, furniture, porcelain, glassware, jewellery — exhibited in a beautiful setting: an old 19th-century *chai*.

There are examples of both antique and modern art at Mouton-Rothschild. The visitor can admire a Mycenaean wine cup of the 13th century BC; a Greek lecythus on a white base decorated with the figure of Dionysus; decorative pieces of Renaissance goldwork; English and Italian furniture; Japanese, Chinese, pre-Columbian and Venetian pieces; Roman busts; and contemporary works by Man Ray, Chadwick, Soulages, César, Morris Graves and Tchelitchev, wine being of course the common source of inspiration in this permanent exhibition.

A temple to wine

Our last port of call is the small island of Bendor just outside Bandol, in Var. On the initiative of Paul Ricard, the Exposition Universelle des Vins et Spiriteux (Universal Exhibition of Wines and Spirits) was opened here in 1958. Since then, several million people — tourists and professionals, French and foreign visitors alike — have visited it. This permanent exhibition-cum-museum, regarded as a world 'temple of wines and spirits', is situated in that part of the Mediterranean which is the cradle of wine culture, dedicated to Bacchus and to Dionysus since the times of antiquity.

The modern buildings cover an area of 875sq m, and have been decorated with some 500sq m of frescos by young artists under 30 years old at the time of commission. It was the wish of Paul Ricard that this exhibition should express the modern character of wine culture.

Visiting these five important museums is certainly not enough for those who want to immerse themselves fully in the regional specificity of each wine-growing area. This brief tour of France does, though, show that wine continues to be a permanent link between rural tradition, art and a prosperous future, from generation to generation.

Tâche, La

The vineyard of La Tâche in the commune of Vosne-Romanée on the Côte de Nuits has a formidable reputation throughout the world. Certain connoisseurs go so far as to revere this wine as the greatest of the Grands Crus of Vosne-Romanée, claiming it to be superior to Romanée-Conti. The source of this justified passion is a pocket-sized vineyard of only 1.5ha, or 6ha when parcels in the neighbouring Premier Cru vineyards of Gaudichots and la Grande Rue are included, situated to the south of La Romanée and Romanée-Conti. These few magical hectares are regulated by the decree of 11 September 1936, which imposes the following conditions of production: a minimum alcoholic strength of 11.5° and a maximum yield of 30hl/ha. Lovers of fine red burgundy look forward keenly to the release of the 1,700 or so cases of this wine each year. It is rounded and full, with a bouquet of violets and an exceptionally distinguished taste. Here is one of the princes of Burgundy, if not the king himself.

Tannat

Synonyms: *Tanat*, *Tannat Gros*, *Tannat Mâle*, *Moustrou*, *Moustroun*, *Moustron* in Landes, *Madiran* in the Adour basin, *Bordeleza Belcha* in the Basque country.

Growing tips open, felty white with carmine margins.

Young leaves downy, bullate, with bronze-coloured patches.

Leaves medium sized, truncate, dark green, coarsely bullate, wavy, with the edge of the blade convex, three-lobed with upper lateral sinuses wide, acute at base, petiolar sinus with overlapping edges; petiolar junction pink; dentation convex, wide; underside of blade arachnoid. The leaves redden fully in the autumn.

Green shoots ribbed, red at nodes and brown on the side exposed to the sun; tendrils thin, small.

Bunches held by a long peduncle, medium sized, cylindrical with two shoulders, compact; grapes spherical or slightly ovoid when compressed in the bunch, medium sized, very dark red-purple to blue-black, thin skinned, rich in colouring matter, flesh juicy with a grassy or leafy taste, slightly astringent; ripening period: third epoch.

This is a very vigorous vine with late budbreak; it performs well if stake-trained and pruned long. It is productive and gives a deeply coloured wine, rich in tannins, which needs several years to mature before it is drinkable. By then it has lost its harshness and has acquired an aroma reminiscent of raspberries. In the Madiran AOC, it may not be used for more than 60 per cent of the blend, the remainder being provided by the Cabernet Franc (locally known as the Bouchy) and the Fer (locally known as the Pinenc). These other varieties soften the Tannat.

Seven registered clones have been approved, the most useful being numbers 398 and 474. Classified as 'recommended' in the South West, Languedoc and Provence, the Tannat now covers 3,225ha in contrast to the 4,192ha occupied in 1958. It is used for the AOCs of Béarn, Madiran and Irouléguy, and the VDQS *appellations* of Tursan and Côtes de Saint-Mont, in the following *départements*: Gers (1,546ha), Landes (527ha), Pyrénées-Atlantiques (604ha), Hautes-Pyrénées (122ha). It is also cultivated in Lot (75ha), Lot-et-Garonne (128ha), Tarn-et-Garonne (178ha), Haute-Garonne (18ha) and Aude (38ha).

One of the five Grands Crus in the commune of Vosne-Romanée is the vineyard of La Tâche, which produces a fine red wine with a splendid bouquet.

Tarabassie

Synonym: *Taraboussié* in Aveyron.

This Aveyron variety is grown in the Lot valley, at Nauviale, Estaing and Saint-Côme-d'Olt. It is vigorous, with average productivity. Unclassified.

Tavel

Vines have been cultivated here since at least 887, initially by the monks of Saint-André-de-Villeneuve. But it was in the 14th century, with the approbation of Popes Clement VII and Benedict XIII, that Tavel became a vineyard area of repute, first as a wine-growing village in its own right, then as the leading area of the Côte du Rhône Gardoise.

We still do not really know where the tradition of rosé wine-making — rosé being the only wine type produced in Tavel — came from. Some have suggested that a mishap in vinification produced such a felicitous result that efforts were made to reproduce it. Others maintain, and this seems more likely, that the soil of Tavel, like the soils of all the Côte du Rhône vineyards in Gard, has always produced wines of a lighter colour and body than the vineyards of the left bank.

The *appellation d'origine contrôlée* was ratified by decree on 15 May 1936 for the commune of Tavel and a few plots at Roquemaure. The vineyard area occupies 870ha, and produces on average 3,500hl a year, of which 1,500hl are made by the cooperative at Tavel.

The grape varieties used are typically Mediterranean. The Grenache dominates, with smaller amounts of Cinsaut and Syrah; and white varieties are also cultivated: Clairette, Bourboulenc, and Piquepoul Blanc.

The soils consist of poor, thin sands, red clays mixed with white calcareous pebbles, and a large terrace of water-borne quartz pebbles — debris of alpine origin.

Some of the grape varieties are lightly crushed, while others are used whole; they are then macerated for several hours. The musts undergo centrifugation to clean and settle them before fermentation, which takes place under temperature-controlled conditions (between 15° C and 20° C).

Typical features of the rosé wines of Tavel are their rosé colour, which is very pure initially, later acquiring hints of gold as the wine ages. The bouquet has distinctive odours of summer fruit and fresh almonds. They are surprisingly dry, with charm and length.

The vineyards of Tavel, planted in poor, stony soil, produce a velvety, full-bodied rosé wine with an intense colour.

Teinturier

Synonyms: *Teinturier du Cher, Gros Noir, Gros Noir de Villebarou* in Loir-et-Cher, *Bourguignon Noir, Noir d'Orléans, Auvernat Teint* in Loiret, *Noir à Tacher, Teinturier Mâle Tachant* in Puy-de-Dôme.

Growing tips felty white with carmine margins and red stipules.

Young leaves downy, completely red with underside of blade felty white.

Leaves orbicular, bullate, crimped at the petiolar junction with the edges of the blade red and red veins, deeply five-lobed with lateral sinuses concave and wide at base, petiolar sinus lyrate, more or less narrow, dentation convex, medium sized; underside of blade downy-pubescent with pubescent veins. The leaves become speckled with red from June, and by the autumn this reddening is complete.

Green shoots ribbed, mahogany-red, brown on the side exposed to the sun; tendrils small, thin, red. Bunches small, cylindrical-conical, compact; grapes small, spherical or slightly ovoid, black with deeply coloured juice; ripening period: first epoch.

This red-fleshed variety played a large role in the past in the vineyards of the Loire valley, mainly in the Orléans area, where it produced wines with a deep colour. These were transported to Paris during the 17th and 18th centuries where they were used by merchants there for blending with other wines. The soubriquet '*Dix fois coloré*' (Ten times coloured) was given to the grapes to indicate that they could colour 10 times their own volume of white wine to a passable red.

The variety was tried out in the Midi, where its lack of vigour and its small bunches led Louis Bouschet to cross it with various southern varieties to produce new Teinturier strains, wrongly called Bouschet hybrids. Later one of these, the Alicante Bouschet, was used by Ganzin to produce the Alicante Ganzin, a Teinturier variety subsequently used by other hybridizers such as Seibel and Seyve-Villard. The Teinturier itself has not been classified, and only a few hectares of it remain.

The Teinturier Femelle is distinguished from the Teinturier Mâle by its bronze-coloured young leaves; its adult leaves more deeply lobed, reddening later; its more lightly coloured green shoots and its more lightly coloured juice, as indicated by its own soubriquet '*Cinq fois coloré*' (Five times coloured).

Tempranillo

Bunches medium sized to large, cylindrical, long, narrow, sometimes winged, compact;

grapes medium sized, spherical, blue-black, skin quite thick, pulp fleshy, juicy; ripening period: third epoch.

This is a Spanish variety with midseason budbreak; its grapes ripen several days before those of the Carignan. Its productivity is satisfactory and regular. It produces wines which are strong in alcohol, powerfully aromatic, deeply coloured, which keep well and are of better quality than those from the Carignan, although at the expense of lower yields. Seven registered clones have been approved, the best being number 771. Classed as 'recommended' in the whole of the Midi, this variety is in fact only planted in Hérault and Aude.

Téoulier

Synonyms: *Téoulié*, *Petit Téoulier*, *Grand Téoulier*, *Thuillier*, *Petit Thuillier*, *Thuillier Noir* in Alpes-de-Haute-Provence, *Plant Dufour* in Hautes-Alpes, *Plant de Manosque*, *Plant de Porto* at Marseille, *Manosquen*, *Taurier*, *Teinturier Téoulier*, *Trouillère*.

Bunches medium sized, conical, compact, with two shoulders, short; grapes ovoid, blue-black; ripening period: second epoch.

The Téoulier has early budbreak, which exposes it to spring frosts, and this variety can also be affected by very severe winter frosts, as in 1956. It is somewhat prone to oidium (powdery mildew) but has better resistance to downy mildew. Its grapes keep well but do not have much juice. Its wine is very deeply coloured, hence its name of Teinturier Téoulier, and it contributes both colour and solidity to blends. This grape, long cultivated in Provence in the Manosque region, was grown less and less widely as the Bouschet hybrids proliferated during the post-phylloxera reconstruction of the vineyards. Classed as 'recommended' in Bouches-du-Rhône, where it is one of the specified varieties for AOC Palette, and in Hautes-Alpes and Alpes-de-Haute-Provence, there are now only a few hectares of it left in cultivation.

Terret Gris

Synonyms: *Tarret*, *Terrain*, *Terret-Bourret*.

Growing tips open, felty white with carmine margins. Young leaves downy, bullate, with bronze-coloured patches.

Leaves medium sized, truncate, soft, contorted, smooth, five-lobed with upper lateral sinuses deep, concave and quite wide at base, petiolar sinus lyrate, narrow with overlapping edges; dentation convex, medium; underside of blade arachnoid and pubescent.

Green shoots markedly ribbed, arachnoid at the tip, pale green, with faint red streaks; tendrils small, thin.

Bunches medium sized to large, conical, compact, winged; grapes oblong or slightly ellipsoidal, grey, skin firm, flesh juicy; ripening period: third epoch.

This is a vigorous variety with an upright habit and late budbreak, susceptible to diseases. Its productivity is satisfactory, reaching 100-150hl/ha on fertile ground and 50-80hl/ha on hill slopes. The wine is fresh, light, dry, with a medium alcoholic strength. It has no great individuality, and is used as a base wine for making vermouth. In the past, it was distilled to produce *eaux-de-vie* in Languedoc.

Classed as 'recommended' in Languedoc and 'authorized' in Provence, the Terret Gris, together with the Terret Blanc, covers nearly 9,000ha, mainly in Hérault (7,658ha) and in Aude (1,215ha).

The Terret Blanc, sometimes called Bourret Blanc, has the same qualities as the Terret Gris, but it is only cultivated on the edges of the Bassin de Thau, whereas the Terret Gris is more widely spread throughout Languedoc, and particularly in the Hérault valley. The Terret Blanc is classed as 'recommended' in Languedoc and 'authorized' in Provence.

The Terret Noir has foliage which reddens slightly in the autumn. It is less productive than the Terrets Blanc and Gris, giving a pale, fresh, light, fragrant wine which blends well with more full-bodied, firmer wines such as those from Grenache or Mourvèdre grapes. Classed as 'authorized' in Provence and 'recommended' in Languedoc and in Vaucluse, it is used for the Châteauneuf-du-Pape, Côtes du Rhône, Coteaux du Languedoc, Corbières, Costières du Gard and Fitou AOCs. As a result of this, its cultivation is spreading: Hérault (782ha), Aude (268ha) and Gard (73ha) in 1985, making a total of 1,150ha compared to 131ha in 1958.

Thouarsais, Vins du

There is little demand for this *appellation*, classified VDQS on 10 August 1966. The area declared for the appellation varies between 15ha and 20ha from year to year. About 450hl of white wine are produced and 350hl of red and rosé. The white wine is based on the Chenin Blanc grape (with up to 20 per cent Chardonnay) and the red wine on the two Cabernet varieties (with some Gamay). The area of production extends over 16 communes or parts of communes in Deux-Sèvres.

The colour of the whites is quite deep. The reds have a carmine hue, while the rosés are rather paler. The white wines and the rosés are delicate and lively; the red wines supple and without astringency. These are simple but distinguished wines. They mature well in the bottle.

Tibouren

Synonyms: *Tiboulen, Antiboulen, Antibouren, Antibois, Tibourin, Gaysserin, Geysserin.*

Bunches medium sized to large, conical, winged, not very tightly packed; grapes medium-sized, ovoid, black, juicy; ripening period: second epoch.

This is probably a vine of eastern origin because the lobing of the leaves and the luxuriant felting on the blade is very similar to certain grape varieties of the Eastern Mediterranean. Its budbreak is midseason and its grapes, which make a pleasant table variety, ripen in the last two weeks of August. The Tibouren is susceptible to downy mildew, anthracnose and *coulure* (flower abortion). It is a fertile vine producing 30-60hl/ha on slopes, with a high alcoholic strength of 12° to 14°, while on flat ground it can produce as much as 100hl/ha. Its wine is fine, delicate, light in colour and should be drunk in the year of production. Classed as 'recommended' in Provence, it was in the past the basic variety used for wine growing around Saint-Tropez. Since then, its cultivation has extended within Var (448ha) and a little into Bouches-du-Rhône (3ha), where it is one of the specified varieties for the Côtes de Provence and Palette AOCs, and the VDQS of Coteaux Varois.

Touraine *See* page 530 for the Touraine regional entry.

At Panzoult near Chinon, in the heart of Touraine, the vineyards are situated on tufa, a chalky rock giving the wine a slightly mineral character.

Touraine

This vineyard area of about 4,000ha was classed AOC by decree on 24 December 1939. It produces an annual total volume of 240,000hl. This includes 26,000hl of white wine from the Sauvignon Blanc variety and between 20,000 and 50,000hl from the Chenin Blanc and Arbois varieties. Some 30,000hl of rosé wine is produced every year from the Cabernet Franc (locally known as the Breton), Cabernet Sauvignon, Côt, Pinot Noir, Meunier, Pinot Gris, Gamay, Pineau d'Aunis and Grolleau varieties. The Teinturier varieties Gamay de Chaudenay and Gamay de Bouze are also allowed up to a limit of 10 per cent. Annual production of red wine is around 15,000hl, from the Cabernet Franc, Cabernet Sauvignon, Côt, Pinot Noir, Meunier, Pinot Gris and Gamay varieties. The Pineau d'Aunis may also be used, but for *primeur* wines only. The area of production extends over the *départements* of Indre-et-Loire, Loir-et-Cher and Indre, covering a total of 70 communes or parts of communes.

The rosés are dry, full and fresh. The whites made from the Sauvignon Blanc (sold as Sauvignon de Touraine) are dry, full and lively with a characteristic blackcurrant-leaf aroma. The other whites of Touraine (with no grape variety specified on the label) are dry, quite firm, lively and full.

Red Touraine *primeur* wines are light, fruity and lively, with a cheerful, rustic character. The ordinary red wines are tasty, with good tannin levels, permitting development in bottle. Their colour is of medium depth, with crimson and redcurrant hues. The white wines are straw yellow in colour, and the rosés are a pale pink. Characteristic of all of the wines is a vegetal, fruity and floral aromatic range, sometimes with mineral hints. The taste is always well balanced, always lively.

Touraine-Amboise

This vineyard was classed AOC by decree on 24 December 1939, with revisions being made to the decree on 15 July 1955 and then on 7 November 1966. It covers 160ha. The grape varieties used are the Chenin Blanc for white wines and the two Cabernet varieties, Côt and Gamay for red and rosé wines.

Average annual production is around 2,800hl of white wine, 4,800hl of red wine and 1,500hl of rosé. The area of production extends over the following communes or parts of communes: Amboise, Chargé, Cangey, Limeray, Mosnes, Nazelles, Pocé-sur-Cisse, Saint-Ouen-les-Vignes.

The whites are straw yellow to amber yellow in colour. Their aroma is fruity, floral and well developed. After sunny years, the wines are full and solid, well balanced, off-dry to medium dry. They keep well in bottle.

The red wines are full, supple and lively with a firm structure. They mature well. The rosés are dry, well structured and elegant.

Touraine-Azay-le-Rideau

This vineyard area, classed AOC by decree on 24 December 1939, extends over 50ha. The Chenin Blanc variety is used for white wines. For rosé wines the grape varieties used are the Grolleau (to a minimum of 60 per cent), with the Gamay, Côt, Cabernet Franc and Cabernet Sauvignon (to a maximum of 10 per cent). The average production of white wine is 1,300hl per year, and of rosé 950hl per year.

The area of production covers the following communes: Azay-le-Rideau, Artannes, Cheillé, Lignières-de-Touraine, Rivarennes, Saché, Thilouze, and Vallères.

The white wines are straw yellow in colour, becoming golden as they age. They have a fruity and floral aroma, sometimes with mineral hints. They are supple, delicate and lively, and age well in bottle. The rosés are delicate, elegant and tasty. They are pale pink in colour.

Touraine-Mesland

This vineyard area, classed AOC by decree on 24 December 1939, with modifications to the decree on 20 November 1962, covers some 200ha. The grape variety used for white wines here is the Chenin Blanc, and the varieties used for red and rosé wines are the Gamay, Côt, Cabernet Franc and Cabernet Sauvignon. Annual production is around 1,200hl of white wine, 8,000hl of red wine and 1,000hl of rosé.

The area of production covers the communes or parts of the communes of Mesland, Chambon-sur-Cisse, Chouzy-sur-Cisse, Molineuf, Monteaux and Onzain.

The red wines are a beautiful ruby red in colour. They have a well-developed fruity aroma. They are firmly structured and cleanly flavoured. The rosé wines are lively and supple. The whites are dry and firm.

Touraine Mousseux

The vineyard area for this AOC, classed by decree on 16 October 1946, covers the same 70 communes or parts of communes as the Touraine AOC, for white and rosé sparkling wines only. Red sparkling wines to be sold as Touraine Mousseux are grown in the same communes or parts of communes as for the Bourgueil, Saint-Nicolas-de-Bourgueil and Chinon AOCs. Production is around 30,000hl of sparkling white wine and 800hl of sparkling rosé wine. Tiny quantities of sparkling red wine are also produced.

Azay-le-Rideau produces fruity white wines and light and supple rosés.

Various grape varieties are used. For white wine, the Chenin Blanc and Arbois are the main varieties used, with a maximum of 20 per cent Chardonnay and a maximum of 30 per cent Cabernet Franc, Cabernet Sauvignon, Pinot Noir, Pinot Gris, Meunier, Pineau d'Aunis, Côt and Grolleau. For the rosé wines, the grape varieties used are the Cabernet Franc, Pinot Noir, Gamay and Grolleau. The Cabernet Franc alone is used for sparkling red wines.

White Touraine Mousseux is a full-bodied but refreshing wine. The rosé is supple and lively; while the red wine is an interesting curiosity. It allies finesse and delicacy with the firmness of the Cabernet.

Touraine Pétillant

This lightly sparkling wine AOC was created by decree on 24 December 1939, with modifications to the decree being made in July 1959. Production is modest — only 5 per cent of the Touraine Mousseux total. The grape varieties used are the same as for the Touraine *appellation*, and the areas of production are the same as for the Touraine Mousseux AOC.

Tourbat

Synonyms: *Malvoisie du Roussillon*, *Malvoisie des Pyrénées-Orientales*.

Growing tips open, felty white with carmine margins.

Young leaves downy, yellowish with bronze-coloured patches and felty pink-white underside.

Leaves medium to large, orbicular, contorted, finely bullate, five-lobed, with lobes of average size and definition, sinuses shallow and narrow, petiolar sinus lyrate, narrow or with slightly overlapping edges; dentation medium sized, ogival; underside of blade arachnoid-pubescent. Green shoots ribbed, glabrous, with brown longitudinal striations.

Bunches medium sized, cylindrical, sometimes winged, loose; grapes medium sized, ovoid, white to slightly pink in colour when overripe, juicy; ripening period: third epoch.

Classed as 'recommended' in Aude, Hérault and Pyrénées-Orientales, the Tourbat is one of the varieties specified for the *vins doux naturels* (sweet fortified wines) of Banyuls, Maury and Rivesaltes, but it is little cultivated (only 20ha) as it is very degenerate. The introduction of Sardinian stock has enabled new experiments to be carried out with the variety in Roussillon. VDN wines produced from the Tourbat have finesse and a characteristic bouquet, and are of generally high quality. The wines have quite a deep golden-yellow colour with fairly high acidity, higher than that of other VDN varieties.

The Tourbat is of average vigour, often with a bushy habit, and with fairly good fertility. It is susceptible to oidium (powdery mildew) and to magnesium deficiency. It is also cultivated in Sardinia, where it is thought to have been of Iberian origin.

Tressot

Synonyms: *Tresseau*, *Ancien Tresseau*, *Tréceau*, *Tréceault*, *Tressiot* in Auxerre, *Irancy*, *Vérot*, *Verrot de Coulanges*, *Petit Vérot* at Joigny, *Nérien*, *Nairien* or *Noirien* at Bar-sur-Aube, *Nerre* or *Petite Nerre* in Haute-Marne, *Pendoulat* at Brienne.

Growing tips open, felty white with carmine margins. Young leaves downy, orange, with bronze-coloured patches.

Leaves medium sized, truncate, finely bullate, crimped at the petiolar junction, with convex edges, five-lobed with lateral sinuses open, deep, concave at base, sometimes with a single tooth at the bottom of the sinus; petiolar sinus lyrate with overlapping edges; dentation pointed, medium sized, not very prominent; underside of blade downy white.

Green shoots ribbed, light green with pale pink nodes; tendrils long, light green.

Bunches medium-sized, cylindrical, compact; grapes small, spherical, black; ripening period: second epoch, early.

This is a variety from the Auxerre region of Burgundy. It is very susceptible to oidium (powdery mildew), and it grafts badly, and these factors have led to a decrease in its cultivation. It is productive, yielding an agreeable wine which brings acidity and tannin to blends with the Gamay and Pinot Noir varieties. Although classed as 'authorized' in Yonne, it is now grown on less than one hectare there. The Tressot Blanc differs from the Tressot Noir only in the white colour of its grapes.

The Tressot Panaché (Variegated Tressot) is a curiosity: either its grapes have white, grey and black stripes on them, arranged like melon slices; or they have a variegated coloration of either red speckles on white or the reverse.

Trousseau

Synonyms: *Triffault*, *Toussot* at Besançon, *Troussé* at Salins, *Trusseau* in the Vosges, *Trussiau*, *Trussiaux* in the Loue valley, *Cruchenton Rouge* and *Capbreton Rouge* in Landes, *Sémillon Rouge* in Gironde.

Growing tips open, felty white with carmine margins.

Leaves large, orbicular, extremely bullate, crimped at the petiolar junction, slightly five-lobed with upper lateral sinuses acute and narrow at base, lower lateral sinuses barely defined, petiolar sinus lyrate, narrow, with overlapping edges; dentation convex, medium sized; underside of blade arachnoid. The foliage reddens in autumn.

Green shoots faintly ribbed, green with some longitudinal brown striations and pink nodes; tendrils fleshy, medium sized.

Bunches small, cylindrical, compact, winged; grapes small, slightly ovoid, black with soft pulp; ripening period: second epoch.

This very vigorous variety has to be pruned long. It is susceptible to anthracnose, grey rot (botrytis) and winter frosts. Production is good, passing 100hl/ha on occasion. The Trousseau gives a dark purple, full-bodied wine that keeps well if yields have not been too high. Wine from the Trousseau is best blended with that from the Poulsard: the latter contributes finesse, while the former ensures a long life in bottle.

Six registered clones have been approved, of which the best are numbers 302, 476 and 590. Classed as 'recommended' in Jura and Doubs, there are now only 74ha in Jura.

Troyen

Synonyms: *Troyen Noir* in Aube and Côte-d'Or, *Galbot* in Aube, *Framboise* at Arrentières (Aube), *Gamery*, *Gamelin*, *Gamay Vert* in the Aube valley, *Petit Gamay* in the Marne valley, *Vert Plant* in the Ornain valley, *Jacquemart* in the Côtes de Toul, *Varenne Noire* and *Plant de Varennes* in Meuse, *Fontanet, Gouligny, Gamay de Rolampont* in the south of Haute-Marne, *Liverdun, Faux Liverdun, Ericé Noir, Petit Ericey, Ricey de Bourgogne* in Moselle and the Vosges, *Renard* in Meurthe.

Bunches small, cylindrical, compact, sometimes winged; grapes small, spherical, blue-black; ripening period: first epoch.

The Troyen is an old grape variety of the Aube and Yonne areas, equally widespread in Meuse, the Vosges and Moselle. It has, though, practically disappeared from cultivation as it has not been classified. It is fertile and productive, giving a light wine.

The vineyards of Tursan in Landes have been in existence since antiquity.

Tursan

This vineyard area of 350ha extends over 41 communes in the southeast of Landes, together with a small area in Gers. Situated on the left bank of the river Adour, the vines nestle in the foothills of the Pyrenees, with the picturesque town of Geaune in their centre. They acquired VDQS status with the decree of 11 July 1958.

The vineyards of Tursan have been in existence since earliest antiquity. After 1152, the wines of Tursan were exported to England and also to Cordova and Seville. From the 15th to the 18th centuries, they were popular in Holland and Germany too. Then they went into a long decline. The renaissance of the vineyards began in 1950, as a result, in particular, of the cooperative movement in the area.

Maritime influences dominate the climatic regime of Tursan. Winters are mild; there is considerable rainfall in spring; summers are hot and dry; autumns are long and sunny, which helps the grapes to ripen perfectly. The average annual amount of sunshine is 1,700 hours, with 900mm of rainfall.

The wine-growing slopes, mostly sited between 100m and 150m, consist of siliceous clay soils on top of a base of limestone molasse or pebbly rubble from Pyrenean fan deltas. These permeable soils are very suitable for wine growing.

A number of grape varieties are used, most of which are characteristic of the vineyards of the western Pyrenees. For the white wines, the main grape is an old local variety, the Baroque; the Marsanne, Raffiat de Moncade, Petit Manseng and Gros Manseng are also used. For the reds and rosés, the Tannat is the main variety used, together with the Cinsaut, Cabernet Franc (locally called the Bouchy) and Cabernet Sauvignon.

Production has increased regularly since 1981, reaching an annual total of 1,100hl in 1985. Sixty per cent of the harvest provides red and rosé wines and 40 per cent white wines.

The white wines have a fine, bright colour, and taste of ripe fruit with a hint of sweet almonds. The rosé wines have a bright redcurrant colour, a delicate fruity taste and are supple and silky. The red wines have an attractively deep purple colour. They are well structured, tannic but supple, with a hint of incense and of resin in their flavour.

LE VIN DES SABLES

In earlier times, the Landes département *possessed some vineyards of great repute, planted in the sands between the dunes and the forests at Capbreton on the Landes coast (producing* vins des sables *or 'sand wines'). There are still many vines left at the foot of the dunes today, the relics of vineyards which disappeared as a result of the major earth-moving works of Louis de Foix, who altered the course of the river Adour.*

During the 1980s, agricultural and forestry workers, accompanied by a team of ampelographers from INRA, and technical advisers and oenologists, have been making efforts to revive some plots of these pleasant, delicately aromatic wines. There now exists a small centre of production of wines from the sands at Messanges, some 20km to the north of Capbreton. If the initiative is successful, vins des sables *could once again play a part in the rural economy of the Landes coast.*

TOURAINE

Under the pastel blue sky of Touraine, in this 'garden of France', with its fertile soils and slowly turning seasons, the relationship between man and vine could not fail to blossom. The wines of Touraine express the full measure of this rich friendship.

Like every part of the Loire region, Touraine has long been inhabited and vines have undoubtedly been growing there for centuries. Celtic monuments, of which there are more in Touraine than anywhere else in France except Brittany, are proof of very early human presence here, although there is no evidence that these ancient inhabitants of Touraine made or drank wine.

At the time of the Roman invasion, there would have been more than 100,000 people living in Touraine. The Emperor Domitian's edict of AD92, ordering the uprooting of half the vines of the provinces of the Roman empire, was particularly grievous in this region, where the hills lend themselves so admirably to vine cultivation; thus, as soon as Probus allowed the Gauls to plant vines again, in 280, there was an immediate renaissance of the Touraine vineyards. In their celebrations of wine, François Rabelais and Pierre de Ronsard — both of whom came from Touraine — testified to the permanence of the vine's presence in the region. Traces of many a lively wine-growing tradition can be found. At the Château de Chenonceau, a vine tended by Marie de Medici may be seen. At the Château de Meaulevrier at Lerné near la Devinière, beside the house where Rabelais was born, you can see a vine which has withstood phylloxera. There are some Cabernet Franc vines in Touraine that are several hundred years old. In 1893, the wine growers of Touraine founded the Union Viticole. In 1911, this organization contained more than 700 vineyard owners and growers.

The town of Chinon, around which the historic vineyards of this appellation *have developed.*

The soils of Touraine

Touraine has not always been the fertile garden it is today. At the time of the Jurassic period, about 180 million years ago, the ocean was slowly covering the region with the sedimentary deposits that now swathe it. During the following Cretaceous period, Touraine remained submerged. Deposits of green sandstone were laid down, covered with calcareous tufa, the thickness of which varies today between 175m and 200m.

At the end of the Cretaceous period, a natural upheaval in the earth's crust meant that the part of Touraine situated to the south of the present-day course of the river Vienne emerged from the ocean. A lacustrine period followed, with vast areas of fresh water accumulating in the districts of Château-la-Vallière, Montbazon, Luynes and Bléré. A further upheaval of white sedimentary rock called *feluns* took place, followed by a final upheaval which created the Touraine of today, making viticulture possible.

Most of the vineyards are planted in calcareous tufa soils, covered by Tertiary period sands partially mixed with siliceous clay produced during the decalcification of the limestone rock. The vines' roots have to penetrate a deep layer (30cm to 1m thick) of this mixture before reaching the calcareous tufa. This limestone rock gives the wine a certain softness. The valleys of the Loir, Loire, Cher, Indre and Vienne, which flow from east to west, and their tributaries, which flow from north to south, provide the region's vineyards with broadly similar situations and aspects. But the wines differ slightly in character from one another due to differences in individual vineyard sites and microclimates.

At Bourgueil and Chinon, for example, there are relatively deep banks of ancient gravels which collect solar energy, making the production of quite strong red wines possible.

Further up the hillside, there is a band several hundred metres wide of siliceous limestone and clay soil known as *aubuis*. This

According to the vintage and its climatic peculiarities, the vineyards of Vouvray produce dry, medium dry or sweet wines.

gives fine, solid white wines from the Chenin Blanc grape variety, one that is particularly successful here. Deeper clay soils with a siliceous top layer, known as *perruches*, produce more firmly structured wines. The pattern of soils along the valley floors is more or less stony, calcareous or siliceous; each is appropriate to viticulture, and root penetration is limited on these sites, reducing yields — always a prerequisite for quality.

The Touraine region never suffers from drought. The limestone rock acts as a reservoir of water, feeding the soil by capillary action, and the closeness of the valley sides promotes the formation of dews, which refresh the vines during periods of fine weather.

The grape varieties

The white wines come from three grape varieties: the Chenin Blanc (locally called the Pineau Blanc de la Loire), the Sauvignon Blanc and the Arbois. The most extensively used grape variety is the Chenin Blanc, thought to be native to the Loire valley. As in Anjou, it is very versatile and can produce a range of white wines from sparkling to still, dry to sweet, depending on the weather conditions during the year.

The Sauvignon Blanc is the main grape variety in the eastern part of Touraine, and it is known as the Surin there. It produces dry wines with well-developed, typically musky aromas reminiscent of blackcurrant leaf.

The Arbois variety has no connection with the town of the same name in the Jura. It is, in fact, a relation of the Chenin Blanc. It is only found in Touraine, where it is also called the Menu Pineau.

The grape varieties used for red wines are more diverse still. These have arrived in Touraine from two directions: northwards up the Rhône valley, and eastwards down the Loire valley from Nantes, at which port they arrived from Aquitaine.

Touraine is the only region in France which produces wines from the Cabernet Franc alone (locally called the Breton). The Cabernet Sauvignon is also grown, but produces ordinary wines here except where it is planted in certain gravelly soils. It is not widespread.

The Côt (also known as the Malbec) was introduced to Touraine a long time ago. It is not an easy vine to grow, as it has a tendency to *coulure* (flower abortion). It brings fruitiness to blends.

The Grolleau, another variety probably native to the region, can be vinified into red, rosé or white wine, and is also particularly well-suited to the production of sparkling wine. It has good resistance to grey rot (botrytis). Its wines are very fine and delicate, without tannin or aggressive acidity.

The Pineau d'Aunis is a moderately aromatic grape variety. Small amounts of Pinot Noir, Pinot Gris and Meunier can also be found in the region.

The climate

Touraine has one of the most stable and moderate climates in France. The average rainfall, measured over a century, produces a figure of around 50mm for every month. This even, regular distribution reinforces the popular image of Touraine as a garden.

The warmth of summer, like the cold of winter, is never excessive here. Maritime influences are fading at this point, and the north winds are blocked by the Loir hills. The

The length of life of Vouvray wines can be over 100 years, as with the 1858, 1874, 1921, 1947 and 1959 vintages. These are wines of great breeding.

microclimates of the different river valleys give individual accents to the wines.

Despite the regularity in climatic conditions from month to month, annual climatic variations can be considerable, giving the wines a profile that changes regularly.

The style of the wines

The wine growers of Touraine like their wines to be a very faithful reflection both of the local vineyards and of the year's climatic conditions.

Touraine

To produce the red wines of the Touraine AOC, the Gamay is used for fruit, the Cabernet Franc and Cabernet Sauvignon for structure, the Grolleau for finesse and the Côt for flavour and richness. This combination produces a light, lively, firm wine with a characteristic freshness, and aromas of summer fruits and spice. The red *primeur* wines are made from the Gamay alone, and are very fruity, pleasant and sound.

The white wines of the Touraine AOC, when made from the Chenin Blanc, are dry or off-dry and well structured. In the eastern sector of Touraine, the Sauvignon Blanc is used, and this variety produces a dry white wine with characteristically vegetal aromas.

The rosés are generally dry. They are made from one or several different grape varieties, each of which will contribute different characteristics to a wine according to the nature of the soil. For example, in south-facing *perruche* soils (deep clay with a siliceous topsoil), the Côt will provide structure, the Gamay will soften the wine, the Cabernet Franc will ensure its aromatic development, and the Grolleau will bring finesse. According to each specific vineyard and its microclimate, 'man the gardener' plays with combinations of different grape varieties just as an organist plays several notes together. A harmonious result, happily reflecting the vineyard environment, is achieved.

The sparkling wine of Touraine is the result of secondary fermentation in bottle, taking place over a minimum of one year, as prescribed by law. Because of the size of the region, many grape varieties can be used. The Chenin Blanc, though, is the main grape variety, and the one that gives the best results here. Most of the sparkling wine is Brut, but some (less dry) Sec is also produced. There are some beautifully elegant sparkling rosé wines produced in Touraine too.

Touraine-Mesland

The red wine of this AOC is produced on rather stony and more or less siliceous soil which suits the Gamay perfectly. It produces a 'complete' wine and there is no need for other grape varieties to be used. The prime importance of *terroir* is well demonstrated here; the grape variety itself is of secondary importance.

A rosé wine is produced in small quantities here, and is dry and full, especially if made by the *saignée* method, in which a part of the must is macerated with the grape skins prior to

Cabernet Franc vines on the former terraces of the Vienne between Cravant-les-Coteaux and Panzoult.

fermentation. White wines, dry in style, are produced in tiny quantities.

Touraine-Amboise

The area of production of this *appellation* extends to both sides of the Loire, and red, white and rosé wines are produced.

White wines are principally produced in the part of the zone that lies adjacent to the Vouvray *appellation*. They are the product of just one grape, the Chenin Blanc, and are dry to medium dry, or even sweet after very sunny vintages, such as 1959, 1964 and 1976. They mature well in the bottle.

The rosés are dry or sometimes just off-dry. They are fine and delicate, particularly when the Côt has played a part in their preparation.

Gamay is usually the dominant variety for the red wines. The Côt and the two Cabernet varieties stiffen and bolster the blend, which then develops perfectly in bottle.

Touraine-Azay-le-Rideau

The white wines, made from the Chenin Blanc alone, are off-dry, their hint of sweetness varying according to climatic conditions from year to year. They mature well in bottle.

The rosés, made from at least 60 per cent Grolleau, are delicate and pleasant.

Montlouis

All of the white wines of Montlouis are made from the Chenin Blanc. They can be dry, medium dry, or sweet depending upon the weather conditions of the year: dry if the summer has been only moderately good; sweet if the summer has been fine and sunny. When young, these wines are both supple and full, and very lively. They mature very well in bottle, developing a bouquet reminiscent of the scent of robinia flowers.

In years when there has been little sun during the summer, much of the *appellation* harvest will be vinified as sparkling white wine of structure and breed.

Vouvray

The white wines of Vouvray are made exclusively from the Chenin Blanc, as tradition dictates. But the annual weather conditions produce a great variety of wines. So it is indispensable when discussing Vouvray, as indeed all Touraine wine, to relate wines to vintages in order to understand their style: dry, medium dry or sweet. It is, of course, the sweet wines that have given Vouvray the fame it enjoys.

The sparkling Vouvray Mousseux wines are made according to traditional quality practices, but the lightly sparkling Pétillant wines have, if anything, more character than the Mousseux, and greater longevity. Nature plays a leading role in the manufacture of these wines in that the wine growers prepare them from the musts of less sunny years, ideally suited to sparkling-wine manufacture.

The former homes of cave dwellers hollowed out of the tufa in the Montlouis area, where the Chenin Blanc grows so successfully.

Bourgueil

This wine, made from the Cabernet Franc variety, is of two distinct kinds. When it is grown on gravel terraces, it has strength, finesse and the friendly, smoky aroma of the hearth, mixed with the scent of red summer fruits. When it comes from the cooler growing conditions found on the limestone slopes, the tannin in the wine is more pronounced, but is soft in texture, thanks to the action of the limestone.

Saint-Nicolas-de-Bourgueil

This wine is a neighbour of the preceding one and comes from the same grape variety. But the vineyards are a little further from the Loire and have their own microclimate. This led the wine growers to claim a separate *appellation*. The wines are a little less dense than those of Bourgueil, but have finesse.

Chinon

The main grape variety used here is also the Cabernet Franc. The production zone benefits from the favourable climatic conditions on the left bank of the Loire, and on both banks of the Vienne. As at Bourgueil, two main kinds of wine are produced, depending on soil type: those grown on gravelly soil, and those grown on the mainly limestone and clay *aubuis* soils. The wines may be enjoyed both very young and after long years of maturing in bottle. If the year has been a sunny one, then the wine will have a greater propensity for longevity.

Coteaux du Vendômois

The white wine of this VDQS is dry. It is produced from the Chenin Blanc and the

Chardonnay varieties. The Pineau d'Aunis produces a supple red or rosé wine with spicy aromas.

Coteaux du Loir

Red, white and rosé wines are grown on the hills or *coteaux* of the Loir valley. The white wines, made from the Chenin Blanc, are generally dry. The Pineau d'Aunis is the main variety used for the red and rosé wines and it gives them a very attractive spicy flavour. The wines are in general light and elegant.

Jasnières

The vineyards of AOC Jasnières are situated on a slope which overlooks the right bank of the Loir. The wines, which are made from the Chenin Blanc, are fine and full, with an excellent length of life in the bottle.

Vins du Haut-Poitou

The light, tasty red wines of this VDQS *appellation* are produced from various grape varieties, including the Gamay, Pinot Noir, Cabernet Franc, Cabernet Sauvignon and Côt. The white wines are dry, full and delicate.

Vinification in Touraine

White wine vinification

A special feature of the vinification of white wines in Touraine is the retention of malic acid. The wine-making practices used, based

THE WINE OF MY ROOTS

Burning bundles of twigs in heaps at the end of the rows to warm our hands, scraping wooden clogs clean twenty times a day with the end of a little stick, these were my first contacts with the vine . . . It was in 1925 . . . Just after the war . . . In this part of Touraine, near Bourgueil, orphan children worked from one end of the year to the other in the vineyards! . . . At that time, wine was cheaper than bread and served as our nourishment . . . The vine was a mother's breast to us . . .

When I was twelve years old, I was apprenticed to a cooper. In the autumn he used to put me in his Marne taxi and we went to gather grapes, pick apples or collect chestnuts. It was from him that I learned to put wine into bottles . . . Bourgueil, Vouvray . . . While travelling we drank a little . . .

But it was cooking that really brought me to wine. I researched, experimented and compared. After the Second World War, I opened a little restaurant. I had to offer my customers wines that they would like . . . I spent whole days tasting . . . Once again, wine came to be associated with hard work for me. Nevertheless it allowed me to build up a very good cellar of local Loire wines . . . Vouvray, Chinon, the wines of the Coteaux du Loir which hardly exist any more . . . Little by little, I got to know all the wines of the Loire. I opened my cellar to Anjou, to Muscadet, to the wines of the Cher valley . . . To Quincy and Reuilly, with their characteristic 'goût de genêt' ('taste of broom') . . . Then I discovered the wines of Bordeaux — which at that time I found distinctly inferior to our Loire wines! — then the wines of Burgundy . . . I went to the vineyards . . . visited them . . . In all, that lasted ten years.

At present, I pride myself on a good knowledge of the wines of France. But it is those of the Touraine that I prefer to all others and, even more than just those of the Touraine, those of my childhood, the wines of Vouvray, then of Bourgueil. They have remained as I knew them. Less amiable than those of Chinon, these are virile wines, tannic, hard and tense like the clay and limestone soil from which they come. The terroir *. . . That is what I want to re-create in my cooking . . . I have many friends who are wine growers . . . They are the most upright, true and sincere men that I know. Whereas many people think that outward appearances are all that matter, those men have remained true to the less visible part of themselves — their roots. And how right they are for, in the end, what else is there left of real interest apart from our roots? . . .*

My whole conception of cooking with red wine derives from the notion that I have developed about wine. A favourite trick of mine is to cook saltwater fish and freshwater fish with red wine. Why always fall back on white wine with fish? It was, in fact, with carp à la Chambord, *cooked in red wine, that I was successful in the 'Best Chef of France' competition . . . I particularly like using wine lees for sauces. Only lees give the consistency and the fragrance that wine, generally over-filtered, is no longer able to give.*

In principle, I never suggest that customers should drink the same wine which was used to make the sauce with the dish. It would be bad for this single note to be sustained so lengthily . . . On the contrary, reduced and heady food essences need a good crack of the whip. They need to be accompanied by fresh-tasting wines, young wines, even cloudy new wines . . . For example, I served my coq au vin de Chinon 1982 *with a Chinon 1985.*

But wine is much more than a simple gastronomic pleasure. It is a symbol of communion. I have a particularly dear friend that I seldom get to see . . . For many years, I'd been saving a rather rare bottle . . . A Château d'Yquem 1916, the year of my birth . . . One day when he came we drank it. This wine was gold; for us, as we drank it, it was a symbol, the perfect embodiment of our friendship . . . What is extraordinary is that wine ages much better than we do, however much care of ourselves we have taken. It can live on for years and give pleasure to several generations . . . For me, that is the most wonderful proof of the superiority of things over beings.

Charles Barrier

on research into low fermentation temperatures, aim to prevent lactic bacteria from multiplying and initiating malolactic fermentation.

Another important point of note is that new presses have been introduced during the 1980s. These are horizontal presses, and they permit easier handling of the grapes and the marc. At the same time, the way in which the must is extracted in these presses produces results which are comparable to or even better than those achieved using the old presses.

Pressing times are still long, four hours on average. During pressing, must selection is practised: juice which has been subjected to oxidization, or which contains impurities, will be set aside and fermented separately. Every year and every day, the wine grower carries out his pressing differently. It is a mixture of art and craft, and responds to the ever-changing conditions of the grape harvest.

The finest wines of Touraine are fermented in casks or large casks housed in caves hollowed out of the tufa rock where the temperature is a constant 12°C. Fermentation under these conditions continues for one, two, even three months. It is sometimes necessary to heat the caves to bring fermentation to completion. Some of the other white wines, and the sparkling wines, are fermented in vats, and in this case, cooling methods are used to ensure a long fermentation time.

The wines are then racked three times before the month of March. For cask-fermented wines, a sulphured wick is burned in the cask on each occasion. The weight of the burned wick is determined by the type of wine to be produced. This very old and simple practice has three different purposes: to protect the wine from contact with the air, to prevent unwanted yeasts and bacteria from multiplying in the cask, and to aid the eventual clarification of the wine.

Before bottling, which generally takes place in March, the wines are filtered. The old fining agents of the past need no longer be used thanks to the more efficient equipment and materials available today.

The wines then develop in bottle; this is an important particularity. The white wines, especially, undergo *élevage* as well as acquiring maturity in bottle. The length of time they need in bottle depends upon the vintage, in other words the amount of sun the grapes received during the year. Bottles are always stored in caves hollowed out of the rock in Touraine, and thus remain at a constant temperature, sheltered from light and from vibrations. Relative humidity is likewise a constant 100 per cent. This, too, helps the wine's development by permitting the cork to keep itself moist from the surrounding air and not from the wine, which in turn minimizes the development of an air gap between the wine and the cork.

Cellars in Vouvray where sparkling wines are prepared and stored.

Rosé wine vinification

Most of the rosé wines of Touraine are obtained by the direct pressing of red grapes, but the practice of *saignée*, in which a part of the must is macerated with the grape skins prior to fermentation, is also used, particularly in years of abundance.

After fermentation, three rackings and the customary filtration treatments, the wines are bottled in March. In certain cases, bottling is postponed until September, but this is not generally a good idea since the wines lose their freshness and their finesse in the intervening period.

Appellation regulations permit the marketing of Touraine rosés as *primeurs*. Growers have not fully exploited this opportunity yet, which is a pity.

Red wine vinification

There are two main approaches to red wine vinification in Touraine. One is used for the Cabernet Franc wines of the *appellations* Bourgueil, Saint-Nicolas-de-Bourgueil and Chinon, and also for the Gamay-based wines of AOC Touraine. The other is a special technique used for the preparation of red *primeur* wines.

The production of Touraine *primeurs* relies partially or completely on carbonic maceration, a vinification practice ancient in principle but for the first time fully understood today,

A double-walled oval cask on arched supports, with oak wood outside and acacia wood inside. Exhibition piece by Raymond Besnard, known as 'Blois — L'Ami-des-Arts'.

TOURAINE'S PRODUCTION PROFILE	White	Red	Rosé	Sparkling
AOC				
Touraine	52 000(1)	94 000	2 000	30 000
Touraine-Amboise	2 800	4 600	1 500	
Touraine-Azay-le-Rideau	1 300		950	
Touraine-Mesland	1 200	8 000	1 000	
Chinon	250	47 000	800	
Bourgueil		39 500	800	
Saint-Nicolas-de-Bourgueil		24 500	400	
Vouvray	49 000			31 000(2)
Montlouis	8 400			4 800(2)
Coteaux du Loir	300	800	200	
Jasnières	900			
VDQS				
Coteaux du Vendômois	550	1 300	2 700	
Vins du Haut-Poitou	13 000	15 000	2 500	
TOTAL (in hectolitres)	**129 700**	**234 700**	**12 850**	**65 800**

(1) Half of this total is sold as Sauvignon de Touraine.
(2) Some 30-40 per cent of this total is sold as Pétillant. The potential annual production of these two appellations is some 440,000hl.

and thus better mastered. It requires whole grapes. Maceration and fermentation take place over 8-15 days, during which time the colouring matter and other substances in the grape skins are transferred to the pulp. To end fermentation, the juice is extracted. After one racking and fining, the wines are ready for sale in November.

The techniques used for producing the red wines of AOC Touraine are more classical, designed to give a wine that will improve in bottle for some years. The harvested grapes are first destalked. The principal fermentation can be in part by carbonic maceration. This is advisable in years when the grapes are not fully ripe. The length of fermentation rarely exceeds two weeks. After its finish, the wine receives the same treatment as most other quality wines: racking, fining with egg white or blood, filtering, bottling in March — or in September for especially firmly structured wines. The wines mature for the most part in caves hollowed out of the tufa rock of the region.

The use of the Cabernet Franc variety in Bourgueil-Chinon, and the excellent ageing potential of the wines of this area, have both influenced production methods: careful testing is carried out to ensure the optimum ripeness of the harvest, the crop is destalked, and fermentation takes place with a large proportion (at least 70 per cent) of whole grapes. This makes possible the crushing of the grapes (*foulage*) during fermentation, and this is traditionally done by the feet of the grape treaders or by staves breaking up the 'cap' of skins and pips that form in the fermenting vat, and is nowadays accomplished by mechanical means. The grape bursts at the point when its skin has yielded up its constituents to the must. This form of grape crushing is ideal, because contact with the air (and must oxidization) is avoided.

Fermentation in the vat generally lasts one month. Malolactic fermentation is encouraged before the wine leaves the vat. Thus, when it is

Sixteenth-century press in the Cave de la Dive Bouteille (Cellar of the Holy Bottle — a Rabelaisian reference) in Bourgueil, today a vine and wine museum.

run off, the wine is in a state of microbiological stability. It simply needs time to develop. It is stored in *demi-muids* or large oak casks of 40hl-80hl capacity.

The casks are usually stored in caves hollowed out of the tufa rock. Thus the wine benefits from a naturally regulated low environmental temperature. Depending upon the wine and the vintage, its *élevage* in cask generally lasts for 6-18 months, during which time it will be racked once or twice, before and after the summer. In most cases, *élevage* lasts one year and the wine is bottled in September. The bottles are also stored in the tufa rock caves. The steady, cool temperature of these natural cellars is well suited to help the wine improve and develop its unique character.

The economic structure of the Touraine wine trade

Quite a number of cooperatives are concentrated in the Cher valley, an important centre of Touraine production. By contrast, production at Chinon is completely in private hands. At Saint-Nicolas-de-Bourgueil, the picture is similar; while there is one cooperative at Bourgueil itself. In Vouvray there are two cooperatives, of which one produces wine . . .

The reasons for this mixed picture lie in the desire to offer consumers wines with as much individuality and local character as possible. This is often the case in areas with long-established wine-growing traditions, where wine is appreciated for itself rather than regarded as just another agricultural product. It should be added that this state of affairs is helped by the production equipment available today to wine producers, whatever their size. A good many growers prefer to work on their own, with their families, in small-sized but well-situated *appellation* areas and sell their wine in bottles, rather than be part of a much larger grouping with the obligations that this entails, and where there is a risk that the true character of the wine will be lost.

Wine's role in Touraine life

The wine producers of Touraine have always enjoyed going out and meeting their customers. They also like to welcome visitors, and all over the region are signs inviting passers-by to come in and taste their wines.

The local wine *confréries* hold frequent chapter meetings. This allows celebrities of all sorts, attending the numerous international conferences held in Touraine, to be kept in contact with Touraine's wines.

There are two museums of note. One is in Tours, the theme of which is 'Man's relationship with the vine and with wine' (*see* page 521), and the other is at Chinon. Here, wax figures act out the life of the wine grower and the history of the cooper's craft.

There are also numerous *caveaux d'exposition* (exhibition cellars), where, in addition to tasting wine, the visitor can see something of the way it is made, at Montlouis, Chambord, Thésée, Saint-Aignan, Chaumont-sur-Loire, Amboise and Azay-le-Rideau.

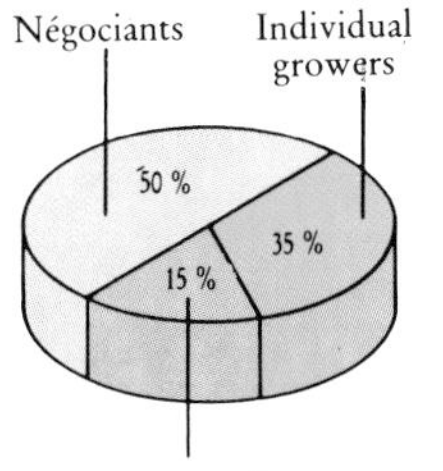

THE TOURAINE WINE TRADE

Confrérie des Entonneurs Rabelaisiens de Chinon* and the Commanderie de la Dive Bouteille de Bourgueil et Saint-Nicolas-de-Bourgueil**

The waters of the Loire may divide Chinon from Bourgueil and Saint-Nicolas-de-Bourgueil, but they are one in the quality of their respective wines and in their dedication to Rabelais, expressed via their respective confréries. *The joyous and purifying laughter of this illustrious native of Chinon still resounds through his town and in its famous Caves Painctes, while Bourgueil has the honour of having been chosen as the site of the Abbey of Thélème. Reference to Rabelais should nevertheless be interpreted properly. It is homage paid to a great humanist with an insatiable curiosity and a great spirit of tolerance — virtues in complete harmony with the art of tippling! Founded in 1962, the Confrérie des Entonneurs Rabelaisiens has more than four thousand members, all of whom came to the celebrated Caves Painctes to take an oath committing them to fight 'against those who abuse wine by adding water to it and who drink it without reason'.*

The Commanderie de la Dive Bouteille, created in 1977, does not yet have as long a roll as its Chinon counterpart, but its Chevaliers are already numerous and have undertaken, with no less conviction, to serve the noble cause of wine and to promote with dignity the taste for good drinking.

Each confrérie, *in its own way and in the same spirit, with humour drawn from the same good source, contributes to a better knowledge of wine and of man's relationship with it.*

*Brotherhood of the Rabelaisian Songsters of Chinon
**Order of the Holy Bottle of Bourgueil and Saint-Nicolas-de-Bourgueil

THE FUTURE OF WINE

How can we gauge the future of wine? Perhaps it is enough to look carefully at its past, to the facts of its presence in the world. From such data, we can cautiously sketch out a future evolution for it, and form an idea of the wine that — after it has negotiated the straits of fashion and economic constraint — we might be drinking in years to come ...

Whereas Hesiod's *Works and Days*, in describing wine making at the time of Homer, leads us to believe that little has changed in the making of sweet wines from sun-shrivelled grapes, who can say exactly what kind of wine the Romans drank, with its mixture of spices, aromatics and honey? What sort of wines did the Phocaeans introduce to the South of France using their own grape varieties, six centuries before the birth of Christ? What were the wines that the Pharaohs of Egypt used to drink? Who knows what Mesopotamian wine was like, so many centuries ago? ...

Wine will evolve as it has always evolved, by following popular taste, or more exactly popular taste constrained by the uncertainties of vinification and storage: in ancient times, wine was sealed in buried amphoras to mature; sometimes it was diluted; the Greeks even mixed their wines with sea water to stabilize them.

For a long time spices were used in wine. Was it for their aromatic and preservative qualities as wine-embalmers? And in which wines? ... Whatever the case, well after the appearance of plugs made from sheets of cork to seal the amphoras for storage, and even after the introduction of wooden casks, invented by the Gauls, wine making suffered a dark age, like everything else, following the fall of the Roman Empire. The use of corks seems to have been lost. Wine was no longer matured, and it reverted to what had been its sole purpose at the start of its evolution, namely to become vinegar if left untended! After all the early efforts to mature and store wine in order to improve it, it was once again being drunk within the year, so that there was only a tenuous link between one wine harvest and the next, just as is the case with *primeur* wines today ...

A return to sources

Everywhere Christianity spread, that small but tenacious creeper, the vine, followed. It was planted wherever there was a religious community, priory or abbey, to make the wine needed for liturgical celebrations. It seems certain that, in many a region where archives and stained-glass images in churches and cathedrals are now the only evidence left of wine growing and making, the wine used for this purpose would by today's standards be scarcely worth drinking ...

However this rapid development in vine cultivation was accompanied in more forward regions by similar progress in wine making, thanks to the cellarers of the abbeys. By means of observant selection over successive generations, the new miracle of matching grape varieties to particular soils and sites, with the help of technical progress, resulted in wines with some degree of nobility again, with a pedigree ... the seeds of *appellations d'origine contrôlée*. This is the heritage that has come down to us, and we will certainly develop it further.

The Bassin de Bacchus fountain at Versailles. Since the 17th century, wines, like man and like life itself, have changed, and we can do no more than imagine the flavour of those that were worthy of honouring the table of the Sun King, Louis XIV.

In any final analysis, though, we would have to admit that we do not know very much about the very early history of wine except that the wines were very different then. We are part of a tradition that is felt as much as known.

Concerning more recent times, we can place our wines in tradition with more exactitude. Bordeaux wines, for example, were only *vins clairets*, that is, lightly macerated, deep rosé wines. It was the same in other vineyard areas, too. Burgundy wines were more often *'oeil-de-perdrix'* (light tawny red) than ruby. The wine of Champagne had nothing in common with the wine from which its present glory comes. The wines of the South undoubtedly soured quickly. Only the Loire wines, though harvested earlier than at present, might have been producing their full vinous flavour from the *'purée septembrale'* (September mash) so memorably celebrated by Rabelais.

Furthermore, what became the customary and conventional 'taste' could also be the result of chance or necessity. If wines had to travel, they were fortified with *eau-de-vie* to reduce the risk of their spoiling. This halting of fermentation soon became the usual practice in some regions, especially those where wines had long distances to travel to reach their markets. Port and Madeira, for example, have for several centuries been completely different from the dry table wines that they once were.

Another example of the happy issue of chance occurred in Tokay, in Hungary, where *Botrytis cinerea* (long before it was recognized as such) transformed an accidental and potentially catastrophic delay in harvesting into a superb wine. The same discovery would be made again, later, in Sauternes, in almost the same way; the sublime Château d'Yquem is the legacy of this accident.

Thus new wines are born. Champagne was born when Dom Pérignon took on the risk of effervescence, controlled it, and produced a *'vin diable'*, a devilish drink as some Englishmen cursed it, but enchantment for those with refined tastes ...

More history, but this time a terrible misfortune, came with *Phylloxera vastatrix*, the vine blight, an American pest that caused havoc in the vineyards of the world. Inherent justice saw to it that the saving remedy also came from the western side of the Atlantic, but only after much experiment with American rootstocks.

A new start was once again necessary; everything had to be relearned. The authentic and typical character of the wines of noble tradition had to be fought for amid the trends of the time, which favoured high productivity and standardization, trends that could easily have reduced entire, historic regions to commonplace mediocrity. This zeal to rediscover and return to origins is still present in French wine growing today and is, if anything, growing stronger with each passing year.

'Vintages of the century' by the dozen

Men have changed; life too. It is certain that our children and grandchildren will no longer have any knowledge of the wines that we have had the good fortune to taste on rare occasions. But it is equally certain that wines in general are much better now than they were two or three generations ago. They will improve further.

An amphora exhibited in the Musée d'Ensérune in Hérault. Amphoras such as these were lined with pitch on the inside and were stopped with cork plugs, to ensure a long life for the syrupy and heavily spiced wines of the time.

Once there were a few 'vintages of the century', confirmed as such only after half a century or more. Now whenever there is a year of auspicious climatic conditions, a new 'vintage of the century' is hailed, sometimes even before the harvest! Wine has become, for better or worse, a 'media product'. (Often for the better.)

In former times, there was little public discussion of wine except in the wine-growing areas, and then such discussion was confined to the agricultural columns of the local newspapers. There were but one or two specialized publications dealing with wine. Now wine is discussed everywhere, and events in the wine world are often reported in a deliberately sensational way, in almost all newspapers and almost throughout the whole world. Too bad, and so much the better. Any publicity is good publicity. Information creates curiosity. Curiosity leads to the acquisition of knowledge, which in turn stimulates demand.

The evolution of wine

In the lists of the great wine merchants of the end of the 19th century, it is astonishing to see that the wines of Hermitage, in the northern Rhône valley, were classed as highly as the greatest first growths of Bordeaux and the greatest or rarest wines of Burgundy. Does that show an evolution in our taste? It certainly shows an evolution in the market for fine wines. For Hermitage is assuredly a very fine wine; but it was Imperial Russia that esteemed it so highly, imported it and, by this devotion, stimulated demand in general. Much later the American market was to exert the same pressure on Bordeaux production. Market forces, therefore, go hand in hand with tastes in wine.

This evolution is still taking place today and will perhaps

develop further. At the beginning of the 20th century, a very long time after Dom Pérignon's perfection of the *méthode champenoise*, who would have thought it possible that dry champagne would one day be universally appreciated? But so it is today, and so it will continue to be. In 1900, not so long ago, the only champagne marketed and appreciated was that which had been heavily dosed with *liqueur d'expédition*, labelled Doux (sweet).

Public interest in wine, including the interest of younger people in whose hands the future of wine lies, none the less tends towards a judicious balance. This interest is continually in development, continually striving to discover the nature and authentic character of a *terroir* and its wine. Nothing will stop connoisseurs from seeking out the truth, from discovering for themselves, from tasting rather than simply drinking.

The development of wine consumption

In earlier times, wine was only drunk on festive occasions and within the family, the quality of wine consumed being determined by social class. It was probably an everyday drink only in the wine-growing regions.

Fortunately this has ceased to be the case. Mass consumption is bringing with it a growing popular awareness of the mystery of wine. People now readily distinguish between wine with no identity or origin — unpleasant and possibly unhealthy industrially-made wine — and that wine which Pasteur confirmed as nourishing and as the healthiest and most hygienic of drinks. Wine is increasingly regarded today as a composite organic product, containing trace elements, mineral salts, vitamins, and the less readily definable power that stems from the very soil in which it has grown — an expression of its authentic and profound nature.

Consumption of branded table wines is therefore receding fast in the face of greater consumption of wines of *appellation d'origine contrôlée*. We are undoubtedly drinking less, but we are drinking better. Wine drinkers everywhere are ignoring wines that are anonymous in favour of those that speak their name, and make clear that behind this name lies one family with one origin, one history and one identity.

The motor forces of wine consumption

There are more and more specialist wine journals and magazines available today containing lots of glossy paper, spectacular photos and more or less repetitive articles. But for all their faults and excesses, they perform a service for wine. There is likewise an increasing number of clubs, associations and schools of wine tasting ...

The wine *confréries* (fraternities), with their endearingly eccentric customs, continue to do good work in popularizing the local characteristics and cultural traditions of a region, thereby maintaining and strengthening the identity of their wine-growing *terroir*.

Restaurateurs, too, are looking around and finding out about wine for themselves. There are fewer and fewer of them who are simply content to trust the first sales representative who comes along, or the grandest-sounding label. They are learning to read labels and find out about wines for themselves. They are increasingly employing *sommeliers* (wine waiters), certain of whom have become well known in their own right thanks to regional, national, indeed even worldwide competitions to establish reputations.

Even though wine is still sometimes ill-treated in restaurants by being served at the wrong temperature, it now receives the same recognition in them as does cuisine.

There are still some old bistros where the *patron* will go looking for simple but genuine wines, often from his own vineyard, to complement the true dishes of his local region. The fashion for wine bars is generally a frothy, sometimes caricatural, reproduction of this time-honoured practice, the soundness of which is ever more evident today.

At the highest level, great restaurateurs pursue the goal of

Innkeeper's outfit. An allegorical illustration in the style of Nicolas de l'Armessin. 17th-century engraving.

Bottles of Château d'Yquem of different ages. This, the finest wine of Sauternes, is the sublime result of a mould long considered noxious: Botrytis cinerea.

pure and harmonious compatibility between dishes and wines. The most prestigious wine lists are no longer just collections on display. Rather they are becoming the instrumental means to greater gastronomic enjoyment since through them, the pursuit of harmony can be refined.

It is certain that, as well as in the great historic regions where the birth of wine took place in Europe, the new vineyards of the world will create their own traditions, too, and develop wines of nobility. The United States, South Africa, Australia and Chile already have established vineyards. Once their special, authentic characters are fully established, wine drinkers will want to experience them too, whatever their origins, in just the same way as they wish to taste the products of the greatest European vineyards. Travel, trade, curiosity, pleasure and competition — all these factors will help the wines of the new world to become as widely known as those of the old.

Mythical wines

By contrast, certain wines will all but disappear because they have assumed a mythical status. There has undoubtedly always been a certain mythology about a small number of very great French wines. The ordinary wine lover can now scarcely hope to come into contact with them, and his or her chances of doing so will only diminish in the future. The prices of such wines are already astronomical.

Is this just financial speculation? Or is it the law of supply and demand? What effect will such mythologizing have on the future of wine? What part does the taste of such a wine play in this process? How much is simply image-making?

When a wine is good, it is appreciated and sought after. If it is also rare, emotional elements — indeed even irrational ones — combine to create a growing pressure on supplies of such a wine. Those who buy the wine generally intend to drink it. But if their thoughts are of investment and not of desire and love, and if they are speculating with this wine as a precious commodity, even if they are few in number, their action becomes dangerous. They will soon monopolize and stockpile the limited production of the greatest wines, and this will impoverish the wine world as a whole.

One unfortunate consequence of this might be that the top-class wine taster will run the risk of never again being able to renew or make acquaintance with the greatest wines due to their extreme rarity, if little is produced and that little becomes a commodity for speculation.

However, despite their expense and inaccessibility, the great *crus* remain the symbolic standards of their region. Romanée-Conti, for example, which produces around 25hl from its 1ha or so, will always be the image *par excellence* of Burgundy. When a glass of it is sold for 800 francs in a Sapporo wine bar in Japan, it is certainly the wine's image that the new consumers are interested in and willing to pay for.

As for us simple wine lovers, we will recount and describe the memorable wine tastings of the past to our grandchildren and they will drink to our memories ...

But they, too, will learn how to build memorable tastings for themselves, when they discover the remnants of our cellars, and when they find themselves in the company of wine growers and knowledgeable wine lovers, in vineyards, in cellars, in France and around the world; when they discover the great growths but also the simple and genuine wines that are good, pleasant and faithful table companions.

They will accede in this way to an understanding of the '*vécu du vin*' (wine's historical and symbolic thread), that profoundly humanizing and civilizing dimension of its being that will never cease to assert itself.

Wine has its prescribed place in the universe. It gives us the physical pleasure of conviviality. It is composed of a thousand complex elements, all of them matters of biology and chemistry, yet rich in the subtlety and unpredictability characteristic of living things.

It is a mysterious catalyst of passions, excesses, of divine bliss as well as fanatical hatred, of fear as well as joy and communion, of drunken dissipation as well as exultant intoxication or exquisite euphoria, of the most profound insights and truths as well as of snobbery, fashion-consciousness, trend-following, cynical commercial considerations and outright speculation ... All of this composes the heritage of wine, and constitutes its future.

This is the label of one of the most famous wines of the world, the red burgundy Grand Cru Romanée-Conti.

WINE AND HEALTH

THE CONSUMPTION OF WINE AND ITS EFFECT ON THE BEHAVIOUR OF MAN AND ON HIS HEALTH

Any thorough work about wine growing and wine must concern itself with the relationship between wine and man, of the action of the one upon the behaviour and health of the other. This is not an easy subject to elucidate, but the truth should be sought because the modern consumer is increasingly preoccupied with health and anxious to understand the effect on the body of what he or she consumes, and the bearing that lifestyle and environment have on health.

Wine consumption, with its beneficial but also harmful effects, is a subject that interests every individual. The beneficial aspects are linked to the origin of wine itself, a natural drink rich in numerous constituents present in the grape, formed by alcoholic fermentation; a drink that the wine grower and the oenologist know how to shape for our greater pleasure, through control of grape varieties, *terroirs* and the techniques of production and storage.

Unfortunately we know about its harmful aspects, too.

Wine growers know that wine is a healthy and natural drink which can bring great pleasure without necessarily leading to a loss of senses or health.

They are linked to the presence of alcohol. Although this substance plays a vital part in wine making by helping to dissolve the numerous constituents of the grape and at the same time giving indispensable support to the aroma, its effects on the human body make it the limiting factor in wine consumption — all the more so because the boundary between acceptable and harmful doses of alcohol is blurred as it varies from individual to individual.

The effects of excessive alcohol consumption, which do not always show themselves as intoxication or obvious drunkenness, change the behaviour of man and have potentially tragic consequences. Statistics show that 40 per cent of fatal road accidents in France are caused by drivers who have alcohol in their bloodstream.

An excessive and regular absorption of alcohol very often leads to insidious alcoholism. For the individual, his family and society at large the consequences of this are serious and damaging.

There are, of course, numerous alcoholic beverages other than wine, and the responsibility of these in causing drunkenness and alcoholism must be taken into account. The effects of alcohol are always the same, regardless of the drink that acts as the vehicle for alcohol. That is why wine consumers, like all drinkers, should be informed of the risks they are running.

In order to appreciate both the beneficial and harmful effects of wine, and thus to acquire the elementary knowledge that will allow anyone who likes wine to enjoy himself or herself without losing either senses or health, it is necessary to know about the composition of wine and the grape from which it is produced.

The composition of the grape

Bunches of grapes are the sole raw material from which wine is made. These are crushed to obtain must, and must is fermented into wine.

The essential parts of the grape for wine making are the pulp and the skin, and these constitute, respectively, 83-91 per cent and 7-11 per cent of the grape, depending upon variety, with the remaining 2-6 per cent being the pips. The constituents of the pulp, skin and pips are listed in the table on the next page. This table allows the basic composition of the two main parts of the grape (the skin and pulp) to be grasped in so far as they affect the composition of must and then of wine. More detail is given in the tables on pages 546–547.

The pulp

As the source of grape juice, the pulp is primarily the supplier of water and sugars. The water contained in the cells of the grape has been drawn from the soil by the roots. It is a very pure plant water. The sugars are, essentially, glucose and fructose, present in practically equal proportions when the fruit is mature. They are transformed into alcohol during fermentation.

Among the organic acids, the presence of tartaric acid should be emphasized since it is a characteristic of the fruit of the vine, whereas malic acid and citric acid are present in all fruits.

The mineral substances that subsequently pass in solution into the juice and then into the wine are firstly potassium, a characteristic cation of the grape and wine, and then, in order of decreasing importance, calcium and magnesium, sodium, iron, copper, zinc and lastly all the trace elements present in fruits and their juices.

The pulp of certain red grape varieties (Teinturiers) contains phenolic compounds, anthocyanins, which colour the wine. But in most red varieties it is only the skin that contains colouring compounds.

COMPARISON OF THE COMPOSITION OF THE PULP, THE SKIN AND THE PIPS OF GRAPES

Grape	Constituents	
Pulp	Water	70-78%
	Sugars	10-25%
	Organic acids (tartaric, malic, citric)	0.2-0.5%
	Mineral matter	2-3%
	Nitrogenous and pectic matter	0.05-1%
Skin	Water	78-80%
	Organic acids	1-1.5%
	Mineral matter	1.5-2%
	Nitrogenous and pectic matter	1.5-2%
	Polyphenolic matter, aromatic substances and their precursors	1-2%
Pips	Water	36-40%
	Fats	10-12%
	Nitrogenous matter	5%
	Mineral matter	1-2%
	Tannins	7-8%
	Hydrocarbons	34-36%

The skin

There are two groups of constituents in the composition of the skin that play an essential role in the quality of the future wine. The first of these groups is that of the phenolic compounds, essentially made up of colouring substances called anthocyanins, which give their colour to red and rosé wines, but also including procyanidols, which give wine its body and its particular organoleptic properties.

Apart from these phenolic compounds, grape skins also contain aromatic substances and their chemical precursors, which come into evidence during wine's fermentation and maturation.

The pips

The pips are present in the must of red wines during alcoholic fermentation, and they release tannins and nitrogenous substances into the must in quantities that depend on the duration and temperature of fermentation. Any breaking of the pips during *foulage* (crushing) should be avoided to limit the release of their constituents, especially fat droplets. Eventually the pips will be taken out of the marc so that grape oil, with its recognized dietary properties, can be extracted from them.

The composition of wine

The conversion of grapes by means of alcoholic fermentation into wine involves the conversion of the sugars glucose and fructose, present in the original grape matter, into alcohol. It also involves the formation of secondary products, among them glycerol, various organic acids and other constituents not present as such when the grapes were harvested.

The composition of wine is therefore even more complex than that of the grape. The tables on pages 546–547, which are based on the research of Pascal Ribéreau-Gayon, lists more than two hundred constituents. Since those constituents were isolated, the use of very powerful analytical techniques has made it possible to increase this total four- or fivefold, mostly thanks to the discovery of trace constituents, generally volatile substances playing a role in the wine's aroma — an extremely complex entity.

The water in wine

Water of plant origin is the major constituent of wine (85-90 per cent) and it comes directly from the grape. It helps to supply human fluid requirements when wine is drunk.

Organic acids

These acids contribute to the acidity of wine, its average pH being 3.3. This is close to that of gastric juice (pH 2–2.5). Despite this high acidity level, the acid flavour of wine is not at all disagreeable since it is balanced and softened by the presence of alcohol.

This acidity corresponds to the optimum for protein digestion. Wine therefore combines perfectly with proteinaceous foods. Appreciation of its digestive qualities makes it a widely appreciated table drink.

There has been much discussion about wine as a food and source of nourishment in its own right, because it provides calorific energy through the body's combustion of alcohol, and because it supplies needed amino acids, vitamins, mineral substances and trace elements. However the nutritive value of wine is negligible. In fact, as will be seen from pages 546–547, wine contains only meagre quantities of amino acids and vitamins, and it is not as good a source of these substances as unfermented grape juice or other fruit juices.

The mineral content of wine is more noteworthy, and here the dominant cation is potassium. Provided there is no contra-indication, wine can be consumed in low salt diets, for the potassium salts, in particular the sulphates, favour diuresis.

The other mineral constituents of wine — calcium, magnesium and trace elements — along with numerous other products of natural origin, are able to contribute to human daily requirements.

The procyanidols

One group of constituents in wine that warrants our attention because of certain specific properties is the group of phenolic compounds, particularly tannins with procyanidols. These substances, responsible for the astringency of unripe fruits, are abundant in plants. The grape is no exception.

The procyanidols of the grape are mainly found in the pips and a longish maceration will dissolve them into the wine, where they can reach a concentration of 1-2g per litre. It was in 1955 that Professor Masquelier first detected them in wine.

Since that date he has made a study of these substances following their extraction from grape pips, and provided evidence of their effects in areas as varied as vascular protection, the biosynthesis of collagen and mucopolysaccharides, fat metabolism, the atherogenic process and the release of histamine.

Taking as an example the action of the procyanidols in the blood vessels, Professor Masquelier has written: 'These substances have their effect on two levels: their action is catabolic in the circulating blood, and parietal in the artery wall.

'In the blood, they accelerate the elimination of cholesterol. This is the hypocholesterolaemiant power of wine that I described in 1961. This phenomenon causes the intervention of vitamin C, which initiates the transformation of cholesterol into biliary acids. The procyanidols are involved in preserving the vitamin C of the organism.

'In the arterial cell wall, the procyanidols perform a double tissular action. On the one hand, they stabilize the collagen fibres which support the various layers of the vessel wall. This collagen strengthening is due to the formation of bridges between the polypeptide chains. On the other hand, they inhibit the enzyme histidine decarboxylase (HD), and this inhibitory action prevents the overproduction of histamine in response to stress. It is known that any excess histamine increases the permeability of the wall, facilitates its penetration and initiates the atherogenic process.'

This could be the explanation of the protective power of wine against cardiovascular disease. This was the conclusion of an enquiry carried out in 18 developed countries in 1979 by American researchers, which produced evidence of a correlation between habitual and moderate wine consumption and a lessened heart attack mortality rate.

However Professor Masquelier himself believes that his work on the procyanidols, grape pip extracts and phenolic compounds — although they possess sufficiently promising pharmaceutical properties to form the active principle of a cardiovascular medicine — 'does not, thus far, permit us to consider wine as a remedy for heart attacks.'

The procyanidols of wine are only present in significant quantities in certain types of wine, particularly red wine. Is their average concentration in wines sufficient to have a verifiable pharmacological effect? Moreover, how are they influenced by the numerous other substances that accompany them in wine?

The procyanidols as constituents of the grape and wine are being thoroughly researched at the INRA experimental laboratory of Pech Rouge at Narbonne.

Professor Masquelier's work should be followed up to clarify the effect on man of procyanidols absorbed at the time of wine consumption and so allow us to answer these questions. While we wait, we should refrain from coming to hasty conclusions.

However, the characteristics of wine and its constituents described above are obviously of great interest.

Alcohol

After water, the second main constituent of wine is alcohol. It is an indispensable element in the production of wine, both as a solvent of the basic constituents and for its organoleptic qualities, for which there is no substitute.

There have been a number of attempts in the 1980s to produce 'alcohol-free wines' but these products no longer have the characteristics of wine. Even low-alcohol wines, from which a part of the alcohol has been removed, no longer resemble the base wines used to make them. Wine-based products, known as coolers in the U.S.A. or 'cocktails' in France, are new products which taste nothing like wine. They are interesting because they are produced, at least in part, from grapes. But none of them replaces wine — which is only wine because of its alcohol, with all the constraints that this places on its drinker.

To understand the effects of alcohol on the human body, we will follow its passage through the organism, concentrating particularly on its effects on the liver and central nervous system. We will study its absorption, its diffusion, its metabolism, and the consequences of excess alcohol in the bloodstream.

Alcohol absorption

Some 20-30 per cent of the alcohol introduced orally into the body is absorbed by the stomach and 70-80 per cent by the small intestine. This absorption is total. No ethanol (alcohol) is found in the faeces. Absorption is rapid: the maximum blood alcohol content is reached between 30 and 60 minutes after ingestion.

A certain number of factors modify the digestive absorption of alcohol. It is important to be aware of these because each factor that slows down this absorption leads to a lower peak of blood alcohol, and helps in its metabolism.

▷ *Digestive factors*

An empty stomach accelerates the absorption of alcohol. The presence of food slows it. The actual nature of a meal, moreover, plays a role. It is with proteinaceous foods and carbohydrates that the rise in the blood alcohol level is at its lowest. Pathological factors such as gastritis, or cases where a gastrectomy has been carried out, lead to an abnormally accelerated rate of absorption.

▷ *The role played by the type of alcoholic drink*
The speed of absorption is roughly proportional to the alcohol content of the drink being consumed. For a fixed amount of alcohol, dilution leads to lower alcohol levels in the blood than when the alcohol concentration is high.

Drinks of high buffering ability, rich in dissolved substances such as certain types of wine rich in dry extract, prolong the gastric phase and lead to lower blood alcohol levels than is otherwise the case.

▷ *Rapidity of ingestion*
The more lengthy the period over which alcohol intake is spread, the lower the blood alcohol level will be. The same quantity of alcohol ingested in a few minutes or in over an hour will lead to very different blood alcohol levels.

So, from a health perspective, it is advisable to take only moderately alcoholic drinks, to consume them during meals, to have a balanced diet during periods of alcoholic consumption, and to be especially careful where digestive ailments are concerned.

The diffusion of alcohol in the body

Alcohol, transported by the bloodstream, reaches all the organs, but it is in the liver that most alcohol is metabolized. A very small percentage of the absorbed alcohol will be eliminated without modification. Two to three per cent is exhaled by the lungs; it is this alcohol that serves as a basis for police alcohol test equipment. A similar percentage is eliminated in urine, and minute quantities pass through the skin in sweat.

The metabolism of alcohol

The metabolism of alcohol depends on the amount consumed. If intake is moderate, metabolism occurs in the normal way (see below). In the case of a more substantial ingestion, secondary processes intervene. It is worth adding that the border between moderate alcohol intake and substantial or excessive intake is blurred because it varies from one individual to another. It is not possible to fix an absolute threshold without misleading those whose bodies, and principally livers, are less tolerant of alcohol than is customary.
▷ In the normal process of metabolism, the alcohol (ethanol) is oxidized to acetaldehyde (ethanal), catalysed by the enzyme alcohol-dehydrogenase (ADH) in an oxidation-reduction reaction, with nicotinamide adenine dinucleotide (NAD) as the reducing agent, leading to the reduced form NADH.

During the second stage of normal metabolism, acetate, the preferred cellular fuel, is oxidized by the Krebs cycle to CO_2 + H_2O coupled to the NAD/NADH system. This combustion produces 7 calories per gram of alcohol. It is this energy supply that has led to classification of alcohol amongst the nutrients. This is true, as long as this energy supply does not lead, as a result of excessive alcohol consumption, to the displacement of the nutritional equilibrium. A new constraint with regard to alcohol therefore becomes apparent. Moderation is necessary to ensure that the energy provided by the combustion of alcohol is not excessive in relation to our daily calorific requirements.
▷ The secondary processes of metabolism intervene when the quantity of alcohol to be metabolized is too high for the normal route of degradation by ADH. Two other enzymatic systems then come into play — the MEOS (microsomal ethanol oxidizing system) and the catalase system.

Excessive consumption of alcohol leads to a laxity in behaviour, as exemplified by the typical attitudes that Nicolas Lancret (1690–1743) captured in Le déjeuner de jambon *(The Ham Lunch).*

GENERAL COMPOSITION OF MUSTS AND WINES

Constituent	Must	Wine
	expressed in grams per litre	
Water	750-850	750-900
Alcohols		
Ethyl alcohol (ethanol)	0	45-160
Propanol	0	0.001-0.03
Isopropyl alcohol	0	0.001-0.03
Isoamyl alcohol	0	0.10-0.35
Isopropylcarbinol	0	0.05-0.2
Methanol	0	0.02-0.2
Polyalcohols		
Glycerol	0	4-20
2,3 Butanediol	0	0.3-1.35
Sorbitol	0.1	0.1
Mannitol	0	spoiled wines
Myoinositol	0.2-0.7	0.2-0.7
Crotyl alcohol	0	0.002-0.02
Monosaccharides		
Glucose	50-150	traces only in dry wines
Fructose	50-150	presence in sweet wines
Arabinose	0.36-150	0.36-2
Thamnose	0.15-0.3	0.15-0.3
Xylose	0.05	0.05
Sucrose	0-2	0
Gums and pectins		
Polysaccharides	3-5	
Nitrogenous substances		
Proteins	+	traces
Peptones and albumoses	traces	
Polypeptides	2-4	2-4
Free amino acids	see analysis below	see analysis below
Amides	traces	traces
Ammonia	0.001-0.07	0.005-0.02
Vitamins		
Thiamine	200-500	5-40
Riboflavin	10-60	60-360
Pantothenic acid	500-700	500-1200

Constituent	Must	Wine
	expressed in grams per litre	
Vitamins (continued)		
Nicotinic acid	1200-3000	800-1900
Biotin	1.5-4	0.6-4.6
Myoinositol	0.2-0.7	0.2-0.7
Pyridoxine	100-450	100-450
Ascorbic acid		1-1.5
Cyanocobalamin		0.05-0.16

Constituent	Must	White wine	Red wine
	expressed in micrograms per litre		
Amino acids			
Arginine	327	46	47
Aspartic acid	2	38	31
Glutamic acid	173	200	221
Cystine	0	25	17
Glycine	22	26	28
Histidine	11	14	14
Isoleucine	7	29	26
Leucine	20	19	19
Lysine	16	40	47
Methionine	1	4	5
Phenylalanine	5	16	19
Proline	264	201	72
Serine	69	54	49
Threonine	258	111	187
Tryptophan	0.6	0	2.5
Tyrosine	0	13	11
Valine	6	36	45

The Breathalyzer measures alcohol in the bloodstream by means of exhaled air.

GENERAL COMPOSITION OF MUSTS AND WINES

Constituent	Must	Wine
	expressed in grams per litre	
Aldehydes		
Ethanal		
Propanal		
Vanillin		
Cinnamic aldehyde		
Acetal		
Volatile neutral esters		
Ethyl acetate		
Ethyl lactate		
Esters of fatty acids	0.1-0.2	
Acid ethyl esters		
Tartaric, malic, succinic and citric acids (nonvolatile, odourless)	0.1	
Organic acids		
Tartaric acid	3-7	2-5
Malic acid	5-20	0-10
Citric acid	0.2-0.5	0-0.5
Succinic acid	0	0.5-1.5
Lactic acid	0	1-12
Citramalic acid	0	0.5-1
Galacturonic acid	0.5-1	0.5-1
Mucic acid	0-0.5	0-0.5
Gluconic acid	present in musts and wines made from rotten grapes	
Pyruvic acid	0.02-0.07	0.02-0.07
∝-Ketoglutaric acid	0.01-0.04	0.01-0.04
Glycolic acid		traces possible
Mesoxalic acid		traces possible
Glyceric acid		traces possible
Glyoxylic acid		traces possible
Saccharic acid		traces possible
Volatile acids		
Acetic acid	0	0.2-0.5
Formic acid	0	0.01-0.1
Butyric acid	0	traces
Propionic acid	0	traces

Constituent	Must	Wine
	expressed in grams per litre	
Phenolic acids		
Ferulic acid		0.001
Vanillic acid		0.015
Syringic acid		0.030
Para-coumaric acid		0.030
Ortho-hydroxybenzoic acid		0-0.0015
Gentistic acid		0.0001
Para-hydroxybenzoic acid		0.0001
Caffeic acid		0.015
Gallic acid		0.012
Protocatechic acid		0.008
Anthocyanins		0.1-5
Flavones		0-0.05
Tannins		0.1-5
Mineral cations		
Potassium	1-2.5	0.7-1.6
Calcium	0.05-0.2	
Magnesium	0.05-0.14	
Sodium	0.02-0.25	
Aluminium	0.05	
Iron	0.002-0.01	
Copper	0.0008-0.001	
Zinc	0.0001-0.005	
Manganese	0.0003-0.005	
Lead	0.00005-0.0004	
Arsenic	0.00001-0.001	
Cobalt	0.00002-0.000015	
Mineral anions		
Sulphate	0.15-0.7	
Chloride	0.025-0.2	
Phosphate	0.08-0.5	
Borate	0.005-0.06	
Fluoride	0.00005-0.005	
Bromide	0.0001-0.0007	
Iodide	0.0001-0.0006	

The MEOS is a special system that increases enzyme activity, while the catalase system converts ethanol to ethanal, but to do this it consumes oxygen and cellular proteins vital for the survival of hepatic cells.

The consequences of excess ethanol (alcohol)

Too much ethanol in the body has the following consequences:

▷ There is competition for the same co-factor, NAD, at the metabolic stages of the normal metabolic process. Any excess alcohol blocks the hepatic NAD to its advantage. The acetate formed can no longer be used, because of the lack of NAD, in the Krebs cycle. The liver will use this acetate for the synthesis of fatty acids, cholesterol, lipids; steatosis begins, accompanied by hyperlipidemia.

▷ The pyruvate-lactate system is called on for the oxidation of NADH to NAD necessary for the oxidation of alcohol. The lactate formed is preferentially eliminated by the kidneys instead of uric acid, the increasing blood concentration of which provokes the bouts of gout frequent amongst alcoholics.

▷ The excess acetaldehyde formed is very toxic to the hepatic cells and is responsible for the formation of fibrous tissues or fibrosis in the liver.

▷ Anoxia provoked by the consumption of oxygen and proteins vital for the life of hepatic cells leads to their destruction and to acute hepatitis; with continued alcohol dependence, cirrhosis of the liver may result.

Alcohol and the central nervous system

Alcohol, above all, acts on the central nervous system and the extent of this action is in proportion to the concentration of alcohol in the blood.

Alcohol can be considered as a depressant of the nerve cells. A small dose of alcohol will therefore at first involve a weakening of self-control, a dimming of critical faculties, less restraint and a higher regard of oneself and of one's capacities.

These first effects are accompanied by a feeling of well-being and euphoria. Alcohol diminishes excessive timidity and releases over-strong intellectual or emotional tension. It can therefore greatly help social intercourse and encourage conviviality.

If alcohol is consumed to excess, the drinker runs the danger of losing control of himself. As paralysis of the superior centres of the brain increases, the inhibition that they normally exercise over the other parts of the brain is lifted. Consequently excitation increases, often manifesting itself in garrulousness and an inability to stay still. The individual more or less loses control of his actions, but his physical capacities remain intact. This explains the occasionally dangerous initiatives undertaken by intoxicated persons, which frequently involve scuffles or accidents. This phase is also characterized by a certain clumsiness and imprecision of movement, sometimes accompanied by incoherent speech, difficulty in walking, or a pale or contorted face.

With repeated ingestion, intoxication will either be limited to the previously described symptoms, or will lead to an alcoholic coma after a phase of uncoordinated movement or characteristic drunkenness with disorders in speech, thought, walking and general behaviour.

The description of the stages of alcohol's effect upon the nervous system is a strong argument for moderation, the exact realization of which will vary from individual to individual, according to his or her personal reaction to alcohol. Moreover this effect is directly dependent upon the concentration of alcohol in the blood, and it will be favourably affected by all the factors listed above which tend to diminish or dilute this concentration.

Alcohol tolerance

It has been shown that alcohol induces biosynthesis of alkyl molecules in the body which have morphinic and hallucinogenic properties. These molecules could be responsible for alcohol dependence, analogous to drug addiction. This aspect of alcohol is important to mention. The consumer of wine and of all alcoholic drinks should necessarily break a pattern of habitual drinking and plan alcohol-free days.

This simplified sketch of the effects of alcohol on the body shows the importance of the body's enzymatic processes in the elimination of alcohol. The efficiency of these enzyme systems, though, varies greatly from one individual to another, depending on genetic make-up.

As far as alcohol intake is concerned, then, all men are not equal. One will be drunk after a single glass of champagne, while another may drink a whole bottle without any apparent difficulty. It is not therefore possible to fix an optimum level of consumption. Each individual must be aware of his or her own personal limits.

The effects of alcohol on the body, and in particular its almost immediate effect on the central nervous system, are directly connected with the amount of alcohol in the blood, which is itself linked to the gastrointestinal absorption of alcohol. So, for this reason, all consumption of alcoholic drinks on an empty stomach should be avoided.

If an aperitif is taken, perhaps a sweet wine, dry wine mixed with fruit syrup, or champagne, it is advisable to accompany it particularly with carbohydrates and above all to prolong the time of its absorption. It is also recommended that a glass of water is drunk at the beginning of a meal. This will result in a dilution of the alcohol in the wine ingested later.

Even if fully aware of his or her limits, the wine lover must take care to drink in moderation. The risk of destroying nutritional equilibrium by giving the body excess calories in the form of alcohol each day is ever-present.

The observation of days of abstinence allows one to drink in a relaxed manner and to avoid alcohol addiction, which so often comes about insidiously.

The occasional wine drinker, however, should also be vigilant, since he does not know his limits or knows them only vaguely. The advice given above is of prime importance to such a drinker.

The information given here should lead the consumer to establish a balance in his or her consumption of wine. Once achieved, he or she will be able to benefit from the enjoyment of a little wine with daily meals, and from the pleasure of discovering outstanding wines through their organoleptic qualities, sought and analysed in association with food.

U V

Ugni Blanc

Synonyms: *Clairette à Grains Ronds* or *Clairette Ronde* in Provence, *Buan* and *Beou* in Alpes-Maritimes, *Rossola* on Corsica, *Grédelin* in Vaucluse, *Saint-Émilion* in the two Charentes *départements*, *Saint-Émilion-des-Charentes*, *Chatar*, *Cadillac*, *Cadillate*, *Castillonne*, *Muscadet* in Gironde, *Queue de Renard*, *Roussan* in Nice.

Growing tips felty white with carmine margins, crook shaped; axis downy.

Leaves large, orbicular, extremely bullate, thick, contorted, coarsely textured with concave edges, five-lobed with generally shallow lateral sinuses, narrow and acute at base, petiolar sinus lyrate, more or less closed; dentation convex, medium sized.

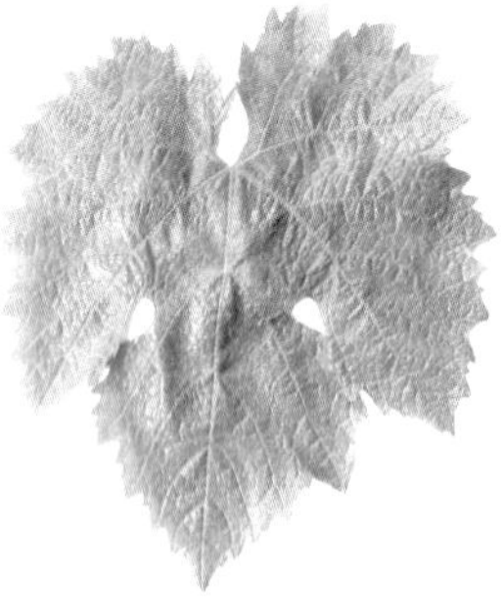

Leaf of the Ugni Blanc. This grape is one of the varieties used for the white wines of Bordeaux and for the base wines for distillation into armagnac.

Green shoots very large, flattened at nodes, deeply ribbed, arachnoid at tips, brown on the side exposed to the sun, with dark nodes; tendrils large, highly developed.

Bunches very large, winged, cylindrical, very long and narrow, with peduncles which are lignified at the base; grapes spherical, medium sized, golden yellow becoming more or less amber coloured if exposed to plenty of sunlight, finally turning pink or even copper-red; skin thin but tough, flesh juicy, abundant; ripening period: third epoch, late.

The Ugni Blanc has late budbreak, which protects it from spring frosts; on the other hand, it is very sensitive to hard winter frosts. It has good resistance to oidium (powdery mildew) and grey rot, but it is susceptible to downy mildew and eelworms. This vine can be pruned in a number of ways but it has always to be remembered that its green shoots are vulnerable to winds and can easily break.

Ugni Blanc green shoot.

The Ugni Blanc is a very vigorous vine, of upright habit, regularly producing 100-150hl/ha with satisfactory alcoholic strength (11°–12°) in the Midi. It is high-yielding, too, in the vineyards of the Cognac region, but here its alcoholic strength is much lower (7°–9° on average) because this late-ripening variety is at the limits of its cultivation. The wines produced in Cognac are, for the same reason, very acidic, while in the Mediterranean region, neutral, bland white wines are produced which are improved by being blended with better quality grape varieties: Clairette, Grenache Blanc, Sauvignon Blanc.

Eleven registered clones have been approved, the most common being numbers 479, 384, 483 and 482. Classed as 'recommended' in all the southern French *départements*, this is the most widely grown white grape variety in France, with 127,470ha under cultivation in 1980, of which 95,000ha were planted in the two Charentes *départements*, providing white wines destined for distillation into cognac.

In Gironde, the Ugni Blanc covers 6,500ha and is one of the specified white grape varieties of AOC Bordeaux, Entre-Deux-Mers and Sainte-Foy-Bordeaux. In the South West there are slightly more than 10,000ha planted for the production of armagnac, divided between Gers (8,860ha), Lot-et-Garonne (1,053ha) and Landes (709ha).

In Languedoc, the Ugni Blanc is among the specified white grape varieties of AOC Coteaux du Languedoc and Costières du Gard, and of the Vins de Pays des Sables du Golfe du Lion. It is also used for the preparation of non-*appellation* white table wines. There are about 4,000ha in all in Languedoc: in Hérault (1,507ha), Gard (1,619ha) and Aude (714ha).

In Provence, this variety is also important: Var (6,587ha), Vaucluse (1,686ha), Bouches-du-Rhône (1,410ha) and Alpes-de-Haute-Provence (77ha), making a total of 9,760ha for the white wines of AOC Bandol, Côtes de Provence, Cassis, Palette, Coteaux d'Aix-en-Provence, Côtes du Rhône, Côtes du Ventoux and for VDQS Coteaux Varois, Coteaux de Pierrevert and Côtes du Lubéron.

In Corsica, the Ugni Blanc (600ha) is used for the white wines of the Vin de Corse and Ajaccio AOCs.

Valais Noir

Synonyms: *Valet* at Salins and Poligny, *Tauquet* at Dole, *Salem*, *Mourlans Noir*, *Trousset*, *Troussé*, *Troussey* or *Troussais*.

Bunches small, cylindrical, compact, grapes spherical or slightly ovoid, small, black; ripening period: second epoch.

Settlers from Valais probably took this vine with them to the Jura around 1650. It is very productive, giving a mediocre wine, flat, though deeply coloured. Frosts do not present a problem for this variety, as it readily regrows fruiting canes; it is pruned long. Unclassified, less than 1ha remains in Jura.

Valdiguié

Synonyms: *Valdiguier*, *Plant de la Roxo* at Montpezat-de-Quercy, *Aramon du Sud-Ouest*, *Gros Auxerrois* in the Quercy area, *Cahors* in Gironde, *Isabelle* at Puylaroque (Tarn-et-Garonne), *Jan Pierrou* at Sauzet in Lot, *Moutet* at Cazès-Mondenard (Tarn-et-Garonne), *Noir de Chartres* in Charente, *Plant du Midi* at Marcillac in Aveyron, *Quercy* in the Blaye area, *Plant de Cros* in Lot, *Brocol* in Haute-Garonne.

Growing tips open, felty white with carmine margins.

Young leaves downy, yellowish, bullate, with lightly bronze-coloured patches, underside of blade felty white.

Leaves large, dull green, orbicular, thick, concave, extremely bullate, without lobes or slightly three-lobed, sometimes with upper lateral sinuses narrow, acute at base; petiolar sinus closed with parallel or overlapping edges; dentation convex, wide, not very prominent; underside of the blade slightly downy, veins lightly pubescent. The foliage reddens partially in autumn.

Green shoots ribbed, with marked red-brown striations, red nodes; tendrils small, thin.

Bunches large, voluminous, conical, compact; grapes ellipsoidal, large, blue-black, skin quite thick, pulp soft, juicy, abundant; ripening period: third epoch.

Little is known about the origins of this variety from the South West. It is probably a natural seedling of the Mérille, first noted by a wine grower called Valdiguié or Valdéguier who bred it for its great fertility. It is in fact a very vigorous vine of semi-erect habit and early budbreak. Thanks to its large bunches and its fertility, yields easily reach 100hl/ha, but the grapes only ripen well in warm climates.

The wine produced is ordinary, without any special qualities, deeply coloured, not very alcoholic and sometimes astringent. The variety is quite resistant to oidium (powdery mildew) but susceptible to downy mildew, *coulure* (flower abortion) and strong winds. Classed as 'authorized' in the Midi and South West, only one registered clone has been approved: number 385. Its cultivation is decreasing: it now only occupies 836ha, compared with 4,908ha in 1958.

It is mainly found in Tarn (275ha), Tarn-et-Garonne, Lot, Ardèche and in some small areas in Hérault, Var, Vaucluse and Aveyron.

Valdiguié leaf.

Branch of the Valdiguié, a fertile and vigorous grape variety. It is found principally in the Midi and South West.

Valençay

This vineyard area, classed VDQS by decree on 10 August 1970, covers 120ha and produces around 4,200hl of red wine, 950hl of rosé wine and 900hl of white wine annually.

The white grape varieties used are the Arbois, Chardonnay and Sauvignon Blanc (to a total of 60 per cent); the secondary varieties, permitted to a maximum of 40 per cent, are the Pinot Blanc and Romorantin.

For red and rosé wine, at least 75 per cent of the blend should be from the Cabernet Sauvignon, Cabernet Franc, Côt, Gamay and Pinot Noir varieties. Subsidiary varieties are the Gascon, Pineau d'Aunis, Grolleau and Gamay de Chaudenay (the last-named to a maximum of 10 per cent).

The area of production covers 14 communes in Indre and a single commune in Loir-et-Cher.

Bunch of Valdiguié grapes.

The red wines have a light colour. They are supple, but with a good rustic solidity. The rosés are clean and dry. The whites are dry with a well-developed aroma, and are full and fresh to taste. All these wines should be drunk young; but wines produced following a sunny vintage will keep well in bottle.

Valérien

Synonym: 23 410 *Seyve-Villard*.

Bunches medium sized, cylindrical, elongated; grapes small, slightly ovoid, white; ripening period: first epoch.

This variety is a vigorous hybrid, susceptible to *coulure* (flower abortion) and to high winds. It has late budbreak. The Valérien produces a *vin ordinaire*. It is classed as 'authorized' in Vendée, where it covers 60ha.

Varousset

Synonym: 23 657 *Seyve-Villard.*

Leaves orbicular-reniform, dark green, slightly five-lobed with upper lateral sinuses narrow, acute at base, petiolar sinus U-shaped, sometimes naked at base; dentation convex, medium sized; underside of blade pubescent.

Bunches large, cylindrical, narrow; grapes medium sized, slightly ovoid, black; ripening period: first epoch, late.

This vigorous hybrid grafts well, but is not very resistant to disease. It must be sited in a sheltered area if its grapes are to ripen properly. Its yield is satisfactory and it gives an alcoholic, pale, rather flat wine. Classed as 'authorized' in the Midi, 335 hectares of it remain in cultivation.

Velteliner Rouge Précoce

Bunches small with green stalks, cylindrical, loose; grapes small, ovoid, pink, flesh juicy; ripening period: first epoch.

This is a very vigorous variety, susceptible to downy mildew, oidium (powdery mildew) and grey rot (botrytis); its grapes are too small to be eaten, although it is often regarded as a dual-purpose vine. Its wine is neutral. Classed as 'recommended' in Savoie, it is cultivated a little in the Chautagne area (2ha). A Velteliner Rose also exists.

Verdesse

Synonyms *Verdèche*, *Verdesse Muscade*, *Muscadelle* at Claix, *Verdèze Musquée*, *Étraire Blanche* around Grenoble, *Dongine* in Ain.

Leaves small, orbicular-reniform, with convex edges, deeply three-lobed with lateral sinuses club shaped, acute at base, forming a wasp-waisted middle lobe, the lateral lobes themselves being divided by secondary sinuses, petiolar sinus in open U-shape; dentation convex, narrow; underside of blade pubescent.

Bunches small, conical, loose, winged; grapes small, ellipsoidal, golden white, juicy; ripening period: second epoch, late.

This is a vigorous vine, which must be trained on trellises when pruned long, as it grows rapidly in the alluvial soils along the Isère, where it is cultivated at Sainte-Marie-d'Alloix. Under the name of Dongine, it is found in the vineyards of Bugey around Culoz. The wine is of good quality, alcoholic, with a pronounced, individual flavour. The Verdesse has been classed as 'recommended' in Isère and Savoie.

Vermentino

Synonyms: *Malvoisie de Corse*, *Malvoisie à Gros Grains*, *Malvoisie Précoce d'Espagne*, *Malvasia* at Bonifacio.

Leaves medium sized, orbicular, contorted, blue-green, finely bullate, deeply five-lobed with lateral sinuses narrow and acute at base, petiolar sinus lyrate, closed; dentation pointed, narrow; underside of blade downy.

Bunches medium to large, conical, generally with one well-developed wing; grapes medium sized, slightly ellipsoidal, white, becoming pink when overripe; ripening period: third epoch, late.

This variety has two uses. The grapes can be eaten fresh or even dried, as raisins. But its principal use is for a good, pleasing white Corsican wine. Four registered clones have been approved: numbers 639, 640, 766 and 795. The variety is classed as 'recommended' in the Midi and in Corsica.

Villard Blanc

Synonym: 12 375 *Seyve-Villard.*

Growing tips arachnoid white.

Young leaves glossy, very bronzed, almost red. Leaves medium sized, orbicular-reniform, very glossy, smooth, undulating, five-lobed with lobes of average size and definition, lateral sinuses narrow, acute at base, petiolar sinus lyrate, open; dentation convex, very long, very narrow; underside of blade glabrous.

Leaf of the Villard Blanc. This variety produces yellow, slightly bitter wine.

Green shoots finely ribbed, glabrous, with inconspicuous nodes.

Bunches large, conical, loose; grapes ovoid, large, golden yellow, flesh soft, with large pips; ripening period: second epoch, late.

This hybrid is the result of a crossing of Seibel 6468 × Seibel 6905 in order to ally the vigour of the first with the fertility of the second, and it was this variety that provided the greatest commercial success for the Seyve-Villard concern. It occupied more than 21,000ha in 1968. Classed as 'authorized' in the Midi and the South West as far north as Charente, there now remains less than 6,000ha of it in cultivation. It is a very vigorous vine that can be grown ungrafted in many soils, but it is better grafted, preferably on to *Riparia-Berlandieri*. Its spreading habit means that it has to be wire-trained. It has good resistance to downy mildew but is more sensitive to oidium (powdery mildew).

Its productivity is good, generally between 80hl/ha and 100hl/ha, though it can produce more than 150hl/ha on fertile ground. Its wine is pale yellow in colour, a little bitter with a strange aroma, but it is of acceptable quality for immediate drinking.

Villard Noir

Synonym: 18 315 *Seyve-Villard.*

Young leaves glabrous, bullate, slightly bronze in colour.

Leaves cuneiform, strongly concave and markedly crimped around the petiolar junction; without lobes; petiolar sinus narrowly lyrate, but in fact generally overlapping because of the concave form of the leaves; dentation pointed, narrow; underside of blade slightly pubescent.

Bunches medium sized, cylindrical-conical, compact; grapes ovoid, medium sized, black, thick skinned, flesh pulpy, with a leafy or stalky taste; ripening period: first epoch, late.

This variety is a cross of Seibel 7053 × Seibel 6905. It is of average vigour, and always requires grafting on to *Berlandieri* hybrids. It does not grow well when grafted on to *Rupestris* or 3 309C. Its budbreak is in midseason. It is almost wholly resistant to downy mildew, but is slightly susceptible to oidium (powdery mildew) and grey rot (botrytis). Its fertility is good, with an average production of 50-80hl/ha of deeply coloured, alcoholic, astringent wine with a leafy or stalky taste. The Villard Noir was widely grown at one time, occupying more than 30,000ha in 1968. There are now only 7,800ha left.

Bunch of Villard Noir grapes.

Vin de Blanquette

This AOC was ratified by decree on 13 April 1981 for sparkling white wines produced in the *appellation* area of Blanquette de Limoux, made only from white Mauzac grapes by the *méthode rurale* of secondary fermentation in bottle without disgorgement.

Green shoot of the Villard Noir. This variety produces a deeply coloured, astringent wine.

Vin de Corse

Certain wine-growing zones of Corsica only are permitted to use the regional *appellation d'origine contrôlée* Vin de Corse, following the decree of 2 April 1976.

This applies to the traditional wine-growing region of Corte in central Corsica, but above all to the area of alluvial deposits on the eastern Tyrrhenian seaboard between Bastia and Solenzara. Within this area, the Aléria region expanded production enormously from 1959–60 onwards, whereas the small regions of la Marana and la Casinca close to the urban area of Bastia are ancient agricultural areas in which grape growing has always had an important place.

The wines are of average quality and individuality. They come from the Nielluccio, Grenache, Cinsaut and Carignan grapes. They are fruity and to be drunk young, particularly the white and rosé wines. The reds can be aged for two or three years.

Vin de Corse-Calvi

This wine is produced in the Balagne area around Calvi on some 260ha, classed AOC by decree on 2 April 1976. The vineyards are situated among the sand and pebbles of the hillsides and plains at the foot of the highest uplands of Corsica. Many vines have been uprooted during the 1970s and 1980s, greatly reducing the productive capacity of this beautiful region.

The grape varieties used are not predominantly Corsican (only 26 per cent of the vines are Vermentino, Sciaccarello and Nielluccio), but are of generally good quality.

The white wines have finesse. The pale rosés are very aromatic and the reds are distinguished.

Vin de Corse-Coteaux du Cap Corse

This *appellation d'origine contrôlée*, classed by decree on 2 April 1976, covers the smallest area of any of Corsica's AOCs — 28ha — and has the smallest production — about 300hl; but the wines are some of the most sought-after on the island.

Vines at Morsiglia, in the Cap Corse zone. These vineyards, once very extensive, occupy no more than a few dozen hectares today, producing fine dry white wines and sweet Muscat wines.

At the end of the 18th century, vineyards here extended over 2,700ha. The wine growers were also sailors and merchants and they transported their wine to Pisa, Livorno and Genoa.

Today, little of this past remains, but the Vermentino, Ugni Blanc and Codivarte varieties still combine to produce an exceptional white wine. The wine growers also produce an unfortified sweet Muscat wine from partly dried grapes, and a *vin de liqueur* called Rappu, made by fortifying unfermented musts of various local white varieties.

Vin de Corse-Figari

These are the southernmost vineyards of Corsica and therefore of France, too. The vineyard area covers 200ha, and was classed AOC by decree on 2 April 1976.

The light, shallow, well-drained soils; the hot, dry climate; the strong, persistent winds: all these factors hardly provide suitable conditions for the cultivation of the vine. But there are small, sheltered areas here where the vine has prospered for centuries.

Extensive uprooting of the vines (80 per cent of the area) during the early 1980s has resulted in a fall in production from 12,890hl of AOC wine in 1979 to 5,141hl in 1983.

The wines have lightness and finesse. An unusual red grape variety is found here, the Carcajolo Noir. Trials are in progress to establish whether or not it will become the equal of Sciaccarello or Nielluccio, the two other leading red Corsican grape varieties.

Vin de Corse-Porto-Vecchio

This beautiful region of brush and pinewoods has a few traditional vineyards. But in the 1960s, great numbers of vines were planted here, eventually covering 1,500ha. Today a large number of these vineyards have been uprooted. Wine enjoying AOC classification, following the decree of 2 April 1976, was initially grown on a hundred hectares or so, producing 8,670hl in 1977–8, then declining to an average of around 1,600hl since 1980.

As in all the Vin de Corse named wine-growing areas, three main Corsican varieties are used: the Sciaccarello, Nielluccio and Vermentino, with the Midi varieties Syrah and Mourvèdre in a secondary role. The white wines are fresh, the rosés have finesse and the reds are well balanced.

Vin de Corse-Sartène

This old wine-growing *terroir* was classed AOC by decree on 2 April 1976. At the end of the 19th century there were three large estates sited here, and these were at the forefront of the technical developments of the time.

Today, the vineyards cover 400ha, sited in the three river valleys of the Baracci, the Rizzanèse and the Ortolo. Production is relatively stable, the total being over 10,000hl annually. The range of grape varieties is traditional and relies to a great extent on Corsican vines: Sciaccarello, Montanaccia (a clone of the Sciaccarello adapted to high slope sites), the Barbarossa and the Vermentino. However in the vineyards planted after 1960, less emphasis has been placed on local grape varieties.

The wines are characterful and strong. The whites are full-bodied, the rosés are sturdy, and the reds are full and well structured.

Vin de Savoie

This *appellation*, classed AOC by decree on 4 September 1973, covers 50 or so communes in the *départements* of Savoie, Haute-Savoie, Isère and Ain.

The different *terroirs* and grape varieties of AOC Vin de Savoie produce unusual and distinctive white, red and rosé wines. In 1986, this *appellation* produced 19,000hl of white wine from the Jacquère, Chardonnay, Chasselas, Pinot Gris and Aligoté grapes. The red grape varieties Gamay, Mondeuse, Pinot Noir, Persan and Cabernet Sauvignon produced a total of 18,000hl of Vin de Savoie red and rosé wine in the same year.

Vin de Savoie followed by a *cru* name

This *appellation d'origine contrôlée* was ratified by the decrees of 4 September 1973 and 27 August 1986, and the following *cru* names may be used.

Abymes

The vineyard area of this *cru* covers approximately 200ha, divided among four communes situated at the foot of Mont Granier, to the south of Chambéry: Apremont, les Marches, Myans in Savoie and Chapareillan in Isére.

The principal white grape variety used here is the Jacquère. It likes the east-facing slopes on which it is grown, these being formed of marlacious limestone. They were produced by a landslide on Mont Granier in 1248.

Abymes is a dry, light, supple, discreetly flowery white wine. Production was 12,000hl in 1986.

After being kept on its lees during the winter, the wine is quickly bottled in spring to preserve its very slight effervescence and fresh aromas. To best appreciate its youthful charms, it should be drunk as soon as possible, preferably within a year of its vintage.

Apremont

These vineyards cover nearly 300ha on the steepest scree slopes of Mont Granier. They face east and southeast, and lie at a height of at least 500m in the communes of Apremont, Saint-André-les-Marches and Saint-Baldoph, all of them in Savoie.

There are many private growers in this part of the Vin de Savoie area. There is also a cooperative at Apremont, and this produces more than 2,500hl annually of white wine under the Apremont or Abymes *cru* names.

Arbin

Situated in the Combe de Savoie beside the river Isère, along the bottom of the Massif des Bauges, the commune of Arbin next to Montmélian is fortunate in having one of the best wine-growing areas for the Mondeuse variety, a grape that likes south-facing slopes of limestone and marlacious limestone scree.

The red wines of the *cru* of Arbin are produced in comparatively small quantities: 2,000hl in 1986, for example. Classic red wine vinification methods produce a tannic wine of pronounced character, for laying down for a few years. The deep red colour of Arbin wine often has purple and blackish notes to it. Depending on the vintage, the wine's aromas may suggest strawberries, raspberries, blackcurrants, violets and sometimes even spices. This wine improves greatly by being given a period of three to five years' bottle ageing.

Ayze (Mousseux and Pétillant)

The vineyards of the Ayze *cru* are situated on the right bank of the Arve in Haute-Savoie, southeast of Geneva, and cover around 40ha divided between the communes of Ayze (or Ayse), Bonneville and Marignier. The vineyards lie on the southeast and southwest slopes of the mountain of le Môle and they are planted in soils which combine molasse and glacial alluvial screes.

A combination of two white grape varieties is used: first and foremost the Gringet, supplemented by the Roussette d'Ayse. Production reached 900hl in 1986. Only white wines given their sparkle by secondary fermentation in bottle are permitted to use the *cru* name. To achieve this, a local method called *fermentation spontanée* (spontaneous fermentation) may be used. Ayze is usually sold as a Brut *vin mousseux*.

Chautagne

From the northern point of the Lac du Bourget in the direction of Seyssel, the vineyards of the Vin de Savoie *cru* of Chautagne cover 45ha of the communes of Chindrieux, Ruffieux, Serrières-en-Chautagne and Motz. The red grape variety Gamay Noir à Jus Blanc, and to a lesser extent Pinot Noir and Mondeuse, produced some 8,000hl of red Chautagne in 1986. Chautagne also produces white wines, based on the Jacquère, Aligoté and Pinot Gris varieties: 3,000hl of these were marketed in 1986. But it is above all for its full-bodied, warm, varietal Gamay wines, coming from vines on the west-facing limestone screes and molasse grits of the Montagne du Gros Foug, that Chautagne is known. This wine requires two or three years' ageing before it reaches its best.

Chignin
The commune of Chignin, situated to the southeast of Chambéry, circumscribes 150ha of vineyards situated on the limestone and marlacious limestone screes of the south-facing slopes of the Massif des Bauges. In 1986, 8,000hl of white wine and 1,500hl of red wine were produced, the main grape varieties being the Jacquère for white wines and the Gamay, Mondeuse and Pinot Noir for red wines.

There are two types of white wine produced (largely by individual growers rather than cooperatives) here. On the one hand, there are delicate, fresh, dry white wines that have not undergone malolactic fermentation; on the other, there are those that have undergone malolactic fermentation, and that are deeper in colour and aromatic nuance, rounder and slightly softer. In both cases, the wines are best drunk young.

Chignin-Bergeron
This white-wine *cru* is sited in three communes in the Combe de Savoie, southeast of Chambéry: Chignin, Montmélian and Francin. Some 600hl were produced here in 1986. The Roussanne (locally called the Bergeron) variety is planted on the sunniest parts of the limestone screes of these communes for Chignin-Bergeron. This grape is a native of Drôme and has difficulty in ripening; very careful vinification is therefore necessary to obtain a characteristically generous, feminine wine with aromas of hawthorn blossom, able to retain its qualities for two or three years.

Cruet
Northeast of Arbin on the right bank of the river Isère lies the commune of Cruet, with its excellent *terroir* of clay-limestone scree and rubble, facing southeast from the slopes of the Massif des Bauges. White wine from the Jacquère grape variety is the principal production of the *appellation* Cruet. This dry wine is full of the charm of youth; some 1,400hl are marketed on average each year.

Jongieux
The exact area of this new *cru* is in the process of being officially defined, but it will include vineyard parcels from the communes of Jongieux, Billième, Lucey, Saint-Jean-de-Chevelu and Yenne, lying to the west of the Lac du Bourget. The west-facing vineyards spread out at the foot of the Mont de la Charvaz, between the Mont du Chat and the left bank of the river Rhône. They consist principally of screes and pebbly moraines on which the red grape varieties Gamay, Mondeuse and Pinot Noir, and the white grape variety Altesse, predominate. The subtlety of the red wines develops from their first year onwards, and those produced from the Mondeuse are best at two to four years.

Marignan
Northeast of Douvaine on the edge of Lac Léman (Lake Geneva) lie a few hectares of

Vines near Ruffieux, north of Lac du Bourget, within the appellation *area of Vin de Savoie-Chautagne. The Grand Colombier peak is visible in the background.*

pebbly moraines in the commune of Sciez (Haute-Savoie), planted with the Chasselas grape variety. Marignan, a dry white wine similar in character to Crépy, is produced from these.

Marin

The exact area of this new white-wine *cru* is in the process of being officially defined, but it will contain vineyard parcels from the communes of Marin and Publier which overlook Lac Léman (Lake Geneva), lying east of Thonon-les-Bains in Haute-Savoie. On glacial moraines and pebbly alluvial soils, the Chasselas (locally known as the Fendant) grape variety produces a dry, *perlant* (very slightly sparkling), light and zesty wine.

Montmélian

A restricted area, lying below the Roche du Guet (Massif des Bauges) in the communes of Montmélian and Francin, southeast of Chambéry, produces less than 500hl of white wine annually, from the Jacquère grape, for the *cru* Montmélian. It should be drunk young, and is similar in character to Chignin. Very small quantities of red wine are also produced here.

Ripaille

The estate of the Château de Ripaille in the commune of Thonon-les-Bains on Lac Léman (Lake Geneva) covers about 15ha of west-facing pebbly lacustrine terraces. In 1986, 1,000hl of white wine from the Chasselas (Fendant) grape variety were produced here. Ripaille is a light, easy, supple white wine.

Saint-Baldoph

This is the Vin de Savoie *cru* with the largest production. The wines are based on the Jacquère grape variety, and 22,000hl were produced in 1986. Saint-Baldoph is a predominantly fresh, light, slightly flowery dry white wine. It is almost always very slightly sparkling due to its slow fermentation, and to having been left on its lees during the winter before early spring bottling. Just like the neighbouring *cru* of Abymes, it should be drunk in the year following the harvest.

Saint-Jean-de-la-Porte

This is the final *cru* of the right bank of the Isère, lying in the commune of Saint-Jean-de-la-Porte, on the slopes of the Massif des Bauges southeast of Chambéry. The name is little used, and annual production is only a few hundred hectolitres of red wine from the Mondeuse. This wine improves with age.

Saint-Jeoire-Prieuré

Adjacent to Chignin in the direction of Chambéry is the *cru* of Saint-Jeoire-Prieuré, known for small quantities of dry white wine produced each year from the Jacquère grape. This wine is similar to Chignin in character.

Vin de Savoie-Ayze Mousseux and Pétillant

See Vin de Savoie followed by a *cru* name.

Vin de Savoie Mousseux and Pétillant

The Mousseux and Pétillant wines of Savoie, produced by the *méthode champenoise*, come mainly from the Jacquère grape variety. The sometimes delicate production techniques needed to produce good sparkling wines and, to an even greater extent, good slightly sparkling wines, means that their manufacture is mostly in the hands of specialized producers. These refreshing sparkling wines enjoy deserved success.

Vin du Bugey

The development of the Bugey vineyards reached a peak under Roman occupation, before being almost obliterated by repeated barbarian invasions. In the Middle Ages, the monks showed great interest in vineyard cultivation, selecting grape varieties suitable to the area which resulted in the creation of remarkable vineyards alongside abbeys, such as that known as 'la Chèvrerie' at Culoz.

Since then, the wines of Bugey (the region from which the famous gastronome Brillat-Savarin came) have always been highly appreciated. In 1963, production methods were regulated by VDQS *appellation* requirements. The area under vines has risen from 250ha in 1982 to almost 300ha in 1986, producing about 15,000hl of white, red and rosé wine each year, half of this figure as sparkling wine.

Bugey is situated in the southeast corner of the *département* of Ain, and borders both Savoie and Haute-Savoie, along the twists and turns of the upper Rhône. The most favourably exposed slopes, at the base of the Jurassic period uplands in the *arrondissement* of Belley, and in the area around Pont-d'Ain some 50km to the northwest of Belley, form quite different *terroirs*. Among the soil types found in the Bugey area are marls, marlacious limestones, limestone and molasse, all of which suit the production of dry white wine.

In this neighbouring region to Savoie, the principal grape varieties are those of Burgundy and Savoie itself. For white wines, the Chardonnay, Altesse, Aligoté, Mondeuse Blanche (locally known as the Dongine) and Jacquère are used, either singly or in combination. These wines are characteristically fresh and lively. The same range of varieties is responsible for the excellent sparkling (*mousseux*) and slightly sparkling (*pétillant*) wines of Bugey (see overleaf). Roussette du Bugey is based on a blend of Altesse and Chardonnay grapes.

The Gamay grape variety gives its youthful and fruity character to the red and rosé wines of Bugey. With the addition of small proportions of wine made from the Poulsard variety, the medium-dry rosé *mousseux* or *pétillant* wines of the Bugey *cru* Cerdon are produced by means of the *méthode champenoise* or *méthode naturelle* (with secondary fermentation in bottle). The Pinot Noir is used for its elegance in the red wines of the *cru* Manicle. The Mondeuse is also used in red Vins du Bugey for its personality and richness.

Vin du Bugey followed by a *cru* name

Following the decree of 27 September 1963, three Vin du Bugey *crus* were classed as VDQS, and permitted the use of their name with that of the main *appellation*.

Cerdon

The *appellation* covers eight communes surrounding Cerdon, lying between Nantua and Pont d'Ain. There are about 200ha of vineyards in the *cru* zone, but only 2,500 to 3,000hl of AOC Vin du Bugey-Cerdon are produced each year. Most of the wine produced here is carbonated sparkling wine, and cannot therefore claim an AOC.

The vineyards of Cerdon are all sited on very steep slopes. The main grape variety is the Gamay.

The sparkling wine of Cerdon can be made by only two methods. The first method is called the *méthode naturelle* or *traditionnelle* (natural or traditional method). For this, the fermentation of the wine is slowed by filtration, natural winter cold and centrifugation, while a certain amount of sugar (40–60g per litre) still remains in the wine. The wine is then bottled in January or February, and allowed to develop a partial effervescence in bottle by the fermentation of some of this sugar. It is then filtered under pressure to remove the yeast deposit. The resulting wine is most often a slightly sparkling rosé. It retains 30–40g per litre of grape sugar, and it has a low alcoholic strength, around 8°. This is the authentic Cerdon of tradition.

The *méthode champenoise* is, though, also used. This yields more consistent results and produces sound sparkling wines, but their typicality and regional character is much inferior to that of wine produced by the *méthode naturelle*. Moreover the *liqueur d'expédition* (sweetening wine added after the removal of the deposit) contains saccharose, which is very different from the fruit sugars left in wine produced by the *méthode naturelle*.

Manicle

In the locality of Manicle, situated to the southwest of Virieu-le-Grand, was the vineyard of the famous gastronome Brillat-Savarin, who also had a cellar there. The wines of Manicle have always had a great reputation in the Bugey area.

They are mentioned in 19th-century documents, and were often featured in the menus of banquets served at the best restaurants of the region. Today, however, the vineyard area is only 2–3ha in size, and the volume of its production, 150hl in 1986, is of little significance.

The white wine of Manicle is made from a combination of Chardonnay (70 per cent) and Pinot Gris. It is characterful: rich, supple and vigorous. Red wines come exclusively from the Pinot Noir grape variety. The vineyards of Manicle are south-facing and quite steeply sloping; the soil is light and gravelly.

Montagnieu

The splendid slopes of Montagnieu stretch over the three communes of Seillonnaz, Briord and Montagnieu, situated some 15km west of Belley, and consist today of about 30ha of vines.

The Altesse, Mondeuse Blanche and one or two other white grape varieties are the most commonly used types. The Montagnieu slopes have made their reputation with VDQS Roussette du Bugey-Montagnieu, made from the Altesse. But this grape variety is now losing ground to other varieties.

The white wines of Montagnieu are strongly perfumed, just off-dry, and often with an agreeable natural *pétillance* (very slight sparkle). Since about 1965, it is sparkling wines made by the *méthode champenoise* that have maintained and developed the reputation of Montagnieu, particularly in the Lyon area. It is now these sparkling wines that form the major part of production of Vin du Bugey-Montagnieu.

Vin du Bugey Mousseux and Pétillant

The production of sparkling wines in Bugey has a long tradition. In the 19th century, members of the well-to-do middle classes used to impress their guests by serving them 'Champagne du Bugey'. But it was from the beginning of the 20th century, and especially following the First World War, that production of these wines was developed. The Vins du Bugey Mousseux and Pétillant received VDQS classification by decree in 1963.

The *méthode champenoise* (with secondary fermentation in bottle) is used for these wines. The basic grape variety is the Chardonnay, with other grape varieties like the Aligoté and, especially, the Molette used in a secondary role. In 1986, about 50 per cent of the wine marketed under the Vin du Bugey name was either Mousseux or Pétillant.

Vins d'Entraygues et du Fel

This small, mountainous vineyard area, characterized by its narrow terraces or banks adjacent to the Lot and the Truyère, would first have been cultivated in the 9th century by the monks of the abbey of Conges. Throughout the Middle Ages, the vineyards had a local reputation. The phylloxera catastrophe in the 19th century devastated them, however, and they remained in decline until 1960. Following this date, a plan to restructure them was initiated, to bring the area back on to the wine-producing map.

The vineyards cover 68ha but, at the present time, only 14ha produce wine that meets *appellation* regulations.

Nearly all (90 per cent) of the vineyards classed VDQS by decree on 18 February 1965 are found in the commune of Entraygues-sur-Truyère, although eight communes or parts of communes have a right to the *appellation*.

Because of the severity of the climate in northern Aveyron, the vines are planted in tiers between 200m and 400m where the two rivers (Truyère and Lot) that surround the town of Entraygues flow together, amid outcrops of bare rock.

To the west, the vineyard soils are schistous and well drained. To the east, decomposing granites have given rise to siliceous soils and sandy clays.

VDQS classification was achieved on the basis of a simplification of grape variety mix used. For red wines, these varieties are the Fer (25 per cent maximum), the two Cabernet varieties, the Gamay, Jurançon Noir, Merlot, Négrette, Pinot Noir and Mouyssaguès. The rosé wines are based on the Gamay (up to 25 per cent) and on the other red varieties listed above.

The white wines are produced from the Chenin Blanc (80 per cent minimum) and the Mauzac. A yield of 45hl/ha is authorized.

There was little noticeable increase in production during the 1970s, but by 1988, total production reached 1,250hl, 45 per cent of this figure as red wine, 22 per cent as rosé wine and 33 per cent white wine.

The red wines are deep in colour and firm, and they owe their tannic character and distinctive aroma to the Fer grape variety. The high proportion of Chenin Blanc grapes in the white wine accounts for its finesse and freshness.

This vineyard of newly planted vines at Entraygues has been created under the local restructuring plan.

Vins d'Estaing

Some 35km northwest of Rodez, between Espalion and Entraygues, the 10ha of Vins d'Estaing produce wines classed VDQS by the decree of 4 November 1965.

The south-facing slopes of this area are divided into narrow terraces. The main grape varieties for red and rosé wine production here are the Fer and the Négrette. The Gamay, which was largely replaced by the Fer during vineyard redevelopment, is now coming back into favour with wine growers. Another local red grape variety, the Mouyssaguès, is valued for its productivity. Also present, though in small quantities only, are the Cabernet Franc, Cabernet Sauvignon, Merlot, Abouriou Noir, Jurançon Noir, Duras, Castets and Pinot Noir. The red wines of Estaing are deeply coloured, powerfully aromatic and acquire finesse with bottle age.

For the white wines, the main grape used is a local variety of the Chenin Blanc known as the Gamet Blanc, together with the Roussellou, another local variety. The white wines of the Gamet are rather dry and acid, but clean tasting. The Roussetou produces a wine with a taste reminiscent of gun flint.

Annual production was 111hl in 1966, and rose to 562hl in 1983. It reached 1,200hl in 1988, with 46 per cent of the wines being red, 20 per cent white and 34 per cent rosé.

Vins de Lavilledieu

Classified VDQS by decree on 22 January 1954, the Vins de Lavilledieu are mainly rosé and red, and are similar in style to the wines of the neighbouring Côtes du Frontonnais.

The Lavilledieu growing zone is situated on gravelly ground between the rivers Tarn and Garonne in the centre of the Tarn-et-Garonne *département*. Thirteen communes are included in the *appellation*.

The vineyards were in a poor state after 1950, and so a team of wine growers and technicians, supported by the local cooperative, embarked on the production of a quality wine based on the Négrette grape variety. The Tannat variety is now equally used, contributing colour, acidity, tannins and ageing potential to blends. This little *appellation*, controlled by an association that vigorously protects the interests of the wine growers, looks set to enjoy success in the future.

Vins de Marcillac

The Marcillac vineyard area was classed VDQS by decree on 4 November 1965. Situated 25 km northwest of Rodez, the Marcillac zone is made up of a series of valleys formed by the river Dourdou and its tributaries, which flow into the Lot. The valley sides are steeply sloped, and are particularly favourable to the cultivation of the vine.

The total vineyard area occupies more than 500ha, of which 108ha are classed VDQS.

Vines have grown in the Marcillac area since the 10th century. The devastation caused by phylloxera towards the end of the 19th century led to vineyards falling into disuse. It is only since the creation of a wine-growing cooperative here in 1963 that the vineyards have again been developed and maintained.

The soils are varied: limestone, clay and siliceous types are all found here. The most important of these is a red clay deposit known as *terre des Causses* (Causses earth): this plays the role of mother rock in combination with local limestones.

More than 85 per cent of plantings are of the Fer variety. Other grape varieties are all diminishing in importance here. Occasionally Gamay, a little Merlot and Jurançon Noir are found in the vineyards. The Mouyssaguès, a variety which had an important place in Mercillac before the onset of phylloxera, has now become extremely rare. The Valdiguié is also seldom seen in vineyards here nowadays thanks to its irregular productivity.

A very small number of white wines are produced in Marcillac from Clairette, Mauzac and Muscat à Petits Grains Blancs.

The best wines are those grown on soils with a high limestone content. In general, Marcillac's red wines are noted for their dark, intense colour: red-black with purple glints. They have an aromatic range that includes scents of strawberry and blackcurrant. Rosé wines are also produced in Marcillac, and these are light, very fruity and lively. All Marcillac wines are best drunk young.

Since 1966, production has increased steadily and is now close on 5,000hl per year.

The Vins de Moselle vineyards have shrunk greatly following damage suffered during the First and Second World Wars.

Vins de Moselle

These wines, classed VDQS by decree on 9 August 1951, and very popular in former times, have restricted production today. A great deal of grubbing up of vines took place during the two World Wars as German growers feared competition from the wines of the French Moselle. The area of production covers 15 communes, and red, white and light rosé wines are all produced in limited quantities.

Vins de l'Orléanais

This vineyard area, classed VDQS by decree on 9 August 1951, covers about 100ha. For white wines, the varieties used are the Chardonnay (known locally as the Auvernat Blanc) and Pinot Gris (known locally as the Auvernat Gris); the red and rosé varieties are the Pinot Noir, Meunier and the Cabernet Franc.

Average annual production is 3,500hl of red wine, 500hl of rosé and 200hl of white. The area of production covers 26 communes.

The reds are light, straightforward and

smooth. The rosés are light in colour, dry and lively. The whites are dry but well rounded.

Vins du Haut-Poitou

This vineyard area, classed VDQS by decree on 23 October 1970, covers roughly 500ha. The white grape varieties grown here are the Sauvignon Blanc, Chardonnay, Pinot Blanc and Chenin Blanc (the last named to form no more than 20 per cent of blends); the red and rosé varieties grown are the Pinot Noir, Gamay, Merlot, Côt, Cabernet Franc, Cabernet Sauvignon, Gamay de Chaudenay and Grolleau (the last two varieties to form no more than 20 per cent of blends in each case). Production is around 15,000hl of red wine, 13,000hl of white and 2,500hl of rosé annually. The area of production extends over 45 communes or parts of communes in Vienne and Deux-Sèvres.

The white wines are at once dry, light and rounded, with fresh, sustained aromas. The rosé wines are similar in style to the white wines, though a little firmer.

The red wines are light in colour with a redcurrant hue. They have a fruity aroma and are smooth, round, lively, with little astringence. They are best drunk young.

Vins de Thouarsais *See* Thouarsais.

Viognier

Synonyms: *Vionnier*, *Petit Vionnier*, *Viogné*, *Galopine* at la Tronche, near Grenoble.

Young leaves arachnoid, with bronze-coloured patches.

Leaves medium sized, orbicular, bullate, contorted, five-lobed with narrow lateral sinuses, acute at base, petiolar sinus in open U-shape; dentation convex, narrow; underside of blade downy. Branches ribbed, light green, slightly brown on the side exposed to the sun; tendrils long and fleshy.

Bunches medium sized, conical, compact, sometimes winged; grapes small, spherical or slightly ovoid, amber white, thick skinned, slightly musky taste; ripening period: second epoch.

This is a variety of poor fertility, and it has to be pruned long; when vinified on its own, it produces fragrant white wines of great quality, most notably those that are harvested on the right bank of the Rhône in AOC Condrieu and Château Grillet. A single registered clone has been approved: number 642. Classed as 'recommended' in Rhône, Loire, Isère, Drôme and Ardèche; in these *départements* some 20ha are under cultivation.

Volnay

The secret of the finesse of Volnay's wines is buried in its soil. Siliceous limestone soils, white marls and iron oxide are all found there: an ideal environment for the vine. The *appellation d'origine contrôlée* of this village on the Côte de Beaune, classed by decree on 9 September 1937, covers 213ha, of which 115ha are Premier Cru, divided among over 20 vineyard sites.

Volnay's red wines are based on the Pinot Noir and Pinot Gris, with the Pinot Liébault, a clone of the Pinot Noir, also being specified in the regulations; minimum alcoholic

A small path between the vines at Volnay. The seductive red wines of this Côte de Beaune village are characterized by exquisite scents of violet and raspberry.

Vosne-Romanée, a village known the world over for its Grands Crus, and for its other elegant and balanced red wines.

strength is 10.5°, with 11° for the Premiers Crus. The base yield is 40hl/ha, producing an annual average harvest of 7,000hl of exclusively red wine.

White wines produced here can only be sold under the Meursault *appellation*.

Volnay's wines are delicate, perhaps the most elegant of those of the Côte de Beaune; gentle, supple and rounded, they often possess a particularly fine aroma, reminiscent of strawberries. Volnay reaches its peak of maturity comparatively quickly, but nevertheless ages well.

The cuverie *(vat room) of the Château de Vougeot, built in the 12th century, contains four magnificent presses, in addition to numerous wooden vats.*

Volnay-Santenots

The paradox of this *appellation d'origine contrôlée*, one of the best of the Côte de Beaune, is that the red wines harvested in the vineyard sites of Santenots-Blancs, Santenots-du-Milieu, Santenots-Dessous, Pétures or Eptures, and Santenots are entitled to the Volnay-Santenots AOC while being situated in the commune of Meursault.

The vineyards cover 29ha, and are subject to the customary requirements of red burgundy of this quality level: an alcoholic strength of 11° and a yield of 35hl/ha.

The wines of Volnay-Santenots possess the same qualities as the 'village' or 'commune' wines of Volnay, but with additional aroma, bouquet and longevity.

Vosne-Romanée

This is the most prestigious AOC village name of Burgundy, ratified by decree on 11 September 1936; it constitutes what is almost a separate family, as its vineyard sites and parcels are so rich in variety and quality. Obviously at first the name conjures those of its world-renowned Grands Crus: Romanée-Saint-Vivant, Richebourg, Romanée-Conti, La Romanée, La Tâche, each described under its own heading, but one should not overlook the glorious range of Premiers Crus of Vosne-Romanée which, from 58ha of this Côte de Nuits village, produce wines of luscious power. The soils found here are on the whole calcareous and ferruginous. The minimum alcoholic strengths are 11.5° for the Grands Crus, 11° for the Premier Crus and 10.5° for the 'village' or 'commune' wines; yields are between 30hl/ha and 35hl/ha, and average annual production is 4,000hl.

It has generally been agreed that the wines of Vosné-Romanée qualify as '*vins complets*' ('complete wines'), as all great burgundies are. Especially appreciated is the velvety finesse and delicate, inspiring balance of these wines of breeding.

Vougeot

Following the decree of 8 December 1936, the *appellation d'origine contrôlée* area of Vougeot on the Côte des Nuits was specified as covering 17ha, of which 10ha are Premiers Crus. Annual harvests are small: 50hl of white wines and 370hl of red wines. The base yield is 35hl/ha, with minimum alcoholic strengths of 10.5° for the red wines and 11° for the red Premiers Crus, and of 11° for the white wines, with 11.5° for the white Premiers Crus. The

Vouvray. The vines put down their roots in a thin cultivable soil layer known as aubuis; *this covers the limestone tufa bedrock in which the famous 'troglodytic' dwellings of Vouvray are built.*

red wines of Vougeot are appreciated for their dark ruby colour and their powerful aroma of truffles, violets and wild herbs. The same qualities are found more vividly in the famous Grand Cru Clos de Vougeot. The white wines of the Clos Blanc (or Vigne Blanche) have a light hazelnut taste.

Vouvray

This vineyard area covers about 1,200ha, and the sole grape variety used is the Chenin Blanc (or Pineau Blanc de la Loire). Annual production is around 49,000hl.

The area of production, classed *appellation d'origine contrôlée* by decree on 8 December 1936, extends over the communes or parts of communes of Vouvray, Rochecorbon, Vernou-sur-Brenne, Sainte-Radegonde, Chançay, Noizay, Reugny and Parçay-Meslay.

Depending on the weather pattern during the year, the richness of the grape in sugars results in either the production of dry wines (after cold summers, as in 1980) or sweet wines (after warm summers, as in 1976).

Generally speaking, the wines are deeply coloured: straw yellow turning to golden yellow with age. The aromas are fruity and floral, with a mineral hint in certain cases. When mature, the wines are characterized by aromatic suggestions of quince.

The wines are full, very supple, delicate and lively, with the characteristic astringence of the Chenin Blanc often present. They age extremely well, especially those produced after sunny summers. The very finest Vouvray wines can last a hundred years or more.

Vouvray Mousseux

This *appellation* area covers about 550ha, though the exact figure varies from year to year; and the sole grape variety used is the Chenin Blanc. The AOC classification was by decree on 8 December 1936, and the area of production extends over the same communes or parts of the communes as are specified for the Vouvray *appellation*.

Annual production is around 31,000hl. During a very sunny year, when fine still wines can readily be made, production of sparkling wines sinks to 21,000hl or so.

The colour of Vouvray Mousseux is a deep straw yellow turning to amber yellow in the case of mature wines. These sparkling wines are full, delicate and lively. They keep well.

Vouvray Pétillant

This AOC classification dates from the decree of 8 December 1936, modified by the decree of 20 July 1959. Around 40 per cent of all sparkling wine production in Vouvray is in Pétillant (slightly sparkling) form.

The area of production extends over the same communes or parts of communes as the Vouvray *appellation*. Vouvray Pétillant is balanced, delicate and lively.

The white wine of Vouvray, whether sparkling, slightly sparkling or still, and often an excellent vin de garde *(wine for long keeping), matures perfectly in caves hollowed in the rock.*

VINS DU CENTRE

From the Côtes d'Auvergne to Valençay, a mosaic of vineyards united under the name 'Vins du Centre' (Wines of Central France) flourishes along the banks of the river Loire. Subject to a continental climate, each of the* appellations *produces wines similar in nature: dry whites, and light red wines low in tannin.

The Vins du Centre, scattered along the upper reaches of the Loire, each have a different history, since every vineyard area has developed in its own time, by its own rhythm and according to the vicissitudes of the particular locale in which it is found. The vineyards of Reuilly were given to the abbey of Saint-Denis de France in Seine-Saint-Denis by the Merovingian king Dagobert I (605-639) ... By 820, the wine production of Sancerre was already subject to local rulings ... The wines of the Côtes du Forez and of Saint-Pourçain appeared at great feasts during the Middle Ages, and later at the tables of the kings of France ... The wines of the Orléans area were celebrated by Rabelais (1483-1553) ... The Côte Roannaise, one of France's oldest vineyard areas, underwent considerable expansion following the opening of the Briare canal in 1642, then the Loing canal in 1723 ...

At the foot of the hill of Sancerre, the river Loire turns westwards and begins its journey towards Touraine.

The 15 appellations of the Vins du Centre — both AOC and VDQS — may have experienced different rhythms of development, but nevertheless they can all lay claim to a long history attested by local traditions and the development of individual *terroirs*.

The vineyard zones and their soils

The soils of the Côtes d'Auvergne are all of volcanic origin. The vines, sited on slopes of south-southeasterly exposure, are planted in a number of different soil types. Depending on the exact site, sandy soils of grantic origin, marls, limestones, and fragments of lava are all found. All the soils are dry and well drained. These factors explain the finesse and fruitiness of the wines of the Côtes d'Auvergne.

The soils of the Côtes du Forez tend to be clayey and siliceous. The vineyards run along the sides of the rivers Lignon and Onzon. The wines are light and firm. The Côte Roannaise zone has similar kinds of soil, and the wines are light and fruity.

The Saint-Pourçain vineyards lie along a line of hills about 30km long and a few kilometres wide. The soils are varied. The influence of marl and limestone brings pleasing fullness to the wines.

Soils of siliceous gravels and sands bring finesse to the wines of Quincy, a fairly flat vineyard area situated in the Cher valley.

The Reuilly vineyards lie to each side of the river Arnon, on semi-sloping and sloping sites, giving fullness to the wines. The vineyards of Menetou-Salon are situated on hills northeast of Bourges enjoying south-southwesterly aspects. The soils are primarily limestone based, giving delicate wines.

The vines of the Côtes de Gien grow on hill slopes, but also on gravel terraces rich in silica, giving the wines finesse.

At Sancerre, the vineyards occupy a very picturesque setting. The dry, limestone soils of the area are known locally as *caillottes*. On higher ground, more limestone soils of the type locally called *terres blanches*, belonging to the same Kimmeridgian stage of the Jurassic period as the finest soils of Chablis, are found. These limestone soils give a supple structure to the wines of Sancerre. Around Sancerre itself the soils are clayey and siliceous.

The Pouilly vineyard zone stretches along charming hills at around 350m in altitude, which means that the vines can be nipped by late frosts and the potential area of the vineyards is restricted. The soils are varied, but the marls and especially the compact Kimmeridgian limestones give wines of finesse and fullness.

The little vineyard area of Cheverny borders the Sologne district. The wines are fine and light, thanks to the siliceous soils.

The soils of the Vins de l'Orléanais vary, as does the exposure of the vines. The conditions change almost from commune to commune, but in general the wines are light.

The grape varieties

This region is the kingdom of the Sauvignon Blanc. It is found in almost all of the *appellations* of the Vins du Centre. Other white grape varieties grown here include the Romorantin, especially in the Cheverny area at Mont-près-Chambord; Aligoté in Saint-Pourçain; Sacy (locally known as Tressalier), which produces very well-balanced wines in Saint-Pourçain; and the Saint-Pierre Doré, which is also grown in Saint-Pourçain.

For red wines, the Pinot Noir produces a fine, supple wine, low in tannin, able to express faithfully the nature of the *terroir* in which it grows. The Gamay Noir à Jus Blanc is also widespread here, and is favoured for the production of light, fruity wines for early drinking. The Meunier produces a *vin gris* (very pale rosé) in the Orléans area.

The style of the wines

The wines grown in this region undoubtedly share certain characteristics, and the main reason for this is a degree of climatic uniformity. Nevertheless, soils, grape varieties and the factor of human intervention, together with microclimatic differences, succeed in creating a range of wines of distinct individuality.

Côtes d'Auvergne

Most wine produced here is red, and the Gamay is the basic grape variety used. Pinot Noir is also authorized but seldom planted. On the predominantly acidic soils of this area, the main characteristic of the wines is always finesse complemented by a greater or lesser tannic firmness depending on the weather conditions of the year. The rosé wines are smooth, dry and fruity. Almost no white wine is produced in Côtes d'Auvergne.

Côtes du Forez

Both the red and rosé wines of the Côtes du Forez are produced from the Gamay. The red wines are low in tannin and fruity. The rosé wines are dry, supple and lively.

Côte Roannaise

The Gamay is used here to produce red wines which are both light and firmly structured, a characteristic combination in red *'vins de montagne'* (mountain wines). A few rosés are also made from the Gamay: they are light in colour and supple.

Saint-Pourçain

The red wines, made from the Gamay and Pinot Noir varieties, are garnet in colour. They are full and fine. The aroma is of dried fruit, with a characteristic, appealing freshness. They mature well in bottle.

The rosé wines are produced from the same two varieties as the red wines; they are light in colour, dry, firm, lively, and have finesse.

The white wines are dry and full, and are made from a characterful blend of Chardonnay, Sacy (locally called the Tressalier) and Saint-Pierre Doré varieties. Sparkling wines, made from the Sacy, account for a very tiny proportion of production.

Pouilly-Fumé

This is a dry white wine produced from the Sauvignon Blanc variety. The pebbly soil contains varying amounts of silica, clay and limestone, a mixture that gives a fine balance to the wine. It is powerful without losing balance, lively but still firm, and the whole is crowned by characteristically forthcoming, musky aromas. This wine matures well in bottle.

Pouilly, on the right bank of the Loire, has produced well-reputed dry white wines since the Middle Ages.

Pouilly-sur-Loire

The main grape variety used here is the Chasselas. Unfortunately, it may be blended with the Sauvignon Blanc, and this makes it a heavier and less graceful wine. At its best it is fine, dry, lively, with great breeding: a very good example of what the Chasselas can produce from siliceous soils in France. Those growers who have remained faithful to the Chasselas alone are owed a debt of thanks.

Sancerre
The white wines of Sancerre are produced from the Sauvignon Blanc variety alone, and they are what have earned Sancerre its reputation. The presence of limestone in the vineyards gives the wines an attractive shapeliness. They have an incomparable, pungent aroma, and are dry and lively. This wine ages well in bottle where it acquires attractive secondary aromas, less 'virile' and more floral than its primary aromas.

A single grape variety, the Pinot Noir, is used for the red wines of Sancerre, and it is grown on soils more siliceous and clayey than those in which the Sauvignon Blanc is planted. The silica gives the wines finesse, and the clay gives them firmness. Their overall character is fruity, floral, and then animal after a few years.

The rosé wine of Sancerre is also made from the Pinot Noir. It is dry and floral in character. It, too, ages well in bottle.

Menetou-Salon
The only grape variety used for the white wines is Sauvignon Blanc. The vineyards are sited on predominantly calcareous soils, so the wines are quite full. This fullness is balanced by firmness and liveliness, and the wines have the characteristically musky aroma of the Sauvignon Blanc, as well as mineral hints.

The Pinot Noir is used for the red wines of Menetou-Salon, which are supple but solidly textured. Their fruity aroma is pronounced, and they age well in bottle, acquiring delicacy as they do so. Rosé wines, based on the Pinot Noir, are dry and light.

Quincy
The vineyards of Quincy are sited on siliceous soils, so the white wines produced here, from Sauvignon Blanc, are characterized by greater lightness of body and more accentuated aromas than in Sancerre and Menetou-Salon.

Reuilly
Reuilly is also marked by limestone soils, and the white wines produced here, based on Sauvignon Blanc, have both fullness and finesse. The breeding of this wine is notable, as is its capacity to mature well in bottle.

The red wines of Reuilly are made from the Pinot Noir and are full bodied. They have fruity and floral aromas.

Pinot Gris is blended with Pinot Noir to produce dry, powerful, but nonetheless charming rosé wines.

Valençay
A number of grape varieties are used for the red wines of Valençay, among them the Gamay, Côt and Pinot Noir. The red wine of Valençay is moderately tannic, but still light and fresh. It is fruity, with an authentically rustic tang to it.

The rosé wines can be made from the same range of varieties as the red wines. They are dry, supple and smooth, sometimes with a hint of sweetness after very sunny years.

The Arbois, Sauvignon Blanc and Chardonnay varieties make up 60 per cent of the white wine blend, with the Chenin Blanc and Romorantin providing the balance. The wines are dry, quite full, with a lively touch to them.

Châteaumeillant
The main variety grown for red wines here is the Gamay (85 per cent of plantings), with the Pinot Noir providing the balance. The wine has a ruby colour. It is light, fresh and tasty, and keeps these qualities in bottle.

The balance of grape varieties used for the very light rosé '*vins gris*' of Châteaumeillant is similar to that used for the reds. *Vin gris* is in fact an older term than 'rosé', and it is one that has always been used here. The wines are dry, fresh and fruity.

Côtes de Gien
The grape varieties used for the red wines of the Côtes de Gien are Gamay (75 per cent of plantings) and Pinot Noir (25 per cent of plantings). The vineyards are sited on hillocks or terraces, and the siliceous soils give the wines both power and finesse.

The rosés are dry and light, and more or less lively depending on how fully the weather conditions of the year have ripened the grapes.

The white wines are based on the Sauvignon Blanc with the addition of a little Chenin Blanc. They are dry and well structured, with a characteristic musky aroma.

Vins de l'Orléanais
For the red wines, Meunier and Cabernet Franc are blended with about 10 per cent Pinot Noir. Three influences meet in this blend: the northeast (Champagne) with the Meunier; the west (Touraine) with the Cabernet Franc, and the east (Burgundy) with the Pinot Noir. The wine makers here try to produce, from siliceous soils with a greater or lesser admixture of clay, light and fruity wines with a touch of firmness.

The rosé wines are made from the same blend of varieties, and are light and lively.

The white wines are made from the Chardonnay and Pinot Gris varieties.

Cheverny
The association of Gamay and silica in the Cheverny area produces a very smooth and elegant red wine. It is lively, fruity and keeps well in bottle. Rosé wines, also generally Gamay based, are smooth and lively.

For the white wines, Sauvignon Blanc is mixed with Arbois, Petit Meslier, Romorantin and Chardonnay to give fine, dry and fruity wines which keep well in bottle.

The vineyards of Chavignol, even if subsumed within the Sancerre appellation, produce wines with a character of their own.

AVERAGE ANNUAL PRODUCTION OF THE VINS DU CENTRE AOCs				
APPELLATION	WHITE	RED	ROSÉ	SPARKLING
AOC				
Pouilly-Fumé	30 000			
Pouilly-sur-Loire	4 000			
Sancerre	75 000	5 000	10 000	
Menetou-Salon	2 600	1 200	400	
Quincy	3 500			
Reuilly	900	140	260	
VDQS				
Côtes du Forez		4 000	2 000	
Côte Roannaise		3 800	200	
Côtes d'Auvergne	10	14 000	7 000	
Saint-Pourçain	5 000	14 000	7 000	200
Valençay	900	4 200	950	
Châteaumeillant		2 700	1 800	
Côtes de Gien	400	3 000	500	
Vins de l'Orléanais	200	3 500	500	
Cheverny	6 000	5 500	600	700
	128 510	61 040	31 210	900
Total	221 660 hectolitres			

Sparkling wines are also produced from a range of varieties that may include Chardonnay, Arbois and Petit Meslier. They have to be made carefully to give them the finesse and lightness required of a sparkling wine today.

Climate

The climate of this large region is continental. No risk is therefore feared more by the growers than the late frosts of April and May. This problem is one of the reasons for the decline of wine-growing here. Well-protected slopes are sought for the planting of new vineyards.

Vinification

Optimum maturity is aimed for, without the overripening the Sauvignon Blanc is given in sunny years elsewhere. Concentration of the grape sugars would give the wines of this region an uncharacteristic, heavy quality.

After juice extraction by the most delicate pressing possible, the white wine must is run into 220-litre wooden casks to ferment. Vats are also used, preferably made of stainless steel. Long fermentation periods of about a month are preferred. Rosé and red wine vinification follows classic northern French lines with the red grapes being destalked before maceration, and with the rosé colour being produced by direct pressing of the red grapes.

After two or three rackings and filtration, the white wines are bottled in March.

Red wines made from the Pinot Noir are often matured in oak vats for a year before being bottled in September. Wines from Gamay are bottled earlier, before the beginning of summer.

The regional wine trade

This is a region of small wine businesses. Direct sales to local customers or tourists are therefore important.

Production is spread evenly between cooperatives and independent growers. The role played by the *négociant-éleveur* (a merchant with wine-growing and -making interests) is modest, although nevertheless important in Sancerre, Pouilly, Quincy, Saint-Pourçain and the Côtes d'Auvergne.

Wine organizations and festivities

Activities organized to celebrate the role of wine in this region are numerous, and it has one of the greatest concentrations of *confréries* in France. Among other gatherings, two of the most memorable are the great Foire aux Sorciers et Birettes (Fair of Sorcerors and Magicians — a local wine *confrérie*'s annual celebration) at Bué near Sancerre on the first Sunday of August; and the Fête de la Saint-Vincent at Chavignol in January, when the patron saint of wine growers is honoured with solemnity and fitting respect for traditions which go back to the Middle Ages.

Caveaux de dégustation ***(cellars where one can taste and try wines) are numerous in this region, and they enable the traveller to meet wine growers of all sorts — mischievous, frank, larger-than-life; men fashioned by the vine and vineyard work, the earth, the region's climate.***

THE ECONOMICS OF AOC WINES

The system of appellation d'origine contrôlée *wines, since its establishment in 1935, has been, year after year and without ever faltering, one of the great successes of the agriculture and food sectors of the French economy, as much on the home market as abroad.*

It is customary in France to oppose *vins de table* to *vins d'appellation d'origine contrôlée*, erroneously assuming the first signifies mediocrity and the second quality. The reality is quite different; quality is by no means limited to AOC wines. Does not every interested consumer know some excellent *vins de table*? And any wish to view French viticulture as being homogenized or uniform is superficial; it is rather characterized by its differences and its variousness.

In fact, rather than a Manichean or dualist vision rigorously opposing good and bad, a better approach is one which recognizes policy differences. French wine-growing is made up of complementary initiatives built on differing economic structures and strategies, resulting in products of great diversity. Just as there is no absolute definition of wine quality, so there is no single policy of quality. The *appellation d'origine contrôlée* system is certainly one way of achieving quality, but it is not the only one. It rubs shoulders with other policy strategies, such as *vins de pays*, varietal wines (made from a single grape variety) or branded wines. Each of these strategies produces a different result, and each has its own criteria for economic success.

When the consumer is faced with a full range of food and drink products on offer in a supermarket, he or she does not realize that a specific economic organization lies behind each one, and that each organization has its own unique structure and way of thinking. Nevertheless, this is so. One organization in particular, that which oversees the French system of *appellations d'origine contrôlée*, merits description here.

A flourishing economy

There are one million hectares of vineyards in France, and AOC vines occupy 375,000ha, or 35 per cent of the total area. Of the known 600,000 wine producers, 90,000 are understood to produce *appellation d'origine contrôlée* wines. The average area cultivated by an AOC wine producer therefore comes to a little more than 4ha.

The volume of AOC wine produced in 1986 was 21.2 million hl out of a total of 73.2 million hl of wine produced in France in the same year. A simple inference is that, since 37 per cent of French vineyards were responsible for 29 per cent of production, yields are lower for AOC wines (56hl/ha) than for other wines (83hl/ha).

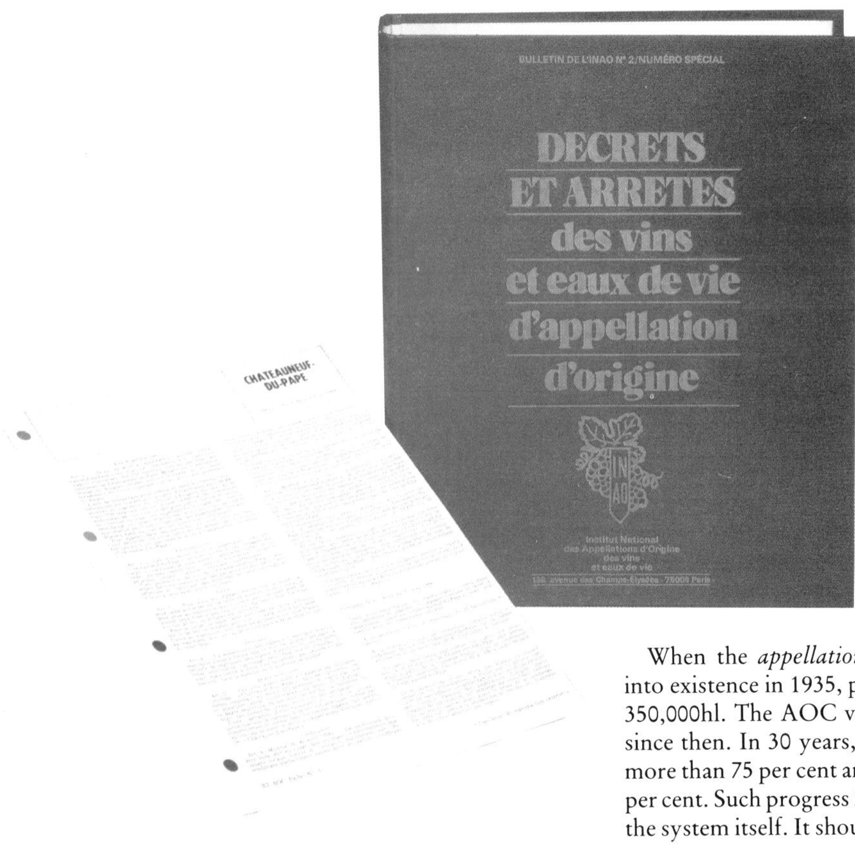

The volume of **décrets et arrêtés** *(decrees and orders) of INAO contains the rules and specifications for every AOC of France. The page shown refers to Châteauneuf-du-Pape, one of the first AOCs to have been granted.*

When the *appellation d'origine contrôlée* system came into existence in 1935, production of AOC wines was only 350,000hl. The AOC vineyard area has expanded steadily since then. In 30 years, the growing area has increased by more than 75 per cent and the volume of production by 140 per cent. Such progress incontestably points to the health of the system itself. It should also be noted that in 1986, 65 per cent of AOC wines produced were red or rosé, in contrast with 35 per cent white.

The contribution of AOC wine production to general French wine production has risen from 36 to 62 per cent in 30 years; AOC wines, which produce 19 billion francs on average annually, contribute nearly 6 per cent of the total value of French agricultural production.

The demand for AOC wines has fortunately responded to the increase in supply, and this has been the case on the French market as well as abroad. French consumers drank five times more AOC wine in 1985 than in 1950. During the same period, the volume of AOC wines exported has multiplied tenfold. It is hard to find equally good results in other agriculture and food sectors. The average French citizen currently consumes 20 litres of AOC wine per year; 63 per cent of the money a French household spends on wine is on French AOC wines.

If we remember that the value of AOC wine exports went up by 15 billion francs in 1986 alone, and that the wines of Champagne and Bordeaux are exported to more than 160 countries, we can easily understand why the AOC wine economy can be described as flourishing.

A complex economy

On 1 January 1987, a total of 390 *appellations d'origine contrôlée* were in existence on French territory. The single characteristric common to this mosaic of products lies in their common access to the AOC seal of authority, which acts as a unifying bond. But these products, scattered as they are about a space of multiple dimensions, obviously have personalities with other, very diverse characteristics. Since 1935, when the AOC system was created, the establishment of new *appellation d'origine contrôlée* wines has been spread out over intervals in time. Each *appellation* has its history, each its own rhythm of development. There are the old *appellations* and the new, and sometimes conflicts arise between the generations, as happens quite naturally in the heart of any family.

Space

Spread over an area of 375,000ha, the 390 *appellations* form a range of products of widely varying geographical origin. Sometimes Mediterranean influences are dominant, at other times Atlantic or continental influences. Every region has, in any case, its own customs and traditions, and it is from these that the specific *savoir-faire* that is essential to the individuality of each product comes. Each *appellation* is therefore the focus of a particular decree which lays down its specific conditions of production (grape varieties, yield, method of vine training ...).

Volume of production

There is little logic in stating an average annual production volume, as this varies so greatly from *appellation* to *appellation*: quantities produced in 1985 ranged from 43hl of AOC Romanée-Conti to 1,508,575hl of AOC Bordeaux.

Price

Prices are what the consumer is most directly aware of and yet, for the same reason as given above, it is difficult to speak of an average price. Both the production processes, which determine the cost price, and the reputation of a wine, which determines the profit margin, vary enormously.

Organoleptic characteristics

These 'taste and smell' characteristics result from the subtle combination of grape variety, *terroir*, and ever-changing climatic conditions, all of these factors being delicately adjusted by the human hand.

Other aspects

Other elements, too, accentuate the heterogeneity of the wine-growing landscape that lies behind the *appellation d'origine contrôlée* system. Emphasis, for example, should be placed on the large structural differences in wine marketing channels in different AOC regions. There is no strict division of labour observable in every region among those involved in marketing wine.

During the 1970s and 1980s, a trend has developed whereby producers sell their wine directly to the public. In the same way, the selling of wine by cooperatives has also grown. These trends have not, though, followed an identical pattern in different regions. Some regions still have many *négociants*, and in such regions cooperatives tend to play a role in production only; in others, on the contrary, *négociants* have disappeared, and the marketing of the region's wines is exclusively in the hands of the cooperatives.

Some commentators see in this complex situation a handicap to future development. It is true that this structural fragmentation is an important evolution, and the challenges posed by the increase in international competition will have to be met by better internal organization and increasingly refined marketing strategies.

What is clear, however, is that this complexity is also an important and positive consequence of the *appellation d'origine contrôlée* system itself. The system has been able to withstand all kinds of harmful centralization, congestive central planning and standardization, precisely because of the system's diversity, based on the principle of delegation to local professionals of the responsibility for their own AOC region. These professionals alone take their destiny in their own hands.

So can diversity really be considered a handicap for the future? If we look at recent trends in food distribution and consumption, we see that *appellation d'origine contrôlée* wines occupy a position outside the norms laid down in French industrial and commercial planning. The *appellation d'origine contrôlée* strategy can hardly be included in the dominant industrial and commercial processes that have, notably, guided the reorganization of agricultural and food production networks, or the transformation of the structures of distribution. The increase in mass distribution, accompanied by a considerable diversification of products, has contributed to the creation of new consumer buying habits. But these new products are also products of mass consumption, and diversification in this instance is linked with standardization, even with a reduction in quality and authenticity. A parallel development is that of intense urbanization, together with an unprecedented acceleration in the pace of life. In this new consumer universe, the quality and authenticity of *appellation d'origine contrôlée* wines mean that they take on a more than habitually attractive flavour. Excessive standardization has created a need for non-standardized products, products that flourish outside the general trend of development.

Arbois was, chronologically, the first AOC. It was ratified on 15 May 1936.

Appellation d'origine contrôlée wines, products of charm, thus become products of refuge for discerning consumers, indispensible thanks to their originality, diversity and authenticity.

Economic organization

The genesis of the *appellation d'origine contrôlée* principle, on which the whole current economic organization of this sector is based, was particularly slow; generation after generation toyed with notions of quality wine legislation until finally the *appellation d'origine contrôlée* system was established by decree on 30 July 1935.

The legislation was not imposed by any government body; it was and remains a result of initiatives of the wine professionals themselves. After successive failures in getting the state and judicial systems to accept *appellations*, a coherent legal system was eventually established and placed in the hands of qualified representatives of the profession. Success, therefore, did not come immediately, but this slow evolution meant that a particular mentality was forged that could eventually be sensibly assimilated into a professional code of practice. At the heart of the *appellation d'origine contrôlée* system lies a coherent philosophy that guides and organizes every decision concerning this sector, and every step aimed at maintaining and developing it.

This philosophy is characterized essentially by a noble conception of what quality in wine should be. In order to define this specific notion of quality, it was necessary to formulate a technical and statutory framework, judged by some to be too rigid, but which has met the demands of the consumer admirably.

Everyone knows how much the definition of quality changes, varying among individuals, businesses and contexts. But it is these very differences in appreciation that have allowed each product to find its place and each marketing strategy to be given a chance. The establishment of the *appellation d'origine contrôlée* system takes into account the realities of today, by rejecting the principle of a single standard of quality in favour of a framework, for the very simple reason that the *terroir* in its broad sense — the soil, subsoil, microclimate and human environment — is the very foundation of quality, and this is obviously rich and various in its potentialities.

The businessmen of the food sector have accustomed us today to processed, sophisticated products, in which the role of agriculture has become minor. The situation is reversed with *appellation d'origine contrôlée* wines, for in them it is *terroir* that predominates. Technology only intervenes in the later stages to ensure the optimum extraction of quality elements present in the association of *terroir* and grape variety. The range of AOC wines is therefore constituted by a repertoire of authentic and typical products.

This scheme of priorities accords nature a primary place. Instead of combating nature and trying to eliminate its unpredictable interventions, its role is encouraged. At the same time AOC viticulture remains completely open to technology, in so far as technology can favour the full expressivity of the characteristics of *terroir* and grape variety. The very particular code of practice that professionals in this sector have to respect, though, makes them only turn to technology advisedly. The product is thus defined 'from the top', by its quality, rather than 'from the bottom', by its greater or lesser adaptability to consumer demand. This collective discipline is freely agreed to because it was deliberately created by the professionals themselves. It is thanks to this concord as to a quality abstract that a network of AOC wine growing has been able to establish itself right across France, and the sector has managed to survive, grow and flourish. Discipline and agreement have also led to the creation of a specific structure serving to maintain collective progress: the Institut National des Appellations d'Origine des Vins et Eaux-de-Vie (INAO); and of others to organize on a local basis the economics of the different *appellations d'origine contrôlée*: the interprofessional committees. In both cases, the AOC system is conceived as one providing responsibility, freedom and self-determination.

The role of the INAO

The Institut National des Appellations d'Origine des Vins et Eaux-de-Vie is, in particular, the body responsible for laying down the rules of production and for setting standards. As an interprofessional organization, it allows representatives of the diverse professions of the wine-growing world — growers, *négociants*, *courtiers* (brokers) — to sit around a table and develop a notion of quality. The INAO is first and foremost an organization of growers and *négociants*; the *syndicats de défense des appellations d'origine contrôlée* (committees for the protection of individual *appellations*) constitute its skeleton. Within the INAO, decisions are not made at the top and then imposed on the base; instead there is a willingness at base level to accept a certain number of disciplines, and respect for these, with a consideration of the requirements of the Brigades Fiscales de Contrôle (tax offices), is judged to be beneficial for all. This method of organization necessitates a structure capable of provoking a high degree of cooperation among wine growers. This is why the *syndicats* were created, to enable growers to translate their opinions into propositions which can eventually become part of the written regulations.

The National Committee of the INAO has to take into consideration local policies in as much as these affect certain principles or general rules. In all its decisions connected with the specification of AOC regulations, and in particular in the specification of a yield appropriate to a particular *appellation*, or in the requirement of submission of wines to analytic and organoleptic examination before they are permitted on to the market, the National Committee has to take account of regional policies.

This consultative process demonstrates how decentralized the system is. There is an overall procedure forming the operational basis of the *appellation d'origine contrôlée* system; this is then subdivided into 390 local procedures from which come the 390 different AOC products.

The *terroir*, the combination of *terroir* and grape variety, and the importance given to the *savoir-faire* of the producer, these are the factors that generate the individuality of AOC wines. The actual quality of production in any one case is linked to the product itself, and generalizations about this are not possible. Quantity also varies from *appellation* to *appellation*. It is fixed according to the base yield specified in the decree of each *appellation*, but this may be modified if local weather conditions warrant. Local decision-making of this sort again shows the importance of decentralized organization of each *appellation d'origine contrôlée*.

AOC, a factor of unity

Another virtue of the *appellation d'origine contrôlée* system is that it allows the different professional families involved in wine to work together. This is, of course, in the best interests of all those involved, for it permits the preservation and maintenance of the economic standing of each *appellation*; this is done in practice by interprofessional committees, referred to in everyday language as *interprofessions*. The essential goal of these committees is to acquire a perfect knowledge of wine products and potential markets; to acquire total control, or better still constant improvement, of quality; and to ensure sound financial management and marketing of their own products. The *interprofession* is the ideal forum for growers and *négociants* to meet. Here, joint decisions can be made by the professional families involved in the production of an AOC wine to promote the best development of the chain of production from grower to consumer. These decisions are an expression of the collective responsibility of the partners involved in AOC production, in the context of collective management of the regional economy. The partners abide by their decisions, and individual interests are subsumed in order to strengthen collective ones. Regional identity and character are also priorities of the highest order for the *interprofessions*. As in the INAO, government intervenes neither on a national nor a regional level. The system is based on voluntary service and the awareness of mutual responsibility among the professional families. One of the great principles of the AOC system is that short-term management is conducted without damage to long-term policy, and one of the ways in which this has been achieved is by allowing the INAO to establish the legal structure while letting the *interprofessions* concentrate on the socio-economic structure. If the function of the INAO is to safeguard the interests of future generations of wine growers, then the *interprofessions* are there to strengthen a present-day chain made up of solid links, but one that is always in danger of breakage owing to dissimilar short-term planning objectives. Producers do not necessarily think in the same way as *négociants*. In the simplest terms, the INAO looks to the long term, while the *interprofessions* look to the short term, and manage on a day-to-day basis.

The future

The benefits gained so far by the whole of the AOC wine-growing network can only bear fruit if the sector manages to follow the goal it has set itself, namely to continue producing quality wines. AOC products are sought-after for their special qualities as much in France as abroad. The law of supply and demand has meant that AOC wines are highly and profitably priced. This is particularly true because supply has remained limited by virtue of the quality of the product. In the AOC sector, total profit is not the result of a slender profit margin multiplied by large quantity — a principle applied in the case of products of mass consumption — but of a wider profit margin multiplied by lower quantity. Quality therefore constitutes the primary source of revenue in this sector, and it is in quality that the future lies. In a few years time, the delimitations of AOC zones will be complete, and France will by then be able to offer everything she possesses in terms of *terroirs* suitable for the production of *appellation d'origine* wines ... It will be necessary, though, to carefully guard over the authenticity and specificity of wines produced in the AOC system throughout this process.

THE FUTURE OF THE VINE AND OF WINE

If it is true to say that the long history of a practice is the guarantee of its future, then the drinking of wine has many centuries' development ahead of it. Nevertheless, important changes in consumer behaviour, debate over whether wine should be the sole product of the vine, and competition from other drinks all leave a very real threat hanging over the future development of wine growing and of wine itself.

Wine occupies an eminent place in the history of Europe. The vine, naturally growing on the perimeter of the Mediterranean, has spread from the coastland of '*mare nostrum*' to more northerly regions of the continent, where its cultivable limits lie.

Since Christianity consecrated wine and the Koran forbade it, the vine has not experienced the same fate on both sides of the Mediterranean. It has remained a typical part of European culture, introduced into other countries on other continents during periods of colonization. The Spanish planted it in South America, the English in North America and Australasia, the Dutch in South Africa, and the French in North Africa. Wherever the vine has taken root, its wine has been drunk, and wherever wine has been drunk, a viti- and vinicultural history has followed, and traditions intimately connected with wine have developed.

There have been many points of contact between the history of wine and French history, including what seem to be relatively recent events whose origins go back a long way through the twists and turns of history. For example, even in Cicero's times, there was a *guerre du vin* (wine war) between France and Italy, just as there was in the 1970s and 1980s. The Roman senate restricted the establishment of vineyards in Gallic Septimania as they would have competed unfavourably with wine production in Italy.

The role of the clergy in the development of wine production is revealed by numerous historical facts. In French feudal times, vines would surround the abbey, monastery or convent where there was an established tradition of hospitality. Charlemagne acknowledged the merits of a monk in these words, written on parchment: 'He built churches and planted vines.' The monks of Saint-Germain, after being chased from their monastery by the Normans in 845, later dedicated themselves with renewed fervour to God and Saint-Germain because they came back to the monastery to find their casks still full.

Royal courts have often contributed to spreading the taste for wine. The English court was partly responsible for the fame of wine from Bordeaux, and the French court also revered wine. The French people are well aware of the significance of wine in the wars that their country has waged. The battle of Waterloo could be seen, at the time, to be the collision of two worlds then opposed by essential cultural differences that might be assimilated to the drinking of beer and the drinking of wine.

The search for quality in the growing and production of wine also has historical roots. The French geographer Galtier explains the historical development of the French vineyard areas in terms of zones '*de conquête de la vigne*' ('of vine conquest'). These are found in conditions favourable to viticulture and in historically important corridors, such as waterways (the Bordeaux region, the Rhine

The** clos **(walled vineyard) of the abbey of Bourgueil has been producing wines for a thousand years.

valley), or natural crossroads or passages often used by armies (Burgundy, Champagne). If the greatest *crus* have managed to evolve, it is not just because of the quality of the *terroir* but also thanks to the historical collaboration of industrious viticulture with a traditional, dynamic commercial sector, the interests of this sector often being linked to those of the wine-growing bourgeoisie.

It is thanks to these combined efforts that the selection of 'noble' grape varieties has been possible in France; these varieties are, moreover, found all over the world today, wherever the production of quality wine is required.

The place of wine in history surely provides an element of explanation of the development of wine–growing traditions, and justifies the survival and popularity of one of the oldest drinks in the world. We might understand from this that wine is not just a product in the 'marketing' sense of the word. It is very much more than a liquid produced merely to satisfy or fulfil some basic need.

The patterns behind wine drinking

Access to French national statistics and surveys, as well as the data of the Institut National de la Statistique et des Études Économiques (INSEE), enables us to perceive quantitive and qualitative developments in wine-drinking evolution, trace the trajectory this evolution has followed, and situate wine within the context of other foods and drinks.

Quantitive slippage and qualitative gain

Two phenomena are apparent from the table shown below. The total consumption of wine in France is decreasing, while the consumption of quality wines is increasing.

DEVELOPMENTS IN WINE DRINKING AND WINE PRICING IN FRANCE

Years	Number of litres per person	Percentage of appellation wines	Indices (base 100 in 1970) Home wine consumption	Real prices of wine
1970	107.5	13.2	100	100
1976	102.8	17.5	99.5	94.3
1980	95.8	23.5	93.2	96.8
1984	88.6	27.0	87.3	98.0

Source: Direction Générale des Impôts, ONIVINS-INSEE.

From the table we can see that the amount of wine drunk per head, which reached an annual maximum of 140 litres in 1954, has diminished subsequently, with a particularly sharp decline between 1970 and 1984. A parallel development is that the proportion of *appellation* wines (AOC and VDQS) consumed is growing rapidly. We should also note the decrease in home (as opposed to bar or restaurant) wine consumption, while the average, inflation-corrected price of wine, which had been in steady decline since the late 1950s, has risen back almost to what it was in 1970; this seems to be due to the 'quality effect'.

The improvement in the average quality of wines drunk is confirmed by the development in home wine consumption indicated by the statistics below.

HOME WINE CONSUMPTION AT MEALTIMES (as a percentage of the number of individuals over 10 years of age)

Periods	Vins de Table	Vins de Pays	VDQS	AOC	Not sure
1979-80	70.0	8.8	3.6	10.0	7.6
1981-85	58.2	14.9	4.5	18.4	6.0

Source: INRA-ONIVINS.

We can see an important increase in the proportion of AOC, VDQS, and *vins de pays* wines drunk, all of which are tending to replace *vins de table* (the famous *vins ordinaires*). At the same time, the proportion of cork-stopped wines (*vins bouchés*) consumed at home meal tables has increased from 23.6 per cent in 1980 to 34.7 per cent in 1985, to the detriment of capped wines (*vins capsulés*); the drinking of these has gone down in the same space of time from 45.8 per cent to 33.4 per cent. The image of wine in cap-topped bottles — very much that of an everyday product — is losing its value in favour of cork-stopped wines, the cork itself being a symbol of quality.

It should also be noted that the demand for quality wines is greater on social dinner occasions than for ordinary meals, and more apparent in restaurants than at home. The differences in consumer attitudes, of course, are a consequence of the image and social status of a wine. This explains two further phenomena: the decline in the daily drinking of wine in favour of special, circumstance-related drinking, permitting heightened appreciation of the product; and the competition that wine has felt from manufactured cold drinks designed primarily to quench thirst.

The decline in daily wine-drinking

As the following table shows, the decline in the drinking of wine with meals is very noticeable.

FREQUENCY OF WINE DRINKING IN FRANCE

	1980	1985	Variation
Regular drinkers	46.0%	37.7%	– 16.1%
Occasional drinkers (2 times per week at least)	29.0%	31.4%	+ 8.4%
Total consumers	75.0%	69.1%	– 6.6%
Abstainers	23.2%	29.9%	+ 28.9%
No reply to question	1.8%	1.0%	

Source: INRA-ONIVINS.

According to a survey by the Institut National de Recherche Agronomique (INRA) and the Office National Interprofessional de Vins (ONIVINS) only one French citizen out of three was drinking wine on a regular basis in 1985. Regular wine drinking is being abandoned in favour of occasional drinking, while the percentage of non-drinkers is increasing. The survey emphasizes that the proportion of regular drinkers is smallest among those aged under 30, but that it has regressed in every age group during the period 1980 to 1985. Regular drinkers who disappear are thus only partially replaced by new ones. The number of non-drinkers is increasing thanks to regular waves of young people who do not adopt their parents' habits.

These conclusions confirm the results of a survey carried out in Toulouse in 1976 by the Chambre Régionale d'Agriculture de Midi-Pyrénées. According to this survey, wine is drunk at mealtimes in 78 out of 100 households, but the proportion of daily drinkers varies according to age: 29 out of 100 young people under 30, 66 out of 100 people over 30. The proportion of wine-drinkers at mealtimes came close to 70 out of 100 in 1978 according to a survey conducted by the Société Française d'Études Statistiques (SOFRES), and 58 out of 100 according to a survey conducted by the Groupe de Recherches et d'Études sur les Statistiques Agro-alimentaires de Jouy-en-Josas (Yvelines).

So a strong trend against daily consumption can be observed, encouraged by the replacement of generations of daily drinkers by young people who drink wine only occasionally or not at all. This trend can, of course, be attributed to social causes: a reduction in the number of manual workers for whom wine is a nourishing and energy-giving drink; and a corresponding increase in the total number of workers in the tertiary industries, and sedentary workers, who look only for pleasure in wine drinking. But it also seems linked to the appearance on the market of a number of drinks currently competing with wine; to the separation of the different generations which makes the education of the young by their elders difficult; to urbanization; to the growth in travel that has introduced young French people to drinks other than wine, and to the struggle against alcohol which has clearly affected wine-drinking habits.

If we examine the development of wine drinking throughout the world, we can see it declining regularly in the great wine-producing countries (where annual consumption per person exceeds 60 litres per year); instead it is the quality of wines that is in increasing demand.

In countries with moderate consumption (15 to 50 litres per person per year), there is a tendency for wine-drinking to increase, at least to a level of 35 to 45 litres, depending on the country. Here, wine is almost always finding new consumers, anxious to enjoy products of quality.

In countries with low consumption (less than 25 litres per person per year), the demand for wine is generally progressing, but by a limited amount each year; or it remains constant, as in the United States and in the USSR in 1986, for example. Wine is gaining converts, but it still hardly figures among the drinks consumed during daily meals.

These worldwide trends confirm the pattern observed in France: more and more occasional drinking for pleasure rather than as a habit.

HOUSEHOLD SPENDING (inflation-adjusted)

Years	Total	Food	Non-alcoholic drinks	Alcoholic drinks excluding wine	Wine
1970	100	100	100	100	100
1976	127,6	113,8	155,2	138,9	93,8
1980	142,6	121,1	138,1	142,4	89,0
1980	163.6	125.0	153.7	140.4	85.3

The table above shows that French household consumption of food is increasing at a slower rate than consumption in general, but that the consumption of drinks other than wine is progressing faster than consumption in general. The figures for wine seem, in fact, to be going down, but this has a lot to do with the increase in its average price resulting from the 'quality effect'. The budgetary coefficient of wine (i.e. the value of wine purchased, expressed as a percentage of total household expenditure) sank from 3.81 in 1970 to 1.29 in 1984; in 14 years, therefore, while the real expenditure of households has doubled, the contribution of wine to this expenditure has gone down by two thirds. The real value of household wine purchases has lowered, but moderately.

The hypothesis of demand swinging from alcoholic to non-alcoholic drinks, as the choice of drinks available to households becomes more diversified, is substantiated by these statistics.

Wine is feeling the brunt of ever greater competition from factory-made drinks and others more or less strong in alcohol; as an accompaniment to a daily meal, it has to compete with water, occasionally with other fermented drinks, and with soft drinks. The growing tendency is to reserve wine for certain special meals, when particular qualities, even significance and a symbolic value, are looked for. At this point, certain attributes of wine take on an increasing importance for the consumer, while others no longer attract him or may even put him off a particular product.

The character of wine and wine drinking

Wine is not a simple foodstuff, nor can it expect to compete with soft drinks in a thirst-quenching role; it is therefore becoming more and more popular for the pleasure and interest its drinking holds. Wine drinking, moreover, often occurs in a group context, and this emphasizes its social and cultural dimension.

The ambiguous status of wine as a source of nourishment

The nutritive properties of wine have in the past proved beneficial to labourers, once a substantial proportion of the population, as well as during food shortages, as occurred in the wine-growing parts of the Midi during the Second World War. But, with today's improved storage facilities, grapes may just as well be eaten as such without being transformed into wine. At the moment the nutritive value of wine (560 calories for a litre of wine of 10°, and more for wines of greater alcoholic strength) seems to be regarded as a fault. The advertising for light wines with low levels of alcohol in the United States is founded on their reduced calorific value.

It is sometimes regretted that, owing to commercial reasons (improvement in the shelf life of the product and its ability to withstand the shocks of travel), attempts have been made so often to raise the alcoholic strength of *vins de table*. Such an attitude has surely gone against the wishes of the consumer and dietary sense.

However, apart from its basic calorific value, it should also be emphasized that wine contains elements with particular properties useful to the human body (*see* pages 542-548).

Wine's declining use as a thirst-quenching drink

It can be argued, though not without opposition, that wine is ceding its everyday role as a thirst-quenching drink to the role traditionally played by fine wine, something drunk essentially for its enjoyable taste. The development of taste accounts for this transition.

In fact, if a wine is acid and sufficiently low in alcohol, people who consume it regularly with meals still enjoy it as a thirst-quenching drink, often with the addition of water. But in this role it is being gradually replaced by tap water, which has grown in popularity since the installation of running water in French households, or by mineral water, soft drinks and other beverages.

The ban on television advertising,for alcoholic drinks in certain countries (including France); the huge advertising budgets enjoyed by factory-made drinks in contrast to the modest resources of organizations seeking to promote wine-drinking; and the pressure placed on drinkers by anti-alcohol campaigners have all contributed to speeding up this transition. Even in conservative South American countries, everyday wine-drinking is declining, again to the benefit of branded drinks with worldwide markets, advertised on television every day. The official attitude to drinks advertising might lead one to believe that old-fashioned products are only allowed old-fashioned channels of publicity, while fashionable, modern drinks have exclusive rights to the new media.

Wine's undisputed quality as a pleasure-bringing drink

Proof of the pleasure experienced by the wine consumer lies in the fact that general sensitivity to nuances in the quality of this product is broadening and developing. This sensitivity is finding more and more eloquent means of expression as the consumer's standard of living improves. It is also crossing social frontiers and winning over new social groups, thanks to the improvements in society's communicative means: contacts brought by travel, and images and information transmitted into every home by the media.

Thus a perception of differences in the quality of wine, which seems to have come from deep in the traditions of the wine-growing regions, appears now to have penetrated all consumer societies. Everyone in such societies acknowledges the differences between wines, and these are conveyed in various ways: labelling, presentation and especially pricing, all these factors resulting from the verdict of connoisseurs. The latter exchange impressions of wines in terms little understood outside their group. But by simplifying these impressions, they can transmit them to amateurs equipped with a modest wine-tasting vocabulary, and in turn these amateurs are able to express basic differences between wines (bouquet, fruitiness, body, length of taste, taste and aroma characteristics).

In general terms, consumers acknowledge and accept the differences they note from external factors: price, the presentation of the bottle, the label (possibly giving an indication of the place of production), the producer's name or brand name, and other signs of good quality. The importance that these aspects take on suggest that wine is more and more drunk for pleasure, consumed on particular occasions and at a frequency depending on social grouping and individual preferences; moreover each individual or household shows a more or less strong desire to broaden their choice of product or, occasionally, to remain faithful to a particular one.

Wine and social life

It has often been said and written that wine brings men together and acts as a catalyst for conviviality, for warm relations and favourable intercourse between members of a group. Certainly there are not many drinks which, when consumed in moderation, are known for the positive and friendly atmosphere that wine can bring to a party of people.

In popular and literary reference we visualize wine offered at the abbey to visitors in the evening, or a gourd passing from hand to hand during festive nights when old

An illustration from a children's book published at the beginning of the 20th century to warn against alcohol.

friends or soldiers get together. Wine has enlivened many a village evening, and after certain wars, wine was reputed to have kept up the morale of the troops.

If modern man, with so many choices before him, always goes back to wine, it is, according to Boisset, to 'instinctively rediscover the vestiges of an environment whose loss he is beginning to lament: the wine of family joy, of friendship, of a time when man was not alone'. Traditionally, wine flows at the celebration of a happy event and the French term *vin d'honneur* (meaning 'a reception') fuses in one phrase the idea of nobility and the name of a drink.

The symbolic and cultural dimension of wine

Research into the consumption of food and drink has shown that the exact pattern set by a household is a product of history and culture in its various aspects, and is especially influenced by the social class to which the household belongs.

Homer, in the 8th century BC, already refers to wine, describing refined people 'who extract from the vine products of considerable worth, thanks to the art of wine growing and the tending of vines and of wine'. Wine, more than any other drink, can evoke certain impressions, call to mind certain symbols that are to be found in every society where this drink has an honoured place.

We can easily understand that wine occupies a privileged position in French national and regional traditions linked with the wine harvests — particularly the start and end of the harvest — and in customs that take on a legendary dimension, such as that *chabrot* strengthens the blood (*chabrot* is the traditional way of finishing the hearty soup called *garbure* in South West France: wine is poured into the last of the broth, and the mixture is then drunk), or the '*libre prise au tonneau*' ('drink what you will') during village feasts, which restored strength of body. Think, too, of all those recipes that need wine . . .

Wine is mentioned more than any other drink in French popular songs, such as the 'Coupo Santo' of Provence, the 'Vignerons Champenois', the 'Enfants de la Bourgogne' or the 'Vin de Saint-Émilion'. We are familiar with the rites of the wine *confréries*, through which the local history of a wine can be traced, as well as those of the Chevaliers du Tastevin, guardians of the French cult of the vine. Cellars are dotted along 'wine circuits' in the wine-growing regions, and the many harvest celebrations are full of life.

Apart from the religious symbolism it holds in Christian civilization, wine has created in the mind of the consumer a direct link between its own characteristics and the work of the wine grower or cellarmaster who produced it. It is thus seen more as a product of art than of technique. This imaginative way of seeing wine allows the consumer to create his own picture of the *terroir* from which a wine comes, and this forms an essential element in his perception of the differences between wines.

For a long time now, the *terroir* has been the basic factor in identifying the quality of French wine, rightly or

Le déjeuner des canotiers *(River Picnic) by Pierre-Auguste Renoir (1841-1919) illustrates the importance of wine in popular festivals.*

Chabrot, *the finishing of soup broth with wine, remains a very strong tradition in the South West of France.*

wrongly, as numerous historical facts prove. A Burgundian edict of 1446 prohibiting the importation of '*vins du Sud*' (from the Lyon region) to Burgundy, and, later, the rejection by Parisian doctors of wines from Auxerre produced beyond the *pont de Sens* (Sens bridge, in Yonne) as being 'noxious', are two examples of this.

Finally, we also know that it is on the basis of a connection between a particular *terroir* and the quality of the wines produced from it that the French regulations concerning *appellations d'origine contrôlée* have been established; the success this system has had has inspired many other countries to follow suit.

These regulations lead the consumer of *appellation* wines into linking the quality of the wine he drinks with the image of a particular area of production. Some companies in France have tried to cash in on this by using brand names for table wines which, by the way they sound or by word association, seem to belong to a particular region: Margnat-Village, Baptistin Caracous, Vincent Racanel, Vieux-Papes . . .

It seems highly unlikely that rapid urbanization will weaken the link between wine and *terroir* in the minds of French consumers looking for their 'roots'. Consumers are always receptive to the idea of *terroir*; and the growing trend for direct buying from producers only serves to reinforce this notion.

The future of the vine and of wines

Wine comes from the depths of history. It is an integral part of French culture, of indisputable symbolic richness, and it is drunk more and more for pleasure. It must therefore find a special niche for itself among the great diversity of products available today that often rely on loud and strident advertising.

The changes noted above in the drinking of wine during the last few decades seem to confirm consumers' acceptance of this special position. If wine's worldwide reputation is to grow, then the qualities we have attempted to isolate here must still be found tomorrow in the wines produced from French *terroirs*.

These *terroirs* will, it seems, never be able to produce a uniform and anonymous manufactured drink if acceptable economic, social and cultural conditions are to be maintained. So what kind of economically viable innovations are to be expected from French vineyards and cellars in the future?

A bipolar orientation in viticulture

Specialists believe that vines, while continuing to thrive and maintain the quality of the old *terroirs*, could be planted elsewhere to produce drinks of a manufactured kind, or juices to be used as a base for other kinds of beverage. Thus two viticultures could coexist: one 'noble', the other productive.

▷ The former would be limited to producing fine wines for discerning consumers, and would be established over a limited area, so that the relative rarity of the products would contribute to their value, not only in monetary terms but also in social and symbolic terms. The direct relationship between *terroir* and quality produce would be unquestioned.

▷ The latter form of viticulture, with very high yields, could produce a large quantity of wine-based beverages at fairly low prices, and these could compete, on their own or mixed with other ingredients, with thirst-quenching drinks of all sorts.

For this to happen, the cheap production of wines low in alcohol would be necessary, and this could be achieved under the following conditions:

- The use of productive grape varieties with good resistance to disease, in order to cut the costs of cultivation for the growers.
- Growing the vines on deep soils, preferably with irrigation, and training them by high systems to increase yields.
- The use of oenological techniques, legalized for this type of wine only, to correct the characteristics of the product as necessary, for example by increasing its acid or sugar levels.
- Seeking to develop and plant vineyards in places where the ratio of cost to yield would be as low as possible, such as in areas where labour is cheap and easily available.

However the development of very productive vineyards with a view to the mass production of everyday wine-based products similar to other thirst-quenching drinks would, in fact, be very difficult to put into practice.

The grower would have to obtain a revenue per hectare sufficient for himself, while selling at very low prices, by developing an enormous and highly productive estate. This would, without doubt, be more competitive outside France, in countries with a cheap labour force, and with new terrain that could be given over to vines. The large national and multinational drinks corporations, who are the only organizations capable of distributing such products effectively, would need to show an interest in this type of wine. But this interest seems to be conditional on the hope for a profit margin at least equal to the margin made on other manufactured soft drinks, which would suppose a very low price paid for the raw material.

Mass export would also have to be organized along the lines used for the sale of other drink products abroad, assuming in the first place that the wine-based product (wine being a 'living item') could bear long transportation without excessive cost.

Shop owners and stockists would also have to be made aware (probably with the help of advertising) of the refreshing and thirst-quenching character of the grape-based product offered to them, and of the two different images of wine that would need to be communicated: that of thirst-quenching wine (*vin désaltérant*) and that of quality wine to be enjoyed as such (*vin d'agrément*).

These conditions would not be easy to fulfil, and thus the possibility of successfully producing cheap, thirst-quenching, wine-based drinks on a scale of massive proportions in France seems remote.

A unipolar orientation for viticulture

Another kind of orientation in viticulture is more probable. Under such a scheme there would be a continuous progression from ordinary, honest *vins de table* to the very finest wines right at the top of the hierarchy, and each level of quality would be represented. In the context of the necessary differentiation between categories of wine, and in acknowledgement of wine's special product image, the following observations should be made:

▷ The distinction between fine wines and table wines is a real one, but it does not imply a complete separation between their two markets. Indeed, it has been noted in France that a considerable increase in the price of certain quality wines has led a proportion of customers into buying the better grades of table wines instead, such as the *vins de pays*.

▷ The search for quality is carried out at different levels for quality wines and table wines, but with similar objectives in mind, and in both cases by almost identical means: the search for good soil conditions and exposure for the vineyards, along with improvements in choice of grape varieties and growing techniques.

Maintaining the existence of staggered or progressive viticultures with links between each level can be carried out if the following conditions apply:

▷ There is a possibility of giving the product a value that will allow the grower to bear the relatively high costs resulting from his efforts to produce a quality product. This currently happens with the majority of fine wines.

▷ There is cooperation between those involved in viticulture and those involved in distribution to ensure that justice is done to the product and that it will be properly appreciated by the consumer.

▷ There is a firm maintenance of the image of wine, linked to the pleasure of its consumption, even if this pleasure seems greater with some categories than with others.

This second model of viticulture seems to relate more closely than the first to current developments in France and in the world. The future of viticulture as practised in developed countries, where the grower tries to obtain a certain revenue which depends on his product fulfilling the desires of the consumer, is thus conditioned by the degree of quality of the wine.

Finally, it seems that in most wine-growing countries the kind of viticulture developing at present, and that will continue developing, is one that is capable of producing and offering the consumer wines way above the acceptable quality threshold, at relatively high prices.

In France, the question of the future of viticulture centres around whether we should leave room for innovation and change, or whether we should limit ourselves, for some time to come, to producing a similar range of wines to that which we offer at present.

The future of wine and grape-based drinks

As outlined above, the development of a very productive viticulture which allows for the creation of wine-based drinks, or drinks in which wine is a constituent, seems difficult and dangerous. Yet the socio-cultural dimensions of wine must continue to develop. This does not exclude research into new grape-based products, but the way in which these are presented to the consumer should not differ radically from that of wines themselves, with all their regional particularities and specificities.

Seen in this perspective, the market opened up for *appellation* wines — followed by *vins de pays* — is bound to grow larger, with countries other than France seeking to create an *appellation d'origine contrôlée* sector more or less different from the French model. In the countries where such a sector already exists, new *terroirs* will, as time goes by, come to benefit from an *appellation*. At an international sales level, it will greatly help the buyer to find his way among the multitude of *appellations* if a generally well-known generic placename, serving almost as a brand name, is adopted, along with the more specific *appellation* for the most knowledgeable consumers. It hardly seems likely that, side by side with wines sold by *cru*, we will see the development of varietal wines, except perhaps in the case of two or three 'noble' varieties well known throughout the world (Cabernet Sauvignon, Merlot, Chardonnay); indeed there are risks involved here. If the Americans, who claim not to acknowledge the notion of *terroir* (and yet do not refute it either), produce primarily varietal wines, it is because they feel the need to give their wines some point of reference. But if the *terroir* gives us this point of reference, why resort to the grape variety to switch this point and risk creating confusion in the mind of the consumer?

Admittedly, for the category of wines without any geo-

Improved plantings and blends of grape varieties, together with progress in growing techniques on appropriate terroirs, *should safeguard the future of the vines and the wines of France.*

graphical denomination, mass-produced by increasingly refined technical means, the grape variety can serve as a useful reference point for consumers. However we believe that, owing to the obligatory severity of regulations concerning varietal wines, those produced in large quantities would be better identified by brand names. These wines should be quite rich in aroma, fairly low in alcohol and well balanced, since they will be drunk more often than not on an occasional rather than on an everyday basis. We should also realize that they will be the wines responsible for attracting new consumers.

Besides the wines of *terroir* (*appellation* wines) and branded wines, the other grape-based products that might be put on the market will have to satisfy two conditions: firstly, that they should not compete with the preceding categories, and secondly that they should not tarnish the image of wine and its social and cultural attributes.

Within these constraints, one could imagine the development of, for example, sparkling wines low in alcohol or slightly sparkling grape juices extremely low in alcohol, providing the costs of production could be kept down with the help of new techniques, thus ensuring competitivity.

In respect of grape juice, it seems that research into low-calorie juices offers future possibilities, but this is only if processing methods can be found to keep production costs low enough to be competitive on the fruit juice market.

The production of alcohol-free wines is at present in its infancy, and the manufacturing techniques (especially that of aroma preservation) are too newly developed to allow an accurate assessment of the future of such wines to be made; this will depend on how they are received on large international markets and how their price structure evolves.

The future of *vins aromatisés* (flavoured wines) seems to be complex. Fortified aperitifs and vermouths may have been able to hold on to their share of the market, but this is less true of drinks with a wine base, low in alcohol, mixed with natural fruit-flavoured products. Such drinks, which were subject to trials on the French market in 1975, have been commercialized with success in America (wine coolers). Demand continues to grow on the other side of the Atlantic, thanks to enormous promotional budgets, and this has enabled the decline in American wine-drinking dating from 1986 to be counteracted. But we must examine the role played by wine in the composition of these products, and ask ourselves whether they could not be produced with low-quality wine made from very high-yielding vines, without any detriment to the quality of the finished product. Here we are returning to the notion of a bipolar viticulture discussed above. If so, the cost of such a product would make it a serious competitor to other industrially produced drinks, but the image of wine, *produit noble*, would be dangerously tarnished.

Moreover, if grape products are being used as a simple flavouring addition to such drinks, it might be worth experimenting with other products such as fermented apple juice in order to cut costs further. Wine might be eliminated from the manufacturing process without the name of the product even having to be modified, at least in countries whose food and drink labelling legislation is lax.

New, alternative uses of vine products should therefore be given careful scrutiny, especially if we believe in maintaining a particular status for wine. For the future of the vine in France and in the world is linked to this status, and its erosion might bring about the disappearance, over the long or short term, of vineyards in countries with ancient wine-growing traditions.

VINS DE TABLE AND VINS DE PAYS

The notion of vin de pays *(country wine) is close to the heart of every French citizen. It evokes the important concept of* terroir *and the ability of a* terroir *to create wine in its own image. Often chanced upon down some country lane while holidaying,* vins de pays *express, in all their diversity, the viticultural wealth of France.*

Wine is a complete and complex world. The starting point that all wines have in common, though, is the precise definition found in the French Code du Vin, and also found in European Community regulations: the drink known in France as wine 'comes exclusively from the fermentation of fresh grapes or of the juice of fresh grapes' — this is true for all wines, whether or not they have an *appellation d'origine*.

Wine is made in the image of the fruit from which it comes: the grape. As with all agricultural products, it is the reflection of an area, of the soil that nourishes the plant, and the climate that governs its development. Above all, it is the product of human endeavour, of over 500,000 French men and women who select and grow vine varieties suitable for the production of balanced grapes and wines, in accordance with the nature of the area where such cultivation takes place. The actual making of the wine is an important part of this endeavour, a harmonization of the vine, the soil, the sun, the wind, the rain ... and the time taken for this living being called wine to mature plays a part, too ... even if the result is not always as good as hoped!

So we can see why there is not wine but wines, each representing an originality, an individual style or a dominant note associated with the grape varieties used and the nature of a *terroir*. We can also see why it is logical that the same *terroir* produces a different wine each year, since the weather conditions — rainfall, the amount of sun, the strength of the wind, the rhythm of seasonal changes — constantly vary.

It is against this background, therefore, that we are able to note the extreme diversity of wines grown and produced in France from the many *terroirs* and ancient wine-growing traditions which exist. This is the reason why France is the second largest producer of wine in the world (roughly 67 million hl per year in the period 1981–85), and the world's largest wine exporter.

French vineyards cover around 1 million ha, but this area has been reduced by about 20 per cent during the last 30 years. This trend is in line with efforts to improve quality, and has grown in strength since the end of the Second World War in response to the continual consumer demand for better quality and originality in wine.

Cucuron in the Lubéron area, where white Vins de Pays d'Oc are produced from Ugni Blanc, Clairette and Bourboulenc grapes.

Some 55 per cent of the area covered by French vineyards is given over to the production of wines for everyday drinking and of *vins de table* (including *vins de pays*), and 45 per cent for quality wines produced in delimited zones (in EC terms VQPRD wines) constituted in France by VDQS and AOC wines.

The production of *vins de table*

Vins de table are produced in all French wine-growing regions, in a ratio of about 35 million hl of red and rosé to 5 million hl of white. The *départements* on the Mediterranean coast and Corsica provide three quarters of the production of red and rosé *vins de table* (see table, right). The production of white *vins de table* is more equally spread over the whole wine-growing area, though there is a discernible concentration in the South West (see table right, below).

The sources of *vins de table*

The tables opposite give us some idea of the geographical sources of French *vins de table*. These are not cited on labels, which only mention (with certain other obligatory details) the name of the EC country producing the wine (e.g. Vin de Table de France). Alternatively, if the wine is a mixture of wines from different EC countries, the description 'Blend of wines from different countries of the European Community' is given.

These are the only indications that are mandatory, and also the only ones that are authorized, and the consumer often judges them to be too vague, even offputtingly so. This is why professionals — both growers and *négociants* — would like to be able to give more detailed information on the bottle label concerning the origin and composition of *vins de table*, most of which have been produced using the useful oenological technique of *assemblage* (wine blending).

On wine-growing estates or in cooperative cellars, wines are often blended from grape varieties grown on different soils, each contributing a particular characteristic — colour, strength, acidity, aroma — to make a 'whole' wine. This method is not only used for *vins de table* but also for famous wines and spirits such as champagne or cognac, which benefit from the subtle skills of the oenologist or cellarmaster, who is trained to 'construct' a well-balanced product.

Similarly, *négociants* (wholesale wine merchants) take advantage of wines produced throughout France and the EC, with the enormous diversity that this implies, in the preparation of their table wine blends.

The *assemblage* of table wines

In blending together wines of different character, the *négociant* preparing a table wine looks for the traditional quality of balance sought by the consumer, and seeks to provide the consumer with a wine that is pleasant to drink in relation to the area in which it is to be sold, to seasonal preferences, to current eating and drinking habits ...

During the first half of the 20th century and until 1962, table wine vineyards in France and in Algeria were complementary. In the blending process, wines from the Midi contributed body, those from Algeria contributed strength, and wines from the centre of France brought a certain vivacity to the blend.

This is not to say that table wines from the Midi were never drunk on their own, but for the largest consumer markets this particular *assemblage* was well established and gave real satisfaction.

After Algeria achieved independence in 1962, it became a 'third country' with respect to the EC, and so its wines could only be imported and consumed unblended. From then on, French vineyards had to rely on their own or other EC produce.

In order to continue the production of satisfying wines, it

PRODUCTION OF RED AND ROSÉ VINS DE TABLE BY REGION

Average over a five-year period in millions of hectolitres

	(1980/1984)	1985
Languedoc-Roussillon	25.2	23.3
Provence-Côte d'Azur	3.7	3.3
Corsica	1.3	0.9
Aquitaine	0.7	0.6
Midi-Pyrénées	1.8	1.5
Loire Valley/Central France	1.3	1.4
Rhône-Alpes	1.4	1.2
Burgundy	0.1	0.1
Other regions of France	0.6	0.6
Total	36.1	32.9

PRODUCTION OF WHITE VINS DE TABLE BY REGION

Average over a five-year period in millions of hectolitres

	(1980/1984)	1985
Languedoc-Roussillon	0.9	1.1
Provence-Côte d'Azur	0.4	0.4
Aquitaine	1.2	0.9
Midi-Pyrénées	1.9	1.6
Loire Valley/Central France	0.3	0.4
Champagne	0.1	0.03
Alsace	0.005	0.02
Burgundy	0.04	0.03
Other regions of France	0.02	0.02
Total	4.9	4.5

VINS DE PAYS

REGIONAL DENOMINATION

Vin de Pays du Jardin de la France
Vin de Pays du Comté Tolosan
Vin de Pays d'Oc

DEPARTMENTAL DENOMINATION**

Loire Valley

Vin de Pays de la Nièvre*
Vin de Pays du Cher
Vin de Pays de l'Indre*
Vin de Pays du Loiret*
Vin de Pays de la Sarthe*
Vin de Pays du Loir-et-Cher
Vin de Pays de l'Indre-et-Loire
Vin de Pays du Maine-et-Loire
Vin de Pays de la Loire-Atlantique
Vin de Pays de la Vendée
Vin de Pays de la Vienne*
Vin de Pays des Deux-Sèvres
Vin de Pays de l'Allier*

Aquitaine and Charentes

Vin de Pays de la Dordogne
Vin de Pays de la Gironde*
Vin de Pays des Landes

The Garonne Area

Vin de Pays de la Haute-Garonne
Vin de Pays du Tarn-et-Garonne
Vin de Pays des Pyrénées-Atlantiques
Vin de Pays du Gers
Vin de Pays du Lot*

Languedoc and Roussillon

Vin de Pays de l'Aude
Vin de Pays du Gard
Vin de Pays de l'Hérault
Vin de Pays des Pyrénées-Orientales

Provence and Lower Rhône Valley

Vin de Pays du Vaucluse
Vin de Pays des Bouches-du-Rhône
Vin de Pays du Var
Vin de Pays des Alpes-Maritimes
Vin de Pays des Alpes-de-Haute-Provence
Vin de Pays des Hautes-Alpes

The Alps and the Pays Rhodaniens

Vin de Pays de l'Ain*
Vin de Pays de la Drôme
Vin de Pays de l'Ardèche
Vin de Pays du Puy-de-Dôme*

Regions of Eastern France

Vin de Pays du Bas-Rhin*
Vin de Pays de la Côte-d'Or*
Vin de Pays de la Meuse*
Vin de Pays de l'Yonne*
Vin de Pays de la Haute-Marne*

ZONAL DENOMINATION

Loire Valley

1 Vin de Pays des Marches de Bretagne*
2 Vin de Pays de Retz
3 Vin de Pays des Coteaux du Cher et de l'Arnon*
4 Vin de Pays des Coteaux Charitois*
5 Vin de Pays du Bourbonnais

Aquitaine and Charentes

6 Vin de Pays Charentais
7 Vin de Pays de l'Agenais
8 Vin de Pays des Terroirs Landais - Région des Coteaux de Chalosse
9 Vin de Pays des Terroirs Landais - Région des Côtes de l'Adour
10 Vin de Pays des Terroirs Landais - Région des Sables Fauves
11 Vin de Pays des Terroirs Landais - Région des Sables de l'Océan

The Garonne Area

12 Vin de Pays des Côtes du Tarn
13 Vin de Pays des Gorges et Côtes de Millau*
14 Vin de Pays des Coteaux de Glanes
15 Vin de Pays des Coteaux du Quercy
16 Vin de Pays de Saint-Sardos
17 Vin de Pays des Coteaux et Terrasses de Montauban
18 Vin de Pays des Côtes de Gascogne
19 Vin de Pays des Côtes du Condomois
20 Vin de Pays de Montrestruc*
21 Vin de Pays de Bigorre*

* *Vin de pays* produced in very small quantities only.

Corsica, Provence and Lower Rhône Valley

22 Vin de Pays de l'Île de Beauté
23 Vin de Pays de la Principauté d'Orange
24 Vin de Pays de la Petite Crau
25 Vin de Pays de Mont Caume
26 Vin de Pays d'Argens
27 Vin de Pays des Maures

The Alps and the Pays Rhodaniens

28 Vin de Pays d'Allobrogie
29 Vin de Pays des Coteaux du Grésivaudan
30 Vin de Pays des Balmes Dauphinoises*
31 Vin de Pays des Coteaux des Baronnies
32 Vin de Pays du Comté de Grignan
33 Vin de Pays des Collines Rhodaniennes
34 Vin de Pays des Coteaux de l'Ardèche
35 Vin de Pays d'Urfé*

Regions of Eastern France

36 Vin de Pays de Franche-Comté
37 Vin de Pays de Franche-Comté - Coteaux de Champlitte

Languedoc and Roussillon

Département of Pyrénées-Orientales

38 Vin de Pays Catalan
39 Vin de Pays des Côtes Catalanes
40 Vin de Pays de Coteaux des Fenouillèdes
41 Vin de Pays des Vals d'Agly
42 Vin de Pays de la Côte Vermeille

Département of Aude

43 Vin de Pays de la Haute Vallée de l'Aude
44 Vin de Pays des Côtes de Prouille
45 Vin de Pays des Côtes de Lastours
46 Vin de Pays des Coteaux de la Cité de Carcassonne
47 Vin de Pays des Hauts de Badens
48 Vin de Pays des Coteaux de Miramont
49 Vin de Pays des Coteaux du Lézignanais
50 Vin de Pays du Val de Cesse
51 Vin de Pays du Val d'Orbieu
52 Vin de Pays des Coteaux de la Cabrerisse
53 Vin de Pays de Cucugnan
54 Vin de Pays de Hauterive en Pays d'Aude
55 Vin de Pays du Val de Dagne
56 Vin de Pays des Coteaux de Termenès
57 Vin de Pays des Coteaux Cathares
58 Vin de Pays des Coteaux du Littoral Audois
59 Vin de Pays de la Vallée du Paradis
60 Vin de Pays des Coteaux de Narbonne
61 Vin de Pays des Côtes de Pérignan

Départements of Aude and Hérault

62 Vin de Pays des Coteaux de Peyriac

Département of Hérault

63 Vin de Pays des Coteaux d'Ensérune
64 Vin de Pays des Coteaux de Fontcaude
65 Vin de Pays des Côtes de Brian
66 Vin de Pays des Monts de la Grage
67 Vin de Pays de Cessenon*
68 Vin de Pays des Coteaux de Murviel
69 Vin de Pays des Coteaux de Laurens
70 Vin de Pays des Coteaux du Salagou
71 Vin de Pays de la Haute Vallée de l'Orb
72 Vin de Pays du Mont Baudile
73 Vin de Pays des Gorges de l'Hérault
74 Vin de Pays de la Bénovie
75 Vin de Pays du Bérange
76 Vin de Pays des Collines de la Moure
77 Vin de Pays de la Vicomté d'Aumelas
78 Vin de Pays des Côtes du Ceressou
79 Vin de Pays de Caux
80 Vin de Pays de Cassan
81 Vin de Pays de Pézenas
82 Vin de Pays des Côtes de Thongue
83 Vin de Pays des Coteaux de Libron
84 Vin de Pays de Bessan
85 Vin de Pays de l'Ardaillou
86 Vin de Pays des Côtes de Thau

Départements of Hérault and Gard

87 Vin de Pays du Val de Montferrand

** Every *département* in mainland France whose name is not already used in an AOC can, in theory, claim its own departmental denomination. The list above groups together only those *départements* that have officially declared a wine harvest.

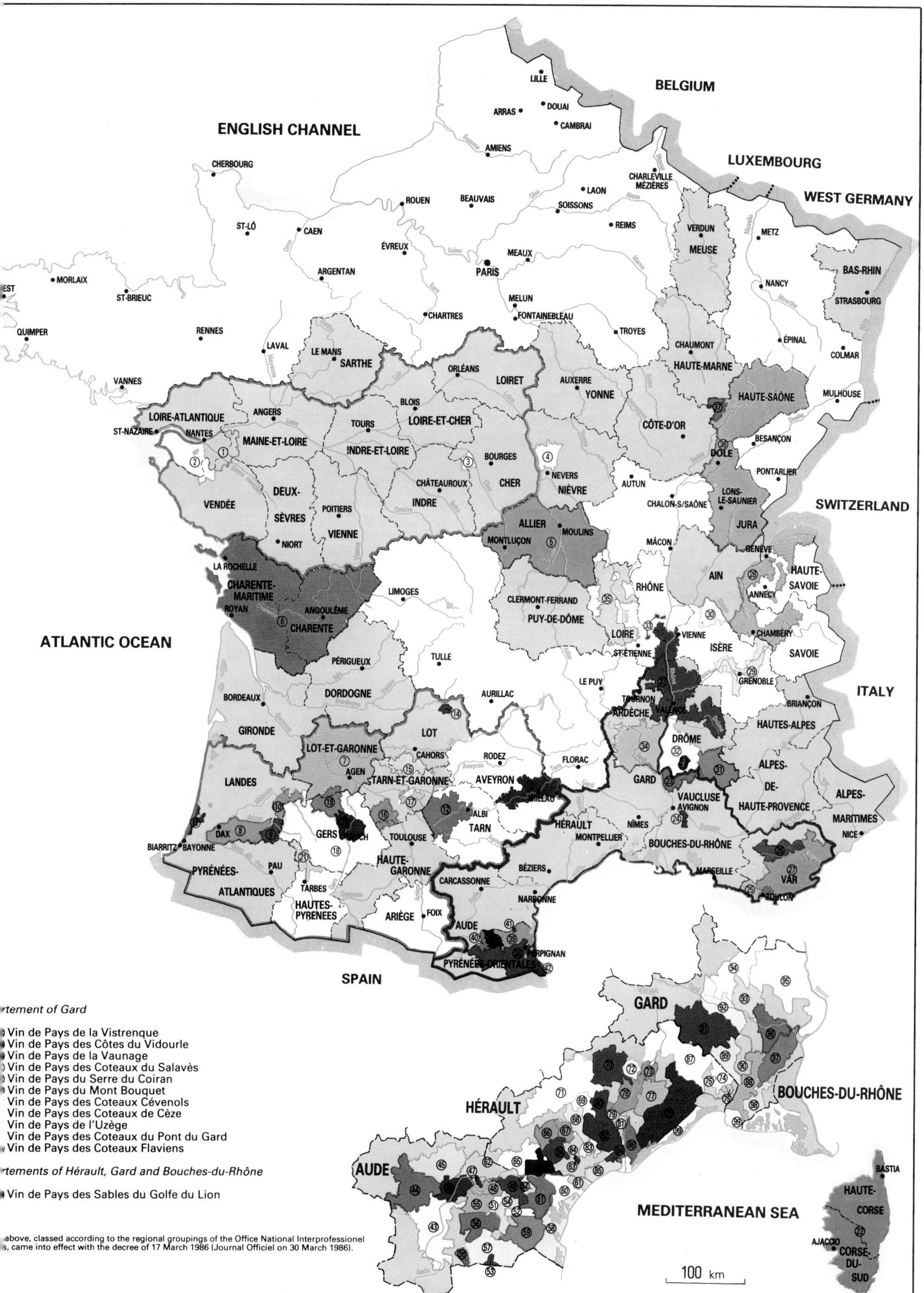

rtement of Gard

- Vin de Pays de la Vistrenque
- Vin de Pays des Côtes du Vidourle
- Vin de Pays de la Vaunage
- Vin de Pays des Coteaux du Salavès
- Vin de Pays du Serre du Coiran
- Vin de Pays du Mont Bouquet
- Vin de Pays des Coteaux Cévenols
- Vin de Pays des Coteaux de Cèze
- Vin de Pays de l'Uzège
- Vin de Pays des Coteaux du Pont du Gard
- Vin de Pays des Coteaux Flaviens

rtements of Hérault, Gard and Bouches-du-Rhône

- Vin de Pays des Sables du Golfe du Lion

above, classed according to the regional groupings of the Office National Interprofessionel
s, came into effect with the decree of 17 March 1986 (Journal Officiel on 30 March 1986).

became necessary to reconsider the mix of grape varieties planted in France, the training methods used for these, and vinification practices. This work has taken a generation to complete, since those involved in wine production are not easily diverted from traditional practices.

The range of French table wines

In the 1970s and 1980s, profound changes occurred in table wine-producing areas and in the attitudes of *négociants* making table wine blends. These were the result of new cellar equipment and vinification methods, and the findings of oenological research that related to *terroirs* and complementary grape varieties.

These new trends provoked a broadening of the range of French table wines on offer to the consumer. Within this range we might distinguish between:

▷ Traditional *vins de table* that meet the demand for wines of recognizable and strong character. They are generally produced from an *assemblage* noted for its quality, though they may include wines from different regions of France or the EC. The French consumer is offered a large variety of these *vins de table*, and they are in general honest, straightforward and individual, bearing no resemblance to standardized manufactured drinks.

▷ Wines which, although included in the category of *vins de table*, are classified as *vins de pays*, since they come from a specific, delimited geographical area, and reflect the traditions and wine-growing practices of their place of origin.

Each one is quite unique, possessing the character of the *pays* it is named after, and often with an indication of the year of its birth. The consumer is therefore faced with another choice: whether to go for traditional *vins de table* that have been tailored to consumer requirements, or whether to explore and experiment with *vins de pays* to find the one most suited to an individual's eating and drinking habits, temperament and the season of the year.

Vin de pays

In everyday French speech, the phrase *vin de pays* has always signified a small, simple wine from a local *terroir*, but one that nevertheless comes from a long wine-growing tradition.

The actual denomination '*vin de pays*' is in much the same spirit. In order to be classed in this category, a wine must conform to four main conditions laid down by law. These regulations concerning *vins de pays* were published in the French government's *Journal officiel* on 8 September 1979:

▷ The production of a *vin de pays* must be in the clearly defined region from which it takes its name, and this must be printed on its label which serves as an 'identity card'.

Regarding geographical zones of origin, the consumer should be aware that there are three separate categories of *vin de pays*:

• *Vins de pays* identified by the name of their *département* of origin (unless this name is already part of an *appellation d'origine*, as is the case with Savoie, Jura or Corse). The number of *départements* that lend their names to *vins de pays* varies slightly from year to year, but it is around 33. The production of each of these is very variable, ranging from hundreds, to hundreds of thousands of hectolitres.

BLENDING A FRENCH TABLE WINE

To create a wine with characteristics appealing to the tastes of regular consumers, the négociant *of the past needed, for example, ten kinds of wine from different regions to make a French table wine of 11°. He might therefore have blended lots as follows:*

Lot 1 — Cooperative A (Hérault): red, 9.5°
Lot 2 — Cooperative B (Ardèche): red, 10.4°
Lot 3 — Private grower A (Aude): red, 9.7°
Lot 4 — Cooperative C (Aude): red, 11.5°
Lot 5 — Cooperative D (Var): red, 11.2°
Lot 6 — Cooperative E (Aude): red, 10.3°
Lot 7 — Cooperative F (Var): red, 11.6°
Lot 8 — Private grower B (Gard): red, 11.5°
Lot 9 — Estate on Corsica: red, 13°
Lot 10 — Private grower C (Hérault): red, 13°

Each type of wine contributed its own particular character to the 'cuvée' *or blend. Some imparted lightness, such as lots 1 and 3; others strength, such as lots 9 and 10; others body, such as lots 4 and 7.*

None of these wines, though, would have been acceptable as an unblended wine. None was made to be drunk in isolation. They needed to be blended together to bring out their best qualities, and to appeal to prevailing consumer tastes.

• *Vins de pays* named after a zone of production that is distinct from the *département*, and generally smaller than the *département*, though occasionally it is bigger. There are now about a hundred of these zones, the amount of territory they cover varying considerably, as does the nature of the wines themselves.

• *Vins de pays* which are 'regional', named after a large zone covering several *départements*. This type plays the role of grouping different wines together, and because of this is subject to regulations that are a little different from those governing the other two types of *vins de pays*. There are three of these large regional zones: the Jardin de la France (covering the Loire valley and its tributaries), the Comté Tolosan in the South West, and the Pays d'Oc on the Mediterranean coast.

The general requirements of production applying to all *vins de pays* named after a *département* are as follows.

▷ The wine must have a natural minimum alcoholic strength of between 9° and 10°, and it must conform to the norms set out in a *bulletin d'analyse* which describes the necessary balance of its constitution.
▷ It must meet with the approval of an officially recognized tasting panel.

Vins de pays from a production zone have to meet even more exacting standards laid down individually for each *vin de pays* by the local Syndicat de Défense des Producteurs (local growers' committee), and formally specified by decree.

Lastly the 'regional' *vins de pays* have their own statute, permitting the *assemblage* of different *vins de pays* from the same region, both by individual wine producers and by *négociants*. This makes it possible to produce large quantities of wine of a uniform but nevertheless regional character, as well as to group a number of wines under a single general identity readily perceived by the consumer.

The production of *vins de pays*

As with all wines, the production of *vins de pays* fluctuates from year to year, although this is within the context of a steadily rising trend. Annual production of *vins de pays* in the years following the initiation of the system in 1979 was around 4 to 6 million hl, whereas in the period 1985–1990 it was around 7 to 10 million hl.

More than 90 per cent of production is spread equally between the departmental and zonal *vins de pays*, the rest (5 to 10 per cent) being regional *vins de pays* from the Jardin de la France, Comté Tolosan or Pays d'Oc. The level of development of *vin de pays* in any given area varies greatly, as is indicated by the very dissimilar levels of production; considerable latitude is given to the producer to choose, for those of his table wines which qualify for a *vin de pays* classification, the exact denomination he feels best characterizes them, while at the same time guaranteeing the authenticity of their origins. But if the producer cannot sell his wines as *vins de pays*, then he can always sell them as *vins de table*. This is why the total consumption of *vins de pays* is

The Château de Montsoreau in Maine-et-Loire. This département *currently produces around 30,000hl of* vin de pays *under the regional denomination Vins de Pays du Jardin de la France.*

La Roque-Gageac. Vin de Pays de Dordogne is produced in all the main wine-growing areas of this département.

still under half of the potential production level.

Around 5 million hl of *vins de pays* were sold or exported as such in 1986, yet production of wines qualifying as *vins de pays* was in the order of 9 million hl. This shows that there is still progress to be made in promoting the reputation and image of these wines.

The panorama of *vins de pays*

Vins de pays are found in most French wine-growing areas, apart from a few where only fine wines are produced.

The ensemble of *vins de pays* can be divided into eight large geographical regions, each being characterized by similar environmental conditions and a common range of grape varieties, as well as by having to meet EC regulations as regards origin, alcoholic strength and acidity levels.

Loire valley

This area extends along the middle and lower reaches of the river Loire and its tributaries, from Nevers as far as the Atlantic. Twelve *départements* are included, each with its own denomination, from Vin de Pays de la Nièvre to Vin de Pays de la Loire-Atlantique.

The regional denomination for the area (Nièvre and Sarthe excepted) is Vin de Pays du Jardin de la France.

There are only three zonal denominations, and two of these are found at the mouth of the river, with one further denomination, little used, in Cher. Fiefs Vendéens was originally a *vins de pays*, but became a VDQS in October 1984.

The production of *vins de pays* in the Loire valley is somewhere between 200,000hl and 400,000hl per annum, depending on climatic variations. Of this total, 50 per cent is red, 30 per cent white and 20 per cent rosé. Two thirds of the wines come from a single grape variety, and the variety will be mentioned on the label. The recommended grape varieties are those traditionally found in the Loire valley. Among the white varieties Sauvignon Blanc is notable, producing dry wines with a strong bouquet and great finesse; and Chenin Blanc, the traditional variety of Touraine and Anjou, which produces dry, fine and fruity wines. The Arbois (locally known as the Menu Pineau) is also used.

For the red and rosé wines there is the Gamay, a grape variety originating in Beaujolais, producing fruity, light and fresh wines that are ideal for drinking very young (*en primeur*); Cabernet Franc (locally called the Breton), which is frequently blended with Cabernet Sauvignon to produce fuller-bodied wines with a deep colour; Grolleau, for fresh and light wines; and Pineau d'Aunis, for pale and slightly peppery rosés.

Aquitaine and Charentes

In the six *départements* included in this region, only three benefit from a departmental denomination: Dordogne and Gironde, mainly for white *vins de pays*, and Landes, especially for reds and rosés.

Charente and Charente-Maritime together make up the area of the Vins de Pays Charentais, which are mostly white and mainly produced from the Ugni Blanc grape variety, with a little Colombard and Sauvignon Blanc. The wines are generally light, dry and aromatic.

The zonal denomination of Vins de Pays de l'Agenais, from Lot-et-Garonne, produces mainly red wines from Bordeaux grape varieties — Merlot, Cabernet Franc, Cabernet Sauvignon, Côt — as well as from more 'rustic' regional varieties, such as Tannat, Bouchalès and Fer.

Production of *vins de pays* in this region is around 60,000hl per year.

The Garonne area

This area constitutes an important part of the Midi-Pyrénées region, together with Pyrénées-Atlantiques.

The production of *vins de pays* here is around 200,000hl annually, mostly reds and rosés, with an important minority production of white wine in Gers, Tarn and Béarn.

The eight *départements* of this area, along with Landes, Lot-et-Garonne and Ariège, make up the total production area of the regional denomination Vins de Pays du Comté Tolosan. These are typical wines of the South West.

Three of the eight *départements* have their own departmental denomination: Vins de Pays de la Haute-Garonne, du Tarn-et-Garonne and des Pyrénées-Atlantiques, and each produces mainly red wines.

There are also 10 zonal denominations: Vins de Pays des Côtes du Tarn, des Gorges et Côtes de Millau, des Coteaux de Glanes, des Coteaux du Quercy, de Saint-Sardos, des Coteaux et Terrasses de Montauban, des Côtes de Gascogne, des Côtes du Condomois, des Côtes de Montestruc and lastly de Bigorre.

The style of these wines varies greatly owing to changing weather conditions from west to east, the influence of the Atlantic and the Mediterranean and, above all, the diversity of grape varieties used.

For red wines, the tendency is to cultivate the best-known 'noble' grape varieties (Gamay, the two Cabernet varieties, Merlot and Syrah) to balance and fill out the local varieties.

For white wines, the main varieties used are Ugni Blanc, which gives a light wine, and Colombard, which has more character, in Gers; in Tarn, Mauzac is blended with Len de l'El, a variety that brings finesse; and in Pyrénées-Atlantiques and surroundings, the Gros Manseng is used to produce structured wines, strong in alcohol but with an important level of fixed acidity.

Languedoc and Roussillon

This region produces two thirds of all the *vins de table* and *vins de pays* of France. Of this very large total, 75 per cent of the wines are red, 20 per cent rosé and 5 per cent white. The *vins de pays* are produced by separate vinification of selected fruit, and the main grape varieties are those approved in the four *départements* on the west coast of the Mediterranean, from the Rhône to the Pyrenees (Aude, Gard, Hérault, Pyrénées-Orientales). Each variety makes its own special contribution to the construction of the wine.

For the red and rosé wines, Carignan is the most important variety cultivated, and it gives them the body and structure they need in order to appeal to consumers. Carbonic maceration, a special vinification technique (*see* page 246), keeps the berries intact during fermentation in an atmosphere of carbon dioxide, and this brings out all of their fruity qualities. The Grenache produces generous wines which combine finesse with high alcoholic strength and bouquet. Cinsaut gives the suppleness and fruit that consumers look for in wines to be drunk young.

These three grape varieties form the basis of the red *vins de pays* in this region, but increasingly they are being supplemented by other varieties of more pronounced character, such as Merlot, Cabernet Sauvignon and Syrah.

For white wines, the principal grape varieties are Clairette (Gard and Hérault), Grenache Blanc and Macabeu (Pyrénées-Orientales and Aude), all of which produce fine wines high in alcohol; and Ugni Blanc and Carignan Blanc, which produce livelier, fresher wines; the addition of Sauvignon Blanc in sandy soil conditions further strengthens aromatic character. The *vins de pays* are made from these different varieties in varying proportions, depending on the *terroirs* and area of production. Now, however, some pure varietal wines are being made, especially from the more aromatic varieties, such as Merlot, Cabernet Sauvignon and Syrah; these are sold under the variety's name. During the autumn and winter that follows the grape harvest, more and more *vins primeurs* (wines to be drunk very young) are being produced.

The regional denomination for this group, which also includes Ardèche, Bouches-du-Rhône, Var and Vaucluse, is that of Vins de Pays d'Oc.

Each of the four *départements* (Aude, Gard, Hérault and Pyrénées-Orientales) has its own departmental denomination.

There are no less than 20 zonal denominations in Aude, 12 in Gard, 27 in Hérault, and 5 in Pyrénées-Orientales (for the full list of names, *see* pages 582–583).

The production area of Vins de Pays des Coteaux de la Cité de Carcassonne is spread over 11 communes around the medieval city.

Corsica

Under the single regional denomination of Vins de Pays de l'Île de Beauté, the eight wine-growing sectors on the island produce 120,000hl to 150,000hl of red or rosé *vins de pays* annually, 65 per cent of which is produced from traditional local grape varieties, with the balance being provided by other French varieties. Nielluccio produces a darkly coloured, structured wine with a very pronounced bouquet; it blends well with the Grenache and Cinsaut. Sciaccarello is well suited to the granitic soils of parts of the island, and produces a wine with a very characteristic bouquet and peppery taste. Its wine is light in colour.

For the white wines (5 per cent of production), Vermentino — a variety with high quality potential — is used, in combination with the Ugni Blanc.

Provence and the lower Rhône valley

This southern French area is the second largest producer of *vins de table* and *vins de pays*: some 700,000hl to 900,000hl of the latter are produced annually, with red wines making up 70 per cent of the total, rosés 25 per cent and whites 5 per cent.

The basic grape varieties used here are the Carignan, which gives wines of structure and solidity; the Grenache, which brings power and depth of colour; and the Cinsaut, which contributes finesse and suppleness. The Ugni Blanc is used to produce lively white wines of average alcoholic strength.

Individuality is brought to the *vins de pays* of this region by blending the wines of traditional local grape varieties with those of varieties from other regions.

The five *départements* found here each possess their own denomination. The Vins de Pays du Vaucluse, des Bouches-du-Rhône and du Var make up most of production. The Vins de Pays des Alpes-Maritimes and des Alpes de Haute-Provence produce only 6,000hl to 8,000hl a year each.

In addition to this, there are five zonal denominations. Vin de Pays de la Principauté d'Orange produces only red wines; Vin de Pays de la Petite Crau produces 70 per cent red wine and 15 per cent each of rosé and white wine; Vin de Pays du Mont Caume produces 55 per cent red wine, 40 per cent rosé and 5 per cent white; Vin de Pays d'Argens produces 80 per cent red wine and 20 per cent rosé; and Vin de Pays des Maures produces two thirds red and one third rosé.

The Alps and the Pays Rhodaniens

This group is made up of the central part of the Rhône valley, broadening out to the foothills of the Massif Central and to the lower slopes of Savoie and the Dauphiné.

Within this region traditional grape varieties form the basis of plantings. For the red wines, Syrah produces characterful, deeply coloured and tannic wines; the Mondeuse, originally from Savoie, produces purple-red wines with a characteristic bouquet; the Étraire de la Dui, a curiosity of the Isère valley, is also used.

The grape varieties used for the white wines are the Marsanne, giving a light, dry wine, sometimes blended with the Roussanne, which brings added bouquet and finesse; the Jacquère with its particular '*pierre à fusil*' or 'gunflint' aroma; Molette with its slightly leafy or stalky flavour; and the Chasselas (locally known as the Fendant) giving a dry wine, often *perlant* (very slightly sparkling).

Burgundian grape varieties are also found here, such as Pinot Noir, Gamay, Chardonnay; as well as varieties from the Midi, such as Grenache, Cinsaut, Carignan, Clairette and Ugni Blanc. Each brings its own characteristics, yet each is influenced by the new environment in which it finds itself. All these varieties may be blended or vinified on their own to give fruity, distinctive and moderately aromatic wines.

Among the ten *départements* in this group are four with a departmental denomination: Ain, Drôme, Ardèche and Puy-de-Dôme.

There are also eight zonal denominations (*see* the list on page 582).

Regions of eastern France

These are a number of further departmental and zonal denominations situated in eastern France, including Vin de Pays de la Meuse, Vin de Pays de l'Yonne and Vin de Pays de Franche-Comté.

The wines produced here are grown on the periphery of the more important *appellations* of the region, on old *terroirs* that were ruined at the beginning of the century by phylloxera.

The production of this group of *vins de pays* is around 3,000hl annually and is slowly increasing.

The major part of production is of white wines, owing to the prevailing soil and weather conditions, and these are light, pleasant, fresh and aromatic.

VINS DE PAYS AND FOOD

The great majority of *vins de pays* accompany food admirably, but there are a few simple rules that are worth following:

▷ Dry white *vins de pays* (and there are very few medium dry or sweet white *vins de pays*) should be served chilled (5°C to 10°C) and drunk with hors d'oeuvre, cold *entrées*, seafood, fish . . . Some people enjoy them with *fromage frais* or hard-paste cheeses. They can also be drunk as an aperitif, if wished, with a dash of Crème de Cassis or Framboise.

▷ Rosé *vins de pays* should also be served chilled, but they are best drunk with the same dishes as light red wines (see below); they also go well with a whole meal if only one wine is available, especially during sunny weather and for outdoor eating.

▷ Light red *vins de pays* are increasingly drunk chilled (8°C to 12°C). They accompany *charcuterie*, hot *entrées*, white meat, poultry, hard-paste cheeses.

▷ The fuller red *vins de pays* should be served at room temperature (15°C to 18°C) and can accompany red meats, sauced meats, game dishes and soft cheeses very well.

GLOSSARY OF FRENCH TASTING TERMS AND TECHNICAL GLOSSARY

Glossary of French Tasting Terms

***ABRICOT*/APRICOT**
Aromatic characteristic of certain white wines, especially those of the Rhône valley; particularly associated with the Viognier grape variety when it has achieved full ripeness.
***ACACIA*/ACACIA**
The very pleasant smell of acacia flowers is characteristic of the aroma of young wines made from the Chardonnay and Chasselas grape varieties, especially those that are not too high in acidity. It belongs to the group of aromas described in French as *miellés* (honeyed).
***ACCIDENT*/SPOILAGE**
In French wine terminology, the general term *accident* is used of any unexpected modification that upsets the visual, olfactory or gustative state of the wine (haziness, a bad taste, re-fermentation, formation of sediment, etc.).
***ACERBE*/ACERBIC**
Tasting term expressing the 'biting' character of a wine, resulting from high acidity intensified by the presence of unripe tannins.
***ACESCENCE*/ACESCENCE**
State or characteristic of wines in which acetic bacteria (vinegar bacteria) have developed. The consequences of acescence depend on the duration and intensity of the contamination. If this is slight, then there is no difference in the wine's smell, but the aftertaste will leave a vinegar-like sensation perceptible to the experienced wine taster. If the contamination is more serious, the acetic acid produced by acescence partially combines with the alcohol in the wine to give ethyl acetate, which has a smell similar to paint thinners or nail varnish. In this state, the wine is already unsuitable for drinking, and less still for tasting! If the acescence worsens to an even greater extent, the wine turns partly to vinegar. (*See also* Technical Glossary.)
***ACIDE, ACIDITÉ*/ACID, ACIDITY**
Acidity is one of the four basic flavours distinguished in the mouth by the papillae on the surface of the tongue. In wine, this flavour is made up of a group of organic acids: tartaric, malic, citric, lactic, succinic, pyruvic, etc. In the buccal cavity, these acids are sensed not only by the tongue, but also indicated by the secretion of parotid saliva stimulated by the acids via the corrosive sensation they have on the mucous membranes of the palate, cheeks and gums. During wine tasting, acidity plays a fundamental role in defining the wine's presence in the mouth and the general balance of flavours. It counterbalances and partially eclipses the constituents that give the wine its richness (sugar, alcohol, glycerine); when combined with tannin, both acid and astringent sensations are intensified. When it appears in excess, or when its presence is insufficiently balanced out by other components, the acidity of the wine is felt first as *vivacité* (vivacity), then as *verdeur* (greenness) and finally as *âcreté* (acridity). Conversely, a lack of acidity or low level of balancing acidity is perceived as *mollesse* (softness) or *lourdeur* (heaviness). If the acidity is marginally dominant, it creates an impression of *fraîcheur* (freshness); if marginally understated, of *souplesse* (suppleness).
***ÂCRETÉ*/ACRIDITY**
Intensification of acerbic character.
***AÉRATION, AÉRER*/AERATION, TO AERATE**
During wine's storage phase, and before it is bottled, air is considered an enemy as it causes oxidization and spoilage or acescence. It has been proven, however, that total air deprivation during this period leads to the opposite effect of oxidization. This is called reduction, and it results in a loss of colour, of body and, especially, of bouquet. So a happy medium has to be found between total or excessive aeration and total air deprivation. This is the reason why wine is periodically racked (moved from container to container) before bottling.

Nevertheless, the negative effects of reduction may also be apparent in wines that have been bottled for several years with a quality cork and capsule. If their character is not already too impoverished by this, a substantial aeration should be enough to revive the colour and, above all, the bouquet of the wine. The extent and duration of this aeration are difficult to determine beforehand, since they depend on the age, grape variety and condition of the wine. One case concerned a Cabernet Sauvignon from Trentino in Italy which, after twenty years in the bottle, had lost all its aroma due to severe reduction; however, after a week in its part-emptied, corked bottle all the bouquet had returned, and this bouquet was particularly intense and subtle. It has also been reported that following a few years' storage in bottle, Chateau Grillet develops its full aromatic richness only half a day after its cork has been pulled.
***AÉRIEN*/ETHEREAL**
Term referring to a wine's bouquet and signifying that it is intense, fine and light, giving the impression of spreading easily in the air.
***AFFAIBLI*/WEAKENED**
Term indicating that a wine has lost part of its texture or particular, original character.
***AGRESSIF*/AGGRESSIVE**
Characteristic of a wine that seems to attack the mucous membranes through an excess of acidity or astringency, or both.
***AIGRE*/SHARP**
Characteristic of a wine (and of other comestible products, such as milk) in which acidity of an acetic or lactic kind dominates, often associated with the beginnings of deterioration or spoilage.
***AIGRE-DOUX*/SOUR-SWEET**
Gustative character of substances (including certain wines) possessing both high acidity and a large amount of sugar or sweet substances. When this is the case, the two groups of flavours, acidity and richness, no longer balance one another but dissociate into opposition. This kind of mixture is sometimes sought by consumers fond of strong sensations. Concentrated tomato sauces, both sugary and vinegary, belong to this category; they are forms of violence and provocation transposed to a sensory level.

***AIMABLE*/PLEASANT**
Character attributed to a pleasing wine, but one without any further pretensions.

***ALCOOL*/ALCOHOL**
After water, alcohol (ethanol) is the main constituent of wine. A wine's alcoholic degree expresses the proportion of alcohol in wine as a percentage. From a gustative point of view, alcohol is generally identified with a burning or even asphyxiating quality, as found in *eaux-de-vie* and other spirits where it constitutes 30 per cent to 45 per cent of the drink. Less widely appreciated is the fact that when alcohol makes up only 10 per cent to 13 per cent of a drink, as is the case with wine, it loses its burning, dehydrating qualities and instead lends a very sugary taste to the drink. It constitutes the major part of the richness or sweetness found in dry wines.

***ALTÉRATION*/SPOILAGE**
Development in a wine, generally resulting from bad storage conditions, which impairs its quality or even makes it unsuitable to drink. This term has a legal standing in France.

***AMANDE, AMANDIER*/ALMOND**
The aromatic qualities associated with the almond appear in different ways in wine:
▷ The smell of almond blossom has sometimes been detected in white wines made from the Sauvignon Blanc, the Sylvaner and other grape varieties.
▷ The aroma of almonds themselves, close to the smell of vanilla, is fairly common in Chardonnay wines of some age.
▷ A bitter almond characteristic is present in many new white wines, and is also part of the discreet taste of fruit kernels found in certain old red wines.

***AMBRE, AMBRÉ*/AMBER**
These terms are used metaphorically to refer both to the visual attributes and to the bouquet of the wine.
▷ Amber colouring, of an intense yellow akin to that of lager, is associated with aged sweet wines, and also with dry or almost dry white wines of fine vintages that age without oxidizing or drying out.
▷ A slight smell of amber — a sweetly resinous scent — is occasionally found in the great Chardonnay-based wines of Champagne, Chablis and the Côte d'Or, as well as in a few great dessert wines of the South West. It is an aromatic constituent of very great distinction.

***AMER, AMERTUME*/BITTER, BITTERNESS**
▷ Physiologists count bitterness as one of the four basic flavours sensed by the papillae on the tongue, and it is measured using quinine as a reference point. By this standard, it is not apparent in wine, except possibly on a transitory basis and to a very light degree in a few red wines. Otherwise it is an unacceptable anomaly. However, as a sensation, it is not far removed from astringency. If a dissolution of tannin is made in slightly acid water it is perceived as astringent, while if the same dissolution is made in alkaline water (Vichy) the result is perceived as distinctly bitter.
▷ There also exists a bacterial disease of wine called *la maladie de l'amer* or *amertume* which especially attacks old red wines in bottle, giving them a very bitter taste resulting from acrolein formed by bacteria. (*See also* Technical Glossary.)

***AMPLE, AMPLEUR*/FULL, FULLNESS**
These are terms applicable to wines which seem to fill the mouth pleasantly, giving the impression of roundness and presence but without any heaviness or weightiness.

***ANANAS*/PINEAPPLE**
An aromatic characteristic found in a large number of white wines following a harvest of grapes that have matured well, both physiologically and in terms of aromatic compounds. It is generally associated with other exotic fruit characteristics.

***ANALYSE SENSORIELLE*/SENSORY ANALYSIS**
Name currently given to the methodical tasting and codifying of drinks and other comestible substances. As the term suggests, not only taste but smell and appearance are taken into account.

***ANGULEUX, ANGULOSITÉ*/BONY, BONINESS**
A characteristic of red wines when an acid and more or less tannic dominance is not balanced by any *rondeur* (roundness or smoothness). (The Burgundians call wines with this quality *pointu* — pointed.)

***ANHYDRIDE*/ANHYDRIDE**
Anhydrides are oxides of non-metals which, when dissolved in water, produce acids. Sulphur anhydride (SO_2), customarily referred to as sulphur dioxide, is the only antiseptic substance permitted in wine conservation. It is generally added at the bottling stage, and is still perceptible to the taste a few weeks or months afterwards, depending on the wine and the quantity present. If wine containing high levels of sulphur dioxide is drunk, it can cause very painful migraines.

***ANIMAL, ANIMALITÉ*/ANIMAL**
Generic terms designating a category of bouquets dominated to various degrees by animal or 'farmyard' smells, ranging from a hint of fur to manure or dung. Generally speaking, these smells are attributable to very volatile compounds formed by reduction, and they vanish after a few moments of aeration.

***ANIS*/ANISEED**
An aromatic characteristic of which traces are found in the bouquet of certain white wines that have reached full maturity.

***ANORMAL, ANOMALIE*/ABNORMAL, ANOMALY**
Terms applied to gustatory qualities that should not be present in a particular wine. It is necessary to place great emphasis on the relative character of all gustative anomalies, since a quality which is abnormal in a particular wine might be perfectly acceptable in another food substance or indeed wine. Thus the smell of acetate, unacceptable in a wine, is completely normal in vinegar; the smell of aldehyde, indicative of oxidization in a new wine, is desirable in *vin jaune* from the Jura; the presence of carbonic gas, unpleasant in red wines, is essential in sparkling wines; a strong concentration of sugar would be out of place in a Chablis, but is quite normal in a Monbazillac, and so on.

***ÂPRE, ÂPRETÉ*/HARSH, HARSHNESS**
The Latin root of *âpre* is *asper* (rough), a root common to *aspérité* (asperity), this complex suggesting roughness and coarseness of contact. In wine, harshness describes a combination of astringency and greenness, together with a more or less repulsive coarseness.

AROMATIQUE/AROMATIC

This term has been given several meanings in the wine context.

▷ It is applied to a certain number of French grape varieties known as *cépages aromatiques*, which include the Sauvignon Blanc, the Muscat varieties and grape varieties from the Rhône. The must of varieties of this sort has a primary (grape or fruit) aroma, while the must of other varieties is aromatically neutral before alcoholic fermentation.

▷ Chauvet and Brechot have termed the anaerobic or 'semi-carbonic' phase in the vinification of Beaujolais 'aromatic fermentation', as it is during this that a large part of the wine's aroma develops.

ARÔME/AROMA

A word of Greek origin applied to the odorous qualities that emanate from natural substances, mainly vegetal (flowers, fruits, essential oils), but also animal (musk). Certain writers have suggested restricting the meaning of the word to the buccal phase of olfactory perception (retronasal aroma), thus implicitly limiting the term to substances that can be consumed. This limitation seems unjustified. The Hellenic root does not license any restriction of this kind, and the pioneering organic chemists of the last century gave the name 'aromatic series' to benzine derivatives more than a hundred years ago, owing to their strongly odorous quality. Distinctions between the French words forming a semantic cluster around the concept of 'aroma' in the wine context might be drawn along the following lines:

Odeur (smell): a generic term designating any emanation from a substance which affects the sense of smell by passage through the air, without prejudging the quality or nature of this emanation.

Parfum (scent): an essentially pleasant smell, generally quite strong, specific to one natural given substance (most often to a flower). Also designates an industrial compound (a perfume) formed by a blend of various aromatic essences.

Essence (aromatic essence): a very volatile, odorous product obtained by distillation.

Senteur (perfume, used in a general sense): a more or less diffuse smell, spreading in the atmosphere and perceptible at a certain distance.

Effluve (fragrance): a subtle emanation which applies not only to the sense of smell, but also in other physical domains (hence the word's secondary significance of 'exhalation'). On an olfactory level, *effluves* or fragrances are faint, intermittent smells, perceptible at a short distance.

Arome (aroma): a specific smell of a natural substance, though this is defined in a broader sense than scent, and the notion of aroma is intimately linked to an implied taste. An aroma is desired for the sensory pleasure it brings and the psychological associations it holds.

Flaveur (flavour): a neologism sometimes used in current French specialist writings, but not yet recorded in French dictionaries. The word has been borrowed from the English word 'flavour', describing all of the sensations perceived in the mouth, making no distinction between aroma and taste. (*See also* Technical Glossary.)

ARRIÈRE-GOÛT/AFTERTASTE

The sensory impressions that certain drinks and foods leave in the mouth after swallowing. Protein substances (cheese, fish, salted meats and salted fish), mild spices (bay leaf, nutmeg, cinnamon), and bitter or astringent substances of various origins, can all leave an aftertaste lasting several minutes. In general, the aftertaste is located at the back of the mouth and runs its course without being perceived as such, unless it is unpleasant or is being consciously analysed as part of a tasting.

ASTRINGENCE, ASTRINGENT/ASTRINGENCY, ASTRINGENT

Astringency is the physico-chemical phenomenon that initiates a contraction of the mucous membrances when they come into contact with certain substances. The most familiar standards of reference for this are the effects of alum, sloe or an infusion of bramble leaves.

In wine, astringency is a fundamental aspect of the taste of tannin. It is usually non-existent in white wines due to the absence of maceration with grape skins during vinification, but traces of it can be found in white wines that have been stored in new oak vats. In rosé wines, its presence is equally discreet, owing to the wine only having undergone a brief maceration period. In red wines, it is caused by a greater or lesser maceration of the solid matter of the grape during vinification. In finished red wines, tannin is present in variable quantities of anything up to 4 or 5g per litre of gallic tannin.

The examination and sensory analysis of several thousands of red wines of diverse origin have shown that astringency is not a simple phenomenon. Three lines of analysis can be followed: intensity, linked to the degree of tannin present; acuity, sensed as a more or less pronounced hardness; and persistence, which is perceived as a lingering fur or thickness on the tongue. During the ageing of wine, the sensations of hardness and thickness associated with astringency are reduced as the tannin 'wears off' and loses its intensity. For drinking purposes, the moment must be seized when this attenuation is matched by the wine's attainment of its optimum gustative qualities.

ATTAQUE/ATTACK

A term frequently used by wine writers and journalists to express the immediate initial contact of the wine with the mouth. The word seems to reflect an overly critical, even aggressive, attitude, looking from the outset for some kind of fault or reason for reproach, rather than beginning the tasting in an open-minded and sympathetic way. The expression 'initial contact' would certainly be preferable.

AUBÉPINE/HAWTHORN

A fairly common aromatic quality of young white wines that are very dry and slightly green, especially those made from the Sauvignon Blanc variety.

AUSTÈRE/AUSTERE

A term applied to red wines in which tannin dominates, supported by acidity, but in the absence of a bouquet that would give the wine some charm.

BADIANE/STAR ANISE

This aroma is close to true (green) aniseed, yet it is stronger in smell and easier to produce. Used with fennel seeds in the making of aniseed-flavoured drinks.

BALSAMIQUE/BALSAMIC
An adjective used to indicate the smell of a balm (an odorous resin obtained from certain trees). These resins were once used to perfume and disinfect the atmosphere in the form of incense, or used in the preparation of antiseptic medicines. In the wine context, the word 'balsamic' is employed to describe more or less resinous smells like those of pine, cedar, sandalwood, juniper, incense, fresh oak, cypress, and so on. When such aromas occur in an evolved and refined way, they add considerable distinction and class to the wines that possess them, most often red wines.

BANANE/BANANA
Used analogously, this term describes the smell of isoamyl acetate, often present in new or young wines, and most intense in wines that have undergone carbonic maceration. To preserve the harmony and quality of the bouquet, this aromatic ingredient must be tempered with other floral and fruity aromas, as it is in Beaujolais or Mâcon Blanc, otherwise the wine's aroma will bring to mind nail varnish, cheap confectionery or chewing gum.

BERGAMOTE/BERGAMOT
An essence with a very pleasant smell extracted from the bergamot orange, a citrus fruit with brightly coloured zest. The essence, richer and more complex than that derived from other citrus fruits, adds terpenic and balsamic nuances to the limonenes of citrus, so it is useful in perfumery and confectionery. This scent is found in aromatic wines at a certain stage of maturity in bottle.

BEURRE/BUTTER
Aromatic nuance mainly constituted by diacetyl, and also found in fresh hazelnut and certain beers. This aroma is sometimes present in white wines made from very ripe fruit, low in acid and very richly flavoured.

BIÈRE/BEER
A smell similar to beer is sometimes found in white wines made from the Chasselas grape variety when they start to lose their freshness.

BLANC DE NOIRS/BLANC DE NOIRS
The majority of consumers believe that white wines come uniquely from white grapes. However, this is not their only possible source of origin. Most black grapes have white juice, and can therefore produce white wines if they are pressed quickly, whole, without having been crushed first. This is the case with certain wines from Champagne, and *crémant* wines from other regions; these are then termed *blancs de noirs* as opposed to the traditional *blancs de blancs*, made from white grapes only. White wines made from black grape varieties have a different character to true white wines. They are less lively, a little more supple, with a strong bouquet reminiscent of the aroma of *reinette* apples. Non-vintage champagne is mostly made from black grapes.

BOISÉ/WOODY, OAKY
An aromatic characteristic taken on by wines during a storage period in oak casks. The degree to which this characteristic is present depends on the volume and age of the casks, and how long the wine stays in them. New casks provide the greatest oakiness; the oak aroma is often out of harmony with the wine at first, then it becomes amalgamated with it, lessening in aggression and blending into the bouquet, giving it balsamic nuances.

BONBON ACIDULÉ/ACID DROP
An aromatic characteristic produced by isoamyl acetate (*see* Banana).

BOTRYTIS/BOTRYTIS
See Technical Glossary.

BOUCHE/MOUTH
In French wine writing, the word *bouche* is used to designate all the sensations connected with the mouth, so, for example, a wine is said to have a '*bouche agréable*' (meaning a 'pleasant taste'), or a '*bouche soutenue*' (meaning a 'full flavour'), and so on.

BOUCHON/CORK
In its general sense, *goût de bouchon* (literally a 'taste of cork', designating a 'corked' wine) means the highly unpleasant taste of spoilt, rotten cork impregnating a wine. In fact, cork in its various states contributes much more than is customarily thought to both the good and bad smells of wine. In Champagne, for example, after the Second World War, the scarcity of real corks resulted in their replacement by synthetic ones; this led to the discovery that the aroma of fresh cork, slightly resinous and almost balsamic, was actually part of the bouquet of champagnes bottled before the war. A similar phenomenon occurs in old red wines that have been sealed with very long, high quality corks: they give off a markedly resinous aroma. (*See also Liège, Liégeux*.)

BOUQUET/BOUQUET
This term is familiarly used to group the aromatic qualities of a wine together, in as far as they make up a coherent, homogenous and characteristic whole.

Yet the word 'bouquet' also expresses, by the nature of its image, the diversity of aromatic types contained in the wine, as well as the idea of an agency that blends them into a whole. Clearly the bouquet is not static. It includes the primary aromas of the grape variety itself, as well as those secondary aromas resulting from alcoholic fermentation; then those that form during the wine's *élevage* in the cellar; and finally the aromas that develop after bottling. These various nuances succeed one another, overlapping and slowly eliminating the ones that preceded them. This evolution coincides with the development of tastes and the overall development of the wine.

There are various factors which have a positive or negative influence on this process. The three most favourable are: a low temperature (10°C to 12°C), darkness, and the absence of movement or vibration in the cellar. For bottled wines, cellar humidity is not very important; heavy damp is harmful, however, since the labels may slip from the bottles and the corks may rot.

BRILLANCE, BRILLANT/BRILLIANCE, BRILLIANT
Brilliance, or luminosity, is one of the visual attributes a wine may possess.

It is caused by the acidity of the wine (or rather its pH value). Acid wines have a very brilliant colour, while wines low in acidity look very matt.

BRÛLÉ/BURNT
An aromatic characteristic termed empyreumatic by specialists, bringing to mind the smell of charred substances such as burnt toast, burnt wood or caramel.

CACAO/COCOA
An aromatic nuance occasionally found in wines with a fruity and spicy bouquet when they reach full maturity.
CAFÉ/CAFÉ, COFFEE
▷ The term *'vins de café'* is used in France to describe red wines that have undergone only a brief maceration period, with adequate colour but low in tannin, destined to be consumed in bulk.
▷ The aroma of coffee is an aromatic nuance found in the bouquet of red wines of quality. It is a more or less constant characteristic of most of the wines of the Côte de Nuits.
CANNELLE/CINNAMON
A spice of fine aromatic quality, the smell of which, or something very like it, is found in the best sweet white wines (Jurançon, Sauternes, Barsac), as well as in the best dry ones (Pouilly-Fuissé, Corton-Charlemagne).
CAPITEUX/HEADY
A characteristic of wines whose richness of flavour is matched by a high alcohol content.
CARAFE/CARAFE
▷ As opposed to *vins de garde* (wines to be laid down to mature for a number of years), *vins de carafe* (literally 'carafe wines') are destined to be drunk quickly and in bulk. They are characterized by their fruitiness, freshness and smoothness. Wines falling into this category are Bourgogne Passetoutgrains, Bourgogne Aligoté, Muscadet, rosé wines of all sorts, Gamay wines, including 'ordinary' Beaujolais, Alsace Sylvaner and Edelzwicker, Fendant (Chasselas) from Switzerland, and so on.
▷ The carafe, as a means of serving wine, is used as a container for wines that have been decanted to separate them from sediment or cardon dioxide or both. In order to obtain better results, or through affectation, carafes of crystal are also used, with long necks and spherical bowls, with or without stoppers. (*See Décantation*.)
CARAMEL/CARAMEL
A coarse aromatic characteristic of fading, oxidized white wines, or intentionally maderized white wines. The chemical standard of reference for the smell is that of hydroxymethyl-furfurol (HMF), produced from the oxidization of fructose.
CARBONIQUE (GAZ)/CARBON DIOXIDE
See Technical Glossary.
CASSE, CASSÉ/CASSE, SPOILED
Terms of professional and technical origin, commonly used in France to designate any deterioration in the appearance and limpidity of the wine, and evoking the notion of rupture and breakage. (*See* Technical Glossary.)
CASSIS/BLACKCURRANT
The aroma of the juice and the fruit of blackcurrant is an integral part of the bouquet of the Cabernet Sauvignon grape variety, wherever it is grown. It is also occasionally found in the fruity character of a large number of other red grape varieties (Pinot Noir, Merlot, Cinsaut, Syrah, Mourvèdre, etc.) when they reach maturity.
CAUDALIE/CAUDALIE
Term created by A. Vedel to serve as a unit of measurement for the gustative persistence of wine. One *caudalie* is equivalent to one second's persistence.
CERISE/CHERRY
The aromas of different varieties of cherry frequently form part of the bouquet of red wines. Cherries may be recalled either in their fresh state (*griotte* or black cherries) or in a preserved state, with an aromatic hint of kernels (as in cherry brandy), this aroma being more common in ageing wines; or in the form of the smell of kirsch, well known as the main aromatic characteristic of the wine of the Beaujolais *cru* of Morgon.
CHAIR/FLESH
Name attributed to the elements of richness in a wine (alcohol, glycerine, sugar), and especially applicable to red wines when this group of elements is slightly dominant, brought into prominence by a muted presence of hard, astringent elements. This 'fleshy' character does not imply a lack of acidity (if this was the case, the result would be limpness or flabbiness).
CHALEUREUX/WARM
This term expresses the sensation of warmth felt in the mouth consequent on the presence of alcohol in wine. It does not indicate a strong wine so much as a heady one (*see Capiteux*).
CHAMBRER/TO BRING TO ROOM TEMPERATURE
In former times, when cellars were chilly and meals were eaten in rooms which were not constantly heated, *chambrer* meant to take red wine from a cellar in advance in order to bring it to room temperature. This rarely exceeded 18°C during most of the year. Today, if red wine is brought to the temperature of modern, centrally heated rooms, disappointment ensues since, above 20°C, red wines rapidly lose the best part of their bouquet. Only wines from the Mediterranean region, produced in a hot climate, can resist such warmth. It is more judicious today to open red wines at their storage temperature and let them slowly heat up in the glass.
CHAMPIGNON/MUSHROOM
▷ A smell similar to that of agaric mushrooms, or of mushroom stalks in general, is occasionally perceptible in wines whose grapes have suffered from grey rot (botrytis), or in wines that have just undergone lactic fermentation, but it is temporary and disappears after aeration in the glass.
Just as it is an important aromatic component of *haute cuisine*, so the scent of the truffle is present in a number of aromatic nuances of ageing white and red wines (*see Truffe*).
CHARPENTÉ/STRUCTURED
This term applies to red wines with high levels of moderately hard tannins, balanced by richness and acidity. The main grape varieties tending to impart this character are: Mourvèdre, Syrah, Cabernet Franc, Tannat, and Pinot Noir if given long maceration during vinification. The French term suggests an analogy between the tannin in the wine and the structure of a building or the skeleton of a living being.
CHÈVREFEUILLE/HONEYSUCKLE
An aromatic characteristic sometimes found in white wines made from the Chardonnay or Sauvignon Blanc varieties, and of other light, aromatic grape varieties.
CIDRE/CIDER
A smell similar to that of cider is occasionally found in white

wines that have oxidized and deteriorated (such wines often have a cider-like colour, too).

CIRE/WAX

The smell of wax or beeswax is quite common in great white wines made from the Chardonnay grape variety, particularly those of Pouilly-Fuissé and of Chablis, and in white Graves.

CITRON, CITRONELLE/LEMON, LEMON BALM

The aroma of lemon is quite common in young, acid and light white wines, contributing to the ethereal character of their bouquets. The aroma of lemon balm is a finer aroma than that of lemon, and is sometimes found in light red *primeur* wines.

COING/QUINCE

An aromatic quality perceptible in richly dry or sweet white wines, and often found together with other very ripe or preserved fruit aromas.

COMMUN/COMMON

A term applied to wines devoid of character, either as *vins de table* or as quality, *cru* wines that lack distinction and typicality.

COMPLET/COMPLETE

A characteristic that may become discernible as a wine is tasted in the mouth, when the flavours as a whole give the impression of fullness, without there being an excess or deficiency of any particular one. The word implies both substantial richness and balance.

CONTACT/CONTACT

The expression '*sensations de contact*' (contact sensations) was used by Max Léglise to designate all the gustatory reactions that occur in the mouth — flavours, tactile reactions, salivation — as opposed to the olfactory sensations perceived at a distance. The expression 'initial contact' would be a good substitute for 'attack' in describing the moment at which the wine meets the mouth.

CORPS/BODY

Among the anthropomorphic analogies that are used to describe the 'shape' of red wines, the word '*corps*' (body), the adjective '*corsé*' (well constituted, robust, stocky) and the quality of '*corpulence*' (corpulence) all apply to wines characterized by the two dominant elements of tannin and richness, that is to say possessing both '*charpente*' (structure) and '*chair*' (flesh). The adjective *corsé* also implies a moderate to high level of alcohol.

COULANT/PLEASANT, SUPPLE

This is a term used of wines that are easy to drink, partly because of an absence of astringency, and partly because of a fine balance between fresh acidity and richness without heaviness.

COULEUR/COLOUR

The coloration of red and rosé wines comes from the pigments or anthocyanins in red grapes, extracted to varying degrees during vinification. The colouring matter in white wines is still not fully understood by researchers, but it is presumed to have something to do with xanthophyll, the yellow colouring matter in vegetable tissue and the twin sister of chlorophyll.

For professional wine tasters, coloration, with its intensity, nuances and other various qualities, is a rich source of information regarding the constitution and maturity of a wine (*see* page 408 ff.). In much French wine writing, the colour of the wine is called its '*robe*' (dress or robe: q.v.).

COUPAGE/BLENDING

See Technical Glossary.

COURT/SHORT

Term applied to wines which have a low gustatory persistence or length in the mouth compared to the usual length of wines in their category. A carafe wine might be said to be short if its gustatory persistence lasts two to three seconds; for a great wine, persistence of between four and five seconds would be regarded as short.

CRÉMANT/CRÉMANT

See Technical Glossary.

CRÉOSOTE/CREOSOTE

A strongly empyreumatic substance extracted from wood tar and used pharmaceutically for its antiseptic qualities. The smell is similar to chimney soot, and it is frequently found in South African, Swiss and Alsace Pinot Noir wines, though more rarely in those from Burgundy. It is also constantly found in Beaujolais (made from the Gamay grape variety).

CREUX/HOLLOW

This adjective may be used of an inconsistent wine which, despite certain indications to the contrary, finally seems '*vide*' (empty), as opposed to '*plein*' (full).

CROUPI/STAGNANT

Smell of brine left in warm, dark places and colonized by mould and fungi which breed in it. The same process can occur in vats or casks when unsterilized water has been left in them. Wine stored in such containers will very easily acquire a *goût de croupi* (stagnant taste).

CRU/RAW

In the sense of being in a raw state, this term applies to young wines that have hardly developed, and still have the vegetal character of the grape in them.

CUIR/LEATHER

Diverse smells of leather are quite often present in certain red wines of quality when a few years old (for example Bandol, Châteauneuf-du-Pape, Madiran, Corton, Hermitage, Chambertin . . .). An explanation for this lies in the fact that leather is a combination of proteins and tannin; red wines, too, are substances naturally rich in tannin, and they absorb proteinaceous substances during the time in which they are aged on their lees. Among the different types of leather of which hints may be found in wines are: fresh leather, morocco, rawhide, Russian leather . . .

CUVE (GOÛT DE)/VAT (TASTE OF)

This is a synonym for *goût de croupi* (*see* above).

DÉCANTATION/DECANTING

This is an operation that consists of removing the wine from the sediment that may have formed while it has been in bottle. It may be carried out at different stages of the wine's journey from its cellar of origin to the customer's table.

▷ Important growers and *négociants* who deal in very old wines which may have thrown sediment often decant their wines themselves, before transporting them over long distances, in order to prevent the sediment being shaken up during transport. The operation is a delicate one, and not without its drawbacks: it has to be done very carefully, usually by using a kind of seesaw mechanism to ensure that no sediment mixes with the wine during decanting, otherwise the whole process would be a waste of time. It necessitates decanting the wine into a new bottle, leaving the sediment in the original one; the wine is substantially aerated as this happens, and this can result in oxidization to a varying degree, depending on the resistance of the wine, even if the bottles are filled up fully again. In order to avoid these drawbacks, the Burgundy *négociant* Louis Latour at Aloxe-Corton created a means of decanting Corton wines without actually moving the liquid from one bottle to another. This is achieved by using a silver-plated metal siphon placed in bottles that have already been standing vertically for a few days to allow the sediment to collect at the bottom. The siphon sucks away the sediment. This method became increasingly popular in wine-producing circles during the 1920s, 1930s and 1950s.

▷ The most effective decanting, though, is that carried out just before drinking, at a restaurant or at home, by transferring the wine to a carafe or decanter. This is just as delicate an operation as the preceding one, since the sediment must be prevented from becoming suspended in the liquid again, and this is not easy if the wine has been stored in a horizontal position until the moment when it is put on the table.

Luxurious instruments called decanting cradles, now more often seen in antique shops or museums than in private homes, are perhaps the most effective means of decanting. A decanting cradle consists of a bottle basket that can be slowly and steadily upended by means of an Archimedes' screw. It avoids the total transfer of liquid from the beginning of the operation, and unites the advantages of both the carafe and the *panier-verseur* (q.v.). As far as aeration is concerned, decanting just before serving does not have the drawbacks of the previous method. On the contrary, it generally amplifies and stimulates the bouquet of red wines to great advantage. Some connoisseurs of old wines still practise this, even if there is no sediment present in the bottle. It is a well-known fact that if wines are deprived of oxygen for too long then the reverse of oxidization occurs, namely reduction. In a mild form, this can deprive red wines of colour and aroma. The brief aeration undergone in decanting counteracts these effects.

***DÉCHARNÉ*/EMACIATED**

This term is applicable solely to red wines when they have literally lost their flesh, their richness, and are distressingly thin. This is generally owing to excessive ageing or ageing in inappropriate conditions.

***DÉFAUT*/FLAW**

▷ When a flaw is specified, it signifies some element missing in the constitution of the wine, such as a flaw in the colour, acidity or persistence. When referring to an absent quality, the word *manque* (lack) is used instead — a lack of finesse, or a lack of freshness. The opposite of this is an *excès* (excess).

▷ A flaw with no further specification refers to an anomaly concerning the appearance, smell or taste of the wine. A hazy wine, wine with a smell of sulphur or the taste of rotten cork are all flawed.

***DÉLICAT*/DELICATE**

▷ A term applied to wines that are finely structured, provoking mild reactions in the taster, but not implying a lack of appeal or character.

▷ The word is also used as a synonym for 'fragile', describing a wine that has not yet been stabilized and must be treated with care.

***DÉPÔT*/SEDIMENT**

This term refers to the insoluble substances which deposit themselves on the sides or on the bottom of a wine bottle after having been suspended in the liquid for some time. The causes of sediment deposition in bottle are very varied, and depending on these causes the nature, appearance and behaviour of the precipitates will differ greatly. In white and rosé wines that are low in phenolic polymerized substances, sediments are rare and are generally caused either by *casse cuivrique* (*see* Technical Glossary), by the coagulation of proteins after bottling, or by tartrate crystals which are deposited if the bottle is knocked or shaken. These mishaps are not serious: *casse cuivrique* (copper casse) is a consequence of reduction, and the sediment can be redissolved when the wine is aerated; while decanting the wine off protein and tartar deposits is easy. In red wines, mishaps resulting in haziness and deposits of sediment are more frequent. These may be due to bacterial action, perhaps harmless, such as lactic fermentation, but also possibly more serious, as in the case of *tourne* (tartaric fermentation) or *amertume* (bitterness) (*see* Technical Glossary). Precipitations of colouring matter or tartaric crystals can result from excessive filtration or cold. Then there is the more traditional, classic formation of sediment of oxidized tannins or hydrolyzed colouring matter which, in certain cases, adheres to the glass forming a layer over the inside of the bottle.

Bacterial deposits are fine, and it is difficult to decant wine off these, especially if they are still active and generating carbon dioxide. Wine can easily be decanted off deposits of colouring matter or tannin.

***DÉPOUILLÉ*/SETTLED, DENUDED**

This term is used to describe two stages in the life of a wine:

▷ When wines are still young and are clarifying themselves, they are said to have 'settled' when the substances which were previously in suspension during fermentation have been deposited.

▷ When aged red wines have lightened in colour and flavour they are said to be *dépouillé* (denuded).

***DÉSÉQUILIBRE*/LACK OF BALANCE**

This characteristic is found in wines whose harmony has been broken by the serious excess or lack of a particular element, or by some other anomaly.

***DESSÉCHÉ*/DRYING, DRIED**

The process of 'drying' in a wine signifies the double effect of a paucity of richness and a harshness induced by the oxydization of tannin. A wine is said to be dried out when, after having a normal gustatory constitution, it begins to weaken with age, becoming more harsh owing to the increasing prominence of its tannin.

***DISTINGUÉ*/DISTINGUISHED**

An anthropomorphic analogy referring to a wine that is both remarkable and refined. *Élégant* (elegant) is also used.

DOUCEUR/SOFTNESS
This is an attribute of slightly sweet wines in which the sugar provides smoothness without being noticeable as such.
DOUX/SWEET
See Technical Glossary.
DUR, DURETÉ/HARD, HARDNESS
This is a quality attributed to red wine in which tannin and acidity clearly dominate, imparting both astringency and aggressiveness. The paucity or inadequacy of richness in such wines exacerbates this quality of hardness. It is occasionally also found in white wines recently stored in new casks that have not been adequately rinsed out.

ÉCORCE/BARK
Apart from the oaky aromas that red wines acquire during the time they spend in wooden casks, they may also possess smells reminiscent of tree bark. The most common of these is oak bark, often charged by the smell of lichen that perfumers call *mousse de chêne* (oak moss). In strongly leafy or stalky wines, smells are often found close to those of elder bark or bloodwort. Light red wines, vinified without wood contact and in large quantities, have a bouquet reminiscent of lime bark when young. The smell of cinchona bark may be found in very old wines from Roussillon, central Italy and Burgundy.
ÉDULCORER/TO SWEETEN
The sweetening of wine consists of carefully enriching it with sugar after fermentation, in order to impart and conserve richness. In France, this sweetening process is only permitted for white and rosé wines, using concentrated must and excluding sucrose. In Germany, Austria and Croatia, the sweetening of red wines in this way is also authorized and appreciated. Synthetic sweeteners (saccharine, dulcine, cyclamates) are forbidden.
ÉGLANTINE/DOG ROSE
This aroma is sometimes present in light, very delicate wines.
ÉLÉGANT/ELEGANT
A term applied to wine by analogy with the attribute as a human quality. Apart from the idea of charm and the satisfaction of formal aesthetic criteria it implies, it also indicates the absence of heaviness in wine, together with a certain originality. The term *distingué* (distinguished) might be regarded as synonymous.
EMPYREUMATIQUE/EMPYREUMATIC
This word describes the smell of anything that has been charred or simply toasted. Included in this category are the smells of tar, soot, burnt wood, caramel, burnt toast and also, in a less overt form, tea, coffee, cocoa, tobacco, rusk, etc. This scientific term is rarely used in the everyday language of wine tasting, the terms preferred being *grillé* (grilled), *brûlé* (burnt), or *fumé* (smoked).
ENCENS/INCENSE
This is a smell with a balsamic (q.v.) character, produced by the calcination of aromatic resins like myrrh, benzoin and especially frankincense. In red wines, the smell of incense seems to be the long-term incarnation of the oak aroma of wines stored in new vats that have not been adequately rinsed out. It is an aromatic nuance of great class, and is often found alongside that of sandalwood in the finest southern French wines.
ENVELOPPÉ/SHROUDED
This term is rarely used. It applies particularly to red wines with all their harshness removed, and with a slightly dominant richness.
ÉPAIS/THICK
A quality of red wines in which richness blended with tannin dominates the balance to the exclusion of finesse and harmony.
ÉPANOUI/OPEN, IN BLOOM
This term is applied to wine that seems to offer an unlimited range of olfactory and gustatory qualities within a balanced and attractive whole.
ÉPICES/SPICES
This term covers a wide range of aromatic nuances, including a range of culinary spices that are detected in an unsystematic way by tasters in various white and red wines of a good gustatory maturity.
ÉQUILIBRE, ÉQUILIBRÉ/BALANCE, BALANCED
Terms used during the buccal phase of wine tasting, meaning that the different groups of flavours match one another in a satisfactory way, so that none is dominant or deficient, subjectively creating the impression of balance. In white wines this relates to acidity and richness; in red wines, to tannin, acidity and richness. This structural and quantitive notion should be distinguished from harmony (q.v.), which is aesthetic and qualitative. A light or very powerful wine may be harmonious, whereas balance implies the idea of equal quantities of constituents being present.
ÉTEINT/FADED
A term describing the temporary or permanent eclipse of the aromatic qualities of the wine, most often following transportation or exposure to extremes of temperature.
ÉTHANOL/ETHANOL
See Alcool.
ÉTOFFÉ/RICHLY TEXTURED
Refers to a red wine well supplied with richness and tannin, but not to excess; such a wine gives the impression of being well textured and of substantial richness.
ÉVENT/STALENESS
A characteristic smell of wines that have been left on ullage and unprotected. The wine is said to be *éventé* (stale, musty), and the formation of this smell is generally accompanied by the loss of other aromatic qualities of the wine.

FADE/BLAND, INSIPID
Refers to a substance weak in flavours and aromas, and the term may be applied to wines with such negative qualities.
FAIBLE/WEAK
When applied to wine, this term implies in part a deficiency in alcohol, and in part a constitutional poverty indicating fragility and problems of conservation.
FANÉ/FADED
By analogy with a flower or leaf, a faded wine is one that has lost its freshness, brilliance and some of its best aromas. The term *défraîchi* means much the same thing, and may also be used.

***FATIGUÉ*/TIRED**
By anthropomorphic analogy, a wine that is tired is one that has temporarily lost its coherence and tone. This occurs particularly after transportation or any other kind of physical disturbance. The comparison can be taken further by specifying a period of *repos* (rest) to recover from the effects of tiredness.

***FAUVE*/ANIMALITY, FOXINESS, MUSKINESS**
Fauve is an animal nuance that can characterize the bouquet of old red wines to varying degrees. In its lightest form, only the smell of animal fur (or stuffed animals) is perceptible. The smell of wildfowl or fox is strong in old Pinot Noir wines, which are accurately said to *'renarder'* ('to fox', meaning to become fox-like). Other old Pinot Noir wines develop scents of venison or even the smell of intestines known as *ventre de lièvre* (hare's stomach). These smells are all formed by reduction, and disappear quite quickly once the wine is aerated (c.f. *Foxé*).

***FAUX GOÛT*/OFF TASTE**
This term is used to describe a gustatory characteristic that clashes with the general impression of a given wine and is sensed as an anomaly.

***FÉMININ*/FEMININE**
Term applied to wines dominated by soft, delicate, perhaps very slightly sweet aroma and flavour constituents, devoid of *nervosité* (internal tensions) or hardness.

***FENOUIL*/FENNEL**
Umbelliferous plant whose seeds are an industrial source for the scent and taste of aniseed (q.v.). This aromatic nuance is sometimes found in very mature dry white wines.

***FERMÉ*/CLOSED**
As opposed to *ouvert* (open), this term refers to a wine whose bouquet refuses to emerge from the glass, and whose flavours may be similarly terse.

***FERMENT*/FERMENTATION AGENTS**
This is a generic term designating all the microbial agents responsible for fermentation (yeast, bacteria ...).

In wine tasting, the taste of fermentation agents is not a desirable one, being close to that of vitamin B_1 or thiamine. It originates from the decomposition of yeast during the storing of wine on its sediment, when the wine is very young.

***FERMETÉ*/FIRMNESS**
This is chiefly a red wine characteristic, indicating that tannin and acidity are slightly dominant in the wine's composition.

***FEUILLE MORTE*/DEAD LEAF**
▷ A term used to describe the colour of certain old red wines. This plant analogy is preferable to comparisons with brick or tile.
▷ An aromatic characteristic, close to the smell of humus or undergrowth, found in certain very mature Cabernet Sauvignon, Cabernet Franc and Pinot Noir wines, generally accompanied by attenuated flavours.

***FIGUE*/FIG**
The aroma of dried fig, frequently found alongside that of cooked or preserved strawberries, is a normal constituent of fortified red wines like port or Banyuls, yet also of old, dry red wines of years in which the fruit was harvested in a very ripe state.

***FIN DE BOUCHE*/FINISH**
This is the terminal stage of the buccal phase of tasting, during which gustatory persistence is monitored. It precedes the aftertaste. In the wine's finish, gustatory particularities or failings may emerge that were not apparent in the previous stages (off tastes, bitterness, metallic tastes, a mousy taste, and so on).

***FLASQUE*/FLACCID**
The term *flasque* is synonymous with *mou* (soft), but it also implies a lack of texture which is not necessarily implicit in *mollesse* (softness).

***FLAVEUR*/FLAVOUR**
Flaveur is a French neologism borrowed from the English word 'flavour'; it does not appear in French dictionaries yet. It is a general term for all the flavours and aromas sensed in the mouth (*see Arôme*).

***FLORAL*/FLORAL**
This is a general characteristic of a wine whose bouquet is dominated by the aroma of flowers.

***FLOU*/HAZY**
This is a visual disturbance of the sort found in wines that seem clear when exposed to a direct line of light, yet that go slightly hazy when lit from the side, due to the Tyndall effect (q.v.).

***FOIN COUPÉ*/MOWN HAY**
An aromatic nuance particular to red wines, and especially apparent in the transitional phase when the wine is passing from the aromas of fermentation to those of gustatory maturity. Older oenological studies identify this smell, in chemical terms, with coumarin, but Émile Peynaud has identified it as a methylboluidic ketone.

***FONDU*/MELTED, SUCCULENT**
A descriptive term used of red wines in which a slightly dominant richness envelops all other sensations.

***FORT*/STRONG**
A term little used by tasters today; in everyday language it signifies a wine rich in alcohol.

***FOUGÈRE*/FERN**
An aromatic quality found in white wines of very high quality, contributing to their fine, ethereal bouquet.

***FOURRURE*/FUR**
A group of smells particular to aged red wines, and belonging to the group of aromas termed 'animal' (*see Animal, Fauve*).

***FOXÉ*/FOXY**
An aromatic quality, not animal but vegetal in character, particular to the 'fox' grapes of native American vine varieties and to a few of their hybrids (such as the Noah, Clinton or Isabelle), the chemical reference for which is methyl anthranilate.

***FRAIS*/FRESH**
By way of analogy, the aromas termed 'fresh', like mint and lemon balm, are those that produce sensations suggesting coolness or a refreshing effect. In a broader sense equally relevant to wine, the term implies newness, youth, lightness and fluidity in the aromas experienced on both the olfactory and buccal level.

***FRAISE*/STRAWBERRY**
▷ The aromatic nuance *fraise des bois* (wild strawberry) is quite common in young red wines, along with aromas of

other small red fruits.
▷ The aroma of cooked or crystallized strawberry is often found together with that of dried fig in sweet, fortified wines and old, dry red wines.

***FRAMBOISE*/RASPBERRY**
The aroma of raspberry is a very important part of the fruity bouquet of the Pinot Noir wines of the Côte de Beaune, and also of numerous aromatic red wines, often *primeur* but not necessarily so (Beaujolais, Côtes du Rhône . . .).

***FRANC*/HONEST, STRAIGHTFORWARD**
Used of a wine presenting its smells and flavours without any aromatic or gustative ambiguity, and with no anomalies present. The word *net* (clear, precise) may also be used of such wines.

***FRAPPÉ*/ICED**
This term is used to describe a wine that has been rapidly (and brutally) chilled in an ice bucket or fridge freezer. Sparkling wines tolerate such treatment. However, it is very harmful to still wines, giving both white and rosé wines a bitter finish, and destroying the balance and definition of the bouquet of red wines, which often emerge cloudy from such treatment.

***FRIAND*/TASTY**
Tasty wines are those that are pleasant to taste in the same way as food delicacies are — light, vivacious and fresh.

***FRUITÉ*/FRUIT, FRUITINESS**
▷ This characteristic marks the first stage in the development of a wine's bouquet after alcoholic fermentation, when the aromas are dominated by the character of fresh fruit.
▷ These terms can also be applied to wines with the aromatic characteristics outlined above. It is used more often of red and rosé wines than of whites, although these may also possess strong fruit smells, such as those of apple, lemon, banana, and so on.

***FUMÉ*/SMOKY**
▷ This term is applied to wines made from the Sauvignon Blanc grape variety in the vineyards of Pouilly-sur-Loire.
▷ It is also an aromatic quality reminiscent of the smell of certain smoked foods (fish, ham, sausage) encountered in certain quality red wines in maturity.

***FUMÉE*/SMOKE**
A smell evoking chimney soot, and a kind of amplification of the preceding quality, almost always present in wines from the *crus* of Beaujolais, and intermittently present in wines made from the Pinot Noir.

In French analytical wine tasting, the smell of smoke tends to be designated as either creosote (q.v.) or wood tar (*see Goudron*). All of these aromas belong to the category of empyreumatic smells (q.v.).

***FUMET*/AROMA**
This word is generally used to suggest the aroma of food being prepared, especially cooked. In certain parts of France, the word *fumet* is used to designate the bouquet of wines, especially when aged.

***FÛT (GOÛT DE)*/CASK (TASTE OF)**
A *goût de fût* is a bad taste imparted to wine owing to negligent upkeep, when empty, of the cask in which the wine has been stored, which may have become tainted with rot or acescence, or acquired a stagnant taste.

When the quality of the cask wood in the vat imparts a positive and attractive taste to the wine, then the term *boisé* (oaky) is used instead of *goût de fût*.

***GARRIGUE*/GARRIGUE**
The garrigue is the arid hill scrubland of Provence and the Midi, covered with stunted vegetation and very dry in the summer. This word can be used analogously to describe the smells of dry grass and wild herbs that are sometimes found in wines of middle maturity.

***GÉNÉREUX*/GENEROUS**
This term is used less and less frequently today; it has traditionally been applied to wines strong in alcohol, or to fortified wines.

***GENÊT*/BROOM**
The yellow flowers of broom have a strong, sweet scent, quite close to that of stock, and such a scent forms part of the fine aromatic range of wines made from the Chardonnay.

***GENIÈVRE*/JUNIPER**
The distinctive smell of juniper berries is found in certain aromatic wines of quality.

***GÉRANIUM*/GERANIUM**
▷ In the strict botanical sense, this term refers to the odour of plants of the *Geranium* genus, such as herb Robert. From these is produced an essence called geraniol that makes up a good part of the perfumer's 'rose essence'. Oenological analysis has identified it in the aroma of certain Muscat wines.
▷ In its more popular and familiar sense, 'geranium' refers to plants of the *Pelargonium* genus. The characteristic smell of this plant is occasionally found in small traces in very old red wines, or in disagreeably large amounts in wines that have been treated with potassium sorbate or sorbic acid.

***GIBIER (ODEUR DE)*/GAME (SMELL OF)**
This is an animal characteristic of greater or lesser foxiness or muskiness, sometimes suggesting marinaded game, found in wines that have undergone a certain degree of reduction in bottle (*venaison* — venison — is a synonym for this aroma). The characteristic generally disappears a few moments after the wine has been aerated.

***GIROFLE*/CLOVE**
A nail-shaped spice used in cooking. Its essence — eugenol — has a very strong and dominating smell, hints of which are found in quality red wines of the Rhône valley after a few years in bottle.

***GIROFLÉE*/STOCK**
Small, ornamental, cruciferous flower whose smell, close to that of broom, is suggested by the aromas of the best wines made from the Chardonnay grape variety.

***GLYCÉROL*/GLYCEROL**
This is the technical name for glycerine. Like alcohol, it is a secondary product of alcoholic fermentation, and only alcohol is produced in larger quantities — 5g to 10g of glycerol are produced for every 100g of alcohol, depending on the conditions of fermentation and the type of yeast used. However, the musts expressed from grapes affected by *pourriture noble* (noble rot) may already contain up to 20g per litre before fermentation.

The flavour of glycerol is sweet and its texture is viscous; in fact it has considerable acridity in its pure state. It tributes to the sensation of richness in a wine, intensely so in naturally sweet dessert wines, and lightly so in dry wines. In the latter its primary role is to help attenuate the burning quality of alcohol. (*See also* Technical Glossary.)

GOUDRON/TAR

▷ This is an abnormal smell in wine if it is reminiscent of the coal tar or bitumen used to cover roads. Such a smell in wine used to be caused by tar vapours infecting the grapes or coming into contact with the casks. This problem has almost disappeared today since tar can now be laid on road surfaces in cold layers.

▷ The smell of wood tar or creosote is similar to certain aromatic components common in the wines of a number of red grape varieties.

GOULEYANT/GULPABLE

A word from the same semantic family as *goulée* (gulp) and *goulot* (bottle neck), and used to describe a wine that is very easy and pleasant to drink.

GOÛT/TASTE

According to the original and basic meaning of the term, taste is one of the five senses, together with sight, hearing, smell and touch, and taste is perceived in the mouth. In the 19th century, sensory physiology defined its strict limits, that of the perception of the four elementary flavours: saltiness, sweetness, acidity and bitterness, thus limiting its scope to the papillae of the tongue.

Currently the word is used in a broader sense again, akin to the original one, describing all those sensations perceived in the mouth, and including aromas as well as flavours. To cover this meaning one might use the English word 'flavour', from which the French neologism *flaveur* has been derived.

GRAIN/GRAIN

This term is used in certain French regions to express the quality of the contact between wine and mouth. The wine is then said to be fine-grained or coarsely grained.

GRAPPE (GOÛT DE)/GRAPE BUNCH (TASTE OF)

An unpleasant taste that is acerbic and stalky to varying degrees, caused by prolonged maceration during vinification of red grapes without the grape bunch stems having been removed.

GRAS/FAT

A term referring to the richness of a wine when it reaches a clearly perceptible level, with no other element sufficiently present to detract from this richness.

GRAVELLE/GRAVELLE

Crystalline, tartaric sediment that forms in bottled wines, particularly white and rosé wines, with the mobile, transparent and shiny appearance of sand. This sediment is generally composed of calcium tartrate.

GRÊLE (GOÛT DE)/HAIL (TASTE OF)

The traumatic effects of hail on grapes during the months preceding the harvest take the form of scars composed of corky tissue which dries out and is invaded by mould. Affected grapes may be vinified with healthy grapes after the harvest, and this results in what is called a 'taste of hail', similar to the dry, rotten and bitter taste of corked wine (*goût de bouchon*). The risk of this can be eliminated by sorting the grapes when they are gathered and removing the damaged fruit.

GRENADINE/GRENADINE

A suggestion of the aroma of this syrup made from pomegranate juice may be found in rosé wines from the Côtes du Rhône and from Provence.

GRILLÉ/TOASTED

An aromatic nuance generally qualifying another. The aroma of *pain grillé* (toast) is found in certain red wines of quality, while *amande grillée* (toasted almond) is one of the finest aromas of great white wines when they are beginning their reduction phase of maturation in bottle.

GROSEILLE/REDCURRANT

An aromatic characteristic occasionally found in *clairets* (very pale red wines) or red *primeur* wines.

GUSTATIF/GUSTATIVE

This word may be used of everything relevant to the sense of taste: gustatory examination, gustatory characteristics, a gustatory anomaly, the gustatory phase of tasting, gustatory aptitude, gustatory qualities, and so on.

HARMONIE, HARMONIEUX/HARMONY, HARMONIOUS

In the complex sensory domains of sight, sound, smell and taste, harmony is the phenomenon in which satisfactory relationships are established between the constituent elements of the object being sensed. These may be elementary, simple, obvious, correct, pleasant or any other realization implying a certain minimum of accord, or exclusion of disaccord. This concept of sensory harmony is actually less simple than it sounds, since it is acquired by us through practice from childhood onwards, via family customs, upbringing and our general cultural context. It is therefore subject to variation in time, and from one country to another. At the highest level, it is part of the philosophical problem of aesthetics.

As far as wine tasting is concerned, a wine is considered to be harmonious if it meets several conditions:

▷ Each group of flavours considered separately (acidity, richness, tannin) must not have any intrinsically disagreeable factor that might clash with and impair the general impression of the whole (for example bitter tannin, or vinegar-like acidity, or richness founded too exclusively on alcohol).

▷ Each of these groups of flavours must be present in a favourable quantity with respect to others, to create an impression of structure and balanced aesthetic style. This situation is rarely attained by equal proportions of groups of flavours (balance is different from harmony), but more often by a graduated hierarchy of the three groups.

In French gastronomy, the word *harmonie* is occasionally used to describe the relationship between the dishes and the wines that accompany them. As this relationship is essentially a mobile and fugitive one, it is quite wrong to name it 'harmony'; it is simply the pairing of the moment.

HAVANE/CIGAR LEAF

The smell of cigar leaf is evoked by nuances found in the aromas of very fine red wines.

HÉDONISME/HEDONISM

▷ In a technical sense, *hédonisme* is an area of French psychology in which the effects of sensations are studied in

terms of pleasure (the word is derived from the Greek *haidôn*, meaning 'pleasure').
▷ Philosophically, hedonism refers to the ethical doctrine that the pursuit of pleasure is the highest good.
▷ In a more general sense, the word hedonism is used to signify the pursuit of pleasure for pleasure's sake. The sensory analysis of wine-tasting is a form of disciplined hedonism.

HERBACÉ/HERBACEOUS, LEAFY OR STALKY QUALITY
This gustatory characteristic is of imprecise chemical origin; the word *herbacé* is used to refer to smells and tastes reminiscent of mown grass, or of green plant organs. These are considered unpleasant nuances when specified in this way.

HUILE, HUILEUX/OIL, OILY
This refers to the viscoid physical appearance that certain wines adopt during youth under the effect of viscous lactic fermentation. From a gustatory point of view, the wine has an oily texture in the mouth and an insipid character. This *maladie de la graisse* is not permanent, and the wine soon recovers.

HUMUS/HUMUS
An aromatic characteristic, also known as *sous-bois* (undergrowth), or *feuille morte* (dead leaf), found in good quality red wines.

'IMPITOYABLES'/'IMPITOYABLES'
This is the brand name of a series of wine-tasting glasses of a large and original shape used for the detailed, in-depth analysis of aromas in wines of all types.

INDOLE/INDOLE
Chemical compound with a fetid smell, present in small traces in animal odours and their wine equivalents.

IODE, IODÉ/IODINE, IODIZED
Terms applicable to wines whose smell contains elements reminiscent of street gutters or salt marshes.

JACINTHE/HYACINTH
This is a floral odour frequently encountered in white wines made from aromatic grape varieties after a few years in bottle (for example in wines made from the Sauvignon Blanc, in white Rhône wines made from local varieties, and in the finest Muscat wines).

JAMBES/LEGS
Descending droplets, also called *larmes* (tears), that form on the sides of the glass after wine has been swirled in it or after drinking. This phenomenon is a result of the difference of evaporation speeds of water and alcohol.

JASMIN/JASMINE
A floral aroma of great finesse often found in wines containing active quantities of linalol and geraniol.

JAUNE (VIN)/JAUNE (VIN)
This is a special type of wine whose ageing process takes place over several years, under a layer of yeast, in wooden casks. For French professional wine tasters, the word *jaune* (yellow) designates not only the colour of the wine (which in fact often remains quite pale), but also the aromatic complex of wines aged in this way, resulting from controlled oxidization and the furannic syntheses of fatty acids and ketones, evoking among other smells that of walnut.

In France, *vin jaune* is a speciality of the Jura; in Spain, fino sherry from Jerez, and manzanilla from Sanlúcar de Barrameda, are both produced in this way. *Vin jaune* has a remarkable role to play in cuisine as well, being finer in this respect than Madeira and similar wines produced by heat processes; *vin jaune* combines admirably with black truffle.

JEUNE/YOUNG
If used with no further qualification, one might describe any wine that has retained a fair proportion of the fruity aromas and fresh flavours resulting from its vinification as young.

LACTIQUE/LACTIC
▷ Lactic acid is a product of the secondary or malolactic fermentation of wine; it is produced from malic acid. Its gustatory qualities play a part in the overall taste impression left on the palate by old wines.
▷ A lactic smell is one produced by lactic acid, either through an unwanted development during lactic fermentation, or thanks to some indeterminate combinations more or less reminiscent of the smell of *fromage frais* or fermented cheeses. (*See also* Lactic Acid in the Technical Glossary.)

LAITERIE (ODEUR DE)/DAIRY (SMELL OF)
The presence in wine of a smell reminiscent of a dairy is the result of various possible lactic impairments.

LARMES/TEARS
The phenomenon of descending droplets of liquid that form on the sides of the glass after drinking is indicated by this word. The term *jambes* (legs, q.v.) is also used to describe this phenomenon.

LAURIER/BAY LEAF
The spicy aroma of bay leaf characterizes the wines of certain southern French grape varieties, notably the Syrah and the Grenache, after a few years in bottle.

LÉGER/LIGHT
A quality attributed to wines that have little substance, yet remain harmonious and balanced.

LEVURES/YEAST
▷ Yeast deposits: these take the form of a finely textured whitish sediment that is found in bottles, consequent on the development of yeast cells due to refermentation or the formation of a yeast scum after bottling. This deposit does not affect the taste of the wine, provided the wine is carefully decanted beforehand.
▷ A yeasty taste: this is a taste imparted to the wine by the decomposition of dead yeast cells while the wine is still being stored on its sediment. This taste is reminiscent of vitamin B_1 when the deposits in the wine are still in a good state; when these are starting to decay, the taste takes on an acetamide character (mousy smell).

LICHEN/LICHEN
An aromatic quality similar to that found in the aromas of certain types of red wine. The perfumer's expression *mousse de chêne* (oak moss) is also used.

LIÈGE, LIÉGEUX/CORK, CORKY
▷ Cork is the substance traditionally used to seal wine in the bottle. It could only be replaced in the future by a substance having the same level of permeability to air and

moisture, and the same neutrality of taste.

▷ *Liégeux* (corky) is an abnormal gustatory quality reminiscent of the smell of damp, rotten cork. It generally comes from a completely different source, most often from the accumulation of tartar deposits in badly maintained vats or casks, but also from the growth of green mould on the floors and walls of wine storage areas.

LIERRE/IVY

The smell of ivy leaves is close to that olfactory quality found in the early postfermentation aroma of many Cabernet Franc and Cabernet Sauvignon wines.

LIMPIDITÉ/LIMPIDITY, CLARITY

Defined as the 'absence of cloudiness', limpidity plays an important role in wine tasting in that it is an essential precondition for sensory analysis or detailed wine tasting. The presence of the suspended particles causing cloudiness spoils the subtle perception of flavours in the mouth by obstructing nerve endings on the tongue.

When there is cloudiness present in wine, the difficulty for the wine taster is in situating it on a scale of intensity, and deciding at what point it becomes unacceptable. In fact the observation of the limpidity of a wine should be carried out not only in a direct line of light but also lit from the side, to see if the Tyndall effect (q.v.) is coming into play. It is often the case that cloudiness not visible in direct light is clearly perceptible when lit from the side, due to the Tyndall effect. If cloudiness is present, its intensity can be expressed using the following scale: *voilé* (veiled), *nébuleux* (misty), *louche* (hazy), *trouble* (cloudy), *opalescent* (opalescent), *laiteux* (milky).

LONG/LONG

Refers to a wine that has long aromatic persistence in the mouth after tasting.

LOURD/HEAVY

This attribute may be used of a wine overladen with the three main groups of flavours, and in particular tannin and richness, to such an extent as to deprive it of any lightness, smoothness or freshness.

LUMIÈRE/LIGHT

Wines, especially white wines, are substantially photosensitive: a bottle exposed to the rising sun for a few minutes has its oxidation-reduction potential reduced by around a hundred millivolts over the days and weeks which follow. Our wine-making predecessors, who observed these phenomena by non-scientific means, realized that wine must be sheltered from light, hence its storage in cellars, wooden vats and dark bottles ...

One of the most common light-exposure accidents occurring in recently bottled champagne and white wine is known as *goût de lumière* (literally a 'taste of light'). It is the result of simultaneous reduction and oxidation of various constituents of the wine under the effect of light, and it takes the form of a slightly sulphurous smell somewhere between that of garlic and vulcanized rubber.

MÂCHE/CHEWINESS

To say that a wine has *de la mâche* (chewiness) may simply mean that it is rich in substance, giving the impression that it could be 'chewed'. For professionals, though, it generally signifies that the wine possesses considerable astringency, necessitating several mastications before the wine can easily be swallowed.

MADÉRISATION/MADERIZATION

This is a form of oxidization that causes a wine to take on the organoleptic qualities of madeira: a browning in colour, the formation of ethyl acetate and its compounds, the acquisition of the characteristic taste of madeira. Normally this is considered a crippling fault in wines that have suffered it, except in the case of *vins jaunes*, when it is considered a normal phase of development.

MAIGRE/THIN

This term is applied anthropomorphically to wines of little substance, lacking any *gras* (fat) or *moelleux* (richness).

MATURATION/MATURATION

This term should be used to designate the phase characterized by the formation of the bouquet during the first years of conservation in bottle. It is more appropriate than the word *vieillissement* (ageing), which rather defines the phase following maturity.

MÉLISSE/BALM

This herbaceous annual plant has an essence reminiscent of lemon zest, but more ethereal and less acid. This aromatic nuance is found in numerous young white wines.

MENTHE/MINT

An aromatic, herbaceous plant whose essence is one of those most commonly used in food and drink substances. There are two main variants: peppermint and spearmint. Traces of these aromas are found in certain white wines, contributing to the freshness and vivacity of their bouquets.

MERCAPTAN/MERCAPTAN

This substance is technically known as thiol, thialcohol, or ethyl hydrogen sulphide. The compound results from the combination of alcohol with hydrogen sulphide, and it is characterized by a very strong and unpleasant sulphurous smell.

Among professionals, there is a tendency to describe (a little too hastily) any manifestation of sulphur as 'mercaptan'. There are in fact four types of sulphurous presence found in wine: 1. Hydrogen sulphide, or H_2S, the primary form with the smell of rotten eggs. 2. True mercaptan, or C_2H_5-SH, which has the smell of lamp gas. 3. Diethyl sulphide or $(C_2H_5)_2S$, an 'encrustation' of the two preceding forms, with an alliaceous or garlic-like smell. 4. The sulphurous compound(s) of aldehyde, still inadequately defined, with the smell of vulcanized rubber. The two first forms appear in wines stored in bulk on their lees. The third results from not applying corrective treatments to eliminate the first two. The fourth is one of the manifestations of the *goût de lumière* (*see Lumière*).

MIEL/HONEY

Apart from the essences gathered by bees (flowers, lavender, pine ...), the smell of honey is characterized particularly by the beeswax in which it is formed. This aromatic characteristic is often suggested by the wines of white grape varieties that age well (Sauvignon Blanc, Marsanne, Viognier, Savagnin, Chardonnay).

MINCE/SLENDER

This term is applied to wines of weak constitution, relatively poor in various elements. *Minceur* (slenderness) is different to *maigreur* (thinness), which implies above all a deficiency in richness, and *légèreté* (lightness), which implies the qualities of fluidity and finesse.

***MIRABELLE*/GOLDEN PLUM**

This is an aromatic quality found in white wines made during years in which the grapes achieved great ripeness. It is generally found within a rich aromatic ensemble, to which it adds an enticing note.

***MOELLEUX*/RICHNESS, SWEETNESS**

▷ In the primitive, original sense of the word, *moelleux* means having the consistency and unctuosity of bone marrow.

▷ For white and rosé wines, the word *moelleux* is used to describe those having a perceptible level of residual sugar, resulting in a gustatory impression of *douceur* (softness, implying sweetness).

▷ As a noun, the term can be used to describe the whole range of sweet substances present in wine: alcohol, glycerol, sugar. This is one of the three groups of basic flavours found in wine (the other two are acidity, and tannin/astringency).

***MOISI*/ROTTEN**

Odorous and gustatory character resulting from mould that may have grown at different times and in different places during the manufacture and storage of the wine (on the grapes, in the vats, in the transfer pipes and pumps, in the corks . . .).

***MOLLESSE, MOU*/SOFTNESS, SOFT**

A characteristic of wines that lack acidity but possess normal levels of richness and tannin.

***MORDANT*/MORDANT**

This word is used to qualify a wine that has a slightly dominant level of acidity and tannin, giving it an edge of aggressiveness, but without *accrochage* (clashing) or even persistence.

***MOUILLÉ*/WATERED**

In food and drink terminology, *mouillé* (watered) designates a natural liquid (wine, milk, cider, fruit juice) which has had water illegally added to it.

***MOUSSE DE CHÊNE*/OAK MOSS**

This is the name given by perfumers to the white, greyish and greenish lichens that grow on oak bark. These have a very particular, strongly vegetal smell, and the equivalent of this aroma is found in numerous red wines when their fruitiness is starting to fade.

***MUET*/DUMB**

▷ In certain French regions, when applied to wine, this word is a synonym for *muté* (literally 'muted', meaning stabilized against further fermentation by sulphur treatment or by fortification with alcohol).

▷ By extension of the previous sense, the word *muet* may also signify a still wine as opposed to an effervescent one.

▷ More generally, a wine is said to be dumb if, when tasted, '*il ne parle pas*' ('it does not speak'), i.e. if it is poor in aromatic expression, or even totally deprived of any kind of character.

***MÛRE SAUVAGE*/(WILD) BLACKBERRY**

This is an aromatic quality resembling that found in very mature red wines endowed with a rich and varied fruitiness.

***MUSCADE*/NUTMEG**

An aromatic spice, suggestions of the aroma of which are found in mature white dessert wines.

***MUSQUÉ, MUSC*/MUSKY, MUSK**

This aromatic quality is similar to that of the animal secretion of the same name. In wine, it is slightly fetid in a state of reduction, but very pleasant if aerated. It is found in various great red wines of middle maturity.

***MYRTILLE*/BILBERRY**

The aroma of bilberries is often associated with that of blackberries, and it is found in wines similar to those in which the aroma of blackberries is suggested.

***NÉBULEUX*/MISTY**

This is the second degree on the scale of cloudiness contrasting with limpidity (q.v.), signifying a wine cloudier than *voilé* (veiled), but a little less cloudy than *louche* (hazy).

***NERVEUX*/VIGOROUS, VITAL**

This is a physical quality attributed especially to white wines, and sometimes also to reds, in which strong levels of acidity and richness create the impression of opposition and tension, suggesting the literal meaning of *nerveux*, nervousness.

***NET*/CLEAR, PRECISE**

This word is used of wine in which the aromatic and gustatory sensations are straightforward and precise, without any ambiguity or complications.

***NEUTRE*/NEUTRAL**

A term applied to wines which lack personality and specific character traits.

***NEZ*/NOSE**

▷ The sensory organ of olfaction, or smell.

▷ By extension of this meaning, the faculty of smell itself, as in the phrase '*avoir un bon nez*' ('to have a good nose').

▷ By extension again, the totality of olfactory qualities of an odorous product, such as '*le nez du vin*' (the smell of wine) or, in a specific wine, '*un nez floral*' (a floral smell).

***NOISETTE*/HAZELNUT**

An aromatic quality quite common in good white wines that are several years old, particularly those based on the Chardonnay grape variety.

***NOYAU*/KERNEL**

This is an aromatic characteristic grouping together various nuances, such as cherry and peach kernels, as well as the industrial flavouring identified with kernels (benzoic aldehyde). This smell is characteristic of the developed bouquet of red wines whose early fruitiness resembled that of stoned fruits, such as cherry or plum.

***NOYER (FEUILLE DE)*/WALNUT (LEAF)**

This olfactory characteristic serves as a useful analogy for the aromatic consequences of a light oxidization combined with the formation of aldehyde and a certain staleness. Especially common in white wines.

***NUANCE*/NUANCE**

This word is used to describe a variation within a basic aroma or colour. For example, nuances of red might include purple, carmine, puce, vermilion or garnet; while those of yellow might include straw, gold or canary yellow. Nuances of colour are one of the means of evaluating the condition and level of development of a wine.

ODEUR/SMELL
A volatile emanation from a natural or synthetic substance that spreads in the air and is perceived by the sense of smell. *See Arôme* for distinctions between smell, fragrance, scent, perfume, aroma and so on.
OEIL/EYE
Certain wine tasters use this word as a synonym for the appearance of a wine.
OEIL-DE-PERDRIX/PARTRIDGE EYE
This is a colour nuance of vague definition, applying in general to rosé wines. In the French-speaking parts of Switzerland, this expression designates a specific wine: rosé made from the Pinot Noir grape variety. The colour of this wine is exactly the nuanced pale orange that characterizes the colour of a partridge's eye.
OEILLET/CARNATION
An aromatic nuance similar to that found in certain red wines with a somewhat austere bouquet.
OENOTHÈQUE/WINE LIBRARY
A neologism derived from *oenologie* (oenology) and *bibliothèque* (library), signifying a collection of wines.
OEUFS PUNAIS/ROTTEN EGGS
A sulphurous smell caused by spoilage of wines stored on their sediment (*see Mercaptan*).
OIGNON (ODEUR DE)/ONION (SMELL OF)
An aromatic characteristic caused by chemical reduction and therefore found in some very old red wines.
ONCTUEUX/UNCTUOUS
This signifies the physical quality of a wine that has high viscosity due to an ample degree of richness, against a background in which tannin and acidity are not readily distinguishable.
ORANGE (PEAU DE)/ORANGE (PEEL)
When orange peel is slightly dried, it can lend a very flattering smell to food products in which it is used, and a similar quality can also be found in young white wines produced from very ripe grapes.
ORANGER (FLEUR DE)/ORANGE BLOSSOM
This is an aromatic characteristic sometimes found in the bouquet of wines made from the Sauvignon Blanc and other white, aromatic grape varieties.
ORGANOLEPTIQUE/ORGANOLEPTIC
The meaning of this scientific, technical word is 'that which is able to stimulate an organ, especially a sense organ'. The organoleptic characteristics of a wine are therefore those that can be apprehended via the senses: appearance, smell and the totality of buccal sensations.
OXYDATION/OXIDIZATION
Various substances contained in wine are liable to combine permanently and irreversibly with oxygen. This process is known as oxidization, and its symptoms are a brown appearance, a stale smell, a deterioration of bouquet, a hardening of tastes. Oxidization is considered as a fault or as a spoilage in the majority of wines, yet it is sought after and induced in a controlled manner in certain special wines, such as *vin jaune*, sherry and madeira.

Note that oxidization should not be confused with oxygenation, which is the rapid and temporary aeration of wine while it is in carafe, a few moments before drinking. Oxygenation stimulates and opens up bouquet.

PAMPLEMOUSSE/GRAPEFRUIT
An aromatic quality suggested in certain sparkling white wines during manufacture, when they are still very acid and have not yet rid themselves of their fermenting agents. This quality disappears during secondary fermentation and clarification.
PANIER-VERSEUR/BOTTLE BASKET
An accessory in which bottles, which have been stored horizontally and which contain sediment, may be placed horizontally, there being no wish to decant them. This basket enables the wine to be carefully poured out while leaving the sediment behind in the bottle.
PARFUM/SCENT, PERFUME
▷ A pleasant odour produced by a flower or some other natural substance.
▷ A composition created by a perfumer using aromatic essences (*see Arôme*).
PARFUMÉ/SCENTED, PERFUMED
This word signifies that which naturally possesses perfume or has had perfume added to it.
PATEUX/PASTY, THICK
An adjective used to describe wines whose heaviness is worsened by a large dose of astringency.
PÊCHE/PEACH
The taste and aroma of white or yellow peaches, as well as their kernels, are often found in red wines from the Côtes du Rhône, or Beaujolais *cru* wines.
PÊCHER (FLEUR DE)/PEACH BLOSSOM
This is a very delicate aromatic nuance, close to the smell of pistachio or bitter almond, and occasionally found in young, fresh, aromatic white wines.
PÉLARGONIUM/PELARGONIUM
The crushed leaf of the pelargonium (commonly known as the geranium) has a very strong and unpleasant smell, similar to that found in wines that have been treated with potassium sorbate or sorbic acid. This smell is also found in minute quantities in certain very old red wines of attenuated colour and flavour.
PELURE D'OIGNON/ONIONSKIN
This is a russet-like colour nuance of vague definition, particularly with regard to its intensity, which lies somewhere between rosé and red, and is similar to that of onions.
PERSISTANCE/PERSISTENCE
Gustatory persistence is the impression a wine leaves in the mouth after drinking. It is measured in seconds or *caudalies*, and in general terms the longer the persistence the better the quality of the wine.
PETIT/SMALL
A term used to describe a wine that is poor in its various constituents and low in alcohol.
PHÉNOLIQUE, PHÉNIQUÉ/PHENOLIC
These words describe a smell reminiscent of phenol, found in red wines of inferior quality in the process of oxidization.
PIERRE À FUSIL/GUNFLINT
The term *goût de pierre à fusil* (taste of gunflint) is used improperly to describe the odorous quality characteristic of

a few light and lively white wines made from the Sauvignon Blanc, Melon, Aligoté and Jacquère grape varieties. A better term would be *odeur d'éclat de silex* (smell of flint splinter).

***PIN*/PINE**
An aromatic characteristic composed of pinene, bornyl acetate, or of a mixture of both. The aroma of pine may be detected in certain very fine red wines.

***PIQUÉ*/PRICKED**
Refers to a wine spoilt by high volatile acidity.

***PIQUETTE*/PIQUETTE**
A drink that wine growers used to make for their personal consumption, by adding water and sugar to the marc left in the vats after the wine had been run off.

Due to the overproduction of wine, this practice was banned in France in 1945 and subsequently in Europe by EC regulations.

***PISTACHE*/PISTACHIO**
A very fine smell, similar to bitter almond but more delicate. It is occasionally found in red wines with subtle, nuanced bouquets.

***PIVOINE*/PEONY**
▷ The intense purple colour of red peony is a useful analogy for describing new red wines that are very deeply coloured.
▷ The slightly peppery smell of this flower is found also in wines that have such a colour. This double connection is probably linked to the presence of peonidol, or peony colouring, in the colouring matter of certain red grape varieties.

***PLAT*/FLAT**
This term is used to describe a wine lacking in contours, owing to the paucity of its constituents.

***PLEIN*/FULL**
An adjective used to describe a wine that seems to fill the mouth with a substantial, balanced richness, giving the impression of plenitude.

***PLOMBÉ*/LEADEN**
A term used to refer to wines that have turned greyish in colour as a result of cloudiness.

***POIRE*/PEAR**
The aromatic nuance of various varieties of pear is often found in supple white wines with a fruity bouquet.

***POIVRE*/PEPPER**
An aromatic characteristic very common to numerous red wines of quality, found in the most ethereal and subtle part of the wine's aroma as well as in the final buccal phase, from which it is often prolonged into the aftertaste.

***POIVRON*/SWEET PEPPER**
An aromatic nuance notably detectable in the mouth, forming part of the retronasal aroma, and characteristic of red grape varieties rich in tannin, whose youthful fruitiness is comparatively subdued.

***POMME*/APPLE**
The different varieties of apple have particular aromas and flavours found in varying degrees of intensity in numerous white wines from the Chardonnay and Sauvignon Blanc grape varieties: the smell of Golden Delicious apples, for example, in light and *primeur* wines; the aroma of fine dessert apples in Meursault wines; the taste of apple compote in some champagnes . . .

***POURRI*/ROTTEN**
Ripe, dry grapes which are attacked by mould can give wine the taste of *pourri sec* (dry rot), which has a mouldy and bitter character, if the affected grapes are not removed from the bunches before vinification.

***PRUNEAU*/PRUNE**
An aromatic characteristic combining fruit with the smell of roasting or toasting, forming part of the bouquet of old wines; if present in excess, it is a sign of permanent oxidization (in red wines only).

***PUISSANT*/POWERFUL**
Wine rich in substance and very full bodied, with high alcoholic strength.

***QUALITÉ*/QUALITY**
This noun has multiple and varied meanings. In the context of French wine terminology it is used in two general senses.
▷ As a notion of intrinsic or absolute quality, expressing a certain level of sensory richness at or above which a wine is situated.
▷ In the phrase *vin de qualité* (quality wine), 'quality' is taken to be synonymous with wine from a particular *cru* and probably vintage, as opposed to *vin de table* or *de consommation courante* (table wine or wine for everyday drinking).

***RACÉ*/WITH BREED, BREEDING**
Another term used in an anthropomorphic sense, this attribute describes a batch or a vat of a particular wine that has great class, distinction and quality.

***RAFLE (GOÛT DE)*/STALKY TASTE**
The *rafle* is the framework of the grape bunch. If it is not removed before the wine is vinified, or if it undergoes prolonged maceration during vinification, it can give the wine an astringent and stalky quality known as *goût de rafle*.

***RAIDE*/STIFF**
A physical characteristic ascribed to red wines in which both tannin and acidity dominate to excess.

***RAISIN SEC (GOÛT DE)*/RAISIN (TASTE OF)**
When the grapes have been partially dried on the vine by the wind, by great heat or by the action of parasites before harvesting, the resulting wines occasionally smell and taste of raisins (a common characteristic in many 1983 wines, for example).

***RANCIO*/RANCIO**
This is a Spanish term, commonly used in French, meaning both 'old' and 'rancid'. It is applied especially to dry red wines or *vins doux naturels* (sweet, fortified wines) from Roussillon that are allowed to maderize as they age.

***RÂPEUX* /ROUGH**
This term signifies a condition of excessive astringence occurring when wine tannin rasps against the mucous membranes in the mouth, resulting in an exaggerated intensity and persistence.

***RÊCHE*/HARSH**
Another term signifying a high degree of astringency.

***RÉGLISSE*/LIQUORICE**
An aromatic quality often found at the end of the buccal phase in a certain number of red wines.

***RENARD*/FOX**
This wild animal smell is very typical of certain red wines from Burgundy. The wine is then said to '*renarder*' ('to fox', meaning to become fox-like). The smell disappears when the wine has had a few moments of aeration in the glass. (C.f. *Foxé*.)

***RÉSINE*/RESIN**
An aromatic characteristic of a balsamic nature that is part of the bouquet of fine, distinguished red wines.

***ROBE*/ROBE**
A term used, in a metaphorical sense, to signify the colour of a wine.

***ROND*/ROUND**
A term applicable to wines without any *angulosité* (boniness), dominated by richness, yet supple and without heaviness.

***ROSE*/ROSE**
This aromatic nuance is made up of substances as diverse as geraniol, phenylethylic alcohol, and rhodinol. It is suggested by the primary aroma of the various varieties of Muscat. The nuance of faded rose is a delicate part of the bouquet of certain old, fine red wines.

***RUBIS*/RUBY**
A precious red stone, brilliant in colour with a slightly purple hue. It is used metaphorically by certain wine tasters to describe the colour of red wines.

***RUDE*/COARSE, HARSH**
A characteristic of a wine whose various sensations lack refinement and jar the tastebuds.

***SANTAL*/SANDALWOOD**
A precious wood from India with a very strong smell that features in certain types of incense. Its scent is suggested by certain very fine wines, both French and foreign. It belongs to the group of balsamic smells.

***SAUVAGE*/WILD**
▷ Describes a wine whose flavours are still raw and unrefined.
▷ On an olfactory level, *sauvage* is a synonym for *fauve* (animal).

***SAVEURS*/TASTES**
In a strictly physiological sense, these are sensations received by the tongue via specialized papillae. Four sensations only are involved: saltiness, sweetness, acidity and bitterness. In more common use, *saveur* is employed interchangeably with *goût* (both meaning 'taste', and implying everything that is perceived in the mouth).

***SEATOL*/SEATOL**
A methyl derivative of indole with a putrid smell, found in small traces in certain 'animal' smells present in wines.

***SEC*/DRY**
A term applied to white wines without perceptible levels of sugar. On the level of detailed analytical wine tasting, a white wine is said to be dry when its richness is discreet or slightly recessive, but without affecting the harmony of the whole.

***SÉCHER*/TO DRY**
In the context of French wine tasting, this verb expresses the way certain wines develop, seeming to lose their fatness and richness, becoming thin and dry with a certain acridity. Such wines may also be said to *se dessécher* (dry out) and to become *desséché* (dried out).

***SENSORIEL*/SENSORY**
A term relating to the activity of sense organs. Sensory analysis is a series of judgments made through sight, smell and taste on an edible or drinkable substance. This expression has a broader application than the term *dégustation* (tasting), which in its strict sense only applies to sensations perceived in the mouth by the sense of taste.

***SERPILLIÈRE (ODEUR ET GOÛT DE)*/FLOOR-CLOTH (SMELL AND TASTE OF)**
This refers to odorous characteristics that develop in damp cloth material that has become stagnant and hosts mould or fungi. This anomaly is found in white wines stored in casks that have not been properly filled, so allowing the bung cloths to rot.

Note that, while this characteristic is homologous with *goût de croupi* (a stagnant taste), it is used more of white wines, while the word *croupi* (stagnant) is used more of red wines.

***SÈVE*/SAP**
A professional wine-tasting term of Bordeaux origin, which has slowly become common in general use. It expresses the characteristic expansion of aromas and fullness of tastes while the wine is in the mouth.

***SÉVÈRE*/SEVERE**
A wine with the double dominant of tannin and acidity is said to be severe, possessing austere aromas and in an overall sense being deprived of joviality.

***SILEX*/FLINT**
This is a synonym for gunflint (*see Pierre à fusil*).

***SOLIDE*/SOLID**
A term that may be used of a red wine possessing a dominant tannin factor, together with a considerable subdominant factor of richness, combining to imply structure and substance.

***SOUPLE, SOUPLESSE*/SUPPLE, SUPPLENESS**
A gustatory quality linked to limited amounts of tannin and acidity, allowing the natural richness of the wine to emerge, but not excessively so.

***SOURIS (GOÛT DE)*/MOUSY TASTE**
A metaphorical expression signifying a smell similar to that of acetamide, appearing a few seconds after drinking, in the aftertaste of a wine that had been stored on decayed or spoiled sediment.

***SOUS-BOIS*/UNDERGROWTH**
An odorous quality similar to that of humus and dead leaves, sometimes found in very old red wines. Certain wines are predisposed towards this, such as those of Saint-Émilion or Vosne-Romanée.

***SOYEUX*/SILKY**
A quality expressing great fineness of contact of the wine in the mouth, by analogy with the feel of silk.

***SPIRITUEUX*/SPIRITUOUS**
See Technical Glossary.

***SUITE*/CONCLUSION**
This word refers to the group of residual sensory impressions left after actual tasting, made up of aromatic persistence (finish) and aftertaste.

TABAC/TOBACCO
Fragrances of green or unburnt tobacco, very close to that scent described by perfumers as *havane* (cigar leaf), are occasionally found in very fine, high quality red wines.
TACHÉ/STAINED
This word is applied to a white wine produced from a red grape variety in cases when a slight must coloration results from the pressing process.
TACT/TACTILE SENSATION
Tact is a synonym for *toucher* (touch), one of the five senses. Sensations received by the internal mucous membranes of the mouth may be so described.
TANIN/TANNIN
See Technical Glossary.
TÂTER/TO TRY (TASTE)
This verb is an old French synonym for *goûter* (to taste), and as such forms part of the term *tastevin* (*see* Technical Glossary).
TEMPÉRATURE/TEMPERATURE
Temperature is a crucial factor with reference to wine, not only in terms of its storage but also in terms of vinification, and tasting and serving.
TENDRE/DELICATE
Describes a wine that offers no resistance in the mouth, due to a low level of tannin and a very fluid type of *moelleux* (richness).
TENUE/BEARING, DEMEANOUR
This term is used to describe the 'behaviour' of a wine in the mouth.
TERROIR/TERROIR
This term is used to signify an area of ground planted with vines and possessing particular characteristics. The term *goût de terroir*, however, which literally means a 'taste of the *terroir*', is loosely used to describe anomalies in wine. These are supposedly linked to the *terroir*, always in a pejorative sense. In fact these tastes can more often be traced back to a problem with the fruit or grape variety rather than the *terroir* itself. (*See also* Technical Glossary.)
THYM/THYME
This aromatic nuance is often found in wines from Provence and Haute-Provence.
TILLEUL (FLEUR DE)/LIME BLOSSOM
An aromatic nuance found in certain white wines with a very fine bouquet.
TOUCHER/TOUCH
A synonym for *tact* (q.v.).
TROUBLE/CLOUDINESS
See Limpidité and 'Cloudiness' in Technical Glossary.
TRUFFE/TRUFFLE
This is a highly prized aromatic nuance found in old, high quality red wines. The black truffle is meant when the term is unqualified. *Truffe blanche* (white truffle) has a smell identical to that of pyradine and is found in white wines of particular vintages, due to a chemical reduction associated with ageing.
TUILÉ/TILE RED
This word is used to describe the appearance of a red wine when its strong brown colour is reminiscent of old red roof tiles.
TURBIDITÉ/TURBIDITY
A general state of cloudiness (for degrees of cloudiness, *see Limpidité*).
TYNDALL (EFFET)/TYNDALL EFFECT
Named after John Tyndall (1820–1893), the Irish physicist who defined it, this is an optical effect whereby a colloidal solution that is seemingly limpid when light is shone directly through it, is actually shown to be slightly cloudy when laterally or indirectly lit. This phenomenon is found in wine, and knowledge and use of the Tyndall effect permits potential problems of cloudiness to be identified and rectified.
TYPICITÉ/TYPICALITY
This term refers to a group of sensory characteristics that enable the origin of a wine to be identified, in accordance with the customs and conventions of the period during which the wine was produced.

USÉ/TIRED
Describes a wine that has lost its qualities and is past its best.

VANILLE/VANILLA
This aroma is a basic element in the bouquet of numerous red and white wines. It has a natural source in the ligneous parts of the grape or in the oak from which the casks are made.
VÉGÉTAL/VEGETAL
In the context of wine tasting, the vegetal (as opposed to animal) characteristics are those that may be attributed to elements in the bouquet reminiscent of plant smells, distinguished in turn from fruits, flowers and aromatic essences.
VELOUTÉ/VELVETY
A term used to describe a wine that evokes the touch of velvet when in the mouth (due to a slightly dominant richness and the absence of any acidity).
VENAISON/VENISON
This is a smell of the animal type reminiscent of game, found in very old red wines. It quickly disappears following aeration.
VERT, VERDEUR/GREEN, GREENNESS
By analogy with the sharp flavour of green fruits, this term is used to refer to a very acid white wine, with a low level of richness exposing an excess of acidity.
VIEILLARDÉ/SENESCENT
This term is used to describe a wine which has aged badly or prematurely.
VIF/LIVELY
An adjective used of a wine with a slightly dominant acidity, yet without any loss of harmony or balance.
VIGOUREUX/VIGOROUS
This term describes a powerful, lively wine provoking a strong reaction in the mouth due to its high alcoholic strength and its acidity.

VINEUX/VINEUX
Vineux is used to describe a wine whose alcoholic strength is so high that it acts as a factor of disharmony.

VIRIL/VIRILE
An attribute that, in wine-tasting terminology, implies a certain strength, substance and full-bodied quality in a wine.

VOILÉ/VEILED
Describes a wine that is very slightly cloudy, especially under the scrutiny that a knowledge of the Tyndall effect (q.v.) makes possible. This condition constitutes the first level on the scale of cloudiness (*see Limpidité*).

VOLTIGEURS/FINE PARTICLES
The word *voltigeurs* (which literally means 'acrobats') is used to describe light, solid particles present in a bottle of wine that remain in suspension for some time after it has been shaken. They are generally made up of residues of fining agents, filter particles or dead yeasts, and they do not impair the quality of the wine in any way.

TECHNICAL GLOSSARY

ACESCENCE
A disease of wine also known in French as *piqûre acétique*. Aerobic, acetic bacteria transform the alcohol in the wine into acetic acid. The acetic acid that is formed partially esterifies the ethanol to form ethyl acetate, which is the cause of the acetic smell of *vin piqué*. This deterioration eventually produces vinegar. The disease is often present in containers that have been left empty; it can be avoided by keeping wine away from air and heat. There is no cure for wines that have become affected by acescence. (*See also* Glossary of French Tasting Terms.)
ACETIC ACID
A product present in wine, either owing to the breakdown of ethanol by acetic bacteria (*piqûre acétique*), or the breakdown of sugars by lactic bacteria (*piqûre lactique*). A small quantity of acetic acid may be produced by the yeast during normal alcoholic fermentation. The complete transformation of ethanol to acetic acid by acetic bacteria produces vinegar.
ACETIC BACTERIA
These are aerobic, Gram negative bacteria. They develop in wine left exposed to the air. They then break down the ethanol in the wine and produce acetic acid. Eventually the wine turns to vinegar. This unwanted development is avoided by protecting the wine from air and heat, or by preserving it beneath inert gas or with sulphur dioxide.
ACIDIFICATION
This is the name for an exceptional treatment given to must or to fermenting wines that are not considered sufficiently acid. This practice, which is strictly controlled, is reserved for wines from the South of France. It is forbidden in any wine that has been chaptalized. Only tartaric acid may be used for this correction.
ACIDITY
Wine is rich in organic acids. In order to quantify the acidity of a wine, several assessment tasks are performed in the laboratory. The pH value expresses the concentration of free protons in the wine medium and represents the true acidity of the wine. This can vary from 2.8 (for very acidic wines) to 3.8 (for only slightly acidic wines). The total acidity of the wine measures the number of acid molecules that can be neutralized with a strong base, when going from the actual pH of the wine to neutrality (pH7).

Volatile acidity is the fraction of acidity constituted by volatile acids, and in particular by acetic acid. The measurement of this allows the degree of damage done by *piqûre acétique* or *lactique* (acescence or lactic acescence) to be gauged. However other acidic compounds can cause errors in this measurement if certain precautions are not taken to eliminate them. This is the case with carbonic, lactic and succinic acid, and sulphur dioxide. Corrected volatile acidity is the end result of this process of measurement and correction, after substances such as sulphur dioxide have been taken into account and their levels diminished.

The fixed acidity is the non-volatile fraction of total acidity. This is equal to the difference between total acidity and volatile acidity.
AGEING
Ageing is the development that a wine undergoes as it gets older. 'Aged' was at one time invariably a term of approbation, but is less so today.
ALCOHOL
The alcohol in wine is ethanol or ethyl alcohol. It is produced by transformation of sugar during alcoholic yeast fermentation. It can also be produced by the intracellular fermentation of grape matter during carbonic maceration.
ALCOHOLIC FERMENTATION
The conversion of sugars (glucose, fructose) into ethanol and carbon dioxide under the action of yeast. This reaction characterizes the transformation of must into wine.
ALCOHOLIC STRENGTH
The degree (q.v.) of alcohol in a drink is its alcoholic strength. This represents the percentage by volume of ethanol at 20°C.
ALDEHYDE
In organic chemistry, aldehydes are the products of the more or less spontaneous, moderate oxidization of alcohols. They constitute an intermediate stage between alcohols and their corresponding fatty acids. Ethanol in wine may oxidize in this manner. Aldehyde begins to form when wine is kept in part-empty containers, catalyzed by sunlight, traces of metal, or by a brutal aeration. Its smell is strong and characteristic, similar to the metaldehyde used to fire some camping stoves. When diluted, it is reminiscent of the smell of walnut leaf and walnut shell. This strong smell, together with a high volatility, makes aldehyde perceptible in wine even when it is present in quantities of only a few mg per litre. In its simple and primitive state, this olfactory characteristic is that of the stale smell of empty bottles or casks. Aldehyde is a vigorously active chemical substance and tends to combine with numerous ingredients in wine (colouring matter, tannins, sugars), as well as with sulphur dioxide, whose action it weakens. This kind of conjunctive development, when monitored, is the basis of the maderization that produces *vins jaunes* and the *rancio* wines of Roussillon.
AMERTUME *See* Bitterness.
AMPELOGRAPHY
Science that describes the different species of vine and grape variety.
ANTHOCYANINS
Phenolic compounds responsible for the red or purple colour of young wines and, to a reduced extent, of old wines.
AOC
The widely used abbreviation for *appellation d'origine contrôlée* (q.v.).
AOÛTEMENT
A physiological phenomenon that occurs on the green

shoots (*rameaux*) of vines at the end of summer. The green surface of the shoot turns a red ochre colour and dries out, forming a protective layer. The shoot hardens and turns woody at the same time, becoming a cane (*sarment*).

APERITIF

A noun derived from the Latin verb *aperire* meaning 'to open', and historically used to describe any plant-based liquid medicine designed to stimulate the appetite. It applies today to any natural or specially prepared wine offered before a meal to stimulate the appetite.

APPELLATION D'ORIGINE

This is a very old notion emphasizing the importance of a complex milieu in the creation of a wine or food product with particular characteristics. The factors involved in this are geographical, historical and human.

APPELLATION D'ORIGINE CONTRÔLÉE

First conceived around 1900, France's *appellations d'origine contrôlée* have been established by law since 1935, under the aegis of the INAO (Institut National des Appellations d'Origine des Vins et Eaux-de-Vie). Each *appellation* is defined by a *délimitation parcellaire* (circumscription of the vineyard areas able to claim the *appellation*), specified grape varieties, methods of cultivation and vinification, and by analytically established characteristics of the wines. *Appellation* wines are submitted to tasting panels before sale.

AROMAS

Aromas are a large group of organic compounds in wines, sufficiently volatile and odoriferous to be perceived by the sense of smell. These compounds may come from the grape (primary aromas) or be produced during alcoholic fermentation (secondary aromas). During ageing, the wine undergoes further development, leading to the production of a bouquet (tertiary aromas). Chemically, these compounds have very variable structures: they may be alcohols, esters, terpenes, aldehydes, and so on. The quantity present is very low, and the human nose is often a far more sensitive detector for them than laboratory equipment. This explains the prime importance of the wine-tasting process. (*See also* Glossary of French Tasting Terms.)

ASSEMBLAGE

Assemblage is an operation consisting of mixing together carefully chosen proportions of different wines or *eaux-de-vie*. These *assemblages* are practised according to traditional guidelines in certain *appellation* regions (Champagne, Bordeaux, Cognac, Armagnac), allowing the representative characteristics of the region's products to be obtained.

BAN DES VENDANGES

In times past, this was the date on which the grape harvest began. Now it is the date from which chaptalization is permitted. This date is proposed by the INAO and local growers' committee, and formally decided by a representative of the French state.

BARRIQUE

This is a wine container with a capacity of about 220 litres. The exact capacity of a *barrique* varies from region to region. It is usually made of oak or chestnut. *Barriques* can be used both for transporting and for the *élevage* of wine.

BERNACHE

This is the name given to white wine must during vigorous fermentation. *Bernache* is milky in appearance and very sweet to taste; it is often drunk as such, as an autumn treat, for example with roast chestnuts.

BITTERNESS

One of the four basic tastes. The French word for bitterness, *amertume*, is also used to describe a disease of wine in which lactic bacteria break down glycerol to produce acrolein, which has a strongly bitter taste. This disease has become quite rare nowadays.

BLANC DE BLANCS

White wine produced solely from white grapes. This term is often used to describe sparkling wines of such an origin.

BLANC DE NOIRS

White wine produced from red grapes that have white juice. Expressing the juice requires very delicate pressure to avoid any form of maceration and must staining.

BLOOM

The bloom (*pruine*) is the waxy layer found on the surface of grapes.

BORDEAUX MIXTURE

This is a preparation based on copper sulphate and lime, perfected by Pierre-Marie-Alexis Millardet (1838–1902) during the 19th century to combat downy mildew. It is being replaced more and more often today by synthetic products containing copper.

BOTRYTIS CINEREA

A filamentous fungus and grape parasite. Depending on local climate or atmospheric conditions, it may produce *pourriture noble* (noble rot) in the grape (necessary in the manufacture of Sauternes and similar dessert wines); but it may also produce *pourriture grise* (grey rot or botrytis, resulting in a loss of quantity and quality in the harvest). In the form of *pourriture noble*, the fungus — among other actions — substantially increases the glycerine content in the grape even before it is picked, thus developing its *moelleux* (richness). In *pourriture grise*, it forms oxydases that will eventually turn the must brown; these develop during the damp phase of the rotting process. Apart from this inconvenience, grey rot arrested at this phase does not generate a bad taste in the wine. But unfortunately the disease is progressive and not static, so if not arrested it will slowly empty the grapes of their pulp and form a dry rot that spreads like grey ash through the stems and dried grape skins. Unlike the rot of the preceding phase, this type can impart a very bad taste to the wine, akin to mouldiness. This can be avoided by sorting through the harvest to eliminate the affected bunches and parts of bunches.

BOTTLING

A number of bottling descriptions are authorized for French wines. These include '*mis en bouteilles au château*', '*mise d'origine*', '*mis en bouteilles à la propriété*, or '*mis en bouteilles au domaine*'. All of these descriptions imply that the wine has remained in its place of production until it was bottled. Wines bearing the description '*mis en bouteilles dans la région de production*' must have been bottled in the *département* in which most of the vineyards of the *appellation* to which they are entitled lie.

BRUT

▷ A term applied to wines that have just finished fermentation, before any clarification occurs.

▷ A category of champagne, *crémant*, or other sparkling wine that has had the minimum quantity of *vin de liqueur* (q.v.) added after disgorgement and therefore contains less than 12g of sugar per litre (although this figure has no legal standing). The description Brut Zéro or Extra Brut also exists, implying the total absence of any added sugar in the form of *vin de liqueur*. Wines prepared in this way have perhaps more authenticity for the connoisseur, but keeping them for any length of time can be risky.

BUDBREAK

Budbreak marks the recommencement of the vine's vegetative activity in spring. The buds burst open and tiny leaves appear.

BUDS

Organs carried on green shoots at each node. Two sorts are generally found: prompt buds which, during the summer, produce secondary unproductive shoots called *entre-coeurs*; and latent buds which, if left in place during pruning, will produce new, productive, green shoots the following spring. The bud includes within itself the forms of each organ to which it gives birth: leaves, internodes, bunches and tendrils.

BUNCH

A bunch of grapes is the result of the development of the inflorescence of the vine, appearing on the green shoots that develop during the spring. Inflorescences are already present in the bud before it breaks, and they develop at the same time as the leaves of the new green shoot. The bunches mature by passing through different stages: flowering, *véraison* and rot (qq.v.).

CAP

The cap or *chapeau* is the term used to refer to all the solid parts of the grape (skins, stalks, pips) that undergo maceration during the fermentation of red wine. Under the effect of carbon dioxide, these solid particles collect on the surface of the liquid in the vat — hence the name 'cap'. *Remontage* (pumping wine over the top of the cap), *pigeage* (breaking up the cap and forcing it back into the liquid), and *brassage à l'azote* (nitrogen mixing) all help to maximize contact between the must and the solid matter, thereby improving the extraction of colour and tannin.

CAPSULE

The capsule is the sheath made of metal or other material which goes over the cork and top of the bottle. It was originally made of a tin alloy, but it also now exists in plastic.

This term also refers to the *bouchon couronne* (crown cap) that is used to stop champagne bottles during the *prise de mousse* (secondary fermentation in bottle) stage of their manufacture.

CAPSULE CONGÉ

A seal is printed on the top of capsules of French wines to be sold in France, and this *capsule congé* indicates that transport duties have been paid.

CARBON DIOXIDE

As carbon dioxide (*gaz carbonique*) is present in all wines, and not only in sparkling wines, a few remarks are appropriate concerning the origin, properties, sensory effects and presence of this gas.

▷ *Origin*: alcoholic fermentation produces carbon dioxide (CO_2) from sugars, the amount produced being almost equal to the quantity of alcohol present, some 40 to 47 per cent of the total sugars in the must. Thus the fermentation of 50hl of must with a potential alcoholic strength of 12° produces 500kg of carbon dioxide (equivalent to some 250 cubic metres). So it is not surprising that the wine remains saturated with CO_2, and that this saturation is reinforced by later lactic fermentation.

▷ *Properties*: The behaviour of carbon dioxide is linked to its hydro-alcoholic solubility and its physical and chemical properties, and these are influenced by numerous factors: pH value, mineralization, alcohol content, the amount of colloidal substances present, and temperature. This last factor is by far the most important when it is realized that the solubility of this gas in wine diminishes by half between 0°C and 20°C.

Producers and *négociants* eliminate excess carbon dioxide before bottling by carrying out a certain number of rackings (q.v.) in warm surroundings, with or without *brassage* (mixing). More thorough elimination of CO_2 is ensured by introducing a flux of nitrogen gas while the wine is being pumped from one container to another, but on no account can suction techniques be used, since any kind of vacuum causes wine to lose alcohol, and a substantial fraction of the aromatic substances in wine may also be lost during a brutal process of gas extraction. Whatever method is used, complete elimination of the gas is never achieved, the lowest level obtainable in practice being 200mg of CO_2 per litre of wine. This is the residual amount that forms an inseparable part of the substance of wine itself.

▷ *Sensory effects*: it is fortunate, in fact, that carbon dioxide cannot be completely removed from wine, since in imperceptible quantities it plays an essential role in the dynamics of tasting. A wine devoid of carbon dioxide gas would have disarmingly insipid flavours and effect in the mouth. But the presence of CO_2 does not provide any particular organoleptic qualities. It is barely acid. Max Léglise has termed it the *éminence grise* of wine tasting, always present, never visible, always influential. Its main effect is that it expands in the mouth under the effect of heat and mastication, and this expansion produces a multitude of microbubbles that are sensed as a kind of granularity, creating what is called the 'grain' of the wine, and making it more than a simple, flat liquid diluted with alcohol.

This microscopic discharge also has the effect of heightening the wine's aromas by making them pass into the gaseous phase, in which they become perceptible. This sensation is not uniform, however, and is modulated over a long period by the various groups of wine constituents. Carbon dioxide does in fact 'marry well' with the acidity of a wine, and this why it is desirable in light white or *primeur* wines, as it brings out their freshness. With this in mind, *pétillant* (q.v.) wines have been created that are oversaturated with carbon dioxide, and in which it is perceptible.

Carbon dioxide does not blend well with the 'rich' or *moelleux* group of substances (alcohol, glycerine, sugars), since its volatility clashes with their solid or heavy consistency. This is why the presence of carbon dioxide must be kept to a minimum in white wines to be stored for some years, or sweet wines.

Carbon dioxide creates most problems in red wines, since it combines with the tannin, increasing its astringency, and such a combination is extremely unpleasant. Carbon dioxide is therefore acceptable only in red wines low in tannin, such as Beaujolais, Côtes du Rhône *primeur* wines, or wines made from the Mondeuse grape variety. It is tolerable in small amounts in Pinot Noir wines and wines from other moderately tannic grape varieties; it is quite repellant, though, in great Cabernet Sauvignon wines, giving the impression of *raideur* (stiffness).

▷ *Presence*: the presence of carbon dioxide is adjusted to the following levels for different wines:

- 200mg/l maximum for the Premiers Crus Classés of Médoc and Graves.
- 400mg/l for the red wines of the Loire valley, like Chinon and Bourgueil, as well as for wines from the South West such as Madiran and Côtes du Roussillon-Villages.
- 400 to 500mg/l in most wines from Burgundy and the Rhône valley.
- 500 to 600mg/l in red *primeur* wines and classic dry white wines.
- 600 to 800mg/l in white *primeur* wines and aromatic white wines.

Beyond 800mg/l lies the category of *perlant* and *pétillants* (very slightly sparkling and slightly sparkling wines). The gas remains invisible when the wine is deeply refrigerated, but it appears as a chain of fine bubbles as soon as it is brought to room temperature.

CARBONIC MACERATION

This is a method of red wine vinification that involves placing the grapes in an inert atmosphere at a moderately high temperature (30°C).

The normally aerobic metabolism of grape cells becomes an anaerobic one, resulting in the production of some degrees of alcohol without the intervention of yeast, and in a migration of anthocyanins (colouring matter) in the pulp. After about a week, the grapes are then pressed. The must obtained from this pressing finishes fermenting under the action of yeast, at a low temperature (20°C), in order to preserve the aromas acquired by the wine in the first phase. This vinification technique is particularly suitable for *primeur* wines. (*See also* page 246.)

CASSES

These are anomalies affecting a wine through defects in appearance, chiefly cloudiness and modifications in colour.

Casse blanche is iron *casse* in white wines.

Casse bleue is iron *casse* in red wines.

Casse brune, also called oxidasic *casse*, is caused by the irreversible breakdown of phenolic compounds in white and red wines. It gives an ochre colour to white wines and a brown colour to red wines.

Casse cuivrique is a reddish-brown precipitate that may appear in bottled white or rosé wines containing excessive levels of copper.

Casse ferrique takes the form of a white cloudiness that appears in white wines, or blue in red wines, owing to the insolubility of excessive iron levels in such wines.

Casse protéique is a whitish cloudiness that can appear in white wines rich in proteins during cold conditions.

CAVAILLON

The *cavaillon* is a longitudinal mound of earth lying along the base of vine stocks. It is formed in late autumn by *chaussage* (q.v.). The *cavaillon* is left intact after *déchaussage* (q.v.) or spring ploughing, as the wine grower's plough does not actually pass under the stocks. In order to flatten the *cavaillon*, an operation called *decavaillonage* (q.v.) is undertaken, either by pulling the earth back down with a hand tool, or by using a specially designed machine for the task called a *decavailloneuse*. This enables all the weeds that have grown on the *cavaillon* to be eradicated, as well as any roots growing on the grafted vine itself, or any green shoots growing on the rootstock.

CELLAR

A place where the wine is produced and stored. The etymology of the French word for a cellar, *cave* (from the Latin *cavum*, meaning a cavity) suggests a subterranean space, and implies that a cellar should be underground. By an extension of meaning, the word *cave* is now used in France to denote all wine-producing buildings, whether underground or not, that act as stores or stockrooms.

CENTRIFUGATION

An operation performed to clarify must or new wine using centrifugal force to eliminate heavy particles. This process is also used to eliminate fining deposits. Machines are now available to perform continuous centrifugation; however their high price only allows them to be purchased by very large businesses (such as *négociants* or cooperatives).

CHABROT

This is a custom in the South West of France that involves adding wine to the soup broth remaining in the bottom of one's bowl and drinking the mixture. Such an action is called *faire chabrot* (to make *chabrot*).

CHAI

A term used in the South, South West and West of France to describe the buildings used for vinifying and storing wines.

CHAMPAGNISATION

This means the process of producing sparkling wines by secondary fermentation in bottle of the sugar contained in the *liqueur de tirage* (a sugar and yeast solution added as the wine is bottled). After a period of storage in bottle during which the wine acquires a sparkle, it is carefully and regularly turned to allow the yeast deposits to gather at the neck (*remuage*), then the bottle is opened and the sediment that has formed during the secondary fermentation is removed (*dégorgement*).

CHAPTALIZATION

This is the process of adding sugar to must. It is carried out when grape maturity (and hence natural sugar levels) are not adequate to provide a satisfactorily balanced wine. The technique was prescribed by the chemist Jean Antoine Chaptal, and named after him. Permitted additives for chaptalization are saccharose (ordinary sugar), concentrated must, and rectified grape sugars. Between 1.7kg and 1.9kg of saccharose are required per hl of must to increase the alcoholic strength of the finished wine by one degree. This operation must be declared to the French Tax Office, and tax has to be paid on it. The maximum quantities of sugar permitted to be added to must are specified by the EC, and fixed on a zonal basis (A, B, C1, C2, C3) that decreases from north to south. Chaptalization is forbidden in Mediterranean zones. While chaptalization certainly increases the alcoholic strength of a wine, it does not add anything to the aromas or other organoleptic qualities of the wine.

CHARPENTE

This term, in addition to referring to a well-structured wine, rich in extracts, also refers to the trunk and branches of a vine stock.

CHÂTEAU

This term, when followed by a proper name, is the Bordeaux equivalent of a brand name for a wine. Many châteaux are indeed 'castles' (the English meaning of the word *château*), but many others are simply names given to a group of vineyard parcels.

CHAUFFERETTE

A type of heater used in certain regions to guard against the damaging effects of spring frosts. The heaters are placed between the rows of vines and heat up the air in the vineyard during cold nights in April and May.

CHAUSSAGE

An operation performed on vineyard soils that involves piling earth up into a *cavaillon* (q.v.) with the help of a plough just before winter. The earthing-up protects the vine stocks from winter frost and enables the winter rainwater to drain effectively.

CITRIC ACID

Citric acid is naturally found in wines in quantities of up to 300mg per litre. This can be broken down in the same way as malic acid during malolactic fermentation. Citric acid has an acid taste, contributing only slightly to the taste of the wine. Due to the presence of three acid functions that are negatively charged to the pH of the wine, it has the property of complexing the iron and keeping it in solution, thus avoiding *casse ferrique* (iron *casse*). For this reason it can be used as a stabilizing agent in wines, provided it is not present in quantities of more than 1g per litre.

CLAIRET

A deep rosé wine produced in the Bordeaux region by short maceration; equivalent to a *vin d'une nuit* (q.v.). *Clairet* is also found in other French regions.

CLARET

A term used by the British to describe red bordeaux.

CLARIFICATION

This term refers to the group of operations that produce limpidity in a wine. Different processes may be adopted: centrifugation, filtration, fining. Clarification must be supplemented by microbiological and physico-chemical stabilization in order to avoid the later formation of cloudiness and deposits.

CLAVELIN

A traditional, squat bottle used for the *vins jaunes* of the Jura, containing 62cl.

CLIMAT

In Burgundy, this term describes not only the atmospheric conditions in the region, but also various small vineyard parcels (*lieux-dits*) registered in each village, some of which enjoy Premier Cru status while others remain unclassified. The names of the latter can, however, appear on wine labels under the 'village' or 'communal' *appellation*, provided they are not liable to be confused with the Premiers Crus. So in Meursault, for example, les Bouchères is a Premier Cru *climat* and is so described on wine labels, while les Narvaux is an unclassified *climat*, sold (and, if wished, named) under the Meursault AOC.

CLONE

Group of vines originating from a single vine. Cloning allows healthy, virus-free vines, each identical to the next, to be reproduced.

CLOS

This word signifies a vineyard, or a number of vineyard parcels, surrounded by a wall. In an *appellation d'origine contrôlée* context, the word *clos* can only be used to describe wines coming exclusively from vines situated within a *clos*. Even if the walls have disappeared during the course of centuries, such a wine may still appear under the *clos* name, if this name has traditionally been used.

CLOUDINESS

Cloudy wines are those that contain visibly suspended matter. Cloudiness has various causes of a chemical nature — these are called casses (q.v.) — or of a microbiological nature, in which case they are the result of yeast and bacterial action.

COLLOIDS

These are macromolecular compounds of a carbohydrate or proteinaceous nature. Their complex structure can rarely be described in detail. They used to be known as gums or mucilages. Their stability in wine is variable. They may flocculate and form a deposit at the bottom of the vats during *élevage*. The main problem they cause is that they block filters very quickly. They can be eliminated by pectolytic enzymes that break them up into smaller molecules, or by fining, or by bentonite treatment (in the case of proteinaceous colloids).

Gum arabic is a protective colloid that, when added to wine, maintains unstable compounds in solution. It is used to prevent casses (q.v.) and thus to preserve clarity in wine.

COLOURING MATTER

Colouring matter in wine is made up of phenolic compounds constituted by anthocyanins, tannins and polymers of tannin and anthocyanins. The colour in young red wines is due to free anthocyanins. During the ageing process, anthocyanins combine with tannins that then condense, imparting a tile-red colour to the wine.

COMPORTES

These are wooden containers with handles, used in the South West for transporting the grape harvest. Their capacity is between 50 litres and 100 litres.

CONGÉ

This is a fiscal document that must accompany alcoholic beverages during transportation in France. These documents can be obtained from *buralistes* (offices authorized by the French finance ministry to supply wine and spirit transport permits). Certain producers and *négociants* have bond registers supplied to them by the *buraliste*. Others use the *capsule-congé* (q.v.) system.

COOPERATIVE

A professional grouping of growers who pool their harvests so that these can be vinified and commercialized with maximum efficiency. Cooperatives are particularly numerous in the Midi. While their structure enables them to make an impact on important markets owing to the considerable volume of wine produced, it does not always encourage research and progress into achieving the best possible quality of wine.

Cooperatives also control, advise and provide direction for their members. Their ceaseless efforts have in certain cases brought about spectacular results, even giving life back to certain appellations that would be forgotten today had it not been for cooperative activity.

CORKS

These are cylinder-shaped pieces of cork oak, or sometimes similarly shaped synthetic materials, used to seal bottles hermetically. The quality of cork varies. Corks of an inferior quality are composed of cork paste. Usually, corks are lightly paraffined to help them enter (and leave) the bottle.

CORRECTION

This signifies improvements made to must or to the wine during fermentation. Notable corrections include chaptalization, acidification, deacidification, or the addition of products designed to stimulate yeast activity, such as nitrogen or vitamin B_1.

COULARD

This term is used of a grape variety susceptible to *coulure* (q.v.).

COULEUSE

This word is used to designate a bottle that has not been hermetically sealed, and from which wine seeps. This can be due to a fault in the corking process, or to excess pressure caused by an insufficient air space having been left between the wine and the bottom of the cork.

COULURE

Coulure is caused by poor fertilization of vine flowers, leading to abortion. *Coulure* generally occurs after a period of cold or dampness at flowering time. Certain grape varieties are particularly susceptible to this, due to the structure and formation of their flowers. Lack of vigour or excessive vigour in vines, as well as certain vine deficiencies or diseases, can also encourage *coulure*.

COUPAGE

This activity consists of blending wines of different origins or grape varieties together, with the idea of creating a product with specific characteristics. This operation is different from *assemblage* (q.v.), which is the blending of different wines of the same regional origin or vintage.

COURTIER

The *courtier* (wine broker) is an intermediary between the seller and the buyer of wines. His job is to inspect vineyards and offer samples to wine buyers. Any transaction organized by a *courtier* is carried out directly between buyer and seller. The *courtier* is remunerated with a *courtage* (brokerage), half of which is paid by each of the parties involved in the transaction.

There are fifty 'Courtiers Jurés Piqueurs de Paris' (Paris Wine Brokers and Tasters) forming a guild of experts, the foundation of which dates back to 1322.

CRÉMANT

▷ Crémant firstly describes a type of champagne in which the pressure in the bottle is weaker than it is in ordinary champagne (3.5 bars minimum, instead of 4.5). The word *crémant* means 'creaming' or 'that which produces cream', 'cream' here signifying a fine, abundant, moderately exuberant sparkle. The word should not be confused with Cramant, which is the name of a *cru* in Champagne, the fruit of which achieves 100 per cent of the nominated annual grape price (*see* panel on page 172).

▷ More generally, *crémant* describes a sparkling wine produced with the addition of *liqueur de tirage* (q.v.) containing less sugar than is used for ordinary *vin mousseux*, but whose ageing period *sur latte* (q.v.) is extended.

▷ In 1974, the *appellation* term Crémant was given legal standing and closely defined to apply to regional sparkling wines, thereby replacing the old term '*mousseux*' which had variable meanings from region to region. These regional sparkling wines are now called Crémant d'Alsace, Crémant de Bourgogne and Crémant de Loire. Their conditions of production are as rigorous as those of champagne, with regulations governing everything from fruit quality in the vineyard to the adding of the *liqueur d'expédition* (q.v.); traditional grape varieties are used in each region, and all Crémants of this sort have to pass a tasting panel before they can be sold. These regulations have resulted in considerable growth in the production of regional sparkling wines.

CRÈME DE TÊTE

This is an expression used in Sauternes to describe wines that come from the first harvest sweep through the vineyards. Produced from grapes rotted to the maximum extent, and described as *confits* (literally 'preserved' — *see* pages 96–97), such wines are particularly rich and unctuous.

CREUX

This term, meaning a 'hollow', is used to describe the volume of air or inert gas under the cork of a bottle. This *creux* is necessary, owing to the fact that the wine may increase in volume when the temperature increases.

The term *creux de rente* is used to describe the quantity of wine that is lost when it is transported in bulk.

CRU

The first meaning of this term is that of a delimited zone capable of producing a particular, original wine. The Burgundian term *climat* is currently synonymous with *cru*, although this has not always been so. However, in Bordeaux, the concept of *cru* is associated with an individual viticultural estate, and consequently as much with a certain blend of grape varieties and with human expertise as with the soil itself. It is the estate, the 'château' and everything that its name implies, that makes up the Bordeaux *cru*. In Champagne, a hierarchy of *crus* exists and it is with respect to this that the price of the grape harvest is specified anew each year (*see* panel, page 172). The notion of *cru* in Champagne refers more to the vineyards of a complete village than to a smaller area.

Various *cru* hierarchies (Grand Cru, Premier Cru, Cru Classé) exist in harness with certain *appellations*. These qualifications are defined by the *appellation* decrees and are based on particular conditions of production (as for the Grands Crus and Premiers Crus of Burgundy), or classifications that have been approved by the French Ministry of Agriculture. Such classifications exist for the Médoc, Graves, Sauternes and Saint-Émilion areas.

CRUSHING

Crushing (*foulage*) is an optional, pre-fermentation process that involves bursting the skins of the grapes to liberate their juice. Crushing must be done very delicately to avoid break-up of the solid parts of the grape, as in some cases this action could impair the quality of the wine.

CRYPTOGAMIC DISEASES

These are fungal vine diseases. The best known are oidium (powdery mildew), downy mildew, black rot, phomopsis, brenner (*rougeot*) and grey rot (botrytis).

CUBITAINER

This is a plastic container protected by an envelope of cardboard, commonly used to sell wine wholesale to individuals. The capacity of such containers varies from 5 litres to 33 litres. Since they are not completely airtight, *cubitainers* can only be used to store wine temporarily.

CUVÉE

▷ The primary meaning of this term is 'the contents of a vat' (*cuve*). By an extension of this meaning, and in its most frequently used sense, the word describes a lot of wine with a very particular identity, and perhaps one which is personalized and commemorative, such as the Cuvée Nicolas Rolin of the Hospices de Beaune, a Cuvée du Cinquantenaire (for the fiftieth anniversary) of INAO in 1985, Cuvées created for the coronation of Queen Elizabeth II in 1953, and so on.

▷ In Champagne, the *cuvée* is the first of the four portions of must obtained during the pressing of a batch of grapes. Theoretically, 20hl of *cuvée* are obtained from each 4,000kg pressing of grapes. The *cuvée* is the best-quality must.

▷ The word *cuvée* is also used, in Champagne and elsewhere, to describe a particular *assemblage* (q.v.). Terms such as Cuvée Réservée or Cuvée Spéciale are often used in such circumstances.

▷ In the case of white wines in general, the word *cuvée* designates must or wine obtained during the first pressing of grapes or marc. In Burgundy, the words *première cuvée* or *deuxième cuvée* are sometimes used to describe Premier Cru wines and 'village' or 'commune' wines respectively.

▷ A *cuvée* is the name given to the result of an *assemblage* (q.v.) of small lots of wine of the same quality or origin, blended in the same vat (*cuve*), with a view to making a larger lot of wine of greater commercial value.

▷ *Cuvée ronde* is an ironical expression used in wine-producing or commercial establishments to describe a mixture of *vins récupération* (unbottled, unsold wines remaining after blending operations) to be reused as *vins de table*.

DEACIDIFICATION

This means the lowering of acidity in a must or in a wine. This can be done chemically, with the aid of calcium carbonate, for example. Such a treatment has to be carried out in conformity with a number of regulations, and so is only useful in very particular cases. Deacidification also happens as a result of malolactic fermentation in the wine. This process is desirable for all red wines, and for certain white wines such as fine white burgundies.

DÉBOURBAGE

Débourbage (settling or purging) generally refers to the process of racking a vat of must a few hours after it has been filled. The aim of *débourbage* is to eliminate undesirable solid matter from the must before fermentation. The residues (particles of earth, pips, etc.) are termed *bourbes*. Wines produced from must that has been *débourbé* (settled or purged) possess more finesse and clarity of flavour than those that have not. *Débourbage* also permits part of the iron in the must to be eliminated, and slows down any tendency towards over-rapid fermentation. If production is on a large scale, *débourbage* can be carried out by centrifugation of the must.

DECANTING

See Décantation in the Glossary of French Tasting Terms.

DÉCAVAILLONAGE

This term signifies the practice of raking down the *cavaillon* (q.v.) between the rows of vines.

DÉCHAUSSAGE

Déchaussage is the form of ploughing carried out at the end of winter, turning the soil between the rows. This is carried out when there is no further threat of frost.

DECLASSIFICATION

Declassification involves withdrawing the *appellation d'origine* entitlement from a wine. This can be done either by the free choice of the producer, or decided by government officials following the advice of experts. These decisions are taken when a wine has been irreversibly spoiled. In some cases, a producer can demand a more general *appellation* for his wine than the one he would otherwise have a right to; this is known as a *repli* (literally 'withdrawal', meaning 'downgrading').

DÉCUVAISON, DÉCUVAGE

These two words both signify the operation of emptying a vat (*cuve*) after fermentation. White wine is simply racked. Red wine is first allowed to drain out on its own, producing the free-run wine (*vin de goutte*). The marc stays in the bottom of the vat and is then removed and pressed to obtain the press wine (*vin de presse*).

DEGREE

The alcoholic 'degree' (°) in use in France, and in this book, is the percentage by volume of ethyl alcohol in a wine.

DEMI-SEC

The Demi-Sec category of sparkling wine usually contains between 35g and 50g of saccharose per litre (hydrolysed to a varying degree), this sugar coming from the 7 to 10 per cent addition of *liqueur d'expédition* (q.v.) after disgorgement.

DENSITY OF VINE PLANTINGS

The number of vine stocks planted per hectare can range from a few hundred to several tens of thousands. In earlier times, the density was very high, and up to 50,000 vines per ha seem to have been planted.

This is only a rough estimate, however, since vines before phylloxera were planted without any grafting stock, and were reproduced *in situ* by simple layering; consequently the rows — when such existed — were not as ordered as those found today. The necessity of grafting and the abandonment of purely manual vineyard work have led to a better organization of plantations.

Strongly traditional vineyard areas maintain quite a high density of planting, between 6,000 and 10,000 vines per ha, or even more. On the other hand, the need to cut costs via vineyard mechanization has led to a wider spacing of rows to facilitate mechanical work, and when this is the case, density falls severely. The quality of the wine generally also falls as a consequence of this. In order to overcome this problem, new vine-training methods have been developed. Costly high tractors able to straddle vines may, too, be used in areas where it is wished to maintain high densities.

DESSERT WINE

The French equivalent of this term, *vin de dessert*, is used to describe *mistelles* (q.v.), as well as *moelleux* (q.v.) and *liquoreux* wines, and *vins cuits* (q.v.). These wines are often drunk in France as an aperitif or at the beginning of a meal, as well as at its conclusion.

DESTALKING

Destalking, called *égrappage* or *éraflage* in French, is an operation that involves separating the body of the grape from its green and ligneous stalk (*rafle*).

In white wine vinification, destalking is not much practised since the stalks help to facilitate must drainage during pressing. In red wine vinification, however, destalking is performed more and more often, since the stalk is generally tannic and acidic, and when macerated it imparts a very harsh astringency to red wines, which then require a long ageing period to soften and attenuate this harshness. Only vinification involving whole grapes (for example the Beaujolais method of vinification, or carbonic maceration) do not involve any destalking at all.

DISGORGEMENT

Disgorgement, known as *dégorgement* or *dégorgeage* in French, is a phase in the champagne-making process which involves eliminating the fermentation and yeast deposits produced during secondary fermentation in bottle. To do this, the bottle has to be turned upside down (*sur pointe*) for several months, so that the sediment gathers in the neck of the bottle. The traditional technique of disgorgement in the champagne method is entirely manual. It is carried out after the *remuage* (regular twisting towards the vertical) of the bottles, this process having moved the sediment into the bottle neck.

One of two operations is then performed: either pressure disgorgement (*dégorgement à la volée*), in which the pressure inside the bottle is used to expel the sediment at cellar temperature when the bottle is opened; or ice disgorgement (*dégorgement à la glace*) in which the bottle necks are frozen in brine, thus imprisoning the sediment in a small block of ice that is removed when the bottle is opened. This stage of *champagnisation* was once done by hand, but it has mostly been mechanized now. Industrial methods that involve filtration while passing wine from one bottle to another after secondary fermentation do not merit being described as disgorgement. French regulations regarding champagnes and *crémants* specify that the bottles should be *sur pointe* for at least nine months before disgorgement.

DISTILLATION

Distillation is the separation, by heating, of the various constituents of a liquid that have different boiling points.

Distillation allows alcohol and other volatile products to be extracted from a fermented liquid, in order to produce *eaux-de-vie* (spirits).

DOMAINE

A term describing an autonomous wine-producing entity. Such wording, if used on a label, has to correspond to a real wine-growing estate.

DOSAGE

This is the term used to describe the addition of sugar in the form of *liqueur d'expédition* (q.v.) to wines made by the champagne method. The operation is performed after disgorgement.

DOUX

An expression (meaning 'sweet') used to describe wines with a medium to high residual sugar level. For sparkling wines, this level must not be lower than 50g per litre.

DOWNY MILDEW

Cryptogamic disease whose agent is *Peronospera viticola*. This fungus, which originated in the USA, was introduced to France in 1878. It caused great damage until the perfecting of bordeaux mixture (q.v.) by Millardet, using a base of copper sulphate and slaked lime. Plant organs attacked by the fungus spores go brown, dry up and die. Synthetic products with or without copper are slowly replacing bordeaux mixture.

DRAPEAU

A *drapeau* is a device used in cellars to warm or cool a wine. It consists of a coil through which wine is run; cooling is carried out by sprinkling water on the coil. Some of these devices can also be plunged in the wine; hot or cold water is then run through them to achieve similar ends.

EAU-DE-VIE

Eau-de-vie, or spirit, is the result of distilling a fermented product. After removal from the still, *eaux-de-vie* are between 50° to 70°. Most often this level is reduced to around 40° or 50° by the addition of distilled water. If aged in wooden casks, *eaux-de-vie* eventually reach a similar strength without dilution with water, while at the same time mellowing considerably and undergoing important aromatic developments.

Eaux-de-vie without any *appellation* entitlement can be sold with a minimum strength of 30°. *Eaux-de-vie* with an *appellation* entitlement must have an alcoholic strength of at least 40°. They can be distilled from wine (brandy), as are cognac and armagnac, or from marc or wine lees.

ÉCHELLE DES CRUS

The phrase refers to the classification of the grape-producing communes of Champagne for the purposes of deciding the annual price of grapes. The best *crus* receive 100 per cent of the nominated price; the least renowned only 70 per cent.

ÉCOULAGE

Écoulage (draining) refers to the phase of red wine vinification that involves drawing the liquid part of the wine out of the bottom of the vat, leaving the marc.

EDELZWICKER

This is an Alsatian word describing an AOC wine obtained by blending together wines of different grape varieties.

ÉLEVAGE
The term *élevage* (which literally means the 'raising' or 'nurturing' of a wine) is generally used to refer to the group of operations that follow vinification. During the months of *élevage*, the wine should clarify, stabilize physico-chemically and biologically, and mature, thus preparing it for harmonious ageing in bottle.
ENCÉPAGEMENT
The French word *encépagement* refers to the exact varietal composition of an area in which different grape varieties are grown. Thus a small *domaine*, or a large region, may both have a particular *encépagement*. One variety or many may be included.

The use of several grape varieties enables wines with different nuances to be produced. In Champagne, Chardonnay is used for its finesse and lightness, while the Pinot Noir and Meunier impart body and fullness. In other regions, like Alsace, multiple *encépagement* allows for the production of a spectrum of wines.
ENRICHISSEMENT
The term signifies chaptalization (q.v.) or the addition of concentrated must to wine musts.
ÉPLUCHAGE
This operation involves sorting rotten grapes from healthy ones after the harvest, a traditional practice in Champagne.
ESTER
An ester is the product of the combination of an alcohol with a carboxylic acid.

Wine esters are almost always ethanol esters. These are strong-smelling substances, a certain number of which (particularly acetates) contribute to the typical fruity aromas that wine possesses.

In wines, a few esters form during alcoholic fermentation, contributing to the bouquet of *primeur* wines (particularly isoamyl acetate). Others form during the ageing of wine, through the combination of succinic, lactic and malic acids with ethanol. These contribute to the bouquet of old wines.

Through spoilage, or if the wine has been stored badly, ethyl acetate may also form, which is the odorous symptom of acescence (q.v.).
ETHANOL
Also known as ethyl alcohol. This is the technical name for alcohol, as found in wine and other fermented drinks and *eaux-de-vie*.
ETHYL ACETATE
A chemical compound from the family of esters produced by the combination of an acetic acid molecule with an ethanol molecule. This compound forms in wines that have been attacked by *piqûre acétique* (acescence) or *piqûre lactique* (lactic acescence) and gives off the characteristically piquant smell of vinegar.
EXTRA DRY
This expression is used to describe a sparkling wine with moderate to low levels of residual sugar (12g to 20g per litre); it is also sometimes used to describe very dry still wines.
EYE
A term used to describe a vine bud that, at the moment of budbreak, bursts open producing a new shoot with leaves and flower clusters.

FAÇONS
This French word (which literally means 'ways') is a general term used to refer to all the different operations involved in vine growing: ploughing, *décavaillonage* (q.v.), *chaussage* (q.v.), weeding, *rognage* (q.v.), pruning (q.v.), and so on.
FILLETTE
A Loire valley bottle with a capacity of 35cl.
FILTRATION
This is a process of clarification that consists in halting the particles that impede clarity with a physical barrier. Such a barrier may be a layer of kieselguhr (diatomaceous earth), cellulose-based plates or synthetic membranes.
FINE
The term *fine* is used in France to refer to an *eau-de-vie de vin* (brandy) produced in certain regions, such as Fine Bourgogne or Fine Bordeaux, the latter being an *appellation réglementée*. The word *fine* has a regulated use in the Cognac area (*see* panel, page 188).
FINE WINES
As opposed to *vins de table* (table wines) and *vins de consommation courante* (wines for everyday drinking), *vins fins* (fine wines) is another term for quality wines produced most often in *appellation contrôlée* areas, sold in bottles, and meant to be aged for some time.

The characteristic of finesse, by contrast, applies more particularly to delicate wines whose flavours and aromas are devoid of any aggressiveness or harshness.
FINING
This is the process of clarifying a wine by adding a fining agent to it; such agents have the property of precipitating through the wine, taking the particles that prevent clarity in wine with them. Most fining agents (known as *colles* in French) are made up of natural proteins: gelatine, egg white (albumen), blood, casein, isinglass. Some of these proteins require tannin to be present before they will precipitate (gelatine, egg white, blood); others precipitate solely under the influence of the acidity in the wine (casein). By an extension of meaning, *collage* (fining) is also used to refer to treatment with bentonite, a natural clay that has the property of eliminating proteins in wine.
FLEUR
In oenological terms, *la fleur* is the veil of yeast that forms on the surface of wines that have been left, deliberately or accidentally, on ullage. In France, this yeast is of the species *Candida mycoderma*, a microscopic, unicellular fungus whose development produces acetaldehyde, with its characteristic smell of *event* (*see* Glossary of French Tasting Terms). This very old, professional terminology draws on the same vein of inspiration as do cheese makers, when they refer to cheeses covered with a white veil of yeast (such as Brie or Camembert) as *fleuries* (flowery). This particular yeast development imparts special, desirable aromas to the wine. This is the case with fino sherry from Jerez or *vins jaunes* from the Jura, for example.
FLOWERING
This is the phase in the growth of a vine when the 'bunches' are fertilized, allowing grapes to form. Flowering occurs between the beginning of June and the middle of July. If

flowering occurs early, then a good vintage is likely, as maturity is easily reached during the three to four months that follow.

FREE-RUN WINE

The free-run wine, or *vin de goutte*, is that which can be run off from a red-wine vinification tank after fermentation has been completed. It is differentiated from the press wine or *vin de presse* that results from the pressing of the marc left at the bottom of such tanks after the free-run wine has been drained off.

FRELATÉ, FALSIFIÉ

Frelaté (adulterated) and '*falsifié*' (falsified), in addition to their primary meanings, also involve the idea of a denaturation that can make a wine harmful.

FROSTS

Winter frosts can damage vines if the temperature drops below −15°C. Young vines are the most adversely affected under such circumstances, as their buds are destroyed. *Chaussage* (q.v.) of the stocks can lessen the effects of winter frosts. In 1956, large areas of French vineyards were destroyed by winter frosts.

Spring frosts are even more dangerous because they come later, when the vine's vegetative cycle has begun. The most destructive frosts are those that occur in May. The risks of late frost attack are closely linked to local relief, with the bottoms of valleys and hollows the most frost-prone zones. Damage begins at temperatures below −2°C. These frosts can be avoided by planting trees to alter local air flows, pruning late to retard budbreak, and warming the air with stoves.

FRUIT CANES

These are the lignified shoots remaining on the vine after winter pruning. Short canes with 1, 2 or 3 eyes are called *coursons* or *côts*, while long canes with 4 to 14 eyes are called *astes*, *long-bois* or *baguettes*, depending on the region in question. After pruning, a particular number of long or short fruit canes are left on the vine, according to the vine training method used. The fertility along the fruit cane depends on the grape variety. Generally speaking, one eye will produce two bunches of grapes, so pruning is the fundamental means of determining yield per hectare.

FÛT, FUTAILLE

These are generic terms for wooden wine containers (casks or barrels).

GAZÉIFIÉ

This term refers to a sparkling wine produced *en cuve close* (in a pressurized vat) by the addition of carbon dioxide, instead of yeast-induced secondary fermentation in bottle, as in the champagne method. *Appellation contrôlée* sparkling wines cannot be *gazéifié*.

GAZEUX

A term applied to wines that show an unwanted saturation of carbon dioxide when the bottles are uncorked or the wine is removed from the vats.

GLYCEROL, GLYCERINE

This substance is the third most important constituent of wine after water and alcohol. The presence of '*jambes*' ('legs') or '*larmes*' (tears) (*see* Glossary of French Tasting Terms) on the sides of a glass are often, wrongly, attributed to glycerol (alcohol alone is the cause of this).

GRAFTING

Grafting refers to the uniting of two different vines. One vine constitutes the rooted part, the other vine the aerial part carrying leaves and fruit. Since the phylloxera louse devastated French vineyards in the second half of the 19th century, European vines (*Vitis vinifera*) have had to be grafted on to rootstocks of American origin that are resistant to this parasite. The grafts (single or double whip grafts, omega grafts) are made at a grafting bench. When completed, they are potted in earth to form roots before being planted in the vineyard.

GRAISSE

La graisse is a disease of wine caused by the growth of mucilaginous lactic bacteria. It does not impair the taste of wine, but causes it to flow abnormally, like oil.

GRAND VIN

▷ This term should describe a wine of very high quality (a 'great wine'). However it has been so abused in the commercial world that its use has been limited by French law to *appellation d'origine contrôlée* wines that benefit from some kind of classification.

▷ This term is used of free-run wine (q.v.) in Bordeaux.

GRAPE

The grape itself is the fruit of the vine. Each grape comes from the fertilization of a single flower. The grape is of variable shape, and is composed of a cuticle covered with bloom, and pulp that is mainly made up of juice, with pips connected to the pedicel or peduncle by the brush. There can be up to four pips; sometimes there are none (in which case the grape is said to be *apyrène* or seedless). There is a relationship between the number of pips and the size of the berry.

GRAPE SKIN

The skin protects the grape. It also contains the anthocyanins responsible for the colour of black grapes (and red and rosé wines), and for wine aromas.

GRAPE VARIETY

This signifies a variety of vine belonging to the *Vitis vinifera* species. Grape varieties, though, are really vine groups sharing a number of very similar features. Each 'single variety' will present a greater or lesser variability from area to area, vine to vine. Some French wines are sold under the name of the variety they are made from (varietal wines); those of Alsace are an example.

GRAPE VARIETY CLASSIFICATION

Different methods of classification of grape varieties have been established:

▷ By precocity. Victor Pulliat (1827–1896) defined a scale of precocity using the Chasselas grape variety as a reference point (*see* page 42). Grape varieties are assigned to the first, second, third and fourth epochs, those of the first epoch being the most precocious with regard to maturity.

▷ According to use. Grape varieties may be destined for fermentation, for distillation, to be eaten at table, or to be dried. Some varieties may be multi-purpose.

▷ Legally enforced classification of grape varieties according to their suitability for a particular *terroir*. Differences are drawn between 'recommended', 'authorized' and 'temporarily tolerated' grape varieties. Such a classification has been established for each wine-growing region.

▷ By family. Ampelographers are able to class grape varieties in families: the Cabernet family, the Pinot family, and so on. The varieties in each family have shared characteristics and origins.

GRAVES

Graves is a term used to refer to areas, or even vineyard sites, where the soil is made up of gravel. This soil type often produces wines of great quality.

GREEN SHOOT

A green shoot (*rameau*) is a vine organ that grows anew with each annual cycle.

GRILLAGE

Grillage (roasting) is a phenomenon that sometimes occurs during great heat. Parts of the grapes and leaves exposed directly to the sun may be damaged.

GUMS

Gums are colloidal substances found in wine that inconveniently block up filters. They are carbohydrates that form a precipitate in alcohol; their exact structure varies depending on their origin.

HAIL

Hail can cause considerable damage to vineyards. It can damage leaves, grapes, shoots and canes, causing plant traumata that can substantially retard fruit maturation. Often the resulting wounds provide a route of access for vine parasites and, particularly, cryptogamic disease. Immediate treatment after hail storms is crucial. Anti-hail guns occasionally provide a defence, but they are often inadequate.

HALF BOTTLE

A half bottle contains 37.5 centilitres.

HYBRID

A hybrid is a vine produced by crossing different species. As a consequence of the phylloxera attack, numerous hybrids have been achieved, some for use as rootstocks, others for ungrafted use as hybrid direct producers. The latter tend to give perfumed, coarsely flavoured wines that are sometimes harmful to health. Hybrids, which for many years created great disorder in French viticulture, have now been banned.

INAO

Institut National des Appellations d'Origine des Vins et Eaux-de-Vie. Founded in 1938, this organization is responsible for defining the rules of production for wines and *eaux-de-vie*, and making sure these are followed. It works in coordination with professionals from the wine-growing regions. Currently, regulations for 260 AOC wines, 2 AOC and 30 *appellation réglementée eaux-de-vie*, and 60 VDQS wines have been drawn up by members of the INAO. These regulations take into account the traditions and customs of the various areas of production.

INERT GAS

This is a type of gas that does not cause any chemical or microbiological transformation in the wine. Two inert gases are permitted for wine use: carbon dioxide and nitrogen. While carbon dioxide on its own may saturate wine, making it unintentionally sparkling, nitrogen can have the reverse effect, making it a little flat. So in practice a small percentage of carbon dioxide is added to nitrogen for wine use. This mixture can, for example, be used to blanket wines in storage and prevent them spoiling in any way.

INSECT PESTS

A number of insects attack vines, and these are known collectively in French as *ennemis de la vigne* (vine enemies). They include caterpillars, spider mites, and other insects such as the phylloxera louse. These insects are kept at bay by the use of insecticides, or by grafting susceptible *vinifera* vines on to resistant rootstocks.

INTERPROFESSIONAL COMMITTEES

These are semi-public regional bodies involved in the marketing and development of local *appellations d'origine contrôlée*. There are 23 of these committees in France. They are responsible for the marketing of wines in their region, the organization of markets, and appropriate studies or viticultural and oenological research.

JEROBOAM

Wine bottle equivalent to a double magnum, in other words four normal bottles, or three litres.

LACTIC ACESCENCE

Formation of acetic acid by heterofermentative lactic bacteria, when they are left to develop in the presence of sugars.

LACTIC ACID

This acid is not present in the must, but it appears during malolactic fermentation due to the breakdown of malic acid. It has only a very slightly acid taste, and this explains the smoothness of wines that have undergone malolactic fermentation. (*See also* Glossary of French Tasting Terms.)

LACTIC BACTERIA

These are aerobic, Gram positive bacteria. In wine, they are responsible for malolactic fermentation. This makes wines more supple, and is systematically encouraged in red wines. It also modifies wine aroma.

LATTE

Lattes (laths) are small strips of wood used to stabilize the stacking of wine bottles. The term '*vieillissement sur latte*' is used of the stage of sparkling wine production by the champagne method when the wine rests in bottle with its secondary fermentation deposits. This improves quality; and the bottles at this time are stocked in piles stabilized by *lattes*.

LAYERING

This is a process of propagation of certain ligneous plants, vines included, which involves bending a shoot back into the soil where it will take root. Once the shoot has taken root, it is separated from its parent, and then constitutes a new plant. Vines were generally propagated in this way before phylloxera (q.v.).

LEES

Lees are the deposits formed in wine by the sedimentation of fermenting agents, mainly yeasts, when their fermentation activity has ceased. (Lees — *la lie* — must not be confused with *bourbes*, which is the solid, expendable material that finds its way into must during pressing, and which also precipitates as a sediment — *see Débourbage*. Yeast lees are slightly greyish, while *bourbes* are coloured and tend to be darker.)

The word 'lees' normally carries a pejorative connotation, yet it is a 'noble' part of wine, and its redissolution is desirable in some wines to enrich them with aromas associated with ageing, and with nitrogenous substances. The nine-month period *sur pointe* (with the bottle inverted) for champagnes and *crémants* is based on this principle. In Burgundy, great white wines are stored in casks *sur lie* (on their lees) until these have been redissolved. The lees are generally full of yeast, bacteria and tartar crystals. It is a speciality of certain white wines to be bottled *sur lie* (directly off their lees); this is true of Muscadet, Gros Plant du Pays Nantais, and Vin de Pays des Sables du Golfe de Lion. Such wines are not racked off their sediment after alcoholic fermentation, and they remain saturated with carbon dioxide, giving them a very slightly sparkling (*perlant*) appearance and allowing them to be bottled with little sulphur dioxide. Wines bottled *sur lie* before or during July in the year that follows their harvest have to display their vintage on their label.

LEVAGE

This is the name given to the operation of lifting up (and tying) vine shoots that have been growing horizontally.

LIQUEUR DE TIRAGE

This is a cane sugar syrup added to base wines to be made sparkling by *champagnisation* (q.v.) at the moment of their initial bottling. This sugar, fermented by the yeast still present in the wine, produces up to 1.5° alcohol and an equal quantity of carbon dioxide, responsible for effervescence. About 25g of *liqueur* per litre of wine is added for *vins mousseux* (sparkling wines). *Vins pétillants* (slightly sparkling wines) receive about half this amount.

LIQUEUR D'EXPÉDITION

This is a wine syrup with a cane sugar base added after the disgorgement (q.v.) of sparkling wines, champagnes or *crémants*. This addition brings the sugar in the wine to the desired level for its category (Extra Dry, Brut, Sec or Demi-Sec), and also permits the addition of stabilizing products if necessary, such as citric acid or sulphur dioxide.

MACERATION

Maceration is a phase in red wine vinification, and sometimes in rosé vinification, during which the solid matter of the grape (skin and pips) is soaked or steeped in the must before or during alcoholic fermentation, in order to extract colour, aroma, tannin and various other substances. Maceration is a principal concern of wine makers, and the question of maceration is one that all techniques aiming to improve red wine vinification must address.

MAGNUM

A double-sized wine bottle, containing a litre and a half.

MAÎTRE DE CHAI

The *maître de chai* or cellar master is the person in charge of the different operations that are carried out in the *chai* (q.v.), both during vinification and *élevage* (q.v.).

MALIC ACID

This is an acid naturally present in the grape. The quantity present diminishes during maturation. In must, it is present in quantities of between 2g and 5g per litre. The yeast may break it down slightly. Bacteria are then able to completely transform it into lactic acid (malolactic fermentation). During vinification by carbonic maceration, the level of malic acid present in the must drops substantially.

MALOLACTIC FERMENTATION

The breakdown of malic acid into lactic acid and carbon dioxide by lactic bacteria. This transformation brings about a partial deacidification of the wine, making it suppler to the taste. This secondary fermentation, sometimes difficult to initiate, is desirable for all red wines and some white wines.

MARC

▷ Marc is the solid grape matter present during, and remaining after, vinification.

▷ Marc is also the name of an *eau-de-vie* obtained by the distillation of this dry residue, produced by pressing.

MAS

A *mas* is a farmhouse or country house in the Midi, and the word may be used to describe a wine of specific origin, coming from a particular wine-growing domain with its own means of production.

MATURATION

Maturation is the period in the life of a vine between *véraison* (when the grapes begin to colour) and full maturity. During this period the berries do not grow much in size. Instead, sugars are accumulated and acids diminish. Once these two processes slow, and the substances reach an equilibrium, the term physiological maturity is used. Beyond this stage lies overmaturation and its associated phenomena: *passerillage* (q.v.) and *pourriture noble* (q.v.), both desired states in certain vineyard areas.

MATURITY

Maturity is a physiological stage of the vine. Physiological maturity is said to have occurred when the grape pips are capable of germination. This type of maturity precedes the technical maturity required by the wine grower. This is an optimum quality level of variable definition, depending on the grape variety and the wines to be produced. For example, 'aromatic maturity' is sought after in grapes destined to produce white wines rich in primary, fruit aromas.

MÉCHAGE

This is an operation that involves burning a wick (*mèche*) or a pastille of sulphur to produce sulphur dioxide. This practice is a way of sulphurating the wine, though it is not a very thorough way; it is also a method of keeping empty casks in good condition.

MERCAPTAN *See* Glossary of French Tasting Terms.

MESOCLIMATE, MICROCLIMATE

As applied to viticulture, these two terms refer to the climatic conditions that permanently dominate a local area and a very small, local sector respectively. These may be different from the macroclimate or general climate of the region, and they may create a privileged situation for a particular *cru* or part of a *cru*.

MÉTHODE CHAMPENOISE see Champagnisation.

MÉTHODE RURALE

The *méthode rurale* is a means of producing sparkling wines by bottling while the wine still has residual sugar in it before alcoholic fermentation has finished. This is completed in bottle, producing a carbon dioxide sparkle. This method was once used in numerous regions where *champagnisation* (q.v.) has now been adopted.

METHUSELAH

A wine bottle containing six litres.

MILLERANDAGE

Millerandage or failed grape development is a phenomenon resulting from the partial abortion of fertilization at the moment of flowering. This ultimately results in the presence within the bunches of a varying proportion of very small grapes without pips. This is a very favourable development for the quality of red wines.

MIRER

This is an operation involving the observation of the limpidity of a wine in bottle or at its exit from a filtration system.

MISTELLE

Mistelles are products made by adding wine alcohol to grape must, usually in a proportion of two thirds must to one third *eau-de-vie* (of around 50°). The resulting mixture is between 15° and 18° alcohol, and is stabilized (by the alcohol) against fermentation. Its sugar level is between 120g and 150g per litre. A number of traditional, regional *mistelles* are produced with *eau-de-vie de marc*; these include Ratafia in Champagne and Burgundy, Macvin in the Jura, and Carthagène in Languedoc-Roussillon.

Certain *mistelles* have been classed with an AOC as *vins de liqueur*, such as Pineau des Charentes and certain Muscat wines from Frontignan.

MOELLEUX

When specified on the label or neck label of a wine bottle, this term signifies a sweet wine, without the level of residual sugar being specified (except in the case of Côtes de Bergerac Moelleux: *see* page 66). (*See also* Glossary of French Tasting Terms.)

MOUSSEUX

This term used to be that used in France to describe sparkling wines, wines that contain carbon dioxide under pressure in bottle, producing *mousse* (froth) when uncorked. This term is now out of date and has been replaced by the term *effervescent* in all official texts.

MUID

A large cask, the exact capacity of which varies from region to region.

MUST

Must is juice expressed by grapes before fermentation occurs. This term is also used to describe a wine in process of fermentation.

MUSTIMÈTRE

The *mustimètre* is an instrument that measures sugar levels in must.

MUTAGE

An operation that involves preventing or arresting alcoholic fermentation, either by the addition of alcohol (as for *vins de liqueur* or *vins doux naturels*) or by the addition of sulphur dioxide (as for most unfortified sweet wines).

MUTER

This verb means to stabilize must, or wine that still contains unfermented sugar, against fermentation, by adding sulphur dioxide or alcohol, or by pasteurization. Home-made fruit juices are often stabilized with benzoate or sodium salicylate, though these substances are forbidden for commercial use.

MYCODERMES

This is a generic name used in France for yeasts that grow as a veil on the surface of liquids.

NATURE

This term is used to describe non-sparkling wines from regions that produce sparkling wines. It is no longer authorized for use in *appellation* names.

NEBUCHADNEZZAR

A wine bottle with a capacity of 15 litres.

NECK LABEL

This label, known as a *collerette* in French, often shows the vintage of a wine.

NÉGOCIANT

Merchant who buys wines to distribute and market them. *Négociants-éleveurs* are also involved in making wine. In particular, they carry out blending, clarification and bottling. *Négociants-manipulants*, in Champagne, are merchant-producers who buy grapes, must or base wine, and carry out the *champagnisation* of these raw materials.

NITROGEN

Nitrogen is an inert gas constituting 80 per cent of air. It is used in vinification installations, together with carbon dioxide, as a preservative gas. It is also employed in a red-wine vinification process known as *brassage à l'azote* (nitrogen mixing). It can, additionally, be used to remove any excess carbon dioxide in a wine before bottling, via the process known as *dégazage à l'azote* (nitrogen degassing).

NOBLE

'Noble' is a term used to refer to quality grape varieties and *cru* wines, as opposed to *vins de table* made from common grape varieties, and, in former times, to wines made from hybrid grape varieties which became popular after phylloxera.

NOUAISON

A phenological stage that the vine passes through during which the newly fertilized grape pips are perfectly attached to the stem. Visually, the transformation of flowers to berries marks *nouaison*.

NOUVEAU (VIN)

A term referring to wines of recent origin. Before they may be marketed, such wines must have been officially approved by the INAO. They must wait for their legal launching date: this is 1 December for *vins de pays* and VDQS wines, and 15 December for AOC wines. *Primeurs* (q.v.), such as Beaujolais Nouveau, are launched on the third Thursday of November.

This term *vin nouveau* may also be used to mean:

▷ In certain areas, a must that is not yet fermented. The term *bourru* may also be used in this way.

▷ Newly fermented wine, prior to its first racking.

▷ Completed wine at the end of vinification, clarified and filtered, ready for drinking as a *primeur* wine.

OENOLOGIST

A specialist in the science of wine and wine making. This profession was recognized in France by a state diploma created by a law passed on 9 March 1955. Oenological training in France lasts four years. Courses are provided by the universities of Bordeaux, Dijon, Montpellier, Reims and Toulouse. Certain oenological practices can only be carried out under the supervision of an oenologist.

OENOLOGY

The science of wine and wine making.

OENOPHILE

A person who appreciates and seeks to understand wine.

OFFICE INTERNATIONAL DE LA VIGNE ET DU VIN (OIV)

This is an international organization, created in 1924. The number of member countries is 28. The OIV studies scientific, economic and technical subjects related to the vine and its derivative products: wine, *eaux-de-vie*, grape juices, table grapes, and raisins and sultanas.

OFFICE NATIONAL INTERPROFESSIONNEL DES VINS (ONIVINS)

This French organization was created in 1983 to provide a technical and economic framework for the production and marketing of table wines.

OIDIUM

Oidium, or powdery mildew, is a cryptogamic disease that develops on the green organs of the vine. The first symptom is the appearance of a whitish down, followed by tissue decay. This disease first appeared in France during the 19th century, after downy mildew. The fungus is combated by the application of sulphur in powdered form, or in solution.

OUILLAGE

An operation that consists of completely filling wine containers, so that the wine does not stay in contact with oxygen in the air.

OVERRIPENING

Physiological stage of the vine that occurs after the normal maturity of the grape. Overripening (*surmaturation*) is characterized by the phenomena of biological concentration caused by *pourriture noble* (*see* Rot). Overripening of white grapes permits the production of sweet or dessert wines.

OXIDIZATION

Chemical reaction in which a molecule loses one electron or more. In wine, numerous compounds are susceptible to oxidization, causing organoleptic faults of varying seriousness: mustiness, *casse brune* and acescence. Oxidization is prevented by *ouillage* (q.v.), storage of wine beneath a blanket of inert gas, and maintaining sufficient levels of sulphur dioxide in wine. (*See also* Glossary of French Tasting Terms.)

PASSERILLAGE

When grapes start to wither on the vine before they are picked due to the natural process of dehydration, their sugar concentration increases substantially. This is called *passerillage*, and is the main method of producing naturally sweet wines, alongside, but to be distinguished from, *pourriture noble* (noble rot).

PASSETOUTGRAINS

A carafe wine produced in Burgundy by mixed vinification of the Gamay Noir à Jus Blanc and the Pinot Noir, the latter constituting at least a third of the blend.

PASTEUR, LOUIS (1822–1895)

French scientist who contributed susbstantially to an understanding of wine microbiology.

PASTEURIZATION

A process aimed at achieving the biological stabilization of food products, based on the sensitivity of micro-organisms to heat. Degrees of pasteurization are defined both in relation to temperature and to length of application.

Treatment of wine by pasteurization is effective, but it does not allow the wine to develop well during ageing and should therefore be reserved for wines that are to be drunk young.

PAULÉE

A wine growers' celebration at the end of the harvest. The most famous of such celebrations is the Paulée de Meursault in Burgundy. The Paulée de Paris and the Paulée du Val de Loire are of more recent origin.

PEDICEL OR PEDUNCLE

The pedicel or peduncle is the part of the grape bunch from which the grape hangs.

PERLANT

A wine is said to be *perlant* (very slightly sparkling) when it releases a small quantity of carbon dioxide when uncorked. This is a smaller quantity still — a mere prickle — than is found in *pétillant* (slightly sparkling) wines, which are regarded as the least sparkling member of the family of *vins effervescents*. Wines that are bottled with a high carbon dioxide content, such as those bottled *sur lie* (like Muscadet), are often *perlant*.

PÉTILLANT

This is a category of *vin effervescent* (sparkling wine) produced by the champagne method, but with half the carbon dioxide level usual in sparkling wines (so 'slightly sparkling'). *Pétillant* sparkling wines are traditional in certain areas, such as Montlouis or Vouvray.

PHENOLIC COMPOUNDS

Chemical compounds that have a phenol radical in their formula. In wines, these compounds are present in quantities of between 1g and 2g per litre. They are responsible for colour and astringency. There are various kinds of phenolic compounds: phenolic acids, anthocyanins (red pigments), flavones (yellow pigments) and tannins.

PHENOLOGICAL STAGES

Stages in the growth of the green shoots and fruiting parts of the vine. Perfect knowledge of these stages allows for the application of phytosanitary treatments at the correct time, and for the prediction of the probable date of grape maturity.

PHYLLOXERA

Phylloxera vastatrix (*see* page 41) is an insect that attacks the roots of European (*Vitis vinifera*) vines. It is of American origin, and first appeared in France in 1864 in Gard, following the introduction of American vines there. Identified by Jean-Étienne Planchon in 1868, it progressively attacked all the vineyard areas of France and Europe. Grafting *vinifera* vines on to resistant American rootstocks has enabled the devastation caused by phylloxera to be halted.

Phylloxera appears in two forms. One, the gall-living form, attacks foliage. French vines are not very susceptible to it, and it only causes damage in rootstock breeding plantations. The other form is root-living, and attacks the roots. It is this type that caused the near total destruction of the French vineyards at the end of the 19th century. The grafting of French *vinifera* vines on to American rootstocks was one solution, and it was with enormous effort that the vineyards were reconstituted in this way. Another solution was to plant hybrid direct producers which did not require grafting. The second method has now been abandoned owing to the mediocrity of the wines such hybrids produced.

PIÈCE

A *pièce* is a volume unit of wine, generally a cask, that varies from region to region, but that has a capacity of between 180 litres and 260 litres.

PIED DE CUVE

Name given to wine yeast leaven or starter. It is prepared by allowing yeasts to multiply and ferment in a small volume of must in advance.

PIGEAGE

Pigeage is an operation performed during red wine vinification that involves pushing the layer of marc that forms on the surface of fermenting must back down into the liquid. The purpose of this action is to renew contact between the must and the grape skins, thus favouring the extraction of the anthocyanins responsible for colour, and of tannins. It also limits the risk of the cap (q.v.) of grape skins becoming subject to acescence, which can happen if it stays in contact with the air for too long. Formerly carried out manually, *pigeage* is now mechanized in special vats called *cuves à pigeage*.

PIGMENTS

Pigments are colouring substances. In the grape, these pigments are chiefly anthocyanins.

PINARDIER

A French term used to denote a ship used for transporting wine, as well as a harbour from which wine is shipped.

PIQUÉ

A term used to describe a wine with high volatile acidity.

PIQÛRE ACÉTIQUE see Acescence.

PIQÛRE LACTIQUE see Lactic Acescence.

POT

A bottle with a capacity of 46.5cl, found in Beaujolais.

PRESS

Apparatus for extracting must for white wine vinification and for pressing marc following red wine vinification. There are several types, manual and mechanical. Among the latter, a distinction is made between continuous presses, discontinuous presses and pneumatic presses (*see* pages 241 and 249). The results can be very different with each.

PRESS WINE

Press wine is the wine expressed by the squeezing action of the press, as opposed to the free-run wine (q.v.) that flows spontaneously during the draining of fermentation vats. Since the marc is pressed several times, there are several degrees and qualities of press wine (*vins de première presse*, *de deuxième presse* and *de troisième presse*) each being murkier and more astringent than that which preceded it.

PRESSING

Pressing is the action of squeezing grapes or grape pulp by means of a press in order to extract liquid. For white and rosé wines, fresh grapes, crushed or uncrushed, are pressed before fermentation, and the liquid that emerges is must or juice; for red wines, pressing (of marc) takes place after fermentation, and the liquid that emerges is press wine.

PRIMEUR (VIN DE)

Vins de primeur are wines produced with the intention of being drunk young. They are fairly light, and are put on the market on the third Thursday of November with the words '*primeur*' or '*nouveau*' on the label. They are generally characterized by suppleness and freshness and they have plentiful aromas.

PROTEIN

Proteins are organic compounds made up of a chain of amino acids. Each protein is characterized by the nature and order of amino acids that form it. These compounds, found in all living beings, play various roles (for example they may be structural proteins or enzymes). When they are present in wine in excess, they can precipitate, causing the wine to become cloudy; this condition is known as *casse protéique*.

PRUNING

Pruning (*la taille*) allows the growth of the vine to be directed according to a required pattern, and ensures that the number of fruit buds with which each vine starts the new year is compatible with its strength and the yield required. Pruning also allows the growth of green shoots to be controlled by *rognage* (q.v.) and topping.

PULP

Pulp is the tissue containing the juice of a grape.

QUART

A *quart* is a bottle containing 25cl.

RACKING

Racking (*soutirage*) has two purposes.

▷ To transfer wine from one container to another. This is not, in fact, simply a change of container, since racking adds the fraction of oxygen necessary for the wine's development, while eliminating any excess of carbon dioxide, separating the wine from any deposits that may have formed, and providing a certain physico-chemical stability.

▷ To separate the wine from its sediment during *élevage*. Racking may be carried out by gravity or by pumping. Profitable use can be made of the racking process to give the wine aeration or adjust its level of sulphur dioxide.

RATAFIA

A *vin de liqueur* (*see Mistelle*), generally consumed as an aperitif, produced in Champagne and Burgundy by fortifying fresh grape must with *eau-de-vie de marc*, in an approximate proportion of two thirds must to one third *eau-de-vie*.

REBÊCHE

The *rebêche* is the final juice extracted from a pressing cycle, and it is of the lowest quality. In Champagne, the *rebêche* is not used. *Rebêche* also signifies the operation of crumbling marc between pressings.

RÉCHAUFFEMENT

Réchauffement (reheating) of must expressed from grapes gathered in cold weather is often necessary to start alcoholic fermentation.

RÉCOLTANT-MANIPULANT
This term is used in Champagne to refer to a grower who produces champagne with his own grapes.
RECTIFIÉE
Rectifiée is a spirit whose purity and alcoholic strength have been increased by elimination of the least volatile fractions during distillation.
RED WINE
Wine with a red colour obtained by maceration of must with the solid parts of the grape, its skin and pips, to extract colour, aroma and tannin. The grape crop is usually destalked first. The maceration period can last a few days or several weeks. The exact colour of the wine will depend on genetic factors (the grape variety or varieties used), the climatic conditions of the year and the soils in which the grapes were grown.
REDUCTION
This physico-chemical phenomenon is the opposite or inverse of oxidization, although it is always associated with it. In wine, reduction is caused by prolonged deprivation of oxygen, the wine being a natural reducer. Reduction poses no danger to the conservation of wine — quite the contrary, in fact — but it encourages the formation of more or less fetid animal odours and various sulphur compounds, while also eclipsing the bouquet of the wine to a varying degree. These drawbacks are easily overcome by giving the wine a brief aeration before drinking.
REFERMENTATION
Refermentation signifies a usually unwanted resumption of alcoholic fermentation. This phenomenon can occur in sweetened wines that have not been properly stabilized.
REFRIGERATION
Refrigeration is a physical process used to stabilize wines. The cold impedes the biological reactions that occur in wine. Furthermore it favours the precipitation of unstable compounds, particularly tartaric acid.
REMONTAGE
Remontage is a process that occurs during red wine vinification, involving pumping wine from the bottom to the top of the vat to wash through the cap (q.v.) and so improve colour extraction.
REMUAGE
This operation is applicable to sparkling wines made by the champagne method. *Remuage* is a way of ensuring that the yeast deposits formed during secondary fermentation collect in the neck of the bottle next to the cork or cap, from where they can easily be removed.
RÉSERVE
A description that, on its own, may only be used of an *appellation* wine that has been specially selected by the bottler, distributor or establishment in which it is served. Descriptions such as 'Réserve de la Maison' or 'Réserve du Patron' may be freely used.
RESIDUAL SUGARS
Residual sugars are those that remain after fermentation and are left intact by the yeast. Wines that are found to have less than 2g of residual sugar per litre of wine are considered to be dry (*sec*).
ROGNAGE
Rognage is a vineyard task that involves trimming the vines' vegetative growth during the summer to avoid the loss of sap caused by the growth of new green shoots. In particular, if this is not carried out at the moment of flowering, *coulure* (flower abortion) can occur, leading to a reduced crop.
ROOTSTOCK
The rootstock (or *porte-greffe* in French) is the part of a vine that is underground and has been grafted. Following the phylloxera epidemic, European vines were grafted on to phylloxera-resistant rootstocks of American origin.
ROSÉ WINE
Wine with a pink colour. This pink can be of various shades, and is obtained either by the direct pressing of a red grape variety, or by crushing and cold maceration for a few hours before pressing, or by very short and incomplete normal maceration before being pressed. Those rosé wines made by methods that involve maceration tend to have a more intense fruitiness than do those made by direct pressing.
ROT
Rot (*pourriture*) is a cryptogamic disease caused by *Botrytis cinerea*. This fungus grows in humid, warm conditions. The greatest damage is found on bunches at the approach of the harvest. Botrytis attacks are encouraged by the wounds left in grapes and bunches by caterpillars or hail. This disease is currently of great concern, since botrytis strains resistant to anti-rot treatments have appeared in vineyards. No reliable and effective means of fighting this disease is available at present.

Vine susceptibility to rot can be minimized by aerating the parts of the vine where the bunches are, by special vine training methods or by leaf thinning. Grapes attacked by rot produce must and wine susceptible to *casse brune*. They must therefore be vinified and stored with special care.

A particular form of *Botrytis cinerea* leads to the formation of noble rot (*pourriture noble*). In this case, the fungus mycelium invades the berry without damaging it. The result is rot-affected grapes known as *rôti* in French (*see* pages 96–97) which, little by little, increase their richness and sugar content without the acid level rising to a corresponding degree. This development is accompanied by the formation of characteristic aromas. *Pourriture noble* wines are produced in France in certain areas only: Alsace, Anjou, Monbazillac, Sauternes, Touraine. The harvest is carried out by making a number of sweeps through the vineyards to pick only the grapes that have reached the desired degree of maturity. The yields are low and the labour involved is substantial, which makes the wines rare and sought after.

Grey rot (*pourriture grise*) is a stage of botrytis that goes beyond *pourriture noble*, and which dries out the grape, eventually leading to *pourri sec* (dry rot). *Pourri sec* marks the stage of deterioration at which the dehydrated grape is attacked by mould.
ROW
A line of vines in a vineyard. Rows of vines are most favourably disposed in a north–south direction, as this ensures that they get maximum sunlight.

SACCHAROSE
Beet sugar or cane sugar used for chaptalization. Saccharose is made up of a molecule of glucose joined to a molecule of

fructose. Glucose and fructose are the principal sugars in grape juice.

SARMENT

Sarments are vine canes. When the green shoots have passed the stage of *aoûtement* (q.v.), they lignify, and are then known as *sarments*. *Sarments* are part of the vine's annual growth, and are generally removed in winter pruning.

SEC

Term used to describe a wine low in residual sugar. In fact, the level of sugar should be no more than 4g per litre, or 9g per litre if the total acidity expressed in grams per litre of tartaric acid is less than 2g lower than the total residual sugar level. Sparkling wines described as 'Sec', however, may contain between 15g and 35g of sugar per litre. (*See also* Glossary of French Tasting Terms.)

SEDIMENT

Solid particles that form at the bottom of wine containers. The deposits produced by new wines are largest. They are eliminated by racking (q.v.).

SÉLECTION DE GRAINS NOBLES

This description may appear on the bottle labels of certain *appellations*: Alsace, Sauternes, Barsac, Cadillac, Cérons, Loupiac, Sainte-Croix-du-Mont, Graves Supérieures, Monbazillac, Bonnezeaux, Quarts de Chaume, Coteaux du Layon, Coteaux de l'Aubance, Jurançon. Wines so described must be produced from selected grapes affected by *pourriture noble* (*see* Rot). In Alsace, wines made from the Gewürztraminer and Pinot Gris can be so described only if their natural sugar level has reached 279g per litre. Riesling and Muscat wines must contain 256g per litre of sugar to be so described. The vintage must be mentioned on the bottle and the wine must not be enriched in any way.

SPARKLING (WINE)

This term describes bottled wine containing carbon dioxide under pressure that expands with effervescence the moment the bottle is opened. The term *effervescent* is, in fact, destined to replace the older term *mousseux* in France; *mousseux* does not, international discussions have revealed, have an exact equivalent in other European languages. Outside France, the words used to describe such wines refer more to the idea of 'foam' (*Schaumwein*, *spumante*, *espumoso*) or 'sparkle' (as in the English phrase 'sparkling wine').

Sparkling wines can be produced by various methods:

▷ with secondary fermentation in bottle, for champagne, *crémants* and various other traditional *appellation* sparkling wines;

▷ fermentation in pressurized vats (*cuve close sous pression*), the method used for most non-*appellation* branded sparkling wines;

▷ carbonation (*gazéification*) by saturation with carbon dioxide (producing a sort of lemonade made with wine), an industrial process used for very cheap products.

A process using elements of the first two systems allows for fermentation in the bottle, but substitutes traditional disgorgement with filtration and rebottling.

Wines termed *perlant* (very slightly sparkling) and *pétillant* (slightly sparkling), with a gaseous pressure lower than 2.5 bars, are included in the category of *vins effervescents*, although they were excluded from that of *vins mousseux*. Reference to the *méthode champenoise* on a sparkling wine label indicates that the wine so labelled has been produced by fermentation in bottle with individual disgorgement.

SPIRITUEUX

A spirit or a product made with spirit, such as *eau-de-vie*, *vin de liqueur*, *vin doux naturel*, vermouth, and so on.

STABILIZATION

Wines are stabilized during *élevage* to avoid precipitation, harmful chemical reactions, or the development of micro-organisms occurring during transport or storage in bottle.

STALK

The stalk (*rafle*) is the skeleton of the grape bunch. It is made of ligneous tissues rich in phenolic compounds liable to release substances with an stalky, astringent taste in wine.

STILL

Wine is said to be 'still' as opposed to 'sparkling'; still wines are therefore those with no perceptible trace of carbon dioxide.

SUGARS

The main fermentable sugars in the grape are glucose and fructose. In chaptalization, saccharose from beet or cane sugar is added. These sugars are fermented by yeast to produce alcohol.

SULFATAGE

Vine treatment that involves spraying the foliage with bordeaux mixture (q.v.). This is based on copper sulphate. Nowadays *sulfatage* is understood to refer to the application of a large number of synthetic products which do not contain copper sulphate.

SULFITAGE

▷ A strictly monitored operation that involves the addition of sulphur dioxide to a wine to ensure its chemical and microbial stability.

▷ The result of this operation, and the level of SO_2 in the wine.

SULPHIDES

Compounds of sulphur formed by chemical reduction, with an unpleasant smell. They are found in wine in the following forms: H_2S or hydrogen sulphide; C_2H_5–SH, or ethyl hydrogen sulphide (mercaptan); $(C_2H_5)_2S$, or diethyl sulphide; and various complex compounds that are not at present clearly defined (*see* Mercaptan in the Glossary of French Tasting Terms).

SULPHUR DIOXIDE

A chemical compound with the formula SO_2, widely used in cellars and wineries for its numerous properties. It is simultaneously an anti-oxidant, anti-oxidase and antiseptic, very effective against bacteria, a little less so against yeasts; it also has a dissolving effect on phenolic compounds. It is used in different forms: as a wick or a pastille of sulphur that is burnt, as a compressed gas, as a solution in water, or as potassium salts. Some types of yeast can produce sulphur dioxide. Its use is officially controlled. (*See also Anhydride* in Glossary of French Tasting Terms.)

SWEETENING

An operation that involves enriching the must with sugar before fermentation in order to increase its final alcoholic strength. In technical language, the word used is chaptalization (q.v.). This practice is regulated according to the geographical area and categories of wine in question. It is currently carried out by adding beet or cane saccharose, or concentrated must. These will soon be replaced by grape sugar or rectified concentrated must.

SYNDICAT VITICOLE

Each *appellation* has a *syndicate viticole* whose members are the wine growers themselves. The role of such *syndicats* is to protect the *appellations* by agreeing production regulations in accordance with the INAO, and by taking legal action in cases of fraud concerning their *appellation*.

TANISAGE

A wine treatment that involves adding oenologically suitable tannins to wine. This operation is carried out, for example, during the fining of white wines, the dose used being a few grams per hl.

TANNIC

A term used to describe a wine rich in tannins, giving — at the very least — an impression of astringency during tasting.

TARTAR

Tartar is a substance that crystallizes on the sides of the vats, casks and bottles. Tartar is made up of salts of tartaric acid. It is almost tasteless.

TARTARIC ACID

A natural acid in grapes and wine, but one that is not otherwise very common in the plant world. Its level diminishes during grape maturation. It diminishes again during alcoholic fermentation owing to its poor solubility in alcohol. New wines are saturated with tartaric acid, causing precipitates of potassium hydrogen tartrate (cream of tartar) to form as soon as the wine is placed in the cold. These crystals, known in French as *gravelle*, form on the sides of wine containers, or even in bottles if the wine is bottled early. Cold treatment of wine during *élevage* is necessary to avoid this problem. Tartaric acid that remains in finished wine already stabilized by cold treatment proves resistant to attack by micro-organisms. In wines that are left untreated, however, tartaric acid may be broken down by certain lactic bacteria, causing the disease known as tartaric fermentation or *tourne* (q.v.).

TASTER

A taster is a person capable of describing the different organoleptic characteristics of a food or drink.

TASTEVIN

The *tastevin* is a small, shallow metallic dish used by cellarmen, mainly for observing the colour and limpidity of the wine, and thus for deciding on any modifications or treatments. Intended for use in cellars for bulk wines, its role as a tasting tool was originally negligible.

TASTEVINAGE

A quality seal awarded to certain wines of Burgundy by the Confrérie des Chevaliers du Tastevin. The seal is awarded only after careful tasting, and it may be shown on a special numbered label that the bottles are given.

TASTING CARD

A tasting card (or *fiche de dégustation*) allows the wine taster to record his impressions methodically. These cards generally separate the visual, olfactory, tactile and gustatory sensations.

TEINTURIER

A red grape variety with red juice (most red grape varieties have white juice). The wines of such varieties were often used to bring colour to blends, hence the name (which literally means 'dyer').

TEMPERATURE

The temperature of must and wine plays a fundamental role in oenology, as much during vinification as during storage. The mastery of temperature control is one of the great advances of modern oenology.

TENUE

The *tenue* of a wine is its capacity to remain stable when exposed to extreme conditions of, for example, exposure to air (*tenue à l'air*) or to cold (*tenue au froid*). Laboratory tests concerning *tenue* are carried out in order to predict a wine's eventual need of curative treatments.

TERROIR

A *terroir* is a distinct pedoclimatic environment that can produce an original, quality product. The notion of *terroir* is one of the basic tenets of the *appellation d'origine contrôlée* system.

TIRAGE

Tirage is an operation involving the emptying of a vat of wine into other containers, such as casks or bottles.

TONNEAU

The word *tonneau* (barrel) is often used synonymously with *fût* (cask). In Bordeaux, the *tonneau* is a wine container equivalent to four *barriques*, or 900 litres.

TOURNE

Tourne, or tartaric fermentation, is a wine disease caused by lactic bacteria. It occurs in wines that have been insufficiently treated with sulphur and is characterized by the breakdown of tartaric acid and the production of carbon dioxide and, in particular, acetic acid. When tasted, the wine is dull, gassy, and has a mousy taste (*goût de souris*).

TRAVAUX EN VERT

The *travaux en vert* are all the vineyard tasks that wine growers carry out on the vine during the growing period. These include *ébourgeonnage* (bud-nipping), *épamprage* (thinning of young shoots), *pincement* (pinching out), *écimage* (topping), *rognage* (trimming), *effeuillage* (leaf thinning) and *incision annulaire* (annular incision-making). The chief aim of all of these tasks is the restriction of growth of the green shoots in order to favour the maturation of the grape bunches.

TRIES

The *vendange par tries* is a selective form of harvesting in which only overripe grapes are picked or, conversely, only green or rotten ones. The former type of harvesting is undertaken to produce sweet wines; the latter type to avoid contamination of an otherwise healthy crop.

TUN

A tun (*foudre*) is a large, vat-shaped wine container with a capacity from 30hl to several hundred hl. Some tuns have a round base, others an oval one. They are usually made of wood. In the eastern regions of France where they are most commonly used, some are very finely finished and are true works of art.

ULLAGE

Ullage is a pocket of air left in tanks, barrels or bottles

containing wine. It is the main cause of spoilage and oxidization of wines. Ullage may be remedied either by filling the container fully (*ouillage*), or by replacing the air in the container with an inert gas (such as nitrogen, argon, or carbon dioxide).

VACUOLES
Parts of vegetable cells where dissolved substances, such as sugars, acids and salts, are found.

VATS
Vats (*cuves*) are wine containers of variable size, ranging from 10hl to several thousand hl capacity. They are used as much for the *élevage* and storing of wine as for its vinification. Numerous materials are used for their construction: wood, stone, concrete, coated steel, stainless steel, glass, fibreglass, plastics. Vinification vats may be fitted with various accessories to carry out *pigeage* or *remontage* (qq.v.).

VATTING
Vatting (*cuvaison*) is the main phase of the vinification of red wines, in which fermentation of the must occurs in large vats, together with maceration of the solid parts of the grape (skin and pips) so that colour, tannins, aromatic substances and various secondary constituents of wine can be extracted.

The vatting time is one of the main conditioning factors on which the type of wine to be produced depends, short vatting times of three or four days being used for *primeur* wines, with longer vatting times of more than a week being suitable for wines to be aged for a long period. However, this factor is not the only one of importance in the vatting process; fermentation temperatures play just as important a role in terms of the level of solid grape substance extracted.

VDN *See Vin Doux Naturel.*

VDQS *See Vin Délimité de Qualité Supérieure.*

VENDANGE TARDIVE
An expression, meaning 'late harvest', used in wine law to refer to certain wines, particularly those of Alsace. It may be used of AOC wines made from the Gewürztraminer and Pinot Gris grape varieties if their natural sugar levels reach 243g per litre, and of AOC wines of the Riesling and Muscat grape varieties if their natural sugar levels reach 220g per litre. Musts may not be chaptalized, and mention of the vintage is obligatory on the labels.

VÉRAISON
Véraison is the stage of the grape maturation process when the red grapes begin to acquire colour and the white grapes start to soften and become translucent. It marks the beginning of ripening.

VERMOUTH
A fortified wine aromatized with plants and seeds by a process of maceration. Good Chambéry and Turin vermouths may contain up to forty natural aromatic essences.

VIEUX
▷ A term that may be officially used to describe AOC wines after 1 September of the second year following their harvest.
▷ More generally, this term is used to refer to a wine that is not only old, but one which shows qualities of advanced development linked to this age.

VINAGE
Addition of wine alcohol or neutral alcohol to wine, either for industrial ends, or for the preparation of *vins doux naturels* and *vins de liqueur*. The practice is forbidden in wines for consumption except in the last two cases.

VIN BOURRU
Vin bourru (literally 'gruff wine') is new wine that is still cloudy after fermentation.

VIN CUIT
Vin cuit is a wine obtained from a must that has been concentrated by heating.

VIN DELIMITÉ DE QUALITÉ SUPÉRIEURE
An *appellation d'origine* wine whose regulations and areas of production are different from AOC ones. They are produced in regions with a lower qualifying potential than that of AOC regions. The production of VDQS wine is 10 to 15 per cent of that of AOC wine.

VIN DE LIQUEUR (VDL) *See Mistelle.*

VIN DE PAILLE
Vin de paille (straw wine) is a sweet wine produced from grapes that have been left on beds of straw (hence the name) to dehydrate. Their concentration of sugar increases without a corresponding increase in acidity. These wines can achieve over 14° natural alcohol and may be kept for a very long period. They are mainly produced in Jura and in the Côtes du Rhône.

VIN DE PAYS
Vins de pays are *vins de table* that conform to strict regulations (*see* pages 580–588). The grape varieties used, and the maturity and quality of the wines are all controlled, and the wines are sold with their *département* or area of origin mentioned on the label. Blending wines of different origins is forbidden for *vins de pays*.

VIN DE QUALITÉ PRODUIT DANS UNE RÉGION DÉTERMINÉE (VQPRD)
A European Community definition for wines of AOC and VDQS status.

VIN DE SABLE
Wine harvested on sandy soils near the coast.

VIN DE TABLE
Vin de table is a wine without any particular quality classification, intended for everyday drinking. In order for this wine category to have a minimum intrinsic quality though, EC regulations have laid down precise guidelines as to the grape varieties that may be used, alcoholic strength (8.5° or 9° minimum) and acidity (4.5g per litre minimum). Whether or not the wine has a brand name, the label must indicate that the wine is *vin de table*, and include specification of its alcoholic strength.

VIN DOUX NATUREL (VDN)
The initial sugar level of *vin doux naturel* musts should be at least 252g per litre. During alcoholic fermentation, the must is fortified by the addition of a quantity of alcohol equal to 5 to 10 per cent of the volume of must. Fermentation then ceases, with the wine retaining a considerable quantity of residual sugar. Included in this category are the AOC wines of Banyuls, Maury, Rivesaltes, the Muscat wines of Beaumes-de-Venise, and some of the Muscat wines of Frontignan.

VIN D'UNE NUIT
A dark rosé wine produced by a brief maceration period of between 12 and 24 hours in the presence of the grape skins, pips and pulp.
VIN GRIS
Vin gris is a pale variety of rosé wine obtained by the rapid crushing and quick, direct pressing of red grapes containing white juice. No maceration takes place. In certain lights, the colour of these wines can take on a faint purplish tinge that suggests grey — hence the name.
VIN JAUNE
This is a wine produced in the Jura with a distinctive golden colour. Its nutty aromas are due to the growth of a veil of yeast on the surface of the wine during *élevage*. (*See also Jaune* (*Vin*) in Glossary of French Tasting Terms.)
VINE
The vine is a plant belonging to the genus *Vitis*. European vines belong to a single species, *Vitis vinifera*, but the grape varieties of this species form a very broad spectrum. American vines make up 18 species, the best known in France belonging to the species *riparia*, *rupestris* and *berlandieri*. The hybrids and varieties that come from these species are used as grafting stocks for European vines, or in the case of the hybrids on their own as direct producers. Asian vines include 19 species, but none of these are used for making wine. Garden 'vines' such as Russian vine or Virginia creeper belong to other botanical genera.
VINE STOCK
The woody part of a vine plant, over a year old (known in French as *cep* or *souche*). Modern grafted vines have a rooted part that is distinct from the part growing above ground. Vine stocks can live for as long as a century.
VINIFICATION
Phase in the production of wine that takes place between the gathering of the grapes and the end of alcoholic fermentation.
VINS DE MARQUE
Vins de marque are branded wines, usually produced in large quantities, of consistent character, the brand name normally being the most important element of the label. Such a name may be completely imaginary, or it may simply be a company name. Wines sold in this way may be anything from a blend of selected table wines, enhanced by a small proportion of wine from a superior grape variety, to sophisticated blends of wines of different regions that consequently lose their *appellation* in favour of the brand name, but which will appeal to the tastes of a large range of consumers. Another possibility is the blending of a large volume of regional or communal *appellation* wine, in which the *appellation* name is linked, but in a secondary position, with the brand name: 'Bordeaux X . . .', 'Champagne Y . . .', 'Burgundy Z . . .'
VINTAGE
A wine vintage is both the year of harvest of a grape crop and the group of organoleptic and physical characteristics that belong to the wines of this harvest. It is also used to signify the harvest itself, as in phrases such as 'The 1959 vintage was a very large one in France'. A certain number of publications periodically produce tables that indicate, with figures or stars, the relative values of vintages that come from different wine-producing regions.
VITACEAE
A family of plants, also called *Ampelidaceae*. It comprises roughly ten genera, incuding the genus *Vitis*. Within the *Vitis* genus are found American species that serve as grafting stocks for the European vine *Vitis vinifera* (the 'wine vine').
VITICULTURE
Viticulture means the cultivation of the vine. In French, *la viticulture* may also be used as a group noun to describe the professionals working in this area.
VITIS VINIFERA
The botanical name for the European vine.
VQPRD
See Vin de Qualité Produit dans une Région Déterminée.

WEEDING
Weeding (*désherbage*) of vines involves the elimination of all self-propagated vegetation around the stocks during the period of growth and maturation of the grapes. This operation used to be carried out entirely by ploughing and hoeing, but now the tendency is to weed chemically. This requires expertise, given the large number of different plant species present, some of which can prove stubborn to remove.
WHITE WINE
Wine that comes from the white juice of white or red grapes, after the extraction of juice or must, followed by alcoholic fermentation.
WINE
In French law, wine is a product obtained exclusively from the total or partial alcoholic fermentation of fresh grapes, crushed or not, or from grape must.
WINE CLASSIFICATION
A number of wine hierarchies exist in certain regions to establish a scale of quality and value among the wines of those regions. The first and most famous classification was made in 1855 in Bordeaux, by the Chambre de Commerce pour la Gironde; in 1860 a Burgundy equivalent was drawn up, using a chart of *crus* of the Côte d'Or formulated by the Comité d'Agriculture. The present-day equivalent of these classifications are the official decisions published under the auspices of the INAO, in the form of decrees, since 1935.
WINE DISEASES
By analogy with irregularities in the health of man, wine diseases refer to microbial developments that spoil the good condition of wine. Spoilage of this sort is generally characterized by three developments: cloudiness, oversaturation with carbon dioxide, and possible acescence.
WINE STORAGE
Wine is an unstable medium that can deteriorate unless certain storage rules are strictly adhered to. These rules are designed to protect the wine from bacterial attack, especially by acetic bacteria, and from physico-chemical impairments due above all to air and heat.

Once bottled, the length of time that a wine may be kept depends, of course, on the suitability of the cellar, but also on the wine itself.

Primeur wines should be drunk within a year of their vintage. They do not improve with age. But many other wines can develop favourably over the course of years. They change and acquire new gustatory balance. The colour evolves and the aromas are modified, often shedding a floral and fruity character and acquiring an empyreumatic or animal one. After reaching a peak, such wines decline and lose interest. Their lifespan ranges from two to more than fifty years.

YEASTS

Microscopic fungi, most often elliptical in shape, but occasionally apiculate. Their length is around 10 microns. They are present in numbers of between 1 and 10 million per ml in fermenting must. Yeasts are responsible for alcoholic fermentation, but also for a number of forms of wine spoilage.

INDEX

Page numbers in *italics* refer to the illustrations

D

E

T

U

V

W

Y

Z

PHOTOGRAPHY CREDITS

15: SCOPE - M. Guillard — **16**: P. Galet — **17**: CEDRI - C. Sappa — **18**: TOP - J. Ducange — **20**: CEDRI - C. Sappa — **22 h**: DIAF - J.-C. Pratt — **22 bg** et **bd**: DIAF - J.-P. Duchêne - SCOPE - J. Guillard — **23 h**: EXPLORER - F. Jalain — **24 h**: SCOPE - J. Guillard — **24 b**: G. Dagli Orti — **25**: DIAF - J. Louvet — **26**: EXPLORER - N. Thibaut — **28**: SCOPE - J.-D. Sudres — **30**: P. Galet — **32**: SCOPE - J.-L. Barde — **33**: GAMMA - J.-P. Paireault — **34**: EXPLORER - J.-P. Ferrero — **35**: GAMMA - J.-P. Paireault — **38**: MAGNUM - E. Lessing — **39**: G. Dagli Orti — **40**: Larousse — **43** et **47**: P. Galet — **49**: EXPLORER - C. Cuny — **50**: I.T.V. — **51**: EXPLORER - Hug — **53**: P. Galet — **53**: Collection Paul Bocuse — **54**: SCOPE - J. Guillard — **55**: SCOPE - J.-D. Sudres — **56**: TOP - G. Marineau — **57 h**: DIAF - J.-P. Langeland — **57 b**: EXPLORER - J.-Y. Loirat — **58 h**: Photo P.M. — **58 b, 60 b** et **61**: SCOPE - J.-L. Barde — **62**: Collection Paul Bocuse — **63**: EXPLORER - C. Errath — **64 h**: EXPLORER - F. Jalain. © A.D.A.G.P. 1987 — **64 b**: J. Verroust — **67**: EXPLORER - R. Truchot — **68** et **69**: SCOPE - J.-D. Sudres — **70**: SCOPE - J.-L. Barde — **71 h**: SCOPE - J. Guillard — **71 b**: SCOPE - M. Guillard — **72**: DIAF - D. Thierry — **73, 74, 75, 77** et **85**: SCOPE - M. Guillard — **86**: GAMMA - J.-P. Paireault — **87**: PIX - La Cigogne — **89**: SCOPE - M. Guillard — **90 h**: J.-L. Charmet — **90 b**: GIRAUDON - Lauros — **91, 92, 93, 96, 97** et **99**: SCOPE - M. Guillard — **100**: GAMMA - J.-P. Paireault — **106**: EXPLORER - G. Boutin — **108**: SCOPE - Guillard — **109**: SCOPE - M. Guillard — **110**: P. Galet — **111**: SCOPE - M. Guillard — **112**: EXPLORER - J. Dupont — **114**: G. Dagli Orti — **115**: SCOPE - J. Guillard — **116**: SCOPE - J. Guillard — **117**: EXPLORER - J. Mathiaut — **118**: EXPLORER - F. Jalain — **119**: EXPLORER - C. Errath — **120**: SCOPE - J. Guillard — **123 h**: SCOPE - P. Beuzen — **123 b**: Photo P.M. — **124**: DIAF - D. Thierry — **125**: S. Marmounier — **127**: SCOPE - J.-D. Sudres — **128 h**: DIAF - J.-P. Durand — **128 b**: SCOPE - J.-D. Sudres — **130 b**: EXPLORER - F. Jalain — **132**: EXPLORER - F. Jalain — **133**: TOP - J. Ducange — **134**: SCOPE - J.-L. Barde — **138**: EXPLORER - F. Jalain — **139** et **140**: SCOPE - M. Guillard — **141 g, cg,** et **cd**: I.T.V. — **141 d**: SCOPE - M. Guillard — **142**: EXPLORER - F. Jalain — **144 h**: SCOPE - J.-D. Sudres — **144 b**: SCOPE - J. Guillard — **145 h**: SCOPE - M. Guillard — **145 b**: EXPLORER - H. Veiller — **146 h**: SCOPE - J. Guillard — **146 b**: J. Verroust — **147**: SCOPE - M. Guillard — **148**: DIAF - A. Le Bot — **149 h**: I.T.V. — **149 b**: SCOPE - M. Guillard — **151**: P. Galet — **152 h**: SCOPE - J. -D. Sudres — **152 b** et **153**: P. Galet — **155**: SCOPE - J.-D. Sudres — **156**: SCOPE - M. Guillard — **157**: P. Galet — **159** et **160 h**: EXPLORER - F. Jalain — **160 b**: M. Garanger — **162 h**: EXPLORER - F. Jalain — **162 b**: Photo P.M. — **163**: SCOPE - J. Guillard — **164**: Champagne Moët et Chandon — **166 h**: EXPLORER - Hug — **166 b**: SCOPE - F. Hadengue — **167 h**: Moët et Chandon — **167 b**: EXPLORER - Danrigal — **168, 169, 170** et **171**: Champagne Moët et Chandon — **172 h**: SCOPE - F. Hadengue - Mosaïques ornant le fronton des caves du Champagne JACQUART à Reims — **172 b**: EXPLORER - F. Danrigal — **173**: G. Boyer — **174 h, 175** et **176**: P. Galet — **177**: EXPLORER - F. Jalain — **179** et **180**: SCOPE - J.-L. Barde — **181**: SCOPE - J.-D. Sudres — **182** et **183**: P. Galet — **185**: EXPLORER - H. Berthoule — **186**: SCOPE - M. Guillard — **187 h**: SCOPE - J. Sierpinski — **187 b**: Comité Interprofessionnel du Cognac — **188**: J.-Y. Boyer — **190**: SCOPE - M. Guillard — **191**: EXPLORER - F. Jalain — **192 h**: SCOPE - D. Faure — **192 b**: EXPLORER - F. Jalain — **193**: SCOPE - J. Guillard — **194**: SCOPE - J. Sierpinski — **196 h**: EXPLORER - F. Jalain — **196 b**: EXPLORER - Jean-Paul — **197**: EXPLORER - J.-M. Labat — **198**: S. Marmounier — **199 h**: EXPLORER - F. Jalain — **199 b**: SCOPE - M. Guillard — **200**: SCOPE - J. Guillard — **201**: EXPLORER - R. Truchot — **202 h**: Photo P.M. — **202 b** et **203**: SCOPE - J. Guillard — **204**: EXPLORER - H. Berthoule — **211, 212** et **213**: SCOPE - J. Guillard — **213 b**: EXPLORER - Hug — **214**: SCOPE - J.-D. Sudres — **216** et **217**: SCOPE - D. Faure — **219 h**: TOP - R. Mazin — **219 b**: SCOPE - J.-D. Sudres — **220**: SCOPE - J.-L. Barde — **222** et **223**: SCOPE - J. Guillard — **225**: EXPLORER - E. Sampers — **226**: GIRAUDON - Lauros — **228**: SCOPE - J.-D. Sudres — **229 h**: EXPLORER - F. Jalain — **229 b**: J. Verroust — **230**: EXPLORER - L. Girard — **231**: SCOPE - J.-D. Sudres — **232 h**: M. Garanger — **232 b**: EXPLORER - F. Jalain — **234**: SCOPE - J.-D. Sudres — **235**: EXPLORER - F. Jalain — **236**: PIX - Gauthier — **239**: P. Galet — **240**: EXPLORER - P. Sauvage — **241**: DIAF - J. Louvet — **242 h**: INRA, Colmar — **242 b**: SCOPE - M. Guillard — **243**: Larousse — **244**: GIRAUDON — **246**: SCOPE - M. Guillard — **248**: DIAF - F. Louvet — **250**: I.T.V. — **251**: SCOPE - J.-D. Sudres — **252**: J.-L. Charmet - Bibl. des Arts décoratifs, Paris — **255**: SCOPE - J.-L. Barde — **258**: SCOPE - J. Guillard — **259**: DIAF - A. Reffet — **260**: INRA — **261** et **262**: I.T.V. — **271**: SCOPE - D. Faure — **272**: SCOPE - J. Guillard — **272 b**: DIAF - J.-P. Langeland — **273 g**: SCOPE - M. Guillard — **273 b**: P. Galet — **274**: M. Taransaud — **275**: G. Dagli Orti — **276**: SCOPE - J.-D. Sudres — **277** et **278**: D.R. — **279**: M. Taransaud — **281, 282** et **283**: EXPLORER - N. Thibaut — **283**: EXPLORER - F. Danrigal — **285**: SCOPE - J.-L. Barde — **287**: P. Galet — **289** et **290**: SCOPE - J. Guillard — **292**: SCOPE - M. Guillard — **293**: P. Galet — **294**: EXPLORER - R. Truchot — **295**: DIAF - A. Le Bot — **296**: J.-L. Charmet - Bibl. des Arts décoratifs, Paris — **298, 299** et **300**: B.S.N. — **302**: SCOPE - J.-D. Sudres — **303**: RAPHO - F. Ducasse — **304**: S. Marmounier — **305**: SCOPE - J.-L. Barde — **306**: EXPLORER - F. Jalain — **307**: TOP - R. Mazin — **308**: SCOPE - J. Sierpinski — **309**: EXPLORER - F. Jalain — **310, 311, 312** et **313**: Larousse — **318**: SCOPE - J.-L. Barde — **319**: EXPLORER - F. Gohier — **320 h**: J. Verroust — **320 b**: EXPLORER - E. Sampers — **322**: S. Marmounier — **323, 324,** et **325**: SCOPE - J. Guillard — **327 hg**: Larousse — **327 hd**: EXPLORER - E. Sampers — **327 bd**: Larousse — **329**: P. Galet — **330**: SCOPE - D. Faure — **332** et **339**: SCOPE - J. Guillard — **333**: Larousse — **339**: SCOPE - J. Guillard — **340**: SCOPE - J.-D. Sudres — **341**: Les Caves Harnois — **344**: SCOPE - J. Guillard — **345 h**: EXPLORER - A. Nadeau — **345 b**: SCOPE - J. Guillard — **346**: SCOPE - J. Sierpinski — **348 h**: Giraudon — **348 b**: SCOPE - J. Guillard — **349**: R. Baillaud — **350**: SCOPE - D. Faure — **351**: SCOPE - J.-D. Sudres — **353**: SCOPE - D. Faure — **354**: SCOPE - J. Guillard — **356**: DIAF - J.-C. Pratt-Pries — **357**: EXPLORER - A. Wolf — **360**: EXPLORER - F. Jalain — **361 h**: EXPLORER - C. Delu — **361 b**: EXPLORER - F. Jalain — **362**: SCOPE - J. Guillard — **367**: EXPLORE - N. Thibaut — **368** et **369**: DIAF - A. Le Bot — **370**: CEDRI - G. Sioën — **372**: Larousse — **373**: Larousse — **373 b**: Giraudon — **374 h**: Giraudon - Lauros — **374**: Cliché réunion des Musées nationaux — **375** et **377**: SCOPE - M. Guillard — **379**: EXPLORER - H. Veiller — **380**: EXPLORER - C. Cuny — **381 h**: J. Verroust — **381 b**: EXPLORER - C. Delu — **382**: SCOPE - J. Sierpinski — **383**: SCOPE - M. Guillard — **384**: SCOPE - D. Faure — **385**: P. Galet — **386**: SCOPE - M. Guillard — **387 g**: P. Galet — **387 d**: EXPLORER — **388** et **389**: P. Galet — **390**: SCOPE - J. Guillard — **391 h**: EXPLORER - H. Veiller — **391 b**: EXPLORER - F. Jalain — **393 h**: SCOPE - J. Guillard — **393 b**: SCOPE - J.-D. Sudres — **394**: SCOPE - J.-L. Barde — **395**: SCOPE - J. Guillard — **396 h**: SCOPE - J. Guillard — **397** et **398**: P. Galet — **399** et **400**: SCOPE - J. Guillard — **401 h**: DIAF - A. Le Bot — **401 bd**: EXPLORER - D. Clément — **402** et **403**: SCOPE - J. Guillard — **404** et **405 h**: P. Galet — **405 b**: SCOPE - J. Sierpinski — **406 h**: EXPLORER - F. Jalain — **406 b** et **407**: SCOPE - J. Guillard — **408**: Larousse — **412 h**: SCOPE - J. Guillard — **412 b**: EXPLORER - F. Jalain — **413**: Larousse — **417**: SCOPE - M. Guillard — **421**: SCOPE - J. Guillard — **423, 426, 427, 428** et **429**: Larousse — **436**: EXPLORER - G. Boutin — **437**: EXPLORER - F. Jalain — **438**: SCOPE - M. Guillard — **439** et **440**: SCOPE - J. Guillard — **442**: SCOPE - M. Guillard — **443** et **444**: P. Galet — **445**: EXPLORER - P. Roy — **446 h**: SCOPE - J. Guillard — **446 b**: EXPLORER - P. Thomas — **447**: JERRICAN - Daudier — **448**: EXPLORER - F. Jalain — **450**: SCOPE - J. Guillard — **452**: EXPLORER - F. Jalain — **453** et **454 h**: SCOPE - J. Guillard — **454 b**: EXPLORER - H. Berthoule — **455 b**: SCOPE - J. Guillard — **456**: J.-L. Charmet — **457**: SCOPE - J. Sierpinski — **458**: C. Lénars — **459**: Giraudon — **460, 461** et **462**: G. Dagli Orti — **463**: Collection Chandon-Moët - Photo Sélection du Reader's Digest — **464**: PIX - Protet — **465**: Photo Bibl. nat., Paris — **467**: SCOPE - J. Guillard — **468**: EXPLORER - F. Jalain — **469**: P. Galet — **470**: SCOPE - J.-D. Sudres — **471**: EXPLORER - H. Berthoule — **473**: SCOPE - J. Guillard — **474**: RAPHO - E. Bright — **475**: SCOPE - F. Hadengue — **476**: C. Lénars — **477 h**: J. Verroust — **477 b**: G. Dagli-Orti — **478**: Larousse — **479**: Giraudon — **480**: Larousse — **481 h**: DIAF - D. Thierry — **482**: Larousse — **483**: TOP - A. Valtat — **485**: SCOPE - J.-L. Barde — **486**: SCOPE - D. Faure — **487 bg**: SCOPE - M. Guillard — **487 cd**: EXPLORER - F. Jalain — **488**: SCOPE - J.-D. Sudres — **489**: SCOPE - M. Guillard — **490**: SCOPE - J. Guillard — **491**: PIX - Chenot — **492**: PIX - Cauchetier — **493**: SCOPE - M. Guillard — **494 g**: P. Galet — **494 d**: SCOPE - J. Marthelot — **496**: S. Marmounier — **498 h**: extrait de l'ouvrage de Roger GIREL, *le Vignoble savoyard* © Editions Glénat 1985 — **498 b**: S. Marmounier — **500 h** et **b**: extraits de l'ouvrage de Roger GIREL *le Vignoble savoyard* © Editions Glénat 1985 — **503**: P. Galet — **504**: EXPLORER - B. et J. Dupont — **506**: EXPLORER - P. Roy — **507**: EXPLORER - F. Jalain — **508**: C. Lénars — **509**: Musée Martin von Wagner, Würzburg — **511**: J.-L. Charmet - © by SPADEM 1987 — **512**: G. Dagli Orti — **513**: Bulloz — **514**: Giraudon — **516**: H. Josse - © by A.D.A.G.P. 1987 — **518 h**: Giraudon - © by S.P.A.D.E.M. 1987 — **518 b**: PIX - Musée de l'Ermitage, Léningrad — **519**: G. Dagli Orti — **520 h**: D. Hecquet — **520 b**: SCOPE - J.-L. Barde — **523**: EXPLORER - H. Berthoule — **524**: EXPLORER - F. Jalain — **526**: TOP - J. Ducange — **527**: SCOPE - M. Guillard — **530**: SCRIPTO — **530**: SCOPE - J.-D. Sudres — **531**: TOP - R. Mazin — **532**: TOP - J. Ducange — **533**: DIAF - J.-C. Pratt — **535 h**: SCOPE - J.-D. Sudres — **535 b**: collection J. Taransand — **536**: EXPLORER - H. Veiller — **538**: TOP - R. Mazin — **539**: R. Baillaud — **540**: J.-L. Charmet — **541**: SCOPE - M. Guillard — **542**: RAPHO - Arcis — **545**: Giraudon — **546**: D.S.C.R. - F. Cepas — **550, 551, 552** et **553**: P. Galet — **554**: SCOPE - M. Guillard — **556**: DIAF - B. Belly — **559**: SCOPE - J.-D. Sudres — **560**: TAPABOR - Kharbine — **561**: EXPLORER - F. Jalain — **562 h**: SCOPE - J. Guillard — **562 b**: EXPLORER - H. Veiller — **563 h**: SCOPE - J.-D. Sudres — **563 b**: SCOPE - J. Guillard — **564**: EXPLORER - L. Salou — **565**: SCOPE - J. Guillard — **566**: EXPLORER - F. Jalain — **570**: EXPLORER - Danrigal — **572**: PIX - J. Labbé — **575**: J.-L. Charmet - collection particulière — **576**: Giraudon — **577**: SCOPE - J.-D. Sudres — **579** et **580**: EXPLORER - H. Veiller — **585**: EXPLORER - C. Delu — **586**: SCOPE - J. Guillard — **587**: EXPLORER - L. Salou